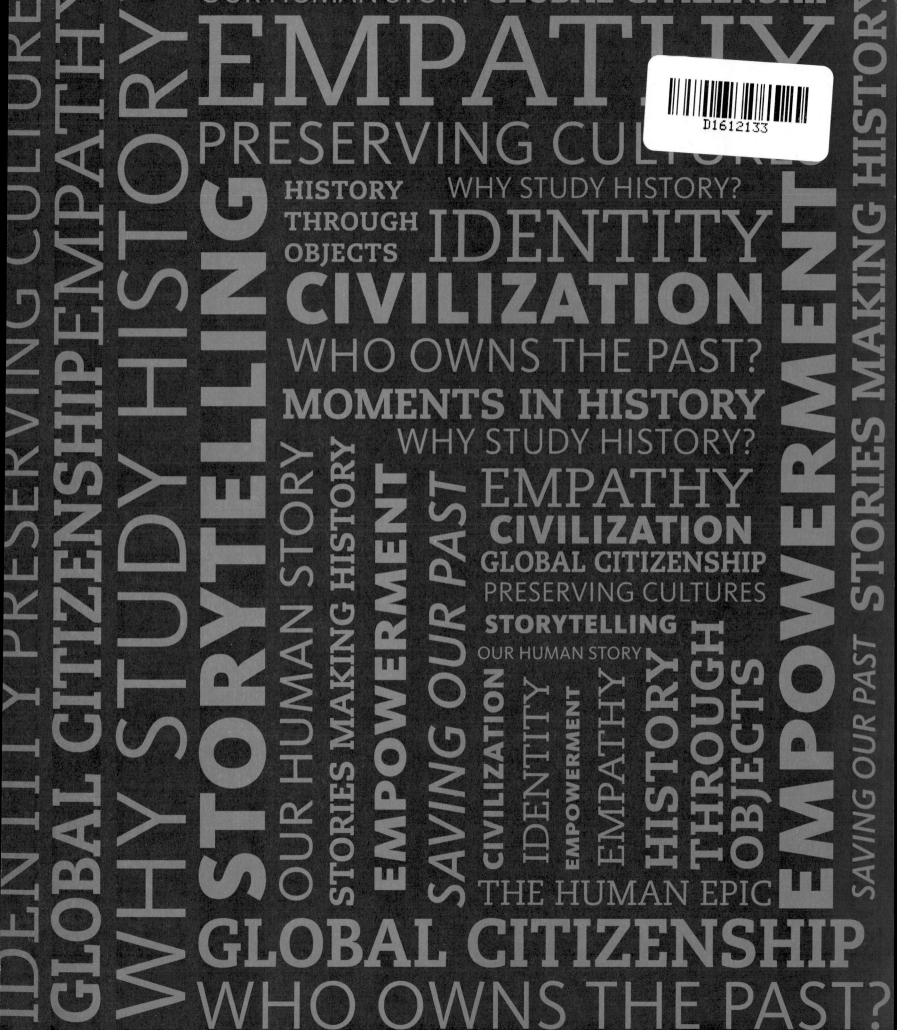

EMPATHY

PRESERVING CULTURES

HISTORY THROUGH OBJECTS

WHY STUDY HISTORY?

IDENTITY

CIVILIZATION

WHO OWNS THE PAST?

MOMENTS IN HISTORY

WHY STUDY HISTORY?

EMPATHY

CIVILIZATION

GLOBAL CITIZENSHIP

PRESERVING CULTURES

STORYTELLING

OUR HUMAN STORY

STORYTELLING

EMPOWERMENT

SAVING OUR PAST

OUR HUMAN STORY

STORIES MAKING HISTORY

CIVILIZATION

IDENTITY

EMPOWERMENT

EMPATHY

HISTORY

THROUGH OBJECTS

THE HUMAN EPIC

GLOBAL CITIZENSHIP

WHO OWNS THE PAST?

EMPOWERMENT

STORIES MAKING HISTORY

SAVING OUR PAST

THE HUMAN EPIC GLOBAL CITIZENSHIP

STORYTELLING

WHY STUDY HISTORY? EMPATHY

IDENTITY CIVILIZATION

STORIES MAKING HISTORY

EMPOWERMENT

SAVING OUR PAST

EMPATHY

HISTORY THROUGH OBJECTS

CIVILIZATION

PRESERVING CULTURES

GLOBAL CITIZENSHIP

PRESERVING CULTURES

EMPATHY

OUR HUMAN STORY

CIVILIZATION THE HUMAN EPIC

WHO OWNS THE PAST?

STORIES MAKING HISTORY

EMPOWERMENT

GLOBAL CITIZENSHIP

SAVING *OUR PAST*

EMPOWERMENT

PRESERVING CULTURES

SAVING OUR PAST

WHY STUDY HISTORY?

GLOBAL CITIZENSHIP

IDENTITY

THE HUMAN EPIC

STORYTELLING

OUR HUMAN STORY

EMPOWERMENT

MOMENTS IN HISTORY

IDENTITY *SAVING OUR PAST*

GLOBAL CITIZENSHIP

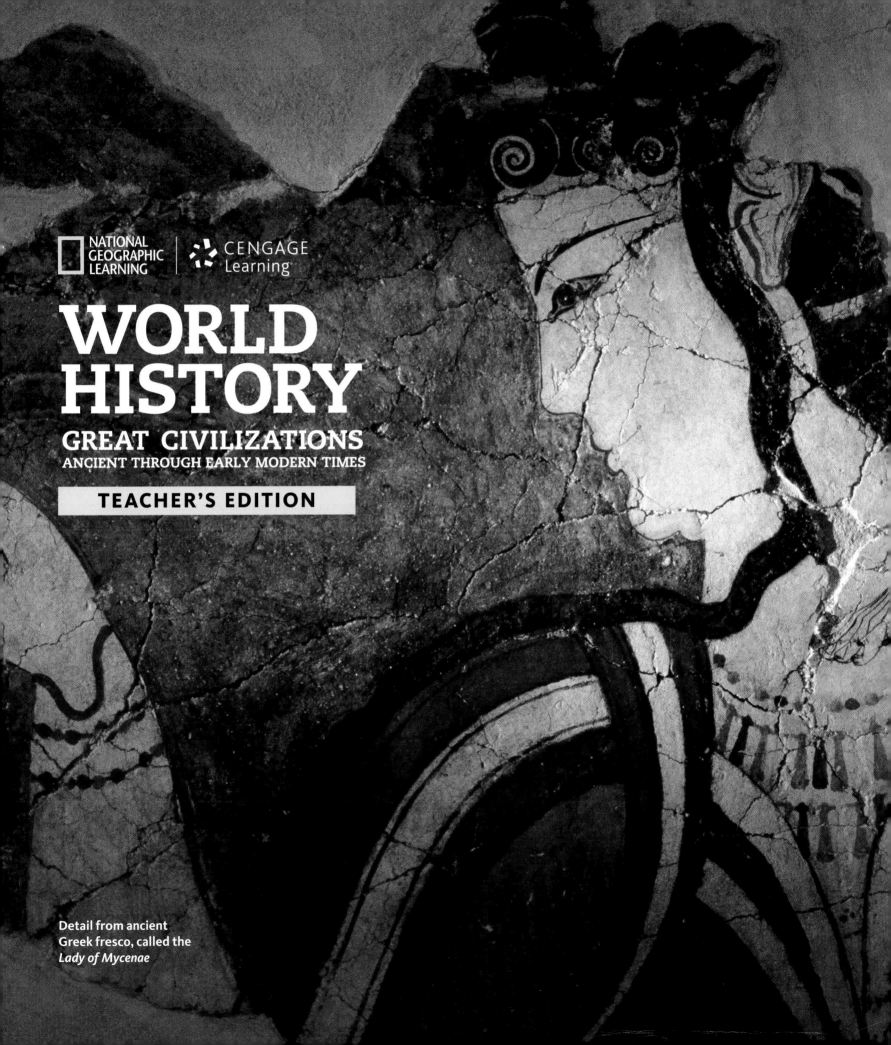

NATIONAL GEOGRAPHIC LEARNING | CENGAGE Learning

WORLD HISTORY

GREAT CIVILIZATIONS

ANCIENT THROUGH EARLY MODERN TIMES

TEACHER'S EDITION

Detail from ancient
Greek fresco, called the
Lady of Mycenae

For product information and technology assistance, contact us at Customer & Sales Support, 888-915-3276

For permission to use material from this text or product, submit all requests online at **www.cengage.com/permissions**

Further permissions questions can be emailed to **permissionrequest@cengage.com**

National Geographic Learning | Cengage Learning
1 N. State Street, Suite 900
Chicago, IL 60602

Cengage Learning is a leading provider of customized learning solutions with office locations around the globe, including Singapore, the United Kingdom, Australia, Mexico, Brazil, and Japan. Locate your local office at **www.cengage.com/global.**

Visit National Geographic Learning online at **NGL.Cengage.com**

Visit our corporate website at **www.cengage.com**

Student Edition
Print Edition ISBN: 978-12853-52312
One-Year Digital Subscription ISBN: 978-13056-59339
Six-Year Digital Subscription ISBN: 978-13056-59025

Teacher's Edition
Print Edition ISBN: 978-13370-99882
One-Year Digital Subscription ISBN: 978-13056-59353
Six-Year Digital Subscription ISBN: 978-13056-59049

Acknowledgments

Grateful acknowledgment is given to the authors, artists, photographers, museums, publishers, and agents for permission to reprint copyrighted material. Every effort has been made to secure the appropriate permission. If any omissions have been made or if corrections are required, please contact the Publisher.

Photographic Credits

Front Cover: ©James L. Stanfield/National Geographic Creative

Acknowledgments and credits continue on page R37

Printed in the USA.
RR Donnelley, Willard, OH

Print Number: 01
Print Year: 2016

PROGRAM CONSULTANTS

Fredrik Hiebert

Dr. Fred Hiebert is a National Geographic Explorer and Archaeology Fellow. He has led archaeological expeditions at ancient Silk Roads sites across Asia and underwater in the Black Sea. Hiebert rediscovered the lost Bactrian gold in Afghanistan in 2004 and was curator of National Geographic's exhibition *Afghanistan: Hidden Treasures from the National Museum, Kabul*, which toured museums throughout the world. Hiebert curated National Geographic's exhibition *Peruvian Gold: Ancient Treasures Unearthed* and, most recently, the exhibition *The Greeks: Agamemnon to Alexander the Great.*

Christopher P. Thornton

Dr. Chris Thornton is the Lead Program Officer of Research, Conservation, and Exploration at the National Geographic Society, and Director of the UNESCO World Heritage Site of Bat in the Sultanate of Oman. Thornton works closely with NGS media to promote grantees and other scientists, overseeing research grants in anthropology, archaeology, astronomy, geography, geology, and paleontology. He also manages the Society's relationship with academic conferences around the world.

Jeremy McInerney

Dr. Jeremy McInerney is chairman of the Department of Classical Studies at the University of Pennsylvania. McInerney recently spent a year as Whitehead Professor in the American School of Classical Studies in Athens, Greece. He has excavated at Corinth, on Crete, and in Israel. Author of *The Cattle of the Sun: Cows and Culture in the World of the Ancient Greeks* (2010), McInerney has received top teaching awards, including the Lindback Award for Distinguished Teaching.

PROGRAM CONSULTANTS

Michael W. Smith

Dr. Michael Smith is the Associate Dean for Faculty Development and Academic Affairs in the College of Education at Temple University. He became a college teacher after 11 years of teaching high school English. His research focuses on how experienced readers read and talk about texts, as well as what motivates adolescents' reading and writing. Smith has written many books and monographs, including the award-winning *"Reading Don't Fix No Chevys": Literacy in the Lives of Young Men*.

Peggy Altoff

Peggy Altoff's long career includes teaching middle school and high school students, supervising teachers, and serving as adjunct university faculty. Peggy served as a state social studies specialist in Maryland and as a K–12 coordinator in Colorado Springs. She was president of the National Council for the Social Studies (NCSS) in 2006–2007 and was on the task force for the 2012 NCSS National Curriculum Standards.

David W. Moore

Dr. David Moore is a Professor Emeritus of Education at Arizona State University. He taught high school social studies and reading before entering college teaching. His noteworthy co-authored publications include the *Handbook of Reading Research* chapter on secondary school reading, the first International Reading Association position statement on adolescent literacy, and *Developing Readers and Writers in the Content Areas (6e)*.

PROGRAM WRITER

Special thanks to Jon Heggie for his extensive contributions to *National Geographic World History: Great Civilizations (Ancient Through Early Modern Times)*. Heggie became fascinated with history as a small child, a passion nurtured by his parents and educators. He studied history at Oxford University and received his Post Graduate Certificate in Education from Bristol University. Heggie has taught English and History at a number of schools in the UK and has written for *National Geographic* magazine for the past ten years. He is currently working on a number of history projects and serving as the editor of the recently launched National Geographic *History* magazine.

REVIEWERS OF RELIGIOUS CONTENT

The following individuals reviewed the treatment of religious content in selected pages of the text.

Murali Balaji
Hindu American Foundation
Washington, D.C.

Dr. Charles C. Haynes
Director, Religious Freedom
Center of the Newseum Institute
Washington, D.C.

Munir Shaikh
Institute on Religion and
Civic Values
Fountain Valley, California

NATIONAL GEOGRAPHIC SOCIETY

The National Geographic Society contributed significantly to *National Geographic World History: Great Civilizations (Ancient Through Early Modern Times)*. Our collaboration with each of the following has been a pleasure and a privilege: National Geographic Maps, National Geographic Education and Children's Media, National Geographic Missions programs, and National Geographic Studios. We thank the Society for its guidance and support.

We BELIEVE in the power of science, exploration, and storytelling to change the world.

ACTIVE LEARNING in the HISTORY CLASSROOM

Easily influenced by peers and distracted by text messaging and the lure of the latest handheld device, middle school learners can be challenging to reach. A class of middle school students is a highly diverse group of learners with myriad personalities and learning styles. Learners may be enthusiastic today and disengaged tomorrow, conversational one day and sullen the next.

Peggy Altoff

As you know from experience, a middle school teacher must be fully prepared to engage students each day and flexible enough to change plans at a moment's notice with the shifting classroom dynamic. National Geographic's *World History* program contains a wealth of teaching options that are perfect for the active teacher— and his or her active students.

VARIETY AND FLEXIBILITY

An expansive repertoire of proven strategies and appropriate activities provides the best preparation for each day's teaching. The structure of the Student Edition in this program is specifically designed to provide options that engage students in meaningful learning activities. The two-page format of each lesson in a chapter allows for several approaches, including

- selecting lessons and sections that are most appropriate for any given class of learners;

- focusing on one lesson each day to provide a depth of content knowledge;

- using cooperative learning activities that allow students to teach and learn from each other.

In a cooperative learning activity, for example, students can participate in a Jigsaw strategy in which groups of students become experts on one lesson in a chapter. Next, all expert groups switch into new groups with each new group having one "expert" on each lesson. Each expert is then responsible for teaching the others in the group about the lesson. (See *Cooperative Learning Strategies* in the Teacher's Edition for a complete explanation of the Jigsaw strategy.)

Another cooperative learning possibility involves breaking a lesson into segments by subheading. Most of the lessons in the Student Edition have two subheadings. This makes it easy for students to work in pairs, with each student reading and learning about information in one segment and then sharing and discussing with the other.

You may also consider having students work in pairs or small groups to discuss a **Review & Assess** question, a **Critical Viewing** question, or other text-based features. Experience suggests that each grouping strategy requires practice with students so that they can meet teacher expectations for appropriate conduct while acquiring knowledge of the content presented.

Student Edition activities are intended to address a variety of learning styles. The **Reading Strategy** at the beginning of each chapter provides students with a plan to organize and analyze what they are about to read. The **Review & Assess** questions at the end of each lesson provide skill practice with interpreting maps, analyzing visuals, sequencing events, and so on that can be completed individually, in small groups, or as a class. **Chapter Reviews** include a **Write About History** activity that requires students to demonstrate what they have learned through writing. A **Unit Wrap-Up** at the end of each unit offers students insight into the work of archaeologists, scientists, writers, and other experts. It also includes a **Unit Inquiry** assignment that asks students to present what they've learned using many different formats, including writing, video, and multimedia.

COMPONENTS FOR THE TEACHER

The Teacher's Edition of the *World History* program presents many possibilities for active learning and student engagement.

Cooperative Learning Strategies offers a preview of the types of strategies located throughout the Teacher's Edition with a clear explanation of how to implement each one. For the highly experienced teacher, this may offer a review of practical procedures. Those new to the profession will probably want to return to these pages frequently to plan new experiences for students.

The **Chapter Planner** in the Teacher's Edition provides an overview of the lesson support in each chapter and contains references to such tools as **Reading and Note-Taking, Vocabulary Practice, Social Studies Skills Lessons, Section Quizzes,** and **Formal Assessment Tests** (available online with a digital subscription to myNGconnect). The **Strategies for Differentiation** section offers ideas that engage striving readers, inclusion students, English language learners, gifted and talented students, and those in pre-Advanced Placement. You can decide how to apply each of these strategies to individual learners.

For daily planning, refer to each lesson's **Plan**, **Teach**, and **Differentiate** sections. The Teach section includes discussion questions and activities that help students summarize and analyze the lesson. It also contains an **Active Options** feature that especially engages students with **Critical Viewing**, **National Geographic Learning Framework**, and (my personal favorite) **On Your Feet** activities. We know that middle school students are constantly moving and doing, and this feature provides you with ways to channel that bounding energy meaningfully.

Think carefully about how to select the options that are appropriate for your students. For me, Rule #1 in working with middle school students has always been to start simple and move toward the complex. It may not be a good idea, for example, to try to implement all of the available strategies and activities in one lesson. Start with those that make the most sense to you and gradually experiment with others. Inform students when you attempt a new strategy or activity and get their feedback on ways to improve it the next time. The activities and strategies found in this program are not meant to provide a recipe for success. Instead, they form a menu of options that support daily decision-making based on your own abilities and preferences and those of your students.

Striking images, graphics, and detailed maps engage and inform students.

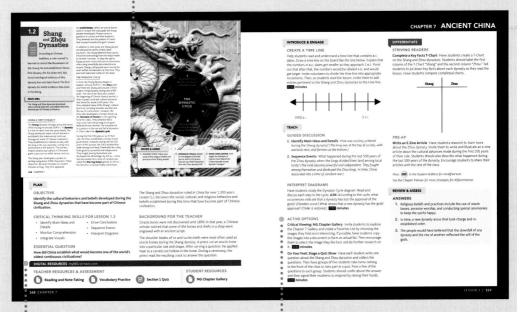

References to digital resources show what is available on myNGconnect.

Teacher Notes in every lesson include extensive teacher and student resources.

SUPPORTING HISTORY
LEARNERS WITH TEXTS

As they study history, students learn how and where civilizations developed through the centuries. They learn how to think about the world and discover the ways in which cultures and civilizations are similar—and how they are unique. They come to understand that knowing why a civilization developed can help them interpret the past, analyze the present, and anticipate the future.

David W. Moore

History texts are major resources for middle school students, who are just learning to think and act like historians. Print and digital texts bring to life cultures, governments, and economic and geographic phenomena that often are too big, distant, and complex for students to experience firsthand. These texts also contribute insights and ways of thinking that deepen understandings of phenomena that can be experienced directly.

Research reviews published during the 2000s (Carnegie Council on Advancing Adolescent Literacy, 2010; Kamil et al., 2008; Torgeson et al., 2007) point to effective ways to support middle school instruction using texts. Two principles derived from these reviews underlie National Geographic's *World History* program: engage learners with considerate texts and engage learners in active processing.

ENGAGE LEARNERS
WITH CONSIDERATE TEXTS

Considerate texts are reader-friendly materials that learners find understandable and memorable (Armbruster & Anderson, 1985). A key feature of such texts is the way in which they present important relationships (Armbruster, 2002). At a global level, this means helping readers see how big ideas and overarching themes unify what is presented (Goldman & Rakestraw, 2000). For example, the *World History* Teacher's Edition presents an essential question in each chapter, such as "What factors contributed to the development of civilization?" Teachers can use the questions to help students integrate concepts and bring structure to supporting details.

At a local level, considerate texts are well organized and clearly guide readers through their content (Goldman & Rakestraw, 2000).

This means providing explicit main idea statements, introductory paragraphs, and headings and subheadings and combining verbal and visual information (Mayer, 2001). For instance, a lesson in the program on ancient Egypt's daily life and religion begins with an introduction to the civilization's early religious practices. The headings that follow indicate that daily life in Egyptian society and Egyptian gods will be discussed one at a time. An image featuring ancient Egyptian gods and hieroglyphs is included to illustrate religious beliefs.

A considerate text is also appropriate for its audience: it connects with its readers' prior knowledge and interests (Armbruster, 2002). For example, a lesson in the program on changing environments during the Paleolithic Age explains how climate changes thousands of years ago altered the landscape in which Paleolithic people lived, forcing them to find new homes and adapt to new conditions. The lesson may interest students on several levels, encouraging them to reflect on the climate change many scientists believe is occurring today and recalling some of the adaptations they may have made when they moved to new places.

As digital communication technologies have emerged, definitions of texts have broadened (Coiro, Knobel, Lankshear, & Leu, 2008). Today, tools such as video screens, Web sites, and podcasts are merging with and often replacing books, paper, and pencils. Considerate digital texts offer readers the opportunity to combine information, including print and images. In line with these new digital resources, the *World History* program provides videos, a digital Student Edition, online handbooks, and interactive whiteboard materials and map tools.

ENGAGE LEARNERS IN ACTIVE PROCESSING

Considerate texts are crucial parts of instruction, but they are effective only when learners actively process them (Israel & Duffy, 2008; McNamara, 2007). For instance, learners actively process texts when they preview a lesson's contents, summarize what they have read, and synthesize what they have just learned with what they already know.

Texts can prompt learners to engage in active processing in several ways (Hartley, 2004). Interspersed questions are especially effective (Wood, Lapp, Flood, & Taylor, 2008). The *World History* program uses several types of questions. **Critical Viewing** questions regularly prompt learners to interpret images. **Review & Assess** questions at the end of each lesson encourage students to assess their understanding and think critically about what they have just read and viewed in the lesson. **Chapter Review** questions at the end of each chapter encourage active reconsideration of the chapter's main ideas, concepts, and visuals.

Text prompts that involve learners in writing and discussion also engage learners in active processing (Newell, 2008; Nystrand,

2006). *World History* provides regular opportunities for learners to write about texts through **Write About History** and **Synthesize and Write** prompts, structured reading and note-taking, and other social studies writing activities. The program also offers regular opportunities for learners to write and talk about texts through active options based on cooperative learning strategies.

Finally, differentiated text prompts generate active processing by accommodating learners with different levels of academic preparedness and approaches to learning (Tomlinson, 2005). The program's Teacher's Edition includes instructional strategies appropriate for English language learners, gifted and talented students, inclusion students, pre-Advanced Placement students, and striving readers.

The two principles underlying *World History* are complementary. Engaging learners with considerate texts goes far in promoting active processing, and engaging learners in active processing occurs best with considerate texts. As a result, the program provides middle school students with a meaningful introduction to history.

REFERENCES

Armbruster, B. B. 2002. Considerate text. In *Literacy in America: An encyclopedia of history, theory, and practice*, ed. B. J. Guzzetti, vol. 1, 97–99. Santa Barbara, Calif: ABC-CLIO.

Armbruster, B. B., and T. H. Anderson. 1985. Producing "considerate" expository text: Or, easy reading is damned hard writing. *Journal of Curriculum Studies* 17: 247–274.

Carnegie Council on Advancing Adolescent Literacy. 2010. *Time to act: An agenda for advancing adolescent literacy for college and career success.* New York: Carnegie Corporation of New York.

Coiro, J., M. Knobel, C. Lankshear, and D. J. Leu, eds. 2008. *Handbook of research on new literacies.* New York: Routledge.

Goldman, S. R., and J. A. Rakestraw, Jr. 2000. Structural aspects of constructing meaning from text. In *Handbook of reading research*, ed. M. L. Kamil, P. Mosenthal, P. D. Pearson, and R. Barr, vol. 3, 311–335. Mahwah, N.J.: Erlbaum.

Hartley, J. 2004. Designing instructional and informational text. In *Handbook of research in educational communications and technology*, ed. D. H. Jonassen, 917–947. 2d ed. Mahwah, N.J.: Erlbaum.

Hattie, J. 2009. *Visible learning: A synthesis of over 800 meta-analyses relating to achievement.* New York: Routledge.

Israel, S. E., and G. Duffy, eds. 2008. *Handbook of research on reading comprehension.* New York: Routledge.

Kamil, M. L., G. D. Borman, J. Dole, C. C. Kral, T. Salinger, and J. Torgesen. 2008. *Improving adolescent literacy: Effective classroom and intervention practices: A practice guide.* Washington, D.C.: Institute of Education Sciences, U.S. Department of Education. http://ies.ed.gov/ncee/wwc.

Mayer, R. E. 2001. *Multimedia learning.* New York: Cambridge University Press.

McNamara, D. S., ed. 2007. *Reading comprehension strategies: Theories, interventions, and technologies.* Mahwah, N.J.: Erlbaum.

Newell, G. E. 2008. Writing to learn: How alternative theories of school writing account for student performance. In *Handbook of writing research*, ed. C. A. MacArthur, S. Graham, and J. Fitzgerald, 235–247. New York: The Guilford Press.

Nystrand, M. 2006. Research on the role of discussion as it affects reading comprehension. *Research in the Teaching of English* 40: 392–412.

Tomlinson, C., ed. 2005. Differentiated instruction [special issue]. *Theory into Practice* 44(3).

Torgesen, J. K., D. D. Houston, L. M. Rissman, S. M. Decker, G. Roberts, S. Vaughn, J. Wexler, D. J. Francis, M. O. Rivera, and N. Lesaux. 2007. *Academic literacy instruction for adolescents: A guidance document from the Center on Instruction.* Portsmouth, N.H.: RMC Research Corporation, Center on Instruction. www.centeroninstruction.org.

Wood, K. D., D. Lapp, J. Flood, and D. B. Taylor. 2008. *Guiding readers through text: Strategy guides for new times.* Newark, Del: International Reading Association.

FOSTERING STUDENTS'
ABILITY TO WRITE ARGUMENTS

When the great Roman statesman, Cicero, and other supporters of the Roman Republic spoke about the role of government, they debated such questions as: What limits should be placed on the state's leaders? Who should have a say in making and passing the state's laws? What benefits should citizens in the state enjoy? What is their civic duty?

Michael W. Smith

These questions still resonate today. People have offered different answers to the questions and have provided arguments in their attempt to convince others to share their views. Arguments have always been central to public discourse. As Richard Andrews notes, "Imagine, for a moment, a world without argument. It would either be an authoritarian or tyrannical state. . . . [T]o be fully conscious, is to be ready for argumentation; for discussion 'with edge'" (2009, pp. 3–4).

Just as we want our society to be a place where intellect and differences are celebrated, so too do we want our classrooms to provide forums for vibrant intellectual exchanges. It is little wonder that schools place such an emphasis on argumentation. Turning to Andrews again: "[Argument] also refers to the most highly prized type of academic discourse: something that is deemed essential to a thesis, to an article in a research journal, to a dissertation, essay, and to many other kinds of writing within schools and the academy" (2009, p. 1).

In National Geographic's *World History* program, students do a variety of writing, but much of our instructional focus is on argument. If students are to understand why history matters, they need to engage in arguments that depend on historical knowledge. In so doing, they learn skills that prepare them not only for their future schooling but also for their lives outside of school.

THE RIGHT APPROACH

The **Social Studies Skills Writing Lessons** in the *World History* program teach students to write effective arguments by articulating the strategies experienced writers employ when they develop arguments. Students are then given extended practice in employing these strategies on their own.

The approach is in line with the recommendation of the *Writing Next* report, which found that the most powerful kind of writing instruction involves "explicitly and systematically teaching steps necessary for planning, revising, and/or editing text" (Graham & Perin, 2007, p. 15). The research of George Hillocks helps explain why this is so (cf. 1986, 1995, 2007, 2011). Throughout his writing, Hillocks draws a distinction between declarative knowledge, or knowledge that can be said, and procedural knowledge, or a kind of knowledge that has to be performed. That distinction is crucially important for, as Hillocks demonstrates again and again, declarative knowledge doesn't result in procedural knowledge. Knowing historical concepts does not mean that students can use them effectively in their writing. They have to be taught how to use them.

Unfortunately, much of the writing instruction students receive is not designed to help them develop procedural knowledge. Think back on how you were taught writing. My bet is that most of your teachers used what I call the Assign and Assess method. That is, you worked in class to develop knowledge on whatever the content of the class was and then your teachers assigned writing exercises that allowed you to display that knowledge. Finally, some weeks later, you received a grade on the assignment along with a few comments justifying the grade and providing instruction for future work.

Not only is the Assign and Assess method inadequate in helping students develop procedural knowledge, but it also may cause students to resist a teacher's efforts to help them improve. In his landmark study on childhood, psychoanalyst Erik Erikson offers an explanation for why students who need their teachers' help the most often do not seek it (1963). He identifies the central psychosocial conflict of school-age students, the stage of most students beginning middle school, as industry versus inferiority.

Middle school students are struggling to assert their competence. Pointing out where they went astray doesn't help them develop it.

My co-author Jeff Wilhelm and I repeatedly saw the importance of fostering students' competence in our study of the literate life of adolescent boys both in school and out (Smith & Wilhelm 2002). One young man provided what could have been a mantra for the whole group when we asked him why he liked playing lacrosse, his favorite outside-of-school activity: "I just like being good at it." If the young men in our study didn't feel competent in an activity, they chose not to engage in it.

Yet they did want to engage in argumentation. The young men we studied "did not want to play 'guess what the teacher already knows.' They wanted to solve problems, debate, and argue in ways through which they could stake their identity and develop both ideas and functional tools that they could share and use with others in very immediate ways. They wanted to develop the competence and capacities of real experts" (Smith & Wilhelm, p. 57).

AN ARGUMENTATION MODEL

The *World History* program helps students develop their expertise in writing effective arguments in several ways. First, Toulmin's model of argumentation, the one that informs the approach the program takes, is built on an understanding of how oral argumentation works in the real world (1958). Anyone who has spent any time with adolescents knows that they are avid and excellent arguers. The program helps them develop an articulated understanding of what they do all the time in their everyday life and then apply it to their writing. The National Commission on Writing calls for curricula to build bridges between students' in-school and out-of-school lives. This program does so.

Second, we provide lots of instruction and practice. Along with the **Social Studies Skills Writing Lessons**, the program contains **Write About History** and **Synthesize and Write** prompts that give students practice in mastering each element of Toulmin's model. We give them practice developing clear, specific, and reasonable claims. We help them understand how to provide specific evidence and how to explain the connection between the evidence and the claim. We work with them to anticipate and respond to counterarguments. We also help them master the sentence structures they will need to effectively express themselves. We then work with students to apply what they have learned to a variety of different kinds of arguments.

Third, we provide explicit instruction to help students successfully complete particular assignments. They learn to unpack the prompt, plan their paper, assess its effectiveness, and revise their argument.

A final thought experiment: Think of some complex activity you have mastered. Mastering it probably took time and instruction and practice. Writing arguments is a crucial and complex skill. *World History* provides students the time, instruction, and practice they need to become competent at it. No comparable textbook does the same.

REFERENCES

Andrews, R. 1979. *The importance of argument in education*. London: Institute of Education, University of London.

Erikson, E. 1963. *Childhood and society*, 2d ed. New York: Norton.

Hillocks, G., Jr. 1986. *Research on written composition: New directions for teaching*. Urbana, Ill: ERIC and National Conference for Research in English.

Hillocks, G., Jr. 1995. *Teaching writing as reflective practice*. New York: Teachers College Press.

Hillocks, G., Jr. 2007. *Narrative writing: Learning a new model for teaching*. Portsmouth, N.H.: Heinemann.

Hillocks, G., Jr. 2011. *Teaching argument writing: Supporting claims with relevant evidence and clear reasoning*. Portsmouth, N.H.: Heinemann.

National Commission on Writing. *Writing and school reform*. http://www. writingcommission.org.

Smith, M. W., and J. Wilhelm. 2002. *"Reading don't fix no Chevys": Literacy in the lives of young men*. Portsmouth, N.H.: Heinemann.

Smith, M. W., and J. Wilhelm. 2006. *Going with the flow: How to engage boys (and girls) in their literacy learning*. Portsmouth, N.H.: Heinemann.

Toulmin, S. 1958. *The uses of argument*. Cambridge, England: Cambridge University Press.

NATIONAL GEOGRAPHIC

Unit Explorers

Each unit in this book opens and closes with a National Geographic Explorer discussing the content presented in the unit and explaining his or her own related work in the field. Within the Student eEdition, you can watch video footage of each Unit Explorer "on location" to expand and enhance your world history learning experience.

Christopher DeCorse
Archaeologist
National Geographic
Grantee

Steven Ellis
Archaeologist
National Geographic
Grantee

Francisco Estrada-Belli
Archaeologist
National Geographic
Grantee

Fredrik Hiebert
Archaeologist
National Geographic
Fellow

Louise Leakey
Paleontologist
National Geographic
Explorer-in-Residence

Albert Lin
Research Scientist/Engineer
National Geographic
Emerging Explorer

Jodi Magness
Archaeologist
National Geographic
Grantee

William Parkinson
Archaeologist
National Geographic
Grantee

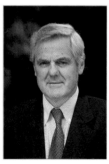

Maurizio Seracini
Cultural Heritage
Engineer
National Geographic
Fellow

Christopher Thornton
Archaeologist
National Geographic
Lead Program Officer of Research,
Conservation, and Exploration

NATIONAL GEOGRAPHIC

CHAPTER EXPLORERS

In the chapters of this book, National Geographic Explorers tell the story of their work as it relates to the time in history you're learning about. Archaeologists, photographers, and writers explain their historical and cultural findings and the process involved in making the important discoveries that help us understand more about the past—and the future.

Caroline Alexander
National Geographic
Writer/Journalist

Beverly Goodman
Geo-Archaeologist
National Geographic
Emerging Explorer

Fredrik Hiebert
Archaeologist
National Geographic
Fellow

Patrick Hunt
Archaeologist
National Geographic
Grantee

Christine Lee
Bio-Archaeologist
National Geographic
Emerging Explorer

Sarah Parcak
Archaeologist
National Geographic
Fellow

Jeffrey Rose
Archaeologist
National Geographic
Emerging Explorer

William Saturno
Archaeologist
National Geographic
Grantee

Hayat Sindi
Science Entrepreneur
National Geographic
Emerging Explorer

Dave Yoder
Photojournalist
National Geographic
Grantee

NATIONAL GEOGRAPHIC

FEATURED EXPLORERS

Throughout the Student eEdition, National Geographic Featured Explorers take part in informal "video chat" style interviews to explain and discuss their fieldwork and explore high-interest topics covered in the book. Other Featured Explorers tell the story of important and ongoing world events in the Stories Making History section.

Salam Al Kuntar
Archaeologist
National Geographic
Emerging Explorer

Nicole Boivin
Archaeologist
National Geographic
Grantee

Steve Boyes
Conservation Biologist
National Geographic
Emerging Explorer

Michael Cosmopoulos
Archaeologist, National
Geographic Grantee

Sarah Parcak
Archaeologist
National Geographic
Fellow

Thomas Parker
Archaeologist
National Geographic
Grantee

Matt Piscitelli
Archaeologist
National Geographic
Grantee

Max Salomon
National Geographic
Producer

Anna Secor
Political Geographer
National Geographic
Grantee

Shah Selbe
Conservation Technologist
National Geographic
Emerging Explorer

Soultana Maria Valamoti
Archaeologist, National
Geographic Grantee

Xiaobai Angela Yao
Geographer
National Geographic
Grantee

The National Geographic Learning book series, *Explore* and *Global Issues*, align with much of the content of *World History: Great Civilizations*. Use these lists to see which *Explore* and *Global Issues* titles can be used to compliment *World History* chapters and lessons.

EXPLORE SERIES

EXPLORE THE AMAZON
aligns to these sections of World History

Chapter 17, Section 1
Peruvian Cultures

Chapter 23, Lesson 3.2
Portugal's Empire

EXPLORE ANCIENT EGYPT
aligns to these sections of World History

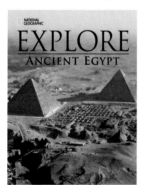

Chapter 4, Section 1
A Society on the Nile

Chapter 4, Section 2
The Old and Middle Kingdoms

Chapter 4, Section 3
The New Kingdom

Chapter 4, Section 4
The Egyptian Legacy

Stories Making History
Our Shared History

EXPLORE ARCHAEOLOGY
aligns to these sections of World History

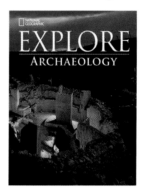

Chapter 2
Origins of Civilization

Chapter 3
Ancient Mesopotamia

Chapter 4 Ancient Egypt

Chapter 7 Ancient China

Chapter 8 Ancient Greece

Chapter 9 Classical Greece

Chapter 10 The Roman Republic

Chapter 11 The Roman Empire and Christianity

Chapter 12 The Byzantine Empire

Chapter 18 Dynasties of China

Chapter 21, Lesson 1.3 Investigating a Mysterious Treasure

Stories Making History Saving Cultural Heritage

Stories Making History Our Shared History

EXPLORE BIG CATS
aligns to these sections of World History

Stories Making History
Into the Okavango: A Live-Data Expedition

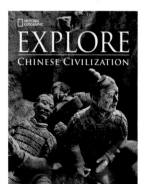
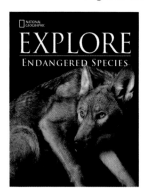

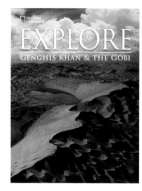
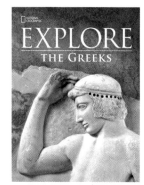

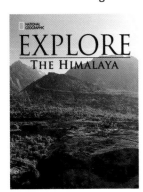
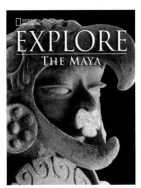
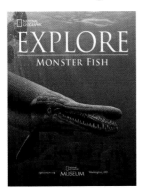
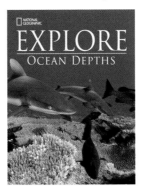
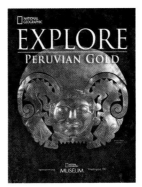

GLOBAL ISSUES

GLOBAL ISSUES: POPULATION GROWTH

aligns to these sections of World History

ALL LEVELS

NG at Work: New Plants to Feed the World

Chapter 1, Lesson 2.2
The Beginnings of Domestication

Chapter 1, Lesson 2.3
The Agricultural Revolution

Chapter 2, Lesson 1.4
Mesoamerica: Oaxaca

Chapter 4, Lesson 1.2 Agriculture Develops

Chapter 23, Lesson 2.5
The Columbian Exchange

ABOVE LEVEL

South Korea's Aging Population

Chapter 20, Lesson 1.4 Korea's Culture

GLOBAL ISSUES: GLOBALIZATION

aligns to these sections of World History

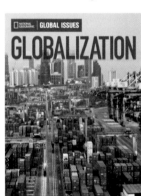

AT LEVEL

South Korea: Toward a Brighter Future

Chapter 20, Lesson 1.4
Korea's Culture

GLOBAL ISSUES: STANDARD OF LIVING

aligns to these sections of World History

BELOW LEVEL

Haiti's Struggle to Overcome Poverty

Chapter 23, Lesson 2.1
An Expanding World

ON LEVEL

Living Well in Costa Rica

Chapter 23, Lesson 2.1
An Expanding World

ABOVE LEVEL

Slow Progress in the Dominican Republic

Chapter 23, Lesson 2.1 An Expanding World

GLOBAL ISSUES: FOOD SUPPLY

aligns to these sections of World History

ALL LEVELS

NG at Work: A "Green" Approach to Relieving Hunger

Chapter 1, Lesson 2.2
The Beginnings of Domestication

Chapter 1, Lesson 2.3
The Agricultural Revolution

Chapter 2, Lesson 1.4 Mesoamerica: Oaxaca

Chapter 4, Lesson 1.2 Agriculture Develops

Chapter 23, Lesson 2.5 The Columbian Exchange

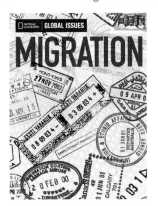
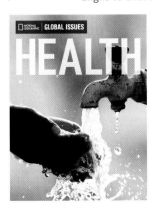
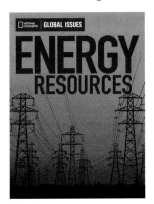
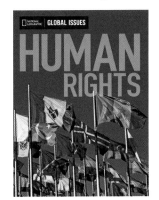

GLOBAL ISSUES: WATER RESOURCES

aligns to these sections of World History

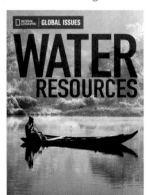

ALL LEVELS

NG at Work: Marine Protected Areas and Water Pollution

> **Stories Making History**
> Into the Okavango:
> A Live-Data Expedition

BELOW LEVEL

Cleaning Up Lake Titicaca

> **Chapter 17, Lesson 1.3** Inca Society and Government
>
> **Chapter 23, Lesson 3.1** The Spanish Conquest

Dolphins in Danger in the Mekong

> **Chapter 20, Lesson 2.1** Vietnamese Kingdoms
>
> **Stories Making History** Into the Okavango: A Live-Data Expedition

ON LEVEL

Protecting the Amazon

> **Chapter 23, Lesson 3.2** Portugal's Empire

China's Powerful Rivers

> **Chapter 2, Lesson 1.3** China: Banpo
>
> **Chapter 7, Lesson 1.1** The Geography of Ancient China

ABOVE LEVEL

Rescuing Lake Maracaibo

> **Chapter 23, Lesson 3.1** The Spanish Conquest
>
> **Stories Making History** Into the Okavango: A Live-Data Expedition

GLOBAL ISSUES: CLIMATE CHANGE

aligns to these sections of World History

ALL LEVELS

NG at Work: Exploring Antarctica's Ocean

> **Chapter 1, Lesson 1.3**
> Changing Environments
>
> **Chapter 1, Lesson 1.4**
> Moving into New Environments

WRITE ABOUT HISTORY

In order to succeed in their academic and professional lives, students must be able to write clearly and effectively in a variety of different modes—convincing arguments, meaningful informational/explanatory texts, and compelling narratives. Strong writers also need to take task, purpose, and audience into consideration and choose their words, information, organization, and format accordingly.

The "Write About History" prompts in the *National Geographic World History: Great Civilizations* Student Edition give students the opportunity to practice writing and defending claims while simultaneously showing what they have learned about events in world history. Each Chapter Review ends with a prompt that provides the support necessary to produce a well-crafted piece of academic writing.

Students are asked to produce one of three forms: a narrative, an informational/explanatory text, or an argument.

Instructions provide students with context for task, purpose, and audience.

Tips provide instruction on how to create the final product.

WRITE ABOUT HISTORY

26. **ARGUMENT** What arguments might a senator favoring Julius Caesar's assassination make? What arguments might a senator opposing his assassination make? Create an outline that lists points supporting each side.

TIPS

- Take notes from the chapter about Caesar's actions as a ruler and the manner of his death.

- Consider who benefited from Caesar's reforms and who benefited from his death.

- Consider how the Romans might have felt when Caesar declared himself dictator for life.

- Use vocabulary from the chapter in your outline.

- List the points that support assassination in the first part of your outline. List the points that support opposition to the assassination in the second part.

INTRODUCING
NATIONAL GEOGRAPHIC
LEARNING FRAMEWORK

The *National Geographic World History: Great Civilizations* program is one of the first products to feature the National Geographic Learning Framework. The Learning Framework is an educational foundation based on research and perspectives from diverse fields of knowledge. It recognizes the distinct core principles and focus areas established at National Geographic along with the values held by families, communities, educators, and cultures.

The Learning Framework provides a common language that defines learning along three dimensions: the **Attitudes**, **Skills**, and **Knowledge** (A.S.K.) of "explorers" of all types, from the National Geographic Explorers featured in this World History program, to curious students exploring the world around them. The Learning Framework provides a way to ensure that educators, parents, and the National Geographic Society are working toward common learning goals, and informs how we measure the impact of National Geographic products and resources.

THE LEARNING FRAMEWORK'S A.S.K. DIMENSIONS

The chart below outlines the Attitudes, Skills, and Knowledge (A.S.K.) dimensions of the National Geographic Learning Framework, as it applies to the *World History* program.

ATTITUDES Feelings we want students to express and experience during the activity	SKILLS What we want students to do during the activity	KNOWLEDGE The type of content the activity pertains to
Curiosity	Observation	Our Human Story
Responsibility	Communication	Our Living Planet
Empowerment	Collaboration	Critical Species
	Problem-Solving	New Frontiers

ATTITUDES

Curiosity. An explorer remains curious about how the world works throughout his or her life. An explorer is adventurous, seeking out new and challenging experiences.

Responsibility. An explorer has concern and empathy for the welfare of other people, cultural resources, and the natural world. An explorer is respectful, considers multiple perspectives, and honors others regardless of differences. An explorer is a global citizen.

Empowerment. An explorer acts on curiosity, respect, responsibility, and adventurousness and persists in the face of challenges.

SKILLS

Observation. An explorer notices and documents the world around her or him and is able to make sense of those observations.

Communication. An explorer is a storyteller, communicating experiences and ideas effectively through language and media. An explorer has literacy skills, interpreting and creating new understanding from spoken language, writing, and a wide variety of visual and audio media.

Collaboration. An explorer works effectively with others to achieve goals.

Problem Solving. An explorer is able to generate, evaluate, and implement solutions to problems. An explorer is a capable decision-maker—able to identify alternatives and weigh trade-offs to make a well-reasoned decision.

KNOWLEDGE

In addition to the skills and attitudes of an explorer, people need to understand how our ever-changing and interconnected world works in order to function effectively and act responsibly as a global citizen. Critical knowledge required of explorers can be expressed through the four National Geographic key focus areas:

Our Human Story. Exploring where we came from, how we live today, and where we may find ourselves tomorrow.

Our Living Planet. Understanding the amazing, intricate, and interconnected systems of the changing planet we live on, its geography, and how the planet impacts living organisms and cultures.

Critical Species. Revealing, celebrating, and helping to protect the amazing and diverse species with which we share our world. Appreciating the impact human history has had on other species.

New Frontiers. Throughout history, searching every day for the "new" and the "next," using the latest technology and science to go places no one has ever been and find answers no one has ever found.

NATIONAL GEOGRAPHIC LEARNING FRAMEWORK AND WORLD HISTORY

The *National Geographic World History: Great Civilizations* Teacher's eEdition includes in-depth material for planning and instruction, as well as a variety of differentiated activities for each lesson. Activities based on the National Geographic Learning Framework (see examples below) are part of the "Active Options" section of each lesson. They provide students with the opportunity to engage with the world history content within the dimensions of the Learning Framework.

National Geographic Learning Framework:

Compare Soldiers' Gear

ATTITUDES **Responsibility**

SKILLS **Collaboration, Communication**

Pair students up and instruct them to use a Venn Diagram to compare a Roman soldier's gear to a modern soldier's gear and discuss the similarities and differences. Have each group present their similarity findings to the rest of the class.

National Geographic Learning Framework:

Learn More About Tsunamis

SKILLS **Collaboration**

KNOWLEDGE **Our Living Planet**

Encourage students to work together to find out more about tsunamis. Place them in pairs and have them use the Internet to find out more about what causes tsunamis, where they have occurred, and how they affect the environment after they occur. Call on student pairs to present their findings to the class. Encourage them to include a minimum of two visuals with their oral reports.

National Geographic Learning Framework:

Write About Craftmanship

ATTITUDES **Curiosity**

KNOWLEDGE **Our Human Story**

Have students select one of the forms of craftsmanship or artistic expression (such as pottery or metallurgy) that they are still curious about after reading this chapter. Instruct them to write a short description of this form of craftsmanship or artistic expression using information from the chapter and additional source material.

National Geographic Learning Framework:

Write an Epic Poem

ATTITUDES **Curiosity**

SKILLS **Communication**

Invite students to think of an adventure they have experienced that could be the subject of a modern epic poem. Have them sketch out an outline of the events, heroes and heroines, and problems that they encountered in their adventures. Encourage students to tell their stories with a partner or in small groups.

National Geographic Learning Framework:

Teach Your Methods

ATTITUDES **Responsibility**

SKILLS **Collaboration**

Assign students to several small groups. Ask each group to come up with a method of doing something they do everyday (such as doing making their lunch, making their bed, or doing their homework). Then have groups share their methods with other groups. Encourage groups to use good listening skills and have them take notes on the different methods presented. To conclude the activity, ask the original groups to reconsider their methods and discuss how they might change them based on other groups' ideas.

National Geographic Learning Framework:

Rank the Traits

ATTITUDES **Empowerment**

SKILLS **Problem-Solving**

Invite students to review the text and visuals in Lesson 2.2. Ask students to consider the five traits of civilization and then rank them in order of importance. Once they have completed their list of rankings, encourage students to share their lists with the class. Write their responses on the board and have students explain how they decided to rank their traits.

NATIONAL GEOGRAPHIC STUDENTS ARE...
- Curious and adventurous
- Responsible for others and the natural world
- Empowered and persistent in the face of challenges

NATIONAL GEOGRAPHIC STUDENTS CAN...
- Observe the world around them
- Communicate effectively through language and media
- Work effectively with others
- Solve problems they encounter

NATIONAL GEOGRAPHIC
Students are
Explorers!

COOPERATIVE LEARNING STRATEGIES

Cooperative learning strategies transform today's classroom diversity into a vital resource for promoting students' acquisition of both challenging academic content and language. These strategies promote active engagement and social motivation for all students.

STRUCTURE & GRAPHIC	DESCRIPTION	BENEFITS & PURPOSES
CORNERS A strongly agree B disagree C agree D strongly disagree	• Corners of the classroom are designated for focused discussion of four aspects of a topic. • Students individually think and write about the topic for a short time. • Students group into the corner of their choice and discuss the topic. • At least one student from each corner shares about the corner discussion.	• By "voting" with their feet, students literally take a position about a topic. • Focused discussion develops deeper thought about a topic. • Students experience many valid points of view about a topic.
FISHBOWL	• Part of the class sits in a close circle facing inward; the other part of the class sits in a larger circle around them. • Students on the inside discuss a topic while those outside listen for new information and/or evaluate the discussion according to pre-established criteria. • Groups reverse positions.	• Focused listening enhances knowledge acquisition and listening skills. • Peer evaluation supports development of specific discussion skills. • Identification of criteria for evaluation promotes self-monitoring.
INSIDE-OUTSIDE CIRCLE	• Students stand in concentric circles facing each other. • Students in the outside circle ask questions; those inside answer. • On a signal, students rotate to create new partnerships. • On another signal, students trade inside/outside roles.	• Talking one-on-one with a variety of partners gives risk-free practice in speaking skills. • Interactions can be structured to focus on specific speaking skills. • Students practice both speaking and active listening.
JIGSAW Expert Group 1 — A's Expert Group 2 — B's Expert Group 3 — C's Expert Group 4 — D's	• Group students evenly into "expert" groups. • Expert groups study one topic or aspect of a topic in depth. • Regroup students so that each new group has at least one member from each expert group. • Experts report on their study. Other students learn from the experts.	• Becoming an expert provides in-depth understanding in one aspect of study. • Learning from peers provides breadth of understanding of over-arching concepts.

STRUCTURE & GRAPHIC	DESCRIPTION	BENEFITS & PURPOSES
NUMBERED HEADS 	· Students number off within each group. · Teacher prompts or gives a directive. · Students think individually about the topic. · Groups discuss the topic so that any member of the group can report for the group. · Teacher calls a number and the student with that number reports for the group.	· Group discussion of topics provides each student with language and concept understanding. · Random recitation provides an opportunity for evaluation of both individual and group progress.
ROUNDTABLE 	· Seat students around a table in groups of four. · Teacher asks a question with many possible answers. · Each student around the table answers the question a different way.	· Encouraging elaboration creates appreciation for diversity of opinion and thought. · Eliciting multiple answers enhances language fluency.
TEAM WORD WEBBING 	· Provide each team with a single large piece of paper. Give each student a different colored marker. · Teacher assigns a topic for a word web. · Each student adds to the part of the web nearest to him/her. · On a signal, students rotate the paper and each student adds to the nearest part again.	· Individual input to a group product ensures participation by all students. · Shifting point of view support both broad and in-depth understanding of concepts.
THINK, PAIR, SHARE 	· Students think about a topic suggested by the teacher. · Pairs discuss the topic. · Students individually share information with the class.	· The opportunity for self-talk during the individual think time allows the student to formulate thoughts before speaking. · Discussion with a partner reduces performance anxiety and enhances understanding.
THREE-STEP INTERVIEW 	· Students form pairs. · Student A interviews Student B about a topic. · Partners reverse roles. · Student A shares with the class information from Student B; then B shares information from Student A.	· Interviewing supports language acquisition by providing scripts for expression. · Responding provides opportunities for structured self-expression.

WORLD HISTORY
GREAT CIVILIZATIONS

TEACHER'S EDITION

This easy-to-navigate Teacher's Edition follows a predictable pattern of units, chapters, and lessons. Easily readable Student Edition pages are included alongside the corresponding teacher material.

UNIT INTRODUCTION AND WRAP-UP

Each unit opens with six pages of introductory material, including an introduction by a National Geographic Explorer and a time line and map that relate to the historical period featured in the unit.

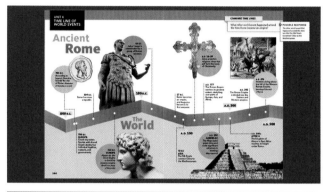

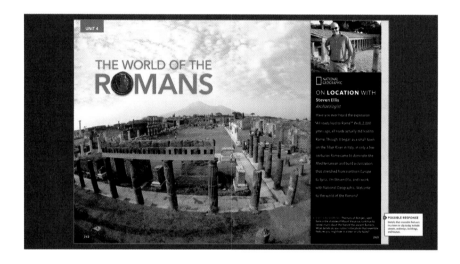

The unit wraps up with four pages of National Geographic-related content, including a feature on the Unit Explorer and his/her work, an adapted National Geographic article, and a Unit Inquiry project (with evaluation rubric).

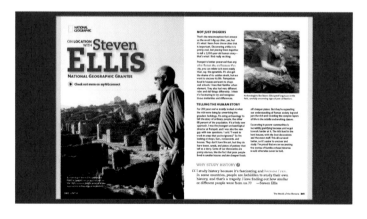

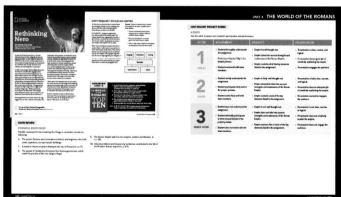

CHAPTER PLANNER

The two-page Chapter Planner outlines the instructional material that exists at the Unit, Chapter, and Lesson levels, including digital resources that are accessible on myNGconnect.

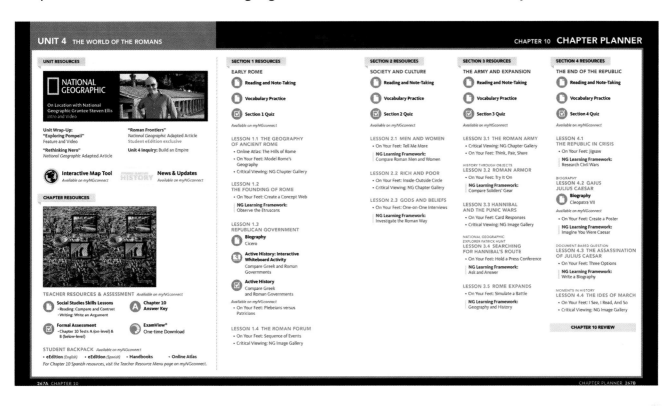

STRATEGIES FOR DIFFERENTIATION

Every student learns in his or her unique way. Five different types of Strategies for Differentiation help teachers appropriately engage every learner with the program content.

- Striving Readers
- Inclusion
- English Language Learners
- Gifted & Talented
- Pre-AP

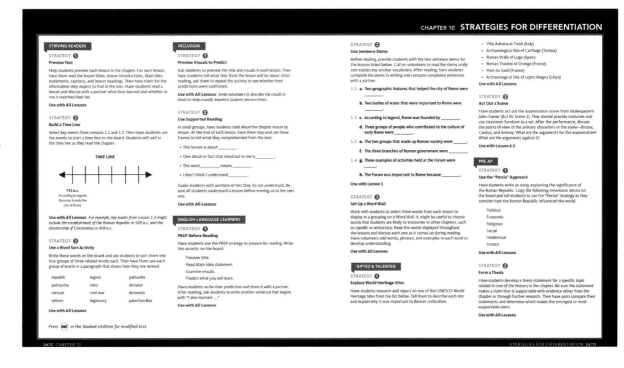

CHAPTER INTRODUCTION

The Chapter Introduction provides an entry point into the chapter, along with introductory activities and questions about the content.

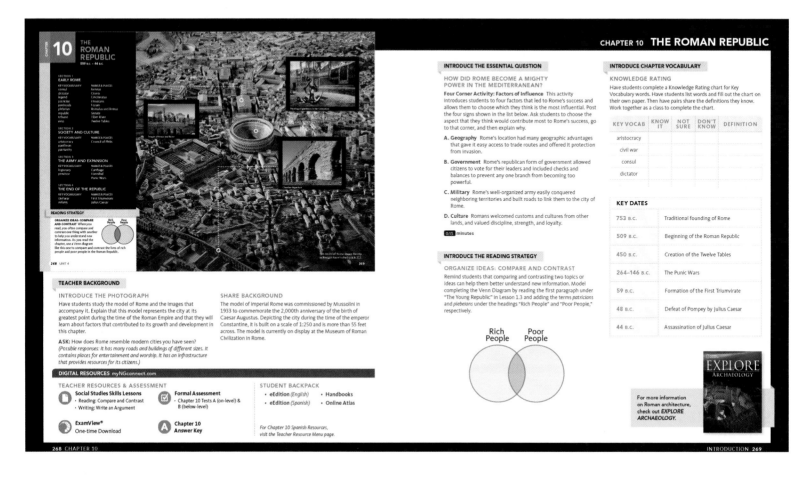

Teacher Background

- Background information helps introduce the Chapter Introduction visual.
- Supporting digital resources are available on myNGconnect.

Introduce the Essential Question

- A cooperative learning activity introduces the Essential Question and provides options for further inquiry.

Introduce the Reading Strategy

- A graphic organizer helps students focus their reading based on the chapter reading strategy.

Introduce Chapter Vocabulary

- A strategy-based activity helps introduce students to content-area vocabulary.

Key Dates

- Key dates correspond to the content in the chapter and serve as a handy chronological reference.

CHAPTER LESSONS

Lessons provide rich teacher material alongside Student Edition pages
to make planning, teaching, and differentiating instruction easy.

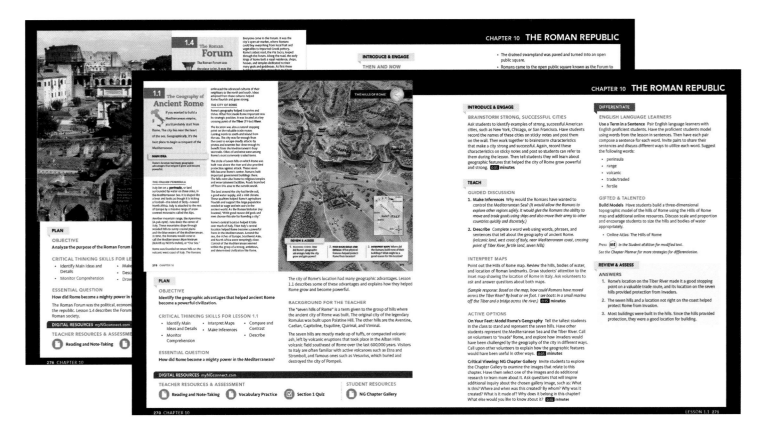

Plan

- Strong lessons center around a clear objective and critical thinking skills.
- Consider the chapter's Essential Question as you teach each lesson.
- Valuable background information helps teachers prep for instruction.
- Supporting digital resources are available at myNGconnect.

Introduce & Engage

- A quick activity invites student participation and serves as an entry point for lesson instruction.

Teach

- Guided Discussion questions build on lesson content.
- A lesson-based activity provides an option for students to interact with visuals or further process information.
- Active Options activities allow students to get up and move or explore the digital resources available at myNGconnect.

Differentiate

- Activities tailored to specific learning groups help all students explore the content appropriately and effectively.

Review & Assess

- Answers to Student Edition questions are provided for easy assessment of student comprehension.

CHAPTER REVIEW

The answers to Chapter Review questions are conveniently provided alongside the Student Edition pages so teachers can easily refer to chapter questions and answers.

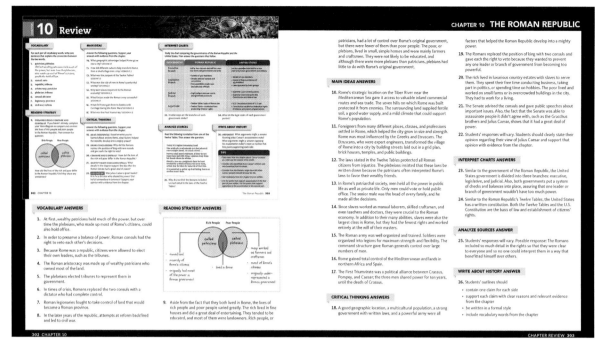

ANCILLARIES AND ASSESSMENT

In addition to the content in this Teacher's Edition, a wealth of supporting ancillaries and formal assessment options are provided at myNGconnect (available with a digital subscription).

Unit Resources
- National Geographic Explorer videos
- Additional adapted National Geographic articles
- Interactive Map Tool

Chapter Resources
- Social Studies Skills Lessons (reading and writing)
- Formal Assessment Chapter Tests (two leveled versions)
- Chapter Answer Key (for ancillaries and assessment)
- ExamView® Assessment Software
- Backpack Page (containing Handbooks and the Online Atlas)

Lesson Resources
- Section Quizzes
- Reading and Note-Taking activities
- Vocabulary Practice activities
- Biographies
- Active History lessons (available as printable activity sheets or interactive whiteboard activities)

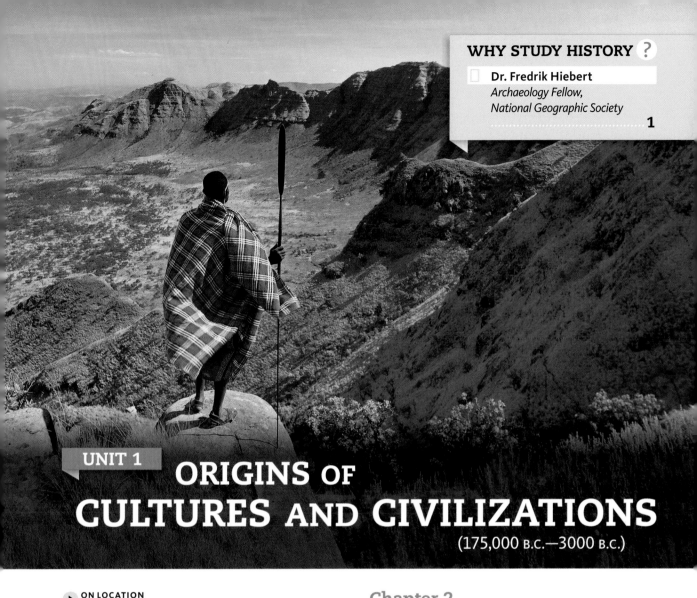

UNIT 1

ORIGINS OF CULTURES AND CIVILIZATIONS

(175,000 B.C.—3000 B.C.)

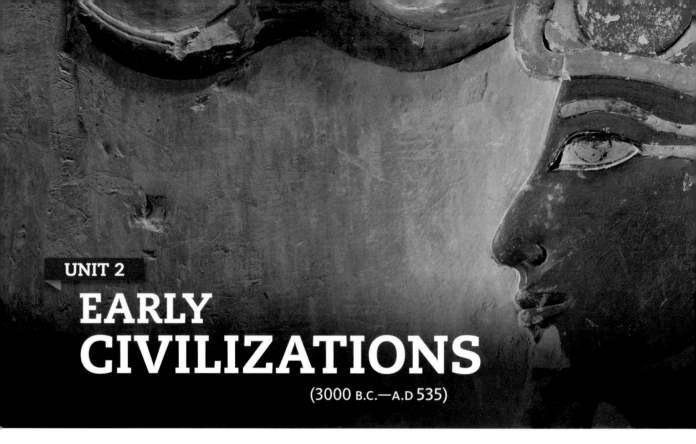

UNIT 2
EARLY CIVILIZATIONS
(3000 B.C.—A.D 535)

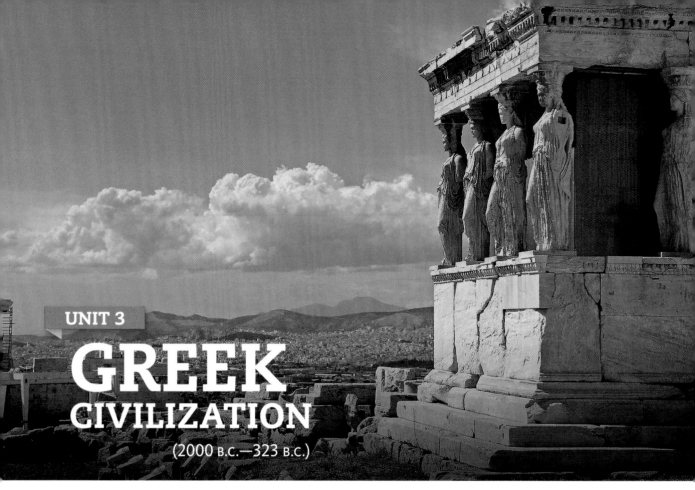

UNIT 3
GREEK CIVILIZATION
(2000 B.C.—323 B.C.)

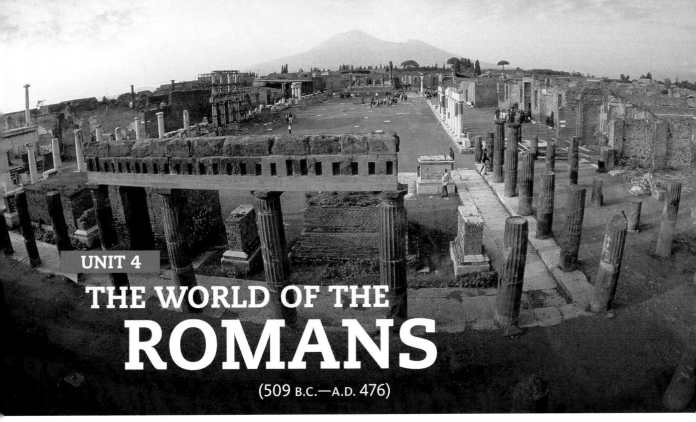

UNIT 5
BYZANTINE AND ISLAMIC CIVILIZATIONS
(330—1858)

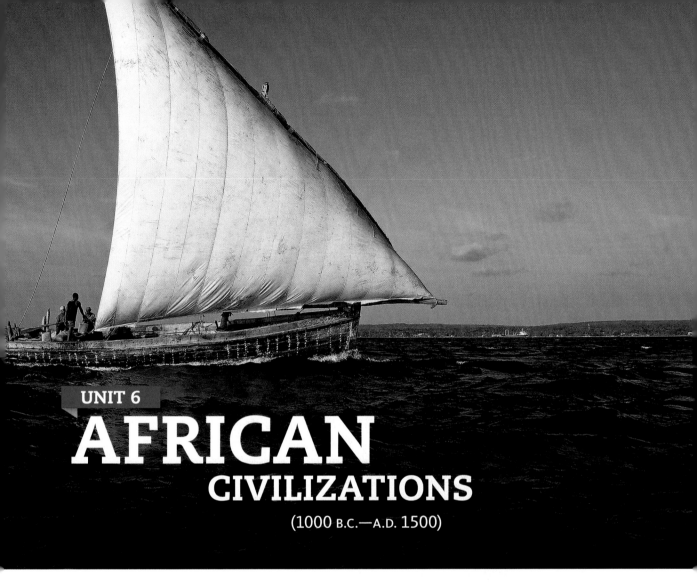

UNIT 6
AFRICAN
CIVILIZATIONS
(1000 B.C.—A.D. 1500)

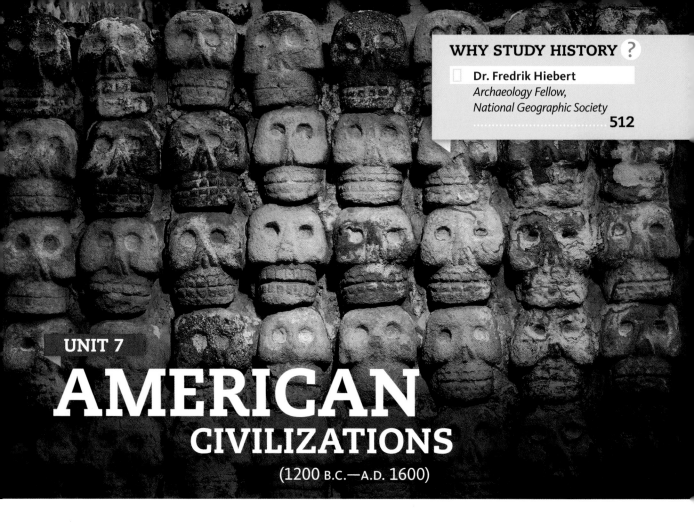

UNIT 7

AMERICAN
CIVILIZATIONS

(1200 B.C.—A.D. 1600)

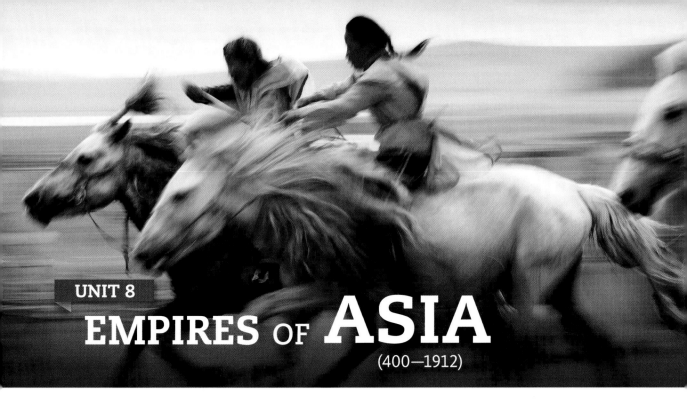

WHY STUDY HISTORY **?**

Dr. Fredrik Hiebert
*Archaeology Fellow,
National Geographic Society*
.... **690**

UNIT 9

MEDIEVAL AND RENAISSANCE EUROPE

(500—1700)

The world changes on a daily basis, and National Geographic is there. Join five National Geographic voices as they tell the stories of five current global events. Learn about these newsworthy topics, discuss what might come next, and think about how these events impact you, the place you live, and the people you know—your global citizenship.

SPECIAL FEATURES

NATIONAL GEOGRAPHIC EXPLORER LESSONS

Hayat Sindi

PRIMARY AND SECONDARY SOURCES: OBJECTS AND EXCERPTS

Passport Medallion

Statue of Julius Caesar

MAPS

DOCUMENT-BASED QUESTIONS

TIME LINES, CHARTS, MODELS, GRAPHS, INFOGRAPHICS

Feudal Society

MOMENTS IN HISTORY

Terra Cotta Warriors

WHY STUDY HISTORY ?

Hi! I'm Fred Hiebert, National Geographic's Archaeology Fellow. We're about to embark on a journey all over the world and back through time—the history of the world as we know it today.

So why do we study past civilizations? The basis of civilization is identity—who we are and what we stand for. We express identity by creating unique ways to be housed and fed and to thrive. The basic building blocks of civilization are the same around the world: what kinds of plants and animals to tend and consume, how to find enough water, and how to survive the changes of the seasons. All core civilizations— from China, India, and Mesopotamia, to Europe and Mesoamerica— struggled with these issues.

Look at the sculptures shown below. These prehistoric "selfies" reveal a universal need to think about ourselves—in relation to the environment, the future, our religious beliefs—that dates from the earliest civilizations.

THE HUMAN EPIC

Historians, archaeologists, and anthropologists constantly update the story of human civilizations as new data surfaces from the latest dig site or the most recent scholarship. The Framework of World History at right is only one way to think about how human identity developed—there are many pathways from the past to the present.

I've lived and worked all over the world in lots of different cultures, and I know first-hand that you and others your age are more alike than you are different. You share the same need to understand yourself, your family, and your community and the same urge to hope and plan for your future. Your generation may be one of the first to truly be considered global citizens.

◀ **ARTEMIS**
This Greek marble sculpture dating back to the 4th century B.C. is known as *Artemis Hunting*.

◀ **NEFERTITI**
The bust of this famous Egyptian queen and wife of Pharaoh Akhenaten was sculpted more than 3,300 years ago.

Fred Hiebert
▶ Watch the Why Study History video

The ancient cave painting in the background is located in Snake Cave in Australia. An Aboriginal artist created it by blowing pigment over his or her hand, leaving a blank hand shape.

◀ **TERRA COTTA BUDDHA**
This 5-foot tall statue was discovered at the site of Hadda in Afghanistan.

FRAMEWORK OF WORLD HISTORY

The model below is one way to view the development of civilizations. For all cultures, it's not just the famous leaders who make history—it's all of us, through small actions that grow into world-changing events and ideas.

1 ## CORE CIVILIZATIONS
Humans begin to think about where they live, what they eat, and what they believe in—and plan for the future. Across the centuries and in all world cultures, humans use these building blocks to think about who they are and where they come from—the beginning of identity.

2 ## PRIMARY CIVILIZATIONS
Humans develop more effective responses to their environment, creating irrigation and other farming methods that make agriculture more predictable and more productive. People are able to form groups and move together, and eventually cities develop.

3 ## SECONDARY CIVILIZATIONS
Human understanding of identity comes into focus, and writing develops partly as an expression of identity. Codes of law and better rulers come to the forefront as cultures take on characteristics that embody those identities.

4 ## WORLD SYSTEMS
Civilizations reach out to each other, and trade develops along what would eventually be called the Silk Roads. The urge to move results in new road systems, new country borders with border guards, and new systems of taxation.

1

WHY STUDY HISTORY ?

TO BECOME A GLOBAL CITIZEN

As you study world history, you're going to meet some National Geographic Explorers along the way—men and women who are making incredible contributions to our lives through their work. Studying world history is part of what they do because they believe they can add to our understanding of the human story. Here are just a few.

MICHAEL COSMOPOULOS ▶
Cosmopoulos directs two major excavations exploring the origins of states and social complexity in Greece.

◀ WILLIAM SATURNO
Saturno supervises excavations in the jungles of Guatemala and determines the architectural history of a site by studying the little pieces that remain.

LOUISE LEAKEY ▲
Paleontologist Louise Leakey is responsible for some of the most important hominid fossils discovered in East Africa in the past two decades.

BECOME PART OF THE GLOBAL CONVERSATION!

Think About It

1. In what ways are you a global citizen?

2. Describe a situation or problem in which you think people should strive for global citizenship. What actions do you think should be taken to solve the problem?

3. Pick one action you named above and explain how you would go about accomplishing it. Develop a detailed action plan that could be put in place to make this happen.

STEVEN ELLIS ▶
Ellis directs the excavation of a working-class district in Pompeii, focusing on the use of public and private space and the role of ordinary people in the life of the ancient city.

◀ SARAH PARCAK
Parcak combines advanced technology such as satellite archaeology with good old-fashioned digging to reveal new Egyptian sites, including temples, pyramids, and tombs.

FUTURE EXPLORER ▶
WILL THIS BE YOU?

Write About It

SYNTHESIZE What does **identity** mean to you? Answer this question in two or three paragraphs in your notebook. Be sure to include your definition of identity, explain the various parts that make up your identity, and describe how you express your identity. Then designate a spot in your notebook where you can record how your understanding of identity changes as you read each chapter.

MAKE CONNECTIONS What different types of identities do you notice in your school and community? Create a chart that represents these identities and write your description of each.

ASK AND ANSWER QUESTIONS Imagine that you are at a panel discussion that includes the Explorers shown above. Write three questions you would like to ask the panel, including specific questions for individual Explorers.

+ PREVIEW UNITS 1 AND 2

As they read Units 1 and 2 in their textbook, have students complete pages 9-15 in their Field Journal to process the material in these units. Remind students that they will use their Field Journal as they read each Why Study History? section and explore the historical record. They will record their thoughts about what they've read and fit them into the larger picture of world history. They will also use the journal to consider how they fit into that big picture and what it means to be a global citizen.

ORIGINS OF
CULTURES AND
CIVILIZATIONS

NATIONAL
GEOGRAPHIC

ON **LOCATION** WITH

Louise Leakey
Paleontologist

One of the first jobs of a paleontologist is finding a good place to dig. We look for places where fossilized bones, buried long ago by rivers and lakes, have been brought to the surface by tectonic activity and erosion. Lake Turkana in Kenya's Great Rift Valley is the world's best field laboratory for fossil discoveries going back several million years. My family has been working in this profession for three generations, uncovering the bones of human ancestors and other animals that lived in this region in the past. I'm Louise Leakey, and I help investigate and share the human story.

 CRITICAL VIEWING A shepherd gazes out over East Africa's Great Rift Valley. How might the geography of the valley help archaeologists carry out their work?

+ POSSIBLE RESPONSE

The valley is relatively flat and empty of vegetation, so it provides a clear site in which to dig.

The World

c. 10,000 B.C.
As the last Ice Age comes to an end, animals such as the woolly mammoth die out.

c. 15,000 B.C.
Lascaux Cave paintings are created.

c. 68,000 B.C.
Groups of modern humans begin to migrate out of Africa.

20,000 B.C.

175,000 B.C.

c. 9600 B.C.
Göbekli Tepe, the world's first temple, is built in present-day Turkey.
(Göbekli Tepe pillar)

What similar events took place within 1,000 years in Egypt and Mesopotamia?

+ POSSIBLE RESPONSE
Agriculture began in both places.

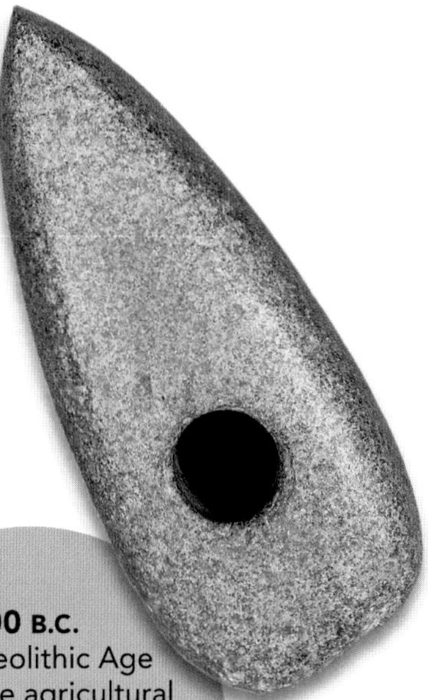

c. 5000 B.C.
Yangshao culture flourishes along the Huang and Wei rivers in China.
(Yangshao pottery)

c. 9000 B.C.
The Neolithic Age and the agricultural revolution begin. Farmers develop tools made of sharpened stone.

c. 5200 B.C.
Egypt's earliest farming community develops at Faiyum.

5000 B.C.

4500 B.C.

c. 7400 B.C.
Çatalhöyük develops in present-day Turkey.

c. 4250 B.C.
The maize revolution begins in Mesoamerica.

7

THE LAST
ICE AGE
18,000 B.C.–10,000 B.C.

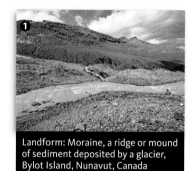

Landform: Moraine, a ridge or mound of sediment deposited by a glacier, Bylot Island, Nunavut, Canada

Landform: Glacier cave, Patagonia, Argentina

For much of history, Earth has been a cold place. It has endured long periods, called Ice Ages, during which temperatures dropped and slow-moving masses of ice called glaciers formed. The last Ice Age, which began more than two million years ago, reached its height in 18,000 B.C. Around this time, glaciers covered large areas of the world. By 12,000 B.C., the overall temperature of Earth had warmed, and much of the ice had melted. By 10,000 B.C., our world looked much the way it does now and had a climate similar to today's. As you can see in the photos, glacial movement also formed bodies of water and landforms that still make up Earth's landscape.

What continents were not affected by the last Ice Age? How can you tell?

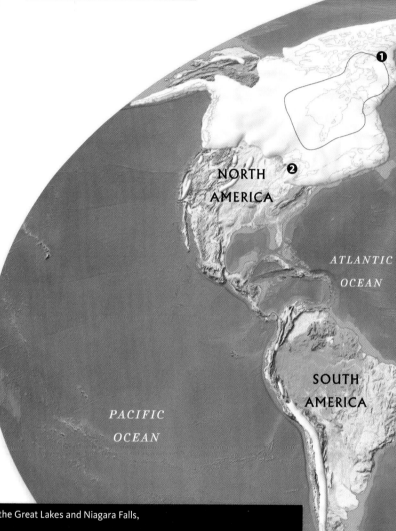

NORTH AMERICA

ATLANTIC OCEAN

SOUTH AMERICA

PACIFIC OCEAN

This series shows how moving ice sheets formed the Great Lakes and Niagara Falls, a process that took thousands of years.

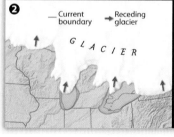

Current boundary — Receding glacier

GLACIER

GLACIER

Lake Superior — Ontario
Wisconsin
Lake Michigan
Lake Huron
Niagara Falls, N.Y.
Lake Ontario
Illinois
Indiana
Ohio
Lake Erie
Finger Lakes
Pennsylvania

Landform: Fjord, a deep glacial trough that filled with seawater, Norway

Landform: Glacial valley, Fagaras Mountains, Romania

Landform: Sediment-filled glacier, Karakoram, Himalaya

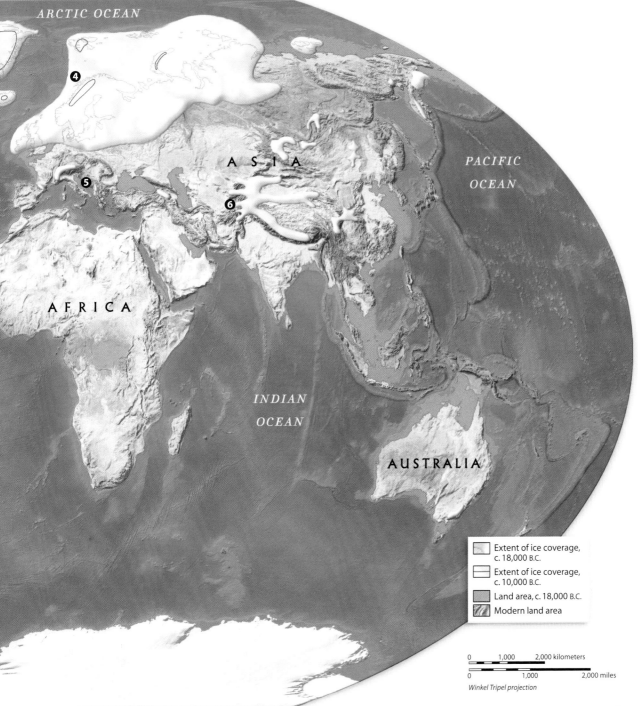

ARCTIC OCEAN

ASIA

PACIFIC OCEAN

AFRICA

INDIAN OCEAN

AUSTRALIA

Extent of ice coverage, c. 18,000 B.C.

Extent of ice coverage, c. 10,000 B.C.

Land area, c. 18,000 B.C.

Modern land area

0   1,000   2,000 kilometers

0   1,000   2,000 miles

Winkel Tripel projection

UNIT RESOURCES

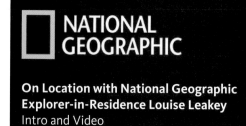

NATIONAL GEOGRAPHIC

On Location with National Geographic
Explorer-in-Residence Louise Leakey
Intro and Video

**Interactive
Map Tool**

**STORIES MAKING
HISTORY** **News
& Updates**

Available on myNGconnect

**Unit Wrap-Up:
"Discovering Our Ancestors"**
Feature and Video

"First Americans"
National Geographic Adapted Article
Student eEdition exclusive

"Scotland's Stone Age Ruins"
National Geographic Adapted Article

Unit 1 Inquiry:
Create a Cultural Symbol

CHAPTER RESOURCES

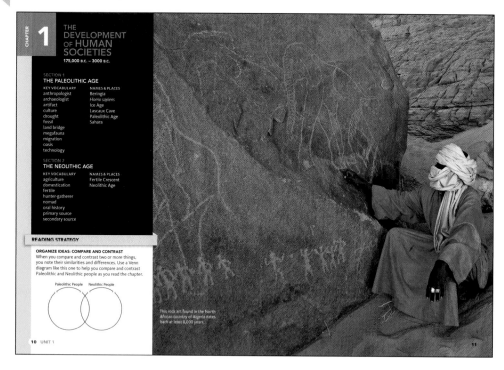

CHAPTER **1**

THE
DEVELOPMENT
OF HUMAN
SOCIETIES
175,000 B.C. – 3000 B.C.

SECTION 1
THE PALEOLITHIC AGE
KEY VOCABULARY
anthropologist
archaeologist
artifact
culture
drought
fossil
land bridge
megafauna
migration
oasis
technology

NAMES & PLACES
Beringia
Homo sapiens
Ice Age
Lascaux Cave
Paleolithic Age
Sahara

SECTION 2
THE NEOLITHIC AGE
KEY VOCABULARY
agriculture
domestication
fertile
hunter-gatherer
nomad
oral history
primary source
secondary source

NAMES & PLACES
Fertile Crescent
Neolithic Age

READING STRATEGY

ORGANIZE IDEAS: COMPARE AND CONTRAST
When you compare and contrast two or more things,
you note their similarities and differences. Use a Venn
diagram like this one to help you compare and contrast
Paleolithic and Neolithic people as you read the chapter.

Paleolithic People   Neolithic People

This rock art found in the North
African country of Algeria dates
back at least 8,000 years.

10 UNIT 1

11

TEACHER RESOURCES & ASSESSMENT

Available on myNGconnect

 Social Studies Skills Lessons
• Reading: Compare and Contrast
• Writing: Write an Explanation

 Formal Assessment
• Chapter 1 Tests A (on-level) & B (below-level)

 **Chapter 1
Answer Key**

 ExamView®
One-time Download

STUDENT BACKPACK *Available on myNGconnect*

• **eEdition** *(English)*   • **eEdition** *(Spanish)*   • **Handbooks**   • **Online Atlas**

For Chapter 1 Spanish resources, visit the Teacher Resource Menu page on myNGconnect.

SECTION 1 RESOURCES

THE PALEOLITHIC AGE

 Reading and Note-Taking

 Vocabulary Practice

 Section 1 Quiz

Available on myNGconnect

LESSON 1.1 DISCOVERING PREHISTORY

 Biography
Richard Leakey   *Available on myNGconnect*
- On Your Feet: Inside-Outside Circle
- Critical Viewing: NG Chapter Gallery

LESSON 1.2 THE ELEMENTS OF CULTURE

- On Your Feet: Four Corners
- Critical Viewing: NG Image Gallery

LESSON 1.3 CHANGING ENVIRONMENTS

- On Your Feet: Three-Step Interview
- Critical Viewing: NG Chapter Gallery

LESSON 1.4 MOVING INTO NEW ENVIRONMENTS

 Active History: Interactive Whiteboard Activity
Compare Past and Present Land Areas

 Active History
Compare Past and Present Land Areas

Available on myNGconnect

| **NG Learning Framework:**
Research a Critical Species

NATIONAL GEOGRAPHIC
EXPLORER JEFFREY ROSE
LESSON 1.5 TRACKING MIGRATION OUT OF AFRICA

- On Your Feet: Rotating Discussion

| **NG Learning Framework:**
Write a Biography

LESSON 1.6 CAVE ART

- On Your Feet: Question and Answer
- Critical Viewing: NG Image Gallery

SECTION 2 RESOURCES

THE NEOLITHIC AGE

 Reading and Note-Taking

 Vocabulary Practice

 Section 2 Quiz

Available on myNGconnect

LESSON 2.1 NOMADIC HUNTER-GATHERERS

- On Your Feet: Word Chain

| **NG Learning Framework:**
Hunting and Gathering

LESSON 2.2 THE BEGINNINGS OF DOMESTICATION

- On Your Feet: Turn and Talk on Topic
- Critical Viewing: NG Chapter Gallery

LESSON 2.3 THE AGRICULTURAL REVOLUTION

 Biography
Dame Kathleen Kenyon

Available on myNGconnect

- On Your Feet: Numbered Heads

| **NG Learning Framework:**
Observe, Exchange, and Discuss

LESSON 2.4 STUDYING THE PAST

- On Your Feet: Three Corners
- Critical Viewing: NG Chapter Gallery

CHAPTER 1 REVIEW

STRATEGY ①
Turn Titles into Questions

To help students set a purpose for reading, have them read the title of each lesson in a section and then turn that title into a question they believe will be answered in the lesson. Students can record their questions and write their own answers, or they can ask each other their questions.

Use with All Lessons *For example, in Lesson 1.2 the question could be, "What are the elements of culture?"*

STRATEGY ②
Use a TASKS Approach

Help students get information from visuals by using the following TASKS strategy:

> **T** Look for a **title** that may give the main idea.
>
> **A** **Ask** yourself what the visual is trying to show.
>
> **S** Determine how **symbols** are used.
>
> **K** Look for a **key** or legend.
>
> **S** **Summarize** what you learned.

Use with All Lessons

STRATEGY ③
Play the "I Am . . ." Game

To reinforce the meanings of key terms and names, assign every student one term or name that appears in the chapter and have them write a one-sentence clue beginning with "I am." Have students take turns reading clues and calling on other students to guess answers.

Use with All Lessons

Press *in the Student eEdition for modified text.*

STRATEGY ①
Provide Terms and Names on Audio

Decide which of the terms and names are important for mastery and have a volunteer record the pronunciations and a short sentence defining each word. Encourage students to listen to the recording as often as necessary.

Use with All Lessons *You might also use the recordings to quiz students on their mastery of the terms. Play one definition at a time from the recording and ask students to identify the term or name described.*

STRATEGY ②
Preview Maps

Use the following suggestions to preview maps with students.

- Explain that some maps are political maps and show country boundaries and names.

- Remind students that physical maps highlight geographic features such as mountain ranges and bodies of land and water.

- Discuss what thematic maps do: show resources, population movement, historical boundaries, and other specialized information.

Use with Lessons 1.4, 1.5, 2.3, and the Chapter Review *For Lessons 1.4 and 2.3, have students explain what the thematic maps are showing. Have students make connections between the maps in Lesson 1.5 and the Chapter Review.*

ENGLISH LANGUAGE LEARNERS

STRATEGY 1

Create a Word Web

To activate prior knowledge and build vocabulary, work with students to create a Word Web for the word *culture* before beginning Section 1 and the word *agriculture* before beginning Section 2.

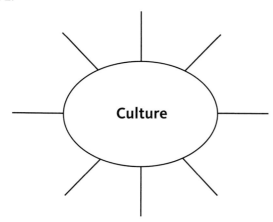

Use with Lessons 1.2 and 2.3 *For the web for* culture, *encourage students to offer words from their own backgrounds related to customs, holidays, food, music, religion, and celebrations.*

STRATEGY 2

Pair Partners for Dictation

After students read each lesson in the chapter, have them write a sentence summarizing its main idea. Have students get together in pairs and dictate their sentences to each other. Then have them work together to check the sentences for accuracy and spelling.

Use with All Lessons

STRATEGY 3

Use Visuals to Predict Content

Before reading, ask students to read the lesson title and look at any visuals. Then ask them to write a sentence that predicts how the visual is related to the lesson title. Repeat the exercise after reading and ask volunteers to read their sentences.

Use with All Lessons

GIFTED & TALENTED

STRATEGY 1

Teach a Class

Before beginning the chapter, allow students to choose one of the lessons listed below and prepare to teach the content to the class. Give them a set amount of time in which to present their lesson. Suggest that students think about any visuals or activities they want to use when they teach.

Use with Lessons 1.2, 1.4, 1.6, and 2.1–2.3

STRATEGY 2

Present a Museum Exhibit

Have groups of students prepare a museum exhibit featuring the paintings of Lascaux Cave in France. Have them photocopy images of the paintings and write museum-style captions for each one. Once students have compiled their exhibits, have them place the images on the wall and present them to the class. Encourage students to introduce the exhibit with some background information on Lascaux. Tell them that they should also be prepared to answer questions as their classmates view the exhibit.

Use with Lesson 1.6

PRE-AP

STRATEGY 1

Consider Two Sides

Tell students that some archaeologists believe the agricultural revolution was a catastrophe for the human race. Have pairs of students research the issue and make a chart listing the positive and negative effects of the revolution. Have students share and discuss their chart with the class.

Use with Lesson 2.3

STRATEGY 2

Create an Archaeology Time Line

Have pairs of students work together to create a time line identifying the archaeologists who have found fossils of modern humans. Tell students that the time line should begin with Richard Leakey's discovery in 1967.

Use with Lesson 1.1 *Encourage students to illustrate their time line with images of the expeditions and their findings.*

1

THE DEVELOPMENT OF HUMAN SOCIETIES

175,000 B.C. – 3000 B.C.

SECTION 1
THE PALEOLITHIC AGE

KEY VOCABULARY	NAMES & PLACES
anthropologist	Beringia
archaeologist	*Homo sapiens*
artifact	Ice Age
culture	Lascaux Cave
drought	Paleolithic Age
fossil	Sahara
land bridge	
megafauna	
migration	
oasis	
technology	

SECTION 2
THE NEOLITHIC AGE

KEY VOCABULARY	NAMES & PLACES
agriculture	Fertile Crescent
domestication	Neolithic Age
fertile	
hunter-gatherer	
nomad	
oral history	
primary source	
secondary source	

READING STRATEGY

ORGANIZE IDEAS: COMPARE AND CONTRAST
When you compare and contrast two or more things, you note their similarities and differences. Use a Venn diagram like this one to help you compare and contrast Paleolithic and Neolithic people as you read the chapter.

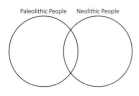

Paleolithic People   Neolithic People

This rock art found in the North African country of Algeria dates back at least 8,000 years.

TEACHER BACKGROUND

INTRODUCE THE PHOTOGRAPH

Have students study the photograph of rock art in Algeria. Explain that people who lived in prehistoric times carved these elephants into the rock. Tell students that, in this chapter, they will learn about the development and achievements of early humans who lived in that time—our ancestors. Then have students examine the tiny human figures in the foreground of the image.

ASK: What do you think is going on between the humans and elephants? *(Possible response: The human figures are preparing to kill the elephants.)*

SHARE BACKGROUND

This rock art was carved into Algeria's Tadrart Plateau, located in the Sahara. Today, of course, the Sahara is a dry region filled with sand, rocks, and mountains, but that's because the climate changed over the last 8,000 years or so. At the time these rocks were carved, the region was a lush savanna, and elephants, giraffes, ostriches, and camels made their home there.

DIGITAL RESOURCES myNGconnect.com

TEACHER RESOURCES & ASSESSMENT

 Social Studies Skills Lessons
· Reading: Compare and Contrast
· Writing: Write an Explanation

ExamView®
One-time Download

 Formal Assessment
Chapter 1 Tests A (on-level) & B (below-level)

A **Chapter 1 Answer Key**

STUDENT BACKPACK

· **eEdition** *(English)*   · **Handbooks**
· **eEdition** *(Spanish)*   · **Online Atlas**

For Chapter 1 Spanish Resources, visit the Teacher Resource Menu page.

INTRODUCE THE ESSENTIAL QUESTION

HOW DID PEOPLE MANAGE TO SURVIVE AND THRIVE TENS OF THOUSANDS OF YEARS AGO?

Roundtable Activity: Factors of Influence This activity allows students to discuss four factors that helped early humans survive and thrive: adaptability, culture, technology, and intelligence. Divide the class into four groups and have each group sit at a table. Assign the following questions to the groups:

Group 1: Why might adaptability have been a key factor in early human survival?

Group 2: What role did culture play in helping early humans deal with daily life?

Group 3: How did technology help early humans improve their lives?

Group 4: Why did early humans need to possess intelligence?

Have students at each table take turns answering the question. When they have finished their discussion, ask a representative from each table to summarize that group's answers.

`0:15` **minutes**

INTRODUCE THE READING STRATEGY

ORGANIZE IDEAS: COMPARE AND CONTRAST

Remind students that comparing and contrasting two topics or ideas can help them better understand new information. Model completing the Venn Diagram. Point out the two sections of the chapter and preview the meaning of the words "Paleolithic" and "Neolithic" ("Old Stone Age" and "New Stone Age"). Model filling in the Venn Diagram with information that describes Paleolithic and Neolithic people.

INTRODUCE CHAPTER VOCABULARY

WORD WALL

Have students complete a Word Wall for Key Vocabulary words as they read the chapter. Have students write each word on a piece of paper, draw a picture that helps clarify its meaning, and write its definition. At the end of the chapter, ask students what they learned about each word.

KEY DATES	
c. 2.5 million B.C.	Beginning of the Paleolithic Age
c. 200,000 B.C.	*Homo sapiens* first appear
c. 100,000 B.C.	Migration out of Africa begins
c. 10,000 B.C.	Beginning of the Neolithic Age
c. 8000 B.C.	Beginning of the agricultural revolution
c. 5000 B.C.	Agriculture established in Fertile Crescent and Indus River Valley
c. 3000 B.C.	Agriculture established in Nile River Valley and Huang He River Valley

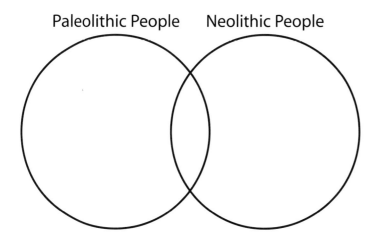

Paleolithic People   Neolithic People

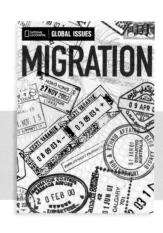

For more on modern human migration, see *GLOBAL ISSUES MIGRATION.*

1.1 Discovering
Prehistory

You probably think your parents are pretty old. Well, think again. They actually belong to the newest human species on the planet—*Homo sapiens*, or "wise man"—and so do you. We'll begin our story with this species.

MAIN IDEA

The evidence uncovered by scientists helps us learn about our early human history.

Great Rift Valley

A rift valley is created in places where Earth's outer layer, or crust, has split apart. In East Africa's Great Rift Valley, this action has produced valleys that average 30 to 40 miles wide. The area has provided archaeologists with a wealth of human fossils because the soil in the valley helped preserve the remains.

GEOLOGIC AND ARCHAEOLOGICAL TIME

Earth is incredibly old: somewhere around 4.5 billion years old. Yet **Homo sapiens** (HOH-moh SAY-pee-uhnz) has existed for only about the last 200,000 years. Scientists know this because they have found fossils and artifacts that belonged to this species. **Fossils** are the remains, such as bones and teeth, of organisms that lived long ago. **Artifacts** are human-made objects, such as stone tools. These items provide some of the best clues to prehistory, or the time before written records existed.

Scientists called **archaeologists** search for, discover, and then interpret fossils and artifacts left behind by *Homo sapiens*. Archaeologists are like the crime scene investigators of history.

They piece together evidence that tells the story of what happened at a site hundreds, thousands, or even hundreds of thousands of years ago.

Archaeologists sometimes use geologic techniques to find out how old fossils and artifacts are. For example, they can figure out how old an artifact is based on how deeply it is buried in layers of dirt. In a site that hasn't been disturbed over time, dirt builds up in layers, with younger layers covering the older ones. Archaeologists know that fossils and artifacts lying in the deepest layers are the oldest.

ORIGINS IN AFRICA

Early *Homo sapiens* looked very much like humans do today. It is now widely accepted that the species first appeared in Africa. Earlier homonins, or human-like species, are believed to have lived in Africa for millions of years before *Homo sapiens*.

In 1967, a team of archaeologists led by Richard Leakey found the earliest fossils of modern humans. The team discovered two *Homo sapiens* skulls near the Omo River in the Great Rift Valley of East Africa. The skulls were originally thought to be 130,000 years old, but a more recent dating has determined them to be about 195,000 years old.

Homo sapiens lived during the **Paleolithic** (pay-lee-uh-LIHTH-ihk) **Age**, a period that began around 2.5 million B.C. and ended around 8000 B.C. The period is also called the Old Stone Age because the people living then made simple tools and weapons out of stone. It was a time of dramatic changes in geography and climate. It was also a time when modern human development—and human history—began.

Homo sapiens fossils have been found in East Africa's Great Rift Valley, shown here.

REVIEW & ASSESS

1. **READING CHECK** What kinds of evidence do archaeologists uncover to learn about early modern humans?

2. **DETERMINE WORD MEANINGS** *Paleo* means "old." What do you suppose *lithic* means?

3. **MAKE INFERENCES** What does the fact that early *Homo sapiens* made tools suggest about this group?

OBJECTIVE

Learn what scientists have uncovered about our early history.

CRITICAL THINKING SKILLS FOR LESSON 1.1

- Identify Main Ideas and Details
- Monitor Comprehension
- Determine Word Meanings
- Make Inferences
- Describe
- Draw Conclusions
- Analyze Visuals

ESSENTIAL QUESTION

How did people manage to survive and thrive tens of thousands of years ago?

Early *Homo sapiens* lived in a time of dramatic changes in geography and climate. Lesson 1.1 discusses the simple stone tools and weapons *Homo sapiens* made to survive in their harsh environment.

BACKGROUND FOR THE TEACHER

Before archaeologists begin digging for artifacts at a site, they have to know who lived in the area, what structures might have been built there, and how the geography of the land has changed over time. Archaeologists then survey the area to look for artifacts on and just below the surface. If what they find is intriguing, then the fun begins.

DIGITAL RESOURCES myNGconnect.com

TEACHER RESOURCES & ASSESSMENT

 Reading and Note-Taking

 Vocabulary Practice

 Section 1 Quiz

STUDENT RESOURCES

 Biography

INTERPRET MODELS

Point out the photograph of East Africa's Great Rift Valley. To show students how the valley was formed, have pairs of students place two paperback books of equal thickness lengthwise between them. Then have them pull the books until they are about a half inch away from each other. Explain that the books represent plates of land that pull apart, leaving deep valleys between them. Tell students that the Great Rift Valley formed this way. **0:05** minutes

TEACH

GUIDED DISCUSSION

1. **Describe** What is one of the geologic techniques archaeologists use to find out how old artifacts are? *(Archaeologists often date artifacts based on how deeply they are buried in the dirt. Artifacts lying in the deepest layers are the oldest.)*

2. **Draw Conclusions** Why do archaeologists have to depend on finding artifacts to uncover information about early *Homo sapiens*? *(There are no written records made by early* Homo sapiens, *so archaeologists must depend on the physical materials these early people left behind for information.)*

ANALYZE VISUALS

Have students examine the photo of East Africa's Great Rift Valley. Point out the shepherd in the foreground of the photo. Tell students that much of the region supports shepherds whose camels, sheep, and goats graze there. **ASK:** What do you think life is like for the shepherds and their flocks in this environment?

(Sample response: The rocky, mountainous landscape probably makes traveling through the valley difficult, but it looks as though there is enough vegetation for the animals to eat.) **0:10** minutes

ACTIVE OPTIONS

On Your Feet: Inside-Outside Circle Use the Inside-Outside Circle strategy to check students' understanding of artifacts and fossils. Have students in the outer circle pose questions (for example, "Which of the following is not an artifact: tool, cup, bone?"), and have students in the inner circle answer them. Then have students trade inside/outside roles and rotate to create new partnerships. **0:10** minutes

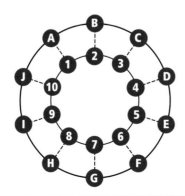

Critical Viewing: NG Chapter Gallery Invite students to explore the Chapter Gallery to examine the images that relate to Chapter 1. Have them select one of the images and do additional research to learn more about it. Ask questions that will inspire additional inquiry about the chosen gallery image, such as: What is this? Where and when was this created? By whom? Why was it created? What is it made of? Why does it belong in this chapter? What else would you like to know about it? **0:10** minutes

DIFFERENTIATE

ENGLISH LANGUAGE LEARNERS

Identify Facts Divide the class into small groups and have the groups conduct a Round Robin activity to review what they have learned in the lesson. Ask groups to generate facts for about 3–5 minutes, with all students contributing. Finally, invite one student from each group to share his or her group's responses. Write all the facts on the board.

GIFTED & TALENTED

Perform a Play Have a group of students learn more about the discovery of early *Homo sapiens* fossils by Richard Leakey and his team in 1967. Then have the group present what they have learned to the class in a short play. Provide the following guidelines for the group:

- Assign each member of the group a role, including that of narrator.
- Compose dialogue that moves the action along.
- Heighten dramatic interest by providing a conflict.
- Convey the challenges and excitement of the dig.
- Use props, if possible, for the digging tools and fossils.
- Have the narrator or a character summarize the recent dating of the fossils.

Press **mt** *in the Student eEdition for modified text.*

See the Chapter Planner for more strategies for differentiation.

REVIEW & ASSESS

ANSWERS

1. Archaeologists study artifacts to understand and learn more about early modern humans.

2. *Lithic* means "stone."

3. The fact that early humans were making tools suggests that they were intelligent.

+ POSSIBLE RESPONSE

The people in the community celebrate by enjoying a large meal together; they eat certain foods; they eat using chopsticks; they enjoy nature.

Critical Viewing Friends and neighbors in a community in China sit down to a lavish banquet. What do details in the photo tell you about the community's cultural behaviors?

1.2 The Elements of Culture

Maybe you've heard the saying "You are what you eat," but did you know that you are also what you speak, what you wear, and what you believe? All of these behaviors—and many others—help identify you with your particular blend of cultures.

MAIN IDEA

Studying the culture of *Homo sapiens* in the Paleolithic Age helps reveal how people lived.

WHAT IS CULTURE?

Culture is a big part of human development. All the elements that contribute to the way of life of a particular group of people make up culture. These elements include language, clothing, music, art, law, religion, government, and family structure. Culture is passed down from parents to children and greatly affects our behaviors and beliefs. It influences people to do things in a particular way, such as eating or avoiding certain foods. It unifies a group and distinguishes that group from others.

Language, art, toolmaking, and religion are the elements that were most important in defining early cultures. Even early *Homo sapiens* communicated through speech, created cave paintings, made and used tools, and buried the dead. However, groups of people often did things slightly differently. These differences reflect each group's technical knowledge, artistic styles, and available natural resources.

WHY STUDY CULTURE?

As you've learned, cultural behaviors are passed down from generation to generation, but they can also change over time or—like the ability to make stone tools—be nearly lost altogether. In part, scientists study prehistoric cultures to learn how these cultures differ from modern cultures and discover what they all have in common. Information about modern cultures is often provided by archaeologists called **anthropologists**.

The artifacts archaeologists uncover help them piece together a picture of early humans' cultural behavior and daily life. For example, by studying tools uncovered at a prehistoric site, archaeologists learn how advanced the people who made them were and what jobs they needed to do. In addition, comparing artifacts from different sites can explain why one group was more successful than another.

Comparing artifacts from different time periods helps explain how people changed and developed. This knowledge helps us see thousands of years into the past so we can better understand the present and predict the future.

REVIEW & ASSESS

1. **READING CHECK** What do artifacts, such as stone tools, reveal about the culture of early *Homo sapiens*?

2. **SUMMARIZE** How do archaeologists and anthropologists work together?

3. **DRAW CONCLUSIONS** What might the discovery of tools used primarily as weapons suggest about a group of early humans?

PLAN

OBJECTIVE

Identify cultural elements of *Homo sapiens* in the Paleolithic Age.

CRITICAL THINKING SKILLS FOR LESSON 1.2

- Identify Main Ideas and Details
- Monitor Comprehension
- Summarize
- Draw Conclusions
- Identify Main Ideas and Details
- Make Inferences
- Make Connections

ESSENTIAL QUESTION

How did people manage to survive and thrive tens of thousands of years ago?

Groups of early *Homo sapiens* developed cultural behaviors that helped them survive and advance. Lesson 1.2 discusses the early cultural elements that developed during the Paleolithic Age.

BACKGROUND FOR THE TEACHER

Understanding and talking about human culture is part of the job of anthropologists. Anthropology can go beyond just looking at artifacts. Margaret Mead is one of the most famous anthropologists in history. It is through Mead that many people first learned about the science of anthropology. She popularized the study of human development through a cross-cultural perspective. Mead also showed that modern societies could learn from so-called "primitive" societies. The study of past peoples helps us understand ourselves.

DIGITAL RESOURCES myNGconnect.com

TEACHER RESOURCES & ASSESSMENT

 Reading and Note-Taking   **Vocabulary Practice**   **Section 1 Quiz**

STUDENT RESOURCES

 NG Chapter Gallery

INTRODUCE & ENGAGE

MAKE A LIST

Write the following headings on the board: Food, Holidays, Clothing, Recreational Activities. Ask students to write each heading on a piece of paper and list examples from their own lives. Then have the class share and discuss their lists. Explain that what they have listed are elements of culture. Tell students that culture reflects how a group of people lives, believes, and thinks. **0:05 minutes**

TEACH

GUIDED DISCUSSION

1. **Identify Main Ideas and Details** What elements were most important in defining early human cultures, and how were these elements part of people's lives? *(The most important elements were agriculture and subsistence, language, art, toolmaking, and religion. People needed to survive and feed themselves, communicated through speech, created cave paintings, made and used tools, and buried their dead.)*

2. **Make Inferences** What kinds of cultural behaviors, passed down from generation to generation, might have helped groups of early *Homo sapiens* survive? *(strategies for keeping warm, farming, irrigation, killing animals in a hunt, escaping danger)*

MAKE CONNECTIONS

Have students spend 20 minutes watching a television show or reading a magazine, a blog, or entries in a social networking site. Ask them to list five facts about culture in the United States that they observe in the media. The facts could relate to any element of culture, including customs, food, language, the arts, and religion. Once students have finished the assignment, have them share their observations and facts with the class. **0:20 minutes**

ACTIVE OPTIONS

On Your Feet: Four Corners Create four signs with the following labels: Arts, Religion, Customs, Language. Tape one sign to each corner of the room. Then distribute magazines to students and ask them to cut out images that reflect these elements of culture. Have students tape each image to the appropriate corner of the room. **0:10 minutes**

Critical Viewing: NG Image Gallery Have students explore the entire NG Image Gallery and choose two images that illustrate culture. Then have students compare and contrast the images, either in written form or verbally, with a partner. Ask questions that will inspire this process, such as: How are these images alike? How are they different? What aspect of culture do they represent? Why did you select these two items? How do they relate in history? **0:10 minutes**

DIFFERENTIATE

ENGLISH LANGUAGE LEARNERS

Outline and Take Notes To help students develop their comprehension skills, ask them to work in pairs to write an outline of this lesson. The following format can help them start writing their outlines.

I. Culture and Cultural Elements

    A.

    B.

II. Elements of Early Cultures

    A.

    B.

III. Cultural Study

    A.

    B.

IV. What Archaeologists Learn

    A.

    B.

STRIVING READERS

Use Examples Define and review some of the words used in this lesson, using context clues or outside dictionaries if necessary: *blend, unifies, generation*, and *site*. Provide examples of each one that are recognizable and familiar to students. Then ask students to use each word in a sentence.

Press **mt** *in the Student eEdition for modified text.*

See the Chapter Planner for more strategies for differentiation.

REVIEW & ASSESS

ANSWERS

1. The artifacts reveal how technologically advanced they were, what jobs they needed to do, and what their daily life was like.

2. Anthropologists provide archaeologists with information about modern cultures. Archaeologists use this information to compare modern cultures with prehistoric ones.

3. The discovery might suggest that these early humans were accomplished hunters and that hunting was important in their culture.

Changing Environments

Today, climate change is forcing us all to make some adjustments—from switching off lights to turning off faucets. Still, we're not the first humans to be affected by shifting climate patterns. A big change in their environment drove Paleolithic people to take steps that would transform the world forever.

MAIN IDEA

A changing climate forced Paleolithic people to move to new places and develop new tools to survive.

+ POSSIBLE RESPONSE

The savannas Paleolithic people lived on would have been lush, green, and flat, with trees for shade and animals to eat.

Critical Viewing Paleolithic people first lived on savannas like this one. Savannas are areas of flat grassland where animals roam. What might have made the savanna a welcoming environment?

FINDING NEW HOMES

About 100,000 years ago, much of Africa had a very unstable climate. Some places became warmer and wetter, while others became hot and dry. These climate changes greatly altered the landscape in which Paleolithic people lived.

Archaeologists have discovered that East Africa suffered a terrible **drought** between 100,000 and 75,000 years ago. This long period of dry, hot weather had a huge impact on the landscape. Rivers and vast lakes shrank and left people struggling for survival. The plants they ate became scarce, and the animals they hunted disappeared. At the

COMPARING TOOLS

The stone tool on the left was made about 100,000 years ago. The fishhook made from bone on the right dates back about 42,000 years. You can see that early humans' technical skill had come a long way in about 60,000 years.

same time, previously uninhabitable areas became livable and attractive. For example, the **Sahara**, which is one of the harshest deserts on Earth today, turned into an **oasis**, or a green area where plants can grow. These environmental changes may have encouraged some of the 10,000 Paleolithic people living in East Africa at the time to leave their homeland. They began their long **migration**, or movement, first to the Sahara in North Africa and then into the wider world.

ADAPTING TO NEW CONDITIONS

As people migrated, they responded to some of the challenges of their new environments by using technology. **Technology** is the application of knowledge, tools, and inventions to meet people's needs.

The ability to capture and control fire was a particularly valuable technology. In addition to providing much-needed warmth and light, fire helped Paleolithic people scare away enemies and drive animals into traps. Cooking meat made it easier to digest and killed bacteria.

Paleolithic people also used technology to develop tools that helped them adapt to new environments and climates. Simple tools had been used for millions of years, but *Homo sapiens* refined them to create

a really effective tool kit. A hard stone called flint was especially useful, as it could be split into hard, razor-sharp flakes. Early humans learned to design a tool to perform a particular task, such as chopping wood, carving meat, or skinning animals.

Over time, tools grew increasingly advanced. Humans crafted fishhooks out of bone and sewing needles out of ivory. These specialized tools helped our ancestors survive in an amazing range of new habitats and climates—from arctic areas to deserts.

REVIEW & ASSESS

1. **READING CHECK** What led some Paleolithic people to leave their home in East Africa thousands of years ago and migrate to new places?

2. **DETERMINE WORD MEANINGS** What context clues tell you that *uninhabitable* means "unlivable"?

3. **MAKE INFERENCES** Think about the adaptations Paleolithic people made to survive in new conditions. What can you infer about their intelligence?

PLAN

OBJECTIVE

Discuss the impact of climate change and the challenges of new environments on Paleolithic people.

CRITICAL THINKING SKILLS FOR LESSON 1.3

- Identify Main Ideas and Details
- Monitor Comprehension
- Determine Word Meanings
- Make Inferences
- Analyze Cause and Effect
- Draw Conclusions
- Analyze Visuals

ESSENTIAL QUESTION

How did people manage to survive and thrive tens of thousands of years ago?

When climate change altered the landscape in which Paleolithic people lived, they moved and adapted to the new environments. Lesson 1.3 discusses the technology Paleolithic people developed to survive in a range of new habitats and climates.

BACKGROUND FOR THE TEACHER

The Sahara is a classic example of how environments can change over time. The Sahara, which means "great desert" in Arabic, is the third largest desert in the world and covers most of North Africa. Dry for most of its history, the Sahara undergoes a humid period every 100,000 years. These humid periods last about 5,000 years, during which the desert becomes lush savanna—as it did during the Paleolithic Age. The last humid period began about 12,000 years ago. Later, the Sahara evolved back to desert over thousands of years.

DIGITAL RESOURCES myNGconnect.com

TEACHER RESOURCES & ASSESSMENT

 Reading and Note-Taking

 Vocabulary Practice

 Section 1 Quiz

STUDENT RESOURCES

 NG Chapter Gallery

INTRODUCE & ENGAGE

TOP TEN

Read the following definition of *technology* aloud to students: the application of knowledge, tools, and inventions to meet people's needs. Then have students make a top ten list of their favorite technological inventions. Ask them to jot down how each one meets people's needs. Tell students that Paleolithic people used technology to help them survive. **0:05** minutes

TEACH

GUIDED DISCUSSION

1. **Analyze Cause and Effect** What happened to the landscape of East Africa as a result of a drought that occurred between 100,000 and 75,000 years ago? *(Rivers and vast lakes shrank, plants became scarce, and many animals disappeared.)*

2. **Draw Conclusions** Once Paleolithic people had to move to colder climates, why was it important to develop a tool for skinning animals? *(They would have needed the animal skins to help them keep warm.)*

ANALYZE VISUALS

Have students study the images of early tools. Ask them to think like archaeologists and consider the following questions: What do you think the older tool was used for? How do you think the toolmaker was able to sharpen the points on the fishhook? How do you think the tools were used? Were they thrown or thrust? Were they attached to a handle or string? How much skill was probably needed to use the tools? If possible, discuss the questions and answers in class. **0:10** minutes

ACTIVE OPTIONS

On Your Feet: Three-Step Interview Have students work in pairs to discuss the following question: *What was daily life probably like for Paleolithic people?* Instruct them to use more detailed questions to interview one another about specific aspects of the question. For example, "How much time did Paleolithic people spend hunting and cooking?" "How did they keep warm?" "Did groups of people work together?" "Where did they live?" "Did they have any free time and, if so, how did they fill it?" Remind students to listen closely to their partner so that they can report back to the class. **0:20** minutes

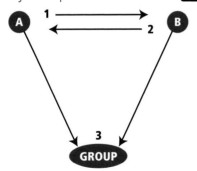

Critical Viewing: NG Chapter Gallery Have students examine the contents of the Chapter Gallery for this lesson. Then invite them to brainstorm additional images they believe would fit within the gallery. Instruct them to do online research to find examples of actual images. Have students explain why these images would belong in the gallery. **0:20** minutes

DIFFERENTIATE

ENGLISH LANGUAGE LEARNERS

Create Word Charts Help students understand the vocabulary words in this lesson. Display the chart below and write the four vocabulary words above it. Ask students to copy and complete the four parts of the chart for each vocabulary word.

drought   migration
oasis   technology

Definition of _____:	Draw a visual.
Tell how it relates to region.	Use it in a sentence.

PRE-AP

Compare Desert Formation Have students conduct online research on a desert area in the United States or another country that used to be green and lush. For example, fossils of rain forest plants have been found in some deserts in the United States. Once they've chosen a desert area, have them find the answers to the following questions: How does the desert today compare with the region at an earlier time? How did scientists learn what the region used to be like? Have students summarize their findings in a brief report comparing the desert today with the region in the past.

Press (**mt**) *in the Student eEdition for modified text.*

See the Chapter Planner for more strategies for differentiation.

REVIEW & ASSESS

ANSWERS

1. The changing, unstable climate, which left *Homo sapiens* struggling for survival, led them to migrate and settle in more habitable places.

2. The preceding phrase, "previously uninhabitable areas became livable and attractive" suggests that *uninhabitable* means "unlivable" or "not fit to live in."

3. Students should infer that Paleolithic people were highly intelligent and creative.

Moving into New Environments

More than 60,000 years ago, the world witnessed movement on a scale never seen before as our restless ancestors began leaving Africa in waves. They set out on a worldwide migration that would permanently populate the entire planet.

MAIN IDEA

Between 70,000 and 10,000 B.C., Paleolithic people migrated from Africa and settled throughout the world.

SPREAD OF EARLY HUMANS

As you have learned, the changing climate made Paleolithic people search for homes outside of Africa. They first migrated into Southwest Asia around 70,000 years ago. The region was warm and tropical and provided lush vegetation and abundant wildlife.

In time, people spread across the rest of the world. From Asia they reached Australia around 50,000 years ago. By about 40,000 years ago, early humans

had arrived in Europe. Around 30,000 years ago, *Homo sapiens* reached Siberia on the edge of eastern Asia.

The last continents to be populated were the Americas. This final migration may have been made possible by the **Ice Age**. At its height around 20,000 years ago, the Ice Age trapped so much water as ice that the sea level was nearly 400 feet lower than it is today. This trapped ice created **land bridges** that allowed humans to walk across continents. Many scientists have proposed the theory that hunters crossed the **Beringia** (beh-RIN-gee-uh) land bridge, which connected Siberia with North America, in a series of migrations between 20,000 and 15,000 years ago.

Scientists believe that during a period of glacial melting around 12,000 years ago, more travelers pushed southward through Central America and South America. However, new evidence has emerged that challenges this timing. The genes of some South American people suggest that their ancestors arrived from Australia 35,000 years ago, and *Homo sapiens* footprints in Central America have been dated to 40,000 years ago. These findings might support the theory that the earliest Americans arrived in boats, rather than by land bridge.

IN SEARCH OF FOOD

People migrated to many of these places, possibly in hot pursuit of the animals they liked to eat. Some of these creatures were **megafauna**, which means "large animals." Megafauna included the woolly mammoth, giant ground sloth, and saber-toothed cat, which are shown below.

Megafauna
Humans hunted herds of woolly mammoths in northern Asia and parts of Europe and North America. The giant ground sloth and saber-toothed cat lived primarily in North and South America.

Woolly Mammoth

Giant Ground Sloth

Saber-Toothed Cat

EARLY HUMAN MIGRATION: 100,000–14,000 YEARS AGO

This map shows what Earth might have looked like many thousands of years ago. The purple shading indicates areas that were covered in ice from the Ice Age. The green shading shows land that once existed but has since eroded, or worn away.

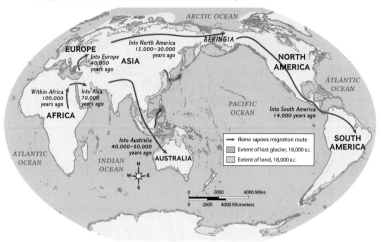

The woolly mammoth, a relative of the modern elephant, was one of the largest megafauna. It stood between 9 and 11 feet tall and weighed as much as six tons. Its curved tusks grew up to 13 feet long.

At five tons, the giant ground sloth wasn't much smaller than the woolly mammoth. However, the sloth was fairly harmless. It mostly used its long claws to tear leaves and bark, not other animals.

There was more reason to fear the saber-toothed cat with its two huge, swordlike teeth. This creature was smaller than a modern lion but much heavier, weighing more than 400 pounds.

These megafauna became extinct, or died out, about 11,000 years ago. Many scientists believe they were overhunted or wiped out by climate change as the Ice Age began to come to a close.

REVIEW & ASSESS

1. **READING CHECK** What food did Paleolithic people eat when they migrated to Asia and other parts of the world?

2. **INTERPRET MAPS** What challenges do you think people encountered as they moved into the new environments shown on the map?

3. **FORM OPINIONS** Do you think the Americas became populated by land bridge, by boat, or by a combination of the two? Explain your position.

PLAN

OBJECTIVE

Identify where Paleolithic people migrated and some of the food they found there.

Over tens of thousands of years, many Paleolithic people left Africa and populated the world. Lesson 1.4 discusses their search for habitable environments and plentiful supplies of food.

CRITICAL THINKING SKILLS FOR LESSON 1.4

- Identify Main Ideas and Details
- Monitor Comprehension
- Interpret Maps
- Form Opinions
- Analyze Cause and Effect
- Make Inferences

BACKGROUND FOR THE TEACHER

In the previous lesson, students learned that climates change over time. Add the impact of humans, and additional changes occur. Woolly mammoths and other megafauna all died out around the same time. Most scientists offer two main reasons for their extinction. Primarily, scientists point to climate change. Experts argue that woolly mammoths, with their heavy coats, could not handle the warming climate. Hotter temperatures may also have destroyed plants that the mammoths—who were herbivores—depended on for survival.

ESSENTIAL QUESTION

How did people manage to survive and thrive tens of thousands of years ago?

DIGITAL RESOURCES myNGconnect.com

TEACHER RESOURCES & ASSESSMENT

 Reading and Note-Taking

 Vocabulary Practice

 Section 1 Quiz

STUDENT RESOURCES

 Active History

INTRODUCE & ENGAGE

CLIMATE QUICKWRITE

Have students take a few minutes to write about their most memorable climate-related experience. Then ask volunteers to share what they wrote. **ASK:** How does climate affect your everyday life? How do you adapt to changes in the climate? *(Sample response: The climate affects how I dress. In the summer, I usually wear shorts, while in the winter, I have to wear a coat.)* Explain to students that in this lesson, they will learn how climate-related changes affected Paleolithic people. **0:05 minutes**

TEACH

GUIDED DISCUSSION

1. **Analyze Cause and Effect** What do scientists believe happened as a result of the Ice Age? *(So much water was trapped as ice that the sea level lowered significantly.)*

2. **Make Inferences** What probably allowed Paleolithic people to successfully hunt and kill woolly mammoths? *(their improved tools and weapons)*

INTERPRET MAPS

Have students study the early human migration map and trace the migrations with their finger. Point out the Beringia land bridge and the green shading that indicates land that existed about 20,000 years ago. Then have them find the areas that were covered by glaciers during this period. **ASK:** What do you think the climate was like in the northern part of North America? *(probably very cold)* Where do you think people settled in North America? *(south of the glacial area)* Why do you think South America was the last continent to be populated by humans? *(It is farthest away from Africa.)* **0:10 minutes**

ACTIVE OPTIONS

Active History: Compare Past and Present Land Areas Extend the lesson by using either the PDF or Whiteboard version of the activity. These activities take a deeper look at a topic from, or related to, the lesson. Explore the activities as a class, turn them into group assignments, or even assign them individually. **0:10 minutes**

NG Learning Framework: Research a Critical Species

ATTITUDE: **Curiosity**
KNOWLEDGE: **Critical Species**

Have students select one of the megafauna creatures they are still curious about after learning about them in this chapter. Instruct them to write a short essay about this creature using information from the chapter and additional source material. Extend the activity by having students research a modern animal on the verge of extinction and write about why it is important to try and preserve as much biodiversity on the planet as possible. **0:15 minutes**

DIFFERENTIATE

STRIVING READERS

Use a TASKS Approach Help students understand the map by using the following TASKS strategy:

T Read the **title**, which explains the subject of the map.
A **Ask** yourself what the map is trying to show.
S Determine how **symbols** are used.
K Look at the **key**, or legend.
S **Summarize** what you learned.

INCLUSION

Make a Time Line Pair each student with a proficient reader. Ask proficient readers to read aloud from the lesson and discuss the information in the map. Then have the partners work together to create a time line based on the information in the lesson and map.

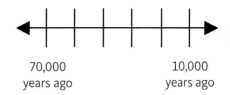

70,000 years ago   10,000 years ago

Press (**mt**) *in the Student eEdition for modified text.*

See the Chapter Planner for more strategies for differentiation.

REVIEW & ASSESS

ANSWERS

1. They fed on the vegetation and megafauna.

2. Paleolithic people must have encountered hostile climates, unfamiliar animals, and rugged landscapes in their new environments.

3. Some students will favor the land bridge theory because sailing on primitive boats for such long distances seems unlikely. Others will support the boat theory because traveling across ice on foot doesn't seem possible. Still others will support a combination of the two theories.

1.5 NATIONAL GEOGRAPHIC EXPLORER **JEFFREY ROSE**

Tracking Migration Out of Africa

Archaeologist Jeffrey Rose lives in a desert truck stop in the Southwest Asian country of Oman. He spends his days with his team of experts, sifting through rocks in 100-degree heat. Occasionally, he finds what he's looking for: small, sharp, egg-shaped stones. That may not sound like much, but his finds may dramatically rewrite our earliest history. Rose is looking for evidence to support his theory about who first migrated out of Africa and what route was taken. After years of exploration, he thinks he might have found the answer.

^ Jeffrey Rose has conducted work in many parts of Southwest Asia, including this desert outside of Dubai, United Arab Emirates.

MAIN IDEA

Jeffrey Rose has found evidence to support a new theory about which Paleolithic people first left Africa and what route they took.

LOOKING FOR EVIDENCE

National Geographic Explorer Jeffrey Rose conducted his search in Oman. Geneticists—scientists who study DNA and heredity—have suggested that the first humans to leave Africa traveled through Ethiopia to Yemen and Oman, following the coast of the Arabian Peninsula. Rose went to Oman hoping to find archaeological evidence of this migration.

He recorded the earliest traces of humans: discarded flint tools. "Our geologist constantly reads the landscape to tell us where Paleolithic humans would have found water and flint. Find those and you find early people," Rose says. However, after years of surveying, he'd found no African-style artifacts and no evidence of Paleolithic humans on the Arabian Peninsula coast.

OUT OF AFRICA

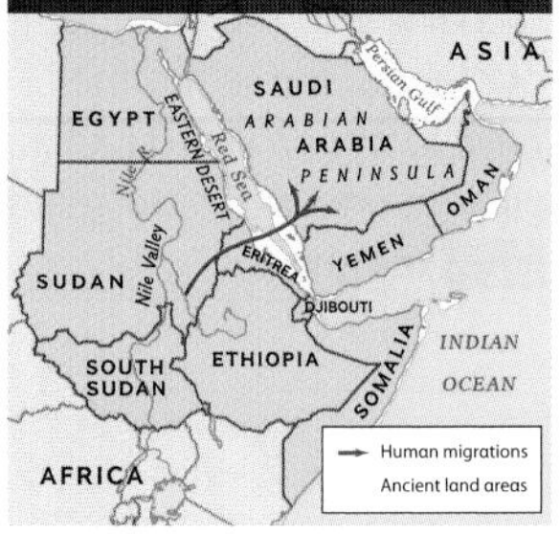
ASIA
SAUDI ARABIA
ARABIAN PENINSULA
Persian Gulf
EGYPT
EASTERN DESERT
Nile
Red Sea
OMAN
YEMEN
ERITREA
DJIBOUTI
SUDAN
Nile Valley
SOUTH SUDAN
ETHIOPIA
SOMALIA
INDIAN OCEAN
AFRICA
Human migrations
Ancient land areas

HITTING THE JACKPOT

Then in 2010, on the final day at the last site on his list, Rose hit the jackpot. He found a stone spear point with a design unique to people of the Nubian Complex, who had lived in the Nile Valley in North Africa. "We had never considered that the link to Africa would come from the Nile Valley and that their route would be through the middle of the Arabian Peninsula rather than along the coast," says Rose. Yet it made sense that people would migrate to Arabia from the Nile Valley. As Rose points out, "It's logical that people moved from an environment they knew to another that mirrored it." By the end of 2013, he had found more than 250 Nubian Complex sites in Oman.

When Rose dated the artifacts, he discovered they were roughly 106,000 years old, a point in time when people of the Nubian Complex flourished in Africa. The puzzle pieces fit. "Geneticists have shown that the modern human family tree began to branch out more than 60,000 years ago," says Rose. "I'm not questioning *when* it happened, but *where*. I suggest the great modern human expansion to the rest of the world was launched from Arabia rather than Africa." Rose's evidence suggests that perhaps it was a two-stage process. Paleolithic people might have left North Africa for Arabia more than 100,000 years ago. Then about 40,000 years later, they left Arabia and began to settle the rest of the world.

Now Rose wants to know why it was people of the Nubian Complex who spread from Africa. "What was it about their technology and culture that enabled them to expand so successfully," he wonders, "and what happened next?" As Rose says, "We've always looked to the beginning and wanted to understand how we got here. That's what it means to be human."

REVIEW & ASSESS

1. **READING CHECK** What theory has Jeffrey Rose proposed about the migration of Paleolithic people?
2. **INTERPRET MAPS** What body of water did the Nubians cross to get to the Arabian Peninsula?
3. **MAKE INFERENCES** Why would resources of water and flint have been important to early humans?

PLAN

OBJECTIVE

Evaluate a theory about which Paleolithic people first left Africa and what route they took.

CRITICAL THINKING SKILLS FOR LESSON 1.5

- Identify Main Ideas and Details
- Monitor Comprehension
- Interpret Maps
- Make Inferences
- Explain
- Sequence Events

ESSENTIAL QUESTION

How did people manage to survive and thrive tens of thousands of years ago?

Explorer Jeffrey Rose believes that the human migration out of Africa was launched from the Arabian Peninsula. Lesson 1.5 describes the evidence discovered by Rose, who believes that early humans living in the Nile Valley eventually moved to a similarly hospitable environment in Arabia.

BACKGROUND FOR THE TEACHER

Understanding the ancient environment of the Nile Valley gives Jeffrey Rose's work some context. Scientists believe that hominins first began living in the Nile Valley more than 500,000 years ago. During the last Ice Age, however, the changing climate had a big impact on the Nile Valley. Less rain fell, and the river became smaller. Although there were still important food resources, some of the large animals left or vanished from the region. Perhaps it was these dwindling resources that motivated people to leave the valley and search for a new home in Arabia.

DIGITAL RESOURCES myNGconnect.com

TEACHER RESOURCES & ASSESSMENT

Reading and Note-Taking

Vocabulary Practice

Section 1 Quiz

STUDENT RESOURCES

NG Chapter Gallery

INTRODUCE & ENGAGE

PREVIEW THE MAP

Have students examine the Out of Africa map in the lesson. Ask volunteers to use the key to identify what the red lines represent and trace them on the map. **ASK:** Where does the red line begin? *(in the Nile Valley in present-day Sudan)* On what continent is this place located? *(Africa)* Where does the line end? *(on the Arabian Peninsula)* On what continent is this place located? *(Asia)* Tell students that the map represents National Geographic Explorer Jeffrey Rose's theory about the first human migration out of Africa. `0:05` minutes

TEACH

GUIDED DISCUSSION

1. **Explain** Why did Jeffrey Rose first go to Oman to search for archaeological evidence of the early human migration out of Africa? *(Geneticists believed that the first humans to leave Africa traveled through Ethiopia to Yemen and Oman, following the coast of the Arabian Peninsula.)*

2. **Sequence Events** According to Jeffrey Rose, what two events launched the great modern human expansion from Africa? *(Paleolithic people left North Africa more than 100,000 years ago. Then about 40,000 years later, they left Arabia and began to settle in the rest of the world.)*

MAKE INFERENCES

Direct students to the quote from Jeffrey Rose at the end of the lesson. **ASK:** What does Rose mean by the last sentence of the quote: "That's what it means to be human"? *(Possible response: He means that it's human to be curious and want to know as much as we can about our history and where we came from.)* `0:10` minutes

ACTIVE OPTIONS

On Your Feet: Rotating Discussion Assign students to one of four corners in the room. Then have each team think of several questions about Jeffrey Rose's search and theory. Start the discussion by tossing a bean bag or other soft object to Team A and asking a question. When Team A answers the question, have them toss the bean bag to another team while asking one of their prepared questions. Continue until teams have exhausted their questions. `0:25` minutes

NG Learning Framework: Write a Biography

ATTITUDE: **Curiosity**
KNOWLEDGE: **Our Human Story**

Have students learn more about archaeologist Jeffrey Rose. Instruct them to write a short biography or profile about Rose using information from the chapter and additional source material. `0:10` minutes

DIFFERENTIATE

STRIVING READERS

Complete Sentence Starters Provide these sentence starters for students to complete after reading. You may also have students preview the starters to set a purpose for reading.

- The earliest traces of humans are _____.

- In Oman, Rose found a stone spear point with a design unique to _____.

- Rose believes that about 100,000 years ago, Paleolithic people left North Africa for _____.

- About 40,000 years later, they began to settle _____.

ENGLISH LANGUAGE LEARNERS

Make Vocabulary Cards Have students make and use flash cards to learn and practice unfamiliar words they encounter in this lesson. On one side of each card, they should write the target word. On the other, they should write related words they are familiar with, draw or glue images that will help them recall the meaning of the target word, or write out other mnemonic devices. Encourage students to use their flash cards for review.

Press **mt** *in the Student eEdition for modified text.*

See the Chapter Planner for more strategies for differentiation.

REVIEW & ASSESS

ANSWERS

1. He suggests that Paleolithic people first migrated from Africa to Arabia and, from there, expanded to the rest of the world.

2. The Nubians crossed the Red Sea to get to the Arabian Peninsula.

3. Early humans needed water to survive, and they used flint to make tools and spark fires.

Cave Art

It wasn't all about tools in the Paleolithic Age. Early humans had an artistic side as well. Prehistoric graffiti appears on cave walls all over the world. It turns out that the urge for artistic expression is almost as old as humankind itself.

MAIN IDEA

Cave paintings reveal much about Paleolithic people and their world.

ANCIENT ARTISTS

Art is an important part of culture. It shows a capacity for creativity, which separates humans from animals. Very early humans may have collected pretty rocks, carved wood, or painted pictures of themselves and their surroundings.

However, around 35,000 years ago, an artistic explosion occurred when humans began painting detailed images on cave walls. Examples have been found across the world, but it took archaeologists a long time to accept that the cave paintings had been created during the Paleolithic Age. They found it hard to believe that prehistoric people had the ability, time, or desire to produce such beautiful works of art.

The subjects of these cave paintings vary quite a bit, which is not surprising since they were created over a span of 25,000 years. The paintings often depict side-view images of animals, including woolly mammoths and horses. Some images feature everyday scenes, such as deer being hunted by men with spears. Other images consist of lines, circles, and geometric patterns.

One type of image that appears all over the world is considered by many to be one of the most moving: handprints. An artist often created this image by blowing paint through a reed over the hands—leaving behind the imprint of people who lived thousands of years ago.

GLIMPSE INTO AN EARLY WORLD

The **Lascaux Cave** in France has some of Europe's most amazing cave paintings, which were created about 17,000 years ago. The cave contains about 600 beautifully clear paintings, mostly of animals, many in shades of red, yellow, and brown. Some of the animals, including a nearly 17-foot-long bull-like creature, are now extinct.

Spectacular cave and rock paintings in Australia's Kakadu National Park show details of daily life and also reflect the spiritual beliefs of Aborigines, the earliest people who lived in Australia. These beliefs include a strong connection to the land and nature, which is still shared by the people who live in the region today.

The Sahara is also rich in rock art. The Tassili-n-Ajjer (tuh-sill-ee-nah-JAIR) mountain range in North Africa has spectacular paintings showing the once abundant wildlife and grasslands of this now barren desert. The Cave of the Hands in Argentina contains an incredible wall of handprints, as shown on the next page.

Despite many theories, it is unclear why Paleolithic people created such beautiful images in dark and hard-to-reach caves. Some researchers believe that most early art was actually created outdoors but has long since faded away. While we are unlikely to ever fully understand the meaning of Paleolithic art, it does provide insight into the lives and culture of our ancestors.

Researchers believe that this painting from the Cave of the Hands in Argentina shows the handprints of 13-year-old boys.

REVIEW & ASSESS

1. **READING CHECK** What do cave paintings reveal about Paleolithic people?

2. **INTEGRATE VISUALS** What different purposes might cave art have served in the Paleolithic world?

3. **COMPARE AND CONTRAST** What does the rock art in North Africa reveal about how that region has changed from the Paleolithic Age to today?

23

PLAN

OBJECTIVE

Learn what cave art reveals about the lives and culture of Paleolithic people.

CRITICAL THINKING SKILLS FOR LESSON 1.6

- Identify Main Ideas and Details
- Monitor Comprehension
- Integrate Visuals
- Compare and Contrast
- Summarize
- Draw Conclusions

ESSENTIAL QUESTION

How did people manage to survive and thrive tens of thousands of years ago?

Paleolithic people created beautiful works of art that have been preserved in caves throughout the world. Lesson 1.6 describes some of the Paleolithic art archaeologists have found, and suggests that the urge for artistic expression is almost as old as humankind itself.

BACKGROUND FOR THE TEACHER

Archaeologists did not discover the cave paintings in Lascaux Cave. Instead, a group of French teenage boys stumbled upon them. In their village, they had heard people talk about a secret underground passage that was supposed to contain a hidden treasure. In the countryside, the boys discovered an opening that led to a long vertical shaft. They were amazed at what they found: rooms of paintings featuring colorful animals. Scientists told the teenagers that they were probably the first humans to see the paintings in 17,000 years.

DIGITAL RESOURCES myNGconnect.com

TEACHER RESOURCES & ASSESSMENT

 Reading and Note-Taking

 Vocabulary Practice

 Section 1 Quiz

STUDENT RESOURCES

 NG Chapter Gallery

ANALYZE VISUALS

Have students examine the image from the Cave of the Hands in Argentina. Tell students that the artist blew paint through a reed over the hands to create a stencil, which he or she then filled in. Then ask them to outline their left or right hand. Once students have created their outlines and filled them in, use the drawings to create a collage of handprints. Discuss with students the similarities between the collage and the image from the Cave of the Hands. **ASK:** What emotions and impressions does the ancient image inspire? *(Possible responses: awe, joy, and sadness; The hands help bring the subjects and the age to life.)* **0:15** minutes

TEACH

GUIDED DISCUSSION

1. **Summarize** Why didn't archaeologists believe at first that the cave paintings they'd found all over the world had been created by Paleolithic people? *(They found it hard to believe that prehistoric people had the ability, time, or desire to produce such beautiful works of art.)*

2. **Draw Conclusions** What can archaeologists learn about Paleolithic people by studying their art? *(Possible response: They can learn about animals that are now extinct, and they can learn what the world's climate was like tens of thousands of years ago.)*

MORE INFORMATION

Australia's Aborigines The Aborigines are considered the oldest continuous human culture in the world. Their customs and beliefs are based largely on their close relationship with the land. According to their belief system, ancestral beings shaped the world during an era often referred to as *Dreamtime*. Dreamtime has a constant presence in the lives of Aborigines and is manifested in every aspect of nature. For Aborigines, Dreamtime connects the individual in the present to ancestors in the past.

ACTIVE OPTIONS

On Your Feet: Question and Answer Have half the class write True-False questions based on information in Lesson 1.6. Ask the other half to create answer cards, with "True" written on one side and "False" on the other. As each question is read aloud, students in the second group should stand and display the correct answer to the question. When discrepancies occur, review the question and discuss which answer is correct. **0:15** minutes

Critical Viewing: NG Image Gallery Invite students to explore the NG Image Gallery for Section 1 of this chapter and create a Favorites List by choosing the images they find most interesting. If possible, have students copy the images into a document to form an actual list. Then encourage them to select the image they like best and do further research on it. **0:10** minutes

ENGLISH LANGUAGE LEARNERS

Use a Main Idea Cluster Have students use a Main Idea Cluster to help them comprehend the text in this lesson. Assign students to pairs, and have each student read one part of the lesson. Student pairs can fill in a Main Idea Cluster with the main idea statement and supporting details. Encourage student pairs to include at least four details per cluster.

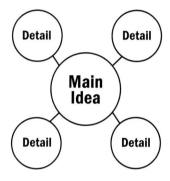

INCLUSION

Clarify Text Have visually impaired students work with sighted partners. As they listen to an audio recording of the text, have the visually impaired students indicate if there are words or passages they do not understand. Their partners can clarify meanings by repeating passages, emphasizing context clues, and paraphrasing.

Press **mt** *in the Student eEdition for modified text.*

See the Chapter Planner for more strategies for differentiation.

ANSWERS

1. The cave paintings reveal the creativity and artistic talent of early humans. The subjects of the paintings also reveal the importance of animals and nature in their world.

2. Artists might have created the art to communicate with others, to use in religious ceremonies, or simply to express themselves.

3. Rock art in the Tassili-n-Ajjer mountain range in North Africa shows a region once abundant with wildlife and grasslands. Today, it lies in the barren Sahara.

Nomadic Hunter-Gatherers

When you're hungry, you probably raid the fridge or head for the store. When Paleolithic people were hungry, they tracked down an animal, killed it with their handmade weapons, and then cooked it over a fire they had to carefully start and keep going. That's what it took to survive every day.

MAIN IDEA

Paleolithic people were constantly on the move to find food.

MOVING WITH THE SEASONS

The Paleolithic world had no farms or stores, but it did have a rich variety of foods. People just had to search them out. During the Paleolithic Age, humans lived as hunter-gatherers. A **hunter-gatherer** hunts animals and gathers wild plants to eat. These tasks were made easier and safer by the fact that early humans worked together and shared the jobs.

Most hunter-gatherer groups were small—around 30 people. The men hunted, often herding large animals into traps or over cliffs. Meanwhile, the women and young children gathered fruits and nuts. Scientists have learned a great deal about hunter-gatherers by studying the body and belongings of a later hunter known as the Iceman, seen at right.

Because the animal herds moved with the seasons, so did the groups hunting them. People who move from place to place like this are called **nomads**. Nomadic hunter-gatherers traveled light. They carried all their possessions with them, including stone tools and clothing.

As hunter-gatherers traveled in areas outside of Africa, they learned to adapt to their new environments—especially the cold. They made needles that enabled them to sew warm clothes out of animal skins. Caves offered the best protection from the worst winter weather. However, people also made shelters of wood, bone, and animal skins, which provided temporary camps.

FOLLOWING THE HERDS

Nomadic hunter-gatherers followed herds of megafauna as the animals moved from place to place. The herds migrated with the seasons and entered new environments created by the changeable Ice Age climate. For example, the Beringia land bridge allowed herds of woolly mammoths to cross into North America, with hunter-gatherers following close behind.

It wasn't easy to kill an animal as big as a woolly mammoth. It took intelligence, teamwork, and special tools. Paleolithic people developed deadly new weapons, including barbed harpoons, spear-throwers, and bows and arrows. These weapons allowed them to kill from a distance, which made the task safer and more efficient. The rewards were also great. A woolly mammoth could feed the group for months.

As humans spread around the world, various human groups competed for resources. Conflict would have been most common during cold periods when food and shelter were scarce. It's likely that in warmer periods of plentiful food, human groups interacted more happily, sharing their technology and culture. This interaction helped spread new ideas and paved the way for a remarkable new stage in human development.

THE ICEMAN

The Iceman lived around 3300 B.C. More than 5,000 years later, hikers found his frozen body in the Alps in Europe. His clothing, his tools, and even the contents of his stomach have helped scientists understand how prehistoric people lived. The graphic here offers some clues as to how he might have died.

❶ The Iceman perches on a cliff. He tests the copper blade of his ax and the flint points of his dagger with satisfaction. They're razor sharp. He searches below for his prey. With any luck, he'll bring goat meat back to his community tonight.

❷ Suddenly an arrow pierces the Iceman's shoulder. Another hunter has shot him from behind. The Iceman falls off the cliff into the snowbank below.

❸ Desperately the Iceman rises and struggles to fight off his attacker, but he's too weak. He falls back down but manages to crawl into a cave in the ice. As the Iceman dies, snow begins to fall. Snow and ice will hide him from view for the next 5,000 years.

REVIEW & ASSESS

1. **READING CHECK** Why were Paleolithic people constantly moving from place to place?

2. **INTEGRATE VISUALS** What words would you use to describe hunter-gatherers such as the Iceman?

3. **ANALYZE CAUSE AND EFFECT** What impact did the changing climate have on hunter-gatherers?

PLAN

OBJECTIVE

Learn how Paleolithic people moved with the seasons and followed herds of animals to hunt and gather food.

CRITICAL THINKING SKILLS FOR LESSON 2.1

- Identify Main Ideas and Details
- Monitor Comprehension
- Integrate Visuals
- Analyze Cause and Effect
- Describe

ESSENTIAL QUESTION

How did people manage to survive and thrive tens of thousands of years ago?

Paleolithic people hunted animals and gathered wild plants for food. Lesson 2.1 describes how nomadic hunter-gatherers moved from place to place to survive.

BACKGROUND FOR THE TEACHER

The Iceman, also known as Ötzi, provided a remarkable glimpse into the lives of Neolithic hunter-gatherers who lived more than 5,000 years ago. His clothing and equipment were of particular interest to archaeologists since, under normal conditions, these would have disintegrated long ago. Ötzi was wearing leggings and a coat made of goat skin. His shoes were insulated with grass and hay, while the outside was made of deerskin. He was well equipped for hunting with an ax, dagger, bow, and arrows. Researchers also found a simple first-aid kit.

TEACHER RESOURCES & ASSESSMENT

 Reading and Note-Taking

 Vocabulary Practice

 Section 2 Quiz

STUDENT RESOURCES

 NG Chapter Gallery

INTRODUCE & ENGAGE

PREVIEW TERMS

Introduce the concept of nomadism by asking students to imagine what their lives would be like if they were constantly on the move. Point out that nomads carry all of their belongings with them. Ask students what items they'd take with them if they were part of a nomadic family. Tell students that some people live as nomads today. For example, describe the nomads of Mongolia who carry and set up their *gers*, or portable tents, wherever they go.
0:10 minutes

TEACH

GUIDED DISCUSSION

1. **Describe** How did nomadic hunters kill a woolly mammoth? *(They worked in groups and used weapons, such as spear-throwers and bows and arrows, to kill the animal from a distance.)*

2. **Analyze Cause and Effect** What happened when human groups enjoyed warm weather and found plentiful food? *(Groups may have interacted, sharing their culture and technology.)*

INTEGRATE VISUALS

Have students study the illustration. Then have volunteers read the introduction and captions aloud. **ASK:** Based on the drawings, what was the climate probably like for the Iceman? *(cold and snowy)* Do you think animals were plentiful or scarce while the Iceman was hunting? *(scarce)* Why do you think the other hunter killed the Iceman? *(to eliminate competition for game; to steal his equipment)*
0:10 minutes

ACTIVE OPTIONS

On Your Feet: Word Chain Have students form three lines. Hand a piece of paper to the first person in each line with one of these words or terms from the text: *hunter-gatherer, nomad, specialized tools.* The first student in line adds a word to the list that relates to the original word. Students pass the paper from person to person, each one adding a word or phrase they associate with the previously written word. Have a volunteer from each group read off the word chain and ask the rest of the class to listen for any words that were used in more than one or any that may not connect correctly.
0:20 minutes

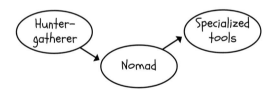

NG Learning Framework: Hunting and Gathering

ATTITUDE: Curiosity
SKILL: Problem-Solving

Have students get together in groups. Ask them to imagine they are hunter-gatherers during the Paleolithic Age and they must either hunt or gather some food. Have each group come up with a plan for finding edible plants or hunting and killing an animal. Once the groups have devised a plan, have them share it with the class.
0:10 minutes

DIFFERENTIATE

STRIVING READERS

Monitor Comprehension Have students work in small groups, reading aloud the text paragraph by paragraph. At the end of each paragraph, have them stop and use these sentence frames:

- This paragraph is about _____.

- One detail that stood out to me is _____.

- The word _____ means _____.

- I don't think I understand _____.

GIFTED & TALENTED

Create Graphics Have students work in groups to create a graphic illustrating another scene in the Iceman's life. Tell students to decide on the scene—for example, the Iceman on a successful hunt, the Iceman returning to his community from a hunt, or the Iceman interacting with his community. Then have students draft their ideas for the scene on a storyboard. The storyboard should include sketches of the scene as well as captions and dialogue bubbles that tell what's going on in each frame. Students should then use the storyboard to create their final graphic. Display the finished graphics in the classroom.

Press **mt** *in the Student eEdition for modified text.*

See the Chapter Planner for more strategies for differentiation.

REVIEW & ASSESS

ANSWERS

1. Paleolithic people were constantly moving in search of food. They hunted animals and gathered wild plants to eat.

2. Examples of words to describe hunter-gatherers might include *hardworking, tough, vulnerable, brave, adaptable,* and *intelligent.*

3. Herds of animals moved into new environments. Hunter-gatherers followed them and had to learn to adapt to the challenging conditions.

2.2 The Beginnings of Domestication

A pet poodle might lick your hand and follow you everywhere, but dogs weren't always man's best friend. All dogs are descended from wolves. Humans transformed some of these wild animals into loyal helpers, which marked a major breakthrough in learning to control their environment.

MAIN IDEA

Early humans took control of their environment by raising useful plants and taming animals.

+ ## POSSIBLE RESPONSE

The sheep are standing or walking peacefully around the girls, who seem to be in control of the herd.

Critical Viewing Young nomadic girls corral sheep for milking in northeastern Afghanistan. What details in the photo tell you that the animals have been domesticated?

CHANGING CLIMATE

Around 14,000 years ago, Earth grew warmer, and the ice sheets melted. These changes raised sea levels, created freshwater lakes, and increased global rainfall. Large areas of land became covered with water. As a result, land bridges disappeared, and coastal waters formed that were full of fish. Animals moved, adapted, or died as their habitats, or environments, changed.

These environmental changes also began to transform the ways that hunter-gatherers lived in some areas. The warmer, wetter climate encouraged the development of forests and grasslands and resulted in longer growing seasons. These conditions proved to be perfect for the growth of grasses. In time, people learned to raise other plants and animals, making them useful to humans. This development, called **domestication**, led to the beginning of farming.

TAMING PLANTS AND ANIMALS

Hunter-gatherers had grown plants to increase their productivity long before the ice began to melt. Now the improved climate made growing plants even easier. After scattering seeds in wet ground, hunter-gatherers knew they could return and harvest the plants the following year. Some foods, especially grains from cereals such as wheat and barley, could be stored to feed people and animals year-round.

At about the same time, humans began to tame animals. The earliest domesticated animals were dogs. All around the world, wild wolf pups were caught and bred for hunting and protection. Other animals were domesticated for food: first sheep and goats, then pigs and cattle. As well as providing meat, milk, and wool, some domesticated animals could carry heavy loads and pull carts.

Although most humans remained nomadic, the warmer climate provided certain areas with such abundant resources that some hunter-gatherer groups decided to settle down. For example, areas around estuaries made perfect places to live. An estuary is formed where a river feeds into the ocean. The combination of fresh water, salt water, and land provided people with a year-round supply of food. Settling down to live permanently in such places would bring about a great change that allowed humans to make their next big leap forward.

REVIEW & ASSESS

1. **READING CHECK** How did humans use the plants and animals they domesticated?

2. **ANALYZE CAUSE AND EFFECT** How did the warmer climate and increased rainfall in some places affect people's ability to grow plants for food?

3. **FORM OPINIONS** What do you think were some of the advantages of the settled life over the nomadic one?

PLAN

OBJECTIVE

Discover how early humans took control of their environment by raising plants and taming animals.

CRITICAL THINKING SKILLS FOR LESSON 2.2

- Identify Main Ideas and Details
- Monitor Comprehension
- Analyze Cause and Effect
- Form Opinions
- Make Predictions
- Make Connections
- Analyze Visuals

ESSENTIAL QUESTION

How did people manage to survive and thrive tens of thousands of years ago?

Environmental changes allowed early humans to raise and grow certain plants. At the same time, they began to tame animals. Lesson 2.2 describes how learning to domesticate plants and animals began to make life easier for early humans.

BACKGROUND FOR THE TEACHER

Some scientists believe that early humans didn't domesticate wolves. Instead, these scientists say that wolves domesticated humans. A friendly, rather than aggressive, wolf may have approached humans while it was scavenging around a human settlement for food. Because of the animal's friendliness, humans may have begun to tolerate the wolf and adopt it. After a few generations, scientists say, these friendly wolves adopted by hunter-gatherers would have begun to look different from wild wolves.

DIGITAL RESOURCES myNGconnect.com

TEACHER RESOURCES & ASSESSMENT

 Reading and Note-Taking

 Vocabulary Practice

 Section 2 Quiz

STUDENT RESOURCES

NG Chapter Gallery

K-W-L CHART

Provide each student with a K-W-L chart. Have students brainstorm what they already know about domesticated animals, such as listing domesticated species and describing these animals' behavior. Then ask them to write questions that they would like to answer as they study the lesson, such as "How are animals domesticated?" Allow time at the end of the lesson for students to fill in what they have learned. `0:15` minutes

K What Do I Know?	W What Do I Want To Learn?	L What Did I Learn?

TEACH

GUIDED DISCUSSION

1. **Make Predictions** How did the disappearance of land bridges probably affect human migration to North America? *(Possible response: It would have made migration more difficult. Instead of being able to walk over land to reach North America from Asia, people probably had to travel across the water.)*

2. **Make Connections** How do people use domesticated animals today? *(Possible response: They still use them on the farm. Domesticated animals are also kept as pets and used to guide and help people with disabilities.)*

ANALYZE VISUALS

Preview the image in the lesson by asking volunteers to describe what they see in the photo. Then read the image caption aloud. Ask students to come up with a definition of *domesticated* based on what they see in the photo. `0:10` minutes

ACTIVE OPTIONS

On Your Feet: Turn and Talk on Topic Have students form three lines. Give each group this topic sentence: *The lives of early humans changed when they learned to domesticate plants and animals.* Tell

them to build a paragraph on that topic by having each student in the line add one sentence. Allow each group to present its paragraph to the class by having each student read his or her statement. `0:15` minutes

Critical Viewing: NG Chapter Gallery Ask students to choose one image from the Chapter Gallery and become an expert on it. They should do additional research to learn all about it. Then, students should share their findings with a partner, small group, or the class. `0:20` minutes

ENGLISH LANGUAGE LEARNERS

Pose and Answer Questions Have students work in pairs to read Lesson 2.2. Instruct them to pause after each paragraph and ask one another *who, what, when, where,* or *why* questions about what they have just read. Suggest students use a 5Ws Chart to help organize their questions and answers.

INCLUSION

Work in Pairs Allow students with disabilities to work with other students who can read the lesson aloud to them. Encourage the partner without disabilities to describe the visual as well. Have students work together to determine their answers to the Critical Viewing and Review & Assess questions. You may also want to give students the option of recording their answers rather than writing them out.

Press (**mt**) *in the Student eEdition for modified text.*

See the Chapter Planner for more strategies for differentiation.

ANSWERS

1. They domesticated and grew plants that they could store to feed them all year round. They domesticated animals for hunting and protection, to provide food and wool, and to carry heavy loads.

2. The warmer climate and increased rainfall made it easier to scatter and grow seeds in the wet ground. Later, the plants, especially certain grains, could be harvested and stored.

3. Some advantages might include greater security, stability, and comfort and the opportunity to share one's culture and knowledge with other groups.

The Agricultural Revolution

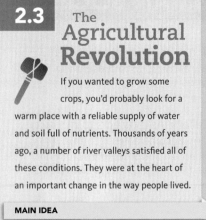

If you wanted to grow some crops, you'd probably look for a warm place with a reliable supply of water and soil full of nutrients. Thousands of years ago, a number of river valleys satisfied all of these conditions. They were at the heart of an important change in the way people lived.

MAIN IDEA

Humans settled down and farmed along river valleys and developed new farm tools and methods.

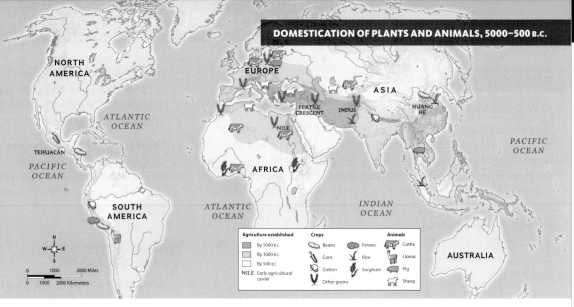

DOMESTICATION OF PLANTS AND ANIMALS, 5000–500 B.C.

Agriculture established
- By 5000 B.C.
- By 3000 B.C.
- By 500 B.C.
- NILE Early agricultural center

Crops: Beans, Potato, Corn, Rice, Cotton, Sorghum, Other grains

Animals: Cattle, Llama, Pig, Sheep

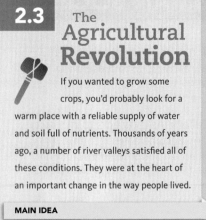

THE SICKLE
The sickle, which developed during the Neolithic Age, was crucial to harvesting certain grains. The tool was so important that in some places, people made sickles all the same size so that the tools could be repaired easily and quickly.

FERTILE RIVER VALLEYS

Imagine that a great change took place all over the world and transformed forever the way people lived. That is exactly what happened when farming largely replaced hunting and gathering. The slow shift to growing food began around 10,000 B.C. and ended around 8000 B.C. By then, many people had discovered that they could live year-round on what they farmed, rather than on what they found.

This shift in the way people lived is called the agricultural revolution. **Agriculture** is the practice of growing plants and rearing animals for food. The shift to agriculture also ushered in a new period known as the **Neolithic Age**, which began somewhere between 10,000 B.C. and 8000 B.C. In the early stages of this period, people began to build farming villages.

Many of the earliest farming villages were in an area called the **Fertile Crescent**. This region stretches from the Persian Gulf to the Mediterranean Sea. It includes the fertile, flat floodplains along the Tigris and Euphrates rivers in Southwest Asia. **Fertile** soil encourages the growth of crops and plants. The region provided a steady food supply. People were able to settle down and enjoy a much more comfortable lifestyle.

NEW FARM TOOLS AND METHODS

Even so, farming was very hard work. To make it easier, Neolithic people developed specialized tools. They fashioned hoes for digging the soil and plows for preparing the land to plant seeds. They also made curved sickles that cut through the stalks of grain and millstones that ground the grain into flour.

Farmers used domesticated animals to make their new tools more efficient. For example, they tied cattle to the plows and led the animals up and down the rows. In addition to helping turn over the soil, the cattle left behind manure that fertilized the land.

Neolithic people also developed new technology for the home. They made clay pots and hardened them in kilns, or ovens. The kilns could also be used to heat and melt the metal from rocks—a process called smelting. The liquid metal was then cast in molds to create metal tools, which eventually began to replace stone tools. The Stone Age had come to a close.

REVIEW & ASSESS

1. **READING CHECK** What new farm tools did humans develop during the agricultural revolution?

2. **INTERPRET MAPS** Along what geographic feature had most agriculture developed by 5000 B.C.?

3. **DRAW CONCLUSIONS** In what ways was the agricultural revolution an important breakthrough in human history?

PLAN

OBJECTIVE

Describe how humans settled down and farmed along river valleys and developed new farm tools and methods.

As humans moved into fertile river valleys, they began to settle down and replace hunting and gathering with farming. Lesson 2.3 describes the new tools and techniques humans developed to succeed in their new environments.

CRITICAL THINKING SKILLS FOR LESSON 2.3

- Identify Main Ideas and Details
- Monitor Comprehension
- Interpret Maps
- Draw Conclusions
- Compare and Contrast
- Make Inferences

BACKGROUND FOR THE TEACHER

With the development of agriculture, the Fertile Crescent had most of the natural resources it needed to flourish. There was little wood, metal, or stone, however. What the region did have in abundance was clay. It was used for mud bricks for building and for figurines and pottery. Eventually, the soft clay was also used as a medium for writing.

ESSENTIAL QUESTION

How did people manage to survive and thrive tens of thousands of years ago?

DIGITAL RESOURCES myNGconnect.com

TEACHER RESOURCES & ASSESSMENT

 Reading and Note-Taking   **Vocabulary Practice**   **Section 2 Quiz**

STUDENT RESOURCES

 Biography

INTRODUCE & ENGAGE

ANALYZE VISUALS

Bring in an image showing agriculture along the Tigris and Euphrates rivers and show it to the class. Have students discuss what they observe in the photo. **ASK**: What does this photo suggest about one benefit from the Tigris and Euphrates rivers? (*The rivers provide water for crops.*) Tell students that, in this lesson, they will learn about the role these rivers played in bringing about a fundamental change in the way people lived. **0:10 minutes**

TEACH

GUIDED DISCUSSION

1. **Compare and Contrast** How does the life of a hunter-gatherer compare with that of a settled farmer? (*Possible responses: A hunter-gatherer is always on the move, while a farmer lives in one place. A hunter-gatherer searches out his food, while a farmer grows or raises most of his. A hunter-gatherer may live in a cave or other temporary home, while a farmer lives in a permanent home he built.*)

2. **Make Inferences** What new challenges might people have encountered as they built and lived together in farming villages? (*Possible responses: growing enough food for everyone, having enough building and other resources for everyone, living in close proximity and getting along*)

INTERPRET MAPS

Have students study the map and its key. Make sure students understand the symbols by asking them to identify different crops and animals on the map. Make sure, too, they understand that the early agricultural centers appear all over the world—not just along the Nile. **ASK**: In which river valleys was agriculture established by 5000 B.C.? (*Fertile Crescent and Indus*) When had agriculture been established in Huang He? (*by 3000 B.C.*) Where else had agriculture been established by this time? (*Nile*) In which river valley did agriculture develop last? (*Tehuacán*) **0:10 minutes**

ACTIVE OPTIONS

On Your Feet: Numbered Heads Organize students into groups of four. Tell students to think about and discuss a response to this question: How did the agricultural revolution change people's lives? Then call a number and have the student from each group with that number report for the group. **0:15 minutes**

NG Learning Framework: Observe, Exchange, and Discuss
SKILLS: Observation, Collaboration
KNOWLEDGE: **Our Living Planet**

Have students revisit Lessons 2.2 and 2.3, specifically the information about the domestication of plants and animals and the agricultural revolution. They should work in pairs to create a list of observations about Neolithic people and how their lives changed as a result of domestication and organized agriculture. Once they have completed their list of observations, each pair should exchange lists with another pair and discuss the new list. **0:15 minutes**

DIFFERENTIATE

STRIVING READERS

Create Word Squares Have students complete Word Squares for the words *agriculture* and *fertile*.

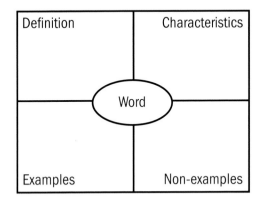

PRE-AP

Research River Valleys Divide the class into four groups and have each learn about one of the four river valleys shown on the map: Tehuacán, Fertile Crescent, Indus, and Huang He. Have them learn about the people who first settled there, what they grew, and how they lived. Tell students that they can present their findings in any form they choose, including a written report or multimedia presentation.

Press (**mt**) *in the Student eEdition for modified text.*
See the Chapter Planner for more strategies for differentiation.

REVIEW & ASSESS

ANSWERS

1. Humans developed new tools such as axes, hoes, plows, sickles, and millstones during the agricultural revolution.

2. Most agriculture had developed along rivers.

3. The agricultural revolution saw the shift from the nomadic life to a settled one. It also led to the development of new and specialized tools, some of which would replace stone tools. The revolution marked the end of the Old Stone Age.

2.4 Studying the Past

Look around. Everything you can see tells a story. At a glance, the shape, size, age, and use of a particular object provide some clues to its history. However, with a team of scientists, you could learn a whole lot more.

MAIN IDEA

Archaeologists, historians, and other specialists gather and study evidence to tell the story of human history.

SCIENTIFIC DATA

As you have learned by reading this chapter, archaeologists piece together clues to tell the story of what happened in a particular place at a particular time. It is detective work, and like detectives, they rely on other specialists to help them find and analyze the evidence.

Some of these specialists include geologists, who can tell the story of a landscape by analyzing rocks and fossils. When geologists investigate rock layers, they sometimes uncover prehistoric plant and animal remains. These remains can reveal what the environment was like. The bones they find provide information about human health and diet. Geologists can also help archaeologists locate deeply buried artifacts.

Other specialists called radiologists study x-ray images to look beneath the surface of objects to show what the eye cannot see, especially in bones and rusty metal. An advanced x-ray called a CT scan provides detailed images that can be manipulated on a computer and turned into three-dimensional representations.

As you may recall, geneticists are scientists who study genes, the biological blueprints for all living things. Genes are made up of DNA, which is encoded in every cell and transmitted from parent to child. *Encode* means "to put a message into a code," or set of symbols. By studying modern DNA patterns, geneticists can trace human ancestry back thousands of years to see how people spread around the world.

HISTORICAL SOURCES

Historians also work to understand the past. They take evidence from many different sources to explain what happened and when and why it did.

Some of the sources historians use include primary sources. A **primary source** is an artifact or piece of writing that was created by someone who witnessed or lived through a historical event. These sources include letters, maps, paintings, and tools. Primary sources are very important, but they are not always completely reliable. The opinions of the author may distort, or misrepresent, the facts.

Historians also use **secondary sources**, artifacts or writings created after an event by someone who did not see it or live during the time when it occurred. These are interpretations of events, often based on primary sources. History books and biographies are secondary sources. **Oral history** is an unwritten account of events that is often passed down through the generations as stories or songs.

Different historians can interpret the same evidence in very different ways. In addition, new evidence is continually being discovered. That means that history—especially the details—is always changing.

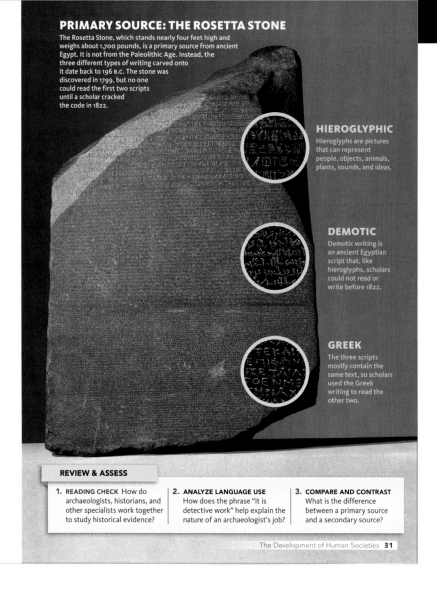

PRIMARY SOURCE: THE ROSETTA STONE

The Rosetta Stone, which stands nearly four feet high and weighs about 1,700 pounds, is a primary source from ancient Egypt. It is not from the Paleolithic Age. Instead, the three different types of writing carved onto it date back to 196 B.C. The stone was discovered in 1799, but no one could read the first two scripts until a scholar cracked the code in 1822.

HIEROGLYPHIC
Hieroglyphs are pictures that can represent people, objects, animals, plants, sounds, and ideas.

DEMOTIC
Demotic writing is an ancient Egyptian script that, like hieroglyphs, scholars could not read or write before 1822.

GREEK
The three scripts mostly contain the same text, so scholars used the Greek writing to read the other two.

REVIEW & ASSESS

1. **READING CHECK** How do archaeologists, historians, and other specialists work together to study historical evidence?

2. **ANALYZE LANGUAGE USE** How does the phrase "it is detective work" help explain the nature of an archaeologist's job?

3. **COMPARE AND CONTRAST** What is the difference between a primary source and a secondary source?

OBJECTIVE

Describe how archaeologists, historians, and other specialists gather and study scientific data and historical sources.

CRITICAL THINKING SKILLS FOR LESSON 2.4

- Identify Main Ideas and Details
- Monitor Comprehension
- Analyze Language Use
- Compare and Contrast
- Make Inferences
- Identify Problems and Solutions
- Analyze Visuals

ESSENTIAL QUESTION

How did people manage to survive and thrive tens of thousands of years ago?

Archaeologists, historians, and other specialists piece together clues from the past to tell the human story. Lesson 2.4 describes how these specialists analyze and interpret the evidence to find out how humans survived and thrived.

BACKGROUND FOR THE TEACHER

The scholar who cracked the code of the Rosetta Stone was a French historian named Jean-François Champollion. In 1808, at the age of 18, he began his first attempts at deciphering the hieroglyphs on the Rosetta Stone. However, his breakthrough didn't come until 1822, when Champollion concluded that the hieroglyphs were not only symbols but functioned as an alphabet and a phonetic language.

DIGITAL RESOURCES myNGconnect.com

TEACHER RESOURCES & ASSESSMENT

 Reading and Note-Taking   **Vocabulary Practice**   **Section 2 Quiz**

STUDENT RESOURCES

 NG Chapter Gallery

INTRODUCE & ENGAGE

IDENTIFY CLUES

Ask a student volunteer to bring his or her backpack to the front of the classroom. Hold the backpack up so students can study it and ask them what they can learn about it just by looking. **ASK:** How old do you think the backpack is? How can you tell? How many compartments and pockets does the backpack have? What does that tell you about its owner? Has the owner attached stickers, buttons, or other items to the pack? What does that tell you? Then tell students that these are the types of questions archaeologists might ask as they study an early artifact. Tell them that they will learn more about how archaeologists and other experts study the past in this lesson. **0:10** minutes

TEACH

GUIDED DISCUSSION

1. **Make Inferences** Why do you think archaeologists are interested to know what a geologist discovers about an early environment? *(Possible response: The information might shed light on what kinds of food were available in the environment, what the climate was like, what challenges the people living there faced.)*

2. **Identify Problems and Solutions** What challenges do historians face when they sift through primary sources? *(Possible response: The sources may be biased or tell only part of a story.)*

ANALYZE VISUALS

Have students examine the image of the Rosetta Stone. Tell them that the yellow circles contain magnified samples of writing from the stone. Point out that the word *hieroglyphic* comes from Greek words meaning "sacred carving." Point out, too, the size and weight of the stone, which are provided in the caption. Then ask students who they think had the writing carved on the stone and what the subject of the writing might be. After their discussion, tell students that an Egyptian ruler had the writing carved on the stone, and the text discusses his power and the responsibilities of Egyptian priests. **0:10** minutes

ACTIVE OPTIONS

On Your Feet: Three Corners Post these signs in three corners of the classroom: Primary Source, Secondary Source, Oral History. Organize students into groups around each sign and have them discuss that historical source and come up with examples of it. Then have students from the primary source group travel to explain their historical source to each of the other two groups. Have the secondary source and oral history groups repeat the process. **0:15** minutes

Critical Viewing: NG Chapter Gallery Invite students to explore the Chapter Gallery and choose one image they feel best represents their understanding of Chapter 1. Have students provide a written explanation of why they selected that particular image. **0:15** minutes

DIFFERENTIATE

STRIVING READERS

Use Reciprocal Teaching Have partners take turns reading each paragraph of the lesson aloud. At the end of the paragraph, the reading student should ask the listening student questions about the paragraph. Students may ask their partners to state the main idea, identify important details that support the main idea, or summarize the paragraph in their own words. Then have students work together to answer the "Review & Assess" questions.

INCLUSION

Summarize Information Use a Fishbowl activity to review the lesson. Place students of mixed ability levels in each circle. Call on more advanced students to take turns summarizing the lesson content. When the first group of students has concluded its summary, switch positions and have inclusion students review the lesson content.

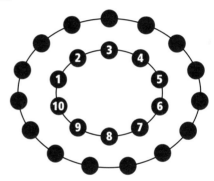

Press **mt** *in the Student eEdition for modified text.*

See the Chapter Planner for more strategies for differentiation.

REVIEW & ASSESS

ANSWERS

1. Archaeologists, geologists, radiologists, geneticists, and historians all use their expertise to study evidence from many different sources to understand what happened in the past and explain when and why it did.

2. The phrase conveys the idea that archaeologists must search for answers by sifting through many clues.

3. A primary source is a document or other source—such as a letter, map, or painting—created by someone who witnessed or lived through a historical event. In contrast, a secondary source is a document or other source created by someone who did not witness the event or live during the time it occurred.

VOCABULARY

For each pair of vocabulary words, write one sentence that explains the connection between the two words.

1. **fossil; artifact**
   Both fossils, the remains of living organisms, and artifacts, human-made objects, provide helpful clues to understanding our history.
2. **archaeologist; anthropologist**
3. **culture; oral history**
4. **anthropologist; culture**
5. **hunter-gatherer; nomad**
6. **migration; land bridge**
7. **agriculture; fertile**
8. **primary source; secondary source**

READING STRATEGY

9. **ORGANIZE IDEAS: COMPARE AND CONTRAST** If you haven't already, complete your Venn diagram to compare and contrast the lives of Paleolithic and Neolithic people. Then answer the question.

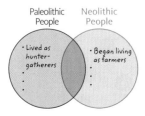

Paleolithic People | Neolithic People
• Lived as hunter-gatherers
• Began living as farmers

In what ways did the lives of Paleolithic and Neolithic people differ? In what ways were they the same?

MAIN IDEAS

Answer the following questions. Support your answers with evidence from the chapter.

10. What do archaeologists learn about early modern humans by studying their fossils and artifacts? LESSON 1.1
11. What effect did a catastrophic drought in East Africa have on *Homo sapiens* thousands of years ago? LESSON 1.3
12. Why were the Paleolithic people who left Africa probably attracted to the region of Southwest Asia? LESSON 1.4
13. How did groups of hunter-gatherers work together? LESSON 2.1
14. What were some of the first plants and animals domesticated by humans? LESSON 2.2
15. Why is the development of farming called the agricultural revolution? LESSON 2.3
16. What sources do historians use to study the past? LESSON 2.4

CRITICAL THINKING

Answer the following questions. Support your answers with evidence from the chapter.

17. **MAKE INFERENCES** What factors do you think were essential to the survival of humankind?
18. **COMPARE AND CONTRAST** How was the culture of prehistoric *Homo sapiens* similar to our own?
19. **DRAW CONCLUSIONS** What does the domestication of plants and animals suggest about the development of humans?
20. **YOU DECIDE** Some historians think that the agricultural revolution was the most important event in human history. Others claim that the ability to control fire was the most important. Which development do you think was more important? Support your opinion.

INTERPRET MAPS

Study the map of the Fertile Crescent. Then use the map to answer the questions that follow.

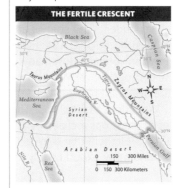

THE FERTILE CRESCENT

21. The Fertile Crescent is the area shown in green on the map. Why do you think the Fertile Crescent was so narrow?
22. What rivers were vital to the development of early farming in the Fertile Crescent?
23. What bodies of water bordering the region probably contributed to its fertility?
24. **MAP ACTIVITY** Sketch your own physical map of the Fertile Crescent. Be sure to label all bodies of water, deserts, and mountains. Use a different color for each type of physical feature. How does your map help you visualize the Fertile Crescent and its surrounding area?

ANALYZE SOURCES

Study this cave painting of two bison, or buffalo-like animals, from the Lascaux Cave in France. Then answer the question.

25. What details in the cave painting suggest that the Paleolithic artist who created it was highly skilled?

WRITE ABOUT HISTORY

26. **EXPLANATORY** Many new developments occurred during the Neolithic Age. Write a paragraph in which you describe one important development and explain how it changed the way people lived during that period.

TIPS

- Take notes from the chapter on the development your chose.
- State your main idea clearly at the beginning of the paragraph.
- Support your main idea with relevant facts, definitions, specific details, and examples.
- Use vocabulary you learned from the chapter.
- Provide a concluding statement about the significance of the development your chose.

VOCABULARY ANSWERS

1. Both fossils, the remains of living organisms, and artifacts, human-made objects, provide helpful clues to understanding our history.

2. An archaeologist digs up fossils and artifacts at an early settlement, and an anthropologist is an archaeologist who studies these objects to understand the culture of the people who once lived there.

3. The songs and stories that make up the oral history of a group of people are an important part of the group's culture.

4. An anthropologist is an archaeologist who studies culture.

5. To survive, hunter-gatherers lived as nomads, moving with the seasons to hunt herds of animals and gather fruits, nuts, roots, and seeds to eat.

6. During the Ice Age, land bridges formed that enabled the migration of *Homo sapiens* from one continent to another.

7. The rich nutrients in the fertile soil of the river valleys in the Fertile Crescent allowed people to practice agriculture, or the practice of growing plants and rearing animals for food.

8. Historians study primary sources, such as letters and tools, and secondary sources, such as biographies and history books, to understand and interpret historical events.

READING STRATEGY ANSWERS

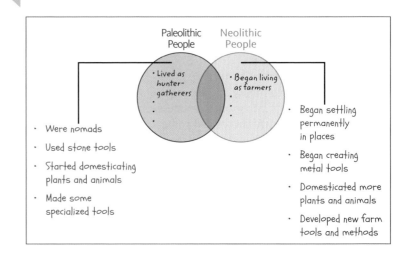

Paleolithic People | Neolithic People

• Lived as hunter-gatherers
• Began living as farmers

- Were nomads
- Used stone tools
- Started domesticating plants and animals
- Made some specialized tools

- Began settling permanently in places
- Began creating metal tools
- Domesticated more plants and animals
- Developed new farm tools and methods

9. Paleolithic and Neolithic peoples both lived in groups, used tools, and learned to adapt to new conditions by developing specialized tools. However, the way of life for Neolithic people changed when many abandoned the nomadic life of hunter-gatherers and began living as settled farmers. They also developed even more sophisticated and specialized tools and materials than Paleolithic people.

MAIN IDEAS ANSWERS

10. Fossils and artifacts tell us when and how early modern humans lived.

11. The drought in East Africa dried up rivers and lakes, made edible plants scarce, and left *Homo sapiens* struggling for survival. Some began migrating to more habitable locations.

12. They were attracted to Southwest Asia because of its lush vegetation and abundant wildlife.

13. Men in the groups went out to hunt while the women and young children gathered fruits, nuts, roots, and seeds.

14. Some of the first plants were grasses and grains. Some of the first animals were dogs, sheep, goats, pigs, and cattle.

15. It's called a revolution because it resulted in a major change in the way people lived.

16. Historians use primary and secondary sources and oral history.

CRITICAL THINKING ANSWERS

17. Increased intelligence and the ability to adapt to new situations and environments might have been most essential to the survival of humankind.

18. Like early *Homo sapiens*, people today use language, create art, practice religion, and develop technology.

19. The domestication of plants and animals suggests that humans were learning how to control their environment rather than simply reacting to it.

20. Students' responses will vary. Students who believe that the agricultural revolution was more important may point out that it radically changed people's way of life and led to the settled population patterns that we still see today. Students who believe that capturing and controlling fire was more important may say that this ability allowed humans to warm themselves, conquer the dark, and cook food, thereby helping to ensure the survival of humankind.

INTERPRET MAPS ANSWERS

21. The Fertile Crescent was narrow because it was bounded by deserts and mountains.

22. The Tigris and Euphrates rivers were vital to the development of early farming.

23. The Mediterranean Sea and the Persian Gulf probably contributed to the region's fertility.

24. Maps and answers will vary. Students' maps should label all bodies of water, deserts, and mountains and use a different color for each.

ANALYZE SOURCES ANSWER

25. Students' responses will vary. Possible response: The artist's use of color, the suggestion of movement, the realistic depiction, and the use of perspective in the crossed hind legs of the two bison reveal a high level of skill.

WRITE ABOUT HISTORY ANSWER

26. Students' paragraphs should
   - provide a clear explanation of one development that changed the way people lived during the Neolithic Age
   - support the explanation with evidence about the tools, methods, and materials developed during the period
   - be written in a formal style
   - include vocabulary words from the chapter

UNIT RESOURCES

On Location with National Geographic Explorer-in-Residence Louise Leakey
Intro and Video

Interactive Map Tool

News & Updates

Available on myNGconnect

Unit Wrap-Up:
"Discovering Our Ancestors"
Feature and Video

"Scotland's Stone Age Ruins"
National Geographic Adapted Article

"First Americans"
National Geographic Adapted Article
Student eEdition exclusive

Unit 1 Inquiry:
Create a Cultural Symbol

CHAPTER RESOURCES

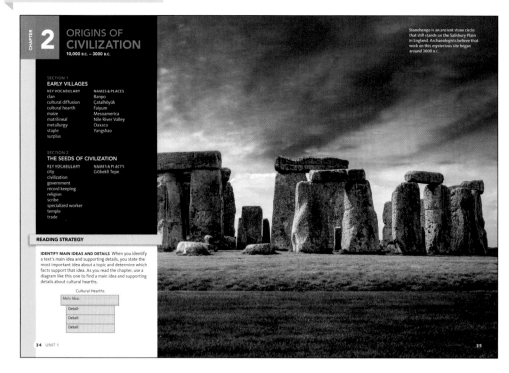

TEACHER RESOURCES & ASSESSMENT

Available on myNGconnect

Social Studies Skills Lessons
• Reading: Identify Main Ideas and Details
• Writing: Write an Explanatory Essay

Formal Assessment
• Chapter 2 Tests A (on-level) &
  B (below-level)

(A) Chapter 2 Answer Key

ExamView®
One time Download

STUDENT BACKPACK *Available on myNGconnect*

• **eEdition** *(English)*   • **eEdition** *(Spanish)*   • **Handbooks**   • **Online Atlas**

For Chapter 2 Spanish resources, visit the Teacher Resource Menu page on myNGconnect.

SECTION 1 RESOURCES

EARLY VILLAGES

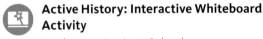 Reading and Note-Taking

Vocabulary Practice

Section 1 Quiz

Available on myNGconnect

LESSON 1.1 CENTERS OF NEW IDEAS

Active History: Interactive Whiteboard Activity
Analyze an Ancient Calendar

Active History
Analyze an Ancient Calendar

Available on myNGconnect

- On Your Feet: Four Corners

LESSON 1.2 SOUTHWEST ASIA: ÇATALHÖYÜK

Biography
James Mellaart

Available on myNGconnect

- On Your Feet: Inside-Outside Circle
- Critical Viewing: NG Chapter Gallery

LESSON 1.3 CHINA: BANPO

- On Your Feet: Question and Answer

| **NG Learning Framework:**
Write About Craftsmanship

LESSON 1.4 MESOAMERICA: OAXACA

- On Your Feet: Think, Pair, Share
- Critical Viewing: NG Chapter Gallery

LESSON 1.5 NORTH AFRICA: FAIYUM

- On Your Feet: One-on-One Interviews

| **NG Learning Framework:**
Teach Your Methods

SECTION 2 RESOURCES

THE SEEDS OF CIVILIZATION

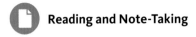 Reading and Note-Taking

 Vocabulary Practice

 Section 2 Quiz

Available on myNGconnect

LESSON 2.1 PATHS TO CIVILIZATION: GÖBEKLI TEPE

- On Your Feet: Living Flow Chart

| **NG Learning Framework:**
Rewrite in Your Own Words

LESSON 2.2 TRAITS OF CIVILIZATION

- On Your Feet: Build a Civilization

| **NG Learning Framework:**
Rank the Traits

HISTORY THROUGH OBJECTS
LESSON 2.3 NEW TECHNOLOGY

- On Your Feet: Make a Tool
- Critical Viewing: NG Image Gallery

CHAPTER 2 REVIEW

STRATEGY ❶

Make Summary Statements

Before reading, have students look at the blue subheadings in each lesson. After reading, direct students to use each subheading to begin a statement that summarizes the information about the subheadings.

Use with All Lessons *For Lesson 1.1, suggest that students use these sentence starters: A cultural hearth is _____ . Four cultural hearths that developed during the Neolithic period were _____ .*

STRATEGY ❷

Play Vocabulary Tic-Tac-Toe

Write nine Key Vocabulary words on a tic-tac-toe grid on the board. Position the words on the grid so that an X or O can be written below each word. Player A chooses a word. If the player correctly pronounces, defines, and uses the word in a sentence, he or she can put an X or O in the insert box in that square. Play alternates until one person has a row of Xs or Os.

Use with All Lessons *This game can also be played using teams. Divide the class into two teams, Team A and Team B, and alternate play until one team has a row of Xs or Os.*

STRATEGY ❸

Use Exit Slips

For a quick, informal assessment tool, direct students to respond in writing to a single question at the end of a lesson. Preview the questions before reading each lesson. Pass out strips of paper. Have students write their responses on the paper strips. Then ask students to turn in their written responses as they exit the class.

2.1 Where was Göbekli Tepe located? *(southeast Turkey, on the edge of the Fertile Crescent)*

2.2 What are two traits of civilizations? *(Students should name two of the following: cities, complex institutions, specialized workers, record keeping, improved technology.)*

2.3 What development allowed people to make tools out of metal instead of just stone? *(metallurgy)*

Use with Lessons 2.1–2.3

Press (mt) *in the Student eEdition for modified text.*

STRATEGY ❶

Preview Content with a Map

Use the following suggestions to preview content using a map.

• Explain that this map is a topical map, meant to show the location of four cultural hearths.

• Remind students that they can identify continents and bodies of water by their labels on the map.

• Tell students to draw lines with their fingers from the four inset maps to their appropriate locations on the world map.

• Explain that these four inset maps give more information than is shown on the main map, including names of rivers, river valleys, and archaeological sites.

Use with Lesson 1.1 *Invite volunteers to describe the visuals in detail to help visually impaired students see them.*

STRATEGY ❷

Modify Main Idea Statements

Have each student work with a partner to preview the chapter by reading and copying each lesson's Main Idea statement onto a sheet of paper. Then have students look at any maps, photos, and illustrations in the text and add to each lesson's Main Idea. They can write complete sentences or notes on the page.

Use with Lessons 1.1–1.5 and 2.1–2.2 *For Lesson 1.2, have students describe the illustration of Çatalhöyük. For Lesson 1.5, have students include details from the photo of Faiyum today.*

STRATEGY ❶

Create Four-Square Word Charts

Give students the following list of vocabulary words and display the Word Chart model. Ask students to complete the four parts of the chart for each word on the list.

city	clan
maize	metallurgy
record keeping	scribe
temple	trade

Definition of *city* *A city is a political, social, and cultural center where a lot of people live.*	Draw a visual. 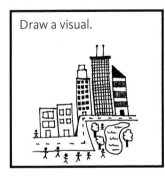
Tell how it relates to the text. *Cities were important in the formation of civilizations.*	Use it in a sentence. *Ur was a major trade center and one of the busiest cities in the ancient world.*

Use with Lessons 1.2–1.4 and 2.1–2.2

STRATEGY ❷
Build Concept Clusters

Write the Key Vocabulary words *cultural hearth* and *civilization* on the board and ask students for words, phrases, or pictures that come to mind. Have volunteers write the words and draw simple pictures around the words *cultural hearth* and *civilization* to build two Concept Clusters. Call on students to create sentences about the words and pictures. Then have each student ask a question they would like to have answered about the Key Vocabulary words.

Use with Lessons 1.1 and 2.2 *You may wish to place students in groups with various levels of language proficiency and have more advanced students assist less advanced students with their Concept Clusters.*

STRATEGY ❸
Find Someone Who Knows

After reading, give students a time limit and tell them to find classmates who can provide the answer to each question below. Each person should write the answer and sign his or her name.

1. What jobs do specialized workers do? (*jobs other than agriculture, such as making pottery or metalworking*)
2. What is trade? (*the exchange of goods*)

3. What material were early needles made of? (*bone; some students might also guess wood*)
4. What is flint? (*a hard stone that can be shaped into a sharp point*)

Use with Lessons 2.2–2.3

STRATEGY ❶
Investigate an Archaeological Site

Direct students to choose one of the archaeological sites listed below and investigate its history in more depth. Have them assemble their findings in a report that includes both visuals and text.

Çatalhöyük   Faiyum   Banpo   Oaxaca   Göbekli Tepe

Use with Lessons 1.1–1.5 and 2.1 *Encourage students to include a map showing the location of their chosen site.*

STRATEGY ❶
Annotate a Time Line

Suggest that student annotate a time line that situates each location and event listed below. Have students include at least two details per location and event on their time lines.

- cultural hearths form
- climate in Sahara changes drastically
- maize revolution takes place
- Yangshao culture thrives
- Göbekli Tepe is built
- Çatalhöyük begins to develop
- Faiyum is established

Use with Lessons 1.1–1.5 and 2.1 *Some students may wish to develop a more complex time line on a specific cultural hearth. Encourage them to conduct research to identify the most significant dates.*

2 ORIGINS OF CIVILIZATION

10,000 B.C. – 3000 B.C.

Stonehenge is an ancient stone circle that still stands on the Salisbury Plain in England. Archaeologists believe that work on this mysterious site began around 3000 B.C.

SECTION 1
EARLY VILLAGES

KEY VOCABULARY	NAMES & PLACES
clan	Banpo
cultural diffusion	Çatalhöyük
cultural hearth	Faiyum
maize	Mesoamerica
matrilineal	Nile River Valley
metallurgy	Oaxaca
staple	Yangshao
surplus	

SECTION 2
THE SEEDS OF CIVILIZATION

KEY VOCABULARY	NAMES & PLACES
city	Göbekli Tepe
civilization	
government	
record keeping	
religion	
scribe	
specialized worker	
temple	
trade	

READING STRATEGY

IDENTIFY MAIN IDEAS AND DETAILS When you identify a text's main idea and supporting details, you state the most important idea about a topic and determine which facts support that idea. As you read the chapter, use a diagram like this one to find a main idea and supporting details about cultural hearths.

Cultural Hearths

Main Idea:
Detail:
Detail:
Detail:

TEACHER BACKGROUND

INTRODUCE THE PHOTOGRAPH

Have students study the photograph of Stonehenge. Encourage them to notice the shapes of the different parts of the structure and the shape of the structure itself.

ASK: What do you think this structure might have been used for? *(Possible responses: Perhaps the site was a meeting place, maybe for religious expression.)*

Explain that because it is round (which may not be obvious from the photograph), people may have gathered there for ceremonial purposes.

SHARE BACKGROUND

Work began on this structure around 3000 B.C., and it went through six different stages of construction, ending in 1520 B.C. Its name, Stonehenge, comes from the Saxon *sten-hangen* and means "stone hanging." It is one of the most impressive prehistoric megaliths, or stone monuments, in the world. Theories abound regarding its purpose, ranging from use for astronomy to healing to a seasonal meeting place for Neolithic and Bronze Age groups in the area.

DIGITAL RESOURCES myNGconnect.com

TEACHER RESOURCES & ASSESSMENT

 Social Studies Skills Lessons
- Reading: Identify Main Ideas and Details
- Writing: Write an Explanatory Essay

 Formal Assessment
- Chapter 2 Tests A (on-level) & B (below-level)

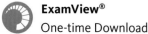 **ExamView®**
One-time Download

 **Chapter 2 Answer Key**

STUDENT BACKPACK

- **eEdition** *(English)*
- **eEdition** *(Spanish)*
- **Handbooks**
- **Online Atlas**

For Chapter 2 Spanish Resources, visit the Teacher Resource Menu page.

WHAT FACTORS CONTRIBUTED TO THE DEVELOPMENT OF CIVILIZATION?

Brainstorming Activity: Characteristics of Civilization Introduce students to the concept of civilization by inviting them to brainstorm different characteristics of civilizations. Record student responses in a Concept Cluster. If students need help getting started, encourage them to think about these topics:

A. **Food and Workers** In order for a civilization to thrive, it must have a reliable way to feed its people, and it must have people who can do specific jobs.

B. **Places to Live** Settlements lead to villages and then to cities from which civilizations expand.

C. **Institutions** One characteristic of civilizations is the formation of institutions such as government and religion.

D. **Writing** Writing down and keeping track of information in an ordered way is important in any civilization.

E. **Technology** Developing new ways to do or produce things involves technology, which improves as civilizations emerge.

`0:15` minutes

IDENTIFY MAIN IDEAS AND DETAILS

Remind students that identifying a main idea and determining which facts support that idea helps them understand the text. Model finding the main idea of the first paragraph under "What is a cultural hearth?" in Lesson 1.1 and add it to the Main Idea Diagram.

Cultural Hearths

Main Idea:
Detail:
Detail:
Detail:

WORD SORT CHART

Have students use a Word Sort strategy for the chapter's Key Vocabulary. Tell them to sort the words into categories (see examples provided below), and then list the words under the heading with which they associate the most. Encourage students to discuss the reasoning behind their sorts.

PEOPLE	FOOD	SKILLS	SOCIETY	CONCEPTS

KEY DATES	
9500 B.C.	Temples at Göbekli Tepe first built
8000 B.C.	Cultural hearths around the world begin to take form
7400 B.C.	Çatalhöyük, a settlement in present-day Turkey, is founded
5200 B.C.	Egypt's earliest farming community, Faiyum, is established
5000–3000 B.C.	Yangshao culture in northern China thrives
4250–2000 B.C.	Domestication of maize in Mesoamerica

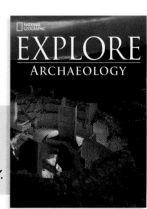

NATIONAL GEOGRAPHIC
EXPLORE
ARCHAEOLOGY

For more on Göbekli Tepe and other wonderful archaeology stories, see **EXPLORE ARCHAEOLOGY.**

Centers of New Ideas

Where do new ideas come from, and how do they spread? Today's trends start with ideas that catch on all over the world. About 12,000 years ago, ideas began to spread in the same way. Groups of people living in different places invented new ways of doing things. These groups created the world's early cultural hearths.

MAIN IDEA

Cultural hearths promoted the spread of new ideas, practices, and technology in different parts of the world.

WHAT IS A CULTURAL HEARTH?

New ideas, practices, and technology began in places called **cultural hearths**. Remember that culture is a group's way of life, including the group's behaviors, beliefs, language, and customs. Ancient cultural hearths spread ideas and practices that influenced the way people did everyday things, from planting crops to burying their dead.

New practices emerged in several cultural hearths around the same time. Between 8000 and 5000 B.C., people living in different parts of the world began to develop new ways of community living. They began to practice new methods of domesticating animals and plants and living in settled communities. As settled societies thrived, they began to form organized governments. People living in settled communities also built places of worship and expressed themselves artistically.

Despite being separated by thousands of miles, ancient cultural hearths shared similar geographic features. These features included mild climates, fertile land, and access to rivers. Such favorable conditions allowed agriculture to flourish and attracted new people to the area. As populations grew and migrated to other places, they took the new cultural practices with them.

FOUR CULTURAL HEARTHS

Several cultural hearths developed during the Neolithic period. In this chapter, you will learn about four of them, specifically the cultural hearths that emerged in Southwest Asia, China, Mesoamerica, and North Africa.

As you can see on the map, these cultural hearths were located in widely scattered parts of the world. For example, Mesoamerica, in present-day Mexico and Central America, was thousands of miles away from Banpo, in China. Keep in mind that people living in these cultural hearths did not have the benefit of modern communication or transportation. Thousands of years ago, new ideas and practices emerged in and spread from very different places around the same time—without the benefit of the Internet or air travel.

Each of these cultural hearths made an important contribution to surrounding cultures and regions. Simultaneously, the people living in these cultural hearths accepted new ideas themselves. They learned new ways of doing things from people who traveled from other places, and they absorbed the new ideas into their own cultures. Later cultures would build upon the foundations established by these ancient cultural hearths.

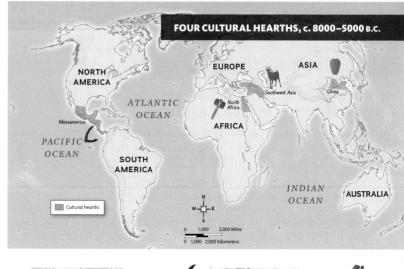

FOUR CULTURAL HEARTHS, c. 8000–5000 B.C.

Cultural hearths

Mesoamerica: Oaxaca
Farmers in Oaxaca introduced an important new crop: maize.

North Africa: Faiyum
Faiyum farmers adopted techniques from cultures across the Mediterranean.

Southwest Asia: Çatalhöyük
Builders at Çatalhöyük demonstrated advanced construction techniques.

China: Banpo
Yangshao potters at Banpo created functional, beautiful pottery.

REVIEW & ASSESS

1. **READING CHECK** What is a cultural hearth?

2. **DESCRIBE** What geographic features did ancient cultural hearths share?

3. **INTERPRET MAPS** Near what rivers did these four ancient cultural hearths emerge?

PLAN

OBJECTIVE

Learn how new ideas, practices, and technology spread from cultural hearths to different parts of the world.

CRITICAL THINKING SKILLS FOR LESSON 1.1

- Identify Main Ideas and Details
- Monitor Comprehension
- Describe
- Interpret Maps
- Analyze Cause and Effect

ESSENTIAL QUESTION

What factors contributed to the development of civilization?

Cultural hearths formed the foundation upon which later civilizations were built. Lesson 1.1 discusses four different cultural hearths that emerged at about the same time.

BACKGROUND FOR THE TEACHER

Some of the new ideas that developed were focused on tools. The sickle was an indispensable tool in the Neolithic-period domestication of plants. It was one of the most ancient tools used in the harvest of grains and other plants. Sickles usually had curved metal blades and short wooden handles, and they were hand held. This meant the person doing the harvesting had to be stooped or bent over near the plants. Longer-handled tools came later, in the form of scythes. Sickles were simple tools, but effective, and they are still used today.

DIGITAL RESOURCES myNGconnect.com

TEACHER RESOURCES & ASSESSMENT

 Reading and Note-Taking

 Vocabulary Practice

 Section 1 Quiz

STUDENT RESOURCES

 Active History

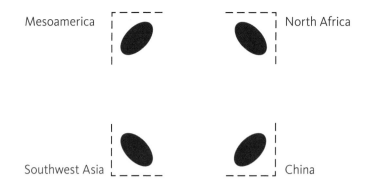

Mesoamerica · North Africa
Southwest Asia · China

INTRODUCE & ENGAGE

PREVIEW CONTENT WITH MAPS

Direct students' attention to the Four Cultural Hearths map. Ask students to locate where four cultural hearths developed. **ASK:** Which of the four cultural hearths is in North America? *(Mesoamerica, in present-day Mexico and Central America)* **ASK:** Which is in North Africa? *(Faiyum, in present-day Egypt)* Explain to students that they will learn about cultural hearths in four different parts of the world. **0:05 minutes**

TEACH

GUIDED DISCUSSION

1. **Monitor Comprehension** When did the cultural hearths discussed in the text develop? *(They developed between 8000 and 5000 B.C., during the Neolithic period.)*

2. **Analyze Cause and Effect** What happened in cultural hearths when people developed a way of domesticating plants and animals? *(The domestication of plants and animals meant settled societies could thrive, which led to organized government and religion.)*

INTERPRET MAPS

Have students study the Four Cultural Hearths map. Ask for volunteers to identify river valleys on the map. *(Students should note the Tehuacán Valley, the Nile River Valley, and the Wei Huang Valley.)*

ASK: What is unique about the location of Çatalhöyük and Göbekli Tepe? *(Çatalhöyük and Göbekli Tepe were located in Southwest Asia, on the edge of the Fertile Crescent. Explain that the Fertile Crescent describes the area between and around the Tigris and Euphrates rivers because it provided fertile lands in the shape of a curve.)* **0:10 minutes**

ACTIVE OPTIONS

Active History: Analyze an Ancient Calendar Extend the lesson by using either the PDF or Whiteboard version of the activity. These activities take a deeper look at a topic from, or related to, the lesson. Explore the activities as a class, turn them into group assignments, or assign them individually. **0:10 minutes**

On Your Feet: Four Corners Assign students to one of four corners in the room, labeled Mesoamerica, North Africa, Southwest Asia, and China. Then have each group brainstorm four questions they have about their group's cultural hearth. Have each group of students present three of the group's questions to the other corners. Start the discussion by tossing a bean bag or other soft object to one team and asking, "What question do you have about your cultural hearth?" When the first team states its question, have them toss the bean bag to another team to hear one of their prepared questions. Continue until teams have listed all their questions. **0:15 minutes**

DIFFERENTIATE

STRIVING READERS

Set a Purpose for Reading Before reading, have students use the subheadings in the lesson to create purpose-setting questions:

- What is the definition of a cultural hearth?
- What are the four cultural hearths introduced in the lesson?

After reading, have student pairs answer the questions. Then ask for student volunteers to share their answers.

GIFTED & TALENTED

Investigate Cultural Hearths Have students conduct independent research on one additional cultural hearth. Direct them to the following locations:

- Indus and Ganges river valleys
- Andean South America
- West Africa

Ask students to prepare a short presentation about the cultural hearth they researched. Explain that these cultural hearths developed at slightly different times, and that in their research, they should note similarities and differences to the cultural hearths in their textbook.

Press **(mt)** *in the Student eEdition for modified text.*
See the Chapter Planner for more strategies for differentiation.

REVIEW & ASSESS

ANSWERS

1. A cultural hearth is a place from which new ideas, practices, and technology spread.

2. Cultural hearths shared similar geographic features, including mild climates, fertile land, and access to rivers.

3. Southwest Asia: Tigris and Euphrates; North Africa: Nile; China: Huang He and Chang Jiang; Mesoamerica: Balsas

Imagine you are a traveler crossing central Turkey 9,000 years ago. Suddenly, you stumble on an amazing sight: hundreds of houses surrounded by fields of ripening wheat and barley, enclosures of cattle, and thousands of people—more people than you ever imagined existed. What is this strange place? It's Çatalhöyük.

MAIN IDEA

Çatalhöyük was an advanced settlement and an early cultural hearth in Southwest Asia.

AN AGRICULTURAL VILLAGE

By modern standards, the Neolithic village of **Çatalhöyük** (chah-tuhl-HOO-yuk) was small and simple. To Neolithic people, though, it was incredibly advanced. Çatalhöyük developed in present-day Turkey beginning around 7400 B.C. This settlement was large, both in size and population. Çatalhöyük still fascinates people thousands of years later because of the rich cultural material left behind by those who lived there.

The people who built Çatalhöyük relied on farming for food. A stable food supply contributed to population growth and Çatalhöyük's agriculture eventually supported as many as 10,000 people.

Farmers grew barley and wheat. They also raised livestock such as sheep, goats, and cattle for meat, milk, and clothing. Çatalhöyük's villagers hunted and fished, too, but farming produced more food. The **surplus**, or extra, food was stored for later use.

EARLY CULTURE

Çatalhöyük is one of the world's oldest known permanent settlements. It is also one of the largest and most advanced settlements yet discovered from this time period. Its physical structure covered more than 30 acres (or 27 football fields) and included thousands of permanent mud brick buildings. Houses were packed together so tightly that there were no streets or yards between them. Instead, the flat rooftops served as a public plaza, or an open square, reached by ladders. Because the houses were built so close together, they formed a protective wall that enclosed the settlement.

People entered their homes through doors in the roofs. Most homes had a single main room where families cooked, ate, and slept. The main room had built-in benches and a fireplace. Plastered walls were covered with murals showing scenes of hunting, daily life, and important events.

At Çatalhöyük, archaeologists found evidence of religious practices and artistic expression. Horned bulls' heads mounted on walls and symbolic clay figures suggest that the villagers worshipped gods. Villagers also buried their dead, a fact revealed by human remains discovered beneath the floors of homes. The presence of pottery, cloth, cups, and bone utensils as well as tools and jewelry shows artistic expression. Archaeologists even found lead and copper, a sign of very early **metallurgy**, or metalworking. This was an important technological advance.

Discoveries at Çatalhöyük continue even today. Each new find sheds more light on the people who lived in this ancient settlement.

IMAGINING ÇATALHÖYÜK

Çatalhöyük was unknown to modern people until its discovery in the 1950s. Since then, archaeologists have carefully excavated the site. Their discoveries have revealed details of a unique settlement and culture. This illustration shows what archaeologists think Çatalhöyük might have been like. The cutaways let you peek inside the homes.

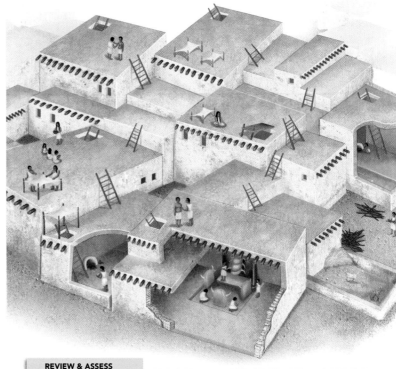

REVIEW & ASSESS

1. **READING CHECK** What archaeological evidence demonstrates that Çatalhöyük was an advanced culture?

2. **IDENTIFY MAIN IDEAS AND DETAILS** Why did the people of Çatalhöyük build their dwellings so close together?

3. **ANALYZE VISUALS** Based on the illustration, what might have been some advantages to living at Çatalhöyük?

OBJECTIVE

Explore the settlement of Çatalhöyük, an early cultural hearth in Southwest Asia.

CRITICAL THINKING SKILLS FOR LESSON 1.2

- Identify Main Ideas and Details
- Monitor Comprehension
- Analyze Visuals
- Draw Conclusions
- Make Inferences

ESSENTIAL QUESTION

What factors contributed to the development of civilization?

Different groups of people began to settle in permanent communities. Lesson 1.2 describes the settlement at Çatalhöyük, in present-day Turkey.

BACKGROUND FOR THE TEACHER

A British archaeologist named James Mellaart discovered Çatalhöyük in the late 1950s and conducted a series of excavations in the 1960s. However, his excavations were halted because Mellaart and his team realized they could not safely preserve the site. In the 1990s, another British archaeologist, Ian Hodder, restarted excavations. Today, Hodder and his team of international archaeologists protect the dig site with tents to shield it from rain and sun. They also remove artifacts, fragile parts of the buildings, and mural paintings to stabilize and conserve them.

INTRODUCE & ENGAGE

TEAM UP

Tell students to imagine that they will be building a settlement that will house several hundred people. Have them brainstorm in groups what they would build and the features they want their settlement to have. Tell them to use an Idea Web to list out the structures and features of their settlement after brainstorming. Tell students to keep in mind things such as security, efficiency, and comfort. **0:05** minutes

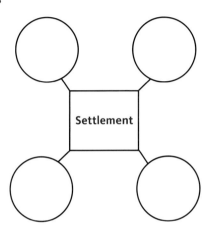

TEACH

GUIDED DISCUSSION

1. **Draw Conclusions** How important was a stable food supply at Çatalhöyük? *(A stable food supply led to population growth. The surplus, or extra, food produced by farmers at Çatalhöyük could be stored for later use.)*

2. **Make Inferences** Why do archaeologists believe that the people at Çatalhöyük practiced some form of religion? *(Archaeologists discovered symbolic clay figures and mounted bull heads at Çatalhöyük, both of which point to the worship of gods or goddesses.)*

ANALYZE VISUALS

Ask students to study the diagram of Çatalhöyük. Elicit student descriptions of the structure depicted. **ASK:** What similarities and differences do you see between Çatalhöyük and modern apartment or condominium buildings? *(The illustration of Çatalhöyük shows a number of individual dwellings that share walls with other dwellings, like modern apartment or condominium buildings. Unlike modern dwellings, though, people entered through the roofs and used the roof space as public plazas.)* **0:10** minutes

ACTIVE OPTIONS

On Your Feet: Inside-Outside Circle Have students form concentric circles facing each other. Allow students time to write questions about the location, purpose, and construction of

Çatalhöyük. Then have students in the inside circle pose questions to students in the outside circle. Have students switch roles. Students may ask for help from other students in their circle if they are unable to answer a question. **0:20** minutes

Critical Viewing: NG Chapter Gallery Invite students to explore the Chapter Gallery to examine the images that relate to this chapter. Have them select one of the images and do additional research to learn more about it. Ask questions that will inspire additional inquiry about the chosen gallery image, such as: What is this? Where and when was this created? By whom? Why was it created? What is it made of? Why does it belong in this chapter? What else would you like to know about it? **0:15** minutes

DIFFERENTIATE

ENGLISH LANGUAGE LEARNERS

Clarify Word Meaning Make sure students understand the word *metallurgy*. Explain that when they encounter new and confusing words, they can look for a root word. Write *metallurgy* on the board and underline the root word *metal*. Ask for examples of different metals. Tell students that clues to word meaning can often be found in the word itself. Review and expand on the definition of *metallurgy*, which is metalworking or the technology used in working with the production of metals.

STRIVING READERS

Summarize Have students work in pairs and assign each student a paragraph to read aloud. The partner should summarize what he or she hears in one or two spoken sentences. Encourage students to ask each other questions as they come across complex information.

Press **mt** *in the Student eEdition for modified text.*

See the Chapter Planner for more strategies for differentiation.

REVIEW & ASSESS

ANSWERS

1. Archaeologists have discovered evidence of worship, burial practices, creation of artistic and useful objects, and metallurgy there.

2. They built their houses close together for protection.

3. The settlement would have provided security, a stable food source, and a community for its residents.

1.3 China: Banpo

About 1,000 years after the development at Çatalhöyük, a lightbulb went off on the other side of the world. Thousands of miles from Southwest Asia, another center of new ideas developed in China's rich river valleys.

MAIN IDEA

The Yangshao culture developed as a cultural hearth in northern China.

RIVER VALLEY AGRICULTURE

Around 5000 B.C., warmer, wetter weather prompted the development of cultural hearths in the fertile river valleys of China. As in Çatalhöyük, people here domesticated pigs, chickens, and dogs. They hunted and fished, too.

In southern China, which has a relatively warm climate, people began to settle in villages. Farmers grew rice, which they had domesticated from the wild rice that grew in the Chang Jiang (chahng jyahng) Basin.

Farming villages also developed farther north in the Huang He (hwahng huh) Basin. However, the colder, drier climate in the north was less favorable for growing rice. Farmers there domesticated wild millet instead. Millet is a tiny, yellow grain. It grows fast and is a low-maintenance, or easy-to-grow, crop. It was an important part of the diet of ancient people in northern China.

YANGSHAO CULTURE

The **Yangshao** (yahng-shou) culture was one of China's Neolithic cultural hearths. The Yangshao lived along the Huang and Wei (way) rivers from about 5000 to 3000 B.C. Archaeologists have discovered more than 1,000 Yangshao sites in northern China.

One of the best-known Yangshao sites is **Banpo**, a large farming village. This village contained many small houses that faced a community building in a central square. Archaeologists determined that Banpo houses were rebuilt many times. People may have abandoned the village when the fields were exhausted of nutrients and then later returned when the land recovered. Banpo villagers grew millet as their **staple**, or main crop. They also grew a fibrous plant called hemp and cultivated silk, which they crafted into textiles.

The Yangshao at Banpo left behind a unique style of pottery that demonstrates their artistry. Yangshao potters created bowls and vessels, or containers, that they formed by hand and baked in kilns, or ovens, just outside Banpo village. The Yangshao's painted pottery commonly features geometric designs. Other examples include shaped vessels used for food storage.

Archaeologists found many of these vessels and other useful items buried with the dead in neatly arranged graves. These "grave goods," as they are called, suggest that the Yangshao people believed in a link between the living and the dead, though their specific religious beliefs remain unknown. Because most graves contained similar grave goods, archaeologists believe that most people probably had equal status in society.

Early Yangshao graves also suggest that people were arranged into **clans**, or family groupings, when buried. These clans were **matrilineal**, which means they traced descendants through the mother rather than the father.

The Huang He in China provided fertile soil for ancient Yangshao farmers.

By about 3200 B.C. Yangshao culture had evolved into Longshan (lung-shan) culture. The Longshan crafted useful tools and beautiful objects from jade—a hard green or white stone. Longshan artists produced a distinctive black pottery using pottery wheels, and craftspeople made tools out of copper. The Longshan also established trade networks on which later Chinese cultures would build.

Yangshao Pottery

Formed in the shape of an owl, this tripod pottery vessel was used to serve food.

REVIEW & ASSESS

1. **READING CHECK** What is unique about the Yangshao culture?

2. **COMPARE AND CONTRAST** Why did farmers grow different types of crops in the southern and northern river basins of China?

3. **DETERMINE WORD MEANINGS** Based on its definition, what does the word part *matri-* mean?

PLAN

OBJECTIVE

Learn how the Yangshao culture developed as a cultural hearth in northern China.

CRITICAL THINKING SKILLS FOR LESSON 1.3

- Identify Main Ideas and Details
- Monitor Comprehension
- Compare and Contrast
- Determine Word Meanings
- Analyze Visuals
- Summarize

ESSENTIAL QUESTION

What factors contributed to the development of civilization?

People in various cultural hearths developed new farming techniques, ways of organizing their societies, and forms of artistic expression. Lesson 1.3 describes the farming, societal organization, and pottery of the Yangshao culture in northern China.

BACKGROUND FOR THE TEACHER

The great river valley civilizations of East Asia developed along the Huang He. The Huang He is sometimes called the Yellow River. It is the main river in northern China, and because of a long history of settlement near it, it is believed to be the cradle of Chinese civilization. It is China's second longest river, winding more than 3,000 miles through the country. The Huang He flows east from the Plateau of Tibet into the Yellow Sea. The Huang He Basin is heavily populated today, as the river continues to support human settlement.

DIGITAL RESOURCES myNGconnect.com

TEACHER RESOURCES & ASSESSMENT

 Reading and Note-Taking

 Vocabulary Practice

 Section 1 Quiz

STUDENT RESOURCES

 NG Chapter Gallery

ACTIVATE PRIOR KNOWLEDGE

Write the word *domesticate* on the board. Elicit student definitions of the word. **ASK:** What does the word domesticate mean? *(In this historical context, domesticate means to tame an animal for farm produce or to cultivate a wild plant for food.)* **ASK:** What is the adjective form of the word? *(The adjective form of the word is* domestic, *which refers to the running of a home or existing inside a particular country. It can also mean something made at home, not abroad, and it can describe animals that are tame.)* Explain that they will encounter this word frequently when studying cultural hearths and early societies. **0:05** minutes

TEACH

GUIDED DISCUSSION

1. **Analyze Visuals** What do the shape and detail of the pottery vessel featured on the page reveal about the Yangshao culture? *(The fact that the Yangshao were making kiln-fired pottery indicates that they possessed an advanced technology and the resources and artisans to devote to pottery making. Crafting the vessel in the shape of the bird would take time and skill beyond making a basic vessel.)*

2. **Summarize** What have archaeologists learned about the Yangshao from their burial practices? *(The Yangshao buried their dead with grave goods, which indicates a belief in a link between the living and the dead. Most graves had similar grave goods, which showed equal social status among the villagers. People were also buried in family groupings.)*

ANALYZE LOCATION

Have students work in groups of four. Tell each group to review the text and images for the lesson. Then, as a class, come up with as many descriptions of the area around the Huang He in China as possible. Write groups' descriptions on the board, keeping track of the number of responses per group. *(Descriptions might include fertile, flat, green, populated with trees, perhaps in a valley. Other descriptions might focus on the width of the river and the dedicated spaces for farming.)* **0:10** minutes

ACTIVE OPTIONS

On Your Feet: Question and Answer Have half the class write True-False questions based on the information about the Yangshao culture and Banpo. Ask the other half to create answer cards, with "True" written on one side and "False" on the other. Have the question-writing students read their questions aloud. Students in the second group should display the correct answer to each question. When discrepancies occur, review the question and discuss which answer is correct. **0:15** minutes

NG Learning Framework: Write About Craftsmanship

ATTITUDE: **Curiosity**
KNOWLEDGE: **Our Human Story**

Have students select one of the forms of craftsmanship or artistic expression (such as pottery or metallurgy) that they are still curious about after reading this chapter. Instruct them to write a short description of this form of craftsmanship or artistic expression using information from the chapter and additional source material. **0:10** minutes

GIFTED & TALENTED

Create a Vessel Have students draw a vessel that they can then (if time permits) shape out of clay. Encourage students to create the vessel with the Yangshao culture in mind. They can conduct independent research on the designs commonly found in Yangshao pottery as inspiration for their own designs. Have the students explain their creation to the class upon completion.

INCLUSION

Monitor Comprehension Have students work in small groups reading aloud the text paragraph by paragraph. At the end of each paragraph, have them stop and use these sentence frames:

- This paragraph is about _____.

- One detail that stood out to me is _____.

- The word _____ means _____.

- I don't think I understand _____.

Press **mt** *in the Student eEdition for modified text.*

See the Chapter Planner for more strategies for differentiation.

ANSWERS

1. The Yangshao culture is distinct in its domestication of millet, the textiles and pottery it created, its belief in a link between the living and the dead, and its matrilineal organization.

2. In the south, Neolithic farmers were able to domesticate and farm wild rice in the wetlands of the Chang Jiang Basin. In the north, however, the climate was cooler and drier, which were not good conditions for growing rice, so instead farmers planted millet in the Huang He Basin.

3. The word part *matri-* means *mother, woman,* or *female.*

Oaxaca

Around the time the Yangshao were farming in China, another cultural hearth was forming across the Pacific in Mesoamerica. The people there were developing an important crop that you might recognize—corn.

MAIN IDEA

Maize domestication helped make Mesoamerica an important cultural hearth.

MESOAMERICAN NOMADS

Mesoamerica, which means "middle America," refers to the ancient geographic and cultural region that reached from central Mexico south through Central America. This region was another important Neolithic cultural hearth, similar in some ways to Çatalhöyük in Southwest Asia and Banpo in China.

For thousands of years, Mesoamericans traveled in small nomadic groups, moving from place to place with the seasons. They gathered wild plants but did little farming. For brief periods, these Mesoamericans may have tended small patches of land. However, they didn't settle in permanent sites, build permanent homes, or form villages. Eventually, though, Mesoamericans began to domesticate wild plants. In this way, they resembled people living in cultural hearths in other parts of the world.

CRADLE OF THE MAIZE REVOLUTION

One of the main plants Mesoamericans domesticated was **maize**, or what we know as corn. A cave is an unlikely place to find clues about an important development in farming, but that is where archaeologists found traces of an ancient plant. In fact, caves and rock shelters scattered across southern Mexico revealed the earliest signs of domestication in North America.

Archaeologists found prehistoric corncob fragments in the highland caves of **Oaxaca** (wah-HAH-kah) and the Tehuacán (tay-wah-KAHN) Valley. The pieces had been preserved for thousands of years by the region's hot, dry conditions. These fragments, which date to around 4250 B.C., came from an early variety of domesticated maize. Archaeologists also found stone tools for grinding the hard maize kernels into flour for baking. The first varieties of maize were probably neither juicy nor yellow, but they were easily harvested and stored, which made them a useful food source.

So where did maize come from? After decades of debate, scientists believe that maize was domesticated from a wild Mexican grass called teosinte (tay-uh-SIN-tay) that is native to the area around the Balsas River. Teosinte kernels are easily knocked off the plant, making it a difficult crop to harvest. However, hundreds of years of domestication solved this problem. Domestication also increased the number and size of kernels on the teosinte plant. Over time, it came to resemble modern corn.

As maize became a more productive crop, Mesoamericans relied on it for their annual food supply. By 2000 B.C., the maize revolution had taken place, and maize farming was widespread in Mesoamerica. Little did these farmers know they had invented a food that people would still enjoy thousands of years later.

DOMESTICATING CORN

Teosinte, the wild relative of modern corn, produced much smaller kernels. Note the size of the cobs of the teosinte plant as compared to a quarter. Now compare a quarter to the size of modern corn. In domesticating this plant, ancient farmers slowly began to encourage fewer branches on the plant. Less branching meant the plant could divert more energy into fewer cobs, which then grew larger. In addition, the hard kernel of the teosinte plant eventually gave way to the softer kernel we recognize as modern corn.

TEOSINTE

MODERN CORN

REVIEW & ASSESS

1. **READING CHECK** How did the domestication of maize help Mesoamerica become a cultural hearth?

2. **SUMMARIZE** How do archaeologists know that Mesoamericans domesticated maize?

3. **INTEGRATE VISUALS** Based on the illustration and text, what changes did domestication bring about to teosinte?

OBJECTIVE

Describe how the domestication of maize helped Mesoamerica develop as a cultural hearth.

CRITICAL THINKING SKILLS FOR LESSON 1.4

- Identify Main Ideas and Details
- Monitor Comprehension
- Summarize
- Integrate Visuals
- Evaluate
- Synthesize

ESSENTIAL QUESTION

What factors contributed to the development of civilization?

People in cultural hearths domesticated wild plants in order to have a stable food supply. Lesson 1.4 describes how Mesoamericans domesticated maize, or corn.

BACKGROUND FOR THE TEACHER

Understanding that the achievements of ancient cultures affect us today can be difficult for students. This is not surprising considering it is also sometimes difficult to prove. Reaching the conclusion that maize came from domesticated teosinte was not easy. Geneticist George Beadle first investigated the connection between these two plants in the 1930s. He crossbred teosinte and maize and grew 50,000 plants. Eventually, he pinpointed just four or five genes that differentiate the two plants.

DIGITAL RESOURCES myNGconnect.com

TEACHER RESOURCES & ASSESSMENT

 Reading and Note-Taking

 Vocabulary Practice

 Section 1 Quiz

STUDENT RESOURCES

 NG Chapter Gallery

INTRODUCE & ENGAGE

PREVIEW WITH VISUALS

Direct students' attention to the illustration of teosinte and modern corn. Call on volunteers to predict what they will learn in the lesson based on what they see in the illustration. At the end of the lesson, have students review the illustration to see how accurate their predictions were. `0:05` minutes

TEACH

GUIDED DISCUSSION

1. **Summarize** Why was teosinte a difficult plant to harvest? *(The kernels on the teosinte plant are easily knocked off if the plant is jostled, which makes collecting usable parts of the plant difficult.)*

2. **Evaluate** Why would the domestication of a single plant be important in the development of Mesoamerican civilizations? *(With the development of a hardy crop like maize, which can be used in a variety of foods, large populations would have a steady food supply. Larger populations lead to the formation of cities and, eventually, advanced civilizations.)*

SYNTHESIZE

Using the illustration and the text, have students create brief group presentations that synthesize what they have learned about Mesoamerica, Oaxaca, and maize domestication. Make sure they answer the five Ws: Who, What, Where, When, and Why it Matters.

ACTIVE OPTIONS

On Your Feet: Think, Pair, Share Have students think of a food that they would invent, much like the Mesoamericans "invented" maize, that could help solve a hunger problem in one part of the world. Ask them to form pairs and discuss their ideas. Then call on individuals to share their ideas for new foods. `0:15` minutes

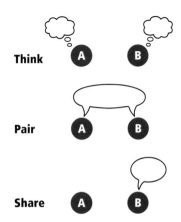

Critical Viewing: NG Chapter Gallery Ask students to choose one image from the Chapter Gallery and become an expert on it. Have them do additional research to learn more about the image. Then,

invite students to share their findings with a partner, small group, or the class. `0:10` minutes

DIFFERENTIATE

STRIVING READERS

Summarize Have students summarize Lesson 1.4 by creating two Word Webs with the terms *teosinte* and *maize* in the center ovals. Ask them to complete each web with relevant information from the lesson.

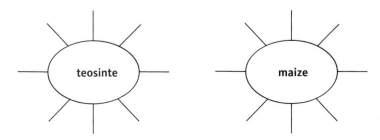

PRE-AP

Investigate Wild Grains Have students pick a grain such as wheat, barley, or oats and then research its history. Encourage them to utilize scholarly sources, such as science and university sites. Tell students they will share their findings with the class in a presentation that uses visuals to illustrate their research.

Press **mt** *in the Student eEdition for modified text.*

See the Chapter Planner for more strategies for differentiation.

REVIEW & ASSESS

ANSWERS

1. The domestication of maize made it possible for early inhabitants to stop foraging and to start farming a useful food source that could support permanent farming villages. Eventually, this led to widespread settlement throughout Mesoamerica.

2. Archaeologists discovered evidence of prehistoric corncob fragments in caves in Oaxaca. They also found stone tools for grinding maize.

3. Domestication seems to have made teosinte a taller plant with fewer branches and larger corncobs with larger kernels.

This photo of Faiyum today shows how access to a water source determines where crops can grow and people can live.

1.5

North Africa:
Faiyum

Long before building their extraordinary pyramids, the ancient Egyptians laid the building blocks of an advanced culture on the floodplains of the Nile River in North Africa. As in other cultural hearths, agriculture was at the root of cultural development in ancient Egypt, whose farmers adapted ideas from places far and wide.

MAIN IDEA

Early farmers established the Nile River Valley as an important cultural hearth.

MIGRANTS FROM THE SAHARA

As you may recall from the previous chapter, the Sahara was a tropical grassland 10,000 years ago. Then the climate changed drastically. Seasonal rains shifted south, and the grasslands dried into desert. This dramatic change forced people to migrate to more fertile lands with steadier water supplies.

The same climate shift that transformed the Sahara transformed the narrow **Nile River Valley**. Its swamps dried up, making the land usable and this fertile valley a perfect place for farming. The Nile floodplain was ideal for the agriculture that would later support a large population.

EGYPT'S EARLIEST FARMING VILLAGE

Faiyum (fy-YOOM) is an oasis about 50 miles south of present-day Cairo. Dating from around 5200 B.C., it is considered Egypt's earliest farming community. At Faiyum, archaeologists discovered storage pits for grain, postholes for building foundations, and the ruins of clay floors and fireplaces. They also stumbled upon a 7,000-year-old, Neolithic-era wood and flint sickle used for farming and left in a storage bin.

The agricultural practices used at Faiyum were not native to the Nile River Valley, though. According to archaeologists, people from neighboring cultures introduced new practices to Faiyum farmers. Grains of wheat and barley and bones of sheep and pigs found at Faiyum came from across the Mediterranean Sea or the Sinai Desert where domestication was already well established. People from these areas likely brought the domesticated grains and animals to the Nile River Valley.

The process by which cultures interact and spread from one area to another is called **cultural diffusion**. This process allowed Faiyum farmers to benefit from the skills of other cultures. It also helped establish the Nile River Valley as an important cultural hearth.

REVIEW & ASSESS

1. **READING CHECK** Why were early farmers attracted to the Nile River Valley?

2. **SUMMARIZE** How did a climate shift that took place 10,000 years ago change the Sahara and Nile River Valley?

3. **DRAW CONCLUSIONS** What impact did neighboring cultures have on the farmers at Faiyum?

PLAN

OBJECTIVE

Examine how early farmers along the Nile River established a cultural hearth in Egypt.

CRITICAL THINKING SKILLS FOR LESSON 1.5

- Identify Main Ideas and Details
- Monitor Comprehension
- Summarize
- Draw Conclusions
- Make Predictions

ESSENTIAL QUESTION

What factors contributed to the development of civilization?

People in cultural hearths shared ideas, practices, and skills with nearby cultures. Lesson 1.5 describes how people in Egypt's earliest farming village shared ideas with other cultures.

BACKGROUND FOR THE TEACHER

Ninety-five percent of Egypt's population lives in the Nile River Valley today, and agriculture is still an important part of the Egyptian economy. Egyptian farmers grow crops such as citrus fruits, tomatoes, sugar beets, potatoes, rice, wheat, and, cotton. Construction of the Aswan High Dam in 1970 regulated the annual flooding of the Nile, making the growing season year-round instead of flood-dependent. The construction of the dam also led to the reclamation of land to use as farmland through the use of irrigation.

DIGITAL RESOURCES myNGconnect.com

TEACHER RESOURCES & ASSESSMENT

 Reading and Note-Taking

 Vocabulary Practice

 Section 1 Quiz

STUDENT RESOURCES

 NG Chapter Gallery

ANALYZE VISUALS

Direct students' attention to the photo of Faiyum. Ask the following questions:

- What is shown in the photo?
- Based on what you see in the photo, where do you think people live?
- What is making it possible to grow the crops?

`0:05` minutes

TEACH

GUIDED DISCUSSION

1. **Make Predictions** What type of weather event in the modern world might cause farmers to migrate to a new place to live? *(Drought commonly forces farmers to relocate, especially in parts of Saharan and sub-Saharan Africa. Another weather event that might cause farmers to relocate today would be rising sea levels that flood farmland.)*

2. **Draw Conclusions** How did archaeologists know that farming techniques were not native to Faiyum farmers? *(Archaeologists discovered evidence of domesticated wheat and barley and bones of sheep and pigs that would have originated from across the Mediterranean Sea or the Sinai Desert.)*

BUILD VOCABULARY

Explore the word *diffusion* and its other forms to help students build vocabulary skills. Review the definition of *cultural diffusion* in the reading. *(Cultural diffusion is the process by which cultures interact with each other and spread.)* Then ask if students know other forms of the word. Explain that the word *diffuse* can be a verb (meaning "to spread") or an adjective (meaning "spread out"). Tell students to come up with a sentence or question that uses either *diffusion* or *diffuse*. Then ask for student volunteers to share their sentence or question. `0:10` minutes

ACTIVE OPTIONS

On Your Feet: One-on-One Interviews Group students in pairs. Have each pair write three questions about Faiyum based on the information they learned in Lesson 1.5. Have students conduct interviews with each other as if they are on a talk news show, and then have them take questions from the "audience." Students' answers should show an understanding of Faiyum and what archaeologists learned about this early farming village. `0:20` minutes

NG Learning Framework: Teach Your Methods

ATTITUDE: **Responsibility**
SKILL: **Collaboration**

Assign students to several small groups. Ask each group to come up with a method of doing something they do everyday (such as doing homework or chores, getting to school). Then have groups share their methods with other groups. Encourage groups to use good listening skills and have them take notes on the different methods presented. To conclude the activity, ask the original groups to reconsider their methods and discuss how they might change them based on other groups' ideas. `0:15` minutes

GIFTED & TALENTED

Make Connections Have students connect the process of cultural diffusion as it happened in history to the way cultural diffusion happens in the world today. Tell students to think of a practice, skill, or idea that started in one part of the world and then spread to another part of the world. Encourage students to identify how the practice, skill, or idea spread, and what impact it had. Have students write a paragraph about their findings.

ENGLISH LANGUAGE LEARNERS

Identify Main Ideas and Details Lesson 1.5 has two subsections. Pair students and assign each pair a subsection of the text to read together. Encourage students to use a graphic organizer to make notes about the main idea and supporting details in their part of the lesson. After answering their questions, have each pair write a one- or two-sentence summary.

Press (mt) *in the Student eEdition for modified text.*

See the Chapter Planner for more strategies for differentiation.

ANSWERS

1. The Nile River Valley provided a major water source and fertile soils on which to grow crops that could sustain a population. Farmers at Faiyum laid the groundwork for future agriculture and incorporated other cultures' practices and techniques.

2. A climate shift that took place 10,000 years ago changed the once-lush tropical grasslands of the Sahara into a dry desert. At the same time, this climate shift dried up forests and swamps, turning the Nile River Valley into an ideal place for farming.

3. People from neighboring cultures brought new practices and techniques to Faiyum that influenced the crops they grew and animals they raised.

Paths to Civilization:
Göbekli Tepe

An old riddle asks: Which came first, the chicken or the egg? Archaeologists have posed their own riddle: Which came first, organized agriculture or organized religion? Like most riddles, this one can't be easily answered.

MAIN IDEA

Throughout history, different cultures have traveled different paths to civilization.

THE WORLD'S FIRST TEMPLE

Over time, cultural hearths around the world transformed into civilizations. A **civilization** is an advanced and complex society. Two important markers of civilization are agriculture and organized **religion**, or the belief in and worship of gods and goddesses.

About 11,600 years ago in southeast Turkey on the edge of the Fertile Crescent, at least 500 people came together to create **Göbekli Tepe** (guh-bek-LEE TEH-peh), the world's first **temple**, or place of worship. Ancient builders formed massive limestone pillars into T shapes and arranged them into sets of circles.

The tallest pillars stood as high as 18 feet and weighed 16 tons. Keep in mind that Göbekli Tepe's builders did all this before the invention of the wheel. Stone workers carved ferocious animals onto the pillars after they were in place. Once completed,

the immense pillars and the frightening images of deadly animals flickering in the firelight must have been an awesome sight.

Göbekli Tepe represents an important event in the development of organized religion. As one of the first known examples of monumental architecture, or large structures built for an identified purpose, it was specifically dedicated for religious use. Its commanding views over fertile plains, evidence of ceremonies, and high levels of artistic expression all suggest a religious purpose.

Göbekli Tepe is also remarkable because archaeologists believe that hunter-gatherers, not settled farmers, built it. The structures at Göbekli Tepe were constructed miles from any Neolithic settlement, water source, or agricultural land. The absence of harvest symbols found in later farming cultures reinforces the theory that hunter-gatherers—not a settled people—built Göbekli Tepe.

THE MEANING OF GÖBEKLI TEPE

Archaeologists argue over the meaning of Göbekli Tepe. Evidence found there has changed the way some think about the human transition from hunter-gatherer to farmer. For a long time, archaeologists thought that the need to ensure good harvests led to the belief in and worship of gods and goddesses. In other words, agriculture developed before religion. However, Göbekli Tepe turns that argument around, suggesting that here, at least, humans developed organized religion before farming. In this case, perhaps the need to feed religious gatherings led to the development of agriculture.

The fact is that in some places, agriculture came before religion; in others, religion came first. Göbekli Tepe teaches us that different cultures forged different paths to civilization. Either way, by 6000 B.C., both organized religion and agriculture—two of the fundamental building blocks of civilization—had been established in the Fertile Crescent.

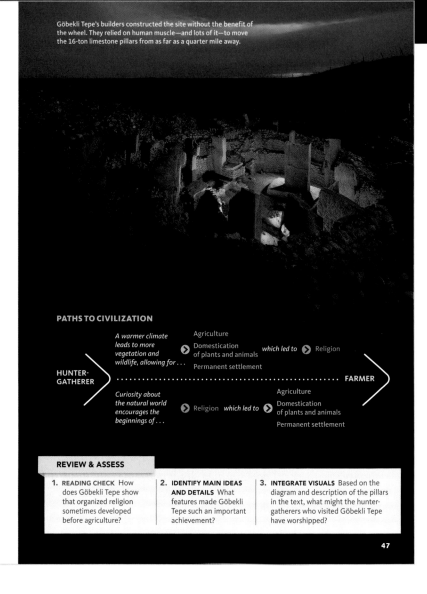

Göbekli Tepe's builders constructed the site without the benefit of the wheel. They relied on human muscle—and lots of it—to move the 16-ton limestone pillars from as far as a quarter mile away.

PATHS TO CIVILIZATION

HUNTER-GATHERER

A warmer climate leads to more vegetation and wildlife, allowing for . . .
→ Agriculture
→ Domestication of plants and animals → *which led to* → Religion
Permanent settlement

Curiosity about the natural world encourages the beginnings of . . .
→ Religion *which led to* → Agriculture
Domestication of plants and animals
Permanent settlement

FARMER

REVIEW & ASSESS

1. **READING CHECK** How does Göbekli Tepe show that organized religion sometimes developed before agriculture?

2. **IDENTIFY MAIN IDEAS AND DETAILS** What features made Göbekli Tepe such an important achievement?

3. **INTEGRATE VISUALS** Based on the diagram and description of the pillars in the text, what might the hunter-gatherers who visited Göbekli Tepe have worshipped?

PLAN

OBJECTIVE

Explore how cultures follow different paths as they develop into civilizations.

CRITICAL THINKING SKILLS FOR LESSON 2.1

- Identify Main Ideas and Details
- Monitor Comprehension
- Integrate Visuals
- Describe
- Explain

ESSENTIAL QUESTION

What factors contributed to the development of civilization?

Two important factors in the development of civilization are religion and agriculture. Lesson 2.1 explores Göbekli Tepe, an ancient temple in present-day Turkey.

BACKGROUND FOR THE TEACHER

Göbekli Tepe, which means "belly hill" in Turkish, predates Stonehenge, the site featured at the beginning of Chapter 2, by about 6,000 years. Anthropologists originally dismissed it in the 1960s, thinking it might be a medieval cemetery. In 1994, German archaeologist Klaus Schmidt was immediately transfixed when he saw the site for the first time while on a dig in the area. He keyed in on its shape: 50 feet high, with a rounded top. Schmidt knew that humans had created it. A year later, he returned with a team and has excavated the site for more than 20 years. Though he has been working there for two decades, he says only about a tenth of the 22-acre site has been explored.

DIGITAL RESOURCES myNGconnect.com

TEACHER RESOURCES & ASSESSMENT

 Reading and Note-Taking

 Vocabulary Practice

 Section 2 Quiz

 STUDENT RESOURCES

NG Chapter Gallery

INTRODUCE & ENGAGE

PREVIEW WITH VISUALS

Direct students' attention to the flow chart and photograph in Lesson 2.1. **ASK:** What do you notice in the photograph? (*Student responses will vary but should focus on the ruins of an ancient building of some sort.*) **ASK:** What is the subject of the flow chart? (*The flow chart shows two different transitions from hunter-gatherer to farmer.*) Explain that in this lesson, they will learn about different theories that explain how ancient people moved from being hunter-gatherers to farmers. **0:05 minutes**

TEACH

GUIDED DISCUSSION

1. **Describe** What do archaeologists think Göbekli Tepe looked like thousands of years ago? (*Massive, T-shaped limestone pillars were arranged in sets of circles. The pillars had carvings of fierce animals on them.*)

2. **Explain** Why do archaeologists believe that hunter-gatherers built Göbekli Tepe? (*Göbekli Tepe was built far from any Neolithic settlement, water source, or agricultural lands. No harvest symbols are present at the site, which would likely have meant a settled community of farmers constructed Göbekli Tepe.*)

MONITOR COMPREHENSION

The concepts presented in this lesson can be challenging to understand. After reading the lesson, devote some class time for a brief question-and-answer session. Ask students to pose questions about what they do not understand. Write questions on the board. Allow time for student volunteers to offer explanations and answers, and write their answers on the board. Clarify any outstanding questions or discrepancies before moving on. **0:10 minutes**

ACTIVE OPTIONS

On Your Feet: Living Flow Chart Have students study the flow chart in Lesson 2.1. Divide the class into two groups, A and B. Assign Group A to the top part of the chart and Group B to the bottom part. Have each group meet for five minutes to review the steps in their "path to civilization." Label one side of the room "Hunter-Gatherer" and the other side "Farmer." Then have each group start at the end of the room labeled "Hunter-Gatherer" and move toward "Farmer" while narrating the steps in between. When groups reach the "Farmer" side of the room, have the class vote on which path seems more logical to them. **0:15 minutes**

NG Learning Framework: Rewrite In Your Own Words

SKILL: Communication

KNOWLEDGE: **Our Human Story**

Have students revisit the text and the flow chart in the lesson. Explain that this flow chart is a visual summary of the text. Then have students rewrite the information in the flow chart using their own words. Encourage students to work in pairs to check each other's work and to help each other understand the two processes described. **0:10 minutes**

DIFFERENTIATE

GIFTED & TALENTED

Build a Model Have students locate an illustration of Göbekli Tepe using a National Geographic resource. Tell them to use the illustration as a guide as they build a 3-D model of the site. They can use modeling clay or another material to "reconstruct" the ancient temple's sets of circles. Students might want to include human figures in their model for scale.

STRIVING READERS

Complete Sequence Chains In order to reinforce comprehension of the flow chart in the lesson, have students reproduce it using the Sequence Chain graphic organizer below. Tell students to fill in two separate chains demonstrating two different paths to civilization. When students have completed their Sequence Chains, have them review each other's work and then gather as a group to check the chains for accuracy.

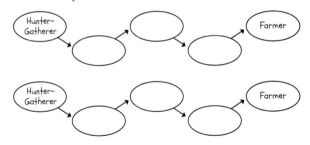

Press (**mt**) *in the Student eEdition for modified text.*

See the Chapter Planner for more strategies for differentiation.

REVIEW & ASSESS

ANSWERS

1. Archaeologists believe that hunter-gatherers built Göbekli Tepe as a place of worship. Therefore, in this particular location, early humans developed organized religion before farming and other stepping-stones of civilization.

2. Göbekli Tepe is an enormous achievement because it was built 11,500 years ago, before large-scale social organization, before organized religion, before farming surpluses to support builders, before advanced construction techniques, before the invention of the wheel, and before writing, metal, and pottery.

3. Because they were hunter-gatherers and fierce animals were depicted on the pillars, visitors might have worshipped animals.

2.2 Traits of Civilization

You might hear the word *civilization* a lot, but do you understand what it means? All civilizations, whether past or present, have certain things in common. So, what is a civilization?

MAIN IDEA

A civilization is a complex society that is defined by five key traits.

Cultural hearths prepared the way for the next development in human history: civilization. Ancient cultures around the world transformed into complex civilizations at about the same time, and they had five traits, or characteristics, in common: cities, complex institutions, specialized workers, record keeping, and improved technology.

CITIES

The first civilizations were born in **cities**. More than just large population centers, early cities were political, economic, and cultural centers for the surrounding areas. Cities often contained monumental architecture usually dedicated to religion or government. The city's heart was its trading center, where farmers and merchants met to conduct business. **Trade**, or the exchange of goods, allowed some civilizations to grow very rich. Some merchants traveled long distances to trade goods with other groups. Over time, they established trade routes, which helped spread ideas and practices.

COMPLEX INSTITUTIONS

As cities developed, complex institutions such as government and organized religion emerged as ways to manage resources and populations. **Government**, or an organization set up to make and enforce rules in a society, provided leadership and laws. Organized religion bound communities together through shared beliefs.

SPECIALIZED WORKERS

Food surpluses made possible by the agricultural revolution led to settled communities and to another key characteristic of civilizations: **specialized workers**. Specialized workers performed jobs other than farming. Some people specialized in pottery, metalworking, weaving, or toolmaking. Others became government officials, priests, teachers, soldiers, or merchants.

RECORD KEEPING

As societies developed, they had to manage information. **Record keeping**, or organizing and storing information, became an important job. Specialized workers called **scribes** recorded business transactions, important events, customs, traditions, and laws. The first writing systems used pictographs that looked like the things they represented, such as wavy lines for water. Eventually, complex writing systems helped people record important information and abstract ideas. As writing developed, so did calendar keeping.

IMPROVED TECHNOLOGY

The fifth key characteristic civilizations have in common is improved technology. As cultures became more complex, people developed new tools and techniques to solve problems and survive. Advances in technology included metalworking methods, inventions such as the wheel and the plow, and tools to create everyday items, such as the potter's wheel.

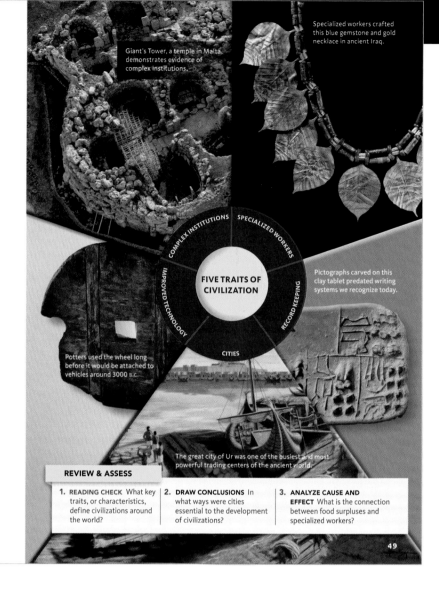

Giant's Tower, a temple in Malta, demonstrates evidence of complex institutions.

Specialized workers crafted this blue gemstone and gold necklace in ancient Iraq.

Pictographs carved on this clay tablet predated writing systems we recognize today.

Potters used the wheel long before it would be attached to vehicles around 3000 B.C.

The great city of Ur was one of the busiest and most powerful trading centers of the ancient world.

FIVE TRAITS OF CIVILIZATION

COMPLEX INSTITUTIONS · SPECIALIZED WORKERS · RECORD KEEPING · CITIES · IMPROVED TECHNOLOGY

REVIEW & ASSESS

1. **READING CHECK** What key traits, or characteristics, define civilizations around the world?

2. **DRAW CONCLUSIONS** In what ways were cities essential to the development of civilizations?

3. **ANALYZE CAUSE AND EFFECT** What is the connection between food surpluses and specialized workers?

OBJECTIVE

Analyze the characteristics of civilizations.

CRITICAL THINKING SKILLS FOR LESSON 2.2

- Identify Main Ideas and Details
- Monitor Comprehension
- Draw Conclusions
- Analyze Cause and Effect
- Evaluate
- Form and Support Opinions
- Analyze Visuals

ESSENTIAL QUESTION

What factors contributed to the development of civilization?

Civilizations are complex societies that share certain characteristics. Lesson 2.2 describes five characteristics found among civilizations.

BACKGROUND FOR THE TEACHER

Civilization is a big word and an important one in the study of human history. The root of *civilization* is *civil*, an adjective from the Latin *civilis*, meaning "relating to a citizen, relating to public life." To be "civil" or "civilized" was to have polite manners. By the 1850s, the word *civilization* began to be used to describe a "human society in a civilized condition, considered as a whole."

DIGITAL RESOURCES myNGconnect.com

TEACHER RESOURCES & ASSESSMENT

 Reading and Note-Taking

 Vocabulary Practice

 Section 2 Quiz

STUDENT RESOURCES

 NG Chapter Gallery

INTRODUCE & ENGAGE

HOW DO YOU KNOW?

Help students practice identifying common characteristics by listing common traits of mammals. Ask students to identify four characteristics of mammals. (*Mammals are vertebrates, which means they have a backbone or spine; they are endothermic, or warm-blooded; most mammals have hair on their bodies; they produce milk to feed their young.*) List the characteristics on the board. Then list different kinds of mammals and, as a class, confirm that each mammal has these characteristics. Explain that like mammals, civilizations also share common characteristics. **0:05** minutes

TEACH

GUIDED DISCUSSION

1. **Evaluate** Why might cities be considered the birthplaces of civilizations? (*In order to emerge, civilizations need people. Cities gathered lots of people together in one place. Therefore, the opportunities for other characteristics of civilizations to develop were plentiful, such as the development of specialized workers, complex institutions, record keeping, and improved technology.*)

2. **Form and Support Opinions** Which trait of civilization do you think is least important? (*Responses will vary, but students should base their opinions on information they learn from the reading.*)

ANALYZE VISUALS

Direct students' attention to the Five Traits of Civilization wheel in the lesson. For each image or illustration, ask students the following questions:

- What catches your attention first?
- What other details do you notice?
- What does the image tell you about a trait of civilization?

0:10 minutes

ACTIVE OPTIONS

On Your Feet: Build a Civilization Divide the class into five groups and assign each group a trait of civilization covered in Lesson 2.2. Then have each group move to an assigned part of the room. Tell students to create their own form of their assigned trait. For example, the "Record-Keeping" group might come up with an original alphabet or a different way of recording information. Allow students time to brainstorm and collaborate. Encourage them to include interesting details. Then gather the five groups together and have each group present their trait to the class. As a class, come up with a name for this new civilization. **0:20** minutes

NG Learning Framework: Rank the Traits

ATTITUDE: **Empowerment**
SKILL: **Problem-Solving**

Invite students to review the text and visuals in the lesson. Ask students to consider the five traits of civilization and then rank them in order of importance. Once they have completed their list of rankings, encourage students to share their lists with the class. Write their responses on the board and have students explain how they decided to rank their traits. **0:10** minutes

DIFFERENTIATE

INCLUSION

Match Text with Visuals Pair students with mixed ability levels. Have each pair review the text. Then have students match each section of the text with its corresponding image in the Five Traits of Civilization wheel on the opposite page. Encourage students to keep track of their matches by using this sentence frame:

The _____ section of text matches with the image of _____.

PRE-AP

Create a Presentation Have students conduct independent research on the five characteristics of civilization as demonstrated in ancient Egypt, ancient Greece, ancient China, or another ancient civilization that they will learn about in this book. After they have completed research, have students create a presentation that demonstrates through text and visuals the five characteristics of civilization found in their chosen civilization. Encourage students to share their presentations with the class.

Press (**mt**) *in the Student eEdition for modified text.*

See the Chapter Planner for more strategies for differentiation.

REVIEW & ASSESS

ANSWERS

1. Civilizations around the world share these key characteristics: advanced cities, trade, complex institutions, specialized workers, record keeping, and improved technology.

2. With many people living in one place, cities accelerated the cultural advances of ancient civilizations. Cities were also the political, economic, cultural, and social centers for the surrounding areas.

3. Food surpluses supported growing populations and allowed people to specialize in jobs other than farming, such as toolmaking and pottery.

2.3 NEW TECHNOLOGY

Ancient tools and technology reveal much about the cultures that used them. As early cultures advanced toward civilization, the design and manufacture of tools improved. Materials used to make tools also changed. For example, with the development of metallurgy, strong metals such as bronze allowed for the transition from stone to metal tools. Better and more complex tools developed by ancient people demonstrated the emergence of civilization around the world. Based on what you see here, what purpose did many early tools serve?

Harpoon
Reindeer antlers provided the bone for this hunting tool.

Flint Tool
Flint is a hard stone that can be shaped into a sharp point.

Copper Awl
This tool was used to pierce holes in leather and cloth.

Sickle
Hand-held tools called sickles were used to harvest grain.

Spearhead
Metals such as bronze improved a weapon's strength.

Arrowhead
Arrowheads of flint or other stone were tied to arrows and used for hunting.

Stone Hoe
This stone hoe, dated around 7000 B.C., is an example of an early agricultural tool.

Bone Needle
Needles made of bone were used for sewing and weaving.

Wheel
Early wheels were constructed simply: wooden disks with holes for axles.

Kitchen Utensil
This fork-shaped utensil made of bone was found at Çatalhöyük.

Flint Stone
When hit, flint stones helped spark fire.

Pottery
Pottery vessels of all shapes held liquids and food.

Flint Knife
The intricate handle on this knife was carved from a hippopotamus tooth.

Bronze Ax Head
Axes were used for chopping and hunting.

51

OBJECTIVE

Identify the new technology that emerged from cultural hearths.

CRITICAL THINKING SKILLS FOR LESSON 2.3

- Draw Conclusions
- Analyze Visuals
- Form and Support Opinions

ESSENTIAL QUESTION

What factors contributed to the development of civilization?

One characteristic of civilization is the development of new and better technology. Lesson 2.3 shows several tools used by ancient cultures.

BACKGROUND FOR THE TEACHER

One of the most prominent metals used in Neolithic tools was bronze. Bronze is an alloy, or combination of two metals, copper and another metal, usually tin. Bronze is easily melted and shaped, but the cooled metal is stronger than copper. Bronze also resists rust, unlike iron. Most tools and weapons were eventually made from iron, however, because it was more available. In addition to use in tools and weapons, bronze was used in ancient coins and, later, statues and artifacts.

DIGITAL RESOURCES myNGconnect.com

TEACHER RESOURCES & ASSESSMENT

 Reading and Note-Taking

 Vocabulary Practice

 Section 2 Quiz

STUDENT RESOURCES

 NG Chapter Gallery

HISTORY THROUGH OBJECTS

Ask students to reach into their backpacks, desks, or pencil boxes and pull out an item they use every day. If personal objects are not available to them, have students select a "tool" from the classroom. **ASK:** What is your tool used for? Why is it important to you? How might you improve upon your tool? (*Responses will vary. Encourage students to hold up their tool so that others can see it.*) **0:05** minutes

TEACH

GUIDED DISCUSSION

1. **Draw Conclusions** Many of the tools featured in the lesson have sharp points. Why might this be? (*Tools with sharp points would be used for hunting and killing animals for food, chopping wood, or planting and harvesting crops.*)

2. **Form and Support Opinions** Which two tools do you think would have been most important to have and use in a Neolithic cultural hearth? Use what you have learned in this chapter to support your opinion. (*Responses will vary, but answers should rely on information from the chapter.*)

ANALYZE VISUALS

Have students create a Venn Diagram for classifying the ancient tools into categories: *farming, cooking,* and *hunting,* based on their function. Point out that some tools may serve dual purposes. Then have students sort the artifacts into the categories, writing each item in the appropriate part of the diagram. Invite volunteers to share their categories and discuss/debate any alternative categorizing. **0:15** minutes

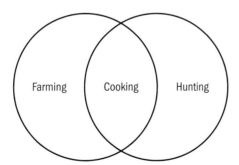

Farming | Cooking | Hunting

ACTIVE OPTIONS

On Your Feet: Make a Tool Divide the class into four or five groups. Have each group draw plans and create a prototype for a tool they might use in their everyday lives. Tools could range in purpose from practical to whimsical. The objective of the task is to define the use for the tool and then create the tool, or at least a mock-up of it. After groups have finished with their plans and prototyping, have each group present its tool to the rest of the class. Encourage students to notice if a particular theme emerges regarding the kinds of tools created. **0:25** minutes

Critical Viewing: NG Image Gallery Invite students to explore the entire NG Image Gallery and create a Favorites List by choosing the images they find most interesting. If possible, have students copy the images into a document to form an actual list. Then encourage them to select the image they like best and do further research on it. **0:10** minutes

DIFFERENTIATE

INCLUSION

Analyze Visuals Pair special needs students with students at a higher proficiency level. Have them reread the lesson. Then have students identify three ancient tools that they find interesting. Have them use the three-column chart below to record each tool, its use, and a similar modern tool.

Ancient Tool	Use	Modern Tool

PRE-AP

Research and Report Have students research and prepare an oral report on the development of metallurgy, the historical transition from stone to metal tools, and where and when this shift happened. Students should explain the significance of the transition in their reports. Have them present their reports to the class and encourage them to take questions from the audience.

Press **mt** *in the Student eEdition for modified text.*

See the Chapter Planner for more strategies for differentiation.

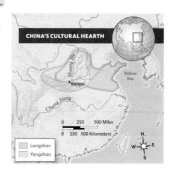

VOCABULARY

Use each of the following vocabulary words in a sentence that shows an understanding of the term's meaning.

1. **cultural hearth**
   A cultural hearth is a place from which new ideas and technology spread to surrounding areas.

2. **surplus**

3. **metallurgy**

4. **matrilineal**

5. **maize**

6. **temple**

7. **cultural diffusion**

8. **government**

9. **specialized worker**

10. **civilization**

READING STRATEGY

11. **IDENTIFY MAIN IDEAS AND DETAILS** If you haven't already, complete your diagram to determine a main idea and supporting details about cultural hearths. Then answer the question.

Cultural Hearths

| Main Idea: *Cultural hearths promoted the spread of new ideas, practices, and technology around the world.* |
| Detail: |
| Detail: |
| Detail: |

What is a cultural hearth? What impact did the four main cultural hearths have on the ancient world?

MAIN IDEAS

Answer the following questions. Support your answers with evidence from the chapter.

12. Why are cultural hearths referred to as centers of new ideas? LESSON 1.1

13. In what way was agriculture central to the people who built Çatalhöyük? LESSON 1.2

14. How did natural resources and climate influence the formation of cultural hearths in China? LESSON 1.3

15. In what ways did the Faiyum farmers demonstrate cultural diffusion? LESSON 1.5

16. What key characteristics do civilizations around the world share? LESSON 2.2

CRITICAL THINKING

Answer the following questions. Support your answers with evidence from the chapter.

17. **EVALUATE** What are some of the factors that contribute to the development of civilization?

18. **DRAW CONCLUSIONS** How did cultural hearths help lead to the emergence of civilization?

19. **MAKE INFERENCES** Why do you think government became necessary as cities developed?

20. **COMPARE AND CONTRAST** How did the lifestyles of hunter-gatherers compare with those of settlers of early agricultural communities?

21. **MAKE INFERENCES** Why is it significant that hunter-gatherers built Göbekli Tepe as a place of worship?

22. **FORM OPINIONS** Do you think agriculture or religion developed first? Support your opinion with evidence from the chapter.

23. **YOU DECIDE** Which of the five traits of civilization do you consider the most important? Support your opinion with evidence from the chapter.

INTERPRET MAPS

Study the map of the locations of the Yangshao and Longshan cultures that developed in China's cultural hearth. Then answer the questions that follow.

24. Which river was vital to the development of the Yangshao culture?

25. Why might the Longshan culture have expanded east from the Yangshao culture?

26. **MAP ACTIVITY** Create your own sketch maps of the other cultural hearths discussed in this chapter. Label the areas and bodies of water. Then study the maps and note the cultural hearths' physical similarities and differences.

ANALYZE SOURCES

The dagger below is made of carved and chipped stone. Archaeologists who discovered it at Çatalhöyük believe it was made around 6000 B.C. Study the artifact. Then answer the question that follows.

27. What information might archaeologists learn about the skills of the Neolithic people who created the dagger? Use evidence from the chapter to support your answer.

WRITE ABOUT HISTORY

28. **EXPLANATORY** Choose two cultures discussed in this chapter. Write a 3-paragraph informative essay that compares and contrasts the cultures in terms of their agricultural and technological developments.

TIPS

- Take notes from the lessons about the two cultures you choose.
- State your main idea and supporting details in a clear, well-organized way.
- Use appropriate transitions to clarify the relationships among ideas.
- Use at least two vocabulary words from the chapter.
- Provide a concluding statement that wraps up the information about the two cultures.

VOCABULARY ANSWERS

1. A cultural hearth is a place from which new ideas and technology spread to surrounding areas.

2. Farming fertile land produced a surplus of food.

3. Archaeologists have found evidence that Neolithic people made advancements in metallurgy, or metalworking.

4. In the Yangshao culture of China, families were grouped into matrilineal clans based on female ancestors.

5. In Mesoamerica, the domestication of maize provided a useful food source that supported permanent farming villages.

6. Göbekli Tepe is one of the world's first temples.

7. Cultural diffusion is the process by which cultures spread and share ideas, practices, and techniques with surrounding cultures.

8. Government is an organization set up to make and enforce rules for a society.

9. Specialized workers such as scribes recorded information.

10. A civilization is an advanced society that has cities, complex institutions, specialized workers, record keeping, and improved technology.

READING STRATEGY ANSWERS

Cultural Hearths

| Main Idea: *Cultural hearths promoted the spread of new ideas, practices, and technology around the world.* |
| Detail: domesticated plants and animals |
| Detail: created artistic pottery |
| Detail: advanced building techniques |
| Detail: adopted new techniques from other cultures |

11. A cultural hearth is place where new ideas, practices, and technology spread. The four cultural hearths of Oaxaca, Banpo, Çatalhöyük, and Faiyum made important contributions to surrounding cultures and regions. For example, farmers in Oaxaca domesticated maize, which became a staple crop for Mesoamericans. Potters at Banpo created kiln-fired, beautiful pottery. Builders at Çatalhöyük demonstrated advanced architectural techniques.

MAIN IDEAS ANSWERS

12. Ancient cultural hearths were places where people developed new ideas and technologies that then spread to other places. These included new ways of living in communities, complex forms of artistic and religious expression, and pioneering methods of raising animals and domesticating plants.

13. Agriculture was central to the people who built Çatalhöyük because in order to support a large population, they needed a steady food supply.

14. Major rivers were bountiful natural resources for water and fishing. Along these river basins fertile soils and a warmer, wetter climate also provided ideal conditions for farming and settlement, all of which enabled Neolithic cultures, such as the Yangshao and Longshan, to develop China's cultural hearth.

15. The Neolithic farmers who settled Egypt's earliest farming community in Faiyum are a significant example of cultural diffusion because they imported domesticated crops and animals, as well as tools and farming techniques, to places where domestication was already well established. The Faiyum farmers adapted neighboring cultures' ideas to their needs, spreading these ideas from one culture and area to another.

16. Civilizations around the world share the key characteristics of cities, complex institutions, specialized workers, record keeping, and improved technology.

CRITICAL THINKING ANSWERS

17. Factors that contribute to the development of civilization include practices that originate in cultural hearths, the emergence of cities and complex institutions, the establishment of specialized workers and record keeping, and improved technology.

18. They allowed people to become specialized workers; trade of agricultural products helped cities develop and become rich; technology diffused through cultural hearths led to more advanced technology.

19. Rules and laws kept order and controlled the growing population.

20. Hunter-gatherers lived a nomadic lifestyle, following herds of animals to hunt for food and skins and following the seasons to gather edible plants, seeds, and nuts—a difficult life of survival. While settlers of early agricultural communities continued to hunt animals and catch fish, they also domesticated plants and animals, which allowed them to farm and settle into permanent villages.

21. If Göbekli Tepe was built by hunter-gatherers—before farming developed—it reverses the order in which archaeologists and historians believe that most civilizations developed: agriculture first, then religion. By building Göbekli Tepe as a temple of worship, the hunter-gatherers practiced religion before they had developed farming.

22. Students' responses will vary. Students should clearly state their opinions about Göbekli Tepe in terms of its significance in the development of agriculture and religion and support their opinions with evidence from the chapter.

23. Students' responses will vary. Students should clearly state their opinions regarding the most important trait of civilization and support their opinions with evidence from the chapter.

INTERPRET MAPS ANSWERS

24. The Huang He was vital to the development of the Yangshao culture.

25. It seems significant that the Longshan culture evolved from the important Huang He river basin, but expanded toward a larger water resource and outlet, suggesting a growing population and advancements in travel and trade.

26. Students' maps will vary but should be labeled correctly.

ANALYZE SOURCES ANSWER

27. Students' responses will vary. Sample response: The photograph of the dagger reveals a high level of technical skill in shaping the flint dagger and sharp edges. The bone handle of the dagger reveals an interest in artistic expression, as well as a high level of artistic skill in shaping it in the form of an animal's head.

WRITE ABOUT HISTORY ANSWER

28. Students' essays should
   - introduce the topic and develop it with relevant details
   - contain transitions from one idea to another
   - include vocabulary words from the chapter
   - end with a concluding statement that supports the information presented

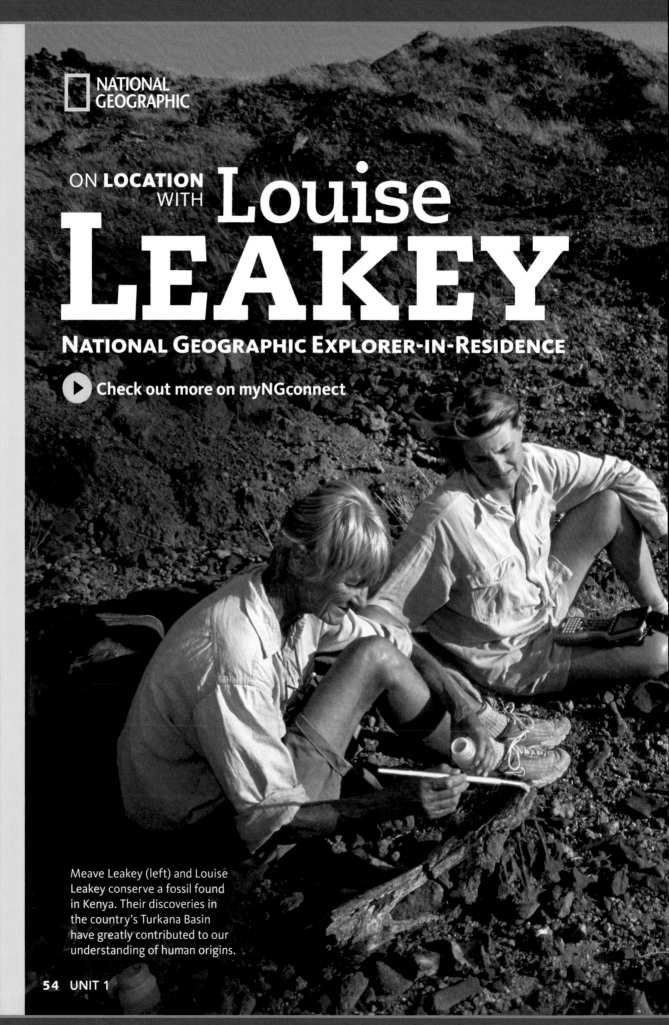

NATIONAL
GEOGRAPHIC

ON **LOCATION**
WITH Louise
LEAKEY

NATIONAL GEOGRAPHIC EXPLORER-IN-RESIDENCE

▶ Check out more on myNGconnect

Meave Leakey (left) and Louise
Leakey conserve a fossil found
in Kenya. Their discoveries in
the country's Turkana Basin
have greatly contributed to our
understanding of human origins.

ALL IN THE FAMILY

I've spent quite a bit of time on my hands and knees, carefully excavating the remains of our ancestors and other animals. I have been fortunate to have done this work alongside my mother, Meave Leakey. She is also a highly acclaimed paleontologist, so there's a lot to live up to! This is what happens when you're born into a family famous for finding prehuman fossils. My grandfather, Louis Leakey, made important discoveries in Tanzania, at Olduvai Gorge, that helped explain the human fossil record. I remember when my father, Richard Leakey, discovered a well-preserved 1.6-million-year-old skeleton of *Homo erectus*, one of our ancestors that left Africa for the first time 1.8 million years ago. I was twelve years old at the time, and they compared my teeth with the teeth of this skeleton, the Nariokotome Boy, to determine that it was about the same age as I was.

EARLY HUMAN FOSSILS

My mother and I continue with our field work, on the east side of Lake Turkana in Kenya's Rift Valley. We organize and coordinate the search for fossil remains in extensive fossil deposits in northern Kenya. During every expedition, we discover and collect exciting new fossils that help us answer important questions about the past. These fossils are kept at the Turkana Basin Institute or in the National Museums of Kenya. In 1999, we

Louise Leakey uses GPS to locate fossils in Kenya. You can explore many of her family's fossil discoveries at www.africanfossils.org.

organized a National Geographic-sponsored expedition to the Turkana Basin. It was there that my mother and I uncovered a 3.3-million-year-old human skull and part of a jaw. The skull is very flat, and that makes it different from anything else ever found. In fact, it is so different that we believe it belongs to an entirely new branch of early human that we named *Kenyanthropus platyops*. To prove this beyond doubt, we still need to find more remains, ideally another intact skull! From this same site, the earliest stone tools known to the world have recently been announced, which strongly suggests that this species was also the earliest tool maker.

WHY STUDY HISTORY ❓

❝ When you look at the state of the world today, with its many conflicts and ethnic divisions, it's hard to believe that we are a single species with a common ancestor. We have to understand our past to contemplate our future. The fossils in east Africa are our *global heritage.* ❞ —Louise Leakey

NATIONAL GEOGRAPHIC

Scotland's Stone Age Ruins

BY ROFF SMITH

Adapted from "Scotland's Stone Age Ruins,"
by Roff Smith, in *National Geographic*, August 2014

Orkney is a fertile, green archipelago off the northern tip of Scotland. Five thousand years ago, people there built something unlike anything they had ever attempted before. They had Stone Age technology, but their vision was millennia ahead of their time.

The ancient people of Orkney quarried thousands of tons of sandstone and transported it several miles to a grassy hill. There they constructed a complex of buildings and surrounded them with imposing walls. The complex featured paved walkways, carved stonework, colored facades, and slate roofs. Many people gathered here for seasonal rituals, feasts, and trade.

Archaeologist Nick Card says the recent discovery of these stunning ruins is turning British prehistory on its head. "This is almost on the scale of some of the great classical sites in the Mediterranean, like the Acropolis in Greece, except these structures are 2,500 years older." Only a small part of the site has been excavated, but this sample has opened a window into the

past. It has also yielded thousands of artifacts, including ceremonial mace heads, polished stone axes, flint knives, stone spatulas, and colored pottery. Archaeologists have also discovered more than 650 pieces of Neolithic art at the site.

"Nowhere else in all Britain or Ireland have such well-preserved stone houses from the Neolithic survived," says archaeologist Antonia Thomas. "To be able to link these structures with art, to see in such a direct and personal way how people embellished their surroundings, is really something."

Sometime around the year 2300 B.C., it all came to an end. Climate change may have played a role. Or perhaps it was the disruptive influence of a new toolmaking material: bronze.

Whatever the reason, the ancient temple was deliberately destroyed and buried under stone and trash. Card surmises, "It seems that they were attempting to erase the site and its importance from memory, perhaps to mark the introduction of new belief systems."

For more from National Geographic
Check out "First Americans" on myNGconnect

UNIT INQUIRY: CREATE A CULTURAL SYMBOL

In this unit, you learned about the origins of early human cultures and civilizations. Based on your understanding of the text, what elements of culture developed in early human societies? How did those elements help make each society unique?

ASSIGNMENT Create a symbol that represents the culture of an early human society you studied in this unit. The symbol should reflect one or more cultural characteristics that made that early society unique. Be prepared to present your cultural symbol and explain its significance to the class.

Plan As you create your symbol, think about specific characteristics that were unique to the society you have selected. For example, what elements of culture defined and unified early Stone Age humans? What customs, social structure, arts, tools, and major achievements distinguished them from other groups of early humans? You might want to use a graphic organizer to help organize your thoughts. Identify the early society and at least one specific detail about different characteristics of its culture. ▶

Produce Use your notes to produce detailed descriptions of the elements of culture that defined the early human society you

selected. You might want to draw or write descriptions of visual icons for each element.

Present Choose a creative way to present your cultural symbol to the class. Consider one of the following options:

- Write an introduction to the cultural symbol that describes the early human society it represents.

- Create a multimedia presentation showing different elements of the society's culture and what made it unique.

- Paint a flag of your symbol using colors that also express significance or meaning to the culture.

Elements of the _____ Culture

- Social Structure
- Major Achievements
- Customs & Beliefs
- Arts & Technology

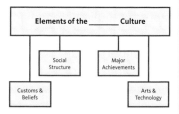

RAPID REVIEW
UNIT 1

ORIGINS OF CULTURES AND CIVILIZATIONS

TOP TEN

1. Humans originated from a common ancestor who lived in Africa 60,000 years ago.

2. For thousands of years, humans lived in small, nomadic groups, hunted wild animals, and gathered edible plants.

3. Farming produced food surpluses that allowed rapid population growth and job specialization.

4. Agriculture encouraged people to group together in villages that grew into more complex cities.

5. Cultural hearths emerged around the world during the Neolithic period.

6-10. **NOW IT'S YOUR TURN** Complete the list with five more things to remember about the origins of cultures and civilizations.

RAPID REVIEW

POSSIBLE RESPONSES

Possible responses for the remaining five things to remember:

6. Societies grew more complex and developed into civilizations.

7. Humans migrated out of Africa and populated most of the world by about 10,000 B.C.

8. Early humans domesticated plants and animals, which led to the agricultural revolution.

9. Domestication and a more temperate climate encouraged settlement in fertile river valleys.

10. Early humans developed new technology, including harnessing fire and inventing specialized tools.

UNIT INQUIRY PROJECT RUBRIC

ASSESS

Use the rubric to assess each student's participation and performance.

SCORE	ASSIGNMENT	PRODUCT	PRESENTATION
3 GREAT	• Student thoroughly understands the assignment. • Student engages fully with the project process. • Student works well independently.	• Cultural symbol is well thought out. • Cultural symbol reflects characteristics of the selected society. • Descriptions of the society's elements of culture are detailed.	• Presentation is clear, concise, and logical. • Presentation does a good job of creatively explaining the cultural symbol and elements of the selected society's culture. • Presentation engages the audience.
2 GOOD	• Student mostly understands the assignment. • Student engages fairly well with the project process. • Student works fairly well independently.	• Cultural symbol is fairly well thought out. • Cultural symbol somewhat reflects characteristics of the selected society. • Descriptions of the society's elements of culture are somewhat detailed.	• Presentation is fairly clear, concise, and logical. • Presentation does an adequate job of creatively explaining the cultural symbol and elements of the selected society's culture. • Presentation somewhat engages the audience.
1 NEEDS WORK	• Student does not understand the assignment. • Student minimally engages or does not engage with the project process. • Student does not work well independently.	• Cultural symbol is not well thought out. • Cultural symbol does not reflect characteristics of the selected society. • Descriptions of the society's elements of culture are few or nonexistent.	• Presentation is not clear, concise, or logical. • Presentation does an inadequate job of creatively explaining the cultural symbol and elements of the selected society's culture. • Presentation does not engage the audience.

EARLY
CIVILIZATIONS

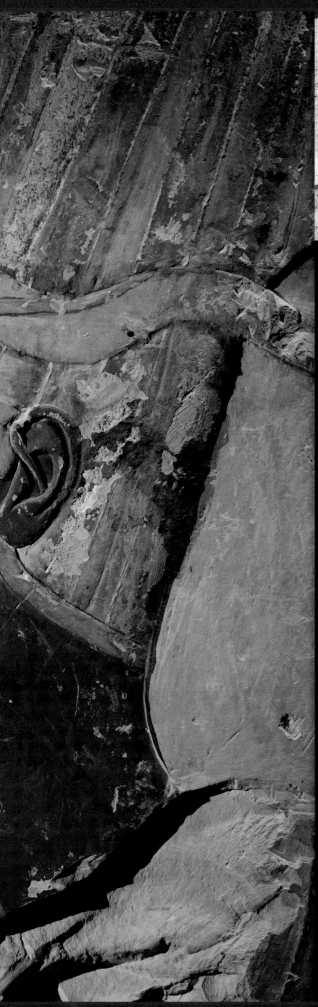

NATIONAL GEOGRAPHIC

ON **LOCATION** WITH

Christopher Thornton
Archaeologist
Lead Program Officer, Research,
Conservation, and Exploration,
National Geographic

The past is a window to the future. Early civilizations differ in many ways from those today, but there are also many similarities between then and now. Studying early civilizations is exciting because of what we can learn from the ancients, and also because what we know—or think we know— is always changing. I'm Christopher Thornton, and I time travel between the past and present. Join me on my journey!

‹ CRITICAL VIEWING This painted bas-relief shows ancient Egyptian king Thutmose III wearing the Atef crown, which was worn during religious rituals. What details in the artwork convey the king's strength and power?

59

⊕ POSSIBLE RESPONSE

Details that convey the king's strength and power include the figure's confident expression, his elaborate headdress and clothing, and his broad shoulders.

Early
Civilizations

**Mesopotamia, Egypt,
Israel, India, and China**

c. 1250 B.C.
Moses leads
the Hebrews
out of Egypt.
(Hebrew text scroll)

c. 1600 B.C.
The Shang dynasty
emerges along the
Huang He in China.

c. 3500 B.C.
The world's first
civilization arises
in Sumer. *(stringed
instrument from Ur)*

1500 B.C.

2334 B.C.
Sargon the Great
conquers Sumer
and creates the
world's first
empire.

c. 1790 B.C.
Hammurabi issues
his Code of Laws
at Babylon.

c. 2500 B.C.
Harappan civilization
develops in the
Indus Valley.

3500 B.C.

c. 1470 B.C.
Hatshepsut becomes
Egypt's first female
pharaoh.

c. 3100 B.C.
Upper and
Lower Egypt are
united under a
single ruler.
*(Horus, Egyptian
sky god)*

c. 1000 B.C.
Aryan civilization spreads
through the northern
Indian subcontinent.

What can you infer about the Qin dynasty in China based on this time line?

c. 269 B.C.
Asoka becomes ruler of the Maurya Empire and eventually rules by Buddhist principles.

A.D. 320
Chandra Gupta I establishes the Gupta Empire, which oversees India's golden age.
(Gupta gold coin)

A.D. 105
The Chinese invent paper.

200 B.C.

563 B.C.
Siddhartha Gautama, the Buddha, is born.

A.D. 100

202 B.C.
The Han dynasty comes to power.
(Han bronze dragon)

600 B.C.

c. 221 B.C.
The Qin dynasty begins with the reign of Shi Huangdi.

587 B.C.
Jerusalem falls to the Babylonians, beginning the Babylonian Exile.

FIRST
CIVILIZATIONS
3500 B.C.–1800 B.C.

Most of the world's earliest civilizations, including Mesopotamia, Egypt, India, and China, developed in fertile river valleys. The good soil made the river valleys ideal for growing crops. By contrast, the Hebrews established their civilization along the Mediterranean. However, what really set them apart was their belief in one God. This belief would influence the rest of the world for centuries.

What landforms separated the civilizations?

➕ POSSIBLE RESPONSE

Mountains and bodies of water separated the civilizations.

ANCIENT MESOPOTAMIA

Water sources:	Tigris and Euphrates rivers, Mediterranean Sea
Civilizations and empires:	Sumer, Akkadia, Babylon, Assyria, Chaldea, Phoenicia, Persia
Significant leaders:	Sargon, Hammurabi, Nebuchadnezzar II, Cyrus
Legacy:	farming, writing, government, law, shipbuilding, math

ANCIENT EGYPT

Water sources:	Nile River
Civilizations and empires:	Egypt, Kush
Significant leaders:	Khufu, Ahmose, Hatshepsut, Ramses II, Piankhi
Legacy:	writing, math, science, medicine, art, architecture

JUDAISM & ISRAELITE KINGDOMS

Water sources:	Mediterranean Sea
Civilizations and empires:	Israel, Judah
Significant leaders:	Abraham, Moses, Saul, David, Solomon
Legacy:	education, religion, philosophy

EUROPE

Black Sea

Caucasus Mts.

Caspian Sea

Mediterranean Sea

Tigris

Mesopotamia

Euphrates

Persian Gulf

Egypt

Nile

Red Sea

AFRICA

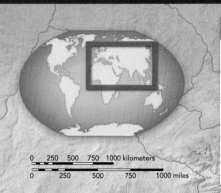

ANCIENT CHINA

Water sources:	Huang He, Chang Jiang
Civilizations and empires:	Shang, Zhou, Qin, Han
Significant leaders:	Shi Huangdi, Liu Bang, Empress Lü, Emperor Wudi
Legacy:	philosophy, government, navigation, farming, writing, textiles, art

0   250   500   750   1000 kilometers

0   250   500   750   1000 miles

A S I A

Himalaya

Huang (Yellow)

China

Chiang Jiang (Yangtze)

Indus

Ganges

India

Arabian Sea

Bay of Bengal

South China Sea

INDIAN OCEAN

ANCIENT INDIA

Water sources:	Indus River, Ganges River, Indian Ocean
Civilizations and empires:	Harappa, Aryan, Maurya, Gupta
Significant leaders:	Chandragupta Maurya, Asoka, Chandra Gupta I
Legacy:	religion, art, medicine, math

63

UNIT RESOURCES

On Location with National Geographic Lead Program Officer Christopher Thornton Intro and Video

Interactive Map Tool

News & Updates

Available on myNGconnect

Unit Wrap-Up:
"Encounters with History"
Feature and Video

"Faces of the Divine"
National Geographic Adapted Article
Student eEdition exclusive

"China's Ancient Lifeline"
National Geographic Adapted Article

Unit 2 Inquiry:
Write a Creation Myth

CHAPTER RESOURCES

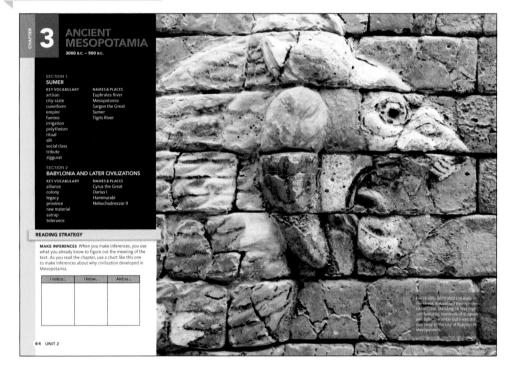

TEACHER RESOURCES & ASSESSMENT

Available on myNGconnect

Social Studies Skills Lessons
• Reading: Make Inferences
• Writing: Write an Argument

Formal Assessment
• Chapter 3 Tests A (on-level) & B (below-level)

Chapter 3 Answer Key

ExamView®
One-time Download

STUDENT BACKPACK *Available on myNGconnect*

• **eEdition** *(English)*   • **eEdition** *(Spanish)*   • **Handbooks**   • **Online Atlas**

For Chapter 3 Spanish resources, visit the Teacher Resource Menu page on myNGconnect.

SECTION 1 RESOURCES

SUMER

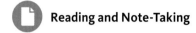 **Reading and Note-Taking**

 **Vocabulary Practice**

 **Section 1 Quiz**

Available on myNGconnect

LESSON 1.1 THE GEOGRAPHY OF ANCIENT MESOPOTAMIA

| **NG Learning Framework:**
Create a Map

• On Your Feet: Inside-Outside Circle

LESSON 1.2 CITY-STATES DEVELOP

| **NG Learning Framework:**
Redesign the City of Ur

• On Your Feet: Create Trade Networks

LESSON 1.3 RELIGION IN SUMER

• Critical Viewing: NG Chapter Gallery
• On Your Feet: Three-Step Interview

DOCUMENT-BASED QUESTION
LESSON 1.4 SUMERIAN WRITING

| **NG Learning Framework:**
Compare Two Writing Systems

• On Your Feet: Telephone

LESSON 1.5 SARGON CONQUERS MESOPOTAMIA

• Critical Viewing: NG Chapter Gallery
• On Your Feet: Fishbowl

SECTION 2 RESOURCES

BABYLONIA AND LATER CIVILIZATIONS

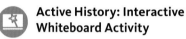 **Reading and Note-Taking**

 **Vocabulary Practice**

 Section 2 Quiz

Available on myNGconnect

LESSON 2.1 HAMMURABI'S CODE OF LAWS

Active History: Interactive Whiteboard Activity
Analyze Primary Sources: Hammurabi's Code

Active History
Analyze Primary Sources: Hammurabi's Code

Available on myNGconnect

• On Your Feet: Code of Laws Roundtable

LESSON 2.2 THE ASSYRIANS AND THE CHALDEANS

• Critical Viewing: NG Chapter Gallery
• On Your Feet: Create a Time Line

LESSON 2.3 THE PHOENICIANS

| **NG Learning Framework:**
Create Your Own Figurehead

• On Your Feet: Three-Step Interview

LESSON 2.4 PERSIAN LEADERS

Biography
Darius I   *Available on myNGconnect*

| **NG Learning Framework:**
Learn More About Persian Leaders

• On Your Feet: Create a Living Time Line

LESSON 2.5 THE LEGACY OF MESOPOTAMIA

• Critical Viewing: NG Chapter Gallery
• On Your Feet: Hold a Debate

CHAPTER 3 REVIEW

STRATEGY ❶
Record and Compare Facts

After reading, ask each student to write at least three facts they can recall from the lesson. Allow pairs of students to compare and check their facts and then combine their facts into one longer list. Challenge students to become the pair with the longest list of accurate facts.

Use with All Lessons

STRATEGY ❷
Turn Headings into Outlines

Model how headings can be made into an outline. Direct students to copy the outline and then read the lesson to record details to complete the outline.

I. New Empire in Mesopotamia

    A.

    B.

    C.

II. Hammurabi's Code

    A.

    B.

    C.

Use with Lesson 2.1

STRATEGY ❸
Identify Chronological Order

Help students track historical events. Explain that dates in the text can be a helpful guide. As students read, they can create a time line to show events in the order in which they happened.

Use with All Lessons

Press **mt** *in the Student eEdition for modified text.*

STRATEGY ❶
Modify Main Idea Statements

Provide these modifications of the Main Idea statements at the beginning of each lesson:

1.1   The rivers, location, and good land helped bring people together as groups and encouraged human social development.

1.2   The group of cities in Sumer, and land surrounding those cities, formed an extended group that allowed for enhanced social development.

Use with Lessons 1.1–1.2

STRATEGY ❷
Use Supported Reading

In small groups, have students read the chapter aloud, lesson by lesson. At the end of each lesson, have them stop and use these frames to tell what they understood from their reading:

This lesson is about _____.

One detail that stood out to me is _____.

The vocabulary word _____ means _____.

I don't think I understand _____.

Guide students through portions of text they do not understand. Be sure all students understand a lesson before moving on to the next one.

Use with All Lessons

ENGLISH LANGUAGE LEARNERS

STRATEGY ❶
Make Word Connections

Display the words below and ask students to talk about what each one means and how the words might be related. Then ask what the words might have to do with the upcoming chapter on Ancient Mesopotamia. Call on volunteers to use one of the words in a sentence about the development of ancient civilizations.

Mesopotamia	city-state	polytheism
silt	social class	rituals
irrigation	artisan	ziggurat

Use with Lessons 1.1–1.3

STRATEGY ❷
Pair Partners for Dictation

After students read each lesson in the chapter, ask them to write a sentence summarizing its main idea. Have students get together in pairs and dictate their sentences to each other. Then have them work together to check the sentences for accuracy and spelling.

Use with All Lessons

STRATEGY ❸
PREP Before Reading

Have students use the PREP strategy to prepare for reading. Write this acrostic on the board:

PREP	**P**review title.
	Read Main Idea statement.
	Examine visuals.
	Predict what you will learn.

Have students write their prediction and share it with a partner. After reading, ask students to write another sentence that begins with "I also learned . . . "

Use with All Lessons

GIFTED & TALENTED

STRATEGY ❶
Write a Dialogue

Tell students to review Lesson 2.4 under the heading "Darius Expands the Empire." Then have them use facts from the text to write a dialogue that might have taken place between Darius I and a satrap in one of the provinces. Encourage students to cover topics that might have been discussed between two officials who governed the people.

Use with Lesson 2.4

STRATEGY ❷
Interview a King

Allow students to work in teams of two to plan, write, and perform a simulated television interview with King Hammurabi of Babylon. Tell students the purpose of the interview is to focus on the achievements of the king during his reign.

Use with Lesson 2.1 *Invite students to use the Internet or library resources to learn more about Hammurabi.*

PRE-AP

STRATEGY ❶
Brainstorm Solutions

Have students reread Lesson 2.5 to understand how Cyrus the Great and Darius I united their empires. Then allow students to work in pairs to brainstorm a list of other ways they could have solved the problem of uniting the people of a large empire. Allow the pairs to share their solutions with the class.

Use with Lesson 2.4

STRATEGY ❷
Create a Travel Brochure

Tell students to create a travel brochure for visitors to the historical Phoenician trading settlement called Carthage. Instruct students to create the brochure as though they are living in 1000 B.C. and trying to attract travelers or traders from around the region. Allow students to create their brochure in a medium of their choosing.

Use with Lesson 2.3

SECTION 1
SUMER

KEY VOCABULARY	NAMES & PLACES
artisan	Euphrates River
city-state	Mesopotamia
cuneiform	Sargon the Great
empire	Sumer
famine	Tigris River
irrigation	
polytheism	
ritual	
silt	
social class	
tribute	
ziggurat	

SECTION 2
BABYLONIA AND LATER CIVILIZATIONS

KEY VOCABULARY	NAMES & PLACES
alliance	Cyrus the Great
colony	Darius I
legacy	Hammurabi
province	Nebuchadnezzar II
raw material	
satrap	
tolerance	

READING STRATEGY

MAKE INFERENCES When you make inferences, you use what you already know to figure out the meaning of the text. As you read the chapter, use a chart like this one to make inferences about why civilization developed in Mesopotamia.

I notice...	I know...	And so...

Fierce lions decorated the walls of the street that passed through the Ishtar Gate. Standing 38 feet high and featuring hundreds of dragons and bulls, the Ishtar Gate was the entryway to the city of Babylon in Mesopotamia.

TEACHER BACKGROUND

INTRODUCE THE PHOTOGRAPH

Have students study the photograph of the lion's head from the walls leading to the Ishtar Gate. The lions here are nearly life-sized on a background of blue- and yellow-glazed bricks. The walls also feature dragons and bulls. Tell students that animals often represent different things in different cultures.

ASK: Using what you know and what you can observe, what do you infer the lion might represent? (*Possible response: The lion looks fierce and like it is about to attack. Lions are known to be protective of their territory and pride, so maybe the lion is supposed to represent the leader of the city.*)

SHARE BACKGROUND

The Ishtar Gate is one of the most famous structures from the ancient world. In the 20th century, archaeologists actually found the walls of the ancient city of Babylon. Though many of the bricks were crumbling, some sections of the walls were in good enough condition to save. Some of the ancient bricks were moved from modern-day Iraq to the Pergamon Museum in Berlin, Germany. There, some of the walls of Babylon were re-created. Curators estimate that about 20 percent of the bricks are original, and the rest were re-created around 1930. Archaeologists believe that the lions represent Ishtar, the Babylonian goddess of love and war.

DIGITAL RESOURCES myNGconnect.com

TEACHER RESOURCES & ASSESSMENT

 Social Studies Skills Lessons
- Reading: Make Inferences
- Writing: Write an Argument

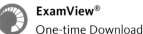 **ExamView®**
One-time Download

Formal Assessment
Chapter 3 Tests A (on-level) & B (below-level)

 Chapter 3 Answer Key

STUDENT BACKPACK

- **eEdition** (*English*)
- **eEdition** (*Spanish*)
- **Handbooks**
- **Online Atlas**

For Chapter 3 Spanish Resources, visit the Teacher Resource Menu page.

INTRODUCE THE ESSENTIAL QUESTION

WHY WAS CIVILIZATION ABLE TO DEVELOP IN ANCIENT MESOPOTAMIA?

Roundtable Activity: Factors of Influence This activity allows students to discuss four factors that allowed civilization to develop in Mesopotamia: geography of the region, aspects of culture, development of empires, and technology. Divide the class into four groups and have each group sit at a table. Assign the following questions to the groups:

Group 1: Why might geography have been a key factor in early civilizations?

Group 2: What role did culture play in helping to build early civilizations?

Group 3: Why did building empires play a key role in developing civilizations?

Group 4: How did technology help spread early civilizations?

Have students at each table take turns answering the question. When they have finished their discussion, ask a representative from each table to summarize that group's answers. **0:15** minutes

INTRODUCE THE READING STRATEGY

MAKE INFERENCES

Remind students that when you make inferences, you use what you already know to figure out the meaning of the text. Use a chart like this one to make inferences about why civilization developed in Mesopotamia by organizing topics or ideas to help students better understand new information. Model completing the chart by reading the paragraphs under "Farming in the Fertile Crescent" in Lesson 1.1 and continue the exercise for each lesson of the chapter.

I notice...	I know...	And so...
farming spread	irrigation was the answer	food surplus

Graphic Organizer
Inference Chart

INTRODUCE CHAPTER VOCABULARY

WORD WEB

Have students complete a Word Web for Key Vocabulary words as they read the chapter. Ask them to write each word in the center of an oval. Have them look through the chapter to find examples, characteristics, and descriptive words that may be associated with the vocabulary word. At the end of the chapter, ask students what they learned about each word.

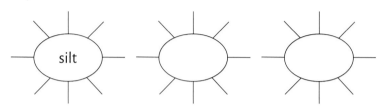

KEY DATES	
c. 8000 B.C.	Beginning of farming in the Fertile Crescent
c. 3500 B.C.	Mesopotamia's first civilization, Sumer, rises
2334 B.C.	Sumer is conquered and becomes part of the Akkadian Empire
1792 B.C.	Hammurabi becomes king of Babylon
c. 650 B.C.	Assyrian army conquers all of Mesopotamia, parts of Asia Minor, and Egypt
539 B.C.	Cyrus the Great captures the Babylonian Empire

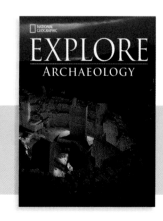

For wonderful archaeology stories, check out *EXPLORE ARCHAEOLOGY*.

The Geography of Ancient Mesopotamia

Long after Çatalhöyük was settled, Southwest Asia was home to another group of people. They lived between two flowing rivers in a fertile land. Because of the advances in government, culture, and technology that took place there, the region is often called a "cradle of civilization."

MAIN IDEA

The geography of Mesopotamia helped create the conditions for civilization.

THE LAND BETWEEN THE RIVERS

As you have learned, the Fertile Crescent sweeps its way across Southwest Asia. In the west it bends down the coast of the Mediterranean. In the east it follows the course of the **Tigris** (TY-gruhs) **River** and the **Euphrates** (yu-FRAY-teez) **River** until they merge and empty into the warm waters of the Persian Gulf. Today this river valley lies mostly in the country of Iraq. Historians call this flat, fertile area **Mesopotamia** (meh-suh-puh-TAY-mee-uh), which means "land between the rivers." The people who once lived there are known as Mesopotamians.

The people of Mesopotamia called the Tigris "swift river" because it flowed fast. The Euphrates flowed more slowly. It frequently changed course, leaving riverside

settlements without water. Both rivers flooded unpredictably. Mesopotamians never knew when or how much water would come. Too much, too little, or too late spelled disaster for crops.

On the plus side, the often-destructive floodwaters deposited **silt**, an especially fine and fertile soil, that was excellent for agriculture. In this way, the rivers brought life to the otherwise dry land of Mesopotamia and supported the early civilization that was developing there. As farming thrived in this river valley, populations grew and cities developed.

FARMING IN THE FERTILE CRESCENT

Farming began as early as 9800 B.C. in the Fertile Crescent. It eventually spread throughout Mesopotamia. However, Mesopotamia was far from perfect for agriculture. In addition to flooding, farmers had to deal with hot summers and unreliable rainfall. However, the region's fertile soils promised plentiful crops, such as wheat, barley, and figs—if the people could come up with a way to control the water supply.

Irrigation, or watering fields using human-made systems, was the answer. Farmers in Mesopotamian villages cooperated to dig and maintain irrigation canals that carried water from the rivers to the fields. Farmers also stored rainwater for later use and built walls from mounds of earth to hold back floodwaters. The people developed important new technology, such as the ox-driven plow, a tool that broke up the hard-baked summer soil and prepared large areas for planting. These creative methods enabled farmers to use the rich soil to their advantage.

The result was a reliable and abundant agricultural surplus. The ample food fed the area's growing population. Because food was plentiful, the people of Mesopotamia could afford to develop art, architecture, and technology. The agricultural surpluses allowed a great civilization to develop.

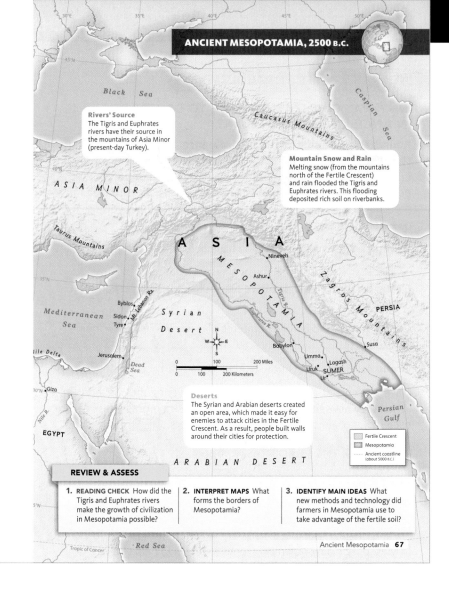

ANCIENT MESOPOTAMIA, 2500 B.C.

Rivers' Source
The Tigris and Euphrates rivers have their source in the mountains of Asia Minor (present-day Turkey).

Mountain Snow and Rain
Melting snow (from the mountains north of the Fertile Crescent) and rain flooded the Tigris and Euphrates rivers. This flooding deposited rich soil on riverbanks.

Deserts
The Syrian and Arabian deserts created an open area, which made it easy for enemies to attack cities in the Fertile Crescent. As a result, people built walls around their cities for protection.

Fertile Crescent
Mesopotamia
---- Ancient coastline (about 5000 B.C.)

REVIEW & ASSESS

1. **READING CHECK** How did the Tigris and Euphrates rivers make the growth of civilization in Mesopotamia possible?

2. **INTERPRET MAPS** What forms the borders of Mesopotamia?

3. **IDENTIFY MAIN IDEAS** What new methods and technology did farmers in Mesopotamia use to take advantage of the fertile soil?

PLAN

OBJECTIVE

Analyze how the geography of Mesopotamia helped create the conditions for civilization to emerge.

CRITICAL THINKING SKILLS FOR LESSON 1.1

- Identify Main Ideas and Details
- Monitor Comprehension
- Interpret Maps
- Identify Main Ideas
- Make Inferences
- Compare and Contrast

ESSENTIAL QUESTION

Why was civilization able to develop in ancient Mesopotamia?

The geography of Mesopotamia helped create favorable conditions for developing civilizations. Lesson 1.1 discusses the Fertile Crescent and how its physical geography allowed for a food surplus.

BACKGROUND FOR THE TEACHER

The Tigris and Euphrates rivers are among the most important features of the physical geography in Southwest Asia. The sources of both of these rivers are in the Taurus Mountains of modern-day Turkey and are only about 50 miles apart. As they flow southeast through modern-day Iraq, toward the Persian Gulf, these rivers are never more than about 250 miles apart. The land between the rivers was historically very fertile because yearly floods deposited silt in the floodplain area.

INTRODUCE & ENGAGE

INTERPRET MAPS

Have students look at the Ancient Mesopotamia map in Lesson 1.1. Explain that the map shows the physical geography of Mesopotamia in 2500 B.C. Remind students that the map legend shows what the green area and red outlines mean. Point out that the ancient coastline was farther inland in 5000 B.C. than it was in 2500 B.C. **ASK:** What role did silt play in changing the coastline of the rivers? *(The rivers deposited so much silt at the mouth of the river that, over time, more land built up on the coast.)* **0:05** minutes

TEACH

GUIDED DISCUSSION

1. **Make Inferences** Review the map of Mesopotamia showing the Tigris and Euphrates rivers. How might the location of the rivers explain why the area is known as the Fertile Crescent? *(Students should notice that the Fertile Crescent is mostly between the rivers. They should make the inference that water played a role in why the region is so fertile.)*

2. **Compare and Contrast** What are the benefits of the Tigris and Euphrates rivers' flooding? What are the drawbacks? *(The benefits are that the floods bring fertile silt to areas that may have poor soil. The drawbacks are that the floods were unpredictable and could lead to destroyed crops.)*

INTERPRET MAPS

Help students interpret the map. **ASK:** What can you infer about the location of the cities in ancient Mesopotamia? *(They were located on or near the rivers, and people probably relied on the rivers for fresh water, food, and transportation.)* **0:10** minutes

ACTIVE OPTIONS

NG Learning Framework: Create a Map

SKILL: Observation
KNOWLEDGE: Our Living Planet

Have students work in pairs. Instruct students to observe the map of ancient Mesopotamia for two minutes. Then instruct them to take five minutes to work with their partner to draw their own map of ancient Mesopotamia. They should include as many landforms, cities, and labels as possible. After the five minutes are up, have students compare their map to the original and make any additions to their map in a different color. Ask students to make observations on the details they now notice compared with their observation at the beginning of this activity. **0:10** minutes

On Your Feet: Inside-Outside Circle Have students form concentric circles facing each other. Allow them time to write questions about the geographic and historical conditions leading to the civilization of ancient Mesopotamia. Then have students in the inside circle pose questions to students in the outside circle. Have students switch roles. Students may ask for help from other students in their circle if they are unable to answer a question. **0:15** minutes

DIFFERENTIATE

ENGLISH LANGUAGE LEARNERS

Identify Facts Have students form small groups and conduct a Round Robin activity to review what they have learned in the lesson. Ask groups to generate facts for about 3–5 minutes, with all students contributing. Finally, invite one student from each group to share his or her group's responses. Write all the facts on the board.

GIFTED & TALENTED

Host a Talk Show Have students assume the roles of a talk show host, a historian, and an economics expert in Southwest Asia. Have students conduct research to learn more about the Tigris and Euphrates rivers. Suggest that they gather information on historical uses of the Fertile Crescent and the types of crops produced in ancient times. Then have them gather statistics on how the Tigris and Euphrates are used today. Include statistics on the types of agricultural products and goods produced and what the modern exports are for the region. Then have students explain how the way people use the land has changed over time.

Press (**mt**) *in the Student eEdition for modified text.*

See the Chapter Planner for more strategies for differentiation.

REVIEW & ASSESS

ANSWERS

1. The rivers were the primary source of fresh water in the region. Using irrigation methods to bring that water to fields allowed farmers to grow an abundance of crops. A better food supply made it possible for people to focus on other aspects of culture, such as art, architecture, and technology.

2. The Zagros Mountains to the north and east, the Euphrates River to the west, and the Persian Gulf to the south form the borders of Mesopotamia.

3. The farmers created irrigation methods and built canals to bring water to fields. They also developed an ox-driven plow to work the soil.

City-States Develop

The present-day location that was once Mesopotamia is made up of windswept deserts. It's hard to imagine that 5,500 years ago this dusty land was filled with people living their busy city lives. The city streets were not just filled with people—there were also buildings and temples so tall they seemed to rise up to the heavens.

THE CITY-STATE OF UR, c. 2000 B.C.

This large temple was built to honor Ur's moon god, Nanna. It was the highest point in Ur and could be seen for miles from outside the city.

Most residents lived in one-story mud houses that were crowded close together along the streets.

Giant surrounding walls protected Ur from attack by other city-states and invaders from outside Mesopotamia.

Ur's residents accessed water from the nearby Euphrates River through a system of canals.

MAIN IDEA

The city-states of Sumer formed Southwest Asia's first civilization.

SUMER

Around 3500 B.C., Mesopotamia's first civilization arose in **Sumer** (SOO-mur), an area in the southern part of the region. (See the map in Lesson 1.1.) Sumer was not controlled by a single, unified government. Instead, the area was made up of a dozen advanced, self-governing city-states. A **city-state** included the city and its surrounding lands and settlements. These units developed when villages united to build major irrigation projects.

Most of Sumer's 12 city-states, including Ur, were built on the Tigris or Euphrates rivers. City-states also clustered close to the coast of the Persian Gulf, where the people developed fishing and trade. Frequent wars were fought between city-states to protect fertile land, limited natural resources, and profitable trade routes.

CENTERS OF CIVILIZATION

Surplus food gave Sumerians time to learn new skills and encouraged trade. Though Sumer had productive farmland, the area lacked important natural resources, such as tin and copper. These resources had to be acquired through trade. When combined, tin and copper produce bronze, a strong metal used by Sumerians to create tools and weapons. Because of the importance of bronze, the period around 3000 B.C. is called the Bronze Age.

Surplus food also led to a growth in population. New government systems had to be established to meet the challenge of managing so many people. Kings arose to provide strong leadership, and administrators supervised taxes and kept order. Because of the wealth created by agricultural surpluses, Sumerians could afford to support these government administrators.

Sumerian society was organized by **social class**, an order based on power and wealth. Kings ruled at the top, with priests just beneath them. Next came administrators, scribes, merchants, and **artisans**, or people who are skilled at making things by hand. These groups in turn looked down on farmers and less-skilled workers. However, even people at the bottom of this system ranked higher than Sumerian slaves.

REVIEW & ASSESS

1. **READING CHECK** How did the organization of Sumerian society affect the way different roles were viewed by others?

2. **INTEGRATE VISUALS** In what ways did the rivers support agriculture and the city-states?

3. **ANALYZE CAUSE AND EFFECT** How did food surpluses encourage local and long-distance trade?

PLAN

OBJECTIVE

Describe how the city-states of Sumer formed Southwest Asia's first civilization.

CRITICAL THINKING SKILLS FOR LESSON 1.2

- Identify Main Ideas and Details
- Monitor Comprehension
- Integrate Visuals
- Analyze Cause and Effect
- Make Inferences
- Draw Conclusions
- Analyze Visuals

ESSENTIAL QUESTION

Why was civilization able to develop in ancient Mesopotamia?

The geography and location of Mesopotamia helped create the conditions that allowed civilization to develop in the region. Lesson 1.2 discusses how the city-states of Sumer formed the first civilization in Southwest Asia.

BACKGROUND FOR THE TEACHER

Human beings have existed for thousands of years with the social structure of small groups. The small groups of people survived for ages as hunter-gatherers when they eventually started cultivating crops. The "land between the rivers," known as Mesopotamia, is one of the earliest areas where large numbers of people settled to farm. There is archaeological evidence of early village settlements by 5000 B.C. By 3000 B.C., a strong urban culture existed with social structures and communities, which was possible because of the agricultural surpluses.

DIGITAL RESOURCES myNGconnect.com

TEACHER RESOURCES & ASSESSMENT

 Reading and Note-Taking

 Vocabulary Practice

 Section 1 Quiz

STUDENT RESOURCES

 NG Chapter Gallery

INTRODUCE & ENGAGE

WORD MAP

Have students discuss the meaning of the word *civilization*. Begin by adding the word to the center of a Word Map. Fill in the map during classroom discussion. Have students consider the root of the word and use a dictionary, if necessary. Revisit this activity at the end of the lesson to fill in any missing details. **0:05** minutes

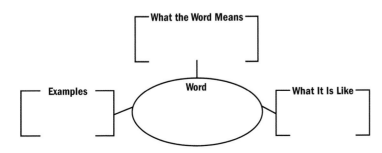

TEACH

GUIDED DISCUSSION

1. **Integrate Visuals** What new information can you observe about the illustration of the city-state of Ur that you did not read about in the text? *(Ur has walls surrounding it. It also appears to have been planned with canals going through it that would allow crops to be moved easily from the fields to the people.)*

2. **Make Inferences** Why might city-states that work together to build canals end up fighting wars? *(They are competing against each other for scarce resources and the best land, and each city-state wanted the best for themselves.)*

3. **Draw Conclusions** What reasons would there be for thick walls around the city? *(The walls are for protection. They may protect against their enemies, or possibly also from flood waters.)*

ANALYZE VISUALS

Have students examine the illustration of the city-state of Ur. Direct them to consider how the physical characteristics of the land influenced how people lived and constructed their buildings. Make a list of the challenges the Sumerians must have faced as they built cities in the region. **0:10** minutes

ACTIVE OPTIONS

NG Learning Framework: Redesign the City of Ur

SKILL: Problem-Solving
KNOWLEDGE: Our Human Story

Have students examine the illustration of the city-state of Ur and point out that the captions show that the city was crowded and surrounded by walls. Additionally, food surpluses meant that the population kept growing. **ASK:** How would you have done things

differently if you were running the city? Have students work in groups to draw their design for the city, or give a description on how they would handle the crowding situation in a walled city in 2000 B.C. **0:10** minutes

On Your Feet: Create Trade Networks On pieces of paper, write the names of commonly traded goods, and indicate if they are goods that are found locally or if they are goods from far away that require trading from a long-distance. (*Examples: figs—local; wheat—local; timber—long distance; copper—long distance, tin—long distance, fish—local, flour—local.*) Hand each student the name of a good to trade, and instruct all students to trade among themselves. Upon completion, lead a discussion about what each student was willing to trade and why students traded their items. **0:15** minutes

DIFFERENTIATE

STRIVING READERS

Complete Sentence Starters Provide these sentence starters for students to complete after reading. You may also have students preview to set a purpose for reading.

- A city and its surrounding lands and settlements was called a _____.
- Ur is among the 12 city-states of _____.
- The order based on wealth by which Sumerian society was organized is called _____.
- People who are skilled at making things by hand are called _____.

Press **mt** in the Student eEdition for modified text.

See the Chapter Planner for more strategies for differentiation.

REVIEW & ASSESS

ANSWERS

1. The organization by social class meant that some people looked down on others who held a lesser status.

2. The water supply from the two rivers was crucial to agriculture in Sumer.

3. Sumerians used their food surpluses to trade for natural resources that they lacked, such as building materials of timber and stone.

Religion
in Sumer

In the blazing sun, Sumerian priests carry food offerings step by step to the top of the great temple. The purpose of this feast is to secure the gods' favor for another day. In the dangerous and unpredictable world of Sumer, it's important to keep the gods on your side.

MAIN IDEA

Sumerians took religion seriously and built monumental structures to please their gods.

VOTIVE STATUES
To demonstrate their devotion to the gods, Sumerians placed small statues called votives in temples. Sumerians believed that while they worked on earthly activities like farming or fishing, the statues would pray on their behalf.

LAND OF MANY GODS

Sumerian lives depended on natural forces they could not control, including rivers that flooded and changed course. The people worshipped hundreds of gods, who they believed could control these forces. A belief in many gods is called **polytheism**.

Sumerians believed that their gods ruled the earth and had created humans to serve them. They also believed that the gods possessed superhuman powers. Unfortunately, the gods could use these powers to cause droughts, floods, and disease. For example, Ishkur was a storm god who was believed to have the power to cause destructive rains and floods whenever he liked.

To keep the gods happy, Sumerian priests tried to please them. Everyone paid a temple tax, which was offered to the gods in elaborate public **rituals**, or formal series of acts always performed in the same way. By observing natural events, including the movement of the sun, moon, and stars, priests tried to predict what the gods were planning. These observations helped the Sumerians develop a calendar, astronomy, and mathematics.

OFFERINGS AT THE TEMPLES

City-states were important religious centers. The most important building within a city-state was a huge pyramid-shaped temple called a **ziggurat** (ZIH-guh-rat). *Ziggurat* means "mountaintop." Every city was dedicated to a major deity, a god or goddess, who was its guardian. Sumerians believed that the deity lived in a shrine, or sacred place, on top of the ziggurat. People reached the shrine by climbing long, external flights of stairs.

Priests were responsible for conducting religious practices at the ziggurat. These practices included various rituals, such as offering food to the city god or goddess. A statue representing the deity was placed in a space called the adytum (A-duh-tuhm), or holy place. A meal was set on a table before the statue. Sumerians believed that the god or goddess would eat the meal.

Priests also performed purification, or cleansing, rituals using holy water. This purification process was often used on kings before they entered shrines where the deities were believed to dwell.

Critical Viewing Priests climbed 100 or more steep steps to the shrine at the top of a ziggurat to worship the city god. Why would the shrine have been positioned so high?

➕ POSSIBLE RESPONSE

When something is important, or has high status, it often is elevated. The gods were thought to have lived on top of the ziggurat because they were important.

REVIEW & ASSESS

1. **READING CHECK** What religious practices did Sumerians observe to serve and please their gods?

2. **DETERMINE WORD MEANINGS** What context clues in the text tell you what *superhuman* means?

3. **MAKE INFERENCES** Why do you think Sumerians thought that cleansing was necessary before entering shrines?

PLAN

OBJECTIVE

Summarize how important religion was to Sumerians and describe the monumental structures they built to please their gods.

CRITICAL THINKING SKILLS FOR LESSON 1.3

- Identify Main Ideas and Details
- Monitor Comprehension
- Determine Word Meanings
- Make Inferences
- Draw Conclusions
- Summarize

ESSENTIAL QUESTION

Why was civilization able to develop in ancient Mesopotamia?

Religion is a part of culture and key to the development of civilization in the Mesopotamian region. Lesson 1.3 discusses how the Sumerians built monuments and carried out rituals to honor their gods.

BACKGROUND FOR THE TEACHER

Religion is defined as an organized system of beliefs, ceremonies, and rules used to worship a god or group of gods. The Sumerians were among the first to engage in an organized system of spiritual practices, which included belief in several gods and goddesses. Sumerians believed in the idea that each of these gods controlled different aspects of everyday life. They also chose to build large and impressive structures to honor the gods. In these structures, they performed rituals to honor and please the gods, hoping to win their favor.

DIGITAL RESOURCES myNGconnect.com

TEACHER RESOURCES & ASSESSMENT

 Reading and Note-Taking

 Vocabulary Practice

 Section 1 Quiz

STUDENT RESOURCES

 NG Chapter Gallery

INTRODUCE & ENGAGE

K-W-L CHART

Provide each student with a K-W-L chart like the one below.

K What Do I Know?	W What Do I Want To Learn?	L What Did I Learn?

Have students brainstorm what they know about religions around the world. Then ask them to write questions that they would like to answer as they study the lesson. Allow time at the end of the lesson for students to fill in what they learned. **0:05** minutes

TEACH

GUIDED DISCUSSION

1. **Make Inferences** What might Sumerians have considered a benefit to developing a calendar? *(The Sumerians observed the movements of the sun, moon, and stars and noticed patterns. They thought that by tracking the movements, they might be able to predict what natural events their gods were planning next.)*

2. **Draw Conclusions** What reason might there have been for the Sumerians to worship so many gods? *(The Sumerians believed that these multiple gods governed the many aspects of their lives.)*

ASK AND ANSWER QUESTIONS

Review the text under the heading "Offerings at the Temple." Ask volunteers to summarize the content by asking the following questions:

1. What is a ziggurat?

2. What is a ritual offering?

3. Why did Sumerians make offerings at the top of ziggurats?

0:05 minutes

ACTIVE OPTIONS

Critical Viewing: NG Chapter Gallery Invite students to explore the Chapter Gallery to examine the images that relate to this chapter. Have them select one of the images and do additional research to learn more about it. Ask questions that will inspire additional inquiry about the chosen gallery image, such as: What

is this? Where and when was this created? By whom? Why was it created? What is it made of? Why does it belong in this chapter? What else would you like to know about it? **0:10** minutes

On Your Feet: Sequence of Events Have students choose a partner. One student should interview the other on the question: Why do you think Sumerians paid a temple tax as part of some rituals? Then have students reverse roles. Finally, each student should share the results of his or her interview with the class **0:10** minutes

DIFFERENTIATE

ENGLISH LANGUAGE LEARNERS

Complete Sentence Frames Use sentence frames such as those below to help students demonstrate their understanding of the main ideas in Lesson 1.3. You may wish to allow students to choose the correct word to fill in the blanks from a list on the board.

- In ancient Sumer, _____ was the practice of worshipping many gods. *(polytheism)*

- A _____ is a small statue of a god that was placed in a temple. *(votive)*

- A series of acts called _____ were performed to honor the gods. *(rituals)*

- Sumerians believed a god, also called a _____, lived on top of the ziggurat. *(deity)*

PRE-AP

Write a Research Paper Have students individually research a deity of a city in Sumer. Tell students that they should use the map in Lesson 1.1 to choose a city before starting their research.

To help organize their paper, students can take notes and complete an outline. Have students use the information in the outline to write an informative paper in which they develop the topic with relevant details. Ask students to close with a concluding statement summarizing the information presented.

Press **mt** *in the Student eEdition for modified text.*

See the Chapter Planner for more strategies for differentiation.

REVIEW & ASSESS

ANSWERS

1. The Sumerians performed rituals to please the gods.

2. The text indicates that the gods could use powers to do things that are outside of the control of a human being—that they could cause big things, good or bad, to happen.

3. Cleansing would be a way of showing respect to something. Rituals were important, and performing ritual cleansing would be an important display of respect to honor the gods.

Sumerian Writing

Sumerians invented the earliest form of writing, known as pictographs, or images of objects. Detailed pictographs evolved into symbols called **cuneiform** (kyoo-NEE-uh-fawrm), which, over time, represented sounds rather than objects. Scribes began forming words and combining them into sentences in religious and scientific works and in stories. This change marked the beginning of written history and a major step forward in the development of civilization.

➕ ANSWERS

DOCUMENT 1
The cuneiform symbols pressed into the clay would have been smudged or smeared if the clay tablets were not dried.

DOCUMENT 2
Cultures like to portray their leaders as strong and brave. Encountering a monster shows that they king is worthy of leading people because he is brave, and able to face a monster, which could represent the king facing enemies.

DOCUMENT 2
Babylonians most likely wanted to tell and record their story of the creation of the world in order to understand their place in the world and in order to pass the story on to future generations.

This 20th-century illustration depicts Gilgamesh arriving at the palace of the goddess Siduri-Sabitu in his search for immortality.

DOCUMENT ONE
Primary Source: Artifact

Cuneiform Tablet, Northern Iraq, c. 600s B.C.
Scribes used reeds, or sharpened blades of grass, to carve the wedge-shaped cuneiform symbols—600 in all—into wet clay tablets that were then dried. This tablet describes a flood scene from *The Epic of Gilgamesh*, explained in more detail below.

CONSTRUCTED RESPONSE Why did the Sumerians dry the clay cuneiform tablets?

DOCUMENT TWO
Primary Source: Epic

from *Gilgamesh*, translated by Stephen Mitchell
The Epic of Gilgamesh is the world's oldest recorded story. The author is unknown. Gilgamesh was probably a real king of Uruk. In the story, he sets off on a fantastic adventure with his loyal friend Enkidu. This passage describes their encounter with a monster.

CONSTRUCTED RESPONSE Why would the Sumerians record a story about their king encountering a monster?

> They came within sight of the monster's den.
> He was waiting inside it. Their blood ran cold.
> He saw the two friends, he grimaced, he bared his teeth, he let out a deafening roar.
> He glared at Gilgamesh. "Young man," he said, "you will never go home. Prepare to die."

DOCUMENT THREE
Primary Source: Creation Story

from *The Epic of Creation*, translated by Stephanie Dalley
This Babylonian creation story by an unknown author explains how the world was formed. In this passage, the chief god, Marduk, creates the stars and a 12-month calendar.

CONSTRUCTED RESPONSE Why might Babylonians want to tell and record their story of the creation of the world?

> He [Marduk] fashioned stands for the great gods.
> As for the stars, he set up constellations corresponding to them.
> He designated the year and marked out its divisions,
> Apportioned three stars each to the twelve months.

SYNTHESIZE & WRITE

1. **REVIEW** Review what you have learned about Sumerian writing and the world's oldest stories.

2. **RECALL** On your own paper, write down the main idea expressed in each document.

3. **CONSTRUCT** Construct a topic sentence that answers this question: What did the Sumerians' cuneiform writing system make possible?

4. **WRITE** Using evidence from the documents, write a paragraph that supports your topic sentence from Step 3.

PLAN

OBJECTIVE

Synthesize information about how the evolution from pictograph symbols to cuneiform marked the beginning of the written word and a major step forward in developing civilizations.

CRITICAL THINKING SKILLS FOR LESSON 1.4

- Make Inferences
- Draw Conclusions
- Form and Support Opinions
- Evaluate

ESSENTIAL QUESTION

Why was civilization able to develop in ancient Mesopotamia?

Cultural advances in the form of writing help spread culture and develop civilizations. Lesson 1.4 discusses how the evolution from pictograph symbols to cuneiform shaped Mesopotamian civilization and eventually world civilizations.

BACKGROUND FOR THE TEACHER

One of the most widely known epic tales ever written stars the character Gilgamesh. This character is believed to be based upon the 5th king of Uruk (a city in the southern region of Sumer), who had such notoriety that the stories of his greatness made him appear divine to the masses. In some tales, he appears alongside Mesopotamian deities. In one poem, he comes to the rescue of the goddess of love and war. His appearance alongside deities shows how highly he was regarded, and explains why, even though he was a human, he was viewed as a god himself.

DIGITAL RESOURCES myNGconnect.com

TEACHER RESOURCES & ASSESSMENT

 Reading and Note-Taking

 Vocabulary Practice

 Section 1 Quiz

STUDENT RESOURCES

 NG Chapter Gallery

INTRODUCE & ENGAGE

PREPARE FOR THE DOCUMENT-BASED QUESTION

Before students start on the activity, briefly preview the three documents and the illustration. Remind students that a constructed response requires full explanations in complete sentences. Emphasize that students should use their knowledge of Mesopotamia and the Mesopotamians' contributions to civilization in addition to the information in the documents. **0:05** minutes

TEACH

GUIDED DISCUSSION

1. **Make Inferences** Why do you think scribes used reeds and clay to record the cuneiform symbols? *(probably because these materials were common)*

2. **Draw Conclusions** Why would it be useful to have cultural tales written down? *(When a story is written, it is more likely that the story will not change much, whereas a story told verbally may be forgotten or the details may change significantly.)*

3. **Form and Support Opinions** Do you think that Gilgamesh really existed? Why or why not? *(Responses will vary. Accept answers that are supported by reasoning.)*

EVALUATE

After students have completed the "Synthesize & Write" activity, allow time for them to exchange paragraphs and read and comment on the work of their peers. Guidelines for comments should be established prior to this activity so that feedback is constructive and encouraging. **0:15** minutes

ACTIVE OPTIONS

NG Learning Framework: Compare Two Writing Systems

ATTITUDE: **Curiosity**
KNOWLEDGE: **Our Human Story**

Have students explore characters and symbols of past and present writing systems. Instruct them to compare and contrast two or three characters and symbols of a writing system from the past, such as cuneiform, with two or three characters and symbols of a writing system from the present, such as Cyrillic, Chinese, or Arabic. Encourage students to share visuals and observations about their comparisons with the class. **0:10** minutes

On Your Feet: Telephone Play a game of telephone to demonstrate the importance of written documents. Divide the class in half and have each group stand in a line. Then write a sentence on a piece of paper and hand it to the first student in each line. Instruct these two students to read the sentence silently. Then have each student whisper the sentence to the student next to her or him. Continue to do so until the last student in line has the message. Ask the last student to repeat out loud what they were told. Compare that sentence with the piece of paper that the first student is holding. Discuss the results with the class. Point out that people tend to write down information when we need to remember the details, and that while the gist of a story may be remembered, written information is valuable for remembering details. **0:10** minutes

DIFFERENTIATE

INCLUSION

Analyze Primary Sources You may choose to have students work in pairs to analyze the primary source excerpts. Provide the steps below to help them with their analysis.

1. Find definitions of words that are unfamiliar and write them down on a piece of paper.

2. Summarize each sentence in your own words and write your summaries on a piece of paper.

PRE-AP

Write Epic Tales Ask students to research what epic tales are and what purpose they served. They can use an epic tale, such as Gilgamesh, as an example of how to structure their tale. Then have students write their own epic tale. Instruct them to write a narrative that is based on either a real or imagined experience. Have them develop their characters and organize a sequence of events. Then they should use their research to establish what other details to include in their tale. Encourage them to share their tale with the class.

Press (**mt**) *in the Student eEdition for modified text.*

See the Chapter Planner for more strategies for differentiation.

SYNTHESIZE & WRITE

ANSWERS

1. Responses will vary.

2. Responses will vary.

3. Possible response: The writing system marked the beginning of the written word, affecting nearly every aspect of civilization.

4. Students' paragraphs should include their topic sentence from Step 3 and provide several details from the documents to support the sentence.

Sargon Conquers Mesopotamia

Have you heard the expression, "Uneasy lies the head that wears a crown"? It applied well to Sargon the Great. He conquered many peoples, lands and cities, including Sumer. As ruler, Sargon was expected to keep his people safe, peaceful, happy, and fed. His role involved much responsibility. It was not easy being in charge of what was, at that time, the world's largest civilization.

MAIN IDEA

Sargon conquered Sumer and other lands in Mesopotamia to create the world's first empire.

AN OUTSIDER TAKES OVER

Sargon the Great was an ancient Mesopotamian ruler who has inspired stories for nearly 4,500 years. It is difficult to separate fact from fiction about his life. According to one story about his childhood, Sargon's mother was a royal priestess who abandoned him as a baby. A humble gardener from Kish raised him after finding him in a basket floating in a river.

Kish was a city-state in Akkad (AH-kahd), an area in central Mesopotamia. Akkadians and Sumerians shared a similar culture but had different ethnic origins and spoke different languages. Before becoming a ruler, Sargon was a servant to the king of Kish. After serving in the royal court, Sargon became a powerful official in Kish and eventually overthrew the king.

While Sargon gained power, Sumer was weakened by internal wars and invasions. In 2334 B.C., Sargon's armies swept through Sumer, conquering it completely. They also took control of northern Mesopotamia. These conquests created the world's first **empire**, a group of different lands and people governed by one ruler. Sargon's empire stretched from the Mediterranean Sea to the Persian Gulf. He ruled the Akkadian Empire from Akkad, his now long-lost capital city.

EMPIRE AND EXPANSION

The Akkadian Empire lasted 150 years, and Sargon ruled for 56 of them. He personally led the fight to expand the empire and claimed to have won 34 battles and taken 50 rulers prisoner. Sargon was an effective warrior and skilled at managing people and projects.

In the lands he conquered, Sargon allowed the people to keep their local rulers and customs. However, they had to obey him and pay a protection tax called a **tribute**. Sargon's policy helped keep peace and win the loyalty of people throughout his empire. He also introduced standard weights and measures and made Akkadian the official language of the government.

Sargon's powerful empire brought prosperity to his people and encouraged trade. Akkad's farmers managed agriculture so well that 100 years went by without **famine**, or widespread hunger. Sargon's wars were spread over large areas. As a result, Akkad traded with distant suppliers for timber, metal, and other raw materials Mesopotamia lacked. His wars concentrated

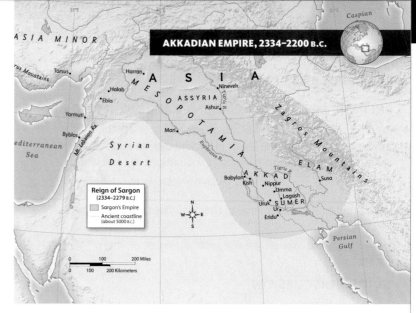

AKKADIAN EMPIRE, 2334–2200 B.C.

Reign of Sargon (2334–2279 B.C.)
▢ Sargon's Empire
····· Ancient coastline (about 5000 B.C.)

0   100   200 Miles
0   100   200 Kilometers

on controlling trade centers and protecting natural resources, such as cedar forests.

Despite Sargon's abilities, the empire became too big to control. After he died, his sons took over but were unable to maintain order. City-states rebelled, and a great deal of time and effort went into trying to keep the peace. Enemies from the northeast raided the empire's unprotected borders. Famine returned, spreading suffering and unrest among the people. By 2200 B.C., the Akkadian Empire had come to an end.

SARGON THE GREAT

To guarantee loyalty from the governors who ruled parts of his empire, Sargon gave trusted relatives powerful positions. To keep control of his army, he created a group of professional soldiers whose sole purpose was to fight for him.

< This sculptured head is believed to depict Sargon with his crown and long beard.

REVIEW & ASSESS

1. **READING CHECK** What measures did Sargon take to unite his empire?

2. **INTERPRET MAPS** Where were most of the cities of the empire located? Why do you think that was so?

3. **DRAW CONCLUSIONS** What conclusions can you draw about Sargon's abilities as a ruler?

PLAN

OBJECTIVE

Identify how Sargon conquered Sumer and other lands in Mesopotamia to create the world's first empire.

CRITICAL THINKING SKILLS FOR LESSON 1.5

- Identify Main Ideas and Details
- Monitor Comprehension
- Interpret Maps
- Draw Conclusions
- Analyze Cause and Effect
- Make Predictions

ESSENTIAL QUESTION

Why was civilization able to develop in ancient Mesopotamia?

Great leaders play important roles in developing civilizations.

Lesson 1.5 discusses how Sargon conquered lands in Mesopotamia to create an empire.

BACKGROUND FOR THE TEACHER

Sargon the Great was a man of legend. His military prowess and strong leadership abilities brought him great fame and power. He was the first person in recorded history to have created an empire. Though stories of his later years are prevalent, very little is really known about his early life. A manuscript describing his early life and rise to power exists. However, there are many gaps in the written version of his story, and it appears to have been written well after his lifetime. Many of the tales of the early years appear to actually be legends.

DIGITAL RESOURCES myNGconnect.com

TEACHER RESOURCES & ASSESSMENT

 Reading and Note-Taking

 Vocabulary Practice

 Section 1 Quiz

STUDENT RESOURCES

 NG Chapter Gallery

DISCUSS GOVERNMENT POWER

Ask students whether they think the government should have the authority to control activities that affect their daily life. Have them discuss what they would think if government legislated the following:

- what language they speak at home
- how much they pay to keep their communities safe
- how to measure the amount of foods they buy

Encourage students to explain why some governments might want to control such activities. Then, at the end of the discussion, tell students that Sargon the Great implemented a protection tax that had to be paid. He also declared an official language and established standard weights and measures. **0:05** minutes

GUIDED DISCUSSION

1. **Analyze Cause and Effect** How did Sargon come to conquer Sumer? *(Sargon was able to invade and conquer Sumer because Sumer had become weak from civil wars between city-states, and other invasions.)*

2. **Make Predictions** Do you think another ruler or empire will take over the land and people of the Akkadian Empire, knowing that this empire ended in 2200 B.C.? *(Students should indicate that it is very likely that another empire will take over where the Akkadian Empire ended. That is generally what happens over the course of time.)*

INTERPRET MAPS

Have students analyze the map of the Akkadian Empire in Lesson 1.5. Then have them compare it to the Ancient Mesopotamia map in Lesson 1.1. Direct them to use the mountains, grid lines, and rivers to compare the size and shape of the Akkadian Empire against the red borders of Mesopotamia in Lesson 1.1. Discuss how much of the Fertile Crescent Sargon had within his empire. **0:10** minutes

ACTIVE OPTIONS

Critical Viewing: NG Chapter Gallery Have students examine the contents of the Chapter Gallery for this lesson. Then invite them to brainstorm additional images they believe would fit for this lesson. Have them write a description of these additional images and provide an explanation of why they would fit within the Chapter Gallery. Then instruct them to do online research to find examples of actual images they would like to add to the gallery. If no images are available, ask why they think the images are not available and what illustrations they would like to see added for this lesson. **0:10** minutes

On Your Feet: Fishbowl Have one half of the class sit in a close circle, facing inward. The other half of the class sits in a larger circle around them. Post the question: What advantages do you think Mesopotamia had when it was an empire united under Sargon? Students in the inner circle should discuss the question for five minutes while those in the outer circle listen to the discussion and evaluate the points made. Then have the groups reverse roles and continue the discussion. **0:10** minutes

INCLUSION

Complete a 5Ws Chart Guide students in completing a 5Ws Chart to help them understand the text. Review vocabulary words that students might have difficulty comprehending, such as *tribute* and *famine*. Review each "W" of the chart as students work through the lesson.

STRIVING READERS

Summarize Read the lesson aloud while students follow along in the text. At the end of each paragraph, ask students to write a sentence on their own paper to summarize what they read.

Press (**mt**) *in the Student eEdition for modified text.*

See the Chapter Planner for more strategies for differentiation.

ANSWERS

1. He allowed people to keep their local rulers and customs. He also standardized weights and measures, making it easier to trade goods and make payments for goods. He also had policies to keep peace in the kingdom.

2. Most of the cities of the empire were located near rivers and near where the coast of the Persian Gulf was at that time. They were located there because of the need for water for farming and trade.

3. Sargon's abilities were effective enough to keep him in power for 56 years. He must have been organized, a fierce warrior, and a leader who commanded respect or instilled fear.

Hammurabi's Code of Laws

Would you know how to play a game if you didn't know its rules? Probably not. This is how people from Mesopotamia must have felt when it came to following laws enforced by rulers. Though they did exist, laws were not laid out in a clear fashion. This changed when a king decided it was time to literally spell out the laws for his people.

MAIN IDEA

Hammurabi changed civilization by organizing laws and displaying them.

NEW EMPIRE IN MESOPOTAMIA

After the fall of Sargon's Akkadian Empire, a tribe called the Amorites invaded western Mesopotamia around 2000 B.C. They established their capital at Babylon (BA-buh-lahn), a city-state overshadowed by powerful neighbors. (See the map in Lesson 1.5.) Then in 1792 B.C., **Hammurabi** (ha-muh-RAH-bee) became the sixth king of Babylon. Hammurabi was Babylon's most influential and powerful ruler. He expanded the kingdom and established his Babylonian Empire across Mesopotamia and other parts of the Fertile Crescent.

Hammurabi spent the first 29 years of his rule working on domestic improvements.

These included directing large projects, such as creating straight streets, strong city walls, magnificent temples, and efficient irrigation canals. Hammurabi also skillfully built up a network of **alliances**, or partnerships. This helped him conquer all of Mesopotamia in just eight years and claim the title "King of Sumer and Akkad."

HAMMURABI'S CODE

Hammurabi was a skillful ruler, but he is best remembered for his Code of Laws. His vast empire contained many different peoples who all followed different laws. To help unite his empire, Hammurabi took the best existing laws, added new rules, and then organized them into a clear, written system. The Code of Laws marked a major step forward for civilization. The code helped bring justice to everyday life. It also serves as an important primary source for historians because it offers insight into Babylonian society, including its structures, priorities, problems, and attitudes.

The Code of Laws was often applied based on a person's social class. For example, landowners could be fined more heavily than slaves. Hammurabi also laid down detailed laws about agriculture and the buying and selling of goods, highlighting the importance of these activities.

Three experienced judges heard cases. They listened to statements, examined evidence, and heard from witnesses. The judges even assumed the defendant's innocence. Guilt had to be proven. (Courts in the United States today also assume that people are innocent until proven guilty.) Hammurabi's Code of Laws influenced later legal systems, including those of ancient Greece and Rome.

After Hammurabi's death in 1750 B.C., the first Babylonian Empire declined rapidly and disappeared about 150 years later. However, Hammurabi's achievements ensured that Babylon remained a center of political, cultural, and religious importance for centuries to come.

CODE OF HAMMURABI

Hammurabi's Code of Laws was carved into an eight-foot-high stone slab, called a stela (STEE-luh), for everyone to see and read. An introduction announced its purpose: "To prevent the strong from oppressing the weak and to see that justice is done to widows and orphans."

The code's 282 laws covered all aspects of life and dictated specific penalties for specific crimes. Punishments were often as brutal as the crime. For example, a son's hand would be cut off for striking his father, and those who robbed burning houses were burned alive. Additional examples of the numbered laws include the following:

196 If a man put out the eye of another man, his eye shall be put out.

197 If he [a man] break another man's bone, his bone shall be broken.

⌄ This top portion of the stela shows King Hammurabi receiving the Babylonian laws from Shamash, the god of justice.

REVIEW & ASSESS

1. **READING CHECK** How was Hammurabi's court system similar to the one we have today?

2. **IDENTIFY MAIN IDEAS AND DETAILS** What details illustrate the improvements Hammurabi made as Babylon's king?

3. **MAKE INFERENCES** Why was Hammurabi's Code of Laws displayed in public for everyone to see?

PLAN

OBJECTIVE

Summarize how Hammurabi changed civilization by organizing and displaying laws.

CRITICAL THINKING SKILLS FOR LESSON 2.1

- Identify Main Ideas and Details
- Monitor Comprehension
- Make Inferences
- Analyze Cause and Effect
- Ask and Answer Questions
- Analyze Visuals

ESSENTIAL QUESTION

Why was civilization able to develop in ancient Mesopotamia?

Having a code of conduct is considered a necessary part of a developing civilization. Lesson 2.1 discusses how Hammurabi developed and enforced the first laws for a civilization.

BACKGROUND FOR THE TEACHER

The familiar phrase "An eye for an eye" is frequently used to describe what justice means to some people. This idea was first put into writing by Hammurabi. While this famous phrase is the takeaway from his ideas, his intent was to create rules in society that he deemed to be fair and just. Hammurabi determined justice by using a system based on social and economic status. He created a system to protect the weak and people of lesser status from suffering and having their status further decreased through wrongdoings by someone else.

DIGITAL RESOURCES myNGconnect.com

TEACHER RESOURCES & ASSESSMENT

 Reading and Note-Taking

 Vocabulary Practice

 Section 2 Quiz

STUDENT RESOURCES

 Active History

INTRODUCE & ENGAGE

K-W-L CHART

Provide each student with a K-W-L Chart.

Have students brainstorm what they know about justice and law from their knowledge of the United States justice system. Then ask them if they know anything about the justice systems in other countries. Ask them to write questions that they would like to have answered as they study the lesson. Allow time at the end of the lesson for students to complete the chart with information they learn in Lesson 2.1. **0:05** minutes

TEACH

GUIDED DISCUSSION

1. **Analyze Cause and Effect** How did the Code of Laws that Hammurabi displayed help to unite the empire? (*The many different peoples and cultures in Hammurabi's empire were following different rules. When Hammurabi displayed the same rules for all to see, they learned how they were expected to behave. The goal of displaying the new rules was to ensure fair treatment for all people.*)

2. **Ask and Answer Questions** What was Hammurabi's Code of Laws? (*Hammurabi's Code of Laws was a system of 282 laws that covered all aspects of life in the Babylonian Empire.*)

ANALYZE VISUALS

Have students analyze the stone slab upon which Hammurabi's Code of Laws is written. Ask students why they think that Hammurabi is shown with Shamash, the god of justice. Ask them to explain what they think that symbolizes. **0:10** minutes

ACTIVE OPTIONS

Active History: Analyze Primary Sources: Hammurabi's Code Have students individually complete the activity by analyzing Hammurabi's code. After they have completed the activity, ask them to form opinions on which of the six laws presented seem the least fair to them. Have students support their opinions with evidence. **0:15** minutes

On Your Feet: Code of Laws Roundtable Divide the class into groups of four. Have students create a "Code of Laws" for their classroom that will provide guidelines for good behavior and the consequences for bad behavior. Tell the first student in each group to write a law on a piece of paper, read it aloud, and pass the paper clockwise to the next student. When the groups have finished writing their laws, invite each group to decide which two laws they think are the most necessary. Then have the class vote on five laws they believe to be the most fair. Post these rules on a bulletin board. **0:10** minutes

DIFFERENTIATE

ENGLISH LANGUAGE LEARNERS

Understand Main Ideas Check students' understanding of the main ideas in Lesson 2.1 by asking them to correctly complete either/or statements such as the following:

- Hammurabi spent [much or little] time making improvements in the empire.
- Hammurabi is best remembered for [uniting or dividing] his empire by using his Code of Laws.
- The Code of Laws punished a landowner [more or less] harshly than a slave for the same offense.
- The panel of judges assumes you are [innocent or guilty].

PRE-AP

Write Hammurabi's Profile Ask an interested group of students to do online research to learn more about Hammurabi. Then tell them to write a social networking profile for Hammurabi, providing a brief summary and "photos" of the king. Have the group share the profile with the rest of the class. Then invite students to "friend" Hammurabi and send him messages about his life and society.

Press (**mt**) *in the Student eEdition for modified text.*

See the Chapter Planner for more strategies for differentiation.

REVIEW & ASSESS

ANSWERS

1. Hammurabi's court system had judges hearing cases from witnesses and examining evidence. It assumed the defendant was innocent until proven guilty.

2. Hammurabi's many domestic improvements included establishing a centralized government and administration, building straight streets and strong city walls, building magnificent temples, and building irrigation canals that boosted Babylon's agriculture and economy.

3. A public display of the Code of Laws made the rules of Babylonian society very clear to everyone—the poor and wealthy, the weak and strong. A public display of the laws also reminded everyone of the purpose of the Code of Laws: "To prevent the strong from oppressing the weak and to see that justice is done to widows and orphans."

The Assyrians and the Chaldeans

For 1,000 years after Hammurabi, Mesopotamia came under the rule of empire after empire. Then around 1000 B.C., the region shook with the sounds of an approaching army: marching feet, pounding hooves, frightening war cries. The Assyrian army had arrived.

MAIN IDEA

The Assyrians and then the Chaldeans conquered Mesopotamia.

THE ASSYRIAN EMPIRE

The Assyrians (uh-SIHR-ee-uhnz) were a people of northern Mesopotamia who developed a different culture. They were united by their worship of the god Ashur, for whom the Assyrian capital was named. (See the map in Lesson 1.5.) A strong agricultural economy and a large professional army helped the Assyrians conquer all of Mesopotamia, parts of Asia Minor, and even the rich state of Egypt by 650 B.C.

Destructive iron weapons gave Assyrian armies an advantage over their enemies, whose weapons were made of a weaker bronze. The armies also had horse-drawn chariots and soldiers who used bows and arrows while riding horses. Assyrian soldiers were experts at capturing cities.

It was not uncommon for soldiers to kill or enslave captured people and then burn their cities to the ground.

Villages, towns, and cities answered to the unforgiving Assyrian king, who held absolute power. Even the highest officials were closely watched. The government sometimes forced rebellious people to move to faraway lands. In time, however, the Assyrian Empire grew too big, and its subjects became tired of being treated so unfairly and violently. By about 626 B.C., the Assyrians were weakened by internal power struggles. This made it possible for a people known as the Chaldeans (kal-DEE-unz) to eventually defeat them.

CHALDEANS OVERTAKE THE ASSYRIANS

The Chaldeans were a seminomadic people who originally came from southern Babylonia. After overthrowing the Assyrians in 612 B.C., the Chaldeans became the ruling power of Babylon and extended their rule over all of Mesopotamia. **Nebuchadnezzar II** (ne-byuh-kuhd-NE-zuhr) was the most famous Chaldean king. Under his rule, which lasted for 43 years, the New Babylonian Empire included Mesopotamia and all of the Fertile Crescent.

Though he was often cruel, Nebuchadnezzar also made improvements to Babylon by rebuilding the city and adding incredible beauty to it. From miles away, the Tower of Babel, a soaring seven-story multicolored ziggurat, inspired awe. Visitors entered the inner city through the colorful Ishtar Gate with its gleaming blue-glazed bricks and images of dragons and bulls.

The king's most famous accomplishment was the Hanging Gardens of Babylon. Pumps operated by slaves irrigated a large, leveled terrace of trees and plants. The terrace formed a green mountain that seemed to float in the city. Although his empire outlasted him by fewer than 25 years, Nebuchadnezzar had built a monumental city fitting its name: Babylon, Gate of God.

Critical Viewing This painting shows what the Hanging Gardens of Babylon might have looked like. What reaction might the gardens have inspired in visitors?

+ POSSIBLE RESPONSE

If this is how the Hanging Gardens might have looked, visitors would have been amazed at its spectacular size and beauty. They may have wondered how it was even possible to build, and how the gardens could grow in a building without much ground for roots to spread out.

REVIEW & ASSESS

1. **READING CHECK** In what ways were the rule of the Assyrians and the Chaldeans similar and different?

2. **MAKE INFERENCES** Why do you think the two empires did not last very long?

3. **ANALYZE LANGUAGE USE** What does "the terrace formed a green mountain that seemed to float in the city" mean?

from *Wonders of the Past*, J. A. Hammerton, ed., 1923

79

OBJECTIVE

Identify how the Assyrians and then the Chaldeans conquered Mesopotamia.

CRITICAL THINKING SKILLS FOR LESSON 2.2

- Identify Main Ideas and Details
- Monitor Comprehension
- Make Inferences
- Analyze Language Use
- Evaluate

ESSENTIAL QUESTION

Why was civilization able to develop in ancient Mesopotamia?

For about 1,000 years after Hammurabi's empire was conquered, Mesopotamia was controlled by a series of empires. Lesson 2.2 discusses how the Assyrians and the Chaldeans each conquered Mesopotamia.

BACKGROUND FOR THE TEACHER

Nebuchadnezzar II was the most famous Babylonian king, but some of his accomplishments are more famous than others. He was the first Babylonian king to rule Egypt. His empire was vast. It included Egypt and Mesopotamia and stretched to the Persian Gulf.

However, Nebuchadnezzar is best known for adding beauty to the city of Babylon, while adding fortification to the city. One of his most famous accomplishments was his palace and the massive walls around Babylon. The Ishtar Gate is one of his greatest feats. It was found by archeologists and a reconstruction of it can be viewed in a museum.

DIGITAL RESOURCES myNGconnect.com

TEACHER RESOURCES & ASSESSMENT

 Reading and Note-Taking

 Vocabulary Practice

 Section 2 Quiz

STUDENT RESOURCES

 NG Chapter Gallery

INTRODUCE & ENGAGE

ANALYZE CHARACTERISTICS OF CIVILIZATIONS

Provide a list of characteristics of powerful, successful civilizations. Some examples are: *a strong army, stable government, meaningful traditions, scientific advances, arts and culture, peace among citizens.* Ask students if they have anything to add. Tell them they will use this list as they compare the Assyrians and Chaldeans. **0:05** minutes

TEACH

GUIDED DISCUSSION

1. **Evaluate** What are some of the advantages that the Assyrians had by having a professional army? (*By having a professional army, the Assyrians were organized and could efficiently plan and execute attacks. The professional army knew what role each person played and they were able to attack an unprepared city and conquer it.*)

2. **Make Inferences** What might have caused the Assyrians to have internal power struggles that led to their defeat? (*The power struggles could have been caused by poor treatment of the people, or the lack of any unifying aspects of culture, such as language or religion. It could have been that the people just didn't like the king. It could have been a combination of these factors.*)

ANALYZE VISUALS

Have students examine the illustration of the Hanging Gardens of Babylon in Lesson 2.2. Explain that historians are not sure what this extraordinary structure looked like, so any illustration is a guess, based on historical texts. **ASK:** Why might people be fascinated with the Hanging Gardens of Babylon, centuries after it existed? (*It was so technologically advanced, so large, and so reportedly beautiful that people many years later remain curious about how it might have looked.*) **0:05** minutes

ACTIVE OPTIONS

Critical Viewing: NG Chapter Gallery Ask students to investigate the image of the Hanging Gardens of Babylon from the Chapter Gallery and become an expert on the subject shown in the image. They should do additional research to learn all about it. Then, students should share their findings with a partner, small group, or the class. **0:10** minutes

On Your Feet: Create a Time Line Have students work in small groups to create a time line of the events from when the Assyrians came to power to after Nebuchadnezzar II's empire ended. When students have completed them, call on volunteers from different groups to explain how each event on the time line led to the eventual fall of the empire. **0:10** minutes

DIFFERENTIATE

STRIVING READERS

Pose and Answer Questions Have students work in pairs to read Lesson 2.2. Instruct them to pause after each paragraph and ask one another *who, what, when, where,* or *why* questions about what they have just read. Advise students to read more slowly and focus on specific details if they have difficulty answering the questions or to reread a paragraph to find the answers.

GIFTED & TALENTED

Build Models Have students review the text description of the Tower of Babel. Then ask them to do research to find more information about what it may have looked like. Students may create a 3-D model, use computer software, draw, or paint their own representation of how they believe the Tower of Babel may have looked. Invite students to share their models with the class.

Press (**mt**) *in the Student eEdition for modified text.*

See the Chapter Planner for more strategies for differentiation.

REVIEW & ASSESS

ANSWERS

1. The Assyrians had a professional army to keep expanding the empire. Their soldiers had iron weapons, horse-drawn chariots, and mounted archers. They also knew how to capture cities. They often killed or enslaved people. The king had absolute power. The Chaldeans were semi-nomadic and not as organized as the Assyrians in warfare. Nebuchadnezzar II was the most famous ruler. He was also known to be cruel and enslaved people. He built grand structures, whereas the Assyrians were destructive.

2. The Assyrian kings held absolute power and ruled with brutal efficiency. Nebuchadnezzar II was also known to be cruel. Cruel rulers usually do not win loyalty from the people they try to control, and the people tend to rebel.

3. The language describes how the Hanging Gardens of Babylon must have looked to a viewer from outside the walls of the city. It was described as an enormous, tiered, terrace of plants and trees. It must have appeared as a lush green wonder in the middle of a desert landscape.

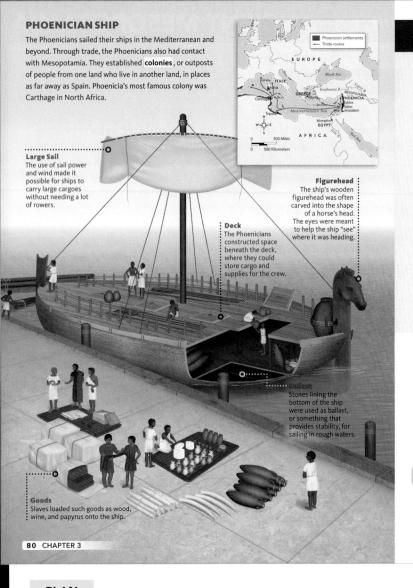

PHOENICIAN SHIP

The Phoenicians sailed their ships in the Mediterranean and beyond. Through trade, the Phoenicians also had contact with Mesopotamia. They established **colonies**, or outposts of people from one land who live in another land, in places as far away as Spain. Phoenicia's most famous colony was Carthage in North Africa.

Large Sail
The use of sail power and wind made it possible for ships to carry large cargoes without needing a lot of rowers.

Figurehead
The ship's wooden figurehead was often carved into the shape of a horse's head. The eyes were meant to help the ship "see" where it was heading.

Deck
The Phoenicians constructed space beneath the deck, where they could store cargo and supplies for the crew.

Stones lining the bottom of the ship were used as ballast, or something that provides stability, for sailing in rough waters.

Goods
Slaves loaded such goods as wood, wine, and papyrus onto the ship.

2.3
The Phoenicians

Do you have a well-traveled friend who always has interesting information about places you've never been? You can think of the Phoenicians as this worldly friend. While conducting trade throughout the Mediterranean and Mesopotamia, the Phoenicians spread cultural practices from one stop on their trade route to the next.

MAIN IDEA

Through their extensive trade network, the Phoenicians spread different cultures throughout the Mediterranean and beyond.

A TRADING PEOPLE

The narrow strip of coast along the eastern Mediterranean (present-day Lebanon) contained many natural resources and had good harbors. This combination was perfect for the development of industry and trade. About 1000 B.C., independent city-states emerged in the area. They shared cultural similarities, including language and a trading economy. The Greeks called the people from these city-states Phoenicians (fih-NEE-shuhnz), which means "purple dye people." The Phoenicians processed local shellfish into a purple dye used to color fabric. This dye was their most famous trade good. They exported wood from their highly desired cedar trees to Egypt and Mesopotamia. From other lands, they imported **raw materials**, or substances from which other things are made. Phoenician artisans crafted these materials into luxury goods for trade.

Phoenicia's most important export was its culture. To record trade transactions, the Phoenicians used their own 22-letter alphabet, which was adapted from Sumerian cuneiform. Each symbol from the Phoenician alphabet stood for a sound. First the ancient Greeks adopted the Phoenician alphabet, then the ancient Romans modified it to form the basis of our modern Western alphabet.

SHIPBUILDERS AND SEAFARERS

The Phoenicians were also skilled shipbuilders and sailors. They built strong, wide ships. Powered mainly by wind and a large, square sail, these ships carried huge cargoes thousands of miles. The Phoenicians became one of the first Mediterranean peoples to sail on the Atlantic Ocean. They sailed north to Britain, west to the Azores (nine volcanic islands located in the mid-Atlantic), and possibly even around Africa.

Despite their talents and enormous wealth, the Phoenicians were militarily weak and were eventually absorbed into the New Babylonian Empire. However, they performed a valuable service by spreading different cultures from one area to another. Their accomplishments show the importance of trade in building civilizations.

REVIEW & ASSESS

1. **READING CHECK** What goods and ideas did the Phoenicians spread through their sea trade network?

2. **ANALYZE VISUALS** Why might ballast have been important to the condition of goods transported by ship?

3. **MAKE INFERENCES** Why would the Phoenicians have established trading colonies in faraway places?

PLAN

OBJECTIVE

Describe how the Phoenicians spread different cultures throughout the Mediterranean and beyond.

CRITICAL THINKING SKILLS FOR LESSON 2.3

- Identify Main Ideas and Details
- Monitor Comprehension
- Analyze Visuals
- Make Inferences
- Make Connections

ESSENTIAL QUESTION

Why was civilization able to develop in ancient Mesopotamia?

Spreading culture through trade interactions is an effective way to develop a civilization. Lesson 2.3 discusses how the Phoenicians spread different cultures throughout the Mediterranean region and beyond.

BACKGROUND FOR THE TEACHER

The Phoenicians lived in a small area of land on the coast of the Mediterranean Sea. The geography of the area dictated their lives and professions. Other than their much sought-after cedar trees, Phoenician land offered little in terms of agriculture. Playing to their geographical strengths, the Phoenicians used the sea extensively. They obtained numerous resources, such as snails used for dye, from the sea. They built boats and traveled for trade.

DIGITAL RESOURCES myNGconnect.com

TEACHER RESOURCES & ASSESSMENT

 Reading and Note-Taking

 Vocabulary Practice

 Section 2 Quiz

STUDENT RESOURCES

 NG Chapter Gallery

INTRODUCE & ENGAGE

SPREADING CULTURE

Examine the map of the Mediterranean region in Lesson 2.3. Ask students to observe where the trade routes and the Phoenician settlements were. Invite students to think about reasons why the settlements were located where they were, and how these settlements could have helped a culture that had much land along a coast and small amounts of land for agriculture. **0:05** minutes

TEACH

GUIDED DISCUSSION

1. **Make Inferences** Why might the Phoenicians have been militarily weak? (*They had good harbors, but only a small amount of land. They spent much time building ships, trading and developing their culture and less time developing a military.*)

2. **Make Connections** How is the alphabet we use today in the Western world related to the Phoenician alphabet? (*The Western alphabet is the result of other alphabets that started with the Phoenician alphabet. The Phoenician alphabet was adapted from the Sumerian cuneiform. Then the Greeks adopted this writing form, then the Romans, and later the Western world.*)

ANALYZE VISUALS

Have students study the illustration of the Phoenician ship in Lesson 2.3. **ASK:** Why do you think it would have been important to use sails instead of many rowers on a cargo ship? (*Possible answer: Cargo ships would have been larger and heavier.*) **0:05** minutes

ACTIVE OPTIONS

NG Learning Framework: Create Your Own Figurehead

ATTITUDE: **Empowerment**
KNOWLEDGE: **Our Human Story**

Review the illustration of the Phoenician ship with students. Discuss the presence and purpose of figureheads. Figureheads were decorative, but they were also symbolic. Have students imagine they are sailors who are empowered to create their own figureheads. They can shape clay, draw, or use a computer to create a figurehead on their own ship. Have students share their figureheads with the class and describe what their figurehead symbolizes. **0:15** minutes

On Your Feet: Three-Step Interview Have students work in pairs. One student should interview the other using this question: *How do you think the Phoenicians became skilled artisans?* Then students should reverse roles. Finally, each student should share the results of his or her interview with the class. **0:10** minutes

DIFFERENTIATE

STRIVING READERS

Summarize Have students read Lesson 2.3 in pairs and write a sentence that restates the main idea of each paragraph as they read. Then have students review those sentences and write a four- or five-sentence paragraph that summarizes the whole lesson. Remind students that they should use their own words in their summary and include only the most important ideas and details.

GIFTED & TALENTED

Write Travel Blogs Explain that a blog is an online journal. Students may want to read some examples of travel blogs to see how they combine facts and personal experiences. Invite students to imagine that they have traveled back in time and are Phoenician sailors traveling to different outposts in the Mediterranean region. Encourage students to refer to the map in Lesson 2.3 and to use the cities as starting points as they do an Internet search to find out more about these places. Then have them tell their story. Remind them to include the basics of a good news story—the 5Ws—as well as vivid sensory details to make the historical trip come alive for readers. An example follows.

November 15: As daylight broke through the clouds, the porters started loading the ship with cedar trees, wine, gold and fine textiles dyed purple. Around noon, we set sail from Byblos, heading west toward Carthage. This will be an exciting journey and I'll get to see the world!

Press (**mt**) *in the Student eEdition for modified text.*

See the Chapter Planner for more strategies for differentiation.

REVIEW & ASSESS

ANSWERS

1. The exported goods included purple dye and wood. They imported raw materials, and artisans created luxury goods out of the raw materials to trade. They also exported their alphabet and culture.

2. Ballast would have been useful to keep the ships upright and keep water from getting in and damaging the goods. It would also keep the ship steady and minimize rocking, keeping the cargo from breaking.

3. Faraway places would have different goods and materials to trade and different raw materials. This would allow the Phoenicians to gain access to more goods that they didn't have access to locally.

Persian Leaders

Palaces in the Persian Empire were built with diverse materials: bricks from Mesopotamia, timber from Phoenicia, ebony and silver from Egypt. This mix of materials was a deliberate celebration of the Persian Empire's rich ethnic diversity—a diversity that was encouraged by the wise leadership of two men.

MAIN IDEA

Under the rule of Cyrus and Darius I, the Persian Empire united different peoples and cultures.

CYRUS THE GREAT

The region of Persia was located in what is present-day southwestern Iran, just east of Mesopotamia. Around 700 B.C., the Persians were ruled by a people called the Medes (meedz). Then in 550 B.C., a Persian king known as **Cyrus the Great** led a successful uprising against the Medes. In 539 B.C., he captured the Babylonian Empire. Cyrus continued to add to his empire until it stretched from Afghanistan to the Aegean Sea, including Mesopotamia. Under Persian rule, these lands enjoyed 200 years of peace and economic well-being.

The secret of Cyrus's success was **tolerance**, or sympathy for the beliefs and practices of others. After winning a war, he showed mercy to conquered kings by allowing them to keep their thrones. Cyrus demanded only tribute that defeated people could afford, sparing them great hardships. He also honored local customs, religions, and institutions. His tolerance won him widespread respect and acceptance from conquered subjects.

DARIUS EXPANDS THE EMPIRE

After Cyrus's death around 529 B.C., his son Cambyses (kam-BY-seez) became king and added Egypt and Libya to the empire. The next king, **Darius I** (duh-RY-uhs), ruled Persia at its height. Darius expanded the empire until it grew to about 2,800 miles, stretching from India in the east to southeastern Europe in the west, with the Fertile Crescent in the middle.

Like Cyrus, Darius was a wise ruler. He avoided problems that had weakened other empires. For example, he divided his empire into 20 smaller **provinces**, or administrative districts, that were ruled by governors called **satraps** (SAY-traps). They helped him maintain control of his huge empire. Darius introduced regular taxation and fixed each province's tribute at only half of what the people could afford to pay. He also introduced a form of currency, which made it easier to pay taxes and buy goods.

Understanding that communications were essential to good government, Darius built the 1,500-mile-long Royal Road, running from Susa in Persia to Sardis in Anatolia (present-day Turkey). Other roads connected all 20 provinces so that messengers could carry his orders anywhere in under 15 days. The roads helped unify the blend of people and cultures that made up the Persian Empire.

Darius also built a new capital, called Persepolis, for his empire. Decorated with palaces and jeweled statues, Persepolis was meant to symbolize the magnificence of the Persian Empire—the largest, most stable, and most powerful empire of ancient Mesopotamia.

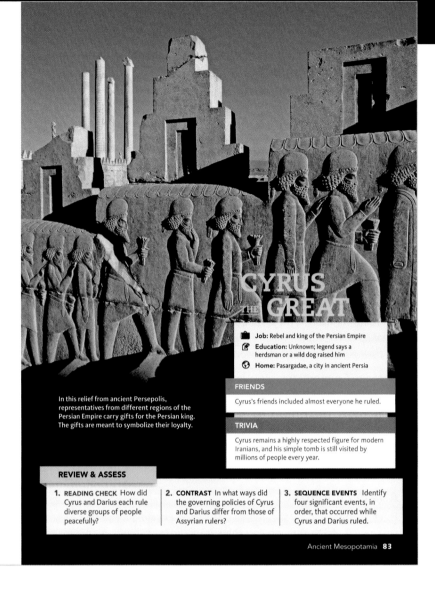

CYRUS THE GREAT

In this relief from ancient Persepolis, representatives from different regions of the Persian Empire carry gifts for the Persian king. The gifts are meant to symbolize their loyalty.

Job: Rebel and king of the Persian Empire

Education: Unknown; legend says a herdsman or a wild dog raised him

Home: Pasargadae, a city in ancient Persia

FRIENDS

Cyrus's friends included almost everyone he ruled.

TRIVIA

Cyrus remains a highly respected figure for modern Iranians, and his simple tomb is still visited by millions of people every year.

REVIEW & ASSESS

1. **READING CHECK** How did Cyrus and Darius each rule diverse groups of people peacefully?

2. **CONTRAST** In what ways did the governing policies of Cyrus and Darius differ from those of Assyrian rulers?

3. **SEQUENCE EVENTS** Identify four significant events, in order, that occurred while Cyrus and Darius ruled.

PLAN

OBJECTIVE

Analyze how Cyrus and Darius I unified different peoples and cultures of the Persian Empire.

CRITICAL THINKING SKILLS FOR LESSON 2.4

- Identify Main Ideas and Details
- Monitor Comprehension
- Contrast
- Sequence Events
- Make Inferences
- Draw Conclusions
- Form and Support Opinions

ESSENTIAL QUESTION

The unification of people and cultures encouraged the development of civilization. Lesson 2.4 discusses how Cyrus the Great and Darius I practiced tolerance to unite the Persian Empire.

BACKGROUND FOR THE TEACHER

The man now known to the world as Cyrus the Great became the king of Persia in 559 B.C. At that time, his kingdom was a small area in what is now southeast Iran. After winning a battle that was instigated by the king of Media, Cyrus acquired much more land for Persia.

After Cyrus invaded Babylonia in 539 B.C., he ruled over an empire that stretched from Egypt, to the eastern part of modern-day Turkey, to Iran. He died while trying to conquer parts of Central Asia in 530 B.C.

DIGITAL RESOURCES myNGconnect.com

TEACHER RESOURCES & ASSESSMENT

 Reading and Note-Taking

 Vocabulary Practice

 Section 2 Quiz

STUDENT RESOURCES

 Biography

THINK, PAIR, SHARE

Have students use a Think, Pair, Share strategy to discuss what they know about the differences between rulers with absolute power and rulers who practice tolerance. Tell students they will explore the reactions of the subject people and levels of success for uniting an empire. `0:05` minutes

TEACH

GUIDED DISCUSSION

1. **Make Inferences** Why would it be important to communicate orders from one province to another in fewer than 15 days? (*In order to keep the empire united, the people in the empire had to have clear, efficient, and consistent communications. All of the satraps had to be aware of what was happening and have clear direction about how to maintain control in their province.*)

2. **Draw Conclusions** How would having one currency be beneficial to an empire? (*It would mean that all the people paid their tribute or taxes with a currency of a consistent value so it ensured that people paid taxes in a fair way.*)

FORM AND SUPPORT OPINIONS

Have students discuss whether they think Cyrus's policy of tolerance while conquering other lands made him a fair ruler. **ASK:** Do you think that Cyrus's tolerance of other cultures won him loyalty? (*Responses will vary, but students may suggest that Cyrus's tolerant approach made him more favored among conquered people.*) `0:10` minutes

ACTIVE OPTIONS

NG Learning Framework: Learn More About Persian Leaders

ATTITUDE: **Curiosity**
SKILL: **Collaboration**

Have students select the leader they are still curious about after learning about the Persian leaders in this lesson. Have students work in pairs and collaborate to write a short biography about this person using information from the chapter and additional source material. `0:10` minutes

On Your Feet: Create a Living Time Line Ask volunteers to create a living time line of the events associated with the unification of the Persian Empire starting with when the Medes ruled the region. Write each of the dates from the time line in Lesson 2.4 on an index card and distribute the cards randomly to volunteers. Have students arrange themselves in a line in correct chronological order. Then have each student in turn explain to the class the significance of the date he or she is holding. `0:10` minutes

STRIVING READERS

Use Reciprocal Teaching Have students read Lesson 2.4 in pairs. Instruct students to take turns reading each paragraph aloud. At the end of the paragraph, the reading student should ask the listening student a question or two about what they have just heard. For example, students may ask their partners to summarize the paragraph in their own words.

ENGLISH LANGUAGE LEARNERS

Make Word Cards Help students make word cards for these three different ideas that helped to unite the Persian Empire: *tolerance*, *provinces*, and *satraps*. For each one, students should list words or phrases related to that word, such as the following:

- tolerance: sympathy for others, accepting beliefs, allowing people to keep their normal lives
- provinces: small parts of the whole empire, administrative parts
- satraps: governors who maintained control of provinces and helped the ruler maintain control

Then ask students to include the words on the cards in brief sentences about each of these ideas.

Press **(mt)** *in the Student eEdition for modified text.*
See the Chapter Planner for more strategies for differentiation.

ANSWERS

1. Cyrus the Great was a tolerant king who won the respect of his conquered subjects. He allowed local rulers to remain in power, he spared defeated people from great hardship, and perhaps most importantly, he honored local customs and religions. Darius was also wise and divided his empire into provinces for more efficient administration, set regular taxes, and built a network of roads.

2. The governing policies of Cyrus and Darius were fair. The Assyrian rulers' governing policies were cruel. For example, Cyrus only asked for tribute that defeated people could afford. People under Darius's rule only had to pay half of what they could afford. Under the Assyrian rulers, failure to pay tribute resulted in severe punishment or death.

3. First: Cyrus demands tribute from defeated people, but only what they could afford. Second: Darius I expands his empire to reach from India to southwestern Europe. Third: Darius I divides his empire into 20 provinces. Fourth: Darius I builds the Royal Road.

The **Legacy** of
Mesopotamia

As you check your calendar, text a friend, or ride your bike, you probably aren't thinking about the people who walked the earth more than 3,000 years ago. But if it weren't for the people of ancient Mesopotamian civilizations, you might not be able to do any of these things.

MAIN IDEA

Mesopotamia civilizations were responsible for major cultural and technological developments.

CULTURAL DEVELOPMENTS

The advances developed in ancient Mesopotamia form the region's **legacy**—or the things, both cultural and technological, left to us from the past. Mesopotamia's cultural legacy touches our lives every day. For example, the written word took important leaps forward with Sumer's development of pictograph and cuneiform writing and then with the spread of the Phoenician alphabet.

Mesopotamia also left us a legacy in forms of government. The city-state unit that developed in Sumer, Babylon, and Phoenicia became an important governmental form in the ancient world. Equally important were the styles of government that emerged. Hammurabi highlighted the importance of law. His Code of Laws influenced later legal systems. Cyrus the Great demonstrated the power of tolerance to future leaders. Finally, the use of provinces, governors, and good communications are still essential to modern governments.

TECHNOLOGICAL ADVANCES

It is easy to take Mesopotamia's technological advances for granted because they seem so commonplace to us today. Yet at the time, Mesopotamian technology clearly furthered the development of human civilization. During the Bronze Age, tools and weapons became more effective than ever before. Strong axes, swords, and daggers were crafted from bronze.

Mesopotamian technology also had an impact on agriculture and on land and sea travel. The ox-drawn plow made it easier to cultivate large areas of land. Irrigation techniques pioneered by the Sumerians are still used around the world. The wheel revolutionized transportation and trade on land. Phoenician shipbuilding and navigation did the same at sea by spreading Phoenicia's Mesopotamian-influenced culture.

With advances like the abacus, people from Mesopotamia laid the foundations of mathematics and science. The abacus is a device that uses sliding beads for counting. The Mesopotamians were also among the first to perform complex calculations and develop a calendar. Additionally, they devised number systems based on 60, which is what we use today to keep track of time.

The application of mathematics made it possible for Mesopotamians to build larger and more complex buildings, including Mesopotamia's cultural and technological masterpiece, the ziggurat. So the next time you ride in a car, use a tool, or see a skyscraper, thank ancient Mesopotamia.

MATCH-UP: THEN AND NOW

These images show Mesopotamian inventions and their current forms—the ones we are familiar with today. Can you pair each Mesopotamian invention with its modern-day match?

MATCH-UP KEY
a. Phoenician merchant ship
b. Text message on cell phone
c. Abacus
d. Message written in cuneiform on clay tablet
e. Cargo ship
f. Tractor
g. Calculator
h. Model of Sumerian plow

REVIEW & ASSESS

1. **READING CHECK** What are examples of Mesopotamia's cultural and technological legacy?

2. **INTEGRATE VISUALS** What other modern items would you add to the images above to illustrate Mesopotamia's legacy?

3. **FORM OPINIONS** Which cultural or technological advance from ancient Mesopotamia do you think is most important? Explain and support your choice.

PLAN

OBJECTIVE

Identify how Mesopotamian civilizations were responsible for major cultural and technological developments.

CRITICAL THINKING SKILLS FOR LESSON 2.5

- Identify Main Ideas and Details
- Monitor Comprehension
- Integrate Visuals
- Form Opinions
- Make Inferences
- Draw Conclusions
- Synthesize

ESSENTIAL QUESTION

Technological advances help spread culture and develop civilization. Lesson 2.5 discusses Mesopotamian civilizations that brought about major cultural and technological advancements.

BACKGROUND FOR THE TEACHER

The Mesopotamians needed to be able to track time in order for their civilization to thrive. Tracking seasons and weather patterns helped them determine when the rivers may have been prone to flooding, or when they could expect crops to be ready. The Mesopotamians used a fairly complicated time tracking system with the number 60 as the base. Historians do not know the exact reason Mesopotamians chose 60 as the base for time. However, the number 60 is divisible by several numbers, including 1, 2, 3, 4, 5, 6, 10, 12, 15, and 30. Given that about half of the day is dark and half of the day is light because of Earth's rotation, they likely chose 60 to allow for a flexible system of tracking time.

DIGITAL RESOURCES myNGconnect.com

TEACHER RESOURCES & ASSESSMENT

 Reading and Note-Taking   **Vocabulary Practice**   **Section 2 Quiz**

STUDENT RESOURCES

 NG Chapter Gallery

INTRODUCE & ENGAGE

IN TIME OR ON TIME?

Show students an analog clock and a calendar showing all 12 months. Ask them what they observe. Do they notice that there are 12 months in a year and there are 12 numbers on the clock? **ASK:** How many minutes are in an hour? Point out to students that the Sumerians had a number system based on 60. Point out that 60 is divisible by several numbers, including 2, 4, and 15, among others. Ask students to discuss why the number 60 would have been a solution to tracking time. Some other topics to discuss may include: How are the numbers on the clock divided? How many seasons are there? How many degrees are there in a circle? How long does it take for Earth to revolve around the Sun? `0:10` **minutes**

TEACH

GUIDED DISCUSSION

1. **Make Inferences** Why would it be useful to have a written alphabet of symbols representing sounds? (*Having specific symbols to represent sounds would be faster and more efficient than drawing a picture of something when a person is trying to communicate. Letters would also be a clear way to communicate an idea.*)

2. **Draw Conclusions** Why would developing a system to keep track of time be important to people? (*Tracking time can be important to everything from knowing when to expect the mountain snows to melt and cause the rivers to flood; when it is time to harvest the crops; when a captain should leave the port with the ship, or how long a journey at sea may take so people can decide how much water and what types of supplies to take on the ship.*)

SYNTHESIZE

Discuss the many ways the advances of Mesopotamian civilizations transformed civilization and how these developments now impact our lives today. Include advances in communication and technology. Then have students imagine they have a time-traveling visitor from Mesopotamia in the classroom to interview. **ASK:** What modern technology do you think a time-traveling Mesopotamian would be most fascinated by? (*Responses will vary, but students should support their opinions with details from the chapter.*) `0:05` **minutes**

ACTIVE OPTIONS

Critical Viewing: NG Chapter Gallery Invite students to explore the Chapter Gallery to examine the images that relate to the Legacy of Mesopotamia. Invite students to choose one image from the gallery they feel best represents their understanding of the Legacy of Mesopotamia and have them provide a written explanation of why they selected the images they chose. `0:10` **minutes**

On Your Feet: Hold a Debate Divide the class into two teams and explain that they will be debating cultural legacies of Mesopotamia, and discussing which one has more impact on our culture today. One side will argue that Hammurabi's Code of Laws is more important to today's society. The other side will argue that Cyrus the Great's legacy of the power of tolerance is more important in today's society. `0:10` **minutes**

DIFFERENTIATE

STRIVING READERS

Create Charts Help students better understand the legacy of Mesopotamian society by creating a chart of technological and cultural inventions. As they read Lesson 2.5 have them complete the chart below. Tell students to use the chart to help them evaluate the positive and negative effects of each invention and to decide which invention they think had the greatest impact on society.

Invention	Effect on Civilization

GIFTED & TALENTED

Describe Inventions Have students think of an idea for an invention of their own. They might come up with a new electronic device, a vehicle, or an item that simply makes everyday life easier. Ask students to write a description of their invention and share it with the class.

Press **(mt)** *in the Student eEdition for modified text.*

See the Chapter Planner for more strategies for differentiation.

REVIEW & ASSESS

ANSWERS

1. Some examples include the city-state, the legal system, writing, calendars, ox-drawn plows, and other math and science foundations.

2. Possibilities might include photos of a calendar, a clock, an irrigation system, and a courthouse.

3. Students' opinions will vary. Accept reasonable responses that are supported by logical reasoning and relevant evidence.

VOCABULARY

Match each word in the first column with its definition in the second column.

WORD	DEFINITION
1. city-state	a. a pyramid-shaped temple with a shrine at the top
2. artisan	b. the governor of a district
3. polytheism	c. an order based on power and wealth
4. ziggurat	d. a person skilled at making things by hand
5. social class	e. an administrative district
6. province	f. a self-governing city that controlled the surrounding land
7. satrap	g. things left to us from the past
8. legacy	h. the belief in many gods

READING STRATEGY

9. MAKE INFERENCES If you haven't already, complete your chart to make inferences about why civilization developed in Mesopotamia. Then answer the question.

I notice . . .	I know . . .	And so . . .
Two rivers flowed through Mesopotamia	Rivers provide water to sustain agriculture.	

Consider the traits of civilization that you learned about in Chapter 2. How did they develop in the region?

MAIN IDEAS

Answer the following questions. Support your answers with evidence from the chapter.

10. How did the geography of Mesopotamia contribute to the development of civilization? **LESSON 1.1**

11. What caused city-states to develop in Sumer and form the world's first civilization? **LESSON 1.2**

12. What purpose did the ziggurat serve in each Sumerian city-state? **LESSON 1.3**

13. What is important about the empire Sargon created in Mesopotamia? **LESSON 1.5**

14. What did Hammurabi establish to help unite his vast empire? **LESSON 2.1**

15. What factors helped the Assyrians of northern Mesopotamia conquer all of Mesopotamia? **LESSON 2.2**

16. How did Phoenician sea traders affect Mesopotamian culture? **LESSON 2.3**

17. In what ways were Cyrus and Darius wise rulers? **LESSON 2.4**

CRITICAL THINKING

Answer the following questions. Support your answers with evidence from the chapter.

18. DRAW CONCLUSIONS How might unpredictable natural forces, such as floods, have influenced the development of polytheism in Sumer?

19. IDENTIFY MAIN IDEAS AND DETAILS What are three details that support the idea that Sargon was a highly skilled administrator?

20. ANALYZE CAUSE AND EFFECT What led to Hammurabi's Code of Laws?

21. SUMMARIZE What were the important achievements of Mesopotamian civilizations?

22. YOU DECIDE Were the punishments in Hammurabi's Code of Laws appropriate? Support your opinion with evidence from the text.

INTERPRET CHARTS

Study the chart comparing letters in the Phoenician, early Greek, early Latin, and modern English alphabets. Then answer the questions that follow.

Phoenician	Early Greek	Early Latin	Modern English
			A
			B
			C
			D
			E
			F
			H

23. Which letter is most similar in all four alphabets?

24. What conclusions can you draw about language in the ancient world?

ANALYZE SOURCES

Read the following translation of an Assyrian king's description of one of his raids. Then answer the question.

I carried off his silver, gold, possessions, property, bronze, iron, tin, . . . captives of the guilty soldiers together with their property, his gods together with their property, precious stone of the mountain, his harnessed chariot, his teams of horses, the equipment of the horses, the equipment of the troops, garments with multi-colored trim, linen garments, fine oil, cedar, fine aromatic plants, cedar shavings, purple wool, red-purple wool, his wagons, his oxen, his sheep—his valuable tribute which, like the stars of heaven, had no number.

25. Based on this passage, what can you conclude about the nature of Assyrian attacks on city-states in Mesopotamia?

WRITE ABOUT HISTORY

26. ARGUMENT Of all the achievements of Mesopotamian civilizations, which one do you think has had the most significant and lasting impact on the modern world? Write a persuasive essay outlining your argument.

TIPS

- Take notes about the many important achievements of Mesopotamian civilizations discussed in the chapter.
- State your argument in a clear, persuasive way.
- Present strong evidence to support your argument.
- Use vocabulary words from the chapter as appropriate.
- Provide a concluding statement that wraps up the argument presented.

VOCABULARY ANSWERS

WORD	DEFINITION
1. city-state f.	a. a pyramid-shaped temple with a shrine at the top
2. artisan d.	b. the governor of a district
3. polytheism h.	c. an order based on power and wealth
4. ziggurat a.	d. a person skilled at making things by hand
5. social class c.	e. an administrative district
6. province e.	f. a self-governing city that controlled the surrounding land
7. satrap b.	g. things left to us from the past
8. legacy g.	h. the belief in many gods

READING STRATEGY ANSWERS

I notice...	I know...	And so...
Two rivers flowed through Mesopotamia.	Rivers provide water to sustain agriculture.	The physical geography of having two rivers helped civilization to develop.

9. The Tigris and Euphrates rivers flowed through Mesopotamia, and the yearly floods brought fertile soil to the land. The river also provided the water needed to sustain agriculture in the region. People settled here because they could grow food. Eventually, groups of people joined together, forming villages. Successful food crops led to larger populations and allowed those people to have free time to develop arts, culture, and technology, including weapons. A succession of rulers used their power to spread culture and unite peoples of different races and religions. These peoples exchanged goods, cultures, and technologies.

MAIN IDEAS ANSWERS

10. Mesopotamia, located between the Tigris and Euphrates rivers, was a flat, fertile river valley that was excellent for agriculture. As farming flourished, populations grew, cities were built, and civilization developed.

11. City-states developed in Sumer when the people in farming villages worked together on major irrigation projects; their collaboration led to united villages that formed city-states.

12. The ziggurat was the heart of each Sumerian city-state. It was a monumental temple, where priests performed rituals to ensure the city-state's well-being.

13. The Akkadian Empire that Sargon created in Mesopotamia was the world's first empire, as well as the world's largest empire.

14. Hammurabi's Code of Laws helped to unite his vast empire.

15. The Assyrians had a strong agricultural economy, which afforded them a large professional army. Armed with iron weapons and skilled at archery, Assyrian armies had the power and force to conquer all of Mesopotamia.

16. As the Phoenicians traveled to different harbors in the Mediterranean for trade, they not only exported goods but they exported their alphabet and other aspects of culture as well.

17. Cyrus and Darius practiced tolerance toward their conquered subjects, allowed conquered kings to keep their thrones, and only charged small tributes. This allowed their conquered kingdoms to be united.

CRITICAL THINKING ANSWERS

18. Unpredictable natural forces, such as destructive floods, might have led to the development of polytheism because this belief helped Sumerians feel more in control in an unpredictable world. With multiple gods governing every aspect of life, Sumerians believed that if they pleased their gods with gifts and ceremonies, they would be protected and spared from such disasters of flooding, drought, and disease.

19. First, Sargon tolerated local rulers and customs of the people he conquered; he introduced standard weights and measures; he unified the whole empire by making Akkadian the official language.

20. Hammurabi had a vast empire that contained many different peoples who all followed different laws. To help bring justice to everyday life, Hammurabi took the best laws of the land, added a few more, and organized the rules. Then he had them written in stone and posted for everyone to see so that everyone had rules to follow.

21. the development of improved agriculture, Sumerian cuneiform writing, the Phoenician alphabet, the city-state, codified laws, metal tools, innovative irrigation techniques, foundations of mathematics and science, and complex building structures

22. Students' responses will vary. Students should support their opinions with evidence from the chapter.

INTERPRET CHARTS ANSWERS

23. The letter "E" is the most similar in all four alphabets.

24. Languages evolve over time, developing further as people come in contact, communicating and sharing elements of different languages.

ANALYZE SOURCES ANSWER

25. Students' responses will vary. Sample response: The excerpt reveals a remarkably detailed list of items taken by the Assyrians. This list includes mention of the highly valued "purple" dyed cloth, so it suggests that the city-state that was raided had traded with the Phoenicians, or were in contact with others who had. This list also reveals how ruthlessly thorough the Assyrians were when raiding city-states; basically, they took absolutely everything of value, leaving nothing for those they had conquered.

WRITE ABOUT HISTORY ANSWER

26. Students' essays will vary, but students should construct a persuasive argument and support it with evidence from the chapter.

Students' outlines should

- contain one claim that they will argue
- support each claim with clear reasons and relevant evidence from the chapter
- be written in a formal style
- include vocabulary words from the chapter

UNIT RESOURCES

NATIONAL GEOGRAPHIC

On Location with National Geographic Lead Program Officer Christopher Thornton
Intro and Video

Unit Wrap-Up:
"Encounters with History"
Feature and Video

"China's Ancient Lifeline"
National Geographic Adapted Article

"Faces of the Divine"
National Geographic Adapted Article
Student eEdition exclusive

Unit 2 Inquiry:
Write a Creation Myth

 Interactive Map Tool
Available on myNGconnect

 **News & Updates**
Available on myNGconnect

CHAPTER RESOURCES

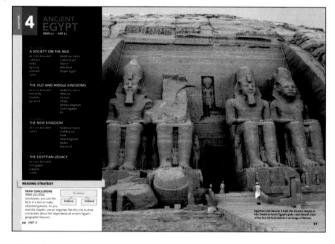

TEACHER RESOURCES & ASSESSMENT *Available on myNGconnect*

 Social Studies Skills Lessons
• Reading: Draw Conclusions
• Writing: Write a Narrative

 Chapter 4
Answer Key

 Formal Assessment
• Chapter 4 Tests A (on-level) & B (below-level)

 ExamView®
One-time Download

STUDENT BACKPACK *Available on myNGconnect*

• eEdition *(English)*   • eEdition *(Spanish)*   • Handbooks   • Online Atlas
For Chapter 4 Spanish resources, visit the Teacher Resource Menu page on myNGconnect.

SECTION 1 RESOURCES

A SOCIETY ON THE NILE

 Reading and Note-Taking

 Vocabulary Practice

 Section 1 Quiz

Available on myNGconnect

LESSON 1.1 THE GEOGRAPHY OF ANCIENT EGYPT
• Critical Viewing: NG Chapter Gallery
• On Your Feet: Think, Pair, Share

LESSON 1.2
AGRICULTURE DEVELOPS

| **NG Learning Framework:**
Observe Upper and Lower Egypt

• On Your Feet: Card Responses

LESSON 1.3 EGYPT UNITES
• Critical Viewing: NG Chapter Gallery
• On Your Feet: Inside-Outside Circle

NATIONAL GEOGRAPHIC
EXPLORER SARAH PARCAK
LESSON 1.4 SENSING UNDER THE SURFACE

| **NG Learning Framework:**
Learn More About Tanis

• On Your Feet: Create a Quiz

SECTION 2 RESOURCES

THE OLD AND MIDDLE KINGDOMS

 Reading and Note-Taking

 Vocabulary Practice

 Section 2 Quiz

Available on myNGconnect

LESSON 2.1 THE OLD KINGDOM

| **NG Learning Framework:**
Discuss the Importance of Pyramids

• On Your Feet: Fishbowl

LESSON 2.2
DAILY LIFE AND RELIGION

• Critical Viewing: NG Chapter Gallery
• On Your Feet: Chart Relay

DOCUMENT BASED QUESTION
LESSON 2.3 LIFE, DEATH, AND RELIGION

| **NG Learning Framework:**
Review Information About the Nile

• On Your Feet: Three Options

LESSON 2.4
THE MIDDLE KINGDOM

| **NG Learning Framework:**
Review Information About the Middle Kingdom

• On Your Feet: Turn and Talk on Topic

SECTION 3 RESOURCES

THE NEW KINGDOM

 Reading and Note-Taking

 Vocabulary Practice

 Section 3 Quiz

Available on myNGconnect

LESSON 3.1 HATSHEPSUT EXPANDS TRADE

 Biography
Hatshepsut

Available on myNGconnect
• Critical Viewing: NG Image Gallery
• On Your Feet: Present a Period of Egyptian History

BIOGRAPHY
LESSON 3.2 RAMSES II

| **NG Learning Framework:**
Compare the Reigns of Ramses II and Hatshepsut

• On Your Feet: Hold a Panel Discussion

HISTORY THROUGH OBJECTS
LESSON 3.3 TUT'S TREASURES

• Critical Viewing: NG Chapter Gallery
• On Your Feet: Three-Step Interview

LESSON 3.4 THE RISE OF KUSH

| **NG Learning Framework:**
Learn More About Life in Kush

• On Your Feet: Create a Concept Web

SECTION 4 RESOURCES

THE EGYPTIAN LEGACY

 Reading and Note-Taking

 Vocabulary Practice

 Section 4 Quiz

Available on myNGconnect

LESSON 4.1
HIEROGLYPHS AND PAPYRUS

 Active History: Interactive Whiteboard Activity
Decipher Egyptian Hieroglyphics

 Active History
Decipher Egyptian Hieroglyphics

Available on myNGconnect
• On Your Feet: Talk and Share

LESSON 4.2 MEDICINE, SCIENCE, AND MATHEMATICS

| **NG Learning Framework:**
Learn More About Medicine in Ancient Egypt

• On Your Feet: Create a Quiz

LESSON 4.3
ART AND ARCHITECTURE

• Critical Viewing: NG Image Gallery
• On Your Feet: Fishbowl

CHAPTER 4 REVIEW

STRATEGY ❶
Focus on Main Idea

Help students locate the Main Idea statements at the beginning of Lessons 1.1, 1.2, 1.3, and 1.4. Explain that these statements summarize the important ideas of the reading and will be useful for helping them pay attention to what matters most in the text.

Use with Lessons 1.1, 1.2, 1.3, and 1.4 *Help students get in the habit of using the Main Idea statements to set a purpose for reading.*

STRATEGY ❷
Play Vocabulary Tic-Tac-Toe

Write nine Key Vocabulary words on a tic-tac-toe grid. Have Player A choose a word. If the player correctly pronounces, defines, and uses the word in a sentence, he or she can put an X in the box. Then have Player B do the same using O. Keep playing until there is a winner.

Use with All Lessons *This activity works well on the Interactive Whiteboard. It can be used to review Key Vocabulary for a single section or the entire chapter.*

STRATEGY ❸
Read and Recall

Allow students to work in groups of two to four. First have each student read the same lesson independently. After reading, students should meet without the book and share ideas they recall. One person should take notes. As a group, students should look at the lesson and decide what should be added or changed in the notes.

Use with All Lessons *For an extension of this strategy, have different groups compare their notes.*

Press *in the Student eEdition for modified text.*

STRATEGY ❶
Preview Visuals to Predict

Ask students to preview the title and visuals in each lesson. Then have students tell what they think the lesson will be about. After reading, ask them to repeat the activity to see whether their predictions were confirmed.

Use with All Lessons *Invite volunteers to describe the visuals in detail to help visually impaired students see them.*

STRATEGY ❷
Complete Cloze Statements

Provide copies of these cloze statements for students to complete during or after reading.

Ancient Egypt had abundant _____ to _____, or exchange, for things the land couldn't produce, especially _____ and exotic luxuries. These goods traveled along _____ routes and pathways established by traders over land and _____. The _____ generated through these expeditions stimulated Egypt's economy and funded great _____ projects.

Use with Lesson 3.1

STRATEGY ❶
PREP Before Reading

Have students use the PREP strategy to prepare for reading. Write this acrostic on the board:

PREP
Preview title.
Read Main Idea statement.
Examine visuals.
Predict what you will learn.

Have students write their prediction and share it with a partner. After reading, ask students to write another sentence that begins "I also learned . . ."

Use with All Lessons

STRATEGY ❷

Pair Partners for Dictation

After students read each lesson in the chapter, have them write a sentence summarizing its main idea. Have students get together in pairs and dictate their sentences to each other. Then have them work together to check the sentences for accuracy and spelling.

Use with All Lessons *For Lessons 4.1, 4.2, and 4.3, monitor students' comprehension of the advances ancient Egyptians made in writing, medicine, science, mathematics, art, and architecture.*

STRATEGY ❸

Set Up a Word Wall

Work with students to choose three words from each section to display in a grouping on a Word Wall. Keep the words displayed throughout the lessons and discuss each one as it comes up during reading. Have volunteers add words, phrases, and examples to each word to develop understanding.

Use with All Lessons

GIFTED & TALENTED

STRATEGY ❶

Write a Dialogue

Tell students to review Lesson 2.4 under the heading "Darius Expands the Empire." Then have them use facts from the text to write a dialogue that might have taken place between Darius I and a satrap in one of the provinces. Encourage students to cover topics that might have been discussed between two officials who governed the people.

Use with Lesson 2.4

STRATEGY ❷

Interview a King

Allow students to work in teams of two to plan, write, and perform a simulated television interview with King Hammurabi of Babylon. Tell students the purpose of the interview is to focus on the achievements of the king during his reign.

Use with Lesson 2.1 *Invite students to use the Internet or library resources to learn more about Hammurabi.*

PRE-AP

STRATEGY ❶

Teach a Class

Before beginning the chapter, allow students to choose one of the lessons listed below and prepare to teach the contents to the class. Give them a set amount of time in which to present their lesson. Suggest that students think about any visuals or activities they want to use when they teach.

Use with Lessons 1.1, 1.2, 2.1, 2.2, 4.1, 4.2, and 4.3

STRATEGY ❷

Debate Contributions

Have students research the many contributions of ancient Egypt to civilization. Tell each student to decide which contribution he or she believes had the greatest impact and make a list of the reasons that support his or her choice. Suggest that students hold a panel discussion to share and debate their decisions.

Use with Lessons 2.1, 2.2, 3.3, 4.1, 4.2, and 4.3 *For Lessons 2.1 and 2.2, suggest that students consider how the pyramids and their contents have influenced what people today know about ancient Egypt.*

4 ANCIENT EGYPT

3000 B.C. – 500 B.C.

Egyptian ruler Ramses II built this massive temple at Abu Simbel to honor Egypt's gods—and himself. Each of the four 66-foot statues is an image of Ramses.

SECTION 1
A SOCIETY ON THE NILE

KEY VOCABULARY	NAMES & PLACES
cataract	Lower Egypt
delta	Menes
dynasty	Nile River
pharaoh	Upper Egypt
vizier	

SECTION 2
THE OLD AND MIDDLE KINGDOMS

KEY VOCABULARY	NAMES & PLACES
hierarchy	Ahmose
mummy	Hyksos
pyramid	Khufu
	Middle Kingdom
	Old Kingdom
	Re

SECTION 3
THE NEW KINGDOM

KEY VOCABULARY	NAMES & PLACES
barter	Hatshepsut
	Kush
	New Kingdom
	Nubia
	Ramses II

SECTION 4
THE EGYPTIAN LEGACY

KEY VOCABULARY
hieroglyph
papyrus
scribe

READING STRATEGY

DRAW CONCLUSIONS
When you draw conclusions, you use the facts in a text to make educated guesses. As you read the chapter, use an organizer like this one to draw conclusions about the importance of ancient Egypt's geographic features.

```
        Conclusion
    ┌──────────────┐
Evidence      Evidence
```

89

TEACHER BACKGROUND

INTRODUCE THE PHOTOGRAPH

Have students study the photograph that shows the four figures of King Ramses II. Point out that two of the figures are located on either side of the entrance to the temple. Tell students that Ramses II had this huge temple carved out of a sandstone cliff on the west bank of the Nile. Explain to students that, in this chapter, they will learn about ancient Egypt–its culture, its religion, and its leaders.

ASK: What does the number and size of the figures of Ramses II indicate about his importance in ancient Egyptian society? *(Possible responses: The number and size of the statues indicate that Ramses II was most likely very important and powerful in ancient Egyptian society.)*

SHARE BACKGROUND

The four statues of King Ramses II at this temple provide an example of ancient Egyptian art. Small figures of Ramses' children, his queen, Nefertari, and his mother, Muttay, are carved around his feet. The temple is dedicated to the sun gods. The temple was built in such a way that, on two days of the year, the first rays of the sun in the morning shine through the length of the building and light up the entire temple.

DIGITAL RESOURCES myNGconnect.com

TEACHER RESOURCES & ASSESSMENT

 Social Studies Skills Lessons
• Reading: Draw Conclusions
• Writing: Write a Narrative

ExamView®
One-time Download

 Formal Assessment
Chapter 4 Tests A (on-level) & B (below-level)

 Chapter 4 Answer Key

STUDENT BACKPACK

• **eEdition** *(English)*   • **Handbooks**
• **eEdition** *(Spanish)*   • **Online Atlas**

For Chapter 4 Spanish Resources, visit the Teacher Resource Menu page.

HOW DID ANCIENT EGYPT'S RULERS USE THE LAND'S RESOURCES AND GEOGRAPHY TO FOUND A CIVILIZATION?

Four Corners Activity: Factors of Influence This activity introduces students to four factors that led to ancient Egypt's success and allows them to choose which factor they think is the most influential. Post the four signs shown in the list below. Ask students to choose the factor that they think contributed most to Egypt's success, go to that corner, and then explain why.

A. Geography The Nile River in Egypt was central to the development of Egyptian civilization, providing water, fertile soil for planting crops, and easy access to trade routes.

B. Government Ancient Egypt was governed by a long series of strong rulers who had complete authority over all religious, civil, and military matters.

C. Military During the New Kingdom, Egypt grew powerful and its army expanded the empire. Egypt became rich from war and taxes from conquered lands.

D. Knowledge of Medicine, Science, and Mathematics Ancient Egyptian advances in medicine, science, and mathematics helped the Egyptians understand human anatomy, treat illnesses, develop a calendar, design buildings, and become successful in trade.

0:15 minutes

DRAW CONCLUSIONS

Explain to students that when you draw conclusions, you use the facts in a text to make educated guesses. Model filling out the graphic organizer by reading aloud the section "The Gift of the Nile" in Lesson 1.1. Add a fact about the Nile from the text to the first "Evidence" box of the organizer. Tell students that they can add more evidence about the Nile as they read the chapter. Then they can use the evidence to help them draw a conclusion about the importance of the Nile River to the civilization of ancient Egypt.

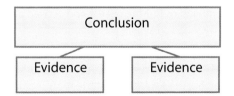

KNOWLEDGE RATING

Have students complete a Knowledge-Rating Chart for Key Vocabulary words. Have students list words and fill out the chart. Work together as a class to complete the chart.

KEY VOCAB	KNOW IT	NOT SURE	DON'T KNOW	DEFINITION
barter				
cataract				
delta				
dynasty				

KEY DATES	
3200 B.C.	Separate kingdoms of Upper Egypt and Lower Egypt
3100 B.C.	Unification of Upper Egypt and Lower Egypt
2700 B.C.–2200 B.C.	The Old Kingdom
2040 B.C.	The Middle Kingdom
1550 B.C.–1070 B.C.	The New Kingdom
728 B.C.	Egypt under Kushite rule
30 B.C.	Conquest of Egypt by Rome

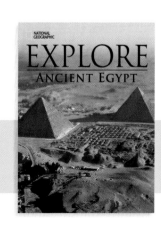

For more on ancient Egypt, see *EXPLORE ANCIENT EGYPT.*

1.1

The Geography of
Ancient Egypt

"Hail to thee, O Nile! Who manifests thyself over this land and comes to give life to Egypt!" These words written 4,000 years ago emphasize the importance of the Nile River to Egyptians: No Nile, no life, no Egypt. It was that simple.

MAIN IDEA

The Nile was the source of life in Egypt's dry, barren deserts.

+ POSSIBLE RESPONSE

The photo shows that the soil alongside the Nile River is rich enough to support the growth of plants.

Critical Viewing This photo shows the fertile land alongside the Nile River. How does it illustrate the way Egyptians depended on the Nile?

THE GIFT OF THE NILE

The **Nile River** was central to the civilization that developed in Egypt. At around 4,132 miles in length, it is the world's longest river. It flows northward from sources deep in Africa to the Mediterranean Sea. Six **cataracts**, rock formations that create churning rapids, break the river's smooth course. The 550 miles from the most northerly cataract to the Mediterranean Sea formed ancient Egypt's heartland, which was divided into two distinct regions: the Upper (southern) Nile and the Lower (northern) Nile. The Lower Nile region included the Nile Delta, next to the Mediterranean. A **delta** is an area where a river fans out into various branches as it flows into a body of water.

The Nile was generally a peaceful river. Its current carried ships gently downstream, while the winds above it usually blew upstream, making it easy for ships to row downstream or sail upstream.

Water was the Nile's greatest gift. Without it there could be no agriculture in Egypt's desert. Every year faraway rains sent a surge of water downstream to Egypt, swelling the river with the annual flood.

Unlike the rivers of Mesopotamia, the Nile's flood was predictable, occurring every summer. The waters spilled over the riverbanks, depositing another great gift: silt, or very fine particles carried from upriver. The silt-enriched soil was fertile, or full of nutrients to support abundant crops. This soil made agriculture extremely productive—a key to the development of Egyptian civilization. With good management and a little luck, the soil delivered huge harvests.

THE BLACK LAND AND THE RED LAND

Egypt's climate was consistently dry, and sunshine was plentiful. Seven months of hot, sunny weather were followed by a winter of mild, sunny weather. The lack of rainfall created a landscape of striking contrast, made up of regions called the "black land" and the "red land."

The black land was the narrow stretch that ran along both sides of the Nile. There, the river's waters and nourishing dark silt allowed plants to grow and people to live.

The red land was a vast, scorching desert that surrounded the Nile. This desert formed a powerful barrier against invasion and helped separate Egypt from the world beyond. The seemingly empty desert also held a treasure trove of raw materials, including stone for building and gold. The only major resource Egypt lacked was timber.

Egypt's geography, its climate, and—above all—the Nile River all played parts in the kind of civilization that Egypt would become. The land was rich in resources, produced a huge food surplus, and had well-protected borders. In addition, Egypt was a crossroads for trade, lying along important trade routes connecting Africa, the Mediterranean, the Red Sea, and the Middle East. The scene was set for Africa's most famous civilization of ancient times.

REVIEW & ASSESS

1. **READING CHECK** Why was the Nile River essential to life in ancient Egypt?

2. **ANALYZE CAUSE AND EFFECT** What effect did the annual flooding of the Nile River have on the development of agriculture in Egypt?

3. **COMPARE AND CONTRAST** What did the black and red lands have in common? How were they different?

PLAN

OBJECTIVE

Identify the Nile River as the source of life in Egypt's dry deserts.

CRITICAL THINKING SKILLS FOR LESSON 1.1

- Identify Main Ideas and Details
- Monitor Comprehension
- Analyze Cause and Effect
- Compare and Contrast
- Make Inferences
- Draw Conclusions
- Analyze Visuals

ESSENTIAL QUESTION

How did ancient Egypt's rulers use the land's resources and geography to found a civilization?

The Nile River provided fresh water that sustained plant and animal life. Lesson 1.1 discusses how the Nile was a source of life in Egypt's deserts.

BACKGROUND FOR THE TEACHER

The Sahara's climate has changed dramatically over time. Nearly 10,000 years ago, the Sahara was a tropical grassland. Around 5300 B.C., seasonal rains that watered the Sahara began shifting southward. Over time, the Sahara became a desert. People living in the Sahara moved out of the desert and settled in the Nile River Valley where they had a reliable water source.

The Nile's main sources are the Blue Nile River and the White Nile River. The Nile River flows north because the southern sources of the river are higher in elevation than the mouth of the river on the Mediterranean Sea.

DIGITAL RESOURCES myNGconnect.com

TEACHER RESOURCES & ASSESSMENT

 Reading and Note-Taking   **Vocabulary Practice**   **Section 1 Quiz**

STUDENT RESOURCES

 NG Chapter Gallery

INTRODUCE & ENGAGE

ACTIVATE PRIOR KNOWLEDGE

Have students work in teams to brainstorm ways in which the climate in which they live affects their school, family, and community. Ask them to consider the effect of physical features such as mountains and deserts, as well as proximity to bodies of water. Invite students to share their ideas with the class. Tell students they will learn about climate and physical features of ancient Egypt in this lesson. **0:05** minutes

TEACH

GUIDED DISCUSSION

1. **Make Inferences** In what way did the Sahara protect Egypt from invasion? (*It would have been difficult to travel across such a hot dry place. Invading enemies would also have to bring food, water, and animals for themselves to survive because there was no water source and crops could not grow in the desert.*)

2. **Draw Conclusions** How do you think the development of civilization in Egypt would have been different without the Nile River? (*The land would not have supported settled farming without the Nile. Without the wealth from farming and the trade made possible by transportation on the Nile, civilization would probably not have developed in the same way.*)

ANALYZE VISUALS

Have students examine the photo of the land alongside the Nile River. Ask them to write sentences to describe what they see in the photo. **0:10** minutes

ACTIVE OPTIONS

Critical Viewing: NG Chapter Gallery Invite students to explore the Chapter Gallery to examine the images that relate to this chapter. Have them select one of the images and do additional research to learn more about it. Ask questions that will inspire additional inquiry about the chosen gallery image, such as: What is this? Where and when was it created? By whom? Why was it created? Why does it belong in this chapter? What else would you like to know about it? **0:10** minutes

On Your Feet: Think, Pair, Share Have students work in pairs to discuss the Reading Check question. Then have each pair meet with another pair to compare answers. Call on volunteers to share and compare their answers with the class. **0:10** minutes

DIFFERENTIATE

STRIVING READERS

Use an Anticipation Guide Write the following statements on the board:

3. The Nile River was important to the development of civilization in ancient Egypt.

4. Egypt's geography made trade with other countries very difficult.

5. Fertile soil that resulted from the flooding of the Nile led to productive agriculture.

6. The desert that surrounded the Nile helped separate Egypt from the world and helped protect it from invasion.

7. Flooding of the Nile River occurred rarely.

Before reading the lesson, ask students to copy each statement and put an A (agree) or D (disagree) before it. After students read Lesson 1.1, allow volunteers to explain why each statement is correct or incorrect.

PRE-AP

Present a Skit Have students work in small groups to create a skit in which they take the roles of ancient Egyptians who lived in the black land and those who lived in the red land. Ask students to highlight ways in which life in the two areas would have been alike and different. Have students present their skits to the class.

Press **mt** *in the Student eEdition for modified text.*

See the Chapter Planner for more strategies for differentiation.

REVIEW & ASSESS

ANSWERS

1. The Nile River provided the water necessary for life in Egypt's arid desert.

2. The annual flooding of the Nile River deposited silt on the riverbanks. This fertile soil made agriculture along the Nile River very productive.

3. Both lands received very little rainfall. The black land, however, was very fertile because it straddled the Nile River. The location of the black land meant it benefited from the floodwaters and silt, creating a fertile landscape for plants to grow and people to live. In contrast, the red land was located in the desert area surrounding the Nile, far from access to water.

1.2 Agriculture Develops

It's August, and all that can be seen of the flooded fields is water lapping at the stones marking each farmer's boundary. In the dark of night, a farmer paddles nervously out and shifts the stones to steal a few feet from his neighbor. It's a profitable but serious crime—the penalty is death. Farmland in Egypt is so valuable that some are willing to risk it.

MAIN IDEA

Agriculture encouraged the development of communities and kingdoms in Egypt.

THE FERTILE NILE DELTA

Five thousand years ago, the lives of most Egyptians revolved around farming. Along with raising livestock, Egyptians grew a wide variety of crops such as wheat, barley, beans, lentils, peas, onions, and leeks. Fruits included grapes, dates, figs, and watermelons. Farmers grew flax to make cloth. Fish and birds were plentiful, and even poor Egyptians could eat well.

The cycles of the river dictated the farming year. From July to October, the fields were flooded, so farmers did other work. When the floods receded, farmers plowed the soft ground, scattered seeds, and used animals to trample the seeds into the soil. The growing crops were carefully watered through

irrigation. Farmers captured floodwater in artificial lakes and channeled it to the fields. Later, the shaduf (shuh-DOOF) made irrigation easier. This tool was a long pole with a bucket on one end and a weight on the other. Farmers could use a shaduf to effortlessly lift water to their fields. The grain harvest started in mid-March. During the hot summer that followed, farmers prepared their fields before the next flood.

Irrigation and the Nile's fertile soil allowed for extremely productive farming. As in Mesopotamia, successful farming generated surpluses, which led to population growth, trade, and specialized jobs. Building and maintaining irrigation networks took a lot of labor, so farmers grouped together to create larger communities. Leadership was needed to coordinate and manage these increasingly complex societies. As villages grew into towns, village chiefs became kings.

TWO KINGDOMS ARISE

Some historians believe that by around 3200 B.C., two kings ruled over two separate kingdoms—**Upper Egypt** and **Lower Egypt**. Lower Egypt was the Nile Delta region with its wide expanse of fertile land and access to the Mediterranean Sea. Upper Egypt was the long, narrow stretch of the Nile south of modern Cairo and hemmed in by desert.

The Nile served as a superhighway, encouraging contact between Upper and Lower Egypt. Movement along the Nile was easy, and all the villages and towns were located near the great river. Goods and ideas were traded freely between the kingdoms, unifying Egyptians economically and culturally. Unlike Mesopotamia, Egypt would come to be a strong, unified state rather than a group of city-states.

However, Upper Egypt and Lower Egypt remained proudly distinct. Even after Egypt was united, it was represented by a double crown. Every time Egypt descended into disorder, the two kingdoms were usually on opposite sides of the power struggle.

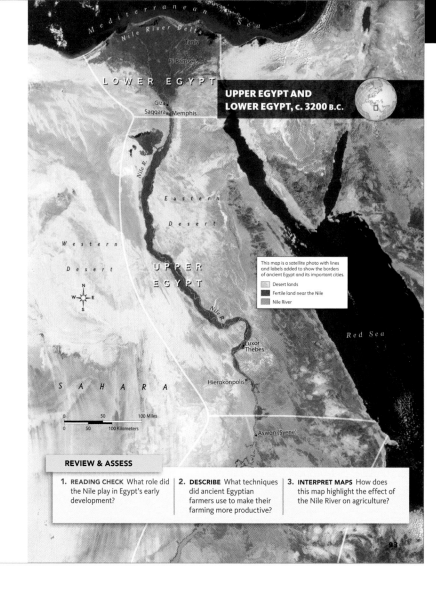

UPPER EGYPT AND LOWER EGYPT, c. 3200 B.C.

This map is a satellite photo with lines and labels added to show the borders of ancient Egypt and its important cities.

- Desert lands
- Fertile land near the Nile
- Nile River

REVIEW & ASSESS

1. **READING CHECK** What role did the Nile play in Egypt's early development?

2. **DESCRIBE** What techniques did ancient Egyptian farmers use to make their farming more productive?

3. **INTERPRET MAPS** How does this map highlight the effect of the Nile River on agriculture?

PLAN

OBJECTIVE

Explain how agriculture encouraged the development of communities and kingdoms in Egypt.

CRITICAL THINKING SKILLS FOR LESSON 1.2

- Identify Main Ideas and Details
- Monitor Comprehension
- Describe
- Interpret Maps
- Summarize
- Draw Conclusions

ESSENTIAL QUESTION

How did ancient Egypt's rulers use the land's resources and geography to found a civilization?

Egypt was rich in natural resources. Lesson 1.2 discusses how the resources and geography influenced the development of the Egyptian civilization in ancient times.

BACKGROUND FOR THE TEACHER

One of the crops Egyptians grew in the fertile Nile Valley was flax. They used the fibers from the stems of the plants. These fibers were split length-wise and spun into thread. The Egyptians wove the thread into sheets of linen they used for clothing. Another plant, papyrus, grew in marshy areas around the Nile River. Ancient Egyptians used papyrus to make paper, rope, sandals, and baskets.

DIGITAL RESOURCES myNGconnect.com

TEACHER RESOURCES & ASSESSMENT

 Reading and Note-Taking

 Vocabulary Practice

 Section 1 Quiz

STUDENT RESOURCES

 NG Chapter Gallery

INTRODUCE & ENGAGE

COMPARE AND CONTRAST

Have students begin a Venn Diagram to compare and contrast the farming methods used in ancient Egypt with farming methods used today. Have them write about farming methods today in the left circle. Then, as they read the lesson, ask them to write details about the methods used in ancient Egypt in the right circle. They should write details about how the methods are alike where the circles overlap. **0:10** minutes

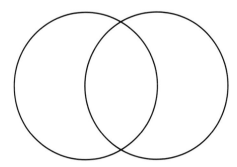

TEACH

GUIDED DISCUSSION

1. **Summarize** What types of crops did the ancient Egyptians grow? (*They grew wheat, barley, beans, lentils, peas, onions, leeks, grapes, dates, figs, and watermelon.*)

2. **Draw Conclusions** How did the Nile River encourage contact between Upper Egypt and Lower Egypt? (*It was easy to travel along the Nile. People traded goods and ideas.*)

INTERPRET MAPS

Point out the map of Upper Egypt and Lower Egypt. Explain that the the map is based on a satellite photo of the region. Have students identify desert lands, fertile lands near the Nile River, and the Nile itself. Remind students that the Nile flows from south to north. **0:10** minutes

ACTIVE OPTIONS

NG Learning Framework: Observe Upper and Lower Egypt

ATTITUDE: **Curiosity**
KNOWLEDGE: **Our Human Story**

Have students observe the map showing Lower Egypt and Upper Egypt. Ask students to think of questions they might have about the two kingdoms of ancient Egypt. Then have them use information from the chapter and additional source material to write sentences comparing and contrasting ways of life in the two kingdoms. **0:10** minutes

On Your Feet: Card Responses Have half the class write six true-false questions based on the lesson. Have the other half create answer cards, writing "True" on one side and "False" on the other. Students from the first group should take turns asking their questions. Students from the second group should hold up their cards, showing either "True" or "False" in response to the questions. Have students keep track of their correct answers. **0:10** minutes

DIFFERENTIATE

INCLUSION

Use Echo Reading Pair students so that there is a proficient reader in each pair. Have the proficient reader read aloud the Main Idea statement at the beginning of the lesson. Have the other student "echo" the same statement in their own words.

GIFTED & TALENTED

Create a Travel Brochure Have students work in small groups to create a travel brochure encouraging people to visit Lower Egypt. Have students describe the kinds of work Egyptians were doing, tell what kind of food to expect, and include information about travel and trade at the time. Ask students to illustrate their brochures. Have each group present its travel brochure to the class.

Press (**mt**) *in the Student eEdition for modified text.*

See the Chapter Planner for more strategies for differentiation.

REVIEW & ASSESS

ANSWERS

1. As agriculture became more productive because of the Nile and farmers began to accumulate surpluses of food, populations grew and farmers grouped together to create larger communities. These growing villages and towns eventually became two kingdoms—Upper Egypt and Lower Egypt.

2. Ancient Egyptian farmers used irrigation to water their crops with floodwater saved in reservoirs and channeled through canals. They also used a tool called a *shaduf*, which made irrigation easier.

3. The land along the Nile is green on the map. It is green because of the vegetation that grows in the fertile black soil.

Egypt
Unites

Egypt's ancient civilization was unified for close to 3,000 years—twelve times as long as the United States has been a country. Of course, ancient Egypt witnessed its share of good rulers and good times and bad rulers and bad times. Still, ancient Egypt will be long remembered for its wealth and power.

MAIN IDEA

Strong kings united Egypt and ruled with the authority of gods.

DYNASTIES BEGIN

Egypt was governed by a long series of strong rulers. Exactly how Egypt united under a single ruler is uncertain. Tradition says that around 3100 B.C., the king of Upper Egypt conquered Lower Egypt and became ruler of all Egypt. Historians believe this king was called **Menes** (MEH-nehz). The complete unification of Egypt was probably a process that took place over the reigns of the kings who followed Menes. A double crown that combined the white crown of Upper Egypt with the red crown of Lower Egypt symbolized the newly unified country.

During this early period, the Egyptians built a magnificent new capital city at Memphis (MEHM-fihs). They also established the foundations of Egypt's political, economic, technological, artistic, and religious practices. The first kings founded a ruling **dynasty** (DY-nuh-stee)—a series of rulers from the same family. Egypt had 31 dynasties and was ruled by a total of more than 330 kings.

PHARAOHS RULE

Even though Egyptians did not call their kings **pharaoh** (FEHR-oh) until after 1000 B.C., the title is generally used for all Egyptian kings. The people used the term because they were afraid to speak the king's name. Why did the pharaoh inspire such fear in his subjects? He had complete authority over all religious, civil, and military matters. He exercised absolute power of life and death over everyone. A pharaoh was more than a man; he was worshipped as the son of Egypt's gods and a living god himself.

In Egypt, religion and government strongly overlapped. The pharaoh's main religious role was to keep harmony by maintaining communication between Egypt's people and their gods. He was high priest of every temple and led the most important ceremonies, especially the New Year rituals to ensure bountiful harvests. With this godly role came risk. Success reinforced the pharaoh's power. Defeat, disease, or famine threatened his authority.

On the government side, the pharaoh dictated all the important decisions. He also led his armies into battle as commander-in-chief. However, much of his day-to-day work was actually done by his **viziers** (vuh-ZEERZ), or chief officials. At first each pharaoh had one vizier. Later pharaohs had two viziers—one ran Upper Egypt and the other ran Lower Egypt. Thousands of lesser officials supported the viziers.

Most pharaohs were men and had many wives. Commonly, the eldest son of the pharaoh's principal wife inherited the throne. He often ruled alongside his father, learning on the job and ensuring a smooth succession (the passing of the throne to the next ruler) when the pharaoh died.

+ POSSIBLE RESPONSE
The double crown symbolized the uniting of Upper Egypt and Lower Egypt into one country.

Critical Viewing This carving shows a pharaoh wearing the double crown of Egypt. Why was it important for the pharaohs to wear the double crown?

REVIEW & ASSESS

1. **READING CHECK** What made the pharaohs of ancient Egypt so strong and powerful?

2. **DRAW CONCLUSIONS** Why would disease or famine threaten the pharaoh's authority over the people?

3. **ANALYZE LANGUAGE USE** Why does the text refer to Egypt's rulers as *strong*?

95

OBJECTIVE

Explain how strong kings united Egypt and ruled with the authority of gods.

CRITICAL THINKING SKILLS FOR LESSON 1.3

- Identify Main Ideas and Details
- Monitor Comprehension
- Draw Conclusions
- Analyze Language Use
- Analyze Cause and Effect
- Make Inferences
- Analyze Visuals

ESSENTIAL QUESTION

How did ancient Egypt's rulers use the land's resources and geography to found a civilization?

Egypt had strong kings. Lesson 1.3 explains how the kings had complete authority over all religious, civil, and military matters.

BACKGROUND FOR THE TEACHER

In addition to crediting Menes with the unification of Egypt, he is also considered the founder of the capital, Memphis, near present-day Cairo. Memphis was an important center during much of Egyptian history. It is located south of the Nile River delta, on the west bank of the river, about 24 kilometers (15 miles) south of modern Cairo. As a series of dynasties ruled Egypt for nearly three millennia, Egyptian culture flourished and remained distinctively Egyptian in its religion, arts, language, and customs.

DIGITAL RESOURCES myNGconnect.com

TEACHER RESOURCES & ASSESSMENT

 Reading and Note-Taking

 Vocabulary Practice

 Section 1 Quiz

STUDENT RESOURCES

 NG Chapter Gallery

INTRODUCE & ENGAGE

THINK, TALK, AND SHARE

Have students work in small groups. Ask each group to think about an elected government position in the United States. Then have students briefly tell about the kinds and amounts of authority an elected official in the United States has. Have them compare the authority of that elected official with the authority a pharaoh had. Ask one student from each group to present their ideas to the class. Tell students they will learn more about the rulers of Egypt in this lesson. **0:05** minutes

TEACH

GUIDED DISCUSSION

1. **Analyze Cause and Effect** For what reasons did ancient Egyptians respect the pharaoh's authority in the area of religion? (*A pharaoh was worshipped as the son of Egypt's gods and a living god himself. His main religious role was to maintain communication between Egypt's people and their gods.*)

2. **Make Inferences** Why might some of Egypt's pharaohs have been very capable and others less capable? (*The pharaohs were not chosen because of their intelligence or abilities. They inherited the throne regardless of their strengths and weaknesses.*)

ANALYZE VISUALS

Have students examine the photo of the carving showing a pharaoh wearing the double crown of Egypt. Invite volunteers to describe the crown. Make sure students understand that the crown represents the unification of Egypt. **0:10** minutes

ACTIVE OPTIONS

Critical Viewing: NG Chapter Gallery Invite students to explore the entire NG Image Gallery and create a Favorites List by choosing the images they find most interesting. If possible, have students copy the images into a document to form an actual list. Then encourage them to select the image they like best and do further research on it. **0:10** minutes

On Your Feet: Inside-Outside Circle Have students form concentric circles facing each other. Allow students time to write questions about the power and responsibilities of the pharaoh. Then have students in the inside circle pose questions to students in the outside circle. Have students switch roles. Students may ask for help from other students in their circle if they are unable to answer a question. **0:10** minutes

DIFFERENTIATE

INCLUSION

Expand the Main Idea Statement Pair each student with a proficient reader. Provide students with the expanded Main Idea statement below. Have students ask any clarifying questions before reading the lesson. To expand the Main Idea even further, ask students to add a sentence to the expanded statement after reading the lesson.

Historians believe the king of Upper Egypt conquered Lower Egypt and became ruler of all Egypt. This king and the rulers that followed had complete power over all matters in Egypt and were worshipped like gods.

ENGLISH LANGUAGE LEARNERS

Monitor Comprehension Monitor students' comprehension of important details in the lesson by asking them to answer either/or questions such as the following:

- Did the double crown represent Upper Egypt, Lower Egypt, or both Upper and Lower Egypt? (*both Upper and Lower Egypt*)

- Is a dynasty a series of rulers from different families or from the same family? (*the same family*)

- Did the pharaoh share power over religious matters or did he hold all the power? (*He held all the power.*)

- Did the pharaoh make important military decisions alone or with help from his lesser officials? (*alone*)

Press **(mt)** *in the Student eEdition for modified text.*

See the Chapter Planner for more strategies for differentiation.

REVIEW & ASSESS

ANSWERS

1. Pharaohs had complete authority over all aspects of governments and the power of life and death over all Egyptians. Egyptians believed pharaohs were living gods.

2. The pharaoh was supposed to control natural events, such as disease and crops. If he failed, that might mean he was not keeping the other gods happy.

3. In this sense of the word, *strong* means "powerful." Because the pharaoh had complete power in Egypt, he must be considered "strong."

Sensing Under the Surface

"Indiana Jones is so old school," laughs National Geographic Explorer Sarah Parcak. "I'm sorry, Indy, but things have moved on!" Parcak should know—she's a leading specialist in satellite archaeology. She is pioneering technology that archaeologists never would have dreamed of decades ago.

After identifying the likely location of an ancient city, Sarah Parcak and her team head for the site to begin the hands-on excavation. Together, technology and muscle power are revealing ancient Egypt.

MAIN IDEA

Sarah Parcak uses satellite imagery to guide her archaeological excavations in Egypt.

SATELLITE TECHNOLOGY

Sarah Parcak prepares for another tough day of searching beneath Egypt's desert for evidence of ancient Egyptian civilization and its people's daily lives. However, instead of digging, she boots up her laptop.

Parcak relies on remote sensing, using powerful infrared cameras mounted on satellites. These cameras use invisible rays of light to pinpoint even small objects buried beneath sand, soil, vegetation, or new buildings. "The Egyptians built with mud-bricks, which are denser than the surrounding soil," explains Parcak. "The infrared picks out this denser material. Computer programs refine the detail until we start to see recognizable shapes— houses, streets, temples, tombs, and pyramids. It's a real 'wow' moment."

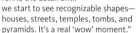
A satellite image of the Great Pyramid of Giza

Yet these revelations only happen after painstaking processing and analysis. "We don't just grab an image, flip it into the computer, and press a button. I've spent more than 10,000 hours of my life staring at satellite imagery to understand what I'm seeing," says Parcak. This effort pays off, saving enormous amounts of time and money. Before leading an expedition to Egypt, Parcak analyzed satellite imagery to figure out exactly where to dig. Within three weeks, she found about 70 sites. With traditional methods, this research would have taken around three and a half years.

MAPPING TANIS

Parcak's hard work has uncovered the main settlement area of Tanis, an important city in the eastern part of the Nile Delta. Over the centuries, Tanis was flooded and buried beneath Nile silt. Until recently only a tiny area had been excavated, but archaeologists, with the help of remote sensing, are changing that. Parcak turned the cameras onto Tanis with startling results. "We've created a map of this ancient city that's so clear it looks like something you'd use to navigate a town today," she says.

Excavations on the ground are proving the value of remote sensing. Scientists found an 80 percent match between the satellite image and the houses they unearthed. "This isn't just another 'gee whiz' toy," Parcak claims. "Less than one percent of ancient Egypt has been discovered and excavated, and, with the pressures of urbanization [the growth of cities], we're in a race against time. We need to use the most advanced tools to explore, map, and protect our past." Right now, satellites are just the tools for the job.

REVIEW & ASSESS

1. **READING CHECK** How does satellite imagery help guide Sarah Parcak's archaeological excavations in Egypt?

2. **COMPARE AND CONTRAST** What advantages does satellite archaeology have compared to more traditional methods of archaeology?

3. **MAKE INFERENCES** Why do you think urbanization creates a problem for the discovery and exploration of ancient Egyptian sites?

PLAN

OBJECTIVE

Explain how National Geographic Explorer Sarah Parcak uses satellite imagery to guide her archaeological excavations in Egypt.

CRITICAL THINKING SKILLS FOR LESSON 1.4

- Identify Main Ideas and Details
- Monitor Comprehension
- Compare and Contrast
- Make Inferences
- Evaluate
- Draw Conclusions
- Analyze Visuals

ESSENTIAL QUESTION

How did ancient Egypt's rulers use the land's resources and geography to found a civilization?

Egypt's geography and its resources affected the development of its civilization. Lesson 1.4 explains how National Geographic Explorer Sarah Parcak uses satellite imagery to get information about the land, geography, and civilization in ancient Egypt.

BACKGROUND FOR THE TEACHER

Sarah Parcak received her Bachelor's degree in Egyptology and Archaeological Studies from Yale University and her Ph.D. from Cambridge University. Parcak is an American archaeologist, space archaeologist, and Egyptologist who uses satellite imaging to identify potential archaeological sites in Egypt and Rome. Parcak believes that one of her most important contributions, however, is writing the first methodology book on satellite archaeology, which will allow the next generation of students to learn and advance the new field.

DIGITAL RESOURCES myNGconnect.com

TEACHER RESOURCES & ASSESSMENT

 Reading and Note-Taking   **Vocabulary Practice**   **Section 1 Quiz**

STUDENT RESOURCES

 NG Chapter Gallery

INTRODUCE & ENGAGE

NUMBERED HEADS

Organize students into groups of four and assign each student a number: one, two, three, or four. Tell students to think about and discuss a response to this question: *What would you like to learn about an ancient city in Egypt and the people who lived there?* Then call a number and have the student from each group with that number explain their group's response to the question. If time permits, repeat the process with an additional question: *What types of ancient artifacts from a region might give information about an ancient city and the people who lived there?* Tell students they will learn about the work of National Geographic Explorer Sarah Parcak in this lesson.

0:10 minutes

TEACH

GUIDED DISCUSSION

1. **Evaluate** How might the use of satellite imagery affect scientists' abilities to learn details about ancient civilizations? (*Satellite imagery can pinpoint even very small objects under the surface of the earth. This imagery can give accurate information to scientists about where to dig and what they might expect to find. It helps scientists explore and map things from the past in a way that saves much time and money.*)

2. **Draw Conclusions** Why might uncovering a city such as Tanis provide a wealth of information about ancient Egyptian society? (*The satellite imagery helped scientists map the ancient city of Tanis in great detail. It led to excavations that included unearthing many houses, which helped scientists understand more about how ancient Egyptians lived.*)

ANALYZE VISUALS

Have students examine the satellite image of the Great Pyramid of Giza. Ask students to describe what they see in the image. Then initiate a class discussion on the benefits of using satellite images in archaeology. **0:10** minutes

ACTIVE OPTIONS

NG Learning Framework: Learn More About Tanis

ATTITUDE: **Curiosity**
KNOWLEDGE: **Our Human Story**

Have students review the information about National Geographic Explorer Sarah Parcak. Then have them do research about the ancient city of Tanis and the tombs and treasures archaeologists have found there. **ASK:** What can scientists learn about ancient Egypt and its people from the burial chambers and the objects found at Tanis? **0:10** minutes

On Your Feet: Create a Quiz Organize students into two teams and have each team write ten True-False questions about using satellite imagery to guide archaeological excavations in Egypt. Then have each team answer the questions the other team created. Review the student answers as a class and have teams keep track of their number of correct answers. **0:15** minutes

DIFFERENTIATE

STRIVING READERS

Pose and Answer Questions Have students work in pairs to read the lesson. Instruct them to pause after each paragraph and ask one another a *who, what, when, where,* or *why* question about what they have just read. Suggest students use a 5Ws Chart to help organize their questions and answers.

GIFTED & TALENTED

Write a Documentary Script Have students conduct research about the work of Sarah Parcak. Tell them to write a five-minute documentary about Sarah that focuses on her use of satellite imagery to guide her archaeological excavations. Students should include information about the value of satellite imagery as well as the importance of doing hands-on excavations. Have students present their documentary scripts to the class.

Press (**mt**) *in the Student eEdition for modified text.*

See the Chapter Planner for more strategies for differentiation.

REVIEW & ASSESS

ANSWERS

1. Satellite imagery helps Sarah Parcak figure out where to dig by revealing details of objects, houses, streets, temples, tombs, and pyramids buried beneath sand, soil, vegetation, or new buildings.

2. Because of the accuracy of the satellite imagery captured by powerful infrared cameras, space archaeology can save archaeologists enormous amounts of time and money in locating excavation sites.

3. With urbanization, large populations of people need more land and resources and more buildings in which to live. That means people are always building new structures over ancient Egyptian sites that have not yet been excavated. Urbanization could literally pave over the past of ancient Egypt.

2.1

The Old Kingdom

It is taller than the Statue of Liberty, twice the area of the U.S. Capitol building, double the volume of the Rose Bowl Stadium, and 4,500 years older than all of them. For thousands of years, the Great Pyramid of Khufu was the largest structure on the planet.

MAIN IDEA

Old Kingdom pharaohs demonstrated their power by building monumental pyramids.

The great pyramids of Giza dwarf the human figures nearby. These imposing structures would have awed the average Egyptian in ancient times, just as they amaze visitors today.

PYRAMIDS ALONG THE NILE

The **Old Kingdom** was Egypt's first great period of unity and prosperity, lasting from around 2700 B.C. to 2200 B.C. During these centuries, Egypt prospered under effective pharaohs, a strong central government, and an efficient administration. As Egyptian power grew, trade, technology, building, writing, and art also flourished. The pharaohs used their enormous wealth and power to build the **pyramids** (PEER-uh-mihdz), massive monumental tombs to house their dead bodies. The pyramids represented the Egyptian belief that life is a passageway to the afterlife, an existence believed to follow death. As a result, people made careful preparations for death.

Egyptian kings were originally buried beneath low mud-brick buildings. Around 2650 B.C., King Djoser (JOH-sur) took this idea to the next level—literally. Djoser's talented vizier, Imhotep (ihm-HOH-tehp), designed a 200-foot-high tomb made of giant steps. Beneath this step pyramid was a maze of chambers packed with items for the pharaoh's spirit to use in the afterlife. A huge complex of buildings and temples surrounded the step pyramid, creating a palace where the king's spirit could live in luxury for eternity.

THE GREAT PYRAMID

In Giza (GEE-zuh), near Cairo, the Great Pyramid of **Khufu** (KOO-foo) dominates the skyline. It is so extraordinarily huge that historians once assumed Khufu had been a cruel tyrant who used brutal methods to build it. In fact, he probably employed farmers unable to farm during the annual floods. Even so, Khufu must have commanded exceptional power and wealth to build his Great Pyramid.

The pyramids were an impressive achievement for a civilization with limited technology. Using copper tools, ropes, sleds, and ramps, some 18,000 workers quarried, cut, and precisely placed 2.3 million two-and-a-half-ton limestone and granite blocks. It took 20 years. The pyramid they built was symmetrical—all sides were the same. It covered 571,158 square feet and stood 481 feet high. Deep inside were Khufu's tomb and treasure. Two other large pyramids were built in Giza by Khufu's successors, Menkaure (mehn-KO-ray) and Khafre (KAH-fray). Khafre also built the Great Sphinx

(sfihnks), a symbol of divine power with a lion's body and Khafre's head. The sphinx was carved out of a huge piece of limestone.

The Great Pyramid was a powerful symbol of the pharaoh's status as a living god and the unity of religion and government in Egypt. A proper burial within the great tomb would ensure the pharaoh's smooth passage to life after death. Until then, a vast city of pyramid builders surrounded Giza. Here, too, were palaces and government buildings that allowed the pharaoh to run the country while building his home for the afterlife.

REVIEW & ASSESS

1. **READING CHECK** Why did Old Kingdom pharaohs build pyramids?

2. **DESCRIBE** What was new and different about the design of King Djoser's burial building?

3. **DRAW CONCLUSIONS** What do the pyramids reveal about Egyptian society?

98 CHAPTER 4

Ancient Egypt **99**

PLAN

OBJECTIVE

Explain how Old Kingdom pharaohs demonstrated their power by building monumental pyramids.

CRITICAL THINKING SKILLS FOR LESSON 2.1

- Identify Main Ideas and Details
- Monitor Comprehension
- Describe
- Draw Conclusions
- Summarize
- Make Inferences
- Analyze Visuals

ESSENTIAL QUESTION

How did ancient Egypt's rulers use the land's resources and geography to found a civilization?

The Egyptian pyramids remain today as evidence of an advanced civilization. Lesson 2.1 discusses the purpose of the pyramids, explains how they were built, and describes the largest of them.

BACKGROUND FOR THE TEACHER

Initially, the Great Pyramid of Khufu stood 481 feet high. Over time, erosion has worn away the limestone and granite surface that once covered the outside of the pyramid. As a result, today the Great Pyramid is only 449 feet tall.

The interior of the Great Pyramid has three separate burial chambers. Ancient Egyptians believed that the dead could enjoy earthly possessions, so they filled burial chambers with clothes, food, and furniture for that purpose.

DIGITAL RESOURCES myNGconnect.com

TEACHER RESOURCES & ASSESSMENT

 Reading and Note-Taking

 Vocabulary Practice

 Section 2 Quiz

STUDENT RESOURCES

 NG Chapter Gallery

98 CHAPTER 4

INTRODUCE & ENGAGE

TEAM WORD WEBBING

Organize students into teams of four and give each team a large sheet of paper, like the one shown, with the word *pyramids* in the center. Give each student a different colored marker. Encourage students to write what they already know about the pyramids. Prompt students to rotate the paper clockwise every 60 seconds. After students have written on all four sides of the paper, have a spokesperson from each team summarize what the team knows about the pyramids. Tell students they will learn more about Egyptian pyramids in this lesson. At the conclusion of the lesson, you may want to return to this activity to verify accuracy of the information students offered. **0:05** minutes

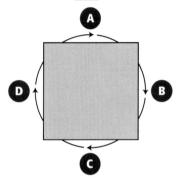

TEACH

GUIDED DISCUSSION

1. **Summarize** How did Egyptian workers build monumental pyramids with limited technology? *(Approximately 18,000 workers used copper tools, ropes, sleds, and ramps to quarry, cut, move, and place the heavy stone blocks that were used to build the pyramids.)*

2. **Make Inferences** Why did cities arise near Giza? *(Many workers were needed to build the pyramids at Giza. They needed places to live, leaders, and government services located close to the place at which they were working.)*

ANALYZE VISUALS

Have students examine the photo of the great pyramids of Giza. Ask small groups of students to brainstorm a list of adjectives that describe the pyramids. Have students share their adjectives with the class. **0:10** minutes

ACTIVE OPTIONS

NG Learning Framework: Discuss the Importance of Pyramids

ATTITUDE: **Responsibility**
SKILL: **Collaboration**

Invite small groups of students to discuss the importance of the pyramids in ancient Egypt. **ASK:** What do the pyramids tell us about the respect the ancient Egyptians had for their pharaohs?

What do the pyramids tell us about the importance of religion in Egyptian society? Ask each person in every group to contribute his or her ideas. Encourage students to listen quietly and politely when another person is talking. **0:10** minutes

On Your Feet: Fishbowl Use a Fishbowl strategy to have students discuss the pyramids in ancient Egypt. Instruct students in the inside circle to discuss the significance of the pyramids while the outside circle listens. Then call on volunteers in the outside circle to summarize what they heard. Have students switch places and ask those now on the inside to discuss how the pyramids were built and how the building of the pyramids affected the growth of communities. The outside circle should listen and then summarize what they heard. **0:10** minutes

DIFFERENTIATE

GIFTED & TALENTED

Build Models Work with students to build three-dimensional paper models of the pyramids. Pair students up and give each pair a large sheet of paper and a template for a six-inch square and a six-inch equilateral triangle. Instruct them to trace the square in the middle of the paper. Next, have them trace an equilateral triangle off of each side of the square, so that the base of each triangle is one of the sides of the square. Now tell them to cut out the diagram and then fold each triangle along the edge attached to the square. They will see how the points come together to form the pyramid. Students may use tape to hold the sides in place.

Press **mt** *in the Student eEdition for modified text.*

See the Chapter Planner for more strategies for differentiation.

REVIEW & ASSESS

ANSWERS

1. Old Kingdom pharaohs used their wealth and power to build the pyramids as monumental tombs where their dead bodies could be guarded and their immortal spirits could live in luxury for eternity.

2. King Djoser's pyramid was the first completely stone building. Its design looked like a series of giant steps.

3. The pyramids reveal much about ancient Egyptian culture and religion. They also demonstrate the engineering skills of ancient Egyptians.

Daily Life and Religion

There's a saying that "you can't take it with you" when you die. But Egyptians did! In fact, they were buried with everything they might need in the afterlife. The graves of wealthy Egyptians contained food, furniture, and jewelry. The Egyptians were ready for anything.

MAIN IDEA

The Egyptians had strong beliefs about religion and burial that affected all social classes.

Eight Gods of Ancient Egypt

Horus Sky god

Hathor Goddess of love, birth, and death

Re God of the sun (sometimes called Ra)

Nut Sky goddess

Anubis God of the dead

Osiris God of agriculture and judge of the dead

Isis Wife of Osiris and mother of Horus

Thoth God of writing, counting, and wisdom

EGYPTIAN SOCIETY

Ancient Egypt's society was a **hierarchy** (HY-rar-kee), meaning that people belonged to different social classes and each class had a rank in society. The social structure resembled Egypt's pyramids. At the top was the pharaoh, the all-powerful ruler and living god.

Beneath the pharaoh came the priests and nobles who ran the country and army. At the next step in the pyramid were all the officials and scribes who kept the government running smoothly by collecting taxes, organizing building projects, and keeping records. Beneath the officials and scribes were craftsmen and merchants. Farmers formed the next layer, and at the bottom came unskilled laborers and slaves who did all the hardest work.

Unlike in Mesopotamia, Egyptian women shared some rights with men. They could own property, conduct business, and take part in court cases. Poorer women often worked alongside their husbands, but they could do almost any job. Still, a woman's main role was to be a wife and raise children.

EGYPTIAN GODS

Like the people of Mesopotamia, the Egyptians believed in multiple gods. Modern scholars know 1,500 of them by name. The Egyptians believed that the gods controlled every aspect of life and death. The most important god was **Re** (RAY), the sun god, who created the world. The Egyptians also worshipped Osiris (oh-SY-rihs), the god of the underworld. The god Anubis (uh-NOO-bihs) weighed each dead person's heart against the weight of an ostrich feather. If the person was good, his or her heart would weigh the same as the feather, and the person would be admitted to the afterlife.

These beliefs encouraged Egyptians to lead good lives and take burial seriously. They believed a dead person's spirit needed food and a body to live in. The spirit would need to recognize the body after death. That is why the bodies of pharaohs and other powerful people were preserved as **mummies**. Specialized workers removed and preserved the internal organs (except for the heart, which Anubis had to weigh). Then the workers dried out the body and wrapped it in linen. Last, the body was placed in a coffin, and priests performed special rituals that were intended to give life to the mummy.

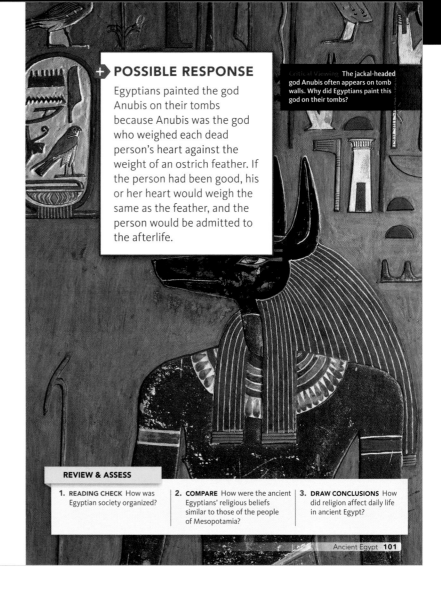

Critical Viewing The jackal-headed god Anubis often appears on tomb walls. Why did Egyptians paint this god on their tombs?

✛ POSSIBLE RESPONSE

Egyptians painted the god Anubis on their tombs because Anubis was the god who weighed each dead person's heart against the weight of an ostrich feather. If the person had been good, his or her heart would weigh the same as the feather, and the person would be admitted to the afterlife.

REVIEW & ASSESS

1. **READING CHECK** How was Egyptian society organized?

2. **COMPARE** How were the ancient Egyptians' religious beliefs similar to those of the people of Mesopotamia?

3. **DRAW CONCLUSIONS** How did religion affect daily life in ancient Egypt?

PLAN

OBJECTIVE

Explain how the strong beliefs the Egyptians had about religion and burial affected all social classes.

CRITICAL THINKING SKILLS FOR LESSON 2.2

- Identify Main Ideas and Details
- Monitor Comprehension
- Compare
- Draw Conclusions
- Describe
- Summarize
- Analyze Visuals

ESSENTIAL QUESTION

How did ancient Egypt's rulers use the land's resources and geography to found a civilization?

The Egyptians' strong beliefs about religion and burial affected all parts of their society. Lesson 2.2 discusses the hierarchy in Egyptian society and the importance of religion and burial in Egyptian civilization.

BACKGROUND FOR THE TEACHER

When they preserved mummies, the Egyptians began by covering the body with a salty substance to dry it out. Once the body was dry, they used lotions on the skin to preserve it. The heart was left in the body because it was considered to be the center of intelligence. They then wrapped the entire body in layers of linen and glued the layers together. The total process could take up to 40 days. Once the body was all wrapped, it was covered in a sheet and placed in a stone coffin called a sarcophagus.

DIGITAL RESOURCES myNGconnect.com

TEACHER RESOURCES & ASSESSMENT

 Reading and Note-Taking   **Vocabulary Practice**   **Section 2 Quiz**

STUDENT RESOURCES

 NG Chapter Gallery

CORNERS

Divide the class into four groups. Then give each group one of the following concepts:

- Lives of pharaohs
- Lives of everyday people
- Religion
- Building of pyramids

Have each group of students create a list of questions about their topic. Then have at least one student from each group share the group's questions with the class. Tell students they will learn about daily life and religion in ancient Egypt. After students read the lesson, have them answer their questions. **0:10** minutes

TEACH

GUIDED DISCUSSION

1. **Describe** What was the role of women in ancient Egyptian society? (*Women shared some rights with men. They could own property and do almost any job. However, their main role was to be a wife and mother.*)

2. **Summarize** For what reason were bodies of pharaohs and other important people preserved as mummies? (*The Egyptians believed that a dead person's spirit needed a body in which to live. They also believed that the spirit would need to recognize the body after death.*)

ANALYZE VISUALS

Have students examine the picture of the tomb wall. Ask them to discuss the images that relate to nature and make inferences about the significance of these images. **0:10** minutes

ACTIVE OPTIONS

Critical Viewing: NG Chapter Gallery Ask students to choose one image from the Chapter Gallery and become an expert on it. They should do additional research to learn all about it. Then, students should share their findings with a partner, small group, or the class. **0:10** minutes

On Your Feet: Chart Relay Tape large pieces of paper to the wall in different locations of the classroom. Have students work in teams of three. Provide each team with a bold marker and one of the sheets of paper. Tell them to label three columns on their paper: Egyptian Hierarchy, Egyptian Gods, and Mummies. Allow teams to think of three facts about each topic. Individual team members are each responsible for one fact. Then, on your signal, have teams write their facts on the charts. The first team that finishes wins. **0:15** minutes

DIFFERENTIATE

STRIVING READERS

Use Exit Slips Preview the following questions before reading the lesson.

- What does it mean when we say that ancient Egypt's society was a hierarchy?
- Who was at the top of the Egyptian hierarchy?
- What do you know about whether the Egyptians believed in gods?

After reading the lesson, direct students to provide a written response to each question. Pass out strips of paper. Have students write their responses on the paper strips. Then ask students to turn in their written responses as they exit the class.

PRE-AP

Research an Egyptian God Have students do research to learn more about one of the eight gods of ancient Egypt. Then have them write and illustrate a book about the god. Have them include ideas about how the god may have influenced Egyptian life.

Press (**mt**) *in the Student eEdition for modified text.*
See the Chapter Planner for more strategies for differentiation.

REVIEW & ASSESS

ANSWERS

1. Ancient Egypt's society was a hierarchy. People belonged to different social classes and each class had a rank in society. The social structure resembled a pyramid. At the top was the pharaoh, then priests and nobles, then the officials and scribes, then the craftsmen and merchants, then farmers. At the bottom were unskilled laborers and slaves who did the hardest work.

2. Similar to the Mesopotamians, ancient Egyptians practiced polytheism. They believed in many different gods and goddesses who controlled every aspect of life and death.

3. Religious beliefs encouraged Egyptians to lead good lives and take burial seriously.

DOCUMENT-BASED QUESTION
Life, Death, and Religion

The majority of ancient Egyptians could not read or write. Still, a vast amount of writing has survived in the form of official records, business transactions, religious texts, technical manuals, and stories. These documents tell us a lot about life in ancient Egypt.

ANSWERS

DOCUMENT 1
By reciting this religious poem in praise of the Nile River each year, ancient Egyptians probably hoped to ensure another successful flooding of the Nile, which brought them much needed water and fertile soil.

DOCUMENT 2
It suggests that Re is responsible for causing the sun to rise and for keeping the world running.

DOCUMENT 3
It can be inferred that Egyptians associated Re with other forms of nature in addition to the sun. It shows that Re was connected with all parts of the natural world.

The ancient Egyptian *Book of the Dead* helped archaeologists learn much about the civilization's religious beliefs. Here, a section of the book illustrates a vision of the afterlife that closely resembles the living world.

DOCUMENT ONE
Primary Source: Poem

from *Hymn to the Nile*, c. 2100 B.C., translated by Paul Guieysse
Hymn to the Nile is a religious poem. It may have been read aloud at festivals celebrating the annual Nile flood. It has about 200 lines divided into 14 verses, although historians are not sure how the verses should be read. The hymn praises the Nile as the source of all life in Egypt. It expresses the people's joy when the flood brings water and silt and their misery when the flood fails. The author is unknown.

> Hail to thee, O Nile!
> Who manifests [reveals] thyself over this land, and comes to give life to Egypt!
> Mysterious is thy issuing forth from the darkness, on this day whereon it is celebrated!
> Watering the orchards created by Re, to cause all the cattle to live, you give the earth to drink, inexhaustible one!

CONSTRUCTED RESPONSE Why might ancient Egyptians have wanted to praise the Nile River each year by reciting this religious poem?

DOCUMENT TWO
Primary Source: Sacred Text

from the *Book of the Dead*, 1240 B.C., translated by E.A. Wallis Budge
The *Book of the Dead* was a series of texts that contained around 200 spells for helping the dead reach the afterlife. The texts were usually placed in the coffin or in the mummy's wrappings. This passage describes the sun god's journey as he rises and sets each day.

> The gods are glad [when] they see Re in his rising; his beams flood the world with light. The majesty of the god, who is to be feared, sets forth and comes unto the land of Manu [a sacred place]; he makes bright the earth at his birth each day; he comes unto the place where he was yesterday.

CONSTRUCTED RESPONSE What does this passage suggest about Re's role in ancient Egyptian beliefs?

DOCUMENT THREE
Primary Source: Artifact

Sun God Re in Falcon Form, Ancient Egypt
This statue depicts Re, god of the sun and creator of Earth.

CONSTRUCTED RESPONSE What can you infer about Re's connection to nature from his representation in this statue?

SYNTHESIZE & WRITE

1. **REVIEW** Review what you have learned about ancient Egyptian religious beliefs from the text and these documents.

2. **RECALL** On your own paper, write down the main idea expressed in the artifact and in each document.

3. **CONSTRUCT** Construct a topic sentence that answers this question: What did the Egyptians believe about their gods' control of their world?

4. **WRITE** Using the evidence from the artifact and documents, write an informative paragraph that supports your topic sentence in Step 3.

PLAN

OBJECTIVE
Synthesize information about life, death, and religion in ancient Egypt from primary source documents.

CRITICAL THINKING SKILLS FOR LESSON 2.3

- Synthesize
- Identify
- Draw Conclusions
- Describe
- Evaluate

ESSENTIAL QUESTION
How did ancient Egypt's rulers use the land's resources and geography to found a civilization?

The Egyptians had very strong religious beliefs. Lesson 2.3 provides several examples from primary sources of the importance of religion in Egyptian society.

BACKGROUND FOR THE TEACHER
The *Book of the Dead* was an ancient Egyptian funerary text. It contained spells and illustrations that, according to Egyptian belief, gave a dead person the knowledge and power he or she needed to journey safely through the dangers of the netherworld (a place the dead went immediately after death). The spells also spoke of the ultimate goal of every ancient Egyptian—eternal life. Written by many priests over about 1,000 years, the *Book of the Dead* was put into use at the beginning of the New Kingdom.

DIGITAL RESOURCES myNGconnect.com

TEACHER RESOURCES & ASSESSMENT

 Reading and Note-Taking

 Vocabulary Practice

 Section 2 Quiz

STUDENT RESOURCES

 NG Chapter Gallery

INTRODUCE & ENGAGE

PREPARE FOR THE DOCUMENT-BASED QUESTION

Before students start on the activity, briefly preview the three documents. Remind students that a constructed response requires full explanations in complete sentences. Emphasize that students should use their knowledge of ancient Egyptian society and religious beliefs as well as information in the documents. **0:05** minutes

TEACH

GUIDED DISCUSSION

1. **Identify** What does the hymn say about the Egyptian people's responses to the annual Nile flood? *(The hymn says that people are joyful about the annual Nile flood.)*

2. **Draw Conclusions** What does the text from the *Book of the Dead* tell us about the role of religion in the lives of the ancient Egyptians? *(The text indicates that Egyptians had a strong religious belief that life on Earth was a passageway to the afterlife.)*

3. **Describe** Which words or phrases would you use to describe this artifact of Sun God Re? *(Responses will vary. Possible responses: looks like a falcon; has a model of the earth on his head; model or sculpture)*

EVALUATE

After students have completed the "Synthesize & Write" activity, allow time for them to exchange paragraphs and read and comment on the work of their peers. Guidelines for comments should be established prior to this activity so that feedback is constructive and encouraging in nature. **0:15** minutes

ACTIVE OPTIONS

NG Learning Framework: Review Information About the Nile

SKILL: Collaboration
KNOWLEDGE: **Our Living Planet**

Have pairs of students revisit Lessons 1.1 and 1.2 to review information about the Nile River. **ASK:** How was the Nile River important to the development of Egyptian civilization? What does the poem *Hymn to the Nile* tell you about how the Egyptians felt about the Nile? **0:10** minutes

On Your Feet: Three Options Label three locations in the room with the name of one of the documents featured in the lesson. Have students reread the lesson and walk to the corner of the room with the document that best helped support their understanding or further their interest in life, death, and religion in ancient Egypt. Have students who chose the same document discuss why they made their selection. Then have volunteers from each group explain what their document is and offer some of the group's reasons for choosing that one. **0:20** minutes

DIFFERENTIATE

INCLUSION

Work in Pairs Consider pairing students with disabilities with students able to read the documents aloud to them. You may also want to give students the option of recording their responses.

PRE-AP

Debate Contributions Ask students to research the many contributions of ancient Egypt to civilization. Tell each student to choose a contribution they believe had the greatest impact and make a list of the reasons that explain why. Suggest that students hold a panel discussion to share and debate their contribution choices.

Press **mt** *in the Student eEdition for modified text.*

See the Chapter Planner for more strategies for differentiation.

SYNTHESIZE & WRITE

ANSWERS

1. Responses will vary but should show a comprehension of the materials.

2. Responses will vary but should specifically reference the sources.

3. Possible response: The Egyptians believed that the gods controlled every aspect of life and death.

4. Students' paragraphs should include their topic sentence from Step 3 and provide several details from the documents to support the sentence.

The Middle Kingdom

First comes the thunder of hooves, then the whistling of arrows. Through the dust of battle bursts a line of horse-drawn chariots. From these wheeled wooden platforms, enemy archers rain arrows into your ranks before crashing through them, scattering your Egyptian army. These foreign war machines are effective; it's time to adopt, adapt, and fight back.

MAIN IDEA

The Middle Kingdom was strong and peaceful between periods of weakness and foreign rule.

CONFLICT AND STABILITY

The peace and prosperity of the Old Kingdom gave way to chaos and war between rival Egyptian groups around 2200 B.C. Building monumental tombs had drained the royal treasury. Water shortages and famines made the people doubt the pharaoh's power as a living god. The kingdom descended into a long period of conflict within its borders.

Then, around 2040 B.C., a king named Mentuhotep II (mehn-too-HOH-tehp) reunited the kingdom and launched a new era of peace and prosperity known as the **Middle Kingdom**. This period

lasted until about 1650 B.C. During the Middle Kingdom, the pharaohs restored the power of the centralized government. Farmers expanded agriculture into new regions, and the building of great monuments, including pyramids, resumed.

The pharaohs also pursued an active foreign policy to increase Egypt's wealth. Trade expanded greatly. Egypt's trade network reached to several nearby lands and possibly as far as East Africa. To support and expand the prosperity of the Middle Kingdom, the pharaohs increased Egypt's military power. In the northeast, they conquered lands along the eastern Mediterranean. They also extended Egypt's southern border further up the Nile by leading successful military campaigns against the kingdoms of Nubia (NOO-bee-uh).

INVADERS

Egypt's wealth made a tempting target. One group of foreigners, the **Hyksos** (HIHK-sohs), came to live in Egypt and rose to power in Lower Egypt. The Hyksos brought an end to the Middle Kingdom.

Hyksos means "rulers of foreign lands," and, from their capital Avaris (AH-var-ihs) in the Nile Delta, they controlled much of Egypt for more than 100 years. The Hyksos probably ruled pretty much as the pharaohs had, adopting native ways and practices. Even so, native Egyptians resented being under foreign rule. Finally, in Upper Egypt, King **Ahmose** (AH-mohz) rebelled. The Hyksos brought to the battlefield deadly new tools including horse-drawn chariots, powerful new bows, curved swords, and body armor. Ahmose adopted these deadly weapons and threw the invaders out of Egypt.

Although Ahmose reunited Egypt under native Egyptian rule, he faced new challenges. Egypt had been largely on its own for centuries, but now the pharaohs had to deal with the wider world. Armed with their new military might, the pharaohs set out to forge an empire.

POSSIBLE RESPONSE

The depiction shows that the Egyptians considered the pharaoh to be the son of Egypt's gods and a living god himself.

Critical Viewing This pendant depicts the pharaoh Ahmose being purified by the gods Re and Amun. Why is the pharaoh shown with the gods?

REVIEW & ASSESS

1. **READING CHECK** Who were the Hyksos?

2. **ANALYZE CAUSE AND EFFECT** Why did the pharaohs lose control of the Old Kingdom?

3. **SEQUENCE EVENTS** What events marked Egypt's movements back and forth between disorder and order?

PLAN

OBJECTIVE

Describe the Middle Kingdom as strong and peaceful between periods of weakness and foreign rule.

CRITICAL THINKING SKILLS FOR LESSON 2.4

- Identify Main Ideas and Details
- Monitor Comprehension
- Analyze Cause and Effect
- Sequence Events
- Describe
- Summarize
- Analyze Visuals

ESSENTIAL QUESTION

How did ancient Egypt's rulers use the land's resources and geography to found a civilization?

The Middle Kingdom had strong and successful periods in which its civilization advanced. It also had periods of weakness and foreign invasion. Lesson 2.4 discusses some of the changes and events that occurred during the Middle Kingdom.

BACKGROUND FOR THE TEACHER

The Egyptians achieved much during the Middle Kingdom. New styles and techniques in art developed, including art that was produced using large blocks of stone. New irrigation projects were also developed on the west bank of the Nile in Lower Egypt, which increased harvests. Writing changed, too. Before the Middle Kingdom, Egyptians used writing for record-keeping and for honoring the gods and goddesses. In the Middle Kingdom, Egyptians began to use writing to tell stories.

DIGITAL RESOURCES myNGconnect.com

TEACHER RESOURCES & ASSESSMENT

 Reading and Note-Taking

 Vocabulary Practice

 Section 2 Quiz

STUDENT RESOURCES

 NG Chapter Gallery

INTRODUCE & ENGAGE

ROUNDTABLE

Have students sit in groups of four. Prompt them to talk about the importance of the Nile River to the development of civilization of Egypt. **ASK:** How might changes in the annual Nile flooding cycle have affected Egypt? Encourage each student to contribute ideas about the effect on Egypt. Tell students they will learn about how changes in the Nile affected the Middle Kingdom in this lesson. `0:05` minutes

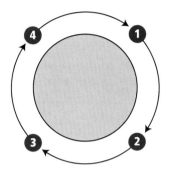

TEACH

GUIDED DISCUSSION

1. **Describe** What was Egypt's trade policy during the Middle Kingdom? *(Trade expanded greatly. The trade network reached to several nearby lands and possibly as far as East Africa.)*

2. **Summarize** How did the pharaoh's increased military power help expand the Middle Kingdom? *(In the northeast, the pharaohs conquered lands along the eastern Mediterranean.They extended Egypt's southern border farther up the Nile by leading successful military campaigns against the kingdoms of Nubia.)*

ANALYZE VISUALS

Have students examine the depiction of Ahmose being purified by the gods. Ask them to discuss the influence and power of the pharaohs in the daily lives of Egyptians. `0:15` minutes

ACTIVE OPTIONS

NG Learning Framework: Review Information About the Middle Kingdom

ATTITUDE: **Empowerment**
SKILL: **Problem-Solving**

Invite students to review the information in Lesson 2.4 about the Middle Kingdom. **ASK:** How might you have done things differently from King Mentuhotep and other kings of the Middle Kingdom? How would your actions have affected the successes in the Middle Kingdom? How would your actions have affected how long the Middle Kingdom controlled Egypt? `0:10` minutes

On Your Feet: Turn and Talk on Topic Have students form three to five groups. Give each group this topic sentence: *When the Hyksos rose to power in Egypt, many changes followed.* Tell students to build a paragraph on that topic by having each student in the group contribute one sentence. Allow each group to present its paragraph to the class by having each student read her or his statement. `0:10` minutes

DIFFERENTIATE

ENGLISH LANGUAGE LEARNERS

Complete Sentence Starters Provide these sentence starters for students to complete after reading.

- At the end of the Old Kingdom, a great deal of money was spent on building monumental tombs called _____.

- Mentuhotep II started an era of peace and prosperity known as the _____.

- A group of outsiders who brought an end to the Middle Kingdom was called the _____.

GIFTED & TALENTED

Present a Report Have students work in small groups to do research about famous pieces of art, artifacts, and buildings inspired by the religion of the ancient Egyptians. Instruct them to prepare a report based on their research. Encourage students to include visuals such as photographs or drawings to illustrate the report. Have each group present its report to the class.

Press (**mt**) *in the Student eEdition for modified text.*

See the Chapter Planner for more strategies for differentiation.

REVIEW & ASSESS

ANSWERS

1. The Hyksos were foreign invaders who seized control of Lower Egypt, made Upper Egypt dependent on them, and controlled much of Egypt for more than 100 years.

2. They had spent too many resources on royal tombs, and the nobility no longer followed them.

3. There was a war between rival groups after the pharaohs lost control of the Old Kingdom. Mentuhotep reunited Egypt and initiated the Middle Kingdom. The next period of disorder was brought about by the invasion of the Hyksos, a group. Then Egypt returned to a time of order when Ahmose reunited the country again.

This statue shows Hatshepsut wearing the false beard traditionally worn by the male pharaohs.

3.1 Hatshepsut Expands Trade

At any grocery store, you can find exotic fruits from distant lands right alongside the crunchy apples from a nearby orchard. Like you, the ancient Egyptians had access to food and other goods from near and far.

MAIN IDEA

Under a great female pharaoh, Egypt grew wealthy through conquest and trade.

EGYPT'S GREAT FEMALE RULER

On the heels of the defeat of the Hyksos came the **New Kingdom**, which spanned nearly 500 years from 1550 B.C. to 1070 B.C. This period of prosperity saw Egypt grow more powerful than ever as it built a mighty empire. Its large professional army expanded the empire northeast into Palestine and south into Nubia. Plunder from war and taxes from conquered lands made Egypt rich, but so did trade. Under the rule of **Hatshepsut** (haht-SHEHP-soot), history's earliest well-known female ruler, trade flourished.

Hatshepsut came to power sometime around 1470 B.C. After her husband the pharaoh died, she ruled with her stepson, Thutmose III (thoot-MOH-suh), who was very young. Hatshepsut played a smart political game and won enough support to be crowned sole king. She performed all the religious, military, and political functions of the pharaoh, and she even dressed as a king.

TRADE AND EXPANSION

Like other pharaohs, Hatshepsut fought wars to expand the empire, but she also promoted trade. Egypt had abundant resources to **barter**, or exchange, for things the land couldn't produce—especially timber and exotic luxuries. These goods traveled along trade routes and pathways established by traders over land and sea. Hatshepsut sent expeditions as far as East Africa. Egyptian merchants and traders bartered Egyptian beer, wine, food, and manufactured goods for myrrh trees, incense, ebony, ivory, leopard skins, and monkeys. The wealth generated through these expeditions stimulated Egypt's economy and funded great building projects.

Back in Egypt, Hatshepsut moved the capital city to Thebes and ordered many great monuments constructed to celebrate her rule. After 15 years in power, she disappeared suspiciously, possibly murdered by her stepson. Thutmose III became a mighty pharaoh in his own right and tried to erase Hatshepsut's name from all monuments and records. Luckily for future generations, he did not entirely succeed. Instead, a solid trail of clues has alowed historians to reconstruct Hatshepsut's remarkable reign.

REVIEW & ASSESS

1. **READING CHECK** In what ways did Egypt prosper during the reign of Hatshepsut?

2. **DRAW CONCLUSIONS** Why did the pharaohs engage in trade with other countries?

3. **FORM AND SUPPORT OPINIONS** What details support the opinion that Hatshepsut was an ambitious leader?

PLAN

OBJECTIVE

Explain how Egypt grew wealthy through conquest and trade under a female pharaoh.

CRITICAL THINKING SKILLS FOR LESSON 3.1

- Identify Main Ideas and Details
- Monitor Comprehension
- Draw Conclusions
- Form and Support Opinions
- Summarize
- Describe

ESSENTIAL QUESTION

How did ancient Egypt's rulers use the land's resources and geography to found a civilization?

Egyptians continued to use their vast resources to further develop their civilization. Lesson 3.1 discusses how Egypt grew wealthy under the leadership of a female pharaoh.

BACKGROUND FOR THE TEACHER

Hatshepsut's rule was a time of prosperity and peace. During this time, magnificent art was produced in Egypt. The time of her reign also included a number of large building projects, including her memorial temple at Deir el-Bahri. She was the widowed queen of the pharaoh Thutmose II. She had been given power after his death to rule for her young stepson, Thutmose III, until he came of age. At first, Hatshepsut acted on her stepson's behalf. But before long, she proclaimed herself pharaoh, the supreme power in Egypt.

DIGITAL RESOURCES myNGconnect.com

TEACHER RESOURCES & ASSESSMENT

 Reading and Note-Taking

 Vocabulary Practice

 Section 3 Quiz

STUDENT RESOURCES

 Biography

INTRODUCE & ENGAGE

ACTIVATE PRIOR KNOWLEDGE

Have students brainstorm ways in which the trading of goods is part of today's society. Have students think about various foods, clothing items, and building materials that come from other parts of the country or from other countries. **ASK:** How did trading food and other goods affect Egyptian society during the New Kingdom? Tell students that, in this lesson, they will learn about trade under the reign of Hatshepsut. `0:05` **minutes**

TEACH

GUIDED DISCUSSION

1. **Summarize** How did Egypt's army contribute toward making Egypt rich? *(The army expanded the empire northeast into Palestine and south into Nubia. Plunder from war and taxes from conquered lands made Egypt rich.)*

2. **Describe** What were some of the resources that Egyptian traders bartered? *(Egyptians bartered Egyptian beer, wine, food, and manufactured goods for myrrh trees, incense, ebony, ivory, leopard skins, and monkeys.)*

MORE INFORMATION

Egypt's Female Rulers Hatshepsut was not the only woman to hold power in ancient Egypt. Several other women ruled either directly as pharaoh or as a regent for a young son. Along with Hatshepsut, the two most famous Egyptian women are probably Nefertiti and Cleopatra VII. Nefertiti co-ruled with her husband, Akhenaten, and is best known for establishing a religion based on the worship of the sun god, Aten. Cleopatra VII was Egypt's last pharaoh and is best known for her relationships with Julius Caesar and Mark Antony.

ACTIVE OPTIONS

Critical Viewing: NG Image Gallery Have students explore the entire NG Image Gallery and choose two of the items to compare and contrast, either in written form or verbally with a partner. Ask questions that will inspire this process, such as: How are these images alike? How are they different? Why did you select these two items? How do they relate in history? `0:15` **minutes**

On Your Feet: Present a Period of Egyptian History Organize students into four groups and assign each group a period of Egyptian history on which they will prepare a short presentation. In every group some students should represent farmers, traders, and pharaohs from each period shown below.

- The early period of dynasties that began under the rule of Menes

- The Old Kingdom
- The Middle Kingdom
- The New Kingdom

`0:15` **minutes**

DIFFERENTIATE

ENGLISH LANGUAGE LEARNERS

PREP Before Reading Have students use the PREP strategy to prepare for reading. Write this acrostic on the board.

PREP	**P**review title.
	Read the Main Idea statement.
	Examine visuals.
	Predict what you will learn.

Have students write their prediction and share it with a partner. After reading, ask students to write another sentence that begins "I also learned . . ."

PRE-AP

Write a Newspaper Article Have students prepare a front-page newspaper article that compares the reigns of Hatshepsut and Ahmose. Have students do research on the kings to ensure that their article includes facts about each king and his or her rule. Ask students to write a headline for their article. Encourage students to share their articles with the class.

Press (**mt**) *in the Student eEdition for modified text.*

See the Chapter Planner for more strategies for differentiation.

REVIEW & ASSESS

ANSWERS

1. Hatshepsut traded items Egypt had in abundance, such as beer, food, and wine, for goods from other lands. She forced Nubia to make trades favorable to the Egyptians, and she gained riches from a trading trip to the land of Punt.

2. They engaged in trade with other countries to obtain things their land couldn't produce—and, thereby, strengthen Egypt.

3. Hatshepsut ruled with her stepson, but she won enough political support from high officials and priests to be crowned pharaoh and perform all of the pharaoh's functions. The expeditions to Punt were difficult and dangerous; the fact that Hatshepsut was willing to take those risks to bring more wealth to Egypt also suggests that she was an ambitious leader.

RAMSES II

RULED
1279 B.C. – 1213 B.C.

The women and children wail, and the men look up to the sun god in desperation. After ruling for 66 years, the pharaoh is dead. Most Egyptians have known no other king, and the dead pharaoh wasn't just any ruler. He was **Ramses II**—also known as Ramses the Great, a man who earned his title. Egypt was never more powerful than during Ramses' long reign.

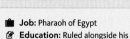

Job: Pharaoh of Egypt
Education: Ruled alongside his father, Seti I
Home: Pi-Ramses

FINEST HOUR
He led Egypt's army against the Hittites at the Battle of Kadesh around 1274 B.C.

WORST MOMENT
He saw 12 of his sons die before he did.

FRIENDS
The people loved him, affectionately calling him Sese (SEH-say), a nickname for "Ramses." He had about 200 wives and more than 100 children.

TRIVIA

His mummified nose was stuffed with peppercorns to keep its distinctive shape. When his mummy was exhibited in Paris, it received the Presidential Guard of Honor reserved for visiting royalty.

Critical [...] Visitors at a museum in Memphis, Egypt, marvel at a statue of Ramses II. What does the size of this statue say about how Ramses was viewed in his day?

＋ POSSIBLE RESPONSE
The huge size of the statue indicates that Ramses was viewed as very powerful and important to his people.

A LONG AND POWERFUL REIGN

Lasting 66 years, Ramses' (RAM-zeez) reign was one of the longest in Egyptian history. Ramses expanded Egypt's empire south into Nubia, west into Libya, and into the eastern Mediterranean. There he clashed with another ancient people, the Hittites (HIH-tyts).

The Hittites had a powerful empire centered around present-day Turkey, and they also sought to control the eastern Mediterranean. In his fifth year as pharaoh, Ramses fought a huge battle against the Hittites at Kadesh (kay-DEHSH). The battle stopped the Hittites' advance, but war with the Hittites dragged on for more than 15 years. At last, Ramses wrote letters to the Hittite king and negotiated a peace treaty. Peace with the Hittites and Egypt's territorial expansion helped Ramses create a strong economy.

Ramses went on to carve his legacy in stone and make himself unforgettable. First he built a new capital city, which he called Pi-Ramses (puh-RAM-zeez). Then he commissioned an awesome number of temples, monuments, and statues. At Abu Simbel (ah-boo SIHM-buhl) in Egyptian-controlled Nubia, Ramses had two cavernous temples carved out of the rock cliff face. His massive tomb at Thebes had a long wait for him—Ramses outlived 12 sons, dying in 1213 B.C. at more than 90 years of age.

THE NEW KINGDOM ENDS

Egypt's power was at its peak under Ramses the Great. After his death, several challenges emerged. Members of the ruling dynasty clashed with each other. In addition, Egypt was repeatedly invaded by a group known as the Sea Peoples.

Although they never conquered Egypt, the Sea Peoples waged a lengthy war that left Egypt's civilization weak and unstable.

In the years following the New Kingdom, Egypt was conquered and controlled by various foreign powers. First the Libyans and then the Nubians siezed large areas of land. Later, another people from Southwest Asia, the Persians, conquered Egypt. After 332 B.C., Egypt came under the control of the Macedonians, a people from the Greek peninsula. The final pharaohs were all Macedonians, right down to the last one, the famous Cleopatra VII. When Rome conquered Egypt in 30 B.C., Cleopatra committed suicide. It was a suitably dramatic end to 3,000 years of pharaohs.

REVIEW & ASSESS

1. **READING CHECK** What weakened Egypt's power after the death of Ramses II?

2. **MAKE INFERENCES** Why did peace with the Hittites help strengthen Egypt's economy?

3. **COMPARE AND CONTRAST** Think about Ramses II and Hatshepsut. What did these two strong pharaohs have in common?

PLAN

OBJECTIVE

Explain how Ramses II was one of the most powerful pharaohs in Egypt.

CRITICAL THINKING SKILLS FOR LESSON 3.2

- Identify Main Ideas and Details
- Monitor Comprehension
- Make Inferences
- Compare and Contrast
- Summarize
- Describe
- Analyze Visuals

ESSENTIAL QUESTION

How did ancient Egypt's rulers use the land's resources and geography to found a civilization?

Ramses II had a long reign as pharaoh. Lesson 3.2 discusses how Ramses II influenced the Egyptian civilization.

BACKGROUND FOR THE TEACHER

Ramses II was the third king of the 19th dynasty of Egypt. He is known for the many temples he built throughout Egypt. The most famous of these are the temple at Abu Simbel, and his mortuary temple at Thebes, the Ramesseum. The tomb of his principal wife, Nefertari, at Thebes is one of the best-preserved royal tombs. The tomb of many of his sons has also recently been found in the Valley of the Kings. Ramses II is known for the many huge statues of him all over Egypt.

DIGITAL RESOURCES myNGconnect.com

TEACHER RESOURCES & ASSESSMENT

 Reading and Note-Taking

 Vocabulary Practice

 Section 3 Quiz

STUDENT RESOURCES

 NG Chapter Gallery

PREVIEW

Call students' attention to the information in the chart about Ramses II. Ask volunteers to predict what they will learn in the lesson based on the information in the chart. Then tell students they will learn about Ramses II and his reign as pharaoh. At the end of the lesson, have students review how accurate their predictions were. `0:05` **minutes**

TEACH

GUIDED DISCUSSION

1. **Summarize** How did Ramses expand Egypt's empire? *(He expanded Egypt's empire south into Nubia, west into Libya, and into the eastern Mediterranean.)*

2. **Describe** How did Ramses carve his legacy in stone? *(Ramses built a new capital city, Pi-Ramses. He commissioned many temples, monuments, and statues. He had a massive tomb built for himself.)*

ANALYZE VISUALS

Have students look at the photo of visitors at a museum in Egypt. Ask students to describe what they see in this photograph and discuss why Ramses is still of interest to museum visitors in the present day. `0:10` **minutes**

ACTIVE OPTIONS

NG Learning Framework: Compare the Reigns of Ramses II and Hatshepsut

SKILLS: Communication, Collaboration
KNOWLEDGE: **Our Human Story**

Invite students to revisit Lessons 3.1 and 3.2. Ask them to work in small groups to discuss how the reigns of Ramses II and Hatshepsut were alike and different. Ask each group to present three of their ideas to the class. `0:10` **minutes**

On Your Feet: Hold a Panel Discussion Have students work in groups of five to conduct a panel discussion. One group member is the moderator, posing the question, "For what reasons did many people consider Ramses II a great pharaoh?" Other group members will contribute ideas about how Ramses earned the title "Ramses the Great." `0:15` **minutes**

STRIVING READERS

Complete Sentence Starters Provide these sentence starters for students to complete after reading. You may also have students preview to set a purpose for reading.

- Ramses' reign as Egyptian pharaoh lasted _____.

- Ramses fought a huge battle at Kadesh against the _____.

- Egypt's power was at its peak under _____.

- When Rome conquered Egypt, it was the end to 3,000 years of _____.

PRE-AP

Interview a Pharaoh Have students work in teams of two to plan, write, and perform a simulated television interview with Pharaoh Ramses II. Tell students that the purpose of the interview is to focus on the many achievements of the pharaoh during his reign.

Press **mt** *in the Student eEdition for modified text.*

See the Chapter Planner for more strategies for differentiation.

REVIEW & ASSESS

ANSWERS

1. After the death of Ramses II, several factors contributed to the decline of Egypt, including weak pharaohs, invasions by the Sea Peoples, and conquests by foreign powers.

2. Peace with the Hittites allowed for Egypt's territorial expansion, which helped Ramses create a strong economy.

3. They both had the ability to form and maintain good trade relationships with neighboring countries, military strength, personal ambition, an urge to build cities and monuments to themselves.

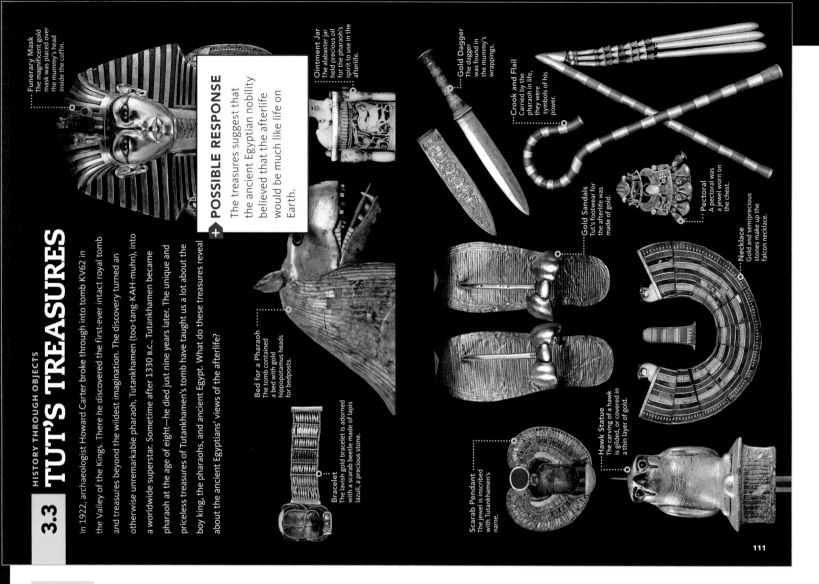

3.3 TUT'S TREASURES

In 1922, archaeologist Howard Carter broke through into tomb KV62 in the Valley of the Kings. There he discovered the first-ever intact royal tomb and treasures beyond the wildest imagination. The discovery turned an otherwise unremarkable pharaoh, Tutankhamen (too-tang-KAH-muhn), into a worldwide superstar. Sometime after 1330 B.C., Tutankhamen became pharaoh at the age of eight—he died just nine years later. The unique and priceless treasures of Tutankhamen's tomb have taught us a lot about the boy king, the pharaohs, and ancient Egypt. What do these treasures reveal about the ancient Egyptians' views of the afterlife?

+ POSSIBLE RESPONSE

The treasures suggest that the ancient Egyptian nobility believed that the afterlife would be much like life on Earth.

Funerary Mask The magnificent gold mask was placed over the mummy's head inside the coffin.

Ointment Jar The alabaster jar held precious oil for the pharaoh's spirit to use in the afterlife.

Gold Dagger The dagger was found in the mummy's wrappings.

Crook and Flail Carried by the pharaoh in life, they were symbols of his power.

Gold Sandals Tut's footwear for the afterlife was made of gold.

Pectoral A pectoral was a jewel worn on the chest.

Necklace Gold and semiprecious stones make up the falcon necklace.

Bed for a Pharaoh The tomb contained a bed with gold hippopotamus heads for bedposts.

Bracelet The lavish gold bracelet is adorned with a scarab beetle made of lapis lazuli, a precious stone.

Scarab Pendant The jewel is inscribed with Tutankhamen's name.

Hawk Statue The carving of a hawk is gilded, or covered in a thin layer of gold.

111

PLAN

OBJECTIVE

Identify some of the treasures found in the tomb of the pharaoh Tutankhamen.

CRITICAL THINKING SKILLS FOR LESSON 3.3

- Make Inferences
- Draw Conclusions
- Analyze Visuals

ESSENTIAL QUESTION

How did ancient Egypt's rulers use the land's resources and geography to found a civilization?

In ancient Egyptian civilization, pharaohs were honored as gods. Their tombs contained items it was believed the pharaohs' spirits would need in the afterlife. Lesson 3.3 shows some of the items that were found in the tomb of the pharaoh Tutankhamen.

BACKGROUND FOR THE TEACHER

Tutankhamen was an Egyptian pharaoh during the New Kingdom. He is often referred to as King Tut. Press coverage of the 1922 discovery of Tutankhamen's tomb by archaeologist Howard Carter went worldwide. The discovery led to much public interest in ancient Egypt. Tutankhamen is a well-known pharaoh largely because his tomb is among the best preserved and his image and the artifacts in his tomb are the most exhibited, having been displayed all over the world. Probably the best-known exhibition tour ran from 1972 to 1979. More than 1.6 million visitors saw the exhibition.

DIGITAL RESOURCES myNGconnect.com

TEACHER RESOURCES & ASSESSMENT

 Reading and Note-Taking

 Vocabulary Practice

 Section 3 Quiz

STUDENT RESOURCES

 NG Chapter Gallery

INTRODUCE & ENGAGE

HISTORY THROUGH OBJECTS

Ask students to form small groups and brainstorm a list of items that they think Egyptians would consider important to include in a pharaoh's tomb. Reconvene as a class and ask each group to share their list. Use the group lists to create a master list on the whiteboard. Then tell students that, in this lesson, they will learn about some of the items that were found in the tomb of the pharaoh Tutankhamen, or King Tut. **0:05** minutes

TEACH

GUIDED DISCUSSION

1. **Make Inferences** Why do you think Egyptians might have included items such as the crook and flail in the tomb? *(Possible response: Egyptians believed that the pharaoh's spirit may have needed these symbols of power in the afterlife.)*

2. **Draw Conclusions** What do the treasures from the tomb of Tutankhamen tell you about the status of the pharaoh in Egyptian society? *(The tomb contained gold and other riches, indicating that the pharaoh was considered to have a very high status in Egyptian society.)*

ANALYZE VISUALS

Have students reform their small groups from the Introduce & Engage activity. Have each group of students revisit their list and examine the artifacts shown here from the tomb of King Tut. Then they should discuss why each of these items may have been included in the tomb. Then have each group share its ideas with the class. **0:10** minutes

ACTIVE OPTIONS

Critical Viewing: NG Chapter Gallery Have students examine the contents of the Chapter Gallery for this chapter. Then invite them to brainstorm additional images they believe would fit within the Chapter Gallery. Have them write a description of these additional images and provide an explanation of why they would fit within the Chapter Gallery. Then instruct them to do online research to find examples of actual images they would like to add to the gallery. **0:15** minutes

On Your Feet: Three-Step Interview Have students choose a partner from the opposite side of the classroom. One student should interview the other on the topic of King Tut and the treasures found in his tomb. Then have students reverse roles. Finally, invite each student to share the results of his or her interview with the class. **0:15** minutes

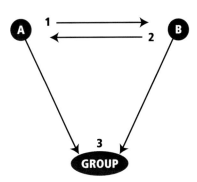

DIFFERENTIATE

PRE-AP

Create a Magazine Ad Have students create an ad for a magazine inviting people to come to an exhibit of some of the treasures found in King Tut's tomb. Students may want to illustrate their written ads with drawings or other images.

GIFTED & TALENTED

Host a Talk Show Have students assume the roles of a talk show host and an expert on the reign of King Tut. Have students do research to determine the appropriate questions for the host to ask and the appropriate responses from the expert. Have students present their talk show to the class.

Press **mt** *in the Student eEdition for modified text.*

See the Chapter Planner for more strategies for differentiation.

3.4 The Rise of Kush

How well do you know your neighbors? How do their lives affect yours? From annoyingly loud parties to borrowing tools or exchanging gifts, neighbors interact. Egypt couldn't ignore its closest neighbor, Nubia.

MAIN IDEA

The Nubian kingdom of Kush followed Egypt as a center of power, culture, and trade.

KUSH CONTROLS EGYPT

Just south of Egypt, across the first cataract of the Nile, lay the land of **Nubia**. Rich in gold, copper, and other important resources needed by Egypt, Nubia also provided a critical trade route for exotic goods from central Africa. This helps explain why the histories of Egypt and Nubia are so deeply connected. Early Nubia was a collection of chiefdoms dominated by Egypt. Later, when stronger Nubian kingdoms emerged, Egypt took more active control of its southern neighbor. It conquered and colonized large areas of Nubia, and Nubia's people adopted many Egyptian practices and customs during a thousand years of direct rule. Eventually, however, the tables were turned.

In the generations following the reign of Ramses II, the Nubian kingdom of **Kush** asserted its independence. It grew strong and ambitious. The Kushite king, Piankhi, invaded Egypt, sweeping north to take control of Thebes, Memphis, and Upper and Lower Egypt. In 728 B.C., Piankhi united the kingdoms of Egypt and Kush under a new line of Kushite kings.

Piankhi did not think of himself as a foreign conqueror but as a traditional pharaoh reviving Egyptian traditions. The Kushite kings styled themselves as pharaohs and continued classic Egyptian religious, social, and political practices. They built pyramids, mummified their dead, and worshipped Egyptian gods.

Eventually, the Kushite kings came into conflict with the iron-weapon wielding superpower of Assyria to the northeast of Egypt. In the course of the war, Kush lost control of Egypt to the Assyrians. Some of the fighting was fierce; the city of Thebes was destroyed before the Kushite kings abandoned Egypt.

TRADE IN IRON AND GOLD

After being pushed out of Egypt, Kush continued to flourish as an independent power. Its capital, Napata (nah-PAH-tuh), had a palace and a temple to the Egyptian god Amun (AH-muhn), one of the creator gods. The city's strategic location across two major trade routes ensured that Kush remained an important center of international trade. The Kushites had stores of gold, and they began to mine and produce iron as well.

Around 590 B.C., the Kushite capital moved south to another important trading city called Meroë (MAIR-oh-ee). Here the Egyptian influence continued with royal pyramids and temples to Amun and the goddess Isis. The Nubians expanded their kingdom and opened up many new trading routes, especially for iron.

Iron was increasingly important in the ancient world because it was used to make strong tools, and Meroë had abundant supplies of iron ore. Because of its resources, the city remained an important economic and political center for several centuries.

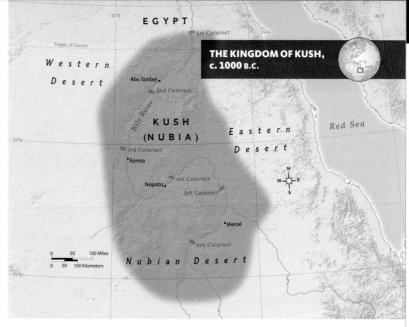

THE KINGDOM OF KUSH, c. 1000 B.C.

GOLD
The importance of gold to Nubia is clear from its name. *Nub* was the Egyptian word for gold, and Nubia was rich with it. Skilled goldsmiths turned gold ore into intricate jewelry, such as this pendant of the goddess Isis.

REVIEW & ASSESS

1. **READING CHECK** In what ways did Kush follow Egypt as a center of power, culture, and trade in Africa?

2. **MAKE INFERENCES** Would life have changed a great deal for Egyptians living under the rule of the Kushite kings? Why or why not?

3. **INTERPRET MAPS** Why do you think Kushite kings established the kingdom's two capital cities—Napata and later Meroë—along the Nile River?

PLAN

OBJECTIVE

Explain how the Nubian kingdom of Kush followed Egypt as a center of power, culture, and trade.

CRITICAL THINKING SKILLS FOR LESSON 3.4

- Identify Main Ideas and Details
- Monitor Comprehension
- Make Inferences
- Interpret Maps
- Summarize
- Draw Conclusions
- Create Graphic Organizers

ESSENTIAL QUESTION

How did ancient Egypt's rulers use the land's resources and geography to found a civilization?

The Nubian kingdom of Kush was a neighbor of Egypt. Lesson 3.4 discusses how Kush used the land's resources to become a center of power.

BACKGROUND FOR THE TEACHER

The Nubian kingdom of Kush was the empire to the south of Egypt. Kush was built at the base of the mountains near the beginning of the Nile River. The location along the Nile River was important for communication and trade routes both within the kingdom and throughout northeastern Africa. The people of Kush enjoyed plenty of rainfall throughout the year, so their crops grew well. Kush also had gold mines, iron ore, and ivory.

DIGITAL RESOURCES myNGconnect.com

TEACHER RESOURCES & ASSESSMENT

 Reading and Note-Taking

 Vocabulary Practice

 Section 3 Quiz

STUDENT RESOURCES

 NG Chapter Gallery

INTRODUCE & ENGAGE

ASK QUESTIONS

Have students form groups of four and come up with a list of three questions about the Nubian kingdom of Kush. After the lesson, review the questions and have students from each group answer the questions they listed or give them the opportunity to research answers if their particular question was not addressed in the text. Have each group share its questions and answers with the class. **0:05** minutes

TEACH

GUIDED DISCUSSION

1. **Summarize** How did the Nubian kingdom of Kush assert its independence? *(The Kushite king, Piankhi, invaded and took control of Egypt.)*

2. **Draw Conclusions** How was the abundance of iron ore important to the economic development of Nubia? *(Iron was increasingly important in the ancient world because it was used to make strong tools. Nubia opened up trading routes, especially for iron.)*

CREATE GRAPHIC ORGANIZERS

As a class, complete the following graphic organizer to help students understand the sequence of events that led to the rise and fall of Kush. **0:10** minutes

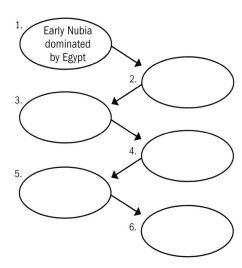

ACTIVE OPTIONS

NG Learning Framework: Learn More About Life in Kush

ATTITUDE: **Curiosity**
KNOWLEDGE: **Our Human Story**

Invite students to list three things they would like to know about life in the kingdom of Kush. Then have them use information from the chapter and additional source material to find answers to their questions about Kush. **0:10** minutes

On Your Feet: Create a Concept Web Have students form groups of four around a section of a bulletin board or a table. Provide each group with a large sheet of paper. Have group members take turns contributing a concept or phrase to a Concept Web with the words *The Nubian kingdom of Kush* at the center. When time for the activity has elapsed, call on volunteers from each group to share their webs. **0:10** minutes

DIFFERENTIATE

INCLUSION

Preview Maps Have students identify the location of the Nile River in the kingdom of Nubia. Divide the class into three groups of mixed ability levels. Ask each group to brainstorm two explanations for how the location of Nubia affected the growth of crops and the growth of trade in the kingdom of Nubia. Have one member from each group share their explanations with the class.

PRE-AP

Create a Group Presentation Have students work in small groups to discuss life in the Nubian kingdom of Kush. Students should include information about its rulers, religious beliefs, and use of resources. Have each group give a presentation to the class.

Press (**mt**) *in the Student eEdition for modified text.*

See the Chapter Planner for more strategies for differentiation.

REVIEW & ASSESS

ANSWERS

1. Kush invaded and conquered Egypt, continued Egyptian religious, social, and political practices, and became an important center of international trade.

2. No, because the Kushite kings came from a culture that was very Egyptianized, and the first Kushite king saw himself as a pharaoh in the Egyptian tradition.

3. It was important for the kingdom to have access to the Nile River for transportation. Trade routes to other countries probably went along the Nile.

4.1
Hieroglyphs and Papyrus

You might be able to guess the meaning of some foreign words. But try reading a store bar code. The seemingly random arrangement of lines is actually a unique writing system telling you the product and price. To read it, you need to crack the code. Egyptian writing was just as baffling until archaeologists discovered the key—a slab of rock called the Rosetta Stone.

MAIN IDEA

The Egyptians valued writing and wrote for many purposes.

Critical Viewing This carving shows a pair of scribes at work during the Old Kingdom. What does the image tell you about a scribe's job?

+ POSSIBLE RESPONSE

The image shows that a scribe's job involved writing and sharing information.

COMMON HIEROGLYPHS

Sun (or day)

R (a mouth symbol)

S (a folded cloth symbol)

N (water ripple)

WRITING AND WRITERS

Egyptian writing developed sometime before 3000 B.C., and it used **hieroglyphs** (HY-ruh-glihfs) instead of letters. A hieroglyph could be a picture representing an object, or it could represent a sound or an idea. By combining hieroglyphs, the Egyptians formed words and sentences.

The hieroglyphic writing system was very complex. There were nearly 800 hieroglyphs, no vowels, and very complicated rules. Few people mastered the skill of writing in hieroglyphs.

These special people were known as **scribes**, or professional writers, and they were among the most highly respected people in Egypt. It took five years of intense training to become a scribe, but the benefits made up for the hard work. Scribes were powerful, well paid, and had many privileges.

Reading and writing were just part of a scribe's job. Scribes were also skilled in art, mathematics, bookkeeping, law, engineering, and architecture. All scribes were important, but a really talented scribe could move up in Egypt's social hierarchy. One royal scribe eventually became the pharaoh Horemheb.

PAPER AND THE ROSETTA STONE

Hieroglyphs were painted and carved on tombs, temples, and monuments. For important documents, the Egyptians used sheets of a paperlike material called **papyrus** (puh-PY-ruhs), made from reeds that grew along the banks of the Nile. Sheets of papyrus could be glued together to make scrolls—some scrolls were several yards long. Papyrus was light and easy for a scribe to carry.

Eventually, the Egyptians abandoned the old forms of writing. For many years, scholars tried to crack the code of the hieroglyphs. Then, in A.D. 1799, a slab of rock was discovered near Rosetta, Egypt. On it was carved the same text in hieroglyphs, another form of writing, and Greek. Because scholars understood Greek, they were able to figure out what the hieroglyphs meant. Thanks to the Rosetta Stone, historians can read hieroglyphs and learn about the lives of the people who produced them.

REVIEW & ASSESS

1. **READING CHECK** How much time did it take to become a scribe in ancient Egypt?

2. **IDENTIFY MAIN IDEAS AND DETAILS** What details support the idea that scribes were among the most highly respected people in Egypt?

3. **MAKE INFERENCES** What does the complexity of the hieroglyphic writing system tell us about the role of scribes?

PLAN

OBJECTIVE

Explain that the Egyptians valued writing and wrote for many purposes.

Writing was an important part of Egyptian civilization. Lesson 4.1 discusses hieroglyphs, the use of papyrus, and the importance of the Rosetta Stone.

CRITICAL THINKING SKILLS FOR LESSON 4.1

- Identify Main Ideas and Details
- Monitor Comprehension
- Make Inferences
- Describe
- Summarize

ESSENTIAL QUESTION

How did ancient Egypt's rulers use the land's resources and geography to found a civilization?

BACKGROUND FOR THE TEACHER

Art from ancient Egypt often depicts scribes carrying the tools of their craft, such as pigments, water pots, and pens. Scribes handled such things as personal letters, government communications and proclamations, legal documents, and religious documents. The closing phrase of many ancient letters, "May you be well when you hear this," implies that the scribes not only wrote but also read communications between people. The training of the scribes was rigorous and the harsh treatment of apprentices is recorded in both in texts and representations.

DIGITAL RESOURCES myNGconnect.com

TEACHER RESOURCES & ASSESSMENT

 Reading and Note-Taking

 Vocabulary Practice

 Section 4 Quiz

STUDENT RESOURCES

 Active History

INTRODUCE & ENGAGE

ROUNDTABLE

Have students sit in groups of four. Ask the groups to brainstorm and then list different forms of communication. Have each group share its ideas with the class. Tell students they will learn more about written communication in ancient Egypt in this lesson. `0:05` minutes

TEACH

GUIDED DISCUSSION

1. **Describe** What is a hieroglyph? (*A hieroglyph could be a picture representing an object, or it could represent a sound or an idea.*)

2. **Summarize** What is the importance of the Rosetta Stone? (*On the Rosetta Stone, the same text was carved in hieroglyphs and in Greek. Because scholars understood Greek, they were able to figure out what the hieroglyphs meant.*)

MORE INFORMATION

The Rosetta Stone The scholar who cracked the code of the Rosetta Stone was a French historian named Jean-François Champollion. In 1808, at the age of 18, he began his first attempts at deciphering the hieroglyphs on the Rosetta Stone. However, his breakthrough didn't come until 1822, when Champollion concluded that the hieroglyphs were not only symbols but functioned as an alphabet and a phonetic language. Applying this strategy, he was able to successfully decipher the names of two ancient Egyptian rulers written on the stone: Ramses and Thutmos. Using what he learned, he was then able to decipher common nouns.

ACTIVE OPTIONS

Active History: Decipher Egyptian Hieroglyphics Extend the lesson by using either the PDF or Whiteboard version of Decipher Egyptian Hieroglyphics. These activities take a deeper look at a topic from, or related to, the lesson. Explore the activities as a class, turn them into group assignments, or even assign them individually. `0:10` minutes

On Your Feet: Talk and Share Ask students to work in small groups. Ask each group to think about the importance of finding the Rosetta Stone. Have each group list things historians have learned about life in ancient Egypt because of the discovery of the Rosetta Stone. Have each group share its list with the class. `0:10` minutes

DIFFERENTIATE

ENGLISH LANGUAGE LEARNERS

Create Four-Square Word Charts Give students the following list of words and display the chart below. Ask students to copy and complete the four parts of the chart for each word on the list.

- hieroglyph
- scribe
- papyrus

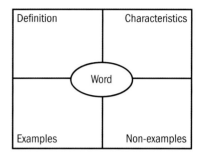

STRIVING READERS

Use a Word Splash Present the words below on the board in a random arrangement (splash) as shown, and ask students to choose four pairs of words that are related to each other. Have students use this sentence starter to write how each pair of words is related.

Press (**mt**) *in the Student eEdition for modified text.*

See the Chapter Planner for more strategies for differentiation.

REVIEW & ASSESS

ANSWERS

1. It took five years of training to become a scribe.

2. The scribes were powerful, well paid, and earned many privileges that other Egyptians did not have. Scribes could rise to high office.

3. Scribes were important and powerful people in society. They were probably among the best and brightest people in the society.

4.2 Medicine, Science, and Mathematics

The priest chants magic spells while the doctor applies a fragrant lotion to your wound. He carefully bandages it and gives you a foul-smelling medicine sweetened with honey. You gag on it, but the chances are you'll live. The ancient Egyptians were advanced medical practitioners for their time.

MAIN IDEA

Egyptians put their advanced knowledge of medicine, science, and mathematics to practical use.

CANOPIC JARS

Canopic (kuh-NOH-pihk) jars contained the internal organs of a mummified body. The head-shaped lids on the jars represent the sons of the god Horus.

MEDICINE

Egypt had the most advanced medical practices in the ancient world. Some ancient Egyptian science was so accurate that it formed the foundation of later medical practices in Europe. The Egyptians had developed a detailed understanding of anatomy through mummifying bodies. They identified the heart as the most important organ and the pulse as its "voice."

Doctors provided medicines made from plants and minerals, set broken bones, and even performed surgery. Researchers have found medical texts written on papyrus that give doctors instructions and advice for treating a variety of illnesses. Texts and carvings also show some of the surgical tools that doctors used to treat their patients. Magical spells to heal different illnesses were also considered part of medical treatment.

SCIENCE AND MATHEMATICS

Ancient Egyptians were gifted astronomers as well as talented doctors. Astronomy is the branch of science that studies the sun, moon, stars, planets, and space. By making observations of the moon, ancient Egyptian astronomers developed a 365-day calendar. It had 24-hour days, 10-day weeks, 3-week months, and 12-month years. The extra five days were added as birthdays for five gods and were considered unlucky.

The Egyptians were also excellent mathematicians. Like us, they used a decimal counting system that included fractions. However, they did not use zero. Egyptian mathematicians established several key principles of geometry, accurately calculating angles and areas. They could calculate the area of a circle and the volume of a pyramid or cylinder. These skills made it possible to design big buildings like the pyramids.

Less visible but equally impressive was their mastery of the mathematics needed to run an empire. Scribes accurately calculated how many workers would be needed for building projects and how much food they would eat. Similar assessments estimated trade profits, crop yields, and taxes. Along with trade and military might, math and science were foundations of ancient Egypt's civilization.

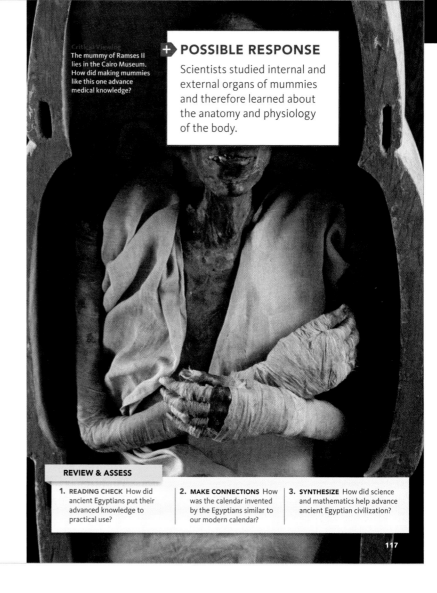

Critical Viewing The mummy of Ramses II lies in the Cairo Museum. How did making mummies like this one advance medical knowledge?

+ POSSIBLE RESPONSE

Scientists studied internal and external organs of mummies and therefore learned about the anatomy and physiology of the body.

REVIEW & ASSESS

1. **READING CHECK** How did ancient Egyptians put their advanced knowledge to practical use?

2. **MAKE CONNECTIONS** How was the calendar invented by the Egyptians similar to our modern calendar?

3. **SYNTHESIZE** How did science and mathematics help advance ancient Egyptian civilization?

PLAN

OBJECTIVE

Explain how Egyptians put their advanced knowledge of medicine, science, and mathematics to practical use.

CRITICAL THINKING SKILLS FOR LESSON 4.2

- Identify Main Ideas and Details
- Monitor Comprehension
- Make Connections
- Synthesize
- Describe
- Summarize
- Create Graphic Organizers

ESSENTIAL QUESTION

How did ancient Egypt's rulers use the land's resources and geography to found a civilization?

Egyptian rulers worked to advance knowledge in their society. Lesson 4.2 discusses how important knowledge of medicine, science, and mathematics was to the Egyptian civilization.

BACKGROUND FOR THE TEACHER

The ancient Egyptians have provided modern historians with a great deal of information about the medical knowledge that they had. Some of the information comes from writings found in papyruses discovered during archaeological searches. Historians have determined that some Egyptian beliefs about medicine were based on myths. However, ancient writings indicate that Egyptians had discovered many things about how the human body worked. For example, evidence shows that Egyptian physicians were aware of the connection between a person's pulse and heart.

DIGITAL RESOURCES myNGconnect.com

TEACHER RESOURCES & ASSESSMENT

 Reading and Note-Taking   **Vocabulary Practice**   **Section 4 Quiz**

STUDENT RESOURCES

 NG Chapter Gallery

INTRODUCE & ENGAGE

USE A K-W-L CHART

Provide each student with a K-W-L Chart like the one shown. Have students use their prior knowledge to brainstorm ideas about how ancient Egyptians might have learned about medicine, science, and mathematics. Ask students to write questions that they would like to have answered as they study the lesson. Allow time at the end of the lesson for students to fill in what they have learned.
0:05 minutes

K What Do I Know?	W What Do I Want To Learn?	L What Did I Learn?

TEACH

GUIDED DISCUSSION

1. **Describe** How did the ancient Egyptians develop a detailed understanding of anatomy? (*They learned about anatomy through mummifying bodies.*)

2. **Summarize** How did mastery of mathematics help scribes contribute to the advancement of the Egyptian empire? (*Ancient Egyptians were able to calculate how many workers would be needed for building projects and how much food they would eat. They estimated trade profits, crop yields, and taxes.*)

CREATE GRAPHIC ORGANIZERS

Have students form groups of four around a section of a bulletin board or a table. Provide each group with a large sheet of paper. Have group members take turns contributing a concept or phrase to a Concept Web with the words *Medicine, Science, and Mathematics* at the center. When time for the activity has elapsed, call on volunteers from each group to share their webs. **0:10** minutes

ACTIVE OPTIONS

NG Learning Framework: Learn More About Medicine in Ancient Egypt

ATTITUDE: **Curiosity**
KNOWLEDGE: **Our Human Story**

Ask students to select one or more medical practices used in ancient Egypt about which they would like to learn more. Then have students do research about the practices and present their findings to the class. **0:10** minutes

On Your Feet: Create a Quiz Organize students into two teams and have each team write ten True-False questions about ancient Egypt's contributions to the fields of medicine, science, and mathematics. Then have each team answer the questions created by the other team. Review student answers as a class and have teams keep track of their number of correct answers. **0:10** minutes

DIFFERENTIATE

STRIVING READERS

Make Summary Statements Have students look at the subheadings in the lesson. After reading the lesson, direct students to use each subheading to begin a statement that summarizes the information about the subheading.

Press (**mt**) *in the Student eEdition for modified text.*

See the Chapter Planner for more strategies for differentiation.

REVIEW & ASSESS

ANSWERS

1. The ancient Egyptian doctors provided medicines, set broken bones, and performed surgery. They treated a variety of illnesses. They gained a detailed understanding of human anatomy. They studied astronomy and used information they learned to develop a calendar. They used math to calculate geometry and help them efficiently handle large building projects.

2. Like our modern calendar, the Egyptian calendar had 365 days. It had 24-hour days, and 12-month years.

3. In order to build the pyramids, Egyptians needed to solve difficult problems, including calculating angles, areas, and volumes for various shapes and forms. Solving these mathematical problems led to some of the first developments of geometry. The study of medicine in ancient Egypt helped them understand human anatomy and physiology.

Egyptian architects used their knowledge of proportion and shapes to create these impressive columns in the temple of Amun Re at Karnak. The columns were decorated with hieroglyphs and carved figures.

4.3 Art and Architecture

The figures in ancient Egyptian paintings look awkward with their bodies facing the viewer, heads and feet facing right. Surely the artist didn't believe people really look like this!

MAIN IDEA

The ancient Egyptians created distinctive art and architecture.

A DISTINCTIVE ART STYLE

Ancient Egyptian art is easily recognizable. That is because artists used a distinctive style called frontalism. According to this style, the head and legs were drawn in profile, but the shoulders, chest, and arms were drawn as if they were facing front. The result looked pretty unnatural, but realism wasn't the goal. Most portraits were painted for religious purposes, which made it important to show as much of the body as possible. Frontalism achieved this goal.

Artists arranged each figure in a painting precisely to achieve balance and order. To get the sizes and proportions right, they followed a strict formula. Typically the human body was divided into three equal parts: from foot to knee, from knee to elbow, and from elbow to hairline. A figure's waist appeared exactly halfway up the body.

Most paintings showed scenes from everyday life. These included pharaohs performing religious rituals, fighting battles, or feasting, and ordinary people at work or play. Artists painted and carved figures and scenes like these in great temples, monuments, and tombs. This ancient art has revealed much about Egyptian life and beliefs.

ARCHITECTURE AND SACRED SHAPES

Egyptian architects also used clever techniques to make their soaring temples and other buildings look impressive. The architects used grid lines to create precise designs. They also applied mathematics to their designs using the "golden ratio." This mathematical formula helped architects achieve the most pleasing proportions—what looks good, in other words. The Greeks borrowed and developed the formula, and the golden ratio is still used today.

Certain geometric shapes, such as squares and triangles, were considered sacred, so architects included these in their designs. The most important shape, though, was the pyramid, which dominated Egyptian architecture throughout the civilization's 3,000-year history. In addition to the Great Pyramid of Khufu, architects built many other pyramids all over Egypt. Small pyramids even topped the tombs of the skilled craftspeople who built Egypt's great monuments.

REVIEW & ASSESS

1. **READING CHECK** What makes ancient Egyptian art and architecture stand out?

2. **DRAW CONCLUSIONS** What do Egyptian art and architecture reveal about the place of religion in ancient Egyptian society?

3. **DETERMINE WORD MEANINGS** How does the base word *front* clarify the meaning of the *frontalism* style of art?

OBJECTIVE

Explain how ancient Egyptians created distinctive art and architecture.

CRITICAL THINKING SKILLS FOR LESSON 4.3

- Identify Main Ideas and Details
- Monitor Comprehension
- Draw Conclusions
- Determine Word Meanings
- Summarize
- Analyze Cause and Effect
- Analyze Visuals

ESSENTIAL QUESTION

How did ancient Egypt's rulers use the land's resources and geography to found a civilization?

Art and architecture were important in Egyptian civilization. Lesson 4.3 discusses these important elements of Egyptian culture.

BACKGROUND FOR THE TEACHER

Egyptian artwork included drawings on walls and pillars. Some of this art was intended to help the dead live forever by giving them instructions they would need as they met up with gods on their way to eternal life. The good deeds of the deceased were often celebrated through artwork. Many artists used colors such as blue, red, orange, and white to create pictures that told about the life of the dead. Sculptors were important artists in Egypt. Artists made statues of kings, queens, scribes, animals, gods, and goddesses.

DIGITAL RESOURCES myNGconnect.com

TEACHER RESOURCES & ASSESSMENT

 Reading and Note-Taking

 Vocabulary Practice

 Section 4 Quiz

STUDENT RESOURCES

 NG Chapter Gallery

INTRODUCE & ENGAGE

CREATE A WORD WEB

Have students use a Word Web like the one shown, with the word *Architecture* in the center. Encourage students to write what they already know about designing and constructing buildings and structures in ancient Egypt. Tell students they will learn more about Egyptian art and architecture in this lesson. **0:05** minutes

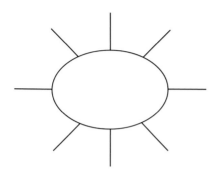

TEACH

GUIDED DISCUSSION

1. **Summarize** How did ancient Egyptian artists determine sizes and proportions of art of the human body when they drew, painted, or sculpted it? (*They followed a mathematical formula that divided the human body into three equal parts: from foot to knee, from knee to elbow, and from elbow to hairline. A figure's waist appeared exactly halfway up the body.*)

2. **Analyze Cause and Effect** How was mathematics used to make temples and other buildings look impressive? (*Architects used grid lines to create precise designs. They used the "golden ratio" mathematical formula to achieve pleasing proportions. This formula is still used today.*)

ANALYZE VISUALS

Have students look at the image of the scribes in Lesson 4.1 and point out the characteristics of frontalism that they read about in the current lesson. Then have students take a few minutes to look back through the chapter and identify other examples of frontalism in chapter photographs. **0:10** minutes

ACTIVE OPTIONS

Critical Viewing: NG Image Gallery Invite students to explore the entire NG Image Gallery and choose one image from the gallery they feel best represents their understanding of each chapter or unit. Have students provide a written explanation of why they selected each of the images they chose. **0:15** minutes

On Your Feet: Fishbowl Have one group of students sit in a close circle facing inward. Have another group sit in a larger circle around

them. Have students on the inside discuss ancient Egyptian art. Then have students on the outside summarize the information they heard. Have groups reverse positions and repeat the same activity. **0:10** minutes

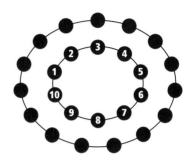

DIFFERENTIATE

STRIVING READERS

Set a Purpose for Reading Direct students to read and find at least three details about ancient Egyptian art and at least three details about ancient Egyptian architecture. After reading, have students record the details on note cards. Encourage partners to compare cards and discuss the details they chose.

PRE-AP

Write Feature Articles Assign students the role of journalist reporting on ancient Egyptian art and architecture. Show students examples of feature articles from newspapers or magazines, and ask students to focus on specific examples of art and architecture and write their own feature article. Then have students share their articles with the class.

Press **mt** *in the Student eEdition for modified text.*

See the Chapter Planner for more strategies for differentiation.

REVIEW & ASSESS

ANSWERS

1. The use of frontalism makes ancient Egyptian art distinctive, with its profile view of the head and legs and frontal view of the shoulders, chest, and arms.

2. In their buildings, ancient Egyptians incorporated shapes such as squares and triangles that they considered sacred. Religious images appear in ancient Egyptian art, even in depictions of everyday life. The art and architecture reveal that religion was very important in ancient Egyptian life.

3. From the base word *front*, one can infer that most of the image of a person was facing toward the front.

VOCABULARY

Use each of the following vocabulary words in a sentence that shows an understanding of the word's meaning.

1. cataract
Cataracts make river travel difficult because boats must navigate around these rapids.

2. dynasty

3. pharaoh

4. hierarchy

5. mummy

6. hieroglyph

7. scribe

8. papyrus

READING SKILL

9. DRAW CONCLUSIONS If you haven't already, complete your organizer to draw conclusions about the importance of ancient Egypt's geographic features. Then answer the question.

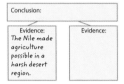

Conclusion:

| Evidence: The Nile made agriculture possible in a harsh desert region. | Evidence: |

How did the Nile River affect civilization in ancient Egypt? Explain.

MAIN IDEAS

Answer the following questions. Support your answers with evidence from the chapter.

10. Why was Egyptian agriculture dependent on the Nile? **LESSON 1.1**

11. What was the relationship between Upper Egypt and Lower Egypt? **LESSON 1.2**

12. What was the role of the pharaoh in Egyptian life? **LESSON 1.3**

13. How did the Great Pyramid of Khufu demonstrate the pharaoh's power? **LESSON 2.1**

14. How were the classes of Egyptian society organized? **LESSON 2.2**

15. What contributions did Hatshepsut make to Egypt during her reign? **LESSON 3.1**

16. In what ways were Kush and Egypt connected? **LESSON 3.4**

17. Why was it desirable to be a scribe in ancient Egypt? **LESSON 4.1**

CRITICAL THINKING

Answer the following questions. Support your answers with evidence from the chapter.

18. SYNTHESIZE How did the pharaohs use Egypt's resources to increase the country's wealth and power?

19. DRAW CONCLUSIONS What impact did the Nile have on Egypt's trade industry?

20. ANALYZE CAUSE AND EFFECT How did the absolute power of the pharaohs contribute to Egypt's cycles of order and disorder?

21. MAKE GENERALIZATIONS What position did women have in Egyptian society?

22. YOU DECIDE The Egyptians had many important achievements in math, science, art, and architecture. Which achievement do you think left the greatest legacy, and why?

INTERPRET DIAGRAMS

Study the cross-section diagram of the interior of King Khufu's Great Pyramid at Giza. Then answer the questions that follow.

GREAT PYRAMID AT GIZA

A **King's Chamber,** where Khufu was buried

B **Queen's Chamber,** which was found empty

C **Grand Gallery,** leading to the King's Chamber

D **Entrance,** which was sealed off by a heavy wall

E **Unfinished Chamber,** built underground, beneath the pyramid

F **Air Vents**

23. What features of the pyramid might help discourage tomb robbers?

24. What features of the pyramid were created to help the workers who built it?

ANALYZE SOURCES

Read the following translation of advice from an ancient Egyptian father to his son, who is training to be a scribe. Then answer the question.

> I have compared the people who are artisans and handicraftsmen [with the scribe], and indeed I am convinced that there is nothing superior to letters. Plunge into the study of Egyptian Learning, as you would plunge into the river, and you will find that this is so. . . . I wish I were able to make you see how beautiful Learning is. It is more important than any trade in the world.

25. What conclusions can you draw about the role of scribes in ancient Egyptian society?

WRITE ABOUT HISTORY

26. NARRATIVE Ramses II was one of the key figures from ancient Egypt. Suppose you were a scribe who was alive then. Write an eyewitness account that tells about the greatest achievements of Ramses II.

TIPS

- Take notes from the chapter about the reign of Ramses II and his achievements.
- Make an outline of the achievements and events you will include.
- Be sure to include details and examples.
- Use at least two vocabulary words from the chapter.
- Provide a concluding statement that summarizes why Ramses II was an effective pharaoh.

VOCABULARY ANSWERS

1. Cataracts make river travel difficult because boats must navigate around these rapids.

2. In an Egyptian dynasty, the throne passed from the pharaoh to his son.

3. Egyptians believed that their king, or pharaoh, was a living god who had absolute power over everyone.

4. In a hierarchy, such as that in ancient Egypt, people belong to different social classes and each class has a rank in society.

5. After death, the body of an Egyptian pharaoh was preserved as a mummy in a royal tomb.

6. Each hieroglyph in the Egyptian writing system represented a sound, an object, or an idea.

7. To become a scribe, an Egyptian trained for five years to acquire the skill of writing.

8. Egyptian scribes wrote on sheets of paper-like material called papyrus.

READING STRATEGY ANSWERS

Conclusion: The Nile was important to the success of Egyptian civilization.

| Evidence: The Nile made agriculture possible in a harsh desert region. | Evidence: The Nile was easy to navigate, making it a good trade route. |

9. The Nile River flooded every year, depositing fertile soil along its banks. For this reason, the Nile made agriculture possible in a harsh desert region. The large harvests and food surpluses were key to the development of Egyptian civilization. The Nile also provided important trade routes for Egypt. Trade was important to the development of Egyptian civilization.

MAIN IDEAS ANSWERS

10. The floods brought water to the crops, as well as silt, which was rich in nutrients. A year with low floodwaters could mean famine.

11. The two kingdoms were next to each other, and goods and ideas were easily traded between them. They probably already shared a culture before being united under the pharaohs. Even so, they maintained their own identities and stood on opposite sides when there were power struggles in Egypt.

12. He went between the people and the gods of ancient Egypt. He was also the absolute ruler of all aspects of government.

13. The Great Pyramid took tremendous resources to build, both in terms of materials and manpower. The pharaoh would have to be very wealthy and powerful to cause such a monumental work to be done.

14. After the pharaoh, the nobles and priests held the most power. Then came the officials and scribes, then the craftsmen and merchants, and then the farmers. At the bottom, came unskilled laborers and slaves.

15. Hatshepsut expanded the Egyptian empire, but her most important contributions were in the promotion and expansion of trade, which greatly increased Egypt's wealth. She risked difficult and dangerous trade expeditions to the coast of East Africa, which further boosted Egypt's wealth and stimulated its economy.

16. Egypt dominated Nubia and Kush for centuries and exploited its resources. During that time, the people of Nubia and Kush adopted Egyptian culture. When Egypt became weak, the Kushites moved in to conquer their former masters.

17. Scribes were important people in society. A scribe could become very powerful, and possibly even a king.

CRITICAL THINKING ANSWERS

18. The pharaohs pursued an active foreign policy to increase Egypt's wealth. They increased trade and military power.

19. Because the Nile River was easily navigable, it became a "superhighway" that encouraged contact and the trade of goods and ideas among different communities along the river.

20. Every aspect of government depended on the pharaoh. That meant that when there was a strong pharaoh, he could maintain order and support trade and expansion. When the pharaoh was weak, there was nobody to impose order on the country.

21. Even though women were first and foremost wives and mothers, they enjoyed many individual rights, including the right to own property, conduct business, participate in legal proceedings, and pursue a great variety of professions.

22. Students' responses will vary. Students should clearly state their opinion regarding their view of which achievement made by the Egyptian civilization left the greatest legacy and support that opinion with evidence from the chapter.

INTERPRET CHARTS ANSWERS

23. The entrance was sealed off by a heavy wall.

24. The air vents helped the workers who built the pyramid.

ANALYZE SOURCES ANSWER

25. Students' responses will vary. Sample response: The advice from the father to his son indicates that learning is valued and that scribes are well-respected in ancient Egyptian society.

WRITE ABOUT HISTORY ANSWER

26. Students' narratives will vary, but should

- include details and examples
- use vocabulary words
- summarize why Ramses II was an effective pharaoh

UNIT 2 EARLY CIVILIZATIONS

UNIT RESOURCES

On Location with National Geographic Lead Program Officer Christopher Thornton Intro and Video

 Interactive Map Tool

 **News & Updates**

Available on myNGconnect

Unit Wrap-Up:
"Encounters with History"
Feature and Video

"China's Ancient Lifeline"
National Geographic Adapted Article

"Faces of the Divine"
National Geographic Adapted Article
Student eEdition exclusive

Unit 2 Inquiry:
Write a Creation Myth

CHAPTER RESOURCES

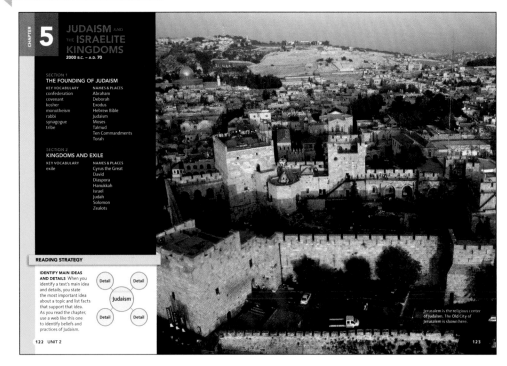

CHAPTER 5

JUDAISM AND THE ISRAELITE KINGDOMS
2000 B.C. – A.D. 70

SECTION 1
THE FOUNDING OF JUDAISM

KEY VOCABULARY
confederation
covenant
kosher
monotheism
rabbi
synagogue
tribe

NAMES & PLACES
Abraham
Deborah
Exodus
Hebrew Bible
Judaism
Moses
Talmud
Ten Commandments
Torah

SECTION 2
KINGDOMS AND EXILE

KEY VOCABULARY
exile

NAMES & PLACES
Cyrus the Great
David
Diaspora
Hanukkah
Israel
Judah
Solomon
Zealots

READING STRATEGY

IDENTIFY MAIN IDEAS AND DETAILS When you identify a text's main idea and details, you state the most important idea about a topic and list facts that support that idea. As you read the chapter, use a web like this one to identify beliefs and practices of Judaism.

Detail — Detail — Judaism — Detail — Detail

122 UNIT 2

Jerusalem is the religious center of Judaism. The Old City of Jerusalem is shown here.

123

TEACHER RESOURCES & ASSESSMENT

Available on myNGconnect

 Social Studies Skills Lessons
• Reading: Identify Main Ideas and Details
• Writing: Write an Argument

 Formal Assessment
• Chapter 5 Tests A (on-level)
  & B (below-level)

 Chapter 5 Answer Key

 ExamView®
One-time Download

STUDENT BACKPACK *Available on myNGconnect*

• **eEdition** *(English)*   • **eEdition** *(Spanish)*   • **Handbooks**   • **Online Atlas**

For Chapter 5 Spanish resources, visit the Teacher Resource Menu page on myNGconnect.

THE FOUNDING OF JUDAISM

 Reading and Note-Taking

 Vocabulary Practice

 Section 1 Quiz

Available on myNGconnect

LESSON 1.1 ABRAHAM AND MOSES
• Critical Viewing: NG Chapter Gallery

NG Learning Framework:
A Man Called Moses

LESSON 1.2 A DISTINCT CULTURE

 Active History: Interactive Whiteboard Activity
Investigate Major Religious Holidays

 Active History
Investigate Major Religious Holidays

Available on myNGconnect

• On Your Feet: Create a Concept Web

LESSON 1.3 BELIEFS AND TEXTS OF JUDAISM
• Critical Viewing: NG Chapter Gallery
• On Your Feet: Inside-Outside Circle

DOCUMENT-BASED QUESTION
LESSON 1.4 WRITINGS FROM THE HEBREW BIBLE
• Critical Viewing: NG Chapter Gallery
• On Your Feet: Two Options

KINGDOMS AND EXILE

 Reading and Note-Taking

 Vocabulary Practice

 Section 2 Quiz

Available on myNGconnect

LESSON 2.1 ISRAEL AND JUDAH

 Biography
Solomon   *Available on myNGconnect*

NG Learning Framework:
Write a Biography

• On Your Feet: Tell Me More

LESSON 2.2 EXILE AND RETURN
• Critical Viewing: NG Chapter Gallery
• On Your Feet: Card Responses

LESSON 2.3 THE DIASPORA
• Critical Viewing: NG Chapter Gallery
• On Your Feet: One-on-One Interviews

NG EXPLORER BEVERLY GOODMAN
LESSON 2.4 UNCOVERING THE STORY OF CAESAREA'S PORT

NG Learning Framework:
Learn More About Tsunamis

• On Your Feet: Three-Step Interview

CHAPTER 5 REVIEW

STRATEGY 1
Preview Text

Help students preview each lesson in the chapter. For each lesson, have them read the lesson titles, lesson introductions, Main Idea statements, captions, and headings. Then have them list the information they expect to find in the text. Have students read a lesson and discuss with a partner what they learned and whether or not it matched their list.

Use with All Lessons

STRATEGY 2
Use Pair-Share Reading

Allow students to work in pairs and divide each two-page lesson into two parts. Have students decide which part each one will handle. Both students will read the first part. The student responsible for it will sum up orally the important information in that part. The second student will make notes and ask a question about the information. The students will switch roles and repeat the procedure with the second part.

Use with Lessons 1.1–1.3 and 2.1–2.3

STRATEGY 3
Turn Lesson Titles into Questions

Before reading each lesson, display the appropriate question based on the lesson title. After reading, have students write the answers to the questions and compare their answers.

1.1 Who were Abraham and Moses?

1.2 How did the Israelites develop a distinct culture?

1.3 What are the beliefs and texts of Judaism?

Use with Lessons 1.1–1.3 *Use the same strategy for the titles in Section 2. Tell students to pay careful attention to words in the titles so that their questions are relevant. For Lessons 2.1–2.3, have students share their questions and answers with classmates.*

Press *in the Student eEdition for modified text.*

STRATEGY 1
Use Supported Reading

In small groups, have students read aloud the chapter lesson by lesson. At the end of each lesson, have them stop and use these frames to tell what they comprehended from the text:

This lesson is about _____.

One detail that stood out to me is _____.

The vocabulary word _____ means _____.

I don't think I understand _____.

Guide students with portions of text they do not understand. Be sure all students understand a lesson before moving on to the next one.

Use with All Lessons

STRATEGY 2
Sequence Events

Write events from Section 2 on index cards. Read the events aloud and then have students put the cards in chronological order.

Use with Lessons 2.1–2.3

STRATEGY 1
PREP Before Reading

Have students use the PREP strategy to prepare for reading. Write this acrostic on the board:

PREP
Preview title.
Read Main Idea statement.
Examine visuals.
Predict what you will learn.

Have students write their prediction and share it with a partner. After reading, ask students to write another sentence that begins "I also learned . . ."

Use with All Lessons

STRATEGY ❷

Pair Partners for Dictation

After students read each lesson in the chapter, have them write a sentence summarizing its main idea. Have students get together in pairs and dictate their sentences to each other. Then have them work together to check the sentences for accuracy and spelling.

Use with All Lessons

STRATEGY ❸

Use Sentence Stems

Before reading, provide students with the two sentence stems for the lessons listed below. Call on volunteers to read the stems orally and explain any unclear vocabulary. After reading, have students complete the stems in writing and compare completed sentences with a partner.

1.1 **a.** The worship of a single God is _____.

b. Abraham's descendants had a special religious agreement, called a _____.

1.2 **a.** The Israelites consisted of 12 extended family units, or _____.

b. The tribes of Israel lived separately but acted as a loose _____.

1.3 **a.** According to religious codes, Jews could eat only _____.

b. In the Hebrew Bible, the five books of Moses make up the _____.

Use with Lessons 1.1–1.3

GIFTED AND TALENTED

STRATEGY ❶

Teach a Class

Before beginning the chapter, allow students to choose one of the two-page lessons listed below and prepare to teach the contents to the class. Give them a set amount of time in which to present their lesson. Suggest that students think about any visuals or activities they want to use when they teach.

Use with Lessons 1.1–1.3 and 2.1–2.3

STRATEGY ❷

Read Historical Biographies

Work with the school librarian to find biographical information about the kings of the Israelites, such as David and Solomon. Allow students to choose one of the kings and read a book or story about the individual and design a way to report on the book or story to the class.

Use with Lessons 2.1–2.4

PRE-AP

STRATEGY ❶

Explain the Significance

Allow students to choose one term below to investigate and design a presentation that explains the significance of the term to the history of the Israelite kingdoms.

David

Solomon

Israel

Judah

Cyrus the Great

Diaspora

Use with Lessons 2.1–2.3

STRATEGY ❷

Form a Thesis

Have students develop a thesis statement for a specific topic related to one of the lessons in the chapter. Be sure the statement makes a claim that is supportable with evidence either from the chapter or through further research. Then have pairs compare their statements and determine which makes the strongest or most supportable claim.

Use with All Lessons

SECTION 1

THE FOUNDING OF JUDAISM

KEY VOCABULARY	NAMES & PLACES
confederation	Abraham
covenant	Deborah
kosher	Exodus
monotheism	Hebrew Bible
rabbi	Judaism
synagogue	Moses
tribe	Talmud
	Ten Commandments
	Torah

SECTION 2

KINGDOMS AND EXILE

KEY VOCABULARY	NAMES & PLACES
exile	Cyrus the Great
	David
	Diaspora
	Hanukkah
	Israel
	Judah
	Solomon
	Zealots

READING STRATEGY

IDENTIFY MAIN IDEAS AND DETAILS When you identify a text's main idea and details, you state the most important idea about a topic and list facts that support that idea. As you read the chapter, use a web like this one to identify beliefs and practices of Judaism.

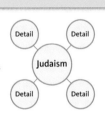

Jerusalem is the religious center of Judaism. The Old City of Jerusalem is shown here.

123

TEACHER BACKGROUND

INTRODUCE THE PHOTOGRAPH

Have students study the photograph of the Old City of Jerusalem. Explain that Jerusalem has held significance for Judaism, Christianity, and Islam for many centuries. While rulers and governments have come and gone, adherents of each religion have maintained a presence in the city because it is holy for Jews, Christians, and Muslims alike. Explain that in this chapter students will learn about the development of Judaism and the significance of Jerusalem in that development.

ASK: Why might people from all over the world travel to Jerusalem? *(Possible responses: They travel to Jerusalem to visit its holy sites and to learn about the city's rich history.)*

SHARE BACKGROUND

The Old City of Jerusalem is a walled area within the modern city of Jerusalem. It made up the entire city of Jerusalem until 1860. The Old City has been continuously inhabited for nearly 5,000 years. It includes important sites of religious significance for three religions: the Dome of the Rock and al-Aqsa Mosque for Muslims, the Church of the Holy Sepulchre for Christians, and the Temple Mount and Western Wall for Jews.

DIGITAL RESOURCES myNGconnect.com

TEACHER RESOURCES & ASSESSMENT

Social Studies Skills Lessons
- Reading: Identify Main Ideas and Details
- Writing: Write an Argument

ExamView®
One-time Download

Formal Assessment
Chapter 5 Tests A (on-level) & B (below-level)

Chapter 5 Answer Key

STUDENT BACKPACK

- **eEdition** *(English)*
- **eEdition** *(Spanish)*
- **Handbooks**
- **Online Atlas**

For Chapter 5 Spanish resources, visit the Teacher Resource Menu page.

INTRODUCE THE ESSENTIAL QUESTION

HOW DID EARLY JEWS DEVELOP AND MAINTAIN A DISTINCT CULTURAL IDENTITY?

Roundtable Activity: Elements of Culture This activity will allow students to explore the Essential Question by discussing what elements make up a culture. Divide the class into groups of four. Have group members position their desks in a circle. Hand each group a sheet of paper with these questions at the top: What elements make up a culture? What are some ways that cultures are different from one another? The first student in each group should write an answer, read it aloud, and then pass the paper clockwise to the next student who may add a new answer. The paper should be circulated around the group until the time is up. After ten minutes, ask for volunteers to read their group's answers to the class. Write groups' responses on the board. *(Possible responses: Culture includes a group's way of life; cultures differ in their foods, customs, and beliefs.)* `0:20` minutes

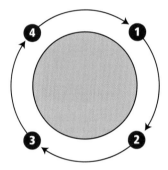

INTRODUCE THE READING STRATEGY

IDENTIFY MAIN IDEAS AND DETAILS

Remind students that the main idea tells what a selection or paragraph is about. Supporting details are facts that support the main idea. Model completing the Main Idea Cluster by reading aloud the first paragraph under "The Promised Land" in Lesson 1.1 and adding the phrase "believed in one God" as one of the details.

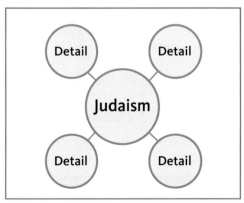

INTRODUCE CHAPTER VOCABULARY

KNOWLEDGE RATING

Have students complete a Knowledge-Rating Chart for Key Vocabulary words. Have students list words and fill out the chart. Then have pairs share the definitions they know. Work together as a class to complete the chart.

KEY VOCAB	KNOW IT	NOT SURE	DON'T KNOW	DEFINITION
confederation				
covenant				
exile				
kosher				

KEY DATES

c. **1290** B.C.	The Exodus: Moses leads the Israelites in their escape from slavery in Egypt
970 B.C.	King Solomon builds his temple in Jerusalem
922 B.C.	Israel is divided into two separate kingdoms: Israel and Judah
722 B.C.	Assyrians conquer the kingdom of Israel
586 B.C.	King Nebuchadnezzar destroys Jerusalem and Solomon's Temple and exiles many Jews
538 B.C.	Cyrus the Great allows thousands of Jews to return to Judah

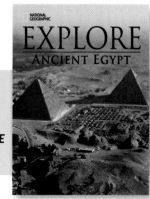

For more about ancient Egyptian pharaohs, such as Ramses II who enslaved the Israelites, see *EXPLORE ANCIENT EGYPT*.

Abraham and Moses

While mighty empires rose and fell, a group of shepherds grew into a small nation. These people never ruled a powerful empire. But they were bound together by a strong religious faith, and their influence has been greater than that of many empires. These people are known by various names, including Hebrews, Israelites, and Jews.

MAIN IDEA

Abraham and Moses were important leaders of Judaism, the first religion based on the worship of a single God.

THE PROMISED LAND

The Hebrews were a people who settled in Canaan (KAY-nuhn) around 1800 B.C. Canaan was on the eastern coast of the Mediterranean Sea. This region was later called Israel and also Palestine. The Hebrews differed from all other ancient people in an important way: they practiced **monotheism**, the worship of a single God. All other ancient people practiced polytheism, which you may recall is the worship of many gods. Monotheism was a significant development in religion and has had a great impact on cultures around the world.

Most of what we know about the Hebrews comes from the **Hebrew Bible**, a collection of ancient religious writings. According to these writings, God told **Abraham**, a Mesopotamian shepherd, to take his family and settle in Canaan. The region would be their Promised Land—a land that would belong to Abraham and his family forever. Abraham's descendants would have a special **covenant** (KUHV-uh-nuhnt), or religious agreement, with God. According to the covenant, God would protect the Hebrews if they accepted no other god and did what God asked.

The early Hebrews led a quiet, seminomadic life in Canaan. Seminomadic people move frequently with their flocks, but they often return to one place where they grow crops.

THE EXODUS

The land of Canaan sometimes became too dry for growing crops. According to the Hebrew Bible, a devastating drought, or dry period, caused such a severe shortage of food that the Hebrews left Canaan and settled in northern Egypt, perhaps around 1650 B.C. Here, the pharaoh enslaved them to work on his building projects. Around this time, the Hebrews became known as the Israelites.

The Hebrew Bible relates that the Israelites endured centuries of suffering before God chose a man named **Moses** to help them escape from Egypt. The Israelites returned to Canaan in a journey from slavery to freedom called the **Exodus**, possibly in the 1200s B.C. According to the Bible, the Israelites traveled through the desert for 40 years before finally returning to Canaan. Along the way Moses climbed Mount Sinai (SY-ny), where God gave him the **Ten Commandments** and other laws. This religious, moral, and civil code reaffirmed and expanded the Israelites' covenant with God. Today, the Ten Commandments form the basis of many modern laws, such as the law against stealing another person's property.

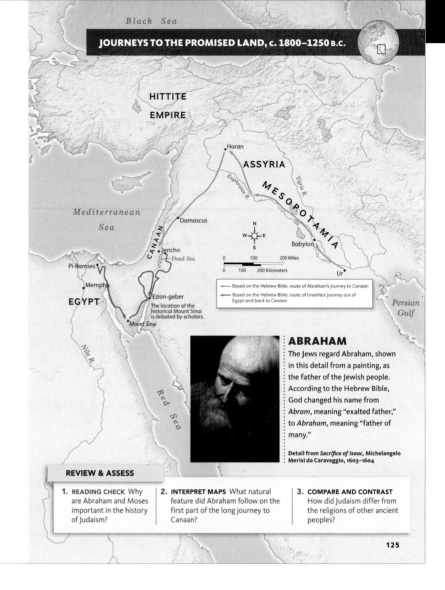

JOURNEYS TO THE PROMISED LAND, c. 1800–1250 B.C.

Based on the Hebrew Bible, route of Abraham's journey to Canaan

Based on the Hebrew Bible, route of Israelites' journey out of Egypt and back to Canaan

ABRAHAM

The Jews regard Abraham, shown in this detail from a painting, as the father of the Jewish people. According to the Hebrew Bible, God changed his name from *Abram*, meaning "exalted father," to *Abraham*, meaning "father of many."

Detail from *Sacrifice of Isaac*, Michelangelo Merisi da Caravaggio, 1603–1604

REVIEW & ASSESS

1. **READING CHECK** Why are Abraham and Moses important in the history of Judaism?

2. **INTERPRET MAPS** What natural feature did Abraham follow on the first part of the long journey to Canaan?

3. **COMPARE AND CONTRAST** How did Judaism differ from the religions of other ancient peoples?

PLAN

OBJECTIVE

Explain why Abraham and Moses were important leaders of Judaism.

CRITICAL THINKING SKILLS FOR LESSON 1.1

- Identify Main Ideas and Details
- Monitor Comprehension
- Interpret Maps
- Compare and Contrast
- Draw Conclusions
- Make Inferences

ESSENTIAL QUESTION

How did early Jews develop and maintain a distinct cultural identity?

Judaism differed from other ancient religions in that it was the first religion based on the worship of a single God. Lesson 1.1 describes the roles of Abraham and Moses in the development of Judaism.

BACKGROUND FOR THE TEACHER

Early Jewish history can be challenging because the Hebrews did not occupy and control a defined territory as many of their contemporaries did. Remind students that what united Hebrews was their belief system. Point out that this can be a much more powerful bond than a common geography. A common belief system can maintain cultural ties across geographic boundaries. Foreshadow the later history of the Jews, including the Diaspora, and point out that the strength of this belief system will become evident.

DIGITAL RESOURCES myNGconnect.com

TEACHER RESOURCES & ASSESSMENT

 Reading and Note-Taking

 Vocabulary Practice

 Section 1 Quiz

STUDENT RESOURCES

 NG Chapter Gallery

INTRODUCE & ENGAGE

BRAINSTORM STRONG LEADERS

Ask students to identify people in history who are considered strong leaders. Students' lists might include George Washington, Abraham Lincoln, or Martin Luther King, Jr. Have students record the names of these leaders on sticky notes and post them on the wall. Then work together to brainstorm characteristics that strong leaders possess. Again, record these characteristics on sticky notes and post. Tell students that in this lesson they will learn about the importance of two strong leaders to Judaism. **0:05 minutes**

TEACH

GUIDED DISCUSSION

1. **Draw Conclusions** What development by the Hebrew people had a great impact on other cultures? *(the development of monotheism)*

2. **Make Inferences** Why was it important for the Israelites to return to Canaan? *(God promised that Canaan would be their Promised Land and would be theirs forever.)*

INTERPRET MAPS

Draw students' attention to the legend and the distance scale on the Journeys to the Promised Land map. Ask students to calculate the distance that Abraham traveled to Canaan and the distance the Israelites traveled out of Egypt and back to Canaan. Have students work with partners to calculate the distances. It might be helpful to use string to follow the lines on the map against the distance scale. *(Abraham's journey is approximately 900 miles. The Israelites' journey is approximately 850 miles.)* **0:15 minutes**

ACTIVE OPTIONS

Critical Viewing: NG Chapter Gallery Have students explore the NG Chapter Gallery and choose two of the items to compare and contrast, either in written form or verbally with a partner. Ask questions that will inspire this process, such as "How are these images alike? How are they different? Why did you select these two items? How do they relate in history?" **0:10 minutes**

NG Learning Framework: A Man Called Moses

ATTITUDE: **Curiosity**
SKILLS: **Communication, Collaboration**

Invite students to reread the information about Moses in Lesson 1.1. Invite them to work in pairs to make a fact sheet about Moses based on the information in the text. Then have each pair pose one additional question about Moses they would like to answer. Have student pairs conduct responsible online research in an attempt to find the answer to their question. Encourage students to add to their Moses fact sheets as they do their research and uncover more information. Have student pairs share their fact sheets with the rest of the class. **0:10 minutes**

DIFFERENTIATE

STRIVING READERS

Summarize Read the lesson aloud while students follow along in their print or digital text. At the end of each paragraph, ask students to summarize what you read in a sentence. Allow them time to write the summary on their own paper.

ENGLISH LANGUAGE LEARNERS

Find Main Ideas and Details Have students form two groups. Give each group a piece of construction paper or a flip chart with the main idea of the lesson written on it: *Abraham and Moses were important leaders of Judaism, the first religion based on the worship of a single God.* Ask each group to list as many details from the lesson as they can to support the main idea. They should write their details on the flip chart or construction paper. Then have the two groups compare their lists.

Press (mt) *in the Student eEdition for modified text.*

See the Chapter Planner for more strategies for differentiation.

REVIEW & ASSESS

ANSWERS

1. Abraham and Moses are important to Judaism because they guided their people in significant ways. Abraham followed God's directive and moved his family to Canaan, which would be their Promised Land. Abraham's descendants would have a covenant with God in which God would protect the Hebrews if they accepted no other god and did what God asked. Moses helped the Israelites escape from Egypt and return to Canaan. Moses also received the Ten Commandments and other laws from God, which expanded the Israelites' covenant with God.

2. Abraham followed the Euphrates River on the first part of his long journey to Canaan.

3. Judaism focused on the worship of only one God, which is called monotheism. In contrast, the religions of other ancient peoples focused on the worship of multiple gods, which is called polytheism.

A Distinct Culture

You need a lot of nerve to go against a common belief. Abraham had this courage. But his strong belief ended up leading his people down a path filled with intolerance and harsh treatment, which continue in some places today. As you will see, acting out of strong belief became an important part of the distinct culture of the Israelites.

MAIN IDEA

As the Israelites fought to win control of their Promised Land, their religious beliefs and practices set them apart from the Canaanites.

Critical Viewing At Mount Tabor, the Israelites battled the Canaanites. This view shows the town of Dabburiya at the foot of Mount Tabor today. Based on this view, how would you describe the terrain of the Promised Land?

DEBORAH

Deborah was the Israelites' only female judge. At the Battle of Mount Tabor around 1125 B.C., she led the Israelites to victory against a Canaanite king.

BELIEF IN ONE GOD

The belief in one God is central to Judaism. This idea may seem normal to many people today, but it was a radical idea in the ancient world. The Israelites were the first people to reject polytheism, making Judaism the world's oldest monotheistic religion.

Belief in one God helped unify the Israelites, but their beliefs and practices also set them apart from other ancient cultures. According to the Hebrew Bible, God gave Moses a code of religious practices that governed most aspects of life. The Israelites did not worship idols, or false gods. They ate only certain foods. They did not work on the Sabbath, a weekly day of rest. While they traded with other peoples, they tried to keep a distinct cultural identity. Most Israelites did not marry outside their faith, and they were careful not to adopt foreign customs. They generally avoided the cultural diffusion, or mixing, that was a major part of many other civilizations.

THE TWELVE TRIBES

According to the Hebrew Bible, when the Israelites returned to Canaan from Egypt, they consisted of 12 **tribes**, or extended family units. Each tribe was descended from a son of Jacob, Abraham's grandson. Since Jacob was also called Israel, the tribes were called the Twelve Tribes of Israel, and Jacob's descendants were called Israelites. They referred to Canaan as the Promised Land.

Moses had died before the Israelites returned to Canaan. The Bible describes how a new leader named Joshua brought the Israelites into the Promised Land around 1250 B.C. Joshua went to war against local people known as the Canaanites, who practiced polytheism. After battling for about 200 years, the Israelites conquered most of Canaan. The tribes then divided up the conquered lands among themselves. They lived separately but acted together as a loose **confederation**, or group of allies. Powerful leaders called judges came to head the confederation of tribes. The judges directed battles, made decisions on policy, and helped keep the tribes united.

REVIEW & ASSESS

1. **READING CHECK** What was a major difference between the Israelites and the Canaanites?

2. **IDENTIFY MAIN IDEAS AND DETAILS** According to the text, how was Israelite society organized?

3. **MAKE INFERENCES** How did the Israelites maintain a distinct cultural identity?

PLAN

OBJECTIVE

Identify how the religious beliefs and practices of the Israelites set them apart from the Canaanites.

CRITICAL THINKING SKILLS FOR LESSON 1.2

- Identify Main Ideas and Details
- Monitor Comprehension
- Make Inferences
- Summarize
- Draw Conclusions
- Analyze Visuals

ESSENTIAL QUESTION

How did early Jews develop and maintain a distinct cultural identity?

The belief in one God helped unify the Israelites. Lesson 1.2 discusses how the Israelites won control of the Promised Land and how their religious beliefs and practices set them apart from the Canaanites.

BACKGROUND FOR THE TEACHER

Understanding where names came from can sometimes help explain connections between people. Different theories exist as to the origin of the term Canaan. The land of Canaan covered an area that today includes Israel, Lebanon, Palestinian territories, and western Jordan. According to the book of Genesis in the Bible, the land was named after a man called Canaan, who was the grandson of Noah. Archaeologists' findings of ancient writings show that the Canaanites were ancestors of later Phoenicians.

DIGITAL RESOURCES myNGconnect.com

TEACHER RESOURCES & ASSESSMENT

 Reading and Note-Taking

 Vocabulary Practice

 Section 1 Quiz

STUDENT RESOURCES

 Active History

INTRODUCE & ENGAGE

ACTIVATE PRIOR KNOWLEDGE

Write the term *tribe* on the board. Ask students to indicate what comes to mind when they hear the term. List students' responses on the board. Students might indicate Native American groups. Discuss the characteristics of a tribe. Students' responses might indicate that a tribe has a leader, shared values, and unique cultural characteristics. Tell students that in this lesson they will learn about the 12 tribes of Israel. **0:05** minutes

TEACH

GUIDED DISCUSSION

1. **Summarize** How did a code of religious practices given to Moses from God govern most aspects of life for the Israelites? *(Under the code, the Israelites did not worship idols, did not work on the Sabbath, did not marry outside their faith, and were careful not to adopt foreign customs.)*

2. **Draw Conclusions** How did Joshua bring the Israelites into the Promised Land? *(Joshua and the Israelites fought the Canaanites; after about 200 years, the Israelites conquered most of Canaan and divided the territory among the tribes.)*

ANALYZE VISUALS

Have students examine the photo of Mount Tabor and the town of Dabburly. Have them read the caption and answer the question. Discuss with students how the Israelites might have reacted when they viewed the Promised Land. Make a list of the reactions as students provide them. **0:10** minutes

ACTIVE OPTIONS

Active History: Investigate Major Religious Holidays Extend the lesson by using either the PDF or Whiteboard version of the activity. These activities take a deeper look at a topic from, or related to, the lesson. Explore the activities as a class, turn them into group assignments, or even assign them individually. **0:10** minutes

On Your Feet: Create a Concept Web Have students form groups of four around a section of a bulletin board or a table. Provide each group with a large sheet of paper. Have group members take turns contributing a concept or phrase to a Concept Web with the words *Distinct Culture* at the center. When time for the activity has elapsed, call on volunteers from each group to share their webs. **0:10** minutes

DIFFERENTIATE

ENGLISH LANGUAGE LEARNERS

Summarize Lesson 1.2 has four paragraphs. Have students work in pairs or small groups and assign each pair or group one paragraph to read together. Then groups should summarize their paragraph in one or two sentences for the class.

PRE-AP

Extend Knowledge Have students conduct Internet research to find out more about the Twelve Tribes of Israel. Their findings should include the names of the tribes, whom each tribe was named after, and where each tribe settled. Ask students to present their findings in an oral report to the class

Press (**mt**) *in the Student eEdition for modified text.*

See the Chapter Planner for more strategies for differentiation.

REVIEW & ASSESS

ANSWERS

1. The Israelites practiced monotheism and the Canaanites practiced polytheism.

2. Israelite society was made up of 12 tribes, or family units, which formed a confederation led by judges who decided on collective policy and kept the tribes organized.

3. The strict code of religious practices reinforced Judaism among Hebrews and set the Israelites apart from everyone else.

Beliefs and Texts of **Judaism**

Your teachers probably have high expectations of you. At the very least, they'd like you to act responsibly and follow the class rules. Likewise, the Israelites believed that God had high expectations of them and wanted them to follow his rules. These rules were written down and covered almost every aspect of their lives.

MAIN IDEA

The Israelites followed religious teachings written down in their holy books.

JEWISH BELIEFS AND PRACTICES

The Hebrew Bible describes how Moses transmitted a religious code that governed the lives of the Israelites. It addressed all aspects of life, including how to worship God, how to treat all members of society well, and what to eat. For example, they could eat only **kosher** foods, foods that were specially prepared according to Jewish dietary laws. According to these laws, animals had to be killed humanely, dairy and meat could not be eaten together, and pork and shellfish were not allowed.

Judaism stressed the importance of treating others well. It promoted social justice, equality, and the holiness of human life. The Israelites also highly valued

education, charity, and hospitality, or the kind treatment of guests. In addition, Israelite women were treated well for the time. Religious teachings told husbands to love and respect their wives, who were considered to be the heart of the family.

In time, Jews began gathering to worship in buildings called **synagogues** (SIHN-uh-gahgs), meaning "places of assembly." A spiritual leader called a **rabbi**, or "teacher," usually conducted services. Rabbis upheld Jewish customs and provided guidance for living a Jewish life.

An important practice of Judaism is the observance of a weekly day of rest known as the Sabbath. It begins at sunset on Friday and ends on Saturday night. On the Sabbath, the Jewish community gathers for prayer and to read from sacred texts. Families enjoy festive meals, and people leave behind weekday work and concerns.

SACRED TEXTS

The Hebrew Bible consists of 24 books in three sections: the **Torah**, Prophets, and Writings. The Torah consists of the five books of Moses. The name *Torah* means "the teachings." Jews believe that the Torah contains the word of God as revealed to Moses on Mount Sinai. The Torah includes religious and moral guidance covering most areas of life. In fact, it forms the basis of all Jewish law. Every synagogue has a Torah scroll, handwritten on parchment, which is treated with enormous respect and read from beginning to end over the course of a year. The Torah and other Jewish laws are discussed and explained in the **Talmud**, a collection of writings by early rabbis.

The books in the Hebrew Bible also make up the Old Testament of the Christian Bible, though the books are ordered, divided, and sometimes named differently. Many stories related in the Hebrew Bible and in the Christian Bible also appear in the Qur'an, the holy book of Islam. For example, stories about Abraham appear in all three texts.

This page from a Hebrew Bible dated 1299 is written in Hebrew script.

REVIEW & ASSESS

1. **READING CHECK** What are some important beliefs and texts of Judaism?

2. **MAKE GENERALIZATIONS** What were important values in Judaism, and why might they have stood out in the ancient world?

3. **DRAW CONCLUSIONS** Why do you think the Torah is treated with great respect by Jews?

PLAN

OBJECTIVE

Describe the religious teachings written down in the religious books of the Israelites.

CRITICAL THINKING SKILLS FOR LESSON 1.3

- Identify Main Ideas and Details
- Monitor Comprehension
- Make Generalizations
- Draw Conclusions
- Form Opinions
- Explain

ESSENTIAL QUESTION

How did early Jews develop and maintain a distinct cultural identity?

The beliefs and teachings of the Jews led to the development of a distinct cultural identity. Lesson 1.3 describes the beliefs and practices and the sacred texts of the Jews.

BACKGROUND FOR THE TEACHER

According to Jewish law, keeping kosher involves three elements. The first is to avoid any non-kosher animals. These include animals that do not chew their cud and have cleft hooves and fish that don't have fins and scales. A second element in keeping kosher is to avoid eating meat and dairy together. The third element involves only eating meat that was slaughtered in a certain way and drained of blood. For Jews, keeping kosher was a way to obey God's laws and to preserve a distinct identity.

DIGITAL RESOURCES myNGconnect.com

TEACHER RESOURCES & ASSESSMENT

 Reading and Note-Taking   **Vocabulary Practice**   **Section 1 Quiz**

STUDENT RESOURCES

 NG Chapter Gallery

INTRODUCE & ENGAGE

CONCEPT EXPLORATION

Display the Concept Web shown here. Discuss the concept of values with the class. Then divide the class into small groups. Have each group discuss what values they think people in their school and community have. Then call on a member from each group to share the values the group elicited. Record the responses in one of the circles of the Concept Web. Tell students that in this lesson they will learn about the values that were important to Judaism. **0:10** minutes

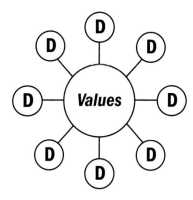

TEACH

GUIDED DISCUSSION

1. **Form Opinions** Judaism included important values and practices that Jews were to follow. Which of the practices and values do you consider to be most important? *(Responses will vary, but students should provide reasons for their opinion.)*

2. **Explain** Why is the Torah important in Judaism? *(Jews believe that the Torah contains the word of God as revealed to Moses on Mount Sinai. It includes religious and moral guidance covering most areas of life and forms the basis of all Jewish law.)*

MORE INFORMATION

Illuminated Manuscript The picture in the lesson is a page from a rare Hebrew manuscript known as the Cervera Bible. The Bible is a manuscript on parchment in Hebrew characters, written and illustrated in Cervera, Spain, between 1299 and 1300. By 1300, Jews had lived in parts of Spain for hundreds of years. The pages in the Bible include ornamental frames and intricate patterns, as well as pictures of mythological creatures such as the unicorn and centaur. The Cervera Bible is richly illustrated, making it one of the most beautiful manuscripts of Medieval Europe. **0:15** minutes

ACTIVE OPTIONS

Critical Viewing: NG Chapter Gallery Invite students to explore the Chapter Gallery to examine the images that relate to this chapter. Have them select one of the images and do additional research to learn more about it. Ask questions that will inspire additional inquiry about the chosen gallery image, such as: What

is this? Where and when was this created? By whom? Why was it created? What is it made of? Why does it belong in this chapter? What else would you like to know about it? **0:10** minutes

On Your Feet: Inside-Outside Circle Arrange students in concentric circles facing each other. Have students in the outside circle ask the students in the inside circle a question about the lesson. Then have the outside circle rotate one position to the right to create new pairings. After five questions, have students switch roles and continue. **0:15** minutes

DIFFERENTIATE

INCLUSION

Use Supported Reading Have students work in pairs and assign each pair one paragraph to read aloud together. At the end of each paragraph, have them use the following sentence frames to tell what they do and do not understand:

This paragraph is about _____.

One fact that stood out to me is _____.

_____ is a word I had trouble understanding, so I figured it out
by _____.

Be sure students understand the content before moving on to the next paragraph.

GIFTED & TALENTED

Create Illuminated Manuscripts Have students research illuminated manuscripts, particularly those from medieval times. Then ask students to choose a page from a favorite book and create their own illuminated pages. Share students' pages in a bulletin-board display.

Press **mt** *in the Student eEdition for modified text.*

See the Chapter Planner for more strategies for differentiation.

REVIEW & ASSESS

ANSWERS

1. Some important beliefs of Judaism include how to worship, live, and even what to wear and eat. Important texts include the 24 books of the Hebrew Bible, consisting of the Torah, Prophets, and Writings, and the Talmud, a collection of writings by early rabbis.

2. Social justice, equality, the holiness of human life, education, charity, and hospitality were important values in Judaism. These values are comparatively modern and would have been unusual in the ancient world.

3. The Torah is treated with great respect by the Jews because the Jews believe that the Torah contains the word of God as revealed to Moses, and it forms the basis of all Jewish laws.

Writings from the Hebrew Bible

Judaism was originally based on an oral tradition, in which stories are passed down by word of mouth. After the Israelites developed writing, they wrote down their religious texts. In 1947, a shepherd discovered a set of texts near the Dead Sea. Later known as the Dead Sea Scrolls, these texts included portions of the Hebrew Bible dating from around 150 B.C.

ANSWERS

DOCUMENT 1
God promises to make Canaan a great nation and to bless Abraham.

DOCUMENT 2
The first four commandments focus on how to worship and show respect to God. The last six commandments tell people how to conduct themselves and interact with others.

In this part of a painting by Italian artist Guido Reni, Moses is shown with one of the two tablets containing the Ten Commandments.

Moses with the Tablets of the Law, Guido Reni, 17th century

130

DOCUMENT ONE
Primary Source: Sacred Text

from the Book of Genesis
Genesis is the first book of the Hebrew Bible. In this excerpt, God speaks to Abraham and tells him to bring his family to the land of Canaan.

CONSTRUCTED RESPONSE What does God promise Abraham?

> Go forth from your native land and from your father's house to the land that I will show you. I will make of you a great nation, and I will bless you.
>
> *Genesis 12:1–2*

DOCUMENT TWO
Primary Source: Sacred Text

from the Book of Exodus
Exodus is the second book of the Hebrew Bible. It describes the oppression of the Israelites in Egypt and their escape from slavery to freedom during the Exodus. It also depicts Moses' experience on Mount Sinai, where God gave Moses the Ten Commandments. According to the Bible, these laws were written on two stone tablets. This excerpt details the Ten Commandments.

CONSTRUCTED RESPONSE What do the first four commandments have in common? What do the last six have in common?

The Great Isaiah Scroll, one of the Dead Sea Scrolls

> **Ten Commandments**
>
> 1. I the Lord am your God. . . . You shall have no other gods besides Me.
> 2. You shall not make for yourself a sculptured image [idol].
> 3. You shall not swear falsely by the name of the Lord your God.
> 4. Remember the Sabbath day and keep it holy.
> 5. Honor your father and your mother.
> 6. You shall not murder.
> 7. You shall not commit adultery.
> 8. You shall not steal.
> 9. You shall not bear false witness against your neighbor.
> 10. You shall not covet [desire] . . . anything that is your neighbor's.
>
> *Exodus 20:2–14*

SYNTHESIZE & WRITE

1. **REVIEW** Review what you have learned about the covenant made between God and the Israelites.

2. **RECALL** On your own paper, write down the main idea expressed in each document above.

3. **CONSTRUCT** Construct a topic sentence that answers this question: What did God promise the Israelites?

4. **WRITE** Using evidence from the documents, write an explanatory paragraph that supports your topic sentence from Step 3.

PLAN

OBJECTIVE

Synthesize information about the Hebrew Bible from primary source documents.

CRITICAL THINKING SKILLS FOR LESSON 1.4

- Synthesize
- Identify
- Make Generalizations
- Evaluate

ESSENTIAL QUESTION

How did early Jews develop and maintain a distinct cultural identity?

The Hebrew Bible forms the basis of all Jewish law. Lesson 1.4 includes excerpts of writings from two books of the Hebrew Bible.

BACKGROUND FOR THE TEACHER

The Dead Sea Scrolls are one of the greatest archaeological finds in modern times. They include about 800 to 900 ancient manuscripts in roughly 15,000 fragments. The fragments were discovered in 11 caves along the northwest shore of the Dead Sea. The scrolls include fragments from almost all the books of the Hebrew Bible. The first seven scrolls were found in 1947 when a shepherd followed a runaway goat into a cave. The decomposed scrolls, made of leather and wrapped in linen cloth, were found inside several large pottery jars. The scrolls show the variety of Jewish thought and practice at the time. For a long time, only a small number of scholars had access to the scrolls. Finally, in the early 1990s, copies of the scrolls were published.

DIGITAL RESOURCES myNGconnect.com

TEACHER RESOURCES & ASSESSMENT

 Reading and Note-Taking   **Vocabulary Practice**   **Section 1 Quiz**

STUDENT RESOURCES

 NG Chapter Gallery

INTRODUCE & ENGAGE

PREPARE FOR THE DOCUMENT-BASED QUESTION

Before students start on the activity, briefly preview the two documents. Remind students that a constructed response requires full explanations in complete sentences. Emphasize that students should use their knowledge of the beliefs and practices of Judaism in addition to the information in the documents. **0:05** minutes

TEACH

GUIDED DISCUSSION

1. **Identify** Which of the Ten Commandments reflect the Hebrew belief in a single God? *(the first and second commandments)*

2. **Make Generalizations** Have students review the Ten Commandments in Document 2. **ASK:** What modern-day laws are reflected in the Ten Commandments? *(Student responses will vary but might point to the sixth, eighth, and ninth commandments.)*

EVALUATE

After students have completed the "Synthesize & Write" activity, allow time for them to exchange paragraphs and read and comment on the work of their peers. Guidelines for comments should be established prior to this activity so that feedback is constructive and encouraging in nature. **0:15** minutes

ACTIVE OPTIONS

Critical Viewing: NG Chapter Gallery Ask students to choose one image from the Chapter Gallery and become an expert on it. They should do additional research to learn all about it. Then students should share their findings with a partner, small group, or the class. **0:10** minutes

On Your Feet: Two Options Label two locations in the room with the name of one of the documents featured in the lesson. Have students reread the lesson and walk to the corner of the room with the document that best helped support their understanding of the importance of the Hebrew Bible to the beliefs and practices of the Israelites. Have students who chose the same document discuss why they made their selection. Then have volunteers from each group explain what their document is and offer some of the group's reasons for choosing that one. **0:20** minutes

DIFFERENTIATE

INCLUSION

Work in Pairs If some students have disabilities, consider pairing them with other students who can read the documents aloud to them. You may also want to give students the option of recording their responses.

PRE-AP

Research Have students conduct Internet research to find out more about the Dead Sea Scrolls. Have them report to the rest of the class about the information that the Dead Sea Scrolls provided archaeologists and historians. Suggest that students include a map showing the location of the findings with their report.

Press **mt** *in the Student eEdition for modified text.*

See the Chapter Planner for more strategies for differentiation.

SYNTHESIZE & WRITE

ANSWERS

1. Responses will vary.

2. Responses will vary.

3. Possible response: God promised the Israelites that they would have a great nation and be blessed if they did what he told them.

4. Students' paragraphs should include their topic sentence from Step 3 and provide several details from the documents to support the sentence.

Israel
and Judah

Twelve friends decide to go to a movie, but everyone has different ideas about what to see. Finally, they agree to put one person in charge—a natural-born leader. His decision is quick and readily accepted. For a similar reason, the Israelites swapped decision-making by judges for rule by a single strong king.

MAIN IDEA

The Israelites united under a line of kings, but they later became divided and were defeated by external powers.

DAVID

David, a simple shepherd, attracted attention when he killed a gigantic warrior called Goliath using only his shepherd's sling and stones. David became one of the Israelites' greatest kings. His emblem, the six-pointed star called the Star of David or Shield of David, became a symbol of Judaism and modern Israel.

A LINE OF KINGS

The Israelites realized they needed greater unity and stronger leadership when they were attacked by another people called the Philistines (FIH-luh-steens), who lived in the area. The Israelites appointed a king named Saul to rule. In 1020 B.C., Saul defended Israel against the Philistines and other enemies.

When Saul died, **David** was crowned king. David united the tribes and continued the fight against the Philistines and other enemies. He captured Jerusalem and made it his capital, starting its transformation into one of history's most important cities.

David's son **Solomon** inherited a peaceful kingdom. He built a great stone temple in Jerusalem. Solomon's Temple became the focus of religious life. Solomon used trade and taxes to fund other huge building projects. However, most of the tax burden fell on the northern tribes, who came to resent Solomon's rule. Once again, trouble began.

Soon war broke out between the northern and southern tribes. Around 922 B.C., Israel was divided into two kingdoms: **Israel** in the north and **Judah** in the south. The northern kingdom consisted of ten of the original tribes, while the southern kingdom consisted of the remaining two. The kingdoms sometimes fought each other and sometimes formed alliances against common enemies. Eventually, Judaism and the Jewish people would be named after Judah.

INVADED AND CONQUERED

In 722 B.C., the Assyrian Empire conquered Israel. The ten tribes of Israel were scattered to other lands and disappeared from history. Judah, though, survived and was able to fight off Assyria.

However, Judah soon found itself the battleground between two warring groups: the Egyptians and the New Babylonians. Egypt conquered Judah first. Then the New Babylonian army, led by King Nebuchadnezzar, overran Judah.

Judah rebelled. In 597 B.C., the king responded by invading Jerusalem. He moved the elite members of society to Babylon, leaving the poor behind. In 586 B.C., Nebuchadnezzar's army destroyed Jerusalem, including Solomon's Temple. For the Jews, the age of kings was over.

SOLOMON'S TEMPLE

According to the Hebrew Bible, King Solomon built a magnificent temple in Jerusalem with walls and a floor of cedarwood overlaid in gold. The Bible indicates that Solomon's Temple housed the Ark of the Covenant, a container holding the stone tablets with the Ten Commandments. This reconstruction is based on descriptions of the Temple in the Hebrew Bible.

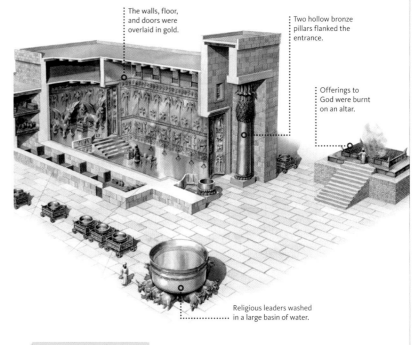

The walls, floor, and doors were overlaid in gold.

Two hollow bronze pillars flanked the entrance.

Offerings to God were burnt on an altar.

Religious leaders washed in a large basin of water.

REVIEW & ASSESS

1. **READING CHECK** What events mark the rise and fall of the Jews' age of kings?

2. **IDENTIFY PROBLEMS** What was one source of conflict between the northern and southern tribes of the Israelites?

3. **MAKE INFERENCES** What do you think the destruction of Solomon's Temple meant to the Israelites?

PLAN

OBJECTIVE

Explain why the Israelites, at first united under a line of kings, later became divided and defeated by external powers.

CRITICAL THINKING SKILLS FOR LESSON 2.1

- Identify Main Ideas and Details
- Monitor Comprehension
- Identify Problems
- Make Inferences
- Draw Conclusions
- Analyze Effects

ESSENTIAL QUESTION

How did early Jews develop and maintain a distinct cultural identity?

The need for greater unity and strong leadership to defend against attacks by another people led the Israelites to appoint a king to rule. Lesson 2.1 discusses the rise of a line of kings of the Israelites, the division of Israel into two kingdoms, and the defeat of the kingdoms by external powers.

BACKGROUND FOR THE TEACHER

Most of what is known about King Solomon comes from the Hebrew Bible. He is known for accumulating enormous wealth while ruling a kingdom that extended from the Euphrates River in the north to Egypt in the south. He is also known for his wisdom, which people from long distances came to hear.

DIGITAL RESOURCES myNGconnect.com

TEACHER RESOURCES & ASSESSMENT

 Reading and Note-Taking

 Vocabulary Practice

 Section 2 Quiz

STUDENT RESOURCES

 Biography

INTRODUCE & ENGAGE

PREVIEW VISUALS

Direct students' attention to the illustration of Solomon's Temple in the lesson. Ask them to read the captions describing the elements of the temple. **ASK:** What was the purpose of the temple? *(It was a place of worship.)* How do you think King Solomon was able to pay for such an elaborate structure? *(Students might indicate that money from trade and taxes collected from his subjects might have been used to pay for building the structure.)* Tell students that in this lesson they will learn about King Solomon and the effect that taxing his subjects had on the Israelite tribes. `0:05` minutes

TEACH

GUIDED DISCUSSION

1. **Draw Conclusions** Why did war break out between the northern and southern tribes? *(People in the northern tribes resented having the greater tax burden placed on them to fund Solomon's huge building project.)*

2. **Analyze Effects** What was the effect of the Assyrian Empire conquering Israel? *(The ten tribes of Israel were scattered to other lands and disappeared from history. Judah survived and fought off Assyria.)*

CREATE TIME LINES

Have students work in pairs to create a time line of events in this lesson. Instruct students to include the dates as discussed in the text and a key event for each date. Work with students to space their dates appropriately on the time line. `0:15` minutes

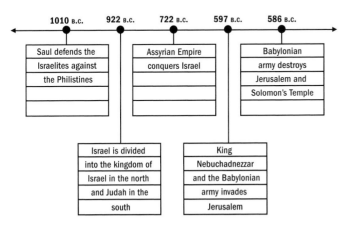

ACTIVE OPTIONS

NG Learning Framework: Write a Biography

ATTITUDE: **Curiosity**
KNOWLEDGE: **Our Human Story**

Have students select one of the people they are still curious about after learning about this individual in this chapter. Instruct them to write a short biography about this person using information from the chapter and additional source material. `0:10` minutes

On Your Feet: Tell Me More Have students form four teams and assign each team one of the following topics:

- King David
- King Solomon
- Israel
- Judah

Each group should write down as many facts about its topic as it can. Have the class reconvene and have each group stand up, one at a time. The rest of the class calls out "Tell me more about [the topic]." The group recites one fact. The class again requests a fact until the group runs out of facts to share. Then the next group presents its facts. `0:10` minutes

DIFFERENTIATE

ENGLISH LANGUAGE LEARNERS

Use Sentence Strips Choose a paragraph from the lesson and make sentence strips out of it. Read the paragraph aloud, having students follow along in their books. Have students close their books and give them the set of sentence strips. Students should put the strips in order and then read the paragraph aloud.

GIFTED & TALENTED

Create Models Have pairs of students work on creating a model of Solomon's Temple. Suggest building materials such as paper, cardboard, or clay. Direct students to use the illustration of the temple in the lesson as well as other sources to make the model. Encourage students to display their models once they have completed them.

Press (**mt**) *in the Student eEdition for modified text.*

See the Chapter Planner for more strategies for differentiation.

REVIEW & ASSESS

ANSWERS

1. The rise of the Jews' age of kings came when the Israelites, realizing that they needed strong leadership to defend against the Philistines, appointed a king named Saul. The fall of the age of kings came when the Babylonian army invaded and destroyed Jerusalem and Solomon's Temple.

2. One source of conflict between the northern and southern tribes was Solomon's taxes, especially on the northern tribes, to pay for his huge building projects. This tax burden caused them to resent Solomon's rule.

3. For the Israelites, the destruction of Solomon's Temple might have meant the end of their religious life and their distinct identity.

Jews come to pray at Jerusalem's Western Wall, a remnant of the Second Temple. Many visitors leave written prayers in cracks in the wall.

2.2 Exile and Return

Psalm 137, from a book in the Hebrew Bible, captures the terrible upheaval the Jews suffered when they were forced to leave Judah and live in Babylon: "By the rivers of Babylon, there we sat, sat and wept, as we thought of Zion [Israel]. How can we sing of the Lord on alien [foreign] soil?" But the Jews found a way, and they grew stronger as a result of the experience.

MAIN IDEA

While in Babylon, the Jews maintained, developed, and strengthened their identity and religion.

BABYLONIAN CAPTIVITY

The removal of some of the Jewish people from their homeland to faraway Babylonia was a deeply distressing experience. Their captivity, called the Babylonian Exile, lasted about 50 years. **Exile** is the forced removal from one's native country. During the exile, Jews built their first synagogues.

Any remaining tribal divisions disappeared, to be replaced by a sense of religious and social unity among the Jewish people. Scribes started writing down the holy texts in a new script that is still used today. Most importantly, the Jews found that it actually was possible to "sing of the Lord on alien soil." Although they had lost control of the Promised Land, the Jews held on to their cultural identity and their religious faith.

CYRUS THE GREAT OF PERSIA

The Jews' efforts to maintain their faith were aided when **Cyrus the Great**, king of the Persian Empire, conquered Babylon in 539 B.C. As you may remember, Cyrus became known as "the Great" because of his impressive military conquests and wise rule. He adopted a policy of tolerance, allowing conquered people to keep their own customs and beliefs.

While Judah remained under Persian control, Cyrus freed the Jewish people in Babylon and encouraged them to return to their homeland and rebuild the Jewish state. Because of his policy of tolerance, Cyrus became a hero to the Jews.

Many of the Jewish people decided to stay in Babylonia. They formed a large Jewish community that thrived for centuries and remains in small numbers in present-day Iran and Iraq. However, in 538 B.C., about 42,000 Jews returned to Judah. There, they began rebuilding the temple in Jerusalem, called the Second Temple. Religious leaders began to refine Judaism into something like its modern form. In particular, they finalized the Hebrew Bible, which became the central document of the Jewish faith, and began public readings of the Torah.

REVIEW & ASSESS

1. **READING CHECK** Why did Cyrus the Great become a hero to the Jews?

2. **IDENTIFY DETAILS** While in exile, how did the Jews maintain their identity?

3. **MAKE INFERENCES** Why did a large number of Jews return to Judah in 538 B.C.?

PLAN

OBJECTIVE

Explain how the Jews maintained, developed, and strengthened their identity and religion while in Babylon.

CRITICAL THINKING SKILLS FOR LESSON 2.2

- Identify Main Ideas and Details
- Monitor Comprehension
- Make Inferences
- Explain
- Analyze Cause and Effect

ESSENTIAL QUESTION

How did early Jews develop and maintain a distinct cultural identity?

The Jewish people were held in captivity in Babylon for about 50 years. Lesson 2.2 explains how the Jews maintained and strengthened their identity and religion.

BACKGROUND FOR THE TEACHER

Cyrus the Great is known for more than just being a great Persian emperor. He is also known as being the epitome of what a great ruler should be. Though he was an impressive military conqueror, Cyrus considered himself a liberator of people and not a conqueror. He treated his subjects equally regardless of religion or ethnicity, allowing them to keep their religion and customs. His rule differed greatly from that of other rulers, such as those of the Assyrians.

DIGITAL RESOURCES myNGconnect.com

TEACHER RESOURCES & ASSESSMENT

 Reading and Note-Taking

 Vocabulary Practice

 Section 2 Quiz

STUDENT RESOURCES

 NG Chapter Gallery

INTRODUCE & ENGAGE

WORD KNOWLEDGE

Ask students if they know what the word *exile* means. Write students' responses on the board. Explain that *exile* is the forced removal from one's native country. Then direct students' attention to the lesson title. Tell students that the title applies to the Jewish people. Ask students what they think the lesson will be about based on the title. **0:10 minutes**

TEACH

GUIDED DISCUSSION

1. **Explain** What was the Babylonian captivity? *(The Babylonian captivity refers to the removal of the Jewish people from Judah to Babylon, where they were held captive for about 50 years.)*

2. **Analyze Cause and Effect** How did the Babylonian Exile affect the Jewish faith? *(It caused the faith to grow stronger as Jews put aside any tribal divisions and wrote down the holy texts.)*

MORE INFORMATION

The Western Wall The Western Wall, sacred to the Jewish people, is a place of prayer in the Old City of Jerusalem. The wall is all that remains of the Second Temple of Jerusalem. Its authenticity has been confirmed by history and archaeological research. What remains of the Western Wall today measures about 160 feet long and about 60 feet high. Jews who visit the wall express sadness over the temple's destruction and pray that it will be restored. Visitors to the Western Wall (pictured in the lesson) often wedge small slips of paper, on which they write prayers and petitions, into the cracks between the stones.

ACTIVE OPTIONS

Critical Viewing: NG Chapter Gallery Have students examine the contents of the Chapter Gallery for this chapter. Then invite them to brainstorm additional images they believe would fit within the Chapter Gallery. Have them write a description of these additional images and provide an explanation of why they would fit within the Chapter Gallery. Then instruct them to do online research to find examples of actual images they would like to add to the gallery. **0:10 minutes**

On Your Feet: Card Responses Have half the class create ten true-false questions based on information in the lesson. Ask the other half to create answer cards, with "True" written on one side and "False" on the other. As each question is read aloud, students in the second group should display the correct answer to the question. **0:10 minutes**

DIFFERENTIATE

STRIVING READERS

Preview Text Help students preview the lesson. Point out the text features, such as the lesson title, Main Idea, and headings. **ASK:** Based on the subheadings, what do you expect this lesson to be about? As students begin reading, help them confirm their understanding of each paragraph before moving on to the next one.

PRE-AP

Research and Present Have students use the Internet to research the life of Cyrus the Great. Students should find out about his early life, his conquests and achievements, and his legacy. Then ask them to write a short biography and share it with the class.

Press **mt** *in the Student eEdition for modified text.*

See the Chapter Planner for more strategies for differentiation.

REVIEW & ASSESS

ANSWERS

1. Cyrus the Great became a hero to the Jews because he freed the Jewish people and encouraged them to return to Judah and rebuild the Jewish state.

2. While living in exile, old tribal divisions disappeared and a sense of unity developed as Jews practiced their religious faith and held onto their cultural identity.

3. A large number of Jews likely returned to Judah in 538 B.C. to reestablish their community and strengthen their identity.

2.3

The Diaspora

If you moved to another country to live, you might adopt its language and customs to get along. But when Jews settled abroad, most tried hard to keep practicing their own religion and customs. The ability of the Jewish people to preserve their religion and heritage has been one of the most remarkable achievements in world history.

MAIN IDEA

The Syrians and then the Romans tried to destroy Judaism but ultimately failed.

YOHANNAN BEN ZAKAI

When the Romans destroyed the Second Temple, a Jewish teacher named Yohannan Ben Zakai asked permission to establish a school to teach Jewish scholars. The school was important in preserving Jewish traditions. Today, Jews regard Zakai as a great hero.

SYRIAN CONTROL

After the Persians, competing foreign powers controlled Judah. By about 300 B.C., Egypt took over the Jewish homeland. The Egyptian rulers tolerated Judaism and largely left Judah alone.

In 198 B.C., a Syrian empire, the Seleucids, conquered Judah. The Seleucids treated the Jews well until 168 B.C., when the Seleucid king tried to force the Jews to worship Greek gods. He dedicated the Second Temple to the Greek god Zeus. Outraged Jews rebelled, led by a family called the Maccabees. Their small army fought hard, defeated the Seleucids, and rededicated the Second Temple to Judaism.

ROMAN RULE

Judah's freedom from foreign rule did not last long. In 63 B.C., Rome seized control of the region. At first the Romans allowed the Jews to rule themselves. In time, however, Rome took direct control of Judah and insisted that Jews worship the Roman gods. Many Jews, including revolutionaries called **Zealots**, favored armed rebellion.

War finally broke out in A.D. 66. Unfortunately, Jewish resistance was no match for the powerful Roman army. Rome's soldiers destroyed much of Jerusalem, including the Second Temple. By A.D. 70, the war was almost over. The Zealots fought on from the mountaintop fortress of Masada, but the Roman army eventually crushed the revolt.

After the rebellion, many Jews were forced to leave Jerusalem and settle in new places. The migration of Jews to places around the world, which began with the Babylonian Exile, is called the **Diaspora** (dy-AS-puh-ruh). Yet even after leaving their homeland, Jews kept their religion alive and maintained a strong connection to the land of Israel. The rabbis transformed Judaism into a home- and synagogue-based religion that could be practiced anywhere. By holding on to their religion and customs, the dispersed Jews ensured Judaism would become a worldwide religion.

The legacy of the Jewish people is important in world history. Judaism was the first monotheistic religion. Its emphasis on justice and morality influenced later religions, including Christianity. Judaism also had a great influence on other aspects of Western civilization, such as law.

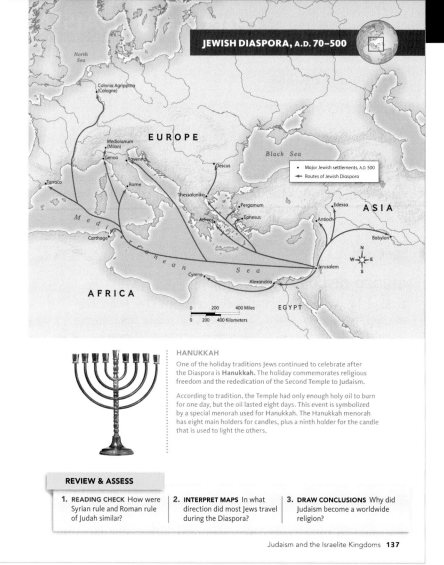

JEWISH DIASPORA, A.D. 70–500

- Major Jewish settlements, A.D. 500
- Routes of Jewish Diaspora

HANUKKAH

One of the holiday traditions Jews continued to celebrate after the Diaspora is **Hanukkah.** The holiday commemorates religious freedom and the rededication of the Second Temple to Judaism.

According to tradition, the Temple had only enough holy oil to burn for one day, but the oil lasted eight days. This event is symbolized by a special menorah used for Hanukkah. The Hanukkah menorah has eight main holders for candles, plus a ninth holder for the candle that is used to light the others.

REVIEW & ASSESS

1. **READING CHECK** How were Syrian rule and Roman rule of Judah similar?

2. **INTERPRET MAPS** In what direction did most Jews travel during the Diaspora?

3. **DRAW CONCLUSIONS** Why did Judaism become a worldwide religion?

PLAN

OBJECTIVE

Explain why the Syrians and the Romans failed in their attempts to destroy Judaism.

CRITICAL THINKING SKILLS FOR LESSON 2.3

- Identify Main Ideas and Details
- Monitor Comprehension
- Interpret Maps
- Draw Conclusions
- Form Opinions

ESSENTIAL QUESTION

How did early Jews develop and maintain a distinct cultural identity?

Syrians and Romans both controlled Judah. Lesson 2.3 examines why their attempts to destroy Judah failed.

BACKGROUND FOR THE TEACHER

Zealots were members of a Jewish sect and an aggressive political party who opposed Roman rule and the Romans' polytheism. Zealots also opposed those Jews who sought improved relations with the Roman authorities. Extremist groups of Zealots turned to terrorism. They would even attack Jews who were friendly to Rome. In A.D. 66–70, Zealots played a leading role in the first revolt against Rome.

DIGITAL RESOURCES myNGconnect.com

TEACHER RESOURCES & ASSESSMENT

 Reading and Note-Taking

 Vocabulary Practice

 Section 2 Quiz

STUDENT RESOURCES

 NG Chapter Gallery

INTRODUCE & ENGAGE

MAKE CONNECTIONS

Present a situation to students in which people have to move from their homes and settle in an unfamiliar place. Discuss with students what issues people might face in making such a move. Students' responses might include issues such as figuring out what to take with them, setting up a new home, getting to know people in the new area, or anxiety about living in an unfamiliar place. Point out to students that in this lesson they will learn why many Jews were forced to move from Jerusalem and where they settled.
0:10 minutes

TEACH

GUIDED DISCUSSION

1. **Draw Conclusions** How were the Jews able to maintain their identity even after being forced to leave their homeland? *(The Jews kept their religion alive and maintained a strong connection to the land of Israel. The rabbis transformed Judaism into a home-based and synagogue-based religion that Jews could practice anywhere.)*

2. **Form Opinions** The legacy of the Jewish people is important in world history. What do you think is their most important legacy? Why do you think so? *(Responses will vary, but students should provide reasons for their opinions. Students might indicate that monotheism was the biggest legacy. Others might indicate Judaism's influence on other religions, particularly Christianity, or its influence on law.)*

INTERPRET MAPS

Draw students' attention to the map of the Jewish Diaspora. Have students review the map legend. **ASK:** What Jewish settlements were located in Africa? *(Alexandria and Cyrene)* What was the main water route for the Diaspora? *(the Mediterranean Sea)*
0:15 minutes

ACTIVE OPTIONS

Critical Viewing: NG Chapter Gallery Invite students to explore the NG Chapter Gallery and choose one image from the gallery they feels best represents their understanding of the chapter. Have students provide a written explanation of why they selected the images they chose. **0:10** minutes

On Your Feet: One-on-One Interviews Group students into pairs. Have both students in each pair write three questions about Syrian and Roman rule of Judah. Start with one student using his or her questions to interview the other student "expert" about Judah under Syrian and Roman rule. Students' answers should show an understanding of the material from the lesson. Once the interview is complete, students should reverse roles. **0:15** minutes

DIFFERENTIATE

INCLUSION

Clarify Text Have visually-impaired students work with sighted partners. As they listen to an audio recording of the text, have the visually-impaired students indicate if there are words or passages they do not understand. Their partners can clarify meaning by repeating passages, emphasizing context clues, and paraphrasing.

GIFTED & TALENTED

Write Journal Entries Have students imagine that they are reporters covering the story of the Diaspora. Ask them to create a set of four or five journal entries that tell why the Jews are moving, Jewish thoughts about the move, and what the Jews hope their life will be like in their new home. Encourage students to use descriptive words and include their personal reactions to the move. Students can then take turns sharing their entries.

Press **mt** in the Student eEdition for modified text.

See the Chapter Planner for more strategies for differentiation.

REVIEW & ASSESS

ANSWERS

1. They were similar in that they both insisted that the Jews worship their gods.

2. Most Jews traveled westward from Jerusalem, spreading throughout the Roman Empire.

3. The Roman destruction of the Second Temple contributed to the dispersal of Jews throughout the world, known as the Diaspora, which spread the Jewish religion worldwide.

Uncovering the Story of Caesarea's Port

In the first century B.C., Judea was a province of Rome and was ruled by a Roman-appointed king named Herod. He founded the city of Caesarea on the coast of what is now Israel. Sometime in the A.D. 100s, the city's port was mysteriously destroyed. That's where National Geographic Explorer Beverly Goodman comes in. Goodman is a geoarchaeologist, a scientist who investigates ancient cultures by applying the tools of earth science. By studying broken seashells, she concluded that a natural disaster destroyed Caesarea's port.

^
Beverly Goodman, shown above, studies archaeological sites along the Mediterranean coast.

MAIN IDEA

Geoarchaeologist Beverly Goodman has shown that a natural disaster likely destroyed the ancient port of Caesarea.

ISRAEL'S ANCIENT COASTLINE

Goodman's research focuses on the complex interaction between nature and humans along coastlines. "No place is more vulnerable than our coasts," she explains. Her findings from the port of Caesarea prove this thesis while ringing alarm bells that echo across 2,000 years.

At the end of the first century B.C., King Herod built a huge harbor at Caesarea to tap into the valuable trade between the East and ancient Rome. Caesarea had no geographic features useful for a harbor, so Herod relied on "modern" technology.

Herod's builders used waterproof concrete to build huge breakwaters, or walls extending out from the coast. These breakwaters created a deepwater harbor where sailing ships could shelter from great storms. Nevertheless, the harbor could not escape the sea's deadliest force. That force came in the form of a tsunami (su-NAH-mee), a giant ocean wave caused by an underwater earthquake, a volcanic eruption, or a landslide. Tsunamis have threatened humans for as long as people have lived on the world's coastlines.

A 2,000-YEAR-OLD DISASTER

Before Goodman began her investigation, no researchers had ever found physical evidence of a major disaster. Scholars had always thought that the harbor had disappeared because of the builders' poor workmanship and inferior materials.

An aerial view of the ruins of Caesarea

However, when Goodman began exploring the coastline, she uncovered an unusual concentration of shell fragments. "Instead of the normal half-inch layer, this band of shells was more than three feet deep!" she said.

To gather more evidence, she developed a new way of taking deep-sea core samples, sinking hollow tubes into the seabed and then pulling them out to show the layers of deposits. The layers can be read like tree rings. Analysis and dating suggested that a single, sudden, and violent event caused the shell concentrations. Goodman concluded that a major tsunami had destroyed Herod's great harbor.

Goodman is now putting her findings to the test. She's examining other archaeological sites around the Mediterranean region, looking for signs of tsunami damage. Goodman's research could help save lives in the future. "Analyzing the causes and effects of ancient environmental events like tsunamis can help tell us which types of coast are at greatest risk, and what kind of damage to expect in the future," Goodman explains. "I hope I'm collecting clues that will help us avoid catastrophic consequences down the line."

REVIEW & ASSESS

1. **READING CHECK** What natural disaster likely destroyed the ancient port of Caesarea?
2. **IDENTIFY MAIN IDEAS AND DETAILS** What findings support Goodman's conclusion about the cause of the port's destruction?
3. **MAKE CONNECTIONS** Why does Goodman's discovery have important implications for other sites on the Mediterranean?

PLAN

OBJECTIVE

Explain how geoarchaeologist Beverly Goodman has shown that a natural disaster likely destroyed the ancient port of Caesarea.

CRITICAL THINKING SKILLS FOR LESSON 2.4

- Identify Main Ideas and Details
- Monitor Comprehension
- Make Connections
- Synthesize
- Describe
- Analyze Visuals

ESSENTIAL QUESTION

How did early Jews develop and maintain a distinct cultural identity?

Rome seized control of Judah in the first century B.C. and appointed a Roman king, Herod, as its ruler. Herod built a huge harbor at Caesarea, along the Mediterranean coast. Lesson 2.4 introduces National Geographic geoarchaeologist Beverly Goodman and describes her investigations into the effects of environmental events on ancient cultures, particularly on Caesarea's port.

BACKGROUND FOR THE TEACHER

The harbor at Caesarea built by King Herod was probably the first harbor ever built entirely in the open sea. It did not have the benefit of a protective bay or peninsula. Instead, huge breakwaters of concrete blocks filled with stone rubble protected the harbor, which was one of the technological marvels of the ancient world. The harbor served as a major port for trade between the Roman Empire and Asia.

DIGITAL RESOURCES myNGconnect.com

TEACHER RESOURCES & ASSESSMENT

 Reading and Note-Taking   **Vocabulary Practice**   **Section 2 Quiz**

STUDENT RESOURCES

 NG Chapter Gallery

INTRODUCE & ENGAGE

ACTIVATE PRIOR KNOWLEDGE

Write the term *tsunami* on the board. Discuss what students know about tsunamis. Students might indicate hearing about tsunamis in Japan and Indonesia on television broadcasts. They might also indicate that they heard about tsunami warnings for places that have experienced earthquakes. Tell students that a tsunami is a giant ocean wave caused by an underwater earthquake, a volcanic eruption, or a landslide. Tell students that in this lesson they will learn how a tsunami affected an ancient port along Israel's Mediterranean coast. `0:05` minutes

TEACH

GUIDED DISCUSSION

1. **Synthesize** How did Beverly Goodman's conclusions differ from previous conclusions about what destroyed the ancient port of Caesarea? *(Previous findings suggested the port disappeared because of the builders' poor workmanship and inferior materials. Goodman's findings pointed to a tsunami as the reason for the port's disappearance.)*

2. **Describe** What evidence led to Beverly Goodman's conclusions about what happened to the ancient port of Caesarea? *(Goodman uncovered a concentration of shells more than three feet deep instead of the usual half inch. She developed a new way of taking deep-sea core samples, sinking hollow tubes into the seabed and then pulling them out to show the layers of deposits. Analysis and dating suggested that a single, sudden, and violent event caused the shell concentrations, leading Goodman to conclude that a tsunami destroyed the ancient port.)*

ANALYZE VISUALS

Have students study the photograph of Beverly Goodman. **ASK:** Where was this photograph apparently taken? *(along the Mediterranean coast)* Does the photograph of this area remind you of anywhere you have been or seen? *(Students' responses will vary.)* Have students offer locations and discuss the similarities and differences between the location shown in the photograph and the location they are thinking about. Students might also offer activities they participated in while at the location. `0:15` minutes

ACTIVE OPTIONS

NG Learning Framework: Learn More About Tsunamis

SKILL: Collaboration
KNOWLEDGE: Our Living Planet

Have students find out more about tsunamis. Have them work in pairs and use the Internet to find out more about what causes tsunamis, where they have occurred, and how they affect the environment after they occur. Call on student pairs to present their findings to the class. Encourage them to include visuals with their oral reports. `0:15` minutes

On Your Feet: Three-Step Interview Have students choose a partner. One student should interview the other on the following question: *Why is the work of geoarchaeologists like Beverly Goodman important to the understanding of past events?* Then they should reverse roles. Finally, each student should share the results of his or her interview with the class. `0:20` minutes

DIFFERENTIATE

ENGLISH LANGUAGE LEARNERS

Teach Compound Words Remind students that two words can be put together to make a new word. Write these words and have students copy them.

deepwater   underwater   earthquake

Ask students to circle the two words within each word. Then help them define each of the two smaller words and the resulting compound word.

PRE-AP

Prepare an Interview Have students prepare a mock interview with Beverly Goodman about her work and about the work of geoarchaeologists in general. Direct students to use the Internet to research the work of geoarchaeologists. After taking notes and gathering information, have pairs of students develop a list of questions to ask Beverly Goodman about her work in the field of geoarchaeology and her work in particular on the interaction between nature and humans along coastlines. Ask pairs of students to act out their interviews for the class.

Press (mt) *in the Student eEdition for modified text.*

See the Chapter Planner for more strategies for differentiation.

REVIEW & ASSESS

ANSWERS

1. A tsunami struck Israel's coast, destroying the ancient port of Caesarea around 200 A.D.

2. Goodman's conclusion is supported by an unusual concentration of shell fragments more than three feet deep, which suggested that a single, sudden, and violent event, like a tsunami, caused the shell concentration.

3. By analyzing the causes and effects of ancient tsunamis, she hopes to find clues about which types of coastlines are at the greatest risk, what kind of damage to expect, and how to avoid catastrophic consequences in the future.

VOCABULARY

Match each word in the first column with its definition in the second column.

WORD	DEFINITION
1. exile	a. a Jewish spiritual leader and teacher
2. tribe	b. the belief in only one God
3. monotheism	c. a place where Jews assemble to worship
4. covenant	d. an extended family unit
5. rabbi	e. a period of forced absence from one's homeland or native country
6. synagogue	f. a religious agreement with God

READING STRATEGY

7. IDENTIFY MAIN IDEAS AND DETAILS If you haven't already, complete your web to identify beliefs and practices of Judaism. Then answer the question.

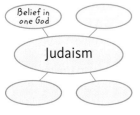

What are some of the beliefs and practices of Judaism? What is one way in which Judaism differs from other ancient religions?

MAIN IDEAS

Answer the following questions. Support your answers with evidence from the chapter.

8. What did the Israelites believe God wanted them to do in order to fulfill their special covenant? **LESSON 1.1**

9. What important religious belief set the Israelites apart from other ancient cultures? **LESSON 1.2**

10. Why is the Torah the most important holy book in Judaism? **LESSON 1.3**

11. What did Saul achieve as the first king of the Israelites? **LESSON 2.1**

12. Who was David, and what were his major accomplishments? **LESSON 2.1**

13. How did Cyrus the Great's policy of tolerance affect Jews during their exile in Babylon? **LESSON 2.2**

14. What was the Diaspora? **LESSON 2.3**

15. What natural disaster likely destroyed King Herod's harbor at Caesarea 2,000 years ago? **LESSON 2.4**

CRITICAL THINKING

Answer the following questions. Support your answers with evidence from the chapter.

16. MAKE CONNECTIONS How did the Jews develop and maintain their cultural identity?

17. DRAW CONCLUSIONS Why did the Israelites believe that the Ten Commandments reaffirmed their covenant with God?

18. EVALUATE Why was the Exodus such an important event in Jewish history?

19. ANALYZE CAUSE AND EFFECT What effect did the Diaspora have on the religion of Judaism?

20. YOU DECIDE Who do you think was the most important person in the history of the Jewish people? Why?

INTERPRET TIME LINES

Study the time line of selected events in Jewish history. Then answer the questions that follow.

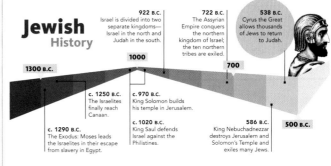

21. Who destroyed the First Temple and exiled the two tribes of Judah to Babylon?

22. Which empire destroyed the northern kingdom of Israel?

ANALYZE SOURCES

Read the following psalm, or sacred song, from the Hebrew Bible. Then answer the question.

> The Lord is my shepherd; I lack nothing. He makes me lie down in green pastures; he leads me to water in places of repose [calm]; he renews my life; he guides me in right paths as befits his name. Though I walk through a valley of deepest darkness, I will fear no harm, for you are with me; your rod and your staff—they comfort me. You spread a table for me in full view of my enemies; you anoint [rub] my head with oil; my drink is abundant. Only goodness and steadfast love shall pursue me all the days of my life, and I shall dwell in the house of the Lord for many long years.
>
> Psalms 23:1–6

23. What qualities does the author attribute to God in this psalm?

WRITE ABOUT HISTORY

24. ARGUMENT Which one of the Ten Commandments do you think has had the greatest impact on society? Make a list of some of its important effects on society.

TIPS

- Reread the Ten Commandments in Lesson 1.4. Choose the one that you think has had the greatest impact on society.
- Write down the commandment. Under it, list at least three effects of this commandment on society.
- If you can think of more than three effects, add them to the list.
- Use vocabulary from the chapter as appropriate.
- If you have difficulty identifying three effects, you might draw evidence from informational texts. For example, you might look up the Ten Commandments in an encyclopedia or another reference book.

VOCABULARY ANSWERS

WORD	DEFINITION
1. exile e	**a.** a Jewish spiritual leader and teacher
2. tribe d	**b.** the belief in only one God
3. monotheism b	**c.** a place where Jews assemble to worship
4. covenant f	**d.** an extended family unit
5. rabbi a	**e.** a period of forced absence from one's homeland or native country
6. synagogue c	**f.** a religious agreement with God

READING STRATEGY ANSWERS

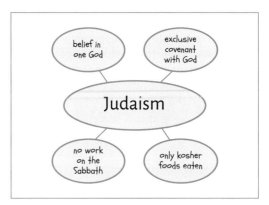

7. Jews practiced monotheism, the worship of a single God. They believed that they had a special covenant with God. They believed that God would protect the Hebrews if they accepted no other god and did what God asked. They did not work on the Sabbath, a weekly holy day. They ate only kosher foods, which were specially prepared according to Jewish dietary laws. Judaism differed from other ancient religions in that it included the worship of a single God.

MAIN IDEAS ANSWERS

8. The Israelites believed they had to obey strict rules in order to keep God's goodwill and the covenant as God's "chosen people."

9. The practice of monotheism—the belief in only one God—set the Israelites apart from other ancient cultures.

10. The Torah is Judaism's most important holy book because Jews believe it contains the word of God as revealed to Moses on Mount Sinai.

11. As the first appointed king of the Israelites, Saul united the Twelve Tribes and successfully defended the Israelites against the Philistines and other enemies.

12. David was crowned the Hebrew king after the death of Saul. As king, David brought peace to Canaan and captured Jerusalem and made it the capital.

13. Cyrus the Great's policy of tolerance helped the Jews maintain their identity and religion. Furthermore, Cyrus encouraged Jews to return to Judah and rebuild their Jewish state.

14. The Diaspora was the dispersal of Jews from their homeland to locations around the world.

15. A tsunami most likely destroyed King Herod's harbor at Caesarea.

CRITICAL THINKING ANSWERS

16. The belief in one God helped unify the Jews, and their beliefs and practices also set them apart from other ancient cultures. They followed a code of religious practices that governed most aspects of life. They did not marry outside their faith and were careful not to adopt foreign customs. The Jews also generally avoided cultural diffusion, which was a major part of many other civilizations.

17. The Israelites believed that the Ten Commandments reaffirmed their covenant with God because the commandments outlined a religious, moral, and civil code that needed to be obeyed in order to stay in God's favor.

18. The Exodus was an important event in Jewish history because it was a journey from slavery in Egypt to freedom in Canaan, the Israelites' Promised Land. According to the Hebrew Bible, in this journey God gave Moses the Ten Commandments and other laws, which reaffirmed the Israelites' covenant with God.

19. During the Diaspora, Jews dispersed to locations around the world, taking with them their religious beliefs and practices, which led to the emergence of Judaism as a world religion.

20. Students' responses will vary. Students should clearly state their opinion regarding their view of which person was most important in the history of the Jewish people and support that opinion with evidence from the chapter.

INTERPRET TIME LINES ANSWERS

21. King Nebuchadnezzar destroyed the first temple and exiled the two tribes of Judah to Babylon.

22. The Assyrian Empire destroyed the northern kingdom of Israel.

ANALYZE SOURCES ANSWER

23. Students' responses will vary. Sample response:
In Psalm 23, the author describes God as generous and benevolent—a shepherd who cares for all the physical and spiritual needs of his followers.

WRITE ABOUT HISTORY ANSWER

24. Students' lists will vary but should include valid effects that had an impact on society.

UNIT RESOURCES

On Location with National Geographic Lead Program Officer Christopher Thornton Intro and Video

Interactive Map Tool

News & Updates

Available on myNGconnect

Unit Wrap-Up:
"Encounters with History"
Feature and Video

"Faces of the Divine"
National Geographic Adapted Article
Student eEdition exclusive

"China's Ancient Lifeline"
National Geographic Adapted Article

Unit 2 Inquiry:
Write a Creation Myth

CHAPTER RESOURCES

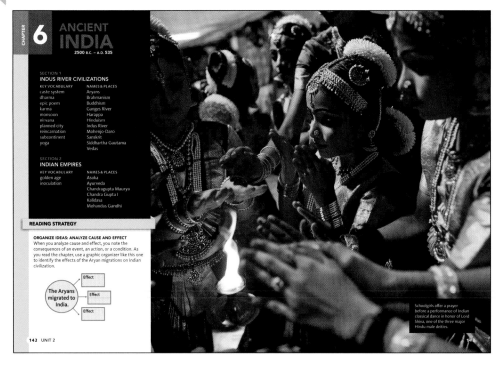

CHAPTER 6 ANCIENT INDIA
2500 B.C. – A.D. 535

SECTION 1
INDUS RIVER CIVILIZATIONS

KEY VOCABULARY
caste system
dharma
epic poem
karma
monsoon
nirvana
planned city
reincarnation
subcontinent
yoga

NAMES & PLACES
Aryans
Brahmanism
Buddhism
Ganges River
Harappa
Hinduism
Indus River
Mohenjo-Daro
Sanskrit
Siddhartha Gautama
Vedas

SECTION 2
INDIAN EMPIRES

KEY VOCABULARY
golden age
inoculation

NAMES & PLACES
Asoka
Ayurveda
Chandragupta Maurya
Chandra Gupta I
Kalidasa
Mohandas Gandhi

READING STRATEGY

ORGANIZE IDEAS: ANALYZE CAUSE AND EFFECT
When you analyze cause and effect, you note the consequences of an event, an action, or a condition. As you read the chapter, use a graphic organizer like this one to identify the effects of the Aryan migrations on Indian civilization.

The Aryans migrated to India. → Effect / Effect / Effect

142 UNIT 2

Schoolgirls offer a prayer before a performance of Indian classical dance in honor of Lord Shiva, one of the three major Hindu male deities.

TEACHER RESOURCES & ASSESSMENT
Available on myNGconnect

Social Studies Skills Lessons
• Reading: Analyze Cause and Effect
• Writing: Write an Informative Text

Formal Assessment
• Chapter 6 Tests A (on-level) & B (below-level)

Chapter 6 Answer Key

ExamView®
One-time Download

STUDENT BACKPACK *Available on myNGconnect*

• **eEdition** *(English)*   • **eEdition** *(Spanish)*   • **Handbooks**   • **Online Atlas**

For Chapter 6 Spanish resources, visit the Teacher Resource Menu page on myNGconnect.

SECTION 1 RESOURCES

INDUS RIVER CIVILIZATIONS

 Reading and Note-Taking

 Vocabulary Practice

 Section 1 Quiz

Available on myNGconnect

LESSON 1.1 THE GEOGRAPHY OF ANCIENT INDIA
- On Your Feet: Fishbowl
- Critical Viewing: NG Chapter Gallery

LESSON 1.2 HARAPPAN CIVILIZATION
- On Your Feet: Card Responses
- Critical Viewing: NG Chapter Gallery

LESSON 1.3 ARYAN MIGRATIONS
- On Your Feet: Create a Quiz

| **NG Learning Framework:**
Research Brahmanism

LESSON 1.4 HINDU BELIEFS AND PRACTICES
- On Your Feet: Numbered Heads
- Critical Viewing: NG Image Gallery

DOCUMENT-BASED QUESTION
LESSON 1.5 HINDU SACRED TEXTS
- On Your Feet: Talk and Share

| **NG Learning Framework:**
Study Primary Sources

LESSON 1.6 SIDDHARTHA AND BUDDHISM

 Active History: Interactive Whiteboard Activity
Map the Spread of Buddhism

 Active History
Map the Spread of Buddhism

Available on myNGconnect

- On Your Feet: One-on-One Interviews

SECTION 2 RESOURCES

INDIAN EMPIRES

 Reading and Note-Taking

 Vocabulary Practice

 Section 2 Quiz

Available on myNGconnect

LESSON 2.1 THE MAURYA EMPIRE

 Biography
Asoka   *Available on myNGconnect*

- On Your Feet: Build a Paragraph
- Critical Viewing: NG Image Gallery

LESSON 2.2 THE GUPTA EMPIRE
- On Your Feet: Present an Empire

| **NG Learning Framework:**
Write a Biography

LESSON 2.3 THE LEGACY OF ANCIENT INDIA
- On Your Feet: Inside-Outside Circle
- Critical Viewing: NG Chapter Gallery

CHAPTER 6 REVIEW

STRATEGY ❶

Use a Word Sort Activity

Write these words on the board and ask students to sort them into four groups of four related words each. Then have them use each group of words in a paragraph that shows how they are related.

subcontinent	medicine	reincarnation	Ganges River
dharma	Hinduism	mathematics	science
yoga	Buddhism	karma	nirvana
moral conduct	Indus River	Himalaya	Asoka

Use with Lessons 1.1, 1.4, 1.6, and 2.3

STRATEGY ❷

Ask Questions

Have students follow the strategy below to increase comprehension of lesson content.

1. Pairs of students read each lesson in the chapter and formulate one question that will help them understand it.

2. Pair One begins by asking Pair Two their question about the first lesson. Pair Two answers the question.

3. Pair One confirms the answer.

4. Pair Two asks Pair Three their question, and so on.

Use with All Lessons *For Lesson 1.1, have students ask questions about the Indus River Valley. For Lesson 2.3, have students ask questions about achievements of ancient India.*

STRATEGY ❸

Summarize Information

Help students summarize information using Idea Webs. Provide the phrase in the middle and have students complete the web using information from the lesson.

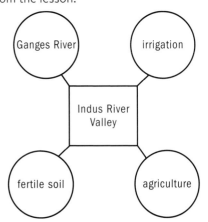

Use with Lessons 1.1, 1.2, 1.3, 1.4, 2.1, 2.2, and 2.3 *For Lesson 1.1, use the phrase "Indus River Valley" and have students fill in related information.*

Press **mt** *in the Student eEdition for modified text.*

STRATEGY ❶

Modify Vocabulary Lists

Limit the number of vocabulary words, terms, and names students will be required to master. Have students write each word from your modified list on a colored sticky note and put it on the page next to where it appears in context.

Use with Lessons 1.1, 1.2, 1.3, 1.4, 1.6, 2.2, and 2.3

STRATEGY ❷

Use Supported Reading

In small groups, have students read aloud the chapter lesson by lesson. At the end of each lesson, have them stop and use these frames to tell what they comprehended from the text:

This lesson is about _____ .

One detail that stood out to me is _____ .

The vocabulary word _____ means _____ .

I don't think I understand _____ .

Guide students with portions of text they do not understand. Be sure all students understand a lesson before moving on to the next one.

Use with Lessons 1.1, 1.2, 1.3, 1.4, 2.2, and 2.3

STRATEGY ❶

Pronounce Words

Provide pronunciations for proper nouns prior to reading. Say and write each word and have students repeat. Then read the passage aloud as a class, assisting as needed.

Use with Lesson 1.1 *Say and write the following words, with students repeating:*

South Asia (south A-zhuh)

Himalaya (HIH-muh-LAY-uh)

Everest (EHV-ruhst)

Nepal (nuh-PAWL)

Ganges (GAN-jeez)

Indus (IN-dus)

Bangladesh (BAHNG-gluh-DEHSH)

STRATEGY ❷
Use Paired Reading

Pairs of students read a passage from the text aloud. Then:

1. Partner 1 reads another passage; Partner 2 retells the passage in his or her own words.

2. Partner 2 reads a different passage; Partner 1 retells it.

3. Pairs repeat the whole exercise, switching roles.

Use with Lessons 1.2, 1.3, 1.4, 1.6, 2.1, 2.2, and 2.3 *For Lesson 1.2, have Partner 1 read the text under the heading "Well-Planned Cities" and have Partner 2 retell the passage. Partners switch places for the text under the heading "An Advanced Culture."*

STRATEGY ❸
Find Someone Who Knows

Give students copies of some or all of the questions below and have them find three different classmates to answer them.

1. What are strong seasonal winds that are important elements of the climate in South Asia? *(monsoons)*

2. What civilization was among the first in the world to have planned cities? *(the Harappan civilization)*

3. Where were Brahmanism's rituals and hymns recorded? *(in sacred texts called the Vedas)*

4. What is the Hindu belief that the soul is reborn in different bodies over different life cycles? *(reincarnation)*

5. What is the oldest of the Hindu sacred texts? *(the Rig Veda)*

6. What is the religion based on the teachings of Siddhartha Gautama? *(Buddhism)*

7. What king in ancient India converted to Buddhism and actively encouraged its spread by sending missionaries to preach abroad? *(Asoka)*

8. What empire brought 200 years of peace and prosperity to India? *(the Gupta Empire)*

9. What Indian leader in the twentieth century led nonviolent protests against British rule in India? *(Mohandas Gandhi)*

Use with All Lessons *Give students a time limit for the activity. When time is up, discuss the questions and their answers in class.*

STRATEGY ❶
Develop a Model

Have students investigate a process of physical geography related to South Asia. Students can create a diagram that illustrates the concept.

Use with Lesson 1.1 *Have students do research about tectonic shifts in the Himalaya. Then have them create a diagram that shows the plate movement. Have students write answers to the following questions: How much are the Himalaya rising each year? What other risks are associated with tectonic shifting?*

STRATEGY ❷
Research a Celebration

Explain to students that it is part of Indian culture to celebrate by having festivals such as Holi, the Festival of Colors, and Diwali, the Festival of Lights. Ask students to write a report including information about the history and traditions of these two festivals.

Use with Lesson 2.3

PRE-AP

STRATEGY ❶
Form a Thesis

Have students develop a thesis statement for a specific topic related to one of the lessons in the chapter. Be sure the statement makes a claim that is supportable with evidence either from the chapter or through further research. Then have pairs compare their statements and determine which makes the strongest or most supportable claim.

Use with All Lessons

STRATEGY ❷
Support an Opinion

Present a challenge to students to decide which two contributions from ancient India made the greatest impact on history. Have them develop a statement that explains their decision.

Use with All Lessons

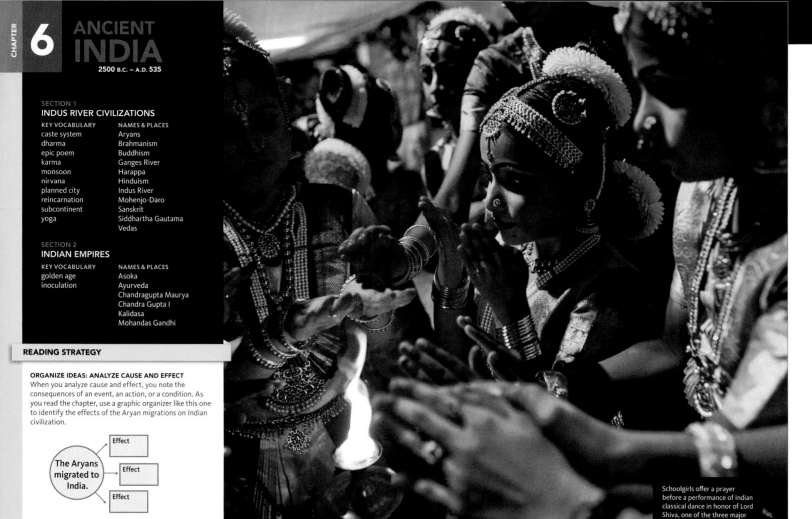

SECTION 1
INDUS RIVER CIVILIZATIONS

KEY VOCABULARY	NAMES & PLACES
caste system	Aryans
dharma	Brahmanism
epic poem	Buddhism
karma	Ganges River
monsoon	Harappa
nirvana	Hinduism
planned city	Indus River
reincarnation	Mohenjo-Daro
subcontinent	Sanskrit
yoga	Siddhartha Gautama
	Vedas

SECTION 2
INDIAN EMPIRES

KEY VOCABULARY	NAMES & PLACES
golden age	Asoka
inoculation	Ayurveda
	Chandragupta Maurya
	Chandra Gupta I
	Kalidasa
	Mohandas Gandhi

READING STRATEGY

ORGANIZE IDEAS: ANALYZE CAUSE AND EFFECT
When you analyze cause and effect, you note the consequences of an event, an action, or a condition. As you read the chapter, use a graphic organizer like this one to identify the effects of the Aryan migrations on Indian civilization.

The Aryans migrated to India. → Effect / Effect / Effect

Schoolgirls offer a prayer before a performance of Indian classical dance in honor of Lord Shiva, one of the three major Hindu male deities.

143

TEACHER BACKGROUND

INTRODUCE THE PHOTOGRAPH

Have students study the photo of the Hindu schoolgirls offering a prayer. Point out that honoring Lord Shiva and the other deities is an important part of the Hindu religion and culture.

ASK: What are some ways people today give honor to their religion in their everyday life? (*Possible response: People say prayers and sing hymns before meals, before sports activities, and before, during, and after many activities of daily life.*)

SHARE BACKGROUND

Hindus show reverence to their deities through rituals, songs, and prayers. Hindus pray in order to make a spiritual connection to their gods. Hindu worship can occur in a variety of settings and on a variety of occasions. Festivals to the gods are held during the year, but prayer may happen whenever an individual wishes. Hindus commonly pray at shrines in temples, in homes, and in outdoor public places.

DIGITAL RESOURCES myNGconnect.com

TEACHER RESOURCES & ASSESSMENT

 Social Studies Skills Lessons
- Reading: Analyze Cause and Effect
- Writing: Write an Informative Text

 Formal Assessment
Chapter 6 Tests A (on-level) & B (below-level)

ExamView®
One-time Download

 Chapter 6 Answer Key

STUDENT BACKPACK
- **eEdition** (*English*)
- **eEdition** (*Spanish*)
- **Handbooks**
- **Online Atlas**

For Chapter 6 Spanish resources, visit the Teacher Resource Menu page.

INTRODUCE THE ESSENTIAL QUESTION

WHAT LED TO THE DEVELOPMENT OF GREAT CIVILIZATIONS IN ANCIENT INDIA?

Think, Pair, Share Have students use the Think, Pair, Share strategy to discuss the Essential Question. Allow students to look through the chapter for clues in photos, maps, titles, and subheadings. Have them focus on each of the following aspects of the question:

A. How mountain ranges and major river systems can influence and restrict settlement

B. How religion can play a role in unifying a people and a nation

C. How traditions can linger after an empire has faded
0:15 minutes

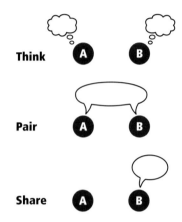

INTRODUCE THE READING STRATEGY

ORGANIZE IDEAS: ANALYZE CAUSE AND EFFECT

Remind students that analyzing cause and effect can help them better understand new information. Model completing the Cause and Effect Web by reading the first paragraph under "Impact on Indian Society" in Lesson 1.3 and adding the phrase *introduced the Sanskrit language* in the first box labeled "Effect."

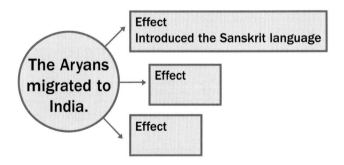

INTRODUCE CHAPTER VOCABULARY

VOCABULARY STUDY CARDS

Have students perform the six steps shown for each Key Vocabulary word in this chapter. It might be helpful to model this strategy for the first vocabulary word. Encourage students to work in pairs as they complete the six steps for the remaining words. Call on volunteers to share examples of their work with the rest of the class.

Vocabulary Word:

1. Write the sentence in which the word appears in your text.
2. Study how the word is used in the sentence. What do you think it means?
3. Now look up the word in a dictionary or use the glossary in your text.
4. Use the word in a sentence of your own.
5. To help you remember the meaning, draw a quick sketch that relates to the word. You might think of an action the word suggests or connect the word to a story or news report.
6. Tell why you chose this way of representing the meaning.

KEY DATES	
2500 B.C.	Development of civilization in the Indus River Valley
1500 B.C.	Immigration of Aryans to India
563 B.C.	Birth of Siddhartha Gautama, the Buddha
325 B.C.	Establishment of the Maurya Empire
A.D. 320	Establishment of the Gupta Empire
A.D. 1947	Independence of India

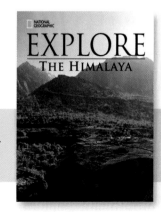

For more information on India, check out **EXPLORE THE HIMALAYA.**

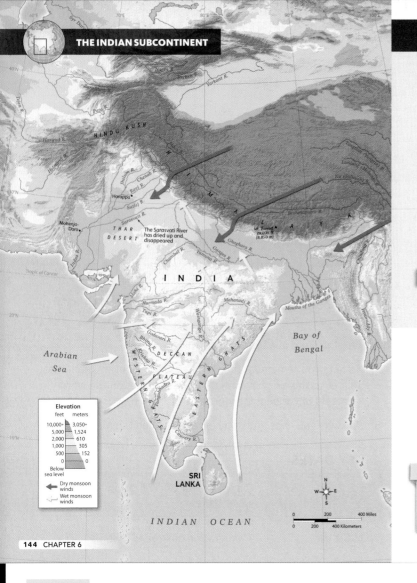

INDIA

Arabian
Sea

Bay of
Bengal

Elevation

feet	meters
10,000+	3,050+
5,000	1,524
2,000	610
1,000	305
500	152
0	0

Below
sea level

← Dry monsoon winds

Wet monsoon winds

SRI LANKA

INDIAN OCEAN

0   200   400 Miles
0   200   400 Kilometers

1.1

The
Geography of
Ancient India

Geographically, India has it all. If you were to travel around India, you could climb snowcapped mountains, cross wide grassy plains, hack through dense tropical forests, sail down mighty rivers, and skirt around sun-scorched deserts. You might travel under a bright blue sky or get soaked by seasonal rains.

MAIN IDEA

South Asia's physical geography affected the development of Indus Valley civilizations.

MOUNTAINS, RIVERS, AND MONSOONS

Present-day India, Bangladesh, Bhutan, Nepal, and Pakistan make up the large landmass, or **subcontinent**, of South Asia. This diamond-shaped landmass was originally an island. However, 40 million years ago, the large moving plates on which the continents lie drove the subcontinent into Asia. As the lands collided, they

pushed Earth's crust upward to form the Himalaya, a 1,500-mile mountain range.

The Himalaya are the world's highest mountains. Many Himalayan peaks rise about 24,000 feet. Thirty peaks, including Mount Everest—Earth's highest point—are over 25,000 feet high.

On either side of the Himalaya lie lower mountain ranges, including the Hindu Kush, which separates what was once northwest India from present-day Afghanistan. These northern mountains form a natural barrier against invaders. The Arabian Sea, Indian Ocean, and Bay of Bengal have provided further protection. The Deccan Plateau, which contains smaller mountain systems, makes up much of southern India.

The two major rivers of northern India, the **Indus** and the **Ganges**, both start in the Himalaya. Like the Tigris and the Euphrates in Mesopotamia, these rivers provide water for irrigation and deposit fertile soil for farming.

Strong seasonal winds called **monsoons** have long been an important element of the subcontinent's climate. These winds bring a dry season in winter. In summer, they bring a wet season with heavy rainfall.

INDUS RIVER VALLEY

Physical characteristics of the Indus River Valley offered nearly ideal conditions for agriculture. The valley's fertile soil and plentiful water supply most likely encouraged nomadic herdsmen to settle there and farm. Villages emerged. Then, around 2500 B.C., some villages grew into cities—and a civilization developed.

REVIEW & ASSESS

1. **READING CHECK** How did physical geography affect the development of Indus Valley civilizations?

2. **INTERPRET MAPS** What physical feature separates India from the continent of Asia?

3. **MAKE INFERENCES** What positive and negative effects might the summer monsoons have had on farmers?

PLAN

OBJECTIVE

Explain how South Asia's physical geography affected the development of Indus Valley civilizations.

CRITICAL THINKING SKILLS FOR LESSON 1.1

- Identify Main Ideas and Details
- Monitor Comprehension
- Interpret Maps
- Make Inferences
- Identify
- Analyze Cause and Effect

ESSENTIAL QUESTION

What led to the development of great civilizations in ancient India?

The physical characteristics of the Indus River Valley included fertile soil and a plentiful water supply. Lesson 1.1 discusses how these physical characteristics led people to settle in the area and led to the growth of villages and cities.

BACKGROUND FOR THE TEACHER

South Asia has some of the most dramatic topography in the world, including the majestic Mount Everest of the Himalaya in Nepal. The plate on which the subcontinent of South Asia is located is still moving northward. As a result, the Himalaya are growing about 5 centimeters (2 inches) higher every year. Sir Edmund Hillary and his Sherpa guide were the first to reach the summit of Mount Everest in 1953. Since then, thousands have made the attempt.

DIGITAL RESOURCES myNGconnect.com

TEACHER RESOURCES & ASSESSMENT

 Reading and Note-Taking

 Vocabulary Practice

 Section 1 Quiz

STUDENT RESOURCES

 NG Chapter Gallery

INTRODUCE & ENGAGE

INTERPRET MODELS

To show students how the Himalaya were formed, have pairs of students place two sheets of paper lengthwise between them, and then push the papers toward each other. Explain that the papers represent plates of land that are forced upward when pushed together, similar to the colliding plates that formed the Himalaya. Tell students they will be learning more about the Himalaya. **0:05** minutes

TEACH

GUIDED DISCUSSION

1. **Identify** What present-day countries make up the subcontinent of South Asia? (*Present-day India, Bangladesh, Bhutan, Nepal, and Pakistan make up the large subcontinent of South Asia.*)

2. **Analyze Cause and Effect** What caused the formation of the Himalaya? (*Large moving plates on which the continents lie drove the subcontinent of South Asia into Asia. As the lands collided, they pushed Earth's crust upward to form the Himalaya mountain range.*)

INTERPRET MAPS

Project the Indian Subcontinent map on a whiteboard or screen. Have volunteers read the lesson aloud while other volunteers point out the geographic features on the map as they are referenced in the text. **0:15** minutes

ACTIVE OPTIONS

On Your Feet: Fishbowl Have students form an inner and outer circle, both facing the center. Use a Fishbowl strategy to have them pose questions and take notes about South Asia's physical features. Then have students switch places to pose questions and take notes about South Asia's climate. **0:10** minutes

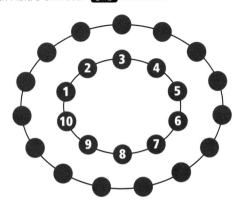

Critical Viewing: NG Chapter Gallery Have students examine the contents of the Chapter Gallery for this chapter. Then invite them to brainstorm additional images they think would fit within the Chapter Gallery. Have them write a description of these additional images and provide an explanation of why they would fit within the Chapter Gallery. Then instruct them to do online research to find examples of actual images they would like to add to the gallery. **0:10** minutes

DIFFERENTIATE

STRIVING READERS

Preview Text Have students preview the lesson. Have them read the title, the Main Idea, subheadings in blue type, map, and questions. Then have them list information about ancient India's geography and climate that they expect to find in the text. Have students read the lesson and discuss with a partner what they learned and whether or not it matched their list.

GIFTED & TALENTED

Create a Presentation Have small groups of students do research to learn more about summer monsoons and winter monsoons in India. Ask students to prepare a presentation explaining the monsoons' effects on farmers, the economy, cities, and coastal communities. Have students share what they learned with the class.

Press (**mt**) *in the Student eEdition for modified text.*

See the Chapter Planner for more strategies for differentiation.

REVIEW & ASSESS

ANSWERS

1. The Indus and Ganges rivers provided fertile soils and a plentiful water supply, essential natural resources that encouraged human settlement and the development of agriculture in ancient India.

2. The Himalaya separates India from the continent of Asia.

3. They bring much needed rain, but they also cause flooding.

1.2 Harappan Civilization

Historians have studied ancient Egyptian civilization for many centuries. But evidence of ancient India's great civilization was not discovered until the early 20th century. Then, in 1921, archaeologists unearthed an Indian culture every bit as vast and sophisticated as that of ancient Egypt: the Harappan civilization.

MAIN IDEA

One of the world's earliest and most advanced civilizations emerged in ancient India's Indus River Valley.

WELL-PLANNED CITIES

Around 2500 B.C., civilization developed in the Indus Valley. Fertile soil and irrigation delivered food surpluses that generated wealth. As populations boomed, villages grew into large cities. **Mohenjo-Daro** (moh-HEHN-joh DAHR-oh), one of the civilization's major cities, covered over 250 acres. Another important city, **Harappa** (huh-RA-puh), gave the Harappan civilization its name. These cities were the largest of their time. Their influence spread across a 500,000-square-mile area, which was greater than that of either ancient Egypt or Mesopotamia.

Indus Valley cities were among the world's first **planned cities**. Many were built with the same layout and the same features. Such cities had an eastern housing and business area guarded by defensive walls. To the west were public buildings, as well as structures that may have been used to store grain. Main roads as straight as rulers intersected at right angles with streets exactly half their width. Wells were another common feature. People used bricks that were all the same size to build houses. Homes had indoor plumbing with a bathroom and a toilet that emptied into excellent underground sewers.

Archaeologists have found similarly styled pottery, jewelry, toys, and tools at more than 1,000 Harappan sites. These similar goods demonstrate strong cultural ties among people living hundreds of miles apart. The similarities also suggest that the Harappan civilization was a single state with a strong central government. However, historians have no idea how it was ruled.

AN ADVANCED CULTURE

In fact, there is a lot historians do not know about Harappan civilization because archaeologists have not figured out its writing system. It seems to be based, at least in part, on pictograms, like Sumerian cuneiform. The only writing found is on small items such as pottery, tools, and tiny square stone seals. Traders probably pressed these seals into soft clay to leave their mark on trading goods. Traders also used stone cubes as standard weights and measures.

The Harappans were long-distance traders, using boats and possibly the world's first wheeled vehicles. Their enormous trade network stretched over the mountains into what are now Afghanistan, Iran, and Iraq. There, archaeologists have found records of Harappan copper, gold, and ivory.

Historians know little about Harappan religion. In fact, much about the Harappans remains a mystery.

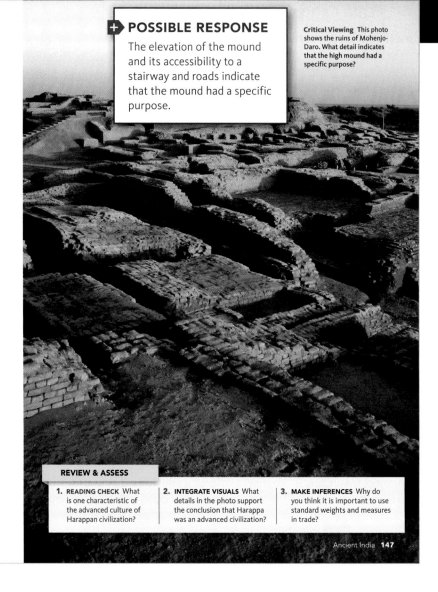

+ POSSIBLE RESPONSE
The elevation of the mound and its accessibility to a stairway and roads indicate that the mound had a specific purpose.

Critical Viewing This photo shows the ruins of Mohenjo-Daro. What detail indicates that the high mound had a specific purpose?

REVIEW & ASSESS

1. **READING CHECK** What is one characteristic of the advanced culture of Harappan civilization?

2. **INTEGRATE VISUALS** What details in the photo support the conclusion that Harappa was an advanced civilization?

3. **MAKE INFERENCES** Why do you think it is important to use standard weights and measures in trade?

PLAN

OBJECTIVE

Explain how one of the world's earliest and most advanced civilizations emerged in ancient India's Indus River Valley.

CRITICAL THINKING SKILLS FOR LESSON 1.2

- Identify Main Ideas and Details
- Monitor Comprehension
- Integrate Visuals
- Make Inferences
- Identify
- Draw Conclusions
- Analyze Visuals

ESSENTIAL QUESTION

What led to the development of great civilizations in ancient India?

The fertile farmland led to food surpluses and wealth. Lesson 1.2 discusses how the productive agriculture led to the growth of cities and the development of civilization in ancient India.

BACKGROUND FOR THE TEACHER

The physical geography of a region often influences its history. The good farmland and geographic isolation of South Asia made the Indus and Ganges river valleys cultural hearths, or centers of civilization from which ideas spread. The first urban civilization in South Asia was the Harappan. It developed along the Indus River in what is now Pakistan. The early cities of Mohenjo-Daro and Harappa provide early examples of organized city planning.

DIGITAL RESOURCES myNGconnect.com

TEACHER RESOURCES & ASSESSMENT

 Reading and Note-Taking   **Vocabulary Practice**   **Section 1 Quiz**

STUDENT RESOURCES

 NG Chapter Gallery

INTRODUCE & ENGAGE

PREVIEW AND PREDICT

Have students read the lesson title, the main idea, and any text in large blue type. Have students use that information to write a sentence that predicts what the lesson is about. Allow pairs of students to compare sentences. `0:05` minutes

TEACH

GUIDED DISCUSSION

1. **Identify** What were the two largest cities at the time of the Harappan civilization? (*Mohenjo-Daro and Harappa*)

2. **Draw Conclusions** What might discoveries of Harappan copper, gold, and ivory in what is now Afghanistan, Iran, and Iraq indicate? (*Harappan people were long-distance traders.*)

ANALYZE VISUALS

Have students study the photograph of Mohenjo-Daro. As a class, fill in a T-Chart to make comparisons between this ancient city and modern cities. `0:10` minutes

Mohenjo-Daro	Modern Cities

ACTIVE OPTIONS

On Your Feet: Card Responses Have half the class write 10 true-false questions based on the lesson. Have the other half create answer cards, writing "True" on one side and "False" on the other side. Students from the first group take turns asking their questions. Students from the second group hold up their cards, showing either "True" or "False." Have students keep track of their correct answers. `0:10` minutes

Critical Viewing: NG Chapter Gallery Invite students to explore the Chapter Gallery to examine the images that relate to this chapter. Have them select one of the images and do additional research to learn more about it. Ask questions that will inspire additional inquiry about the chosen gallery image: What is this? Where and when was this created? By whom? Why was it created? What is it made of? Why does it belong in this chapter? What else would you like to know about it? `0:10` minutes

DIFFERENTIATE

ENGLISH LANGUAGE LEARNERS

Ask Who? What? Where? When? How? Reporters use the questions *Who? What? Where? When?* and *How?* to guide their reporting. Students can use the same questions to understand the information in the lesson. Have students work in pairs to answer the five questions about the Harappan civilization.

STRIVING READERS

Make a Concept Cluster Organize students into teams of four. Invite each team to fill out a graphic organizer like the one shown. Have students write the words *Harappan Civilization* in the center. Have them write the words *Cities, Culture,* and *Trade* in the other ovals. Then encourage students to write words or phrases they know about the cities, the culture, and the trading practices of the Harappans.

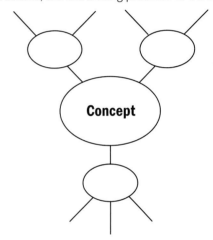

Press (**mt**) *in the Student eEdition for modified text.*

See the Chapter Planner for more strategies for differentiation.

REVIEW & ASSESS

ANSWERS

1. The immense size of the Harappan civilization, its strong cultural influence, its large planned cities, an enormous commercial network, and the use of standard weights and measures all reveal an advanced culture.

2. Straight roads that intersected with other streets, bricks that were the same size, the appearance of a planned city, and defensive walls support the conclusion that Harappa was an advanced civilization.

3. Standard weights and measures help ensure fair and honest trade.

Aryan Migrations

Historians believe the Indus Valley suffered a series of earthquakes from which the Harappan civilization never recovered.

Other forces were also in play. Eventually, migrations of Aryan people from the north led to the establishment of another great Indian civilization.

MAIN IDEA

After the Harappan civilization declined, Aryan immigrants forged a new Indian civilization.

END OF HARAPPA

A combination of natural forces probably contributed to the Harappan civilization's downfall. First agriculture declined when rainfall diminished. Then earthquakes caused flooding and drastically changed the course of rivers. One river, the Sarasvati, no longer flowed near Harappan cities. With reduced access to river water for irrigation, agriculture became more difficult.

As food supplies declined, people abandoned the cities. By 1900 B.C., a simple village way of life had largely replaced the Harappans' advanced urban civilization.

HARAPPAN SEAL

Found at Mohenjo-Daro, this soft stone seal was probably used to mark trade goods. The marks at the top are an example of the Harappan language, which archaeologists have not yet learned to read.

According to many historians, around 1500 B.C., waves of new people began crossing the Hindu Kush into India. The migrants were a collection of tribes called **Aryans**, meaning "noble ones." They belonged to the Indo-European people who had populated central Asia. (Some scholars have begun to dispute this theory, however. They believe that the Aryans were descendants of earlier Indus civilizations and were not foreign invaders at all.)

The Aryans were seminomadic herders of horses and cattle and were also fierce warriors. They built only basic houses but rode horses and used wheeled chariots.

Around 1000 B.C., what became known as Vedic civilization expanded south and east. There the people adopted agriculture, cleared the forests to cultivate crops, and settled down in villages. The villages grouped together into chiefdoms and then into kingdoms. As they conquered and mixed with native people, the Aryans had a huge cultural impact on religion, class, and language.

IMPACT ON INDIAN SOCIETY

The Aryans worshipped many gods from nature. They also had gods for friendship and for moral authority. To keep their gods happy, Aryan priests, or Brahmans, performed complicated rituals in **Sanskrit**, the Aryan language. Their religion came to be called **Brahmanism** (BRAH-muh-nih-zuhm).

In time Brahmanism's rituals and hymns were recorded in sacred texts called the **Vedas**. The oldest text is the Rig Veda, which contains 1,028 melodic hymns.

VEDAS

The Vedas are four sacred texts that were probably composed between 1500 and 1200 B.C. For a thousand years, people passed the Vedas down orally.

After a written form of Sanskrit emerged, people were finally able to write down the Vedas. These texts tell historians what life might have been like in the Vedic period.

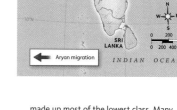

ARYAN MIGRATIONS, c. 1500 B.C.

← Aryan migration

Brahmanism grew powerful because the priests established beneficial relationships with kings. The Brahmans preached that the gods granted the right to rule to the kings. In return the kings upheld the authority of the Brahmans.

Over time, a social class system developed that determined how people lived. Priests were at the top, followed by warriors and nobles. Freemen, farmers, and traders were third in importance. At the bottom were slaves, laborers, and artisans. Non-Aryans made up most of the lowest class. Many centuries later, another group developed that was considered even lower.

The Aryan hierarchy developed into a rigid **caste system** that was hereditary and could never be changed. People's castes dictated the kind of work they did and whom they could marry. The caste system even dictated what people could eat. Such definitions applied to people's children as well.

REVIEW & ASSESS

1. **READING CHECK** Who were the Aryans?

2. **INTERPRET MAPS** What physical features did the Aryan migrations pass through?

3. **DETERMINE WORD MEANINGS** What does *waves* mean in the sentence, "Around 1500 B.C. waves of new people began crossing the Hindu Kush into India"?

PLAN

OBJECTIVE

Identify how, after the Harappan civilization declined, the Aryan immigrants forged a new Indian civilization.

After the Harappan civilization declined, tribes called *Aryans* moved into the region. Lesson 1.3 discusses how the Aryan immigrants built a new civilization in ancient India.

CRITICAL THINKING SKILLS FOR LESSON 1.3

- Identify Main Ideas and Details
- Monitor Comprehension
- Interpret Maps
- Determine Word Meanings
- Analyze Cause and Effect
- Describe
- Create Graphic Organizers

BACKGROUND FOR THE TEACHER

The word *Aryan* comes from the Sanskrit *arya* meaning "noble or distinguished." Many historians believe that *arya* defined a social difference, not an ethnic difference. Hindu society is based on the Aryan caste system. The Hindu legend is that the four groups come from an ancient being: Brahmans—India's priests—come from the mouth; Kshatriyas—warriors and leaders—come from the arms; Vaisyas—farmers, traders, and craftspeople—come from the thighs; and Sudras—workers and servants—come from the feet.

ESSENTIAL QUESTION

What led to the development of great civilizations in ancient India?

DIGITAL RESOURCES myNGconnect.com

TEACHER RESOURCES & ASSESSMENT

 Reading and Note-Taking

 Vocabulary Practice

 Section 1 Quiz

STUDENT RESOURCES

 NG Chapter Gallery

INTRODUCE & ENGAGE

TEAM UP

Have students work in groups of four to brainstorm a list of factors that contribute toward the development of civilization in a particular region. Have students share their lists with the class. Tell students they will learn more about how factors in a region can affect the civilization that lives there. **0:05** minutes

TEACH

GUIDED DISCUSSION

1. **Analyze Cause and Effect** What natural forces contributed to the Harappan civilization's downfall? (*Rainfall diminished causing agriculture to decline. Earthquakes caused flooding and changed the course of rivers. For these reasons, food supplies declined.*)

2. **Describe** What kind of relationship did the Brahmans in ancient India have with the kings? (*The Brahmans preached that the gods granted the right to rule to the kings. The kings upheld the authority of the Brahmans.*)

CREATE GRAPHIC ORGANIZERS

To help students understand the structure of India's ancient caste system, have them work in groups of four to create a graphic that accurately represents each caste. For instance, students might create a pyramid structure with priests at the top, freemen, farmers, and traders at the next level, and so on. **0:15** minutes

ACTIVE OPTIONS

On Your Feet: Create a Quiz Based on what they learned in the lesson, have students work in groups to create a fill-in-the-blank quiz about the Aryan migrations and civilization. Encourage students to use the text to confirm their answers. Then have each group ask another group their questions. Have students keep track of the number of correct answers for their group scores. **0:10** minutes

NG Learning Framework: Research Brahmanism

ATTITUDE: **Curiosity**
KNOWLEDGE: **Our Human Story**

Have students work in small groups. Ask members of each group to think about questions they would like to ask about Brahmanism. Then have them do research to learn more about the religion. Ask students to write short sentences describing what they learned. **0:10** minutes

DIFFERENTIATE

INCLUSION

Use Echo Reading Pair each proficient reader with a student with special needs. Have the proficient reader read aloud the Main Idea statement about the Aryans at the beginning of the lesson. Have his or her partner "echo" by reading the same statement. Repeat for each of the blue subheadings in the lesson.

PRE-AP

Write a Report Have small groups of students do research about the caste system at the time of the Aryans. Have students write a report about how a person's caste affected his or her life in ancient India. Encourage students to share their reports with the class.

Press (**mt**) *in the Student eEdition for modified text.*

See the Chapter Planner for more strategies for differentiation.

REVIEW & ASSESS

ANSWERS

1. The Aryans were a collection of Indo-European tribes who began crossing the Hindu Kush into India in 1500 B.C.

2. The Aryans passed through the Hindu Kush mountains to reach the Indus Valley.

3. In the quoted sentence, *waves* means great numbers of people arriving all at once.

Hindu Beliefs and Practices

If you are into computer games, you might have an online avatar, a character that represents you. The concept of avatars is nothing new. The Hindu god Vishnu had many avatars, including a godlike hero called Krishna. Unlike your avatar, Vishnu's avatars were versions of himself in various forms.

MAIN IDEA

Over 5,000 years, Hinduism absorbed and integrated many beliefs found throughout South Asia.

GODS AND SACRED TEXTS

The religion that grew out of Aryan beliefs and practices is **Hinduism**, the world's third largest religion. Hinduism developed over many centuries. Its many gods and goddesses, or deities, combine to form Brahman, a universal spirit. The three most important Hindu deities are Brahma, Vishnu, and Shiva.

Female deities include Saraswati, goddess of knowledge, science, and the arts, and Parvati, who is both a goddess and the beautiful wife of Shiva. She meditated for years in the Himalaya to attract his attention. Lakshmi, wife of Vishnu, is the goddess of wealth and prosperity. People who seek success worship Lakshmi.

The Vedas are Hinduism's holiest books, but two **epic poems**, or long narrative poems, are also important. One, called *Mahabharata* (mu-HAH-bahr-AH-tuh), teaches the importance of living and acting righteously. The other poem, the *Ramayana* (rah-mah-YAH-nuh), tells the story of Rama, the perfect king, who fought evil forces in the world.

Within the *Mahabharata* is a spiritual poem called Bhagavad Gita (BAH-gah-vuhd GEET-ah), or "Song of the Lord." In this poem Krishna praises duty. He also encourages action over inaction, knowledge over ignorance, belief over disbelief, and good over evil. This poem remains popular as a source of spiritual guidance and inspiration.

BELIEFS AND PRACTICES

Hindus occasionally worship in temples, but the home is the center of religious activity. Many homes have a temple room or corner where family members worship. Many Hindus still observe certain cultural practices related to the caste system, such as marrying within one's caste. They also believe the soul is eternal and is reborn in different bodies over different life cycles. This is known as **reincarnation**.

According to Hindu beliefs, people's actions and conduct create **karma**, which determines the kind of life into which they will be reborn. The karma of someone who leads a good and moral life leads to rebirth into a better life. A life filled with misdeeds creates bad karma, which leads to rebirth into a life of greater hardship and suffering. The ultimate goal of a Hindu is to end this cycle of rebirth by living selflessly and eliminating material desires.

There are many paths to the perfect life. One path involves the practice of **yoga**—a series of exercises intended to help a person achieve spiritual insight. An important idea underlying such practices is to seek and know the truth.

These women in northern India are throwing flowers in the air to celebrate the Hindu festival of Holi, which marks the coming of spring.

HINDU DEITIES

Brahma, *the Creator:* Brahma created the universe, the world, and the human race. His four heads represent the four Vedas.

Vishnu, *the Preserver:* Vishnu contains and balances good and evil. It is his job to maintain the divine order of the universe. If evil is winning, Vishnu comes to Earth in human form to restore the balance.

Shiva, *the Destroyer:* Shiva is responsible for all forms of change, from giving up bad habits to death. He is closely associated with yoga.

REVIEW & ASSESS

1. **READING CHECK** Who are the three most important gods in Hinduism, and what is the role of each?

2. **MAKE INFERENCES** How might the concept of karma guide a Hindu during his or her lifetime?

3. **ANALYZE LANGUAGE USE** How does knowing that *carne* refers to "flesh" help you understand the word *reincarnation*?

OBJECTIVE

Explain how, over 5,000 years, Hinduism absorbed and integrated many beliefs found throughout South Asia.

CRITICAL THINKING SKILLS FOR LESSON 1.4

- Identify Main Ideas and Details
- Monitor Comprehension
- Make Inferences
- Analyze Language Use
- Identify
- Summarize

ESSENTIAL QUESTION

What led to the development of great civilizations in ancient India?

Hinduism developed over many centuries. Lesson 1.4 discusses how Hinduism integrated and absorbed many beliefs found throughout South Asia.

BACKGROUND FOR THE TEACHER

Over many years, the ideas in the Vedas, the sacred texts of Brahmanism, began to blend with ideas from other cultures. For example, people from kingdoms in Central Asia, such as Persia, brought their ideas to India. This mix of ideas, customs, and beliefs eventually led to the religion of Hinduism. Hinduism is one of the oldest religions in the world. Hindus believe that eventually their souls will join the deity Brahma, the creator and universal spirit.

DIGITAL RESOURCES myNGconnect.com

TEACHER RESOURCES & ASSESSMENT

 Reading and Note-Taking

 Vocabulary Practice

 Section 1 Quiz

STUDENT RESOURCES

 NG Chapter Gallery

ASK QUESTIONS

Have students work in in groups of four. Have each group come up with a list of three questions about Hinduism. Tell students that they will learn about some beliefs and practices associated with Hinduism. After the lesson, review the questions and have students from each group answer the questions they listed. Have each group share its questions and answers with the class. **0:05** minutes

TEACH

GUIDED DISCUSSION

1. **Identify** Where do Hindus worship? (*They occasionally worship in temples but the home is the center of religious activity. Many homes have a temple room or corner in which family members worship.*)

2. **Summarize** What is the ultimate goal of a Hindu? (*The ultimate goal is to end the cycle of reincarnation by living selflessly and eliminating material desires.*)

MORE INFORMATION

Hindu Rituals Rituals are an important part of Hinduism. *Pujas*—a type of blessing—and traditional decorations such as henna are two important rituals. Others include ritual bathing, participation in festivals, fasting, and prayer and meditation. Pujas can be performed by priests or by individual worshippers. One common type is *arati*, or the use of a lighted lamp in front of the object, deity, or person to be blessed. Pujas are used under specific circumstances and also as a practice of devotion. **0:15** minutes

ACTIVE OPTIONS

On Your Feet: Numbered Heads Organize students into groups of four and assign each group member a number (1-4). Tell students to think about and discuss a response to this question: *How are the religious beliefs of the Hindus and the Aryans similar?* Then call a number and have the student from each group with that number report for the group. If time permits, repeat the process with an additional question: *How might a caste system have affected the lives of Aryans and many Hindus?* **0:10** minutes

Critical Viewing: NG Image Gallery Invite students to explore the entire NG Image Gallery, including the images for this chapter. Ask students to choose two images they think represent Hindu values or customs and do further research on each of them using this text and using other sources. Then have students present their findings to the class. Prompt students to explain why they chose their two images. **0:10** minutes

ENGLISH LANGUAGE LEARNERS

Create Webs for Key Words Display the word *Hinduism* and draw a circle around it. Allow students to volunteer words they have learned that are related to the Hindu religion. Draw spokes for the circle and write the words suggested at the ends of the spokes. Have students write or say sentences that use any of the words in the web.

STRIVING READERS

Make Lists Have students work in groups of four. Post the title "Four Things I Learned About Hindu Practices and Beliefs." Ask each group to copy the title. Then ask each person in the group to write or say a sentence about the title. Encourage students to share their lists with the class.

Press (**mt**) *in the Student eEdition for modified text.*

See the Chapter Planner for more strategies for differentiation.

ANSWERS

1. In Hinduism, the three most important gods are Brahma the creator, Vishnu the preserver, and Shiva the destroyer and re-creator.

2. The concept of karma determines the kind of life into which Hindus will be reborn. The karma of someone who leads a good and moral life leads to rebirth into a better life.

3. Possible response: Knowing that *carne* means "flesh" helps me understand that reincarnation is related to the body.

Hindu Sacred Texts

The Bhagavad Gita and the *Ramayana* are two of Hinduism's most famous and popular sacred texts. They tell exciting stories about great warriors having heroic adventures, while also teaching important religious and moral lessons. People in ancient India originally memorized these epic poems and passed them down orally, as they did the Vedas.

ANSWERS

DOCUMENT 1
Krishna's words reassure Arjuna that even if he was injured or killed in battle, his soul would live on.

DOCUMENT 2
Rama's brother might be comforted by the idea that life is short and that everyone dies.

DOCUMENT 2
After death, a person becomes one with nature.

This painting shows the Lord Krishna, an avatar of Vishnu, and Prince Arjuna as they head into battle.

152

DOCUMENT ONE
Primary Source: Sacred Text

from the Bhagavad Gita, translated by Stephen Mitchell
The Bhagavad Gita is a 700-verse poem describing a conversation between Vishnu's avatar Krishna and the hero Arjuna. In this excerpt, Krisha speaks to Arjuna before a great battle. Krishna tells the warrior about the soul—the "it" in the poem.

CONSTRUCTED RESPONSE According to Krishna, what is special about a soul?

> The sharpest sword will not pierce it; the hottest flame will not singe [burn] it; water will not make it moist; wind will not cause it to wither [die].
>
> It cannot be pierced or singed, moistened or withered; it is vast, perfect and all-pervading [everywhere], calm, immovable, timeless.

DOCUMENT TWO
Primary Source: Epic Poem

from the *Ramayana*, a retelling by William Buck
The *Ramayana* is a love story in which the good king Rama, an avatar of Vishnu, rescues his kidnapped wife Sita from Ravana, the evil ruler of an island off India's southeastern coast. In this passage, Rama speaks to his brother after they learn that their father has died.

CONSTRUCTED RESPONSE What comfort might his brother take from Rama's words?

> Life is passing as a river ever flowing away, never still, never returning. Life is changeable as the flashing lightning, a pattern of as little meaning, and impermanent. . . . Life is bright and colored for a passing moment like the sunset. Then it is gone and who can prevent it going?

DOCUMENT THREE
Primary Source: Sacred Text

from the Rig Veda, translated by Wendy Doniger
The Rig Veda is a series of 1,028 hymns grouped into 10 books. It is also the oldest of the Hindu sacred texts. This excerpt from a poem in Book 10 addresses a person who has just died.

CONSTRUCTED RESPONSE According to the passage, what happens to a person after death?

> May your eye go to the sun, your life's breath to the wind. Go to the sky or to earth, as is your nature; or go to the waters, if that is your fate. Take root in the plants with your limbs.

SYNTHESIZE & WRITE

1. **REVIEW** Review what you have learned about Hinduism, the Bhagavad Gita, the *Ramayana*, and the Rig Veda.

2. **RECALL** On your own paper, write down the main idea expressed in each document.

3. **CONSTRUCT** Construct a topic sentence that answers this question: What do the passages from the Bhagavad Gita, the *Ramayana*, and the Rig Veda suggest about Hinduism's attitude toward life and death?

4. **WRITE** Using evidence from the documents, write an explanatory paragraph that answers the question in Step 3.

PLAN

OBJECTIVE
Synthesize information about Hindu sacred texts from primary and secondary source documents.

CRITICAL THINKING SKILLS FOR LESSON 1.5
- Synthesize
- Identify
- Make Inferences
- Summarize
- Evaluate

ESSENTIAL QUESTION
What led to the development of great civilizations in ancient India?

The Hindu sacred texts include the Hindu philosophy, verse, and hymns. These texts provided spiritual guidance for Hindus as their civilization developed. Lesson 1.5 provides excerpts from these sacred texts.

BACKGROUND FOR THE TEACHER
The Bhagavad Gita comprises chapters 23 to 40 of Book 6 of the *Mahabharata*. It includes a long conversation between the deity Vishnu and Prince Arjuna. On the eve of a great battle, Arjuna expresses doubts about killing. Vishnu tells Arjuna that because he is a warrior, he must go into battle. However, after death, the soul is released from the body and is transferred to another body. If the soul attains true wisdom, it achieves *moksha*, or release from the cycles of rebirth.

DIGITAL RESOURCES myNGconnect.com

TEACHER RESOURCES & ASSESSMENT

 Reading and Note-Taking

 Vocabulary Practice

 Section 1 Quiz

STUDENT RESOURCES

 NG Chapter Gallery

PREPARE FOR THE DOCUMENT-BASED QUESTION

Before students start on the activity, briefly preview the three documents. Remind students that a constructed response requires full explanations in complete sentences. Emphasize that students should use their knowledge of Hindu beliefs in addition to the information in the documents. **0:05** minutes

TEACH

GUIDED DISCUSSION

1. **Identify** What is the role of Krishna in the Bhagavad Gita? (*Krishna is the avatar of the god Vishnu.*)

2. **Make Inferences** What does the excerpt from the Rig Veda indicate about the importance of nature in the Hindu religion? (*The excerpt includes the words* sun, wind, sky, earth, nature, waters, root, *and* plant. *The use of these words would indicate that nature is very important to the Hindu religion.*)

3. **Summarize** In the *Ramayana*, what does Rama do that makes him a hero? (*He rescues his kidnapped wife, Sita, from Ravana, an evil ruler.*)

EVALUATE

After students have completed the "Synthesize & Write" activity, allow time for them to exchange paragraphs and read and comment on the work of their peers. Guidelines for comments should be established prior to this activity so that feedback is constructive and encouraging in nature. **0:15** minutes

ACTIVE OPTIONS

On Your Feet: Talk and Share Ask students to work in small groups. Ask each group to list things they have learned about the importance of the Hindu sacred texts in the lives of Hindus. Have each group share its list with the class. **0:10** minutes

NG Learning Framework: Study Primary Sources

SKILL: Communication
KNOWLEDGE: **Our Human Story**

Invite students review the text of the primary sources in the lesson. **ASK:** What do these documents reveal about the Hindu attitude toward life, death, and beliefs about a person's soul? Have students write a short paragraph to explain their answer. **0:10** minutes

STRIVING READERS

Write a Tweet Divide students into three groups. Assign one of the documents to each group. Have each group write a tweet that describes the document. Have each group read their tweets to the class.

PRE-AP

Present an Oral Report Ask small groups of students to research and prepare an oral report on the Hindu view of nature, including information about Hindus' respect for animals, plants, and the environment as a whole. Have groups present their findings to the class. Encourage each person in the group to take part in the oral presentation.

Press (**mt**) *in the Student eEdition for modified text.*

See the Chapter Planner for more strategies for differentiation.

ANSWERS

1. Responses will vary.

2. Students should convey and support the main idea with appropriate evidence from the primary sources.

3. Students should construct a clearly written topic sentence that answers the question.

4. Students' paragraphs should include their topic sentence from Step 3 and provide several details from the documents to support the sentence. Students should organize the information in a logical, clearly written paragraph.

Siddhartha and Buddhism

Like many people, you might very much want to own the latest cell phone or tablet. But what if someone told you that your desire for such material possessions would only bring you suffering? That's exactly what a man who lived about 2,500 years ago said.

MAIN IDEA

Buddhism emerged in India around 500 B.C.

Buddhist monks pray before a statue that represents the Buddha.

SIDDHARTHA GAUTAMA

EIGHTFOLD PATH

Right View: See and understand things as they really are

Right Intention: Commit to ethical self-improvement

Right Speech: Tell the truth and speak gently

Right Action: Act kindly, honestly, and respectfully

Right Livelihood: Earn a living in a moral, legal, and peaceful way

Right Effort: Focus your will onto achieving good things

Right Mindfulness: Value a good mind

Right Concentration: Single-mindedness

THE LIFE OF BUDDHA

Earlier in this chapter, you learned about the development of Hinduism in India. Another major religion, called **Buddhism**, also began there. Buddhism is based on the teachings of **Siddhartha Gautama** (sih-DAR-tuh GOW-tuh-muh). According to tradition, Siddartha was born in 563 B.C. He was a prince who lived a life of luxury in what is now Nepal.

Siddhartha enjoyed his life until, at the age of 29, he came across an old man, a sick man, a dead man, and a holy man who was poor but very happy. These men made Siddhartha think about suffering brought on by old age, disease, and death and wonder what had made the holy man so happy. Siddhartha

gave up his wealth, his wife, and his child to search for the answer to this question. Then, after six years of wandering, he meditated beneath a tree and finally understood how to be free from suffering. Because of this revelation, or understanding of truth, Siddhartha came to be known as the Buddha, or "Enlightened One."

BUDDHIST BELIEFS

The Buddha spent the rest of his life teaching what he had learned. Much of what he taught is contained in a set of guidelines called the Four Noble Truths. The first truth teaches that all life is suffering. The second truth is that the cause of suffering is desire. The third truth teaches that the end of desire means the end of suffering; the fourth, that following the Eightfold Path can end suffering. The Eightfold Path is also called the Middle Way because it promotes a

life balanced between happiness and self-denial. Like Hindus, the Buddha believed in reincarnation. He taught that following the Eightfold Path would lead to **nirvana** (nihr-VAH-nuh), a state of bliss or the end of suffering caused by the cycle of rebirth.

The totality of the Buddha's teachings are known as the **dharma** (DUHR-muh), or divine law. The Buddha taught that a person of any caste could attain nirvana, and he also promted nonviolence. Buddhism spread throughout Asia and beyond. After the Buddha died, his remains were buried under eight mound-like structures called stupas.

💼 **Job:** Prince, poor man, Enlightened One, and founder of Buddhism

📖 **Education:** Princely pursuits followed by soul searching

🌐 **Home:** Northeast India

FINEST HOUR
He finally achieved enlightenment after 49 days of intense meditation.

WORST MOMENT
He struggled to find the answers he sought, despite putting himself through much suffering and hardship.

MILESTONE
The Buddha is said to have received enlightenment at the age of 35.

REVIEW & ASSESS

1. **READING CHECK** Who is Siddhartha Gautama and what did he seek to learn?

2. **DRAW CONCLUSIONS** What is the purpose of the Four Noble Truths and the Eightfold Path?

3. **MAKE INFERENCES** Why do you think Buddhism became popular in ancient India?

PLAN

OBJECTIVE

Explain how Buddhism emerged in India around 500 B.C.

CRITICAL THINKING SKILLS FOR LESSON 1.6

- Identify Main Ideas and Details
- Monitor Comprehension
- Draw Conclusions
- Make Inferences
- Identify
- Describe
- Analyze Visuals

ESSENTIAL QUESTION

What led to the development of great civilizations in ancient India?

Buddhism was founded in ancient India. Lesson 1.6 discusses how Buddhism influenced the development of Indian civilization.

BACKGROUND FOR THE TEACHER

The Buddha did not leave written records of his teachings. His early disciples preserved the teachings by transmitting them orally from one generation to the next. Around 80 B.C., followers of the Buddha recorded his teachings in a set of books called the *Tripitaka*, or "Three Baskets." Over a period of centuries, Buddhism spread throughout Asia and other parts of the world. In South Asia today, Buddhism is the main religion of Bhutan and Sri Lanka. Buddhism focuses on helping people end their physical and mental suffering by teaching them to give up worldly possessions.

DIGITAL RESOURCES myNGconnect.com

TEACHER RESOURCES & ASSESSMENT

 Reading and Note-Taking

 Vocabulary Practice

 Section 1 Quiz

STUDENT RESOURCES

 Active History

INTRODUCE & ENGAGE

K-W-L CHART

Provide each student with a K-W-L Chart like the one shown below. Have students brainstorm what they know about religions in ancient India. Then ask them to write questions that they would like to have answered as they learn about Buddhism. Allow time at the end of the lesson for students to fill in what they have learned. **0:05 minutes**

K What Do I Know?	W What Do I Want To Learn?	L What Did I Learn?

TEACH

GUIDED DISCUSSION

1. **Identify** For what reason was the Buddha considered the "Enlightened One?" (*After wandering and then meditating, he finally understood the truth about how to be free from suffering.*)

2. **Describe** What are three teachings of the Buddha? (*Responses can include: the Four Noble Truths, guidelines for ending suffering, the Eightfold Path that leads to nirvana; the attainment of nirvana by a person of any caste; nonviolence; reincarnation.*)

ANALYZE VISUALS

Have students examine the photo of the Buddhist monks. Direct students to write a sentence about how the appearance and dress of the monks might give a clue about their religious beliefs and practices. (*Possible response: The monks are wearing simple robes with no jewelry or other accessories. This indicates that the monks probably lead a simple life with few material possessions.*) **0:10 minutes**

ACTIVE OPTIONS

Active History: Map the Spread of Buddhism Extend the lesson by using either the PDF or Whiteboard version of the activity. These activities take a deeper look at a topic from, or related to, the lesson. Explore the activities as a class, turn them into group assignments, or even assign them individually. **0:10 minutes**

On Your Feet: One-on-One Interviews Group students in pairs. Assign each pair one of the following religions: Brahmanism, Hinduism, or Buddhism. Have one student in each pair write three

questions about the religion. Have that student use the questions to interview the other student about the religion. Students' answers should show an understanding of the religion. **0:10 minutes**

DIFFERENTIATE

INCLUSION

Use Supported Reading In small groups, have students read the lesson aloud. At the end of the lesson, have them stop and use these frames to tell what they understood from the text.

- This lesson is about _____.
- One detail that stood out to me is _____.
- The vocabulary word _____ means _____.
- One thing I would like to understand more clearly is _____.

Guide students through portions of the text they do not understand. Make sure all students understand this lesson before moving on to the next lesson.

GIFTED & TALENTED

Host a Talk Show Have pairs of students assume the roles of a talk show host and Siddhartha Gautama. Ask students to plan, write, and perform a simulated television talk show in which Siddhartha is the guest. Tell students to focus the talk show on Siddhartha's life and his teachings, including the Four Noble Truths and the Eightfold Path.

Press (**mt**) in the Student eEdition for modified text.

See the Chapter Planner for more strategies for differentiation.

REVIEW & ASSESS

ANSWERS

1. Siddhartha was a prince who gave up everything to learn how to be truly happy.

2. Buddhists believe that following the Four Noble Truths and the Eightfold Path will lead to the end of suffering.

3. Buddhism rejects the rigid caste system and favors equality, which most likely appealed to many people, especially those belonging to the lowest social classes in India's caste system.

The Maurya Empire

Bite into oven-hot food and you'll burn your tongue. But nibble away at the cooler edges and you can eventually eat the whole meal. That's the principle one king applied to defeat some weaker kingdoms until he was strong enough to conquer them all.

MAIN IDEA

The Maurya Empire united much of India under a single ruler.

A UNITED INDIA

Earlier in this chapter, you read about the Aryans who migrated to India. The Aryans established many kingdoms in the subcontinent. For hundreds of years, no major power arose. Then, around 550 B.C., a kingdom called Magadha in northeast India grew powerful.

Chandragupta Maurya (chuhn-druh-GUP-tuh MOWR-yuh) became king of Magadha around 325 B.C. Believed to have been a soldier, Chandragupta gained power with the help of Kautilya, a Brahmin who plotted Chandragupta's rise. Once Chandragupta became king, he conquered many of the other kingdoms and established an empire. His Maurya Empire united most of northern India and was the first great Indian empire.

Chandragupta established a strong central government. He used taxes to pay for a network of spies and a large army to crush troublemakers. Then, somewhat surprisingly, Chandragupta gave up the throne in 297 B.C. Instead of continuing to rule his empire, he chose to become a monk committed to nonviolence.

THE BUDDHIST KING

Around 269 B.C., **Asoka** (uh-SHOH-kuh), Chandragupta's grandson, became king. At first he earned a reputation for cruelty. His unprovoked attack on another Indian kingdom caused the deaths of hundreds of thousands of people. In the aftermath of so much violence, Asoka underwent a dramatic change. He converted to Buddhism and began to rule using Buddhist principles about peace.

Asoka made a pilgrimage to all the Buddhist holy places in northern India, preaching to his subjects as he traveled. He actively encouraged the spread of Buddhism by sending missionaries to preach abroad. This practice helped Buddhism reach other countries such as Sri Lanka and China, where it is still very popular today.

Asoka had his Buddhist policies inscribed on rocks and tall pillars across his empire. The inscriptions were written in the appropriate regional languages. These policies encouraged everyone to live good lives. State officials monitored moral conduct.

Asoka built more than 1,000 stupas in honor of the Buddha. He donated to charity and built hospitals for animals as well as for humans. To govern his vast empire effectively, Asoka built good roads with plenty of shade and water. These roads were useful for trade and allowed his instructions, inspectors, and armies to travel quickly.

Although Asoka may have been India's greatest king, his well-run empire did not last long. After his death, the Maurya Empire collapsed into many warring kingdoms.

THE MAURYA EMPIRE, c. 250 B.C.

This pillar is one of many that Asoka had erected during his reign.

REVIEW & ASSESS

1. **READING CHECK** How did Chandragupta Maurya unite much of India into the first great Indian empire?

2. **INTERPRET MAPS** Where was Magadha located?

3. **ANALYZE CAUSE AND EFFECT** What caused Asoka to renounce violence? What was the effect?

PLAN

OBJECTIVE

Describe how the Maurya Empire united much of India under a single ruler.

The Maurya Empire united much of India under Chandragupta Maurya and then his grandson, Asoka. Lesson 2.1 discusses the development and then the decline of the Maurya Empire.

CRITICAL THINKING SKILLS FOR LESSON 2.1

- Identify Main Ideas and Details
- Monitor Comprehension
- Interpret Maps
- Analyze Cause and Effect
- Describe
- Summarize
- Create Graphic Organizers

BACKGROUND FOR THE TEACHER

Chandragupta Maurya was an Indian prince who conquered almost all of northern India and united it into one empire. The Maurya Empire had a complex government. In addition to having spies and an army of around 600,000 soldiers, the government had thousands of chariots and war elephants.

Asoka was a very strong ruler who made the empire powerful and rich. After he died, the kings who followed him were weak. After the Maurya Empire declined, India broke up into several kingdoms.

ESSENTIAL QUESTION

What led to the development of great civilizations in ancient India?

TEACHER RESOURCES & ASSESSMENT

 Reading and Note-Taking

 Vocabulary Practice

 Section 2 Quiz

STUDENT RESOURCES

 NG Chapter Gallery

INTRODUCE & ENGAGE

TEAM WORD WEBBING

Have students sit around a large piece of paper. Give each team member a different colored marker. Give students the following topic for their Word Web: *What are some characteristics of a successful civilization?* Ask students to write words or phrases that answer the topic question. Have each student add to the part of the web nearest to her or him. On a signal, have students rotate the paper and have each student add to the nearest part again. Tell students they will learn about how the Maurya Empire was successful. **0:05** minutes

TEACH

GUIDED DISCUSSION

1. **Describe** What was the government like under Chandragupta? (*It was a strong central government. Taxes paid for a network of spies and a large army.*)

2. **Summarize** What were some ways in which Asoka governed his empire? (*He ruled using Buddhist principles about peace. He had policies to encourage people to lead good lives. He donated to charity and built hospitals for animals and humans. He built good roads that were used for trade and that allowed armies to travel quickly.*)

CREATE GRAPHIC ORGANIZERS

Have students copy and fill in the following chart to help them remember the achievements and accomplishments of the two Maurya rulers mentioned in the lesson. **0:10** minutes

	Political Achievements	Religious Achievements
Chandragupta		
Asoka		

ACTIVE OPTIONS

On Your Feet: Build a Paragraph Direct students to form four lines. Provide each line of students with the same topic sentence: *Asoka may have been India's greatest king.* Each line, or group of students, should build a paragraph about the topic, with each person in line adding one sentence. Then have the groups record and share their paragraphs with the class. **0:10** minutes

Critical Viewing: NG Image Gallery Have students explore the NG Chapter Gallery and then the complete NG Image Gallery. Invite students to choose two images: one from this chapter and one from another chapter. Have students create a T-Chart with the column headings "Similar" and "Different." Students should complete their T-Chart by listing ways the two images are similar and ways they are different. Encourage students to move beyond physical comparison statements such as "one image shows a sculpture and the other shows a painting" by asking students to consider what the item in each gallery image represents, when it was made, and how it reflects the time or location in which it was made. **0:10** minutes

DIFFERENTIATE

ENGLISH LANGUAGE LEARNERS

Ask Yes/No Questions Ask the questions below and have students say or write *yes* or *no* in response. Then reread the questions and ask students to correct the information in any sentence that has *no* as an answer. (*numbers 2, 3, 6, 7*)

1. Did Chandragupta's empire have a strong government?
2. Did Chandragupta rule until the end of his life?
3. Did Chandragupta divide his empire?
4. Did Asoka's government encourage people to lead good lives?
5. Did Asoka help Buddhism reach other countries?
6. Did Asoka convert to Hinduism?
7. Was Asoka a weak ruler?
8. Did Asoka build roads and hospitals?

PRE-AP

Create a Travel Brochure Have pairs of students prepare a travel brochure for India during the rule of Asoka. The brochure should illustrate and describe places or structures that visitors should be sure to see.

Press (**mt**) *in the Student eEdition for modified text.*

See the Chapter Planner for more strategies for differentiation.

REVIEW & ASSESS

ANSWERS

1. First Chandragupta Maurya became king of Magadha, a powerful kingdom in northeast India. From there, he conquered other kingdoms and united them into an empire.

2. Magadha was located in the most northeastern part of the subcontinent.

3. A particularly bloody war caused Asoka to renounce violence. Asoka became a Buddhist and decided to rule India through the peaceful principles of Buddhism, which spread throughout India and other regions.

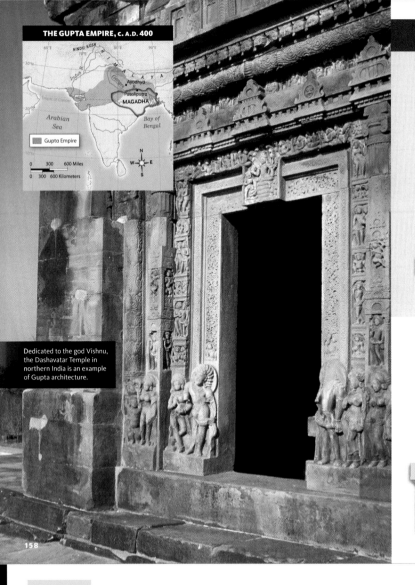

Dedicated to the god Vishnu, the Dashavatar Temple in northern India is an example of Gupta architecture.

2.2

The Gupta Empire

History has some weird coincidences.

Two of India's greatest empires began in Magadha with a king called Chandragupta. But the kings weren't related. And both empires began around 320, although the Maurya Empire began in 320 B.C. and the Gupta in A.D. 320.

MAIN IDEA

The Gupta Empire brought 200 years of peace and prosperity to India.

A WISE RULER

The collapse of the Maurya Empire led to 500 years of fighting in India. Despite this disorder, the period brought continued economic, social, and cultural progress. Then around A.D. 320 a new unifying power arose. A leader in Magadha called **Chandra Gupta I** began gaining new land and established the Gupta Empire. A dynasty of strong Gupta kings continued to expand the empire until it covered most of northern India. Instead of establishing a strong central government like the Mauryas did, the Guptas allowed the defeated kings to continue to rule. In exchange the Guptas required obedience and tribute, or payment, from the defeated kings.

A series of strong, wise, and long-lived Gupta rulers brought India 200 years of political stability, peace, and prosperity. The expanding empire and its extensive trade routes spread Indian cultural influences around Asia and beyond. Hinduism was reestablished and eventually became India's main religion.

A GOLDEN AGE

Chandra Gupta II, grandson of Chandra Gupta I, ruled during India's **golden age**, a period of great cultural achievement. **Kalidasa** (kah-lih-DAH-suh), the greatest poet in Chandra Gupta II's court and one of India's greatest writers, composed poems and plays in Sanskrit. Scribes, or writers, finally wrote down the spoken stories, including the *Mahabharata* and the *Ramayana*.

Indian artists painted and sculpted statues of Hindu deities. Architects designed and built elegant new temples. Metalworking improved dramatically. A 24-foot iron pillar weighing more than 6 tons still stands in Delhi some 1,500 years after being installed.

Medical understanding also increased. **Ayurveda** (y-uhr-VAY-duh), a traditional guide to medicine, diet, exercise, and disease, developed and remains an alternative form of healing. In medicine, as in many other areas, ancient Indian knowledge and culture reached far around the world.

REVIEW & ASSESS

1. **READING CHECK** How did the Gupta kings bring peace to their empire?

2. **INTERPRET MAPS** In which directions did the Gupta Empire spread out from Magadha?

3. **FORM AND SUPPORT OPINIONS** Which achievement during India's golden age do you think was most significant? Explain your answer.

PLAN

OBJECTIVE

Describe how the Gupta Empire brought 200 years of peace and prosperity to India.

CRITICAL THINKING SKILLS FOR LESSON 2.2

- Identify Main Ideas and Details
- Monitor Comprehension
- Interpret Maps
- Form and Support Opinions
- Compare and Contrast
- Identify
- Analyze Visuals

ESSENTIAL QUESTION

What led to the development of great civilizations in ancient India?

The Gupta Empire brought prosperity to India. Lesson 2.2 discusses the development and contributions of the Gupta Empire.

BACKGROUND FOR THE TEACHER

The Gupta Empire began in the fertile Ganges River Valley. Gupta artists and scientists created lasting cultural contributions. Advances in metalworking, literature, mathematics (including the development of the decimal), and astronomy were part of this legacy. Trade helped make the Gupta Empire wealthy. Cloth, salt, and iron were among the goods the Guptas traded. Cities grew along trade routes. People in the kingdom prospered. Eventually, invasions weakened the Guptas, and by A.D. 540 their reign was over.

ACTIVATE PRIOR KNOWLEDGE

Have students work in small groups. Ask students to think about how trading goods and sharing ideas with other countries can influence a country's prosperity, religions, and advances in arts and sciences. Have each group present three ideas to the class. Tell students they will learn about some of the factors that influenced the success of the Gupta civilization. **0:05** minutes

TEACH

GUIDED DISCUSSION

1. **Compare and Contrast** How was the Gupta government similar to and different from the Maurya government? (*Both governments had strong kings who expanded the empires. The Guptas did not establish a strong central government like the Mauryas. They allowed defeated kings to rule. In return, the Guptas required obedience and tribute, or payment, from the defeated kings.*)

2. **Identify** What was India's main religion during the Gupta Empire? (*Hinduism was the main religion in India during the Gupta Empire.*)

ANALYZE VISUALS

Have students examine the photo of part of the Dashavatar Temple in India. Ask them to list adjectives that describe what they see. Ask students what the style of the art and architecture might suggest about the art and architecture of the time. (*Students may respond that the art and architecture are quite elaborate and might indicate that art and architecture were important in the Gupta civilization.*) **0:10** minutes

ACTIVE OPTIONS

On Your Feet: Present an Empire Divide the class into two groups. Assign one group to the Maurya Empire and the other group to the Gupta Empire. Have each group prepare a presentation of "their" empire. The Maurya Empire should include government officials, members of the military, and the leader Asoka. The Gupta Empire should include Hindus, artists, and people who studied medicine. **0:10** minutes

NG Learning Framework: Write a Biography

ATTITUDE: **Curiosity**
KNOWLEDGE: **Our Human Story**

Have students select one of the leaders they are curious about after reading Lessons 2.1 and 2.2. Instruct them to write a short biography about this person using information from the chapter and additional source material. **0:20** minutes

STRIVING READERS

Find Main Ideas and Details Remind students that a main idea is a statement that summarizes the key idea of an article, speech, or paragraph. Details are facts, dates, events, and descriptions that support a main idea. Ask students to write one main idea and four details for the Gupta Empire. They should use their own words. Have students share their ideas when they have finished. The Maurya Empire is shown as an example

The Maurya Empire united much of India under a single ruler.
The king, Chandragupta, conquered many other kingdoms and established an empire.
Chandragupta established a strong central government.
Asoka ruled using Buddhist principles about peace.
Asoka built hospitals and roads.

INCLUSION

Complete Cloze Statements Provide copies of these cloze statements for students to complete during or after reading.

A _____ of strong Gupta kings expanded the empire until it covered most of northern _____. They did not establish a strong central _____. Instead, the Guptas allowed the defeated _____ to continue to _____. The Guptas required _____ and tribute, or _____ from the defeated kings.

Press (**mt**) *in the Student eEdition for modified text.*

See the Chapter Planner for more strategies for differentiation.

ANSWERS

1. The Gupta kings brought peace by allowing rulers of conquered kingdoms to continue to rule.

2. The Gupta Empire spread out to the north and the west of Magadha.

3. Responses will vary. Students may choose achievements in literature, art, metalworking, design and building of structures, or medicine.

The Legacy of Ancient India

Martin Luther King, Jr., championed nonviolent protest to win rights for African Americans. His methods were inspired by the nonviolent protests of Mohandas Gandhi, who helped India gain its independence in 1947. And Gandhi took his nonviolent principles from Hinduism and Buddhism. In that way alone, Indian thinking has had an immense impact on the modern world.

MAIN IDEA

The achievements of ancient India have influenced much of the world.

RELIGION

Two major religions had their origins in India: Hinduism and Buddhism. These religions remain important and influential in much of the modern world. Today four out of five Indians are Hindu, which greatly affects the country's culture. Although the caste system is now officially illegal, some people still observe certain cultural practices according to caste. The idea of reincarnation is especially widespread. Ancient Sanskrit texts continue to teach ethics through stories. Millions of people in many countries practice Hinduism, including more than two million people in the United States alone.

A number of great leaders, including **Mohandas Gandhi** (moh-HUHN-dahs GAHN-dih), have encouraged the Hindu and Buddhist principle of nonviolence. People throughout the world engage in nonviolence to protest injustice. Many vegetarians, people who do not eat meat, follow the Hindu and Buddhist principle of nonviolence toward animals. Today around one percent of India's population is Buddhist. However, Buddhism thrives in countries such as Sri Lanka, Thailand, Vietnam, Japan, Korea, and China. Buddhism also has a following in Europe and in the United States.

ARTS AND SCIENCE

You've learned that religion influenced Indian writing. The *Mahabharata* and the Bhagavad Gita are popular around the world. Religion also influenced Indian architecture, an influence that spread to other parts of the world. The temple of Angkor Wat in Cambodia, a country in Asia, is considered one of the world's greatest architectural achievements. The building's elaborate style evolved from ancient Indian architecture. Similar examples can be found in Myanmar (Burma), Vietnam, and Thailand.

Ancient India also contributed much to the fields of science and mathematics. Indians were among the first to practice **inoculation**, which stimulates mild forms of disease in people so that they do not develop more serious forms. Inoculation has greatly reduced the threat of smallpox.

Indian mathematicians created the decimal system and numerals (the number symbols we use today). They also developed the concept of zero, which is crucial to mathematics and computing. Indian astronomers, scientists who study the sun, moon, stars, and planets, accurately calculated the length of the solar year. They also asserted that Earth traveled around the sun and proved that the world was round 1,000 years before Columbus's voyage to America.

LEGACIES OF ANCIENT INDIA

Moral Conduct

Mohandas Gandhi's understanding of the Bhagavad Gita inspired his nonviolent protests in the mid-twentieth century against the British rule of India.

Science

Ancient astronomers determined that Earth is round. They also correctly calculated the length of the solar year.

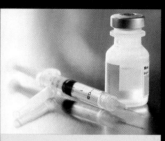

Medicine

Inoculation protects people's health by increasing one's resistance to disease. It has virtually eliminated smallpox.

Mathematics

Mathematicians of ancient India devised both the decimal system and numerals. They were the first to use zero.

REVIEW & ASSESS

1. **READING CHECK** How did ancient India influence religion in other parts of the world?

2. **SEQUENCE EVENTS** How did mathematicians in ancient India contribute to the age of computers?

3. **MAKE CONNECTIONS** What is the legacy of India's ancient Sanskrit texts?

PLAN

OBJECTIVE

Describe how the achievements of ancient India have influenced much of the world.

CRITICAL THINKING SKILLS FOR LESSON 2.3

- Identify Main Ideas and Details
- Monitor Comprehension
- Sequence Events
- Make Connections
- Analyze Cause and Effect
- Identify

ESSENTIAL QUESTION

What led to the development of great civilizations in ancient India?

Achievements in ancient India had a great influence on the rest of the world. Lesson 2.3 discusses some of these achievements in the areas of religion, the arts, and science.

BACKGROUND FOR THE TEACHER

Doctors in ancient India made many advances in medicine. They could perform operations such as removing infected tonsils, removing tumors, and rebuilding broken noses. They treated and stitched wounds and set broken bones. Doctors put much of their medical knowledge in writing. Some of these writings describe ways to make medicines from herbs and minerals. Doctors in ancient India invented a variety of medical tools. At times, they also would cast magic spells to try to cure diseases.

DIGITAL RESOURCES myNGconnect.com

TEACHER RESOURCES & ASSESSMENT

 Reading and Note-Taking

 Vocabulary Practice

 Section 2 Quiz

STUDENT RESOURCES

 NG Chapter Gallery

INTRODUCE & ENGAGE

ROUNDTABLE

Have students sit in groups of four. Ask students to talk about what they know about Hinduism and Buddhism and, if time allows, the effect these religions had on ancient Indian civilization. Encourage each student to contribute ideas about the religions. Tell students they will learn more about the influence of Hinduism and Buddhism on society. They also will learn about Indian contributions to the arts and sciences. **0:05** minutes

TEACH

GUIDED DISCUSSION

1. **Cause and Effect** How does innoculation reduce the occurrence of disease? (*Innoculation stimulates mild forms of a disease in people so they do not develop more serious forms of the disease.*)

2. **Identify** What were some achievements of astronomers in ancient India? (*Astronomers accurately calculated the length of the solar year. They asserted that Earth traveled around the sun. They determined that Earth is round.*)

MORE INFORMATION

Gandhi Mohandas Gandhi is considered to be the father of modern India. His understanding of Hinduism inspired his nonviolent protests against the British rule of India in the first half of the 20th century. One such protest was the Salt March of 1930 in response to Britain's heavy tax on salt. Thousands of Indians followed Gandhi for a distance of some 240 miles. The result of the march was the arrest of nearly 60,000 people, including Gandhi, but his actions won him admiration around the world. After the end of World War II, Britain worked with Gandhi and other leaders to grant India's independence, which was finally achieved in 1947. Sadly, Gandhi did not get to enjoy it for long. In 1948, he was assassinated by a young Hindu extremist who resented Gandhi's work with Muslim leaders.

ACTIVE OPTIONS

On Your Feet: Inside-Outside Circle Arrange students in concentric circles facing each other. Have students in the outside circle ask the students in the inside circle a question about the lesson. Then have the outside circle rotate one position to the right to create new pairings. After five questions, have students switch roles and continue. **0:10** minutes

Critical Viewing: NG Chapter Gallery Invite students to explore the gallery for this chapter. Then have each student think of and research one additional image that would fit within and enhance the Chapter Gallery. Have students provide a written or verbal explanation of why they selected the extra image, how they selected it, and why they feel it would make a valuable addition to the gallery. Be sure students provide a printout or other visual

representation of the image they would like to add to the gallery so their classmates can examine it. **0:10** minutes

DIFFERENTIATE

ENGLISH LANGUAGE LEARNERS

Use Sentence Stems Before reading, provide students with the sentence stems listed below. Call on volunteers to read the stems orally and explain any unclear vocabulary. After reading, have students complete the stems in writing and compare completed sentences with a partner.

1. Two major religions that originated in India are _____ and _____.
2. To protest injustice, Gandhi and other leaders encouraged the principle of _____.
3. Ancient astronomers determined that Earth is _____.
4. The medical practice practiced in ancient India that greatly reduced the threat of smallpox is _____.
5. Ancient mathematicians in India created the concept of the numeral _____.

PRE-AP

Write a Feature Article Have students do research about the temple of Angkor Wat. Have them find information about its religious significance. Ask them to look for interesting details about its history and architecture. Then have them write a feature article describing what they learned.

Press (mt) *in the Student eEdition for modified text.*

See the Chapter Planner for more strategies for differentiation.

REVIEW & ASSESS

ANSWERS

1. Ancient India developed two of the world's great religions, Hinduism and Buddhism. These religions spread to many other countries, where they are still practiced today.
2. Mathematicians in ancient India developed the concept of zero, the decimal system, and numerals, all of which we continue to use today in the age of computers.
3. Religion influenced Indian writing. The ancient texts the *Mahabharata* and the Bhagavad Gita are still popular around the world.

VOCABULARY

On your paper, write the vocabulary word that completes each of the following sentences.

1. Today, five countries make up the Indian _____, which is separated from the rest of Asia by the Himalaya.

2. Strong seasonal winds called _____ shape India's climate.

3. The *Ramayana* is an example of an _____.

4. Ancient Indians had a social hierarchy that developed into a rigid _____.

5. Hindus believe in _____, which means that when a person dies, his or her soul is reborn in another body.

6. According to Hindu teachings, _____ is the practice of breathing exercises as a path to spiritual insight.

7. The totality of the Buddha's teachings are known as the _____, or divine law.

8. Buddhists believe that the Eightfold Path leads to the end of suffering, or _____.

READING STRATEGY

9. If you haven't already, complete your organizer to identify the effects of the Aryan migrations on Indian civilization. Then answer the question.

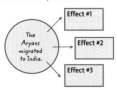

Effect #1

The Aryans migrated to India.

Effect #2

Effect #3

How did the Aryans change civilization in ancient India?

MAIN IDEAS

Answer the following questions. Support your answers with evidence from the chapter.

10. How did geographic features contribute to the development of the Harappan civilization? **LESSON 1.1**

11. In what way were the cities of Mohenjo-Daro and Harappa signs of an advanced civilization? **LESSON 1.2**

12. Who were the Aryans? **LESSON 1.3**

13. How did Hinduism develop in India? **LESSON 1.4**

14. What did Siddhartha Gautama achieve? **LESSON 1.6**

15. How did Asoka spread Buddhism? **LESSON 2.1**

16. In what ways was the reign of Chandra Gupta II a golden age? **LESSON 2.2**

17. What Hindu beliefs and values still deeply influence people's behavior in India today? **LESSON 2.3**

CRITICAL THINKING

Answer the following questions. Support your answers with evidence from the chapter.

18. **ANALYZE CAUSE AND EFFECT** How did the Guptas establish and maintain their empire?

19. **MAKE CONNECTIONS** What did early Indus Valley civilizations have in common with other ancient river valley civilizations?

20. **EVALUATE** How important were the contributions of ancient India to the fields of science and mathematics? Support your evaluation with evidence from the chapter.

21. **COMPARE AND CONTRAST** How are Hindu and Buddhist beliefs similar? How are they different?

22. **YOU DECIDE** What do you think were Asoka's two greatest leadership qualities? Support your opinion with evidence from the chapter.

INTERPRET CHARTS

Study the chart of the caste system that developed in ancient Indian society. Then answer the questions that follow.

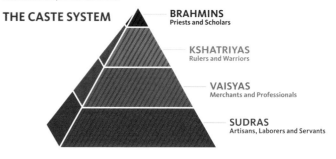

THE CASTE SYSTEM

BRAHMINS
Priests and Scholars

KSHATRIYAS
Rulers and Warriors

VAISYAS
Merchants and Professionals

SUDRAS
Artisans, Laborers and Servants

23. To which caste did most Indians belong?

24. Which caste was the smallest? Why do you think this was so?

ANALYZE SOURCES

Read the following words spoken by the Buddha. Then answer the question.

Hold fast to the truth as a lamp. Hold fast as a refuge [place of safety] to the truth. Look not for refuge to any one besides yourselves. . . .

And whosoever, . . . either now or after I am dead, shall be a lamp unto themselves, . . . shall look not for refuge to any one besides themselves—it is they . . . who shall reach the very topmost Height!—but they must be anxious to learn.

from *The Last Days of Buddha*, trans. T.W. Rhys David

25. In the passage, the Buddha is telling his followers how to act. What is his message?

WRITE ABOUT HISTORY

26. **INFORMATIVE** Suppose you are writing a pamphlet for a museum exhibit about India. Write short essay that explains the lasting influence of ancient India on religion.

TIPS

- Develop an outline that shows how ancient India's influence on religion continues to this day.
- Write the introductory paragraph of your essay using your outline as a guide.
- Develop the topic with relevant, well-chosen facts, concrete details, and examples.
- Use vocabulary from the chapter to explain your ideas.
- Provide a concluding statement that summarizes the information presented.

VOCABULARY ANSWERS

1. subcontinent
2. monsoons
3. epic poem
4. caste system
5. reincarnation
6. yoga
7. dharma
8. nirvana

READING STRATEGY ANSWER

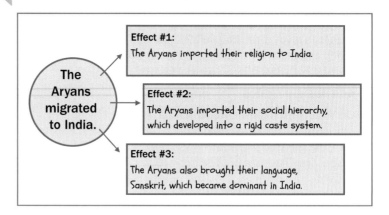

The Aryans migrated to India.

Effect #1:
The Aryans imported their religion to India.

Effect #2:
The Aryans imported their social hierarchy, which developed into a rigid caste system.

Effect #3:
The Aryans also brought their language, Sanskrit, which became dominant in India.

9. The Aryans brought to India their religion, their social hierarchy, and their Sanskrit language, all of which had a great impact on the civilization of ancient India.

MAIN IDEAS ANSWERS

10. Rivers provided water for irrigation and enriched the soil by depositing silt, which led to settlement and farming. Mountain ranges to the north and surrounding oceans helped protect India from invaders.

11. Mohenjo-Daro and Harappa were not only the largest cities of their time, but they were the world's first planned cities, with standardized layouts, buildings, advanced sanitation, and grid-pattern roads.

12. The Aryans were a collection of Indo-European tribes who migrated into India beginning in 1500 B.C. They had a tremendous impact on India's culture, specifically religion, social hierarchy, and language.

13. Over many centuries, Aryan Brahmanism fused with native Indian religions to form Hinduism.

14. Siddhartha Gautama was the founder of Buddhism. He sought to learn the secret of happiness.

15. Asoka helped spread Buddhism by making it the state religion and sending missionaries to other countries to preach and spread Buddhist ideas.

16. Two hundred years of political stability, peace, and prosperity, plus a long line of wise, strong kings greatly stimulated culture and learning during the reign of Chandra Gupta II.

17. The Hindu beliefs in reincarnation and the importance of ethics are still effective influences on people's behavior.

CRITICAL THINKING ANSWERS

18. The Guptas gained new land and established an empire. Strong Gupta kings expanded the empire. The Guptas allowed defeated kings to rule in exchange for obedience and tribute.

19. Like other ancient river valley civilizations, the Indus Valley civilizations enjoyed fertile soil, plentiful water from river sources, and good climate, all of which encouraged settlement and farming.

20. Ancient Indian civilization made many important achievements and contributions in the fields of science and mathematics. In science, these achievements and contributions included proving the world was round and that Earth revolved around the sun. In mathematics, achievements and contributions included the decimal system, numerals, and the concept of zero.

21. Hindus and Buddhists both believe in reincarnation. Buddhists reject the caste system and believe in equality, promoting a nonviolent way of life toward all living things. Hindus believe in a complex array of deities. Buddhists follow a moral way of life based on the Four Noble Truths and the Eightfold Path.

22. Students' responses will vary. Students should cite two of Asoka's leadership qualities and explain their importance with evidence from the chapter.

INTERPRET CHARTS ANSWERS

23. Most people belonged to the Sudra caste.

24. The Brahmin caste was the smallest. The Brahmins established relationships with kings, preaching that the gods gave kings the right to rule. The kings upheld the authority of the Brahmins.

ANALYZE SOURCES ANSWER

25. Students' responses will vary. Sample response: A lamp creates light, illuminating the dark to guide one's way. In comparing truth to a lamp, the Buddha suggests that like a lamp, the truth will illuminate one's thoughts and lead the way to nirvana, the end of suffering.

WRITE ABOUT HISTORY ANSWER

26. Students' essays will vary but should be clear and well organized. Students should use relevant details and examples to support the main points of their essay.

UNIT 2 EARLY CIVILIZATIONS

UNIT RESOURCES

On Location with National Geographic Lead Program Officer Christopher Thornton Intro and Video

Unit Wrap-Up:
"Encounters with History"
Feature and Video

"China's Ancient Lifeline"
National Geographic Adapted Article

"Faces of the Divine"
National Geographic Adapted Article
Student eEdition exclusive

Unit 2 Inquiry:
Write a Creation Myth

Interactive Map Tool

News & Updates

Available on myNGconnect

CHAPTER RESOURCES

TEACHER RESOURCES & ASSESSMENT

Available on myNGconnect

Social Studies Skills Lessons
• Reading: Analyze Language Use
• Writing: Write an Argument

Formal Assessment
• Chapter 7 Tests A (on-level) & B (below-level)

Chapter 7 Answer Key

ExamView®
One-time Download

STUDENT BACKPACK *Available on myNGconnect*

• **eEdition** *(English)*   • **eEdition** *(Spanish)*   • **Handbooks**   • **Online Atlas**

For Chapter 7 Spanish resources, visit the Teacher Resource Menu page on myNGconnect.

SECTION 1 RESOURCES

RIVER DYNASTIES

 Reading and Note-Taking

 Vocabulary Practice

 Section 1 Quiz

Available on myNGconnect

LESSON 1.1 THE GEOGRAPHY OF ANCIENT CHINA
- Critical Viewing: NG Chapter Gallery
- On Your Feet: Fishbowl

LESSON 1.2 SHANG AND ZHOU DYNASTIES
- Critical Viewing: NG Chapter Gallery
- On Your Feet: Stage a Quiz Show

LESSON 1.3 CHINESE PHILOSOPHIES

 Biography
Confucius

Available on myNGconnect
- Critical Viewing: NG Chapter Gallery
- On Your Feet: Code of Conduct Roundtable

DOCUMENT-BASED QUESTION
LESSON 1.4 CONTRASTING BELIEF SYSTEMS

| **NG Learning Framework:**
Learn About Different Chinese Philosophies
- On Your Feet: Use a Jigsaw Strategy

SECTION 2 RESOURCES

CHINA'S EMPIRES

 Reading and Note-Taking

 Vocabulary Practice

 Section 2 Quiz

Available on myNGconnect

BIOGRAPHY
LESSON 2.1 SHI HUANGDI

| **NG Learning Framework:**
Learn About Shi Huangdi
- On Your Feet: Hold a Panel Discussion

LESSON 2.2 THE GREAT WALL

| **NG Learning Framework:**
Learn About the Great Wall
- On Your Feet: Build a Wall

MOMENTS IN HISTORY
LESSON 2.3 TERRA COTTA WARRIORS

| **NG Learning Framework:**
Learn About Shi Huangdi's Army
- On Your Feet: I See, I Read, And So

LESSON 2.4 THE HAN DYNASTY
- Critical Viewing: NG Chapter Gallery
- On Your Feet: Stage a Quiz Show

LESSON 2.5 THE LEGACY OF ANCIENT CHINA
- Critical Viewing: NG Chapter Gallery
- On Your Feet: Inventions and Ideas

SECTION 3 RESOURCES

EAST MEETS WEST

 Reading and Note-Taking

 Vocabulary Practice

 Section 3 Quiz

Available on myNGconnect

LESSON 3.1 THE SILK ROADS

| **NG Learning Framework:**
Learn About the Silk Roads
- On Your Feet: Team Word Webbing

LESSON 3.2 TRADE ON THE SILK ROADS

 Active History: Interactive Whiteboard Activity
Barter on the Silk Roads

 Active History
Barter on the Silk Roads

Available on myNGconnect
- On Your Feet: Inside-Outside Circle

HISTORY THROUGH OBJECTS
LESSON 3.3 GOODS FROM THE SILK ROADS
- Critical Viewing: NG Chapter Gallery
- On Your Feet: Set Up a Market

NG EXPLORER FREDRIK HIEBERT
LESSON 3.4 EXCAVATING ALONG THE SILK ROADS

| **NG Learning Framework:**
Learn About Fredrik Hiebert
- On Your Feet: Tell Me More

CHAPTER 7 REVIEW

STRATEGY 1
Make Predictions About Content

Before students read the lessons listed below, have them examine the headings and visuals in each one and write their predictions on what the lesson will be about. After students read the lessons, have them check to see whether their predictions were accurate.

Use with Lessons 1.3, 2.5, and 3.4 *You might want to pair students whose predictions were inaccurate with students who correctly predicted the content of the lessons and have them compare the conclusions they drew from viewing the subheadings and visuals in each one.*

STRATEGY 2
Use a Word Sort

Display these words and tell students to sort them into groupings and label each group by category. Then have students write a sentence that explains how each group of words is connected.

Shi Huangdi	Confucianism
caravan	filial piety
Han	barter
cultural diffusion	Great Wall
Qin	

Use with Lessons 1.3, 2.1, 2.4, 3.1, and 3.2

STRATEGY 3
Complete a Key Facts T-Chart

Have students create a T-Chart on the early Chinese dynasties. In one column of the T-Chart, students should list the Shang, Zhou, Qin, and Han dynasties. In the other column, students should jot down key facts about each dynasty as they read the lesson. Have students compare completed charts.

Use with Lessons 1.2 and 2.1–2.4 *You might have students use this strategy in other lessons in the chapter.*

Press (mt) *in the Student eEdition for modified text.*

STRATEGY 1
Describe Lesson Visuals

Pair visually challenged students with students who are not visually challenged. Ask the latter to help their partners "see" the visuals in the chapter by describing the images and answering any questions the visually impaired student might have.

Use with All Lessons *For example, for the dynastic cycle diagram in Lesson 1.2, students might describe the dragon around the diagram: its expression, teeth, claws, long, curving tail. Students might also read aloud the captions on the diagram in order.*

STRATEGY 2
Expand Main Idea Statements

After reading, direct students to copy each of the following Main Idea statements and write a paragraph that expands on the statement. Use these starters as examples if needed:

1.1 China's deserts, mountains, and rivers helped shape its civilization. The deserts include _____.

1.2 The Shang and Zhou dynasties developed many cultural behaviors and beliefs that have become part of Chinese civilization. For example, _____.

1.3 Chinese philosophies developed important ideas on how society should be organized. One of these philosophies is called _____.

Use with Lessons 1.1–1.3

STRATEGY 1
Use Paired Reading

Pairs of students read a passage from the text aloud. Then:

1. Partner 1 reads another passage; Partner 2 retells the passage in his or her own words.

2. Partner 2 reads a different passage; Partner 1 retells it.

3. Pairs repeat the whole exercise, switching roles.

Use with All Lessons *For Lesson 1.1, have Partner 1 read the text under the subhead "Natural Barriers" while Partner 2 points to the appropriate landforms on the map. Partners switch roles for the subhead "Major Rivers."*

STRATEGY 2
Brainstorm Vocabulary from Visuals

Before reading, have students examine all the visuals in Lesson 2 and write down words that come to mind while studying the visuals. Ask students to identify words and to write each on a piece of paper. Create a display of words for students to refer to as the lesson is read and discussed.

Use with Lessons 2.1–2.5

STRATEGY ③
Find Someone Who Knows

Give students copies of the questions below and have them find five different classmates to answer them.

1. Between what two rivers did China's civilization develop? *(Huang He and Chang Jiang)*

2. What was China's first dynasty? *(Shang)*

3. Whose teachings have influenced China for centuries? *(Confucius)*

4. Who was China's first emperor? *(Shi Huangdi)*

5. What is the name of the trade routes that connected China and other countries? *(Silk Roads)*

Use with Lessons 1.1–1.3, 2.1, and 3.1

GIFTED & TALENTED

STRATEGY ①
Create a Multimedia Presentation

Have students choose a research topic for ancient China and create a presentation. Students can use photos, maps, and other visuals that they find online or photocopy from written material to support their presentation.

Use with Lessons 2.1–2.3 and 3.1–3.3 *For a presentation on the Silk Roads, students might want to research and include the history of the trade routes during the time of Genghis Khan.*

STRATEGY ②
Interview a Historical Figure

Allow students to work in teams of two to plan, write, and perform a simulated television interview with Shi Huangdi or Confucius. Tell students that the purpose of the interview is to focus on the achievements, actions, and goals of the historical figure.

Use with Lessons 1.3 and 2.1 *Invite students to do research to learn more about the historical figure they have chosen. Encourage them to elicit in-depth answers by asking the historical figures why and how they did the things they did.*

PRE-AP

STRATEGY ①
Form a Thesis

Have students develop a thesis statement for a specific topic related to one of the lessons. Be sure the statement makes a claim that is supportable with evidence either from the lesson or through further research. Then have pairs compare their statements and determine which makes the strongest or most supportable claims.

Use with All Lessons

STRATEGY ②
Explain the Significance

Allow students to choose one term below to investigate and design a presentation that explains the significance of the term to the history of China.

Mandate of Heaven	Great Wall
Confucianism	Han
Legalism	Silk Roads

Use with Lessons 1.2, 1.3, 2.1, 2.2, 2.4, and 3.1

ANCIENT CHINA

2000 B.C. – A.D. 220

SECTION 1
RIVER DYNASTIES

KEY VOCABULARY	NAMES & PLACES
dynastic cycle	Chang Jiang
dynasty	Confucianism
filial piety	Daoism
isolate	Huang He
oracle bone	Legalism
	Mandate of Heaven
	Shang
	Warring States
	Zhou

SECTION 2
CHINA'S EMPIRES

KEY VOCABULARY	NAMES & PLACES
bureaucracy	Great Wall
emperor	Han
peasant	Qin
silk	Shi Huangdi
terra cotta	

SECTION 3
EAST MEETS WEST

KEY VOCABULARY	NAMES & PLACES
barter	Silk Roads
caravan	
cultural diffusion	
maritime	

READING STRATEGY

ANALYZE LANGUAGE USE
When you analyze language use, you note how specific word choices indicate the author's point of view and purpose. As you read the chapter, use concept clusters like this one to analyze the language used to describe the philosophies of Confucianism, Daoism, and Legalism.

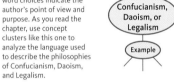

The lion's dance, a Chinese tradition for more than 1,000 years, is performed during a New Year's celebration in Beijing, China's capital.

165

TEACHER BACKGROUND

INTRODUCE THE PHOTOGRAPH

Have students study the photograph of the lion's dance in Beijing. Explain that in Chinese culture, the lion represents power, strength, and stability. The lion's dance, with its firecrackers and banging drums, is believed to chase away evil spirits. Tell students that, in this chapter, they will learn about the culture and civilization of ancient China. Then have students examine the faces of the lions in the photo.

ASK: What details in the lions' faces convey power and strength? *(Possible response: large, fierce eyes; teeth and fangs; menacing expression)*

SHARE BACKGROUND

The lion's dance starts at a temple and proceeds through the streets of the town or city. Performers of the dance often stop at a shop or home during the procession. These visits are thought to bring good luck in the year to come for the owners. The owners will enjoy even greater luck if they are allowed to stick their heads in the lions' mouths. The dance ends at another temple.

DIGITAL RESOURCES myNGconnect.com

TEACHER RESOURCES & ASSESSMENT

Social Studies Skills Lessons
- Reading: Analyze Language Use
- Writing: Write an Argument

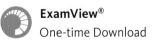
ExamView®
One-time Download

Formal Assessment
Chapter 7 Tests A (on-level) & B (below-level)

Chapter 7 Answer Key

STUDENT BACKPACK

- **eEdition** *(English)*
- **eEdition** *(Spanish)*
- **Handbooks**
- **Online Atlas**

For Chapter 7 Spanish resources, visit the Teacher Resource Menu page.

INTRODUCE THE ESSENTIAL QUESTION

HOW DID CHINA ESTABLISH WHAT WOULD BECOME ONE OF THE WORLD'S OLDEST CONTINUOUS CIVILIZATIONS?

Roundtable Activity: Leaders, Beliefs, Encounters Seat students around tables in groups of four. Ask groups to discuss what they have learned about other ancient civilizations, such as those of Mesopotamia, Egypt, and India. Encourage them to consider the factors that helped these civilizations thrive. If students need help coming up with ideas, have them consider the questions below. After students have finished the activity, tell them that, in this chapter, they will learn about the factors that helped China establish and develop a thriving civilization.

1. **What role did strong leaders play in the ancient civilizations you have learned about?**

2. **What beliefs unified the people of these civilizations?**

3. **How did the civilizations benefit from trade and other encounters with different cultures?** `0:15` minutes

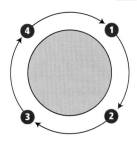

INTRODUCE THE READING STRATEGY

ANALYZE LANGUAGE USE

Tell students that analyzing language use can help them understand an author's meaning, tone, and purpose. Model completing the Concept Cluster by reading the second and third paragraphs under "A Ruthless Ruler" in Lesson 2.1 and writing "punishing anyone who disagreed with him" in the central oval. Then have students discuss the meaning, tone, and purpose of this phrase.

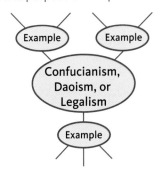

INTRODUCE CHAPTER VOCABULARY

KNOWLEDGE RATING

Have students complete a Knowledge-Rating Chart for Key Vocabulary words. Have students list words and fill out the chart. Then have pairs share the definitions they know. Work together as a class to complete the chart.

KEY VOCAB	KNOW IT	NOT SURE	DON'T KNOW	DEFINITION
barter				
bureaucracy				
caravan				
cultural diffusion				

KEY DATES

c. 1600 B.C.	Shang dynasty, China's first, develops
c. 1045 B.C.	Zhou dynasty overthrows Shang
551 B.C.	Birth of Confucius
221 B.C.	Shi Huangdi becomes first emperor
202 B.C.	Han dynasty begins
100 B.C.	Silk Roads are well established
A.D. 105	Paper invented by the Chinese
A.D. 220	Han dynasty ends

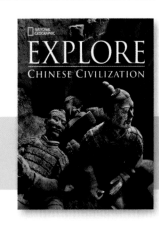

For more articles about China, see *EXPLORE CHINESE CIVILIZATION.*

The Geography of Ancient China

At about 240 years of age, the United States may seem like an old civilization, but it's young compared to China. The Chinese civilization has continued for more than 5,000 years. China's geography helped set the stage for the early development of its civilization.

MAIN IDEA

China's deserts, mountains, and rivers helped shape its civilization.

NATURAL BARRIERS

In the beginning of its growth, natural barriers somewhat **isolated**, or cut off, China's civilization from much of the rest of the world. As a result, ancient China developed differently from other early civilizations, with relatively little outside cultural influence. This early isolation helped unify Chinese culture and allowed China to establish a firm foundation for its civilization.

Some of China's natural barriers included vast deserts. The Gobi to the north and the Taklimakan (tah-kluh-muh-KAHN) to the west discouraged invaders and peaceful immigrants alike. The Himalaya, Tian Shan, and Pamir mountain ranges formed a significant obstacle in the west. The waters of the Pacific Ocean, Yellow Sea, and East China Sea on China's east coast separated the region from its nearest neighbors, Japan and Korea.

MAJOR RIVERS

Like the ancient civilizations of Mesopotamia, Egypt, and India, China's civilization arose along fertile river valleys. It developed on the land between China's two great rivers: the **Huang He** (hwahng huh) and the **Chang Jiang** (chahng jyahng).

The 3,395-mile-long Huang He lies in northern China. It is also called the Yellow River because of its high concentration of yellow silt, or fine, fertile soil. The river deposits this silt along its floodplains, creating good farmland. However, the Huang He is unpredictable. Its course, or the direction in which a river flows, has changed many times. Throughout China's history, heavy rains have also caused the river to flood—with deadly results.

At about 4,000 miles long, the Chang Jiang, or Yangtze, in central China is the third longest river in the world. Like the Huang He, the Chang Jiang carries fertile yellow silt. Unlike the Huang He, the Chang Jiang maintains a relatively predictable course. For thousands of years, the river helped unify China by serving as a useful transportation and trade network within its borders.

The area between the two rivers, called the North China Plain, is the birthplace of Chinese civilization. In Chapter 2, you read about the Yangshao culture, which developed along the Huang He. Another important culture in the area was the Longshan, which developed around 3200 B.C. Other advanced Chinese cultures arose in other river valleys. These cultures include the Liangzhu (lyahng-jew) and the Hongshan. Archaeologists have uncovered beautifully carved jade objects from these cultures in other parts of China. All of these ancient cultures contributed to the development of China's unique civilization and to the rise of its earliest rulers: the Shang and the Zhou.

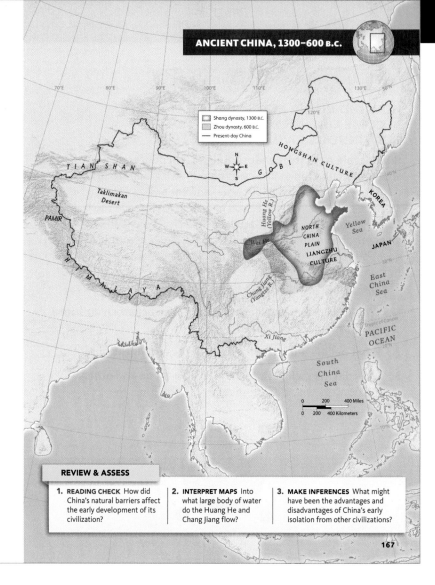

ANCIENT CHINA, 1300–600 B.C.

Shang dynasty, 1300 B.C.
Zhou dynasty, 600 B.C.
Present-day China

REVIEW & ASSESS

1. **READING CHECK** How did China's natural barriers affect the early development of its civilization?

2. **INTERPRET MAPS** Into what large body of water do the Huang He and Chang Jiang flow?

3. **MAKE INFERENCES** What might have been the advantages and disadvantages of China's early isolation from other civilizations?

PLAN

OBJECTIVE

Analyze how China's deserts, mountains, and rivers helped shape its civilization.

CRITICAL THINKING SKILLS FOR LESSON 1.1

- Identify Main Ideas and Details
- Monitor Comprehension
- Interpret Maps
- Make Inferences
- Compare and Contrast

ESSENTIAL QUESTION

How did China establish what would become one of the world's oldest continuous civilizations?

Natural barriers somewhat isolated China's early civilization from much of the rest of the world. Lesson 1.1 discusses the deserts, mountains, and bodies of water that helped unify Chinese culture and allowed China to establish a firm foundation for its civilization.

BACKGROUND FOR THE TEACHER

Gobi means "place without water." The extreme dryness and strong winds that sometimes blow through the desert result in blinding dust storms. At most, only about seven inches of rain fall in the Gobi every year. Some parts receive no rain at all. Temperatures in the desert can reach 113°F in the summer and -40°F in the winter. The temperatures in the Gobi can rise and fall by as much as 60 degrees within the same day.

DIGITAL RESOURCES myNGconnect.com

TEACHER RESOURCES & ASSESSMENT

 Reading and Note-Taking

 Vocabulary Practice

 Section 1 Quiz

STUDENT RESOURCES

 NG Chapter Gallery

INTRODUCE & ENGAGE

DEMONSTRATE LANDFORMS

Use a sheet of unlined paper to help students differentiate among the landforms discussed in the lesson. Tell students that a *plain* is flat like a sheet of paper. Then fold the paper lengthwise and open it as a V. Explain that the sides of the paper are mountains, and the river *valley* is at the bottom. **0:05** minutes

TEACH

GUIDED DISCUSSION

1. **Compare and Contrast** How are the Huang He and Chang Jiang similar? How do they differ? *(Both are long and carry fertile yellow silt. However, while the Chang Jiang maintains a relatively predictable course, the course of the Huang He has changed many times.)*

2. **Make Inferences** Why do you think Chinese civilization developed on the North China Plain? *(The plain lies between the fertile river valleys of the Huang He and Chang Jiang and would have been excellent for growing crops.)*

INTERPRET MAPS

Have students study the map of ancient China. Point out the North China Plain and the two major rivers that flow through it. Have students trace the Huang He on the map. **ASK:** What is the name of the river's tributary that flows through the North China Plain? *(Wei He)* Then point out the general area where the Liangzhu and Hongshan cultures developed. **ASK:** What is unusual about the area where the Hongshan culture developed? *(The Hongshan culture didn't develop around a major river. Instead, it developed in a desert area.)* **0:10** minutes

ACTIVE OPTIONS

Critical Viewing: NG Chapter Gallery Invite students to explore the Chapter Gallery to examine the images that relate to Chapter 7. Have them select one of the images and do additional research to learn more about it. Ask questions that will inspire additional inquiry about the chosen gallery image, such as: What is this? Where and when was this created? By whom? Why was it created? What is it made of? Why does it belong in this chapter? What else would you like to know about it? **0:10** minutes

On Your Feet: Fishbowl Have half the class sit in a close circle, facing inward. Have the other half of the class sit in a larger circle around them. Instruct students in the inside circle to discuss what they know about the Huang He while the outside circle listens. The discussion should include details about the river's location, size, and importance. Then call on volunteers in the outside circle to summarize what they heard. Have students switch places and ask

those now on the inside circle to discuss what they know about the Chang Jiang. The outside circle should listen and then summarize what they heard. **0:10** minutes

DIFFERENTIATE

STRIVING READERS

Take Notes Have students take notes on China's landforms as they read the lesson, using a Concept Cluster. Tell them to add more clusters as needed. Allow students to compare their completed clusters in small groups and make any necessary corrections. Then call on volunteers to use their diagrams to summarize what they know about the landforms.

ENGLISH LANGUAGE LEARNERS

Use Geographic Terms Write the following words on the board: *mountain, desert, plain, river, ocean*. Say each word and have students repeat it after you. Then have students work in pairs and copy the words on individual sticky notes. Next, ask students to place the sticky notes on appropriate places on the map of ancient China. Monitor students as they work and clarify understanding as needed. Finally, invite volunteers to use the words in sentences.

Press (mt) *in the Student eEdition for modified text.*

See the Chapter Planner for more strategies for differentiation.

REVIEW & ASSESS

ANSWERS

1. The deserts, mountain ranges, and water were natural barriers that isolated China physically from other civilizations. As a result, early China developed with relatively little cultural influence from other civilizations.

2. The Huang He and the Chang Jiang flow into the Pacific Ocean.

3. The advantages include protection from invaders and the development of a homogeneous culture. The disadvantages include insulation and the inability to benefit from the ideas of other early cultures.

Shang and Zhou Dynasties

According to Chinese tradition, a ruler named Yu learned to control the floodwaters of the Huang He and established China's first dynasty, the Xia (shee-AH). But no archaeological evidence of this dynasty has ever been found. The first dynasty for which evidence does exist is the Shang.

MAIN IDEA

The Shang and Zhou dynasties developed many cultural behaviors and beliefs that have become part of Chinese civilization.

CHINA'S FIRST DYNASTY

The **Shang** dynasty emerged along the banks of the Huang He around 1600 B.C. A **dynasty** is a line of rulers from the same family. The Shang developed many cultural behaviors and beliefs that rulers would continue throughout much of Chinese civilization. They established an ordered society with the king at the top, warlords coming next, and farmers at the bottom. The farmers helped advance agriculture in China and grew crops such as millet, wheat, and rice.

The Shang also developed a system of writing using about 3,000 characters. These characters became the basis for modern Chinese writing. They first appeared on **oracle bones**, which are animal bones used to consult the many gods the Shang people worshipped. Priests carved a question on a bone and then heated it. They believed that the pattern of cracks that resulted revealed the gods' answer.

In addition to their gods, the Shang people worshipped the spirits of their dead ancestors. The Shang believed these spirits influenced everything from the king's health to farmers' harvests. To keep the spirits happy, priests conducted special ceremonies, often using beautifully decorated bronze vessels. Shang craftspeople were among the most skilled metalworkers at that time. They also built elaborate tombs for the dead.

THE DYNASTIC CYCLE

In time, the Shang dynasty began to weaken. Around 1045 B.C., the **Zhou** (joh) overthrew the Shang and became China's longest ruling dynasty, lasting about 800 years. The rise of the Zhou also marked the beginning of China's classical period, a time of great social and cultural advances that lasted for about 2,000 years. The Zhou adopted many of the Shang's cultural practices, including ancestor worship and the use of oracle bones. However, the Zhou also developed a concept, known as the **Mandate of Heaven**, to be a guiding force for rulers. They believed that a king could rule only as long as the gods believed he was worthy. The mandate led to a pattern in the rise and fall of dynasties in China called the **dynastic cycle**.

During the first 200 years or so of their rule, the Zhou established a strong central government. However, during the last 500 years of the dynasty, the Zhou divided their lands among local lords. Eventually the ruling lords grew too powerful and independent. They fought among themselves and disobeyed the Zhou kings. By 475 B.C., China had descended into a time of constant war called the **Warring States** period. In 256 B.C., the last Zhou king was finally overthrown.

THE DYNASTIC CYCLE

1. The people believe that the gods approve of the new dynasty.
2. The dynasty weakens.
3. Disasters occur.
4. The people believe that the gods no longer approve of the dynasty.
5. The dynasty is overthrown.
6. A new dynasty re-establishes order.

REVIEW & ASSESS

1. **READING CHECK** What were some of the religious beliefs and practices of the Shang people?

2. **INTEGRATE VISUALS** Based on the diagram and what you've read in the lesson, what do you think happened after the Zhou dynasty fell?

3. **DRAW CONCLUSIONS** How might the Mandate of Heaven have helped the Chinese people accept dynastic changes?

169

OBJECTIVE

Identify the cultural behaviors and beliefs developed during the Shang and Zhou dynasties that have become part of Chinese civilization.

The Shang and Zhou dynasties ruled in China for over 1,300 years. Lesson 1.2 discusses the social, cultural, and religious behaviors and beliefs established during this time that have become part of Chinese civilization.

CRITICAL THINKING SKILLS FOR LESSON 1.2

- Identify Main Ideas and Details
- Monitor Comprehension
- Integrate Visuals
- Draw Conclusions
- Sequence Events
- Interpret Diagrams

BACKGROUND FOR THE TEACHER

Oracle bones were not discovered until 1899. In that year, a Chinese scholar noticed that some of the bones and shells in a shop were engraved with an ancient script.

The shoulder blades of ox and turtle shells were most often used as oracle bones during the Shang dynasty. A priest cut an oracle bone into a particular size and shape. After carving a question, he applied heat to a carved-out hollow in the bone. During a ceremony, the priest read the resulting crack to answer the question.

ESSENTIAL QUESTION

How did China establish what would become one of the world's oldest continuous civilizations?

DIGITAL RESOURCES myNGconnect.com

TEACHER RESOURCES & ASSESSMENT

 Reading and Note-Taking   **Vocabulary Practice**   **Section 1 Quiz**

STUDENT RESOURCES

 NG Chapter Gallery

CREATE A TIME LINE

Help students read and understand a time line that contains B.C. dates. Draw a time line on the board like the one below. Explain that the numbers in B.C. dates get smaller as they approach 1 B.C. Point out that after that, the numbers would be labeled A.D. and would get larger. Invite volunteers to divide the time line into appropriate increments. Then, as students read the lesson, invite them to add entries pertinent to the Shang and Zhou dynasties to the time line. ⏱ **minutes**

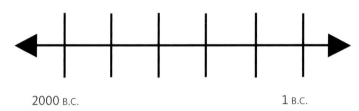

2000 B.C.   1 B.C.

GUIDED DISCUSSION

1. **Identify Main Ideas and Details** How was society ordered during the Shang dynasty? *(The king was at the top of society, with warlords next, and farmers at the bottom.)*

2. **Sequence Events** What happened during the last 500 years of the Zhou dynasty when the kings divided their land among local lords? *(The lords became powerful and independent. They fought among themselves and disobeyed the Zhou kings. In time, China descended into a time of constant war.)*

INTERPRET DIAGRAMS

Have students study the Dynastic Cycle diagram. Read and discuss each step in the cycle. **ASK:** According to the cycle, what occurrences indicate that a dynasty has lost the approval of the gods? *(Disasters occur.)* What shows that a new dynasty has the gods' approval? *(Order is restored.)* ⏱ **minutes**

ACTIVE OPTIONS

Critical Viewing: NG Chapter Gallery Invite students to explore the Chapter 7 Gallery and create a Favorites List by choosing the images they find most interesting. If possible, have students copy the images into a document to form an actual list. Then encourage them to select the image they like best and do further research on it. ⏱ **minutes**

On Your Feet: Stage a Quiz Show Have each student write one question about the Shang and Zhou dynasties and collect the questions. Then have groups of five students take turns coming to the front of the class to take part in a quiz. Pose a few of the questions to each group. Students should confer about the answer and then signal their readiness to respond by raising their hands. ⏱ **minutes**

STRIVING READERS

Complete a Key Facts T-Chart Have students create a T-Chart on the Shang and Zhou dynasties. Students should label the first column of the T-Chart "Shang" and the second column "Zhou." Tell students to jot down key facts about each dynasty as they read the lesson. Have students compare completed charts.

Shang	Zhou

PRE-AP

Write an E-Zine Article Have students research to learn more about the Zhou dynasty. Invite them to write and illustrate an e-zine article about the cultural advances made during the first 200 years of their rule. Students should also describe what happened during the last 500 years of the dynasty. Encourage students to share their articles with the rest of the class.

Press **mt** in the Student eEdition for modified text.

See the Chapter Planner for more strategies for differentiation.

ANSWERS

1. Religious beliefs and practices include the use of oracle bones, ancestor worship, and conducting special ceremonies to keep the spirits happy.

2. In time, a new dynasty arose that took charge and re-established order.

3. The people would have believed that the downfall of one dynasty and the rise of another reflected the will of the gods.

1.3 Chinese Philosophies

"What you do not wish for yourself, do not do to others." Sound familiar? You may have heard this saying before—or another version of it. It's a simple but powerful guide for moral behavior, and it was written 2,500 years ago by a man called Confucius.

MAIN IDEA

Chinese philosophers developed important ideas on how society should be organized.

+ POSSIBLE RESPONSE

The notes indicate that people today still respect and try to follow his teachings.

Critical Viewing Followers write comments and questions to Confucius on notes that bear his image. What do the notes suggest about the lasting influence of Confucius?

CONFUCIANISM

As you've read, China began to fall into disorder during the Zhou dynasty. By the time Confucius was born in 551 B.C., China was already experiencing unrest. A teacher and government official, Confucius believed that Chinese society was breaking down as a result of the constant conflict. In an effort to restore order, he taught that people should respect authority and one another.

Confucius' teachings formed the basis of a belief system known as **Confucianism**. His teachings focused on the duties and responsibilities in the following five relationships: father and son, older brother and younger brother, husband and wife, friend and friend, and ruler and subject. Confucius also promoted education, family unity, and **filial piety**, or the respect children owe their parents and ancestors.

Confucius died believing he had failed to restore order to society. Yet after his death, his students collected his teachings in a book called the *Analects*, and Confucian ideas spread. In time Confucius' teachings became required reading for all government officials. Today Confucianism influences millions of people. The philosophy has been a unifying force in Chinese culture and civilization.

DAOISM AND LEGALISM

Another man called Laozi (low-dzuh) is believed to have lived around the same time as Confucius. He founded a belief system called **Daoism**, which emphasizes living in harmony with nature and the Dao. *Dao* means "the Way" and is believed to be the driving force behind everything that exists. Daoists seek order and balance in their lives by merging, or blending, with nature "like drops of water in a stream."

In contrast with both Confucianism and Daoism, **Legalism** emphasizes order through strong government and strictly enforced laws. Legalism developed after 400 B.C. This philosophy does not have a founder, but Han Feizi (fay-zee) set down its ideas around 260 B.C. He maintained that people were naturally bad and needed to be controlled through the threat of harsh punishment. As you will see, a Chinese dynasty would arise that would govern according to this philosophy.

YIN dark cold soft water

YANG light hot hard fire

DAOIST YIN-AND-YANG SYMBOL
This symbol is often used in Daoism to show how seemingly opposite forces form a whole. Daoists believe that everything contains aspects of both yin and yang. The symbol shows some of the aspects of each force.

REVIEW & ASSESS

1. **READING CHECK** What are the basic beliefs of Confucianism?

2. **ANALYZE LANGUAGE USE** What Daoist idea does the phrase "blending with nature like drops of water in a stream" help convey?

3. **COMPARE AND CONTRAST** How does Legalism's attitude toward people's nature differ from that of both Confucianism and Daoism?

170 CHAPTER 7

Ancient China 171

PLAN

OBJECTIVE

Examine the beliefs and philosophies that developed in Chinese civilization.

CRITICAL THINKING SKILLS FOR LESSON 1.3

- Identify Main Ideas and Details
- Monitor Comprehension
- Analyze Language Use
- Compare and Contrast
- Make Generalizations
- Draw Conclusions

ESSENTIAL QUESTION

How did China establish what would become one of the world's oldest continuous civilizations?

Three different philosophies arose in China around the Warring States period. Lesson 1.3 describes the unifying force of Confucianism in Chinese culture and civilization.

BACKGROUND FOR THE TEACHER

Confucius was born Kong Qiu and often called Kongfuzi (Master Kong) in Chinese. Confucius is the name used by Europeans. He saw teaching as a calling and a way of life. He wanted education to be available to all, not just to rich families who could hire professional tutors for their sons. Confucius found individual masters to teach him the six key arts of ritual, music, archery, charioteering, calligraphy, and arithmetic. He also studied classical Chinese poetry and history and began teaching in his 30s.

DIGITAL RESOURCES myNGconnect.com

TEACHER RESOURCES & ASSESSMENT

 Reading and Note-Taking

 Vocabulary Practice

 Section 1 Quiz

STUDENT RESOURCES

 Biography

170 CHAPTER 7

INTRODUCE & ENGAGE

ANALYZE MORAL CODES

Write this saying of Confucius on the board: "What you do not wish for yourself, do not do to others." Ask students what they think the saying means and if they know of similar sayings from other sources. Explain that this saying is similar to the Golden Rule—"Do unto others as you would have them do unto you"—a guideline for human behavior from Christian scripture. Discuss as a class how students think Confucius' saying applies to their own lives. Then ask students to brainstorm as many sources for rules for good behavior as they can. (*parents or family, teachers, government, religion, philosophy, community organizations*) Write students' responses on the board. Explain that they will learn about an ethical system in China that provided many rules for good behavior. **0:10** minutes

TEACH

GUIDED DISCUSSION

1. **Make Generalizations** How did the society in which Confucius lived influence his teachings? (*Society during the Zhou dynasty was already experiencing unrest. Confucius wanted to use his teachings to restore harmony.*)

2. **Draw Conclusions** What was the guiding principle behind all three Chinese philosophies? (*They all sought to bring order to society.*)

MORE INFORMATION

Yin and Yang The forces of yin and yang not only influence Chinese philosophy. The duality of yin and yang also guides traditional Chinese medicine. The upper body is considered part of yang because it is closer to heaven. The lower body is considered part of yin because it is closer to Earth. Internal organs are also divided into yin and yang aspects. Doctors who practice traditional Chinese medicine try to keep their patients' yin and yang in balance. Yin and yang imbalance within the body is believed to result in disease.

ACTIVE OPTIONS

Critical Viewing: NG Chapter Gallery Have students explore the Chapter 7 Gallery and choose two items that illustrate religion or belief systems in China. Have students compare and contrast the images, either in written form or verbally with a partner. Ask questions that will inspire this process, such as: How are these images alike? How are they different? Why did you select these two items? How do they relate in history? **0:10** minutes

On Your Feet: Code of Conduct Roundtable Divide the class into groups of four. Have the groups move desks together to form a table where they can all sit. Hand each group a sheet of paper with the title *Code of Conduct*. Tell students that they will create a list of rules for their classroom that will provide guidelines for good behavior. Then have the first student in each group write a rule, read it aloud, and pass the paper clockwise to the next student. Each student in each group should write two rules. When the groups have finished writing their codes, invite each group to share their rules. After all groups have shared, have the class vote on the five rules they like best. Post these rules on a bulletin board. **0:20** minutes

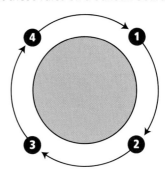

DIFFERENTIATE

ENGLISH LANGUAGE LEARNERS

Find Someone Who Knows Give students copies of the questions below and have them find five different classmates to answer them.

1. Whose teachings have influenced China for centuries? (*Confucius*)

2. What does Dao mean? (*the way*)

3. Which Chinese philosophy emphasizes order through strong government and strict laws? (*Legalism*)

4. Who is the founder of Daoism? (*Laozi*)

5. What book contains the teachings of Confucius? (*the Analects*)

STRIVING READERS

Monitor Comprehension Have students work in pairs to read the lesson, pausing after each paragraph to ask and answer questions about words or passages they did not understand.

Press (**mt**) *in the Student eEdition for modified text.*

See the Chapter Planner for more strategies for differentiation.

REVIEW & ASSESS

ANSWERS

1. Confucianism provides ideas on promoting proper conduct through respect. The belief system also promotes filial piety.

2. The phrase helps convey the idea of achieving harmony with nature.

3. Legalism takes the attitude that people are naturally bad, while Confucianism and Daoism take the attitude that people are generally good.

Contrasting **Belief Systems**

You've seen that the suffering caused by weak government and conflict in China led many to think about the best ways to ensure an orderly and peaceful society. As a result, China produced some of the world's greatest philosophical thinkers and writers. Their ideas were so powerful that they not only shaped the future of China for 2,000 years but also continue to influence world thinking today.

Children dressed in traditional clothing perform in China during a celebration of Confucius' birthday.

➕ ANSWERS

DOCUMENT 1
Confucius tells Lord Ji Kang that in order for the people to be loyal, the ruler himself must set a good example by being a good son and father.

DOCUMENT 2
Powerful people can live peaceful, happy lives by centering themselves in the Dao, becoming content with their simple, everyday lives, and freeing themselves from desire.

DOCUMENT 2
The passage suggests that Legalism supported strong, even ruthless rulers who had no concern for those beneath them.

DOCUMENT ONE
Primary Source: Philosophical Teaching

from *Analects of Confucius*,
translated by Simon Leys
The *Analects*, a collection of Confucius' ideas, sayings, and stories, was probably recorded by many people over many years. In this passage from the *Analects*, a lord asks Confucius (often referred to as "the Master") how to govern his people.

CONSTRUCTED RESPONSE What details in the passage support the idea that Confucius believed rulers had to set a good example for their people?

> Lord Ji Kang asked: "What should I do in order to make the people respectful, loyal, and zealous [enthusiastic]?" The Master said: "Approach them with dignity and they will be respectful. Be yourself a good son and a kind father, and they will be loyal. Raise the good and train the incompetent [those unable to do a good job], and they will be zealous."

DOCUMENT TWO
Primary Source: Philosophical Teaching

from *Dao de Jing*,
translated by Stephen Mitchell
The *Dao de Jing* is a key text of Daoism. In general, it stresses inaction over action and silence over words. This passage explains the power of the Dao.

CONSTRUCTED RESPONSE According to the passage, how can powerful people live peaceful, happy lives?

> The Dao never does anything, yet through it all things are done. If powerful men and women could center themselves in it, the whole world would be transformed by itself, in its natural rhythms. People would be content with their simple, everyday lives, in harmony, and free of desire.

DOCUMENT THREE
Primary Source: Philosophical Teaching

from *Han Feizi: Basic Writings*,
translated by Burton Watson
Han Feizi lived from 280 to 233 B.C. He did not believe Confucianism was the answer to the chaos brought about in China during the Warring States period. In this passage from a collection of his writings, Han Feizi describes the role of rulers.

CONSTRUCTED RESPONSE What does the passage suggest about the kind of ruler and government Legalism supported?

> Discard wisdom, forswear [reject] ability, so that your subordinates [those beneath you] cannot guess what you are about. Stick to your objectives and examine the results to see how they match; take hold of the handles of government carefully and grip them tightly. Destroy all hope, smash all intention of wresting [taking] them [the handles of government] from you; allow no man to covet [desire] them.

SYNTHESIZE & WRITE

1. **REVIEW** Review what you have learned about Confucianism, Daoism, and Legalism.

2. **RECALL** On your own paper, write down the main idea expressed in each document.

3. **CONSTRUCT** Write a topic sentence that answers this question: What ideas about leadership do each of the ancient Chinese philosophies convey?

4. **WRITE** Using evidence from the documents, write a paragraph to support your answer from Step 3.

PLAN

OBJECTIVE

Synthesize the different ideas presented by three Chinese philosophies.

CRITICAL THINKING SKILLS FOR LESSON 1.4

- Synthesize
- Make Inferences
- Form and Support Opinions
- Evaluate
- Draw Conclusions

ESSENTIAL QUESTION

How did China establish what would become one of the world's oldest continuous civilizations?

Confucianism, Daoism, and Legalism have guided the people and rulers of China for centuries. Lesson 1.4 provides primary source excerpts, conveying core ideas of each philosophy.

BACKGROUND FOR THE TEACHER

Many legends have been told about Laozi. One of the most famous tells the story of a meeting—which likely never took place—between Laozi and Confucius. According to the tale, Laozi chastised the other philosopher for his pride and ambition. Confucius is said to have been so impressed with Laozi's insight that he likened him to a dragon riding on the wind and clouds. This was high praise since, in Chinese culture, the dragon symbolizes power, strength, and good luck.

DIGITAL RESOURCES myNGconnect.com

TEACHER RESOURCES & ASSESSMENT

 Reading and Note-Taking   **Vocabulary Practice**   **Section 1 Quiz**

STUDENT RESOURCES

 NG Chapter Gallery

PREPARE FOR THE DOCUMENT-BASED QUESTION

Before students start on the activity, briefly preview the three documents. Remind students that a constructed response requires full explanations in complete sentences. Emphasize that students should use what they have learned about ancient Chinese philosophies in addition to the information in the documents. **0:05** minutes

TEACH

GUIDED DISCUSSION

1. **Form and Support Opinions** Do you support Confucius' ideas about how to make people respectful, loyal, and zealous? *(Responses will vary. Possible responses: Yes, I believe that treating people with respect, setting a good example, and adapting to the needs of individuals will make people respectful, loyal, and zealous; No, I think that some people would take advantage of this kind of leadership and would require more forceful treatment.)*

2. **Draw Conclusions** What does the writer of the *Dao de Jing* suggest about powerful men and women? *(The writer suggests that powerful men and women do not live simple, harmonious lives and are not free of desire.)*

3. **Make Inferences** What emotions would a ruler who lived by the philosophy supported by Han Feizi probably inspire in his people? *(Responses will vary. Possible responses: fear, hatred, distrust)*

EVALUATE

After students have completed the "Synthesize & Write" activity, allow time for them to exchange paragraphs and read and comment on the work of their peers. Guidelines for comments should be established prior to this activity so that feedback is constructive and encouraging in nature. **0:15** minutes

ACTIVE OPTIONS

NG Learning Framework: Learn About Different Chinese Philosophies

SKILLS: Observation, Collaboration
KNOWLEDGE: Our Human Story

Have students revisit Lessons 1.3 and 1.4 and review the information about Confucianism, Daoism, and Legalism. Then ask students to work in pairs to create a list of what they consider the best aspects of each philosophy. Once they have completed their list of observations, each pair should exchange lists with another pair and discuss the new list. **0:10** minutes

On Your Feet: Use a Jigsaw Strategy Organize students into three "expert" groups and have students from each group analyze one

of the documents and summarize the main ideas of the teaching in their own words. Then have the members of each group count off using the letters A, B, C, and so on. Regroup students into three new groups so that each new group has at least one member from each expert group. Have students in the new groups take turns sharing the simplified summaries they came up with in their expert groups. **0:10** minutes

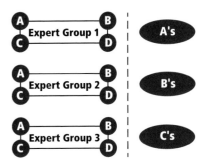

STRIVING READERS

Summarize Read each document aloud to students. Have one group of students work together to reread each document and summarize it for the larger group. After each document is summarized, read the constructed response question with the larger group and make sure all students understand it. Then have volunteers suggest responses.

GIFTED & TALENTED

Write a Profile Ask groups of students to learn more about Confucius, Laozi, and Han Feizi. Then have each group select a philosopher and write a social-networking profile on him, providing a brief summary and "photos." Have the groups share their profiles with the rest of the class. Then invite students to "friend" the philosophers and send them messages about their lives and teachings.

Press **(mt)** *in the Student eEdition for modified text.*

See the Chapter Planner for more strategies for differentiation.

ANSWERS

1. Responses will vary.

2. Responses will vary.

3. Possible response: Confucianism, Daoism, and Legalism have very different ideas about how a leader should rule.

4. Students' paragraphs should include their topic sentence from Step 3 and provide several details from the documents to support the sentence.

SHI HUANGDI

259 B.C. – 210 B.C.

The flames rise higher as officials toss more books onto the fire. Their emperor, Shi Huangdi, has ordered them to burn any writing that contains ideas he doesn't like. High on the list is anything to do with Confucianism. Shi Huangdi is a cruel but skilled ruler—and he intends his dynasty to last for 10,000 generations.

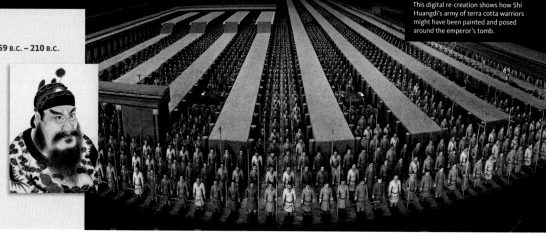
This digital re-creation shows how Shi Huangdi's army of terra cotta warriors might have been painted and posed around the emperor's tomb.

Job: First emperor of China
Home: Kingdom of Qin

FINEST HOUR
After unifying and expanding China, he became its first emperor.

WORST MOMENT
He supposedly died after taking pills he thought would keep him alive forever.

HOBBIES
He built a huge tomb for himself filled with life-size statues of warriors and horses.

GREATEST FEAR
Convinced that his enemies wanted to kill him, he slept in a different apartment in his palace every night.

A RUTHLESS RULER

China's Warring States period finally ended when the leader of the **Qin** (chin) kingdom defeated all other kingdoms around 221 B.C. The leader's name was Ying Zheng, and he united the kingdoms to form an empire. He would come to call himself **Shi Huangdi** (shee hwahng-dee), meaning "first emperor." An **emperor** is the ruler of an empire.

Shi Huangdi established his government based on Legalist ideas. He set up his capital in Xianyang (shee-ahn-yang) and built magnificent palaces in the city to demonstrate his power. The emperor then forced thousands of China's most powerful families to relocate to the capital so he could keep an eye on them.

In addition, Shi Huangdi divided his empire into 36 areas governed by officials he himself had selected. He also followed Legalist ideas by punishing anyone who disagreed with or criticized him. Shi Huangdi is said to have put to death hundreds of Confucian scholars.

A UNIFIED EMPIRE

Although his methods were cruel, Shi Huangdi brought order to China. He made sure units used to weigh and measure items throughout the empire were standardized, or the same, to ensure that buyers were not being cheated. He also brought a single writing system and currency, or form of money, to China.

As Shi Huangdi conquered new lands and expanded his empire, he made further improvements that united his territory. He had thousands of miles of roads built to link different parts of the empire. These roads were all constructed at the same width. He also built canals and irrigation systems. Shi

Huangdi's most famous construction project was the **Great Wall** of China, which you will learn more about in the next lesson. Many historians believe these structures were built by forced labor and funded by high taxes.

Shi Huangdi's rule came to an end when he died in 210 B.C. Throughout his reign, the emperor had feared being murdered by assassins. It seems he believed evil spirits could also attack him in the afterlife. As a result, Shi Huangdi had an army of **terra cotta**, or baked clay, warriors buried beside his tomb to protect him. The burial site probably forms his greatest legacy—an odd twist of fate for a man who spent much of his life trying to cheat death.

REVIEW & ASSESS

1. **READING CHECK** How did Shi Huangdi link the new lands of his empire?

2. **DRAW CONCLUSIONS** What are the benefits of using a single currency within a country?

3. **FORM OPINIONS** What do you think was Shi Huangdi's greatest achievement? Why?

PLAN

OBJECTIVE

Explain how Shi Huangdi ruled his people and united his empire.

CRITICAL THINKING SKILLS FOR LESSON 2.1

- Identify Main Ideas and Details
- Monitor Comprehension
- Draw Conclusions
- Form Opinions
- Make Predictions
- Analyze Visuals

ESSENTIAL QUESTION

How did China establish what would become one of the world's oldest continuous civilizations?

Shi Huangdi united the kingdoms of China to form an empire. Lesson

2.1 discusses the steps Shi Huangdi took to establish and unify his empire and bring order to China.

BACKGROUND FOR THE TEACHER

Shi Huangdi had good reason to fear for his life. Between 227 and 218 B.C., three attempts were made to murder him.

The emperor wanted his dynasty to last for 10,000 generations, but he also wanted his life to continue as long as possible. To that end, Shi Huangdi had his servants search out pills and potions that would prolong his life. He even sent them on missions to find herbs that supposedly had magical properties. Ironically, Shi Huangdi died at the age of 49 after ingesting pills made by his doctors to keep him alive. The pills contained mercury.

DIGITAL RESOURCES myNGconnect.com

TEACHER RESOURCES & ASSESSMENT

 Reading and Note-Taking

 Vocabulary Practice

 Section 2 Quiz

STUDENT RESOURCES

 NG Chapter Gallery

INTRODUCE & ENGAGE

PREVIEW A PROFILE

Before students read the lesson, go over Shi Huangdi's profile with the class. Ask them to share their impressions of the emperor based on the profile entries. `0:05` minutes

TEACH

GUIDED DISCUSSION

1. **Make Predictions** How might Shi Huangdi's rule have been different if he had established his government based on Confucian or Daoist ideas? (*Possible response: His rule wouldn't have been as ruthless, and he might have been more tolerant of those who disagreed with his ideas.*)

2. **Draw Conclusions** Why did Shi Huangdi have all roads constructed at the same width? (*so that vehicles could travel on all the roads throughout the empire*)

ANALYZE VISUALS

Have students compare the photograph of the digital re-creation of the soldiers with the photograph in Lesson 2.3. Have them use the photograph in the other lesson to study the soldiers' faces, clothing, and poses. **ASK:** What do you find most striking about the digital re-creation? (*Possible response: the number of soldiers, the colors, the weapons*) What does the army shown suggest about Shi Huangdi? (*Possible response: He was afraid of death and wanted a huge army to protect him; he was proud and arrogant and believed that he deserved a full army to protect him, even in death.*) `0:10` minutes

ACTIVE OPTIONS

NG Learning Framework: Learn About Shi Huangdi

ATTITUDE: **Empowerment**
SKILL: **Decision-Making**

Invite students to revisit the biography of Shi Huangdi in Lesson 2.1 and imagine they were in the emperor's place. **ASK:** How would you have done things differently from Shi Huangdi? How do you feel these changes would have affected China and the world? `0:10` minutes

On Your Feet: Hold a Panel Discussion Build on the third question in "Review & Assess" by asking volunteers to stage a panel discussion before the rest of the class about Shi Huangdi's greatest achievements. Students can choose any achievement they learned about in the lesson to discuss. `0:20` minutes

DIFFERENTIATE

STRIVING READERS

Use Reciprocal Teaching Have partners take turns reading each paragraph of the lesson aloud. At the end of the paragraph, the reading student should ask the listening student questions about the paragraph. Students may ask their partners to state the main idea of the paragraph, identify important details that support the main idea, or summarize the paragraph in their own words. Then have students work together to answer the Review & Assess questions.

INCLUSION

Summarize Have students complete a Concept Cluster like the one shown to keep track of important details about Shi Huangdi as they read the lesson. Then have students form pairs and use their completed charts to summarize what they learned about Shi Huangdi.

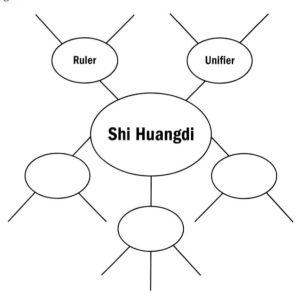

Press (**mt**) *in the Student eEdition for modified text.*

See the Chapter Planner for more strategies for differentiation.

REVIEW & ASSESS

ANSWERS

1. He linked the empire by building roads, canals, and irrigation systems throughout the empire.

2. People within a country do not have to change money into another currency. Prices are easier to compare.

3. Responses will vary, but students may say that bringing a single writing system and currency to China was his greatest achievement.

The Great Wall

Groaning under the weight of another brick, you set it in place on the wall. You didn't volunteer for this work, and you won't be paid very much for it either. It's possible you'll even die working on the wall. But under Shi Huangdi's rule, you do as you're told.

MAIN IDEA

Shi Huangdi began building the Great Wall to keep invaders out of China.

KEEPING OUT INVADERS

While mountains, deserts, and seas protected most of China, part of its northern border was vulnerable, or open to attack. Riding on horseback, nomadic tribes from Central Asia often swept over the border, destroying farms, villages, and towns. Small walls had been built along the border during the Warring States period, but Shi Huangdi decided to join them into one long wall that would stretch over 2,500 miles.

The emperor forced hundreds of thousands of **peasants**, or poor farmers, to build his wall. He also conscripted soldiers and prisoners to perform the backbreaking labor, often in extreme conditions. Many of the laborers died from exhaustion, hunger, and disease. After Shi Huangdi's death, the wall fell into disrepair. However, later rulers built and extended it. In fact, work on the wall continued into the 1600s.

176 CHAPTER 7

+ POSSIBLE RESPONSE

Details include the fortified walls and the rugged mountains that extend for miles.

This photo of the Great Wall shows the structure as it appears today. Little of the original wall built under Shi Huangdi remains. What details in the photo show how the wall would have discouraged invaders?

REVIEW & ASSESS

1. **READING CHECK** What methods did Shi Huangdi use to get his wall built?

2. **INTEGRATE VISUALS** Based on the text and the photo, what "extreme conditions" do you think workers on the wall had to endure?

3. **DETERMINE WORD MEANINGS** What does the word *conscripted* mean as used in the sentence, "He also conscripted soldiers and prisoners to perform the backbreaking labor"?

77

PLAN

OBJECTIVE

Describe and explain the purpose of the Great Wall.

CRITICAL THINKING SKILLS FOR LESSON 2.2

- Identify Main Ideas and Details
- Monitor Comprehension
- Integrate Visuals
- Determine Word Meanings
- Form Opinions

ESSENTIAL QUESTION

How did China establish what would become one of the world's oldest continuous civilizations?

Shi Huangdi undertook a project to join and expand small walls along China's border that had been built during the Warring States period. Lesson 2.2 describes the beginnings of the Great Wall, which would protect China for hundreds of years.

BACKGROUND FOR THE TEACHER

As Chinese rulers after Shi Huangdi extended the Great Wall, they had watchtowers built every 200 or 300 yards along its length. Soldiers manned the towers. When an enemy was sighted, one of these soldiers lit a fire as a signal. The soldier at the next tower saw the smoke and lit a fire in turn. The signal continued along the wall. The smoke alerted troops to the danger.

DIGITAL RESOURCES myNGconnect.com

TEACHER RESOURCES & ASSESSMENT

 Reading and Note-Taking   **Vocabulary Practice**   **Section 2 Quiz**

STUDENT RESOURCES

 NG Chapter Gallery

INTRODUCE & ENGAGE

COMPLETE A K-W-L CHART

Have students use a K-W-L Chart to record what they already know about the Great Wall. Encourage students to draw on what they have learned in school or what they have seen on television or online. Then have students jot down what they would like to learn about the Great Wall. After they have read the lesson, ask them to record what they learned. **0:10** minutes

K What Do I Know?	W What Do I Want To Learn?	L What Did I Learn?

TEACH

GUIDED DISCUSSION

1. **Identify Main Ideas and Details** Who built the wall and under what conditions did they labor? *(Peasants, soldiers, and prisoners worked on the wall, often in extreme conditions. Many died from exhaustion, hunger, and disease.)*

2. **Form Opinions** Do you think the Great Wall was worth the human price it exacted to build? Why or why not? *(Some students may say the wall was worth the toll in human lives because it helped to safeguard China for centuries. Others may say that the construction of the wall could have been carried out in a more humane manner.)*

INTEGRATE VISUALS

Have students study the photograph of the Great Wall as it appears today. Initiate a discussion about the length of the wall, its building materials, and its setting in the photograph. **ASK:** Why do you think the passageway is so wide? *(Possible response: to allow troops of soldiers and vehicles to travel along the wall)* What purpose might the shelter have served? *(Possible response: It might have served as a shelter for soldiers who stopped there for the night. It might have provided a post from which to watch for or fire at the enemy.)* **0:10** minutes

ACTIVE OPTIONS

NG Learning Framework: Learn About the Great Wall

SKILL: Communication
KNOWLEDGE: Our Living Planet

Have students imagine they have been conscripted to work on the Great Wall of China. Ask students to write a letter home telling their family about their experiences and the geographic challenges they encounter as they try to build the wall. **0:10** minutes

On Your Feet: Build a Wall Have students use chairs or blocks to build a wall across the classroom. Remind them that the Great Wall began as a series of small walls that were later joined together. After the wall is complete, **ASK:** How does a wall help a country defend itself? *(A wall forms a barrier that makes it easier for a country's soldiers to guard. Enemies cannot get horses or equipment over a wall easily.)* Invite students to evaluate how effective they think a wall would be today compared to periods in the past. **0:20** minutes

DIFFERENTIATE

INCLUSION

Practice Summarizing Have partners work together to understand the lesson. Ask the pairs to read the first paragraph together. Then have them close the book and write down all the facts they can remember. When students have finished, tell them to open the book and check their facts. Have them repeat the exercise with the second paragraph in the lesson.

GIFTED & TALENTED

Draw the Great Wall Have students research to learn more about the features of the Great Wall: the height and materials of the walls; the battlements, the passageways, and the watchtowers. Then ask them to use what they learn to draw a portion of the Great Wall and label each of the features. Invite students to share their drawings and compare them with the photo in this lesson.

Press (mt) *in the Student eEdition for modified text.*

See the Chapter Planner for more strategies for differentiation.

REVIEW & ASSESS

ANSWERS

1. He forced hundreds of thousands of workers to labor on the wall.

2. They had to endure hauling materials up mountains, laboring in cold, snowy weather, doing everything by hand, and getting little to eat and little rest.

3. It means "to force someone to serve or work."

209 B.C.

On the morning of March 29, 1974, farmers digging a well in a village near Xi'an (shee-ahn), China, made an incredible discovery. They found a body—but one made of baked clay. It was one of an estimated 8,000 life-size terra cotta warriors that had been created to protect Shi Huangdi more than 2,000 years ago. The army of warriors—and their chariots and horses—stood in battle formation, ready to fight Shi Huangdi's battles in the afterlife. Historians estimate that more than 700,000 laborers worked for 38 years to complete the project around 209 B.C. As wonderful as the warriors are, archaeologists believe even greater treasures lie in the emperor's tomb itself, which remains unexplored. What details in the statues help make the warriors look lifelike?

+ POSSIBLE RESPONSE

The warriors' eyes, expressions, hair, clothing, and positions help make them look lifelike.

178

179

PLAN

OBJECTIVE

Describe the terra cotta warriors Shi Huangdi had created and placed around his tomb.

CRITICAL THINKING SKILLS FOR LESSON 2.3

- Describe
- Make Inferences
- Analyze Visuals

ESSENTIAL QUESTION

How did China establish what would become one of the world's oldest continuous civilizations?

Shi Huangdi was China's first and one of its greatest emperors.

Lesson 2.3 provides a glimpse of some of the clay warriors the emperor had buried beside his tomb.

BACKGROUND FOR THE TEACHER

When archaeologists first excavated the site in Xi'an, they found the terra cotta warriors armed with real weapons. These included bronze swords and about 40,000 arrowheads. About 100 of these were tied together to fit in a single quiver. Archaeologists also found life-size clay horses standing four abreast with wooden chariots behind them. Interestingly, Shi Huangdi's body has not yet been found.

DIGITAL RESOURCES myNGconnect.com

TEACHER RESOURCES & ASSESSMENT

 Reading and Note-Taking   **Vocabulary Practice**   **Section 2 Quiz**

STUDENT RESOURCES

 NG Chapter Gallery

INTRODUCE & ENGAGE

ACCESS PRIOR KNOWLEDGE

Invite students to share what they already know or have heard about the terra cotta warriors. Record student responses in a Concept Cluster on the board. Then call on volunteers to use the completed cluster to summarize the class discussion. `0:15` minutes

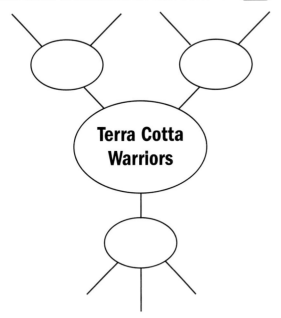

Terra Cotta Warriors

TEACH

GUIDED DISCUSSION

1. **Describe** How would you describe the look on the face of the warrior shown on the right page? *(Responses will vary. Possible response: He looks alert, watchful, confident, ready to do battle.)*

2. **Make Inferences** Why do you think the two warriors shown on the left page are holding their hands up? *(Responses will vary. Possible responses: When they were made, they were probably holding something in their hands, such as a weapon or the reins of a chariot.)*

MORE INFORMATION

Variety of Terra Cotta Figures In the two largest pits, archaeologists uncovered infantry soldiers. The soldiers include archers armed with bows and arrows, armed warriors, and horses ready to pull chariots. Warriors holding long poles were found in the smallest pit. Archaeologists believe this pit was meant to be a command post. Other pits contain non-military figures. Some of these terra cotta figures are civil servants holding knives and tablets to write on. Others appear to be acrobats, probably meant to entertain the emperor in the afterlife. `0:10` minutes

ACTIVE OPTIONS

NG Learning Framework: Learn About Shi Huangdi's Army

ATTITUDE: **Curiosity**
KNOWLEDGE: **Our Human Story**

Have students research to learn more about Shi Huangdi's actual military force. Encourage students to find images of what the real soldiers, weapons, and war machinery would have looked like and compare them with the terra cotta versions. `0:10` minutes

On Your Feet: I See, I Read, And So On a large sheet of chart paper or a whiteboard, create a chart like the one pictured below. As a group, reexamine the photograph of the terra cotta warriors. Have volunteers describe something they observe in the photo and something they have read to draw conclusions about Shi Huangdi and the terra cotta warriors. Record their observations on the chart. `0:15` minutes

I See	I Read	And So

DIFFERENTIATE

ENGLISH LANGUAGE LEARNERS

Develop Vocabulary Spanish-speaking students may recognize the term *terra cotta* because it is similar to the Spanish word for baked clay: *terracota*. Invite students to teach the Spanish term to the class and explain that the parts of the word translate literally as "baked earth."

PRE-AP

Create a Top Ten List Have groups of students research to learn more about the terra cotta warriors. Then have them create a list of ten interesting facts about the warriors and their discovery. Tell groups to list the facts beginning with number ten, the least important, and ending with number one, the most important. Then have the groups take turns reading the lists to the class.

Press **mt** *in the Student eEdition for modified text.*

See the Chapter Planner for more strategies for differentiation.

2.4

The Han Dynasty

Maybe you've gotten in trouble for coming to class late, but that predicament would be nothing next to this: In 209 B.C., some farmers arrived late to sign up for their required military service, and they were sentenced to death. The farmers got away and spurred thousands of others to rebel against the Qin dynasty.

MAIN IDEA

Han dynasty rulers reformed the government, expanded the empire, and brought prosperity to China.

GOVERNMENT

After Shi Huangdi died, his son became emperor but proved to be a weak ruler. The farmers who escaped their death sentence fueled a bloody rebellion that brought about the collapse of the Qin dynasty. Rebels struggled for power until Liu Bang (lee-oo bahng), a peasant from the Han kingdom, seized control and began the **Han** dynasty in 202 B.C.

Han emperors introduced practices that were less cruel than those of Shi Huangdi. They lowered taxes and put an end to laws that were especially harsh. They also required lighter punishments for crimes.

You may recall that Shi Huangdi had forced workers to labor for years on his building projects. The Han, on the other hand, had peasants work for only one month per year to build roads, canals, and irrigation systems.

The Han rulers also replaced Legalism with Confucianism and used Confucius' teachings as a guide. Furthermore, they valued the well-educated and obedient officials Confucianism produced. As a result, the officials they appointed had to pass an examination that tested their knowledge of Confucianism. The rulers established their government based on a **bureaucracy**, in which these appointed officials ran the bureaus, or offices.

Later Han rulers included Liu Bang's wife, who came to be known as Empress Lü. Women were not allowed to rule as emperor in ancient China, but Lü found a way around that restriction. After her husband died in 195 B.C., Lü placed their young son on the throne and ruled in his name. When she outlived her son, she held on to power by crowning a couple of infants emperor and ruling in their place. After Lü died in 180 B.C., all of her relatives were executed by a group of rival court officials. They made sure that no other member of her family could rule again.

Emperor Wudi (woo-dee), who ruled from 141 to 87 B.C., was another notable emperor. He used military conquests to expand the empire's boundaries—nearly to the size of present-day China. His reign lasted 54 years, which set a record that would not be broken for more than 1,800 years.

DAILY LIFE

China prospered under the Han dynasty. Many merchants, government workers, and craftspeople lived in large houses in the cities. Like modern cities, these were crowded places filled with restaurants, businesses, and places of entertainment. Some cities had populations of up to 500,000 people.

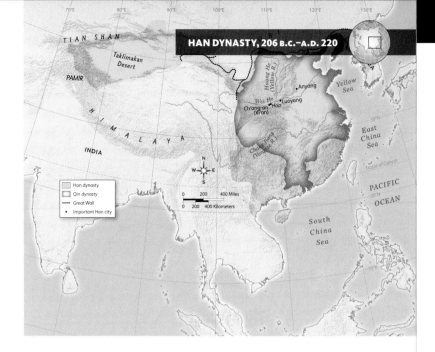

HAN DYNASTY, 206 B.C.–A.D. 220

Most of the Chinese people, however, were peasants. They lived in small mud houses in villages close to their farms. Some peasants could not afford farm animals and so pulled their plows themselves. They had few possessions and barely produced enough to feed their own families. For the most part, peasants lived on the rice, wheat, and vegetables they grew on their farms.

Perhaps because the Han leaders ruled more wisely than Shi Huangdi had, their dynasty lasted about 400 years—until A.D. 220. Most Chinese people today are proud of their ancient civilization and of the contributions made during the Han dynasty in particular. As a result, many Chinese call themselves "people of the Han" in recognition of the dynasty's great achievements.

REVIEW & ASSESS

1. **READING CHECK** What government reforms did the Han rulers put in place?

2. **INTERPRET MAPS** How does the size of the Qin dynasty compare to that of the Han?

3. **COMPARE AND CONTRAST** How did the lives of poor peasants and rich merchants differ?

PLAN

OBJECTIVE

Discuss the ways in which Han dynasty rulers reformed the government, expanded the empire, and brought prosperity to China.

CRITICAL THINKING SKILLS FOR LESSON 2.4

- Identify Main Ideas and Details
- Monitor Comprehension
- Interpret Maps
- Compare and Contrast
- Explain
- Summarize

ESSENTIAL QUESTION

How did China establish what would become one of the world's oldest continuous civilizations?

Han rulers established a dynasty that brought reform and prosperity to China and that lasted for about 400 years. Lesson 2.4 describes the achievements of Han dynasty rulers, which continue to instill pride in Chinese people today.

BACKGROUND FOR THE TEACHER

When Liu Bang died, his 15-year-old son became emperor, but the boy's mother dominated him from the beginning. Empress Lü, as his mother came to be called, had many challengers to her authority murdered, including several of her stepsons. Her actions so frightened the boy emperor that he never dared challenge her himself.

DIGITAL RESOURCES myNGconnect.com

TEACHER RESOURCES & ASSESSMENT

 Reading and Note-Taking

 Vocabulary Practice

 Section 2 Quiz

STUDENT RESOURCES

 NG Chapter Gallery

INTRODUCE & ENGAGE

THINK, PAIR, SHARE

Have students use a Think, Pair, Share strategy to discuss what they have already learned about Confucianism. Tell students that they will learn how Confucianism was implemented into Chinese government in this lesson. **0:10** minutes

TEACH

GUIDED DISCUSSION

1. **Explain** How did Han rulers integrate Confucianism into government? *(They used Confucius' teachings as a guide for their own rule and appointed only government officials who passed an examination that tested their knowledge of Confucianism.)*

2. **Summarize** Who benefited most from the prosperity brought about by the Han dynasty? *(Merchants, government workers, and craftspeople mostly benefited from the prosperity.)*

INTERPRET MAPS

Have students examine the map showing the extent of the Han and Qin dynasties and the Great Wall. Invite students to trace the dynasty boundaries and Great Wall on the map. **ASK:** In which directions did Han rulers extend the empire? *(to the south and west)* Why do you think the Great Wall did not fully extend around the borders of the Han Empire? *(Possible response: because desert and mountains provided a natural obstacle to invaders)* **0:10** minutes

ACTIVE OPTIONS

Critical Viewing: NG Chapter Gallery Invite students to explore the Chapter Gallery and choose one image they feel best represents their understanding of Section 2. Have students provide a written explanation of why they selected that particular image. **0:10** minutes

On Your Feet: Stage a Quiz Show Have each student write one question about the Han dynasty. Then have groups of five students take turns coming to the front of the class to take part in a quiz. Pose a few of the questions to each group. Students should signal their readiness to answer by raising their hands. **0:20** minutes

DIFFERENTIATE

ENGLISH LANGUAGE LEARNERS

Use a Word Square Have pairs of students use context clues to complete a Word Square, like the one shown, for *bureaucracy*. Once they've completed the squares, have pairs present them to the class.

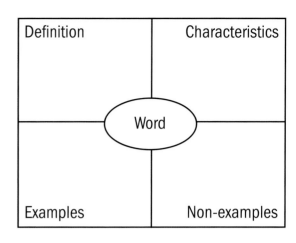

STRIVING READERS

Understand Main Ideas Check students' understanding of the main ideas in Lesson 2.4 by asking them to correctly complete either/or statements such as the following:

- Han rulers introduced practices that were [less cruel or more cruel] than those of Shi Huangdi.
- Under Han rulers, Legalism was [replaced or kept] as a guide for government.
- [Most or a small number] of the Chinese people lived in large houses in the cities during the Han dynasty.
- The Han dynasty [lasted longer or for a briefer amount of time] than the Qin dynasty.

Press **mt** *in the Student eEdition for modified text.*

See the Chapter Planner for more strategies for differentiation.

REVIEW & ASSESS

ANSWERS

1. They lowered taxes, enforced lighter punishments, required shorter periods of labor on building projects, and established their government based on a bureaucracy.

2. The Han dynasty was almost twice as big as the Qin dynasty.

3. Poor farmers lived in small mud houses, had little to eat, and often had to pull their own plows. Rich merchants lived in large houses in the city, where they could eat in restaurants and enjoy entertainment.

THE LEGACY OF CHINA'S EARLY COMPASS

Over the centuries, people have used the technology behind ancient Chinese inventions to develop their own inventions. For example, this Chinese compass from the Han dynasty paved the way for the development of the items shown below. The compass wasn't used for navigation, but it did show direction. The spoon is a special type of magnet that aligns with Earth's poles and can point in the eight main directions marked on the plate.

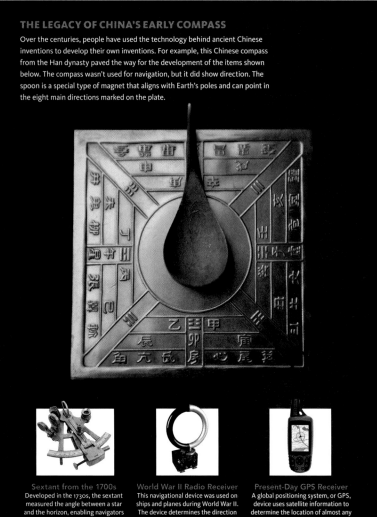

Sextant from the 1700s
Developed in the 1730s, the sextant measured the angle between a star and the horizon, enabling navigators to determine latitude.

World War II Radio Receiver
This navigational device was used on ships and planes during World War II. The device determines the direction of incoming radio signals.

Present-Day GPS Receiver
A global positioning system, or GPS, device uses satellite information to determine the location of almost any place on or near Earth.

2.5

The Legacy of
Ancient China

Ancient China's contributions to world civilization are so many and so varied that it's difficult to know where to begin. But consider that whenever you read a book, you're looking at one of China's most important inventions: paper.

MAIN IDEA

Early Chinese achievements, including inventions, cultural contributions, and ideas, left the world a lasting legacy.

INVENTIONS

Although historians believe the use of paper in China goes back even further, China is officially said to have invented paper in A.D. 105. The invention transformed writing. The ancient Chinese made paper from tree bark, plant fibers, and old rags. It was cheap to produce and easy to write on. The availability of paper allowed ideas to spread farther and faster than ever.

During the Han dynasty, the ancient Chinese also invented the first compass (shown opposite). The Chinese sometimes used the instrument to determine the best location for burials. However, this early compass would eventually lead to the development of the navigational compass, which made exploration of distant lands possible.

As you have learned, most Chinese worked as farmers. Many benefited from early agricultural inventions, such as an improved plow, a wheelbarrow, and a harness that fitted around a horse's neck.

CULTURE AND IDEAS

Not all of ancient China's contributions were strictly practical. One of its most valued inventions is the beautiful textile, or cloth, called **silk**. The Chinese developed the technique for making silk and kept it secret for thousands of years. (Hint: It had something to do with worms.) Demand for silk grew until it became China's most traded good. It is still a prized textile today.

Chinese craftspeople worked in metals as well. Remember reading about the advanced bronze sculptures developed during the Shang dynasty? Hundreds of years later, the Chinese would also teach the world to cast iron. This process involves heating iron until it becomes liquid and then pouring it into a mold to solidify into different shapes.

Finally, Chinese philosophies remain one of ancient China's greatest legacies. One of these philosophies—Confucianism—got a boost from the invention of paper. Confucian ideas were among the first spread by China's new writing material. Today, Confucianism continues to influence thinking, just as Chinese inventions make our lives easier.

REVIEW & ASSESS

1. **READING CHECK** What were a few of the inventions that ancient China contributed to world civilization?

2. **ANALYZE CAUSE AND EFFECT** What impact did agricultural advancements probably have on ancient China's food production and economy?

3. **FORM OPINIONS** Which ancient Chinese invention, cultural development, or idea do you think is the most significant? Explain your reasons.

PLAN

OBJECTIVE
Discuss the lasting legacy of early Chinese achievements.

CRITICAL THINKING SKILLS FOR LESSON 2.5

- Identify Main Ideas and Details
- Monitor Comprehension
- Analyze Cause and Effect
- Form Opinions
- Summarize
- Make Inferences
- Analyze Visuals

ESSENTIAL QUESTION
How did China establish what would become one of the world's oldest continuous civilizations?

The ancient Chinese developed important inventions and cultural ideas that continue to influence thinking today. Lesson 2.5 describes ancient China's legacy, which helped advance and strengthen Chinese civilization.

BACKGROUND FOR THE TEACHER

China's early compass was considered a divining board rather than a compass. The oval bowl that the compass rested on symbolized heaven, while the square plate represented Earth. Its primary use in ancient times was to determine the best location and time for burials. This was an important tool for a society that practiced ancestor worship. In fact, the compass was used for this purpose well into the 1800s.

DIGITAL RESOURCES myNGconnect.com

TEACHER RESOURCES & ASSESSMENT

 Reading and Note-Taking

Vocabulary Practice

✓ **Section 2 Quiz**

STUDENT RESOURCES

NG Chapter Gallery

INTRODUCE & ENGAGE

DISCUSS INVENTIONS

Initiate a class discussion about inventions. Ask students to name some inventions that have had an important impact on people. Then have them discuss inventions that are important in their lives. Finally, open a book and point to a page in it. Tell students that in ancient times, paper was an important development and that China invented it. **0:10 minutes**

TEACH

GUIDED DISCUSSION

1. **Summarize** What did the ancient Chinese use to make paper? *(tree bark, plant fibers, and old rags)*

2. **Make Inferences** Why do you think the Chinese kept the technique for making silk a secret? *(They kept the technique secret so that they could remain the exclusive manufacturers of silk, charge high prices for it, and use it in trade.)*

ANALYZE VISUALS

Help students understand the visual in this lesson. First, read aloud the introduction. Then discuss the central image of the compass. Ask students to identify the eight directions marked on the plate. Emphasize that the magnetized spoon could point in these directions. Finally, read the labels for the smaller images and discuss the items' use. **ASK:** What do all of the items have in common with the early compass? *(They all indicate direction.)* **0:10 minutes**

ACTIVE OPTIONS

Critical Viewing: NG Chapter Gallery Ask students to choose one image from the Chapter Gallery and become an expert on it. They should do additional research to learn all about it. Then, students should share their findings with a partner, small group, or the class. **0:10 minutes**

On Your Feet: Inventions and Ideas Post these signs in the four corners of the classroom: paper, compass, silk, Confucianism. Have students vote for the invention or idea they think is most significant by going to the appropriate corner. Once students have made their decisions, ask each group to defend their choice. **0:20 minutes**

DIFFERENTIATE

STRIVING READERS

Make an Invention Chart Help students answer the third question in "Review & Assess" by completing a chart like the one shown here as they read the lesson. Have students work in pairs to read the lesson and take notes in the chart. Then instruct them to use the chart to help them evaluate the impact on each invention and decide which invention they think was most significant.

Invention	Date	Impact

GIFTED & TALENTED

Describe Inventions Have students think of their own inventions. They might come up with a new electronic device, vehicle, or concept or an item that simply makes everyday life easier. Ask students to write a description of their invention and share it with the class.

Press **(mt)** *in the Student eEdition for modified text.*

See the Chapter Planner for more strategies for differentiation.

REVIEW & ASSESS

ANSWERS

1. Some inventions include paper, the compass, the plow, the wheelbarrow, and silk.

2. Agricultural advancements, such as the plow and wheelbarrow, probably made work easier for farmers and improved agricultural productivity in ancient China.

3. Responses will vary.

The Silk Roads

The desert sun beats down on your back as you trudge wearily across the sand. Peering ahead, all you see is a long line of camels, each loaded with bundles of silk. Still, you know that the profit you'll make from trading these goods will make your journey worthwhile.

MAIN IDEA

The Silk Roads were some of the world's most important international trade routes.

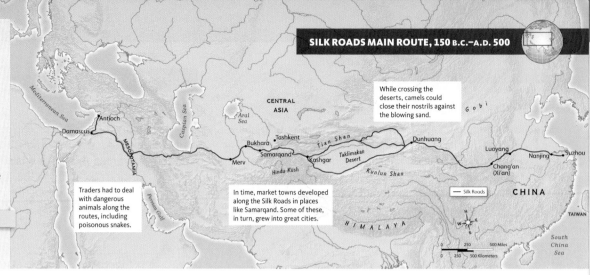

SILK ROADS MAIN ROUTE, 150 B.C.–A.D. 500

While crossing the deserts, camels could close their nostrils against the blowing sand.

Traders had to deal with dangerous animals along the routes, including poisonous snakes.

In time, market towns developed along the Silk Roads in places like Samarqand. Some of these, in turn, grew into great cities.

— Silk Roads

CENTRAL ASIA

CHINA

CAMELS

Camels sometimes bite and spit, but they're terrific on a long journey—like one along the Silk Roads. They can store fat in their humps and survive without eating or drinking for days. When they get a chance to drink, however, they can take in as much as 25 gallons of water at one time.

ROUTES ACROSS ASIA

You have learned about ancient China's legacy of inventions, culture, and ideas. However, a series of international trade routes called the **Silk Roads** is also one of China's great legacies. The Silk Roads had been well established by 100 B.C., but the name for the routes was coined many centuries later. A German geographer came up with the name because silk was the main good China traded on the routes. The Silk Roads brought great wealth to China and its trading partners.

The Silk Roads began as a network of local overland routes. These eventually joined to form a huge network that connected China with the rest of Asia, Europe, and Africa. The main route stretched more than 4,000 miles and ran from China through Central Asia and Mesopotamia. Other land routes branched off the main road. Some of these routes brought traders to northern India.

The Silk Roads also included **maritime**, or sea, routes. Traders could sail along these routes to the Mediterranean Sea and to Europe. Other maritime routes led across the Indian Ocean to East Africa and across the Pacific Ocean to Korea, Japan, and Southeast Asia.

A DEMANDING JOURNEY

Chinese goods might have traveled thousands of miles, but Chinese traders did not. They traded their goods somewhere around Kashgar, near China's western border. They may have passed their goods along to Central Asian nomads. The nomads, in turn, may have gone on to trade the goods with other merchants from Asia, Africa, and Europe. The goods probably changed hands so many times that no one knew where they originated.

Actually, few traders made the entire journey from one end of the main Silk Roads route to the other. The trip over the rugged terrain would have taken at least six months. At best, traders followed rough paths or tracks. At worst, they scaled ice-covered mountain passes or encountered sandstorms as they crossed scorching-hot deserts.

These difficult conditions made camels the ideal pack animals because they were strong, sure-footed, and tough. They could carry huge loads—about 400 to 500 pounds of goods—for long distances in the driest, hottest weather.

The traders on the Silk Roads usually walked alongside the camels and traveled in groups called **caravans**. They found safety in numbers. The valuable caravans created a tempting target for the bandits and thieves who often lay in wait along the routes. After all, a single camel carried more wealth than most people could possibly imagine.

REVIEW & ASSESS

1. **READING CHECK** What continents were connected by the Silk Roads?

2. **INTERPRET MAPS** Why do you think the main route of the Silk Roads divided in two between the cities of Dunhuang and Kashgar?

3. **MAKE INFERENCES** What impact do you think the Silk Roads had on China's economy?

PLAN

OBJECTIVE

Describe the routes and the journey involved on the Silk Roads.

CRITICAL THINKING SKILLS FOR LESSON 3.1

- Identify Main Ideas and Details
- Monitor Comprehension
- Interpret Maps
- Make Inferences
- Make Connections

ESSENTIAL QUESTION

How did China establish what would become one of the world's oldest continuous civilizations?

By 100 B.C., China had established the Silk Roads, trade routes that eventually connected China with the rest of Asia, Europe, and Africa. Lesson 3.1 describes the Silk Roads, which became some of the world's most important international trade routes.

BACKGROUND FOR THE TEACHER

The Silk Roads depended on strong governments to protect travelers and allow trade to flourish. Beyond China, empires in Persia and Rome protected the routes. When the Han dynasty declined after A.D. 204, trade fell off until the time of the Tang dynasty in the 600s to 900s.

After another period of decline, the Mongol empire of Genghis Khan in the 1200s allowed the routes to prosper. The land routes were little used after the mid-1400s. Sea trade, which was safer and faster for large cargo, then became more important.

DIGITAL RESOURCES myNGconnect.com

TEACHER RESOURCES & ASSESSMENT

 Reading and Note-Taking

 Vocabulary Practice

 Section 3 Quiz

STUDENT RESOURCES

 NG Chapter Gallery

ACTIVATE PRIOR KNOWLEDGE

Invite students to share what they know about camels from what they have read or seen on television or at the zoo. Ask these questions and write students' responses on the board:

- What region of the world do camels come from?
- What do camels look like?
- What do camels eat?
- What are camels used for?

Then tell students they will learn more about camels and their role on the trade routes known as the Silk Roads in this lesson. **0:10** minutes

TEACH

GUIDED DISCUSSION

1. **Make Connections** In what way were the Silk Roads a form of global economy? *(Traders from many parts of the world conducted business there.)*

2. **Make Inferences** In addition to being good businesspeople, what skills or qualities did traders on the Silk Roads probably need? *(They would have had to be tough, brave, persuasive, patient, and able to ride a camel.)*

INTERPRET MAPS

Discuss the map of the Silk Roads with students. Have students trace the route on the map and emphasize that the map shows only the main overland route of the Silk Roads. Ask students to use the distance scale to determine the length of the route. Then read aloud and discuss the captions on the map. **ASK:** What physical obstacles did the traders encounter on the main route? *(mountains and deserts)* Over what body of water might goods have traveled from Antioch? *(the Mediterranean Sea)* **0:10** minutes

ACTIVE OPTIONS

NG Learning Framework: Learn About the Silk Roads

SKILLS: Collaboration, Communication
KNOWLEDGE: **Our Human Story**

Have groups of students work together to create a storyboard about a caravan on the Silk Roads. For example, students might illustrate and tell the story of traders scaling a mountain, dealing with their camels, or encountering thieves. Tell students to include captions and dialogue in their storyboards. **0:10** minutes

On Your Feet: Team Word Webbing Organize students into teams of four and have them record what they know about the Silk Roads on a piece of paper. Encourage students to build on their teammates' entries as they rotate the paper from one member

to the next. Then call on volunteers from each group to make statements about the Silk Roads based on their webs. **0:15** minutes

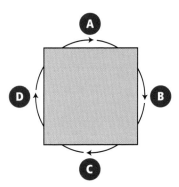

STRIVING READERS

Ask and Answer Questions Have students work in pairs to understand the lesson by turning the subheadings in the lesson into questions and then reading to find the answers. Instruct students to use the words *who, what, when, where, why,* and *how* to begin their questions. For example, students might turn the subheading "Routes Across Asia" into questions such as the following:

- What were the routes across Asia called?
- How far did the routes extend?
- What were the routes used for?

PRE-AP

Prepare Oral Reports Have groups of students use online sources to learn more about the maritime routes of the Silk Roads. Groups should find a map of the routes to photocopy or trace. They should also learn who used the routes, what trade items they carried, and what challenges the traders encountered on the sea routes. Ask students to prepare a brief report on the maritime routes that they will deliver to the class.

Press (**mt**) *in the Student eEdition for modified text.*

See the Chapter Planner for more strategies for differentiation.

ANSWERS

1. Asia, Africa, and Europe were connected by the Silk Roads.

2. It divided to bypass the most difficult area of the Taklimakan Desert.

3. The Silk Roads probably greatly improved China's economy and wealth.

3.2

Trade
on the
Silk Roads

In the late 1930s, archaeologists discovered two sealed rooms in Begram, Afghanistan, an ancient city on the Silk Roads. Inside they found decorative bowls from China, ivory statues from India, and glassware from Europe. Stored away about 2,000 years ago, the objects illustrate the worldwide trade that flowed along the Silk Roads.

MAIN IDEA

Many different goods and ideas from three continents were traded on the Silk Roads.

GOODS

As you have learned, silk was China's chief trade good. Production of the fabric was not easy, though. Silk is made from the cocoons, or protective coverings, of silkworms, which live only on mulberry trees. Chinese workers had to remove strands of silk from the cocoons by hand and spin them into thread. Even so, the process was worth the trouble. Demand for the rare fabric allowed Chinese merchants to charge high prices for it. In fact, silk was so valuable that the Chinese government sometimes used it to pay its soldiers.

In addition to silk, China traded paper, highly polished decorative items called lacquerware, and objects made of iron or bronze. In return for these goods, Chinese merchants often sought gold, silver, and olive oil. One of the items the Chinese especially valued was Central Asian horses.

Market towns sprang up all along the Silk Roads. Major market towns in China included Chang'an, where the main route began, and Kashgar. A dazzling variety of items, including Central Asian rugs, Indian spices, and European wool, landed in the stalls in these towns. Traders from these and many other places used different currencies. Many had no money at all. As a result, the traders often **bartered**, or exchanged, items for other goods.

INVENTIONS AND IDEAS

Goods were not all that passed along the Silk Roads. With so many traders from so many parts of the world, the routes served as a network for the exchange of inventions and ideas as well. You have already learned that the process by which ideas spread from one culture to another is called **cultural diffusion**. By this process, Chinese ideas about papermaking, metalwork, and farming techniques began to spread beyond China's borders. In time, these ideas and inventions reached as far as Western Europe.

China also absorbed new ideas. Chief among these was Buddhism. You might remember that Buddhism began in India around 500 B.C. Indian merchants introduced Buddhist ideas to Chinese traders and even established Buddhist shrines along the Silk Roads.

Buddhism's ideas about ending suffering appealed to the Chinese, and eventually the religion became an important part of Chinese life. Many Chinese blended its practices with Confucianism. From China, Buddhism would spread throughout East Asia. Other ideas also reached China, including Greek and Indian styles in sculpture, painting, and temple building. All of these ideas enriched Chinese culture and civilization.

Critical Viewing: It took artists more than 90 years to carve this Giant Buddha in southwest China, the largest carved stone Buddha in the world. What qualities does the Buddha's face convey?

→ **POSSIBLE RESPONSE**

The Buddha's face seems still, peaceful, contemplative, patient, and solemn.

REVIEW & ASSESS

1. **READING CHECK** What were some of the goods and ideas exchanged on the Silk Roads?

2. **DRAW CONCLUSIONS** Why do you think Buddhism's ideas about ending suffering might have appealed to the ancient Chinese?

3. **MAKE INFERENCES** Why were Chinese traders able to demand high prices for their silk?

187

PLAN

OBJECTIVE

Describe the goods and ideas that were traded on the Silk Roads.

CRITICAL THINKING SKILLS FOR LESSON 3.2

- Identify Main Ideas and Details
- Monitor Comprehension
- Draw Conclusions
- Make Inferences
- Analyze Cause and Effect

ESSENTIAL QUESTION

How did China establish what would become one of the world's oldest continuous civilizations?

Many different goods and ideas were traded on the Silk Roads. Lesson 3.2 discusses the goods and ideas traded on the Silk Roads, all of which enriched Chinese culture and civilization.

BACKGROUND FOR THE TEACHER

According to legend, a Chinese queen first got the idea for making silk in the 2000s B.C. The empress was drinking tea when a silkworm cocoon from a mulberry tree fell into her cup. She picked up the cocoon and discovered that it was made of a strong, soft thread. Intrigued by the thread, the empress is said to have figured out how to extract it and invented a loom to weave it into cloth.

When production of silk first began in ancient China, only the king and his family could wear clothes made of the fabric. Eventually, members of the nobility were allowed to wear silk. However, people of the merchant and peasant class could not wear silk clothing.

DIGITAL RESOURCES myNGconnect.com

TEACHER RESOURCES & ASSESSMENT

 Reading and Note-Taking

 Vocabulary Practice

 Section 3 Quiz

STUDENT RESOURCES

 Active History

INTRODUCE & ENGAGE

POSE QUESTIONS

Have students use an Idea Web to jot down questions about trade on the Silk Roads that they think the lesson will answer. If needed, start them off with an example, such as *What items were traded on the Silk Roads?* **0:15** minutes

TEACH

GUIDED DISCUSSION

1. **Analyze Cause and Effect** Why did many traders on the Silk Roads engage in bartering? *(because traders were from different places and used different currencies and because some traders had no money at all)*

2. **Make Inferences** Why do you think market towns such as Kashgar developed into thriving cities? *(Trade brought people and wealth to the towns. In time, the towns would have grown larger and developed into cities as trade increased.)*

MORE INFORMATION

Buddhism in East Asia The branch of Buddhism mainly practiced in East Asia is Mahayana Buddhism, which teaches that ordinary people can be released from suffering without having to become monks or nuns. Buddhists in East Asia created many large sculptures of the Buddha and other wise beings called bodhisattvas (boh-duh-SUHT-vuhz). Buddhist temples are similar to Confucian and Daoist temples, and many temples contain deities from both Buddhist and Daoist traditions. Many Chinese Buddhist temples feature pagodas.

ACTIVE OPTIONS

Active History: Barter on the Silk Roads Extend the lesson by using either the PDF or Whiteboard version of the activity. These activities take a deeper look at a topic from, or related to, the lesson. Explore the activities as a class, turn them into group assignments, or even assign them individually. **0:10** minutes

On Your Feet: Inside-Outside Circle Have students stand in concentric circles facing each other. Have students in the outside circle ask students in the inside circle a question about the lesson. Then have the outside circle rotate one position to the right to create new pairings. After five questions, have students switch roles and continue. **0:15** minutes

DIFFERENTIATE

STRIVING READERS

Understand Bartering Help students understand the concept of bartering. Give students index cards or pieces of paper with names and drawings of some of the goods traded on the Silk Roads, such as silk, spices, wool, horses, gold, and olive oil. Have pairs of students trade their goods by bartering. Explain that they will decide the value of their goods and what they should receive in exchange for them. For example, in exchange for gold, students might insist on receiving silk and wool. At the conclusion of the activity, have students discuss any difficulties they encountered.

GIFTED & TALENTED

Write a Skit Have students prepare a short skit dramatizing a trading encounter on the Silk Roads. Students may wish to conduct research to learn more about traders on the Silk Roads before writing their scripts. A sample script is started below.

> **Chinese Trader:** I have silks of every color imaginable for sale.
>
> **Indian Trader:** I have never seen such fine cloth! I will give you these precious stones for a yard of the material.
>
> **Chinese Trader:** Throw in those spices and we'll have a deal.

Press **mt** *in the Student eEdition for modified text.*

See the Chapter Planner for more strategies for differentiation.

REVIEW & ASSESS

ANSWERS

1. Goods and ideas exchanged on the Silk Roads included silk, paper, lacquerware, iron and bronze objects, papermaking, metalwork, and farming techniques from China; rugs from Central Asia; ivory, spices, and Buddhism from India; and glassware and wool from Europe.

2. Buddhism's ideas about ending suffering might have appealed to the ancient Chinese because their lives were very hard.

3. Chinese traders were able to demand high prices for their silk because China held the secret for silk production.

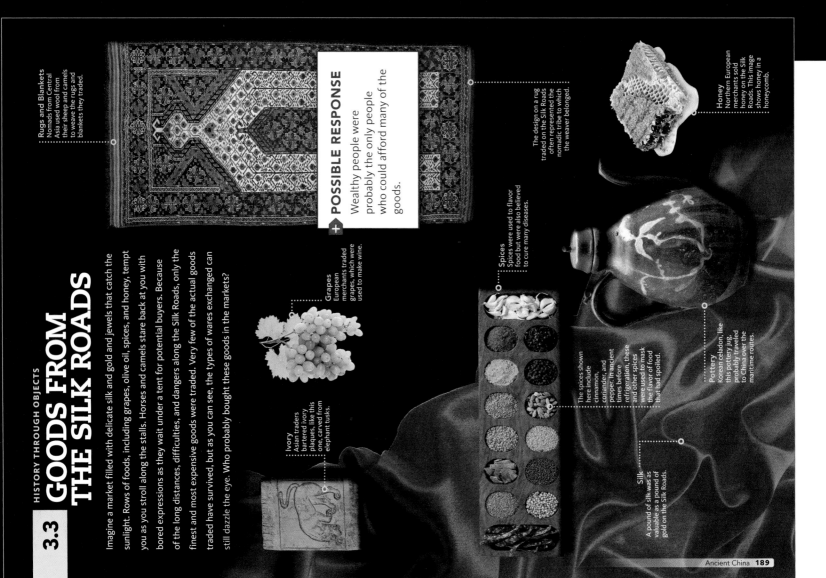

3.3 GOODS FROM THE SILK ROADS

Imagine a market filled with delicate silk and gold and jewels that catch the sunlight. Rows of foods, including grapes, olive oil, spices, and honey, tempt you as you stroll along the stalls. Horses and camels stare back at you with bored expressions as they wait under a tent for potential buyers. Because of the long distances, difficulties, and dangers along the Silk Roads, only the finest and most expensive goods were traded. Very few of the actual goods traded have survived, but as you can see, the types of wares exchanged can still dazzle the eye. Who probably bought these goods in the markets?

Rugs and Blankets Nomads from Central Asia used wool from their sheep and camels to weave the rugs and blankets they traded.

+ POSSIBLE RESPONSE Wealthy people were probably the only people who could afford many of the goods.

The design on a rug traded on the Silk Roads often represented the nomadic tribe to which the weaver belonged.

Honey Northern European merchants sold honey on the Silk Roads. This image shows honey in a honeycomb.

Grapes European merchants traded grapes, which were used to make wine.

Spices Spices were used to flavor food but were also believed to cure many diseases.

Ivory Asian traders bartered ivory plaques, like this one, carved from elephant tusks.

The spices shown here include cinnamon, coriander, and pepper. In ancient times before refrigeration, these and other spices were used to mask the flavor of food that had spoiled.

Pottery Korean celadon, like this pottery jug, probably traveled to China over the maritime routes.

Silk A pound of silk was as valuable as a pound of gold on the Silk Roads.

Ancient China **189**

PLAN

OBJECTIVE

Identify some of the goods traded on the Silk Roads.

CRITICAL THINKING SKILLS FOR LESSON 3.3

- Form Opinions
- Make Inferences
- Analyze Visuals

ESSENTIAL QUESTION

How did China establish what would become one of the world's oldest continuous civilizations?

Many different goods from three continents were traded on the Silk Roads. Lesson 3.3 shows some of the trade goods that enriched and influenced Chinese civilization and culture.

BACKGROUND FOR THE TEACHER

Ivory is still greatly in demand on the international market. The good is obtained mainly from elephant tusks, as it was when traders bartered it on the Silk Roads. However, in modern times, there has been an outcry against this harvesting, which results in the death of thousands of elephants every year. In 2012, more than 25,000 elephants were killed in Africa alone. In 1989, a ban on ivory trade put a halt to the killing and resulted in a rebound in the elephant population. The ban was somewhat lifted, though, in 1999 and 2008. Bowing to pressure from countries in Asia and southern Africa, sales of ivory in limited markets were allowed once again.

DIGITAL RESOURCES myNGconnect.com

TEACHER RESOURCES & ASSESSMENT

 Reading and Note-Taking

 Vocabulary Practice

 Section 3 Quiz

STUDENT RESOURCES

 NG Chapter Gallery

INTRODUCE & ENGAGE

HISTORY THROUGH OBJECTS

Initiate a discussion about international trade today. Tell students that the goods that one country receives from another for sale or distribution are called imports, while those that one country sends to another for sale or distribution are called exports. For example, the United States imports many cars and other vehicles from other countries and exports computers around the world. Ask students if they can name other goods the United States—or another country they are familiar with—imports and exports. Point out that most of these goods arrive at their destinations on ships. Then tell students that, in this lesson, they will see some of the goods that were traded on the Silk Roads—carried on foot, on camels, or on ships. **0:05** minutes

TEACH

GUIDED DISCUSSION

1. **Form Opinions** Which item would you have been interested in buying? Explain why. *(Responses will vary. Possible response: I would have bought the rug because it is both beautiful and useful.)*

2. **Make Inferences** Which item could probably have been bartered to purchase all the other items combined? Why? *(Possible response: Silk could probably have been used to buy all the other items because it was literally worth its weight in gold.)*

ANALYZE VISUALS

Have students create a three-column chart for classifying the Silk Roads goods into the following categories: *food or drink, useful items, luxury items.* (Or, as a class, brainstorm different headings that could be used to categorize the goods.) Then have students sort the goods into the categories, writing each item in the appropriate column. Point out that some goods could belong in more than one category. End the activity by inviting volunteers to share their categories and discuss/debate any alternative categorizing. **0:15** minutes

Food or Drink	Useful Items	Luxury Items

ACTIVE OPTIONS

Critical Viewing: NG Chapter Gallery Have students examine the contents of the Chapter Gallery for this chapter. Then invite them to brainstorm additional images they believe would fit within the Chapter Gallery. Have them write a description of these additional images and provide an explanation of why they would fit within the Chapter Gallery. Then instruct them to do online research to find examples of actual images they would like to add to the gallery. **0:10** minutes

On Your Feet: Set Up a Market Photocopy full-page images of the types of goods shown in this lesson. Distribute several copies of the goods to four small groups of students. Have these groups set up a market in each corner of the classroom. Then have the remaining students act as buyers. Encourage the sellers to try to attract the buyers' interest by "pitching" their goods—extolling their value, usefulness, beauty, or flavor. The buyers should make their choices and "buy" each good with a pen, pencil, or paper clip. At the end of the activity, tally up the money to see which market sold the most goods. **0:15** minutes

DIFFERENTIATE

INCLUSION

Help Students See This lesson might pose a challenge to the visually impaired. Have students who are not visually challenged help their classmates see the goods shown in the lesson by describing them in detail—their colors, shapes, patterns, and designs. You might also bring some of the items to class so the visually impaired can feel, smell, and taste the goods, too.

PRE-AP

Research Silk Roads Goods Have students research to find out more about goods traded on the Silk Roads and where they came from. Ask students to sketch a map showing the items and their place of origin. They should also prepare a poster or digital presentation, featuring images of the goods.

Press **mt** in the Student eEdition for modified text.

See the Chapter Planner for more strategies for differentiation.

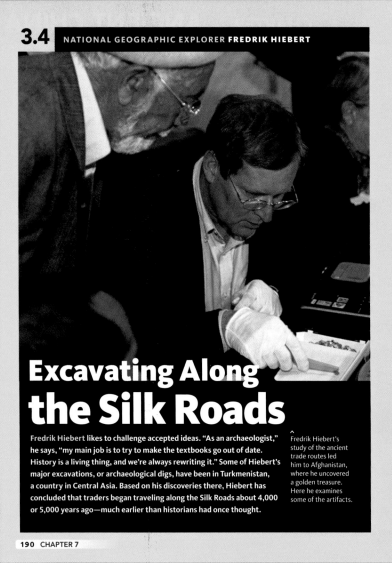

Excavating Along the Silk Roads

Fredrik Hiebert likes to challenge accepted ideas. "As an archaeologist," he says, "my main job is to try to make the textbooks go out of date. History is a living thing, and we're always rewriting it." Some of Hiebert's major excavations, or archaeological digs, have been in Turkmenistan, a country in Central Asia. Based on his discoveries there, Hiebert has concluded that traders began traveling along the Silk Roads about 4,000 or 5,000 years ago—much earlier than historians had once thought.

^
Fredrik Hiebert's study of the ancient trade routes led him to Afghanistan, where he uncovered a golden treasure. Here he examines some of the artifacts.

MAIN IDEA

Archaeologist Fredrik Hiebert's explorations have uncovered lost gold and challenged ideas about when trading began on the Silk Roads.

CONNECTED CULTURES

National Geographic Explorer Fredrik Hiebert has been conducting excavations at Silk Roads sites—like cities in Turkmenistan—for more than 20 years. "Historians thought the Silk Roads had emerged about 100 B.C.," says Hiebert. "But when we dug deeper into Silk Roads cities, we found they'd been built on much older Bronze Age settlements, which contained artifacts from as far away as India and Mesopotamia. This means that long-distance trade along the Silk Roads took place 2,000 years before we'd thought it had started."

The realization didn't surprise Hiebert. He believes that ancient cultures were always connected. "It's easy to argue that ancient cultures were isolated by geography and the lack of transport," he claims, "but that really didn't stop people from traveling and trading. They just did it more slowly."

Necklace from the Bactrian Hoard

LOST GOLD

Hiebert's explorations of the Silk Roads have also taken him to Afghanistan, which borders Turkmenistan in the south. In 1988, a Russian archaeologist told him about 21,000 pieces of ancient gold that he'd excavated ten years earlier near the Afghan region of Bactria. He later showed Hiebert photos of the collection, which came to be known as the Bactrian Hoard. The gold had belonged to nomads who herded and traded along the Silk Roads around the first century B.C. The collection

was placed in a museum in Afghanistan. However, after war erupted in the country in 1978, the gold disappeared. The Russian archaeologist believed it was lost forever.

"Fast-forward to 2003 when I heard rumors of ancient gold hidden in the Afghan presidential palace," Hiebert continues the story. "I thought: Could it be the Bactrian Hoard?" Working with the National Geographic Society, Hiebert persuaded the Afghan authorities to let him open the safes where he thought the treasure might be found. Inside were all 21,000 pieces of gold, including a necklace, shown here, that Hiebert recognized from the photos he had seen of the hoard.

"Against all odds it had survived intact, thanks to a few dedicated museum workers who had kept it secret for so many years," Hiebert says. His study of the gold revealed more evidence of cultural connections. The items were imitations of Chinese, Greek, and Indian artifacts traded on the Silk Roads. The gold is beautiful and valuable beyond measure, but that's not what most interests Hiebert. As he says, "We don't actually search for treasure. We search for knowledge—that's our real gold."

REVIEW & ASSESS

1. **READING CHECK** When does Hiebert believe trade along the Silk Roads first took place?

2. **IDENTIFY MAIN IDEAS AND DETAILS** What evidence did Hiebert find to support his ideas about cultural connections on the Silk Roads?

3. **ANALYZE LANGUAGE USE** What does Hiebert suggest about knowledge when he compares it to gold?

PLAN

OBJECTIVE

Describe the findings and explorations of archaeologist Fredrik Hiebert on the Silk Roads.

CRITICAL THINKING SKILLS FOR LESSON 3.4

- Identify Main Ideas and Details
- Monitor Comprehension
- Analyze Language Use
- Explain
- Sequence Events
- Make Inferences

ESSENTIAL QUESTION

How did China establish what would become one of the world's oldest continuous civilizations?

Explorer Fred Hiebert has excavated the Silk Roads for more than 20 years. Lesson 3.4 describes the evidence he has uncovered, suggesting that trade along the Silk Roads began about 2,000 years earlier than formerly believed.

BACKGROUND FOR THE TEACHER

Much of the Bactrian hoard was secreted in trunks in the Central Bank treasury vault in the presidential palace. In 2001, the Taliban, which had taken control of the Afghan government, destroyed thousands of priceless items—but they didn't find everything.

In 2003, after the Taliban had been overthrown, the Central Bank announced that the trunks in the vault had not been broken into. Dr. Fredrik Hiebert and Russian archaeologist Viktor Sarianidi were both present at the opening of the vault.

DIGITAL RESOURCES myNGconnect.com

TEACHER RESOURCES & ASSESSMENT

 Reading and Note-Taking

 Vocabulary Practice

 Section 3 Quiz

STUDENT RESOURCES

 NG Chapter Gallery

INTRODUCE & ENGAGE

HIDING AND FINDING A TREASURE

Ask students where they would hide a prized possession for safekeeping. Would they hide it under a bed or in a drawer? Would they bury it? Then ask students if they have ever gone on a treasure hunt. If so, how did they feel when they discovered the treasure? Tell students that, in this lesson, they will learn how a priceless golden treasure traded on the Silk Roads was hidden for years and then found. **0:05** minutes

TEACH

GUIDED DISCUSSION

1. **Explain** What evidence did Fredrik Hiebert find that suggested long-distance trade on the Silk Roads had begun 2,000 years earlier than archaeologists had thought? *(He found that Silk Roads cities in present-day Turkmenistan had been built on settlements from the later Bronze Age.)*

2. **Sequence Events** What happened shortly after a Russian archaeologist had excavated the Bactrian Hoard? *(War broke out in Afghanistan, and the hoard disappeared.)*

MAKE INFERENCES

Direct students to the quote from Fredrik Hiebert on the first page of the lesson. **ASK:** What does Hiebert mean when he says, "As an archaeologist, my main job is to try to make the textbooks go out of date"? *(Possible response: He means that he wants to find new evidence and information that challenge and overturn accepted ideas.)* **0:10** minutes

ACTIVE OPTIONS

NG Learning Framework: Learn About Fredrik Hiebert

ATTITUDE: **Curiosity**
KNOWLEDGE: **Our Human Story**

Have students learn more about archaeologist Fredrik Hiebert. Instruct them to write a short biography or profile about this person using information from the chapter and additional source material. **0:10** minutes

On Your Feet: Tell Me More Have students form two teams and assign each team one of the following topics: *Trade on the Silk Roads* and *Finding Hidden Gold*. Each group should write down as many facts about their topic as they can. Have the class reconvene and have each group stand up, one at a time. The sitting group calls out, "Tell me more about [Trade on the Silk Roads or Finding Hidden Gold]!" The standing group recites one fact. The sitting group should keep calling, "Tell me more!" until the standing group runs out of facts to share. Then have the groups switch places. **0:15** minutes

DIFFERENTIATE

ENGLISH LANGUAGE LEARNERS

Give a Thumbs Up or Thumbs Down Write a set of true-false statements about the lesson, such as "Trade along the Silk Roads began about 2,000 years before archaeologists thought it had started." Read the lesson aloud with students following along in their books. Then have them close the books and listen as you read the true-false statements. Students should give a thumbs up if a statement is true and a thumbs down if a statement is false.

STRIVING READERS

Use a Five-Ws Chart Students may have trouble understanding that the lesson describes the results of two different archaeological expeditions. To help students clarify and organize their reading, have them take notes for the text under each subheading using a 5Ws Chart.

What?
Who?
Where?
When?
Why?

Press (**mt**) *in the Student eEdition for modified text.*

See the Chapter Planner for more strategies for differentiation.

REVIEW & ASSESS

ANSWERS

1. He believes trade along the Silk Roads first took place about 2,000 years before originally believed.

2. In Turkmenistan, he found very early artifacts that had been made in India and Mesopotamia. In Afghanistan he found that the Bactrian gold items were local imitations of Chinese, Greek, and Indian artifacts.

3. He suggests that knowledge is as valuable as gold.

VOCABULARY

Complete each of the following sentences using one of the vocabulary words from the chapter.

1. During China's early development, physical features such as mountains and deserts helped _isolate_ China.

2. The Han dynasty's government was based on a _____ run by appointed officials.

3. Rather than sell silk for money, Chinese merchants would _____ it for gold.

4. According to the _____, a dynasty is overthrown once it has lost the approval of the gods.

5. Many historians believe that hundreds of thousands of _____ were forced to build the Great Wall.

6. Confucius taught that children should show their parents _____.

7. Traders on the Silk Roads often traveled in groups called _____.

READING STRATEGY

8. **ANALYZE LANGUAGE USE** If you haven't already, complete your concept clusters to analyze language used to describe Confucianism, Daoism, and Legalism. Then answer the question.

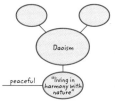

Based on the author's choice of words, how would you describe the overall theme of each philosophy?

MAIN IDEAS

Answer the following questions. Support your answers with evidence from the chapter.

9. Why did civilization in ancient China first develop with relatively little cultural influence from the outside world? **LESSON 1.1**

10. What was the Mandate of Heaven? **LESSON 1.2**

11. How did Shi Huangdi organize his empire? **LESSON 2.1**

12. Why did Shi Huangdi begin building the Great Wall? **LESSON 2.2**

13. How did Han rulers bring Confucianism into their government? **LESSON 2.4**

14. What were the benefits of traveling on the Silk Roads in camel caravans? **LESSON 3.1**

15. How did trade on the Silk Roads encourage the process of cultural diffusion? **LESSON 3.2**

CRITICAL THINKING

Answer the following questions. Support your answers with evidence from the chapter.

16. **SUMMARIZE** How did China establish one of the world's oldest continuous civilizations?

17. **DRAW CONCLUSIONS** How did the dynastic cycle help ensure the rise of new dynasties throughout China's early history?

18. **MAKE INFERENCES** Why do you think Shi Huangdi was drawn to Legalist ideas rather than Confucian ideas?

19. **COMPARE AND CONTRAST** What did the governments under the Qin and Han dynasties have in common? How did they differ?

20. **MAKE INFERENCES** What role do you think the Silk Roads played in the Han dynasty's prosperity?

21. **YOU DECIDE** Do you think Shi Huangdi was an effective emperor? Why or why not? Support your opinion with evidence from the chapter.

INTERPRET MAPS

Study the map showing the spread of Buddhism. Then answer the questions that follow.

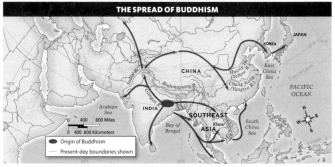

THE SPREAD OF BUDDHISM

22. Why do you think Buddhism spread to China before Korea and Japan?

23. What other region shown on the map was influenced by Buddhism?

ANALYZE SOURCES

Study this bronze statue of a flying horse, one of the finest examples of art from the Han dynasty. Then answer the question.

24. What details in the statue make it appear as if the horse is actually flying?

WRITE ABOUT HISTORY

25. **ARGUMENT** Which Chinese philosophy might be most effective as the basis for a governing policy? Choose one of the philosophies—Confucianism, Daoism, or Legalism—and create a bulleted list of arguments you might use in a debate on the subject.

TIPS

- Take notes from the lessons about each philosophy and its application in ancient Chinese government.

- Study the excerpt from each philosophy's teachings in Lesson 1.4.

- Consider what each philosophy offers governments and the people they rule.

- Use vocabulary terms from the chapter.

- Organize your ideas into a bulleted list of arguments. Include points that might counter, or answer, arguments proposed by the opposing side.

VOCABULARY ANSWERS

1. isolate
2. bureaucracy
3. barter
4. dynastic cycle
5. peasants
6. filial piety
7. caravans

READING STRATEGY ANSWERS

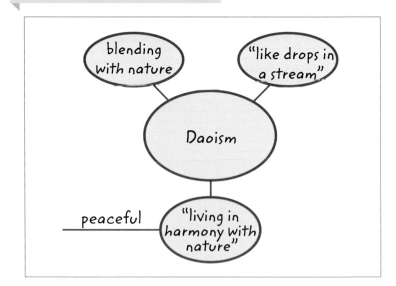

8. Daoism: People should blend with nature; Confucianism: People should respect authority and one another; Legalism: Order comes from strong government and law enforcements.

MAIN IDEAS ANSWERS

9. Civilization in ancient China developed with relatively little cultural influence from the outside world because of formidable geographical barriers that isolated much of China.

10. The Mandate of Heaven was the idea that a king could rule only as long as the gods believed he was worthy. If he ruled badly, the gods would withdraw their approval, and a good ruler would overthrow him.

11. He divided his empire into 36 areas governed by officials he had selected.

12. Shi Huangdi built the Great Wall to protect China's weak northern border from attack by nomadic tribes from Central Asia.

13. They only appointed government officials who had passed an exam that tested their knowledge of Confucianism.

14. The camels could endure the rough conditions of the routes, and the caravans helped protect the traders from bandits and thieves.

15. As people from different parts of the world came in contact with one another on the Silk Roads, they exchanged ideas, which greatly encouraged cultural diffusion.

CRITICAL THINKING ANSWERS

16. In its early history, mountains and deserts protected China from invaders and isolated its people from other cultures. Strong rulers unified and expanded China's empire and established effective governments. The philosophical ideas of Confucianism, Daoism, and Legalism and the religious ideas of Buddhism strengthened government and helped stabilize society. Inventions improved all aspects of life in China and influenced other civilizations. The Silk Roads brought wealth and new ideas to China.

17. According to the dynastic cycle, the rise and fall of dynasties was natural and the will of the gods.

18. Shi Huangdi probably didn't believe that he needed to respect his people or lead them by his good example. He wanted to remain in control, punish those who disobeyed his laws or were opposed to him, and keep a tight rein on those beneath him.

19. Governments under both dynasties were strong and expected peasants to work on building projects for the state. However, the Han emperors based their government on Confucianism rather than Legalism and were less harsh in their dealings with the Chinese people.

20. The trade of goods it promoted—particularly China's expensive silk—must have brought in a good deal of wealth and greatly bolstered the empire's economy.

21. Students' responses will vary. Students should clearly state their opinion of Shi Huangdi's effectiveness and support it with evidence from the chapter.

INTERPRET MAPS ANSWERS

22. China was geographically closer to India, and Buddhism was carried along China's Silk Roads.

23. Southeast Asia

ANALYZE SOURCES ANSWER

24. Students' responses will vary. Possible response: The horse is balanced on one hoof; its other hooves are raised above the ground; the horse's tail is lifted in the air.

WRITE ABOUT HISTORY ANSWER

25. Students' bulleted arguments should
- explain why one of the philosophies would be effective as the basis for a governing policy
- present the information clearly and logically
- include points that might counter opposing arguments
- include vocabulary words from the chapter

ON **LOCATION** WITH

Christopher
THORNTON

NATIONAL GEOGRAPHIC LEAD PROGRAM OFFICER, RESEARCH, CONSERVATION, AND EXPLORATION

▶ Check out more on myNGconnect

Christopher Thornton directs
excavations at the archaeological
site of Bat in Oman. He has
uncovered information that is
providing new insights into the
social history of the region.

EARLY PASSION

I'd always planned to major in chemistry in college, but in my freshman year, I took a seminar on archaeological chemistry and got hooked! From that moment on, archaeology became my passion and my career.

Today I specialize in late prehistory in Southwest Asia, from the beginning of agriculture to the rise of empires. I love working in this region because, while people's lives have been modernized, their cultures remain fairly traditional. You get a sense of "the old ways" while still enjoying hot showers!

Chris Thornton works near a 4,500-year-old Bronze Age monument in northwestern Oman at the site of Bat.

DIGGING FOR CLUES

Because this region had very limited literacy during the late prehistoric and early historic periods, it needs an archaeologist's eye to investigate and figure out what was going on then. One of the key questions I'm trying to answer is how and why people living in harsh regions like present-day Oman managed to create relatively large settlements 4,000 years ago but, 1,000 or so years later, were content to live in much smaller areas. A clue lies in copper.

Mesopotamian texts from the Bronze Age refer to modern Oman as "Magan," noting that it was then a major producer of copper for the entire region. Most archaeologists believed that the people of Magan were being exploited by traders from Mesopotamia and the Indus Valley. However, for nine years, my team and I have been excavating a site called Bat in northwestern Oman. In the course of our digs, we've discovered not only evidence of copper production, but also indications of the local use of copper in tools, weapons, and jewelery. This suggests that despite the harsh geography of the region, the people of Magan were a very important part of the Bronze Age economic trade networks that led to the rise of cities. This puts a whole new slant on the history of the region.

Now we hope to find clues that will help us understand how the adoption of farming led to early settled villages in Magan, and how these eventually grew into the large centers we find by 2200 B.C. These are the kind of answers we keep digging for.

WHY STUDY HISTORY ?

" History helps us *to understand the similarities* **between apparently different nations, peoples, and cultures. Studying history lets us look back on all that we have accomplished and to consider where we are going now! "** —Christopher Thornton

NATIONAL GEOGRAPHIC

China's Ancient Lifeline

BY IAN JOHNSON

Adapted from "China's Ancient Lifeline,"
by Ian Johnson, in *National Geographic*, May 2013

Barges sailing the Grand Canal have knit China together for 14 centuries. They carried grain, soldiers, and ideas between the economic heartland in the south and the political capitals in the north.

Old Zhu, as everyone calls him, is a modern barge captain. Barge captains live by tough calculations that determine whether they get rich or are ruined. One captain said, "The product owners set the price, the moneylenders set the interest, and the government officials set the fees. All we can do is nod and continue working."

On paper, the Grand Canal runs 1,100 miles between Beijing and the southern city of Hangzhou. But for nearly forty years, part of its course has been too dry for shipping. Today, the waterway's main commercial section is the 325 miles from Jining to the Yangtze.

Emperor Yang of the Sui dynasty built the original canal system. Ancient China's main rivers ran west to east, and he needed a way to move rice from south to north to feed his armies. The emperor forced one million workers to build the canal. It took six years to complete and many workers died, but goods began to flow. The Grand Canal also moved culture. Emperors inspecting the canal took some local customs back to the capital.

Along one section, Old Zhu pointed and said, "That's the old Grand Canal, or what's left of it," pointing to a channel about 15 feet wide curving between a small island and the bank. Today, local governments aim to boost tourism and development by beautifying the canal. But beautification can also destroy. In Yangzhou, the makeover required leveling nearly every canal-side building.

In 2005, a small group of citizens campaigned for the Grand Canal to become a UNESCO World Heritage site. "Every generation wants the next generation to look at its monuments," said Zhu Bingren, who co-wrote the proposal. "But if we wipe out the previous generations' work, what will following generations think of us?"

For more from National Geographic
Check out "Faces of the Divine" on myNGconnect

UNIT INQUIRY: WRITE A CREATION MYTH

In this unit, you learned about the development of early civilizations in Mesopotamia, Egypt, India, and China. Based on your understanding of the text, what crucial roles did geography and natural resources play in the development of early civilizations? What other factors were important to their growth and longevity?

ASSIGNMENT Write a creation myth for one of the civilizations you learned about in this unit. The narrator of your creation myth should be a geographic feature or a natural resource—such as a river—that was vital to the civilization's development. Be prepared to present your creation myth to the class and explain your choice of narrator.

Plan As you write your creation myth, think about the essential roles geography and natural resources played in that civilization's development. To describe the civilization, answer from the narrator's point of view the questions *Who? What? Where? When? Why?* and *How?* Try to incorporate these descriptions in your myth. You might want to use a graphic organizer to help organize your thoughts. ►

Produce Use your notes to produce detailed descriptions of the factors that were important in the development of the civilization you selected. Begin your creation myth with an engaging introduction to capture your audience's attention.

Present Choose a creative way to present your myth to the class. Consider one of these options:

- Create a multimedia presentation using illustrations or photographs of the civilization's geography to produce a sense of place.

- Dress in costume and play the role of an ancient storyteller for an oral presentation of the myth.

- Illustrate cover art featuring the narrator of the creation myth.

Who?	_____
What?	_____
Where?	_____
When?	_____
Why?	_____
How?	_____

RAPID REVIEW
UNIT 2

EARLY CIVILIZATIONS

TOP TEN

1. Farming in the fertile lands of Mesopotamia led to the emergence of city-states such as Sumer and Ur.

2. The fertile farmland along the Nile River enabled the development of ancient Egyptian civilization.

3. Judaism was the first monotheistic religion.

4. Several important religions developed in India, including Hinduism and Buddhism.

5. Ancient China spread innovative forms of government, philosophy, technology, writing, and art via trade routes.

6-10. **NOW IT'S YOUR TURN** Complete the list with five more things to remember about early civilizations.

POSSIBLE RESPONSES

Possible responses for the remaining five things to remember:

6. Rulers in ancient China believed they had divine authority but that the people had the right to rise up and replace them.

7. Mesopotamia's city-states were centers of learning, commerce, religion, and culture.

8. Pharaohs ruled with absolute authority and were believed to be intermediaries with ancient Egyptian gods.

9. Because their homeland was repeatedly conquered, Jews dispersed around the world.

10. Nomadic Aryans who brought their language, religious beliefs, and class system, replaced the Harappan civilization in India's Indus Valley.

UNIT INQUIRY PROJECT RUBRIC

ASSESS

Use the rubric to assess each student's participation and performance.

SCORE	ASSIGNMENT	PRODUCT	PRESENTATION
3 GREAT	• Student thoroughly understands the assignment. • Student engages fully with the project process. • Student works well independently.	• Creation myth is well thought out. • Creation myth reflects the essential roles played by geography and natural resources in the selected civilization's development. • Creation myth contains all of the key elements listed in the assignment.	• Presentation is clear, concise, and logical. • Presentation does a good job of creatively presenting the creation myth. • Presentation engages the audience.
2 GOOD	• Student mostly understands the assignment. • Student engages fairly well with the project process. • Student works fairly independently.	• Creation myth is fairly well thought out. • Creation myth somewhat reflects the essential roles played by geography and natural resources in the selected civilization's development. • Creation myth contains some of the key elements listed in the assignment.	• Presentation is fairly clear, concise, and logical. • Presentation does an adequate job of creatively presenting the creation myth. • Presentation somewhat engages the audience.
1 NEEDS WORK	• Student does not understand the assignment. • Student minimally engages or does not engage with the project process. • Student does not work independently.	• Creation myth is not well thought out. • Creation myth does not reflect the essential roles played by geography and natural resources in the selected civilization's development. • Creation myth contains few or none of the key elements listed in the assignment.	• Presentation is not clear, concise, or logical. • Presentation does not creatively present the creation myth. • Presentation does not engage the audience.

TURN AND TALK

One of the themes in this Why Study History? text is "establishing identity." Write the word *identity* in the center of a Concept Cluster circle and draw lines coming out from the circle. Ask volunteers to add words that relate to and help define the concept of identity. Then place students in small groups and have them discuss what their own personal identity means to them and how they make their identity known to others.

WHY STUDY HISTORY ?

TO LEARN ABOUT THE BUILDING BLOCKS OF CIVILIZATION

In Units 1 and 2, you've learned about the origins of culture and how the building blocks of civilization allowed humans to move from individuals struggling to survive to groups creating a life together. All early civilizations faced the same challenges—and the urge to establish an identity was key to their survival.

The record of human occupation involves the study of stones, bones, and artifacts that go back hundreds of thousands of years. Archaeologists rely on that record to learn about the way we've lived on this earth. Artifacts represent people's identity. When an artifact is looted, or excavated illegally, we lose the context for that artifact—where it was found and who created it. It becomes lost to history. The human record is a non-renewable resource that can never be replaced.

Fred Hiebert
▶ Watch the Why Study History video

PREVIEW UPCOMING UNITS

Have students examine the images at the bottom of the Why Study History? spread, and read the labels on each photograph. Invite volunteers to make observations and predictions about what the upcoming units (3-7) will bring.

WHAT COMES NEXT? PREVIEW UNITS 3–7

3

ACROPOLIS

4

POMPEII

5

MOSAIC, HUQOQ, ISRAEL

GREEK CIVILIZATION

Learn how the Greeks left a legacy in government, art, and architecture that would have an impact on all civilizations.

THE WORLD OF THE ROMANS

See how the Roman developments in government, engineering, and religion continue to affect your life today.

BYZANTINE AND ISLAMIC CIVILIZATIONS

Explore the judicial and artistic contributions of the Byzantine civilizations and the rise of Islamic traditions and empires.

KEY TAKEAWAYS UNITS 1 AND 2

PATTERNS IN HISTORY: SIMILAR DEVELOPMENTS ACROSS LOCATIONS

All centers of civilization develop the same basic structures:

- the beginnings of social organization that lead to governments
- origins of religion as a way to make sense of the world
- the development of crafts that lead to technology
- basic economies that lead to today's economy

GOVERNMENT

Advancements include the rise of dynasties, such as those in Egypt and China; the creation of laws, including Hammurabi's Code; and the building of cities.

MOVEMENT OF PEOPLE AND IDEAS

People adapt to new places, environments, and climates, from the earliest exodus from Africa to migrations in India.

TRADE

Peoples and cultures gradually intermingle, a first step toward global citizenship.

ARTISTIC EXPRESSION

Cave art, including the handprints shown here, become early expressions of identity.

TECHNOLOGY & INNOVATION

Tools, settlements, and the development of agriculture increase chances of survival.

+ GUIDED DISCUSSION

In Units 1 and 2, students learned about the origins of culture and the earliest civilizations. All early civilizations faced the same challenges—and the urge to establish an identity was key to their survival.

1. **Time Out for a Definition!**
   The word—"looting"—is sadly one students will come across frequently as they study world history. What it refers to in a historical context is the stealing of cultural artifacts, typically during a time of unrest. As you teach each unit, ask students to assess and discuss the effects of looting on a civilization or culture. If time permits, invite them to conduct a responsible Internet search for news stories relating to looting in the present-day. Discuss why groups or individuals might be motivated to steal artifacts from a culture—either their own or someone else's.

2. **Technologies and Innovations** Invite students to consider the different types of tools and innovations, including agricultural advances, that increased the chances of survival and shaped the earliest civilizations. Have students choose one of these innovations and create a one-page explanation of it, including an illustration or other visual and one or two paragraphs of explanatory text.

DHOW

AZTEC SKULLS

AFRICAN CIVILIZATIONS

Learn how African peoples successfully adapted to the extreme environments in which they lived to found great trading civilizations.

AMERICAN CIVILIZATIONS

Study the sophisticated cultures that developed in the Americas and their similarities and differences to earlier cultures.

AS YOU READ ON

History is more than just one fact after another. Keep in mind the key takeaways from Units 1 and 2. Be sure to ask "how" and "why," and not just "what." Watch as the human story continues with the civilizations that may be most familiar to you: the Greek, Roman, Byzantine, and Islamic civilizations.

+ REFLECT ON UNITS 3–7

As they read Units 3 through 7 in their textbook, have students complete pages 20-36 in their Field Journal to process the material in these units. Remind students that they will use their Field Journal as they read each Why Study History? section and explore the historical record. They will record their thoughts about what they've read and fit them into the larger picture of world history. They will also use the journal to consider how they fit into that big picture and what it means to be a global citizen.

GREEK
CIVILIZATION

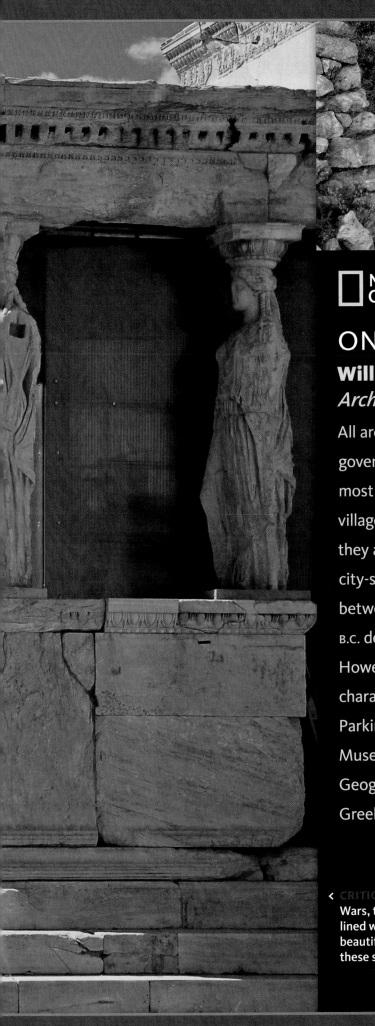

ON **LOCATION** WITH

William Parkinson
Archaeologist

All around the world, before there were governments and formal countries, most people lived in small farming villages. As individual societies grew, they also became more complex. The city-states that emerged in Greece between the ninth and sixth centuries B.C. developed as distinct cultures. However, they were united by certain characteristics, too. I'm William Parkinson, and I work with the Field Museum in Chicago and National Geographic. Welcome to the world of Greek civilization!

< CRITICAL VIEWING Built during the Peloponnesian Wars, the Caryatid Porch of the Erechtheion is lined with statues of maidens. It is one of the most beautiful features of the Acropolis. What function do these statues serve in the porch?

+ POSSIBLE RESPONSE

The statues are holding up the top of that portion of the Erechtheion.

Greek
Civilization

c. 1450 B.C.
Mycenaean civilization thrives on the Greek mainland and takes control of Crete, ending Minoan civilization.
(Lion Gate of Mycenae)

c. 2000 B.C.
Minoan civilization flourishes on the island of Crete.
(a lady of the Minoan court)

1500 B.C.

2000 B.C.

c. 2000 B.C.
EUROPE
Stonehenge is built in England.

1790 B.C.
ASIA
Hammurabi's Code is issued in the Babylonian Empire.

1300 B.C.
ASIA
The kingdom of Israel is established by the Hebrews.

1279 B.C.
AFRICA
Ramses II begins 66-year reign in Egypt.

The
World

1200 B.C.
AMERICAS
Olmec culture rises in the Americas.
(Olmec stone head)

What happened in the world just before democracy was established in Athens?

➕ **POSSIBLE RESPONSE**
The Roman Republic was established just before democracy was established in Athens.

800 B.C.
Greeks begin using an alphabet. Literature is written down, including the *Iliad* and *Odyssey*.

431 B.C.
The Peloponnesian War between Athens and Sparta begins. *(Greek pot with scene from Peloponnesian War)*

334 B.C.
Alexander the Great enters Asia Minor in order to conquer Persia. He dies in 323 B.C., marking the end of the Classic Age. *(gold coin with Alexander's profile)*

1000 B.C.

c. 750 B.C.
Phoenicia develops into wealthy city-states, including the colony of Carthage.

c. 500 B.C.
The first democracy is established in Athens.

1100s B.C.
ASIA
The Zhou dynasty rules China.
(Zhou vessel)

500 B.C.

509 B.C.
EUROPE
The Roman Republic is established.

551 B.C.
Confucius is born in China.

ANCIENT GREECE c. 500 B.C.

The area colored orange on the map may look like a small and fragmented collection of peninsulas and islands, but these areas of land formed one of the most sophisticated cultures and civilizations the world has ever known: the civilization of ancient Greece. Not even its geography stood in Greece's way. Greek traders used the waters of the Mediterranean to secure and control trade routes. Mountains made travel and communication difficult, but independent city-states formed around them. The city-states are labeled with dots on the map. In the city-state called Athens, a form of government developed that would change the world: democracy.

What empire might have challenged Greek power in the region?

+ **POSSIBLE RESPONSE**

The Persian Empire might have challenged Greek power in the region.

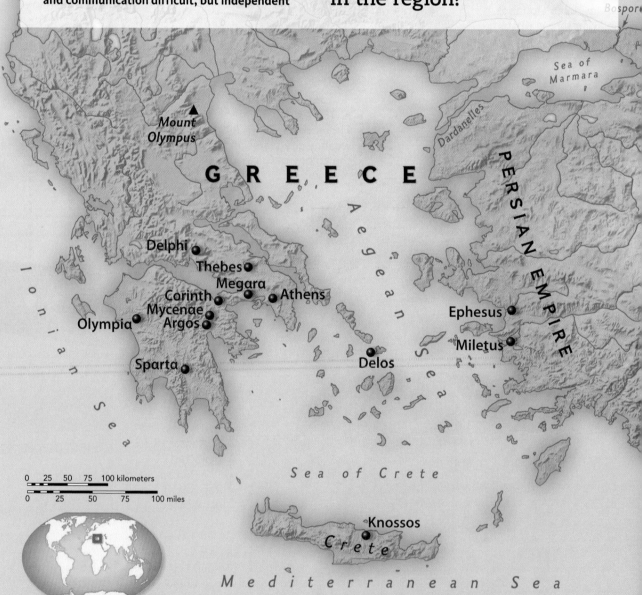

204

THE OLYMPICS

The first Olympic Games took place in 775 B.C. and lasted one day. Today's games include 28 different sports in summer and 7 in winter and last a couple of weeks. The early games had just a few events, not all of which are played today. You can read about the original events in the early Greek Olympics below. Emperor Theodosius banned the games in A.D. 393, calling them a "pagan cult." The first modern Olympics took place in 1896.

 Running   Contestants ran the 200-meter dash, 400-meter dash, and long distance events.

 Jumping   Athletes carried stone weights that they threw at the end of their jump to increase their distance.

 Discus   Athletes tossed a heavy disk made of stone, or later, of heavy metal.

 Boxing   Athletes fought one another using wrapped straps around their hands to strengthen their punches.

 Equestrian   Horse races and chariot-driven races took place in the Hippodrome, an ancient Greek stadium.

 Pentathlon   The pentathlon included five events: long jump, javelin throw, discus throw, foot race, and wrestling.

 Pankration   This event was a blend of wrestling and boxing and had few rules.

UNIT 3 GREEK CIVILIZATION

UNIT RESOURCES

**On Location with National Geographic
Grantee William Parkinson** Intro and
Video

Unit Wrap-Up:
"The Emergence of Cities"
Feature and Video

"Greek Statues Sparkle Once Again"
National Geographic Adapted Article

"Behind the Tomb"
National Geographic Adapted Article
Student eEdition exclusive

Unit 3 Inquiry:
Define Good Citizenship

**Interactive
Map Tool**

**News
& Updates**

Available on myNGconnect

CHAPTER RESOURCES

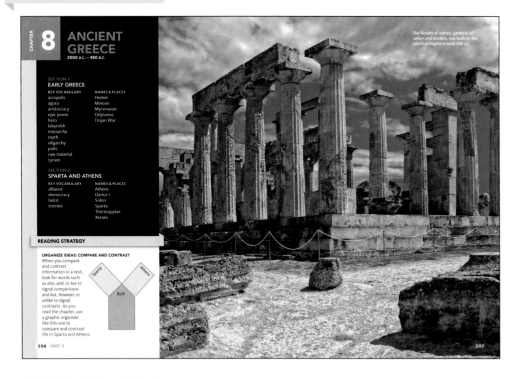

**TEACHER RESOURCES
& ASSESSMENT**

Available on myNGconnect

Social Studies Skills Lessons
  • Reading: Compare and Contrast
  • Writing: Write an Informative Paragraph

Formal Assessment
  • Chapter 8 Tests A (on-level)
    & B (below-level)

A **Chapter 8
Answer Key**

ExamView®
One-time Download

STUDENT BACKPACK *Available on myNGconnect*

• **eEdition** *(English)* • **eEdition** *(Spanish)* • **Handbooks** • **Online Atlas**

For Chapter 8 Spanish resources, visit the Teacher Resource Menu page on myNGconnect.

SECTION 1 RESOURCES

EARLY GREECE

 Reading and Note-Taking

Vocabulary Practice

 Section 1 Quiz

Available on myNGconnect

LESSON 1.1 MYSTERIOUS MINOANS
- Critical Viewing: NG Chapter Gallery
- On Your Feet: Card Responses

LESSON 1.2 MYCENAEAN CIVILIZATION
NG Learning Framework:
Learn More About Greek Origins
- On Your Feet: Chart Relay

LESSON 1.3 THE AGE OF HEROES
Biography
Homer

Available on myNGconnect

NG Learning Framework:
Write an Epic Poem
- On Your Feet: Conduct Talk Show Interviews

LESSON 1.4 CITY-STATES
- Critical Viewing: NG Chapter Gallery
- On Your Feet: Tell Me More

LESSON 1.5 COLONIZATION AND TRADE
NG Learning Framework:
Advertise a New Colony
- On Your Feet: Create Trade Networks

SECTION 2 RESOURCES

SPARTA AND ATHENS

 Reading and Note-Taking

 Vocabulary Practice

 Section 2 Quiz

Available on myNGconnect

LESSON 2.1 SPARTA'S MILITARY SOCIETY
NG Learning Framework:
Create a Government
- On Your Feet: In This Corner

LESSON 2.2 ATHENS'S DEMOCRATIC SOCIETY
 Active History: Interactive
Whiteboard Activity
Analyze Primary Sources: Democracy

 Active History
Analyze Primary Sources: Democracy

Available on myNGconnect

- On Your Feet: Create a Concept Web

LESSON 2.3 UNITING AGAINST THE PERSIANS
NG Learning Framework:
Learn More About Triremes
- On Your Feet: Inside-Outside Circle

MOMENTS IN HISTORY
LESSON 2.4 THE BATTLE OF THERMOPYLAE
- Critical Viewing: NG Chapter Gallery
- On Your Feet: I See, I Read, And So

CHAPTER 8 REVIEW

STRATEGY ❶

Set a Purpose for Reading

Before students read a lesson, help them set a purpose for reading by turning the Main Idea statement into a question. Tell students to answer the question in writing after they read. Below are sample questions for Section 1.

1.1 Who established the earliest civilization in ancient Greece?

1.2 Why did the Mycenaeans copy and then conquer the Minoans?

1.3 What strong tradition did the ancient Greeks create?

1.4 How did city-states establish different ways of governing?

1.5 How did the ancient Greeks spread their culture throughout the region?

Use with All Lessons

STRATEGY ❷

Make Predictions About Content

Before students read the lessons listed below, have them examine the headings and visuals in each one and write their prediction on what the lesson will be about. After students read the lessons, have them check to see whether their predictions were accurate.

Use with Lessons 2.1–2.4 *Pair students whose predictions were inaccurate with students who correctly predicted the content of the lessons and have them compare the conclusions they drew from viewing the subheadings and visuals in each one.*

STRATEGY ❸

Make a "Top Five Facts" List

Assign a lesson to be read. After reading, have students write in their own words five important facts that they have learned. Let them meet with a partner to compare lists and consolidate the two lists into one final list. Call on students to offer facts from their lists.

Use with All Lessons

Press **mt** *in the Student eEdition for modified text.*

STRATEGY ❶

Modify Vocabulary Lists

Using your standards as a guide, limit the number of vocabulary words that students will be required to master. As they read, have students create a vocabulary card for each word in the modified list. Students may create a picture to illustrate each word or write definitions, synonyms, or examples. Encourage students to refer to their vocabulary cards often as they read.

Use with All Lessons *You may want to focus on the content-specific words that may be the most unfamiliar with students, including acropolis, agora, polis, helot, and trireme, and possibly others.*

STRATEGY ❷

Build a Time Line

Select key events from Lessons 1.1, 1.2, 2.2, and 2.3. Then have students use the events to start a time line on the board. Students will add to the time line as they read the chapter.

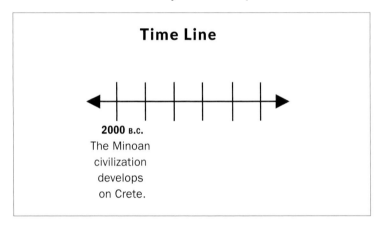

Time Line

2000 B.C.
The Minoan civilization develops on Crete.

Use with All Lessons *A key event from each lesson could be included on the time line. For example, in Lesson 1.4, students might add 750 B.C. Greek city-states emerge. Explain that some dates may carry multiple events.*

STRATEGY ❶

Activate Prior Knowledge

Display the words below in a random "splash" arrangement and ask students to talk about what the words bring to mind. Then have them work in pairs and write sentences using two of the words in each sentence.

Use with Lessons 1.1–1.5 *Challenge students to create their own word splash for words they encounter in Lessons 2.1–2.4.*

STRATEGY ❷
Provide Sentence Frames

Have pairs of students read the lessons and complete the sentences below.

1.1 The Minoans were expert _____.

1.2 The _____ conquered the Minoans.

1.3 The Odyssey is an _____ _____.

1.4 The highest point in a Greek city was called the _____.

1.5 The ancient Greeks established _____ all over the Mediterranean region.

Use with All Lessons *For Lessons 2.1–2.4, have students work in pairs to write their own sentence frames for each lesson. Pairs can then trade sentence frames with another pair and complete them together.*

STRATEGY ❸
Set Up a Word Wall

Work with students to identify three words from each section to display in a grouping on a Word Wall. It might be useful to choose words that students are likely to encounter in other chapters, such as *city-state or democracy*. Keep the words displayed throughout the lessons and discuss each one as it comes up during reading. Have volunteers add words, phrases, and examples to each word to develop understanding.

Use with All Lessons

STRATEGY ❶
Act Out a Scene

Have students act out the Trojan Horse scene from the *Odyssey*. They should provide costumes and use classroom furniture as a set. After the performance, discuss the points of view of the primary characters in the scene—Odysseus, the Greeks, the Trojans, and Helen. Encourage students to read the relevant passages from the epic poem to create their dialogue and stage directions. Have the group appoint a Director and a Stage Manager. Reinforce the importance of leadership and teamwork as students rehearse their scene.

Use with Lesson 1.3

STRATEGY ❷
Write a Historic Dialogue

Tell students to use the fact they have learned to write a dialogue that might have taken place between Xerxes, emperor of Persia, and King Leonidas of Sparta. Encourage students to convey Xerxes' outrage at the rebelling Greeks and Leonidas' commanding direction as he marched into battle. Students may want to augment their dialogues with additional research. Remind them to use academic sources in their research.

Use with Lessons 2.3 and 2.4

STRATEGY ❶
Use the "Persia" Approach

Have students write an essay explaining the significance of the ancient Greeks from 2000 B.C. to 480 B.C. Copy the following mnemonic on the board and tell students to use the "Persia" strategy:

Political

Economic

Religious

Social

Intellectual

Artistic

Use with All Lessons *Offer bonus points to those students who integrate the name of this exercise into their essays.*

ANCIENT GREECE

2000 B.C. – 480 B.C.

SECTION 1
EARLY GREECE

KEY VOCABULARY	NAMES & PLACES
acropolis	Homer
agora	Minoan
aristocracy	Mycenaean
epic poem	Odysseus
hero	Trojan War
labyrinth	
monarchy	
myth	
oligarchy	
polis	
raw material	
tyrant	

SECTION 2
SPARTA AND ATHENS

KEY VOCABULARY	NAMES & PLACES
alliance	Athens
democracy	Darius I
helot	Solon
trireme	Sparta
	Thermopylae
	Xerxes

READING STRATEGY

ORGANIZE IDEAS: COMPARE AND CONTRAST
When you compare and contrast information in a text, look for words such as *also, and,* or *too* to signal comparisons and *but, however,* or *unlike* to signal contrasts. As you read the chapter, use a graphic organizer like this one to compare and contrast life in Sparta and Athens.

The Temple of Aphaia, goddess of sailors and hunters, was built on the island of Aegina around 500 B.C.

TEACHER BACKGROUND

INTRODUCE THE PHOTOGRAPH

Have students study the photograph of the Temple of Aphaia. Explain that in the study of ancient Greece, they will encounter a number of temples. **ASK:** What is a temple? *(A temple is a building used for worship.)* What does the presence of temples tell us about a civilization? *(Temples are evidence of the practice of religious beliefs.)*

SHARE BACKGROUND

The Temple of Aphaia shown in the photograph was built on the Greek island of Aegina around 500 B.C. Aphaia was a local goddess whose worship eventually became blended with that of the more recognizable Athena, the Greek goddess of wisdom and war. The temple is an example of Doric architecture and a precursor to the more famous Parthenon of Athens.

DIGITAL RESOURCES myNGconnect.com

TEACHER RESOURCES & ASSESSMENT

 Social Studies Skills Lessons
- Reading: Compare and Contrast
- Writing: Write an Informative Paragraph

 Formal Assessment
Chapter 8 Tests A (on-level) & B (below-level)

ExamView®
One-time Download

 Chapter 8 Answer Key

STUDENT BACKPACK

- **eEdition** *(English)*
- **eEdition** *(Spanish)*
- **Handbooks**
- **Online Atlas**

For Chapter 8 Spanish resources, visit the Teacher Resource Menu page.

INTRODUCE THE ESSENTIAL QUESTION

HOW DID A CULTURED AND INFLUENTIAL CIVILIZATION ARISE IN GREECE?

Four Corner Activity: Civilization Traits This activity introduces students to the culture and influence of ancient Greek civilization. Tell students that in this chapter, they will learn about the formation of early Greece, which led to the development of a civilization that continues to influence the world today. Remind students that civilizations have particular traits in common. **ASK:** What are some common traits among civilizations? Historians and archaeologists study these traits to learn about a civilization as a whole. Designate a section of the room to each of the traits below and have students move to the area that interests them most. Once students are organized into their groups, have them discuss the questions below. Then call on volunteers from each group to summarize their thoughts for the class.

1. **Government** What is government? Why is it important? What kind of government does the United States have?

2. **Art** What can we learn about a culture or civilization through its art? What kinds of art do you enjoy?

3. **Trade** What is trade? What kinds of goods are traded? What do you use to trade for goods?

4. **Cities** Do you like to visit cities? What are some important cities in the world? What can you find in cities?

`0:15` minutes

INTRODUCE THE READING STRATEGY

ORGANIZE IDEAS: COMPARE AND CONTRAST

Remind students when they compare and contrast information in a text, they should look for words such as *also, and,* or *too* to signal comparisons and *but, however,* or *unlike* to signal contrasts. Model finding signal words in the introductory paragraph in Lesson 2.1. Show students how to fill out a Y-Notes Chart.

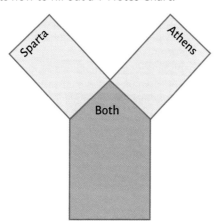

INTRODUCE CHAPTER VOCABULARY

KNOWLEDGE RATING

Have students complete a Knowledge-Rating Chart for Key Vocabulary words. Have students list words and fill out the chart. Then have pairs share the definitions they know. Work together as a class to complete the chart.

KEY VOCAB	KNOW IT	NOT SURE	DON'T KNOW	DEFINITION
acropolis				
agora				
aristocracy				
epic poem				

KEY DATES	
2000 B.C.	Minoan civilization emerges
1450 B.C.	Mycenaeans conquer Minoans
750 B.C.	Greek bard Homer creates epic poems
750 B.C.	Greek city-states form
508 B.C.	Athenians establish democracy
480 B.C.	Battle of Thermopylae
479 B.C.	Greeks defeat Persians

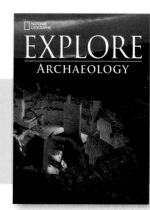

For more about how archaeologists study other ancient civilizations, see *EXPLORE ARCHAEOLOGY.*

1.1

Mysterious
Minoans

You step forward and grasp the horns of the huge panting bull. Its head twitches; your muscles tighten in anticipation. Blocking out the cheers of the crowd, you spring over the bull's back and land behind the enormous animal. In ancient Crete such deadly games as bull-leaping are your way of worship.

MAIN IDEA

The Minoans established the earliest civilization in ancient Greece.

ANCIENT DISASTER

Around 1600 B.C., a volcano called Thira (THIH-ruh) erupted on an island 70 miles north of Crete. The eruption destroyed most of the island and caused death and destruction across the Mediterranean.

Scholars disagree about whether this eruption caused the decline of Minoan civilization, but this is one possibility.

MINOAN CIVILIZATION

Historians trace the origins of Greek civilization to Crete, a mountainous island about 150 miles off the coast of mainland Greece. Neolithic farmers settled there around 7000 B.C. and agriculture flourished. By 2000 B.C., a sophisticated **Minoan** (mih-NOH-uhn) civilization had emerged, centered on cities governed from magnificent royal palaces.

Though the Minoans left behind written records, historians cannot read their language. Their knowledge of Minoan civilization is pieced together through archaeology and the writings of ancient Greek historians. There are also many myths about this civilization. **Myths** are very old stories told to explain events or to justify beliefs and actions. The word *Minoan* comes from a mythical Cretan king named Minos (MY-nuhs). According to the myth, Minos built a **labyrinth** (LAB-uh-rinth), or maze, beneath his palace. A monstrous Minotaur (MIHN-uh-tawr)—half man, half bull—lived in this labyrinth and was offered regular sacrifices of unlucky humans. Unlikely? Perhaps, but archaeological evidence confirms that a powerful Minoan king built a labyrinth-like palace, and Minoans did in fact worship bulls and perform sacrifices.

CITIES AND CULTURE

The Minoans grew wealthy through trade across the Mediterranean. One of the Minoans' strengths was that they were expert sailors. Their well-built ships carried olive oil, wine, cloth, pottery, and metalwork to Greece, Egypt, Cyprus, and Spain. The Minoans returned from trading voyages with important **raw materials**, or substances from which other products are made, such as tin, gold, pearls, and ivory. Minoans spread their culture throughout Greece and along the coasts of the Aegean (ee-JEE-uhn) Sea. Their strong navy controlled the seas, making the Minoans feel so safe they did not build city walls.

The great palace at Knossos (NAW-suhss) dominated Crete. The size and complexity of the palace may have encouraged some people to believe it was Minos's labyrinth. Home to almost 20,000 people, Knossos was more like a city than a palace. It was the center of Minoan culture, religion, and economy. The palace included a central courtyard for ceremonies, hundreds of rooms,

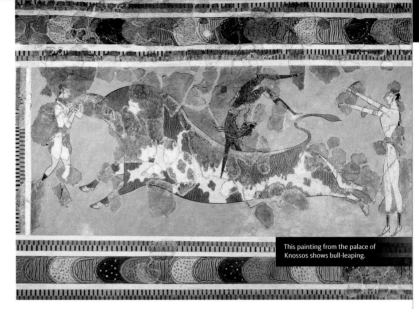

This painting from the palace of Knossos shows bull-leaping.

and even advanced plumbing. It also provided workshops for Minoan artisans and storerooms for surplus crops, such as grains. Minoans worked to support the palace and enjoyed a relatively prosperous life.

Minoan religion was polytheistic, which means that people believed in many gods and goddesses. Lifelike Minoan wall paintings suggest forms of worship involving bull-leaping, boxing, wrestling, and dancing as well as sacrifices to pacify the gods.

Mysteries surround the end of the Minoans. Around 1500 B.C., Minoan civilization declined sharply and its palaces fell into ruins. Possible causes for their collapse include natural disasters such as earthquakes, tidal waves, or volcanic eruptions. Some historians think all three factors—as well as an invasion by people from mainland Greece—contributed to the Minoans' decline. By 1450 B.C., a new civilization would overtake the Minoans.

REVIEW & ASSESS

1. **READING CHECK** What were some of the traits of the earliest civilization in ancient Greece?

2. **DRAW CONCLUSIONS** What does the great palace at Knossos reveal about the Minoan civilization?

3. **ANALYZE CAUSE AND EFFECT** How did trade help the Minoans develop wealth?

PLAN

OBJECTIVE

Identify the origins of ancient Greek civilization.

CRITICAL THINKING SKILLS FOR LESSON 1.1

- Identify Main Ideas and Details
- Monitor Comprehension
- Draw Conclusions
- Analyze Cause and Effect
- Describe
- Evaluate
- Analyze Visuals

ESSENTIAL QUESTION

How did a cultured and influential civilization arise in Greece?

Historians and archaeologists trace the origins of different civilizations. Lesson 1.1 discusses the earliest civilization in ancient Greece, the Minoans.

BACKGROUND FOR THE TEACHER

A British archaeologist named Sir Arthur Evans first excavated the ruins of Knossos at the turn of the 20th century. Evans had earlier theorized that Mycenaean civilization originated on the island of Crete. He began a formal archaeological dig at Knossos, revealing an ancient cultural capital. Because he believed King Minos once ruled the palace at Knossos, he named this civilization *Minoan*. Evans tried to decipher the hieroglyphic-like symbols and the writing system, called Linear A, used by the Minoans, but he was unsuccessful. To date, later archaeologists and historians have not been able to, either.

DIGITAL RESOURCES myNGconnect.com

TEACHER RESOURCES & ASSESSMENT

 Reading and Note-Taking

 Vocabulary Practice

 Section 1 Quiz

STUDENT RESOURCES

 NG Chapter Gallery

INTRODUCE & ENGAGE

ACTIVATE PRIOR KNOWLEDGE

Direct students' attention to a map of the present-day map of the Mediterranean region. Ask a volunteer to point out Greece, another to point out Crete, and another to identify the Mediterranean Sea and the Aegean Sea. **ASK:** What types of geographic features can you identify in Greece? *(islands, mountains, coastlines, cities)* Where is Crete in relation to the mainland? *(It is located in the Mediterranean off the southern coast of the mainland of Greece.)* What kind of skills might ancient people who lived in this part of the Mediterranean have to have had to thrive? *(Because of their location on the Mediterranean Sea, they would have had to be good sailors and good fishermen.)* **0:05** minutes

TEACH

GUIDED DISCUSSION

1. **Describe** Who was King Minos and why is he important in understanding Minoan civilization? *(Minos was a mythological king of Crete. According to myth, he built a labyrinth under a great palace where he kept a Minotaur. His name is also the base of the word Minoan.)*

2. **Evaluate** What factors do you think led to the decline of Minoan civilization, natural disasters or invasions? Support your answer with evidence from the text. *(Minoan civilization was centered on Crete, an island in the Mediterranean, which might make it vulnerable to natural disasters such as volcanic eruptions, earthquakes, and tidal waves. Or, invasions by outside groups may have led to collapse. The Minoans did not build walls around their city and may have not expected outsiders could overpower their navy.)*

ANALYZE VISUALS

Have students examine the painting from the palace of Knossos. Tell the class that analyzing details about a piece of art can help us understand a past culture. Ask students to describe the details they see in the painting of bull-leaping. Have a volunteer record students' observations on the board. Then, as a class, create a description of Minoans based on details students mention. Compare that description to the text and point out similarities or discrepancies between them. **0:10** minutes

ACTIVE OPTIONS

Critical Viewing: NG Chapter Gallery Have students explore the NG Chapter Gallery and choose two of the items to compare and contrast, either in written form or verbally with a partner. Ask questions that will inspire this process, such as: How are these images alike? How are they different? Why did you select these two items? How do they relate in history? **0:10** minutes

On Your Feet: Card Responses Have half the class create ten true-false questions based on information in the lesson. Ask the other half to create answer cards, with "True" written on one side and "False" on the other. As each question is read aloud, students in the second group should display the correct answer to the question. **0:20** minutes

DIFFERENTIATE

ENGLISH LANGUAGE LEARNERS

Summarize This lesson has two sections. Pair students and assign each pair a section of the text to read together. Encourage students to use a graphic organizer to make notes about their part of the lesson, including questions they have about vocabulary or idioms. After answering their questions, have each pair write a one- to two-sentence summary.

PRE-AP

Explore Mythology Have students conduct research on the myth of the labyrinth of Minos and the Minotaur. Direct them to investigate the basic questions of *who, what, where,* and *when,* but also to explore *why* bulls play such a prominent role in the myths of this civilization. Encourage students to research and integrate visuals, such as the mosaic in the lesson, in a short oral presentation for the class.

Press (**mt**) *in the Student eEdition for modified text.*

See the Chapter Planner for more strategies for differentiation.

REVIEW & ASSESS

ANSWERS

1. The Minoans established city-states, built great palaces, engaged in agriculture and extensive trade, and practiced religion.

2. The great palace at Knossos reveals a highly skilled and wealthy civilization that enjoyed cultural advancements of religion, architecture, and art, as well as a stable, central government and a prosperous economy.

3. Trade helped the Minoans develop wealth because they returned from voyages with raw materials with which they produced goods.

1.2 Mycenaean Civilization

The fascinating thing about history is often what we *don't* know.

Though we know the Mycenaeans overtook the Minoans, we don't know for sure what caused their own violent end. Along with the Minoans, the Mycenaeans helped lay the foundation of Greek civilization.

MAIN IDEA

After copying Minoan culture, the Mycenaeans conquered the Minoan people.

CONQUERORS

Around 2000 B.C., a new group of people from farther east settled in mainland Greece. They became known as **Mycenaeans** (my-SEE-nee-uhnz) based on the name of their main city, Mycenae (my-SEE-nee). The early Mycenaeans established villages throughout Greece, picked up influences from Minoan culture which had spread there, and spoke an early version of the Greek language.

After invading Crete in 1500 B.C, the Mycenaeans adopted Minoan culture. The Mycenaeans copied Minoan art, architecture, religion, writing, trade, metalworking, and shipbuilding. Elements of Minoan and Myceanaen culture became part of the foundation of Greek civilization.

The Mycenaeans had an aggressive streak, though, and they eventually turned against the Minoans. The Mycenaeans seized and conquered lands across the eastern Mediterranean and Greece. Around 1450 B.C. they conquered the Minoans, taking their treasure, land, people, and palaces.

RICH KINGS

The city of Mycenae was the center of Mycenaean civilization. Built high on a hill, the city was surrounded by thick walls that protected houses, storerooms, and a grand palace. The Mycenaeans protected Mycenae and other cities with great stone walls—so huge that later Greeks believed they were built by mythical giants called Cyclopes (SY-klohps). A network of good roads connected Mycenae to other important cities.

While most Mycenaean farmers lived in simple mud-brick houses in the countryside, important officials, artisans, and traders lived in three-story stone houses in cities. Warriors had it even better. Mycenaean kings gave elite warriors fine houses and lands to rule. Everyone else worked to support the warriors.

Extensive trade and wars made Mycenaean kings rich. The fierce Mycenaean military, wearing metal armor and driving fast-moving chariots, raided and conquered surrounding people. Yet at the height of its power, around 1200 B.C., the Mycenaean civilization came to a violent end. Suddenly most Mycenaean cities and towns were mysteriously destroyed.

Historians have several theories about why Mycenaean civilization declined. One theory suggests that natural disasters caused shortages that turned cities against one another or led to peasant uprisings. Another theory suggests that Mycenaean cities were invaded by the mysterious Sea Peoples. The Sea Peoples were seaborne and land raiders who had also attacked the ancient Egyptians and fought the Hittites of Mesopotamia.

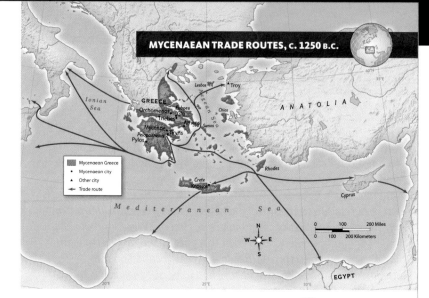

MYCENAEAN TRADE ROUTES, C. 1250 B.C.

Whatever the cause of the collapse, the end of Mycenaean civilization meant that ancient Greece entered a period of decline that lasted until about 950 B.C. The people abandoned cities, trade halted, and the economy floundered. During this time, the ancient Greeks also stopped keeping written records.

Without written records, historians know little about this 400-year period of Greek history. Luckily, though, the Greeks would learn to write again and record some of the greatest stories ever told.

MASK OF AGAMEMNON
This gold funeral mask discovered at Mycenae in 1876 is called the Mask of Agamemnon, named after the mythical Greek king. The mask most likely covered the face of a Mycenaean leader, though archaeologists are unsure which leader it was.

REVIEW & ASSESS

1. **READING CHECK** How did the Mycenaeans become so powerful?

2. **COMPARE AND CONTRAST** In what ways were the Mycenaeans similar to and different from the Minoans?

3. **INTERPRET MAPS** Describe the route Mycenaean traders used to reach Egypt from Tiryns.

PLAN

OBJECTIVE

Determine the influence of the Mycenaeans in ancient Greek civilization.

CRITICAL THINKING SKILLS FOR LESSON 1.2

- Identify Main Ideas and Details
- Monitor Comprehension
- Compare and Contrast
- Interpret Maps
- Explain
- Make Inferences

ESSENTIAL QUESTION

How did a cultured and influential civilization arise in Greece?

Civilizations develop by adopting practices, culture, and from other civilizations. Lesson 1.2 explores the Mycenaeans, who adopted Minoan culture and then conquered them.

BACKGROUND FOR THE TEACHER

As the photo of the Mask of Agamemnon shows, the Mycenaeans were wonderful metalworkers. They shaped gold, silver, and bronze into fine gold jewelry, intricate drinking cups and ritual vessels, and strong armor and weapons, such as daggers made of bronze. They also pounded sheets of gold into thin and detailed funeral masks like the one in Lesson 1.2. Metalworkers used metals from Greek rivers and mines as well as from trade with surrounding civilizations.

DIGITAL RESOURCES myNGconnect.com

TEACHER RESOURCES & ASSESSMENT

 Reading and Note-Taking   **Vocabulary Practice**   **Section 1 Quiz**

STUDENT RESOURCES

 NG Chapter Gallery

INTRODUCE & ENGAGE

TEAM UP

Tell students to imagine they will be building a powerful civilization in a prime location in a region with seas, extensive and accessible coastlines, and inhabited by many different cultures. Have them brainstorm in groups. Tell them to use an Idea Web to list what they would build and the features they want their civilization to have. Tell students that the Mycenaeans had created a powerful maritime civilization in the Mediterranean region by around 1450 B.C. **0:05** minutes

TEACH

GUIDED DISCUSSION

1. **Explain** Why might the Mycenaeans have been interested in conquering Crete? *(As an island in the Mediterranean, Crete's location would have been strategic and advantageous for Mycenaeans to control.)*

2. **Make Inferences** In what ways can trade and warfare make a civilization strong? *(Trade and warfare can make civilizations strong by building wealth through the exchange of goods and through conquering people and taking their treasures and land.)*

INTERPRET MAPS

Help students interpret the map of Mycenaean trade routes. **ASK:** Based on the map and information in the text, what can you infer about the location of Mycenae, the main city of Mycenaeans? *(Mycenae was located slightly inland and on a high hill. This location would keep the city safe from invaders. Also, the city was protected with high walls.)* **ASK:** If you lived in Mycenae and wanted to trade with someone in Troy, how would you get there? *(You could leave from the port of Tiryns, sail north and east between various islands, and cross the Aegean Sea to land on the Anatolian coast.)* **0:10** minutes

ACTIVE OPTIONS

NG Learning Framework: Learn More About Greek Origins

ATTITUDE: **Curiosity**
SKILL: **Collaboration**

Have pairs or small groups of students review Lessons 1.1 and 1.2. Ask them to consider a group or event from those lessons that they are still curious about. Instruct them to collaborate in writing five questions about their group or event that they would like to answer. If time allows, encourage students to pursue answers to their questions through research at the library or online. **0:15** minutes

On Your Feet: Chart Relay Tape large pieces of paper to the wall in different locations of the classroom. Have students work in teams of four. Provide each team with a bold marker. Tell them to make four columns on their paper: City, Trade, War, and Invasions. Allow teams time to come up with three facts about each topic. Individual team members are each responsible for one topic. Then, on your signal, have teams write their facts on the charts. The first team that finishes wins. **0:25** minutes

DIFFERENTIATE

STRIVING READERS

Complete Sentence Starters Provide these sentence starters for students to complete after reading. You may also have students preview to set a purpose for reading.

- The Mycenaeans conquered the _____ in 1450 B.C.

- The city of _____ was the center of Mycenaean civilization.

- Later Greeks believed that _____ had built the great stone walls around Mycenaean cities.

- The Mycenaean civilization came to a violent end around _____ B.C.

Press **mt** *in the Student eEdition for modified text.*

See the Chapter Planner for more strategies for differentiation.

REVIEW & ASSESS

ANSWERS

1. The Mycenaeans settled in mainland Greece, copied Minoan culture, conquered the Minoans and surrounding cultures, and grew wealthy through trade and wars.

2. The Minoan and Mycenaean cultures were similar in many ways because after the Mycenaeans settled in mainland Greece, they adopted and copied virtually every aspect of Minoan culture, including art, architecture, government, religion, writing, shipbuilding, and trade. The Mycenaeans were different from the Minoans in that they seemed to be more focused on conquering other people.

3. Mycenaean traders set sail from Tiryns on the shores of the Aegean Sea and then sailed southeast across the Mediterranean Sea to Egypt.

1.3

The Age of Heroes

A good story needs an exciting plot, a little suspense, fascinating characters, and an exotic location. The ancient Greeks knew this and invented stories filled with adventure, romance, revenge, and intense action. This was the age of heroes.

MAIN IDEA

The ancient Greeks created a strong storytelling tradition.

HOMER'S EPIC POEMS

The ancient Greeks believed in many gods, goddesses, monsters, and heroes. Stories about these characters were told and retold. About 750 B.C., a man named **Homer** emerged. Historians do not know much about Homer, but tradition says he was a blind bard who lived in ancient Greece. A bard is a poet who tells stories as a rhythmic chant accompanied by music.

Homer composed two of the world's greatest stories, the *Iliad* and the *Odyssey*. Both are **epic poems**, or long poetic stories. Every epic poem has a **hero**, or a character who faces a challenge that demands courage, strength, and intelligence. Homer's epic poems dramatized how gods and goddesses influenced the lives of humans. They also helped establish the characteristics of Greek gods and goddesses.

The *Iliad* and the *Odyssey* followed a strong Greek storytelling tradition that mixed history, religion, and fantasy. These epic poems also united the Greeks through pride in their shared past and set the stage for future Western literature.

HEROIC DEEDS

The setting for Homer's epic poems was the **Trojan War**, which historians believe was fought between the Greeks and the Anatolian city of Troy around 1200 B.C. The *Iliad* tells of events in the final weeks of the war. According to the story, the Trojan War started because Paris, the prince of Troy, ran away with Helen, the wife of Menelaus (mehn-uh-LAY-uhs), the king of Sparta.

The *Odyssey* tells the story of the Greek hero **Odysseus** (oh-DIH-see-uhs). After ten years of fighting the Trojan War, Odysseus suggests that the Greeks play a trick on the Trojans. The Greeks leave a huge wooden horse as a gift and pretend to sail away from Troy. The Trojans drag the horse into the city, not knowing that Odysseus and his men hiding inside. That night, Odysseus and his men sneak out of the horse. They open the city gates to Greek soldiers waiting outside. The Greeks take the city and recover Helen.

The *Odyssey* also tells the story of Odysseus's journey home after the war. He has many adventures involving creatures such as a one-eyed Cyclops and the Sirens—women whose singing lures sailors to crash their ships onto rocks.

FACT OR FICTION?

For thousands of years Troy and the Trojan War were considered nothing more than myths. However, Homer's stories inspired archaeologists to explore Greece. In the 1820s, they discovered the remains of a great city in Turkey. It matched Homer's description of Troy and had been violently destroyed about the same time, so Homer's war may have actually happened.

Critical Viewing The *Odyssey* captured artists' imaginations long after Homer lived. What part of the action does this painting depict?

➕ POSSIBLE RESPONSE

The painting depicts the point at which the Trojans are pulling the Trojan Horse into the city gates.

The Trojan Horse, Henri Motte, painted 1874

REVIEW & ASSESS

1. **READING CHECK** What is the setting for Homer's epic poems, the *Iliad* and the *Odyssey*?

2. **IDENTIFY MAIN IDEAS AND DETAILS** In Greek epic poems, why do heroes take action and what traits do they have?

3. **FORM AND SUPPORT OPINIONS** What details about the Trojan War do you think are fact and which are fiction?

213

PLAN

OBJECTIVE

Understand the role of the epic hero in ancient Greek culture.

CRITICAL THINKING SKILLS FOR LESSON 1.3

- Identify Main Ideas and Details
- Monitor Comprehension
- Form and Support Opinions
- Compare and Contrast
- Make Inferences
- Make Connections

ESSENTIAL QUESTION

How did a cultured and influential civilization arise in Greece?

Myths and storytelling are key elements of cultural development in a civilization. Lesson 1.3 discusses the importance of the epic poem and Homer in ancient Greek culture.

BACKGROUND FOR THE TEACHER

Though historians attribute the *Iliad* and *Odyssey* to Homer, he did not write his epic poems down. Instead, he composed and told or "sang" his epics. In fact, Homer's word for poet—*aoidos*—means "singer." Homer's style differed from other poetic singers because his stories took longer to tell than simply a performance at a festival, feast, or other gathering. Homer's poems were longer and more expansive. Perhaps that characteristic is why they have endured through the centuries.

TEACHER RESOURCES & ASSESSMENT

 Reading and Note-Taking   **Vocabulary Practice**   **Section 1 Quiz**

STUDENT RESOURCES

 Biography

INTRODUCE & ENGAGE

PREVIEW USING VISUALS

Call students' attention to the art in the lesson. Ask students to come up with one or two words that describe what they see in the painting. Write their responses on the board. Then ask for a volunteer to read the Critical Viewing caption and question on the page. Tell students that they will be able to answer the question after they read. `0:05` minutes

TEACH

GUIDED DISCUSSION

1. **Compare and Contrast** What are some similarities and differences between oral and written stories? *(Stories told orally have to be passed down directly from one person to another. Written stories can be read at any time. Oral stories may change in details as they move through a culture. Written stories might tend to stay mostly the same.)*

2. **Make Inferences** Why might war be a good topic for an epic poem? *(A topic of war would provide an author like Homer many opportunities to describe actions of a hero up against difficult challenges. It would also be a topic an audience would recognize as part of their own experience.)*

MAKE CONNECTIONS

Explain to students that Homer's idea of the Trojan Horse has fascinated people for centuries. Today, in the world of modern computing and connectivity, a "Trojan horse virus" refers to malware, or destructive software, which once downloaded onto a computer or computer system, can do great damage. Trojan horse viruses can attack millions of computers at the same time and can completely disable entire systems. The virus is disguised as something helpful, entertaining, or otherwise innocent, much like the Greeks' gift to the Trojans. However, once opened, the virus attacks computer hardware and can destroy its components. `0:10` minutes

ACTIVE OPTIONS

NG Learning Framework: Write an Epic Poem

ATTITUDE: **Curiosity**
SKILLS: **Communication, Problem-Solving**

Invite students to think of an adventure they have experienced that could be the subject of a modern epic poem. Have them sketch out an outline of the events, heroes and heroines, and problems that they encountered in their adventures. Encourage students to tell their stories with a partner or in small groups. `0:25` minutes

On Your Feet: Conduct Talk Show Interviews Have teams of three students conduct talk show interviews on Homer and epic poems. Student 1, the interviewer, develops a question to ask the show's "guest." Student 2, an "expert" on Homer and epic poems, answers the question, citing information from Lesson 1.3. Student 3, a member of the studio audience, asks a spin-off question that the whole class can answer. Have participants ask and answer several questions to ensure a solid review of the topic. `0:15` minutes

DIFFERENTIATE

INCLUSION

Analyze Visuals Provide concrete questions to help students describe the painting of the Trojan Horse. **ASK:** How big is the Trojan Horse compared to a real horse? What are the warriors in the painting doing? Does this painting look like it represents the Trojan Horse story before or after the Greek warriors inside escape and fight the Trojans? Encourage students to point to details that they don't understand and help them frame questions about these details.

GIFTED & TALENTED

Storyboard an Epic Poem Have artistically inclined students storyboard an epic poem of their own creation. Students might base their storyboards on a current news story, a tall tale, or even on an event in their own community or school. Encourage students to identify a hero or heroine, a challenge, and a set of gods, goddesses, or otherworldly beings with which the hero or heroine must interact. Then tell the students to create a storyboard of their epics. Have them include sketches of characters and a clear direction for the storyline.

Press **mt** *in the Student eEdition for modified text.*

See the Chapter Planner for more strategies for differentiation.

REVIEW & ASSESS

ANSWERS

1. The *Iliad* and the *Odyssey* are set during the Trojan War.

2. Heroes in Greek epic poems are characters who take action to meet challenges relying on the traits of extraordinary courage, strength, and intelligence.

3. Details about the Trojan War that may be factual are when and where it was fought. The idea that a horse filled with men was key to the victory of the Greeks is fiction. Students should support their answers with evidence from the text.

1.4 City-States

Though ancient Greek cities seemed to lie quiet for 400 years, around 800 B.C. they began to thrive again. Eventually they would extend their influence across the Mediterranean.

MAIN IDEA

Ancient Greek city-states established different ways of governing as they gained power.

Critical Viewing The ruins of a temple called the Parthenon still stand atop the Acropolis in Athens. What details in this photo convey the advantages of the Acropolis's location?

+ POSSIBLE RESPONSE

The Acropolis's location is advantageous because it seems one could see for miles around, especially to be alerted to invading enemies.

CITIES AND CITY-STATES

As population, trade, and wealth grew, the ancient Greeks began to build cities near coastlines for trade and on hilltops for defense. Greek cities were distinct from one another, each with its own personality. However, these ancient cities shared certain similarities, too.

The highest point in an ancient Greek city was the **acropolis** (uh-KRAHP-uh-lihs), or upper city. This stone-walled fortress was the city's last line of defense against invasion. From the acropolis one could see houses and narrow streets and easily spot the open space of the **agora**, the city's marketplace and social center for sports, festivals, and meetings.

A powerful city grew into an even more powerful city-state, also called a **polis** (POH-luhs). As you may recall, a city-state is an independent political unit in which a dominant city rules the surrounding area. A number of Greek city-states emerged after 750 B.C. Some city-states grew larger than others. Smaller towns and villages supplied food, trade goods, labor, and soldiers for the city-states.

Geographic isolation influenced how city-states developed in ancient Greece. High mountains surrounded plains and valleys, separating cities from one another. The mountains made it more challenging for some city-states to communicate and engage in trade with other city-states.

City-states developed at the same time all over ancient Greece, but they did so in different ways. Although they shared a common language, religion, heritage, and culture, city-states remained independent from one another. Each city-state had its own sets of customs and laws. Even more, citizens identified themselves as Athenians or Spartans—not as Greeks.

EARLY GOVERNMENT

Greek city-states were as different as they were independent. Each city-state established its own way of governing its citizens. One form of governing was a **monarchy**, a government ruled by a single person, such as a king. Another form was an **aristocracy**, a government ruled by a small group of elite, landowning families.

Aristocratic rule was soon challenged by a growing merchant class. As trade expanded, the merchants became more powerful. The 600s saw increasing tensions involving aristocratic landowners and an uneven distribution of wealth. These tensions led to fighting and civil strife. Sometimes powerful men took advantage of the situation and seized power as **tyrants**. Some tyrants were ruthless, but others made positive changes, including giving farms to the landless and work to the unemployed. Not everyone favored their rule, though. In order to take power from tyrants, merchants formed an **oligarchy**, or a government ruled by a few powerful citizens.

Eventually, some city-states, such as Athens, wanted to give citizens a greater voice and began to experiment with a new type of government. You will read more about this government later in the chapter.

REVIEW & ASSESS

1. **READING CHECK** How were ancient Greek city-states alike and different?

2. **DETERMINE WORD MEANING** Based on what you have read, from what ancient Greek word do you think the word *politics* originates?

3. **ANALYZE CAUSE AND EFFECT** How did the geography of Greece influence the development of city-states?

PLAN

OBJECTIVE

Learn about the formation and importance of city-states.

CRITICAL THINKING SKILLS FOR LESSON 1.4

- Identify Main Ideas and Details
- Monitor Comprehension
- Determine Word Meaning
- Analyze Cause and Effect
- Make Inferences
- Compare and Contrast

ESSENTIAL QUESTION

How did a cultured and influential civilization arise in Greece?

An important component of civilization is organized government. Lesson 1.4 discusses the development of city-states and different forms of governing in ancient Greece.

BACKGROUND FOR THE TEACHER

The word *acropolis* means "city at the top" in Greek. The ancient Greeks founded their cities on the highest points for military and religious reasons. Militarily, having a city located up high would allow citizens to spot and prepare for invaders. Cities were also built in high places because for the Greeks, establishing a city involved invoking their gods for protection, and the city was to provide an earthly home for the gods.

DIGITAL RESOURCES myNGconnect.com

TEACHER RESOURCES & ASSESSMENT

 Reading and Note-Taking

 Vocabulary Practice

 Section 1 Quiz

STUDENT RESOURCES

 NG Chapter Gallery

INTRODUCE & ENGAGE

ACTIVATE PRIOR KNOWLEDGE

Explain that in this lesson, students will learn about the development of Greek city-states and early government in ancient Greece. Ask students to draw on what they already know about cities and states to discuss these questions.

- What is a city? (*A city is a place where a number of people live and interact.*)
- What is a state? (*A state is a formal political unit.*)
- Based on your understanding of cities and states and on what you have read in previous chapters, what do you think a city-state is? (*A city-state is an independent political unit in which a dominant city rules the surrounding area.*) **0:05** minutes

TEACH

GUIDED DISCUSSION

1. **Make Inferences** Why do you think citizens of city-states identified with their city-states more than as Greeks? (*The city-state, not a larger, more inclusive country, was the central political unit. As such, ancient Greeks identified as Athenians or Spartans instead of as Greeks. Explain that this identity might be like citizens of the United States identifying as Texans or Californians rather than as Americans.*)

2. **Compare and Contrast** What are similarities and differences between aristocracies and oligarchies? (*Both aristocracies and oligarchies are forms of government in which small groups of people make decisions. Aristocracies are based on heredity, elite status, and land ownership; oligarchies are formed from small groups of powerful people, but not necessarily based on wealth or land ownership.*)

MORE INFORMATION

Geography of Greece Three particular physical features—specifically the mountains, the lowlands, and the coastline—impacted the development of independent city-states in ancient Greece. About 80 percent of the land is mountainous; the remaining 20 percent is lowlands. Several mountain chains run through the mainland, creating steep valleys. These mountains and valleys separated some parts of ancient Greece from one another, which some historians theorize led to more independent development. Greece also has many miles of coastline and no interior land is more than 50 miles from the coast. City-states' proximity to the Mediterranean, Ionian, and Aegean seas helped shape ancient Greece as a maritime power in the region.

ACTIVE OPTIONS

Critical Viewing: NG Chapter Gallery Ask students to choose one image from the Chapter Gallery and become an expert on it. They should do additional research to learn all about it. Then, students should share their findings with a partner, small group, or the class. **0:15** minutes

On Your Feet: Tell Me More Have students form three teams and assign each team one of the following topics:

- Geography of Greece
- City-States of Ancient Greece
- Forms of Government in Early Greece

Each group should write down as many facts about their topic as they can. Have the class reconvene, and have each group stand up, one at a time. The rest of the class calls out, "Tell me more about [the topic]!" A spokesperson for the group recites one fact. The class again calls, "Tell me more!" until the group runs out of facts to share. Then the next group presents its facts. Keep track of which group has shared the most facts on its topic. **0:15** minutes

DIFFERENTIATE

STRIVING READERS

Chart Forms of Government Have students record the different governments that ruled in ancient Greece using a chart such as the one shown below. In the rows, they should write a short description of the way each form of government shaped ancient Greece. Allow students to work in pairs to read the lesson. Have them read the text once and fill in their charts. Then have them read the text a second time and check their work. Have students share their charts with the rest of the group and add any information they might have missed to their own charts.

Monarchy	Aristocracy	Tyranny	Oligarchy

Press **mt** in the Student eEdition for modified text.

See the Chapter Planner for more strategies for differentiation.

REVIEW & ASSESS

ANSWERS

1. Ancient Greek city-states were alike because many were organized around an acropolis above an agora, and they shared a common language, religion, and culture. City-states were different because of the way each governed.

2. The word *politics* is based on the ancient Greek word, *polis*.

3. High mountains and surrounding plains and valleys separated cities from one another, which encouraged tightly knit communities and distinct identities as city-states.

1.5

Colonization and Trade

The ancient Greeks were always on the look out for fertile land and materials such as timber, metals, and luxury goods. Together these prompted the Greeks to trade and settle around parts of the Mediterranean where they could control the land.

MAIN IDEA

Ancient Greeks spread their culture around the Mediterranean and Black seas.

NEW SETTLEMENTS

Growing city-states meant growing populations and new problems. The hot, dry, and mountainous Greek countryside did not have enough usable farmland to feed everyone. As hunger fueled unrest, the leaders of city-states had two choices. They could fight other city-states for space or they could reduce their own populations.

Most did both. Between 750 and 550 B.C., the city-states waged wars with one another for control over limited natural resources. They also sent people overseas to establish new colonies in places with better farmland and valuable raw materials. Remember, a colony is an area controlled by a distant ruler. City-states selected their colonists by lottery and often prevented them from returning to Greece. The rulers wanted to make sure the new colonies would stay populated.

Greek city-states established hundreds of colonies in the Mediterranean region. Most colonies were situated on or near the coastlines of the Black and Mediterranean seas. They were located in present-day Spain, France, and Italy, in North Africa, and on the islands of Sardinia, Corsica, and Cyprus.

The new colonies were self-governing, but they maintained close political and economic links with their parent city-states. Although colonists adopted some local ways, they remained proudly Greek in their culture and outlook. They shared a common language, worshipped the same gods, and took part in Greek festivals such as the Olympic Games.

WATER HIGHWAYS

Colonies served many purposes for the ancient Greeks. Overall, they allowed access to land and resources not available in Greece. Some colonies were specifically set up to secure and control trade routes.

The Mediterranean and Black seas were relatively easy to navigate. Because most colonies were positioned near good harbors, sea trade flourished throughout the region. Expert sailors on well-built merchant ships carried raw materials such as silver and tin from present-day Spain and France back to Greece.

The flow of new resources to and from these colonies stimulated the production of goods. These goods were then traded at home and abroad. Trade boosted Greece's growing economy, as did the introduction of coins after 600 B.C.

Wide-ranging sea trade also encouraged cultural diffusion, or the spread of ideas from one culture to another. This dual exchange of goods and ideas was important in shaping civilizations in the ancient world. For example, the ancient Egyptians welcomed learning about Greek military skills. Ancient Greece had a strong cultural influence on early Rome and carried Mediterranean culture as far away as

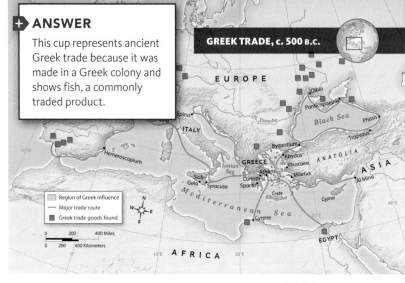

ANSWER
This cup represents ancient Greek trade because it was made in a Greek colony and shows fish, a commonly traded product.

GREEK TRADE, c. 500 B.C.

Region of Greek influence
Major trade route
Greek trade goods found

present-day France. The ancient Greeks also incorporated ideas from other cultures. Elements of Egyptian culture influenced Greek art and architecture. Some historians think that ancient Greeks may have gotten their ideas of city-states, colonization, and sea trade from the Phoenicians.

One of the major effects of cultural diffusion in the ancient Mediterranean was the Greek adoption of the Phoenician alphabet. The Greeks made changes to the Phoenician alphabet, which then became the foundation of the modern alphabet we use today.

GREEK POTTERY IN ITALY
Tuna fish decorate this pottery cup found in the Apulia region, in the heel of Italy's boot. The cup may have been produced there by Greek colonists, or it may have been a trade good. Archaeologists believe the cup dates to about 500 B.C. In what ways does this cup represent Greek colonization and trade?

REVIEW & ASSESS

1. **READING CHECK** Why did the ancient Greeks establish colonies in the Mediterranean region?

2. **ANALYZE CAUSE AND EFFECT** In what ways did trade and cultural diffusion shape the ancient Greek world?

3. **INTERPRET MAPS** How far north did Greek influence reach as a result of trade?

PLAN

OBJECTIVE

Explore the impact of colonization and trade in ancient Greece.

CRITICAL THINKING SKILLS FOR LESSON 1.5

- Identify Main Ideas and Details
- Monitor Comprehension
- Analyze Cause and Effect
- Interpret Maps
- Identify
- Evaluate

ESSENTIAL QUESTION

How did a cultured and influential civilization arise in Greece?

The creation of colonies and the exchange of goods in the Mediterranean region transformed ancient Greece into a regional power. Lesson 1.5 explores colonization and trade routes in ancient Greece.

BACKGROUND FOR THE TEACHER

Colonization and trade was intensely competitive in the ancient Mediterranean. Greek city-states competed with each other, sometimes to the point of war, over access to resources and for claims to new locations that would help relieve population pressures. At the same time, the Greeks competed with the Phoenicians and the Carthaginians over resources and power in the seas. Despite the competition, the ancient Greeks greatly expanded their power and influence in the region between 750 and 500 B.C. through colonization and trade.

DIGITAL RESOURCES myNGconnect.com

TEACHER RESOURCES & ASSESSMENT

 Reading and Note-Taking

 Vocabulary Practice

 Section 1 Quiz

STUDENT RESOURCES

 NG Chapter Gallery

INTRODUCE & ENGAGE

PREVIEW CONTENT WITH MAPS

Direct students' attention to the map of Greek trade. Have them scan the title, legend, and other map features to determine the upcoming content. **ASK:** What do you think this map shows? (*The map shows trade routes of ancient Greeks.*) **ASK:** What three features on the map do you notice right away? (*Students may say the parts of land colored green, the green lines, and the purple squares.*) Ask for volunteers to identify what each map feature represents. **0:05** minutes

TEACH

GUIDED DISCUSSION

1. **Identify** What stresses did increased populations put on ancient Greek city-states by 750 B.C.? (*Growing populations meant that more people needed food, which was hard to produce on hot, dry lands in Greece. Hunger began to fuel unrest and city-states began to fight with one another over resources and space.*)

2. **Evaluate** In what ways did Greek colonization and trade foster cultural diffusion in the Mediterranean region? (*Colonization introduced people from different cultures to each other, and trade brought merchants, seamen, and travelers into contact with one another. Cultural diffusion, or the exchange of ideas among cultures, was in some ways inevitable because people had to interact with one another to set up colonies and to trade.*)

INTERPRET MAPS

Have students study the map of Greek trade. **ASK:** What does the presence of Greek trade goods in places far away from Greece indicate about the extent and strength of ancient Greek trade? (*Greek trade goods found in Egypt and the city of Cyrene make sense, because these places were located on major trade routes. However, trade goods found in places much farther away, and off major trade routes, as in parts of present-day France and even Russia, could indicate that the goods traded were valuable and had a long trade life, or it could indicate that traders involved in ancient Greek networks traded with many different groups.*) **0:10** minutes

ACTIVE OPTIONS

NG Learning Framework: Advertise a New Colony

SKILL: Collaboration
KNOWLEDGE: Our Human Story

Invite students to imagine that they are in charge of an ad campaign announcing a new colony in ancient Greece. Have them work in small groups to collaborate on a poster that could advertise the new colony and that might persuade citizens of the mainland to move there. Encourage groups to share their posters with the class. **0:15** minutes

On Your Feet: Create Trade Networks Have students work with two or three partners and create a description of a product or good they could trade with other groups. When each group is ready, replicate the Mediterranean region by assigning groups to separate parts of the room, leaving the middle of the room fairly empty. Then have groups trade their goods with each other. Some may trade one good for another good, and some may require a form of currency. Allow students to explore different methods. Some groups may grow wealthy; others may run out of products to trade. After each group has traded with at least three other groups, come back together as a class to discuss the experience of trading. Ask students if they preferred one exchange system over another, or if their group formed an alliance with another group to benefit as trade partners. **0:25** minutes

DIFFERENTIATE

ENGLISH LANGUAGE LEARNERS

Ask the Five Ws Reporters use the questions *What?, Who?, Where?, When?,* and *Why?* to guide their reporting. Students can use the same questions to understand nonfiction text. Have students work in pairs to answer the five questions about colonization and trade in ancient Greece.

GIFTED & TALENTED

Explore Greek Trade Have students research five products or goods exchanged along ancient Greek trade routes. Encourage students to use a visual such as a map or flow chart to show the origin and movement of the traded products and goods. Have students show their maps or flow charts to the class and to describe their findings.

Press **mt** *in the Student eEdition for modified text.*

See the Chapter Planner for more strategies for differentiation.

REVIEW & ASSESS

ANSWERS

1. Ancient Greeks established colonies in the Mediterranean region to relieve overcrowding and find places with better farmland and resources.

2. The colonies stimulated sea trade as well as the production of manufactured goods that were traded at home and abroad—all of which boosted Greece's growing economy. Trade stimulated the production of manufactured goods that were traded at home and abroad. This trade boosted Greece's growing economy. Cultural diffusion meant that ideas and practices from Greece spread to other civilizations in the ancient world, and vice versa.

3. Greek influence reached as far north as Olbia, on the northern shore of the Black Sea.

2.1 Sparta's Military Society

One of the greatest rivalries in the ancient world was between the city-states of Athens and Sparta. The Athenians, whom you'll learn about in the next lesson, emphasized culture and learning. The Spartans, though, were the fierce warriors of ancient Greece. They fought hard and could handle more pain than anyone. They were almost unbeatable, thanks to tough military training.

MAIN IDEA

Sparta was a powerful ancient Greek city-state devoted to war.

STRONG WOMEN

This bronze sculpture from Sparta reflects the expectation that Spartan girls and women be tough. Girls' education focused on physical strength and athletic skills, and Spartan girls learned how to defend themselves.

SPARTAN SOCIETY

The Spartans lived in one of the most fertile areas of southern Greece. The city-state of **Sparta** was located in the Eurotas river valley, protected by mountains that made attacking this city-state difficult. This physical separation may have led to an outlook and values in sharp contrast with those of other ancient Greek city-states.

Spartan government was an unusual blend of rule by kings, elected officials, and the ruling class. Two kings who shared power ruled Sparta. Together, they led Sparta's armies into battle. Real power rested with the five officials who were elected each year by an assembly of Spartan citizens. In addition, the two kings and a council of elders, made up of 28 men over 60 years of age, proposed laws. The Spartans' unique government helped maintain a balance of power and prevent revolts.

Spartan society was a rigid hierarchy. Groups of citizens were ranked by importance based on wealth and power. Elite, landowning families of Sparta formed the upper class. A second class included free noncitizens from the villages around Sparta. They were farmers and traders and sometimes served in the army.

The lowest social class was made up of the **helots**, or state-owned slaves captured from conquered lands. Helots farmed the Spartans' land and were only allowed to keep a tiny portion of their harvest. The helots outnumbered the Spartans, and fear of helot uprisings was a main reason for Sparta's military society. The army was at the center of everything in Sparta—and everything in Sparta was centered on the army.

DAILY LIFE

Spartan soldiers considered it an honor to die in battle for Sparta, but they did not die easily. At seven years of age, all boys were taken from their families and raised by the state to be soldiers. Their training was brutal. They wore thin tunics and no shoes, even in winter. Their meals were purposely small and nasty so that they had to steal food to survive but were punished if caught.

Such intense physical training and endless military drills created strong and obedient

Critical Viewing: King Leonidas of Sparta was a heroic Spartan soldier. How does this statue of him celebrate Spartan values?

+ POSSIBLE RESPONSE

The statue of Leonidas celebrates strength, militarism, and readiness for war.

soldiers. At age 20, they joined a military mess, or regiment, a commitment that dominated the rest of their lives.

Family life supported Sparta's military values. Women's primary role was to produce future soldiers for the state, and husbands and wives spent much time apart. One result of this separation was that Spartan women lived their daily lives independent of men. Spartan women could also own property.

Sparta's extraordinary commitment to war transformed this city-state into an ancient power, but this success came at a price. Although Sparta boasted the best soldiers, it claimed few artists, philosophers, or scientists, unlike its rival Athens.

REVIEW & ASSESS

1. **READING CHECK** What was one reason Sparta developed a military society?

2. **SUMMARIZE** In what ways was Sparta's government unique?

3. **ANALYZE CAUSE AND EFFECT** What effect did Sparta's commitment to the military have on other aspects of its society and culture?

PLAN

OBJECTIVE

Learn about Spartan society in ancient Greece.

CRITICAL THINKING SKILLS FOR LESSON 2.1

- Identify Main Ideas and Details
- Monitor Comprehension
- Summarize
- Analyze Cause and Effect
- Describe
- Make Inferences
- Compare and Contrast

ESSENTIAL QUESTION

How did a cultured and influential civilization arise in Greece?

Many different groups contributed to the development of civilization in ancient Greece. Lesson 2.1 discusses the Spartans and their military society.

BACKGROUND FOR THE TEACHER

The rigorous military training Spartan boys endured was called *agoge*. One reason for the training was to maintain control over the helots, or state-owned slaves. This dynamic led to a self-perpetuating cycle: training Spartan warriors to control slaves working to provide food (and time) for Spartan warriors to train. This training and approach set Sparta quite apart from other ancient Greek city-states. As they became more committed to this approach, Spartans turned away from any artistic expression or development to focus solely on the development of the military and its warriors.

DIGITAL RESOURCES myNGconnect.com

TEACHER RESOURCES & ASSESSMENT

 Reading and Note-Taking

 Vocabulary Practice

 Section 2 Quiz

STUDENT RESOURCES

 NG Chapter Gallery

INTRODUCE & ENGAGE

WORD RECOGNITION

Ask students if they're familiar with the word *spartan* and ask them to volunteer guesses about its meaning. Write student guesses on the board. Explain that the word means, "showing or characterized by a lack of comfort or luxury." The word comes from the name of a group of ancient Greeks called Spartans who were known for their indifference to comfort and luxury. The word is used today to describe things that are bare and without frills, or things that are stern or rigorous. Encourage students to look for uses of the word *spartan*. **0:05** minutes

TEACH

GUIDED DISCUSSION

1. **Describe** What different social classes existed in Sparta? *(Elite, landowning families formed the upper class; a second class included free noncitizens; the lowest social class was made up of helots.)*

2. **Make Inferences** How might the rigid hierarchy of Spartan society have been mirrored in its military? *(Any military is characterized by rank, so a Spartan citizen would understand the hierarchy in the Spartan military.)*

COMPARE AND CONTRAST

Have students examine the photograph of King Leonidas. **ASK:** What elements of the statue show military strength? *(The sword, shield, helmet, and armor of Leonidas demonstrate a powerful soldier.)* Have students compare the photo of Leonidas to photos of modern soldiers in battle uniform. **ASK:** What are some similarities between Spartan soldier uniforms and modern soldier uniforms? *(Spartan soldiers and modern soldiers wear helmets and armor, have a standardized uniform, and carry weapons.)* What are some differences between Spartan and military uniforms? *(In the photo in Lesson 2.1, Leonidas is depicted in a short tunic; modern soldiers wear long pants to protect their legs. Modern soldiers also don't carry metal shields or wear heavy adornments on their helmets.)* **0:10** minutes

ACTIVE OPTIONS

NG Learning Framework: Create a Government

ATTITUDE: **Responsibility**
SKILL: **Decision-Making**

Invite students to imagine that they are responsible for leading a new society. Have them select one of the groups discussed in this chapter and use it as a model or example for how they might structure their society's government and societal roles. **ASK:** Why did you decide to use this group as your model? What characteristics do you want your government to have? How are leaders chosen? What kinds of responsibilities do citizens in your society have? **0:10** minutes

On Your Feet: In This Corner Place cards in two corners of the room, one labeled "Spartan Warrior" and the other labeled "Helot." Call on individual students, giving each a word or phrase—such as *farmer, soldier, slave, battle, uprising, war, majority, minority*. Students are to go to one of the two labeled areas and explain why their word or phrase fits the label. As a class, discuss any differences in opinion about how students have categorized terms. **0:10** minutes

DIFFERENTIATE

INCLUSION

Identify Main Ideas and Details Have pairs of students use the graphic organizer shown to identify the main idea and supporting details in the lesson. First, they should write the lesson's Main Idea statement in the Main Idea box. Then have students work together to identify and write supporting details.

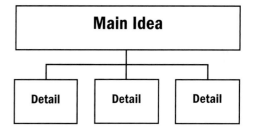

GIFTED & TALENTED

Write Journal Entries Have students conduct research to learn about the life of a helot, a Spartan man, or a young Spartan girl. Then have them write a series of journal entries from the perspective of their chosen person. Students should include factual information from their research in their journal entries. Ask for volunteers to read some entries aloud.

Press **(mt)** *in the Student eEdition for modified text.*
See the Chapter Planner for more strategies for differentiation.

REVIEW & ASSESS

ANSWERS

1. They developed a military society in order to control the helots—slaves captured from conquered countries—and to prevent uprisings.

2. Sparta's government was made up of a unique combination of monarchy, democracy, and oligarchy that helped to maintain a balance of power and suppress radical politics.

3. Sparta's commitment to its military strength meant that other aspects of society and culture—such as the arts and sciences—were not developed. Therefore, Sparta produced the strongest and most obedient soldiers, but very few artists, poets, musicians, philosophers, or scientists.

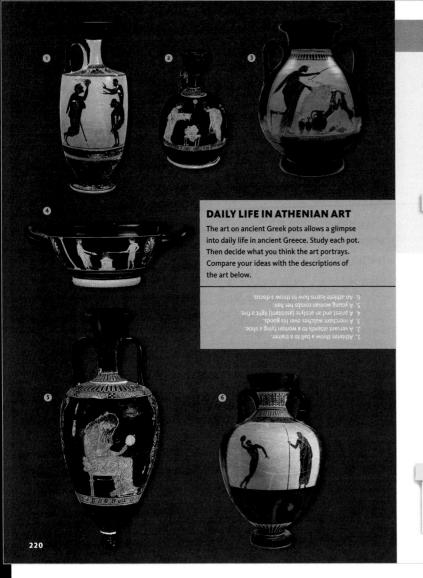

DAILY LIFE IN ATHENIAN ART

The art on ancient Greek pots allows a glimpse into daily life in ancient Greece. Study each pot. Then decide what you think the art portrays. Compare your ideas with the descriptions of the art below.

1. Athletes throw a ball to a trainer.
2. A servant attends to a woman tying a shoe.
3. A merchant watches over his goods.
4. A priest and an acolyte (assistant) light a fire.
5. A young woman combs her hair.
6. An athlete learns how to throw a discus.

2.2 Athens's Democratic Society

The city-state of Athens was named for its devotion to Athena, the Greek goddess of wisdom. Ancient Athenians developed one of the world's great forms of government.

MAIN IDEA

The culturally rich city-state of Athens developed democracy.

DAILY LIFE

The daily lives of people in ancient **Athens** helped shape their approach to governing. Citizenship was open to adult men who had been born in Athens. Foreign-born residents could live in Athens. However, they did not generally become citizens, vote, or own property—even though they paid taxes and fought in the army. Slaves were at the bottom of society.

Athenian women were firmly controlled by their husbands. Wealthy women ran the household and raised children, but they could not go out alone. Poorer women had more freedom but had to work for wages.

Children were raised much differently in Athens than in Sparta. Athenians valued education, and boys attended school if their families could afford it. After a well-rounded education, Athenian boys went through two years of military training in preparation for citizenship. Athenian girls did not attend school, but they learned household skills at home. Poor children worked from an early age.

BEGINNINGS OF DEMOCRACY

Even as the city-state of Athens thrived, many Athenians felt they had little voice in their government. Unlike Sparta, Athens replaced its monarchy with an aristocracy. Trouble arose when aristocratic families began to fight with each other and farmers started to protest decreasing wealth and land. A time of increasing strife and, on occasion, violence in Athens followed. A harsh code of laws made things worse.

In 594 B.C., the aristocrats responded to the crisis by granting special powers to a trusted man named **Solon**. He improved conditions for the poor by limiting the power of the aristocracy and allowing an assembly of free citizens to pass laws. In 508 B.C., Athens established **democracy**, a form of government in which citizens have a direct role in governing.

Athenians were less devoted to war than were Spartans. Although their citizen-soldiers were capable, they did not form a professional army. To defend itself, Athens joined forces with other city-states, including Sparta. In 490 B.C., the Persians attacked Greece from the east. The resulting war would test Spartans and Athenians alike.

REVIEW & ASSESS

1. **READING CHECK** What role do citizens play in a democracy?

2. **ANALYZE CAUSE AND EFFECT** What steps did Solon take to reform Athens's government?

3. **INTEGRATE VISUALS** How do the depictions of ancient Greek women on the pots fit with the text's description of them?

PLAN

OBJECTIVE

Explore the culture and society of ancient Athens.

CRITICAL THINKING SKILLS FOR LESSON 2.2

- Identify Main Ideas and Details
- Monitor Comprehension
- Analyze Cause and Effect
- Integrate Visuals
- Identify
- Compare and Contrast
- Analyze Visuals

ESSENTIAL QUESTION

How did a cultured and influential civilization arise in Greece?

Ancient Athens provided a fertile environment for cultural and artistic expression to thrive. Lesson 2.2 describes Athens's democratic society.

BACKGROUND FOR THE TEACHER

Black-and-red pottery is an iconic ancient Greek art form. First, potters shaped and fired, or baked, the vessels in a kiln. Some pots had handles on one or both sides. Sometimes vessels were tall vases and sometimes they were bowls. Plain, undecorated vessels were used for everyday tasks, such as food service and preparation, beverages, or washing. Finely painted pots such as the ones shown in Lesson 2.2 were reserved for more important occasions. Illustrations on the pots depicted myths and stories, seemingly unimportant tasks such as combing hair, as well as athletic training and contests, musical performances, historical events, and students listening to teachers.

DIGITAL RESOURCES myNGconnect.com

TEACHER RESOURCES & ASSESSMENT

 Reading and Note-Taking

 Vocabulary Practice

 Section 2 Quiz

STUDENT RESOURCES

 Active History

INTRODUCE & ENGAGE

COMPLETE A K-W-L CHART

Provide each student with a K-W-L Chart like the one shown. Have students brainstorm what they know about ancient Athens and the development of democracy. Then ask them to write questions that they would like to have answered as they study the lesson. Allow time at the end of the lesson for students to fill in what they have learned. **0:10** minutes

K What Do I Know?	W What Do I Want To Learn?	L What Did I Learn?

TEACH

GUIDED DISCUSSION

1. **Identify** To whom was citizenship available in ancient Athens? *(Citizenship was open to adult men who had been born in Athens.)* **ASK:** Could Athenian women be citizens? *(No.)*

2. **Compare and Contrast** How did life differ between young Spartan and young Athenian boys? *(Spartan boys went into military training and then became soldiers. Athenian boys had some military training but they also received well-rounded educations.)*

ANALYZE VISUALS

Have students examine the ancient Greek pots shown in the lesson. As a class, work through their responses to the prompt asking them to describe what they think the art on the pots portrays. If students offer different answers than those listed, ask them to explain what they think the art depicts. Ask students to think of objects that they own or use that depict ordinary events. Allow time for students to make a connection between modern and ancient expressions of the everyday. **0:10** minutes

ACTIVE OPTIONS

Analyze Primary Sources: Democracy Extend Lesson 2.2 on the beginnings of democracy in ancient Greece by using either the PDF or Whiteboard version of the activity. These activities take a deeper look at a topic from, or related to, the lesson. Explore the activities

as a class, turn them into group assignments, or even assign them individually. **0:10** minutes

On Your Feet: Create a Concept Web Have students form groups of four around a section of a bulletin board or a table. Provide each group with a large sheet of paper. Have group members take turns contributing a concept or phrase to a Concept Web with the words *Early Greeks* at the center. When time for the activity has elapsed, call on volunteers from each group to share their webs. **0:10** minutes

DIFFERENTIATE

ENGLISH LANGUAGE LEARNERS

Teach and Learn Pair English language learners with English-proficient students. Have English-proficient students teach words from the lesson that appear in various forms throughout Lesson 2.2. Have pairs compose a sentence for each word and then share their sentences with the class. Suggest the following words:

- aristocracy, aristocratic
- wealth, wealthy
- citizen, citizenship
- governing, government

PRE-AP

Create an Exhibit Have students research a type of ancient Greek art and create a virtual exhibit of the artifacts they bring together. Students should create a theme and title for their exhibit, write accurate labels for each artifact, and represent each object through a photograph.

Press (**mt**) *in the Student eEdition for modified text.*

See the Chapter Planner for more strategies for differentiation.

REVIEW & ASSESS

ANSWERS

1. In a democracy, citizens have a direct role in governing themselves or elect representatives to lead them.

2. Solon established a limited democracy by reducing the power of the aristocracy and empowering an assembly made up of free citizens, which led to a growing equality among the people of Athens (excluding women, children, foreigners, and slaves).

3. The art on the pots idealizes Athenian women as focused on the home and children and on personal beauty. This depiction matches with the text, which asserts that women were centered on the home and childrearing and that girls had little education.

2.3 Uniting Against the Persians

When the Persians attacked Greece, they triggered the Persian Wars. We know much about these wars from the ancient Greek historian Herodotus. Modern historians consider him to be reliable even though it's likely that he exaggerated the size of the Persian threat. Whatever the numbers, these wars changed the course of Greek history.

MAIN IDEA

City-states in ancient Greece united to drive back invasions by the Persian Empire.

26.2

The modern marathon has its roots in the Persian Wars. According to one legend, upon defeating the Persians at Marathon, Militiades sent his best runner to Athens to announce the victory. After he reported the news, the runner collapsed and died.

The distance from Marathon to Athens was just over 24 miles. Today's race measures 26.2 miles.

IONIAN REVOLT

In 546 B.C., the Persian Empire conquered Ionia, an area of Greek colonies on the west coast of present-day Turkey. Life under Persian rule was not especially harsh, but the Ionians wanted to regain their independence. They rebelled in 499 B.C. with the support of Athens. Despite Athenian help, Persia crushed the Ionian revolt in 494 B.C. The Persian emperor **Darius I** vowed to punish Athens as revenge for helping Ionia.

In 490 B.C., the Persian army landed at Marathon, just over 24 miles east of Athens. Knowing they were outnumbered by at least two to one, the Athenians knew their strategy would have to be clever—and bold. As the Persian foot soldiers stood in formation, the Greek general Militiades (mihl-ih-tee-AH-deez) ordered his troops to lock shields and advance at a full run. The Greeks charged into the surprised Persians, forced them back to their ships, and claimed victory over them.

DEFEAT OF THE PERSIAN EMPIRE

Ten years after the Battle at Marathon, **Xerxes** (ZURK-seez), Darius's successor, invaded Athens. In 480 B.C., hundreds of Persian ships and more than 150,000 soldiers went on the attack. Athens was ready this time—and it did not have to face the Persians alone. Athens had forged strong **alliances**, or partnerships, with other Greek city-states, including Sparta. Because the Athenians needed more time to prepare for battle, King Leonidas of Sparta occupied the important mountain pass of **Thermopylae** (thur-MAHP-uh-lee). Leonidas's small army fought off the Persians, giving the Greeks time to assemble further south.

The Athenians fought on. At the Battle of Salamis (SAL-uh-mihs) a small fleet of Greek warships called **triremes** (try-REEMZ) faced the Persian navy. The Greeks lured the Persians into a trap in the strait at Salamis and destroyed nearly a third of the Persian fleet. In 479 B.C., a large and united Greek army finally defeated the Persians at the Battle of Plataea. After this, the Persians left Greece and never invaded again. Although the war flared on and off for a few more decades, Greece was safe. Athens and Sparta emerged triumphant as the most powerful city-states in Greece.

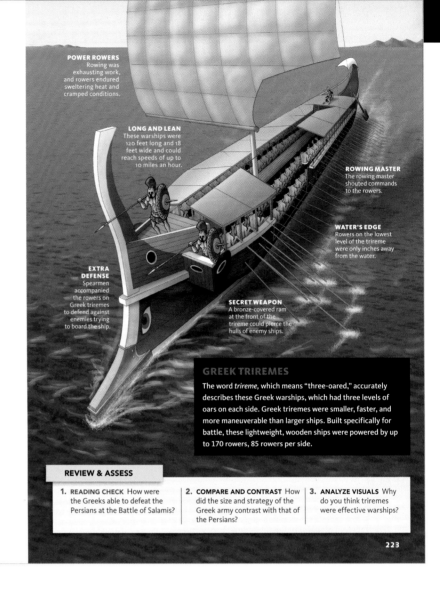

POWER ROWERS Rowing was exhausting work, and rowers endured sweltering heat and cramped conditions.

LONG AND LEAN These warships were 120 feet long and 18 feet wide and could reach speeds of up to 10 miles an hour.

ROWING MASTER The rowing master shouted commands to the rowers.

WATER'S EDGE Rowers on the lowest level of the trireme were only inches away from the water.

EXTRA DEFENSE Spearmen accompanied the rowers on Greek triremes to defend against enemies trying to board the ship.

SECRET WEAPON A bronze-covered ram at the front of the trireme could pierce the hulls of enemy ships.

GREEK TRIREMES

The word *trireme*, which means "three-oared," accurately describes these Greek warships, which had three levels of oars on each side. Greek triremes were smaller, faster, and more maneuverable than larger ships. Built specifically for battle, these lightweight, wooden ships were powered by up to 170 rowers, 85 rowers per side.

REVIEW & ASSESS

1. **READING CHECK** How were the Greeks able to defeat the Persians at the Battle of Salamis?

2. **COMPARE AND CONTRAST** How did the size and strategy of the Greek army contrast with that of the Persians?

3. **ANALYZE VISUALS** Why do you think triremes were effective warships?

PLAN

OBJECTIVE

Learn about military victories by the ancient Greeks.

CRITICAL THINKING SKILLS FOR LESSON 2.3

- Identify Main Ideas and Details
- Monitor Comprehension
- Compare and Contrast
- Analyze Visuals
- Summarize
- Form and Support Opinions

ESSENTIAL QUESTION

How did a cultured and influential civilization arise in Greece?

As the ancient Greeks became more powerful, they clashed with powers in the region. Lesson 2.3 describes the events of the Persian Wars.

BACKGROUND FOR THE TEACHER

The defeat of the Persian Empire at the hands of the ancient Greeks was the underdog story of its day. The Persian Empire dwarfed the Greek armies in size and power. After his embarrassing defeat at Thermopylae, the Persian emperor Xerxes wanted to totally destroy the Greeks. At the Battle of Salamis, the size of the Persian military and its ships became a detriment rather than a guarantee of victory. Persian ships were large and difficult to maneuver. The Greeks were able to navigate between the Persian ships, setting them on fire. Spartans waiting at water's edge killed the Persians who abandoned ship and made it to shore.

DIGITAL RESOURCES myNGconnect.com

TEACHER RESOURCES & ASSESSMENT

 Reading and Note-Taking

 Vocabulary Practice

 Section 2 Quiz

STUDENT RESOURCES

 NG Chapter Gallery

PREVIEW WITH VISUALS

Direct students' attention to the illustration of the Greek trireme. Ask volunteers to read the main caption and the smaller captions. **ASK:** Based on what you see and what you've heard, what do you think Lesson 2.3 will be about? *(Students' responses will vary, but should focus on Greek warships and soldiers.)* Encourage students to refer to the illustration as they read the last paragraph of the text. **0:05** minutes

TEACH

GUIDED DISCUSSION

1. **Summarize** Why did the Persians attack the Greeks at the Battle of Marathon? *(The Persian emperor wanted to punish Athens for helping Ionia revolt against Persian rule.)*

2. **Form and Support Opinions** What do you think helped the Greeks more as they defended themselves against the Persians: their size or their alliances? Use details in the reading to support your opinion. *(Students' responses will vary but should be supported by details in the reading.)*

ANALYZE VISUALS

As a class, review the illustration of the Greek trireme. **ASK:** Based on the illustration's captions, what do you think it might have been like to be a rower on a Greek trireme? *(Students responses will vary, but may note that the ships were probably very hot, that it was hard to hear, that rowers probably couldn't see what was going on, and that it was probably quite frightening to engage in battle with much larger ships.)* **0:10** minutes

ACTIVE OPTIONS

NG Learning Framework: Learn More About Triremes

ATTITUDE: Curiosity
SKILL: Problem-Solving

Invite students to review the text and illustration in the lesson. Encourage them to share their observations about how the triremes were constructed, how rowers had to work together, and how wind and water conditions might affect a battle. **ASK:** What might be one of the problems a rower on a trireme would have had to solve? **0:10** minutes

On Your Feet: Inside-Outside Circle Have students form concentric circles facing each other. Allow students time to write questions about the events of the Persian Wars. Then have students in the inside circle pose questions to students in the outside circle. Have students switch roles. Students may ask for help from other students in their circle if they are unable to answer a question. **0:20** minutes

STRIVING READERS

Set a Purpose for Reading Before reading, have students use the lesson subheadings and the illustration to create purpose-setting questions:

- Who were the Ionians? Why did they revolt?
- Who defeated the Persian Empire? How did they do it?
- What is a trireme?

After reading, have student pairs answer the questions. Then ask for student volunteers to share their answers.

PRE-AP

Annotate a Time Line Have students annotate a time line of the Persian Wars. They should conduct independent research to support the reading in the lesson and to include more details and dates. Their time lines should extend from 546 B.C. to 479 B.C. Encourage students to include visuals on their time lines that might help illustrate events. Have students post their time lines on the wall in the classroom.

Press **mt** *in the Student eEdition for modified text.*

See the Chapter Planner for more strategies for differentiation.

ANSWERS

1. Greek city-states had formed alliances with each other so were better prepared for battle. The use of the triremes was a strategic advantage for the Greeks because of their small size and speed.

2. The Greek army was vastly smaller than the Persian army. The Greeks relied on surprise attacks and clever maneuvers, while the Persians relied on size and might.

3. Greek triremes were effective warships probably because they were maneuverable, fast, and lightweight. The rams could also pierce enemy ships' hulls.

+ POSSIBLE RESPONSE

The actions of Leonidas and the 300 reflect the culture of Sparta because the soldiers fought to the death to protect against the invading Persians and they sacrificed themselves for the good of the Greek city-states.

480 B.C.

Heroic events inspire exciting movies. Here, outnumbered Spartan soldiers force Persians over a cliff in a scene from the 2007 film *300*. At the Battle of Thermopylae in 480 B.C., 6,000 Greek soldiers led by Spartans fought off more than 100,000 Persian soldiers. Exhausted, the soldiers battled bravely, but their strength was running out. King Leonidas of Sparta realized the battle was lost and ordered most of the soldiers to withdraw. He and his 300 elite Spartans stayed behind to protect the retreating army and delay the Persians. It meant certain death. The ensuing battle was fierce. When swords broke, the Spartans fought with bare hands. None escaped alive. Thanks to the sacrifice of the 300, the Greeks were able to regroup and eventually defeat the Persians. How do the actions of Leonidas and the 300 reflect the culture of Sparta?

PLAN

OBJECTIVE

Explore the drama of the Battle of Thermopylae.

CRITICAL THINKING SKILLS FOR LESSON 2.4

- Analyze Visuals
- Make Connections

ESSENTIAL QUESTION

How did a cultured and influential civilization arise in Greece?

As they grew from small city-states into an advanced civilization, the ancient Greeks often clashed with regional powers. Lesson 2.4 provides a modern, cinematic interpretation of the events of the Battle of Thermopylae in 480 B.C. between the Persians and the Greeks.

BACKGROUND FOR THE TEACHER

The Persian Empire was mighty. When the ancient Greeks defeated this military giant, a definite shift in power took place in the region. The epic battle at Thermopylae has captured the attention of historians and military buffs alike for centuries. The notion of a tiny, scrappy army defeating one of the most powerful empires in the region strikes a chord with audiences, even today. The actual pass at Thermopylae is about four miles long, and 480 B.C. was not the last time the location would see battle. The Greeks fought off the Celts there in 279 B.C. and the Seleucids defended against the Romans in 191 B.C.

DIGITAL RESOURCES myNGconnect.com

TEACHER RESOURCES & ASSESSMENT

 Reading and Note-Taking   **Vocabulary Practice**   **Section 2 Quiz**

STUDENT RESOURCES

 NG Chapter Gallery

INTRODUCE & ENGAGE

MAKE PREDICTIONS USING VISUALS

Ask students to look at the photograph in the lesson. Then ask for volunteers to describe what is happening in the photograph and what mood the photo strikes. **ASK:** Which group of soldiers has the upper hand in this scene? *(the Spartans, who are pushing the Persians over a cliff)* `0:05` minutes

TEACH

GUIDED DISCUSSION

1. **Analyze Visuals** What details in the photo help the viewer know who the Spartans are? *(The Spartans are identifiable by their characteristic helmets.)*

2. **Make Connections** The Battle of Thermopylae has come to represent courage in battle and victory in the face of overwhelming odds. Can you think of another instance, not necessarily based on war, in which the underdog emerged victorious against seemingly insurmountable odds? *(Responses will vary. Possible responses: The American colonies defeat of the British Empire in the American Revolution; the victory of the English navy over the Spanish Armada; the victory of the U.S. Olympic hockey team over the Soviets in 1980; Billy Mills' come-from-behind win in the 10,000-meter race in the 1964 Olympics in Tokyo.)*

MORE INFORMATION

King Leonidas As leader of the Spartans, King Leonidas took charge of the strategy at Thermopylae. In order to protect retreating Greeks, he and his elite team of 300 stayed behind to fight off the Persians. The Greek historian Herodotus wrote that Leonidas handpicked his soldiers for the mission at Thermopylae. All the soldiers he selected were fathers, perhaps because they were considered reliable and battle-tested. When Leonidas first understood the huge size of the army that awaited him and his Spartans, he had second thoughts, according to Herodotus. In the end, all the Spartans died, including Leonidas, but not without first demonstrating courage, sacrifice, and heroism.

ACTIVE OPTIONS

Critical Viewing: NG Chapter Gallery Invite students to explore the entire NG Image Gallery and choose one image from the gallery they feel best represents their understanding of each chapter or the unit. Have students provide a written explanation of why they selected each of the images they chose. `0:15` minutes

On Your Feet: I See, I Read, And So On a large sheet of chart paper or a whiteboard, create a chart like the one pictured. As a group, re-examine the movie scene of the Battle of Thermopylae. Have volunteers describe something they observe in the photo and something they have read to draw conclusions about the Battle of

Thermopylae and the ultimate defeat of the Spartans in 480 B.C. Record their observations on the chart. `0:15` minutes

I See	I Read	And So

DIFFERENTIATE

STRIVING READERS

Analyze Visuals Provide concrete questions to help students of different ability levels process the photograph. Make sure students understand that the photo is a movie still and not a representation of the actual battle. **ASK:** Which soldiers in the photo represent the Persians? Which represent the Spartans? Encourage students to point to things they don't understand about the photo and help them frame questions about these details.

GIFTED & TALENTED

Offer an Alternative Ending Have students offer an alternate outcome for the Battle of Thermopylae. Encourage them to imagine what might have happened if the Spartans had somehow pushed the Persians back and, ultimately, out of Greece? Have students discuss different outcomes with each other and then select one to present to the class. Then have the class ask questions and offer suggestions about other outcomes.

Press (**mt**) *in the Student eEdition for modified text.*

See the Chapter Planner for more strategies for differentiation.

8 Review

VOCABULARY

Complete each of the following sentences using one of the vocabulary words from the chapter.

1. According to an ancient myth, King Minos of Crete built a large maze, or _____, beneath his palace.

2. The *Odyssey* is a(n) _____ that was written by Homer and tells the many adventures of Odysseus.

3. _____ is the Greek word for city-state.

4. In ancient Greek city-states, the _____ was the city's marketplace and social center.

5. Typically built on a hilltop, the _____ was a city's last line of defense.

6. During the Persian Wars, Athens formed _____ with other Greek city-states.

7. In Spartan society, _____ were slaves from conquered regions.

8. Gold and tin are examples of _____.

READING STRATEGY

9. **ORGANIZE IDEAS: COMPARE AND CONTRAST** If you haven't already, complete your graphic organizer to compare and contrast life in Sparta and Athens. Then answer the question.

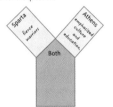

How was life in Sparta and Athens similar? How was it different?

MAIN IDEAS

Answer the following questions. Support your answers with evidence from the chapter.

10. Where did the Minoan civilization settle and flourish? LESSON 1.1

11. How did the Mycenaeans gain wealth and power in the Mediterranean? LESSON 1.2

12. What are epic poems and what kinds of stories do they tell? LESSON 1.3

13. What was the function of the polis as it developed in Greek civilization? LESSON 1.4

14. How did sea trade affect ancient Greek civilization? LESSON 1.5

15. What were the advantages and disadvantages of Sparta's military society? LESSON 2.1

16. How did the roles of Athenian men and women differ? LESSON 2.2

17. What caused the Persian Wars? LESSON 2.3

CRITICAL THINKING

Answer the following questions. Support your answers with evidence from the chapter.

18. **SYNTHESIZE** What were some of the developments that led to the establishment of a cultured and influential civilization in ancient Greece?

19. **COMPARE AND CONTRAST** How were the Minoan and Mycenaean civilizations alike? How were they different?

20. **DRAW CONCLUSIONS** Why were epic poems and their heroes important to the ancient Greeks?

21. **EVALUATE** Why was the Greek adoption of the Phoenician alphabet an important development?

22. **YOU DECIDE** Which city-state—Athens or Sparta—had the most effective system of government? Support your opinion with evidence from the chapter.

INTERPRET MAPS

Study the map of the Persian Wars. Then answer the questions that follow.

23. How did the routes of the first and second Persian invasions differ?

24. Which of the major battles shown was a naval battle?

ANALYZE SOURCES

Read the following description of Darius I, the emperor of Persia, written by Herodotus after the Ionian revolt.

> Darius did, however, ask who the Athenians were, and after receiving the answer, he called for his bow. This he took and, placing an arrow on it, shot it into the sky, praying as he sent it aloft, "O Zeus, grant me vengeance on the Athenians."
>
> Then he ordered one of his servants to say to him three times whenever dinner was set before him, "Master, remember the Athenians."

25. What does this description of Darius I reveal about him?

WRITE ABOUT HISTORY

26. **INFORMATIVE** Suppose you have been asked to participate in a radio program that examines important topics from history. Write a paragraph to inform your audience about the beginnings of democracy in ancient Greece between 600 and 500 B.C.

TIPS

- Take notes from the lesson about Athens's democratic society.
- Introduce the topic clearly.
- Develop the topic with relevant, well-chosen facts, concrete details, and examples.
- Use vocabulary from the chapter to explain democratic ideas.
- Provide a concluding statement that summarizes the information presented.

VOCABULARY ANSWERS

1. labyrinth
2. epic poem
3. Polis
4. agora
5. acropolis
6. alliances
7. helots
8. raw materials

READING STRATEGY ANSWER

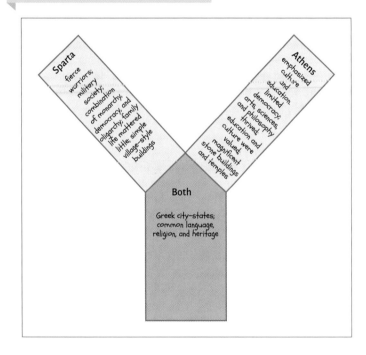

9. Both Sparta and Athens were Greek city-states that shared a common language, religion, and heritage, but that is where their similarities ended. Each Greek city-state developed differently due to their relative isolation. Sparta developed a military society with a rigid hierarchy—every element of Sparta's society was devoted to war and maintaining firm control over the helots. Athens, on the other hand, valued arts, sciences, and education in their more liberal society, where a limited democracy developed. Athens was a beautiful city-state with many magnificent stone buildings and temples.

MAIN IDEAS ANSWERS

10. Minoan civilization settled and flourished on the island of Crete in the Mediterranean.

11. The Mycenaeans gained wealth and power by waging war and conquering lands across the Mediterranean and through trade.

12. Epic poems are long, poetic stories that tell of a hero's adventures with humans and with gods and goddesses.

13. The polis, or city-state, was a small, independent unit in which a dominant city—such as Athens, Sparta, or Thebes—ruled the surrounding area from a centralized location.

14. Sea trade helped early Greeks spread their culture throughout the Mediterranean by establishing hundreds of new colonies and by their wide-ranging trade in the region.

15. The advantages of a military society included being able to control the helots and the general population and to wage effective wars. The disadvantages included harsh living conditions and childhoods.

16. Athenian men could be citizens and received educations; Athenian women were not considered citizens and were not educated. Men's roles centered on the city-state; women's roles centered on the home.

17. The Persian Wars were caused by Athens, who encouraged the Ionians to rebel against the Persians. To punish Athens, the Persians invaded Greece.

CRITICAL THINKING ANSWERS

18. The Minoans and Mycenaeans established the foundation for ancient Greek civilization. Later, ancient Greek city-states developed unique cultures, various types of government, and established a complex and rich trade network in the Mediterranean. The ancient Greeks also developed strong militaries that enabled them to defend themselves against huge empires such as the Persians.

19. The Minoans and Mycenaean civilizations were alike in terms of culture. After they settled in mainland Greece, the Mycenaeans copied nearly all aspects of Minoan culture, including government, religion, architecture, shipbuilding, and trade. The Minoans focused on building ships and trading, while the Mycenaeans were a warring people who used their military power to seize other lands and expand their power in the region.

20. Epic poems united the Greeks through pride in their shared past.

21. The Greek adoption of the Phoenician alphabet was important because after the Greeks adopted the Phoenician alphabet, they improved it, eventually making it the Greek alphabet. This alphabet was in turn adopted and became the basis of the modern alphabet used today.

22. Students' responses will vary. Students should clearly state their opinion regarding their view of government in Sparta and Athens and support that opinion with evidence from the chapter.

INTERPRET MAPS ANSWERS

23. In the first invasion the Persians attacked Greece from the south, by sea. In the second invasion, the Persians attacked from the north, by both land and sea.

24. The Battle of Salamis was a naval battle.

ANALYZE SOURCES ANSWER

25. Students' responses will vary. Sample response: The description reveals how fiercely angry Darius I is toward the Athenians for their role in the Ionian revolt. Details such as Darius shooting an arrow, swearing to God, and wanting to be reminded of the Athenians all show the extent of his anger and determination to punish the Athenians.

WRITE ABOUT HISTORY ANSWER

26. Students' informative paragraphs will vary, but students should present the information in a clear, logical manner that explains how democracy began to form in ancient Greece between 600 and 500 B.C.

UNIT RESOURCES

On Location with National Geographic Grantee William Parkinson Intro and Video

Unit Wrap-Up:
"The Emergence of Cities"
Feature and Video

"Greek Statues Sparkle Once Again"
National Geographic Adapted Article

"Behind the Tomb"
National Geographic Adapted Article
Student eEdition exclusive

Unit 3 Inquiry:
Define Good Citizenship

 Interactive Map Tool
Available on myNGconnect

 **News & Updates**
Available on myNGconnect

CHAPTER RESOURCES

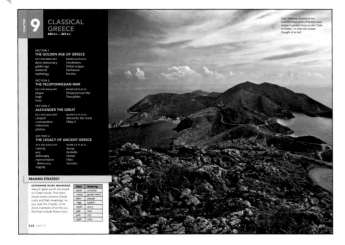

TEACHER RESOURCES & ASSESSMENT *Available on myNGconnect*

 Social Studies Skills Lessons
• Reading: Determine Word Meanings
• Writing: Write an Informative Text

Chapter 9
Answer Key

 Formal Assessment
• Chapter 9 Tests A (on-level) &
  B (below-level)

 ExamView®
One-time Download

STUDENT BACKPACK *Available on myNGconnect*

• **eEdition** *(English)* • **eEdition** *(Spanish)* • **Handbooks** • **Online Atlas**
For Chapter 9 Spanish resources, visit the Teacher Resource Menu page on myNGconnect.

SECTION 1 RESOURCES

THE GOLDEN AGE OF GREECE

 Reading and Note-Taking

 Vocabulary Practice

 Section 1 Quiz

Available on myNGconnect

LESSON 1.1 PERICLES AND DEMOCRACY

 Biography
Cleisthenes

Available on myNGconnect

• On Your Feet: Small Groups

NG Learning Framework:
Democracy in Action

LESSON 1.2 THE ATHENIAN EMPIRE

• On Your Feet: Debate

NG Learning Framework:
Research the Acropolis

LESSON 1.3 RELIGION AND THE GODS

• On Your Feet: Play a Game of Telephone

NG Learning Framework:
Retell a Myth

SECTION 2 RESOURCES

THE PELOPONNESIAN WAR

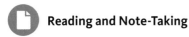 Reading and Note-Taking

 Vocabulary Practice

 Section 2 Quiz

Available on myNGconnect

LESSON 2.1 WAR BREAKS OUT
- On Your Feet: Inside-Outside Circle
- Critical Viewing: NG Chapter Gallery

LESSON 2.2 THE DEFEAT OF ATHENS
- On Your Feet: Identifying Issues
- Critical Viewing: NG Image Gallery

DOCUMENT-BASED QUESTION
LESSON 2.3 ATHENIAN DEMOCRACY
- On Your Feet: Jigsaw

| NG Learning Framework:
| Attitudes Toward Democracy

SECTION 3 RESOURCES

ALEXANDER THE GREAT

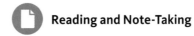 Reading and Note-Taking

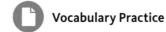 Vocabulary Practice

Section 3 Quiz

Available on myNGconnect

LESSON 3.1 PHILIP OF MACEDONIA
- On Your Feet: Tell Me More

| NG Learning Framework:
| Role-Play

BIOGRAPHY
LESSON 3.2 ALEXANDER THE GREAT
- On Your Feet: Make Inferences About Character
- Critical Viewing: NG Image Gallery

LESSON 3.3 THE SPREAD OF HELLENISTIC CULTURE
- On Your Feet: Culture Roundtable
- Critical Viewing: NG Chapter Gallery

SECTION 4 RESOURCES

THE LEGACY OF ANCIENT GREECE

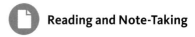 Reading and Note-Taking

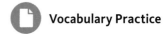 Vocabulary Practice

 Section 4 Quiz

Available on myNGconnect

LESSON 4.1 PHILOSOPHY AND LITERATURE

 **Biography**
Aristotle

Available on myNGconnect
- Critical Viewing: NG Image Gallery
- On Your Feet: Understand Multiple Perspectives

LESSON 4.2 ARTS AND ARCHITECTURE
- On Your Feet: Small Groups

| NG Learning Framework:
| Write a Play

MOMENTS IN HISTORY
LESSON 4.3 THE PARTHENON
- On Your Feet: Debate
- Critical Viewing: NG Chapter Gallery

LESSON 4.4 DEMOCRACY AND LAW

 Active History: Interactive Whiteboard Activity
Research Ancient Greek Contributions

 Active History
Research Ancient Greek Contributions

Available on myNGconnect
- On Your Feet: Democracy from Scratch

CHAPTER 9 REVIEW

STRATEGY ❶

Use a TASKS Approach

Help students get information from visuals by using the following TASKS strategy:

T Look for a **title** that may give the main idea.

A **Ask** yourself what the visual is trying to show.

S Determine how **symbols** are used.

K Look for a **key** or legend.

S **Summarize** what you learned.

Use with All Lessons

STRATEGY ❷

Make Summary Statements

Before reading, have students look at the blue subheadings within the lessons. After reading, direct students to use each subheading to begin a statement that summarizes the information about the subheading.

Use with Lesson 1.2 *Suggest that students use these sentence starters: Athens and other states banded together to form the _____, to defend themselves from Persia. Athens used money from the Delian League to _____.*

STRATEGY ❸

Play the "I Am . . ." Game

To reinforce the meanings of key terms and names, assign every student one term or name that appears in the chapter and have them write a one-sentence clue beginning with "I am." Have students take turns reading clues and calling on other students to guess answers.

Use with All Lessons

Press (**mt**) *in the Student eEdition for modified text.*

STRATEGY ❶

Provide Terms and Names on Audio

Decide which of the terms and names are important for mastery and have a volunteer record the pronunciations and a short sentence defining each word. Encourage students to listen to the recording as often as necessary.

Use with All Lessons *You might also use the recordings to quiz students on their mastery of the terms. Play one definition at a time from the recording and ask students to identify the term or name described.*

STRATEGY ❷

Preview Visuals to Predict

Ask students to preview the title and visuals in each lesson. Then have students tell what they think the lesson will be about. After reading, ask them to repeat the activity to see whether their predictions were confirmed.

Use with All Lessons *Invite volunteers to describe the visuals in detail to help visually impaired students see them.*

STRATEGY ❶

PREP Before Reading

Have students use the PREP strategy to prepare for reading. Write this acrostic on the board:

PREP   **P**review title.

                     Read Main Idea statement.

                     Examine visuals.

                     Predict what you will learn.

Have students write their prediction and share it with a partner. After reading, ask students to write another sentence that begins "I also learned . . ."

Use with All Lessons

STRATEGY ②
Use Visuals to Puzzle Through Vocabulary

Ask students to look at the visuals and try to figure out what clues they might offer about the key vocabulary words in the text. In Lesson 1.3 have them work out the meaning of the word *mythology*, while in Lesson 2.2 see if the visual helps them understand the word *siege*.

Use with Lessons 1.3 and 2.2

STRATEGY ③
Speak, Listen, and Learn

After students have read several lessons, divide the class into small groups and conduct a round-robin activity to review the material students have learned. Write the topic of the lesson on the board and have groups generate facts for about three to five minutes, with all students contributing. Then have one student from each group share the group's responses without repeating any fact already stated by another group. Have the volunteer write the fact on the board.

Use with Lessons 3.1, 3.3, and 4.4

GIFTED & TALENTED

STRATEGY ①
Teach a Class

Before beginning the chapter, allow students to choose one of the lessons listed below and prepare to teach the content to the class. Give them a set amount of time in which to present their lesson. Suggest that students think about any visuals or activities they want to use when they teach.

Use with Lessons 1.2, 1.4, 1.6, and 2.1–2.3

STRATEGY ②
Create a Fan Zine for a Classical Greek Author or Philosopher

Using any author or philosopher mentioned in the text, suggest that students create a comic or zine to celebrate and teach about the person. Tell students to use both visuals and text, quotations from the thinker, and examples illustrating his ideas.

Use with Lessons 2.3, 4.1, and 4.2

PRE-AP

STRATEGY ①
Consider Two Sides

Tell students that some people believe that direct democracy is superior to representative democracy, or the type of democracy that is practiced in the United States. Have pairs of students research the issue and make a chart listing the positive and negative aspects of the two types of democracy. Have students share and discuss their chart with the class.

Use with Lessons 1.1 and 4.4

STRATEGY ②
Read Literature

Work with the school librarian to find and display a variety of titles from the period of classical Greece or historical fiction about that period. Allow students to choose a book (or part of a book) to read and design a way to report on the book to the class.

Use with All Lessons

CLASSICAL GREECE
480 B.C. – 323 B.C.

SECTION 1
THE GOLDEN AGE OF GREECE

KEY VOCABULARY	NAMES & PLACES
direct democracy	Cleisthenes
golden age	Delian League
immortal	Parthenon
mythology	Pericles

SECTION 2
THE PELOPONNESIAN WAR

KEY VOCABULARY	NAMES & PLACES
plague	Peloponnesian War
siege	Thucydides
truce	

SECTION 3
ALEXANDER THE GREAT

KEY VOCABULARY	NAMES & PLACES
catapult	Alexander the Great
cosmopolitan	Philip II
Hellenistic	
phalanx	

SECTION 4
THE LEGACY OF ANCIENT GREECE

KEY VOCABULARY	NAMES & PLACES
comedy	Aesop
jury	Aristotle
philosophy	Homer
representative	Plato
democracy	Socrates
tragedy	

READING STRATEGY

DETERMINE WORD MEANINGS
Many English words are based on Greek words. This chart shows some common Greek roots and their meanings. As you read the chapter, write down examples of words you find that include these roots.

Root	Meaning
cosm-	universe
-cracy	government
dem-	people
-logy	speech
myth-	story
phil-	love
poli-	city
soph-	wise

Cape Tainaron, located at the southernmost point of Greece, was known in ancient times as the "Gate to Hades," or what the Greeks thought of as hell.

TEACHER BACKGROUND

INTRODUCE THE PHOTOGRAPH

Have students study the photograph of Cape Tainaron. Explain that a cape is a large extension of land that sticks out into a body of water. Explain that the geography of Greece influenced its history and culture and that students will learn more about these characteristics in the chapter.

ASK: What can you tell about the geography of Greece from this picture? *(Possible response: It is hilly, rocky, and near water.)*

SHARE BACKGROUND

Hades was the name of both the Greek underworld—the place where souls went after death—and its god. After death, a soul journeyed to the underworld through a cave thought to be on Cape Tainaron. There the soul was greeted by Charon, the ferryman who took souls across the river Styx to the gates of Hades. Each soul then appeared before a panel of judges who passed sentence according to deeds performed during the previous life. Good souls went to the Elysian Fields, a type of paradise, while bad souls remained in Hades and were punished for eternity.

DIGITAL RESOURCES myNGconnect.com

TEACHER RESOURCES & ASSESSMENT

 Social Studies Skills Lessons
- Reading: Determine Word Meanings
- Writing: Write an Informative Text

 Formal Assessment
- Chapter 9 Tests A (on-level) & B (below-level)

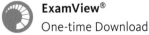 **ExamView®**
One-time Download

 **Chapter 9 Answer Key**

STUDENT BACKPACK

- **eEdition** *(English)*
- **eEdition** *(Spanish)*
- **Handbooks**
- **Online Atlas**

For Chapter 9 Spanish Resources, visit the Teacher Resource Menu page.

WHAT LASTING INFLUENCES DID ANCIENT GREEK CULTURE HAVE ON THE MODERN WORLD?

Jigsaw: Cultural Influence This activity introduces students to four factors of culture in order to differentiate the various influences that classical Greek civilization has had on modern society. Have students form four expert groups and then tell them to research and brainstorm one aspect of Greek culture and how it has influenced a modern culture. Students may focus on religion, government, customs and traditions, arts and recreation, or some other aspect. Then have students regroup so that one member from each expert group is in the new group. Each expert should then report on his or her topic of study to the members of the new group. **0:15** minutes

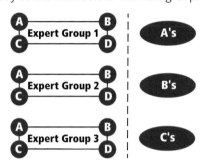

DETERMINE WORD MEANINGS

Read through the chart of Greek roots and their meanings with students. Model the strategy by using knowledge of the roots *dem-* and *-cracy* to determine the meaning of the word *democracy*, or government of the people.

Root	Meaning
cosm-	universe
-cracy	government
dem-	people
-logy	speech
myth-	story
phil-	love
poli-	city
soph-	wise

KNOWLEDGE RATING

Have students complete a Knowledge-Rating Chart for Key Vocabulary words. Have students list words and fill out the chart. Then have pairs share the definitions they know. Work together as a class to complete the chart.

KEY VOCAB	KNOW IT	NOT SURE	DON'T KNOW	DEFINITION
catapult				
comedy				
cosmopolitan				
direct democracy				

KEY DATES

c. 500 B.C.	Development of democracy in Athens
478 B.C.	Creation of the Delian League
431 B.C.	Beginning of the Peloponnesian War; Pericles' funeral oration
414 B.C.	Athens's siege of Syracuse
404 B.C.	End of the Peloponnesian War; the defeat of Athens
338 B.C.	Unification of Greece under Philip of Macedonia
331 B.C.	Conquest of the Persian Empire by Alexander the Great

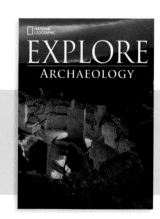

For more about how archaeologists study other ancient cultures, check out *EXPLORE ARCHAEOLOGY*.

Pericles and Democracy

When you go out with your friends after school, how does your group decide what to do? Does one friend make this decision? Do two or three take charge? Or do you all have a say? If you all weigh in, that's democracy, a concept that began in Athens more than 2,500 years ago.

MAIN IDEA

Athens established the world's first democracy.

ELECTED BY LOTTERY

Athenians used this machine, known as a *kleroterion*, to elect officials. Each eligible male placed a token with his name on it in one of the slots. A series of balls were then released from a tube to determine whose tokens would be chosen.

SEEDS OF DEMOCRACY

As you may recall from the previous chapter, the leader Solon made life better for the poor. He cancelled their debts, freed enslaved farmers, and abolished unfair payments to greedy landowners.

Solon also reduced the power of the aristocracy. He organized citizens into four classes based on wealth. Rich men still had more power, but all male citizens, rich and poor, were allowed to join the assembly and help elect leaders. Solon also created a council chosen by lottery, or chance, from the assembly. Solon made Athenian government fairer, but it was not yet a true democracy.

Around 500 B.C., a leader named **Cleisthenes** (KLYS-thuh-neez) took things further. Under his rule, the assembly members debated openly and heard court cases. Citizens were organized into groups based on where they lived. Each group sent 50 representatives a year to the Council of 500. The council proposed laws and debated policies, and the assembly voted on them. The citizens were now fully engaged in government. This was democracy—but a limited one. Only male property owners born in Athens could participate. Women, foreigners, and slaves had no political rights.

ATHENS'S GREATEST LEADER

Pericles (PEHR-uh-kleez), one of Athens's greatest leaders, expanded this limited democracy into one that would allow all male citizens to participate in government. He transferred the remaining powers of the aristocrats to the assembly. He paid jurors, which allowed poor citizens to take time off to serve the state. This idea was later extended to all public officials, who previously were unpaid. Pericles also opened up powerful political positions to the middle classes. Neither social class nor poverty was a barrier to political power anymore. Athens now had a **direct democracy**, in which citizens gathered together to vote on laws and policies.

Pericles was also determined to glorify Athens by transforming it from a city ravaged by the Persian Wars to a center of learning, creativity, and beauty. By encouraging the work of great thinkers and artists, Pericles guided Athens through a **golden age**—a period of great cultural achievement.

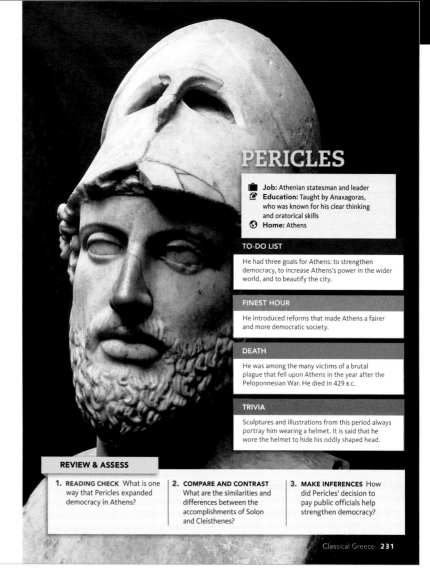

PERICLES

- **Job:** Athenian statesman and leader
- **Education:** Taught by Anaxagoras, who was known for his clear thinking and oratorical skills
- **Home:** Athens

TO-DO LIST

He had three goals for Athens: to strengthen democracy, to increase Athens's power in the wider world, and to beautify the city.

FINEST HOUR

He introduced reforms that made Athens a fairer and more democratic society.

DEATH

He was among the many victims of a brutal plague that fell upon Athens in the year after the Peloponnesian War. He died in 429 B.C.

TRIVIA

Sculptures and illustrations from this period always portray him wearing a helmet. It is said that he wore the helmet to hide his oddly shaped head.

REVIEW & ASSESS

1. **READING CHECK** What is one way that Pericles expanded democracy in Athens?

2. **COMPARE AND CONTRAST** What are the similarities and differences between the accomplishments of Solon and Cleisthenes?

3. **MAKE INFERENCES** How did Pericles' decision to pay public officials help strengthen democracy?

PLAN

OBJECTIVE

Identify the process by which Athens became a democracy.

CRITICAL THINKING SKILLS FOR LESSON 1.1

- Identify Main Ideas and Details
- Compare and Contrast
- Analyze Causes
- Analyze Visuals
- Monitor Comprehension
- Make Inferences

ESSENTIAL QUESTION

What lasting influences did ancient Greek culture have on the modern world?

Greece introduced the world to the concept of democracy. Lesson 1.1 describes the evolution of Greece's democratic government.

BACKGROUND FOR THE TEACHER

Athens is credited with having the first direct democracy in history. Democracy comes from two Greek words—*kratos*, meaning "rule" and *demos*, meaning "village or people." The idea that not just the rich and powerful should have a say in government gave rise to the idea of the assembly. The assembly gave the normal people more say in government and made it harder for corrupt individuals to use power for personal gain. It was used to check the power of the council, the full-time government of Athens that ran the daily affairs of the city. The council was elected by lottery and changed every year.

DIGITAL RESOURCES myNGconnect.com

TEACHER RESOURCES & ASSESSMENT

 Reading and Note-Taking   **Vocabulary Practice**   **Section 1 Quiz**

STUDENT RESOURCES

 Biography

INTRODUCE & ENGAGE

COMPLETE A K-W-L CHART

Provide each student with a K-W-L Chart. Have students brainstorm what they know about Pericles and democracy. Then ask them to write questions that they would like to have answered as they study Lesson 1.1. Allow time at the end of the lesson for students to fill in what they have learned. **0:05** minutes

TEACH

GUIDED DISCUSSION

1. **Make Inferences** Why might a leader like Solon have wanted to reduce the power of the aristocracy and improve the lives of the poor? *(because he wanted to improve the lives of the poor, gaining their approval and reducing discontent, as well as strengthening his own position)*

2. **Analyze Causes** What was the motivation to pay jurors under Pericles' leadership? *(Paying jurors allowed poor citizens to serve on juries. Otherwise they could not afford to take time off from their jobs.)*

ANALYZE VISUALS

Direct students' attention to the photo of the statue of Pericles. **ASK:** What can you tell about the style of Greek sculpture? How does it compare to figures created by the ancient Egyptians? *(Greek sculpture is very realistic with lots of attention to detail. Egyptian figures were less detailed and more symbolic in appearance.)* **0:10** minutes

ACTIVE OPTIONS

On Your Feet: Small Groups Have students form small groups. Have each group find a different country that has some form of democracy today and report to the class some details about the country's system, including whether it is a limited or unlimited democracy, a mix, a republic, or perhaps, a democracy with a monarch. **0:10** minutes

NG Learning Framework: Democracy in Action

ATTITUDES: **Empowerment, Responsibility**
SKILLS: **Collaboration, Problem-Solving**

Have students observe Athenian direct democracy in action by letting them vote on some aspect of the day's instruction or the classroom layout. For example, they might vote on whether or not to answer lesson questions in groups or on whether or not to arrange desks in a circle for the day. Students should give a yes or no vote on the aspect and a simple majority should determine whether the measure passes. After the vote, discuss the strengths and weaknesses of this form of government. **0:10** minutes

DIFFERENTIATE

STRIVING READERS

Chart Athenian Leaders Have students use the chart to keep track of reforms made by the three leaders in Lesson 1.1.

	Solon	Cleisthenes	Pericles
Let only male property owners participate in government	✓	✓	
Made life better for the poor	✓		
Allowed women to participate in government			
Organized citizens into classes	✓		
Paid jurors and public officials			✓
Created a council by lottery	✓		
Guided Athens to a golden age			✓
Created a limited democracy		✓	

PRE-AP

Write Reports Use Lesson 1.1 as a starting point to have students explore the concept of democracy further. Tell students to research the characteristics of limited and unlimited democracies, finding historical and contemporary examples for each. Then direct students to write a short report about the advantages and disadvantages of both types of democracy. Encourage volunteers to share their reports with the class.

Press (mt) *in the Student eEdition for modified text.*
See the Chapter Planner for more strategies for differentiation.

REVIEW & ASSESS

ANSWERS

1. Pericles expanded democracy by transferring the remaining powers of the aristocrats to the assembly, opening up powerful political positions to the middle classes, and establishing a direct democracy.

2. Both Solon and Cleisthenes made life fairer for the poor. But under Solon's rule, wealthy men still had more power. Cleisthenes reduced wealthy men's power by reorganizing citizens into classes based on location, not wealth.

3. Paying public officials strengthened democracy by allowing all men, not just wealthy ones, to have the opportunity to hold government positions.

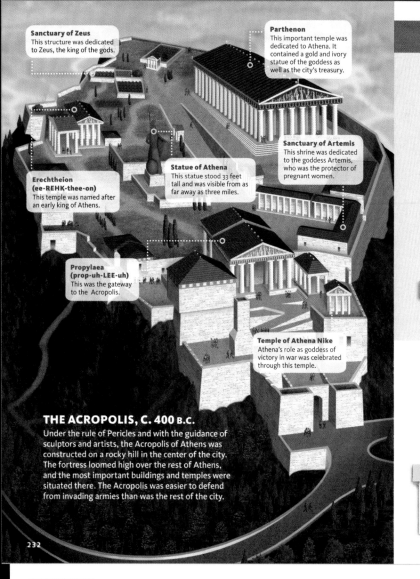

Sanctuary of Zeus
This structure was dedicated to Zeus, the king of the gods.

Parthenon
This important temple was dedicated to Athena. It contained a gold and ivory statue of the goddess as well as the city's treasury.

Sanctuary of Artemis
This shrine was dedicated to the goddess Artemis, who was the protector of pregnant women.

Statue of Athena
This statue stood 33 feet tall and was visible from as far away as three miles.

**Erechtheion
(ee-REHK-thee-on)**
This temple was named after an early king of Athens.

**Propylaea
(prop-uh-LEE-uh)**
This was the gateway to the Acropolis.

Temple of Athena Nike
Athena's role as goddess of victory in war was celebrated through this temple.

THE ACROPOLIS, C. 400 B.C.

Under the rule of Pericles and with the guidance of sculptors and artists, the Acropolis of Athens was constructed on a rocky hill in the center of the city. The fortress loomed high over the rest of Athens, and the most important buildings and temples were situated there. The Acropolis was easier to defend from invading armies than was the rest of the city.

1.2

The Athenian Empire

The war with Persia made the Greeks realize that there really is strength in numbers. So Athens and numerous other city-states joined forces to protect themselves against enemies. But Athens was always the strongest of the city-states, and it soon became apparent that Athenians had their own interests in mind.

MAIN IDEA

Athens grew into a powerful empire and was rebuilt to reflect its important status.

THE DELIAN LEAGUE

To defend themselves from Persia, which still posed a possible threat, Athens and the other city-states formed an anti-Persian alliance. The **Delian** (DEE-lee-uhn) **League**, formed in 478 B.C., was based on the island of Delos, where funds were kept to fight future wars with Persia.

Each city-state contributed cash, ships, or soldiers and had equal votes in the league's council. However, Athens was always the league's leader and took control over the other city-states in the alliance.

Pericles used the league's money to build Athens's powerful navy. This naval force allowed Athens to rule the Mediterranean region and the Delian League. In 454 B.C., the league's treasury was moved from the island of Delos to Athens. The other city-states in the alliance were now powerless against Athens.

The Spartans were not happy that the Athenians were gaining so much power. Although distracted by regular slave revolts, Sparta remained a major power. It established its own network of alliances called the Peloponnesian League. Resentment built between the two leagues, causing tension to run dangerously high.

REBUILDING THE CITY

Meanwhile, Athens was still in ruins from the Persian Wars. The Delian League began funding the rebuilding of Athens, which would be grander than ever.

The city walls were rebuilt. Then Pericles rebuilt the Acropolis with richly decorated temples and monuments. One structure on the Acropolis was the **Parthenon** (PAHR-thuh-nahn), the awe-inspiring temple that was dedicated to Athens's goddess, Athena. The city's leaders poured money into beautifying the city with the finest architecture, art, and sculpture. Pericles transformed Athens into one of the most magnificent cities in the ancient world. It was a fitting capital for a powerful empire.

REVIEW & ASSESS

1. **READING CHECK** How did the Delian League make Athens more powerful?

2. **ANALYZE CAUSE AND EFFECT** How did the Spartans respond to the creation of the Delian League?

3. **INTEGRATE VISUALS** Why do you think the Parthenon was located on the Acropolis?

PLAN

OBJECTIVE

Understand Athens's transformation into a powerful empire.

CRITICAL THINKING SKILLS FOR LESSON 1.2

- Identify Main Ideas and Details
- Monitor Comprehension
- Analyze Cause and Effect
- Integrate Visuals
- Form and Support Opinions

ESSENTIAL QUESTION

What lasting influences did ancient Greek culture have on the modern world?

The Acropolis of Athens and its buildings and temples, especially the Parthenon, continue to attract visitors today. The Athenian city on a hill is known for its architectural beauty. Lesson 1.2 explains how the rebuilding of the Acropolis became a symbol of Athens's power and glory.

BACKGROUND FOR THE TEACHER

The word *acropolis* means "high city" in Greek. Most city-states had an acropolis at their center—a rocky mound or hill that housed important temples and served as a fortress during an attack. Undoubtedly, the most famous acropolis is the one in Athens. Most of its early temples were destroyed by the Persians in 480 B.C., which paved the way for its rebuilding under the leadership of Pericles.

DIGITAL RESOURCES myNGconnect.com

TEACHER RESOURCES & ASSESSMENT

 Reading and Note-Taking

 Vocabulary Practice

 Section 1 Quiz

STUDENT RESOURCES

 NG Chapter Gallery

PREVIEW WITH PROBLEM-SOLVING

Describe the following scenario to students: Imagine that you and a group of friends decided to pool your money together to order pizza. One friend volunteers to hold all the money until it is time to order, but then you find out that this friend used the money to buy a new video game for him- or herself instead. Have students discuss how this action would make them feel toward their friend. Explain that in Lesson 1.2 they will learn how Athens behaved in a similar way toward its fellow city-states. `0:05` minutes

TEACH

GUIDED DISCUSSION

1. **Analyze Cause and Effect** When Athens began using its power to control the Delian League, what was the effect on the other city-states? *(They felt powerless against Athens, and Sparta established its own Peloponnesian League.)*

2. **Form and Support Opinions** Was Athens right to use Delian League money to build a navy and rebuild the city? *(yes, because a strong Athens would help protect all the city-states; no, because the money was not distributed fairly to help the defenses of all the city-states who contributed to it)*

INTEGRATE VISUALS

Direct students' attention to the illustration of the Acropolis. Ask them to consider how the physical characteristics of the land influenced how people lived and constructed their buildings. As a class, make a list of the challenges the Athenians must have faced as they built structures on the hill. `0:10` minutes

ACTIVE OPTIONS

On Your Feet: Debate Divide the class into two groups. Have one side represent Athens and the other Sparta. Offer the issue of Athens's growing power under the Delian League as a topic of debate. Alternatively, come up with a different topic as a class. Then, have the groups use the information from Lesson 1.2 to organize the strongest arguments in favor of their group's position. Each group should also generate some suggestions to address the concerns of the other group. Then give the two groups a chance to debate the topic by taking turns presenting their arguments and offering their suggestions. Encourage the class to reach consensus on one or two suggestions. `0:10` minutes

NG Learning Framework: Research the Acropolis

ATTITUDES: **Curiosity, Empowerment**
KNOWLEDGE: **Our Human Story**

Have pairs of students research a building at the Acropolis other than the Parthenon. They should determine what the building looked like, what it was used for, and what it tells us about ancient Greek society. Then have pairs share their information by giving a brief presentation with visuals. `0:20` minutes

STRIVING READERS

Complete Sentence Starters Provide these sentence starters for students to complete after reading. You may also have students preview to set a purpose for reading.

• The Delian League was formed because _____.

• Pericles used the league's money to _____.

• The _____ were not happy about Athens's rising power.

• Sparta established its own network of alliances, called the _____.

• The _____ funded the rebuilding of the Acropolis.

GIFTED & TALENTED

Build a Model Have students work in groups to create a three-dimensional model of the Acropolis for the classroom. Encourage them to explore different materials to use for their model and to draft plans for the model before trying to build it. Some groups may want to select a particular feature to highlight. Other groups might want to situate the Acropolis by building it on a hill as part of their model.

Press (**mt**) *in the Student eEdition for modified text.*

See the Chapter Planner for more strategies for differentiation.

ANSWERS

1. Pericles used money from the Delian League to build a powerful navy. This gave Athens enough power to become an empire. Pericles also used money from the league to rebuild, strengthen, and beautify Athens.

2. The Spartans formed a rival alliance called the Peloponnesian League, which increased tensions between the two leagues in the Mediterranean.

3. The Parthenon was sacred to Athenians because it was dedicated to their goddess, Athena. By locating the Parthenon high up on the Acropolis, it would be easier for Athenians to defend the temple from enemies.

Religion and the Gods

Greek gods and goddesses may seem more like cartoon superheroes than divine deities. According to Greek belief, the gods looked and acted like humans: They married, had children, got jealous, and started wars. But they did it all with fantastic superpowers! Ordinary people had to either keep them happy or face their wrath.

MAIN IDEA

The Greeks believed that the many gods they worshipped could strongly influence daily life.

BELIEFS

Greek gods played an important role in ancient Greece. The gods were considered **immortal**, or able to live forever. Like the Mesopotamians and Egyptians, the Greeks believed that

The 12 Olympians

Zeus King of the gods

Hera Queen of the gods

Aphrodite Goddess of love and beauty

Apollo God of the sun and music

Ares God of war

Artemis Goddess of the moon and hunting

Athena Goddess of wisdom and war

Demeter Goddess of the harvest

Dionysus God of wine

Hephaestus God of fire and metalworking

Hermes Messenger of the gods

Poseidon God of the sea

unhappy gods showed their displeasure by causing problems in people's lives. Greeks obtained the gods' help by leaving offerings outside temples—the gods' earthly homes. Temples were usually impressive stone buildings housing a statue of the god. A city's biggest temple was dedicated to its patron god, who protected it.

There were hundreds of Greek gods. According to Greek belief, the top 12 gods were the Olympians, or the ones who lived in luxury on Mount Olympus, the highest mountain in Greece. A holy day, celebrated with colorful and noisy public festivals, was dedicated to each god and goddess. These special days involved great processions, offerings, poetry recitals, and competitive sports, including the original Olympic Games. For private worship, most Greek homes had small altars where people would pray to the gods.

MYTHS

The Greeks had a close relationship with their gods, who often got involved in human affairs. This is how Greek religion blended with **mythology**—a collection of stories that explained events, beliefs, or actions. In Greek myths, the gods, kings, heroes, and ordinary people had amazing adventures together. The gods often rewarded or punished humans for their deeds. These stories were written down to form a group of exciting tales that are still popular today. One of these myths appears on the next page.

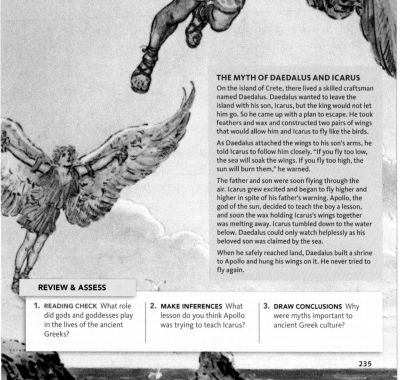

THE MYTH OF DAEDALUS AND ICARUS

On the island of Crete, there lived a skilled craftsman named Daedalus. Daedalus wanted to leave the island with his son, Icarus, but the king would not let him go. So he came up with a plan to escape. He took feathers and wax and constructed two pairs of wings that would allow him and Icarus to fly like the birds.

As Daedalus attached the wings to his son's arms, he told Icarus to follow him closely. "If you fly too low, the sea will soak the wings. If you fly too high, the sun will burn them," he warned.

The father and son were soon flying through the air. Icarus grew excited and began to fly higher and higher in spite of his father's warning. Apollo, the god of the sun, decided to teach the boy a lesson, and soon the wax holding Icarus's wings together was melting away. Icarus tumbled down to the water below. Daedalus could only watch helplessly as his beloved son was claimed by the sea.

When he safely reached land, Daedalus built a shrine to Apollo and hung his wings on it. He never tried to fly again.

REVIEW & ASSESS

1. **READING CHECK** What role did gods and goddesses play in the lives of the ancient Greeks?

2. **MAKE INFERENCES** What lesson do you think Apollo was trying to teach Icarus?

3. **DRAW CONCLUSIONS** Why were myths important to ancient Greek culture?

PLAN

OBJECTIVE

Understand religious beliefs of the ancient Greeks.

CRITICAL THINKING SKILLS FOR LESSON 1.3

- Identify Main Ideas and Details
- Monitor Comprehension
- Make Inferences
- Draw Conclusions
- Explain

ESSENTIAL QUESTION

What lasting influences did ancient Greek culture have on the modern world?

The ancient Greeks believed that their gods and goddesses played an active role in their daily life. Lesson 1.3 introduces important Greek

deities and describes how ancient beliefs have carried over to the present day.

BACKGROUND FOR THE TEACHER

Religion was central to culture in ancient Greece. All Greeks worshipped the same gods and goddesses, who looked and behaved like humans, but had superpowers. Each god controlled a particular area of life. For example, the Greeks prayed to the goddess Artemis when they needed help with hunting.

Some Greeks visited an oracle, or a priest or priestess who was believed to speak on behalf of a god or goddess. People visited oracles in shrines located deep below temples and would ask questions about their future.

DIGITAL RESOURCES myNGconnect.com

TEACHER RESOURCES & ASSESSMENT

 Reading and Note-Taking

 Vocabulary Practice

 Section 1 Quiz

STUDENT RESOURCES

 NG Chapter Gallery

INTRODUCE & ENGAGE

ACTIVATE PRIOR KNOWLEDGE

Greek heroes, gods, and goddesses have been portrayed in comics, electronic games, films, and novels. Ask students if they are familiar with any Greek myths. Discuss why the dramatic stories of the Greeks continue to fire our imaginations many centuries later. **0:05** minutes

TEACH

GUIDED DISCUSSION

1. **Explain** How did the gods interact with ordinary mortals, both positively and negatively, in Greek myths? *(Humans left offerings to the gods to win their favor and assistance. Gods showed their displeasure by causing problems for humans.)*

2. **Make Inferences** What was the lesson of the myth of Daedalus and Icarus retold in the lesson? *(Possible response: Don't try to reach too high, too soon, especially if you are in unfamiliar circumstances. Stay humble, or you might start to think you can go higher than you can.)*

MORE INFORMATION

Greek vs. Roman Mythology The Romans took much of Greek mythology and made it their own. Every major Greek god has a Roman counterpart: Zeus is Jupiter; Hera is Juno; Aphrodite is Venus; and Ares is Mars. Notice that many of these Latin names were used to name both the planets in our solar system and days of the week (such as Saturday).

ACTIVE OPTIONS

On Your Feet: Play a Game of Telephone Ask students to retell a myth. First tell one student the myth, and then have that student tell another student, and so on. The last student should tell the myth out loud. Have students discuss how the story changed from one person to the next. Explain that this is an example of how stories can morph through multiple tellings. **0:15** minutes

NG Learning Framework: Retell a Myth

ATTITUDES: **Curiosity, Empowerment**
KNOWLEDGE: **Our Human Story**

Have students research and read a Greek myth other than the one that appears in the lesson. Some ideas include "Pygmalion," "King Midas," "Arachne," or "Echo and Narcissus." Ask volunteers to narrate their particular myth for the rest of the class. Some students may want to work in groups and act out a particular myth. After each student or group presents their myth, discuss what event, belief, or action the myth was created to explain. **0:25** minutes

DIFFERENTIATE

ENGLISH LANGUAGE LEARNERS

Create Vocabulary Cards Post the words *immortal* and *mythology* on the board. Have students make vocabulary cards for these two words. On the front of each card, they should copy the word. On the back, they should write the definition of the word.

GIFTED & TALENTED

Rewrite an Ancient Myth Have students research ancient Greek myths. Have each student choose a different myth and rewrite it for the present day. Students may want to illustrate their myths or present them as short plays or videos. Make sure students include the usual mythical figures: humans, heroes, gods, and demi-gods. Encourage students share their present-day myths with the class.

Press (mt) *in the Student eEdition for modified text.*

See the Chapter Planner for more strategies for differentiation.

REVIEW & ASSESS

ANSWERS

1. Greeks believed that if they didn't keep their gods happy, bad things would happen. They kept the gods happy by leaving them offerings, celebrating them during public festivals, and worshipping them privately.

2. Apollo was trying to teach Icarus to listen to his father and not fly too high for his own good.

3. Greek myths about gods, kings, and heroes helped the people of ancient Greece understand their world and gave explanations for how things came to be the way they were.

War Breaks Out

As Athens became wealthier and more powerful, other city-states, especially Sparta, became suspicious and fearful of Athens's future plans. Athens and Sparta had created very different societies. Athens championed a democratic government, while Sparta focused on military strength. These differences contributed to a growing distrust that exploded into war.

MAIN IDEA

Rivalry between Sparta and Athens plunged Greece into war.

TENSIONS RISE

In addition to societal differences, Sparta resented Athens's use of money from the Delian League. Remember, Athens had used this money, intended to protect all of the city-states, for its own benefit. When the city-states protested this inequality and attempted to free themselves from Athenian rule, Pericles punished them. By 431 B.C., Sparta had had enough of Athenian aggression and declared war on Athens. The **Peloponnesian War** had begun.

Sparta had a strong army and Athens had a strong navy. This contrast in military strength forced the two sides to develop very different plans for winning the war. Athens, under Pericles, avoided fighting Sparta and its allies on land and planned to attack from the sea. Athens withdrew behind its strong city walls. Its ships kept the city stocked with supplies and were also used to raid its enemies' land.

Meanwhile, Sparta marched its army into Athenian lands expecting a big battle, but the Athenian army stayed protected behind the city walls. The frustrated Spartans attempted to weaken the Athenian economy by burning its crops. Though the walls protected Athenians from the Spartans, they could not prevent a devastating attack from an unexpected enemy.

A PLAGUE STRIKES ATHENS

In 430 B.C., Athenians began suffering from rashes, headaches, vomiting, and fever. This was probably an outbreak of typhoid fever, a highly infectious disease. In the narrow streets of Athens, overcrowded with refugees from the countryside, the fever quickly became a deadly **plague**, or a disease that causes many deaths. In four years the plague killed one in three Athenians—about 60,000 people—including Pericles. Disease was doing more damage than Sparta's soldiers.

Elsewhere the war raged on with brutal acts committed by both sides. It was typical for a captured city to have all its male citizens executed and its women and children enslaved. Despite all the deaths, the war seemed unwinnable. Athens was dominant at sea and Sparta ruled on land, but neither was able to overpower the other. In 421 B.C., Athens signed a **truce**, or an agreement to stop fighting. Sparta and Athens entered a period of peace, but it would not last for long.

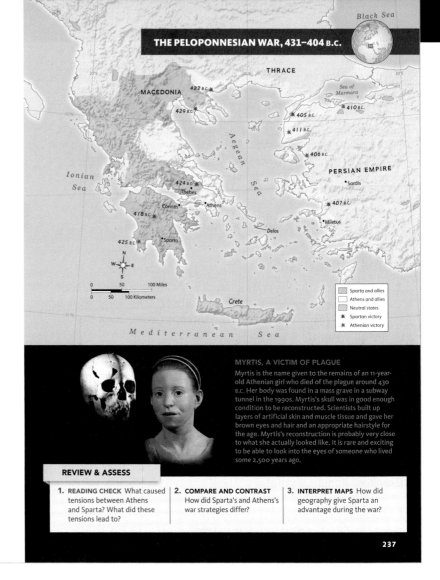

THE PELOPONNESIAN WAR, 431–404 B.C.

- Sparta and allies
- Athens and allies
- Neutral states
- ★ Spartan victory
- ✦ Athenian victory

MYRTIS, A VICTIM OF PLAGUE
Myrtis is the name given to the remains of an 11-year-old Athenian girl who died of the plague around 430 B.C. Her body was found in a mass grave in a subway tunnel in the 1990s. Myrtis's skull was in good enough condition to be reconstructed. Scientists built up layers of artificial skin and muscle tissue and gave her brown eyes and hair and an appropriate hairstyle for the age. Myrtis's reconstruction is probably very close to what she actually looked like. It is rare and exciting to be able to look into the eyes of someone who lived some 2,500 years ago.

REVIEW & ASSESS

1. **READING CHECK** What caused tensions between Athens and Sparta? What did these tensions lead to?

2. **COMPARE AND CONTRAST** How did Sparta's and Athens's war strategies differ?

3. **INTERPRET MAPS** How did geography give Sparta an advantage during the war?

PLAN

OBJECTIVE

Understand the factors that led to war between Athens and Sparta.

CRITICAL THINKING SKILLS FOR LESSON 2.1

- Identify Main Ideas and Details
- Monitor Comprehension
- Compare and Contrast
- Interpret Maps
- Sequence Events
- Draw Conclusions

ESSENTIAL QUESTION

What lasting influences did ancient Greek culture have on the modern world?

The war between Sparta and Athens was a turning point in the classical period, when Athens's power began to wane. Lesson 2.1 explains the events that led up to the war.

BACKGROUND FOR THE TEACHER

The Peloponnesian War is remembered and its details so well known because of one main account, Thucydides' *History of the Peloponnesian War*. Thucydides was a historian and an Athenian general during the war, and he wrote a chronological account containing the speeches of leaders and generals. The most famous of these is Pericles' funeral oration for Athenian soldiers who died during the war. An excerpt from Thucydides' work is included later in this chapter.

DIGITAL RESOURCES myNGconnect.com

TEACHER RESOURCES & ASSESSMENT

 Reading and Note-Taking

 Vocabulary Practice

 Section 2 Quiz

STUDENT RESOURCES

 NG Chapter Gallery

INTRODUCE & ENGAGE

ACTIVATE PRIOR KNOWLEDGE

The differences between Sparta and Athens were both military and cultural. Remind students of the development of the city-states, discussed in Chapter 8 and what they learned about Sparta's military society. **ASK:** How might Sparta's military society have caused the city-state to conflict with Athens and its democratic society? **0:05** minutes

TEACH

GUIDED DISCUSSION

1. **Sequence Events** Complete the Sequence Chain with four events that occurred after the Peloponnesian War began. *(Athens has a strong navy, and Sparta has a strong army. Athens withdraws behind the city walls to avoid a land war. Sparta ruins Athens's food source. Athenians begin to be affected by the plague.)*

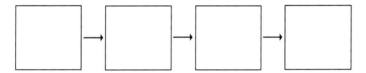

2. **Draw Conclusions** What were the reasons for the truce that ended the Peloponnesian War? *(The deaths caused by plague and war became so great, and both sides were equally matched, so both sides decided to stop fighting and declare a truce.)*

INTERPRET MAPS

Have students study the map of the Peloponnesian War. **ASK:** Would you rather have land or sea power (army or navy) in this particular geographic area? Have students give reasons to support their opinion. **0:10** minutes

ACTIVE OPTIONS

On Your Feet: Inside-Outside Circle Have students stand in concentric circles facing each other. Have students in the outside circle ask students in the inside circle a question about the lesson. Then have the outside circle rotate one position to the right to create new pairings. After five questions, have students switch roles and continue. **0:15** minutes

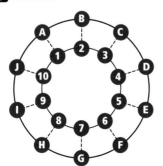

Critical Viewing: NG Chapter Gallery Invite students to explore the Chapter Gallery to examine the images that relate to this chapter. Have them select one of the images and do additional inquiry about the chosen gallery image, such as: What is this? Where and when was this created? By whom? Why was it created? What is it made of? Why does it belong in this chapter? What else would you like to know about it? **0:10** minutes

DIFFERENTIATE

INCLUSION

Work in Pairs Pair students who have visual or learning disabilities with partners who are proficient readers. Have the proficient student read the section titled "Tensions Rise" aloud. After reading each paragraph, the reader should stop and his or her partner should retell the same information in his or her own words to check comprehension.

PRE-AP

Hold a Panel Discussion Have groups of students do research and find out different ways that the plague affected Greek society. Ask them to present a panel discussion about the sickness. Encourage students to cover the following points in their discussion:

- the plague's physical effects
- the percent of the total population that was afflicted
- the effect of the plague on the war for Athens

Press **mt** *in the Student eEdition for modified text.*

See the Chapter Planner for more strategies for differentiation.

REVIEW & ASSESS

ANSWERS

1. Tensions rose between Athens and Sparta because of societal differences, Sparta's mistrust of Athens's increase in wealth and power, and Sparta's resentment toward Athens's use of Delian League money.

2. Sparta relied on its strong army to march into Athenian lands. Athens avoided a land battle by staying behind strong city walls. Athens used its powerful navy to raid enemy land.

3. Because of Sparta's location farther inland, Sparta was probably less vulnerable to an attack from Athens's powerful navy.

2.2 The Defeat of Athens

Both Sparta and Athens wanted to control all of Greece. Sparta thought its soldiers, with their strict military training, would crush any opponent. Athens attempted to dominate the region by building a powerful navy. But Sparta and Athens failed to notice that their constant warring was causing Greece to slowly fall apart.

MAIN IDEA

After many years of fighting, Greece found itself in a weakened and vulnerable state.

THE WAR DRAGS ON

The truce was supposed to last 50 years. Instead it ended in only two. Sparta and Athens were drawn back into war over the rich lands of Sicily, a fertile island near Italy that the Greeks had colonized. A dispute between a pro-Athenian colony and a pro-Spartan colony prompted Athens to invade.

In 414 B.C., Athens laid **siege** to Syracuse, Sicily's strongest and richest city. In a siege, soldiers surround a city in an attempt to take control of it. The invasion of Syracuse was disorganized, and Athens made many mistakes. Spartan reinforcements arrived and attacked the Athenians on land and sea. The Spartans sank all 200 of Athens's ships, and killed or enslaved 40,000 soldiers.

Meanwhile, Sparta seized control of the land around Athens, cutting off the Athenians' agricultural and economic resources. With Athens weakened, its allies revolted. Athens's situation just kept getting worse. The city-state had no good leaders left, and its naval fleet had been completely destroyed by Sparta.

In 412 B.C., Sparta strengthened its forces by allying with its old enemy Persia. The Spartan army steadily advanced on Athens, deliberately causing refugees to flee to the already overcrowded city. Blocked by Spartans on land and sea, a desperate Athens had only two choices: surrender or starve. In 404 B.C., Athens surrendered and the Peloponnesian War was finally over.

SPARTA IS VICTORIOUS

Sparta's fellow members in the Peloponnesian League wanted Athens to be completely destroyed and its people enslaved, but Sparta rejected these calls for revenge. Still, surrendering to Sparta was humiliating to the proud Athenians. The long walls linking Athens to the sea were torn down, and the Athenian navy was reduced to just 12 ships. As a final insult, Sparta replaced Athenian democracy with an oligarchy, a government made up of a small group of people. It was run by tyrants who ruled in a ruthless and controlling way. This form of leadership caused further conflicts within democracy-loving Athens.

The once powerful city of Athens was reduced to a second-rate state. However, Athens was not alone in its suffering. The long war had been costly in men, money, and resources to all the city-states involved. Greece as a whole was left weakened and vulnerable. To repair the damage, the city-states needed to cooperate with one another. Unfortunately, the end of the war did not stop conflicts from erupting. The city-states were soon warring among themselves again. In its weakened condition, Greece was a prime target for attack.

POSSIBLE RESPONSE Spartan soldiers were well-prepared with battle gear and ordered themselves into organized lines when they attacked.

Critical Viewing Spartan soldiers raise their weapons for battle. What does the illustration suggest about how Spartan soldiers fought?

Spartan Warriors, Howard David Johnson, 2013

REVIEW & ASSESS

1. **READING CHECK** What finally caused Athens to surrender to Sparta, ending the Peloponnesian War?

2. **DETERMINE WORD MEANINGS** How does knowing that *olig-* means "few" and *arch-* means "ruler" clarify the meaning of *oligarchy*?

3. **ANALYZE CAUSE AND EFFECT** What were the effects of the Peloponnesian War on the Greek city-states?

PLAN

OBJECTIVE

Examine the consequences of the Peloponnesian War and their effect on ancient Greece.

CRITICAL THINKING SKILLS FOR LESSON 2.2

- Identify Main Ideas and Details
- Monitor Comprehension
- Determine Word Meanings
- Analyze Cause and Effect
- Make Predictions

ESSENTIAL QUESTION

What lasting influences did ancient Greek culture have on the modern world?

The Peloponnesian War and its contemporary historians have influenced how we write history and wage war today. Lesson 2.2 examines the effects of the war on the cultural center of Athens.

BACKGROUND FOR THE TEACHER

The Athenian siege of Syracuse was the brainchild of the military commander Alcibiades. Athens spent all the money in its treasury to build a large fleet and army for the endeavor. If the siege had succeeded, it would have been a huge victory for Athens. However, it failed. Alcibiades escaped to Sparta, where he betrayed Athens's plans to the Spartans. Athenians looked to their leaders to figure out what had gone wrong. It was the beginning of the end of Athens's power.

DIGITAL RESOURCES myNGconnect.com

TEACHER RESOURCES & ASSESSMENT

 Reading and Note-Taking   **Vocabulary Practice**   **Section 2 Quiz**

STUDENT RESOURCES

 NG Chapter Gallery

INTRODUCE & ENGAGE

IDENTIFY POINTS OF VIEW

Organize the class into small groups. Invite them to discuss two different strategies that military and government leaders use, defensive and offensive. Explain that in ancient Greece, Pericles's strategy against the Spartans was a defensive one. After his death, some government leaders wanted to use a more offensive strategy. Assign half the groups to represent those who support a defensive strategy and assign the other half to represent those who think an offensive strategy is better. Have groups make a three-column chart to list their group's views. In the "Viewpoint" column, groups should list their positions. In the "Support" column, they should list their reasons why. Have groups representing both sides of the argument discuss their viewpoints. Tell groups to complete the "Opposing Viewpoint" column during their discussion. Tell students that they will read about Athens's strategies in its campaign in Sicily in Lesson 2.2. **0:15** minutes

TEACH

GUIDED DISCUSSION

1. **Make Predictions** After reading the lesson, ask students to predict what might happen next among the city-states. *(They might keep fighting each other in small conflicts. Another enemy might target them because they are so disorganized and divided among themselves.)*

2. **Identify Main Ideas and Details** Ask students to pair up and work together. Have them write down the main idea of the first paragraph. Then they should add details that support that main idea. Have them repeat this for two more paragraphs in the lesson.

MORE INFORMATION

Athens's New War Strategy Most historians blame Athens's loss of its dominance in the region on its own decision to enter into war too rashly. Overturning Pericles' policy of staying out of the war and behind their strong city walls, Athenian leaders wanted action—and they plunged ahead despite the superior strength of their opponents. One leader, Nicias, trying to stop the momentum toward war, thought of a plan. He would ask the treasury for such a huge amount of money for the ships and soldiers needed that they would not agree to it. His plan backfired. Nicias was granted his request, and Athens spent all of its money on the plan to attack Syracuse. Most historians think that Athens might have held onto its power in the region if it had just kept going with Pericles' strategy. But in his *History of the Peloponnesian War,* Thucydides makes the case that the war was inevitable, along with the loss of democracy and Athenian power in the region.

ACTIVE OPTIONS

On Your Feet: Identifying Issues Divide students into four groups and have them move to different corners of the classroom. Ask each group to address the following question: *What might be a challenge to upholding a democracy when your country is surrounded by oligarchies?* Encourage students to consider the question individually and then discuss their responses as a group. Suggest that one person in the group act as the recorder. Then invite recorders to take turns stating their group's conclusions. **0:15** minutes

Critical Viewing: NG Image Gallery Have students explore the entire NG Image Gallery and choose two of the items to compare and contrast, either in written form or verbally with a partner. Ask questions that will inspire this process, such as: How are these images alike? How are they different? Why did you select these two items? How do they relate in history? **0:10** minutes

DIFFERENTIATE

STRIVING READERS

Sequence Events Have students summarize the events of the section in chronological order, using a chart like this:

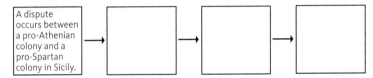

PRE-AP

Research Sieges in History Have students research other sieges in history and compare their findings to the events of the Athenian siege of Syracuse. Then have students write about their findings in a short report. Encourage them to answer three questions: Why did the military leaders attempt a siege? What challenges emerged? How do the outcomes compare?

Press (mt) *in the Student eEdition for modified text.*

See the Chapter Planner for more strategies for differentiation.

REVIEW & ASSESS

ANSWERS

1. Sparta had effectively blocked Athens on land and sea, forcing Athens into choosing between surrendering and starving.

2. The word parts make up a word that means rule by the few.

3. The Peloponnesian War weakened the economies and resources of all the Greek city-states, which left Greece as a whole very vulnerable and open to attack.

Athenian Democracy

In 431 B.C., Pericles delivered an oration, a kind of formal speech, at a large public funeral held in honor of Athenian soldiers who had died fighting in the Peloponnesian War. Pericles used the opportunity to inspire the living to keep fighting for Athens. He talked about the many reasons that Athenians could be proud of their great city, including all of the advantages that came with living in a democratic society.

The Age of Pericles, Philipp von Foltz, 1852

POSSIBLE RESPONSE

The Athenians in the picture have differing reactions, but many seem upset, worried, or expectant.

Critical Viewing An artist imagines what the scene might have looked like as Pericles delivered his oration. How do the Athenians appear to react to Pericles' words?

DOCUMENT ONE

Primary Source: Speech

from *History of the Peloponnesian War*
by Thucydides (translated by Rex Warner)

Thucydides (thoo-SIH-duh-deez) was a Greek historian and general best known for his historical account of the events of the Peloponnesian War. As an Athenian military commander, he failed to prevent the capture of an important city from Sparta and was exiled for 20 years. During this time, he was able to witness events firsthand and interview participants much as a modern journalist would. His account provides a detailed record of Pericles' funeral oration. In this excerpt, Pericles reminds Athenians of the power they have as members of a democratic society.

CONSTRUCTED RESPONSE According to Pericles, what was special about the Athenian system of government?

> Our constitution is called a democracy because power is in the hands not of a minority but of the whole people. When it is a question of settling private disputes, everyone is equal before the law; when it is a question of putting one person before another in positions of public responsibility, what counts is not membership of a particular class, but the actual ability that the man possesses. No one, so long as he has it in him to be of service to the state, is kept in political obscurity because of poverty.

DOCUMENT TWO

Ostracon, Greece, c. 400s B.C.
Ostracism was an enforced banishment. Athenians used to prevent an individual from gaining too much power. Each citizen carved the name of someone he believed to be dangerous on a piece of pottery called an ostracon, seen at right. If the same name appeared often enough, the named person had to leave Athens. He did not lose citizenship, property, or wealth, but he was forbidden to return for ten years.

CONSTRUCTED RESPONSE What does the practice of ostracism tell you about Athenian values?

ANSWERS

DOCUMENT 1
Athenian democracy was special because power was in the hands of the majority of people, not just the rich, creating a more equal society.

DOCUMENT 2
The principles of fairness and democracy were more important than one person's power.

SYNTHESIZE & WRITE

1. **REVIEW** Review what you have learned about democracy in Athens from the text and the sources above.

2. **RECALL** On your own paper, write down the main idea expressed in the speech and artifact.

3. **CONSTRUCT** Write a topic sentence that answers this question: What was most important in Athenian democracy—the individual or the community?

4. **WRITE** Using evidence from the speech and artifact, write an argument to support your answer to the question in Step 3.

PLAN

OBJECTIVE

Synthesize information about Athenian democracy from two primary sources.

CRITICAL THINKING SKILLS FOR LESSON 2.3

- Synthesize
- Make Inferences
- Make Connections
- Evaluate

ESSENTIAL QUESTION

What lasting influences did ancient Greek culture have on the modern world?

Democracy is one of the most widely spread forms of government in the modern world. Lesson 2.3 provides insight into Athenian democracy through the analysis of primary sources.

BACKGROUND FOR THE TEACHER

The practice of ostracism began under Cleisthenes when the democratic-minded leader took power after the last of the Greek tyrants. Ostracism was practiced in the Athenian democracy as a way to check the power of individuals or to punish them for failed policies. Ostracism was used only rarely, and the practice fell into disuse after it was found that some politicians attempted to manipulate the process to their own ends. The similar practice of exile was used in ancient Rome, but it was more of a punishment, involving loss of property and status, and usually lasting for the rest of the person's life.

INTRODUCE & ENGAGE

PREPARE FOR THE DOCUMENT-BASED QUESTION

Before students start on the activity, briefly preview the document and artifact. Remind students that a constructed response requires full explanations in complete sentences. Emphasize that students should use their knowledge of Greek history in addition to the information in the documents. **0:05** minutes

TEACH

GUIDED DISCUSSION

1. **Make Inferences** Why might Pericles have felt the need to make this speech to his people? *(The people might have doubted the validity of democracy or Pericles' leadership after some very hard years of war and plague. They may have been disillusioned that the new system failed to fix anything. Pericles is trying to inspire them again by emphasizing democracy's greater aims and truths.)*

2. **Make Connections** Explain to students that an ostracon is a small clay piece with a name written on it. It was used by Athenians to vote to ostracize a citizen. **ASK:** Can you think of any similar practice in today's world? *(Possible response: Certain clubs and corporate organizations might use a similar process to vote a member out of the group.)*

EVALUATE

After students have completed the "Synthesize & Write" activity, allow time for them to exchange paragraphs and read and comment on the work of their peers. Guidelines for comments should be established prior to this activity so that feedback is constructive and encouraging in nature. **0:15** minutes

ACTIVE OPTIONS

On Your Feet: Jigsaw Divide students into four "expert" groups. Offer each group one of these features of democracy: assembly, checks and balances, paid legislators, or courts. Have groups research their feature using the following steps: 1. Define what their feature is. 2. Find out what problem their feature solved. 3. Identify how their feature reflected democratic ideals. 4. Describe what problems, if any, the feature created. Use the Jigsaw strategy to have experts report their findings to different groups. **0:25** minutes

NG Learning Framework: Attitudes Toward Democracy

SKILL: Collaboration
KNOWLEDGE: Our Human Story

Have students read an excerpt from another speech about democracy, such as John F. Kennedy's inaugural address in 1961 or Ronald Reagan's address for the Goldwater presidential campaign in 1964. Discuss how the democratic principles mentioned in the speech are similar to or different from those in Pericles' funeral oration. **0:15** minutes

DIFFERENTIATE

INCLUSION

Check Understanding Have students write the letters A, B, and C on three separate index cards. Then check students' understanding of the lesson by asking them questions that have three possible answer choices, labeled A, B, and C. Instruct students to hold up the card with the letter that corresponds to the correct answer. Help students find the answers in Lesson 2.3 for any questions that cause them difficulty.

PRE-AP

Research Ostracism Tell students to research the practice of ostracism and some of the men who were ostracized in ancient Greece. Give them the name of Aristides—who was ostracized for being too popular—as a starting point in their research. Tell students to research other men who were ostracized, as well as the rationale behind the practice of ostracism. Encourage students to share their findings with the class.

Press **(mt)** *in the Student eEdition for modified text.*

See the Chapter Planner for more strategies for differentiation.

SYNTHESIZE & WRITE

ANSWERS

1. Responses will vary.

2. Responses will vary but will reflect upon the meaning of democracy.

3. Possible Response: In Athenian democracy, the needs of individuals were less important than what was good for the community. Selfishness was less important than service.

4. Students' arguments should include their topic sentence from Step 3 and provide several details from the documents to support the sentence.

Philip of Macedonia

Your king wants to conquer Greece, located just south of your homeland. Weakened from internal fighting, Greece has become a prime target for attack. You and your fellow soldiers grip your 18-foot-long spears tighter as Greek soldiers approach. You are terrified, but you trust King Philip II. His military skills are extensive. In his capable hands, the act of war is turned into an art.

MAIN IDEA

Greece became unified under the military influence of Philip II.

CONQUEROR OF GREECE

The Greeks didn't think much of the kingdom of Macedonia (ma-suh-DOH-nee-uh), located just north of Greece. They dismissed its residents as uncultured foreigners. However, in 359 B.C., **Philip II** seized the Macedonian throne. He was an intelligent general and a clever politician—skills he combined with ambition, determination, and ruthlessness. An inspiring king, Philip completely controlled all political, military, legal, and religious matters.

Philip admired many things about Greece, including its ideas and art. He set his sights on uniting the Greek city-states with his own kingdom to create a combined kingdom strong enough to conquer the Persian Empire—his ultimate goal.

Philip built a powerful professional army and used new warfare methods. For example, he placed large groups of soldiers close together, forming an almost unstoppable battle formation called a **phalanx** (FAY-langks). Each soldier carried a spear that was much longer than the enemy's. The soldiers stood close to one another so that their shields overlapped, making it difficult for the enemy to attack them. Another new method of waging war was the use of war machines like the **catapult**, which hurled huge stones to shatter city walls.

Philip conquered the lands around Macedonia and seized Greek colonies that were rich in natural resources like gold mines, increasing his wealth. Greek city-states were still weak from the Peloponnesian War and were constantly quarrelling among themselves.

They were no match for Philip's strong army, great wealth, and political skill. By 348 B.C., Philip had won control of much of Greece. Any remaining Greek resistance crumbled when Athens and the strong city-state of Thebes fell to Philip at the Battle of Chaeronea (kair-uh-NEE-uh) in 338 B.C. Philip had united Greece for the first time ever. However, his son, **Alexander the Great**, would soon surpass his achievements.

YOUNG ALEXANDER

Born in 356 B.C., Alexander demonstrated his courage at a young age. One story tells how 12-year-old Alexander bravely stepped up to a nervous wild horse named Bucephalus (byoo-SEHF-uh-luhs), spoke gently to calm him down, and then rode him. Philip proudly announced that Macedonia would never be big enough for such a brave boy—and he was right.

Alexander trained for war with "the companions," a group of aristocratic sons

+ POSSIBLE RESPONSE

In the mosaic, Alexander the Great looks like a young, fearless, and single-minded leader who people would follow.

The Battle of Issus, House of (?)

Critical Viewing
This mosaic fragment shows Alexander the Great in battle. What do the details in this picture help you infer about Alexander's character?

who became his loyal lifelong friends. His most important training came from his father, who took Alexander into battle with him. This gave his son firsthand experience in planning and carrying out a war.

The Greek scientist and great thinker Aristotle (A-ruh-stah-tuhl) was Alexander's tutor. He taught him geography, science, and literature. Alexander was greatly influenced by Homer's *Iliad* and kept a copy of it under his pillow. He wanted to be like the *Iliad's* courageous hero, Achilles (uh-KIH-leez). According to myth, Achilles was one of the greatest warriors Greece had ever known.

Alexander soon became a warrior himself. At the age of 16, he was fighting off invasions and founding cities. In 336 B.C., Philip was assassinated, and 20-year-old Alexander became king.

The people of Thebes rebelled after Philip's death. They thought Macedonia would become weak without him. They could not have been more mistaken. Alexander marched into Greece to assert his leadership. He destroyed Thebes, terrifying all of Greece into submission. Alexander was well on his way to becoming "the Great."

REVIEW & ASSESS

1. **READING CHECK** What was Philip II's key achievement in Greece?

2. **ANALYZE CAUSE AND EFFECT** Why were the Greek city-states unprepared for an attack by Philip II?

3. **IDENTIFY MAIN IDEAS AND DETAILS** What evidence from the text demonstrates that Philip II was an intelligent general?

PLAN

OBJECTIVE

Learn about the fate of Greek city-states after they were conquered by Macedonia.

CRITICAL THINKING SKILLS FOR LESSON 3.1

- Identify Main Ideas and Details
- Monitor Comprehension
- Analyze Cause and Effect
- Make Predictions
- Create Graphic Organizers

ESSENTIAL QUESTION

What lasting influences did ancient Greek culture have on the modern world?

Philip of Macedonia and his son, Alexander the Great, united Greece and helped spread Greek culture throughout the known world. Lesson 3.1 explains how Greece was unified under Macedonian rule.

BACKGROUND FOR THE TEACHER

While the Greek city-states were embroiled in fighting each other during the 27- year-long Peloponnesian War, the kingdom just north of Greece, Macedonia, grew stronger under King Philip II. After seizing the throne and uniting the tribes of Macedonia, Philip turned his attention to Greece. He wanted to bring the Greek city-states under his control in order to build an empire to rival that of the Persians. By 338 B.C., he had succeeded. He allowed the city-states to maintain many freedoms, but for the first time they were unified under one leader.

DIGITAL RESOURCES myNGconnect.com

TEACHER RESOURCES & ASSESSMENT

 Reading and Note-Taking

 Vocabulary Practice

 Section 3 Quiz

STUDENT RESOURCES

 NG Chapter Gallery

INTRODUCE & ENGAGE

ACTIVATE PRIOR KNOWLEDGE

Explain to students that Lesson 3.1 will discuss Philip of Macedonia and his son, Alexander the Great. Ask students if they have ever heard of either man. Discuss any popular culture references they might know. **0:05** minutes

TEACH

GUIDED DISCUSSION

1. **Identify Main Ideas and Details** Ask students to pair up and work together. Have them write down the main idea of the third paragraph. Then they should add details that support that main idea. Have them repeat this for two more paragraphs in the lesson.

2. **Make Predictions** After reading the lesson, ask students to predict what might happen as a result of Alexander's destruction of Thebes. *(Possible response: The rest of the city-states would not dare to oppose Alexander, and he would keep his campaign going to conquer even more territory.)*

BUILD A TIME LINE

Have students build a time line of Philip II's reign. Tell students to record the major events of Philip's reign on a time line that they make themselves. Time lines can be organized horizontally or vertically. Students should include dates and descriptions of events at hash marks in chronological order on their time lines. Encourage students to include pictures or drawings on their time lines. **0:15** minutes

ACTIVE OPTIONS

On Your Feet: Tell Me More Have students form two teams and assign each team one of the following topics: Philip II of Macedonia or Alexander the Great. Each group should write down as many facts about their topic as they can. Have the class reconvene and have each group stand up, one at a time. The sitting group calls out, "Tell me more about [Philip II of Macedonia or Alexander the Great]!" The standing group recites one fact. The sitting group again calls, "Tell me more!" until the standing group runs out of facts to share. Then the groups switch places. **0:15** minutes

NG Learning Framework: Role-Play

ATTITUDE: **Curiosity**
SKILLS: **Observation, Problem-Solving**

Invite students to revisit the information on Alexander the Great in Lesson 3.1 and to imagine that they were in Alexander's place. **ASK:** What made Alexander so successful in expanding his empire? How would you have done things differently from Alexander? What modern aspects of life might change how Alexander behaved if he lived today? **0:10** minutes

DIFFERENTIATE

ENGLISH LANGUAGE LEARNERS

Word Squares Have students create separate Word Squares for the vocabulary words in the text and for at least three other words that are confusing or interesting. Encourage students to write the meaning of the words and to include examples and related words. For example, a Word Square for *phalanx* might include the words and phrases such as those shown below:

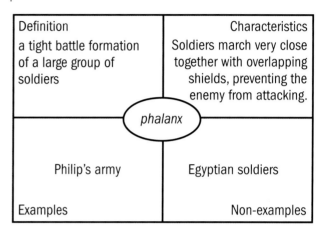

Definition	Characteristics
a tight battle formation of a large group of soldiers	Soldiers march very close together with overlapping shields, preventing the enemy from attacking.
phalanx	
Philip's army	Egyptian soldiers
Examples	Non-examples

STRIVING READERS

Venn Diagram Have students use a Venn Diagram to take notes on Philip and Alexander. Explain that facts unique to either man should be entered in the outer circles with common characteristics placed in the overlapping area. When students have finished, have them make a generalization about the two men.

Press (**mt**) *in the Student eEdition for modified text.*

See the Chapter Planner for more strategies for differentiation.

REVIEW & ASSESS

ANSWERS

1. Philip II conquered all of Greece and unified it for the first time.

2. The Greek city-states were open to attack by Philip II because they were still weak from the Peloponnesian War and constant infighting; they could not unify against an attack by Philip II.

3. Philip II combined military force and wealth to win control of Greece. He built a powerful army using methods such as the phalanx battle formation and catapults. He seized Greek colonies rich in natural resources, which funded his army.

ALEXANDER
THE GREAT 356 B.C. – 323 B.C.

According to legend, the city of Gordium in Asia Minor contained a knot so complex that it was impossible to untie. Whoever could unravel the Gordian knot would conquer Asia. When Alexander saw the knot, he drew his sword and asked, "What does it matter how I untie it?" He then sliced the knot in two.

ALEXANDER'S EMPIRE, c. 323 B.C.

🧳 **Job:** King of Macedonia and general of the army

✏️ **Education:** Taught by Aristotle, the great Greek thinker and scientist

🌐 **Home:** Born in Pella, Macedonia

FINEST HOUR

He led his unbeaten army to conquer lands as far east as India.

WORST MOMENT

In a drunken rage, he murdered his friend Cleitus.

FRIENDS

- Ptolemy (boyhood friend and general in the army)
- Hephaestion (lifelong friend and second-in-command)
- His soldiers

ENEMIES

- Thebans (Greek warriors)
- Darius (Persian king)
- Porus (Indian king)

TRIVIA

To honor his beloved horse, Alexander named a city in present-day India after him: Bucephala.

ALEXANDER'S TRIUMPHS

In 334 B.C., Alexander set out to fulfill his father's plans to conquer Persia. Philip was a skilled politician and general, but Alexander was even more gifted. He was a military genius who never once lost a battle. Alexander invaded and freed Persian-controlled Anatolia (present-day Turkey). Then he marched his army south toward Egypt, taking control of Persia's Mediterranean naval bases along the way. Persia responded with an attack from its huge army. However, Alexander cleverly forced the battle to occur on a narrow coastline, which destroyed Persia's advantage of having more soldiers.

When Alexander arrived in Egypt, the people, who had been living under Persian rule, greeted him as a liberator and crowned him pharaoh. Here, as elsewhere, Alexander won the support of conquered people by honoring local traditions. While in Egypt, he founded Alexandria, the first of many cities to bear his name. As a center of education, culture, and trade, Alexandria was one of the most important cities in the ancient world.

In 331 B.C., Alexander defeated the Persians near Babylon and soon controlled the rest of the Persian Empire. Instead of returning home to celebrate, Alexander and his soldiers continued east. They conquered present-day Afghanistan and Uzbekistan before turning toward what is now India, which was then thought to be the edge of the world. In 326 B.C., Alexander crossed the Indus River and won a number of bloody battles, but his soldiers had had enough. Deeply homesick after 11 years away, they wanted to return home. Alexander reluctantly agreed. Over the course of 13 years, Alexander had carved out an empire stretching 3,000 miles from Europe to India. Legend says that he wept because he had no more worlds to conquer.

ALEXANDER'S DEATH

Thousands of soldiers died during the long trip home. Alexander himself did not survive the return journey. In 323 B.C., he became sick with a fever while in Babylon and died a few days later at the age of 32. His generals fought each other for control of the empire, which eventually fell apart. Alexander's empire was replaced with four kingdoms: the Egyptian, Macedonian, Pergamum (PUR-guh-muhm), and Seleucid (suh-LOO-suhd) kingdoms.

REVIEW & ASSESS

1. **READING CHECK** How did Alexander the Great win the support of the people he conquered?

2. **COMPARE AND CONTRAST** How were Philip II and Alexander similar and different as leaders?

3. **INTERPRET MAPS** What physical feature marks the eastern extent of Alexander's empire?

PLAN

OBJECTIVE

Examine the growth of the Macedonian empire under the reign of Alexander the Great.

CRITICAL THINKING SKILLS FOR LESSON 3.2

- Identify Main Ideas and Details
- Monitor Comprehension
- Compare and Contrast
- Interpret Maps
- Sequence Events
- Form and Support Opinions

ESSENTIAL QUESTION

What lasting influences did ancient Greek culture have on the modern world?

The growth of Alexander's empire, detailed in Lesson 3.2, brought Greek culture into new parts of the world.

BACKGROUND FOR THE TEACHER

By the time Alexander inherited the kingdom of Macedonia, his father had unified the city-state and grown it into a powerful force in the region. Macedonia was mountainous in the west and flatter in the east with gentle hills and plains for farming. It also had warm summers and very cold winters. Though Macedonians spoke Greek, their language had many words that were hard for others to understand, and so they were considered foreign by other Greeks.

DIGITAL RESOURCES myNGconnect.com

TEACHER RESOURCES & ASSESSMENT

 Reading and Note-Taking   **Vocabulary Practice**   **Section 3 Quiz**

STUDENT RESOURCES

 NG Chapter Gallery

INTRODUCE & ENGAGE

INTERPRET MAPS

Have students preview the lesson by studying the map of Alexander's empire. Use the distance scale to estimate how wide the empire was at its greatest extent *(over 2,400 miles)*. **ASK:** How might the growth of Alexander's empire have affected the influence of Greek culture? *(It would have allowed Greek culture to spread south and east.)* `0:05` minutes

TEACH

GUIDED DISCUSSION

1. **Sequence Events** What sequence of events led Alexander to conquer the Persian Empire? *(First Alexander freed Anatolia from Persian control. Then he marched south to take control of Persia's Mediterranean naval bases. After this, he arrived in Egypt, where the people greeted him as a liberator. Finally, Alexander defeated the Persians near Babylon and gained control of the rest of the Persian Empire.)*

2. **Form and Support Opinions** Based on what you read in the lesson, why do you think Alexander was so driven to conquer Persia? Point out ideas or details in the text that support your response. *(Responses will vary but should be supported by examples from the text. Possible responses: He wanted to carry out his father's plans. He had great military genius and a drive to conquer other lands. He wanted to spread Greek culture and trade.)*

MORE INFORMATION

Aristotle and Alexander Aristotle was already a respected Greek philosopher when he was chosen by Philip to tutor Alexander. At the time, Alexander was 13 years old. Aristotle already had a connection with Macedonia, as his father was court physician to a king there. Today, the tutor is as well known as his famous pupil. He taught Alexander literary studies, as well as political theory and history, and possibly natural science, a subject that would fascinate Alexander through his life and travels. But later, Aristotle and Alexander were not close. Alexander became a king and conqueror, while Aristotle believed that the only case where a monarchy would be acceptable was if the person was far superior to others in character and quality of mind. Aristotle never mentioned that Alexander or anyone else he had known was so exceptional.

ACTIVE OPTIONS

On Your Feet: Make Inferences About Character Have students work in pairs to conduct Three-Step Interviews. One student should interview the other using this question: *What might Alexander's actions tell us about his character?* Then students should reverse roles. Finally, each student should share the results of his or her interview with the class. `0:25` minutes

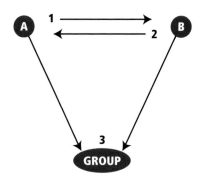

Critical Viewing: NG Image Gallery Invite students to explore the entire NG Image Gallery and choose one image from the gallery they feel best represents their understanding of the unit. Have students provide a written explanation of why they selected the image they chose. `0:10` minutes

DIFFERENTIATE

ENGLISH LANGUAGE LEARNERS

Read a Map Direct students' attention to the map in Lesson 3.2 and ask them questions to ensure they comprehend what the map shows. **ASK:** Did Alexander's empire extend to the Caucasus Mountains? *(No)* Did Alexander conquer Egypt or Babylon first? *(Egypt)* What is one major battle site? *(Chaeronea, Granicus, Issus, Gaugamela)*

STRIVING READERS

Summarize Have students read Lesson 3.2 in pairs. Tell them to write a sentence that restates the main idea of each paragraph as they read. Then have students review those sentences and write a four- or five-sentence paragraph that summarizes the whole lesson. Remind students that they should use their own words in their summary and include only the most important ideas and details. Call on volunteers to share their paragraphs with the class.

Press **mt** *in the Student eEdition for modified text.*

See the Chapter Planner for more strategies for differentiation.

REVIEW & ASSESS

ANSWERS

1. He honored their local traditions.

2. Both Philip II and Alexander were excellent leaders and skilled conquerors. However, as a military genius who never lost a battle, Alexander was even more successful than his father, and he conquered many more lands than Philip II did.

3. Physical features that mark the eastern extent of Alexander's empire include the Arabian Sea, Bucephala, and a river system including the Indus River.

This statue, known as *Winged Victory of Samothrace*, is an example of Hellenistic sculpture from the second century B.C. It depicts Nike, the Greek goddess of victory. The head and arms of the statue have been lost.

3.3 The Spread of
Hellenistic Culture

People enjoy going to museums to check out new exhibits. The library is the perfect quiet spot for research and reading. Sports fans gather in stadiums to be entertained by sporting events. Theaters showcase the latest dramatic play for an eager audience. Thousands of years ago, ancient Greeks enjoyed these very same activities.

MAIN IDEA

Alexander's conquests spread Greek culture across Asia.

CULTURAL BLEND

Hellas is Greek for "Greece," and the three centuries after Alexander's death are called the **Hellenistic** era because the known world was dominated by Greek culture. Alexander founded Greek colonies wherever he went, and Greek culture spread from these centers through cultural diffusion. Thousands of Greek colonists carried Greek practices and ideas to the plains of Persia, deserts of Egypt, mountains of Afghanistan, and river valleys of northern India. Each area adopted and adapted Greek culture differently, blending it with its own culture.

Alexander founded more than 70 cities, each with Greek designs and features such as temples, gymnasiums, and theaters. These cities flourished, cementing Greek influence in faraway places for centuries. The ultimate Hellenistic city was Alexandria, Egypt's new capital.

WORLDLY ALEXANDRIA

Alexandria became one of the largest, wealthiest, and most cultured cities in the ancient world. Many parks and open spaces created a pleasant environment, and the main streets were lined with colonnades, a series of columns that support a roof to provide shade. Alexandria's multiethnic mix of Greeks, Egyptians, Jews, and others created a **cosmopolitan**, or worldly, atmosphere.

In addition to housing Alexander's tomb and countless temples, Alexandria also had many magnificent buildings, including a museum used as a research center and a library known as the Great Library. It boasted a copy of every book written in Greek—some 500,000 scrolls. The library drew scholars and scientists from around the world. Meanwhile, Alexandria's wealth attracted the best artists, sculptors, writers, and musicians. The city was the cultural and trade center of the Hellenistic world.

REVIEW & ASSESS

1. **READING CHECK** How did Alexander spread Greek culture across Asia?

2. **DRAW CONCLUSIONS** What made Hellenistic culture unique?

3. **IDENTIFY MAIN IDEAS AND DETAILS** In what ways was Alexandria the cultural center of the Hellenistic world?

OBJECTIVE
Identify traits of Hellenistic culture.

CRITICAL THINKING SKILLS FOR LESSON 3.3

- Identify Main Ideas and Details
- Monitor Comprehension
- Draw Conclusions
- Analyze Cause and Effect
- Form and Support Opinions
- Analyze Visuals

ESSENTIAL QUESTION
What lasting influences did ancient Greek culture have on the modern world?

Alexander the Great helped spread Greek culture through his conquests of the ancient world. Lesson 3.3 describes the Hellenistic world and its grandest city—Alexandria.

BACKGROUND FOR THE TEACHER

The Great Library of Alexandria attracted a variety of scholars whose work influenced the modern world: Euclid, the father of geometry; Ptolemy, author of the geocentric theory of the universe; Hypatia, a female mathematician and philosopher who expanded upon the works of Plato; and Eratosthenes, who first calculated the circumference of Earth.

DIGITAL RESOURCES myNGconnect.com

TEACHER RESOURCES & ASSESSMENT

 Reading and Note-Taking

 Vocabulary Practice

 Section 3 Quiz

STUDENT RESOURCES

 NG Chapter Gallery

INTRODUCE & ENGAGE

UNDERSTAND CULTURE

Remind students that a culture region is an area unified by language, religion, or other traits. Alexandria had a mix of cultures, which contributed to a cosmopolitan atmosphere. Divide the class into four groups and have each group discuss how one of the following topics might influence cultures in close contact to change.

1. Seeing and learning about other lands, their people, and cultures

2. Creating new styles in art and architecture

3. Adopting and applying ideas to design new inventions

4. Challenging one's assumptions and being open to new explanations

`0:05` minutes

TEACH

GUIDED DISCUSSION

1. **Analyze Cause and Effect** As Greek culture began to spread through the city centers, how did it affect the further spread of Greek culture? *(More people in different places adopted Greek culture, making it even more influential and cross-cultural.)*

2. **Form and Support Opinions** What was the most influential aspect of Greek culture? Use examples from the text to support your opinion.

ANALYZE VISUALS

Direct students' attention to the photo of the *Winged Victory of Samothrace in* Lesson 3.3. As a class, consider how Nike's figure represents Greek culture and its diffusion by exploring the following questions:

- What do you notice most?
- What details do you see?
- What do you see that demonstrates Greek culture?

`0:10` minutes

ACTIVE OPTIONS

On Your Feet: Culture Roundtable Divide the class into groups of four or five. Hand each group a sheet of paper with the question *What does culture mean to you?* on it. The first student in each group should sit at the desk and write an answer, read it aloud, and pass the paper clockwise to the next student. Each student should add at least one answer. The paper should circulate around the table until students run out of answers or time is up. `0:15` minutes

Critical Viewing: NG Chapter Gallery Ask students to choose one image from the Chapter Gallery and become an expert on it. They should do additional research to learn all about it. Then, students should share their findings with a partner, small group, or the class. `0:15` minutes

DIFFERENTIATE

PRE-AP

Research Alexandrias Point out to students the different cities named after Alexander in the text in Lessons 3.2 and 3.3 and on the map in Lesson 3.2. Have students work in four groups to research one of these ancient cities: Alexandria, Egypt; Alexandria Areion; Alexandria Arachoton; Alexandria Eschate. Encourage students to present their findings to the class. After each group presents, determine as a class the similarities and differences among the Alexandrias.

GIFTED & TALENTED

Locate Greek References Encourage students to explore their everyday worlds and locate references to Greek culture that surround them in our modern world. Offer as an example the Nike brand of shoes. Ask students to locate at least three items or ideas that reflect ancient Greek culture. Tell them to bring in examples to share with the class. As students share their examples, list their findings on the board under broad categories, such as *Politics, Sports, Literature, Architecture,* and *Art.*

Press **mt** *in the Student eEdition for modified text.*

See the Chapter Planner for more strategies for differentiation.

REVIEW & ASSESS

ANSWERS

1. Alexander founded Greek colonies in the lands he conquered. Greek culture spread from these colonies through cultural diffusion across Asia.

2. Hellenistic culture was unique in that it influenced arts, sports, architecture, and cities all over the world.

3. Alexandria had a multiethnic population that enjoyed parks, temples, a museum, and a library. This library drew scholars and scientists from all over the world. In this way, the best minds came to Alexandria, making it the cultural center of the Hellenistic world.

Philosophy and Literature

What is right? What is wrong? What is good? What is bad? We all think we know the answers, but do we really? These are some of the questions posed by Greek thinkers over 2,000 years ago. Today we are still searching for the answers.

MAIN IDEA

Greek ideas and writings remain influential today. They are the foundation of Western thought.

SOCRATES, PLATO, AND ARISTOTLE

Philosophy comes from a Greek word meaning "love of wisdom." Philosophers try to understand the universe and our place in it. Instead of explaining the world through gods and myths, they use logic and reason. Greek city-states provided an open environment where philosophers excelled. They also studied and taught other subjects, such as science, math, and biology.

Socrates (SAH-kruh-teez) was an Athenian philosopher interested in ethics, or the study of right and wrong. He challenged people to think more deeply, asking probing questions like, "What is justice?" His question-and-answer teaching style became known as the Socratic method. Socrates' methods made him unpopular among the leaders of Athens. He was accused of not believing in the official gods and of encouraging young

Athenians to rebel. He was put on trial, found guilty, and sentenced to death.

Socrates taught **Plato** (PLAY-toh), one of the most influential philosophers in history. Plato believed that this world was a shadow of a superior world. He disliked democracy, believing instead that philosopher-kings should rule. Plato founded an elite academy, where he taught **Aristotle**, the tutor of Alexander the Great.

Aristotle searched for understanding by examining the world closely. He categorized everything, laying the foundations for the study of biology, law, physics, and politics. Aristotle opened an academy, the Lyceum, where anyone could study a wide range of subjects. Together these three Greek philosophers formed the basis of modern Western philosophy, mathematics, and science and continue to influence our thinking.

EPICS AND HISTORIES

Homer was the most famous writer of epic poetry, a form of poetry that combines elements of drama and narrative. With their mythical beasts, interfering gods, and adventurous heroes, Homer's epics about the Trojan War—the *Iliad* and the *Odyssey*—continue to entertain modern readers. Another Greek writer still popular today was a slave called **Aesop** (EE-sahp). He wrote a series of fables, or short stories with animals as the central characters. Each fable taught a moral lesson.

The Greeks were among the first people to research their past and write it down accurately. When the Greek historian Herodotus (hih-RAH-duh-tuhs) wrote a history of the Persian Wars, he made sure to check his sources and to understand the significance of the events he described. He is considered the father of history. Similarly, Thucydides wrote an accurate account of the Peloponnesian War, while Xenophon (ZEH-nuh-fuhn) described life in Greece. They provided useful insights into ancient Greece and created a model for the future study of history.

THE SCHOOL OF ATHENS (Detail)

The Renaissance artist Raphael worked on this fresco over a three-year period. It was painted on a wall in the pope's palace in Rome. The painting shows the greatest thinkers of classical Greek society. There are mathematicians, natural philosophers, artists, and scientists. They all lived at different times, but Raphael painted them under one roof. The two central figures are Plato and Aristotle, who have had a lasting effect on Western thought.

Detail from *The School of Athens*, Raphael, A.D. 1511

Aristotle
Aristotle believed in studying the world as it is, including politics and biology.

Socrates
Socrates taught his pupils to question everything and to think for themselves.

Plato
Plato believed that all things on Earth were lesser versions of their ideals in heaven.

REVIEW & ASSESS

1. **READING CHECK** What are some of the subjects that ancient Greek thinkers studied and taught?

2. **DRAW CONCLUSIONS** What was unique about Aristotle's philosophy?

3. **ANALYZE CAUSE AND EFFECT** How did Herodotus and Thucydides influence the writing of history?

PLAN

OBJECTIVE

Understand how ancient Greek achievements in philosophy and literature influenced the ancient and modern worlds.

CRITICAL THINKING SKILLS FOR LESSON 4.1

- Identify Main Ideas and Details
- Monitor Comprehension
- Draw Conclusions
- Analyze Cause and Effect
- Explain
- Compare and Contrast
- Analyze Visuals

ESSENTIAL QUESTION

What lasting influences did ancient Greek culture have on the modern world?

The sophisticated thinkers and writers detailed in Lesson 4.1 brought to the study of the world, both metaphysical and scientific, a curiosity, transparency, and logic still valued today.

BACKGROUND FOR THE TEACHER

The Greek philosophical tradition began with the Agora, which means "gathering place" or "assembly." It was a location in the open air where men gathered to discuss the world of politics, nature, and more abstract subjects such as the meaning of life and justice. The first man to be called a philosopher was not Socrates, who is possibly the most famous of the Greek philosophers today, but Pythagoras. A religious cult sprang up around Pythagoras's beliefs. Little is known about these beliefs, as his writings have not survived. We do know that the Pythagoreans believed in the magic of numbers. They also were vegetarians and believed in reincarnation.

DIGITAL RESOURCES myNGconnect.com

TEACHER RESOURCES & ASSESSMENT

 Reading and Note-Taking

 Vocabulary Practice

 Section 4 Quiz

STUDENT RESOURCES

 Biography

INTRODUCE & ENGAGE

THUMBS UP, THUMBS DOWN

Ask students whether they've heard of the philosophers and writers mentioned in the chapter. Have students give each one a thumbs up if they've heard of the person or a thumbs down if they have not. For each figure, ask students who put their thumb up to share any details that they know about the person. Tell students they will learn about the famous philosophers who defined rational thought. `0:05` minutes

TEACH

GUIDED DISCUSSION

1. **Explain** How did Socrates' teaching methods work? *(He asked probing questions to get people to think more deeply.)*

2. **Compare and Contrast** How were the three philosophers mentioned in the lesson alike, and how were they different? *(Possible response: Socrates, Plato, and Aristotle were all deep thinkers and were interested in the reasons behind the way things are in the world. Socrates emphasized thinking for one's self, Plato was more interested in an ideal world, and Aristotle wanted to understand the way in which the world actually worked.)*

ANALYZE VISUALS

Have students examine *The School of Athens*. Tell them that the people depicted did not all live during the same time period. Instead, they reflect the most important minds in Greek philosophy, art, and science throughout ancient Greek history. Ask students to describe the figures and what they are doing. Have them look at the figures of Aristotle and Plato and read the captions to make educated guesses at what they might be talking about. `0:10` minutes

ACTIVE OPTIONS

Critical Viewing: NG Image Gallery Invite students to explore the NG Image Gallery for this chapter and create a Favorites List by choosing the images they find most interesting. If possible, have students copy the images into a document to form an actual list. Then encourage them to select the image they like best and do further research on it. `0:10` minutes

On Your Feet: Understand Multiple Perspectives Divide the class to form two groups, and have them stand on either side of the room. Have one side represent philosophy and the other, science or natural law. Give them some topic ideas and have them decide whether philosophical or scientific perspective is more relevant and helpful to discuss the topic. Start with a term mentioned in the reading, such as "What is justice?" or "What is perfection?" and have students argue whether the philosophers or the scientists can discuss this, or both, and whether they can debate each other on the topic. If not, ask them why not? Then give the two groups a chance to debate the topic by taking turns offering their suggestions.

Encourage the class to reach consensus on at least one topic. Then ask students from the other group to share any concerns as the other group discusses the topic. `0:25` minutes

DIFFERENTIATE

STRIVING READERS

Chart Athenian Thought Leaders Have students complete the following chart to keep track of the ideas of the three philosophers mentioned in the lesson.

	Socrates	Plato	Aristotle
Known for			
Famous Pupil			
Main Interest			

PRE-AP

Write About It Use the lesson as a starting point to research one of the figures shown in *The School of Athens* but not mentioned in the lesson. Have them write a short narrative paragraph about this person. Then have volunteers share their paragraph with the class.

Press (**mt**) *in the Student eEdition for modified text.*

See the Chapter Planner for more strategies for differentiation.

REVIEW & ASSESS

ANSWERS

1. Some of the subjects include philosophy, science, math, and biology.

2. Aristotle used logic to systematically examine, categorize, and understand the world.

3. Herodotus and Thucydides were among the first to apply careful research and accurate written accounts of past events in order to understand the significance of those events from which insights could be gained.

Arts and Architecture

A well-known ancient Greek tyrant cruelly enjoyed burying his enemies alive. Surprisingly, actors performing a Greek play were able to make him cry during sad scenes. The tyrant would weep for the suffering the actors mimicked onstage. Greek drama was powerful.

MAIN IDEA

The Greeks developed forms of art and architecture that are still appreciated today.

POSSIBLE RESPONSE
The amphitheater resembles a baseball stadium.

Critical Viewing This theater in Taormina, Sicily, is one of the best-preserved examples of a Greek amphitheater. What modern structure does this theater resemble?

DRAMA AND SCULPTURE

GREEK MASKS
Greek actors hid their faces with masks that represented the faces of a play's characters. Since three actors played multiple roles, the masks helped the audience recognize character changes.

The Greeks loved the theater. Plays sometimes lasting entire days were performed in huge semicircular theaters, or amphitheaters. Greek drama evolved from plays honoring the god Dionysus (dy-uh-NY-suhs) into two main forms. **Comedy** was humorous and often mocked famous people. **Tragedy** was serious, with characters suffering before an unhappy ending.

Only three male actors performed each play, which required each actor to play many parts. The chorus, a group of actors who spoke, sang, and danced together, narrated the story. Costumes, props, and music brought the action to life.

The greatest Greek playwrights were Sophocles (SAH-fuh-kleez), Aeschylus (EHS-kuh-luhs), and Euripides (yu-RIH-puh-deez), who all wrote tragedies, and Aristophanes (a-ruh-STAH-fuh-neez), who wrote comedy.

Greek sculptors were dedicated to capturing the human form in their art. They carved sculptures from marble, wood, and bronze. The sculptures were painted to look amazingly alive. The Colossus of Rhodes was a 100-foot-tall bronze statue of the sun god Helios, similar in style to the Statue of Liberty. It was once considered one of the Seven Wonders of the Ancient World, but the original no longer stands. In fact, many of the best examples of Greek sculpture are actually newer Roman copies of Greek originals.

COLUMNS AND TEMPLES

Ancient Greek architecture was a democratic art. It expressed beauty and harmony for everyone to enjoy. Temples were designed to be admired from outside, and all followed a similar plan. The temple usually faced east, toward the sunrise. The main room was rectangular and contained a statue of the temple god. Columns supported the roof. The features of Greek architecture continue to influence the style of buildings today. The Supreme Court Building in Washington, D.C., is a good example of this influence.

THREE COLUMN TYPES

Doric
Mainland, western colonies

Corinthian
More rarely found

Ionic
Eastern Greece and the islands

REVIEW & ASSESS

1. **READING CHECK** What art forms did the Greeks develop that we still appreciate today?

2. **COMPARE AND CONTRAST** What is the difference between the two main forms of Greek drama—comedy and tragedy?

3. **IDENTIFY MAIN IDEAS AND DETAILS** The text states that Greek architecture was a democratic art form. What evidence supports this claim?

OBJECTIVE

Explain how classical Greek achievements in the arts and architecture influenced the ancient and modern worlds.

Lesson 4.2 shows the influence of Greece's dramatic and architectural legacy and how these forms are still used in the world today.

CRITICAL THINKING SKILLS FOR LESSON 4.2

- Identify Main Ideas and Details
- Compare and Contrast
- Form and Support Opinions
- Monitor Comprehension
- Describe
- Analyze Visuals

BACKGROUND FOR THE TEACHER

One of the major legacies of the classical Greeks is architecture. Modern theaters and sports arenas are based on the design of the Greek amphitheater, and Greek columns are used to support the roofs of buildings around the world. Three styles of columns are attributed to the Greeks: Doric, which are simple and sturdy with a plain top; Ionic, which are thinner and carved with narrow lines and a scroll style top; and Corinthian, which have tops elaborately decorated with leaves. The U.S. Supreme Court Building is a good example of the influence of ancient Greek architecture.

ESSENTIAL QUESTION

What lasting influences did ancient Greek culture have on the modern world?

DIGITAL RESOURCES myNGconnect.com

TEACHER RESOURCES & ASSESSMENT

 Reading and Note-Taking

 Vocabulary Practice

 Section 4 Quiz

STUDENT RESOURCES

 NG Chapter Gallery

INTRODUCE & ENGAGE

UNDERSTAND CULTURE

Tell students that they probably know a lot of art and architecture that is based on the forms that the classical Greeks invented. Athenian culture emphasized the importance of human experience, the pursuit of knowledge, and harmony and balance in architecture. It was also a religious society, and stories of Greek gods and goddesses occupied a featured place in Greek literature, theater, and architecture, and continue to influence Western literature and film today. In the early fourth century, the philosopher named Aristotle was the most important critic of Greek drama. He analyzed plays, classified types of plays, and defined rules for tragic drama. **0:05** minutes

TEACH

GUIDED DISCUSSION

1. **Describe** Have students look at the columns depicted in the lesson and write a sentence to describe each column's features. *(Doric columns have a simple top; Corinthian columns have an ornate top; and Ionic columns have a scroll-like top.)*

2. **Form and Support Opinions** Ask students whether they like stories that are tragedies or comedies, and have them give some examples or reasons to back up their responses. *(Responses will vary.)*

ANALYZE VISUALS

Direct students' attention to the photograph of the amphitheater in Lesson 4.2. Ask them to consider how the physical characteristics of the land influenced how people lived and constructed such buildings. Make a list of the challenges the Greeks might have faced as they built structures on the mountainous terrain. **0:10** minutes

ACTIVE OPTIONS

On Your Feet: Small Groups Organize students into small groups and have each group read a passage from a play by one of the playwrights mentioned in Lesson 4.2 and discuss its meaning. Then have a volunteer from each group read the passage aloud to the class and give a short summary of the passage. **0:25** minutes

NG Learning Framework: Write a Play

ATTITUDE: **Empowerment**
KNOWLEDGE: **Storytelling**

Have students revisit earlier lessons in the chapter and have them work in small groups to write a short scene (comic or tragic) based on some dramatic event in the chapter. Examples include the plague of Athens, the funeral oration of Pericles, the Peloponnesian War, or Alexander's conquest of Greece. Students should use information from the chapter and their own creativity to build their scenes. Then have them perform the scenes for the class. **0:20** minutes

DIFFERENTIATE

INCLUSION

Describe a Photograph Have students look at the photograph of the amphitheater in Lesson 4.2. Ask them to describe it and then talk about why the shape and features of the building might be good for a performance space.

GIFTED & TALENTED

Write a Short Play Have students research and read a Greek comedy or tragedy, or part of one, and then create their own new play, either wholly invented or partially based on the source play. Have students cast the different parts and act out the play for the class.

Press (**mt**) *in the Student eEdition for modified text.*

See the Chapter Planner for more strategies for differentiation.

REVIEW & ASSESS

ANSWERS

1. The Greeks developed many art forms that we still appreciate today, including drama, sculpture, and architecture.

2. A comedy is funny and often makes fun of famous people; in contrast, a tragedy is serious and includes characters who suffer terribly before an unhappy ending.

3. According to the text, Greek architecture was designed and built for everyone to enjoy.

432 B.C.

POSSIBLE RESPONSE
The columns are sturdy and thick, and the building is beautiful, tall, and intimidating.

The Parthenon, one of the world's most recognizable buildings, was completed in 432 B.C. It took workers almost 15 years to build this magnificent marble temple, which honored Athena, goddess and protector of Athens. Like much Greek architecture, the Parthenon was made to be looked at from the outside. Its elegant proportions communicated a sense of harmony and balance. Inside, towering from floor to ceiling, was a 33-foot gold and ivory statue of Athena. The Parthenon was both an expression of Athens's wealth and a symbol of its cultural, political, and military superiority. What details in the Parthenon's design help convey these ideas?

PLAN

OBJECTIVE

Identify the cultural ideas that found expression in Greek architecture's most stunning example: the Parthenon.

CRITICAL THINKING SKILLS FOR LESSON 4.3

• Describe • Make Connections • Analyze Visuals

ESSENTIAL QUESTION

What lasting influences did ancient Greek culture have on the modern world?

Lesson 4.3 discusses the Parthenon, one of Athens's most magnificent buildings.

BACKGROUND FOR THE TEACHER

Building with stone has it origins in the seventh century B.C., when Greece began to first have knowledge of Egypt and its workers' method of quarrying and constructing stone. By the time the Parthenon was built, the basics of the different styles, or orders, of Greek architecture were well in place. The Parthenon is in the Doric style, which is plain but conveys an essence of power for those gazing upon it. It is one of the most famous—and most studied—buildings on Earth. It was built after the completion of the Persian War to celebrate the war's end and represent Athens's authority in the region.

DIGITAL RESOURCES myNGconnect.com

TEACHER RESOURCES & ASSESSMENT

 Reading and Note-Taking   **Vocabulary Practice**   **Section 4 Quiz**

STUDENT RESOURCES

 NG Chapter Gallery

INTRODUCE & ENGAGE

EXPLORE RENEWAL

Engage students in a discussion about ways that people recover a sense of normalcy and peaceful living after years of long and grueling warfare. Fixing or replacing buildings that were destroyed, having feasts or contests, attending performances, and getting back to normal, everyday routines are some ways societies renew after traumatic events. Then tell students they will learn about a building that was vital to the restoration of Athens's spirit. `0:10` minutes

TEACH

GUIDED DISCUSSION

1. **Describe** How do the details in the Parthenon's design convey power? What other qualities do you think it conveys? *(The columns are sturdy and thick, without many curves or unnecessary designs. The building itself looks very tall, so it would make an observer feel tiny. The building is also slightly raised, with stairs on every side, making it inviting and open, allowing people to approach it freely and without fear.)*

2. **Make Connections** Have you seen other buildings that have a similar look or design style as the Parthenon? *(Responses will vary, but students may cite specific buildings or more general buildings such as government buildings, libraries, colleges, and museums.)*

ANALYZE VISUALS

Give students some background on the Parthenon. Remind them how Athens was burned to the ground during the Persian Wars. Even the olive tree, which according to legend had been a gift to the city from Athena, was dead. But someone saw a tiny leaf growing from the burned tree, and from this sign the Athenians decided to rebuild the city. Ask students why the construction of the Parthenon was such an important moment in Greek history. Encourage students to volunteer their ideas as you add them to the board. Responses will vary but students should make the connection between the building of the Parthenon and Athens becoming a strong force in the region again. `0:15` minutes

ACTIVE OPTIONS

On Your Feet: Debate Divide the class into two groups and have one side discuss reasons why they might support rebuilding Athens, while the other side finds reasons to argue against it. Have students from each group take turns debating the topic, and make sure that they also try to address the concerns of the other group. See if either group can persuade opposing students to change sides. At the end, reward the side with the most remaining students the winner of the debate. `0:20` minutes

Critical Viewing: NG Chapter Gallery Have students examine the contents of the Chapter Gallery for this chapter. Then invite them to brainstorm additional images they believe would fit within the Chapter Gallery. Have them write a description of these additional images and provide an explanation of why they would fit within the Chapter Gallery. Then instruct them to do online research to find examples of actual images they would like to add to the gallery. `0:10` minutes

DIFFERENTIATE

GIFTED & TALENTED

Draw the Parthenon Have students work in pairs on a drawing of the Parthenon based on the photograph in the lesson. Then have them discuss how they would have built the building, starting from the ground up. Remind them that the building took about 15 years to build, and that it had a statue of Athena inside it. They also may try to draw the statue based on their imagination and what they have read or seen of Athena in books or pictures.

PRE-AP

Research Symbols Have students research online to find visual depictions of abstract concepts such as justice, harmony, balance, strength, and mercy, and report on the characteristics usually associated with each one.

Press **mt** *in the Student eEdition for modified text.*

See the Chapter Planner for more strategies for differentiation.

4.4 Democracy and Law

Sometimes we might take our system of government for granted. However, our democracy is a legacy that has been passed down to us from thousands of years ago. Our modern ideas of democracy, justice, and citizenship all have their roots in ancient Greece.

MAIN IDEA

The Constitution of the United States was influenced by ancient Greek ideas.

GOVERNMENT OF THE PEOPLE

Ancient Greece was the birthplace of democracy and citizenship. Thousands of Greek citizens met regularly to vote on policies and laws. Greek colonies in Italy spread democracy to the ancient Romans, who carried it around the ancient world. They firmly established Greek political ideas in Europe. From these ideas evolved our modern ideas about government and civic life.

Ancient Greece also laid the foundations of American constitutional democracy. The cornerstone of Greek democratic ideas was that political power should rest with the people. The Greeks established the concept of citizenship with its rights and responsibilities toward the state and a duty to participate in politics and civic life.

The Greeks also embraced the principle of political equality, in which one citizen has one vote and where officials are paid, allowing the poor to serve as well as the rich. The Greeks put checks and balances into place. They limited terms of office and separated the three key branches of government—lawmaking, executive, and judicial—to prevent any one branch from becoming too powerful.

The **representative democracy** of the United States is based on the Greek system. Because the U.S. population is so large, its millions of citizens cannot vote directly on policies. Instead, citizens exercise their political power by electing representatives to vote on their behalf.

RULE OF LAW

Greek democracy was built on the rule of law. Greek citizens proposed and voted on laws that were enforced in courts. These courts established innocence or guilt through trials by **jury**. A jury is a group of people chosen to decide guilt or innocence in a trial. Greek jurors were selected randomly so that the results would be impartial. They also were paid so that even poor citizens could take part.

In Greek trials, the accuser and the accused represented themselves. There were no lawyers. Both parties had the same amount of time to speak, and both relied on witnesses. Under oath, witnesses sometimes testified to events but usually provided character statements.

Both sides presented their case, but they did not sum up the evidence, as lawyers do in court cases today. Nor was the jury allowed to discuss the case. Instead, jurors voted immediately by placing metal discs called ballots into a pot. The jury also passed sentence. Some penalties were automatic, such as death for murder, but more involved fines. Few people were actually imprisoned. There were no appeals, and the entire process was completed in a day.

+ POSSIBLE RESPONSE

The people in the photograph demonstrate citizenship by standing up for their beliefs and gathering together to discuss or debate public matters.

Critical Viewing Supporters of immigration rights march through downtown Los Angeles. How are these people demonstrating citizenship?

REVIEW & ASSESS

1. **READING CHECK** Why were jury members chosen randomly and why were they paid?

2. **ANALYZE CAUSE AND EFFECT** What ancient Greek ideas laid the foundation for the U.S. system of government?

3. **COMPARE AND CONTRAST** What are the differences between ancient Greek trials and modern trials in the United States?

PLAN

OBJECTIVE

Learn about the influence of Greek ideas on the government of the United States.

CRITICAL THINKING SKILLS FOR LESSON 4.4

- Identify Main Ideas and Details
- Monitor Comprehension
- Analyze Cause and Effect
- Compare and Contrast
- Draw Conclusions
- Analyze visuals

ESSENTIAL QUESTION

What lasting influences did ancient Greek culture have on the modern world?

Lesson 4.4 shows the influence of Greek government, particularly democracy, on the world today.

BACKGROUND FOR THE TEACHER

At first glance, the city-state of Athens had a more democratic government than that of the United States because its government was a direct democracy in which all citizens could vote on laws. Citizenship in Athens was strictly limited to men, however, and women, foreigners, and slaves were excluded. Some scholars estimate that citizens made up only 10 to 15 percent of the population. Nevertheless, the concept of rule by many (citizens/democracy), rather than rule by few (noblemen/oligarchy) or one (king/monarchy), was put into practice.

DIGITAL RESOURCES myNGconnect.com

TEACHER RESOURCES & ASSESSMENT

 Reading and Note-Taking

 Vocabulary Practice

 Section 4 Quiz

STUDENT RESOURCES

 Active History

INTRODUCE & ENGAGE

VENN DIAGRAM

Tell students that they will be reading about Greek democracy. Explain that Lesson 4.4 explores the differences between classical Greek laws and practices and the laws and practices of the United States today. Draw a large Venn diagram on the board and write *democracy* where the circles overlap. Label one side of the diagram *Classical Greece* and the other *United States*. Then have students make their own Venn diagrams that they will complete as they read Lesson 4.4. Once they have finished reading, review their responses as a class and add items to the large diagram on the board. `0:15` minutes

TEACH

GUIDED DISCUSSION

1. **Analyze Causes** Why do you think the United States is a representative democracy instead of a direct democracy? *(Possible response: There are too many people in the country— for everyone to cast a vote directly on every policy would be unworkable.)*

2. **Draw Conclusions** What are some of the benefits and drawbacks of the classical Greek system of law? *(Possible responses: Having trials last only one day would be good because people would not have to wait to stand trial very long. Automatic penalties could be bad because there are different motivations for crimes, and motivations are important.)*

ANALYZE VISUALS

Direct students' attention to the photograph of activists in Los Angeles in Lesson 4.4. Ask the class to describe what they see in the photo and write students' descriptions on the board. Ask students to consider why the flag is an important symbol and why people are holding it up. **ASK:** In what way does the flag symbolize citizenship? What else can a flag symbolize? *(Possible responses: commonality, strength, fairness, justice, idealism, nationalism)* `0:10` minutes

ACTIVE OPTIONS

Active History: Research Ancient Greek Contributions Extend the lesson by using either the PDF or Whiteboard version of the Research Ancient Greek Contributions activity. These activities take a deeper look at a topic from, or related to, the lesson. Explore the activities as a class, turn them into group assignments, or even assign them individually. `0:10` minutes

On Your Feet: Democracy from Scratch Have students gather into small groups to think of what rights and responsibilities they would include in a democracy. Encourage them to be creative and to draw on what they already know about democracy. Have them

share with the class three of their main ideas, and have them explain why each would be important and useful to the people in their nation or state. Encourage other students to ask questions and offer constructive criticism of each other's plans. `0:20` minutes

DIFFERENTIATE

ENGLISH LANGUAGE LEARNERS

Build Vocabulary Help students understand words used in Lesson 4.4 that may be unfamiliar to them. Begin with the Key Vocabulary words for this lesson: *representative democracy* and *jury*. Provide students with index cards or small pieces of paper. Have students write each word and its definition based on context clues in the text on separate index cards. Then have them compare their definitions with definitions in the Glossary. Once students have established solid definitions, encourage them to write sentences using the Key Vocabulary. Other words in Lesson 4.4 that students may need extra practice with include *civic, constitutional, citizenship, equality, trial, innocence,* and *appeal*. Have students refer to a dictionary in the classroom or online to gather definitions for these or other words and then write sentences using the words.

INCLUSION

Work in Pairs Pair students who have visual or learning disabilities with partners who are proficient readers. Have the proficient student read the subsection titled "Government of the People" aloud. After reading each paragraph, the reader should stop and their partner should retell the same information in their own words to check comprehension.

Press (**mt**) *in the Student eEdition for modified text.*

See the Chapter Planner for more strategies for differentiation.

REVIEW & ASSESS

ANSWERS

1. Jury members were chosen randomly so that they would be impartial. They were paid so that poor citizens could also take part.

2. Ancient Greek ideas of citizenship, justice, political equality, rule of law, and the right to vote are among the many ideas that laid the foundation for democracy in the United States.

3. Both sides presented their cases at court, but did not sum up the evidence like lawyers today do. Greek juries did not discuss their vote, as they do today, but simply voted after the evidence was presented. Also the jury passed sentences in Greek democracy, unlike today.

VOCABULARY

Use each of the following vocabulary words in a sentence that shows an understanding of the meaning of the word.

1. **direct democracy**
   Athens's government was a direct democracy, in which citizens voted for or against laws.

2. **immortal**

3. **plague**

4. **siege**

5. **philosophy**

6. **comedy**

7. **tragedy**

8. **jury**

READING STRATEGY

9. **DETERMINE WORD MEANINGS** Copy the chart below and add your examples of words that include each Greek root. Then write a paragraph about Greek culture that includes each word.

Root	Meaning	Example(s)
cosm-	universe	
-cracy	government	democracy
dem-	people	democracy
-logy	speech	
myth-	story	
phil-	love	
poli-	city	
soph-	wise	

MAIN IDEAS

Answer the following questions. Support your answers with evidence from the chapter.

10. How did Athens become a powerful empire after the Persian Wars? LESSON 1.2

11. Why did the Greeks make offerings to the gods and goddesses they worshipped? LESSON 1.3

12. What caused the outbreak of the Peloponnesian War between Athens and Sparta? LESSON 2.1

13. How did Sparta defeat Athens and end the Peloponnesian War? LESSON 2.2

14. What was Phillip II's most important achievement in Greece? LESSON 3.1

15. Why did Alexander's conquests end? LESSON 3.2

16. How is Hellenistic culture an example of cultural diffusion? LESSON 3.3

17. What evidence is there that the ideas of the Greek philosophers and writers are still important today? LESSON 4.1

CRITICAL THINKING

Answer the following questions. Support your answers with evidence from the chapter.

18. **DRAW CONCLUSIONS** What are three ways in which Greek influences are felt today?

19. **ANALYZE CAUSE AND EFFECT** How did the plague contribute to the failure of Pericles' war strategy against the Spartans?

20. **EVALUATE** What factors contributed to Philip II's success in conquering and unifying Greece?

21. **YOU DECIDE** Where would you rather have lived—Athens or Sparta? Why? Support your opinion with details from the chapter.

INTERPRET MAPS

Study the map of the Hellenistic world after Alexander's death, when his empire broke apart. Then answer the questions that follow.

THE HELLENISTIC WORLD, 241 B.C.

22. Into what four kingdoms did Alexander's empire separate?

23. Which kingdom appears to have the least territory?

ANALYZE SOURCES

Read the following excerpt from the American Declaration of Independence. Then answer the question.

We hold these truths to be self-evident, that all men are created equal, that they are endowed by their Creator with certain unalienable Rights, that among these are Life, Liberty, and the pursuit of Happiness.

24. How are the thoughts on democracy expressed by the authors of the Declaration of Independence similar to those of the Athenians?

WRITE ABOUT HISTORY

25. **INFORMATIVE** Write a three-paragraph speech for new American citizens explaining how democratic concepts developed in Greece laid the foundation for democracy in the United States.

TIPS

- Take notes from the lessons about Pericles and democracy and the legacy of ancient Greece.
- Introduce the topic clearly.
- Develop the topic with relevant, well-chosen facts, concrete details, and examples.
- Use vocabulary from the chapter as appropriate.
- Use appropriate transitions to clarify the relationships among concepts.
- Provide a concluding statement that summarizes the information presented.

VOCABULARY ANSWERS

1. Athens's government was a direct democracy, in which citizens voted for or against laws.

2. The Greeks believed that their gods and goddesses were immortal, or lived forever.

3. A deadly plague killed thousands of Athenians, including Pericles.

4. Athens ended the truce with Sparta when it laid siege to Syracuse in Sicily.

5. The study of philosophy has been greatly influenced by the ideas of Socrates, Plato, and Aristotle.

6. One form of Greek drama was comedy, which was funny and often made fun of famous people.

7. Another form of Greek drama was tragedy, in which characters suffered terrible events and tragic endings.

8. At trials, Greeks used a jury, or a group of people chosen to determine whether an accused person is innocent or guilty.

READING STRATEGY ANSWER

Root	Meaning	Example(s)
cosm-	universe	cosmopolitan
-cracy	government	democracy
dem-	people	democracy
-logy	speech	mythology
myth-	story	mythology
phil-	love	philosophy
poli-	city	cosmopolitan
soph-	wise	philosophy

9. Students' paragraphs should include each word and accurately describe Greek culture.

MAIN IDEAS ANSWERS

10. After the Persian Wars, Athens and other Greek city-states formed an alliance called the Delian League, which Athens led. Pericles used funds from the league to build and expand Athens's navy and dominate the Mediterranean. Eventually, the other city-states became part of the Athenian empire.

11. The Greeks believed that they must keep the gods and goddesses happy, otherwise they would become angry and interfere with their lives.

12. The outbreak of war between Athens and Sparta was sparked by an argument between two minor rival states, Corinth and Corfu. Confrontations between Athens and Sparta escalated, and Sparta declared war on Athens in 432 B.C.

13. Sparta effectively blockaded Athens on land and sea, cutting off resources and forcing Athens to make a desperate choice— surrender or starve. Athens surrendered, and the war ended.

14. Philip II conquered all of Greece and unified it for the first time ever.

15. Alexander's conquests ended in India because Alexander's army was homesick and weary of battle after eleven years; they mutinied against Alexander, who reluctantly ordered the men to leave India and return home.

16. Hellenistic culture is an example of cultural diffusion because thousands of Greek colonists spread Greek ideas and practices throughout Asia, with each area adopting and adapting Greek culture differently and blending it with their own cultures.

17. The ideas and writings of Socrates, Plato, and Aristotle formed the basis of modern western philosophy, which continues to influence our way of thinking and examining the world and all areas of study—from law and politics to math and science.

CRITICAL THINKING ANSWERS

18. The legacy of ancient Greek culture is important to the modern world because Greek culture has influenced many different aspects of present-day life around the world. For example, in the United States, the influence of Greek culture is demonstrated in its government, in the architecture of many buildings, in its philosophers and writers, and in its artists and the work they produce.

19. During the Peloponnesian War, a key part of Pericles's war strategy was to take a defensive position on land with Athenians and refugees staying together behind the city's strong walls. The outbreak of the plague quickly spread throughout the overcrowded city, killing thousands of people, including Pericles.

20. After the Peloponnesian War, Greek cities were weak and open to attack by Philip II and his army. In addition, Philip II and his army used new weapons of warfare, such as the phalanx battle formation and catapults to conquer Greek colonies and cities.

21. Students' responses will vary. Students should clearly state their opinion regarding where they would rather live and support that opinion with evidence from the chapter.

INTERPRET MAPS ANSWERS

22. After Alexander's death, his empire separated into the Egyptian Kingdom, Macedonian Kingdom, Pergamum Kingdom, and Seleucid Kingdom.

23. The Macedonian Kingdom has the least amount of territory.

ANALYZE SOURCES ANSWER

24. Students' responses will vary. Sample response: The thoughts on democracy expressed in the U.S. Declaration of Independence shares with Athenian democracy the ideals of rights and an equal voice for all people.

WRITE ABOUT HISTORY ANSWER

25. Students' speeches should

- introduce the topic clearly
- contain relevant, well-chosen facts, concrete details, and examples
- incorporate chapter vocabulary
- include a concluding statement

ON **LOCATION** WITH William PARKINSON

NATIONAL GEOGRAPHIC GRANTEE

▶ **Check out more on myNGconnect**

In the field, Parkinson uses hi-tech equipment like this Real-Time-Kinetic GPS. It makes accurate maps by communicating with multiple satellites at one time.

FROM VILLAGE TO CITY

Like many kids who grew up in the Midwest, I loved searching for arrowheads in the fields and woods. Finding them made me want to learn more about people who lived long ago. Lucky for me, I had excellent college professors who encouraged me to study archaeology, and now I'm living my dream!

Today, I study how small farming villages turned into big cities. From an archaeological perspective, cities are weird. Until about 8,000 years ago humans lived in small groups and moved around as hunter-gatherers. Today, more than half of all humans live in cities. This has dramatic implications for our future. Archaeologists have done a good job explaining human development from hunter-gatherers to settled farmers. However, we still don't really understand how those early villages turned into massive cities.

Bill Parkinson explores a coastline while conducting an archaeological survey in Diros Bay, Greece.

A TEAM SPORT

In Europe and the Near East, the turning point came during the Neolithic and the Bronze Age. My team has been excavating an ancient farming village in Greece, just outside a big cave called Fox Hole Cave. This cave was used for rituals and habitation during the Neolithic period, when the first farmers emerged in southeastern Europe. Greek archaeologists have explored this cave for 40 years, and we wanted to build on their great work. Archaeology is a team sport that relies on the collaboration of many different specialists, so we brought together an international crew to study the cave.

Our excavations show that people built an agricultural settlement at the site about 6,000 years ago. This settlement gives us greater insight into how early agricultural villages developed. I'm studying a similar site from the same time period in Hungary, so we're able to compare and contrast how societies changed over time in different parts of the world. Now we are publishing the results of our research, another crucial part of archaeology. Soon we'll be back in the field, hunting for the next clues about how ancient villages transformed into cities.

WHY STUDY HISTORY ❓

❝ Nothing can describe how exciting it is to put your trowel in the ground and uncover something nobody has seen for several thousand years. *It never gets old.* ❞ —William Parkinson

NATIONAL GEOGRAPHIC

Greek Statues Sparkle Once Again

BY A. R. WILLIAMS

Adapted from "2,500-Year-Old Greek Statues
Sparkle After Facelift," by A. R. Williams,
news.nationalgeographic.com, June 19, 2014

Four marble maidens from ancient Greece have gotten a makeover. Using a specially designed laser, conservators have stripped away the black grime that covered the statues. Sculpted in the late fifth century B.C., the figures served as columns for the Erechtheion, one of the temples that stood on the Acropolis. The maidens, known as the Caryatids, stand more than seven and a half feet tall and hold the roof of the Erechtheion's south porch on their heads.

As Athens rapidly industrialized over the past century, the Caryatids suffered from the effects of air pollution. Their golden hue turned dark, and their features began to dissolve under the constant assault of acid rain. In 1979 the figures were moved to protect them from further damage. Cement replicas were installed in their place on the Erechtheion's porch.

The Caryatids got their makeover in the public gallery of the Acropolis Museum. Conservators focused on one figure at a time in a makeshift room whose walls were sheets of heavy fabric hung from a frame. A video

monitor outside allowed visitors to see the statues slowly changing color. The curtain walls protected museumgoers' eyes from the laser system that conservators, wearing protective goggles, used to clean the statues. This system uses two pulsed beams of radiation—one infrared and the other ultraviolet—to zap away dust, soot, minerals, and metals.

Conservators and technicians considered several different kinds of cleaning, including chemicals and micro-sandblasting. The dual-wavelength laser system was the best option. It allows for safe, controlled cleaning that leaves the marble's ancient patina intact.

A future project may reveal even more of the maidens' original beauty. Their clothing was once brightly painted. However, centuries of winter rain have washed away all visible traces of pigment. Modern imaging techniques can peer into the invisible parts of the light spectrum and find long-faded hues. The result may be even more dazzling than the maidens' current makeover.

For more from National Geographic
Check out "Behind the Tomb" on myNGconnect

UNIT INQUIRY: DEFINE GOOD CITIZENSHIP

In this unit, you learned about ancient Greek civilization and its influence on our modern world. Based on your understanding of the text, what new form of government was central to Greek civilization? What role did citizenship play in Greek civilization and government?

ASSIGNMENT Create your own definition for good citizenship. Your definition should include a clear statement of what constitutes good citizenship and why it is important today. Be prepared to present your definition to the class and explain your reasoning.

Plan As you write your definition, think about the active role citizens played in ancient Greek civilization and government. Also think about the rights and responsibilities ancient Greek citizens had and how those ideas have influenced our ideas about citizenship today. You might want to use a graphic organizer to help organize your thoughts. ▶

Produce Use your notes to produce descriptions of the elements that make up your definition of good citizenship.

Present Choose a creative way to present your definition to the class. Consider one of these options:

- Create a video presentation using examples from everyday life showing good citizens "in action" in their community.

- Design a good citizenship medal to present to someone who exemplifies what it means to be a good citizen.

- Design a good citizenship brochure that outlines citizens' rights and responsibilities.

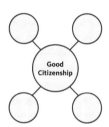

Good Citizenship

RAPID REVIEW
UNIT 3

GREEK CIVILIZATION

TOP TEN

1. The Minoans and the Mycenaeans were the first advanced Greek civilizations.

2. Ancient Greek city-states established colonies and trade networks throughout the Mediterranean.

3. The city-state of Athens developed the world's first democracy.

4. Alexander the Great conquered Persia, Egypt, Afghanistan, and India, building a vast empire that spread Greek culture.

5. The ancient Greeks influenced Western art, architecture, literature, philosophy, science, medicine, government, and law.

6-10. **NOW IT'S YOUR TURN** Complete the list with five more things to remember about Greek civilization.

RAPID REVIEW

POSSIBLE RESPONSES

Possible responses for the remaining five things to remember:

6. Two rival factions of Greek city-states—the Delian League led by Athens and the Peloponnesian League led by Sparta—fought the Peloponnesian War.

7. City-states governed through many forms of government, including monarchies, aristocracies, oligarchies, and tyrannies.

8. Independent city-states in ancient Greece shared a common language and culture but established their own governments, laws, and customs.

9. Athens and Sparta formed an alliance to defeat the Persian Empire in the Persian Wars.

10. The Macedonian general, King Philip II, conquered the Greek city-states and united Greece under his sole control.

UNIT INQUIRY PROJECT RUBRIC

ASSESS

Use the rubric to assess each student's participation and performance.

SCORE	ASSIGNMENT	PRODUCT	PRESENTATION
3 GREAT	• Student thoroughly understands the assignment. • Student engages with the project topic. • Student works well independently.	• Definition is well thought out. • Definition clearly states what constitutes good citizenship and why it is important today. • Definition clearly reflects Greek ideals about citizenship.	• Presentation is clear, concise, and logical. • Presentation does a good job demonstrating good citizenship. • Presentation engages the audience.
2 GOOD	• Student mostly understands the assignment. • Student engages fairly well with the project topic. • Student works fairly independently.	• Definition is fairly well thought out. • Definition somewhat clearly states what constitutes good citizenship and why it is important today. • Definition somewhat clearly reflects Greek ideals about citizenship.	• Presentation is fairly clear, concise, and logical. • Presentation does a fairly good job demonstrating good citizenship. • Presentation somewhat engages the audience.
1 NEEDS WORK	• Student does not understand the assignment. • Student minimally engages or does not engage with the project topic. • Student struggles to work independently.	• Definition is not well thought out. • Definition does not clearly state what constitutes good citizenship and why it is important today. • Definition does not reflect Greek ideals about citizenship.	• Presentation is not clear, concise, or logical. • Presentation does not demonstrate good citizenship. • Presentation does not engage the audience.

THE WORLD OF THE
ROMANS

NATIONAL
GEOGRAPHIC

ON **LOCATION** WITH

Steven Ellis
Archaeologist

Have you ever heard the expression "All roads lead to Rome?" Well, 2,000 years ago, all roads actually did lead to Rome. Though it began as a small town on the Tiber River in Italy, in only a few centuries Rome came to dominate the Mediterranean and build a civilization that stretched from northern Europe to Syria. I'm Steven Ellis, and I work with National Geographic. Welcome to the world of the Romans!

< CRITICAL VIEWING The ruins of Pompeii, seen here in the shadow of Mount Vesuvius, continue to reveal much about the lives of the ancient Romans. What details do you notice in the photo that resemble features you might see in a town or city today?

+ POSSIBLE RESPONSE

Details that resemble features in a town or city today include streets, walkways, buildings, and houses.

Ancient Rome

753 B.C.
According to legend, Romulus founds the city of Rome. *(illustration of Romulus on a coin)*

509 B.C.
Rome becomes a republic.

44 B.C.
Julius Caesar is assassinated by a group of Roman senators.

800 B.C.

100 B.C.

The World

**750 B.C.
EUROPE**
Greek city-states flourish with shared Greek identity but individual loyalties, customs, and governments.

**334 B.C.
EUROPE**
Alexander the Great begins to build his massive empire.
(detail from statue of Alexander)

What other world event happened around the time Rome became an empire?

A.D. 26–29
Jesus preaches religious ideas that will form the basis of Christianity.

A.D. 476
Invasions bring about the fall of the Western Roman Empire.
(painting of the sack of Rome)

A.D. 177
The Roman Empire reaches its greatest extent, stretching over parts of Europe, Asia, and Africa.

A.D. 395
The Roman Empire is divided into the Eastern and Western empires.

27 B.C.
Rome becomes an empire, and Augustus becomes its first emperor.

A.D. 300

A.D. 500

A.D. 100

**A.D. 250
AMERICAS**
The Maya build great cities and make significant advances in learning.
(Maya pyramid)

**A.D. 300s
AFRICA**
The kingdom of Aksum in East Africa reaches its height under Ezana.

**10 B.C
ASIA**
The Silk Roads connect China to the Mediterranean.

265

FROM REPUBLIC TO
EMPIRE
146 B.C.–A.D. 117

Find Rome on the map. That's how it began: as a small dot in a land once known as Italia. Actually, Rome was even smaller, since it began as a village of farmers. But the Romans developed a civilization that grew to become one of the greatest empires the world has ever seen.

At its full extent, the Roman Empire stretched over three continents. It was held together by taxes, the powerful Roman army, and an amazing network of roads. Through periods of peace and war, Rome remained the center of the Western world for hundreds of years.

What body of water probably helped link the Roman Empire?

+ POSSIBLE RESPONSE

The Mediterranean Sea most likely helped link the lands of the Roman Empire.

Hadrian's Wall

North Sea

Caledonia
Hadrian's Wall
Hibernia
BRITANNIA
• Londinium
MAGNA GERMANIA
12 B.C.–A.D. 9
Rhine
GERMANIA INFERIOR
Germa
GERMANIA SUPERIOR
Elbe
Seine
LUGDUNENSIS
BELGICA
Rhine
Danube
RAETIA
NORICUM
Loire
Gallia
Lake Geneva
Rhône
ALPES GRAIAE ET POENINAE
Lake Garda
Po
AQUITANIA
ALPES COTTIAE
Adri
NARBONENSIS
ALPES MARITIMAE
ITALIA
Ebro
CORSICA
Rome ✪
TARRACONENSIS
Tyrrhenian Sea
LUSITANIA
Tagus *Hispania*
SARDINIA
Emerita Augusta •
Balearic Islands
BAETICA
Mediterrane
• Carthage
AFRICA
MAURETANIA TINGITANA
MAURETANIA CAESARIENSIS
Atlantic Ocean
• Volubilis
A   F   R

Time Line of Good and Bad Emperors

"Bad" emperor
Historians traditionally call the first three emperors below "bad" because they abused their power.

"Good" emperor
The other five emperors are considered "good" because, like Augustus, they presided over a period of peace and ruled wisely.

 Caligula
A.D. 37–41

- Reigned as a cruel tyrant
- Insisted on being treated as a god

 Nero
A.D. 54–68

- Committed many murders
- Did nothing while much of Rome burned

Domitian
A.D. 81–96

- Ruled as a dictator
- Murdered many of his enemies

 Nerva
A.D. 96–98

- First emperor chosen for the job
- Tried to end tryannical rule

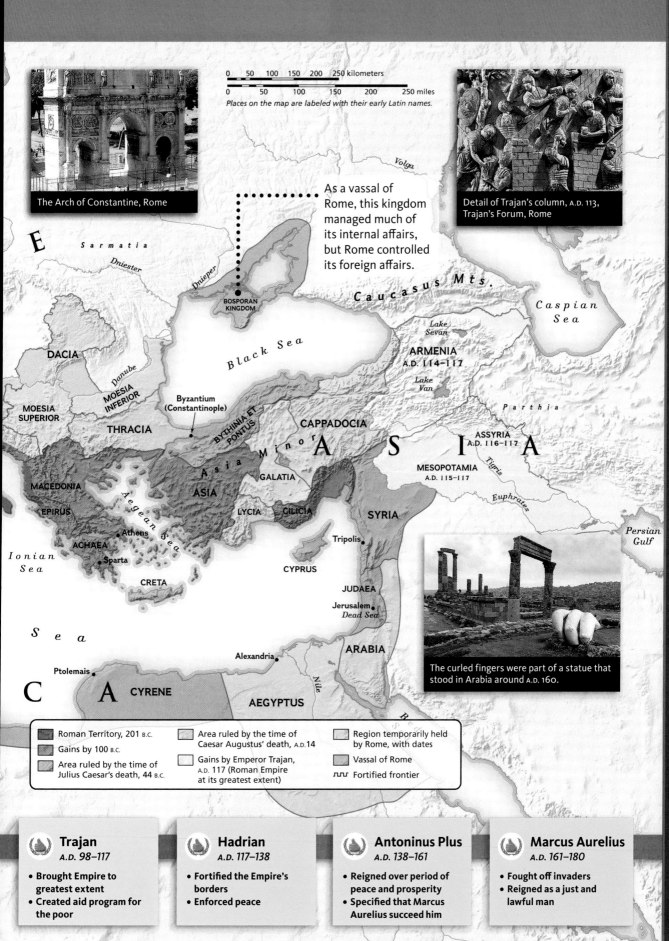

0 50 100 150 200 250 kilometers

0 50 100 150 200 250 miles

Places on the map are labeled with their early Latin names.

The Arch of Constantine, Rome

As a vassal of Rome, this kingdom managed much of its internal affairs, but Rome controlled its foreign affairs.

Detail of Trajan's column, A.D. 113, Trajan's Forum, Rome

E

Sarmatia

Dniester

Dnieper

Volga

BOSPORAN KINGDOM

Black Sea

Caucasus Mts.

Caspian Sea

Lake Sevan

ARMENIA
A.D. 114–117

Lake Van

Parthia

DACIA

Danube

MOESIA INFERIOR

MOESIA SUPERIOR

THRACIA

Byzantium (Constantinople)

BYTHINIA ET PONTUS

CAPPADOCIA

Asia Minor

A **S** **I** **A**

ASSYRIA
A.D. 116–117

MESOPOTAMIA
A.D. 115–117

Tigris

Euphrates

MACEDONIA

Aegean Sea

ASIA

GALATIA

EPIRUS

LYCIA

CILICIA

SYRIA

Persian Gulf

Athens

ACHAEA

Sparta

Ionian Sea

CRETA

CYPRUS

Tripolis

JUDAEA

Jerusalem

Dead Sea

The curled fingers were part of a statue that stood in Arabia around A.D. 160.

S *e* *a*

Ptolemais

C **A** CYRENE

Alexandria

Nile

ARABIA

AEGYPTUS

■ Roman Territory, 201 B.C.	□ Area ruled by the time of Caesar Augustus' death, A.D.14	□ Region temporarily held by Rome, with dates
■ Gains by 100 B.C.	□ Gains by Emperor Trajan, A.D. 117 (Roman Empire at its greatest extent)	□ Vassal of Rome
■ Area ruled by the time of Julius Caesar's death, 44 B.C.		ᴨᴨ Fortified frontier

Trajan
A.D. 98–117

- Brought Empire to greatest extent
- Created aid program for the poor

Hadrian
A.D. 117–138

- Fortified the Empire's borders
- Enforced peace

Antoninus Plus
A.D. 138–161

- Reigned over period of peace and prosperity
- Specified that Marcus Aurelius succeed him

Marcus Aurelius
A.D. 161–180

- Fought off invaders
- Reigned as a just and lawful man

UNIT RESOURCES

On Location with National Geographic Grantee Steven Ellis
Intro and Video

Unit Wrap-Up:
"Exploring Pompeii"
Feature and Video

"Rethinking Nero"
National Geographic Adapted Article

"Roman Frontiers"
National Geographic Adapted Article
Student eEdition exclusive

Unit 4 Inquiry:
Build an Empire

 **Interactive Map Tool**
Available on myNGconnect

 **News & Updates**
Available on myNGconnect

CHAPTER RESOURCES

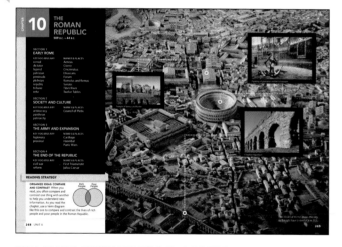

TEACHER RESOURCES & ASSESSMENT *Available on myNGconnect*

 Social Studies Skills Lessons
• Reading: Compare and Contrast
• Writing: Write an Argument

 Chapter 10
Answer Key

 Formal Assessment
• Chapter 10 Tests A (on-level) &
  B (below-level)

 ExamView®
One-time Download

STUDENT BACKPACK *Available on myNGconnect*

• **eEdition** *(English)*   • **eEdition** *(Spanish)*   • **Handbooks**   • **Online Atlas**
For Chapter 10 Spanish resources, visit the Teacher Resource Menu page on myNGconnect.

SECTION 1 RESOURCES

EARLY ROME

 Reading and Note-Taking

 Vocabulary Practice

 Section 1 Quiz

Available on myNGconnect

LESSON 1.1 THE GEOGRAPHY
OF ANCIENT ROME
• Online Atlas: The Hills of Rome
• On Your Feet: Model Rome's
  Geography
• Critical Viewing: NG Chapter Gallery

LESSON 1.2
THE FOUNDING OF ROME
• On Your Feet: Create a Concept Web

NG Learning Framework:
Observe the Etruscans

LESSON 1.3
REPUBLICAN GOVERNMENT

 Biography
Cicero

 Active History: Interactive
Whiteboard Activity
Compare Greek and Roman
Governments

 Active History
Compare Greek
and Roman Governments

Available on myNGconnect
• On Your Feet: Plebeians versus
  Patricians

LESSON 1.4 THE ROMAN FORUM
• On Your Feet: Sequence of Events
• Critical Viewing: NG Image Gallery

SECTION 2 RESOURCES

SOCIETY AND CULTURE

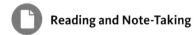 Reading and Note-Taking

Vocabulary Practice

Section 2 Quiz

Available on myNGconnect

LESSON 2.1 MEN AND WOMEN
- On Your Feet: Tell Me More

NG Learning Framework:
Compare Roman Men and Women

LESSON 2.2 RICH AND POOR
- On Your Feet: Inside-Outside Circle
- Critical Viewing: NG Chapter Gallery

LESSON 2.3 GODS AND BELIEFS
- On Your Feet: One-on-One Interviews

NG Learning Framework:
Investigate the Roman Way

SECTION 3 RESOURCES

THE ARMY AND EXPANSION

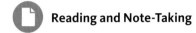 Reading and Note-Taking

Vocabulary Practice

Section 3 Quiz

Available on myNGconnect

LESSON 3.1 THE ROMAN ARMY
- Critical Viewing: NG Chapter Gallery
- On Your Feet: Think, Pair, Share

HISTORY THROUGH OBJECTS
LESSON 3.2 ROMAN ARMOR
- On Your Feet: Try It On

NG Learning Framework:
Compare Soliders' Gear

**LESSON 3.3 HANNIBAL
AND THE PUNIC WARS**
- On Your Feet: Card Responses
- Critical Viewing: NG Image Gallery

NATIONAL GEOGRAPHIC
EXPLORER PATRICK HUNT
**LESSON 3.4 SEARCHING
FOR HANNIBAL'S ROUTE**
- On Your Feet: Hold a Press Conference

NG Learning Framework:
Ask and Answer

LESSON 3.5 ROME EXPANDS
- On Your Feet: Simulate a Battle

NG Learning Framework:
Geography and History

SECTION 4 RESOURCES

THE END OF THE REPUBLIC

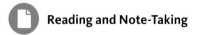 Reading and Note-Taking

Vocabulary Practice

Section 4 Quiz

Available on myNGconnect

**LESSON 4.1
THE REPUBLIC IN CRISIS**
- On Your Feet: Jigsaw

NG Learning Framework:
Research Civil Wars

BIOGRAPHY
**LESSON 4.2 GAIUS
JULIUS CAESAR**

 **Biography**
Cleopatra VII

Available on myNGconnect

- On Your Feet: Create a Poster

NG Learning Framework:
Imagine You Were Caesar

DOCUMENT-BASED QUESTION
**LESSON 4.3 THE ASSASSINATION
OF JULIUS CAESAR**
- On Your Feet: Three Options

NG Learning Framework:
Write a Biography

MOMENTS IN HISTORY
LESSON 4.4 THE IDES OF MARCH
- On Your Feet: I See, I Read, And So
- Critical Viewing: NG Image Gallery

CHAPTER 10 REVIEW

STRIVING READERS

STRATEGY 1
Preview Text

Help students preview each lesson in the chapter. For each lesson, have them read the lesson titles, lesson introductions, Main Idea statements, captions, and lesson headings. Then have them list the information they expect to find in the text. Have students read a lesson and discuss with a partner what they learned and whether or not it matched their list.

Use with All Lessons

STRATEGY 2
Build a Time Line

Select key events from Lessons 1.2 and 1.3. Then have students use the events to start a time line on the board. Students will add to the time line as they read the chapter.

TIME LINE

753 B.C.
According to legend,
Romulus founds the
city of Rome.

Use with All Lessons *For example, key events from Lesson 1.3 might include the establishment of the Roman Republic in 509 B.C. and the dictatorship of Cincinnatus in 458 B.C.*

STRATEGY 3
Use a Word Sort Activity

Write these words on the board and ask students to sort them into four groups of three related words each. Then have them use each group of words in a paragraph that shows how they are related.

republic	legion	palisades
patriarchy	veto	dictator
consuls	civil war	domestic
reform	legionary	paterfamilias

Use with All Lessons

INCLUSION

STRATEGY 1
Preview Visuals to Predict

Ask students to preview the title and visuals in each lesson. Then have students tell what they think the lesson will be about. After reading, ask them to repeat the activity to see whether their predictions were confirmed.

Use with All Lessons *Invite volunteers to describe the visuals in detail to help visually impaired students process them.*

STRATEGY 2
Use Supported Reading

In small groups, have students read aloud the chapter lesson by lesson. At the end of each lesson, have them stop and use these frames to tell what they comprehended from the text:

- This lesson is about _____.

- One detail or fact that stood out to me is _____.

- The word _____ means _____.

- I don't think I understand _____.

Guide students with portions of text they do not understand. Be sure all students understand a lesson before moving on to the next one.

Use with All Lessons

ENGLISH LANGUAGE LEARNERS

STRATEGY 1
PREP Before Reading

Have students use the PREP strategy to prepare for reading. Write this acrostic on the board:

> **P**review title.
> **R**ead Main Idea statement.
> **E**xamine visuals.
> **P**redict what you will learn.

Have students write their prediction and share it with a partner. After reading, ask students to write another sentence that begins with "I also learned . . ."

Use with All Lessons

Press *in the Student eEdition for modified text.*

STRATEGY ❷
Use Sentence Stems

Before reading, provide students with the two sentence stems for the lessons listed below. Call on volunteers to read the stems orally and explain any unclear vocabulary. After reading, have students complete the stems in writing and compare completed sentences with a partner.

1.1 **a.** Two geographic features that helped the city of Rome were _____.

b. Two bodies of water that were important to Rome were _____.

1.2 **c.** According to legend, Rome was founded by _____.

d. Three groups of people who contributed to the culture of early Rome were _____.

1.3 **e.** The two groups that made up Roman society were _____.

f. The three branches of Roman government were _____.

1.4 **g.** Three examples of activities held at the Forum were _____.

h. The Forum was important to Rome because _____.

Use with Lesson 1

STRATEGY ❸
Set Up a Word Wall

Work with students to select three words from each lesson to display in a grouping on a Word Wall. It might be useful to choose words that students are likely to encounter in other chapters, such as *republic* or *aristocracy*. Keep the words displayed throughout the lessons and discuss each one as it comes up during reading. Have volunteers add words, phrases, and examples to each word to develop understanding.

Use with All Lessons

GIFTED & TALENTED

STRATEGY ❶
Explore World Heritage Sites

Have students research and report on one of the UNESCO World Heritage Sites from the list below. Tell them to describe each site and explain why it was important to Roman civilization.

- Villa Adriana at Tivoli (Italy)
- Archaeological Site of Carthage (Tunisia)
- Roman Walls of Lugo (Spain)
- Roman Theatre of Orange (France)
- Pont du Gard (France)
- Archaeological Site of Leptis Magna (Libya)

Use with All Lessons

STRATEGY ❷
Act Out a Scene

Have students act out the assassination scene from Shakespeare's *Julius Caesar* (Act III, Scene 1). They should provide costumes and use classroom furniture as a set. After the performance, discuss the points of view of the primary characters in the scene—Brutus, Cassius, and Antony. What are the arguments for the assassination? What are the arguments against it?

Use with Lesson 4.3

PRE-AP

STRATEGY ❶
Use the "Persia" Approach

Have students write an essay explaining the significance of the Roman Republic. Copy the following mnemonic device on the board and tell students to use the "Persia" strategy as they consider how the Roman Republic influenced the world.

Political
Economic
Religious
Social
Intellectual
Artistic

Use with All Lessons

STRATEGY ❷
Form a Thesis

Have students develop a thesis statement for a specific topic related to one of the lessons in the chapter. Be sure the statement makes a claim that is supportable with evidence either from the chapter or through further research. Then have pairs compare their statements and determine which makes the strongest or most supportable claim.

Use with All Lessons

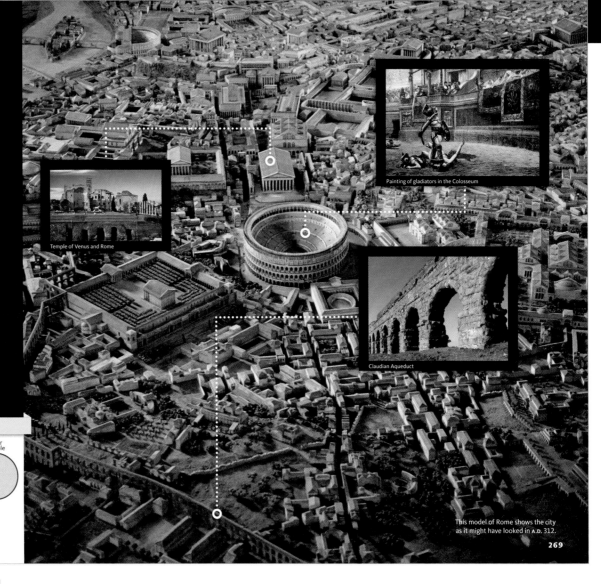

SECTION 1
EARLY ROME

KEY VOCABULARY	NAMES & PLACES
consul	Aeneas
dictator	Cicero
legend	Cincinnatus
patrician	Etruscans
peninsula	Forum
plebeian	Romulus and Remus
republic	Senate
tribune	Tiber River
veto	Twelve Tables

SECTION 2
SOCIETY AND CULTURE

KEY VOCABULARY	NAMES & PLACES
aristocracy	Council of Plebs
pantheon	
patriarchy	

SECTION 3
THE ARMY AND EXPANSION

KEY VOCABULARY	NAMES & PLACES
legionary	Carthage
province	Hannibal
	Punic Wars

SECTION 4
THE END OF THE REPUBLIC

KEY VOCABULARY	NAMES & PLACES
civil war	First Triumvirate
reform	Julius Caesar

READING STRATEGY

ORGANIZE IDEAS: COMPARE AND CONTRAST When you read, you often compare and contrast one thing with another to help you understand new information. As you read the chapter, use a Venn diagram like this one to compare and contrast the lives of rich people and poor people in the Roman Republic.

Rich People / Poor People

Temple of Venus and Rome

Painting of gladiators in the Colosseum

Claudian Aqueduct

This model of Rome shows the city as it might have looked in A.D. 312.

TEACHER BACKGROUND

INTRODUCE THE PHOTOGRAPH

Have students study the model of Rome and the images that accompany it. Explain that this model represents the city at its greatest point during the time of the Roman Empire and that they will learn about factors that contributed to its growth and development in this chapter.

ASK: How does Rome resemble modern cities you have seen? (*Possible responses: It has many roads and buildings of different sizes. It contains places for entertainment and worship. It has an infrastructure that provides resources for its citizens.*)

SHARE BACKGROUND

The model of imperial Rome was commissioned by Mussolini in 1933 to commemorate the 2,000th anniversary of the birth of Caesar Augustus. Depicting the city during the time of the emperor Constantine, it is built on a scale of 1:250 and is more than 55 feet across. The model is currently on display at the Museum of Roman Civilization in Rome.

DIGITAL RESOURCES myNGconnect.com

TEACHER RESOURCES & ASSESSMENT

 Social Studies Skills Lessons
- Reading: Compare and Contrast
- Writing: Write an Argument

 Formal Assessment
- Chapter 10 Tests A (on-level) & B (below-level)

ExamView®
One-time Download

 Chapter 10 Answer Key

STUDENT BACKPACK

- **eEdition** (*English*)
- **eEdition** (*Spanish*)
- **Handbooks**
- **Online Atlas**

For Chapter 10 Spanish Resources, visit the Teacher Resource Menu page.

INTRODUCE THE ESSENTIAL QUESTION

HOW DID ROME BECOME A MIGHTY POWER IN THE MEDITERRANEAN?

Four Corner Activity: Factors of Influence This activity introduces students to four factors that led to Rome's success and allows them to choose which they think is the most influential. Post the four signs shown in the list below. Ask students to choose the aspect that they think would contribute most to Rome's success, go to that corner, and then explain why.

A. Geography Rome's location had many geographic advantages that gave it easy access to trade routes and offered it protection from invasion.

B. Government Rome's republican form of government allowed citizens to vote for their leaders and included checks and balances to prevent any one branch from becoming too powerful.

C. Military Rome's well-organized army easily conquered neighboring territories and built roads to link them to the city of Rome.

D. Culture Romans welcomed customs and cultures from other lands, and valued discipline, strength, and loyalty.

`0:15` minutes

INTRODUCE THE READING STRATEGY

ORGANIZE IDEAS: COMPARE AND CONTRAST

Remind students that comparing and contrasting two topics or ideas can help them better understand new information. Model completing the Venn Diagram by reading the first paragraph under "The Young Republic" in Lesson 1.3 and adding the terms *patricians* and *plebeians* under the headings "Rich People" and "Poor People," respectively.

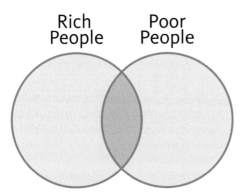

Rich People   Poor People

INTRODUCE CHAPTER VOCABULARY

KNOWLEDGE RATING

Have students complete a Knowledge Rating chart for Key Vocabulary words. Have students list words and fill out the chart on their own paper. Then have pairs share the definitions they know. Work together as a class to complete the chart.

KEY VOCAB	KNOW IT	NOT SURE	DON'T KNOW	DEFINITION
aristocracy				
civil war				
consul				
dictator				

KEY DATES

753 B.C.	Traditional founding of Rome
509 B.C.	Beginning of the Roman Republic
450 B.C.	Creation of the Twelve Tables
264–146 B.C.	The Punic Wars
59 B.C.	Formation of the First Triumvirate
48 B.C.	Defeat of Pompey by Julius Caesar
44 B.C.	Assassination of Julius Caesar

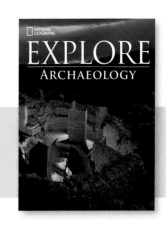

For more information on Roman architecture, check out *EXPLORE ARCHAEOLOGY*.

The Geography of Ancient Rome

If you wanted to build a Mediterranean empire, you'd probably start from Rome. The city lies near the heart of the sea. Geographically, it's the best place to begin a conquest of the Mediterranean.

MAIN IDEA

Rome's location had many geographic advantages that helped it grow and become powerful.

THE ITALIAN PENINSULA

Italy lies on a **peninsula**, or land surrounded by water on three sides, in the Mediterranean Sea. It is shaped like a boot and looks as though it is kicking a football—the island of Sicily—toward North Africa. Italy is attached to the rest of Europe by a massive range of snow-covered mountains called the Alps.

Another mountain range, the Apennines (A-puh-nynz), runs down the center of Italy. These mountains slope through wooded hills to sunny coastal plains and the blue waters of the Mediterranean. In time, the Romans would come to call the Mediterranean *Mare Nostrum* (MAHR-ay NOHS-truhm), or "Our Sea."

Rome was founded on seven hills on the volcanic west coast of Italy. The Romans embraced the advanced cultures of their neighbors to the north and south. Ideas adopted from these cultures helped Rome flourish and grow strong.

THE CITY OF ROME

Rome's geography helped it survive and thrive. What first made Rome important was its strategic position. It was located at a key crossing point of the **Tiber** (TY-bur) **River**.

The location was also a natural stopping point on the valuable trade routes running north to south and inland from the sea. The city was far enough from the coast to escape deadly attacks by pirates and enemies but close enough to benefit from the Mediterranean's busy sea trade. Olive oil and wine were among Rome's most commonly traded items.

The circle of seven hills on which Rome was built rose above the river and also provided protection against attack. These seven hills became Rome's center. Romans built important government buildings there. The hills were also home to religious temples and entertainment facilities. Roads branched off from this area to the outside world.

The land around the city had fertile soil, a good water supply, and a mild climate. These qualities helped Rome's agriculture flourish and support the large population needed to wage and win wars in the ancient world. As the Roman historian Livy boasted, "With good reason did gods and men choose this site for founding a city."

Rome's central location helped it take over much of Italy. Then Italy's central location helped Rome become a powerful force in the Mediterranean. Around the sea, the riches of Europe, Southwest Asia, and North Africa were temptingly close. Control of the Mediterranean seemed within the grasp of a strong, ambitious, and determined civilization like Rome.

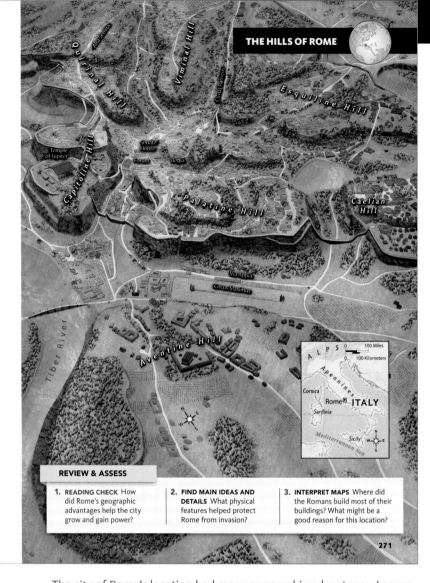

THE HILLS OF ROME

REVIEW & ASSESS

1. **READING CHECK** How did Rome's geographic advantages help the city grow and gain power?

2. **FIND MAIN IDEAS AND DETAILS** What physical features helped protect Rome from invasion?

3. **INTERPRET MAPS** Where did the Romans build most of their buildings? What might be a good reason for this location?

271

PLAN

OBJECTIVE

Identify the geographic advantages that helped ancient Rome become a powerful civilization.

CRITICAL THINKING SKILLS FOR LESSON 1.1

- Identify Main Ideas and Details
- Monitor Comprehension
- Interpret Maps
- Make Inferences
- Compare and Contrast
- Describe

ESSENTIAL QUESTION

How did Rome become a mighty power in the Mediterranean?

The city of Rome's location had many geographic advantages. Lesson 1.1 describes some of these advantages and explains how they helped Rome grow and become powerful.

BACKGROUND FOR THE TEACHER

The "seven hills of Rome" is a term given to the group of hills where the ancient city of Rome was built. The original city of the legendary Romulus was built upon Palatine Hill. The other hills are the Aventine, Caelian, Capitoline, Esquiline, Quirinal, and Viminal.

The seven hills are mostly made up of tuffs, or compacted volcanic ash, left by volcanic eruptions that took place in the Alban Hills volcanic field southeast of Rome over the last 600,000 years. Visitors to Italy are often familiar with active volcanoes such as Etna and Stromboli, and famous ones such as Vesuvius, which buried and destroyed the city of Pompeii.

DIGITAL RESOURCES myNGconnect.com

TEACHER RESOURCES & ASSESSMENT

 Reading and Note-Taking

 Vocabulary Practice

 Section 1 Quiz

STUDENT RESOURCES

 NG Chapter Gallery

INTRODUCE & ENGAGE

BRAINSTORM STRONG, SUCCESSFUL CITIES

Ask students to identify examples of strong, successful American cities, such as New York, Chicago, or San Francisco. Have students record the names of these cities on sticky notes and post them on the wall. Then work together to brainstorm characteristics that make a city strong and successful. Again, record these characteristics on sticky notes and post so students can refer to them during the lesson. Then tell students they will learn about geographic features that helped the city of Rome grow powerful and strong. `0:05` minutes

TEACH

GUIDED DISCUSSION

1. **Make Inferences** Why would the Romans have wanted to control the Mediterranean Sea? *(It would allow the Romans to explore other regions safely. It would give the Romans the ability to move and trade goods using ships and also move their army to other countries quickly and discretely.)*

2. **Describe** Complete a word web using words, phrases, and sentences that tell about the geography of ancient Rome. *(volcanic land, west coast of Italy, near Mediterranean coast, crossing point of Tiber River, fertile land, seven hills)*

INTERPRET MAPS

Point out the Hills of Rome map. Review the hills, bodies of water, and location of Roman landmarks. Draw students' attention to the inset map showing the location of Rome in Italy. Ask volunteers to ask and answer questions about both maps.

(Sample response: Based on the map, how could Romans have moved across the Tiber River? By boat or on foot. I see boats in a small marina off the Tiber and a bridge across the river.) `0:15` minutes

ACTIVE OPTIONS

On Your Feet: Model Rome's Geography Tell the tallest students in the class to stand and represent the seven hills. Have other students represent the Mediterranean Sea and the Tiber River. Call on volunteers to "invade" Rome, and explore how invaders would have been challenged by the geography of the city in different ways. Call upon other volunteers to explain how the geographic features would have been useful in other ways. `0:05` minutes

Critical Viewing: NG Chapter Gallery Invite students to explore the Chapter Gallery to examine the images that relate to this chapter. Have them select one of the images and do additional research to learn more about it. Ask questions that will inspire additional inquiry about the chosen gallery image, such as: What is this? Where and when was this created? By whom? Why was it created? What is it made of? Why does it belong in this chapter? What else would you like to know about it? `0:10` minutes

DIFFERENTIATE

ENGLISH LANGUAGE LEARNERS

Use a Term in a Sentence Pair English language learners with English proficient students. Have the proficient students model using words from the lesson in sentences. Then have each pair compose a sentence for each word. Invite pairs to share their sentences and discuss different ways to utilize each word. Suggest the following words:

- peninsula
- range
- volcanic
- trade/traded
- fertile

GIFTED & TALENTED

Build Models Have students build a three-dimensional topographic model of the hills of Rome using the Hills of Rome map and additional online resources. Discuss scale and proportion and encourage students to size the hills and bodies of water appropriately.

- Online Atlas: The Hills of Rome

Press (**mt**) *in the Student eEdition for modified text.*

See the Chapter Planner for more strategies for differentiation.

REVIEW & ASSESS

ANSWERS

1. Rome's location on the Tiber River made it a good stopping point on a valuable trade route, and its location on the seven hills provided protection from invaders.

2. The seven hills and a location not right on the coast helped protect Rome from invasion.

3. Most buildings were built in the hills. Since the hills provided protection, they were a good location for building.

1.2 The Founding of Rome

Three thousand years ago, a few small huts stood scattered across the hills that overlooked the Tiber River's swampy floodplain. Within just 250 years, this humble landscape was transformed into the heart of a mighty empire.

MAIN IDEA

Rome grew from a tiny village to a city between 753 and 509 B.C.

+ POSSIBLE RESPONSE

It would allow the Romans to see invading enemies from a distance and give them time to prepare a defense.

Critical Viewing Palatine Hill is thought to be the oldest part of the city. How might building on a hill provide security for early Romans?

MYTHICAL BEGINNINGS

The Romans loved stories, especially bloody ones with great heroes. One of the most popular **legends**, or stories about famous people and events in the past, was about the founding of Rome. Not only did the story contain a hero and plenty of blood, but it also linked Rome to the great civilization of ancient Greece.

According to the legend, a Trojan hero named **Aeneas** (ih-NEE-uhs) was the ancestor of Rome's founders—the twin brothers **Romulus** (RAHM-yuh-luhs) and **Remus** (REE-muhs). As babies, the brothers were abandoned. They were rescued by a wolf and raised by a shepherd. When they grew up, the brothers founded their own city. In 753 B.C., Romulus became the first king of the city, which he named Rome, after himself.

Research actually supports a part of the story of Romulus and Remus. Archaeologists have uncovered ruins suggesting that the hills around Rome contained many small villages in 1000 B.C. Some of these villages merged with villages in the valleys to create a larger settlement around 750 B.C. This was early Rome.

EARLY ROMANS

At this time, Italy was a patchwork of different peoples with their own rulers, customs, and languages. Most of Rome's original residents were Latins, who came from an area around the Tiber River called Latium. The Latins were not united, and their many cities were often at war with one another as well as with neighboring peoples. In its early days, Rome was a small village in a violently competitive world.

What helped make Rome strong was that it welcomed people from many different lands. Foreigners of different classes and professions settled in the city and helped it grow in size and strength. The people who most influenced early Rome were the Greeks to the south and the **Etruscans** (ih-TRUHS-kuhnz) to the north.

The Greeks dominated the Mediterranean and had many colonies in southern Italy. Through travel and trade, they introduced the Romans to important advances in agriculture, architecture, and learning.

The Romans learned to grow olives and modified the Greek alphabet for writing. Roman poets copied the Greek style of the long epic poem.

The Etruscans were expert traders, metalworkers, and engineers. Three Etruscan kings who came to rule Rome brought these professional skills with them. They laid out the city's streets in a grid plan around a central square. The Etruscans replaced mud huts with stone houses and built Rome's first temples and public buildings. By 509 B.C., Rome was becoming the city we still see traces of today.

REVIEW & ASSESS

1. **READING CHECK** How did people from different cultures help Rome develop into a city?

2. **IDENTIFY MAIN IDEAS AND DETAILS** According to legend, how was Rome founded?

3. **MAKE INFERENCES** What does the willingness to adopt other peoples' ideas suggest about Roman values?

PLAN

OBJECTIVE

Identify how Rome grew from a village to a large city.

CRITICAL THINKING SKILLS FOR LESSON 1.2

- Identify Main Ideas and Details
- Monitor Comprehension
- Make Inferences
- Explain
- Analyze Visuals

ESSENTIAL QUESTION

How did Rome become a mighty power in the Mediterranean?

Rome welcomed people from other lands and adopted aspects of their culture. Lesson 1.2 discusses how this cultural influence helped Rome grow from a tiny village to a city.

BACKGROUND FOR THE TEACHER

The Etruscans are considered to be the first great rulers of central Italy. Artifacts gathered from the region, primarily from Etruscan tombs, help tell the story of their culture and skills and explain the influence the Etruscans had over the construction of the city of Rome during the 6th century B.C.

The Etruscans, as expert builders and metalworkers, also had a great influence over the layout and construction of the city of Rome. It is thought that the tiled roofs of Rome were first introduced by the Etruscans. The Etruscans are also believed to have influenced religious rituals, Roman numerals, and even the Latin alphabet. Etruscan ruling families such as the Tarquins were eventually replaced by Roman rulers, but their legacy lived on through Roman customs, culture, and architecture.

DIGITAL RESOURCES myNGconnect.com

TEACHER RESOURCES & ASSESSMENT

 Reading and Note-Taking   **Vocabulary Practice**   **Section 1 Quiz**

STUDENT RESOURCES

 NG Chapter Gallery

THUMBS UP, THUMBS DOWN

Ask students to volunteer the names of legends that they've read, heard, or seen a movie about, such as Hercules, Odysseus, or Achilles. Make a list of these legends, then read the list aloud and have students give each one a thumbs up or a thumbs down, depending on whether they know it or like it. Explain that a legend is a story that has been passed on for many generations. A legend usually has important meaning or symbolism, is based somewhat on facts, and contains a hero or heroes. Tell students they will learn about one famous legend that explains how Rome was founded. **0:05** minutes

TEACH

GUIDED DISCUSSION

1. **Explain** Which two peoples had the most influence on early Rome, and what did they contribute to Roman civilization? *(Rome was most influenced by the Greeks to the south and the Etruscans to the north. The Greeks introduced the Romans to important advances in agriculture, architecture, and learning. The Etruscans helped structure Rome's city and built the first stone houses, temples, and public buildings.)*

2. **Make Inferences** What might be the negative effects of a city such as Rome welcoming people from many different lands? *(It could make communication difficult, and could lead to overcrowding and cultural clashes.)*

ANALYZE VISUALS

Have students examine the photo of Palatine Hill. Direct them to consider how the physical characteristics of the land influenced how people lived and constructed their buildings. Make a list of the challenges the Romans must have faced as they built structures on the hill. **0:10** minutes

ACTIVE OPTIONS

On Your Feet: Create a Concept Web Have students form groups of four around a section of a bulletin board or a table. Provide each group with a large sheet of paper. Have group members take turns contributing a concept or phrase to a concept web with the words *Early Romans* at the center. When time for the activity has elapsed, call on volunteers from each group to share their webs. **0:10** minutes

NG Learning Framework: Observe the Etruscans

SKILLS: Observation, Collaboration
KNOWLEDGE: **Our Living Planet**

Have students revisit Lesson 1.2, specifically the information about the Etruscans. They should work in pairs to create a list of observations about the Etruscan people and how their lives were impacted by their environment and nature. Once they have completed their list of observations, each pair should exchange lists with another pair and discuss the new list. **0:10** minutes

STRIVING READERS

Chart Early Roman Influences Have students record the different peoples who influenced early Rome using a chart such as the one shown below. In the rows, they should write a short description of the people and the way they influenced early Rome. Allow students to work in pairs to read the lesson. Have them read the text once and fill in their charts. Then have them read the text a second time and check their work. Have students share their charts with the rest of the group and add any information they might have missed.

Latins	Greeks	Etruscans

PRE-AP

Read a Legend Have students read three different versions of the legend of Romulus and Remus and write about or discuss the following:

- similarities and differences between the different versions of the legend
- facts that support the legend
- mythical elements, locations, and characters within the legend
- heroes or heroism within the legend
- a summary of how the legend explains the founding of Rome

Press (**mt**) *in the Student eEdition for modified text.*

See the Chapter Planner for more strategies for differentiation.

ANSWERS

1. They each brought elements of their own culture, which the Romans adopted as their own.

2. It was founded by the brothers Romulus and Remus.

3. It suggests that the Romans were tolerant of other cultures and open to new ideas.

1.3

Republican
Government

You wouldn't have wanted to meet the Etruscan king Tarquin the Proud in a dark alley. He ruled as a tyrant—a cruel ruler—and had many of his opponents killed. In 509 B.C., the people of Rome overthrew Tarquin and established a new form of government.

MAIN IDEA

Rome developed a republican form of government that protected the rights of ordinary citizens.

THE YOUNG REPUBLIC

In a **republic**, citizens vote for their leaders. Only free adult men were citizens in Rome, but not all citizens were equal. Roman society was divided into two groups: the patricians and the plebeians. The **patricians** (puh-TRIH-shuhnz) were wealthy landowners. The **plebeians** (plih-BEE-uhnz), who included poorer farmers and craftsmen, made up the majority of Rome's citizens but were under-represented in the government.

The plebeians wanted a say in how Rome was run. As a result, in 494 B.C., they went on strike. The plebeians left the city, shutting down Roman shops and businesses, and set up their own government. Economic activity came to a halt. Once the patricians started losing money, they became frightened and agreed to share their power. In time, the plebeians were allowed to elect their own representatives, called **tribunes**, who fought to protect the rights of ordinary citizens.

The plebeians had one more demand. Because Rome's laws were not written down, the patricians often interpreted them to favor their rich friends. The plebeians fought back. They insisted that the laws be not only written down but carved into bronze tablets and displayed for all to see. These laws became known as the **Twelve Tables**. They protected all Roman citizens from injustice. Some of these laws are the basis of our own laws today.

ROMAN GOVERNMENT

Rome's new, more representative government contained three branches. An executive branch led the government and the army, a legislative branch made the laws, and a judicial branch applied the laws.

The Romans put checks and balances in place to prevent any one branch from becoming too powerful. They also replaced the position of king with two leaders called **consuls**. The consuls had the authority of a king but for only one year. They shared power so equally that the consuls had the right to **veto**, or reject, each other's decisions.

The legislative branch was made up of the **Senate**, elected judicial officers, and two assemblies. The Senate advised the consuls. The assemblies represented the plebeians. In the beginning, most of the 300 members of the Senate were patricians. Over time, however, plebeians were also allowed to participate.

Senators often spoke out about issues in the Senate House and in public squares. Delivering such speeches was a highly valued skill in Rome. One of Rome's most brilliant speakers was **Cicero** (SIH-suh-roh), who often used his speeches to attack those who he believed were a threat to the republic.

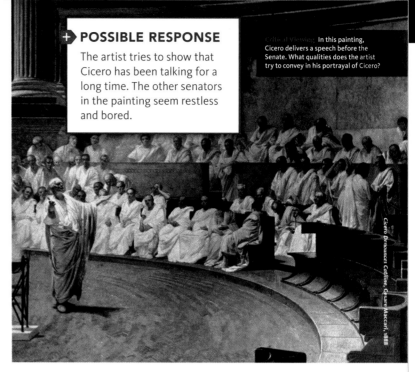

Critical Viewing In this painting, Cicero delivers a speech before the Senate. What qualities does the artist try to convey in his portrayal of Cicero?

Cicero Denounces Catiline, Cesare Maccari, 1888

+ POSSIBLE RESPONSE

The artist tries to show that Cicero has been talking for a long time. The other senators in the painting seem restless and bored.

In times of crisis, the Romans appointed **dictators** who had complete control but were expected to give up power after danger had passed. One such Roman dictator was **Cincinnatus** (sihn-suh-NA-tuhs). In 458 B.C., Rome's army was facing defeat by a fierce enemy, and the Senate wanted Cincinnatus to take charge. He accepted the dictatorship, defeated the enemy, and then surrendered his power and returned to his farm. The example set by Cincinnatus was celebrated by the Romans, who valued the idea of civic duty—putting service to the community ahead of personal interest.

REVIEW & ASSESS

1. **READING CHECK** How did the Roman government come to protect the rights of the citizens?

2. **COMPARE AND CONTRAST** In what ways are the governments of the Roman Republic and the United States similar?

3. **DRAW CONCLUSIONS** Why was it important to the plebeians to have Roman laws written down?

PLAN

OBJECTIVE

Describe the government of the Roman Republic and explain how it protected citizens' rights.

CRITICAL THINKING SKILLS FOR LESSON 1.3

- Identify Main Ideas and Details
- Monitor Comprehension
- Compare and Contrast
- Draw Conclusions
- Make Generalizations
- Make Connections

ESSENTIAL QUESTION

How did Rome become a mighty power in the Mediterranean?

The Romans created a republic with three branches of government and written laws. Lesson 1.3 discusses how the republic protected the rights of ordinary citizens and prevented any one group from becoming too powerful.

BACKGROUND FOR THE TEACHER

Marcus Tullius Cicero was born in 106 B.C. in Latium. He was a famous Roman lawyer, scholar, writer, and orator who devoted himself to upholding the principles of the Roman Republic during the civil wars that ultimately destroyed it. Appointed as consul in 63 B.C., Cicero gave many famous speeches designed to preserve the republic and expose what he viewed to be dangerous civil uprisings. He was considered by some to be the "father of his country."

DIGITAL RESOURCES myNGconnect.com

TEACHER RESOURCES & ASSESSMENT

 Reading and Note-Taking

 Vocabulary Practice

 Section 1 Quiz

STUDENT RESOURCES

 Biography

TOSS AND TELL

Provide students with a soft ball or small beanbag that can be safely tossed. Ask students to think of the branches of the U.S. government. Toss the ball or beanbag to a student and ask him or her to name one of the branches. If the student cannot, he or she can toss the ball or beanbag to someone else. Repeat the tossing and telling throughout the classroom until all three branches have been named. Then tell students they will learn how the Romans developed these three branches of government. **0:05** minutes

TEACH

GUIDED DISCUSSION

1. **Make Generalizations** Were the demands of the Roman plebeians and the way they went about having their demands met reasonable and/or successful? *(Possible response: Yes, their demands were reasonable and successful. The plebeians just wanted to have equal rights to the patricians, and they proved they had a powerful voice in society. There were more plebeians than patricians, and the plebeians provided most of the goods and services to the patricians. When the plebeians closed their shops and businesses, the patricians were forced to listen to their demands.)* How did the plebeian demand for written laws benefit all Romans? *(Having permanent, public laws protected Roman citizens from having laws be interpreted in different ways that benefitted only the friends of powerful people.)*

2. **Draw Conclusions** As shown through Cincinnatus's actions, the Romans valued setting aside personal interests to benefit the community. Do you believe politicians and leaders today are willing to set aside their personal goals, wealth, or interests to benefit their country or community? Why or why not? *(Responses will vary. Students should defend their views using examples.)*

COMPARE AND CONTRAST

ASK: How does the structure of the U.S. government compare to the structure of the representative government of Rome? As a group, work to make two diagrams on large sheets of paper or a whiteboard. One diagram should show the structure of Rome's representative government, and the other should show the structure of the U.S. government. Include the three branches in both, but be sure to acknowledge and draw students' attention to distinguishing features, such as having two Roman consuls versus having one American president. **0:20** minutes

ACTIVE OPTIONS

Active History: Compare Greek and Roman Governments Extend the lesson by using either the PDF or Whiteboard version of the Compare Greek and Roman Governments Active History activity. These activities take a deeper look at a topic from or related to the lesson. Explore the Active History activities as a class, turn them into group assignments, or even assign them individually. **0:15** minutes

On Your Feet: Plebeians versus Patricians Divide the class into two groups: plebeians and patricians. Provide each group with a large sheet of paper, and ask them to imagine it is 495 B.C. Have the groups create a list of their sentiments about the current state of Roman society, including what they like, dislike, fear, and would like to change or keep the same. After ten minutes, ask each group to share their concerns. You may wish to facilitate a debate or dialogue between the groups by asking questions such as, "Patricians, how do you feel about the fact that Rome's laws are not currently written down?" "Plebeians, there are more of you in Rome than patricians, but you are under-represented in the government. Are you satisfied with this arrangement?" **0:20** minutes

STRIVING READERS

Analyze Visuals Have students study the painting of Cicero giving a speech before the Roman Senate. In pairs, have students make a list of observations about the Roman Senate based on what they see in the painting. Encourage students to compare the layout of the Roman Senate to the United States Senate, providing photographs of the latter, if needed.

GIFTED & TALENTED

Become an Orator Many consider Cicero to be the greatest speaker that ever lived. Provide students with topics to speak about, or invite them to select their own. Brainstorm qualities that make a good speech and a successful orator. Remind students that speeches should have a clear theme and details that support the main idea. Guide students to write a short speech of 3–5 minutes and present it to their peers.

Press **mt** *in the Student eEdition for modified text.*

See the Chapter Planner for more strategies for differentiation.

ANSWERS

1. It wrote all laws down on bronze tablets so everyone could see them and not misinterpret them.

2. Both governments have three branches—legislative, executive, and judicial; both have written laws.

3. It was important because the plebeians wanted the laws to be applied equally. They didn't want the patricians to get away with interpreting the laws in different ways that favored themselves.

The ruins of the Roman Forum represent different periods of Rome's ancient history. Here older ruins of buildings surround the Arch of Titus. The Colosseum stands in the background.

1.4 The Roman
Forum

The Roman Forum was the place to be. It was the place to meet, shop, do business, worship, celebrate, and be entertained. This public square was one of the liveliest and most important places in all of Rome.

MAIN IDEA

The Roman Forum was the political, religious, economic, and social center of the Roman Republic.

BURIAL GROUND TO PUBLIC SQUARE

The **Forum** developed over several centuries in a valley between the Palatine and Capitoline hills. In heavy rain, the banks of the Tiber River would burst, flooding the marshy valley. Long before Rome was founded, this scrap of swamp had been used as a burial ground. However, once Rome began to grow and its population spilled down the hills, the swamp became a piece of desirable real estate. Around 600 B.C., an Etruscan king built a sewer to drain the area and created an open public square paved with pebbles. The Roman Forum was born.

Everyone came to the Forum. It was the city's open-air market, where Romans could buy everything from local fruit and vegetables to imported Greek pottery. Rome's oldest road, the Via Sacra, looped through the Forum. Along the road, the early kings of Rome built a royal residence, shops, houses, and temples dedicated to their many gods and goddesses. At first these buildings were little more than mud huts or raised-earth platforms. Over time, these were replaced with permanent structures, and the Forum became the center of Rome's religious, economic, and social activity.

THE CENTER OF ROME

After the republic was founded, the Forum also became the center of Roman politics. Although the Forum's open space remained small, huge public and government buildings sprang up around it. The Temple of Saturn, dedicated to one of Rome's most important gods, became the treasury, holding the growing riches of the republic. The Curia was the meeting place of the Roman Senate. Political activity, ranging from public speeches to rioting mobs, took place at the Forum. Because it was where ordinary Romans gathered, the Forum was the perfect place to display the Twelve Tables.

The Forum also provided a setting for public spectacles. Crowds came to watch theatrical performances and athletic games. Even the funerals of important men were held at the Forum.

In later centuries, the Forum's buildings were transformed from brick to marble, and great bronze statues were added. Later rulers built other public places, but none ever rivaled the importance of the great Roman Forum.

REVIEW & ASSESS

1. **READING CHECK** Why did the ancient Romans gather in the Forum?

2. **IDENTIFY MAIN IDEAS AND DETAILS** How did the Forum change over time?

3. **MAKE INFERENCES** How did the Roman Forum reflect the democratic values of the Roman Republic?

PLAN

OBJECTIVE

Analyze the purpose of the Roman Forum in the Roman Republic.

CRITICAL THINKING SKILLS FOR LESSON 1.4

- Identify Main Ideas and Details
- Monitor Comprehension
- Make Inferences
- Describe
- Draw Conclusions

ESSENTIAL QUESTION

How did Rome become a mighty power in the Mediterranean?

The Roman Forum was the political, economic, and social center of the republic. Lesson 1.4 describes the Forum and explains its place in Roman society.

BACKGROUND FOR THE TEACHER

One of the most famous forms of entertainment offered in the Forum was fighting. The large open space of the rectangular Forum was the perfect place for hand-to-hand combat between trained fighters known as gladiators. Spectators would flock to the Forum to watch the fights from rows of seats that stretched up the Capitoline Hill. One of the most famous early gladiator battles took place in 216 B.C. as part of a series of "funeral games" put on by the sons of the consul Marcus Aemilius Lepidus to honor their late father. Eventually, the Colosseum was constructed just east of the Forum, offering spectators a better view of gladiator fights from higher seats and enclosing the gladiators within an arena to prevent them from leaving.

DIGITAL RESOURCES myNGconnect.com

TEACHER RESOURCES & ASSESSMENT

 Reading and Note-Taking

 Vocabulary Practice

 Section 1 Quiz

STUDENT RESOURCES

 NG Chapter Gallery

INTRODUCE & ENGAGE

THEN AND NOW

Ask students to think about "the" place to hang out in their town, community, or neighborhood—a busy, lively place where they know they'll meet up with friends or family members. Is it a park? A restaurant? A gymnasium? Perhaps it's a community center or a church or temple. Write a list on the whiteboard of the locations students consider to be the important places in their community or neighborhood, and have volunteers describe what happens in these places. `0:05` minutes

TEACH

GUIDED DISCUSSION

1. **Describe** Tell how the Forum was used by the people of Rome. (*It was used as a market and as a religious center. It also became a center for politics and government after the republic was formed. The Senate met in a building in the Forum, the city's riches were housed in another building, and people met in the open spaces to give speeches and express their opinions. Many people also gathered in the Forum to watch performances and games.*)

2. **Draw Conclusions** The Forum served many purposes, but one of its chief roles was as a gathering place. Why is it important for a community to have such a place? (*Possible responses: People in a community feel more connected to each other and the place they live if they have a central place to spend their free time and get important things done. Also, a central gathering place can be a good location to gather, share information, and find safety.*)

MORE INFORMATION

The Arch of Titus Among the surviving structures in the Roman Forum is the Arch of Titus (visible in the photograph in the lesson). This arch is located at the highest point of Rome's oldest road, the Via Sacra. It is one of the most famous monuments in the Forum and the oldest surviving arch in Rome. The Arch of Titus was built to honor the popular Roman emperor Titus, who died in 81 A.D. The carvings on the arch celebrate Titus's famous suppression of a rebellion in Jerusalem.

ACTIVE OPTIONS

On Your Feet: Sequence of Events Provide pairs of students with large sheets of paper with events written on them specific to the development of the Forum over time. Use the following events (but provide them in a scrambled order):

- Heavy rains caused the Tiber River to overflow, making the valley between the Palatine and Capitoline Hills a marshy swamp.
- The swampy land in the valley was used as a burial ground.
- An Etruscan king drained the swampy land in the valley by building a sewer.

- The drained swampland was paved and turned into an open public square.
- Romans came to the open public square known as the Forum to do their shopping out of mud huts and raised-earth platforms.
- Permanent structures were built and the Forum became the center of Rome's religious, economic, and social activity.
- After the republic was founded, the Forum became the center of Rome's politics.
- The Forum's buildings were transformed from brick to marble, and great bronze statues were added.

Have students move around the classroom and read other students' events. Then have students work as a group to place their events in order, consulting their book if desired. Review the events as a class to determine if they are properly arranged. `0:15` minutes

Critical Viewing: NG Image Gallery Have students explore the entire NG Image Gallery and choose two of the items to compare and contrast, either in written form or verbally with a partner. Ask questions that will inspire this process, such as: How are these images alike? How are they different? Why did you select these two items? How do they relate in history? `0:10` minutes

DIFFERENTIATE

INCLUSION

Review Concepts Provide definitions of this key concept from the lesson:

The **Forum** was a public square for shopping, gathering, and working. People came to the **market** at the Forum to buy and sell things like food and pottery. A road called the Via Sacra passed through the Forum, and shops, houses, and **religious temples** were built there. The Forum also had buildings for **government** meetings and storing riches. People came to the Forum to watch actors put on shows and athletes compete in games. **Funerals** were also held there.

Then examine the photo of the Forum and point out some of the features and buildings that are shown.

Press (**mt**) *in the Student eEdition for modified text.*

See the Chapter Planner for more strategies for differentiation.

REVIEW & ASSESS

ANSWERS

1. They gathered in the Forum for religious, economic, political, and social activities.

2. It went from being a swamp and a burial ground to an open-air market. When more permanent structures were built, it became a center for Roman politics and culture. Eventually, the buildings were transformed into marble masterpieces.

3. Everyone had a right to congregate there. Also, the Twelve Tables were on display there.

Men and Women

Growing up in Rome wasn't easy. There were no laws to protect children. Boys were expected to head their own families one day, but most girls never had any real control over their futures.

MAIN IDEA

Men and women had different roles in Roman society.

MEN IN ANCIENT ROME

If you were born a boy in Rome, you already had a head start in life. Rome was a **patriarchy** (PAY-tree-ahr-kee), or a society in which men have all the power. Only men could vote or hold public office, fight in wars, and perform important ceremonies. In Rome's patriarchy, men were in charge of everything—especially the family.

The family was at the core of Roman society. At the head of every family was the senior male, the *paterfamilias* (pa-tur-fuh-MIH-lee-uhs). He made all decisions. He could put family members on trial and punish them—even execute them. The Twelve Tables eventually limited the power of the paterfamilias, but he still had a lot of control over his family.

Boys from poorer families received little education and often could not read or write. Instead they went out to work beginning at an early age. Wealthier families sent their sons to school. Classes started at dawn, and teachers, who were often Greek slaves, taught reading, writing, and arithmetic. Public speaking was another important lesson. Long poems had to be memorized, and mistakes were often punished with a beating.

After the age of 14, boys destined for government jobs continued their education with private tutors at home. At the age of 17, boys were considered to be men and registered as Roman citizens in the Forum.

WOMEN IN ANCIENT ROME

Roman women had more rights than women in ancient Greece, but those still didn't amount to much by modern standards. Roman women were subject to the authority of men—their husbands, fathers, or brothers. They could not vote or hold public office, though they could eventually own property and manage their own businesses and finances. A wife could also manage her husband's business, and women with powerful husbands had some political influence.

In Rome, a woman's main role was to be a good wife and mother. For many, this meant doing the daily domestic chores of spinning yarn, making clothes, cooking, cleaning, and looking after the children. Sometimes women would have paying jobs as well. In wealthier families, the wife managed the household and its finances, but slaves did all the physical labor.

If they were lucky, some girls from wealthy families learned basic reading, writing, and arithmetic at home. However, they mostly learned household skills to prepare them for married life, which could begin when girls were as young as 12. Most marriages had little to do with love but were arranged to benefit the family. However, divorce was easy and acceptable, and ambitious politicians might remarry many times to gain support from increasingly important families.

Critical Viewing: This fresco, a style of painting on fresh plaster, shows a Roman woman and man holding writing tools. Based on the details you can see in the fresco, what conclusions can you draw about these people?

+ POSSIBLE RESPONSE

The man and woman must be from a wealthy family because usually only wealthy people learned to read and write. Also, it is more likely that a woman from a wealthy family would have been educated.

REVIEW & ASSESS

1. **READING CHECK** What was a woman's role in Roman society?

2. **DETERMINE WORD MEANINGS** How does knowing that *pater* is Latin for "father" help clarify what *patriarchy* and *paterfamilias* mean?

3. **COMPARE AND CONTRAST** How did roles differ for boys and girls in Rome?

PLAN

OBJECTIVE

Explain the different roles of men and women in Roman society.

CRITICAL THINKING SKILLS FOR LESSON 2.1

- Identify Main Ideas and Details
- Monitor Comprehension
- Determine Word Meanings
- Compare and Contrast
- Make Inferences
- Form and Support Opinions

ESSENTIAL QUESTION

How did Rome become a mighty power in the Mediterranean?

Men and women in ancient Rome had different rights and responsibilities. Lesson 2.1 describes these differences and explains how men and women each contributed to Roman society.

BACKGROUND FOR THE TEACHER

Roman *patresfamilias* had a surprising amount of power and were the only people who could own property. Even successful married adult sons continued to receive an allowance until their father died. They could not own any property. Still, sons were valued because of the fact that they carried forth the family's name.

Roman women did not have many rights and were not given the educational opportunities that men were given. But they were rewarded for bearing many children. Many babies and children died at a young age during the first century A.D., so if a woman gave birth to three or four children who survived, she was given legal freedom. This allowed her to become independent from men if she wanted to be.

DIGITAL RESOURCES myNGconnect.com

TEACHER RESOURCES & ASSESSMENT

 Reading and Note-Taking   **Vocabulary Practice**   **Section 2 Quiz**

STUDENT RESOURCES

 NG Chapter Gallery

GENDER IN THE WORKPLACE

Ask students to think about the roles of men and women in American culture today. **ASK:** Are there certain jobs that are usually done only by men or only by women? Why? Make a list of such jobs on the whiteboard and discuss possible reasons why one gender might be suited to doing particular jobs or why certain jobs typically attract males or females. Then tell students that in this lesson, they will learn about how men and women were treated differently in Roman society. **0:05** minutes

TEACH

GUIDED DISCUSSION

1. **Make Inferences** How does the ability to get an education affect someone? (*Students might discuss how an education affects job opportunities, social and economic advancement, financial independence, or power.*)

2. **Form and Support Opinions** In your opinion, did women or men have a harder life in the culture of ancient Rome? Support your opinion using facts from the text. (*Possible responses: Men had a harder life because they had to go through more schooling, and the punishments for making mistakes during their lessons were very harsh. Also, men were responsible for stressful tasks like voting, fighting in wars, and leading their families. Women had a harder life because they were usually not as educated as men, and had very few rights. They had to stay home, do household chores, and care for the children, which is very hard work. Also, some girls had to get married by the young age of 12.*)

CREATE GRAPHIC ORGANIZERS

To help students understand important concepts, have them work in small groups and create a graphic organizer. They can use a Concept Cluster to explain a term such as *patriarchy*, or a T-Chart to compare the lifestyle and rights of a wealthy Roman man or woman to the life of a poor one. **0:15** minutes

ACTIVE OPTIONS

On Your Feet: Tell Me More Have students form three teams and assign each team one of the following topics:

- paterfamilias
- education of young people in ancient Rome
- women's rights in ancient Rome

Each group should write down as many facts about their topic as they can. Have the class reconvene and have each group stand up, one at a time. The rest of the class calls out "Tell me more about [the topic]." The group recites one fact. The class again requests a fact until the group runs out of facts to share. Then the next group presents its facts. **0:10** minutes

NG Learning Framework: Compare Roman Men and Women

ATTITUDES: Responsibility, Empowerment
SKILLS: Collaboration, Problem-Solving
KNOWLEDGE: Our Human Story

In small groups, have students review the different roles of men and women in Roman society. Ask each group to create a T-Chart to compare the roles. Then have each student write a paragraph to assess how the roles benefitted Roman society as a whole. Empower students to return to their small groups to discuss how expanding gender roles might have been even more beneficial to Roman society. **0:10** minutes

STRIVING READERS

Compare and Contrast Provide students with slips of paper. Ask them to write a sentence that tells about some facet of how women lived in Roman times on one side of the paper. On the other side, have them write a comparison statement showing how women live today. Invite students to share their contrasting statements with the group.

GIFTED & TALENTED

Make Predictions Have students imagine what daily life would have been like for a 14-year-old girl and a 14-year-old boy living in ancient Rome. Have them work in pairs to write a short narrative, possibly in the form of a diary entry, from the perspective of a Roman girl or boy, telling about a typical day.

Press **mt** *in the Student eEdition for modified text.*

See the Chapter Planner for more strategies for differentiation.

ANSWERS

1. A woman's role in Roman society was to be a good wife and mother.

2. It hints that both words have to do with the head male of a family.

3. They differed extremely. Boys were educated and became citizens who could vote or hold public office. Girls were not usually educated and focused primarily on the home.

2.2 Rich and Poor

If you were rich in Rome, life was good, but if you were poor, life was miserable.

The huge gap between rich and poor was reinforced by a rigid class structure that kept all Romans firmly in their places.

MAIN IDEA

Roman society was divided among different classes of people.

CLASS DIVISIONS

At the top of society was the **aristocracy**, the small group of wealthy patricians who owned most of the land and dominated the government. The majority of citizens were plebeians. Some were well-off and owned farms or businesses, but many were very poor. At the bottom was Rome's huge population of slaves.

The wealthiest families lived in luxurious country estates. These were built around elegant courtyards and decorated with works of fine art. Slaves did the hard work, leaving the homeowners free to conduct business, take part in politics, or spend time on their hobbies.

Most poor Romans lived and worked on small farms. Often, the wealthy used their money to buy up land and create huge farms worked entirely by slaves. This practice forced many farmers off their farms and into the city to look for work. There they

lived in overcrowded buildings and worked at manual labor for very low wages.

Romans' diets also differed greatly. The poor used cheap pottery bowls to eat porridge or bread with vegetables. Meat was a luxury. Only the largest houses had kitchens, so even wealthier plebeians relied on restaurants for hot food. There they could eat fish, cooked meat, and vegetables and perhaps a dessert of sweet pastries. The very rich enjoyed lavish banquets with dozens of courses, including exotic foods.

Around 287 B.C., the plebeians finally achieved political equality when their representative assembly, the **Council of Plebs**, was allowed to make laws for all citizens. However, the patricians continued to dominate society.

SLAVES IN THE REPUBLIC

Slaves were the largest class in Rome, but they had the fewest rights. They were considered property to be bought and sold. Some slaves were prisoners from Rome's conquests. However, most were bought from foreign traders.

Slaves were very useful in Rome's economy. Most worked at manual labor, from household chores to construction work or agriculture. Skilled slaves might be craftspeople, while educated slaves might be teachers, doctors, or managers of their master's business. The worst slave jobs were in the mines or factories, where the work was tough, the conditions were harsh, and the life expectancy was short.

Some slaves were treated well, but others suffered very badly. Excessive punishments could spark rebellion. A slave named Spartacus led the most famous rebellion in 73 B.C. For about two years, his slave army fought the Roman soldiers and controlled large areas of the countryside. When Spartacus was finally defeated, 6,000 of his followers were executed as a warning to other slaves.

A WEALTHY ROMAN FAMILY'S HOME

The diagram below shows four key areas in a house belonging to a wealthy family. While the house contained rooms for the family's private use, much of the space was designed for business and social gatherings.

❶ ENTRANCE HALL
The front door opened up on a large entrance hall. Most mornings clients seeking favors waited here for the chance to pay their respects to their patron, or financial supporter.

❸ OFFICE
This room was located behind the reception area and functioned as the patron's office. The room could also be used for family gatherings.

❹ COURTYARD
A roofed porch enclosed the courtyard garden. The space often included fountains, benches, and sculptures. In the richest homes, the porch's inner walls were often decorated with frescoes.

❷ RECEPTION ROOM
In this large, airy space, the patron showed off his wealth and received visitors. The rectangular space beneath the opening in the roof served to collect rainwater.

REVIEW & ASSESS

1. **READING CHECK** How did the lives of the Roman classes differ?

2. **INTEGRATE VISUALS** In what ways might plebeian or slave homes have differed from the home illustrated above?

3. **MAKE INFERENCES** How do you think the patricians reacted at first to the plebeians' political equality?

PLAN

OBJECTIVE

Compare life in the Roman Republic for people of different social classes.

CRITICAL THINKING SKILLS FOR LESSON 2.2

- Identify Main Ideas and Details
- Monitor Comprehension
- Integrate Visuals
- Make Inferences
- Analyze Cause and Effect
- Compare

ESSENTIAL QUESTION

How did Rome become a mighty power in the Mediterranean?

Roman society was divided among different classes of people. Lesson 2.2 describes these classes and their role in Roman society.

BACKGROUND FOR THE TEACHER

One of the most famous slaves of all time, Spartacus, has served as an inspiration to revolutionary groups throughout history because of his successful, albeit temporary, organized slave revolt. Once a soldier in the Roman army, Spartacus was later sold into slavery and trained as a gladiator. He escaped from slavery in 73 B.C. and assembled a large army of escaped slaves, leading this army to defeat the Romans in a series of attacks. As 72 B.C. drew to a close, Spartacus's rebel forces were finally subdued by the Roman army, and Spartacus was killed.

DIGITAL RESOURCES myNGconnect.com

TEACHER RESOURCES & ASSESSMENT

 Reading and Note-Taking

 Vocabulary Practice

 Section 2 Quiz

STUDENT RESOURCES

 NG Chapter Gallery

INTRODUCE & ENGAGE

HANDS-ON HISTORY

Most students will have some understanding of the history of slavery in the United States. Ask volunteers to offer what they know about American slavery. If appropriate, guide students to discuss topics such as the jobs American slaves did, where they worked, how they lived and were treated, and how they were acquired, so that this activity serves as a precursor to the information students will learn about Roman slaves. **0:10** minutes

TEACH

GUIDED DISCUSSION

1. **Analyze Cause and Effect** How did slaves affect the jobs of farmers? (*When the wealthy used their money to buy up land and create large farms, they oftentimes brought in slaves to work and run the farms. That meant many farmers were forced off their farms and had to move into the city to find work. Many were forced to work manual labor jobs for poor wages.*)

2. **Compare** What types of different jobs did Roman slaves have? (*Most slaves worked in manual labor, doing household chores, construction work, or farm work. Unlucky slaves worked in mines or factories, doing very difficult or unsafe work. Skilled slaves might have been craftspeople. Educated slaves might have been teachers, doctors, or managers of their master's business.*)

CREATE GRAPHIC ORGANIZERS

Place students in small groups and ask each group to create a graphic organizer to show and describe the social classes into which Roman society was divided. (Students should draw a graphic organizer with *aristocracy* at the top of the chart, *plebeians* in the middle, and *slaves* at the bottom (or similar). Students should describe each social class as follows: aristocracy—wealthy patricians who owned most of the land and dominated the government; plebeians—large group of citizens, some of whom were well-off and owned farms or businesses, some of whom were very poor; slaves—largest population in Rome, many worked on farms and in manual labor, most were bought from foreign traders.) **0:10** minutes

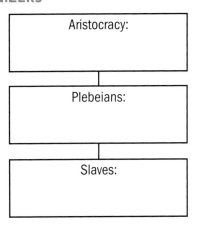

Aristocracy:

Plebeians:

Slaves:

ACTIVE OPTIONS

On Your Feet: Inside-Outside Circle Arrange students in concentric circles facing each other. Have each student in the outside circle ask a question about Roman social classes. Then have each student in the inside circle answer their partner's question. On a signal, have students on the inside circle rotate counterclockwise to meet a new partner and begin again. On a different signal, have students trade roles so those in the inside circle ask the questions and those in the outside circle answer the questions. **0:10** minutes

Critical Viewing: NG Chapter Gallery Ask students to choose one image from the Chapter Gallery and become an expert on it. They should do additional research to learn all about it. Then, students should share their findings with a partner, small group, or the class. **0:10** minutes

DIFFERENTIATE

STRIVING READERS

Use Context Clues Model how to use textual definitions and context to understand key words in this lesson: *aristocracy, Council of Plebs*. Then guide students in using the text to understand other unfamiliar academic vocabulary words such as *exotic, conquests, craftspeople*, and *rebellion*. Students can use a chart like the one below to record their ideas.

Key Vocabulary	Definition From Context

Press **mt** *in the Student eEdition for modified text.*

See the Chapter Planner for more strategies for differentiation.

REVIEW & ASSESS

ANSWERS

1. Patricians owned most of the land and dominated government; some plebeians owned farms or businesses, but most were very poor; slaves had few rights and could be bought and sold.

2. Plebeian or slave homes were probably not as large or fancy. They probably had fewer, simpler rooms and homes that were more practical.

3. They probably reacted harshly because they were used to having all of the power and now had to share it with the plebeians.

Gods and Beliefs

To Romans, the wrath of their gods was always present. They felt that honoring the gods—or at least not upsetting them—was a matter of life and death.

MAIN IDEA

Religious worship was an important part of Roman life.

Ten Gods of Ancient Rome

Jupiter King of the gods

Saturn God of agriculture

Mercury Messenger of the gods

Apollo God of poetry and music

Mars God of war

Neptune God of the sea and earthquakes

Ceres Goddess of the harvest

Juno Goddess of women; wife of Jupiter

Diana Goddess of the moon and the hunt

Venus Goddess of love and beauty

ROMAN WORSHIP

Roman religion was based on a **pantheon** (PAN-thee-ahn), or group of many gods, most adopted from the ancient Greeks. These gods had Roman names and were believed to have human traits and to control areas of Roman life. For example, Jupiter was the king of the gods. Juno was the goddess of women, marriage, childbirth, and children. Mars was the god of war, and Venus was the beautiful goddess of love.

The pantheon constantly grew to include the gods of people Rome conquered. Later, the Romans worshipped their rulers as gods after their death. Some rulers claimed to be living gods, but this claim made them very unpopular.

Romans worshipped their gods almost anywhere. Nearly every home had a shrine where the paterfamilias would make daily offerings to the gods that protected his family and his house. Priests managed temples for the most important gods. The priests conducted the rituals that Romans believed would secure the gods' favor.

The Roman calendar had many religious festivals that attracted huge audiences. The government funded many of them to ensure that the gods granted Rome good harvests or victories in war. These festivals included colorful processions, feasts, music, dance, theater, and sports.

THE ROMAN WAY

Roman gods had human traits that often highlighted the qualities most prized by the Romans. The Romans were a very practical and ambitious people, so they valued qualities that would help them achieve success. They considered the Greek virtues of beauty, grace, and elegance as nice but not essential. Instead, they preferred qualities like discipline, strength, and loyalty. Discipline and strength helped Romans endure hardship and overcome problems. Loyalty bound strong individuals together into even more powerful groups.

These valued qualities emphasize an important aspect of the Roman personality—*gravitas* (GRA-vuh-tahs). Having gravitas means being solemn and serious. Romans respected people who acted with great consideration, determination, and energy. These characteristics helped the people of the Roman Republic accomplish remarkable achievements in war, politics, law, commerce, and engineering. These qualities came to be known as "the Roman Way."

Critical Viewing A statue of Neptune, god of the sea, stands above the flowing water of Rome's Trevi Fountain. What details in the statue convey the qualities that the ancient Romans admired?

Trevi Fountain, Nicola Salvi and Giuseppe Pannini, 1762

➕ POSSIBLE RESPONSE

The statue's face looks solemn and serious, and the body is muscular, illustrating strength.

REVIEW & ASSESS

1. **READING CHECK** Why was the worship of gods an important part of Roman life?

2. **SUMMARIZE** In what ways did the Romans expect the gods to affect daily life?

3. **DRAW CONCLUSIONS** What qualities did the Romans value? Why did they value these qualities more than others?

PLAN

OBJECTIVE

Explain the roles of religion and values in Roman culture.

CRITICAL THINKING SKILLS FOR LESSON 2.3

- Identify Main Ideas and Details
- Monitor Comprehension
- Summarize
- Draw Conclusions
- Compare and Contrast
- Make Inferences
- Synthesize

ESSENTIAL QUESTION

How did Rome become a mighty power in the Mediterranean?

Religion and values were an important part of Roman culture. Lesson 2.3 examines how these aspects contributed to ancient Rome's success.

BACKGROUND FOR THE TEACHER

King of all Roman gods, Jupiter was a god of the sky. His original temple was built in Rome on the Capitoline Hill. For Romans, Jupiter, or Jove as he was also called, symbolized keeping one's promises or oaths to other people and to the Roman state. He was associated with keeping heroes focused on their duties and was considered the protector of the Roman Republic and people.

DIGITAL RESOURCES myNGconnect.com

TEACHER RESOURCES & ASSESSMENT

 Reading and Note-Taking

 Vocabulary Practice

 Section 2 Quiz

STUDENT RESOURCES

 NG Chapter Gallery

INTRODUCE & ENGAGE

MAKE CONNECTIONS

Post descriptions of two different people for students to read. Describe Person A as practical, strong, disciplined, and loyal. Describe Person B as beautiful or handsome, graceful, and elegant. Ask students to predict which individual would be more valued by the Romans, and which would be more valued by the Greeks. Tally students' predictions and post them on the whiteboard. Then have students brainstorm people from today's society who might fit each description, record their names on sticky notes, and post them under the appropriate descriptions. **0:10 minutes**

TEACH

GUIDED DISCUSSION

1. **Compare and Contrast** How is Roman worship similar to and different from the modern religions that you are familiar with today? (*Responses will vary, but may focus on the following points, which may be contrasted or compared to present-day religions: the Romans worshipped many gods and goddesses, not one; the gods had human names and traits and had control over specific facets of daily life, such as music or farming; the Romans added more gods to the pantheon as they conquered different peoples; Roman gods had shrines and temples where people worshipped them; the Romans held festivals in honor of their gods and goddesses.*)

2. **Make Inferences** Given what you know about the Romans' religious beliefs, how might a Roman farmer have gone about ensuring a successful growing season and a good harvest? (*A farmer might have visited the temple for Saturn, the god of agriculture, or Ceres, the goddess of the harvest, and made an offering or said a prayer for a successful growing season. The farmer also might have attended a religious festival funded by the Roman government to honor Ceres or Saturn.*)

SYNTHESIZE

This lesson introduces students to the concept of *gravitas*. Put students into small groups and ask them to create a Concept Web with the term *gravitas* in the center. Students should discuss what they have learned about gravitas in terms of Rome, and then add phrases, words, and examples to the web to explain the term and relate it to Roman culture and values. (*Students' webs will vary but should reflect the word's meaning: solemn and serious.*) **0:15 minutes**

ACTIVE OPTIONS

On Your Feet: One-on-One Interviews Group students into pairs. Have both students in the pair write three questions about Roman religious practices and "the Roman Way." Start with one student using his or her questions to interview the other student "expert" about Roman religion and culture. Students' answers should show an understanding of the material from the lesson. Once the interview is complete, students should reverse roles. **0:15 minutes**

NG Learning Framework: Investigate The Roman Way

ATTITUDE: **Curiosity**
SKILL: **Communication**
KNOWLEDGE: **Our Human Story**

Have students explore local museums or libraries, in person or digitally, to view interesting artifacts or gather information about Rome. Have them write a short paragraph describing how what they found represents the Roman Way. **0:10 minutes**

DIFFERENTIATE

STRIVING READERS

Who's Who? Assign pairs of students one of the ten gods of ancient Rome listed in the lesson. Have the students discuss what the god is known for (doing additional research, if desired) and work together to create a flag, crest, or trading card that represents the deity and his or her role in Roman religion.

GIFTED & TALENTED

Research a Roman God Allow students (or student pairs) to select a Roman god or goddess and conduct further research on him or her in order to create a short presentation for their classmates. Presentations should include information about the following:

- the name of the assigned god or goddess and his or her role in Roman religion
- any relevant connections to Greek gods and goddesses
- festivals or events planned in honor of the god or goddess
- positive and negative qualities of the selected deity
- photographs of artwork, sculptures, architecture, or other representations of the deity

Press (mt) *in the Student eEdition for modified text.*

See the Chapter Planner for more strategies for differentiation.

REVIEW & ASSESS

ANSWERS

1. The worship of gods was important because they controlled areas of Roman life.

2. Romans expected the gods to affect daily life, the harvest, and performance in war.

3. The Romans valued discipline, strength, and loyalty because they felt these qualities would help them endure hardship, overcome problems, and accomplish remarkable achievements.

3.1 The Roman Army

War in the ancient world was extremely physical, and the Romans were good at it. The republic developed a formidable fighting force of well-trained professional soldiers called the legion. It was the ultimate weapon of ancient warfare.

MAIN IDEA

Organization and training brought Rome's army military success.

+ POSSIBLE RESPONSE

It might have been effective because it turned all the individuals in the unit into a solid formation that could easily ram into the enemy. The formation also probably offered additional protection to the soldiers.

Roman Legionaries

Roman soldiers kept fit by running, marching, and practice fighting. They could march 20 miles a day wearing armor, swim or cross rivers in boats, and build bridges.

This photo shows a reenactment of a Roman army battle formation. As you can see, Roman legionaries usually fought in tight lines with their shields held before the attacking enemy. Why might this battle tactic, or strategy, have been effective?

‹ A Roman legionary stands guard in a reenactment of ancient warfare.

THE ROMAN LEGION

It was a privilege to serve in Rome's legions. At first only property-owning citizens could join, and they had to supply their own weapons. A legion contained around 4,200 men, and each consul led an army of two legions. When the battle season finished in October, everybody went home.

Yet as the republic fought longer wars farther from Rome, citizens who owned property became reluctant to serve. In 107 B.C., the consul Marius (MAIR-ee-uhs) found himself short of recruits, so he allowed poor, landless citizens to volunteer. The government supplied their equipment, which included a bronze helmet, mail armor, a short sword, a javelin, and an oval shield. These men became professional soldiers known as **legionaries**.

Marius also reorganized the legions for maximum strength and flexibility. He often grouped squads of men into 100-man centuries, or units. These units, in turn, were grouped into 600-man cohorts, or divisions. Ten cohorts made up a legion, now 6,000 strong. This command structure gave Roman generals control over large numbers of men, and it continues to be a model for modern military organization.

The legions became an efficient military machine that Rome used to conquer its enemies and expand its territory. Rome recruited additional soldiers from the regions it defeated, which led to more military might and manpower. If a Roman army was defeated, Rome would send an even bigger army the next time. This stubborn determination made Rome unstoppable.

LIFE OF A LEGIONARY

Legionaries joined young and served for a maximum of 16 years. A recruit had to pass a physical inspection. Then in front of the legion's revered flag, the eagle, he swore an oath to serve the republic. This oath inspired a powerful sense of duty to comrades, to commanders, and to Rome itself.

Daily life revolved around a squad that trained, marched, and fought together. Soldiers built strong bonds of friendship and loyalty through sharing a tent, duties, and meals. When off duty, a legionary might play games or visit the public baths. However, duty always came first. While bravery led to rewards, failure led to severe punishment.

Training was key to the legions' success. Legionaries learned to carry out complicated instructions in the chaos of battle. At the end of each day, they built a fortified camp with deep ditches and high walls called palisades. Over time, they also built the straight roads and strong bridges that connected the republic and carried its men into battle.

REVIEW & ASSESS

1. **READING CHECK** How did the Roman army's organization and training lead to success?

2. **IDENTIFY MAIN IDEAS AND DETAILS** What were the duties of a legionary?

3. **SUMMARIZE** What changes did Marius make to the Roman army?

PLAN

OBJECTIVE

Explain how the organization and training of Roman soldiers led to Rome's military success.

CRITICAL THINKING SKILLS FOR LESSON 3.1

- Identify Main Ideas and Details
- Monitor Comprehension
- Summarize
- Draw Conclusions
- Make Inferences

ESSENTIAL QUESTION

How did Rome become a mighty power in the Mediterranean?

The organization of Rome's army is still used as a model for modern military units. Lesson 3.1 describes the Roman legion and explains how it contributed to Rome's success.

BACKGROUND FOR THE TEACHER

Professional soldiers, or legionaries, supplied the Roman army with the strength it needed in battle to defend and expand the republic. However, legionaries were not the only type of soldiers in the army, and fighting was not the only thing that Roman soldiers did. Roman auxiliaries were soldiers who weren't Roman citizens, but who were paid a small wage to guard forts and sometimes fight in battles. Artillery soldiers used weapons such as catapults and crossbows against enemies, and cavalry battled on horseback. Other soldiers gathered supplies, constructed buildings and roads, made and repaired weapons and shields, and cared for the wounded.

DIGITAL RESOURCES myNGconnect.com

TEACHER RESOURCES & ASSESSMENT

 Reading and Note-Taking

 Vocabulary Practice

 Section 3 Quiz

STUDENT RESOURCES

 NG Chapter Gallery

INTRODUCE & ENGAGE

JOIN THE RANKS

March students drill-style, through the school, ask them to stand at attention, or spend a few minutes barking orders at them as a drill sergeant might. Ask students to reflect about and share how they might feel about serving their country as a member of the military. What would they like about it? (*travel, education, room and board, pride in serving their country*) What would they dislike? (*being away from family and friends, danger, difficult living conditions, having to take orders*) Record these likes and dislikes on the whiteboard. Then tell students they are going to learn what life was like for soldiers in the Roman army. `0:10` minutes

TEACH

GUIDED DISCUSSION

1. **Draw Conclusions** What were the short-term and long-term impacts of the legionaries on Rome? (*On a daily basis, legionaries protected the city of Rome, conquered enemies, and expanded Rome's territory. They also had a lasting impact on the Roman Republic because they were responsible for building the straight roads and strong bridges that connected the republic and carried soldiers into battle. Many other civilizations modeled their infrastructure after Rome's.*)

2. **Make Inferences** What might have been the advantages and disadvantages of joining the Roman legions as a volunteer? (*For people who were poor and landless, joining the legions provided an opportunity to serve the republic, which instilled in them a deep sense of loyalty and pride. The legionaries were kept very busy and made many friends. Joining the legions also provided volunteers with shelter, food, and military instruction. The disadvantages of joining the legions included the risk of death or injury during battle, hard work under difficult conditions, and severe punishments for failing to perform one's duties.*)

CREATE GRAPHIC ORGANIZERS

To help students understand how the consul Marius organized the Roman legions for maximum effectiveness, have them work together (or as a class) to create a graphic organizer or visual to show how the soldiers were organized. `0:15` minutes

ACTIVE OPTIONS

Critical Viewing: NG Chapter Gallery Have students examine the contents of the Chapter Gallery for this chapter. Then invite them to brainstorm additional images they believe would fit within the Chapter Gallery. Have them write a description of these additional images and provide an explanation of why they would fit within the Chapter Gallery. Then instruct them to do online research to find examples of actual images. `0:10` minutes

On Your Feet: Think, Pair, Share Have students consider the following questions:

- Originally, only property-owning citizens who supplied their own weapons were permitted to join Roman legions as soldiers. By 107 B.C., Marius was forced to allow poor, landless citizens to volunteer as legionaries. What changed in Roman society to require this dramatic shift in how the legions were staffed?

- Do you think legions made up largely of poor volunteers would be any different from legions made up of privileged property-owning citizens? Why or why not? What advantages or disadvantages might each social group bring to their legion?

After students have time to consider the topics individually, place them in pairs to discuss them together. Then invite a volunteer from each pair to share the results of their discussion with the rest of the class. `0:10` minutes

DIFFERENTIATE

ENGLISH LANGUAGE LEARNERS

Summarize Lesson 3.1 has seven paragraphs. Have students work in pairs or small groups, and assign each pair or group one paragraph to read together. Then each group should summarize their paragraph in one or two sentences for the class.

PRE-AP

Comparing Armies Have students do Internet research and create a chart that compares today's U.S. Army and the duties and obligations of the enlisted to those of the Roman legion and its legionaries. Have them consider the following:

- the minimum recruitment age and length of service

- the organization of each army

- the duties and daily lives of the soldiers

ASK: What generalizations can you make about how the two armies compare? Why might some of the differences and similarities exist?

Press **mt** *in the Student eEdition for modified text.*

See the Chapter Planner for more strategies for differentiation.

REVIEW & ASSESS

ANSWERS

1. The army's organization made it easy for generals to control large numbers of men, and the soldiers' training prepared them for the chaos of battle.

2. A legionary served the republic in battle and through various construction projects.

3. Marius allowed poor, landless citizens to volunteer for the army, and he reorganized the structure of the legion.

3.2 ROMAN ARMOR

"The infantry soldier carries so much equipment that he differs little from a mule," said an observer from the first century A.D. Along with his armor, shield, and weapons, which combined weighed some 50 pounds, a soldier had to carry food, tools, and personal belongings that could double the weight. Based on what you see here, what might have been some challenges that Roman soldiers encountered on and off the battlefield?

The ridge protected against vertical sword strikes.

Wide cheek flaps protected the face but left ears exposed to hear orders.

Breastplate Made of steel plates bound by leather straps, it weighed about 20 pounds and was lined with padding for comfort.

Galea, or Helmet The iron helmet followed a design used by warriors from Gaul.

A wide projection shielded the neck and deflected blows from behind.

The shield's iron boss and rim were used as weapons to punch the enemy.

Javelin The heavy javelin was thrown at close range and was designed to bend on impact.

Sword Legionaries wore it on the right; officers wore it on the left.

Sheath Made of wood, it was covered in decorative leather.

Tunic Soldiers wore red wool tunics under armor.

Shield The leather-covered wooden shield weighed over 20 pounds. A legion's unique emblem was painted on the front.

Hooded Cloak Wool kept soldiers warm.

Stake Each soldier carried two to build a palisade.

Iron Pick Picks were used in camp construction.

Canteen Canteens held *posca*, a mixture of vinegar and water.

Rucksack The carryall contained tools and rations.

Around two feet long, the javelin's iron spear had a pyramidal, or arrow-shaped, tip.

Made of ash, the javelin's shaft measured between four and five feet.

Scabbard Made of iron and often engraved, the scabbard had rings to attach it to the belt.

Sandals Sandals were made from a single piece of leather. They had thick soles and were studded with iron tacks.

Ladle Soldiers carried cooking and eating utensils.

Dagger The short dagger had a stone handle and was worn on the hip.

➕ POSSIBLE RESPONSE
Soldiers probably found it challenging to walk long distances while carrying so much heavy equipment. On the battlefield, they might have found it difficult to move quickly with their heavy armor.

The Roman Republic **287**

PLAN

OBJECTIVE

Identify the equipment used to keep Roman soldiers safe and successful on and off the battlefield.

CRITICAL THINKING SKILLS FOR LESSON 3.2

- Describe
- Draw Conclusions
- Analyze Visuals

ESSENTIAL QUESTION

How did Rome become a mighty power in the Mediterranean?

Roman legionaries carried everything they needed to survive on and off the battlefield. Lesson 3.2 shows what Roman soldiers wore and carried, and explains the importance of these items to a soldier's survival.

BACKGROUND FOR THE TEACHER

Not all Roman soldiers were equally well equipped with gear and weaponry. Legionaries posted on the edges of the expanding Roman Republic often found themselves without the supplies they needed as they dealt with dangerous local peoples who were most likely unhappy about the presence of the legions. Like the soldiers of today, Roman legionaries spent their free time writing letters home, sharing details about their work and living conditions, and asking for care packages to be sent to them. Warm clothing and news from home were at the top of their lists.

TEACHER RESOURCES & ASSESSMENT

 Reading and Note-Taking

 Vocabulary Practice

 Section 3 Quiz

STUDENT RESOURCES

 NG Chapter Gallery

HISTORY THROUGH OBJECTS

Ask students to form small groups and brainstorm a list of equipment and items a soldier, explorer, or survivalist would be likely to carry with them to travel on foot over rough terrain and to live outdoors. Reconvene as a class and ask each group to share their list. Use the group lists to create a master list on the whiteboard. Discuss the best way to transport the gear and the challenges this would pose. Then tell students they will learn about equipment that was vital to the survival of Roman soldiers. **0:05** minutes

TEACH

GUIDED DISCUSSION

1. **Describe** How were Roman helmets designed to protect a soldier's head? (*They were made of iron and designed to be similar to helmets worn by successful warriors from Gaul. They had a ridge along the forehead to protect the soldier from vertical sword slashes. They had a wide piece at the back to protect the soldier's neck. Wide flaps on the sides of the helmet protected the soldier's face, but allowed him to hear his superiors.*)
   ASK: What types of problems might Roman soldiers have had with their helmets? (*They were heavy because they were made of iron, which means they were probably uncomfortable. They may have made it hard to see.*)

2. **Draw Conclusions** What do the armor, weapons, and tools used by the Romans tell you about the success of their army? (*Responses will vary. Possible responses: The Roman soldiers had a wide variety of weapons, so they were probably able to adapt to many different challenges in battle. The details on the weapons, such as the engraving on the scabbard and dagger, make me think they took pride in creating well-made weapons. Pieces of heavy armor like the breastplate, shield, and helmet show that soldiers were well-protected as they went into dangerous combat, and that the Romans were fine crafters of armor.*)

ANALYZE VISUALS

Have students create a three-column chart for classifying the Roman artifacts into the following categories: staying warm, staying safe, and daily living, based on their function. (Or, as a class, brainstorm different headings that could be used to categorize the items.) Then have students sort the artifacts into the categories, writing each item in the appropriate column. End the activity by inviting volunteers to share their categories and discuss/debate any alternative categorizing. **0:15** minutes

Staying Warm	Staying Safe	Daily Living

ACTIVE OPTIONS

On Your Feet: Try It On Gather items similar to the armor and gear that Roman soldiers wore and carried, so students can experience how it would feel to wear and carry it. Here are some modern equivalents to traditional Roman gear:

- Steel breastplate = weighted vest, lifejacket, or backpack filled with 20 lbs. of weight, worn on the chest
- Helmet = football helmet or motorcycle helmet
- Shield = 20-pound piece of plywood or flat stone
- Tunic = long t-shirt or short dress
- Javelin = long pole or dowel rod
- Sword = shorter pole or dowel rod
- Rucksack = backpack
- Hooded cloak = poncho or blanket
- Canteen = water bottle

Ask volunteers to wear and carry the equipment around and share their experience. Challenge them to crouch, hop, run, walk, and climb onto a chair carrying all of that gear to simulate what Roman soldiers would have done while they were on the move. **0:20** minutes

NG Learning Framework: Compare Soldiers' Gear

ATTITUDE: **Responsibility**
SKILLS: **Collaboration, Communication**

Pair students up to use a Venn Diagram to compare a Roman soldier's gear to a modern soldier's gear and explore the similarities and differences. Have each group present their similarity findings. **0:20** minutes

DIFFERENTIATE

INCLUSION

Identify New Words Pair special needs students with students at a higher proficiency level. Have them reread the lesson. Then have students identify three pieces of Roman equipment that were unfamiliar to them before they read the lesson. Have them use a two-column chart to record each piece of equipment and its purpose.

Equipment	Purpose

PRE-AP

Research a Roman Weapon Have students research and report on one of the Roman weapons featured in the lesson. Possible concepts to research: how, when, and why the weapon was used, what it was made of, and what it was designed to do.

Press **mt** *in the Student eEdition for modified text.*

See the Chapter Planner for more strategies for differentiation.

3.3 Hannibal and the Punic Wars

To win in the big leagues, you've got to take on the champion. In 264 B.C., Rome turned its might against the Mediterranean superpower of Carthage. The two enemies fought a series of wars, called the **Punic** (PYOO-nihk) **Wars**, that lasted, off and on, for about 100 years.

MAIN IDEA

Rome and Carthage fought the Punic Wars for control of the Mediterranean Sea.

In the early battles, many of the Roman soldiers, who had never seen an elephant before, fled in terror.

War Elephants

Hannibal's war elephants were the "battle tanks" of the ancient world. Their size and power made them a terrifying and innovative battle weapon. Normally gentle creatures, however, the elephants had to be provoked and prodded to attack.

THE FIRST PUNIC WAR

The North African city of **Carthage** was immensely rich. It had grown from a Phoenician colony (*Punic* is Latin for "Phoenician") into a trading empire. Carthage had established colonies and trading ports around the western Mediterranean, and the city controlled valuable mineral resources in North Africa and present-day Spain. In time, Rome began to compete with Carthage for control of the sea.

The First Punic War broke out in 264 B.C. over the strategic island of Sicily (see the map in Section 3.5). The war was fought mainly at sea, but Carthage's navy was vastly superior to

Rome's. After suffering a key defeat, Rome quickly built a fleet of 120 powerful warships that beat the Carthaginian navy in almost every battle. These victories allowed Rome to occupy the important islands of Sicily, Sardinia, and Corsica. In 241 B.C., Carthage surrendered to Rome. Its defeated general was Hamilcar Barca, the father of a young boy named **Hannibal**.

THE SECOND PUNIC WAR

When Hannibal was a child, he promised his father that he would always hate Rome. When he became a Carthaginian general, he made good on that promise. After Hannibal attacked one of Rome's allies in southern Spain, the Second Punic War began in 218 B.C. While the Romans planned a counterattack,

Hannibal outsmarted them. He led about 60,000 soldiers and a herd of war elephants out of Spain and across the Alps to invade the Italian Peninsula by land. This astonishing action caught the Romans by surprise. Hannibal swiftly defeated the Roman army in battle after battle as he swept south toward Rome itself.

By 216 B.C., Hannibal was in southeast Italy, facing a huge Roman army at Cannae (KA-nee). Although outnumbered, Hannibal defeated the legions. His brilliant tactics are still studied at military academies today.

Rome fought on, however, and steadily wore down Hannibal's army. In 205 B.C., the Roman general Scipio (SIHP-ee-oh) was elected consul. He invaded North Africa in a plan devised to draw Hannibal out of Italy. It worked. Hannibal left Italy to defend his homeland. At the Battle of Zama (ZAY-muh) in 202 B.C., Hannibal and Scipio faced each other in a desperate fight. They were both brilliant generals, but after a long, bloody battle, Hannibal was defeated and later fled abroad to Asia Minor in present-day Turkey. In 201 B.C., the Second Punic War ended, and Rome once again ruled the western Mediterranean.

REVIEW & ASSESS

1. **READING CHECK** What events led Rome to fight two wars with Carthage?

2. **COMPARE AND CONTRAST** How were the two Punic Wars alike and how were they different?

3. **DRAW CONCLUSIONS** Why was Hannibal's trek through the Alps such an astonishing accomplishment?

PLAN

OBJECTIVE

Explain the causes and impact of the First and Second Punic Wars on the Roman Republic.

CRITICAL THINKING SKILLS FOR LESSON 3.3

- Identify Main Ideas and Details
- Monitor Comprehension
- Compare and Contrast
- Draw Conclusions
- Identify
- Sequence Events

ESSENTIAL QUESTION

How did Rome become a mighty power in the Mediterranean?

In 264 B.C., Rome challenged the mighty Mediterranean city of

Carthage. Lesson 3.3 explains how the First and Second Punic Wars helped Rome expand its territory along the Mediterranean.

BACKGROUND FOR THE TEACHER

Many wonder how Hannibal was able to bring elephants to Spain as he prepared to attack the Roman army and where those elephants came from. The only evidence that exists is a Carthaginian coin made around the time of the invasion. The physical features of the elephant shown on the coin indicate that Hannibal's elephants were probably small African elephants, not Asian elephants. There is evidence that this smaller African elephant subspecies lived in the Atlas Mountains of present-day Morocco and Algeria, which could be where Hannibal got them.

DIGITAL RESOURCES myNGconnect.com

TEACHER RESOURCES & ASSESSMENT

 Reading and Note-Taking

 Vocabulary Practice

 Section 3 Quiz

STUDENT RESOURCES

 NG Chapter Gallery

POSE AND ANSWER QUESTIONS

Ask students if they think a parent's views and opinions are passed down to their children. Split students into small groups and invite them to discuss this question. Help guide groups to consider how it is possible for a parent's feelings about religion, politics, race, even sports teams to be passed down to a child, and why that happens. Tell them to consider this topic as they read about Hannibal and his father, the Carthaginian general Hamilcar Barca. **0:05** minutes

TEACH

GUIDED DISCUSSION

1. **Identify** How did the Romans respond to their original defeat during the First Punic War? (*They strengthened their navy by building 120 powerful warships. This allowed them to beat the Carthaginian navy in almost every subsequent battle, and occupy the islands of Sicily, Sardinia, and Corsica.*)

2. **Draw Conclusions** Why might modern military academies study the strategies of Hannibal, a general who fought over 2,000 years ago? (*Hannibal led the Carthaginian army to defeat the strong and disciplined Roman army multiple times. He used creative battle tactics, including war elephants and surprise attacks, to outsmart and outfight the Romans. His strategies could be valuable and useful to the military forces of today.*)

SEQUENCE EVENTS

Work as a class to create a time line on chart paper or a whiteboard to document the main events involved during the wars between the Carthaginians and Romans. Be sure to include the following dates and events:

- 264 B.C. First Punic War breaks out over control of Sicily.
- 241 B.C. Carthage surrenders to Rome, who occupied the islands of Sicily, Sardinia, and Corsica.
- 218 B.C. Hannibal attacks Rome's ally in Spain—Second Punic War breaks out. Hannibal surprises the Romans by invading the Italian Peninsula by land using elephants. Romans are defeated.
- 216 B.C. Hannibal defeats Roman legions in Southeast Italy even though he was outnumbered.
- 205 B.C. Roman general Scipio invades North Africa to draw Hannibal back to his homeland.
- 202 B.C. Hannibal is defeated by Scipio in the battle of Zama and flees to present-day Turkey.
- 201 B.C. Second Punic War ends. **0:15** minutes

ACTIVE OPTIONS

On Your Feet: Card Responses Have half the class write 15 true-false or yes-no questions based on the lesson. Have the other half create answer cards, writing "True" or "Yes" on one side of the cards and "False" or "No" on the other side. Students from the question group should take turns asking their questions. Students from the answer group should hold up their cards, showing the correct answer. Have students keep track of their correct answers. **0:15** minutes

Critical Viewing: NG Image Gallery Invite students to explore the entire NG Image Gallery and create a Top Ten List by choosing the images they think are most representative of the Roman Empire. If possible, have students copy the images into a document to form an actual list. Then encourage them to select the image they like best and do further research on it. **0:10** minutes

DIFFERENTIATE

STRIVING READERS

Write About It Tell students to imagine they are Roman soldiers seeing elephants for the first time in their lives during a battle against Hannibal's army. Have them write short narrative paragraphs explaining this experience. Then have volunteers share their paragraphs with the class.

PRE-AP

Sequence Events Have students complete the Sequence Events activity individually or in pairs, without any prompts or suggestions about identifying important events and creating a graphic organizer.

Press (mt) *in the Student eEdition for modified text.*

See the Chapter Planner for more strategies for differentiation.

REVIEW & ASSESS

ANSWERS

1. The events included an argument over possession of the island of Sicily and an attack by Hannibal on one of Rome's allies.

2. Rome won both wars. The first war was fought mainly at sea, and the second was fought primarily on land.

3. It was astonishing because he accomplished it in a cold winter with a large amount of men and elephants.

3.4 NATIONAL GEOGRAPHIC EXPLORER **PATRICK HUNT**

Searching for Hannibal's Route

Patrick Hunt is a man on a mission to solve one of history's mysteries: Where did Hannibal cross the Alps? One of the most daring military maneuvers of all time, Hannibal's invasion of Italy in 218 B.C. required marching about 40,000 men and 37 elephants across these rugged mountains in winter. Hannibal didn't leave a map behind though. "For the last decade plus, we've been trying to pinpoint Hannibal's route," says Hunt. Because of his research, now he's close to an answer.

^ Patrick Hunt theorizes that Hannibal used the Col du Clapier-Savine Coche mountain pass, shown above, to cross the Alps into Italy.

MAIN IDEA

Geoarchaeologist Patrick Hunt is rediscovering the route of Hannibal's army.

HANNIBAL'S FOOTSTEPS

Patrick Hunt is a National Geographic grantee and the director of the Hannibal Expedition. Since 1994, he has used everything from ancient literature to satellite imaging to find the mountain pass Hannibal traveled. "It's like looking for a needle in a haystack," Hunt says, "but it's not just for the sake of mystery." The Alps were considered impassable in winter. Historians know Hannibal crossed them, but they don't know how because they don't know where. If someone were to find the route, historians might begin to understand how Hannibal achieved this amazing military feat.

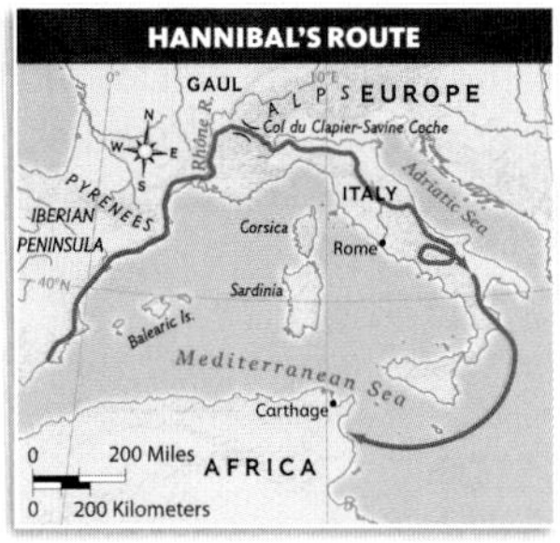

HANNIBAL'S ROUTE
GAUL
ALPS
EUROPE
Col du Clapier-Savine Coche
Rhône R.
PYRENEES
IBERIAN PENINSULA
ITALY
Corsica
Rome
Adriatic Sea
Sardinia
Balearic Is.
Mediterranean Sea
Carthage
AFRICA
0 200 Miles
0 200 Kilometers
40°N

The Roman historians Polybius (puh-LIH-bee-uhs) and Livy (LIH-vee) wrote accounts of Hannibal's campaign. Although they use few place-names, they describe the geographic features Hannibal saw and the distances he traveled each day. Hunt uses these clues to work out probable routes. "It's a bit like sleuthing," he admits. "We've been over close to 30 Alpine passes, mostly on foot, constantly comparing how they fit the descriptions."

A SCIENTIFIC APPROACH

Geoarchaeology applies earth sciences such as geography and geology to archaeology. These sciences are vital to Hunt's search because he has to factor in 2,000 years of change. Mountains may look different because of erosion; climate changes may have moved the snow line. "The first thing we do on-site is to examine the basic rock types to check how stable the geology is," he says. "The more stable it is, the less likely it is to have changed much." It's a scientific approach and a physically challenging one, too. Several team members have suffered broken bones because of the treacherous working conditions.

Through a process of elimination, Hunt is now confident he knows most of Hannibal's route. The view from the summit of the Col du Clapier-Savine Coche fits perfectly with the descriptions in the ancient texts. "Now we're looking for physical evidence, and we are focused on the campsites," he explains. "Ash has a chemical signature that lasts over 2,000 years. We think we've found the ash of Hannibal's camps and have pinpointed a major summit campground. Now we're looking at stone deposits that may mark graves. An elephant burial would be fantastic!"

"Hannibal is very close to my heart," asserts Hunt. "He lost close to 40 percent of his men crossing the Alps. That would be unacceptable today, but Hannibal went on to defeat the Romans multiple times. This is a man who wins battle after battle but ultimately doesn't win the war."

REVIEW & ASSESS

1. **READING CHECK** What tools is Patrick Hunt using to determine Hannibal's route through the Alps?
2. **INTERPRET MAPS** In what ways did the Alps both protect Rome and help Hannibal attempt a sneak attack?
3. **MAKE INFERENCES** What knowledge of geography and maps might Hannibal have had in order to believe his campaign over the Alps could be successful?

PLAN

OBJECTIVE

Describe how and why geoarchaeologist Patrick Hunt is tracing the route of Hannibal's army, and how geoarchaeology can help historians make sense of past events and individuals.

CRITICAL THINKING SKILLS FOR LESSON 3.4

- Identify Main Ideas and Details
- Monitor Comprehension
- Interpret Maps
- Make Inferences
- Synthesize
- Describe
- Analyze Visuals

ESSENTIAL QUESTION

How did Rome become a mighty power in the Mediterranean?

Rome's defeat of Carthage and its brilliant general, Hannibal, was key to the success of the growing republic. Lesson 3.4 introduces National Geographic Grantee, Patrick Hunt, and describes his search for Hannibal's historic route through the Alps.

BACKGROUND FOR THE TEACHER

It's not easy to hike for miles over snowy mountains leading a herd of elephants, and Patrick Hunt is determined to figure out how Hannibal did it. His high-altitude archaeology explorations are done mostly on foot over treacherous Alpine terrain that often reaches elevations of 10,000 feet. Hunt's team searches for confirmation of Hannibal's route as well as signs of human modifications to the Alpine passes, both of which would aid in our understanding of this legendary military leader.

DIGITAL RESOURCES myNGconnect.com

TEACHER RESOURCES & ASSESSMENT

- **Reading and Note-Taking**
- **Vocabulary Practice**
- **Section 3 Quiz**

STUDENT RESOURCES

- **NG Chapter Gallery**

ACTIVATE PRIOR KNOWLEDGE

Discuss what students know about the meaning of the prefix *geo-* and the job of an archaeologist. Invite student volunteers to use a dictionary or other resources as needed. Write the following questions on the whiteboard: What might a geoarchaeologist do that is different from a regular archaeologist? What might be the challenges of this field? Have students brainstorm and discuss answers, and record them on the whiteboard. Tell students that in this lesson they will learn about a geoarchaeologist's search to uncover Hannibal's route across the Alps. **0:05 minutes**

TEACH

GUIDED DISCUSSION

1. **Synthesize** Why is it important to historians to determine Hannibal's route through the Alps? (*Determining where Hannibal crossed through the Alps would help historians understand how Hannibal completed a journey considered to be impossible during the winter, and shed new light on this famous general's knowledge of geography and impressive military tactics.*)

2. **Describe** What types of physical evidence would confirm for Hunt and his team that Hannibal and his troops had passed through a specific region? (*Finding ash from campfires dating back to the time of Hannibal's crossing of the Alps would confirm where he and his army camped during their journey. Gravesites of people or animals, such as elephants, would also confirm the route.*)

ANALYZE VISUALS

Have students study the photograph of Patrick Hunt. Ask them the following questions about the photograph:

- Where was this photograph of Hunt taken? (*the Col du Clapier-Savine Coche in the Alps*)

- How would you describe the terrain shown in this photograph? (*rocky, uneven, grassy, mountainous*)

- How might the terrain have been different when Hannibal crossed through this region to surprise the Romans? (*It was winter when he crossed, so it would have been snowy and icy, hard to see, and hard to climb. Also, years of erosion have probably changed the landscape, altering the shape of the land and the mountains.*)

ASK: Does the photograph of this region remind you of anywhere you have been or seen? Have students offer locations with similar terrain or geography, and discuss the similarities and differences between the location shown in the photograph (the Col du Clapier-Savine Coche in the Alps) and the location they are thinking about. **0:15 minutes**

ACTIVE OPTIONS

On Your Feet: Hold a Press Conference Assign one third of the class the role of geoarchaeologists from Patrick Hunt's team and tell them they have just returned from an expedition through the Alps in search of evidence of Hannibal's path. Assign the remaining students the role of "reporters," and challenge them to write down three questions they'd like to ask the geoarchaeologists. The questions should primarily be based on information from the lesson, but may also include questions they have about Hannibal's route, geoarchaeology, or other related topics. Each reporter should then ask the geoarchaeologists a question, and the geoarchaeologists should respond. Encourage students to draw upon their knowledge from this lesson and the other lessons in the section. **0:15 minutes**

NG Learning Framework: Ask and Answer

ATTITUDES: Curiosity, Responsibility
SKILL: Communication
KNOWLEDGE: Our Human Story

Patrick Hunt is uncovering a centuries-old mystery. After reading the lesson, have students write down one question they would like to have answered about Hunt's work. Tell students to research their question and see if they can find an answer. If not, have them keep their question in a log that they can come back to later and see if they can find an answer then. **0:10 minutes**

DIFFERENTIATE

INCLUSION

Watch a Movie If appropriate, show students the National Geographic documentary Hannibal v. Rome (or clips of it) to help students experience and understand the content in this lesson and subsequent lessons.

Press **mt** *in the Student eEdition for modified text.*

See the Chapter Planner for more strategies for differentiation.

REVIEW & ASSESS

ANSWERS

1. He is using everything from satellite imaging to ancient literature.

2. The Alps were high and hard to cross, which helped protect Rome. However, they also provided places for Hannibal and his men to hide before their attack.

3. He must have known that there were some passes through the mountains. He also must have known about weather conditions there to adapt to them.

3.5 Rome
Expands

The geographic location of Rome made it the perfect place to begin building a Mediterranean empire. By 146 B.C., Rome had proved this point at the expense of its conquered neighbors. Its navy ruled the seas, its army dominated the land, and many once-great countries were now run by a Roman governor.

MAIN IDEA

Between 264 and 146 B.C., Rome's armies conquered a vast amount of land stretching from the Iberian Peninsula to Greece.

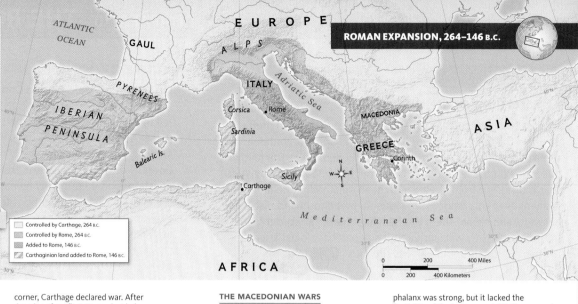

ROMAN EXPANSION, 264–146 B.C.

Controlled by Carthage, 264 B.C.
Controlled by Rome, 264 B.C.
Added to Rome, 146 B.C.
Carthaginian land added to Rome, 146 B.C.

The Catapult

The catapult was one of the Roman army's most effective weapons. It was capable of launching 60-pound rocks, long wooden beams, and even vats of fire. This powerful war machine relied on a system of tension and release to hurl missiles 500 to 1,000 feet across battlefields.

THE THIRD PUNIC WAR

After the Second Punic War, Carthage focused on trade and began to grow very rich. This worried the Romans, who were still suspicious of their old enemy. The famous Roman statesman Cato the Elder visited Carthage and was alarmed by its wealth, which he believed would be used to fight Rome. Cato shared his fears with the Senate in a unique way. Whenever he spoke, whatever the subject, he always ended with the dramatic exclamation "*Carthago delenda est*" ("Carthage must be destroyed").

Roman leaders eventually ordered the city of Carthage to be abandoned. Bullied into a corner, Carthage declared war. After decades of conflict, Rome decided that only the total destruction of its old enemy would do.

In 149 B.C., Rome laid siege to Carthage, surrounding it and stopping its food supply. Roman soldiers battered the city with huge rocks hurled from catapults and then stormed its shattered walls. The starving defenders fought bravely, but the Romans' victory was inevitable—and their revenge was merciless. The Romans sold Carthaginian survivors as slaves and destroyed every building. Carthage ceased to exist. Carthage and its adjoining lands were renamed the Roman **province** of Africa. The Iberian Peninsula, which Carthage had controlled, eventually became the Roman province of Hispania.

THE MACEDONIAN WARS

While Hannibal was rampaging through Italy in the Second Punic War, Philip V of Macedonia launched the First Macedonian War against Rome. Because Rome's army was focused on Hannibal, Rome could not fight against Macedonia and was forced to make peace. However, after Hannibal's defeat, two legions of battle-hardened Roman warriors invaded Macedonia, starting the Second Macedonian War.

The legions were pitched against the Macedonian phalanx, a solid body of troops bristling with long spears. The phalanx was strong, but it lacked the flexibility of the legion—and this flaw proved decisive. Once past the spears, fresh Roman reserves would fight ferociously until they destroyed the enemy army. These tactics defeated Philip's army in 197 B.C., ending the war. Macedonia later became a Roman province. Rome also destroyed the city of Corinth and conquered Greece, turning it into a Roman province in 146 B.C.

Roman power now extended from the Iberian Peninsula to the islands of Greece. Control of this vast area made Rome the new superpower of the ancient world.

REVIEW & ASSESS

1. **READING CHECK** In what order did the events of the Punic and Macedonian wars occur?

2. **INTERPRET MAPS** How did the defeat of Philip of Macedonia help Rome dominate the Mediterranean?

3. **ANALYZE LANGUAGE USE** How does Cato's exclamation about Carthage convey the Romans' fear of their enemy?

PLAN

OBJECTIVE

Explain the causes and impact of the Third Punic War and the Macedonian Wars on the Roman Republic.

CRITICAL THINKING SKILLS FOR LESSON 3.5

- Identify Main Ideas and Details
- Monitor Comprehension
- Interpret Maps
- Analyze Language Use
- Sequence
- Synthesize

ESSENTIAL QUESTION

How did Rome become a mighty power in the Mediterranean?

Through victories over Carthage and Macedonia, the Roman Republic tripled in size. Lesson 3.5 describes the events of the Third Punic War and the First and Second Macedonian Wars.

BACKGROUND FOR THE TEACHER

Beginning around 700 B.C., early Macedonia was populated by a group with unknown ethnic origins who called themselves Macedonians. Between 500 and 400 B.C., the Macedonians formed a unified empire and began speaking Greek. Under the rule of Alexander III, or Alexander the Great, Macedonia expanded its empire into Asia and up to the Nile and Indus rivers, conquering the Persian Empire. This made Macedonia the world's largest empire—even larger than the Roman Republic—spanning lands from Europe to North Africa and India.

DIGITAL RESOURCES myNGconnect.com

TEACHER RESOURCES & ASSESSMENT

 Reading and Note-Taking

 Vocabulary Practice

 Section 3 Quiz

STUDENT RESOURCES

 NG Chapter Gallery

COMPARE MAPS

Show students a current map of the Mediterranean region. Ask them to review the countries that border the Mediterranean Sea and nearby Atlantic Ocean. Remind them that while the physical features of this region have remained largely the same, the region has been organized into empires, republics, territories, and countries and controlled by many different groups in different ways throughout history. Next, preview the map in Lesson 3.5. Invite students to share observations about the names of the different regions during the time of Roman expansion. Finally, study the map key and draw students' attention to how the land changed hands during the period of Roman expansion. **0:10** minutes

TEACH

GUIDED DISCUSSION

1. **Sequence** How did Rome manage to destroy Carthage completely? (*First, Roman soldiers surrounded Carthage and stopped its food supply. Then the soldiers used catapults to batter the city and shatter its walls. The Romans fought the Carthaginians and sold any survivors as slaves. Finally, the Romans tore down all of the Carthaginian buildings and renamed Carthage the Roman province of Africa.*)

2. **Synthesize** How was the defeat of the Macedonians during the Second Macedonian War a victory for the Romans in many different ways? (*Defeating the Macedonians was a military victory for the Romans because they were able to overpower the Macedonian phalanx by recognizing its lack of flexibility. It was a geographic victory for the Romans because they gained Macedonia and Greece as Roman provinces and destroyed the city of Corinth. And it was a victory for the Roman Republic because it was transformed into the new superpower of the world.*)

INTERPRET MAPS

Have students examine the Roman Expansion, 264–146 B.C. map. Help students interpret the map. Explain and discuss the color-coded map legend. **ASK:** Which land was controlled by Rome originally, and where was this land located? (*Students should point to Italy.*) What does the purple color represent on the map? (*land that was added to Rome in 146 B.C.*) Who held most of the islands in this region prior to 146 B.C.? (*Carthage*) What were the largest areas of land that the Romans acquired in 146 B.C.? (*most of the Iberian Peninsula, Greece, Macedonia, and north into the Alps*) **0:15** minutes

ACTIVE OPTIONS

On Your Feet: Simulate a Battle Guide students to use plastic figures (such as army men) to simulate the invasion of Macedonia by Roman warriors at the beginning of the Second Macedonian War. Use one type or color of figures to represent the Roman legions and another type or color to represent the Macedonian phalanx. Help

students simulate the strategic positioning and movement of each army, demonstrating how the phalanx was strong but less flexible than the legion. Once past the phalanx, simulate the defeat of the Macedonian army by the Roman legion. **0:10** minutes

NG Learning Framework: Geography and History

ATTITUDES: **Curiosity, Responsibility**
SKILLS: **Collaboration, Problem-Solving**
KNOWLEDGE: **Our Living Planet**

Have students review Lessons 3.3, 3.4, and 3.5 and examine the relationships between geography and history. Then ask them to work in groups of five to select a topic, research, and produce a visual representation of the relationship between geography and history. Examples might be: a diorama of Hannibal crossing the Alps, a drawing of soldiers using rivers for transport, or a map positioning catapults around Carthage. **0:10** minutes

ENGLISH LANGUAGE LEARNERS

Use a Term in a Sentence To demonstrate their understanding of the terms *province*, *phalanx*, and *catapult*, have students write two sentences using each word appropriately, and draw a picture to go with each word. If needed, show students photographs or illustrations to help them visualize the phalanx and the catapult.

PRE-AP

Build a Catapult Place students in groups and tell them they will be designing and building a simple catapult. First, have each group sketch how their catapult will look. Then discuss the simple supplies needed to build classroom catapults, such as popsicle sticks, paper cups, and string. After obtaining those supplies, allow students time to build their catapults and test them. Finally, organize a contest to see whose catapult can throw an object the farthest.

Press (**mt**) *in the Student eEdition for modified text.*

See the Chapter Planner for more strategies for differentiation.

ANSWERS

1. Hannibal invaded Italy. Meanwhile, Macedonia launched a war against Rome. Rome was forced to make peace with Macedonia. After Hannibal's defeat, Rome invaded Macedonia and defeated Philip's army. Rome ordered Carthage to be abandoned. Carthage declared war on Rome. Rome laid siege to Carthage and destroyed it. Rome destroyed Corinth and conquered Greece.

2. The defeat gave Rome control over more land along the Mediterranean.

3. It shows that the Romans still viewed Carthage as a serious threat to their republic.

The Republic in Crisis

Politics in Rome had often been crooked, selfish, and occasionally even violent. But after 133 B.C., the corruption and greed spiraled out of control and threatened the survival of the republic.

MAIN IDEA

The Roman Republic collapsed into civil war following a series of major events.

ATTEMPTS AT REFORM

Expansion following the Punic Wars brought great wealth to the Roman Republic, but this wealth was not evenly distributed among the people. Roman generals returned with great riches from the conquered territories. They used their new wealth to buy large areas of farmland, which drove many small farmers out of business. Unemployment and poverty became common in the republic, but the rich ignored the problems of the poor.

In 133 B.C., the tribune Tiberius Gracchus (ty-BIHR-ee-uhs GRA-kuhs) proposed a bill to take land from the rich and give it to the poor for farming. He knew the senators would reject his bill, so he had it approved by the plebeian assembly instead.

The Senate was furious at being bypassed. In response, members of the Senate arranged to assassinate, or murder, Tiberius. Ten years later his brother, Gaius (GAY-uhs) Gracchus, tried to introduce **reforms**, or changes to make things better, in the Senate. He, too, was assassinated.

In 107 B.C., the people elected the army general Marius as consul. As you have learned, he allowed landless citizens to join the army. When these soldiers retired, they relied on the generosity of their generals to support them, which made them more loyal to their commanders than to the state.

BATTLES FOR CONTROL

Marius's reforms did not help him when a general named Sulla rose up against him. Sulla was a brilliant general with political ambitions of his own. He marched his army into Rome, starting a **civil war**, or war between groups in the same country, and took control of the Senate. Marius fled, and Sulla set himself up as dictator of Rome. He created a list of his enemies and had many of them killed.

When Sulla left Rome to fight in the east, Marius led his army into Rome and attacked Sulla's supporters. Sulla invaded Rome a second time and regained control. By 81 B.C., he was declared dictator once again.

In the following decades, crises arose that forced the Senate to give extraordinary powers to two generals named Pompey (PAHM-pee) and Crassus. You have read about the slave rebellion that spread throughout the republic in 73 B.C. Pompey and Crassus combined their two large armies to put down the rebellion.

By 63 B.C., the republic was in chaos, and the consul Cicero argued strongly for reducing the powers of the army and restoring the government's system of checks and balances. However, his words failed to persuade Rome's leaders.

FACTORS THAT WEAKENED THE REPUBLIC

- Greed of the rich
- Inequality between rich and poor
- Failed reforms
- Ambitious generals and powerful armies
- Soldiers' shifting loyalty to their generals
- Civil war

Critical Viewing Sulla, shown here on horseback, never lost a battle. What qualities of a successful general are conveyed in this painting?

+ POSSIBLE RESPONSE

His men are gathered around him, which shows that they like and respect him. It also appears that he and his horse are unharmed, which indicates that he is a successful warrior.

REVIEW & ASSESS

1. **READING CHECK** What happened when Marius and Sulla fought over Rome?

2. **IDENTIFY MAIN IDEAS AND DETAILS** What problems led to civil war in Rome?

3. **FORM OPINIONS** Could Roman leaders have helped the republic survive? Why or why not?

PLAN

OBJECTIVE

Explain the factors that weakened the Roman Republic during the transition from republic to empire.

CRITICAL THINKING SKILLS FOR LESSON 4.1

- Identify Main Ideas and Details
- Monitor Comprehension
- Form Opinions
- Identify Problems and Solutions
- Make Inferences
- Analyze Cause and Effect

ESSENTIAL QUESTION

How did Rome become a mighty power in the Mediterranean?

A series of major events led to civil war as the republic began to fall apart. Lesson 4.1 describes these events and explains how they set the stage for the emergence of a strong leader.

BACKGROUND FOR THE TEACHER

Historically, dictators don't have a great reputation, and the verdict is still out among historians on whether Sulla helped or hurt the Roman Republic. As dictator of Rome from 81 to 79 B.C., Sulla held complete power over the Roman military, people, judiciary, and legislature. However, Sulla did use his considerable power to reform and reorganize the republic, restore power to the Senate, and increase the number of courts for criminal trials. He also instituted new laws against treason and for the protection of citizens.

DIGITAL RESOURCES myNGconnect.com

TEACHER RESOURCES & ASSESSMENT

 Reading and Note-Taking

 Vocabulary Practice

 Section 4 Quiz

STUDENT RESOURCES

 NG Chapter Gallery

INTRODUCE & ENGAGE

K-W-L CHART

Have students brainstorm the names of famous dictators and write them on the whiteboard. (Adolf Hitler, Josef Stalin, Saddam Hussein, and Kim Jung Un are possible examples.) Provide students with a K-W-L Chart. Have students think about what they know about dictators. Then ask them to write questions that they would like to have answered as they study the lesson. Allow time at the end of the lesson for students to fill in what they have learned.
`0:10` minutes

TEACH

GUIDED DISCUSSION

1. **Identify Problems and Solutions** Which problem did Tiberius Gracchus try to address through his bill in 133 B.C.? *(Unemployment and poverty became common in the Roman Republic as wealthy Roman generals used their money to buy large areas of farmland, driving small farmers out of business.)*

2. **Make Inferences** While the Roman Republic was in crisis, it was controlled by powerful generals such as Sulla, Pompey, and Crassus. How might having military leaders in control of the republic benefitted Rome? How might it have been damaging? *(Having powerful military leaders would have been helpful during battles and conflicts against other civilizations. However, having generals with so much control also weakened the republic because power was unbalanced and the army was too strong.)*

ANALYZE CAUSE AND EFFECT

This lesson presents opportunities to discuss numerous cause and effect relationships that played a role in the crisis in the Roman Republic. Have students copy the chart and work in pairs to identify and write effects. Ask for volunteers to share their results.
`0:15` minutes

Cause	Effect
Rich generals bought up farmland.	Many small farmers were driven out of business.
Tiberius and Gaius Gracchus tried to introduce reform in the Senate.	They angered the senators and were assassinated.
Retired soldiers had to rely on the generosity of their generals after they retired.	They were loyal to their generals instead of to the state.
Sulla marched his army into Rome.	Civil war began between followers of Marius and followers of Sulla.

ACTIVE OPTIONS

On Your Feet: Jigsaw Divide the class into six groups. Assign each group one of the factors that weakened the Roman Republic:

- Greed of the rich and inequality of the poor
- Failed reforms
- Ambitious generals and powerful armies
- Soldiers' shifting loyalty to their generals
- Civil war

Have each group study their assigned factor and become "experts" on it. Then regroup students so that each new group contains at least one expert from the original groups. As a whole, each new group should discuss the six factors with each group member reporting on their area of expertise. `0:15` minutes

NG Learning Framework: Research Civil Wars

ATTITUDES: Curiosity, Responsibility
SKILLS: Collaboration, Communication

Have students work in groups to research the term *civil war* and do research on another example of a civil war, its causes, timeframe, and outcomes. Have the groups present their findings to the rest of the class. After the presentations, ask the class what similarities they noticed between the civil wars that were discussed.
`0:30` minutes

DIFFERENTIATE

INCLUSION

Match Key Dates and Events Write the key dates and events presented in this lesson on separate note cards. Pair special-needs students with students of a higher proficiency level or with a teacher's aide to reread the passage aloud. Then have students match dates and events and arrange them in chronological order.

Press (**mt**) *in the Student eEdition for modified text.*

See the Chapter Planner for more strategies for differentiation.

REVIEW & ASSESS

ANSWERS

1. A civil war broke out.

2. Problems that led to civil war include an unequal distribution of wealth and the ambition of the generals Marius and Sulla.

3. Possible response: Yes, a strong leader who put the interests of the republic and the people ahead of his own ambition might have been able to provide the leadership necessary to reunite the republic.

GAIUS JULIUS CAESAR
100 B.C. – 44 B.C.

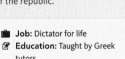

Julius Caesar is by far the most famous Roman. He overcame obstacles to success with his military brilliance, political cunning, and amazing speeches. When his power-sharing triumvirate collapsed, he led his army into Rome and was voted dictator for life by the frightened Senate. Caesar's rule marked the end of the republic.

- 💼 **Job:** Dictator for life
- 📓 **Education:** Taught by Greek tutors
- 🌐 **Home:** Rome

FINEST HOUR
His conquest of Gaul was his most impressive military achievement.

WORST MOMENT
His enemies finally won when dozens of them joined in stabbing him to death.

FRIENDS

‹ Cleopatra VII, Queen of Egypt
- Commoners of Rome
- Veteran soldiers

TRIVIA
His most noted connection was with Egypt's last queen, Cleopatra VII. Both a love affair and a political alliance, their relationship was short lived. It began in 48 B.C. and ended with Caesar's assassination in 44 B.C.

Many movies and television series have focused on the life of Julius Caesar. Here, actor Ciarán Hinds portrays Caesar in the 2005 television series *Rome.*

THE FIRST TRIUMVIRATE

Generals Crassus and Pompey were elected consuls in 70 B.C. However, they soon made themselves unpopular with the Senate by seizing much of its power for themselves. As a result, the Senate turned to a rising political star, **Julius Caesar**.

Caesar had already proved himself as a politician and general. Pompey and Crassus used their influence to have him elected consul. In return, Caesar persuaded the Senate to pass Pompey and Crassus' legislation. This political alliance became known as the **First Triumvirate** (try-UHM-vuh-ruht)—a sharing of power between three people. The triumvirate lasted for about seven years but was always an uneasy alliance full of suspicions and jealousies.

The triumvirate granted Caesar a huge army, which he used to conquer Gaul (present-day France). This conquest extended Roman territory north and made Caesar very popular with the people. He also won immense wealth and the fierce loyalty of his soldiers.

END OF THE REPUBLIC

In 53 B.C., Crassus died, and the triumvirate collapsed. Law and order in Rome broke down. To end the chaos, the Senate appointed Pompey sole consul. This, however, resulted in a power struggle between Caesar in Gaul and Pompey in Rome. To regain control, Caesar led his army into Rome, sparking a bloody civil war. In August 48 B.C., Caesar defeated Pompey and declared victory.

Many Romans expected Caesar to restore the republic, but he had other ideas. Backed by his army, he ruled alone. Caesar declared himself dictator for life and introduced reforms that were popular with the people, such as creating jobs for the poor. But the Senate hated his reforms. On March 15, 44 B.C., a group of senators assassinated Caesar.

Another civil war followed Caesar's death. Fourteen years later, the Roman Republic transformed into a monarchy and, ultimately, an empire.

Et tu, and tu, and tu, and tu, and tu?

Julius Caesar was assassinated by about 60 senators under a statue of his old enemy Pompey. According to legend, as Caesar died, he cried out to a man who he had thought was his friend, *"Et tu, Brute?"* ("And you, Brutus?")

REVIEW & ASSESS

1. **READING CHECK** What were Caesar's major successes and failures?
2. **SUMMARIZE** Why was Caesar assassinated, and what happened after he was killed?
3. **COMPARE AND CONTRAST** How does Caesar's career as a general compare with his role as a leader?

PLAN

OBJECTIVE
Analyze the impact that Julius Caesar had on the Roman Republic and summarize his key achievements.

CRITICAL THINKING SKILLS FOR LESSON 4.2
- Identify Main Ideas and Details
- Monitor Comprehension
- Summarize
- Compare and Contrast
- Analyze Cause and Effect
- Form and Support Opinions

ESSENTIAL QUESTION
How did Rome become a mighty power in the Mediterranean?

The rise of Julius Caesar transformed Rome forever. Lesson 4.2 provides an overview of Caesar's accomplishments and explains how his assassination affected the republic.

BACKGROUND FOR THE TEACHER
Caesar's military victories and legislative reforms gained him admiration from his soldiers and appreciation from the Roman people, but he was not necessarily a beloved ruler. In spite of the surprising generosity Caesar showed toward the opponents he defeated in war, they still disliked him. In fact, his own Senate may have killed him in part because of his generosity toward the people he conquered. Caesar successfully instituted many reforms to benefit his people, at the risk of angering the Senate.

DIGITAL RESOURCES myNGconnect.com

TEACHER RESOURCES & ASSESSMENT

 Reading and Note-Taking   **Vocabulary Practice**   **Section 4 Quiz**

STUDENT RESOURCES

 Biography

INTRODUCE & ENGAGE

IDENTIFY CHARACTERISTICS

As a class, work to brainstorm a list of characteristics of powerful, successful leaders. Have students record their characteristics on sticky notes and post them on the classroom wall. Some examples may include: *respectable, intelligent, experienced, sympathetic, fair.* Tell students they will add to and/or modify this list as they read about Julius Caesar, one of the world's most famous leaders. **0:10** minutes

TEACH

GUIDED DISCUSSION

1. **Analyze Cause and Effect** What were the effects of Caesar's conquest of Gaul? *(Rome's territory was extended north. Caesar became very popular with the people, and very wealthy. Caesar also secured the loyalty of his soldiers because of this victory.)*

2. **Compare and Contrast** Compare the Roman leaders Sulla and Caesar. How were they alike? How were they different? *(Sulla and Caesar were both self-appointed Roman dictators and legendary military leaders. They both came into power due to civil wars in Rome. They are different because Sulla rose up against the current consul, Marius, and Caesar instead formed a political alliance with the consuls, creating the First Triumvirate. Sulla had many of his enemies killed, but Caesar befriended the Roman people.)*

FORM AND SUPPORT OPINIONS

Pose the following question to students: There's no doubt that Caesar was one of the world's most famous leaders, but was he a great leader? Give students a few minutes to think about this question and jot down notes to support their opinion. Then form small groups and invite students to present and support their opinions. You may wish to form groups that contain students who have different views on Caesar's greatness. **0:15** minutes

ACTIVE OPTIONS

On Your Feet: Create a Poster Encourage students to use their knowledge from the lesson to create a poster featuring Julius Caesar. They should focus on what they have learned about the ruler and his accomplishments, and should include a drawing of, or related to, Caesar. Before starting on the poster, students should plan out the content and do a rough sketch, asking themselves: what are the most important things to know about Julius Caesar? **0:20** minutes

NG Learning Framework: Imagine You Were Caesar

ATTITUDE: **Empowerment**
SKILL: **Problem-Solving**

Invite students to revisit the biography of Julius Caesar in Lesson 4.2 and imagine they were in Caesar's place. **ASK:** How would you have done things differently from Caesar? How do you feel these changes would have affected both Rome and your life? **0:10** minutes

DIFFERENTIATE

STRIVING READERS

Identify Main Ideas and Details Remind students that a main idea is a statement that summarizes the key idea of an article, speech, or paragraph. Details are facts, dates, events, and descriptions that support a main idea. Ask students to write one main idea and three or four details for the segment "The First Triumvirate."

Main Idea: The First Triumvirate was a sharing of power between three people: Caesar, Pompey, and Crassus.
Detail: The triumvirate lasted 7 years.
Detail: The three rulers were always suspicious of each other.
Detail: The triumvirate gave Caesar a huge army that he used to conquer Gaul.
Detail: The triumvirate ended when Crassus died.

GIFTED & TALENTED

Write a Biography Have students review the information about Julius Caesar presented in the text. Then instruct them to work in pairs to write a short biography of Caesar. Finally, have them do online research to find additional visuals to pair with their biography.

Press (**mt**) *in the Student eEdition for modified text.*

See the Chapter Planner for more strategies for differentiation.

REVIEW & ASSESS

ANSWERS

1. Major successes include conquering Gaul, beating Pompey in civil war, and introducing popular reforms. Major failures include angering the Senate, not restoring the republic, and getting assassinated.

2. He was assassinated because the Senate hated the reforms he introduced as dictator. After he was killed, civil war broke out.

3. He was a better general in that he was victorious and popular in that role; the same could not be said of him as a leader.

DOCUMENT-BASED QUESTION

The Assassination of
Julius Caesar

Caesar's assassination commanded much attention right after his death—and for many centuries after that. The ancient Romans commemorated, or remembered, the date with special coins. Historians who lived in later years tried to describe Caesar's death, and playwrights dramatized the event. We may never know all the details of his death, but the story and fate of a leader who became too hungry for power still fascinates us.

+ ANSWERS

DOCUMENT 1
Roman leaders wanted people to remember the fate of Julius Caesar when they saw the commemorative coin.

DOCUMENT 2
The violence of Caesar's death shows that the liberators heartily disliked Caesar.

DOCUMENT 3
According to Mark Antony, Caesar was assassinated because of his ambition.

Critical Viewing The woman fainting in the painting is a soothsayer, or a fortune-teller, warning Caesar not to go to the Senate. What elements of this painting forewarn of a terrible event?

Julius ... , c. 1850

+ POSSIBLE RESPONSE
The ominous sky and the fainting woman hanging onto Caesar's clothing are details that forewarn of a terrible event.

DOCUMENT ONE   Primary Source: Artifact

Silver Denarius of Marcus Junius Brutus, Macedonia, 43–42 B.C.
This commemorative coin, called a denarius, shows the profile of Marcus Brutus, Caesar's former friend and assassin. The reverse features two daggers and a "cap of liberty." Underneath are the words EID MAR, or Ides of March. In the Roman calendar, the ides referred to the day that fell in the middle of the month.

CONSTRUCTED RESPONSE What did Roman leaders want people to remember about Caesar when they saw the commemorative coin?

DOCUMENT TWO   Secondary Source: Biography

from *The Lives of the Twelve Caesars*, by Gaius Suetonius Tranquillus, translated by J.C. Rolfe
In Volume 1 of his biography, written in the second century A.D., Suetonius describes Caesar's assassination by a group of senators who called themselves "the liberators."

CONSTRUCTED RESPONSE What does the violence of Caesar's death tell about the liberators' view of Caesar?

> When he saw that he was beset [surrounded] on every side by drawn daggers, he muffled his head in his robe . . . with the lower part of his body also covered . . . [H]e was stabbed with three and twenty wounds, uttering not a word . . . All the conspirators made off, and he lay there lifeless.

DOCUMENT THREE   Secondary Source: Drama

from William Shakespeare's *Julius Caesar*
In this excerpt from Act 3, Scene 2 of Shakespeare's play *Julius Caesar*, written in 1599, Mark Antony, a Roman politician and general, speaks at Caesar's funeral.

CONSTRUCTED RESPONSE According to Mark Antony, why was Caesar assassinated?

> Friends, Romans, countrymen, lend me your ears;
> I come to bury Caesar, not to praise him.
> The evil that men do lives after them;
> The good is oft interred [buried] with their bones;
> So let it be with Caesar. The noble Brutus
> Hath told you Caesar was ambitious:
> If it were so, it was a grievous [serious] fault,
> And grievously hath Caesar answer'd it.

SYNTHESIZE & WRITE

1. **REVIEW** Review what you have learned about the Roman Republic, Julius Caesar, and Caesar's assassination.

2. **RECALL** On your own paper, write down the main idea expressed in each document and in the photograph of the coin.

3. **CONSTRUCT** Construct a topic sentence that answers this question: What do the Roman leaders' actions and words tell about their view of Caesar?

4. **WRITE** Using evidence from the documents, write a paragraph that supports your answer to the question in Step 3.

PLAN

OBJECTIVE
Synthesize information about the assassination of Julius Caesar from primary and secondary source documents.

CRITICAL THINKING SKILLS FOR LESSON 4.3
- Identify
- Draw Conclusions
- Describe
- Synthesize

ESSENTIAL QUESTION
How did Rome become a mighty power in the Mediterranean?

The assassination of Julius Caesar was a turning point in the history of ancient Rome as it moved from a republic to an empire. Lesson 4.3 provides several interpretations of this event from primary and secondary sources.

BACKGROUND FOR THE TEACHER
Shakespeare's play *Julius Caesar* was most likely written in 1599 and is one of the famous playwright's three "Roman plays," all of which take place in ancient Rome. *Julius Caesar* tells the story of the conspiracy against Caesar, the dictator's dramatic assassination, and the defeat of his murderers at the Battle of Philippi. Like many of Shakespeare's plays, *Julius Caesar* was written and performed many years before it was published.

DIGITAL RESOURCES myNGconnect.com

TEACHER RESOURCES & ASSESSMENT

 Reading and Note-Taking

 Vocabulary Practice

 Section 4 Quiz

STUDENT RESOURCES

 NG Chapter Gallery

PREPARE FOR THE DOCUMENT-BASED QUESTION

Before students start on the activity, briefly preview the three documents. Remind students that a constructed response requires full explanations in complete sentences. Emphasize that students should use their knowledge of Julius Caesar and ancient Roman history in addition to the information in the documents. **0:05** minutes

TEACH

GUIDED DISCUSSION

1. **Identify** What is shown on the silver denarius of Marcus Junius Brutus? *(A denarius is a commemorative coin. This one shows the profile of Caesar's friend and murderer, Marcus Brutus on one side, and two daggers, a hat called a "cap of liberty," and the words EID MAR, which means "Ides of March.")*

2. **Draw Conclusions** Can Shakespeare's play be considered a reliable source of historical information about Caesar's assassination? *(A play is a work of fiction, and fiction contains made-up characters, events, and information. Although Shakespeare's play may be about real people and real events, it is still fiction and cannot be considered a reliable source about an event in history. It is still useful, however, to read the play to see how Shakespeare and others interpreted Caesar's assassination.)*

3. **Describe** Which words would you use to describe Suetonius' retelling of Caesar's death? *(Responses will vary. Possible responses: dramatic, violent, scary, sad.)* **ASK:** Based on this excerpt from Suetonius' biography, who do you believe Suetonius sympathized with more: Caesar's assassins or Caesar himself? *(Responses will vary. Possible response: I believe Suetonius sympathized with Caesar more than the assassins. He draws attention to the brutality of the killing and makes you feel sorry for Caesar. At the end of the excerpt, he makes the conspirators sound very mean, sneaking off to let Caesar die alone.)*

PEER REVIEW

After students have completed the Synthesize & Write activity, allow time for them to exchange paragraphs and read and comment on the work of their peers. Guidelines for comments should be established prior to this activity so that feedback is constructive and encouraging in nature. **0:15** minutes

ACTIVE OPTIONS

On Your Feet: Three Options Label three locations in the room with the name of one of the documents featured in the lesson. Have students reread the lesson and walk to the corner of the room with the document that best helped support their understanding or further their interest in Julius Caesar's assassination. Have students who chose the same document discuss why they made their selection. Then have volunteers from each group explain what their document is, and offer some of the group's reasons for choosing that one. **0:20** minutes

NG Learning Framework: Write a Biography

ATTITUDE: **Curiosity**
KNOWLEDGE: **Our Human Story**

Have students select one of the people they are still curious about after learning about this individual in this chapter. Instruct them to write a short biography about this person using information from the chapter and additional source material. **0:10** minutes

INCLUSION

Work in Pairs Consider pairing students with disabilities with other students who can read the documents aloud to them. You may also want to give students the option of recording their responses.

PRE-AP

Research "Et tu, Brute" Ask students to research the famous phrase "Et tu, Brute" from Shakespeare's *Julius Caesar*. Encourage them to report on its meaning, context, and Shakespeare's controversial use of Latin, although it is likely that Caesar primarily spoke in Greek. Encourage students to consider and give examples of modern uses of this antiquated phrase.

Press **mt** *in the Student eEdition for modified text.*

See the Chapter Planner for more strategies for differentiation.

ANSWERS

1. Responses will vary.

2. Responses will vary.

3. Possible response: The actions and words of Roman leaders show that they did not have a good opinion of Julius Caesar.

4. Students' paragraphs should include their topic sentence from Step 3 and provide several details from the documents to support the sentence.

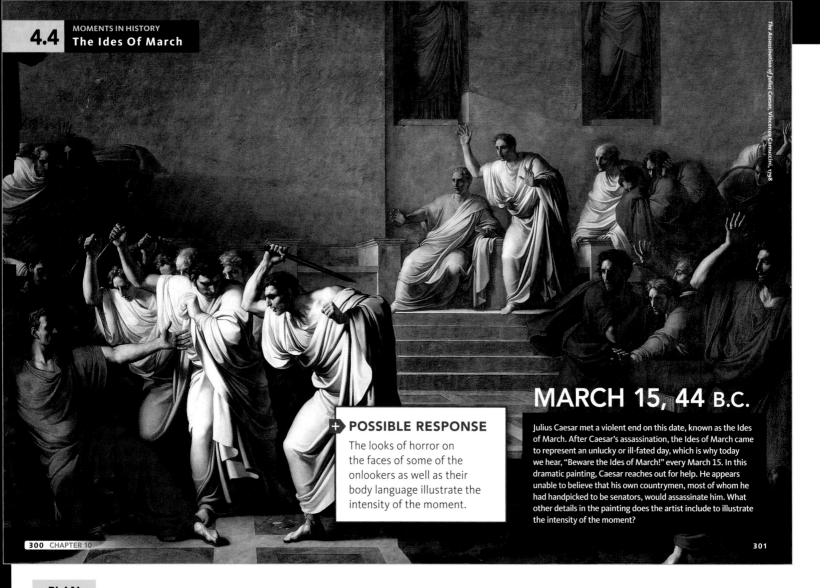

The Assassination of Julius Caesar, Vincenzo Camuccini, 1798

MARCH 15, 44 B.C.

Julius Caesar met a violent end on this date, known as the Ides of March. After Caesar's assassination, the Ides of March came to represent an unlucky or ill-fated day, which is why today we hear, "Beware the Ides of March!" every March 15. In this dramatic painting, Caesar reaches out for help. He appears unable to believe that his own countrymen, most of whom he had handpicked to be senators, would assassinate him. What other details in the painting does the artist include to illustrate the intensity of the moment?

➕ POSSIBLE RESPONSE
The looks of horror on the faces of some of the onlookers as well as their body language illustrate the intensity of the moment.

301

PLAN

OBJECTIVE
Determine the impact of Julius Caesar's assassination on the Roman Republic.

CRITICAL THINKING SKILLS FOR LESSON 4.4
- Analyze Visuals
- Make Connections

ESSENTIAL QUESTION
How did Rome become a mighty power in the Mediterranean?

While Julius Caesar was assassinated because he held too much power, his death ironically paved the way for the end of the republic and the beginning of imperial rule. Lesson 4.4 provides one artist's interpretation of the events of March 15, 44 B.C.

BACKGROUND FOR THE TEACHER
Before the murder of Julius Caesar on March 15, 44 B.C., the word *ides* was simply a term used to mark the full moon on the Roman calendar and not anything to be concerned about. After Caesar's assassination, however, the Ides of March took on a new meaning. It became a reference to a day that brings with it drastic change. For the Romans, that Ides of March completely reshaped their civilization.

DIGITAL RESOURCES myNGconnect.com

TEACHER RESOURCES & ASSESSMENT

 Reading and Note-Taking   **Vocabulary Practice**   **Section 4 Quiz**

STUDENT RESOURCES

 NG Chapter Gallery

ANALYZE DATES

Briefly explain the concept of the Ides of March and its relationship to the anniversary of the assassination of Julius Caesar. Discuss how March 15 still represents an unlucky or ill-fated day, or a day associated with great change. Ask student volunteers to identify other dates that have a negative or a positive connotation or special significance attached to them. Post these dates on the whiteboard. Examples may include being born on a Friday the 13th or a good luck day such as March 17th (Saint Patrick's Day). You may even wish to talk about lucky or unlucky numbers, and why people perceive them that way. `0:05` minutes

TEACH

GUIDED DISCUSSION

1. **Analyze Visuals** Examine Camuccini's painting of Caesar's assassination. What do the onlookers' reactions indicate about the conspiracy to assassinate Caesar? *(Responses will vary. Possible response: Some onlookers seem to be supportive of what is taking place. Some seem shocked and horrified, like they didn't know the murder was going to happen. One onlooker even has his head covered, which might suggest that he is either terrified or feels guilty about what is happening, and therefore doesn't want to watch.)*

2. **Make Connections** Caesar's assassination on the Ides of March in 44 B.C. marked the start of the transition from the Roman Republic to the Roman Empire. What other examples of events can you think of that led to a new era or other type of significant change or reform. *(Responses will vary. Possible responses: The attacks on the World Trade Center on September 11, 2001, led to an era of heightened security and an escalated war on terrorism. Columbus's discovery of the New World began an era of conquest and exploration that led to the creation of the United States of America.)* `0:10` minutes

MORE INFORMATION

The Roman Calendar The first Roman calendar was based on the Greek lunar calendar. It had only 10 months and a year of 304 days and included terms like *Kalends* (new moon), *Nones* (first quarter moon), and *Ides* (full moon). This calendar was revised to add two months: January and February. In 46 B.C., Caesar again revised the calendar, creating a new system of dates called the Julian calendar. The Julian calendar had a 365-day year divided into 12 months of 30 or 31 days, with the exception of the shorter month of February. Interestingly, the Julian calendar wasn't completely adopted until 8 A.D., long after Caesar's assassination. The Ides remained the same as on the Roman calendar.

ACTIVE OPTIONS

On Your Feet: I See, I Read, And So On a large sheet of chart paper or a whiteboard, create a chart like the one pictured below. As a group, reexamine the painting of Caesar's assassination. Have volunteers describe something they observe in the painting and something they have read to draw conclusions about the assassination of Julius Caesar. Record their observations on the chart. `0:15` minutes

I See	I Read	And So

Critical Viewing: NG Image Gallery Invite students to explore the entire NG Image Gallery and look for other images of historical events. Have them choose one and write a paragraph that compares and contrasts it with Pujol's depiction of the Ides of March. `0:10` minutes

STRIVING READERS

Analyze Visuals Provide concrete questions to help students of different ability levels process and interpret the painting.

ASK: Which figure represents Julius Caesar in the painting? Do all of the senators shown in the painting appear to be part of the plot to assassinate him? If no, which ones do and which ones do not? How can you tell? Pick one of the men in the painting and describe how you believe he is reacting to the attack on Caesar. Encourage students to point to things they don't understand about the painting and help them frame questions about these details.

GIFTED & TALENTED

Act Out a Scene As a group, read Act 1, Scene 2 of William Shakespeare's play, *Julius Caesar*, which contains the famous soothsayer's line about the Ides of March. Discuss the characters, setting, and any unfamiliar words or phrases. Then have volunteers do a dramatic reading of the scene.

Press (**mt**) *in the Student eEdition for modified text.*

See the Chapter Planner for more strategies for differentiation.

10 Review

VOCABULARY

For each pair of vocabulary words, write one sentence that explains the connection between the two words.

1. **patrician; plebeian**
   At first wealthy patricians held much of the power, but over time the plebeians, who made up most of Rome's citizens, could also hold office.

2. **consul; veto**

3. **republic; tribune**

4. **aristocracy; patrician**

5. **plebeian; tribune**

6. **consul; dictator**

7. **legionary; province**

8. **civil war; reform**

READING STRATEGY

9. **ORGANIZE IDEAS: COMPARE AND CONTRAST** If you haven't already, complete your Venn diagram to compare and contrast the lives of rich people and poor people in the Roman Republic. Then answer the question.

Rich People   Poor People

called patricians   called plebeians

How did the lives of the rich and poor differ in the Roman Republic? Did they share any similarities?

MAIN IDEAS

Answer the following questions. Support your answers with evidence from the chapter.

10. What geographic advantages helped Rome grow into a city? LESSON 1.1

11. How did different cultures help transform Rome from a small village into a city? LESSON 1.2

12. What was the purpose of the Twelve Tables? LESSON 1.3

13. What was the role of men in Rome's patriarchal society? LESSON 2.1

14. Why were slaves important to the Roman economy? LESSON 2.2

15. What factors made the Roman army successful? LESSON 3.1

16. What did Rome gain from its battles with Carthage during the Punic Wars? LESSON 3.3

17. What was the First Triumvirate? LESSON 4.2

CRITICAL THINKING

Answer the following questions. Support your answers with evidence from the chapter.

18. **MAKE INFERENCES** Based on what you've learned about ancient Rome, what factors helped the republic develop into a mighty power?

19. **DRAW CONCLUSIONS** Why did the Romans replace the position of king with two consuls and give each the right to veto?

20. **COMPARE AND CONTRAST** How did the lives of the rich and poor differ in the Roman Republic?

21. **IDENTIFY MAIN IDEAS AND DETAILS** What details in the chapter support the idea that the Roman Senate had a great deal of power?

22. **YOU DECIDE** Was Julius Caesar a great leader? Was he a dictator who abused his power? Did he fall somewhere in between? Support your opinion with evidence from the chapter.

INTERPRET CHARTS

Study the chart comparing the governments of the Roman Republic and the United States. Then answer the questions that follow.

GOVERNMENT	ROMAN REPUBLIC	UNITED STATES
Executive Branch	Led by two consuls elected for a one-year term; led government and army	Led by a president elected for a four-year term; heads government and military
Legislative Branch	• Senate of 300 members • Senate advised consuls and set policies • Two assemblies made laws and selected officials	• Senate of 100 members • House of Representatives of 435 members • Laws approved by both groups
Judicial Branch	• Eight judges oversaw courts and governed provinces	• Supreme Court of nine justices • Supreme Court interprets the Constitution and federal law
Legal Code	• Twelve Tables basis of Roman law • Twelve Tables established laws protecting citizens' rights	• U.S. Constitution basis of U.S. law • Constitution established individual rights of citizens and powers of government

23. In what ways are the branches of each government similar?

24. What do the legal codes of each government protect?

ANALYZE SOURCES

Read the following translation from one of the Twelve Tables. Then answer the question.

> TABLE VII: Rights Concerning Land
>
> The width of a road extends to 8 feet where it runs straight ahead, 16 round a bend . . .
>
> Persons shall mend roadways. If they do not keep them laid with stone, a person may drive his beasts where he wishes . . .
>
> Should a tree on a neighbor's farm be bent crooked by a wind and lean over your farm, action may be taken for removal of that tree.
>
> It is permitted to gather up fruit falling down on another man's farm.

25. Why do you think the Romans included so much detail in the laws of the Twelve Tables?

WRITE ABOUT HISTORY

26. **ARGUMENT** What arguments might a senator favoring Julius Caesar's assassination make? What arguments might a senator opposing his assassination make? Create an outline that lists points supporting each side.

TIPS

• Take notes from the chapter about Caesar's actions as a ruler and the manner of his death.

• Consider who benefited from Caesar's reforms and who benefited from his death.

• Consider how the Romans might have felt when Caesar declared himself dictator for life.

• Use vocabulary from the chapter in your outline.

• List the points that support assassination in the first part of your outline. List the points that support opposition to the assassination in the second part.

VOCABULARY ANSWERS

1. At first, wealthy patricians held much of the power, but over time the plebeians, who made up most of Rome's citizens, could also hold office.

2. In order to preserve a balance of power, Roman consuls had the right to veto each other's decisions.

3. Because Rome was a republic, citizens were allowed to elect their own leaders, such as the tribunes.

4. The Roman aristocracy was made up of wealthy patricians who owned most of the land.

5. The plebeians elected tribunes to represent them in government.

6. In times of crisis, Romans replaced the two consuls with a dictator who had complete control.

7. Roman legionaries fought to take control of land that would become a Roman province.

8. In the later years of the republic, attempts at reform backfired and led to civil war.

READING STRATEGY ANSWER

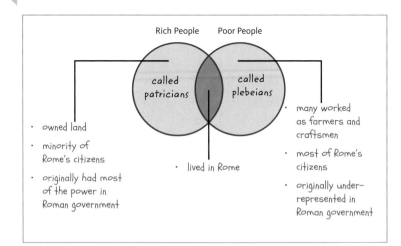

Rich People   Poor People

called patricians   called plebeians

• owned land
• minority of Rome's citizens
• originally had most of the power in Roman government

• lived in Rome

• many worked as farmers and craftsmen
• most of Rome's citizens
• originally under-represented in Roman government

9. Aside from the fact that they both lived in Rome, the lives of rich people and poor people varied greatly. The rich lived in fine houses and did a great deal of entertaining. They tended to be educated, and most of them were landowners. Rich people, or

patricians, had a lot of control over Rome's original government, but there were fewer of them than poor people. The poor, or plebians, lived in small, simple homes and were mainly farmers and craftsmen. They were not likely to be educated, and although there were more plebians than patricians, plebians had little to do with Rome's original government.

MAIN IDEAS ANSWERS

10. Rome's strategic location on the Tiber River near the Mediterranean Sea gave it access to valuable inland commercial routes and sea trade. The seven hills on which Rome was built protected it from enemies. The surrounding land supplied fertile soil, a good water supply, and a mild climate that could support Rome's population.

11. Foreigners from many different places, classes, and professions settled in Rome, which helped the city grow in size and strength. Rome was most influenced by the Greeks and Etruscans. The Etruscans, who were expert engineers, transformed the village of Rome into a city by building streets laid out in a grid plan, brick houses, temples, and public buildings.

12. The laws stated in the Twelve Tables protected all Roman citizens from injustice. The plebeians insisted that these laws be written down because the patricians often interpreted Rome's laws to favor their wealthy friends.

13. In Rome's patriarchal society, men held all the power in public life as well as private life. Only men could vote or hold public office. The senior male was the head of every family, and he made all the decisions.

14. Since slaves worked as manual laborers, skilled craftsmen, and even teachers and doctors, they were crucial to the Roman economy. In addition to their many abilities, slaves were also the largest class in Rome, but they had the fewest rights and worked entirely at the will of their masters.

15. The Roman army was well organized and trained. Soldiers were organized into legions for maximum strength and flexibility. The command structure gave Roman generals control over large numbers of men.

16. Rome gained total control of the Mediterranean and lands in northern Africa and Spain.

17. The First Triumvirate was a political alliance between Crassus, Pompey, and Caesar; the three men shared power for ten years, until the death of Crassus.

CRITICAL THINKING ANSWERS

18. A good geographic location, a multicultural population, a strong government with written laws, and a powerful army were all factors that helped the Roman Republic develop into a mighty power.

19. The Romans replaced the position of king with two consuls and gave each the right to veto because they wanted to prevent any one leader or branch of government from becoming too powerful.

20. The rich lived in luxurious country estates with slaves to serve them. They spent their free time conducting business, taking part in politics, or spending time on hobbies. The poor lived and worked on small farms or in overcrowded buildings in the city. They had to work for a living.

21. The Senate advised the consuls and gave public speeches about important issues. Also, the fact that the Senate was able to assassinate people it didn't agree with, such as the Gracchus brothers and Julius Caesar, shows that it had a great deal of power.

22. Students' responses will vary. Students should clearly state their opinion regarding their view of Julius Caesar and support that opinion with evidence from the chapter.

INTERPRET CHARTS ANSWERS

23. Similar to the government of the Roman Republic, the United States government is divided into three branches: executive, legislative, and judicial. Also, both governments put a system of checks and balances into place, assuring that one leader or branch of government wouldn't have too much power.

24. Similar to the Roman Republic's Twelve Tables, the United States has a written constitution. Both the Twelve Tables and the U.S. Constitution are the basis of law and establishment of citizens' rights.

ANALYZE SOURCES ANSWER

25. Students' responses will vary. Possible response: The Romans included so much detail in the rights so that they were clear to everyone and so no one could interpret them in a way that benefitted himself over others.

WRITE ABOUT HISTORY ANSWER

26. Students' outlines should
   - contain one claim for each side
   - support each claim with clear reasons and relevant evidence from the chapter
   - be written in a formal style
   - include vocabulary words from the chapter

UNIT 4 THE WORLD OF THE ROMANS

UNIT RESOURCES

On Location with National Geographic Grantee Steven Ellis
Intro and Video

Unit Wrap-Up:
"Exploring Pompeii"
Feature and Video

"Rethinking Nero"
National Geographic Adapted Article

"Roman Frontiers"
National Geographic Adapted Article
Student eEdition exclusive

Unit 4 Inquiry:
Build an Empire

 Interactive Map Tool
Available on myNGconnect

 **News & Updates**
Available on myNGconnect

CHAPTER RESOURCES

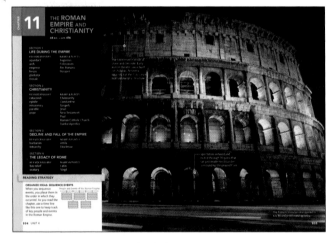

TEACHER RESOURCES & ASSESSMENT *Available on myNGconnect*

 Social Studies Skills Lessons
• Reading: Sequence Events
• Writing: Write an Explanation

 Chapter 11
Answer Key

 Formal Assessment
• Chapter 11 Tests A (on-level) &
  B (below-level)

 ExamView®
One-time Download

STUDENT BACKPACK *Available on myNGconnect*

• **eEdition** *(English)*   • **eEdition** *(Spanish)*   • **Handbooks**   • **Online Atlas**

For Chapter 11 Spanish resources, visit the Teacher Resource Menu page on myNGconnect.

SECTION 1 RESOURCES

LIFE DURING THE EMPIRE

 Reading and Note-Taking

 Vocabulary Practice

 Section 1 Quiz

Available on myNGconnect

**LESSON 1.1 AUGUSTUS
AND THE PAX ROMANA**
• On Your Feet: Numbered Heads

NG Learning Framework:
Evaluate Augustus' Reforms

**LESSON 1.2
GROWTH AND TRADE**
• On Your Feet: Fishbowl
• Critical Viewing: NG Chapter Gallery

**LESSON 1.3
ROMAN ENGINEERING**
• On Your Feet: Three Corners

NG Learning Framework:
Research and Compare

**LESSON 1.4
THE COLOSSEUM**
• On Your Feet: Three-Step Interview

NG Learning Framework:
Write a Brochure

**LESSON 1.5
VILLAS AND FRESCOES**
• On Your Feet: Build a Mosaic

NG Learning Framework:
Write a Travel Guide

LESSON 1.6 POMPEII
• On Your Feet: Card Responses
• Critical Viewing: NG Chapter Gallery

SECTION 2 RESOURCES

CHRISTIANITY

 Reading and Note-Taking

Vocabulary Practice

Section 2 Quiz

Available on myNGconnect

LESSON 2.1 THE ORIGINS OF CHRISTIANITY
- On Your Feet: Roundtable

| NG Learning Framework:
Write a Biography

LESSON 2.2 CHRISTIANITY SPREADS

Biography
Paul

Available on myNGconnect
- On Your Feet: Numbered Heads
- Critical Viewing: NG Chapter Gallery

DOCUMENT-BASED QUESTION
LESSON 2.3 NEW TESTAMENT LITERATURE
- On Your Feet: Think, Pair, Share

| NG Learning Framework:
Ask and Answer

LESSON 2.4 THE EARLY CHRISTIAN CHURCH
- On Your Feet: Research and Present

| NG Learning Framework:
Multimedia Presentation

SECTION 3 RESOURCES

DECLINE AND FALL OF THE EMPIRE

 Reading and Note-Taking

Vocabulary Practice

Section 3 Quiz

Available on myNGconnect

LESSON 3.1 THE THIRD CENTURY CRISIS
- On Your Feet: Four Corners

| NG Learning Framework:
Support an Argument

LESSON 3.2 EASTERN AND WESTERN ROMAN EMPIRES
- On Your Feet: Team Word Webbing
- Critical Viewing: NG Chapter Gallery

LESSON 3.3 END OF THE WESTERN ROMAN EMPIRE

Biography
Attila

Available on myNGconnect
- On Your Feet: Fishbowl

| NG Learning Framework:
Write a Speech

SECTION 4 RESOURCES

THE LEGACY OF ROME

 Reading and Note-Taking

Vocabulary Practice

Section 4 Quiz

Available on myNGconnect

LESSON 4.1 LATIN AND LITERATURE

Active History: Interactive Whiteboard Activity
Analyze the Roots of Modern Languages

Active History
Analyze the Roots of Modern Languages
Available on myNGconnect
- On Your Feet: Word Race

LESSON 4.2 ART, ARCHITECTURE, AND LAW
- On Your Feet: Legacy Debate

| NG Learning Framework:
Compare Observations

MOMENTS IN HISTORY
LESSON 4.3 THE ROMAN AQUEDUCT
- On Your Feet: True-False
- Critical Viewing: NG Chapter Gallery

CHAPTER 11 REVIEW

STRATEGY

Turn Titles into Questions

To help students set a purpose for reading, have them read the title of each lesson in a section and then turn that title into a question they believe will be answered in the lesson. Students can record their questions and write their own answers, or they can ask each other their questions.

Use with All Lessons *For example, in Lesson 1.1, the question could be, "Who was Augustus and what was the Pax Romana?"*

STRATEGY

Play Vocabulary Tic-Tac-Toe

Write nine Key Vocabulary words on a tic-tac-toe grid on the board. Position the words on the grid so that an X or O can be written below each word. Player A chooses a word. If the player correctly pronounces, defines, and uses the word in a sentence, he or she can put an X or O in that square. Play alternates until one person has a row of Xs or Os.

Use with All Lessons *This game can also be played using teams. Divide the class into two teams, Team A and Team B, and alternate play until one team has a row of Xs or Os.*

STRATEGY

Play the "I Am . . ." Game

To reinforce the meanings of key terms and names, assign every student one term or name that appears in the chapter and have them write a one-sentence clue beginning with "I am . . ." Have students take turns reading clues and calling on other students to guess answers.

Use with All Lessons

Press *in the Student eEdition for modified text.*

STRATEGY

Provide Terms and Names on Audio

Decide which of the terms and names are important for mastery and have a volunteer record the pronunciations and a short sentence defining each word. Encourage students to listen to the recording as often as necessary.

Use with All Lessons *You might also use the recordings to quiz students on their mastery of the terms. Play one definition at a time from the recording and ask students to identify the term or name described.*

STRATEGY ❷

Preview Content Using a Map

Use the following suggestions to preview content using a map:

- Point to the map key and discuss the ways it helps to explain the content shown on a map. Discuss that the different colors on the map represent different things.

- Remind students that they can identify continents and bodies of water by their labels on the map.

- Call out specific map features, such as rivers, mountain ranges, oceans, and countries, and ask students to point to them.

Use with Lessons 1.2, 2.2, and 3.2 *Invite volunteers to describe the visuals in detail to help visually impaired students see them.*

STRATEGY ❶

PREP Before Reading

Have students use the PREP strategy to prepare for reading. Write this acrostic on the board:

PREP　　　Preview title.

　　　　　　Read Main Idea statement.

　　　　　　Examine visuals.

　　　　　　Predict what you will learn.

Have students write their prediction and share it with a partner. After reading, ask students to write a sentence that begins with "I also learned . . ."

Use with All Lessons

STRATEGY 2
Pair Partners for Dictation

After students read each lesson in the chapter, have them write a sentence summarizing its main idea. Have students get together in pairs and dictate their sentences to each other. Then have them work together to check the sentences for accuracy and spelling.

Use with All Lessons *For Lessons 1.3, 4.1, 4.2, and 4.3, monitor students' comprehension of the legacy of Rome in language, literature, engineering, government, art, and architecture.*

STRATEGY 3
Use Visuals to Predict Content

Before reading, ask students to read the lesson title and look at any visuals. Then ask them to write a sentence that predicts how the visual is related to the lesson title. Repeat the exercise after reading and ask volunteers to read their sentences.

Use with All Lessons

GIFTED & TALENTED

STRATEGY 1
Teach a Class

Before beginning the chapter, allow students to choose one of the lessons listed below and prepare to teach the content to the class. Give them a set amount of time in which to present their lesson. Suggest that students think about any visuals or activities they want to use when they teach.

Use with Lessons 1.1, 1.2, 1.4, and 1.6

STRATEGY 2
Present a Museum Exhibit

Have groups of students prepare a museum exhibit featuring the ruins of Pompeii. Have them photocopy images of the ruins and write museum-style captions for each one. Once students have compiled their exhibits, have them place the images on the wall and present them to the class. Encourage students to introduce the exhibit with some background information about Pompeii. Tell them that they should also be prepared to answer any questions as their classmates view the exhibit.

Use with Lesson 1.6

PRE-AP

STRATEGY 1
Consider Multiple Sides

Tell students that historians have different opinions about why the Roman Empire came to an end. Have pairs of students research the issue and make a chart listing the different perspectives about the causes of the fall of the Roman Empire. Have students share and discuss their chart with the class.

Use with Lessons 3.1–3.3

STRATEGY 2
Debate Contributions

Have students research the many contributions of Rome to civilization. Tell each student to decide which contribution he or she believes had the greatest impact and make a list of the reasons why. Suggest that students hold a panel discussion to share and debate their decisions.

Use with Lessons 1.3, 1.4, 1.6, 2.4, and 4.1–4.3

THE ROMAN EMPIRE AND CHRISTIANITY

44 B.C. – A.D. 476

SECTION 1
LIFE DURING THE EMPIRE

KEY VOCABULARY
aqueduct
arch
emperor
fresco
gladiator
mosaic

NAMES & PLACES
Augustus
Colosseum
Pax Romana
Pompeii

SECTION 2
CHRISTIANITY

KEY VOCABULARY
catacomb
epistle
missionary
parable
pope

NAMES & PLACES
Christianity
Constantine
Gospels
Jesus
New Testament
Paul
Roman Catholic Church
Twelve Apostles

SECTION 3
DECLINE AND FALL OF THE EMPIRE

KEY VOCABULARY
barbarian
tetrarchy

NAMES & PLACES
Attila
Diocletian

SECTION 4
THE LEGACY OF ROME

KEY VOCABULARY
bas-relief
oratory

NAMES & PLACES
Latin
Virgil

READING STRATEGY

ORGANIZE IDEAS: SEQUENCE EVENTS
When you sequence events, you place them in the order in which they occurred. As you read the chapter, use a time line like this one to keep track of key people and events in the Roman Empire.

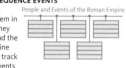

People and Events of the Roman Empire

The Colosseum is made of stone and concrete. Early Roman theaters were built into hillsides for extra support, but the Colosseum is a freestanding structure.

Spectators entered and exited through 76 gates that sat just inside the 80 arches surrounding the ground floor.

The Roman Colosseum was opened in A.D. 80 and is still standing today.

305

TEACHER BACKGROUND

INTRODUCE THE PHOTOGRAPH

Have students study the photograph of the Colosseum in Rome. Explain that this is a modern photo of a structure built nearly 2,000 years ago. Point out that the very existence of these ruins is a testament to the lasting influence of the Roman Empire.

ASK: What type of modern structure does the 2,000-year-old Colosseum resemble? *(Possible response: a sports stadium)*

SHARE BACKGROUND

The Colosseum is one example of Rome's enduring legacy. Romans made significant contributions to art, engineering, and philosophy, and spread Christianity across the ancient world. All of these achievements shaped, and continue to shape, the world today. Ultimately, however, Rome's greatest lesson may not be in its achievements, but rather in its demise—arguably the greatest empire in history did ultimately come to an end.

DIGITAL RESOURCES myNGconnect.com

TEACHER RESOURCES & ASSESSMENT

 Social Studies Skills Lessons
· Reading: Sequence Events
· Writing: Write an Explanation

 Formal Assessment
· Chapter 11 Tests A (on-level) & B (below-level)

 ExamView®
One-time Download

 **Chapter 11 Answer Key**

STUDENT BACKPACK

· **eEdition** *(English)*
· **eEdition** *(Spanish)*
· **Handbooks**
· **Online Atlas**

For Chapter 11 Spanish Resources, visit the Teacher Resource Menu page.

INTRODUCE THE ESSENTIAL QUESTION

WHAT MADE THE ROMAN EMPIRE SO POWERFUL AND LONG LASTING?

Roundtable Activity: International Influence This activity will allow students to explore the question by categorizing types of power and types of lasting influence. Divide the class into groups of four or five students and assign each group a number. Hand the odd numbered groups a sheet of paper with this question at the top: What types of power can one country have over another? Hand the even numbered groups a sheet of paper with this question at the top: What types of lasting influence can countries have? The first student in each group should write an answer and then pass the paper clockwise to the next student, who may add a new answer. The paper should be circulated around the group until the time is up. Students may pass at any time. After ten minutes, ask for volunteers to read their group's answers to the class. `0:15` minutes

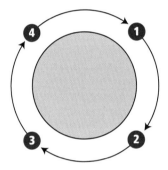

INTRODUCE THE READING STRATEGY

ORGANIZE IDEAS: SEQUENCE EVENTS

Remind students that sequencing events can help them keep track of new information. Model sequencing events by using the first three dates listed in the Key Dates table. Take the opportunity to explain the change between "B.C." and "A.D."

People and Events of the Roman Empire

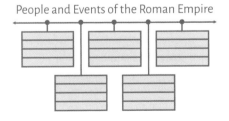

INTRODUCE CHAPTER VOCABULARY

WORD SORT CHART

Divide the class into groups and have them copy each word from the list on a separate note card or slip of paper. Then have the groups discuss what they think the words might mean and sort them into the following categories: art, architecture, people, reading/speaking, government. Groups may also choose their own categories if they prefer. When groups have finished, ask them to explain their categories to the class.

aqueduct	emperor	mosaic
arch	epistle	oratory
barbarian	fresco	parable
bas-relief	gladiator	pope
catacomb	missionary	tetrarchy

KEY DATES	
31 B.C.	Augustus becomes emperor of Rome
c. **6** B.C.	Birth of Jesus
A.D. **79**	Vesuvius erupts, destroying Pompeii
A.D. **80**	Colosseum opens
A.D. **285**	Diocletian divides Roman Empire into East and West
A.D. **312**	Constantine converts to Christianity
A.D. **476**	Last emperor of the Western Roman Empire leaves the throne

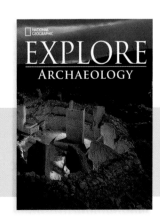

For more information on Roman architecture, check out *EXPLORE ARCHAEOLOGY.*

Augustus and the Pax Romana

When Julius Caesar was assassinated, Romans rolled their eyes and thought, "Here we go again." After decades of dictatorships and civil wars, they hoped for stability in the empire. They got it, but the republic was dead. A new type of leader was about to rule Rome for the next 500 years.

MAIN IDEA

Augustus transformed Rome from a violent republic into a peaceful empire.

A NEW EMPIRE

After Caesar's death, his heir, Octavian, found himself at the center of a deadly power struggle. At 18 years old, he had to kill or be killed. He survived and thrived. Octavian defeated his rivals, killed Caesar's assassins, and crushed revolts. He emerged victorious, immensely rich, and all-powerful. In 31 B.C., he became Rome's sole ruler. Four years later, the Senate gave him the name **Augustus**, or "exalted one."

Augustus was smarter than Caesar had been. He used his wealth and political skill to take control of the army and secure the people's support. He also won over the Senate, which awarded him dictator-like powers. He did all this while working within the law and appearing to uphold republican

ideals. The Senate, among other institutions, continued, but Augustus controlled its decisions. He was the supreme ruler in Rome, or its **emperor**. His powers were granted for life and could be passed to a successor, which was something that made the Romans uneasy. They didn't want to return to the harsh rule of kings. However, the people accepted Augustus because he moved slowly, carefully, and legally. Above all, he finally brought peace to Rome.

PEACE UNDER AUGUSTUS

Augustus' reign began the **Pax Romana**, or "Roman Peace"—200 years of peace and prosperity enjoyed across the empire. The Pax Romana was possible because Augustus tackled some long-standing problems. The poor thanked Augustus for guaranteeing free handouts of grain. Most of the people might not have noticed that Augustus' newly paid officials were improving government. However, everyone took immense pride in his transformation of Rome into an impressive capital with magnificent marble monuments. Meanwhile, Augustus' new laws were restoring order, and he actively encouraged art, literature, and education.

Augustus also cleverly prevented any threat that might have been posed by the army. He cut its size in half but kept out-of-work veterans happy with grants of land. Soldiers still serving were kept constantly busy defending and expanding the empire's frontiers. The army also now had standardized pay and conditions and a new oath of loyalty to the emperor himself.

The elite Praetorian (pree-TAWR-ee-uhn) Guard were the only soldiers stationed in Rome, and they were committed to upholding the emperor's authority. In addition, to protect the empire's coasts and shipping trade, Augustus created Rome's first permanent navy. All of these changes helped ensure long-term stability for the empire and for many Roman emperors to come.

GAIUS OCTAVIAN
AUGUSTUS

💼 **Job:** First emperor of Rome

FINEST HOUR

Augustus was able to peacefully pass on all his imperial powers. He left a secure, stable, and prosperous empire to his adopted son Tiberius.

WORST MOMENT

A major military embarrassment occurred in A.D. 9 when Germanic barbarians destroyed three Roman legions.

TRIVIA

Although often ill, Augustus lived to be 77. Shortly before he died, the month of August was named after him.

Augustus of Pirmaporta, c. 20–17 B.C.

REVIEW & ASSESS

1. **READING CHECK** What is the Pax Romana?

2. **IDENTIFY MAIN IDEAS AND DETAILS** What are three things Augustus did to secure people's support?

3. **MAKE INFERENCES** Why do you think Augustus was careful to reward soldiers and reduce the size of the army?

307

OBJECTIVE

Identify how Augustus secured and solidified his leadership of the Roman Empire and Rome's lasting legacy.

CRITICAL THINKING SKILLS FOR LESSON 1.1

- Identify Main Ideas and Details
- Monitor Comprehension
- Make Inferences
- Explain
- Compare and Contrast

ESSENTIAL QUESTION

What was the power and enduring legacy of the Roman Empire?

Augustus was a smart and strong leader whose name is almost

synonymous with the power and legacy of Rome. Lesson 1.1 discusses how he used his skills to transform Rome and Roman society.

BACKGROUND FOR THE TEACHER

During his reign, Augustus reorganized the government, reforming the administrative structures and beginning the first Roman civil service. These improvements fostered communication and trade and thus helped hold the empire together. He also embarked on a massive public works project of improving Rome. According to the historian Suetonius, Augustus boasted that he found the city built of brick and left it built of marble.

DIGITAL RESOURCES myNGconnect.com

TEACHER RESOURCES & ASSESSMENT

 Reading and Note-Taking

 Vocabulary Practice

 Section 1 Quiz

STUDENT RESOURCES

 NG Chapter Gallery

THREE-STEP INTERVIEW

Ask the class to think about how living in peace-time conditions for 200 years might affect the government. What are possible advantages and disadvantages? Have pairs of students take turns asking each other those questions. Then ask pairs to share their interview results with the class. **0:10** **minutes**

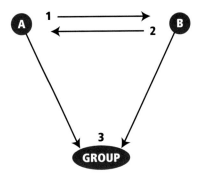

TEACH

GUIDED DISCUSSION

1. **Explain** What personal qualities did Augustus have that helped him secure power? (*Augustus was smart, decisive, and understood that happy people were much easier to manage than dissatisfied ones. His intelligence allowed him to understand and exploit the nuances of Roman government. By taking quick action against his enemies, Augustus was able to stop opposition before it ever got started. Finally, Augustus made the most powerful Romans—the senate and the soldiers—feel that he had their interests at heart. At the same time, Augustus brought peace to the empire, which made Romans from all ranks happy.*)

2. **Make Inferences** How might Augustus' support of art, literature, and education have helped to stabilize Roman society? (*By giving people outlets in other areas, they might be less likely to use their leisure time to cause unrest. Additionally, an educated population might better realize that a strong leader and a stable society brought many practical benefits, such as a reliable food supply and better overall infrastructure.*)

COMPARE AND CONTRAST

Ask students to compare and contrast the leadership of Julius Caesar versus that of Augustus. Suggest they use a Venn Diagram to list the similarities and differences. **0:10** **minutes**

ACTIVE OPTIONS

On Your Feet: Numbered Heads Count students off in groups of four. Have the groups discuss how Augustus contributed to the longevity and lasting influence of the Roman Empire. Choose a number and have the student with that number from each group summarize their discussion for the class. **0:10** **minutes**

NG Learning Framework: Evaluate Augustus' Reforms

ATTITUDE: Responsibility
SKILLS: Communication, Collaboration

Invite students to revisit the biography of Augustus in Lesson 1.1 and his reforms once he was in power. **ASK:** Which reform had the most immediate effect? Which had the longest legacy? Pair up students and have them collaborate on answers to these two questions. Then combine two pairs of students into groups of four and have the small groups discuss their answers respectfully. **0:10** **minutes**

ENGLISH LANGUAGE LEARNERS

Use Sentence Strips Choose a paragraph from the lesson and make sentence strips out of it. Read the paragraph aloud, having students follow along in their books. Have students close their books and give them the set of sentence strips. Students should put the strips in order and then read the paragraph aloud.

GIFTED & TALENTED

Research Roman Emperors Have students research an emperor who came after Augustus. Suggest they create a T-Chart to compare the two leaders as they did with Julius Caesar. Then suggest they develop a table or chart that effectively compares and contrasts the traits of all three leaders.

Press **mt** *in the Student eEdition for modified text.*

See the Chapter Planner for more strategies for differentiation.

ANSWERS

1. The Pax Romana refers to the 200 years of peace and prosperity enjoyed across the Roman Empire.

2. Augustus gave free grain to the poor and land and cash to veteran soldiers. He built monuments that turned Rome into an impressive capital of the empire.

3. An organized army has great power. By rewarding soldiers and reducing the size of the standing army, Augustus made sure this powerful group was happy and less of a threat to his leadership.

1.2 Growth and Trade

During the Pax Romana, you could travel easily and safely across the entire Roman Empire. By A.D. 117, that meant you could cross most of the known western world. It was a merchant's dream, and the economy boomed as Romans enjoyed goods imported from almost everywhere.

MAIN IDEA

As the Roman Empire expanded, trade became easier and the economy boomed.

IMPERIAL EXPANSION

Under Augustus, the Roman army became the mightiest in the world. Its relentless march expanded the empire's frontiers and cultural influence farther than ever before. Soldiers in forts on three continents—Europe, Asia, and Africa—protected the empire's frontiers from attacks by numerous enemies. The soldiers could be soaking in the rains of northern Britain, sweltering in the deserts of southern Egypt, battered by Atlantic winds in western Spain, or swimming in the waters of the Red Sea.

Some of the frontier military camps became permanent settlements. Soldiers stationed at these settlements often stayed in the community when they retired. This practice helped expand Roman culture and influence in the region.

The Roman Empire did not always rely on military conquest to expand its borders. If an area looked like it would be difficult or costly to conquer outright, Augustus would support a local ruler. In return, the territory would be required to provide the empire with military aid if needed. In this way, Augustus was able to expand the empire while saving the expense of an all-out war. This arrangement also made it easier for Augustus to invade the territory in the future if he felt that it was necessary.

A network of roads, bridges, and tunnels built by soldiers connected these far-flung frontiers. It allowed the army to march swiftly across great distances and quickly crush trouble wherever it arose. The roads helped the army keep order, but they also benefited everyone in the empire. The official mail service used the roads to keep information flowing across the empire. Rest areas and inns for overnight stays were built at regular intervals. Everyone in the empire could travel farther, faster, more easily, and more safely than ever before.

A BOOMING ECONOMY

These excellent roads also stimulated the economy by making it easy to transport and sell goods throughout the empire—basic goods as well as luxuries. Even citizens with limited incomes could afford African olive oil and Spanish salted fish. This flow of goods around the empire created a thriving economy as well as a sense of community. Roman merchants gained great benefits from all of this trade.

Rome's craftspeople produced beautiful objects that archaeologists have found as far away as Vietnam, but what flowed out of the empire most was money. The city of Rome itself was the main consumer of imports, or goods brought from other places. Rome especially needed food to feed its huge population. Agriculture, though still Rome's largest industry, was focused on luxuries such as fruit.

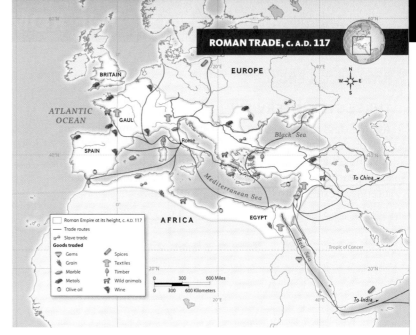

ROMAN TRADE, c. A.D. 117

The most important Roman goods in terms of the quantity traded were wine, olive oil, and grain. Traders moved these bulky goods by ship before transferring them to slower ox-drawn carts. Adventurous traders looked far beyond the empire's borders. These merchants would sail east to India or travel the Silk Roads to China. There they sought to trade wool, gold, and silver for luxuries such as silks, spices, and gems.

The introduction of a standard currency, or money, throughout the empire made it easier to conduct trade as well as collect taxes and pay soldiers. The empire made coins called *denarii* (dih-NAIR-ee) out of silver and *sesterces* (SEHS-tuhrs) out of brass. Roman coins were accepted not only in the empire but also beyond. The expanded empire and the Pax Romana were certainly good for business.

REVIEW & ASSESS

1. **READING CHECK** What factors encouraged trade in the Roman Empire?

2. **INTERPRET MAPS** From which locations in the empire did Rome import grain to feed its citizens?

3. **ANALYZE CAUSE AND EFFECT** What were two positive effects of the flow of goods throughout the empire?

PLAN

OBJECTIVE

Describe how trade contributed to Rome's strength and ability to endure over time.

CRITICAL THINKING SKILLS FOR LESSON 1.2

- Identify Main Ideas and Details
- Monitor Comprehension
- Interpret Maps
- Analyze Cause and Effect
- Explain
- Draw Conclusions

ESSENTIAL QUESTION

What was the power and enduring legacy of the Roman Empire?

Rome controlled trade across the empire, making it easier for local and distant merchants to sell their goods. Lesson 1.2 discusses how Rome's efforts to improve trade led to a booming economy, which in turn made the empire more stable.

BACKGROUND FOR THE TEACHER

Trade was a very significant unifying influence in the early Roman Empire. While military campaigns brought new territories under Roman control, trade brought new goods into the empire. Equally as important, military expansion increased the cultural exchange between Rome proper and the frontiers. This financial and cultural interchange contributed to the empire's prosperity and stability over a huge geographic area.

DIGITAL RESOURCES myNGconnect.com

TEACHER RESOURCES & ASSESSMENT

 Reading and Note-Taking

 Vocabulary Practice

 Section 1 Quiz

STUDENT RESOURCES

 NG Chapter Gallery

INTRODUCE & ENGAGE

CONNECT TO MODERN LIFE

Ask students to consider what they know about trade in today's world: specifically, how do goods get to their home? Explain that modern transportation methods (planes, oceangoing ships, etc.) are the bedrock of international trade. However, in the Roman Empire, road building was the technology that allowed the empire to thrive. **0:10** minutes

TEACH

GUIDED DISCUSSION

1. **Explain** What was the relationship between the Roman army and trade? *(Possible answer: The Roman army built the roads as they conquered new regions. In effect, the army was opening new markets and providing access to those markets.)*

2. **Draw Conclusions** How do you think trade benefited smaller communities far from the empire's capital? *(Possible answer: Smaller communities located far from Rome itself would have benefited from trade in much the same way the capital did: access to a variety of goods was made possible by the security and speed of Roman roads. Additionally, communities located near desirable natural resources such as precious metals or good farmland, could afford to specialize in luxury commodities because they could get the staples needed to support the community through trade.)*

INTERPRET MAPS

Help students interpret the Roman Trade c. A.D. 117 map. Using the map scale, point out that the empire at this time covered tens of thousands of square miles. The ability to move quickly across such a large area was critical to the success of trade as well as the success of the empire itself. Also point out that the importance of trade by water is shown clearly on the map. **0:10** minutes

ACTIVE OPTIONS

On Your Feet: Fishbowl Have one half of the class sit in a close circle, facing inward. The other half of the class sits in a larger circle around them. Pose the question "What was the most important product that was imported to the city of Rome itself?" Students in the inner circle should discuss the question for 10 minutes while those in the outer circle listen to the discussion and evaluate the points made. Then have the groups reverse roles and continue the discussion. **0:20** minutes

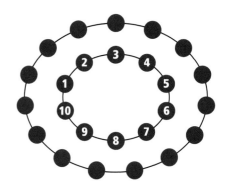

Critical Viewing: NG Chapter Gallery Ask students to choose one image from the Chapter Gallery and become an expert on it. They should do additional research to learn all about it. Then, students should share their findings with a partner, small group, or the class. **0:15** minutes

DIFFERENTIATE

STRIVING READERS

Summarize Read the lesson aloud while students follow along in their books. At the end of each paragraph, ask students to summarize what they read in a sentence. Allow them time to write the summary on their own paper.

INCLUSION

Describe Details in Maps Pair students who are visually impaired with students who are not. Ask the latter to describe the details in the Roman Trade map in detail for their partners. Then have the pairs of students work together to answer the map question in the Review & Assess.

Press (**mt**) *in the Student eEdition for modified text.*

See the Chapter Planner for more strategies for differentiation.

REVIEW & ASSESS

ANSWERS

1. Ease of transportation, security, and potential for profit were all factors that encouraged trade in the Roman Empire.

2. Rome imported grain from North Africa and Eastern Europe.

3. Two positive effects of the flow of goods in the Roman Empire were that goods became more affordable and trade fostered a sense of community across a large area.

Roman Engineering

Step outside your door and you'll see a road. Follow the road and you'll reach a city. In the city, you'll find large concrete buildings. Two thousand years ago, Roman engineers were perfecting the techniques that enabled the building of these "modern" constructions.

MAIN IDEA

The Romans were skilled engineers who helped transform how things were built.

ROMAN INVENTIONS

Arch
A curved structure over an opening

Vault
An extended series of arches

Dome
A rotated series of arches

ROADS

Before the Romans began building their network of roads, travel generally meant following dirt tracks. Rome's first great road was the Appian Way built in 312 B.C. It connected Rome with southern Italy. As the empire expanded, its armies built new roads back to the capital—which is where the saying "All roads lead to Rome" comes from.

The army used specialized tools and lots of human power to build roads. Soldiers marked the route, dug foundations, and built up the road with several layers of material. The center of the road was slightly higher than the edges, which helped rain run into drainage ditches.

Where possible, the soldiers built the road wide and straight, making marches shorter and easier. Engineers developed special techniques to overcome obstacles. Roads sometimes included bridges over rivers or tunnels through hills. Every mile a milestone marked the distance to major cities. By A.D. 300, the Romans had built about 53,000 miles of roads.

ARCHES AND AQUEDUCTS

Concrete is not usually very interesting, but at the time of Augustus it transformed construction. The Romans developed a new, stronger type of concrete and used it to build huge freestanding structures, like the Pantheon in Rome. This building, shown on the next page, was built in 27 B.C. as a temple to all the gods of ancient Rome.

Roman architecture was modeled on Greek architecture, but the use of arches, vaults, and domes created a distinctive Roman style. An **arch**, or curved structure over an opening, is strong and inexpensive to build. Lengthening an arch creates a vault, and joining a circle of arches at their highest point creates a dome.

Long stone channels called **aqueducts** (AK-wih-duhkts) carried clean water from hilltops into cities and towns. The engineers' precise calculations over long distances ensured a steady flow of water. Rome received 35 million cubic feet of water every day. While most of an aqueduct ran underground, sometimes huge arched bridges were built to carry the water across valleys. Many of these magnificent structures still stand as reminders of Roman engineering ability: building big and building to last.

POSSIBLE RESPONSE

Architects created an awe-inspiring mood, as if the opening provided a view to the heavens.

Critical Viewing This interior photo of the Pantheon shows the oculus—the opening in the center of the dome. What mood did Roman architects create using a tall dome with an opening at the top?

REVIEW & ASSESS

1. **READING CHECK** What techniques and constructions did Roman engineers develop?

2. **SUMMARIZE** What was the process Roman soldiers used to build roads?

3. **MAKE INFERENCES** How did aqueducts help unify the empire?

PLAN

OBJECTIVE

Identify Roman contributions to structural engineering.

CRITICAL THINKING SKILLS FOR LESSON 1.3

- Identify Main Ideas and Details
- Monitor Comprehension
- Summarize
- Make Inferences
- Analyze Visuals

ESSENTIAL QUESTION

What was the power and enduring legacy of the Roman Empire?

Roman engineering was not just innovative; it solved practical problems with quality construction that was able to stand for thousands of years. Lesson 1.3 discusses Roman engineering techniques and ideas that are still used today.

BACKGROUND FOR THE TEACHER

The Pantheon is a remarkable building. The dome was the largest in the world until the modern era. It is about 142 feet in diameter and about 77 feet tall. The oculus is 27 feet across and was the only means of lighting the interior. There are arches set on top of one another to support the dome inside the walls, which are 20 feet thick. The entrance has huge bronze double doors that are 24 feet tall—the earliest known examples of the style. All of this gives the Pantheon a feeling of gravitas that can be felt as one gazes up at the beautiful light cascading down from the top of the dome.

DIGITAL RESOURCES myNGconnect.com

TEACHER RESOURCES & ASSESSMENT

 Reading and Note-Taking   **Vocabulary Practice**   **Section 1 Quiz**

STUDENT RESOURCES

 NG Chapter Gallery

INTRODUCE & ENGAGE

BRAINSTORM

Ask students to think about what they already know about Roman architecture. Point out that it might be more than they think. As a class, brainstorm different buildings or architectural features they have seen that use Roman elements (e.g., stadiums, certain monuments, arched doorways, domes, vaults, etc.). Capture the ideas on the board and cross out those that don't apply. There should still be enough items to illustrate that Roman influence in architecture continues today. **0:05** minutes

TEACH

GUIDED DISCUSSION

1. **Make Inferences** Why would Roman ideas about architecture still be used today? *(Possible answer: Because they work—as is evidenced by the fact that buildings such as the Pantheon are still standing.)*

2. **Summarize** What are two examples of Roman engineering that we would consider public works today? *(Possible answer: Roads and aqueducts. Maintaining roads for transportation and delivering water to our homes are two Roman engineering feats that we use today and largely take for granted.)*

ANALYZE VISUALS

Review the Critical Viewing question for the image of the Pantheon with students. Explain to students that the oculus was intentional not only in function (to provide light), but in effect, too. The amount of light that comes in is limited and changes dramatically as the sun moves. This creates a dynamic environment inside the building and some architectural historians believe the Pantheon was one of the first ancient buildings that focused more on interior, rather than exterior, design. **0:10** minutes

ACTIVE OPTIONS

On Your Feet: Three Corners Post three signs in different parts of the room that read: *arch, vault,* and *dome*. Show students different examples of these architectural features and ask them to go to the sign matching the photo. **0:15** minutes

NG Learning Framework: Research and Compare

ATTITUDE: **Responsible**
SKILL: **Observation**
KNOWLEDGE: **New Frontiers**

Have students do responsible online research to find photographs showing architectural features of ancient Roman buildings (e.g. arches, domes, vaults, etc.). Then they should find photographs of modern buildings where they observe the same type of feature. Have them present one of their comparisons to the class. **0:10** minutes

DIFFERENTIATE

ENGLISH LANGUAGE LEARNERS

Pose and Answer Questions Have students pose and answer questions that begin with the 5Ws. Remind them that *Who* refers to people, *What* to events, *Where* to places, *When* to dates or time, and *Why* to reasons. Invite students to share their questions and answers.

GIFTED & TALENTED

Create Multimedia Presentations Instruct students to create a multimedia presentation about Roman engineering using photos, spoken words, and written text. The presentations should describe Roman buildings, roads, and bridges, and modern examples that show Roman influence. Invite students to share their presentations with the class.

Press **mt** *in the Student eEdition for modified text.*

See the Chapter Planner for more strategies for differentiation.

REVIEW & ASSESS

ANSWERS

1. Roman engineers developed roads, bridges, tunnels, arches, vaults, domes, and aqueducts.

2. Soldiers marked the route, dug foundations, and built up the road with several layers of material.

3. Aqueducts helped unify the empire by bringing water directly into major cities, which created a sense of familiarity and modernity across the empire.

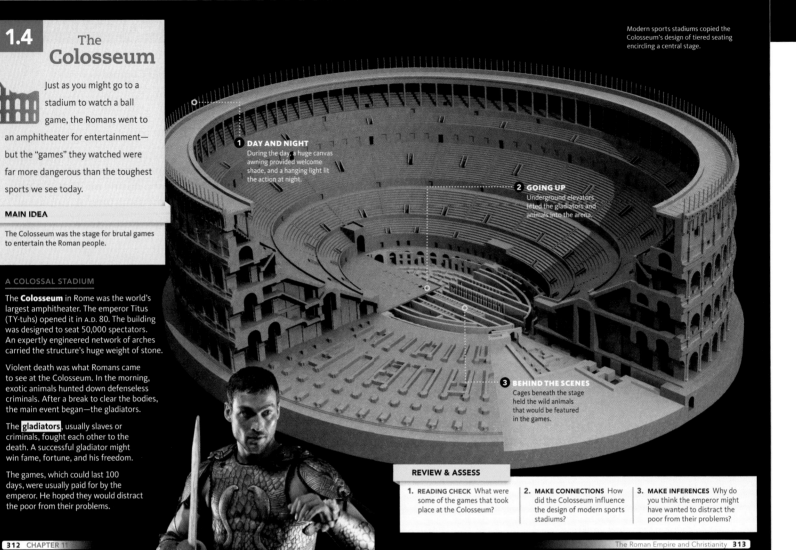

1.4

The Colosseum

Just as you might go to a stadium to watch a ball game, the Romans went to an amphitheater for entertainment—but the "games" they watched were far more dangerous than the toughest sports we see today.

MAIN IDEA

The Colosseum was the stage for brutal games to entertain the Roman people.

A COLOSSAL STADIUM

The **Colosseum** in Rome was the world's largest amphitheater. The emperor Titus (TY-tuhs) opened it in A.D. 80. The building was designed to seat 50,000 spectators. An expertly engineered network of arches carried the structure's huge weight of stone.

Violent death was what Romans came to see at the Colosseum. In the morning, exotic animals hunted down defenseless criminals. After a break to clear the bodies, the main event began—the gladiators.

The gladiators, usually slaves or criminals, fought each other to the death. A successful gladiator might win fame, fortune, and his freedom.

The games, which could last 100 days, were usually paid for by the emperor. He hoped they would distract the poor from their problems.

Modern sports stadiums copied the Colosseum's design of tiered seating encircling a central stage.

1 DAY AND NIGHT
During the day, a huge canvas awning provided welcome shade, and a hanging light lit the action at night.

2 GOING UP
Underground elevators lifted the gladiators and animals into the arena.

3 BEHIND THE SCENES
Cages beneath the stage held the wild animals that would be featured in the games.

REVIEW & ASSESS

1. **READING CHECK** What were some of the games that took place at the Colosseum?

2. **MAKE CONNECTIONS** How did the Colosseum influence the design of modern sports stadiums?

3. **MAKE INFERENCES** Why do you think the emperor might have wanted to distract the poor from their problems?

PLAN

OBJECTIVE

Understand the role of the Colosseum in Rome and its lasting legacy.

CRITICAL THINKING SKILLS FOR LESSON 1.4

- Identify Main Ideas and Details
- Monitor Comprehension
- Make Connections
- Make Inferences
- Identify
- Draw Conclusions

ESSENTIAL QUESTION

What was the power and enduring legacy of the Roman Empire?

The Colosseum was a remarkable feat of engineering that was used for horrifically brutal entertainment. Lesson 1.4 shows the ingenuity—and endurance—of the building and describes some of the blood-sport distractions for which the Colosseum was used.

BACKGROUND FOR THE TEACHER

Construction of the Colosseum was begun by the emperor Vespasian sometime between A.D. 70 and A.D. 72. The site chosen was on the palace grounds of former emperor Nero's estate. The choice of construction site was symbolic—paving over the tyrannical ruler's home. The emperor Titus officially dedicated the Colosseum in A.D. 80, and Domitian completed final construction in A.D. 82.

The Colosseum has long been a major draw for tourists and a source of pride for Romans.

DIGITAL RESOURCES myNGconnect.com

TEACHER RESOURCES & ASSESSMENT

 Reading and Note-Taking

 Vocabulary Practice

 Section 1 Quiz

STUDENT RESOURCES

 NG Chapter Gallery

INTRODUCE & ENGAGE

ANALYZE VISUALS

Have students review the Colosseum illustration and ask volunteers to point out interesting features of the structure. **0:05** minutes

TEACH

GUIDED DISCUSSION

1. **Identify** What was the main use of the Colosseum? *(to host a variety of violent sources of entertainment for the masses)*

2. **Draw Conclusions** What type of society do you think Rome had during this period? *(It would be easy to simply say that Romans were bloodthirsty and violent. Take the opportunity to remind students that judgments about any society based on a single aspect of that society are very likely to be inaccurate. While Roman citizens of the time did flock to see other humans torn apart by animals, this fact alone does not warrant any general statement about Romans.)*

MORE INFORMATION

Naval Battles It is sometimes said that the Colosseum floor could be flooded to hold mock naval battles along with other water-based shows. Archaeological evidence indicates that this may have been possible in the earlier years of the Colosseum's operation. However, later structural modifications to the building appear to have made flooding the amphitheater impossible. At the time, there were other venues in Rome that were built specifically to hold water for such shows. Thus, removing that ability from the Colosseum would have had less of an impact from an entertainment perspective.

ACTIVE OPTIONS

On Your Feet: Three-Step Interview Have student pairs interview each other about this topic: "Roman emperors used games in the Colosseum to distract citizens from other issues. Can you think of any other historical examples where governments or leaders have tried to distract their citizens?" Ask volunteers to report the results of their interview to the class. **0:20** minutes

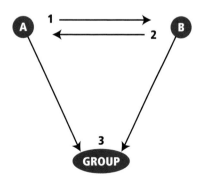

NG Learning Framework: Write a Brochure

ATTITUDE: Curiosity
SKILL: Communication

Have students select an element of the Colosseum that they are still curious about after exploring this lesson. Instruct them to write a short informational brochure about this element using information from additional source material. **0:20** minutes

DIFFERENTIATE

ENGLISH LANGUAGE LEARNERS

Dictation Have students write a sentence summarizing the main idea of the lesson. Then have students get together in pairs and dictate their sentences to each other. Have them work together to check the sentences for accuracy and spelling.

GIFTED & TALENTED

Create Enhanced Illustrations Instruct students to use the book's Colosseum illustration as a foundation for their own, enhanced illustration. Based on reading and other research, have students add historically accurate elements to the illustration. Ask volunteers to present their work to the class.

Press **mt** *in the Student eEdition for modified text.*

See the Chapter Planner for more strategies for differentiation.

REVIEW & ASSESS

ANSWERS

1. Wild animals hunted criminals and gladiators fought each other to death in the Colosseum.

2. Modern sports stadiums copy the design of the Colosseum, including the concept of tiered seating surrounding a central stage.

3. Roman emperors might have wanted to keep the poor distracted so they would not cause trouble over issues the government should be handling, e.g., food shortages, public safety, or corruption.

Villas and Frescoes

Whether you rented rooms in a block of apartments or were rich enough to own a house, summer in the city of Rome was seriously hot for everyone. Summer also brought the risk of deadly diseases. There was no air conditioning to keep you cool and no antibiotics if you got sick. If you were really rich, you'd head for the fresh, clean air of your country home.

MAIN IDEA

Wealthy Romans lived in luxurious country houses called villas.

This detail of a Roman mosaic was uncovered at the ancient Roman town of Zeugma in modern Turkey. It is known as the "Gypsy Girl."

LIFE IN A ROMAN VILLA

Villas were large country houses designed to impress. Visitors entered through huge doors into a bright central courtyard. This was the main living room, where Romans would relax and entertain. They knew their guests would admire expensive features such as fountains, magnificent marble statues, and portraits of important ancestors. Many other rooms for working, eating, and sleeping stood beyond the courtyard.

Roman interior designers favored large rooms with high ceilings. Usually there were only a few pieces of very fine furniture, which were often beautifully carved or decorated. A very expensive design feature in Roman villas was mosaic (moh-ZAY-ihk) floors. A **mosaic** contains tiny colored stone cubes set in mortar to create a picture or design. A mosaic floor was a work of art, and keeping it clean was essential. Villas had many slaves who did all the work, from tending the fields to cleaning, cooking, and serving meals.

The Villa Adriana at Tivoli (TIH-vuh-lee) near Rome is a luxurious example of a country house that is still visible today. Built by the emperor Hadrian, it formed a vast group of 30 buildings, many copied and named after places Hadrian had admired on his travels. Covering an area equal to about 270 football fields, the villa included a theater, a stadium, baths, a library, and a palace.

FRESCOES

The Romans learned the art of painting frescoes from the ancient Greeks. A **fresco** is a picture painted directly onto the wall while the plaster is still wet. Rich Romans covered their walls with these paintings. Talented Greek artists were often employed to paint these frescoes.

Roman frescoes could show a variety of scenes such as landscapes, famous battles, and views of everyday life. Some pictures even included family members, posed to show off wealth and status. The Romans were great lovers of art, which they used to emphasize their position in society. To rich Romans, appearance was everything.

REVIEW & ASSESS

1. **READING CHECK** What kinds of luxurious features did the villas of wealthy Romans often have?

2. **MONITOR COMPREHENSION** For what purpose did wealthy Romans employ talented Greek artists?

3. **SYNTHESIZE** What was the relationship between art and status in Roman culture?

PLAN

OBJECTIVE

Recognize what can be learned about Romans through their art and architecture.

Mosaics and frescoes from the Roman Empire draw us into the world of the Romans. Lesson 1.5 describes how the culture of wealthy Romans is kept alive today through their homes and artwork.

CRITICAL THINKING SKILLS FOR LESSON 1.5

- Identify Main Ideas and Details
- Monitor Comprehension
- Synthesize
- Make Inferences
- Draw Conclusions
- Analyze Visuals

BACKGROUND FOR THE TEACHER

One school of thought holds that Roman homes were as much the owner's place of business as they were private residences. The home was a private, social, and commercial space. As a result, Romans decorated their homes as much to make a statement as they did to please their own eye. Mosaics, by their nature, are more abundant and accessible to modern researchers. Mosaics provide a wealth of material from which to study Roman living spaces and indeed Roman culture itself. How and where mosaics were placed in a particular floor plan can reveal much about the owner and the community.

ESSENTIAL QUESTION

What was the power and enduring legacy of the Roman Empire?

DIGITAL RESOURCES myNGconnect.com

TEACHER RESOURCES & ASSESSMENT

 Reading and Note-Taking

 Vocabulary Practice

 Section 1 Quiz

STUDENT RESOURCES

 NG Chapter Gallery

INTRODUCE & ENGAGE

DISCUSS ART AS HISTORY

Ask students to think about what is hanging on their walls at home. Now ask them to consider what a stranger might learn about them simply by looking at their walls. This is part of what historians and archaeologists try to do. They examine what a person or culture has left behind, including their art, and try to figure out what can be learned about the people and the time in which they lived. **0:10** minutes

TEACH

GUIDED DISCUSSION

1. **Make Inferences** Why might there be more Roman mosaics than other types of Roman art? *(It may be that the way mosaics were created allowed them to hold up better over time than other types of art.)*

2. **Draw Conclusions** Why are mosaics and frescoes a valuable resource for studying ancient Rome? *(Roman mosaics and frescoes are valuable for studying the culture because they were created deliberately for a purpose. Using these artworks in conjunction with other clues can help researchers understand the purpose and meaning behind the art, which can lead to other insights about Roman culture.)*

ANALYZE VISUALS

Have students examine the mosaic called "The Gypsy Girl." Point out that the artist created an image by taking colored rocks and arranging them in a certain way—difficult and time consuming. Ask them to point to one detail they find particularly interesting.

(Possible answers: the color around the eyes possibly indicating makeup, or the single white stone in the iris that shows a reflection of light) **0:10** minutes

ACTIVE OPTIONS

On Your Feet: Build a Mosaic Challenge students to build a mosaic of their own. Bring colored pieces (stones, tile scraps, buttons, candy, pushpins, etc.) and have groups work together to create a mosaic. After they finish, ask students how difficult it was and how long it might take to cover an entire floor. **0:20** minutes

NG Learning Framework: Write a Travel Guide

ATTITUDE: Curiosity
SKILLS: Collaboration, Communication

Have students still curious about Roman villas form a group to research the Villa Adriana at Tivoli. Instruct them to collaborate on writing a travel guide about the site using information from the chapter and additional source material. They can present their work to the class. **0:20** minutes

DIFFERENTIATE

ENGLISH LANGUAGE LEARNERS

Read in Pairs Pair English language learners with native English speakers and have them read the lesson together. Instruct the native speakers to pause whenever they encounter a word or sentence construction that is confusing to their partners. Suggest that the native speakers point out context clues to help their partners understand the meanings of unfamiliar terms. Encourage English language learners to restate sentences in their own words.

PRE-AP

Write Dialogue Assign small groups to research and write a possible dialogue between a Roman homeowner and a friend that describes a particular choice of mosaic and its intended location in his home.

Press **(mt)** *in the Student eEdition for modified text.*

See the Chapter Planner for more strategies for differentiation.

REVIEW & ASSESS

ANSWERS

1. The villas of wealthy Romans often had fountains, magnificent marble statues, and portraits of important ancestors.

2. Wealthy Romans employed talented Greek artists to paint frescoes on the walls of their villas.

3. Art and status were closely linked. Art was used to illustrate and emphasize one's position in society.

1.6

Pompeii

As dawn broke on August 24, A.D. 79, the citizens of **Pompeii** (pahm-PAY) rolled out of bed and dressed for another day. Around noon, a dog was chained to a post, a crate of new pottery waited to be unpacked, and a kettle was filled with water. Then disaster struck. Within days, the whole city became a "living" history—entombed in ash for 1,900 years.

MAIN IDEA

The ruins and remains of Pompeii provide insight into everyday Roman life.

This man died fleeing the eruption of Mount Vesuvius, which rises in the background. Pompeians' final moments were preserved by the ash from the volcano and then revealed using plaster casts.

MODERN VESUVIUS

Mount Vesuvius is still an active volcano, and about 2.4 million people live in nearby Naples and its suburbs.

Vesuvius has erupted several times since the destruction of Pompeii. The last eruption was in 1944. Experts believe it is not a question of *if* the volcano will erupt again, but *when*.

DISASTER STRIKES

Pompeii was an average city resting in the shadow of Mount Vesuvius (vuh-SOO-vee-uhs), a volcano on Italy's western coast. The paved streets of the city followed an orderly pattern, and citizens there had all the civic comforts expected. Some 20,000 people worked, played, ate, slept, and lived within Pompeii's city walls until the afternoon of August 24, A.D. 79.

The Roman writer Pliny the Younger was near Pompeii that day. He had once described the city as "one of the loveliest places on Earth." After the events that occurred in Pompeii, he described a nightmare.

A violent explosion brought the city to a standstill. Pliny watched in horror as Mount Vesuvius erupted, shooting gas mixed with rock and ash high into the sky and creating an immense black cloud that blocked out the sun. Panic-stricken citizens fled as ash rained down.

As lava crept toward the city, fires raged and buildings collapsed. A vast volcanic ash cloud swept in to suffocate the city, burying its people and their possessions nearly 25 feet deep. A cloud of poisonous gas overtook and killed anyone who had not yet escaped. Over the next few days, lightning, earthquakes, and tidal waves followed. Finally after three days, Vesuvius went quiet—as silent as the deserted city of Pompeii.

A CITY PRESERVED

The volcanic ash that buried Pompeii also helped preserve its contents. The city's ruins were first discovered in the late 1500s. By 1861, archaeologists began carefully uncovering and working to protect their extraordinary find. Removing the ash, the scientists found houses, shops, and public buildings that contained mosaics, frescoes, and even graffiti. Many of the items had obviously been abandoned suddenly, in the first moments of the eruption. These artifacts offer a revealing glimpse into everyday Roman life. The ash preserved items such as leather shoes, wooden furniture, food, and a library of scrolls.

The ash also preserved some of its victims. It hardened around the bodies. Over time the bodies decayed and left behind an empty space. By pouring plaster into these spaces, archaeologists created exact casts of people, animals, and plants at their moment of death. All the discoveries are moving reminders of how suddenly death came to the city of Pompeii and froze it in time under a blanket of ash.

REVIEW & ASSESS

1. **READING CHECK** What items in Pompeii were preserved after the eruption?

2. **SEQUENCE EVENTS** What was the order of events that occurred in Pompeii on August 24, A.D. 79?

3. **ANALYZE CAUSE AND EFFECT** How were the ruins of Pompeii preserved?

PLAN

OBJECTIVE

Analyze how the clues found at Pompeii can help us understand daily life in the Roman Empire.

CRITICAL THINKING SKILLS FOR LESSON 1.6

- Identify Main Ideas and Details
- Monitor Comprehension
- Sequence Events
- Analyze Cause and Effect
- Form Opinions
- Make Inferences
- Analyze Visuals

ESSENTIAL QUESTION

What was the power and enduring legacy of the Roman Empire?

Pompeii is one of the most compelling stories of the ancient world: a city destroyed in a matter of days and hidden away for hundreds of years. Lesson 1.6 examines the end of Pompeii and the stories the city tells us about daily life in a Roman town.

BACKGROUND FOR THE TEACHER

Pompeii was a town long before the Romans gained control. Descendants of Neolithic peoples formed the first settlements in the region. Soon after, these settlements came under the influence of Greeks and Etruscans. Then the Samnite people conquered the region toward the end of the 5th century B.C. Soon after 89 B.C., Rome conquered the Samnites. Pompeii was quickly Romanized, but was really only under Roman control less than 100 years before it was destroyed.

DIGITAL RESOURCES myNGconnect.com

TEACHER RESOURCES & ASSESSMENT

 Reading and Note-Taking

 Vocabulary Practice

 Section 1 Quiz

STUDENT RESOURCES

 NG Chapter Gallery

ACTIVATE PRIOR KNOWLEDGE

Ask volunteers to share what they already know about Pompeii. Ask leading questions such as, "What type of natural disaster destroyed the city?" "What types of photos of Pompeii have you seen?" Discuss as a class. **0:10** minutes

TEACH

GUIDED DISCUSSION

1. **Form Opinions** Millions of people still live near Vesuvius today. Why do people live in potential disaster areas? *(Answers to this question will vary widely and there is no right answer. However, people are usually aware of the natural dangers around where they live, but they have judged that they enjoy the area enough to risk facing a possible natural disaster.)*

2. **Make Inferences** Why is discovering a well-preserved city that is hundreds of years old so important for archaeologists and historians? *(Such a city allows researchers to examine not only the details of daily life, but also the daily life of people across a wide range of the socioeconomic spectrum.)*

ANALYZE VISUALS

Give groups of students a selected set of images of Pompeii's ruins. Ask them to look for identifiable features. *(streets, buildings, fountains, temples, etc.)* Also present the groups with selected images of Pompeii's frescoes and mosaics and ask them to speculate if the original art served any purpose beyond the aesthetic. *(for example, the floor mosaics that identified different types of shops in Pompeii)* **0:15** minutes

ACTIVE OPTIONS

On Your Feet: Card Responses Have half the class write 10 true-false questions based on the lesson. Have the other half create answer cards, writing "True" on one side and "False" on the other side. Students from the first group take turns asking their questions. Students from the second group hold up their cards, showing either "True" or "False." Have students keep track of their correct answers. **0:15** minutes

Critical Viewing: NG Chapter Gallery Have students examine the contents of the Chapter Gallery for this chapter. Then invite them to brainstorm additional images they believe would fit within the Chapter Gallery. Have them write a description of these additional images and provide an explanation of why they would fit within the Chapter Gallery. Then instruct them to do online research to find examples of actual images that fit their descriptions. **0:10** minutes

DIFFERENTIATE

STRIVING READERS

Use Your Own Words Have students work in pairs to explain in their own words the story of Pompeii and how it was preserved.

PRE-AP

Research Pompeian Culture Have students research some of the amazing discoveries made in Pompeii. Possible topics include graffiti, art, restaurants, and preserved everyday objects. Students should write a one-page essay with an introduction and a conclusion. Have them work with a partner to exchange and proofread each other's work.

Press (**mt**) *in the Student eEdition for modified text.*

See the Chapter Planner for more strategies for differentiation.

REVIEW & ASSESS

ANSWERS

1. Some of the items that were preserved include buildings, leather shoes, wooden furniture, food, and a library of scrolls.

2. There was an explosion that created a large black cloud. Ash began falling and eventually buried the city. Poison gas also moved through the city, killing anyone who was still alive. Lightning, earthquakes, and tidal waves occurred over the three days following the eruption, and then Vesuvius went quiet.

3. The ash buried everything in the city, protecting it from the weather and looters.

The Origins of Christianity

A man named Jesus who lived in Nazareth was a Jew whose beliefs became a threat to Jewish and Roman leaders. His teachings formed the foundation of a religion that has powerfully shaped the world for over 2,000 years.

MAIN IDEA

Christianity developed in Jewish communities and was based on the teachings of Jesus.

JEWISH ROOTS

As the empire expanded, the Romans were usually tolerant of the many different religions practiced throughout the empire. As long as people worshipped their emperor as a god, they could follow whatever faith they liked. This was not a problem for most religions. The exception was Judaism, the religion of the Jewish people.

As you've already learned, the Romans captured the Jewish city of Jerusalem in 63 B.C. This brought the Jewish people under Roman control. At first the Romans allowed the Jews to worship one God. Over time, tensions grew. Rome began to enforce emperor worship, and the tensions exploded into conflict. In A.D. 70, Rome defeated the Jews, who then scattered throughout the empire. This helped spread a new religion that was developing in the Jewish community: Christianity.

JESUS OF NAZARETH

Christianity is based on the teachings of **Jesus**, a man born into a poor family in Judea around 6 B.C. Most of what we know about Jesus' teachings comes from the four **Gospels**. These books were written after Jesus' death by four of his followers—Matthew, Mark, Luke, and John. The Gospels are part of the **New Testament**, which presents the history, teachings, and beliefs of Christianity. According to historical record, Jesus was a practicing Jew and worked as a carpenter. When he was about 30 years old, he began to teach ideas that differed from Jewish practices. Biblical accounts claim that Jesus could perform miracles, such as healing the sick.

In time, Jesus traveled around Judea preaching and gathering disciples, or followers. He chose his closest followers, known as the **Twelve Apostles**, to help spread his teachings. He often used **parables** (short stories about everyday life) to make his religious or moral points. In his Sermon on the Mount, Jesus declared that love for God and charity toward all people were more important than following Jewish law. He also promised that those who sought God's forgiveness for their sins would go to heaven after death. To his followers, Jesus became Christ, "the anointed one." They believed he was the promised Messiah—the one who would free them.

According to Christian writings, Jesus criticized Jewish practices while visiting Jerusalem during the Jewish observance of Passover. Jesus was arrested and turned over to Roman authorities. Pontius Pilate, the Roman governor of Judea, sentenced Jesus to death by crucifixion—being nailed to a cross and left to die. Jesus' body was buried, and then, according to the Gospel accounts, he was resurrected, or rose from the dead, and ascended into heaven. For Christians, the resurrection signals victory over sin and death. The man called Jesus was gone, but Christianity was just beginning.

The Last Supper, Leonardo da Vinci, 1498

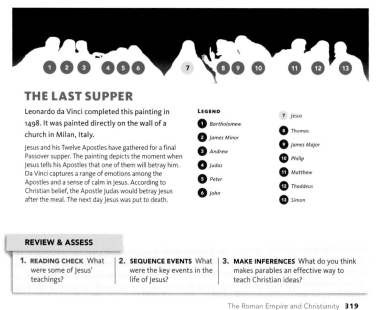

THE LAST SUPPER

Leonardo da Vinci completed this painting in 1498. It was painted directly on the wall of a church in Milan, Italy.

Jesus and his Twelve Apostles have gathered for a final Passover supper. The painting depicts the moment when Jesus tells his Apostles that one of them will betray him. Da Vinci captures a range of emotions among the Apostles and a sense of calm in Jesus. According to Christian belief, the Apostle Judas would betray Jesus after the meal. The next day Jesus was put to death.

LEGEND

1. Bartholomew
2. James Minor
3. Andrew
4. Judas
5. Peter
6. John
7. Jesus
8. Thomas
9. James Major
10. Philip
11. Matthew
12. Thaddeus
13. Simon

REVIEW & ASSESS

1. **READING CHECK** What were some of Jesus' teachings?

2. **SEQUENCE EVENTS** What were the key events in the life of Jesus?

3. **MAKE INFERENCES** What do you think makes parables an effective way to teach Christian ideas?

PLAN

OBJECTIVE

Describe the origins of Christianity and the history and teachings of Jesus.

CRITICAL THINKING SKILLS FOR LESSON 2.1

- Identify Main Ideas and Details
- Monitor Comprehension
- Sequence Events
- Make Inferences
- Explain
- Evaluate
- Analyze Visuals

ESSENTIAL QUESTION

What was the power and enduring legacy of the Roman Empire?

Christianity developed out of the Jewish community during the time of the Roman Empire. Lesson 2.1 discusses the origins of Christianity and the role of Jesus.

BACKGROUND FOR THE TEACHER

The Romans captured Jerusalem and destroyed the Second Temple in A.D. 70. This scattered Jews throughout the Empire, which also spread Christianity. For Jews today, however, this defeat holds one of the greatest sources of national pride. Zealots, a fierce and uncompromising Jewish sect, refused to surrender. They held the fortress of Masada about 33 miles southeast of Jerusalem.

For almost two years, 15,000 Roman soldiers battled a Jewish force of less than 1,000 people including women and children.

DIGITAL RESOURCES myNGconnect.com

TEACHER RESOURCES & ASSESSMENT

 Reading and Note-Taking

 Vocabulary Practice

 Section 2 Quiz

STUDENT RESOURCES

 NG Chapter Gallery

INTRODUCE & ENGAGE

ACTIVATE PRIOR KNOWLEDGE

Ask students to think about any religious images they may have seen. Ask them what similarities and differences they have noticed among the images. Then ask why visual imagery might be important to a religion. *(Possible answer: Images can effectively convey ideas and themes. In other words, they can be an effective teaching tool.)* `0:10` minutes

TEACH

GUIDED DISCUSSION

1. **Explain** Why might the Romans have been fearful of a religion that refused to acknowledge the emperor as a god? *(Followers of a religion that refused to acknowledge the emperor as a god might be more likely to rebel whenever the will of the emperor conflicted with the tenets of the religion.)*

2. **Evaluate** How successful were the apostles at spreading Christianity? *(Given the number of Christians in the world today, the apostles were very successful.)*

ANALYZE VISUALS

Tell students that Leonardo da Vinci's *Last Supper* is considered a masterpiece and one of the most famous paintings in the world. Ask students if they find it compelling. Why or why not?

(Answers will vary. Considered a masterpiece of composition, da Vinci's painting captures the tension of a moment and focuses it through his simple composition and use of one-point perspective.) `0:15` minutes

ACTIVE OPTIONS

On Your Feet: Roundtable Have the class move their desks into a circle and guide a discussion about how and why a religion begins, spreads, and endures. `0:15` minutes

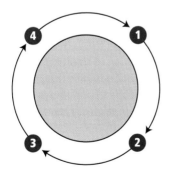

NG Learning Framework: Write a Biography

ATTITUDE: Curiosity
SKILL: Communication

Have students select one of the people they are still curious about after reviewing the painting of the Last Supper. Instruct them to write a short biography about this person using information from additional source material. `0:20` minutes

DIFFERENTIATE

STRIVING READERS

Summarize Have students work in pairs, and assign each pair one paragraph to read together. Encourage students to use a Main Idea and Details Chart to organize their ideas. Then have each pair summarize their paragraph in one or two sentences for the class.

ENGLISH LANGUAGE LEARNERS

Make Vocabulary Cards Have students use flash cards to learn and practice unfamiliar words they encounter in this lesson. On one side of each card they should write the target word. On the other, they should write related words they are familiar with, draw or paste images that will help them recall the meaning of the target word, or write out other mnemonic devices. Encourage students to use their flash cards for review.

Press (**mt**) *in the Student eEdition for modified text.*

See the Chapter Planner for more strategies for differentiation.

REVIEW & ASSESS

ANSWERS

1. Jesus taught that believers should show love for God and charity toward all people. He also taught that those who sought God's forgiveness for their sins would go to heaven after they died.

2. Key events include the following: born in Judaea; worked as a carpenter; began preaching when he was about 30; arrested and executed in Jerusalem.

3. Parables are an effective way to teach Christian ideas because they apply larger moral concepts to relatable, everyday events. Parables make the teachings easy to access.

2.2 Christianity Spreads

Faith is very personal. We follow a particular religion (or no religion) for different reasons. Early Christians were the same way. Christianity had broad appeal and attracted a wide mix of people. They all believed that Jesus was the Messiah.

MAIN IDEA

Christianity attracted many followers and spread throughout the Roman Empire.

THE SPREAD OF CHRISTIANITY, c. A.D. 500

Legend:
— Boundary of Roman Empire, c. A.D. 395
▓ Christian areas, c. A.D. 325
☐ Christian expansion, c. A.D. 500

APPEAL OF CHRISTIANITY

At first all Christians were practicing Jews who still met in synagogues, places for Jewish worship. However, soon Christianity placed less emphasis on the laws of Judaism and welcomed Gentiles (GEHN-tylz), or non-Jews. As a result of the split from Judaism, Christianity grew and developed its own identity.

Christianity appealed to a lot of people. The religion's main appeal was the promise of salvation made possible by the sacrifice of Jesus. Many followers were also attracted by Christianity's rejection of the Roman focus on wealth and image. They preferred Jesus' focus on living simply and peacefully, sharing property, and providing charity to help the less fortunate. The poor liked the way Christian communities shared their wealth and established hospitals, schools, and other public services to improve their lives. Women and slaves liked Christianity because it treated them more like equals than other religions and Roman society did. Finally, many people embraced the idea of a personal relationship with God.

SPREADING THE WORD

In spite of Christianity's broad appeal, the religion's survival was far from certain, and it could easily have faded away. Instead it thrived because Jesus' followers spread his teachings fast and far. Through the Roman road network, Christianity spread rapidly in Jewish communities across the empire. Another big break was that the Romans confused Christianity with Judaism, and so they ignored the new religion, which allowed it to grow.

Even so, life as a Christian wasn't easy. The Romans often persecuted, or punished, Christians for their beliefs. However, one of Christianity's fiercest persecutors, a man named **Paul**, eventually became its biggest champion.

Paul was most responsible for spreading early Christianity. He was a well-educated Jew and a Roman citizen. He converted to Christianity while traveling on the road to Damascus. According to Paul's own account, he had a vision in which Jesus was revealed to him as the Son of God. As a result, Paul became a **missionary**, a person who travels to another country to do religious work.

He began spreading Jesus' teachings. Paul was often arrested, but he always escaped to preach again. He wrote many letters, or **epistles** (ih-PIH-suhls), explaining Jesus' teachings by answering specific questions. According to tradition, Paul was killed in a Roman massacre of Christians in A.D. 64. By then, Roman leaders realized that Christianity was a separate religion from Judaism and a popular religion—too popular. Fearful that Christianity might threaten the stability of the empire, Roman rulers made the religion's practice illegal.

REVIEW & ASSESS

1. **READING CHECK** How did Christianity spread throughout the Roman Empire?

2. **INTERPRET MAPS** What natural features served as the northern border for Christian expansion by A.D. 500?

3. **MAKE INFERENCES** Why was Paul an effective spokesperson for spreading the teachings of Christianity?

PLAN

OBJECTIVE

Analyze how and why Christianity spread across the Roman world.

CRITICAL THINKING SKILLS FOR LESSON 2.2

- Identify Main Ideas and Details
- Monitor Comprehension
- Interpret Maps
- Make Inferences
- Analyze Cause and Effect
- Make Predictions

ESSENTIAL QUESTION

What was the power and enduring legacy of the Roman Empire?

The size and stability of the Roman Empire helped the spread of Christianity. Lesson 2.2 discusses how Christianity spread in the Roman Empire and why Christianity is one of the most powerful legacies of the Roman Empire.

BACKGROUND FOR THE TEACHER

Paul's conversion to Christianity on the road to Damascus came not only with a belief in Christ, but also with a belief that the Gospels should be conveyed to Gentiles without the need for Jewish conversion nor the inclusion of traditional Jewish ceremonies. This put him fundamentally at odds with the Jewish Christian community. Paul acknowledged that the Christian mission was for all people and necessitated a dramatic break from Jewish traditions. This universal, or catholic, belief heavily informed the development of the early Christian church.

DIGITAL RESOURCES myNGconnect.com

TEACHER RESOURCES & ASSESSMENT

 Reading and Note-Taking

 Vocabulary Practice

 Section 2 Quiz

STUDENT RESOURCES

 Biography

INTRODUCE & ENGAGE

PREVIEW

Call students' attention to the map showing the spread of Christianity. Review the map as a class. Call on volunteers to describe what they see. At the end of the lesson, ask students to describe the relationship between the map and the text. **0:10 minutes**

TEACH

GUIDED DISCUSSION

1. **Analyze Cause and Effect** What was the effect of Rome's stability on the spread of Christianity? *(Rome's stability allowed people to travel across the empire in safety, which meant that individuals, such as Paul, who were trying to spread Christianity could move safely over great distances.)*

2. **Make Predictions** Have students consider the future of Christianity from this time period. **ASK:** Based on your knowledge and what you've read, what do you think happened next for Christianity and the Roman Empire? *(Answers will vary, but most students should recognize that Christianity would continue to spread, and they may guess that Christianity would become the official religion of the Roman Empire.)*

INTERPRET MAPS

Point out to students that many of the Christian areas c. A.D. 325 are along coastal areas or along rivers. **ASK:** Why might this be the case? *(Water was one of the most efficient means of travel at this time. As a result, it is not surprising that Christianity spread to coastal areas and along rivers first.)* **0:15 minutes**

ACTIVE OPTIONS

On Your Feet: Numbered Heads Organize students into groups of four and give each student a number. Tell students to think about and discuss a response to this question: Why might Christianity have been so appealing? Then call a number and have the student from each group with that number report for the group. **0:15 minutes**

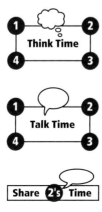

Critical Viewing: NG Chapter Gallery Invite students to explore the Chapter Gallery to examine the images that relate to this chapter. Have them select one of the images and do additional research to learn more about it. Ask questions that will inspire additional inquiry about the chosen gallery image, such as: What is this? Where and when was this created? By whom? Why was it created? What is it made of? Why does it belong in this chapter? What else would you like to know about it? **0:15 minutes**

DIFFERENTIATE

STRIVING READERS

Complete Sentence Starters Provide these sentence starters for students to complete after reading. You may also have students preview to set a purpose for reading.

- Gentiles are _____.

- The poor liked Christian communities because _____.

- The man who became Christianity's biggest champion was _____.

PRE-AP

Draw Conclusions Invite students to meet in small groups to draw conclusions about why Christianity was so appealing to so many people and why Roman leaders would outlaw its practice.

Press **mt** *in the Student eEdition for modified text.*

See the Chapter Planner for more strategies for differentiation.

REVIEW & ASSESS

ANSWERS

1. Christianity spread throughout the Roman Empire fast and far via Roman roads and the relative security of the empire.

2. The Rhine River and the Danube River served as the northern border for expansion.

3. Paul was well educated and a Jew. This gave him a credibility that other early missionaries may not have had.

New Testament Literature

The Christian Bible is made up of two parts: the Old Testament (or Hebrew Bible) and the New Testament. The New Testament includes the Gospel of Luke and Paul's Epistles. At the core of the New Testament teaching is the death and resurrection of Jesus, giving the world a "new covenant" (new testament) that would enable all who repented of their sins to enter the kingdom of heaven.

This painting shows a moment from Jesus' parable of the Prodigal Son.

ANSWERS

DOCUMENT 1
The Samaritan actually stopped to help the beaten man.

DOCUMENT 2
Paul is stating that all Christians are equal.

The Prodigal Son, Lucio Massari, c. 1614

DOCUMENT ONE
Primary Source: Sacred Text

The Parable of the Good Samaritan
This parable was recorded in the Gospel of Luke in the first century A.D. The Samaritans (suh-MEHR-uh-tuhns) were a community of people who were generally distrusted by the Jews, the audience of the parable. According to the Gospel of Luke, Jesus tells this parable to answer the question "Who is my neighbor?"

CONSTRUCTED RESPONSE How does the Samaritan's response to the beaten man differ from the responses of the priest and Levite?

Good Samaritan, Julius Schnorr von Carolsfeld, 1860

A man was going down from Jerusalem to Jericho, when he fell into the hands of robbers. They stripped him of his clothes, beat him, and went away, leaving him half dead. A priest happened to be going down the same road, and when he saw the man, he passed by on the other side. So too, a Levite [a Jew], when he came to the place and saw him, passed by on the other side. But a Samaritan, as he traveled, came where the man was; and when he saw him, he took pity on him. He went to him and bandaged his wounds, pouring on oil and wine. Then he put the man on his own donkey, took him to an inn, and took care of him. The next day he took out two silver coins and gave them to the innkeeper. "Look after him," he said, "and when I return, I will reimburse you for any extra expense you may have."

—Luke 10:30–35

DOCUMENT TWO
Primary Source: Sacred Text

from Paul's Epistle to the Galatians
Paul wrote his letter to the Galatians (guh-LAY-shuhnz) in the first century A.D. The Roman province of Galatia contained a number of early Christian communities. In his letter, Paul stresses some important ideas of the Christian faith.

CONSTRUCTED RESPONSE What important Christian ideas is Paul stating in this epistle?

You all are sons of God through faith in Christ Jesus, for all of you who were baptized . . . have clothed yourselves with Christ. There is neither Jew nor Greek, slave nor free, male nor female, for you are all one in Christ Jesus.

—Galatians 3:26–28

SYNTHESIZE & WRITE

1. **REVIEW** Review the ideas expressed in the parable of the Good Samaritan and Paul's Epistle to the Galatians.

2. **RECALL** On your own paper, write down the main idea expressed in each document.

3. **CONSTRUCT** Write a topic sentence that answers this question: What are some fundamental Christian ideas about how people should treat one another?

4. **WRITE** Using evidence from the documents and from the chapter, write a paragraph that supports your answer to the question in Step 3.

PLAN

OBJECTIVE

Synthesize information about New Testament Literature from primary source documents.

CRITICAL THINKING SKILLS FOR LESSON 2.3

- Synthesize
- Identify
- Draw Conclusions
- Make Inferences
- Evaluate

ESSENTIAL QUESTION

What was the power and enduring legacy of the Roman Empire?

The New Testament is the central element of modern Christianity's sacred text, the Bible. Lesson 2.3 provides a parable and an excerpt from one of Paul's letters as examples from Christianity's sacred text.

BACKGROUND FOR THE TEACHER

The New Testament is a collection of early Christian literature. The four Gospels deal with the life and the teachings of Jesus based on the memories of early Christians. The Book of Acts discusses the resurrection of Jesus to the death of Paul. The Letters, or Epistles, come from early Christian leaders, including Paul. The Epistles applied church teachings to issues facing early Christian communities. There was a large group of apocalyptic literature in early Christian writing. The only one included in the New Testament, however, was The Book of Revelation (the Apocalypse).

DIGITAL RESOURCES myNGconnect.com

TEACHER RESOURCES & ASSESSMENT

 Reading and Note-Taking   **Vocabulary Practice**   **Section 2 Quiz**

STUDENT RESOURCES

 NG Chapter Gallery

INTRODUCE & ENGAGE

PREPARE FOR THE DOCUMENT-BASED QUESTION

Before students start on the activity, briefly preview the two documents. Remind students that a constructed response requires full explanations in complete sentences. Emphasize that students should use what they have learned in the chapter in addition to the information in the documents. **0:05** minutes

TEACH

GUIDED DISCUSSION

1. **Draw Conclusions** Why might the Parable of the Good Samaritan have used a Samaritan—a group that Jews distrusted—as the hero? *(To establish that good can be found everywhere and that global judgments are not always correct)*

2. **Make Inferences** Why would letters be included in a sacred text? *(Responses will vary. Possible responses: Paul's Epistles were written relatively close to the time of Jesus and are valuable sources of information about the beliefs of early Christians. Capturing these beliefs, particularly in the form of letters to real people with real questions, in a sacred text makes sense.)*

EVALUATE

After students have completed the "Synthesize & Write" activity, allow time for them to exchange paragraphs and read and comment on the work of their peers. Guidelines for comments should be established prior to this activity so that feedback is constructive and encouraging in nature. **0:15** minutes

ACTIVE OPTIONS

On Your Feet: Think, Pair, Share Give students a few minutes to think about this question: What is the most effective way to communicate important ideas? Then have students choose partners and talk about the question for five minutes. Finally, allow individual students to share their ideas with the class. **0:20** minutes

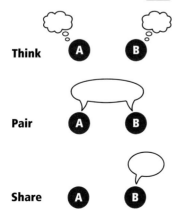

Think **A** **B**

Pair **A** **B**

Share **A** **B**

NG Learning Framework: Ask and Answer

ATTITUDE: Curiosity
SKILL: Communication

Have curious students find another primary source that fits in thematically with those included in the lesson. Have them write and answer a constructed response question of their own. Then have them rewrite their answer for item 4 under "Synthesize & Write," incorporating evidence from their new source. **0:30** minutes

DIFFERENTIATE

INCLUSION

Synthesize Help students minimize distractions by typing the two excerpts on one sheet of paper. Give photocopies of these to students along with highlighters. Tell students to highlight important words that appear in all two documents. Then have them write a summary sentence using several of the words.

PRE-AP

Research the Prodigal Son Ask students to research the parable depicted in the large image on the page, the Prodigal Son. Encourage them to report on this parable and include it in their Synthesize & Write activity.

Press **mt** *in the Student eEdition for modified text.*

See the Chapter Planner for more strategies for differentiation.

SYNTHESIZE & WRITE

ANSWERS

1. Help others; all Christians are equal.

2. Responses will vary.

3. Possible response: People should be kind to others and respect their differences.

4. Students' paragraphs should include their topic sentence from Step 3 and provide several details from the documents to support the sentence.

2.4

The Early Christian Church

Being different can make you a target for attacks. Early Christians were violently attacked, but their courage and determination ensured Christianity's survival.

MAIN IDEA

In time, Christianity became the official religion of the Roman Empire.

< Saint Peter's Basilica, in present-day Vatican City

Catacombs

Catacombs are underground burial chambers. They often have tunnels with spaces cut into the walls for the bodies. Some catacombs also have large chambers where funeral feasts were held. There are about 40 early Christian catacombs around Rome, and they are the most extensive of any known catacomb system in the world. Shown below is the Catacomb of Priscilla in Rome, Italy.

THE CONVERSION OF CONSTANTINE

As you have learned, Christians were often persecuted by their Roman rulers. In A.D. 35, a Christian named Stephen became the first of thousands of Christian victims. He was killed for his religious beliefs. Roman leaders punished Christians for refusing to worship the emperors.

This persecution only got worse. In A.D. 64, the emperor Nero blamed Christians for a great fire that swept through Rome. He had thousands of Christians put to death. Just being a Christian became punishable by death. As a result, worshippers were forced to meet in secret. They buried their dead in hidden underground chambers called **catacombs** (KA-tuh-kohms).

CONSTANTINE

Constantine was very generous to his supporters. Historians have suggested that he could afford to be so generous only because he robbed temples and used tax money for his own purposes. It is also clear that some of his supporters gained favor by faking conversions to Christianity.

In A.D. 312, Christian persecution had reached its highest point when an amazing change began. On the eve of a battle for control of the empire, a young Roman leader named **Constantine** prayed for help. He believed his prayers were answered with a vision of the Christian cross. The vision led him to paint a symbol on his soldiers' shields. Constantine went on to win the battle. As a result, he immediately put an end to Christian persecution.

Constantine made many other changes after he became emperor. He built churches in Roman lands and declared Sunday the Christian day of rest. He even had Christian symbols placed on coins. Constantine ruled for a long time. However, it was only after Constantine's rule that the emperor Theodosius officially closed all the temples to the Roman gods and made Christianity the official religion of Rome.

FORMATION OF THE EARLY CHURCH

With the legalization of Christianity, Christian communities could openly share their beliefs. Church leaders from across the empire held councils, or meetings, to discuss Christianity and the writings of religious scholars. Their discussions helped them define Christian beliefs and practices.

Christian practices were then communicated to Christian churches throughout the empire and beyond. Each church was led by a priest, and groups of churches were overseen by a bishop. The first bishop of Rome, according to Christian tradition, was the apostle Peter, who died for his beliefs in A.D. 64. Constantine had a church, St. Peter's Basilica, built over the apostle's tomb. The photo above shows the basilica, which was rebuilt in the 1600s. In time the bishop of Rome became the most important bishop, or **pope**. He was seen as the leader of the unified church, known as the **Roman Catholic Church**.

Church leaders standardized Christian beliefs into a common creed, or statement of beliefs. One such statement was the definition of God as a Holy Trinity: the union of Father, Son (Jesus), and Holy Spirit. Worship in the Christian church focused on some common sacraments, or religious ceremonies, such as baptism, an individual's acceptance by the church. As Christianity grew more structured and became more organized, it became a powerful religion.

REVIEW & ASSESS

1. **READING CHECK** How did Christianity become the official religion of the Roman Empire?

2. **DESCRIBE** How was the leadership of the early church organized?

3. **DRAW CONCLUSIONS** In what way did their persecution help unite the Christians?

PLAN

OBJECTIVE

Understand the development and formation of the early Christian church.

CRITICAL THINKING SKILLS FOR LESSON 2.4

- Identify Main Ideas and Details
- Monitor Comprehension
- Describe
- Draw Conclusions
- Summarize
- Make Predications
- Analyze Visuals

ESSENTIAL QUESTION

What was the power and enduring legacy of the Roman Empire?

The conversion of Constantine began the process of making Christianity the official religion of the Empire. Lesson 2.4 discusses how Christianity became the religion of Rome and how the early church began to organize itself.

BACKGROUND FOR THE TEACHER

Soon after Constantine converted, he called and presided over the Council of Nicaea. This was a gathering of church leaders who were discussing church problems, specifically, the fact that Arius of Alexandria in the Eastern church had declared that Jesus was not divine, but a "created being." The council ultimately condemned Arius and wrote the Nicene Creed, which established church doctrine on the divinity of Christ.

DIGITAL RESOURCES myNGconnect.com

TEACHER RESOURCES & ASSESSMENT

 Reading and Note-Taking

 Vocabulary Practice

 Section 2 Quiz

STUDENT RESOURCES

 NG Chapter Gallery

INTRODUCE & ENGAGE

PREVIEW

Remind students that the Christian church at this time was growing and still working out its leadership structure. Pose the question: *What challenges does any organization face as it expands?*
0:10 minutes

TEACH

GUIDED DISCUSSION

1. **Summarize** Summarize the events of Constantine's conversion and his actions afterwards. *(Constantine prayed for help on the eve of a battle and saw a vision of a Christian cross. He painted the symbol on his soldiers' shields and was victorious. He converted to Christianity, ended persecution of Christians, built churches, and even put Christian symbols on coins.)*

2. **Make Predictions** What might the long term effects be of Christianity becoming the official religion of the Roman Empire? *(Answers will vary, but most students should recognize that elements of Christian beliefs might start to guide political policy.)*

ANALYZE VISUALS

Point out St. Peter's in the photo. **ASK:** What about this building indicates that it's a church, and a Christian church in particular?

(The large, grand nature of the structure is often an indicator that the building is a church. Note for students that the church also looks like some government buildings. The cross at the top is an indicator that this is probably a Christian church.) **0:15** minutes

ACTIVE OPTIONS

On Your Feet: Research and Present Divide the class into groups of four and ask each group to do research about a specific aspect of Constantine's life. Have each group present their information to the class. **0:20** minutes

NG Learning Framework: Multimedia Presentation

ATTITUDE: **Responsibility**
SKILL: **Communication**
KNOWLEDGE: **Our Human Story**

Have students work in small collaborative groups to research more information about catacombs of early Christians in Rome. Tell students they should be respectful of the topic and of each other. Groups should present their findings to the class in a multimedia format. **0:30** minutes

DIFFERENTIATE

ENGLISH LANGUAGE LEARNERS

Give a Thumbs Up or Thumbs Down Write a set of true-false statements about the lesson, such as "Constantine converted to Christianity." Read the lesson aloud while students follow along in their books. Then have them close the books and listen as you read the true-false statements. Students should give a thumbs up if a statement is true and a thumbs down if a statement is false.

PRE-AP

Research St. Peter's Have students research the history and construction of St. Peter's. Have students pick an aspect of the building's history and write a research paper about it. Encourage students to add visuals or possibly build physical models to illustrate elements of their report.

Press (**mt**) *in the Student eEdition for modified text.*

See the Chapter Planner for more strategies for differentiation.

REVIEW & ASSESS

ANSWERS

1. The emperor Constantine converted to Christianity and stopped the persecution of Christians. The emperor Theodosius made Christianity the official religion of Rome.

2. The leadership of the Roman Catholic Church was organized in a hierarchy, with priests, bishops, and the title of pope for the bishop of Rome.

3. Christian persecution ensured that Christians worked together to maintain their beliefs, which included the creation of secret underground burial areas known as catacombs.

3.1 The Third Century Crisis

Despite the occasional unbalanced emperor, the Roman Empire ran smoothly for 200 years. Then things began to fall apart. Disputes over who should be emperor caused the return of political violence and civil war. In some years, four or even six emperors were on the throne. By A.D. 235, the Roman world had plunged into a crisis.

MAIN IDEA

Military problems led to a crisis in the Roman Empire.

MILITARY PROBLEMS

So what went wrong? Arguably the empire had physically outgrown the emperor's ability to govern it. At its height, the Roman Empire stretched from Scotland to the Sahara, an area about half the size of the United States. This vast expanse, with huge geographic and cultural differences, was very difficult to govern effectively.

Defending such a large area also proved difficult. Rome faced attacks on two fronts at the same time, which drained money and resources all across the empire. In the east, Rome fought the powerful Parthian Empire from Persia, while Germanic tribes raided Rome's northern borders.

Meanwhile, warring groups within the empire once again fought to decide who would be emperor. Civil wars bled the empire of desperately needed food, money, and soldiers. As emperors fought expensive wars they could not win, enemies from outside the empire attacked. With so many Roman soldiers engaged in warfare, the invaders plundered, or stole riches from, the unguarded interior. It was a sure sign of trouble when cities, including Rome, rebuilt their long-neglected defensive walls. These military problems provoked further political and social problems.

POLITICAL, ECONOMIC, AND SOCIAL PROBLEMS

War was not only dangerous for soldiers; it was disruptive for everyone. Emperors were blamed for not protecting the empire, and they were regularly replaced or murdered. Fifty different emperors ruled between A.D. 235 and 285. People living in what would become Spain, France, and Britain preferred to trust local rulers. They broke from Rome to form a separate Gallic Empire. These events weakened imperial authority and prevented the strong, decisive, and long-term action needed to restore order.

This constant warfare also ruined the economy. Trade was interrupted, and the empire had to rely on its inadequate agricultural resources. The people suffered food shortages and higher taxes. Wars are expensive, and the emperors expected the people to pay for them. Even heavier taxes were enforced when the imperial currency lost value. This affected rich and poor but mostly the poor.

Ordinary people grew angry, criminal organizations grew, and outbursts of mob anger increased. It even became difficult to recruit local officials. Nobody wanted these jobs because people risked a beating for doing them. In these unstable times, good citizenship took second place to looking after oneself.

DECLINE OF THE ROMAN EMPIRE

Illustration of a parade honoring victories of Emperor Augustus

Military Reasons
- Fighting the Parthian Empire in the east
- Fighting Germanic tribes in the west
- Fighting civil wars at home

Stone relief showing a government bureaucrat at work

Political Reasons
- Difficult to govern huge empire
- Frequently changing emperors
- Power gained by local leaders

Relief depicting a tax payment

Economic Reasons
- Trade interrupted
- People heavily taxed
- Lower value of currency

Illustration of a Roman party with the poor waiting on the rich

Social Reasons
- Unrest from gap between rich and poor
- More criminal organizations
- Civic responsibility no longer important

REVIEW & ASSESS

1. **READING CHECK** Why did the size of the Roman Empire cause military problems?

2. **ANALYZE CAUSE AND EFFECT** What was the result of the emperors' expensive wars?

3. **DRAW CONCLUSIONS** How did Rome's military problems lead to political, social, and economic problems?

PLAN

OBJECTIVE

Analyze the issues that led to a crisis for the Roman Empire in the third century.

CRITICAL THINKING SKILLS FOR LESSON 3.1

- Identify Main Ideas and Details
- Monitor Comprehension
- Analyze Cause and Effect
- Draw Conclusions
- Form and Support Opinions

ESSENTIAL QUESTION

What was the power and enduring legacy of the Roman Empire?

The power of Rome began to break down in the third century. Lesson 3.1 discusses the various factors that weakened the empire and would ultimately alter it forever.

BACKGROUND FOR THE TEACHER

Historians have debated for centuries the question of why Rome fell. The modern consensus is that there were multiple factors—of varying severity and duration—that converged to make the empire as it had been untenable. Military, political, economic, and social factors all contributed to what is considered the end of the Roman Empire. The truth is that these problems began long before the empire "fell." "The Third Century Crisis" is often identified as the point at which the empire began to unravel.

DIGITAL RESOURCES myNGconnect.com

TEACHER RESOURCES & ASSESSMENT

 Reading and Note-Taking

 Vocabulary Practice

 Section 3 Quiz

STUDENT RESOURCES

 NG Chapter Gallery

INTRODUCE & ENGAGE

ANALYZE VISUALS

Review the feature on the decline of the Roman Empire as a class. Ask students to look for the bullet points in the text as they read. Point out that bullet points can be a good summary, but the text provides context. Specifically, the context in this lesson is that all of Rome's troubles were intertwined. **0:10 minutes**

TEACH

GUIDED DISCUSSION

1. **Analyze Causes** Discuss as a group what sparked the various problems Rome faced in the third century. (*Possible answers: The military was weakened from internal civil wars and from being attacked on two fronts. Frequently changing emperors meant less political stability. War and political infighting inevitably hurt the empire economically. Arguably, the general unrest in other areas of society led to a social breakdown, which led to more crime and further distrust of those in power.*)

2. **Form and Support Opinions** If there were one thing that the Romans could have done differently to prevent the Empire's decline, what would it have been? Explain why. (*Answers will vary. Possible answers: They could have kept a bigger army to fight off their enemies. OR A strong leader could have stopped the political infighting and focused on stabilizing the empire.*)

MORE INFORMATION

Too Many Cooks in the Kitchen Below is a listing of emperors in 238—there were six. Ask students to imagine six different presidents in one year. That's a new president every two months!

Maximinus I 235–238 A.D.
Gordian I 238 A.D.
Gordian II 238 A.D.
Balbinus 238 A.D.
Pupienus 238 A.D.
Gordian III 238–244 A.D.

ACTIVE OPTIONS

On Your Feet: Four Corners Place signs around the room that list each of the four general reasons for the decline of the Roman Empire—military, political, economic, and social. Ask students to move to the sign for the reason that they feel was most responsible for Rome's decline. Have groups confer about their position and select a representative to present their position to the rest of the class. **0:20 minutes**

NG Learning Framework: Support an Argument

SKILL: Collaboration
KNOWLEDGE: **Our Human Story**

Invite students to pair up and choose one of the four topics shown in the "Decline of the Roman Empire" feature that they believe was most responsible for Rome's decline—military, political, economic, or social. Have each pair research support for their choice. Have all the pairs for each topic get together to share their findings and then present the material to the class. **0:30 minutes**

DIFFERENTIATE

ENGLISH LANGUAGE LEARNERS

Use Vocabulary Word Maps Pair beginning and more advanced English Language Learners. Have them use a Word Map for three words they are struggling with in the text. Have groups trade Word Maps and review.

GIFTED & TALENTED

Make a Poster Suggest that students use the text and online research to find reasons for the decline of the Roman Empire. Suggest to students that they visually represent those reasons on a poster. Have students display their final posters in class.

Press (mt) *in the Student eEdition for modified text.*

See the Chapter Planner for more strategies for differentiation.

REVIEW & ASSESS

ANSWERS

1. The vast borders of the Roman Empire meant that it could potentially take Roman soldiers a great deal of time to move from one location to another. This meant that invaders could potentially advance deep into Roman territory before encountering resistance.

2. Expensive wars ruined the economy. Trade was interrupted and emperors raised taxes to pay for the wars, which made life even harder for Roman citizens.

3. Rome's military problems caused hardships for the people and made it very difficult for a single emperor to stay in power for very long. People became increasingly disenchanted and the crime rate rose as people turned to taking what they needed. The constant war was expensive, and emperors used taxes to finance them. War also interrupted trade. So not only did people have less to spend, there were less available resources to buy, such as food.

Eastern and **Western**
Roman Empires

The Roman Empire was too big for one person to manage. Unfortunately that didn't stop ambitious men from trying and failing. Then Rome's luck changed. In A.D. 284, the throne was seized by an emperor who had the sense and strength to make the big changes that could keep the empire alive.

MAIN IDEA

In A.D. 285, the Roman Empire was divided into the Western Roman Empire and the Eastern Roman Empire.

DIOCLETIAN DIVIDES THE EMPIRE

The new emperor was named **Diocletian** (dy-uh-KLEE-shuhn), and he had a lot on his plate. He faced endangered frontiers, overstretched armies, economic collapse, weak imperial authority, and widespread unrest. However, Diocletian had a radical plan: In A.D. 285, he divided the empire in two. Diocletian ruled the Eastern Roman Empire, and his trusted friend Maximian ruled the Western Roman Empire. Each man appointed a junior emperor to rule with him. This rule by four emperors, called a **tetrarchy** (TEH-trahr-kee), worked really well at first.

Each emperor focused on his specific region while cooperating to introduce reforms.

Together they increased the army to 400,000 men and reorganized and strengthened the frontier forces. They also created a mobile field army ready to tackle trouble wherever it broke out. On the political front, Diocletian and Maximian reformed government administration and divided the provinces into more manageable units. To promote unity, they enforced emperor worship and the Latin language everywhere. They encouraged economic recovery by reforming tax laws, controlling inflation, and stabilizing the currency. The empire was on the road to recovery, and after 20 years, Diocletian and Maximian retired, letting the junior emperors take over. However, this was as good as the tetrarchy got.

CONSTANTINE MOVES THE CAPITAL

You've learned that the emperor Constantine made the practice of Christianity legal in the empire. Before he did that, he had to fight to become emperor. Constantine's father was emperor of the Western Roman Empire. When Constantine's father died in A.D. 306, however, the tetrarchy refused his claim to be western emperor, sparking a civil war. Constantine won the war and became emperor of east and west. However, Constantine was more interested in the eastern half of his empire.

Rome's importance had long been decreasing. Emperors no longer lived in Rome, and Italy had lost its privileged status.

The differences between east and west were increasing. The east produced more people, more food, more taxes, and more soldiers, while the west just grew weaker. So Constantine moved the capital from Rome to the ancient Greek city of Byzantium, which he renamed Constantinople. (Today the city is called Istanbul.) He built his new capital on the strategically important Bosporus, a narrow stretch of water separating Europe and Asia.

Constantine also continued the reforms begun by earlier emperors, earning the title "the Great." However, his sons plunged the empire into another civil war. The emperor Theodosius later reunited the empire, but the division of east and west became permanent after his death in A.D. 395. From then on, the fortunes and futures of the two empires were very different.

ROMAN EMPIRE: EAST AND WEST, c. A.D. 395

NATURAL BORDERS The Rhine and Danube rivers on the northern border of the Roman Empire were difficult to cross, which made it easier for the Roman army to defend the empire.

CONSTANTINOPLE Constantine's new capital on the Bosporus provided easy access to many resources and allowed the empire to control trade.

EUROPE

Rhine R.

Danube R.

Black Sea

Bosporus

ATLANTIC OCEAN

Rome

Constantinople

ASIA

ROME Diocletian's decision to rule the Eastern Roman Empire made it clear that Rome was no longer the center of political power.

AFRICA

Mediterranean Sea

Western Roman Empire
Eastern Roman Empire

REVIEW & ASSESS

1. **READING CHECK** Why did Diocletian divide the Roman Empire in two?

2. **INTERPRET MAPS** In what ways was Rome's location similar to that of Constantinople?

3. **IDENTIFY PROBLEMS AND SOLUTIONS** What was Diocletian's plan for ruling the vast empire more efficiently?

PLAN

OBJECTIVE

Explain how and why the Roman Empire was divided and administered.

CRITICAL THINKING SKILLS FOR LESSON 3.2

- Identify Main Ideas and Details
- Monitor Comprehension
- Interpret Maps
- Identify Problems and Solutions
- Compare and Contrast
- Draw Conclusions

ESSENTIAL QUESTION

What was the power and enduring legacy of the Roman Empire?

Diocletian divided the empire administratively so that it could be run more efficiently. Lesson 3.2 discusses Diocletian's division of the empire and Constantine's "reunification" of the empire and subsequent move of the capital to Byzantium, which he named Constantinople.

BACKGROUND FOR THE TEACHER

The division of the Roman Empire happened about 40 years before Constantine came to power. Diocletian did move his administrative capital to the East at Nicomedia—near Constantine's future capital of Byzantium. Maximian ruled the West, but from Milan, not Rome. Although Diocletian found a way to stabilize the empire, it was only a temporary fix that succeeding emperors could not emulate.

DIGITAL RESOURCES myNGconnect.com

TEACHER RESOURCES & ASSESSMENT

 Reading and Note-Taking

 Vocabulary Practice

 Section 3 Quiz

STUDENT RESOURCES

 NG Chapter Gallery

INTRODUCE & ENGAGE

REVIEW

Discuss how much area the Roman Empire covered. Review what students remember about the challenges of ruling such a large area. Ask students if they think ruling the empire might have been easier with some help. It seems obvious, and that's exactly what Diocletian did. **0:05** minutes

TEACH

GUIDED DISCUSSION

1. **Compare and Contrast** Review the reforms of the tetrarchy and Constantine. What similarities and difference do you notice? *(Possible answers for similarities: tried to reform government, believed the power of the empire was in the East; Possible answers for differences: religious beliefs, tetrarchy versus sole emperor.)*

2. **Draw Conclusions** Tell students that the tetrarchy was very successful, but that soon after Diocletian and Maximian retired, the Roman Empire again fell into disarray. **ASK:** What conclusions can you draw about the tetrarchy? *(The success of the tetrarchy was largely due to the people in charge.)*

INTERPRET MAPS

Have students review the map and read the call-outs. Ask volunteers what they find interesting or what questions they have about the material shown on the map.

(Possible notes: rivers as borders in the north; cities next to water; the Roman Empire was on three continents) **0:10** minutes

ACTIVE OPTIONS

On Your Feet: Team Word Webbing Organize students into teams of four and have them record what they know about the division of the Roman Empire into East and West on a piece of paper. Encourage students to build on their teammates' entries as they rotate the paper from one member to the next. Then call on volunteers from each group to make statements about the division of the Roman Empire based on their webs. **0:15** minutes

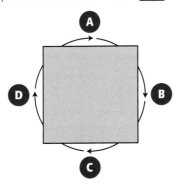

Critical Viewing: NG Chapter Gallery Have students explore the NG Chapter Gallery and choose two of the items to compare and contrast, either in written form or verbally with a partner. Ask questions that will inspire this process, such as: How are these images alike? How are they different? Why did you select these two items? How do they relate in history? **0:10** minutes

DIFFERENTIATE

STRIVING READERS

Pose and Answer Questions Have students work in pairs to read the lesson. Instruct them to pause after each paragraph and ask one another *who, what, when, where,* or *why* questions about what they have just read. Advise students to read more slowly and focus on specific details if they have difficulty answering the questions, or to reread a paragraph to find the answers.

PRE-AP

Map Research Point out the discussion about the Rhine and Danube rivers being natural borders for the Roman Empire. Pair students up and have them research the other borders of the empire and what defined them.

Press **mt** *in the Student eEdition for modified text.*

See the Chapter Planner for more strategies for differentiation.

REVIEW & ASSESS

ANSWERS

1. Diocletian divided the empire so that it could be better managed and defended.

2. The location of Rome and Constantinople were similar in that they were both near water, and they were both near the center of the respective spheres of influence when they were established.

3. Diocletian split the empire in two with four rulers: an eastern and western emperor, each with a junior emperor. Diocletian and Maximian restructured the government and created more manageable territories.

3.3

End of the **Western** Roman Empire

If you lived in the Western Roman Empire in A.D. 375, you'd be unhappy with the way things were going. While the west struggled to rule itself, feed itself, pay its bills, and defend its borders, you would enviously watch the Eastern Roman Empire grow richer, stronger, and more stable. However bad things got, you could never imagine a world without the Roman Empire—but that reality was just 101 years away.

MAIN IDEA

Invaders attacked the Western Roman Empire and caused its downfall.

FOREIGN INVADERS

Diocletian and Constantine only delayed the end of the Western Roman Empire. The end came in the form of **barbarians**, a Greek word Romans used to describe all people outside of the empire. Three main tribes of barbarians would finally tear the Western Roman Empire apart. The Visigoths (VIH-zuh-gahths) and Vandals were Germanic tribes from northern Europe. Looking for better farmland, both groups migrated south toward the Roman frontier.

The Huns formed the third tribe of barbarians. Migrating from Asia, they were nomads, or wandering cattle herders. Their skill with horses and bows made them a ferocious fighting force. Beginning in A.D. 445, a man named **Attila** was their sole ruler.

THE WESTERN ROMAN EMPIRE FALLS

Attila and his army swept into Europe. Forced into the Western Roman Empire by the Huns, the Visigoths soon invaded Italy. Around the same time, the Vandals invaded Gaul and then Spain. By now the emperor, who had few Roman soldiers to call on, had to enlist barbarian fighters to defend the empire.

On August 24, 410, the Visigoths shocked the world by sacking, or destroying, Rome. They then conquered Gaul and Spain, driving the Vandals into North Africa. Then came Attila. The Huns attacked Gaul in A.D. 451, and the emperor relied on barbarian armies to fight them. Rome had lost control. In A.D. 476, the last emperor quietly left the throne.

The Western Roman Empire was broken up into many Germanic kingdoms, and the Eastern Roman Empire became known as the Byzantine Empire. The Roman Empire was over. Historians argue about why the Western Roman Empire fell. Did it end naturally because of internal failings? Was it brought down by external forces? Or was it simply transformed into something new?

POSSIBLE RESPONSE

The artist has used bright colors for Attila and more muted colors in the background, which makes Attila stand out. Attila also has wild-looking eyes and is looking straight out at the viewer, which makes him seem fierce.

Critical Viewing This painting shows Attila the Hun attacking a Roman city. In what ways has the artist made Attila seem very fierce?

REVIEW & ASSESS

1. **READING CHECK** What three barbarian tribes invaded Roman territory, leading to Rome's downfall?

2. **SEQUENCE EVENTS** What events led to the fall of the Western Roman Empire?

3. **DRAW CONCLUSIONS** Why were so many tribes able to invade the Western Roman Empire?

The Roman Empire and Christianity **331**

PLAN

OBJECTIVE

Identify the forces that ultimately brought an end to the Western Roman Empire.

CRITICAL THINKING SKILLS FOR LESSON 3.3

- Identify Main Ideas and Details
- Monitor Comprehension
- Sequence Events
- Draw Conclusions
- Identify
- Make Inferences
- Make Predictions

ESSENTIAL QUESTION

What was the power and enduring legacy of the Roman Empire?

Foreign invaders destroyed the Western Roman Empire. Lesson 3.3 discusses some of the groups involved in ending the Roman Empire.

BACKGROUND FOR THE TEACHER

The decline of the Western Roman Empire is complicated and multifaceted, but the deathblow is clear—the "barbarian" tribes rampaged across the Western Empire, sacking Rome several times. Regardless of the various factors that brought the Western Empire to its low point, once there, a Roman army that was increasingly in disarray could not check the military force of Germanic and Asian invaders. The Western Roman emperor had essentially lost control and the Eastern Roman Empire was not going to get mired in the fight.

TEACHER RESOURCES & ASSESSMENT

 Reading and Note-Taking

 Vocabulary Practice

 Section 3 Quiz

STUDENT RESOURCES

 Biography

INTRODUCE & ENGAGE

ANALYZE VISUALS

Have students look at the painting of Attila in the lesson. Point out that it was painted in 1930—long after the fall of Rome—and that the artist was Italian. **ASK:** What does this painting tell you not only about Attila, but about the artist? **0:05** minutes

TEACH

GUIDED DISCUSSION

1. **Explain** Why would multiple groups attacking the Western Roman Empire at the same time be more challenging to defend against? *(Multiple attackers would mean there was no single leadership with which to negotiate. Additionally, the various groups would have their own motivations for attacking and thus be harder to predict where their forces were headed.)*

2. **Make Inferences** Point out to students that the Eastern Roman Empire does not come to the aid of the Western Roman Empire during this period. Ask students why this might be the case. *(Answers will vary, but the Eastern Roman Empire was under attack as well. However, the East had better leadership and was able to keep invaders at bay through either military strength or negotiation.)*

MAKE PREDICTIONS

The Western Roman Empire was replaced by many smaller Germanic kingdoms. **ASK:** How do you think life in the former empire might have changed for the people who lived there? *(Answers will vary, but point out the loss of a large centralized bureaucracy being a significant change. Use this as an opportunity to foreshadow the Middle Ages.)* **0:10** minutes

ACTIVE OPTIONS

On Your Feet: Fishbowl Use a Fishbowl strategy to reinforce what students have learned. Have half the class sit in an inner circle and discuss the fall of Rome. Have the other half of the class sit in an outer circle, facing inward, and take notes on the discussion. On a signal, have the circles trade places. **0:15** minutes

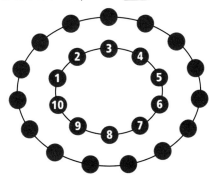

NG Learning Framework: Write a Speech

SKILLS: Collaboration, Communication
KNOWLEDGE: **Our Human Story**

Divide the class into groups—the Visigoths, Vandals, and Huns. Have each group collaborate to research and produce a speech describing their reasons for attacking Rome. Groups should choose a volunteer to read the speech. **0:15** minutes

DIFFERENTIATE

STRIVING READERS

Create Sequence Chains Have students work in pairs to create a Sequence Chain that shows the events leading to the fall of Rome. Remind students to refer to the text to help them. Discuss their Sequence Chains as a group to assess their comprehension.

GIFTED & TALENTED

Create a Multimedia Presentation Ask students to create multimedia presentations about the fall of Rome using photos, text, and audio. Point out to students that their presentations should describe the events that led to the last emperor of Rome leaving the throne. Invite volunteers to share their presentations with the class.

Press (mt) *in the Student eEdition for modified text.*

See the Chapter Planner for more strategies for differentiation.

REVIEW & ASSESS

ANSWERS

1. The Visigoths, Vandals, and Huns invaded Roman territory.

2. The movement of the various tribes caused them to clash with the Romans at different times and places. In 410, the Visigoths destroyed Rome; in 445, Attila became sole leader of the Huns. In 451, the Huns attacked Gaul. In 476, the last emperor of Rome left the throne.

3. So many tribes were able to invade the Western Empire because weak leadership in Rome was unable to provide the support the army needed to fend off the attacks.

Latin and Literature

Students learning Latin have a rhyme: "Latin is a language as dead as dead can be. First it killed the Romans, and now it's killing me." But Latin is not dead. Latin is still used—especially by scientists and doctors. In fact, you use Latin words every day. It's part of Rome's legacy, or heritage.

MAIN IDEA

The Latin language spread across the empire and influences the way we speak and write today.

AN INFLUENTIAL LANGUAGE

As you've learned, the Roman Empire had dozens of languages, but the language spoken in Rome was **Latin**. Although Greek was also commonly used, Latin was established as the official language for international communication, government, law, and trade. It was used for official business from Britain to Egypt.

The Romans brought writing to northern Europe, and we still use the Latin alphabet today. However, back then the alphabet had only 22 letters. The letters *i* and *j* were interchangeable, as were *u* and *v*. The letters *w* and *y* did not exist at all.

After the Roman Empire fell, the Latin language lived on. Over time, new languages, called Romance languages, developed from Latin. These languages include French, Italian, Spanish, and Portuguese. Each language is distinctive but shares a common root in Latin, the "Roman" in *Romance*. The English language was greatly influenced by the Romance languages and uses many Latin words, including *campus, census, curriculum, index, item, sponsor,* and *stadium*.

ORATORY, POETRY, AND PHILOSOPHY

In addition to language, Rome left behind a legacy in literature, featuring speeches, poetry, and philosophical works. **Oratory**, or public speaking, was especially prized, and promising young men were trained in the art of argument and persuasion. As you learned previously, Cicero was one of Rome's greatest orators, and his speeches are still studied by serious students of public speaking.

The Romans also loved poetry, which was based on Greek traditions. The ultimate poem was the epic, a long story describing a hero's adventures. The most celebrated Roman epic was **Virgil's** *Aeneid* (uh-NEE-uhd), which fills 12 volumes. Written between 30 and 19 B.C., it tells the story of Aeneas, the legendary founder of Rome.

Roman philosophy was another extension of Greek ideas. Philosophy is the study of reality, knowledge, and beliefs. Ethical and religious arguments interested Romans more than theory and speculation. The Greek Stoic (STOH-ihk) philosophy was especially influential in Roman life. It stressed a practical approach to life in which people performed their civic duty and accepted their circumstances—good or bad.

The Roman Catholic Church became the keeper of Roman literature for centuries after the empire fell. It preserved works that could be used to educate young men in morality, government, and law. A 15th-century fascination with the ancient world revived the popularity of Roman literature and has ensured its widespread circulation ever since.

LATIN AND ENGLISH

Many English words have Latin roots, or origins. Examine the prefixes and suffixes listed. What words can you add?

-ty, -ity
FORMS NOUNS FROM ADJECTIVES
Similarity
Technicality

Sub-
UNDER
Submarine
Subway

Re-
AGAIN
Rebuild
Remake

-ation
FORMS NOUNS FROM VERBS
Celebration
Formation

Pre-
BEFORE
Preview
Prepay

Dis-
NOT ANY
Disbelief
Disrespect

-ment
FORMS NOUNS FROM VERBS
Entertainment
Statement

-ible, -able
FORMS ADJECTIVES FROM VERBS
∧ *Flexible*
Likable

Post-
AFTER
Postgame
Postwar

-fy, -ify
FORMS VERBS AND MEANS "TO MAKE"
< *Purify*
Humidify

LEGEND
● Prefix ● Prefix Definition ● Suffix ● Suffix Explanation ● Example Words

REVIEW & ASSESS

1. **READING CHECK** How has the English language been influenced by Latin?

2. **SEQUENCE EVENTS** What sequence of events helped keep Latin alive?

3. **MAKE INFERENCES** How did Roman ideas about philosophy support the ancient Roman approach to life?

PLAN

OBJECTIVE

Understand the lasting legacy of Rome in language and literature.

CRITICAL THINKING SKILLS FOR LESSON 4.1

- Identify Main Ideas and Details
- Monitor Comprehension
- Sequence Events
- Make Inferences
- Summarize
- Make Inferences
- Analyze Visuals

ESSENTIAL QUESTION

What was the power and enduring legacy of the Roman Empire?

Latin and literature are Roman legacies that have endured over 2,000 years. Lesson 4.1 discusses the written and spoken legacies of the Roman Empire.

BACKGROUND FOR THE TEACHER

The oldest existing example of written Latin is on a Greek cloak pin from around the 7th century B.C. Small communities along the Tiber River still spoke Latin as Rome began its rise. Latin became the language of Rome and then spread along with Rome's borders. Long after the Empire was gone, Latin was the language used in most major universities. The Roman Catholic church required Latin to be used in religious services until the late 20th century.

DIGITAL RESOURCES myNGconnect.com

TEACHER RESOURCES & ASSESSMENT

 Reading and Note-Taking   **Vocabulary Practice**   **Section 4 Quiz**

STUDENT RESOURCES

 Active History

INTRODUCE & ENGAGE

ACTIVATE PRIOR KNOWLEDGE

Tell students that in this lesson, they will start to learn about some of the enduring legacies of Rome. Ask students to identify aspects of modern culture they know came from Rome. *(Possibilities: our alphabet; a variety of English words—either directly or derived; philosophy; the art of public speaking; art; architecture; law)*
0:05 minutes

TEACH

GUIDED DISCUSSION

1. **Summarize** Tell students that philosophy is a way of looking at the world. As mentioned in the text, Greek Stoic philosophy was influential in Roman culture. Have students summarize their understanding of stoicism and provide an example of what they believe would be a stoic approach to a situation. *(Answers will vary.)*

2. **Make Inferences** Why is language one of the most influential legacies a culture or civilization can leave behind? *(Possible answer: Language is not just an alphabet. Language is also the means by which ideas are passed from one person to another, from one culture to another. A language reflects a world view and if that language survives, carries a significant aspect of that culture into the future.)*

ANALYZE VISUALS

Have students review the prefix and suffix graphic. Walk through the chart as a class and discuss how a prefix or a suffix can change a word. **0:10** minutes

ACTIVE OPTIONS

Active History: Analyze the Roots of Modern Languages Extend the lesson by using either the PDF or Whiteboard version of the Analyze the Roots of Modern Languages Active History lesson. These activities take a deeper look at a topic from, or related to, the lesson. Explore the activities as a class, turn them into group assignments, or even assign them individually. **0:15** minutes

On Your Feet: Word Race Divide the class into two teams and line them up in front of two prepared writing areas. (blackboard, whiteboard, butcher paper, etc.) Write a prefix or a suffix above each team's writing area. On your count, the first student in each line will go up and write a word that uses their assigned prefix or suffix. When finished, they'll go to the back of the line and the next team member goes up, and so forth. Give each team 60 seconds to write as many words as they can. Each correct word scores a point. Add more rounds as desired. **0:20** minutes

DIFFERENTIATE

STRIVING READERS

Strengthen Vocabulary Ask students to write the word *oratory* in a Word Square and then write its definition and characteristics. Have students provide examples and non-examples of it. After students complete the Word Square, ask them to create Word Squares for the other vocabulary words in the lesson.

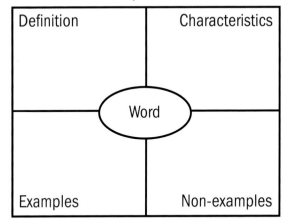

Definition	Characteristics
	Word
Examples	Non-examples

PRE-AP

Research the *Aeneid* Have students find an English translation of Virgil's *Aeneid*. Let them know that it was written in hexameters. Hexameter has not been a very widely-used style in English because the language does not easily lend itself to the format. Ask them to start scanning the text and find a passage that they like. Have them copy this passage and explain to the class what it means to them.

Press **mt** *in the Student eEdition for modified text.*

See the Chapter Planner for more strategies for differentiation.

REVIEW & ASSESS

ANSWERS

1. The English language contains many Latin words that we use everyday. Also, the Romance languages that developed from Latin influenced the English language.

2. Latin's continued use in education, literature, and in the Roman Catholic Church helped keep the language alive.

3. The Greek Stoic philosophy stressed a practical approach to life in which people performed their civic duty and accepted their circumstances—good or bad. This was very much in keeping with Roman society and government, which is why the Romans perpetuated this philosophy.

4.2 Art, Architecture, and Law

The Romans shaped the ancient world for a thousand years. But what have they ever done for us? Well, quite a lot actually. If you know what to look for, you can spot Rome's legacy in modern-day art, architecture, and law.

MAIN IDEA

The Romans developed many ideas that continue to influence our lives today.

This panel from a Roman sarcophagus is an example of bas-relief.

ART AND ARCHITECTURE

As with their philosophy, Romans preferred a realistic approach to art. The paintings and statues that decorated their homes showed people and things as they really looked. Like the Romans, people today often display realistic family portraits, although photos have generally replaced statues.

The Romans also made mosaics and frescoes popular on floors and walls around the world. Roman frescoes can be compared to modern murals and even some street art. The Roman **bas-relief** (bah-ruh-LEEF) is a realistic sculpture with figures raised against a flat background. These sculptures appear on monuments such as the National World War II Memorial in Washington, D.C. The photo on these pages is an example of a Roman bas-relief carved into the side of a sarcophagus, or stone coffin.

Rome's architectural influence is everywhere. Starting from the ground up, the Romans showed the world the benefit of an extensive, well-built, and well-maintained all-weather road network. European roads still follow Roman routes and sometimes cross original Roman bridges.

When a new Roman town was created, city planners took into account the city's climate and geography. The Romans always tried to establish a grid pattern for the streets. That means that the streets formed a network of intersecting horizontal and vertical lines. Many towns and cities use this pattern today.

Like the Romans, modern builders rely on concrete to build strong, tall, and unusual buildings. Roman architectural styles such as columns, arches, and domes can be seen in the the U.S. Capitol and other buildings. Many modern stadiums follow the design perfected in the Colosseum.

LAW AND GOVERNMENT

Rome even influences the way people today live. Roman ideas of civic duty are encouraged in the United States and elsewhere. The structure of the U.S. government reflects elements of the Roman Republic, including representative assemblies and the system of checks and balances. Roman laws are the basis of law codes around the world, including that of the United States. The ideas of a fair judge, presumption of innocence, and equality under the law also come from the Romans.

The Latin language is still very much a part of modern law and other fields and professions. Legal documents, science papers, and memorial inscriptions are rich with Latin text. As you learned earlier, many everyday English words have their roots in Latin. Studying Latin can also make it easier to learn other modern languages that have Latin roots.

So don't just think about the legacy of Rome, search it out. It's in our language, laws, government, art, and architecture. The Romans are everywhere.

REVIEW & ASSESS

1. **READING CHECK** What Roman achievements in art and architecture influence our lives today?

2. **MAKE CONNECTIONS** How has the government of the Roman Republic influenced the structure of the U.S. government?

3. **COMPARE AND CONTRAST** How are the layouts of many towns and cities today similar to those in ancient Rome?

PLAN

OBJECTIVE

Understand the lasting legacy of Rome in modern-day art, architecture, and law.

CRITICAL THINKING SKILLS FOR LESSON 4.2

- Identify Main Ideas and Details
- Monitor Comprehension
- Make Connections
- Compare and Contrast
- Synthesize
- Make Inferences
- Analyze Visuals

ESSENTIAL QUESTION

What was the power and enduring legacy of the Roman Empire?

Roman art, architecture, and law profoundly influenced the development of Western society. Lesson 4.2 discusses these aspects of the Roman Empire and how we can still see them all around us today.

BACKGROUND FOR THE TEACHER

City planning was a deliberate and thoughtful process in the Roman Empire. Wide avenues would run from the mid-point of each side directly across to the opposite side. Side streets were based off that grid. The forum was located near the center of Roman towns. Purpose-driven structures often appeared on the perimeter of the forum, including shops, tax collectors, and temples. Large cities might have multiple forums dedicated to specific activities such as finance or administration.

DIGITAL RESOURCES myNGconnect.com

TEACHER RESOURCES & ASSESSMENT

 Reading and Note-Taking

 Vocabulary Practice

 Section 4 Quiz

STUDENT RESOURCES

 NG Chapter Gallery

BRAINSTORM: WHERE IS ROME?

Tell students that there are legacies of Roman culture that are clearly visible to us every day. As a class, brainstorm modern objects, ideas, art, etc., based on what students have learned so far. *(Select possibilities: language, legal theories, buildings, sculptures, civic duty)* **0:10** minutes

TEACH

GUIDED DISCUSSION

1. **Synthesize** Why are legal concepts such as a fair judge, a presumption of innocence, and equality under the law important? *(Possible answer: All of these concepts are designed to protect the innocent and to ensure that the law is applied the same way from trial to trial.)*

2. **Make Inferences** Why might something such as city planning be such a lasting legacy of the Roman Empire? *(Possible answer: The empire existed for a long time, and there was plenty of time to find out what worked and what didn't. So it makes sense that Romans found useful and efficient ways of doing certain things.)*

ANALYZE VISUALS

Have students review the bas-relief sculpture in the photo and remind them it is made out of stone. Ask them what they find interesting about it. *(Possible answers: the detail, the realism)* **0:05** minutes

ACTIVE OPTIONS

On Your Feet: Legacy Debate Divide the class into three teams: Art, Architecture, and Law. Give the teams some time to develop their reasons for why their Roman legacy is the most enduring aspect of Roman culture today. **0:20** minutes

NG Learning Framework: Compare Observations

SKILLS: Observation, Collaboration
KNOWLEDGE: **Our Human Story, New Frontiers**

Have students review the previous lessons, looking specifically for information about the legacy of Rome. They should work in pairs to create a list of observations about the Roman legacy and why elements of Roman culture have endured. Once they have completed their list of observations, each pair should exchange lists with another pair and discuss the new list. **0:15** minutes

INCLUSION

Summarize by Matching Provide pairs of students with a set of index cards showing the following words and phrases in mixed order: *bas-relief, fresco, mosaic, column, arch, dome, representative assembly, checks and balances, equality.* Then have the students sort the cards into three groups: art, architecture, and government and law.

GIFTED & TALENTED

Describe Roman Art Have students use library resources or online sources to research Roman art. Instruct them to choose a way to describe Roman art. They might create a multimedia presentation with photos and descriptions; create their own sculpture, fresco, or mosaic; create a play or dialogue around Roman art; or write a traditional research paper. **ASK:** What makes Roman art worth preserving and emulating? *(Answers may vary but should include a comment about the enduring nature of art.)*

Press (**mt**) in the Student eEdition for modified text.

See the Chapter Planner for more strategies for differentiation.

ANSWERS

1. Some achievements include mosaics, frescoes, bas-relief, columns, arches, domes, and the use of concrete.

2. Representative assemblies and a checks-and-balances system have been used in the U.S. government.

3. They are based on a grid pattern.

A.D. 52

The system of aqueducts that supplied water to Rome and its empire was a major feat of engineering. In the capital city itself, 11 aqueducts carried fresh water from the area's surrounding rivers and lakes, some as far as 57 miles away. Not all of these structures were architectural masterpieces like the Claudian Aqueduct (shown here), which was completed in A.D. 52. Many consisted of simple underground pipes through which water flowed to various tanks throughout the city. The Roman aqueduct system fell apart after the breakdown of the empire, but the basic engineering principles behind its construction are still in use today.

336 CHAPTER 11   337

PLAN

OBJECTIVE

Understand why aqueducts themselves were important, but also why they are powerful reminders of the once mighty Roman Empire.

CRITICAL THINKING SKILLS FOR LESSON 4.3

- Analyze Visuals
- Make Inferences

ESSENTIAL QUESTION

What was the power and enduring legacy of the Roman Empire?

Sustaining and supporting a growing urban population was a constant effort in ancient Rome. Supplying water was a vital part of that effort.

Lesson 4.3 shows a still-standing aqueduct that began bringing water to the city of Rome around A.D. 52.

BACKGROUND FOR THE TEACHER

Aqueducts are systems for providing water. Although the Roman aqueducts are the most famous water delivery system of the ancient world, they were not the first. Persia, India, and Egypt all had water supply systems in place hundreds of years before Rome. Still, the engineering mastery shown in the system of aqueducts that supplied the city of Rome with water was unmatched in the ancient world and would remain so until modern times.

DIGITAL RESOURCES myNGconnect.com

TEACHER RESOURCES & ASSESSMENT

 Reading and Note-Taking   **Vocabulary Practice**   **Section 4 Quiz**

STUDENT RESOURCES

 NG Chapter Gallery

INTRODUCE & ENGAGE

WHERE'S THE WATER?

Have students consider the topography of their community—hills, valleys, etc.—and ask them to think about the nearest source of water. **ASK:** How would you move enough water for everyone in the community using only gravity? Explain that this was the challenge faced by Roman engineers across the empire. **0:10 minutes**

TEACH

GUIDED DISCUSSION

1. **Analyze Visuals** Examine the photograph of the Claudian Aqueduct. What do you see? *(Responses will vary. Possible response: The structure dwarfs the people in the image. The structure looks old and battered, but still very solid.)*

2. **Make Inferences** What might be a disadvantage to having a water supply system such as this? *(Responses will vary. Possible response: An above-ground water system could be vulnerable to disruption by even minor earthquakes or deliberate attacks by enemy forces.)*

MORE INFORMATION

Roman Engineering Across Europe Roman roads, walls, and aqueducts can be found throughout Europe. Among the things that the Roman army brought with them to conquered lands were ideas about civic improvement and defense. Hadrian's Wall in England; the aqueduct at Segovia, Spain; Roman roads in Portugal—all are examples of Roman engineering that are still visible today. Roman engineers built improvements wherever the empire spread, not with an eye toward a lasting legacy, but rather with the goal of bringing Rome to every part of the empire through stone and mortar.

ACTIVE OPTIONS

On Your Feet: True-False Write a series of true-false questions related to Roman engineering generally and aqueducts specifically. Establish one side of the room as "True" and another side as "False." Ask the questions and have students move to the side of the room that represents their answer. **0:15 minutes**

Critical Viewing: NG Chapter Gallery Invite students to explore the entire NG Chapter Gallery and choose one image from the gallery they feels best represents their understanding of the chapter. Have students provide a written explanation of why they selected the image they chose. **0:10 minutes**

DIFFERENTIATE

ENGLISH LANGUAGE LEARNERS

Examine Related Words Students whose first language is Spanish might quickly understand the word *aqueduct*. The Spanish for aqueduct is *acueducto* and comes from the same Latin roots. In both languages, the roots are from the Latin *aqua*, "water," and *ducere*, "to lead." Point to other vocabulary similarities between languages for terms in the lesson or that you can see on the page.

ENGLISH	LATIN	SPANISH
arch	arch	arco
pipe	pipe	pipa
cloud	nubes	nube

GIFTED & TALENTED

Build Models Have students research an ancient Roman aqueduct—there were 11. Have them use clay, papier-mâché, a drafting program, etc. to build a model of the aqueduct system. Have students display their models in the classroom.

Press **mt** *in the Student eEdition for modified text.*

See the Chapter Planner for more strategies for differentiation.

VOCABULARY

Match each word in the first column with its definition in the second column.

WORD	DEFINITION
1. aqueduct	a. the practice and skill of public speaking
2. fresco	b. thousands of tiny colored stone cubes set in plaster to create a picture or design
3. parable	c. a painting done on plaster walls
4. barbarian	d. a system of government in which there are four rulers
5. oratory	e. a member of a tribe outside the empire
6. bas-relief	f. a simple story told to make a moral point
7. tetrarchy	g. a stone channel that carries water
8. mosaic	h. a sculpture with figures raised against a flat background

READING SKILL

9. ORGANIZE IDEAS: SEQUENCE EVENTS If you haven't already, complete your time line of key people and events in the Roman Empire. Then answer the question.

People and Events in the Roman Empire

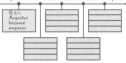

Which person or event do you think had the greatest impact on the Roman Empire? Why?

MAIN IDEAS

Answer the following questions. Support your answers with evidence from the chapter.

10. What was accomplished during the Pax Romana? LESSON 1.1

11. What effect did safe seas and a network of excellent roads have on the Roman Empire's economy? LESSON 1.2

12. What role did Constantine play in the growth of Christianity? LESSON 2.4

13. Why did Diocletian divide the Roman Empire into the Eastern and Western Roman Empires? LESSON 3.2

14. How did Roman ideas about government and law influence the government of the United States? LESSON 4.2

CRITICAL THINKING

Answer the following questions. Support your answers with evidence from the chapter.

15. FORM AND SUPPORT OPINIONS What was the main reason the Roman Empire became so powerful and long lasting?

16. SYNTHESIZE What steps did Augustus take to secure the support of the Roman people and bring peace to the Roman Empire?

17. EVALUATE What role did technology play in Roman architecture?

18. ANALYZE CAUSE AND EFFECT How did the Roman Empire's vast geographic expanse become a serious disadvantage in the third century? What was the effect of this disadvantage?

19. MAKE CONNECTIONS How did the Latin language influence the Romance languages and English?

20. YOU DECIDE Do you think Augustus was a great emperor or a clever politician? Support your opinion with evidence from the chapter.

INTERPRET MAPS

ROAD NETWORK OF THE ROMAN EMPIRE, c. A.D. 117

21. Where is Rome located in relation to the rest of the Roman Empire?

22. In A.D. 117 how far north and how far south did the Roman Empire extend?

ANALYZE SOURCES

Read the following selection from Jesus' Sermon on the Mount. Then answer the question.

> Blessed are the poor in spirit, for theirs is the kingdom of heaven.
>
> Blessed are the meek, for they will inherit the Earth.
>
> Blessed are the merciful, for they will be shown mercy.
>
> Blessed are the pure in heart, for they will see God.
>
> —Matthew 5:3–8

23. SYNTHESIZE How might these teachings from Jesus have helped guide people to lead their lives during the Roman Empire?

WRITE ABOUT HISTORY

24. EXPLANATORY Many social, political, and economic problems contributed to the decline and fall of the Roman Empire. Put yourself in the position of a senator at that time. Write a speech explaining three of these problems.

TIPS

- Take notes as you review the portion of the chapter about the decline and fall of the Roman Empire.
- State your main idea and supporting details in a clear, well-organized way.
- Present evidence to support your explanation.
- Use vocabulary from the chapter to explain the problems.
- Make a concluding statement based on your explanation of and evidence about the decline and fall of the Roman Empire.

VOCABULARY ANSWERS

WORD	DEFINITION
1. aqueduct g	a. the practice and skill of public speaking
2. fresco c	b. thousands of tiny colored stone cubes set in plaster to create a picture or design
3. parable f	c. a painting done on plaster walls
4. barbarian e	d. a system of government in which there are four rulers
5. oratory a	e. a member of a tribe outside the empire
6. bas-relief h	f. a simple story told to make a moral point
7. tetrarchy d	g. a stone channel that carries water
8. mosaic b	h. a sculpture with figures raised against a flat background

READING STRATEGY ANSWER

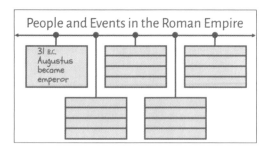

People and Events in the Roman Empire

9. Events and people listed on the time lines will vary, as will the explanations for which was most important and why.

MAIN IDEAS ANSWERS

10. The Pax Romana was a 200-year period of peace that brought great prosperity to the Roman Empire—law and order began to return; art, literature, and education all improved; Rome was transformed into a magnificent capital.

11. Safe seas and a network of excellent roads made it much easier to transport and sell goods throughout the Roman Empire, which greatly stimulated the economy.

12. Constantine believed that the Christian god had helped him win an important battle. In gratitude, he converted to Christianity, stopped persecution of Christians, built churches, and dedicated the new capital of the Roman Empire to Christ.

13. Diocletian divided the vast Roman Empire into the Eastern and Western Empires in order to make governing and defending the vast Roman Empire more efficient, and to restore order and stability.

14. The United States government includes representative assemblies—both houses of Congress—and the constitution outlines the separation of powers among the different branches of government, all of which were important elements of the Roman Republic.

CRITICAL THINKING ANSWERS

15. Answers will vary, but should include recognition of an aspect of Rome's power and endurance with support from the text. Possible aspects: military power; strong governance; advanced technology.

16. Augustus worked within the law to create a hereditary monarchy that upheld ideals of the republic, but he had the supreme power as emperor. He secured people's support by guaranteeing the supply of grain, giving land and money to soldiers, encouraging the arts and education, and transforming Rome into an impressive capital with magnificent marble monuments—all worthy of a powerful empire.

17. They used a new, stronger type of concrete and a combination of multiple arches, vaults, and domes to build huge, free-standing structures.

18. In the third century, the Roman Empire covered such a vast geographic expanse that it became very difficult to govern and defend. Because of its size, the empire was attacked on two fronts along the eastern and western borders, which led to invasions in the empire's interior. The once mighty empire could no longer protect itself.

19. Through local usage, the Latin language corrupted into new languages, including French, Italian, Spanish, and Portuguese, which are known collectively as the Romance languages. The English language has borrowed many Latin words and phrases that are used everyday, as well as written and read by scholars, scientists, doctors, and lawyers.

20. Students' responses will vary. Students should clearly state their opinions regarding their view of Augustus and support that opinion with evidence from the chapter.

INTERPRET MAPS ANSWERS

21. In relation to the rest of the Roman Empire, Rome is located at the center.

22. In A.D. 117 the Roman Empire extended as far north as Britain and as far south as Egypt.

ANALYZE SOURCES ANSWER

23. Students' responses will vary. Sample response: These selections from the Beatitudes offered hope and comfort to the poor and enslaved during the time of the Roman Empire, as well as a guide for how to live a more moral, meaningful life—something that humans continue to strive to do today.

WRITE ABOUT HISTORY ANSWER

24. Students' paragraphs will vary, but they should construct a clear explanation and support that explanation with evidence from the chapter.

NATIONAL GEOGRAPHIC

ON **LOCATION**
WITH Steven
ELLIS

NATIONAL GEOGRAPHIC GRANTEE

▶ Check out more on myNGconnect

Archaeologist Steven Ellis surveys the
ruins of Pompeii. His project focuses on
the city's common people, which is a new
approach to archaeological excavation.

NOT JUST DIGGERS

That's the misconception that annoys us the most! I dig up cities, yes, but it's what I learn from those cities that is important. Discovering artifacts is pretty cool, but piecing them together to tell a 2,000-year-old human story—that's what I find really exciting.

Pompeii is better preserved than any other Roman site, and because it's a city, you can relate to it more easily than, say, the pyramids. It's also got the drama of its sudden death, but we want to uncover its life. Pompeiians lived in houses and went to shops and schools. I love that familiar urban element. They also had very different rules and did things differently. I think it's fascinating to try and recognize those similarities and differences.

Archaeologists like Steven Ellis spend long hours in the field, carefully uncovering signs of past civilizations.

TELLING THE HUMAN STORY

For 200 years we've mostly looked at what the rich were doing by unearthing the grandest buildings. I'm using archaeology to tell the story of ordinary people, the other 98 percent of the population. It's a fairly new approach. I was the youngest archaeological director at Pompeii, and I was also the new guy with new questions. I said, "I want to work in areas that you've ignored." So I'm looking at shops, bars, restaurants, and houses. They don't have fine art, but they do have bones, seeds, and pieces of pottery that tell us a story. Some of our discoveries are pretty obvious, like the fact that poor people lived in smaller houses and ate cheaper foods off cheaper plates. But they're expanding our understanding of Roman society beyond just the rich and revealing the complex layers of life in the middle and working classes.

Excavating in poorer communities is incredibly gratifying because you've got to work harder at it. The rich lived in the best houses, with the best decorations and the most stuff. This all survived better, so it's easier to uncover and study. I'm proud that we are excavating the stories of families whose histories would otherwise never be told.

WHY STUDY HISTORY ?

"I study history because it's fascinating and *because I can*. In some countries, people are forbidden to study their own history, and that's a tragedy. I love finding out how similar or different people were from us." —Steven Ellis

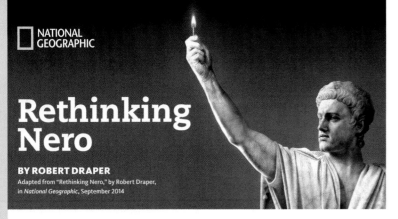

Rethinking Nero

BY ROBERT DRAPER

Adapted from "Rethinking Nero," by Robert Draper, in *National Geographic*, September 2014

As the city of Rome burned in A.D. 64, the infamous emperor Nero allegedly sat around playing his violin. He also may have killed two of his wives, his mother, and his stepbrother. In the accounts of many historians, he is described as a murderer and a lunatic. But now some scholars are rethinking Nero's reputation.

In 2007, archaeologist Fedora Filippi discovered the base of a column while digging under a busy street in Rome. Burrowing further, she encountered a portico and the edge of a pool. After a year of analysis, she concluded that she had discovered the enormous public gymnasium built by Nero a few years before the Great Fire. At first her discovery garnered little attention. But it was an important find. "The gymnasium was part of a big change Nero brought about in Rome," Filippi says. "Before, such baths were only for the aristocrats. This changed social relations because it put everyone on the same level, from senators to the horsemen."

Nero's gymnasium and events early in his reign suggest that he was a reformer who desired the admiration of his people. He ended the secret trials of the previous emperor, issued pardons, and was reluctant to sign death warrants. He praised Greek culture, encouraging Greek-style contests of athletics and poetry. Instead of looting other countries to gain wealth, Nero taxed wealthy Romans to raise funds, a practice that made him unpopular with the most powerful members of society. These early accomplishments likely alienated him from the Roman senators. But his own outrageous behavior later in his reign is the reason why he went down in history as a madman.

"Nero was a fool obsessed with his own power, but a fool can also be charming and interesting," says Roman archaeologist Andrea Carandini. He became powerful by appealing to the popular desires and prejudices of his people. In turn, he cherished the masses who adored him.

Romans themselves were conflicted about their ruler. "He was a monster," says Roberto Gervaso, author of the biographical novel *Nerone*. "But that's not all he was."

For more from National Geographic
Check out "Roman Frontiers" on myNGconnect

UNIT INQUIRY: BUILD AN EMPIRE

In this unit, you learned about ancient Rome and its legacy. Based on your reading, what factors can help make an empire great? What factors can lead to its decline?

ASSIGNMENT Design an empire that you think would be successful today. The empire should have a geographic location, a government, an economy, a social structure, and its own culture. Be prepared to present your empire and explain it to the class.

Plan As you build your empire, think about ancient Rome—what made it successful and what made it grow weak. Make a list of these factors and try to incorporate or avoid them in your own empire. Use a graphic organizer like this one to help organize your thoughts. ▶

Produce Use your notes to produce detailed descriptions of the elements of your empire. Write them in outline or paragraph form.

Present Choose a creative way to present your empire to the class. Consider one of these options:

- Create a multimedia presentation using photos to represent different elements of your empire.
- Write an introduction to a travel guide that describes your empire.
- Draw a map of your empire to accompany the description of its overall structure.

Geography | Government | Economy

My Empire

Social Structure | Culture

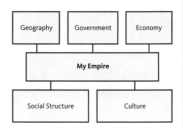

RAPID REVIEW
UNIT 4

THE WORLD OF THE ROMANS

TOP TEN

1. In the Roman Republic, power was shared between elected consuls and assemblies to prevent individuals from becoming too powerful.
2. After many civil wars, Rome became an empire ruled with absolute authority by a single emperor.
3. The wise rule of the emperor Augustus ushered in the Pax Romana, 200 years of peace and prosperity.
4. The Colosseum hosted spectacular and bloody games where gladiators fought to the death.
5. Romans spoke Latin, and we still use many Latin words today.

6-10. **NOW IT'S YOUR TURN** Complete the list with five more things to remember about the world of the Romans.

RAPID REVIEW

POSSIBLE RESPONSES

Possible responses for the remaining five things to remember include the following:

6. The ancient Romans were innovative architects and engineers who built roads, aqueducts, and spectacular buildings.

7. A massive volcanic eruption destroyed the city of Pompeii in A.D. 79.

8. The spread of Christianity threatened the Roman government, which made the practice of this new religion illegal.

9. The Roman Empire split into two empires, Eastern and Western, in A.D. 285.

10. Internal problems and invasions by barbarians contributed to the fall of the Western Roman Empire in A.D. 476.

UNIT INQUIRY PROJECT RUBRIC

ASSESS

Use the rubric to assess each student's participation and performance.

SCORE	ASSIGNMENT	PRODUCT	PRESENTATION
3 GREAT	• Student thoroughly understands the assignment. • Student participates fully in the project process. • Student works well with team members.	• Empire is well thought out. • Empire takes into account strengths and weaknesses of the Roman Empire. • Empire contains all of the key elements listed in the assignment.	• Presentation is clear, concise, and logical. • Presentation does a good job of creatively explaining the empire. • Presentation engages the audience.
2 GOOD	• Student mostly understands the assignment. • Student participates fairly well in the project process. • Student works fairly well with team members.	• Empire is fairly well thought out. • Empire somewhat takes into account strengths and weaknesses of the Roman Empire. • Empire contains some of the key elements listed in the assignment.	• Presentation is fairly clear, concise, and logical. • Presentation does an adequate job of creatively explaining the empire. • Presentation somewhat engages the audience.
1 NEEDS WORK	• Student does not understand the assignment. • Student minimally participates or does not participate in the project process. • Student does not work well with team members.	• Empire is not well thought out. • Empire does not take into account strengths and weaknesses of the Roman Empire. • Empire contains few or none of the key elements listed in the assignment.	• Presentation is not clear, concise, or logical. • Presentation does not creatively explain the empire. • Presentation does not engage the audience.

BYZANTINE AND ISLAMIC CIVILIZATIONS

NATIONAL GEOGRAPHIC

ON **LOCATION** WITH

Jodi Magness
Archaeologist

People say that the Roman Empire fell in 476, and a part of it did. But the Empire lived on in the East. This part became known as the Byzantine Empire, but its citizens called themselves Romans. In the 600s, Muslim Arabs invaded Southwest Asia and conquered some of the territory held by the Byzantines, including Palestine. I'm Jodi Magness, and I excavate archaeological sites in Israel. Join me as we dig through the history of the Byzantine and Islamic civilizations!

‹ CRITICAL VIEWING Magness discovered a 5th-century synagogue and this Byzantine-inspired mosaic of an elephant at a site in Israel. What does the mosaic suggest about the skill of its artist?

POSSIBLE RESPONSE
The mosaic suggests that the artist was highly skilled and inventive.

345

Byzantine and Islamic Civilizations

527
Justinian begins
his rule of the
Byzantine Empire.
(mosaic of Justinian)

630
Muhammad
unites much
of Arabia
under Islam.

750
Muslim rule spreads
Islam over parts
of Asia, Africa,
and Europe.
(page from the Qur'an)

800

1054
Christianity splits,
and the Eastern
Orthodox Church
forms in Byzantium.

500

The World

800
EUROPE
Charlemagne unites
and rules much of
Western Europe.

c. 1000
AMERICAS
Inca civilization
arises in South
America.
(gold Inca figurine)

618
ASIA
Tang dynasty
begins in
China.

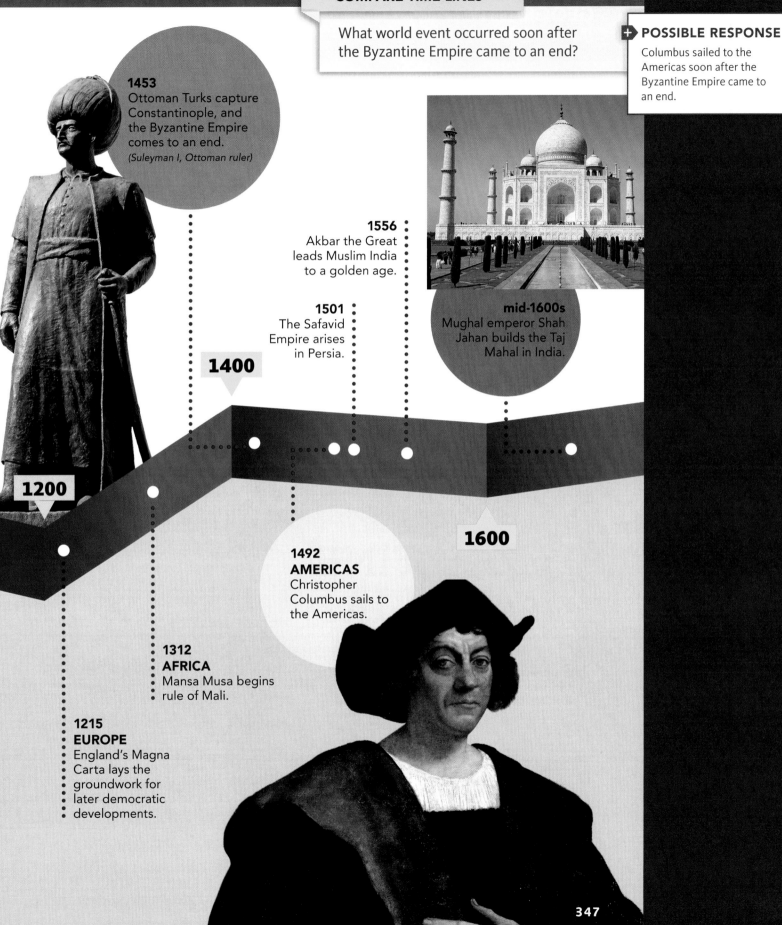

What world event occurred soon after the Byzantine Empire came to an end?

POSSIBLE RESPONSE
Columbus sailed to the Americas soon after the Byzantine Empire came to an end.

1453
Ottoman Turks capture Constantinople, and the Byzantine Empire comes to an end.
(Suleyman I, Ottoman ruler)

1556
Akbar the Great leads Muslim India to a golden age.

1501
The Safavid Empire arises in Persia.

mid-1600s
Mughal emperor Shah Jahan builds the Taj Mahal in India.

1400

1200

1600

1492
AMERICAS
Christopher Columbus sails to the Americas.

1312
AFRICA
Mansa Musa begins rule of Mali.

1215
EUROPE
England's Magna Carta lays the groundwork for later democratic developments.

BYZANTINE AND EARLY MUSLIM EMPIRES, 565–750

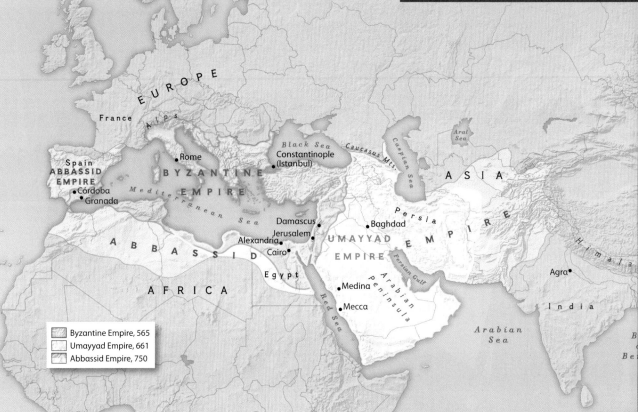

Byzantine Empire, 565
Umayyad Empire, 661
Abbassid Empire, 750

BYZANTINE & MUSLIM
EMPIRES 565–1683

After the Western Roman Empire fell in 476, invaders overran its lands. But the eastern part of the empire, which came to be known as the Byzantine Empire, survived. The empire reached its height in 565.

The Byzantine Empire's power was soon overshadowed by a Muslim state that arose in Arabia. Over many centuries, Muslim armies conquered lands in Europe, Asia, and Africa. Muslim leaders established empires there and spread their Islamic faith.

Byzantine mosaic of a lion from the 5th or 6th century

On which continent were the later Muslim empires mostly located?

+ POSSIBLE RESPONSE
The later Muslim empires were mostly located in Asia.

LATER MUSLIM EMPIRES, 1683

EUROPE

France

Alps

Spain

Córdoba
Granada

Rome

OTTOMAN EMPIRE

Mediterranean Sea

OTTOMAN EMPIRE

AFRICA

Black Sea

Constantinople
(Istanbul)

Caucasus Mts.

Caspian Sea

Aral Sea

ASIA

Persia

SAFAVID EMPIRE

Damascus
Jerusalem
Alexandria
Cairo

Egypt

Baghdad

Persian Gulf

Arabian Peninsula

Red Sea

Medina

Mecca

Arabian Sea

Himalaya

India

Agra

MUGHAL EMPIRE

Bay of Bengal

- Ottoman Empire, 1683
- Safavid Empire, 1683
- Mughal Empire, 1683

0   500   1,000   1,500   2,000 kilometers
0   500   1,000   1,500   2,000 miles

Present-day boundaries are shown on the map.

Alhambra Palace built by Muslim rulers in Granada, Spain

Blue-tiled ceiling of a mosque in Iran

349

UNIT 5 BYZANTINE AND ISLAMIC CIVILIZATIONS

UNIT RESOURCES

On Location with National Geographic Grantee Jodi Magness Intro and Video

Interactive Map Tool

STORIES MAKING HISTORY **News & Updates**

Available on myNGconnect

Unit Wrap-Up:
"History Is a Puzzle"
Feature and Video

"The Stolen Past"
National Geographic Adapted Article

"The Wells of Memory"
National Geographic Adapted Article
Student eEdition exclusive

Unit 5 Inquiry:
Make an Idea Map

CHAPTER RESOURCES

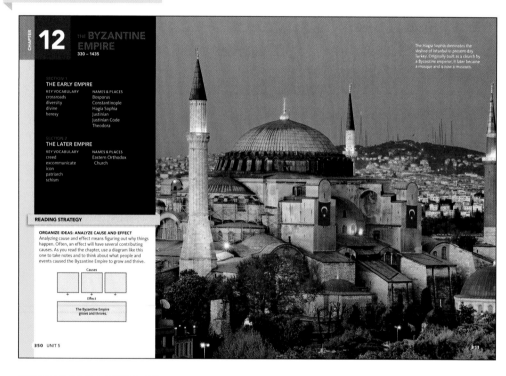

TEACHER RESOURCES & ASSESSMENT

Available on myNGconnect

Social Studies Skills Lessons
 • Reading: Analyze Cause and Effect
 • Writing: Write an Explanation

Formal Assessment
 • Chapter 12 Test A (on-level) & B (below-level)

Chapter 12 Answer Key

ExamView®
One-time Download

STUDENT BACKPACK *Available on myNGconnect*

 • **eEdition** *(English)* • **eEdition** *(Spanish)* • **Handbooks** • **Online Atlas**

For Chapter 12 Spanish resources, visit the Teacher Resource Menu page on myNGconnect.

SECTION 1 RESOURCES

THE EARLY EMPIRE

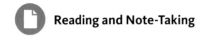 **Reading and Note-Taking**

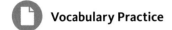 **Vocabulary Practice**

 **Section 1 Quiz**

Available on myNGconnect

LESSON 1.1 THE GEOGRAPHY OF THE BYZANTINE EMPIRE
- On Your Feet: Inside-Outside Circle

NG Learning Framework:
List Geographic Impacts

LESSON 1.2 JUSTINIAN AND THEODORA

 Biography
Theodora   *Available on myNGconnect*

NG Learning Framework:
Write a Biography

- On Your Feet: Card Responses

MOMENTS IN HISTORY
LESSON 1.3 THE HAGIA SOPHIA
- On Your Feet: Descriptive Words
- Critical Viewing: NG Chapter Gallery

LESSON 1.4 LIFE IN CONSTANTINOPLE
- On Your Feet: Three-Step Interview
- Critical Viewing: NG Image Gallery

SECTION 2 RESOURCES

THE LATER EMPIRE

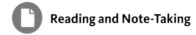 **Reading and Note-Taking**

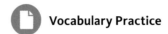 **Vocabulary Practice**

 **Section 2 Quiz**

Available on myNGconnect

LESSON 2.1 THE CHURCH DIVIDES

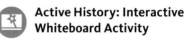 **Active History: Interactive Whiteboard Activity**
Compare Two Branches Of Christianity

 **Active History**
Compare Two Branches Of Christianity

Available on myNGconnect

- On Your Feet: Thumbs Up/Thumbs Down

HISTORY THROUGH OBJECTS
LESSON 2.2 BYZANTINE MOSAICS
- On Your Feet: Four Corners
- Critical Viewing: NG Chapter Gallery

LESSON 2.3 THE END OF AN EMPIRE
- On Your Feet: Turn and Talk on Topic
- Critical Viewing: NG Chapter Gallery

CHAPTER 12 REVIEW

STRIVING READERS

STRATEGY ①
Record and Compare Facts

After reading a lesson, ask students to write two important facts they learned. Allow pairs of students to compare and check their facts and then combine their facts into one longer list. Ask a volunteer from each group to read the most important fact from the list.

Use with All Lessons

STRATEGY ②
Preview and Predict

Before they read, have students preview the lesson. Ask them to locate and read the lesson title, the Main Idea statement, and any text in large blue type. Have students use that information to write a sentence that predicts what the lesson is about.

Use with All Lessons *For Lesson 1.2, tell students to use the lesson title and Main Idea to help them identify who ruled Byzantium during its golden age.*

STRATEGY ③
Use Paired Reading

Pair students and assign each pair two passages in the lesson. Tell them that they will each take one passage, read it, take notes, become an expert on it, and share their expertise with their partner. After students have had time to prepare their passages, have them report on their reading to each other. Tell each listener to write two clarifying questions.

Use with All Lessons

Press *in the Student eEdition for modified text.*

INCLUSION

STRATEGY ①
Modify Main Idea Statements

Have each student work with a partner to preview the chapter by reading and copying each lesson's Main Idea statement onto a sheet of paper. Then have students look at the maps and other visuals in the text and add to each lesson's Main Idea. They can write complete sentences or notes on the page.

Use with Lessons 1.1–1.4 *For Lesson 1.4, have students use the illustration of the city of Constantinople to describe the city.*

STRATEGY ②
Modify Vocabulary Lists

Limit the number of vocabulary words, terms, and names students will be required to master. Have students write each word from your modified list on a colored sticky note and put it on the page next to where it appears in context.

Use with Lessons 2.1–2.3

ENGLISH LANGUAGE LEARNERS

STRATEGY ①
Use Visuals to Predict Content

Before reading, ask students to read the lesson title and look at any visuals. Then ask them to write a sentence that predicts how the visual is related to the lesson title. Repeat the exercise after reading and ask volunteers to read their sentences.

Use with Lessons 1.1–1.4

STRATEGY ②
Use Pronunciation Keys

Preteach the meaning and pronunciation of vocabulary words before beginning each lesson. Give a brief definition or example for each word and then pronounce it slowly and clearly several times. Have students repeat after you. Then have students create a pronunciation key for each word.

After each lesson, have students write simple sentences using each word (for example, "A *creed* is a statement of belief"). Have students refer to their pronunciation keys to help them say the words correctly.

Use with All Lessons

STRATEGY ❸
Predict Vocabulary Meanings

Before reading, give students the following list of words and definitions and have them write the word next to the definition they predict is correct. After reading, have them check and correct any mistakes.

| creed | icons | schism |
| excommunicated | patriarch | |

1. _____ images of Jesus and the saints
2. _____ leader of the Eastern Orthodox Church
3. _____ separation
4. _____ statement of belief
5. _____ no longer part of the church

Use with Lesson 2.1

STRATEGY ❶
Teach a Class

Before beginning the chapter, allow students to choose one of the two-page lessons listed below and prepare to teach the contents to the class. Give them a set amount of time in which to present their lesson. Suggest that students think about any visuals or activities they want to use when they teach.

Use with Lessons 1.1, 1.2, and 1.4

STRATEGY ❷
Create a Brochure

Tell students to imagine that they are living in the city of Constantinople and have been given the job of creating a brochure to encourage people to visit the city. Ask students to work with partners to design the brochure. Direct students to include factual information about the city, important sites, and places of interest. Students should use the information in the lesson as well as other resources to find the information. Have students share completed brochures with the class.

Use with Lesson 1.4

STRATEGY ❶
Write a Feature Article

Have students use the Internet to research Byzantine art and architecture. Have them write a feature article describing what they have learned. Articles should focus on types of art, such as mosaics and frescoes, as well as descriptions of Byzantine architecture. Encourage students to include photos to accompany their articles.

Use with Lessons 1.3 and 2.2

STRATEGY ❷
Support an Opinion

Present a challenge to students to decide which achievement of Justinian made the greatest impact on the Byzantine Empire. Have them develop a thesis statement that explains their decision and write an essay that supports it. Ask students to share their essays with the class.

Use with Lessons 1.1 and 1.2

12

THE BYZANTINE EMPIRE
330 – 1435

SECTION 1
THE EARLY EMPIRE

KEY VOCABULARY
crossroads
diversity
divine
heresy

NAMES & PLACES
Bosporus
Constantinople
Hagia Sophia
Justinian
Justinian Code
Theodora

SECTION 2
THE LATER EMPIRE

KEY VOCABULARY
creed
excommunicate
icon
patriarch
schism

NAMES & PLACES
Eastern Orthodox
 Church

The Hagia Sophia dominates the skyline of Istanbul in present-day Turkey. Originally built as a church by a Byzantine emperor, it later became a mosque and is now a museum.

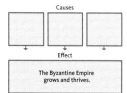

READING STRATEGY

ORGANIZE IDEAS: ANALYZE CAUSE AND EFFECT
Analyzing cause and effect means figuring out why things happen. Often, an effect will have several contributing causes. As you read the chapter, use a diagram like this one to take notes and to think about what people and events caused the Byzantine Empire to grow and thrive.

Causes

Effect

The Byzantine Empire grows and thrives.

351

TEACHER BACKGROUND

INTRODUCE THE PHOTOGRAPH

Have students study the photograph of Istanbul and the Hagia Sophia. Explain that Istanbul was once called Constantinople and was an important city in the Byzantine Empire. Tell students that, in this chapter, they will learn about the factors that contributed to the growth of the Byzantine Empire and the importance of Constantinople to the empire.

ASK: How would you describe the city of Istanbul? *(Possible responses: Istanbul looks like an older city; it is densely populated.)*

SHARE BACKGROUND

Istanbul is the largest city and port in Turkey. The ancient city was known as Constantinople when it was the capital of the Byzantine Empire. Later, Constantinople became the capital city of the Ottoman Empire. The city became known as *Istanbul* off and on after it became the capital of the Ottoman Empire. After the creation of the Turkish Republic in 1923, however, *Istanbul* became the official name of the city. Although no longer its capital, Istanbul remains the cultural center of Turkey.

DIGITAL RESOURCES myNGconnect.com

TEACHER RESOURCES & ASSESSMENT

 Social Studies Skills Lessons
· Reading: Analyze Cause and Effect
· Writing: Write an Explanation

 Formal Assessment
· Chapter 12 Tests A (on-level) &
 B (below-level)

 ExamView®
One-time Download

 **Chapter 12
Answer Key**

STUDENT BACKPACK

· **eEdition** *(English)*
· **eEdition** *(Spanish)*

· **Handbooks**
· **Online Atlas**

For Chapter 12 Spanish Resources, visit the Teacher Resource Menu page.

INTRODUCE THE ESSENTIAL QUESTION

HOW DID THE BYZANTINE EMPIRE CARRY ON THE CULTURE AND TRADITIONS OF THE OLD ROMAN EMPIRE?

Jigsaw Activity: Preview Content This activity will help students preview and make predictions about the topics covered in Chapter 12. Divide the class into seven groups. Assign one lesson from the chapter to each group. Have group members preview the lesson and consider the following questions:

Group 1 What effect might the geography of the Byzantine Empire have had on the empire?

Group 2 Who were Justinian and Theodora? How were they important to the Byzantine Empire?

Group 3 What is the Hagia Sophia? Why was it important to the Byzantine Empire?

Group 4 Where was Constantinople located? What was life like in Constantinople?

Group 5 What religion was important in the Byzantine Empire? What caused the church to divide?

Group 6 What are mosaics? Why are mosaics important in Byzantine art?

Group 7 What led to the decline of the Byzantine Empire? When did it end?

Regroup students so each new grouping has at least one member from each original group. Have students share their preview of their assigned lesson so that other students can learn what to expect from their reading in Chapter 12. **0:20** minutes

INTRODUCE THE READING STRATEGY

ORGANIZE IDEAS: ANALYZE CAUSE AND EFFECT

Remind students that cause and effect involves figuring out why things happen. A cause is an action or condition that makes something else happen. An effect is what happens as a result of the cause. An effect often has several causes. Model completing the diagram by reading the first paragraph under "Connecting East and West" in Lesson 1.1 and adding the phrase *location at crossroads of Europe and Asia* in one of the Cause boxes in the diagram.

Causes

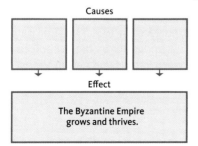

Effect

The Byzantine Empire grows and thrives.

INTRODUCE CHAPTER VOCABULARY

STUMP THE EXPERT

Have students play "Stump the Expert" with the Key Vocabulary words. Give each student a list of words or write the words on the board. Identify a student as the first expert. Have a stumper present a definition or clue. Give the expert a set time to name the word. If the response is correct, the next stumper offers a word challenge. Continue until the expert is stumped or until the expert answers three challenges. The student who stumps the expert becomes the new expert, and the procedure begins again.

KEY DATES	
A.D. **293**	Diocletian divides Roman Empire
A.D. **527**	Justinian becomes emperor of Byzantine Empire
A.D. **537**	Hagia Sophia is officially blessed
A.D. **711**	Arabs conquer parts of Byzantine Empire
A.D. **1054**	Church splits into Roman Catholic Church and Eastern Orthodox Church
A.D. **1204**	Christian Europeans conquer and occupy Constantinople
A.D. **1453**	Constantinople comes under Turkish control

For more information on issues facing present-day Turkey, check out *GLOBAL ISSUES STANDARD OF LIVING.*

1.1

The Geography of the Byzantine Empire

The Western Roman Empire fell in A.D. 476, but that's not the end of its story. For a thousand years after that date, the glory of Rome lived on in the Byzantine Empire.

MAIN IDEA

The Byzantine Empire was well located for trade but open to attack.

CONNECTING EAST AND WEST

From law to architecture, the Byzantine (BIHZ-uhn-teen) Empire's achievements were extraordinary. One reason for those achievements was the empire's location at the **crossroads** of Europe and Asia, the place where the trade routes from each continent met. As a result of the empire's geography, many influences came together to create the Byzantine civilization.

As you may recall from the previous chapter, the emperor Diocletian divided the Roman Empire in A.D. 293. The Eastern Roman Empire became known as the Byzantine Empire because its capital was built on the old Greek town of Byzantium (buh-ZAN-tee-uhm). In fact, the Byzantine Empire is often referred to as Byzantium. By A.D. 330, the emperor Constantine had transformed Byzantium into a grand "New Rome." He named the city **Constantinople**, or city of Constantine. Today it is called Istanbul.

While the Western Roman Empire was ripped apart by invading barbarians, the Byzantine Empire managed to survive similar attacks. A series of strong emperors fought off Byzantium's enemies and strengthened the empire. Thus, the Byzantine Empire continued the traditions of Roman civilization for another thousand years after the collapse of the Western Roman Empire. The people we now call Byzantines proudly called themselves Romans.

Constantinople occupied one of the ancient world's most important geographic locations. At the heart of the empire was the small but important land link between Asia and Europe that permitted trade between east and west. The empire itself reached into both continents. Its heartland was in what are now Greece and Turkey.

Constantinople was also located on the **Bosporus**, a strait that links the Black Sea with the Mediterranean. The city was a major trade center for goods traveling by land and sea from all over the world. Constantinople and the Byzantine Empire grew rich on this trade. The city also attracted people from many parts of the world. They came to trade goods from their homelands and wound up living in the bustling city. These immigrants gave Constantinople the cultural **diversity**, or variety, for which it was famous.

EXPANDING THE EMPIRE

The Byzantine Empire's location brought problems as well as advantages. Although Constantinople itself was well protected, the rest of the empire was surrounded by enemies. To the north and west were many barbarian kingdoms forcefully pressing on Byzantium's borders. To the east was an age-old enemy, the powerful and hostile Persian Empire.

The rich resources and great wealth of Byzantium made it a tempting target for raids and invasions. With no strong geographic barriers to prevent invasion by enemies, the empire was dangerously exposed. Its long borders were constantly under attack by invading neighbors.

The Byzantine Empire needed strong leadership to hold it together in the face of so many threats. Over a thousand years, its borders grew and shrank, depending on the ability of its rulers and the eagerness of its enemies to wage war. At its greatest extent, the empire completely encircled the Mediterranean Sea.

Probably the greatest Byzantine ruler was one of its earliest—**Justinian**, the emperor from A.D. 527 until his death in 565. He not only recaptured lost Byzantine lands but also reconquered large areas of the old Western Roman Empire. His armies defeated the Persians and reconquered North Africa, Italy, and parts of Spain. For a brief time, Justinian reunited the Eastern and Western Roman Empires. He built up the strength of the Byzantine Empire, even while Rome was being overrun by invaders. Justinian's legacy of leadership remained influential throughout the time of the Byzantine Empire and beyond.

THE BYZANTINE EMPIRE, A.D. 527–565

- The Byzantine Empire before Justinian
- Expansion under Justinian

REVIEW & ASSESS

1. **READING CHECK** Why was Constantinople's geographic location an advantage for trade?

2. **ANALYZE CAUSE AND EFFECT** What caused the Persian Empire and other enemies to attack and invade Byzantium?

3. **INTERPRET MAPS** How far west did the borders of the Byzantine Empire expand after Justinian's conquests?

PLAN

OBJECTIVE

Identify the geographic features of the Byzantine Empire.

CRITICAL THINKING SKILLS FOR LESSON 1.1

- Identify Main Ideas and Details
- Analyze Cause and Effect
- Summarize
- Monitor Comprehension
- Interpret Maps
- Draw Conclusions

ESSENTIAL QUESTION

How did the Byzantine Empire carry on the culture and traditions of the old Roman Empire?

When Diocletian divided the Roman Empire, the Eastern Roman Empire became the Byzantine Empire and continued hundreds of years after the end of the Western Roman Empire. Lesson 1.1 explains how the location of the Byzantine Empire made it well located for trade but open to attack.

BACKGROUND FOR THE TEACHER

The Bosporous connects the Sea of Marmara with the Black Sea. It also forms a dividing line between the European and Asian sections of the city of Istanbul. Lining the Bosporous are villages, ancient towers, and summer homes. In the 18th and 19th centuries, various European nations sought to control the strait. In 1923, the strait was internationalized; however, in 1936, the strait came under the control of Turkey. In 1973, a bridge across the Bosporous became the first southern link between Europe and Asia in almost 2,500 years.

DIGITAL RESOURCES myNGconnect.com

TEACHER RESOURCES & ASSESSMENT

 Reading and Note-Taking

 Vocabulary Practice

 Section 1 Quiz

STUDENT RESOURCES

 NG Chapter Gallery

INTRODUCE & ENGAGE

ACTIVATE PRIOR KNOWLEDGE

Ask students to recall ancient civilizations they have learned about, such as those in Egypt and Mesopotamia. Ask them how the location of these civilizations helped make them become important civilizations. Students should indicate that both developed along rivers. Tell students that in Lesson 1.1, they will learn how geographic features contributed to the growth of the Byzantine Empire. **0:05** minutes

TEACH

GUIDED DISCUSSION

1. **Summarize** How did the location of Constantinople make it important for trade both on land and on water? *(Constantinople provided a land link between Asia and Europe, and its location on the Bosporus made Constantinople a major trade center for goods traveling by land and sea from all over the world.)*

2. **Draw Conclusions** Why was having a strong leader especially important for the Byzantine Empire? *(The Byzantine Empire was surrounded by enemies who sought the empire's resources and wealth and had no geographic barriers to prevent attacks and invasions. The empire needed strong leadership to be able to hold it together in the face of these threats.)*

INTERPRET MAPS

Draw students' attention to the map of the Byzantine Empire, focusing on the extent of the empire. Review how to use the distance scale. Ask students to determine the size of the Byzantine Empire at its height, from east to west. *(approximately 2,750 miles)* **0:15** minutes

ACTIVE OPTIONS

On Your Feet: Inside-Outside Circle Arrange students in concentric circles facing each other. Have each student in the outside circle ask a question about the geography of the Byzantine Empire. Then have each student in the inside circle answer his or her partner's question. On a signal, have students on the inside circle rotate counter-clockwise to meet a new partner and begin again. Have students trade roles so those on the inside ask the questions and those on the outside answer the questions. **0:10** minutes

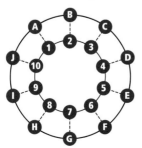

NG Learning Framework: List Geographic Impacts

SKILLS: Observation, Collaboration
KNOWLEDGE: **Our Living Planet**

Have students review Lesson 1.1 about the geography of the Byzantine Empire. They should work in pairs to create a list of observations about the empire's geographic features and how the Byzantine Empire was impacted by its environment. Once they have completed their list of observations, each pair should exchange lists with another pair and discuss the new list. **0:10** minutes

DIFFERENTIATE

STRIVING READERS

Summarize Read the lesson aloud while students follow along in their books. At the end of each paragraph, ask students to summarize what you read in a sentence. Allow them time to write the summary on their own paper.

ENGLISH LANGUAGE LEARNERS

Use Sentence Strips Choose a paragraph from the lesson and make sentence strips out of it. Read the paragraph aloud, having students follow along in their books. Have students close their books and give them the set of sentence strips. Students should put the strips in order and read the paragraph aloud.

Press **(mt)** *in the Student eEdition for modified text.*

See the Chapter Planner for more strategies for differentiation.

REVIEW & ASSESS

ANSWERS

1. Constantinople's location on the Bosporus linked the Black Sea with the Mediterranean, making it ideal for trade between east and west. As a major trade center, Constantinople led to the growth and economic success of the Byzantine Empire.

2. Byzantium's rich natural resources and immense wealth caused the Persian Empire and other enemies to attack and invade.

3. After Justinian's conquests, the borders of the Byzantine Empire expanded as far west as North Africa and the southern tip of Spain.

Justinian and Theodora

There's a popular saying that two heads are better than one.

This was certainly true of Justinian's reign. Justinian became Byzantium's greatest emperor thanks in part to the support and intelligence of his wife, Theodora.

MAIN IDEA

Justinian and Theodora ruled over a golden age for Byzantium.

A POWERFUL RULER

Justinian was born in A.D. 482 or 483 to a peasant farmer. It was a humble beginning, but Justinian's uncle rose to become a great general and then emperor. The uncle educated Justinian, gave him important jobs, and appointed him as his successor. It was a smart choice. Justinian was intelligent, talented, and ambitious. He modeled himself on the old Roman Caesars. After he became emperor in 527, Justinian worked to bring a golden age to Byzantium.

In many ways, Justinian proved to be a powerful and effective leader. As you have read, he greatly expanded the empire's borders. Within those borders, he made major improvements in the areas of government, construction, and law. He reformed Byzantine government to improve efficiency and get rid of corruption. Justinian

also started an ambitious construction program. He ordered the building of the **Hagia Sophia** (HY-uh soh-FEE-uh), a church in Constantinople that today is considered a masterpiece of Byzantine architecture. He also sponsored many other civic projects in the city, including a magnificent new building for the Senate.

Justinian was a dedicated Christian actively involved in issues of faith. He punished those he found guilty of **heresy** (HAIR-uh-see)—beliefs contrary to church teachings—including Jews. For example, he prohibited Jews from building synagogues and reading the Bible in Hebrew.

Justinian also worked hard to settle the differences of opinion that divided the early church. For example, groups within the church had different beliefs about whether Jesus Christ was fully **divine** (having the nature of a god) and should be worshipped as an equal to God. This disagreement continued long after Justinian's death.

Justinian's reform of the law was far more successful. He reorganized and standardized confusing Roman laws and had the surviving laws written down clearly and logically in a single work called the **Justinian Code**. This remarkable work has formed the basis of European law until modern times.

A COURAGEOUS EMPRESS

Of all Justinian's advisors, the most influential was his wife, **Theodora**. An actress when she was young, Theodora was part of a lower social class, so Justinian had to have the law changed to marry her. Together, they formed an unstoppable team who shared power as nearly equal co-rulers.

Theodora was extremely bright and energetic. Justinian admired her intelligence and deeply respected her opinions. As a result, she had a huge influence on imperial policy. Theodora was probably behind the laws passed to protect women, children, and some Christian minority groups.

This sixth-century mosaic shows Justinian in the center with religious leaders on his right and government officials on his left.

Theodora even saved Justinian's crown. In 532, some of Justinian's opponents turned a riot between rival sports fans into a widespread rebellion against his policies. As Justinian prepared to flee the city, Theodora refused to leave. Her courageous determination to stay and fight the rebels inspired Justinian. He ordered the army to crush the rebellion, which led to the deaths of 30,000 protesters. Order was restored, along with the emperor's authority. Following these events, Justinian decided to rule more carefully in the future.

SPORTS, POLITICS, AND PASSIONS

The people of Byzantium passionately followed the sport of chariot racing. More than just entertainment, the races were a focus of life and politics in the city. The people were bitterly divided in their support of the two main chariot teams—the Blues and the Greens. Races were an emotional standoff between supporters who often became violent. Justinian and Theodora both supported the Blues.

REVIEW & ASSESS

1. **READING CHECK** In what areas did Justinian make major improvements during his reign?

2. **IDENTIFY MAIN IDEAS AND DETAILS** What evidence from the text shows that Justinian's law reforms were successful?

3. **ANALYZE VISUALS** What can you infer about Justinian's reign from the people portrayed in the mosaic?

PLAN

OBJECTIVE

Identify key characteristics and events of the reign of Justinian and Theodora.

CRITICAL THINKING SKILLS FOR LESSON 1.2

- Identify Main Ideas and Details
- Monitor Comprehension
- Analyze Visuals
- Synthesize
- Form and Support Opinions

ESSENTIAL QUESTION

How did the Byzantine Empire carry on the culture and traditions of the old Roman Empire?

The emperor Justinian modeled himself after the old Roman Caesars.

Lesson 1.2 discusses Justinian's rule over a golden age for Byzantium.

BACKGROUND FOR THE TEACHER

Theodora, the empress of the Byzantine Empire, was the most powerful woman in Byzantine history. She was born into a poor family, and at one point in her life she made a living as an actress and also as a wool spinner. Theodora's beauty and intelligence attracted Justinian, and they were married in 525. Theodora influenced many of the laws passed during Justinian's rule. She worked to pass laws that enhanced the rights of women, an issue that was not taken up by many governments at that time. She also skillfully handled political affairs, such as meeting with foreign rulers, which previously were actions carried out only by the emperor. Theodora died in 548.

DIGITAL RESOURCES myNGconnect.com

TEACHER RESOURCES & ASSESSMENT

 Reading and Note-Taking

 Vocabulary Practice

 Section 1 Quiz

STUDENT RESOURCES

 Biography

INTRODUCE & ENGAGE

POSE AND ANSWER QUESTIONS

As a class, complete a K-W-L Chart exploring what students know and what they would like to learn about the Byzantine rulers Justinian and Theodora. Write students' ideas on the board in a K-W-L chart. Give students the opportunity to return to the chart and review what they have learned after they have read the lesson. **0:15** minutes

TEACH

GUIDED DISCUSSION

1. **Synthesize** What achievements in government, construction, and law showed Justinian to be a powerful and effective leader? *(Students' responses will vary but should include that in government, Justinian reformed the government to improve efficiency and to get rid of corruption; Justinian started a construction program, ordering the building of the Hagia Sophia and other civic projects in the city; Justinian reorganized and standardized confusing Roman laws and had the remaining laws written down clearly and logically in the Justinian Code.)*

2. **Form and Support Opinions** How important do you think Theodora was to Justinian's success as a ruler? *(Students' responses will vary, but students should provide reasons for their opinions.)*

MORE INFORMATION

Mosaic of Justinian The mosaic of Justinian is located in the Basilica of San Vitale, a church in Ravenna, Italy. It is an important example of early Christian Byzantine art and architecture in Western Europe. In the mosaic, dated A.D. 547, Justinian is clad in a purple toga with a golden halo around his head and a crown on his head. In the mosaic, the military personnel and the government officials are on Justinian's right, and the clergymen are on Justinian's left. Every person in the mosaic is overlapped by someone else except the emperor, showing his importance and power.

ACTIVE OPTIONS

NG Learning Framework: Write a Biography

ATTITUDE: **Curiosity**
KNOWLEDGE: **Our Human Story**

Have students select one of the people they are still curious about after learning about the individual in this chapter. Instruct them to write a short biography about the person using information from the chapter and additional source material. **0:15** minutes

On Your Feet: Card Responses Have half the class write ten true-false or yes-no questions based on the lesson. Have the other half create answer cards, writing "True" or "Yes" on one side of the cards and "False" or "No" on the other side. Students from the question

group should take turns asking their questions. Students from the answer group should hold up their cards, showing the correct answer. Have students keep track of their correct answers. **0:10** minutes

DIFFERENTIATE

INCLUSION

Use Supported Reading Have students work in pairs and assign each pair one paragraph to read aloud together. At the end of each paragraph, have them use the following sentence frames to identify what they do and do not understand:

This paragraph is about _____.

One fact that stood out to me is _____.

_____ is a word I had trouble understanding, so I figured it out by _____.

Be sure all students understand the content before moving on to the next paragraph.

PRE-AP

Extend Knowledge Have students conduct Internet research to find out more about Justinian or Theodora. Direct them to find out about the person's early life as well as more information about his or her accomplishments as a ruler. Encourage students to share their findings in an oral report to the class.

Press **mt** *in the Student eEdition for modified text.*

See the Chapter Planner for more strategies for differentiation.

REVIEW & ASSESS

ANSWERS

1. Justinian expanded the empire by conquering former lands of the Roman Empire in Africa and the west. He undertook major building projects, including the Hagia Sophia in Constantinople. He also reformed Byzantine government to make it more efficient and clarified Roman laws in his Justinian Code.

2. The text states that the Justinian Code clarified and standardized confusing and contradictory Roman laws, organizing them logically in a single work that later formed the basis of European law.

3. Responses will vary. A possible response might be that the number and position of the people behind Justinian indicates that many people helped to run the government and were accountable to him, but that Justinian held all the power.

DECEMBER 27, 537

The newly completed Hagia Sophia, which means "Holy Wisdom," was officially blessed on this date. The church, which still stands, is considered a remarkable achievement in architecture. The centerpiece of the vast building is its extraordinary brick dome, which is 180 feet high and 100 feet across. After the fall of the Byzantine Empire, the Hagia Sophia was converted to a mosque—an Islamic place of worship. Today, it is a museum. In Justinian's time, the church symbolized Byzantine power and wealth.

PLAN

OBJECTIVE

Identify the importance of the Hagia Sophia to the Byzantine Empire.

CRITICAL THINKING SKILLS FOR LESSON 1.3

- Make Inferences
- Make Generalizations
- Analyze Visuals

ESSENTIAL QUESTION

How did the Byzantine Empire carry on the culture and traditions of the old Roman Empire?

The emperor Justinian was known for his huge construction projects. The moment in history featured in Lesson 1.3 was the day that Justinian's major project, the Hagia Sophia, was dedicated.

BACKGROUND FOR THE TEACHER

The Hagia Sophia is actually the third structure constructed on its site. The current structure was built by two renowned architects of the time, ordered by the Emperor Justinian. The current structure was dedicated on December 27, 537. The Hagia Sophia drew on both Greek and Egyptian architectural styles. Its dome was designed by a mathematician and a physicist. The massive dome rests on multiple marble pillars. Earthquakes have damaged the structure, resulting in added reinforcements. The Hagia Sophia was chosen as a world heritage site by UNESCO in 1985, and it is an important site for tourism in Istanbul today.

DIGITAL RESOURCES myNGconnect.com

TEACHER RESOURCES & ASSESSMENT

 Reading and Note-Taking   **Vocabulary Practice**   **Section 1 Quiz**

STUDENT RESOURCES

 NG Chapter Gallery

INTRODUCE & ENGAGE

MAKE CONNECTIONS

Ask students about important and impressive buildings that they have seen or visited. Students might indicate buildings in their community or historical buildings like the U.S. Capitol. Discuss with students what makes these buildings impressive. Tell students that the photo in this lesson is of the Hagia Sophia, a significant and impressive building of the Byzantine Empire. `0:05` minutes

TEACH

GUIDED DISCUSSION

1. **Make Inferences** Why do you think December 27, 537, was a significant day for Emperor Justinian? *(Students might indicate that it was the dedication day for the Hagia Sophia, an ambitious building project completed under the orders of Justinian and a major accomplishment for him.)*

2. **Make Generalizations** Based on the photo of the dome of the Hagia Sophia, what generalization can you make about the condition of the structure today? *(Students' responses might indicate that though the Hagia Sophia is still beautiful and impressive, it is in need of repair and restoration.)*

ANALYZE VISUALS

Have students examine the photo of the dome of the Hagia Sophia. Have them identify the various elements they see in the photo. List students' responses on the board. Discuss with students what the dome indicates about art and architecture in the Byzantine Empire. `0:10` minutes

ACTIVE OPTIONS

On Your Feet: Descriptive Words Hand out two sticky notes to each student. Have students examine the details in the photograph of the dome in the Hagia Sophia. Then have them write a word or phrase on each sticky note that describes the dome and elements of the dome. Have students place their sticky notes on the board and discuss their descriptions. `0:10` minutes

Critical Viewing: NG Chapter Gallery Ask students to choose one image from the Chapter Gallery and become an expert on it. They should do additional research to learn all about it. Then, students should share their findings with a partner, a small group, or the class. `0:10` minutes

DIFFERENTIATE

INCLUSION

Describe Lesson Visuals Pair visually impaired students with students who are not visually challenged. Ask the latter to help their partners "see" the visual in this lesson by describing the elements in the photo and answering questions the visually impaired student might have.

GIFTED & TALENTED

Make a Poster Direct students to read the information about the Hagia Sophia in the lesson. Ask them to imagine that they are in Constantinople and have been tasked with constructing a poster advertising the event on December 27, 537. Have students work with a partner to create the poster, which should urge people to attend the event. Students' posters should include words that create interest in the building and excitement about the event. Display completed posters in the classroom.

Press **mt** *in the Student eEdition for modified text.*

See the Chapter Planner for more strategies for differentiation.

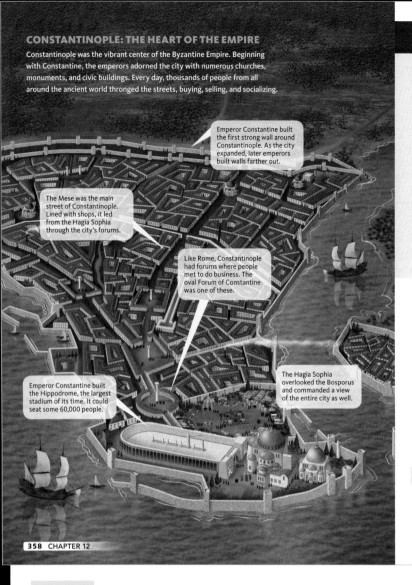

CONSTANTINOPLE: THE HEART OF THE EMPIRE

Constantinople was the vibrant center of the Byzantine Empire. Beginning with Constantine, the emperors adorned the city with numerous churches, monuments, and civic buildings. Every day, thousands of people from all around the ancient world thronged the streets, buying, selling, and socializing.

Emperor Constantine built the first strong wall around Constantinople. As the city expanded, later emperors built walls farther out.

The Mese was the main street of Constantinople. Lined with shops, it led from the Hagia Sophia through the city's forums.

Like Rome, Constantinople had forums where people met to do business. The oval Forum of Constantine was one of these.

Emperor Constantine built the Hippodrome, the largest stadium of its time. It could seat some 60,000 people.

The Hagia Sophia overlooked the Bosporus and commanded a view of the entire city as well.

1.4 Life in Constantinople

You had to like people to enjoy living in Constantinople. It was the world's largest city, with its 500,000 inhabitants packed tightly together. The people of the city considered it the new Rome.

MAIN IDEA

Constantinople was a lively capital city modeled on ancient Rome.

THE CAPITAL CITY

Like Rome, Constantinople relied on resources from outside the city for its survival. The people consumed grain imported from Egypt and water piped in from more than 70 miles away.

Surrounded by the sea on three sides, Constantinople expanded to the west as it constantly attracted new people. Its strategic location on the Bosporus made it the richest and most influential city of its time. Merchants and traders from many parts of Europe and Asia brought in a constant flow of business and goods.

Like the residents of Rome, many of Constantinople's residents lived in poor conditions. They relied on government handouts of bread. Just a short walk away, though, spectacular public buildings and magnificent monuments inspired civic pride. As in Rome, a Senate house, public baths, triumphal arches, columns, and statues reflected the wealth and glory of the empire.

The city's people would frequently cram into the huge Hippodrome, a massive arena almost 1,500 feet long, to watch chariot races. The track was decorated with treasures from ancient Greece and Egypt. The emperor supervised the games from the imperial box, just as in Rome.

ROMAN CULTURAL INFLUENCE

Constantinople reflected everything that was glorious about ancient Rome. Its design, architecture, and monuments all reinforced the fact that the Byzantines considered themselves Roman. They saw themselves as the true inheritors of Roman cultural traditions—far more than Rome itself. Indeed, the Byzantine emperors brought many great monuments from Roman Italy, Africa, and Greece to adorn the capital.

Constantinople was also a center of cultural diversity because it was a center of trade. People who came from abroad to trade sometimes settled in the city. Greece was a strong inflence as well. Greek, not Latin, was the people's language and the official language of the state. However, the Justinian Code, based on Roman law, continued as the basis for the Byzantine legal system. In this way, Byzantium helped preserve Greek and Roman learning for later generations.

REVIEW & ASSESS

1. **READING CHECK** What was one way in which Constantinople modeled itself on ancient Rome?

2. **MAKE INFERENCES** Why was trade with other regions necessary for Constantinople?

3. **INTERPRET VISUALS** What details in the drawing illustrate the idea that Constantinople was a busy, wealthy city?

PLAN

OBJECTIVE

Describe the ways in which Constantinople was modeled on ancient Rome.

CRITICAL THINKING SKILLS FOR LESSON 1.4

- Identify Main Ideas and Details
- Monitor Comprehension
- Make Inferences
- Interpret Visuals
- Draw Conclusions
- Form Opinions

ESSENTIAL QUESTION

How did the Byzantine Empire carry on the culture and traditions of the old Roman Empire?

Constantinople was the capital city of the Byzantine Empire. Lesson 1.4 describes how it was modeled on ancient Rome.

BACKGROUND FOR THE TEACHER

The Hippodrome was the center of Constantinople's social life. People bet huge amounts of money on the four teams that took part in chariot races. Each of the teams was sponsored by a different political party. Each chariot was powered by four horses, and up to eight chariots competed on the racing track. In addition to being sporting events, the races provided rare occasions for the emperor and citizens to come together in a single venue.

DIGITAL RESOURCES myNGconnect.com

TEACHER RESOURCES & ASSESSMENT

 Reading and Note-Taking

 Vocabulary Practice

 Section 1 Quiz

STUDENT RESOURCES

 NG Chapter Gallery

INTRODUCE & ENGAGE

TEAM UP

Tell students to imagine they will be building a city in a prime location near a waterway. Have them brainstorm in groups. Tell them to use an Idea Web to list what they would build and the features they want their city to have. Tell students that in this lesson they will learn about the features the emperor Justinian included in the city of Constantinople. **0:05** minutes

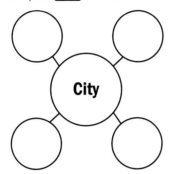

TEACH

GUIDED DISCUSSION

1. **Draw Conclusions** How did being the center of trade also make Constantinople a center of cultural diversity? *(Merchants and traders from many parts of Europe and Asia brought in business. Sometimes people who came from abroad to trade settled in the city, contributing to its diversity.)*

2. **Form Opinions** What factor do you think was most important in making Constantinople a great city? *(Answers will vary. Students should provide reasons for their opinions.)*

INTERPRET VISUALS

Focus students' attention on the drawing of Constantinople. Call on students to read the callouts. Ask students to use the information in the drawing to discuss what daily life might have been like for people living in Constantinople. **0:10** minutes

ACTIVE OPTIONS

On Your Feet: Three-Step Interview Have students choose a partner. One student should interview the other on the question, *In what ways was Constantinople modeled on ancient Rome?* Then they should reverse roles. Finally, each student should share the results of his or her interview with the class. **0:15** minutes

Critical Viewing: NG Image Gallery Invite students to explore the entire NG Image Gallery and create a Favorites List by choosing the images they find most interesting. If possible, have students copy the images into a document to form an actual list. Then encourage them to select the image they like best and do further research on it. **0:20** minutes

DIFFERENTIATE

STRIVING READERS

Outline and Take Notes Have students work in pairs, each pair numbering off from one through six. Assign each pair one paragraph to read together. Encourage student pairs to take notes on their assigned paragraphs. Then have students form larger groups made up of numbered pairs. Have them share their notes so that everyone in their group has notes for all paragraphs. Have pairs or groups work together to create an outline from their notes. Depending on the number of students involved, there may need to be two sets of six pairs.

GIFTED & TALENTED

Compare Architecture Have students use the Internet to conduct research and find examples of structures from the Roman and Byzantine empires. Tell them to download photos and organize them into a presentation that describes the architecture of the periods and compares similarities and differences of the architecture of the two empires.

Press **mt** *in the Student eEdition for modified text.*

See the Chapter Planner for more strategies for differentiation.

REVIEW & ASSESS

ANSWERS

1. Constantinople was modeled after ancient Rome, borrowing Rome's design, architecture, and monuments. Byzantines also continued Roman cultural traditions.

2. Trade was necessary because Constantinople relied on resources from outside the city for its survival.

3. The information about the Mese and the Forum of Constantine illustrate that Constantinople was a busy, wealthy city.

The **Church Divides**

It's Saturday afternoon in the Hagia Sophia. Just before the service, three men burst in, march up to the altar, slam down a piece of paper, shout in a foreign language, and storm out. You've just witnessed the Christian church being split in two—forever.

MAIN IDEA

Christianity in the East and the West developed differently, causing arguments and finally a split.

EAST VERSUS WEST

When the old Roman Empire divided, the cultures of its eastern and western empires developed very differently. Arguments arose over Christian religious practices. In the East, the emperor was seen as God's representative on Earth. The emperor had a great deal of influence over the church and its leader, the **patriarch**. The first patriarchs of Constantinople were bishops under the governance of the pope. Over time, however, they became more independent of Rome.

The West did not have an emperor after 476, when the Roman Empire fell. As you may recall, the pope in Rome grew extremely powerful and claimed absolute authority over all western Christians, even kings. He then claimed authority over the eastern Christians, which led to a long power struggle with the Byzantine emperors.

With different leaders and with very little contact, eastern and western Christians drifted apart in their beliefs and practices.

One key conflict was a disagreement about the Holy Trinity—the Father, the Son, and the Holy Spirit. The western church adopted a **creed**, or statement of belief, that claimed the Holy Spirit comes from the Father and the Son—God and Jesus. The eastern church maintained the belief that the Holy Spirit comes only from the Father.

Another major clash was over **icons**, images of Jesus and the saints. Many Christians had icons, and some began to pray to them. In the East, the emperor banned icons and ordered that they be destroyed. In the West, the pope rebuked the emperor and condemned the destruction of the icons. Religion was an extremely important topic to the Byzantine people. They believed their eternal salvation depended on proper understanding of God and the Bible. As a result, these religious disagreements brought about strong feelings.

THE EAST-WEST SCHISM

Growing disagreements created suspicion and hostility between eastern and western Christians. Finally, the pope's representatives in Constantinople announced that the Byzantine patriarch was **excommunicated**—no longer part of the church. They made this announcement by placing the letter of excommunication on the altar of the Hagia Sophia. The furious patriarch then excommunicated the pope. In 1054, the church split in what is called the East-West Schism (SKIH-zuhm) or the Schism of 1054. A **schism** is a separation. The Roman Catholic Church remained in the West, and the **Eastern Orthodox Church** developed in Byzantium.

Followers of each religion shared some important common ground. They both based their beliefs on Jesus and the Bible, and they both worshipped in churches with services led by priests and bishops. However, in

THE SCHISM OF 1054

Eastern Orthodox Church
Roman Catholic Church

the Roman Catholic Church, the pope had authority over all the clergy and even kings. Priests could not marry, and services were conducted in Latin. In the Eastern Orthodox Church, the emperor had spiritual authority over the clergy, priests could marry, and services were conducted in Greek.

ICONS

The word *icon* comes from the Greek word for "image." Many icons were painted on wood, but some were made from mosaic tiles, ivory, and other materials. Although Byzantine emperors banned icons more than once, people kept them in their homes and businesses and placed them in churches.

REVIEW & ASSESS

1. **READING CHECK** What was one principal difference between the eastern and western churches?

2. **DETERMINE WORD MEANINGS** How does knowing that *ortho* refers to "correct" and *dox* refers to "opinion" clarify the meaning of the word *orthodox*?

3. **INTERPRET MAPS** What does the map add to the text's description of the Schism of 1054?

PLAN

OBJECTIVE

Explain how differences in the development of Christianity in the East and the West led to a split in the church.

CRITICAL THINKING SKILLS FOR LESSON 2.1

- Identify Main Ideas and Details
- Monitor Comprehension
- Determine Word Meanings
- Interpret Maps
- Analyze Cause and Effect
- Compare and Contrast

ESSENTIAL QUESTION

How did the Byzantine Empire carry on the culture and traditions of the old Roman Empire?

Cultures in the eastern and western parts of the old Roman Empire developed differently. Lesson 2.1 describes how differences in religious practices led to a split in the Christian Church.

BACKGROUND FOR THE TEACHER

The split between Christianity in the East and the West had its origin when the Roman Empire was divided into eastern and western parts. The Western Roman Empire was destroyed by the invasions of barbarian tribes, while the Eastern Roman Empire—the Byzantine Empire—thrived. Other differences also caused the two sides to drift apart. The main language in the West was Latin, while Greek was dominant in the East. The Church was also affected by the division between the East and the West, resulting in different rites and views of religious teachings.

DIGITAL RESOURCES myNGconnect.com

TEACHER RESOURCES & ASSESSMENT

 Reading and Note-Taking

 Vocabulary Practice

 Section 2 Quiz

STUDENT RESOURCES

 Active History

ACTIVATE PRIOR KNOWLEDGE

Ask students to recall events in history when the United States experienced a split. Lead students to recall the Civil War and the split between the North and the South and the split between the colonies from Great Britain. Tell students that in this lesson they will learn about the split in Christianity that affected the Byzantine Empire. **0:05** minutes

TEACH

GUIDED DISCUSSION

1. **Analyze Cause and Effect** What was the effect of the excommunication of the Byzantine patriarch and then the excommunication of the pope by the patriarch? *(The effect was the split between the eastern and western churches in what is called the East-West Schism.)*

2. **Compare and Contrast** What are some ways in which the Roman Catholic Church and the Eastern Orthodox Church were alike and ways in which they were different in their beliefs? *(Both churches based their beliefs on Jesus and the Bible, and both worshipped in churches with services led by priests and bishops. They differed in that in the Roman Catholic Church, the pope had authority over all the clergy and even kings, priests could not marry, and services were conducted in Latin, whereas in the Eastern Orthodox Church, the emperor had spiritual authority over the clergy, priests could marry, and services were conducted in Greek.)*

INTERPRET MAPS

Have students examine the Schism of 1054 map. Help students interpret the map. Focus on the map legend. **ASK:** What do the colors used in the map represent? *(The gold color represents the places in which people followed the Roman Catholic religion, and the purple color represents the places in which people followed the Eastern Orthodox religion.)* What would be another way of showing the same information? *(Students might respond that a chart listing the places that followed each religion would be another way to show the information.)* Discuss with students why using a map such as this one is often a more efficient way of showing information. **0:10** minutes

ACTIVE OPTIONS

Active History: Compare Two Branches of Christianity Extend the lesson by using either the PDF or Whiteboard version of the Compare Two Branches of Christianity Active History activity. These activities take a deeper look at a topic from, or related to, the lesson. Explore the activities as a class, turn them into group assignments, or even assign them individually. **0:10** minutes

On Your Feet: Thumbs Up/Thumbs Down Divide the class into groups and have each group write six true-false statements about the lesson with the correct answers included. Collect the questions. Mix them up and read them aloud to the class, skipping any duplicates. Have students give a "thumbs up" for true statements and a "thumbs down" for false statements. Correct any misconceptions. **0:05** minutes

DIFFERENTIATE

ENGLISH LANGUAGE LEARNERS

Match Words and Definitions Give students the following matching exercise. Have them work in pairs to match the words with their definitions and then write a sentence using each one.

1. patriarch	**a.** no longer part of the church
2. creed	**b.** images of Jesus and the saints
3. icons	**c.** separation
4. excommunicated	**d.** leader of the Eastern Orthodox Church
5. schism	**e.** statement of belief

PRE-AP

Write a Report Have students do Internet research in order to write a report about the beliefs and practices of the Eastern Orthodox and the Roman Catholic churches. Direct students to download photos of some of the practices in their reports. Encourage students to include a Venn diagram to illustrate the similarities and the differences between the two religions. Have students share their reports with the class.

Press **mt** *in the Student eEdition for modified text.*

See the Chapter Planner for more strategies for differentiation.

REVIEW & ASSESS

ANSWERS

1. There were principal differences between the eastern and the western churches. The western church claimed the Holy Spirit comes from the Father and the Son, while the eastern church maintained the belief that the Holy Spirit comes only from the Father. Icons were banned and destroyed in the East. In the East, the emperor had a great deal of influence over the church and the patriarch. The West did not have an emperor, and the pope grew very powerful.

2. The word means "having the right opinion."

3. The map indicates the extent of each of the churches and indicates the places that followed each one.

2.2 BYZANTINE MOSAICS

The Byzantine Empire developed an influential artistic culture. Its distinctive style is well represented by the remarkable mosaics found in churches such as the Hagia Sophia.

Covering entire walls and ceilings, Byzantine mosaics stood out for their exceptional quality and craftsmanship. Large expanses of gold-backed glass created a rich glow. Natural stone cubes helped create vibrant, detailed scenes. The breathtaking results still awe viewers today.

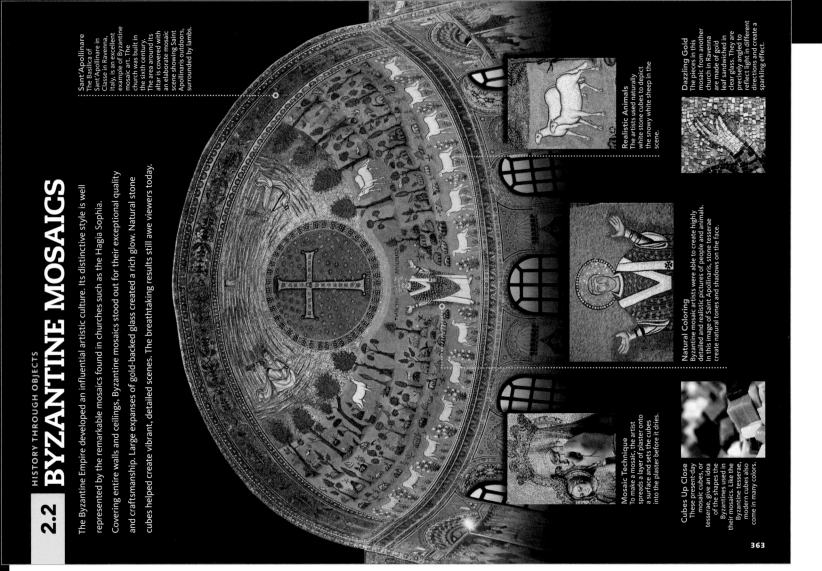

Sant'Apollinare
The Basilica of Sant'Apollinare in Classe in Ravenna, Italy, is an excellent example of Byzantine mosaic art. The church was built in the sixth century. The area around its altar is covered with an elaborate mosaic scene showing Saint Apollinaris outdoors, surrounded by lambs.

Realistic Animals
The artists used naturally white stone cubes to depict the snowy white sheep in the scene.

Dazzling Gold
The pieces in this mosaic from another church in Ravenna are made of gold leaf sandwiched in clear glass. They are precisely angled to reflect light in different directions and create a sparkling effect.

Natural Coloring
Byzantine mosaic artists were able to create highly detailed and realistic pictures of people and animals. In this image of Saint Apollinaris, stone tesserae create natural tones and shadows on the face.

Mosaic Technique
To make a mosaic, the artist spreads a layer of plaster onto a surface and sets the cubes into the plaster before it dries.

Cubes Up Close
These present-day mosaic cubes, or tesserae, give an idea of the shapes the Byzantines used in their mosaics. Like the Byzantine tesserae, modern cubes also come in many colors.

363

PLAN

OBJECTIVE

Describe the distinctive Byzantine style of mosaic art.

CRITICAL THINKING SKILLS FOR LESSON 2.2

- Describe
- Make Generalizations
- Analyze Visuals

ESSENTIAL QUESTION

How did the Byzantine Empire carry on the culture and traditions of the old Roman Empire?

The Byzantine Empire's distinctive style of art is represented by the beautiful mosaics found in several churches throughout the empire. Lesson 2.2 describes some of the aspects of mosaic art.

BACKGROUND FOR THE TEACHER

The Basilica of Sant'Apollinare in Classe is located in Ravenna, Italy. Classe is the main port of Ravenna. Sant'Apollinare in Classe is a significant structure of Byzantine art. It is one of eight Ravenna sites listed on UNESCO's World Heritage List. The huge brick church was consecrated in 549 and dedicated to Saint Apollinaris, the first bishop of Ravenna and Classe.

DIGITAL RESOURCES myNGconnect.com

TEACHER RESOURCES & ASSESSMENT

 Reading and Note-Taking   **Vocabulary Practice**   **Section 2 Quiz**

STUDENT RESOURCES

 NG Chapter Gallery

INTRODUCE & ENGAGE

MAKE CONNECTIONS

Discuss with students their experiences with putting together a jigsaw puzzle. Have them describe the kinds of puzzles they assembled and the number of pieces involved. Ask them how difficult assembling the pieces was and the reason for any difficulty. Tell students that in this lesson they will learn about the art of mosaics, a distinctive style of art of the Byzantine Empire. Tell them that creating a mosaic is similar in part to assembling a jigsaw puzzle in that small pieces form a montage to create a bigger picture. **0:05** minutes

TEACH

GUIDED DISCUSSION

1. **Describe** How do artists make a mosaic? *(They spread a layer of plaster onto a surface and set the cubes into the plaster before it dries.)*

2. **Make Generalizations** What generalization can you make about the characteristics of the people who created the mosaics pictured in the lesson? *(Responses will vary, but might include that the people were creative, artistic, attentive to detail, and imaginative.)*

ANALYZE VISUALS

Have students focus on the mosaic from the Basilica of Sant'Apollinare in Classe in Ravenna. Direct them to read the text and callouts. **ASK:** How were artists able to show different colors in the mosaic? *(They used stone cubes to create natural tones and shadows on faces and white cubes to depict the white sheep. To create a sparkling effect, artists angled cubes to reflect light.)* **0:15** minutes

ACTIVE OPTIONS

On Your Feet: Four Corners Ask students to examine the photos and callouts in the lesson. Post the four signs listed below and have students choose the phrase that best describes their opinion about and reaction to the Byzantine mosaics. Have group members discuss their opinions and reactions. Then ask one member from each group to report to the class. **0:15** minutes

A. amazing   **B.** beautiful   **C.** unrealistic   **D.** not interesting

Critical Viewing: NG Chapter Gallery Have students examine the contents of the Chapter Gallery for this chapter. Then invite them to brainstorm additional images they believe would fit within the Chapter Gallery. Have them write a description of these additional images and provide an explanation of why they would fit within the Chapter Gallery. Then instruct them to do online research to find examples of actual images they would like to add to the gallery. **0:10** minutes

DIFFERENTIATE

INCLUSION

Describe Details in a Photo Pair students who are visually impaired with students who are not. Ask the latter to be their partners' "eyes" and describe the details in the photos of Byzantine mosaics. Students should read the captions of the callouts to the visually impaired students before they describe the details in each one.

GIFTED & TALENTED

Make a Mosaic Have students use the information in the lesson and do additional Internet research to find out more about mosaic art and to find other examples of mosaics. Then have them create their own mosaics. Direct students to first draw an outline of a picture. They might draw a picture of an individual object, such as a flower, or they might draw an abstract design. Students might use small objects such as different-colored beads, sequins, or seeds to fill in their drawing. Display completed mosaics in the classroom.

Press (**mt**) *in the Student eEdition for modified text.*

See the Chapter Planner for more strategies for differentiation.

The End of an Empire

On May 29, 1453, the last Byzantine emperor died fighting as his enemies swarmed through his capital's shattered walls. That day, the Byzantine Empire ended. It was a heroic finale for an empire that had survived against the odds for a thousand years.

MAIN IDEA

After Justinian, the empire experienced invasions and another golden age before it finally collapsed.

GREEK FIRE

The Byzantine army had a secret weapon: Greek fire. It was liquid fire soldiers could propel at enemy troops. It burned with an incredible intensity, and not even water could extinguish it.

The formula for making Greek fire was a closely guarded secret that died with the empire.

DEBTS AND INVASIONS

After Justinian died in 565, the debts the emperor had taken out to pay for his many wars nearly bankrupted the empire. In addition, the plague, which had already attacked during Justinian's time, made a return. Rats arriving aboard grain ships from Egypt carried the deadly disease, and it spread quickly through the overcrowded city. At the height of the plague, perhaps 10,000 people died every day.

As if that weren't enough, Byzantium's old enemies, including the Persians, renewed their attacks on the empire's borders. And then, in 634, the Byzantine Empire confronted a new rival. The religion of

Islam had united Arab tribes, who formed a mighty Muslim army. This army conquered Egypt—a disaster for Constantinople's grain supply. By 711, the Arabs had conquered Syria, Egypt, parts of Southwest Asia, North Africa, and the Persian Empire.

NEW GOLDEN AGE AND FALL

Still, the Byzantine Empire was not yet down or out. By the early 1000s, the empire had entered a new golden age. Under the leadership of Basil II, Byzantium regained more control over trade, restored many of Constantinople's buildings and institutions, and spread Christianity among Slavic peoples to the north.

The empire's prosperity was short-lived, however. In 1096, an army of Christian Europeans launched a series of wars called the Crusades to fight the spread of Islam. The Crusaders soon came into conflict with Byzantine leaders. In 1204, they sacked Constantinople and occupied the city until 1261.

In time, the Byzantine Empire became a shadow of its former power—and then came the Turks, a people who had migrated into the region. By 1450, the Turks, who were Muslims, controlled all the lands around Constantinople. The city stood alone and surrounded.

In 1453, Mehmed II, the Turkish ruler, launched an army of 100,000 men against Constantinople's walls. The city's defenders, in contrast, numbered 7,000. On May 29, 1453, the Turks launched a final assault. They broke through the city's walls and killed the last Byzantine emperor, Constantine XI, as he charged into the invading army. By nightfall, Constantinople was under Turkish control.

+ POSSIBLE RESPONSE

The battle looks brutal and chaotic. The invading army looks well armed.

Critical Viewing This painting shows the invasion of Constantinople by the Crusaders. Based on this painting, how would you describe the battle?

The Capture of Constantinople in 1204, Jacopo Robusti Tintoretto, 16th century

REVIEW & ASSESS

1. **READING CHECK** What was one factor that led to the decline and collapse of the Byzantine Empire?

2. **ANALYZE CAUSE AND EFFECT** Why was the plague able to spread so quickly throughout Constantinople?

3. **SEQUENCE EVENTS** What events took place in Byzantium during the 1000s?

365

PLAN

OBJECTIVE

Explain the factors that weakened the Byzantine Empire and ultimately destroyed it.

CRITICAL THINKING SKILLS FOR LESSON 2.3

- Identify Main Ideas and Details
- Analyze Cause and Effect
- Make Inferences
- Analyze Visuals
- Monitor Comprehension
- Sequence Events

ESSENTIAL QUESTION

How did the Byzantine Empire carry on the culture and traditions of the old Roman Empire?

After the death of Emperor Justinian, the Byzantine Empire began to decline. Lesson 2.3 discusses the events that caused the decline and eventually led to the empire's collapse.

BACKGROUND FOR THE TEACHER

The bubonic plague contributed to the decline of the Byzantine Empire. The plague that hit the empire in the sixth century had a death rate from forty to seventy percent of its cases. The plague lasted four months, during which time daily life and work in the city of Constantinople stopped. The plague had a devastating impact on the empire's economy, which was primarily agricultural. One of the immediate effects was the loss of farmers. This in turn led to a shortage of food and famines after the plague ended. The diminished population resulted in a smaller tax base, which led to financial hardships for the empire.

DIGITAL RESOURCES myNGconnect.com

TEACHER RESOURCES & ASSESSMENT

 Reading and Note-Taking

 Vocabulary Practice

 Section 2 Quiz

STUDENT RESOURCES

 NG Chapter Gallery

INTRODUCE & ENGAGE

WORD KNOWLEDGE

Ask students if they know what the word *decline* means. Write students' responses on the board. Explain that *decline* has more than one meaning, but in this lesson the term means "to grow weaker." Then direct students' attention to the lesson title. Ask students what they think the lesson, based on the title, will be about.
0:05 minutes

TEACH

GUIDED DISCUSSION

1. **Make Inferences** How was the geography of the Byzantine Empire a factor in the invasions that the empire experienced? *(Possible response: The empire's location with few physical barriers left it unprotected. This allowed invasions by Europeans from the north and west and Persians from the east.)*

2. **Analyze Cause and Effect** How do you think the plague contributed to the decline of the Byzantine Empire? *(Possible response might include that the plague killed tens of thousands of people in the Byzantine Empire. The deaths resulted in fewer people able to combat the oncoming invasions.)*

ANALYZE VISUALS

Show and discuss the painting of the invasion of Constantinople. Have students use the painting and the information in the lesson to answer the following questions:

- What does the painting show?
- What details do you see?
- Which two groups are represented in the painting?
- Which group appears to have the upper hand? What details in the painting lead you to think so?

0:15 minutes

ACTIVE OPTIONS

On Your Feet: Turn and Talk on Topic Have students form four lines. Give each group this topic sentence: *The Byzantine Empire grew weaker and shrank until it was finally destroyed.* Tell them to write a paragraph by having each student in the line add a sentence that supports the topic. **0:20** minutes

Critical Viewing: NG Chapter Gallery Invite students to explore the entire NG Image Gallery and choose one image from the gallery they feel best represents their understanding of each chapter or unit. Have students provide a written explanation of why they selected each of the images they chose. **0:10** minutes

DIFFERENTIATE

ENGLISH LANGUAGE LEARNERS

Summarize Lesson 2.3 has six paragraphs. Have students work in pairs or small groups, and assign each pair or group one paragraph to read together. Then each group should summarize their paragraph in one or two sentences for the class.

STRIVING READERS

Create a Time Line Display the events listed below and have students work in pairs to arrange them in the correct order on a time line.

- Christian Europeans conquer Constantinople. (1204)
- Justinian dies. (565)
- The Christian European occupation of Constantinople ends. (1261)
- Constantinople comes under Turkish control. (1453)
- Arabs conquer Syria, Egypt, Mesopotamia, Palestine, North Africa, and the Persian Empire. (711)

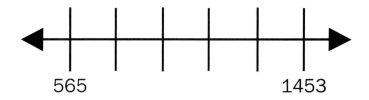

565   1453

Press **mt** *in the Student eEdition for modified text.*

See the Chapter Planner for more strategies for differentiation.

REVIEW & ASSESS

ANSWERS

1. The bubonic plague and enemy attacks and invasions led to the decline and collapse of the Byzantine Empire.

2. The deadly plague, carried by rats, was able to spread quickly because of the city's overcrowded conditions.

3. By the early 1000s, the Byzantine Empire had entered a new golden age. However, in 1096, an army of Christian Europeans launched a series of wars called the Crusades. These Europeans sacked Constantinople in 1204 and occupied the city until 1261. The Crusaders were followed by the Turks, who took control of the city in 1453.

VOCABULARY

Match each word in the first column with its meaning in the second column.

WORD	DEFINITION
1. divine	a. an image of Jesus or another holy figure
2. patriarch	b. a belief that goes against church teachings
3. heresy	c. having the nature of a god
4. icon	d. variety
5. diversity	e. a leader of the Eastern Orthodox Church

READING SKILL

6. **ORGANIZE IDEAS: ANALYZE CAUSE AND EFFECT** If you haven't already, complete your diagram to identify the factors that caused the Byzantine Empire to grow and thrive. Then answer the question.

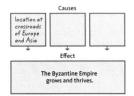

What conditions made it possible for the Byzantine Empire to grow, thrive, and enter a golden age?

MAIN IDEAS

Answer the following questions. Support your answers with evidence from the chapter.

7. In what ways was the location of Constantinople important to the growth of the Byzantine Empire? **LESSON 1.1**

8. In what ways did the Justinian Code improve on the Roman laws that it replaced? **LESSON 1.2**

9. What actions did Justinian take to bring a golden age to Byzantium? **LESSON 1.2**

10. Why did the Byzantines use ancient Rome as the model for their capital city, Constantinople? **LESSON 1.4**

11. How did the Byzantine emperor affect the religious life of the empire? **LESSON 2.1**

12. What effect did the plague have on the Byzantine Empire? **LESSON 2.3**

CRITICAL THINKING

Answer the following questions. Support your answers with evidence from the chapter.

13. **DRAW CONCLUSIONS** How do events that took place during the Byzantine Empire still affect the present-day world?

14. **SYNTHESIZE** How did the Byzantine Empire carry on the culture and traditions of the old Roman Empire?

15. **ANALYZE CAUSE AND EFFECT** Why was the Byzantine Empire a target for invaders throughout its long history?

16. **MAKE GENERALIZATIONS** How does geographic location help determine whether a city will become wealthy and powerful?

17. **YOU DECIDE** What was Justinian's greatest accomplishment? Support your opinion with evidence from the chapter.

INTERPRET DIAGRAMS

Study the diagram below to compare and contrast the two branches of Christianity that developed after the East-West Schism. Then answer the questions that follow.

The East-West Schism

Roman Catholic Church
• Led by the pope
• Pope had authority over all Christians, including kings and emperors
• Priests could not marry
• Services conducted in Latin
• Worship and use of icons promoted by the pope

Similarities
• Faith based on belief in Jesus and the Bible
• Services held in churches led by priests and bishops

Eastern Orthodox Church
• Led by the patriarch
• Emperor had authority over all church officials
• Priests could marry
• Services conducted in Greek
• Some believed the worship of icons should be forbidden

18. In what way did the pope have greater influence in the West than patriarchs did in the East?

19. How were the faiths of both branches of Christianity similar?

ANALYZE SOURCES

The historian Procopius was present at and recorded the events of a rebellion in 532. Read his account of Theodora's speech to Justinian as the emperor prepared to flee Constantinople. Then answer the question that follows.

I believe that flight, now more than ever, is not in our interest even if it should bring us to safety. . . . For one who has reigned it is intolerable to become a fugitive. May I *never* be parted from the purple [the imperial color]! May I *never* live to see the day when I will not be addressed as Mistress by all in my presence! Emperor, if you wish to save yourself, that is easily arranged. . . . But consider whether, after you have saved yourself, you would then gladly exchange safety for death.

20. What does this this speech suggest about Theodora's character and influence?

WRITE ABOUT HISTORY

21. **INFORMATIVE** Suppose you are in the court of the emperor Justinian. Write an explanation for your fellow citizens of how Theodora influences Justinian's rule of the Byzantine Empire.

TIPS

• Take notes from the lessons about Justinian and Theodora.

• Write a topic sentence that clearly introduces your main idea about Theodora and Justinian.

• Choose relevant facts, concrete details, and examples for your explanation.

• Use vocabulary from the chapter where appropriate.

• Organize your details, facts, and examples clearly and logically.

• Provide a concluding statement that summarizes the information presented.

VOCABULARY ANSWERS

WORD	DEFINITION
1. divine c.	**a.** an image of Jesus or another holy figure
2. patriarch e.	**b.** a belief that goes against church teachings
3. heresy b.	**c.** having the nature of a god
4. icon a.	**d.** variety
5. diversity d.	**e.** a leader of the Eastern Orthodox Church

READING STRATEGY ANSWER

Causes

| location at crossroads of Europe and Asia | expansion under Justinian | creation of the Justinian Code |

Effect

The Byzantine Empire grows and thrives.

6. Many factors made it possible for the Byzantine Empire to grow, thrive, and enter a golden age. Constantinople's ideal geographic location, which made it a major trade center, resulted in great wealth and cultural diffusion. Another key factor in the creation of the empire's golden age was Justinian. As emperor, he was dedicated to restoring Byzantium's glory, and he took many steps to do so, including reforming government, undertaking massive building projects, and reforming Roman laws into the Justinian Code.

MAIN IDEA ANSWERS

7. Constantinople's geographic location on the Bosporus linked the Black Sea with the Mediterranean, making the capital city ideal as a major trade center between east and west. This brought great wealth to the Byzantine Empire.

8. The Justinian Code clarified and standardized old Roman laws, making them more practical and easier to understand.

9. Justinian expanded the empire's borders; made major improvements in the areas of government, construction, and law; reformed Byzantine government; started an ambitious construction program; ordered the building of the Hagia Sophia; and sponsored many other civic projects in Constantinople.

10. The Byzantines used ancient Rome as the model for Constantinople because they considered themselves Roman and saw themselves as the true inheritors and keepers of Roman culture.

11. The Byzantine emperor was seen as God's representative on Earth. The emperor had a great deal of influence over the church and the patriarch. The emperor had spiritual authority over the clergy.

12. The plague had a disastrous effect on the Byzantine Empire. At the height of the plague, about 10,000 people died every day in the overcrowded city of Constantinople, weakening the empire.

CRITICAL THINKING ANSWERS

13. Possible response: The city of Constantinople is now Istanbul and still is an important location for trade; the Justinian Code has formed the basis of European law until modern times; the Roman Catholic Church and Eastern Orthodox Church continue today.

14. The Byzantine Empire, like the Roman Empire, extended over a large area; the design, architecture, and monuments of Constantinople reflected those of Rome; the Justinian Code was based on Roman law.

15. The Byzantine Empire was surrounded by enemies and had no strong geographic barriers to prevent invasions; its rich resources and great wealth made the empire a target for raids and invasions.

16. A city that is located on a major waterway or land link that is conducive to trade is more likely to become a center for trade and thereby more likely to become wealthy and powerful.

17. Students' responses will vary. Students should clearly state their opinion regarding their view of Justinian's greatest accomplishment and support that opinion with evidence from the chapter.

INTERPRET DIAGRAMS ANSWERS

18. The pope had greater influence in the west than the patriarch did in the east because the pope had authority over all Christians—including kings and emperors.

19. Both branches of Christianity were based on the belief in Jesus and the Bible.

ANALYZE SOURCES ANSWER

20. Students' responses will vary. Possible responses might include that Theodora was brave and loyal and exerted great influence over Justinian.

WRITE ABOUT HISTORY ANSWER

21. Students' informative essays should
    - contain a topic sentence that introduces the main idea
    - support the topic sentence with facts, details, and examples from the chapter
    - include vocabulary words from the chapter
    - present the information in a clear, logical manner
    - contain a concluding statement

UNIT RESOURCES

On Location with National Geographic Grantee Jodi Magness
Intro and Video

Interactive
Map Tool

News
& Updates

Available on myNGconnect

Unit Wrap-Up:
"History Is a Puzzle"
Feature and Video

"The Wells of Memory"
National Geographic Adapted Article
Student eEdition exclusive

"The Stolen Past"
National Geographic Adapted Article

Unit 5 Inquiry:
Make an Idea Map

CHAPTER RESOURCES

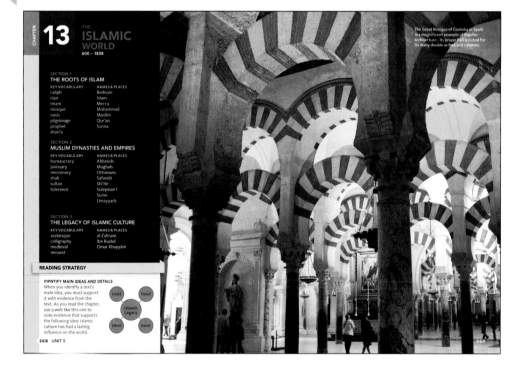

TEACHER RESOURCES
& ASSESSMENT

Available on myNGconnect

Social Studies Skills Lessons
• Reading: Identify Main Ideas and Details
• Writing: Write an Informative Article

Formal Assessment
• Chapter 13 Tests A (on-level)
  & B (below-level)

(A) Chapter 13
Answer Key

ExamView®
One-time Download

STUDENT BACKPACK *Available on myNGconnect*

• **eEdition** *(English)*   • **eEdition** *(Spanish)*   • **Handbooks**   • **Online Atlas**

For Chapter 13 Spanish resources, visit the Teacher Resource Menu page on myNGconnect.

SECTION 1 RESOURCES

THE ROOTS OF ISLAM

 Reading and Note-Taking

 Vocabulary Practice

 Section 1 Quiz

Available on myNGconnect

LESSON 1.1 TRADING CROSSROADS

- On Your Feet: Think, Pair, Share

| NG Learning Framework:
| List Observations

LESSON 1.2 THE PROPHET OF ISLAM

 Biography
Khadijah

Available on myNGconnect

- On Your Feet: Card Responses

| NG Learning Framework:
| Discuss the Umma's Influence

LESSON 1.3 BELIEFS AND LAWS

- On Your Feet: Give Examples
- Critical Viewing: NG Image Gallery

DOCUMENT-BASED QUESTION
LESSON 1.4 THE QUR'AN AND HADITH

- On Your Feet: Three Corners
- Critical Viewing: NG Chapter Gallery

LESSON 1.5 AFTER MUHAMMAD

- On Your Feet: Three-Step Interview

| NG Learning Framework:
| Discuss the Caliphs

SECTION 2 RESOURCES

MUSLIM DYNASTIES AND EMPIRES

 Reading and Note-Taking

 Vocabulary Practice

 Section 2 Quiz

Available on myNGconnect

LESSON 2.1 THE UMAYYADS AND THE ABBASIDS

- On Your Feet: Fishbowl
- Critical Viewing: NG Chapter Gallery

LESSON 2.2 MUSLIM SPAIN

- On Your Feet: Create a Concept Cluster
- Critical Viewing: NG Chapter Gallery

MOMENTS IN HISTORY
LESSON 2.3 THE ALHAMBRA

- On Your Feet: Inside-Outside Circle

| NG Learning Framework:
| Write About an Architectural Example

LESSON 2.4 THE OTTOMAN EMPIRE

 Biography
Suleyman I

 Active History: Interactive Whiteboard Activity
Build a Time Line of Suleyman's Reign

 Active History
Build a Time Line of Suleyman's Reign

Available on myNGconnect

- On Your Feet: Turn and Talk on Topic

LESSON 2.5 THE SAFAVID AND MUGHAL EMPIRES

- On Your Feet: Present a Skit

| NG Learning Framework:
| Give a Presentation

SECTION 3 RESOURCES

THE LEGACY OF ISLAMIC CULTURE

 Reading and Note-Taking

 Vocabulary Practice

 Section 3 Quiz

Available on myNGconnect

LESSON 3.1 SCIENCE AND PHILOSOPHY

 Biography
al-Zahrawi

Available on myNGconnect

- On Your Feet: Stage a Quiz Show

| NG Learning Framework:
| Research Medieval Medical Practices

NG EXPLORER HAYAT SINDI
LESSON 3.2 AIDING PEOPLE THROUGH SCIENCE

- On Your Feet: Play "Ready, Set, Recall"
- Critical Viewing: NG Image Gallery

LESSON 3.3 ARCHITECTURE, THE ARTS, AND LITERATURE

- On Your Feet: Team Word Webbing
- Critical Viewing: NG Image Gallery

HISTORY THROUGH OBJECTS
LESSON 3.4 ISLAMIC ART

- On Your Feet: Question and Answer Chain

| NG Learning Framework:
| Give a Presentation

CHAPTER 13 REVIEW

STRATEGY ❶
Use Pair-Share Reading

Allow students to work in pairs and divide each two-page lesson into two parts. Have students decide which part each one will handle. Both students will read the first part. The student responsible for it will discuss the important information in that part. The second student will make notes and ask a question about the information. The students will then switch roles and repeat the procedure with the second part.

Use with Lessons 1.1, 1.2, 1.3, 1.5, 2.1, 2.2, 2.4, 2.5, 3.1, and 3.3

STRATEGY ❷
Build a Time Line

Select key events from Lessons 1.2 and 1.5. Then have students use the events to create a time line on the board. Students will add to the time line as they read the chapter.

570
Muhammad, the
prophet of Islam, is
born.

Use with Lessons 1.2, 1.5, 2.1, 2.2, 2.4, and 2.5 *For example, key events from Lesson 1.5 might include the death of Muhammad in 632 and the Muslim conquests of new lands by 652.*

STRATEGY ❸
Record and Compare Facts

After reading a lesson, ask students to write two important facts they learned. Allow small groups of students to compare and check their facts and then combine their facts into one longer list. Ask a volunteer from each group to read the most important fact from the list.

Use with All Lessons

Press **(mt)** *in the Student eEdition for modified text.*

STRATEGY ❶
Make Word Connections

Have students write a Key Vocabulary word from the lesson on a sticky note or index card. As they read, ask students to write words from the text or other words they know that are associated with the vocabulary word.

Use with Lessons 1.1, 1.2, 1.3, 1.5, 2.1, 2.2, 2.4, 2.5, 3.1, and 3.3

STRATEGY ❷
Use Supported Reading

In small groups, have students read aloud the chapter lesson by lesson. At the end of each lesson, have them stop and use these frames to tell what they understood from the text:

- This lesson is about _____.
- One detail that stood out to me is _____.
- The vocabulary word _____ means _____.
- I don't think I understand _____.

Guide students through portions of text they do not understand. Be sure all students understand a lesson before moving on to the next one.

Use with All Lessons

STRATEGY ❶
Pair Partners for Dictation

After students read each lesson in the chapter, have them write a sentence summarizing its main idea. Have students get together in pairs and dictate their sentences to each other. Then have them work together to check the sentences for accuracy and spelling.

Use with All Lessons *For Lessons 2.1, 2.2, 2.4, and 2.5, monitor students' comprehension of the main groups discussed in the text. For example, in Lesson 2.1, students should identify how the leadership of the Umayyads and the Abbasids differed.*

STRATEGY ❷
Use Sentence Stems

Before reading, provide students with the two sentence stems for the lessons listed below. After reading, have students complete the stems and compare their completed sentences with a partner.

1.1 a. Many of Arabia's inhabitants in the early 600s made their living as nomadic herders called _____.

    b. An isolated source of water where plants can grow in a desert is called an_____.

1.2 a. Followers of Islam are called _____.

    b. Muhammad taught that loyalty to one's tribe is not as important as loyalty to the _____.

1.3 a. Islamic law is called _____.

    b. A Muslim place of worship is a _____.

1.4 a. The holy book of Islam is the _____.

    b. Accounts of what Muhammad said, did, or approved are called the _____.

1.5 a. After Muhammad's death, Muslim leaders appointed Muhammad's father-in-law, Abu Bakr, to be the successor, or _____.

    b. Abu Bakr's strong leadership kept all of Arabia united under the religion of _____.

Use with Lessons 1.1–1.5

STRATEGY ❸
Review Vocabulary

After reading, write the following words on the board and ask students to write a phrase or draw a picture to describe each word. Then have volunteers use each word in a sentence.

bureaucracy	mercenary	tolerance	janissary
oasis	pilgrimage	clan	prophet
shari'a	mosque	imam	caliph

Use with Lessons 1.1, 1.2, 1.3, 1.5, 2.1, 2.2, 2.4, and 2.5

STRATEGY ❶
Create a Photo Gallery

Have students research to create a gallery of photographs that illustrate Muslim art and architecture. Students should include captions with each photograph.

Use with Lesson 3.3

STRATEGY ❷
Present a Television Documentary

Have students read more about the Blue Mosque, a historic mosque in Istanbul, Turkey, that was built for an Ottoman sultan. Then have students work in small groups to write and present a television documentary about the mosque. Ask students to include information about the origins and history of the mosque as well as its design, features, and architecture. Encourage students to include visuals with the documentary. Invite each group to present their documentary to the class.

Use with Lesson 2.4

STRATEGY ❶
Write a Feature Article

Encourage students to do research to learn more about Suleyman I of the Ottoman Empire. Then have them write a feature article describing what they learned about him and highlighting his talents, contributions, and accomplishments. Encourage students to include photos, drawings, tables, and charts with their article.

Use with Lesson 2.4

STRATEGY ❷
Hold a Panel Discussion

Have students work in small groups to research the many contributions of the medieval Muslim dynasties to world civilization. Ask each group to choose a particular contribution that had a great impact and list reasons why the contribution was so important. Invite students to hold a panel discussion to share their ideas.

Use with Lessons 3.1 and 3.3

13
THE ISLAMIC WORLD
600 – 1858

SECTION 1
THE ROOTS OF ISLAM

KEY VOCABULARY	NAMES & PLACES
caliph	Bedouin
clan	Islam
imam	Mecca
mosque	Muhammad
oasis	Muslim
pilgrimage	Qur'an
prophet	Sunna
shari'a	

SECTION 2
MUSLIM DYNASTIES AND EMPIRES

KEY VOCABULARY	NAMES & PLACES
bureaucracy	Abbasids
janissary	Mughals
mercenary	Ottomans
shah	Safavids
sultan	Shi'ite
tolerance	Suleyman I
	Sunni
	Umayyads

SECTION 3
THE LEGACY OF ISLAMIC CULTURE

KEY VOCABULARY	NAMES & PLACES
arabesque	al-Zahrawi
calligraphy	Ibn Rushd
medieval	Omar Khayyám
minaret	

READING STRATEGY

IDENTIFY MAIN IDEAS AND DETAILS
When you identify a text's main idea, you must support it with evidence from the text. As you read the chapter, use a web like this one to note evidence that supports the following idea: Islamic culture has had a lasting influence on the world.

The Great Mosque of Córdoba in Spain is a magnificent example of Muslim architecture. Its prayer hall is noted for its many double arches and columns.

369

TEACHER BACKGROUND

INTRODUCE THE PHOTOGRAPH

Have students study the photograph of the prayer hall of the Great Mosque of Córdoba. Tell students that the Great Mosque is shaped like a large rectangle. About 850 pillars divide the interior of the building into 19 north-to-south aisles and 29 east-to-west aisles. Pillars are decorated with colored marble. Some walls of the building are inlaid with mosaics and gold. Tell students that in this chapter they will learn about art and architecture in the Islamic world. They will also learn about Islam and Islamic empires. **ASK:** How would you describe the prayer hall? (*Possible responses: It is large. It has columns and arches. It has bright colors and ornate decorations.*)

SHARE BACKGROUND

Tell students that the original structure for the Great Mosque of Córdoba was built from 784 to 786. Additions to the mosque were built in the 9th and 10th centuries, making it one of the largest mosques in the world of Islam. The building has served as a Christian cathedral since the 13th century. In the 16th century, the character of the building was changed with the addition of a central high altar, a cruciform choir, a number of chapels, and a tall belfry.

DIGITAL RESOURCES myNGconnect.com

TEACHER RESOURCES & ASSESSMENT

 Social Studies Skills Lessons
- Reading: Identify Main Ideas and Details
- Writing: Write an Informative Article

 **Formal Assessment**
- Chapter 13 Tests A (on-level) & B (below-level)

 ExamView®
One-time Download

 Chapter 13 Answer Key

STUDENT BACKPACK

- **eEdition** (*English*)
- **eEdition** (*Spanish*)
- **Handbooks**
- **Online Atlas**

For Chapter 13 Spanish Resources, visit the Teacher Resource Menu page.

INTRODUCE THE ESSENTIAL QUESTION

WHAT MAJOR CONTRIBUTIONS DID MEDIEVAL MUSLIM LEADERS AND SCHOLARS MAKE TO WORLD CIVILIZATION?

Cause and Effect Activity: Patterns of Civilization Tell students that throughout history, the development of civilizations or advanced societies have followed similar patterns. Display the Cause-and-Effect Chain below one box at a time to reveal the pattern. At each step, invite students to share anything they know about that topic or to predict what happens next. Summarize the process in this way: People who have moved from place to place to find food discover fertile land near sources of water. They begin to grow their food and settle down. Farming villages grow into cities. Society becomes more complex as people have a variety of jobs and develop new skills and technology. Explain that they will learn how this pattern developed in the Arabian Peninsula. **0:15** minutes

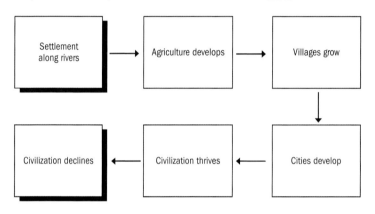

INTRODUCE THE READING STRATEGY

IDENTIFY MAIN IDEAS AND DETAILS

Remind students that when they identify main ideas in a text, they need to support them with details from the text. Model the strategy by reading aloud the first two paragraphs under the subheading "Mathematics and Astronomy" in Lesson 3.1. Fill out the graphic organizer with details from the paragraphs.

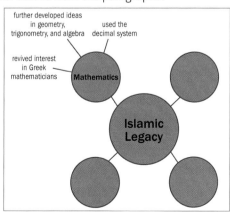

INTRODUCE CHAPTER VOCABULARY

VOC STRATEGY

Have students perform the six steps shown below for each Key Vocabulary word in the chapter. It might be helpful to model this strategy for the first vocabulary word. Encourage students to work in pairs as they complete the six steps for the remaining words. Call on volunteers to share examples of their work with the rest of the class.

VOCABULARY WORD:

1. Write the sentence in which the word appears in your text.

2. Study how the word is used in the sentence. What do you think it means?

3. Look up the word in a dictionary or use the glossary in your text.

4. Use the word in a sentence of your own.

5. To help you remember the meaning, draw a quick sketch that relates to the word. You might think of an action the word suggests, or connect the word to a story or a news report.

6. Tell why you chose this way of representing the meaning.

KEY DATES	
Early 600s	Crossroads for trade in the Arabian Peninsula
613	Muhammad begins to preach Islamic faith
632	Death of Muhammad
652	Muslim conquest of Syria, Palestine, Iraq, Iran, Egypt, and parts of North Africa
661	Rise of the Umayyads
750	Rise of the Abbasids
933	Muslim Spain unifies under abd-al-Rahman
1500s	Rise of the Ottoman Empire, the largest empire in the world
1501	Beginning of the Safavid Empire in Persia
1526	Rise of the Mughal Empire in India

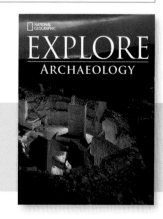

For fascinating archaeology articles, check out *EXPLORE ARCHAEOLOGY*.

Trading
Crossroads

People living on the Arabian Peninsula in the 600s had to be tough. Their homeland was mostly a sea of sun-scorched sand that offered little shelter, shade, or water. But its location—at a spot where three continents meet—proved to be an advantage.

MAIN IDEA

The Arabian Peninsula became an important crossroads for trade among the continents of Asia, Africa, and Europe by the early 600s.

DESERT LIFE

The huge rectangle of the Arabian Peninsula, also known as Arabia, is one of the hottest and driest places on Earth. Almost the entire 1.2 million square miles is scorching desert and dry, flat land. Rain falls in few places, making water scarce and precious. Much of the peninsula gets only three to five inches of rain a year.

The region's harsh climate has long placed limits on farming. Many of Arabia's early inhabitants made their living as nomadic herders called **Bedouin** (BEH-duh-wuhn). They constantly moved their sheep, goats, and cattle among sources of water and grazing land. *Bedouin* is an Arabic word meaning "desert dweller."

In the 600s, the Bedouin were organized into tribes based on **clans**, or groups of

related families who believed they shared a common ancestor. Each tribe formed an extended family to which members were fiercely loyal. Tribe members owned land and most property together, and each tribe had an elected leader called a sheikh (SHAYK). The tribes often fought one another to maintain or gain control of areas of the desert. As a result, the tribesmen became strong and skilled warriors.

GROWTH OF CITIES

The only place life could flourish in Arabia was at an **oasis**. An oasis is an isolated, reliable source of water in a desert where plants can grow. The oases were like stepping stones across the vast desert. They naturally attracted people, who then built permanent settlements. Anyone crossing the desert had to visit the oases, which became useful places to trade.

Because of its central location, Arabia became an important crossroads connecting routes from Asia, Africa, and Europe. Merchants led camels carrying silks, spices, metals, and other products along these trade routes. As a result, some oases grew into rich market towns and then into cities.

Arabia's most important city was **Mecca**, which became a center for both trade and religion. The various Arab tribes worshipped different nature gods. These beliefs were polytheistic, or based on the existence of multiple gods. Most Arabs also recognized the existence of a supreme God, called Allah (AL-luh) in Arabic. According to ancient Islamic tradition, the religious leader known in the Hebrew Bible as Abraham had stopped at Mecca and built a shrine called the Ka'aba (KAH-buh). Although Abraham dedicated the Ka'aba to the one supreme God, the shrine came to include representations of many Arabian tribal gods. Mecca became an important site for polytheistic Arabs. People from all over the peninsula made a **pilgrimage**, or journey, to worship there.

TRADE IN SOUTHWEST ASIA, c. 570

+ **POSSIBLE RESPONSE**
They may have faced attacks from different tribes who lived there and shortages of water for themselves and their animals.

Critical Viewing Sand dunes like these cover much of the Arabian Peninsula. What dangers might traders have faced as they crossed the vast desert?

REVIEW & ASSESS

1. **READING CHECK** How did Arabia's location contribute to its development as an important trading crossroads?

2. **ANALYZE CAUSE AND EFFECT** How did Arabia's physical geography influence the Bedouin's way of life?

3. **INTERPRET MAPS** Find Mecca on the map. Why is Mecca's location good for trade?

PLAN

OBJECTIVE

Explain how the Arabian Peninsula became an important crossroads for trade among the continents of Asia, Africa, and Europe by the early 600s.

CRITICAL THINKING SKILLS FOR LESSON 1.1

- Identify Main Ideas and Details
- Analyze Cause and Effect
- Make Inferences
- Draw Conclusions
- Monitor Comprehension
- Interpret Maps
- Analyze Visuals

ESSENTIAL QUESTION

What major contributions did medieval Muslim leaders and scholars make to world civilization?

The climate of the Arabian Peninsula influenced the way of life of different groups of people who lived there. Lesson 1.1 discusses how certain groups moved from place to place in the desert while others settled in towns that became important for trade.

BACKGROUND FOR THE TEACHER

Most oases have underground water sources called aquifers. Some oases are large enough to support a city and its cropland. Common oasis crops include dates, olives, figs, citrus fruits, cotton, wheat, and corn. Sands blown by desert winds can pollute water in the wells and destroy crops. For this reason, many oasis communities plant strong trees, such as palms, around the oasis to protect the water and the crops from blowing sand.

DIGITAL RESOURCES myNGconnect.com

TEACHER RESOURCES & ASSESSMENT

 Reading and Note-Taking

 Vocabulary Practice

 Section 1 Quiz

STUDENT RESOURCES

 NG Chapter Gallery

INTRODUCE & ENGAGE

TEAM UP

Have students work in groups of four. Ask them to brainstorm ways climate, including temperature and amount of rainfall, affects the way people live. Encourage them to think about participation in activities, ease of travel, effect on farming or gardening, and so on. Tell students they will learn how climate affected the way people lived and where they established cities in the Arabian Peninsula. **0:05 minutes**

TEACH

GUIDED DISCUSSION

1. **Make Inferences** Why did people who lived in the Arabian Peninsula in the 600s build settlements in or near oases? *(Plants could grow in those areas, and people could farm because oases had a source of water.)*

2. **Draw Conclusions** For what reason was Mecca considered the most important city in Arabia? *(It was a center for both trade and religion.)*

ANALYZE VISUALS

Invite students to study the photograph of sand dunes in the lesson. **ASK:** What does this photo suggest about the climate in this area? How might such a climate affect the lives of people who live there? As a class, create a Cause-and-Effect Chart to identify possible effects of the desert climate on people's lives. **0:15 minutes**

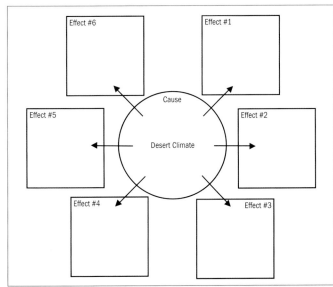

ACTIVE OPTIONS

On Your Feet: Think, Pair, Share Have students work in pairs. Invite each student to think of two questions about the geography

and resources of the Arabian Peninsula. Have one student in each pair pose questions to his or her partner and have the partner answer. Then have students switch roles. Ask volunteers to share their questions and answers with the class. **0:10 minutes**

NG Learning Framework: List Observations

SKILL: Collaboration
KNOWLEDGE: Our Living Planet

Have students review the information in the lesson about living near an oasis. Have students work in pairs to create a list of observations about how people in these areas lived. Ask students to describe how the lives and behaviors of the people were affected by their environment. After students have completed their list of observations, have each pair exchange lists with another pair and discuss the new list. **0:10 minutes**

DIFFERENTIATE

ENGLISH LANGUAGE LEARNERS

Review Vocabulary After reading, write the following words on the board and ask students to write a phrase to describe each word. Then have them use each word in a sentence.

- clan
- oasis
- pilgrimage

PRE-AP

Create a Group Presentation Have students work in small groups to do research about the Bedouin living in Arabia in the 600s. Then ask students to discuss how living in a desert influenced the development of the Bedouin culture. Students should focus on topics such as clothing, housing, food, customs, and livelihoods. Have each group create a report to present to the class.

Press **(mt)** *in the Student eEdition for modified text.*

See the Chapter Planner for more strategies for differentiation.

REVIEW & ASSESS

ANSWERS

1. Because of Arabia's location with regards to Asia, Africa, and Europe, it became an important crossroads connecting trade routes from those continents.

2. With little farmland and scarce water supplies, the Bedouin could not settle in one location and farm, so they became nomadic herders, moving their sheep, goats, and cattle from one water source to another in the desert.

3. Mecca's location is good for trade because land and sea routes connecting Asia, Africa, and Europe intersect there.

1.2

The **Prophet** of **Islam**

An oasis city in Arabia became the birthplace of a major world religion in the 600s. In a cave near Mecca, a middle-aged merchant heard messages that he reported came from an angel named Gabriel. The merchant began preaching those messages and united Arabia under a new religion.

MAIN IDEA

Muhammad was a great religious, political, and military leader who preached the religion of Islam and unified much of Arabia.

THE LIFE OF MUHAMMAD

Today the religion of **Islam** has about 1.5 billion followers worldwide. Its prophet, **Muhammad**, was born into a family of Mecca's ruling tribe about 570. A **prophet** is a teacher believed to be inspired by God. As a young man, Muhammad gained a reputation for intelligence, honesty, and kindness. He worked as a trader for a wealthy widow and merchant named Khadijah (kah-DEE-juh). She was so impressed by Muhammad's virtues that she married him.

Muhammad had a deep interest in religion. He periodically retreated to a cave outside of Mecca to pray. When he was about 40 years old, he had the first of many religious experiences. As he prayed in his cave, he heard a voice that he identified as the angel Gabriel. The main message was that people could achieve salvation, or go to heaven, in the afterlife only by worshipping and obeying the one true God. Muhammad thereafter rejected the polytheism that was common in Mecca. Instead, he followed the teaching attributed to Abraham, who said that there is only one God.

In 613, Muhammad began to preach that only the God of Abraham should be worshipped and obeyed, not the traditional tribal gods. In Arabic, *Islam* means "submission to the will of God." The name for a follower of Islam, **Muslim**, means "one who has submitted to God."

THE LEADERSHIP OF MUHAMMAD

Muhammad's teachings about the one true God threatened Mecca's political leaders. They supported traditional religion and benefitted from the city's position as a pilgrimage center for polytheistic Arabs. The leaders made life difficult for Muhammad and his followers, who then fled to the Arabian city of Yathrib. This event became known as the Hijrah (HEEJ-rah). The year of Muhammad's flight, 622, marks the beginning of the Muslim calendar. Yathrib was later renamed Medina (muh-DEE-nuh).

Muhammad and his followers were given leadership of Medina, where they established an Islamic community called the umma (OO-muh). Muhammad made loyalty to the umma more important than that to a tribe. He began uniting Arabia's many quarrelling tribes under Islam.

The ruling tribes of Mecca tried to crush this movement. However, in 630, Muhammad conquered Mecca, removed all idols at the Ka'aba, and dedicated the shrine to the God of Abraham. This victory and others helped spread Islam. By 632, when Muhammad died, most Arab tribes had joined the umma. Muhammad had proved himself a great religious, political, and military leader.

Muslims from all over the world journey to pray at the Ka'aba. This shrine takes the form of a stone cube and contains a holy rock called the Black Stone.

REVIEW & ASSESS

1. **READING CHECK** On what main belief did Muhammad base the religion of Islam?

2. **ANALYZE CAUSE AND EFFECT** Why did Muhammad and his followers move from Mecca to Medina?

3. **IDENTIFY DETAILS** The text states that Muhammad was a great religious, political, and military leader. What details in the text support this claim?

PLAN

OBJECTIVE

Discuss Muhammad as a great religious, political, and military leader who preached the religion of Islam and unified much of Arabia.

CRITICAL THINKING SKILLS FOR LESSON 1.2

- Identify Main Ideas and Details
- Monitor Comprehension
- Analyze Cause and Effect
- Identify Details
- Describe
- Summarize
- Analyze Visuals

ESSENTIAL QUESTION

What major contributions did medieval Muslim leaders and scholars make to world civilization?

Muhammad was a great religious, military, and political leader in Arabia. Lesson 1.2 discusses how Muhammad united Arabia under the religion of Islam.

BACKGROUND FOR THE TEACHER

When Muhammad ruled Medina, he settled many disputes among people. He made treaties with the nomads who lived in the peninsula. He built an army that defended Medina against attacks. Muhammad believed that all people were equal. He preached that rich people should share their wealth and that living a good life was more important than having money. After Muhammad's death, the religion of Islam spread far beyond the Arabian Peninsula.

DIGITAL RESOURCES myNGconnect.com

TEACHER RESOURCES & ASSESSMENT

 Reading and Note-Taking   **Vocabulary Practice**   **Section 1 Quiz**

STUDENT RESOURCES

 Biography

INTRODUCE & ENGAGE

ACTIVATE PRIOR KNOWLEDGE

Have students work in small groups to create a list of ways in which a person's religion can influence his or her life in terms of religious ceremonies, practices, and holidays as well as other aspects of daily life. Tell students they will learn more about the teachings of Muhammad and how the religion of Islam affected people's lives. **0:05** minutes

TEACH

GUIDED DISCUSSION

1. **Describe** What was the Hijrah? *(The Hijrah refers to the move by Muhammad and his followers to the city of Yathrib, a city later renamed Medina.)*

2. **Summarize** What did Muhammad teach about loyalty to the umma? *(It was more important than loyalty to a tribe.)*

ANALYZE VISUALS

Have students examine the photo of the Ka'aba. **ASK:** What do you observe about the photo? What can you infer from your observations about the importance of this shrine to Muslims? **0:10** minutes

ACTIVE OPTIONS

On Your Feet: Card Responses Have half the class write 10 true-false questions based on the lesson. Have the other half create answer cards, writing "True" on one side and "False" on the other side. Students from the first group should take turns asking their questions. Students from the second group should hold up their cards, showing either "True" or "False." **0:10** minutes

NG Learning Framework: Discuss the Umma's Influence

SKILL: Communication
KNOWLEDGE: Our Human Story

Have students think about the relationships early Muslims had with the umma. Ask students to compare those relationships with those other Arabs may have had with their tribes. Then ask students to discuss how loyalty to the umma changed society in Arabia, empowered Muhammad, and contributed to the rise of Islam in the Arabian Peninsula. **0:10** minutes

DIFFERENTIATE

STRIVING READERS

Use Sentence Starters Provide these sentence starters for students to complete after reading.

1. Muhammad was the prophet of _____ .

2. Muhammad taught that there was only one _____ .

3. The name for a follower of Islam is _____ .

4. The year of the Hijrah, 622, marked the beginning of the Muslim _____ .

5. In Medina, Muhammad established an Islamic community called the _____ .

GIFTED & TALENTED

Interview a Follower of Muhammad Allow students to work in teams of two to plan, write, and perform a simulated interview with an early follower of Muhammad. Tell students the purpose of the interview is to focus on Muhammad's religious beliefs and teachings. Encourage students to include questions and answers about how Muhammad gained and developed his beliefs and how he united many Arab tribes under one religion.

Press **mt** *in the Student eEdition for modified text.*

See the Chapter Planner for more strategies for differentiation.

REVIEW & ASSESS

ANSWERS

1. Muhammad founded the religion of Islam on the belief that salvation in the afterlife could only be achieved through devotion to one true God.

2. The political leaders in Mecca made life difficult for Muhammad because they opposed his monotheistic teachings. So Muhammad and his followers immigrated to Medina—whose pilgrims were impressed with Muhammad's ideas—and established a new Islamic community there.

3. Muhammad founded Islam and united Arabia's many quarreling tribes under Islam. He accomplished this by making loyalty to the umma—the Islamic community—more important than loyalty to a tribe and by conquering Mecca and dedicating the Ka'aba to Islam. These details describe characteristics of a great leader.

1.3

Beliefs
and Laws

Could you point toward the direction of your home no matter where you were, even if you were in a faraway city? Muslims must be able to point toward the holy city of Mecca wherever they happen to be. It's an important aspect of a Muslim's daily life, which revolves around faithfully following Islamic religious practices.

MAIN IDEA

Islamic religious practices are based on Islam's holy book and the life of Muhammad.

THE QUR'AN AND THE SUNNA

The holy book of Islam is called the **Qur'an** (kuh-RAN). Muslims believe that the Qur'an contains the flawless words of Allah as revealed to Muhammad by the angel Gabriel. The Qur'an teaches that there is only one God, whom all Muslims should worship. According to the Qur'an, God is the creator and is merciful and compassionate. Islam teaches that God will judge individuals for their good and bad actions and send them to heaven or hell on a final judgment day. The Qur'an states how Muslims should behave. For example, the Qur'an promotes charity and forbids gambling and drinking alcohol.

Muslims believe that Muhammad demonstrated perfectly how to apply the Qur'an in daily life. The words and actions attributed to Muhammad, called the **Sunna** (SOON-uh), were written down by his followers. Muslims rely on both the Qur'an and the Sunna as guides. For example, the Qur'an instructs Muslims to wash before prayer but does not explain how. However, accounts of the Sunna claim to describe how Muhammad washed for prayer, so Muslims carefully follow this description.

Together, the Qur'an and the Sunna form the basis of Islamic law, which is called **shari'a** (shah-REE-ah). This system of law is comprehensive. It covers all aspects of human behavior, including family life, community life, moral conduct, worship, and business.

Early Muslims recognized Islam's link to the other monotheistic religions of Judaism and Christianity. They regarded Jews and Christians as "people of the book" because they consider Abraham a prophet and had a holy book with teachings similar to those of the Qur'an. Muslims believed the Qur'an was the final book of revelations from the same God that Jews and Christians worshipped. They regarded Muhammad as the final prophet of God.

EVERYDAY PRACTICES

Muslims apply their religious beliefs to their daily lives by following a set of duties called the Five Pillars of Islam. Additional Islamic customs guide their daily lives. For example, Muslims avoid eating certain meats and eat meat only from animals that are killed in a humane way.

Each Islamic community centers on a **mosque**, a Muslim place of worship. The main weekly service is on Friday afternoon. Worshippers wash themselves before entering a mosque and kneel on special prayer mats facing Mecca. A religious teacher called an **imam** leads the weekly service, which includes prayer and a sermon. Mosques also serve as centers of education and social work.

374 CHAPTER 13

+ POSSIBLE RESPONSE

The Muslims should be facing toward Mecca as they pray.

Critical Viewing A group of Bedouin in Saudi Arabia stop for evening prayer. According to the Five Pillars of Islam, in what direction should these Muslims be facing as they pray?

THE FIVE PILLARS OF ISLAM	1	2	3	4	5
All believers of Islam are called upon to carry out the following duties.	Faith **Testify to** this statement of faith: "There is no god but God, and Muhammad is His Prophet."	Prayer **Pray five** times a day, facing toward Mecca.	Alms **Donate a** portion of one's wealth to help people in need.	Fasting **Eat and** drink nothing between dawn and sunset during the Islamic holy month of Ramadan.	Pilgrimage Perform the hajj (haj), or pilgrimage to Mecca, at least once in a lifetime if able.

REVIEW & ASSESS

1. **READING CHECK** What is one practice that Muslims follow based on the Qur'an?

2. **SYNTHESIZE** How are the Qur'an and the Sunna related?

3. **MAKE GENERALIZATIONS** What are some links among Judaism, Christianity, and Islam?

The Islamic World **375**

PLAN

OBJECTIVE

Describe how Islamic religious practices are based on Islam's holy book and the life of Muhammad.

CRITICAL THINKING SKILLS FOR LESSON 1.3

- Identify Main Ideas and Details
- Monitor Comprehension
- Synthesize
- Make Generalizations
- Summarize
- Draw Conclusions
- Analyze Visuals

ESSENTIAL QUESTION

What major contributions did medieval Muslim leaders and scholars make to world civilization?

Following the teachings of Muhammad played an important role in medieval Muslim civilization. Lesson 1.3 discusses how Muslim leaders guided Muslims to follow the Qur'an in their religious practices and everyday life.

BACKGROUND FOR THE TEACHER

Muslims recite passages from the Qur'an at daily prayers and at all important events. Muslims who know the entire Qur'an by heart are given the title *hafiz,* which means "one who has memorized the sacred text." Verses from the Qur'an are inscribed on mosques and other public buildings. These inscriptions show how important it is to Muslims to connect with God in their daily lives. Everything related to the Qur'an is considered sacred to Muslims. The Qur'an is always treated with respect, kept clean, and kept in a place of honor.

DIGITAL RESOURCES myNGconnect.com

TEACHER RESOURCES & ASSESSMENT

 Reading and Note-Taking

 Vocabulary Practice

 Section 1 Quiz

STUDENT RESOURCES

 NG Chapter Gallery

INTRODUCE & ENGAGE

ASK QUESTIONS

Have students work in groups of four. Have each group come up with a list of three questions about Islam. Tell students that they will learn about some beliefs and practices associated with the religion of Islam in this lesson. After the lesson, have groups work together to answer the questions they listed. Then ask each group to share its questions and answers with the class. **0:05** minutes

TEACH

GUIDED DISCUSSION

1. **Summarize** What is Shari'a? *(Shari'a is the system of Islamic law based on the Qur'an and the Sunna that covers all aspects of human behavior including family life, community life, moral conduct, worship, and business.)*

2. **Draw Conclusions** In what way do the Five Pillars of Islam guide the daily lives of Muslims? *(Muslims are called upon to carry out the duties described in the Five Pillars of Islam.)*

ANALYZE VISUALS

Have students get together in small groups and examine the photo of the Bedouin in Saudi Arabia. Then ask the groups to copy the chart shown below and add their own answers to the questions about the photograph. **0:15** minutes

5Ws	Possible Responses
What is being shown in the photograph?	*a desert in Saudi Arabia*
Who is shown in the photograph?	*a group of Bedouin men*
Where was the photograph taken?	*Saudi Arabia*
When was the photograph taken?	*during evening prayer*
Why was the photograph taken?	*to show that Muslims can pray anywhere as long as they are facing Mecca*

ACTIVE OPTIONS

On Your Feet: Give Examples Direct students to form four groups and provide each group with the same topic sentence: *Muhammad taught that Muslims should apply their religious beliefs to their daily lives*. Each group should work together to list three examples related to the topic. Then have the groups share their examples with the class. **0:10** minutes

Critical Viewing: NG Image Gallery Have students explore the entire NG Image Gallery and choose two of the items to compare and contrast, either in written format or verbally with a partner.

Ask questions that will inspire this process, such as: How are these images alike? How are they different? Why did you select these two items? How do they relate in history? **0:10** minutes

DIFFERENTIATE

ENGLISH LANGUAGE LEARNERS

Find Someone Who Knows Give students copies of the questions below and have them find five different classmates to answer them. Give students a time limit for the activity. When time is up, discuss the questions and answers in class.

1. How do Muslims know how Muhammad washed in prayer? *(The Sunna describes how Muhammad washed in prayer.)*

2. According to the Five Pillars of Islam, how are Muslims supposed to help people in need? *(They are supposed to donate part of their wealth to help them.)*

3. How do Muslims change their patterns of eating and drinking during the Islamic holy month of Ramadan? *(They do not eat or drink anything between dawn and sunset.)*

4. What is a mosque? *(A mosque is a Muslim place of worship.)*

5. What does an imam do? *(An imam is a teacher who leads the weekly service, which includes prayer and a sermon.)*

GIFTED & TALENTED

Create a Booklet Have students work in small groups to create an illustrated booklet about the Islamic holy month of Ramadan. Ask students to include information about the significance of Ramadan to the Islamic religion as well as details about ways Muslims observe the holy month.

Press **mt** *in the Student eEdition for modified text.*

See the Chapter Planner for more strategies for differentiation.

REVIEW & ASSESS

ANSWERS

1. Sample response: Based on the Qur'an, Muslims worship only one God. Muslims are expected to lead good lives so that they can go to heaven on judgment day.

2. Both the Qur'an and the Sunna provide a moral guide for how Muslims should behave and worship. The Qur'an is believed to be the words of Allah as revealed to Muhammad by the angel Gabriel, while the Sunna details the words and actions of Muhammad. The Sunna further explains the Qur'an's teachings.

3. Jews and Christians have a holy book with teachings similar to those of the Qur'an. Jews, Christians, and Muslims worship one God.

DOCUMENT-BASED QUESTION

The Qur'an and Hadith

The Qur'an, Islam's holy book, provides religious guidance to Muslims on all aspects of life, from saying prayers to conducting business. Muslims also look to the Sunna, or Muhammad's example, to guide their behavior. Accounts of what Muhammad reportedly said, did, or approved were recorded by his followers after his death and are called hadith (huh-DEETH). The word *hadith* can refer either to a specific account of Muhammad's words and actions or to all the accounts in general.

This Persian painting shows the

ANSWERS

DOCUMENT 1
The noblest human beings are those who are most god-fearing.

DOCUMENT 2
The Qur'an suggests that Allah created a world of diversity in order to "try" people in their ability to be tolerant and do good works in a world where there is variance "in what has come to you."

DOCUMENT 3
According to the hadith, Muslims should not harm their neighbors, they should be generous to their guests, and they should speak only if they have something good to say.

DOCUMENT ONE
Primary Source: Sacred Text

from the Qur'an
Muslims consider the Qur'an to be the words of God revealed in human language. In this excerpt, God speaks using the pronoun *We*, even though God is a single being. This use of *We* serves to emphasize the majesty and authority of God. This excerpt and the following one focus on why God created diversity among people.

CONSTRUCTED RESPONSE According to the Qur'an, who are the noblest human beings?

> O mankind, We have created you male and female, and appointed you groups and tribes, that you may know one another. Surely the noblest among you in the sight of God is the most godfearing of you. God is All-knowing, All-aware.
>
> *Qur'an XLIX:13*

DOCUMENT TWO
Primary Source: Sacred Text

from the Qur'an
As this excerpt suggests, tolerance of diversity is an important value in the Qur'an. In this excerpt, the pronoun *He* is used to refer to God. Muslims believe that God has no gender. The use of *He* is simply a custom.

CONSTRUCTED RESPONSE According to the Qur'an, why did Allah create a world of diversity?

> If God had willed, He could have made you one nation; but [He willed otherwise] that He may try [test] you in what has come to you. So be you forward [active] in good works; unto God shall you return, all together.
>
> *Qur'an V:54*

DOCUMENT THREE
Primary Source: Sacred Text

Hadith
The Qur'an strongly warns Muslims to prepare for a day of judgment, when the worthy will go to paradise and the unworthy will suffer in hell. This hadith offers guidance on how to behave on Earth in order to attain paradise.

CONSTRUCTED RESPONSE According to this hadith, what should Muslims do to be worthy of entering paradise on the Last Day?

> Anyone who believes in God and the Last Day [of Judgment] should not harm his neighbor. Anyone who believes in God and the Last Day should entertain his guest generously. And anyone who believes in God and the Last Day should say what is good or keep quiet.
>
> *Sahih Al-Bukhari, 6018*

SYNTHESIZE & WRITE

1. **REVIEW** Review what you have learned about the Qur'an and hadith.

2. **RECALL** On your own paper, write down the main idea expressed in each of the three documents.

3. **CONSTRUCT** Write a topic sentence that answers this question: According to sacred Islamic writings, how should people behave?

4. **WRITE** Using evidence from the documents, write an informative paragraph that supports your topic sentence.

PLAN

OBJECTIVE
Synthesize information about the Qur'an and hadith from primary source documents.

CRITICAL THINKING SKILLS FOR LESSON 1.4
- Identify
- Explain
- Describe
- Evaluate
- Synthesize

ESSENTIAL QUESTION
What major contributions did medieval Muslim leaders and scholars make to world civilization?

The Qur'an and hadith provide major sources of religious guidance for Muslims. Lesson 1.4 provides several examples of accounts of Muhammad's teachings from primary sources.

BACKGROUND FOR THE TEACHER
The word *hadith* means "to tell about a happening, or to report." A hadith includes reports of the teachings, words, and deeds of Muhammad. In about 846, Imam Muhammad a-Bukhari finished compiling a collection of hadith known as Sahih Al-Bukhari. After that, Bukhari spent the last years of his life traveling to different cities and teaching the hadith he had collected. Thousands of people would gather to hear him. Hadith are regarded as important tools for understanding the Qur'an.

DIGITAL RESOURCES myNGconnect.com

TEACHER RESOURCES & ASSESSMENT

 Reading and Note-Taking

 Vocabulary Practice

 Section 1 Quiz

STUDENT RESOURCES

 NG Chapter Gallery

INTRODUCE & ENGAGE

PREPARE FOR THE DOCUMENT-BASED QUESTION

Before students start on the activity, briefly preview the three documents. Remind students that a constructed response requires full explanations in complete sentences. Emphasize that students should use their knowledge of Muhammad and Islamic religious beliefs as well as information in the documents. **0:05** minutes

TEACH

GUIDED DISCUSSION

1. **Identify** What do Muslims consider the Qur'an to be? *(They consider the Qur'an to be the words of God revealed in human language.)*

2. **Explain** For what reason do Muslims use the word *He* when referring to God? *(The use of "He" when talking about God is simply a custom. Muslims believe that God has no gender.)*

3. **Describe** What do Muslims believe will happen on the day of judgment? *(The worthy will go to paradise, and the unworthy will suffer in hell.)*

EVALUATE

After students have completed the "Synthesize & Write" activity, allow time for them to exchange paragraphs and read and comment on the work of their peers. Guidelines for comments should be established prior to this activity so that feedback is constructive and encouraging in nature. **0:15** minutes

ACTIVE OPTIONS

On Your Feet: Three Corners Label three locations in the room with the name of one of the documents featured in the lesson. Have students reread the lesson and walk to the area of the room displaying the document that best helped support their understanding or furthered their interest in Muhammad and Islam. Have students who chose the same document discuss why they made their selection. Then have volunteers from each group explain what their document discusses, and offer some of the group's reasons for choosing that document. **0:15** minutes

Critical Viewing: NG Chapter Gallery Ask students to choose one image from the Chapter Gallery and become an expert on it. They should do additional research to learn all about it. Then, students should share their findings with a partner, small group, or the class. **0:10** minutes

DIFFERENTIATE

INCLUSION

Work in Pairs Pair visually impaired students with students who can read the documents aloud to them. Ask the visually impaired students to tell what they learned about each document. You may also want to give students the option of recording their responses.

PRE-AP

Present an Oral Report Ask small groups of students to prepare an oral report on how the Qur'an, the Sunna, and hadith are important in the lives of Muslims. Encourage each person in the group to take part in an oral presentation to the class.

Press (**mt**) *in the Student eEdition for modified text.*

See the Chapter Planner for more strategies for differentiation.

SYNTHESIZE & WRITE

ANSWERS

1. Responses will vary.

2. Responses will vary.

3. Possible response: According to sacred Islamic writings, people should respect their neighbors.

4. Students' paragraphs should include their topic sentence from Step 3 and provide several details from the documents to support the sentence.

The Prophet's Mosque in Medina, Saudi Arabia, contains the tomb of Muhammad and is a holy site for Muslims.

1.5 After Muhammad

If your classroom teacher were suddenly called away, is there a student in your class who could take control and keep everyone focused on the lesson? After Muhammad died, Muslims needed a leader to keep the community focused. After a period of uncertainty, the Muslim state met the challenge.

MAIN IDEA

The Muslim state recovered from a period of disorder after Muhammad's death and soon expanded to form a powerful empire.

NEW LEADERS

In 632, the Muslim state in Arabia almost collapsed when Muhammad died without naming a successor. His followers disagreed over how to choose a leader. Then a few leading Muslims acted decisively. They appointed Muhammad's father-in-law, Abu Bakr (uh-boo BA-kuhr), as **caliph** (KAY-lihf), which means "successor." He promised to follow Muhammad's example.

As the first of many caliphs, Abu Bakr served as the supreme religious, political, and military leader of a growing Muslim empire. Though he ruled for just two years, he was critical to the survival of Islam. He crushed rebellions that could have destroyed the young state. His strong leadership kept all of Arabia united under Islam.

ISLAM SPREADS

The early caliphs succeeded in establishing a large Muslim empire that stretched thousands of miles from the Mediterranean region into Central Asia. The Muslims faced two great superpowers in the region. The Byzantine Empire ruled Syria and Egypt, while the Persian Empire ruled Iran and Iraq. However, these two rival empires had become exhausted by fighting long and bitter wars. Meanwhile, the Muslim empire had developed a skilled, disciplined, and enthusiastic army. By 652, just 20 years after Muhammad's death, the Muslims had conquered Syria, Palestine, Iraq, Iran, Egypt, and various parts of North Africa. (A map of Muslim conquests appears in the Chapter Review.)

The Qur'an forbade the conquering caliphs from forcing their new non-Muslim subjects to convert to Islam. Instead of being persecuted, or mistreated, as they had been under Byzantine and Persian rule, Jews, Christians, and those of other faiths were allowed to follow their own religious customs with some restrictions. Even so, many people chose to convert to Islam. Some people were genuinely attracted by Islamic ideas and customs. Other people converted for practical reasons of social, political, and economic gain.

REVIEW & ASSESS

1. **READING CHECK** How did Muhammad's death in 632 affect the Muslim state he had established?

2. **ANALYZE CAUSE AND EFFECT** Why were the Muslims able to conquer the powerful Byzantine and Persian Empires in just 20 years?

3. **MAKE GENERALIZATIONS** Why did many Jews, Christians, and other non-Muslims convert to Islam in the growing Muslim empire?

PLAN

OBJECTIVE

Explain how the Muslim state recovered from a period of disorder after Muhammad's death and expanded to form a powerful empire.

CRITICAL THINKING SKILLS FOR LESSON 1.5

- Identify Main Ideas and Details
- Monitor Comprehension
- Analyze Cause and Effect
- Make Generalizations
- Make Inferences
- Summarize
- Interpret Maps

ESSENTIAL QUESTION

What major contributions did medieval Muslim leaders and scholars make to world civilization?

The leaders who led the Muslim state after Muhammad's death practiced Islam and maintained skillful, well-disciplined armies. Lesson 1.5 discusses how the leaders and their armies helped the Muslim empire expand after the death of Muhammad.

BACKGROUND FOR THE TEACHER

Abu Bakr was a loyal advisor to Muhammad. He was from Mecca and had been an early convert to Islam. After Muhammad died, some Muslims in Arabia refused to obey the law of the land, pay taxes, and follow the principles of Islam. Abu Bakr was a strong leader who used his powerful army to reunite Muslims in Arabia. The rule of Abu Bakr and the rule of the next three caliphs was called a caliphate. The first four caliphs were guided by the principles of the Qur'an.

DIGITAL RESOURCES myNGconnect.com

TEACHER RESOURCES & ASSESSMENT

 Reading and Note-Taking

 Vocabulary Practice

 Section 1 Quiz

STUDENT RESOURCES

 NG Chapter Gallery

INTRODUCE & ENGAGE

K-W-L CHART

Provide each student with a K-W-L Chart like the one shown here. Have students brainstorm what they know about Muhammad's leadership. Then ask them to write questions that they would like to have answered as they learn about the Muslim state after Muhammad's death. Tell students they will learn what happened in the Muslim state after Muhammad's death in this lesson. Allow time at the end of the lesson for students to fill in their charts with the information they have learned. **0:05** minutes

K What Do I Know?	W What Do I Want To Learn?	L What Did I Learn?

TEACH

GUIDED DISCUSSION

1. **Make Inferences** Why was Abu Bakr important to the survival of the Muslim state? *(He followed the practices of Islam. He was a strong leader who led the Muslim state in areas of religion, politics, and military power. He crushed rebellions and kept Arabia united under Islam.)*

2. **Summarize** How did the conquering caliphs treat their non-Muslim subjects? *(They did not persecute or mistreat them. They allowed non-Muslims to follow their own faiths with some restrictions.)*

INTERPRET MAPS

Have students look at the Spread of Islam map in the Chapter Review. **ASK:** How had the Muslim empire grown in size under the first four caliphs? *(It had more than doubled in size.)* **0:10** minutes

ACTIVE OPTIONS

On Your Feet: Three-Step Interview Have students work in pairs to discuss their answers to the "Reading Check" question. Instruct them to use detailed questions to interview one another about specific aspects of the topic, such as, "How did Muhammad's followers react?" Remind students to listen closely to their partner's answers so they can report what they hear to the class. **0:10** minutes

NG Learning Framework: Discuss the Caliphs

SKILL: Communication
KNOWLEDGE: Our Human Story

Have small groups of students discuss the role the caliphs played in the growing Muslim empire. Ask them to talk about ways the caliphs followed the example set by Muhammad. Invite each person in the group to contribute her or his ideas. Encourage students to listen quietly and politely when others are talking. **0:10** minutes

DIFFERENTIATE

STRIVING READERS

Pose and Answer Questions Have students work in pairs to read the lesson. Have one partner ask the other a *what, who, where, when,* or *why* question about what they have just read. Then have partners switch roles and have the other partner ask the questions. Suggest that students use a 5Ws Chart to help organize their questions and answers.

GIFTED & TALENTED

Write a Speech Have students work in small groups to do research about Abu Bakr. Then ask them to write a speech proposing his name as caliph after the death of Muhammad. Invite students to include descriptions of Abu Bakr's experiences and discuss the qualities and ideas that would make him a good leader. Encourage each person in the group to contribute to the speech. Ask a volunteer from each group to present the group's speech to the class.

Press **mt** *in the Student eEdition for modified text.*

See the Chapter Planner for more strategies for differentiation.

REVIEW & ASSESS

ANSWERS

1. His death nearly led to the state's collapse because his followers couldn't agree on a new leader.

2. The Byzantine and Persian empires were rivals and already exhausted from long and bitter wars with each other. They were no match for the Muslim army, made up of skilled, disciplined, and enthusiastic warriors who believed that death assured them a place in paradise.

3. Many Jews, Christians, and other non-Muslims converted to Islam because they were attracted by Islamic ideas and customs or for reasons of social, political, and economic gain.

2.1
The Umayyads and the Abbasids

Running an empire is hard work. There are complicated issues to understand, mountains of paperwork to complete, and tough decisions to make. The caliphs lost interest and let others govern while they enjoyed luxurious livestyles. Their actions lost them both respect and control of their empire.

MAIN IDEA

Opposing groups competed for power in the Muslim empire, and a major split developed in Islam in the late 600s.

UMAYYAD EXPANSION

Despite its military successes, the Muslim community could not maintain unity as various groups struggled for power. The last three of the first four caliphs were assassinated. After the last one, Ali, was murdered in 661, a family known as the **Umayyads** (oo-MY-yadz) gained power.

The Umayyads established a hereditary system of succession, with the title of caliph automatically passing within the clan, usually from father to son. They also moved the capital of the Muslim empire to Damascus in Syria, which made it easier to control conquered lands. However, many Muslims felt the new capital was too far from Islam's heartland near Medina.

These unpopular actions helped split Islam into two branches. The majority group, the **Sunni** (SU-nee), accepted Umayyad rule. They believed that any Muslim could be caliph. The other group, the **Shi'ite** (SHEE-yt), believed that only members of Muhammad's family, especially Ali and his descendants, could rule as caliph. This major division in Islam remains today.

Despite this split, the Umayyads expanded the Muslim empire, which spread Islam into new areas. To govern their growing territory, the Umayyads set up an efficient **bureaucracy**, a system of government with specialized departments. They also divided the empire into provinces governed by Muslim rulers. A postal service connected the provinces, and a strong army kept order. These actions helped unite the diverse empire. However, many Muslims believed that the Umayyads put too much emphasis on gaining wealth and power.

ABBASID RULE

Opposition to the Umayyads grew until rebel groups overthrew them in 750. A rival clan called the **Abbasids** (AB-uh-sihdz), who were descendants of Muhammad's uncle, took control of the empire. Non-Arab converts and Shi'ites lent support to the Abbasids, who moved the capital to Baghdad in central Iraq.

The Abbasids ruled during a prosperous golden age in Muslim history, but the caliphs were isolated from the people. Government was left to trusted advisers who held the empire together through force. They built a huge army that relied on mainly Turkish **mercenaries**, or hired soldiers.

Eventually, a group called the Seljuk (SEHL-jook) Turks converted to Islam and came to control the government of the Muslim empire. Then, in 1258, an invading group from Central Asia called the Mongols stormed Baghdad and killed the last Abbasid caliph.

This painting shows philosophers working in the House of Wisdom, a great library and academy built by the Abbasids in Baghdad about 830.

REVIEW & ASSESS

1. **READING CHECK** What major division in Islam developed after the Umayyads came to power?

2. **IDENTIFY MAIN IDEAS AND DETAILS** How did the Umayyads strengthen the Muslim empire?

3. **EVALUATE** What flaws of the Abbasid caliphs contributed to their downfall?

PLAN

OBJECTIVE

Identify opposing groups that competed for power in the Muslim empire and explain how a major split developed in Islam in the late 600s.

CRITICAL THINKING SKILLS FOR LESSON 2.1

- Monitor Comprehension
- Identify Main Ideas and Details
- Evaluate
- Describe
- Identify
- Interpret Maps

ESSENTIAL QUESTION

What major contributions did medieval Muslim leaders and scholars make to world civilization?

Different groups fought for control of the Muslim empire. Lesson 2.1 discusses what led to the split in Islam in the late 600s.

BACKGROUND FOR THE TEACHER

The first four caliphs after the death of Muhammad thought of themselves as the equals of other Muslims. They did not live extravagant lives or wield their power unfairly. The rulers in the dynasty that followed, the Umayyads, chose to live in a more luxurious way and hold on to power. Many Muslims resented this extravagant lifestyle, believing that it was not consistent with the principles of Islam. These Muslims rebelled against the Umayyads and helped the Abbasids take power.

DIGITAL RESOURCES myNGconnect.com

TEACHER RESOURCES & ASSESSMENT

 Reading and Note-Taking　　 **Vocabulary Practice**　　 **Section 2 Quiz**

STUDENT RESOURCES

 NG Chapter Gallery

INTRODUCE & ENGAGE

NUMBERED HEADS

Organize students into groups of four, giving each student in the group a number from one to four. **ASK:** What would you like to learn about the split that occurred in the Muslim empire in the late 600s? Tell students to think about and discuss a response to the question. Then call a number from one to four and have the student in each group with that number report the group's answer to the class. Tell students they will learn about how the split in Islam occurred in this lesson. **0:05** minutes

TEACH

GUIDED DISCUSSION

1. **Describe** What system of succession was established by the Umayyads? *(They set up a hereditary system of succession with the title of caliph automatically passing within the clan, usually from father to son.)*

2. **Identify** Where did the Abbasids move their capital? *(They moved their capital to Baghdad.)*

INTERPRET MAPS

Have students look at the borders of the Umayyad and Abbasid empires on the map of Byzantine and early Muslim empires from the beginning of the unit. **ASK:** Where did the Abbasids expand the Muslim empire after they came to power? *(They expanded it west to Spain, south to include more of northern Africa, and east into Asia.)* **0:10** minutes

ACTIVE OPTIONS

On Your Feet: Fishbowl Use a Fishbowl strategy to have students discuss groups in the Muslim empire in the late 600s. Instruct students in the inside circle to discuss what they know about the rule of the Umayyads while those in the outside circle listen. Then call on volunteers in the outside circle to summarize what they heard. Have students switch places and ask those now on the inside circle to discuss what they know about the rule of the Abbasids. Students in the outside circle should listen and then summarize what they heard. **0:10** minutes

Critical Viewing: NG Chapter Gallery Have students examine the contents of the Chapter Gallery for this chapter. Then invite them to brainstorm additional images they believe would fit within the Chapter Gallery. Have them write a description of these additional images and provide an explanation of why they would fit within the Chapter Gallery. Then instruct them to do online research to find examples of actual images they would like to add to the gallery. **0:10** minutes

DIFFERENTIATE

STRIVING READERS

Use Exit Slips Preview the following questions before reading the lesson. After reading the lesson, pass out strips of paper. Have students write their responses to the questions on the paper strips. Ask students to turn in their written responses as they exit the class.

1. Which branch of Islam accepted Umayyad rule? *(The Sunni accepted Umayyad rule.)*

2. Why did the Umayyads move the capital of the Muslim empire to Damascus? *(It made it easier to control conquered lands.)*

3. For what reasons did many Muslims criticize the Umayyads? *(Some Muslims believed that the Umayyads emphasized wealth and power too much.)*

4. What was the army like under the rule of the Abbasids? *(The army was huge, it relied on mercenaries, and it held the empire together by force.)*

INCLUSION

Use Supported Reading Pair students so that there is a proficient reader in each pair. Have the proficient reader read the lesson aloud. Then have the other student use these frames to tell what they comprehended from the text:

This lesson is about _____.

Two details that stood out to me were _____ and _____.

The vocabulary word _____ means _____.

I don't think I understand _____.

Press (mt) *in the Student eEdition for modified text.*

See the Chapter Planner for more strategies for differentiation.

REVIEW & ASSESS

ANSWERS

1. Islam split into two opposing sects after the Umayyads came to power. The Sunni majority accepted Umayyad rule, believing that any Muslim could be caliph; the Shi'te minority opposed the Umayyads, believing that only Muhammad's descendants could rule as caliph.

2. The Umayyads spread Islam into new areas. They governed their expanding empire through the establishment of an efficient bureaucracy. They divided the empire into provinces governed by Muslim rulers, established a postal system to connect the provinces, and built a strong army to keep order.

3. The Abbasids ruled their empire by force and relied mainly on Turkish mercenaries. Eventually, the Seljuk Turks converted to Islam and took control of the government of the Muslim empire.

Muslim Spain

When they overthrew the Umayyads in 750, the Abbasids ruthlessly hunted down and killed members of the Umayyad family. But they missed one important person. An Umayyad prince escaped to Spain and soon founded a rival Muslim dynasty that was destined for fame.

The Great Mosque of Córdoba, shown in the background, is today a Catholic cathedral.

MAIN IDEA

The Umayyads transformed Muslim Spain into a center of power, learning, and culture between 756 and 1031.

THE UMAYYADS RETURN

Muslims had first conquered Spain in 711, and much of the region came under Umayyad control by 750. The last surviving Umayyad prince, Abd al-Rahman, fled to this region in 755 and founded an Umayyad dynasty in 756. From the city of Córdoba, he established a powerful, independent state called al-Andalus (al-an-duh-LUS) and refused to acknowledge Abbasid authority in Baghdad.

Al-Andalus flourished under the Umayyad dynasty, developing a thriving economy. The state reached its peak under the leadership of Abd al-Rahman III. At the time he assumed power in 912, rebel Arab leaders had been challenging the authority of the Umayyad dynasty. However, Abd al-Rahman III vigorously fought the rebels and proclaimed himself caliph in 929, directly competing with the Abbasids. His strong leadership preserved Umayyad power, and all of Muslim Spain was united under his rule by 933.

A GREAT CAPITAL

Abd al-Rahman III transformed Córdoba into one of the largest and greatest cities in the world. He built a series of lavish palaces and extended the Great Mosque, one of the most beautiful buildings ever created. Its vast prayer hall could hold over 50,000 worshippers and is famous for its hundreds of soaring arches. (A picture of the prayer hall appears at the beginning of the chapter.)

Córdoba became most celebrated as a center of learning. Its huge library was said to contain about 400,000 books. In Córdoba, Christians, Jews, and Muslims lived together under a government that practiced religious **tolerance**, or sympathy for the beliefs and practices of others. In this rich intellectual environment, many advances in science, philosophy, medicine, and the arts were made.

Muslim rulers of al-Andalus faced many challenges, however. After the death of Abd al-Rahman III in 961, civil war erupted. Al-Andalus split into many small Muslim kingdoms after 1031. The increasingly powerful Christian kings of northern Spain steadily took over more of al-Andalus. In 1492, the Christians captured Granada, Spain's last Muslim city, ending almost 800 years of Muslim rule in western Europe.

REVIEW & ASSESS

1. **READING CHECK** How did the Umayyad dynasty transform Muslim Spain?

2. **DRAW CONCLUSIONS** Why did Córdoba become an international center of learning in the 900s?

3. **SEQUENCE EVENTS** What series of events ended almost 800 years of Muslim rule in Europe?

PLAN

OBJECTIVE

Explain how the Umayyads transformed Muslim Spain into a center of power, learning and culture between 756 and 1031.

CRITICAL THINKING SKILLS FOR LESSON 2.2

- Identify Main Ideas and Details
- Monitor Comprehension
- Draw Conclusions
- Sequence Events
- Describe
- Make Generalizations
- Analyze Visuals

ESSENTIAL QUESTION

What major contributions did medieval Muslim leaders and scholars make to world civilization?

When the Abbasids overthrew the Umayyads, they persecuted them. Lesson 2.2 discusses how the Umayyads moved to Spain and created a powerful Muslim state there.

BACKGROUND FOR THE TEACHER

When Abd al-Rahman first arrived in Spain, different groups of Muslims were fighting for control. People who supported the Umayyads were loyal to Abd al-Rahman. Al-Rahman was able to make treaties with some groups. He attacked and defeated the groups that continued to oppose him. Then he declared himself the ruler of al-Andalus. Word of his success inspired many Muslims who supported the Umayyads to move to Spain. As a result, al-Rahman's government and army became even stronger.

DIGITAL RESOURCES myNGconnect.com

TEACHER RESOURCES & ASSESSMENT

 Reading and Note-Taking

 Vocabulary Practice

 Section 2 Quiz

STUDENT RESOURCES

 NG Chapter Gallery

INTRODUCE & ENGAGE

ROUNDTABLE

Organize students into groups of four. Prompt them to name some cities in the world they know about. **ASK:** What are some characteristics that make a city great? Encourage each student to contribute ideas. Have each group share its ideas with the class. Tell students they will learn about how Córdoba, Spain, was transformed into a great city under the rule of the Umayyad dynasty. **0:05** minutes

TEACH

GUIDED DISCUSSION

1. **Describe** What was the Great Mosque of Córdoba? *(It was a beautiful building with many soaring arches. It had a prayer hall that could hold over 50,000 worshippers.)*

2. **Make Generalizations** How did the Umayyads in Córdoba treat people who did not share their religious beliefs? *(They practiced religious tolerance, or sympathy for the beliefs and practices of others.)*

ANALYZE VISUALS

Have students study the photograph of the Great Mosque that appears in the lesson and the photograph of its interior that appears at the beginning of the chapter. As a class, create an Idea Web to note features of Muslim architecture. **0:10** minutes

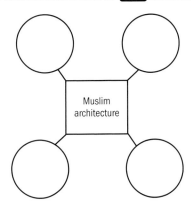

Muslim architecture

ACTIVE OPTIONS

On Your Feet: Create a Concept Cluster Have students form groups of four. Provide each group with a large sheet of paper and ask them to draw a Concept Cluster on it with the words *Córdoba, Spain,* at the center. Have group members take turns contributing a concept or phrase about Córdoba to the Concept Cluster. Call on volunteers from each group to share their webs. **0:10** minutes

Critical Viewing: NG Chapter Gallery Invite students to explore the Chapter Gallery to examine the images that relate to this chapter. Have them select one of the images and do additional research to learn more about it. Ask questions that will inspire additional inquiry about the chosen gallery image, such as: What is this? Where and when was this created? By whom? Why was it created? What is it made of? Why does it belong in this chapter? What else would you like to know about it? **0:10** minutes

DIFFERENTIATE

INCLUSION

Use Echo Reading Pair students so that there is a proficient reader in each pair. Have the proficient reader read aloud the Main Idea statement at the beginning of the lesson. Have the other student "echo" the same statement in his or her own words.

GIFTED & TALENTED

Create a Travel Poster Have students work in small groups. Invite them to do research to create a travel poster encouraging people to visit Córdoba during the rule of Abd al-Rahman III. Encourage students to include information about Córdoba's location and climate, as well as interesting places to visit. Ask students to illustrate their posters.

Press **mt** *in the Student eEdition for modified text.*

See the Chapter Planner for more strategies for differentiation.

REVIEW & ASSESS

ANSWERS

1. The Umayyad dynasty turned Spain into a center of Islamic power, learning, and culture.

2. Córdoba had a huge library. The government practiced religious tolerance, which created an intellectual environment in which Jews, Christians, and Muslims could work together. The city developed a reputation as a center of learning. For all these reasons, the city attracted many scholars and students.

3. After the reign of Rahman III, civil war erupted in al-Andalus, and it grew weaker and more vulnerable to attack. Christian kings of northern Spain became more powerful and succeeded in taking over more of al-Andalus. Then, in 1492, Christians captured Granada, Spain's last Muslim city, ending Islamic rule in that part of Europe.

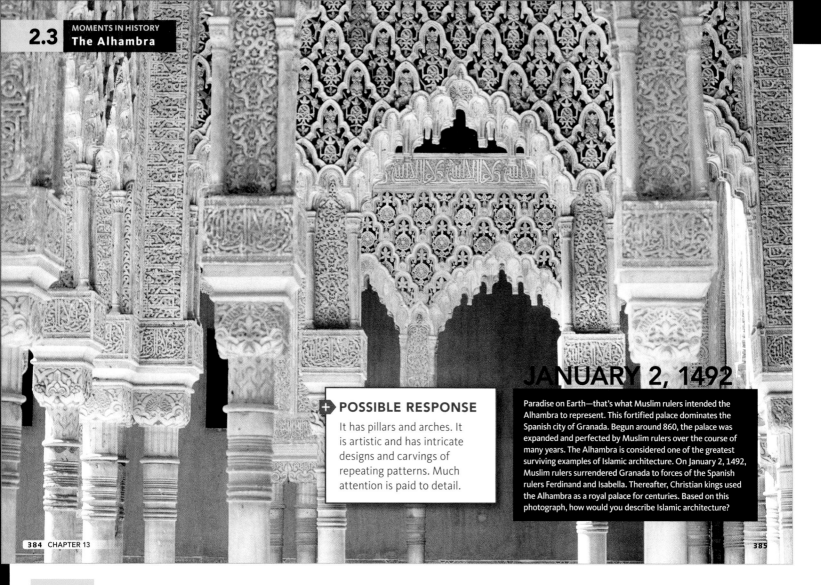

JANUARY 2, 1492

+ POSSIBLE RESPONSE

It has pillars and arches. It is artistic and has intricate designs and carvings of repeating patterns. Much attention is paid to detail.

Paradise on Earth—that's what Muslim rulers intended the Alhambra to represent. This fortified palace dominates the Spanish city of Granada. Begun around 860, the palace was expanded and perfected by Muslim rulers over the course of many years. The Alhambra is considered one of the greatest surviving examples of Islamic architecture. On January 2, 1492, Muslim rulers surrendered Granada to forces of the Spanish rulers Ferdinand and Isabella. Thereafter, Christian kings used the Alhambra as a royal palace for centuries. Based on this photograph, how would you describe Islamic architecture?

385

PLAN

OBJECTIVE

Explain the significance of the Alhambra to both Muslim and Christian rulers.

CRITICAL THINKING SKILLS FOR LESSON 2.3

- Analyze Visuals
- Summarize
- Generalize

ESSENTIAL QUESTION

What major contributions did medieval Muslim leaders and scholars make to world civilization?

Muslim rulers built a large palace, the Alhambra, in the Spanish city of Granada. Lesson 2.3 shows a part of the Alhambra, a great example of Islamic architecture.

BACKGROUND FOR THE TEACHER

Built on a plateau overlooking Granada, the Alhambra is the most famous example of a Muslim palace. The name *Alhambra,* meaning "red" in Arabic, most likely comes from the reddish color of the bricks in the outer walls. The oldest part of the palace is called the citadel. Only its outer walls, towers, and ramparts are left. One of the main courts of the palace is called the Court of the Lions and has the Fountain of the Lions at its center. The fountain is supported by statues of 12 marble lions, which signify courage and strength.

DIGITAL RESOURCES myNGconnect.com

TEACHER RESOURCES & ASSESSMENT

 Reading and Note-Taking   **Vocabulary Practice**   **Section 2 Quiz**

STUDENT RESOURCES

 NG Chapter Gallery

INTRODUCE & ENGAGE

TALK AND SHARE

Have small groups of students talk about different buildings and structures in the world. Encourage them to include buildings and structures they might see today as well as those from earlier times. **ASK:** What are some memorable features of the buildings and structures? Have each group share its ideas with the class. Tell students that in this lesson, they will learn about the Alhambra, a palace that was very important to the Muslims. **0:05** minutes

TEACH

GUIDED DISCUSSION

1. **Summarize** What happened in Granada in 1492? *(Muslim rulers surrendered Granada to Spanish forces.)*

2. **Generalize** In what way did the Alhambra become important to Christian rulers? *(They used it as a royal palace for centuries.)*

MORE INFORMATION

Granada The city's name may have come from the Spanish word for pomegranate, a fruit that grows in the area and is on the city's coat of arms. It is a popular tourist area in Spain because of its interesting and artistic buildings and monuments. Granada has many churches, convents, palaces, and mansions. The tombs of the rulers Ferdinand and Isabella are located in a church in Granada.

ACTIVE OPTIONS

On Your Feet: Inside-Outside Circle Arrange students in concentric circles facing each other. Have students in the outside circle ask the students in the inside circle a question about the lesson. Then have the outside circle rotate one position to the right to create new pairings. After five questions, have students switch roles and continue. **0:10** minutes

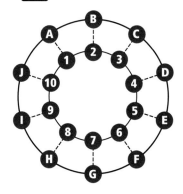

NG Learning Framework: Write About an Architectural Example

ATTITUDE: **Curiosity**
KNOWLEDGE: **Our Human Story**

Have small groups of students investigate other examples of Islamic architecture and choose one example to present to the class. Ask them to write a paragraph about the structure they chose and include photographs or drawings in their presentation. **0:20** minutes

DIFFERENTIATE

INCLUSION

Complete Cloze Statements Pair students so that there is a proficient reader in each pair. Have the proficient reader read each of these cloze statements aloud. Then provide copies of the cloze statements for students to complete during or after reading.

_____ rulers intended the Alhambra to represent _____ on _____. The palace was built in the Spanish city of _____. The palace was extended and perfected over a period of _____. The Alhambra is considered one of the greatest surviving examples of _____ architecture. After 1492, Christian _____ used the Alhambra as a royal _____.

PRE-AP

Present a Report Have students work in small groups to do research about the Alhambra. Instruct them to prepare a report based on their research. Encourage students to include visuals such as photographs or drawings to illustrate the report. Have each group present its report to the class.

Press (**mt**) *in the Student eEdition for modified text.*

See the Chapter Planner for more strategies for differentiation.

The Ottoman Empire

In the 1500s, one Muslim leader became the most powerful monarch in the world. A devout Muslim, Suleyman I oversaw one of the largest empires in history—and one of the longest lasting. This empire included the lands of Persia, Byzantium, and Egypt as well as parts of eastern Europe.

MAIN IDEA

A Muslim state known as the Ottoman Empire became the largest empire in the world in the 1500s.

A VAST EMPIRE

SULEYMAN THE LAWGIVER

Suleyman I reformed the legal system in the Ottoman Empire. He cracked down on corruption and passed laws to protect non-Muslims. His commitment to justice earned him the title Suleyman the Lawgiver.

While al-Andalus was in decline, a new Muslim power was arising to the east. A dynasty of Turkish Muslims, known as the **Ottomans**, emerged as frontier warriors against the Byzantines in Anatolia, or what is now Turkey, around the 1290s. These warriors and their leader, Osman, captured many Byzantine cities, fueling the Ottomans' expansion into the Balkans in southeastern Europe. In 1453, the Ottomans ended the Byzantine Empire by capturing Constantinople. This city, renamed Istanbul, became the Ottomans' capital and the center of their highly efficient government. The Ottomans

continued to build an empire as they challenged the Safavid Empire, a rival Muslim power, and then captured Syria, Palestine, and Egypt from other Muslim rulers.

The Ottoman rulers were called **sultans**. The greatest of them was **Suleyman I**, known as Suleyman the Magnificent. He ruled the Ottoman Empire at the height of its power and grandeur, from 1520 to 1566. He led a powerful navy and a large army well-equipped with guns and cannons, which helped him conquer vast portions of northern Africa and eastern Europe. Only bad weather made him turn back from besieging the Austrian capital of Vienna.

However, military conquest wasn't Suleyman's only interest. He was also a celebrated poet, a talented goldsmith, and a generous patron of the arts. His rule inspired a cultural era that made Istanbul the artistic center of the Muslim lands. Suleyman commissioned work on restoration of the Grand Mosque in Mecca. He built magnificent mosques and palaces, transforming Istanbul's skyline with many buildings still seen there today.

DAILY LIFE

The Ottoman Empire steadily declined after the reign of Suleyman I, but it lasted into the early 1900s. One reason for its long life was its religious tolerance, which helped reduce internal conflict. Jews and Christians enjoyed religious and cultural freedom in return for paying a tax and being loyal to the state. They were organized into large self-governing communities, whose leaders worked with the Ottoman government to ensure positive relations. These communities prospered.

OTTOMAN EMPIRE, c. 1683

Many "people of the book," or Jews and Christians, played important roles in the Ottoman Empire. Like other civilizations, the empire had different social classes. The Ottomans relied heavily on special slaves to staff the government and army. These slaves attained elite status and became rich and powerful. Many senior government officials were technically slaves. Slaves also made up the **janissaries**, a group of highly trained and disciplined soldiers in the Ottoman army who received the best equipment and benefits. To form the janissary corps, the government took young boys from non-Muslim villages, educated them, and trained them to fight for the sultan.

As elsewhere in the world, women in the Ottoman Empire led more restricted lives than men did. Lower-class women had more access to public areas than did upper-class women, who were often kept isolated from the outside world. Upper-class women influenced elite culture and royal policies, and they used their wealth to promote the arts, architecture, and charitable causes.

REVIEW & ASSESS

1. **READING CHECK** What were some of the major achievements of Suleyman I?

2. **MAKE INFERENCES** How did the Ottoman Empire benefit from practicing religious tolerance?

3. **INTERPRET MAPS** Along what major seas did the Ottoman Empire extend?

PLAN

OBJECTIVE

Explain how a Muslim state known as the Ottoman Empire became the largest empire in the world in the 1500s.

CRITICAL THINKING SKILLS FOR LESSON 2.4

- Identify Main Ideas and Details
- Monitor Comprehension
- Make Inferences
- Interpret Maps
- Identify
- Summarize
- Analyze Cause and Effect

ESSENTIAL QUESTION

What major contributions did medieval Muslim leaders and scholars make to world civilization?

The Ottoman Empire was a Muslim state. Lesson 2.4 discusses how the Ottoman Empire became the largest empire in the world.

BACKGROUND FOR THE TEACHER

The decline of the Ottoman Empire accelerated in 1683 when its failed attempt to capture Vienna in Austria put it at odds with European countries. For more than a century after that battle, the Ottomans fought wars with European countries, losing much of their Balkan territory and all the territory on the shores of the Black Sea.

DIGITAL RESOURCES myNGconnect.com

TEACHER RESOURCES & ASSESSMENT

 Reading and Note-Taking

 Vocabulary Practice

 Section 2 Quiz

STUDENT RESOURCES

 Biography

INTRODUCE & ENGAGE

PREVIEW WITH THE MAP

Have students look at the area shaded in orange on the Ottoman Empire map. **ASK:** To what parts of Europe does the empire extend? *(The empire extends into Europe to areas such as Hungary, Poland, the Balkans, Greece, and into the Crimea.)* Tell students that they will learn how this large and powerful empire developed and lasted for more than 500 years. **0:10 minutes**

TEACH

GUIDED DISCUSSION

1. **Identify** What city was the Ottomans' capital and the center of their government? *(The city of Istanbul, formerly called Constantinople, was the Ottomans' capital and the center of their government.)*

2. **Summarize** Who were the janissaries and what role did they have in the Ottoman Empire? *(The janissaries were slaves who were highly trained and disciplined soldiers in the Ottoman army. To form the janissary corps, the government took young boys from non-Muslim villages, educated them, and trained them to fight for the sultan.)*

ANALYZE CAUSE AND EFFECT

Have students look at the Ottoman Empire map. Ask them what they would expect the effects to be of expanding an empire to cover such a large and diverse territory. For example, how would expansion affect the cultures of the conquered peoples? How would it affect relations with neighbors next to the conquered territories? Have students work in pairs to write their responses on a Cause-and-Effect Web. **0:20 minutes**

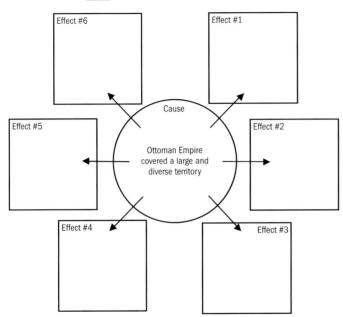

ACTIVE OPTIONS

Active History: Build a Time Line of Suleyman's Reign Extend the lesson by using either the PDF or Whiteboard version of the activity. These activities take a deeper look at a topic from, or related to, the lesson. Explore the activities as a class, turn them into group assignments, or even assign them individually. **0:10 minutes**

On Your Feet: Turn and Talk on Topic Have students form three to five lines. Give each line this topic sentence: *The Ottoman Empire brought many changes to the area that it controlled.* Tell students to build a paragraph on that topic by having each student in the line add one sentence. Allow each line to present its paragraph to the class by having each student read her or his statement. **0:10 minutes**

DIFFERENTIATE

ENGLISH LANGUAGE LEARNERS

Monitor Comprehension Monitor students' comprehension of important details in the lesson by asking them to answer either/or questions such as the following:

- Was the capital of the Ottoman Empire in Istanbul or Rome? *(Istanbul)*
- Was the Ottoman Empire small or large? *(large)*
- Were the Ottomans Muslims or Christians? *(Muslims)*
- Did the Ottoman Empire last about 100 years or about 500 years? *(about 500 years)*

Press **mt** *in the Student eEdition for modified text.*

See the Chapter Planner for more strategies for differentiation.

REVIEW & ASSESS

ANSWERS

1. Suleyman I ruled the largest empire in the world, the Ottoman Empire, in the 1500s. He led a powerful navy and a large, well-equipped army. He conquered lands in northern Africa and eastern Europe. He was a poet, a goldsmith, and a generous patron of the arts. His rule inspired a cultural era that made Istanbul the artistic center of the Muslim lands. He built magnificent mosques and palaces.

2. The Ottoman Empire's religious tolerance helped reduce internal conflict. In return for enjoying religious and cultural freedom, Jews and Christians paid a tax and were loyal to the state. Their leaders worked with the Ottoman government to ensure positive relations. These communities prospered.

3. The Ottoman Empire extended along the Black Sea, the Adriatic Sea, the Mediterranean Sea, the Persian Gulf, and the Red Sea.

2.5

The Safavid and Mughal Empires

As Islam spread over parts of three continents—Asia, Africa, and Europe—rival dynasties arose that challenged one another. The Ottoman Empire was the largest empire of its time, but it faced strong rivals in Persia and India.

MAIN IDEA

Rival Muslim empires arose in Persia and India during the time of the Ottoman Empire.

THE SAFAVID EMPIRE

The Ottomans formed the largest Muslim empire of the time. However, it was not the only one. The **Safavids** (suh-FAH-vihdz), a Shi'ite dynasty, became rivals of the Sunni Ottomans.

The Safavid Empire arose when a youthful leader named Ismail united the Persian kingdoms into an independent state in 1501. He took the Persian title for king, **shah**. Ismail rapidly expanded Persia's borders north and west by boldly invading Ottoman lands. The Safavids and Ottomans went on to fight a long war that lasted more than 100 years. They battled mainly over control of Mesopotamia's fertile plains. Over and over again, the Safavids gained and lost possession of this land.

Located at the center of international trade routes, the Safavid Empire developed a strong economy. The Safavids used their wealth to build fabulous palaces and mosques and schools, hospitals, roads, and bridges. They made their new capital of Esfahan into one of the most magnificent cities in the world. It had more than 160 mosques and more than 270 public baths.

The Safavids also made Persia into a cultural center by encouraging the immigration of Shi'ite scholars and attracting craftspeople, artists, and traders of many nationalities. The government actively supported both art and industry, resulting in a rich mix of beautiful textiles, carpets, and other products. Europeans eagerly imported these products from Safavid merchants.

The Safavids actively spread Shi'ite Islam. They established it as the dominant Islamic faith in the Caucasus (a region between the Black and Caspian Seas) and in western Asia.

The Safavid Empire reached its peak between 1588 and 1629, during the reign of Shah Abbas I. It then declined steadily under the leadership of weak shahs. In 1722, a group of Afghan warriors invaded the Safavid Empire, which resulted in its downfall.

THE MUGHAL EMPIRE

The Safavid Empire was wedged between two other Muslim empires—the Ottoman Empire to the west and the Mughal Empire to the east. The **Mughals** (MOO-guhlz) were nomads from Central Asia who invaded India. In 1526, troops headed by a Mughal leader named Babur swept out of Central Asia and conquered north and central India. Babur laid the foundation of the Mughal Empire, which eventually stretched across almost the entire subcontinent.

In 1556, the Mughal leader Akbar the Great came to the throne at the age of 13 and led Muslim India to a brilliant golden age. Akbar doubled Babur's conquests and stabilized the empire by establishing a loyal governing class and an effective modern

The Safavids built the Shah Mosque in Esfahan, Iran. Considered a masterpiece of Persian architecture, the mosque features a magnificent dome covered with colorful tiles.

government. He also allowed different religions to flourish in the empire. He even tried to end traditional conflicts between Muslims and Hindus by creating a new religion that mixed elements of both. His library was vast and included books in English, Greek, Persian, Hindi, and Arabic, and his court was cultured and learned.

The Mughal Empire reached its peak under Akbar's grandson, Shah Jahan, who reigned from 1628 to 1658. The empire became most famous for its dazzling splendor and wealth. Shah Jahan collected thousands of precious jewels and exported magnificent Indian art to Europe. He commissioned India's most famous building, the Taj Mahal, in memory of his beloved wife, who had died at a young age. Built of white marble, the monument served as a testament to the power and glory of Mughal rule. (This majestic tomb is pictured in Lesson 3.3.)

Mughal power eventually began to decline, however, as rebellious Hindus and European countries sought to gain control of India. In 1857, the British, who by then had gained control, sent the last Mughal ruler into exile.

REVIEW & ASSESS

1. **READING CHECK** What Muslim empires were rivals of the Ottoman Empire, and where were they located?

2. **COMPARE AND CONTRAST** How were the Safavid and Mughal Empires similar? How were they different?

3. **IDENTIFY PROBLEMS AND SOLUTIONS** How did Akbar the Great deal with the problem of religious conflicts?

PLAN

OBJECTIVE

Identify rival Muslim empires that arose in Persia and India during the time of the Ottoman Empire.

Other Muslim empires arose in Persia and India during the time of the Ottoman Empire. Lesson 2.5 discusses the rise of the Safavid Empire and the Mughal Empire.

CRITICAL THINKING SKILLS FOR LESSON 2.5

- Identify Main Ideas and Details
- Monitor Comprehension
- Compare and Contrast
- Identify Problems and Solutions
- Summarize
- Draw Conclusions
- Interpret Maps

ESSENTIAL QUESTION

What major contributions did medieval Muslim leaders and scholars make to world civilization?

BACKGROUND FOR THE TEACHER

The Taj Mahal was built in Agra, India, by the Mughal ruler Shah Jahan. Blending Indian, Islamic, and Persian styles, it is considered to be the finest example of Mughal architecture and one of the most beautiful buildings in the world. The white marble of the Taj Mahal is decorated with many semiprecious stones. Passages from the Qur'an written in calligraphy are used as decorative elements.

DIGITAL RESOURCES myNGconnect.com

TEACHER RESOURCES & ASSESSMENT

 Reading and Note-Taking

 Vocabulary Practice

 Section 2 Quiz

STUDENT RESOURCES

 NG Chapter Gallery

INTRODUCE & ENGAGE

HOLD A PANEL DISCUSSION

Have students work in groups of five to conduct a panel discussion. One group member is the moderator, posing the following questions:

- What characteristics made the empires of the Umayyads, the Abbasids, and the Ottomans powerful?
- Which, if any, of these characteristics are the most important and why?

Tell students they will learn about two other powerful Muslim empires, the Safavid Empire and the Mughal Empire in this lesson. **0:10** minutes

TEACH

GUIDED DISCUSSION

1. **Summarize** How did the Safavids make Persia into a cultural center? *(They encouraged immigration of Shi'ite scholars and attracted craftspeople, artists, and traders. They supported art and industry.)*

2. **Draw Conclusions** Why did the empire under Shah Jahan become famous for its splendor and wealth? *(Shah Jahan collected thousands of precious jewels and exported magnificent Indian art to Europe. He built India's most famous building, the Taj Mahal.)*

INTERPRET MAPS

Have students look at the borders of the Ottoman, Safavid, and Mughal empires on the map of later Muslim empires from the beginning of the unit. Point out how some of the borders overlap. **ASK:** What can you infer about these empires based on the fact that they have overlapping territory? *(They probably fought each other for control of the overlapping territory.)* **0:10** minutes

ACTIVE OPTIONS

On Your Feet: Present a Skit Divide the class into two groups, one for the Safavid Empire and one for the Mughal Empire. Invite each group to present a short skit about the culture in their empire. Students may want to role-play rulers, soldiers, scholars, artists, traders, or other members of each society. **0:10** minutes

NG Learning Framework: Give a Presentation

SKILL: Collaboration

KNOWLEDGE: **Our Human Story**

Have students review the information about the Safavid and Mughal empires. Ask them to work in small groups to discuss how the two empires were alike and different. Ask each group to present two of their ideas to the class. **0:10** minutes

DIFFERENTIATE

STRIVING READERS

Find Main Ideas and Details Remind students that a main idea is a statement that summarizes the key idea of an article, speech, or paragraph. Details are facts, dates, events, and descriptions that support a main idea. Ask students to write one main idea and two details about some aspect of the Safavid Empire and of the Mughal Empire. Students should use their own words. Have students share their ideas when they have finished. The Ottoman Empire is shown as an example.

> **Main Idea:** In the 1500s, the Ottoman Empire was a Muslim state that became the largest empire in the world.
>
> > **Detail:** powerful navy
> >
> > **Detail:** cultural era

PRE-AP

Research Akbar the Great Have students research Akbar the Great. Ask them to prepare and present one-on-one interviews with the leader. One student should role-play Akbar, while the other role-plays an interviewer. Students should indicate how important Akbar was and include information about some of his contributions, such as his use of diplomacy and his influence on art and culture.

Press (**mt**) *in the Student eEdition for modified text.*

See the Chapter Planner for more strategies for differentiation.

REVIEW & ASSESS

ANSWERS

1. The Safavid Empire in Persia and the Mughal Empire in India were rivals of the Ottoman Empire.

2. Both empires were rivals of the Ottoman Empire; they existed over a similar time span; they were centers of wealth and culture; they produced magnificent buildings; rebellions played a role in their decline. The Safavid Empire spread Shi'ite Islam. The empire established it as the dominant Islamic faith in the Caucasus and in western Asia. The Mughal Empire allowed different religions to flourish.

3. Akbar tried to end traditional conflicts between Muslims and Hindus by creating a new religion that mixed elements of the Muslim and Hindu religions.

Science and Philosophy

The knowledge in a book is useless if nobody reads it. But when people read a book and share its knowledge with others, the knowledge can become incredibly valuable. The leaders of various Muslim empires opened up whole libraries and shared their books with the world to stimulate learning. By doing so, Muslim empires advanced both science and philosophy.

MAIN IDEA

Under the leadership of Muslim dynasties, science and philosophy made important advances that spread across the world.

MATHEMATICS AND ASTRONOMY

Medieval times, which spanned from the 500s to the 1500s, saw the rise and fall of many Muslim empires. The vast extent of these empires and their religious tolerance allowed for a unique blending of cultures. Medieval Muslim leaders and scholars played a key role in preserving and building on the intellectual works of ancient Greece, Persia, and India. In this way, they helped build a foundation for modern civilization.

The field of mathematics provides an important example. Muslim scholars revived interest in the works of such Greek

mathematicians as Euclid and Archimedes and further developed their ideas in geometry, trigonometry, and algebra. To simplify mathematics, they used the decimal number system and encouraged its adoption as the world's standard number system.

Muslim scholars also built upon ancient learning to extend their understanding of the universe. They constructed observatories to plot the movement of the stars, which enabled them to calculate dates for religious ceremonies and contributed to advances in navigation.

MEDICINE AND IDEAS

The Muslim quest for knowledge helped make the form of medicine practiced in Muslim lands the most advanced in the world. Following the Qur'an's instruction to care for the sick, Muslims built many hospitals. Muslim, Jewish, and Christian doctors collected the best available medical knowledge and organized it into reference books. These works helped spread the most advanced medical practices of the time throughout much of the world. They provided the basis for many Western medical treatments for centuries.

One of the most influential works was a 30-volume medical encyclopedia produced around 1000 by an Arab Muslim physician in al-Andalus known as **al-Zahrawi** (al-zuh-RAH-wee). This encyclopedia recommended treatments for a wide range of illnesses and included in-depth descriptions of surgeries. Al-Zahrawi pioneered surgical procedures and invented instruments, some of which are still used today.

Another Muslim physician from al-Andalus known as **Ibn Rushd** (ih-buhn RUSHT) wrote influential books on medicine. He was also a famous philosopher. His detailed studies of the Greek philosophers Aristotle and Plato were crucial in keeping alive the works of these two great thinkers. In his writings, Ibn Rushd tried to harmonize the ideas of Aristotle and Plato with Islam.

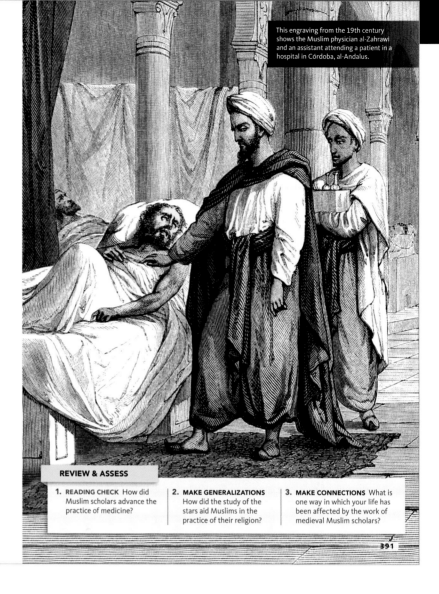

This engraving from the 19th century shows the Muslim physician al-Zahrawi and an assistant attending a patient in a hospital in Córdoba, al-Andalus.

REVIEW & ASSESS

1. **READING CHECK** How did Muslim scholars advance the practice of medicine?

2. **MAKE GENERALIZATIONS** How did the study of the stars aid Muslims in the practice of their religion?

3. **MAKE CONNECTIONS** What is one way in which your life has been affected by the work of medieval Muslim scholars?

PLAN

OBJECTIVE

Describe how, under the leadership of Muslim dynasties, science and philosophy made important advances that spread across the world.

CRITICAL THINKING SKILLS FOR LESSON 3.1

- Identify Main Ideas and Details
- Monitor Comprehension
- Make Generalizations
- Make Connections
- Identify
- Analyze Cause and Effect
- Analyze Visuals

ESSENTIAL QUESTION

What major contributions did medieval Muslim leaders and scholars make to world civilization?

Under the leadership of Muslim dynasties, many important advances were made that spread across the world. Lesson 3.1 discusses some of the advances Muslims made in the fields of mathematics, astronomy, medicine, and philosophy.

BACKGROUND FOR THE TEACHER

Muslims made important advances in the field of science. In astronomy, they measured the size of Earth and studied the sun, moon, and stars. In physics, they explained such phenomena as gravity and light refraction. In medicine, they introduced dissection to study the anatomy and physiology of the human body. They also made advances in finding causes and treatments for certain diseases.

DIGITAL RESOURCES myNGconnect.com

TEACHER RESOURCES & ASSESSMENT

 Reading and Note-Taking   **Vocabulary Practice**   **Section 3 Quiz**

STUDENT RESOURCES

 Biography

SHARE IDEAS

Divide the class into three groups. Assign one of the following topics to each group: mathematics, astronomy, or medicine. Ask each group to talk about how current knowledge and practices related to each of these topics can affect their daily life. Invite each group to share its ideas with the class. **0:05 minutes**

TEACH

GUIDED DISCUSSION

1. **Identify** When did medieval times occur? *(Medieval times spanned from the 500s to the 1500s.)*

2. **Analyze Cause and Effect** What was the Qur'an's instruction about caring for the sick and how did it influence Muslim care of people who were ill? *(The Qur'an instructed Muslims to care for the sick. Muslims built many hospitals and developed advances in the field of medicine to promote health and treat illnesses.)*

ANALYZE VISUALS

Have students look at the engraving of al-Zahrawi that appears in the lesson. Discuss how the scene is similar to and different from what they would see in a modern hospital setting. **0:10 minutes**

ACTIVE OPTIONS

On Your Feet: Stage a Quiz Show Have each student write one question about the advances made in mathematics, astronomy, medicine, or philosophy under the leadership of the Muslim dynasties. Then have groups of five students take turns coming to the front of the class to take part in a quiz. Pose a few of the questions to each group. Students should signal their readiness to answer by raising their hands. **0:10 minutes**

NG Learning Framework: Research Medieval Medical Practices

ATTITUDE: **Curiosity**
KNOWLEDGE: **Our Human Story**

Have small groups of students do research to find out more about medical practices followed and treatments used in Muslim lands in medieval times. Ask each group to present its findings to the class. **0:10 minutes**

STRIVING READERS

Record and Compare Facts After reading the lesson, have groups of students write four important facts they learned. Allow groups to compare and check their facts and then combine their facts into one longer list. Ask a volunteer from each group to read an important fact from the list.

GIFTED & TALENTED

Write an E-Zine Article Have students research to find out more about advances in mathematics, medicine, and other areas of science made under the leadership of Muslim dynasties. Invite students to write and illustrate an e-zine article about the advances Muslims made in one or more of these areas.

Press (**mt**) *in the Student eEdition for modified text.*

See the Chapter Planner for more strategies for differentiation.

ANSWERS

1. They collected and organized medical information into reference books and spread the best-known medical practices throughout the world. They pioneered surgical procedures and invented surgical instruments.

2. Muslims used the study of astronomy to determine the time for prayer and religious celebrations.

3. Answers may vary. Sample response: I use the decimal number system, which was promoted as a standard for the world by Islamic scholars.

Aiding People Through Science

Hayat Sindi is acclaimed as one of the most influential Muslim women in the world. She is proud of her culture and its legacy of learning. "I've always admired people who do something for society," she says. One of her contributions fits on the tip of her finger. It's a tiny piece of paper that is helping save millions of lives around the world.

^ As a co-founder of Diagnostics for All, Hayat Sindi has traveled around the world. This photograph shows her in Brooklyn, New York.

MAIN IDEA

Scientist Hayat Sindi is following Muslim tradition by promoting a medical device that benefits the world's poor people.

MEETING CHALLENGES

A fundamental belief of Islam is that the healthy should care for the sick, just as the wealthy should look after the poor. This belief motivated medieval Muslims to build hospitals and provide medical care to all groups of people at a time when medical care was extremely limited. The work of National Geographic Explorer Hayat Sindi carries on this tradition in the modern world. "Science can be such a powerful way to help humanity," says Sindi, a practicing Muslim from Mecca. "I'm using it to bring easy, affordable health diagnoses to the world's poorest people."

Postage-stamp-sized diagnostic tests developed by a scientific team at Harvard

Sindi was raised in a traditional Muslim family. Her passion for science drove her to leave Saudi Arabia, where women are not allowed to drive or vote. Even taking a job requires a male relative's permission. She traveled to England, where she taught herself English and won a place studying science at King's College in London. She went on to study at the University of Cambridge, the University of Oxford, the Massachusetts Institute of Technology, and Harvard University. "It was quite a journey," she says, "but when people tell me things are impossible, it just gives me energy."

A MISSION TO SAVE LIVES

Sindi's journey was certainly worth it. Today a medical invention she co-invented is helping millions of people from various ethnic groups and religions. "Essentially we've created a medical laboratory that can be taken anywhere because it's made of paper and is the size of a postage stamp," explains Sindi. The paper is etched with tiny channels that carry a single drop of saliva or other body fluid to tiny wells filled with chemicals. The chemicals change color, providing information on medical conditions, such as how well a person's liver is functioning.

The test costs less than a dime and requires no medical training to interpret. It is saving lives by identifying medical conditions early enough to be treated. "It's a tool that allows the poorest people in the most medically challenged places to get the tests they need," explains Sindi.

Just as Muslim physicians compiled books of medical knowledge and pushed the boundaries of medical understanding, Sindi is using the latest technology to ensure that more people receive better care. Sindi believes passionately in bringing science to everyone. "For me science is a universal language that transcends [rises above] nationality, religion, and gender. It can help solve any problem our world faces." Perhaps Muslim scholars before her felt the same way.

REVIEW & ASSESS

1. **READING CHECK** How does the medical device Sindi promotes benefit poor people?

2. **COMPARE AND CONTRAST** How is Sindi's work similar to the work of medieval Muslim physicians?

3. **DISTINGUISH FACT AND OPINION** Is the following statement a fact or an opinion: "[Science] can help solve any problem our world faces"? Explain your answer.

PLAN

OBJECTIVE

Describe how scientist Hayat Sindi is following Muslim tradition by promoting a medical device that benefits the world's poor people.

The Qur'an teaches Muslims that it is important to care for the sick. Lesson 3.2 describes how National Geographic Explorer Hayat Sindi invented a medical device that can provide health diagnoses for the world's poorest people.

CRITICAL THINKING SKILLS FOR LESSON 3.2

- Identify Main Ideas and Details
- Monitor Comprehension
- Compare and Contrast
- Distinguish Fact and Opinion
- Draw Conclusions
- Summarize
- Analyze Cause and Effect

BACKGROUND FOR THE TEACHER

In many areas of the world, people do not have access to care from skilled medical professionals. Sometimes, even when people are able to get to medical clinics, they must wait weeks to get lab results. Hayat Sindi's medical device provides a solution to those problems. Using the device, health care workers can visit hundreds of homes a day, perform tests, and take action to treat illnesses immediately.

ESSENTIAL QUESTION

What major contributions did medieval Muslim leaders and scholars make to world civilization?

DIGITAL RESOURCES myNGconnect.com

TEACHER RESOURCES & ASSESSMENT

 Reading and Note-Taking   **Vocabulary Practice**   **Section 3 Quiz**

STUDENT RESOURCES

 NG Chapter Gallery

INTRODUCE & ENGAGE

GROUP BRAINSTORM

Organize students into small groups. Tell students to think about and discuss a response to this question: *What are some things that scientists, medical workers, and others can do to contribute to society?* Invite students to share their responses. Tell students they will learn about how scientist Hayat Sindi is using a medical device to help promote the health of the world's poorest people. **0:05** minutes

TEACH

GUIDED DISCUSSION

1. **Draw Conclusions** Why is it easy to take Sindi's medical device anywhere? *(It is made of paper and is only the size of a postage stamp. It requires no medical training to interpret.)*

2. **Summarize** How do the chemicals in Sindi's invention change to provide information about medical conditions? *(They change color.)*

ANALYZE CAUSE AND EFFECT

Remind students that an effect of an action or event can also be a cause of another action or event. Have students copy the following Cause-and-Effect Chain and explore a possible chain of effects that could stem from the invention of Sindi's medical test. **0:10** minutes

Test is inexpensive and easy to interpret → →

ACTIVE OPTIONS

On Your Feet: Play "Ready, Set, Recall" After the class has read the lesson, invite small groups of students to list everything they recall. Then have groups, in round-robin order, contribute one item at a time to a class list on the board. When a group runs out of items, it must drop out of the game. However, if that group thinks of a new item, it can get back in the game. **0:10** minutes

Critical Viewing: NG Image Gallery Invite students to explore the entire NG Image Gallery and create a list of favorites by choosing several images they find most interesting and relevant to the chapter. If possible, have students copy the images into a document to form an actual list. Then encourage them to select the image they like best and do further research on it. **0:10** minutes

DIFFERENTIATE

ENGLISH LANGUAGE LEARNERS

Give a Thumbs Up or Thumbs Down Write a set of true-false statements about the lesson, such as "Scientist Hayat Sindi spoke English well when she left Saudi Arabia." Read the lesson aloud with students following along in their books. Then have them close their books and listen as you read the true-false statements. Students should give a thumbs up if a statement is true and a thumbs down if a statement is false.

STRIVING READERS

Make Lists Post the title "Three Things I Know About Hayat Sindi and Her Work." After reading the lesson, ask pairs of students to copy the title you posted and add three sentences about the topic. Ask volunteers to share their sentences with the class.

Press (**mt**) *in the Student eEdition for modified text.*

See the Chapter Planner for more strategies for differentiation.

REVIEW & ASSESS

ANSWERS

1. Her medical innovation is a simple, inexpensive paper test that enables millions of people of various ethnic groups and religions in the world's poorest places to get the medical tests they need.

2. Medieval Muslims built hospitals and provided medical care because Islam taught that the healthy should care for the sick and the wealthy should look after the poor. Sindi is doing the same through her medical device.

3. The statement is an opinion. One could argue that science cannot help solve certain problems. For example, science cannot stop a natural disaster from occurring.

3.3

Architecture, the Arts, and Literature

Have you ever drawn your name or other words in an artistic way? If so, you have something in common with medieval Muslim artists. These artists considered beautiful writing to be one of the highest forms of art and an expression of their religion, Islam. The Qur'an provided the passages for this beautiful writing.

MAIN IDEA

Medieval Muslim dynasties produced distinctive forms of architecture, art, and writing that are highly admired today.

BUILDING AND DESIGN

In medieval Islamic civilization, beautiful writing appeared not only in books but also in buildings. Those buildings, especially mosques, displayed many architectural features that were developed from Roman, Egyptian, Byzantine, and Persian models. However, the style of architecture soon became recognized as distinctly Islamic.

A typical mosque was topped by a large dome and had one or more **minarets**. These extremely tall, slender towers were designed to dominate the skyline and call attention to the importance of the mosque. From a minaret, a Muslim

official known as a muezzin (moo-EH-zuhn) would call out a summons to prayer.

The inside of a mosque also had distinctive features. Under the dome was the prayer hall, a large open area designed to appear spacious and full of light. Set into one wall was the mihrab (MEE-ruhb), an often richly decorated archway that indicated the direction of Mecca. While sharing these common features, mosques also incorporated local influences, so they varied in design in different locations.

The decoration inside a mosque was often elaborate, featuring elegant writing called **calligraphy** and abstract design known as **arabesque**. Arabesque consists of patterns of flowers, leaves, vines, and geometric shapes. The patterns often repeat in a seemingly endless way, representing the Muslim belief in the infinity of God's creation. Muslim artists did not portray human figures or animals. According to an interpretation of the Qur'an, the depiction of people and animals imitates God's act of creation. Muslims feared the display of such works might encourage the worship of images.

LITERATURE

Besides distinctive architecture and art, medieval Islamic civilization also produced significant works of literature. Muslims consider the Qur'an to be the greatest literary work in the Arabic language. The best-known popular work of literature is *The Thousand and One Nights*, a collection of entertaining stories from India, Persia, and Arabia. It features such well-known characters as Aladdin and Sinbad the Sailor.

Muslims admired poetry more than any other form of literature. A four-line rhyming poem known as a quatrain was made popular by the Persian poet **Omar Khayyám** (ky-YAM), who lived from 1048 to 1131. *The Rubáiyát of Omar Khayyám*, a selection of his quatrains, is considered a masterpiece of world literature.

394 CHAPTER 13

POSSIBLE RESPONSE

Features of Muslim architecture apparent in the building's exterior include the minarets, the domes, the geometric shapes, the elaborate designs, the absence of human or animal figures.

Critical Viewing The Taj Mahal in India was built in the mid-1600s by the Mughal emperor Shah Jahan. What features of Muslim architecture are apparent in the building's exterior?

REVIEW & ASSESS

1. **READING CHECK** What is a distinctive feature of the exterior architecture of a typical mosque?

2. **DRAW CONCLUSIONS** Would you expect to find statues in a mosque? Why or why not?

3. **EVALUATE** What qualities of Muslim architecture and art do you find most appealing?

The Islamic World **395**

PLAN

OBJECTIVE

Describe how medieval Muslim dynasties produced distinctive forms of architecture, art, and writing that are highly admired today.

CRITICAL THINKING SKILLS FOR LESSON 3.3

- Identify Main Ideas and Details
- Monitor Comprehension
- Draw Conclusions
- Evaluate
- Make Generalizations
- Identify

ESSENTIAL QUESTION

What major contributions did medieval Muslim leaders and scholars make to world civilization?

Medieval Muslim dynasties produced distinctive forms of architecture, arts, and literature. Lesson 3.3 describes some of the highly admired contributions Muslim dynasties made in these areas.

BACKGROUND FOR THE TEACHER

Omar Khayyám was born in Persia in 1048. He was a mathematician, an astronomer, and poet. In his own country and time, he was well known for his scientific achievements. In the West, he is best known for the poem, *The Rubaiyat of Omar Khayyám*. This poem is a collection of Khayyám's quatrains. In the verses, the poet discusses eternity, the uncertainty of life, and the fleeting beauty of the material world.

DIGITAL RESOURCES myNGconnect.com

TEACHER RESOURCES & ASSESSMENT

 Reading and Note-Taking **Vocabulary Practice** **Section 3 Quiz**

STUDENT RESOURCES

 NG Chapter Gallery

COMPOSE A POEM

Tell students that a quatrain is a four-line stanza. Organize students into groups of four and invite them to write a quatrain with an *aaba* rhyme scheme about a Muslim contribution to civilization. Each member of the group should contribute a line to the quatrain. Encourage groups to share their quatrains with the class. Tell students that they will learn about Muslim contributions in architecture, art, and writing. Explain that they will read about a poem by Omar Khayyám that was composed of quatrains with an *aaba* rhyme scheme. **0:10 minutes**

GUIDED DISCUSSION

1. **Make Generalizations** How do the patterns in arabesque often repeat and what does the repetition represent? *(The patterns often repeat in a seemingly endless way, representing the Muslim belief in the infinity of God's creation.)*

2. **Identify** What do Muslims consider to be the greatest literary work in the Arabic language? *(Muslims consider the Qur'an to be the greatest literary work in the Arabic language.)*

MORE INFORMATION

The Thousand and One Nights Also known as *The Arabian Nights,* this work is a collection of Middle Eastern and Indian tales of uncertain authorship. The tales are tied together by a frame story. It tells of King Shahryar, who marries and kills a new wife every day. When the clever Scheherazade marries him, she postpones her death by telling him a fascinating tale every night for a thousand and one nights until the king realizes he is in love with her and spares her. Some of the stories from the collection have become part of Western folklore, including "The Seven Voyages of Sinbad the Sailor," "Aladdin and the Wonderful Lamp," and "The Forty Thieves."

ACTIVE OPTIONS

On Your Feet: Team Word Webbing Organize students into teams of four and have them record on a piece of paper what they know about literature produced by the medieval Islamic civilization. Encourage students to build on their teammates' entries as they rotate the paper from one member to the next. Then call on volunteers from each group to make statements about medieval Muslim literature based on what they have recorded. **0:10 minutes**

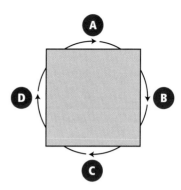

Critical Viewing: NG Image Gallery Invite students to explore the entire NG Image Gallery and choose one image from the gallery they feel best represents their understanding of each chapter or unit. Have students provide a written explanation of why they selected each of the images they chose. **0:10 minutes**

STRIVING READERS

Use Reciprocal Teaching Have students read the lesson in pairs. Instruct them to take turns reading each paragraph aloud. After finishing a paragraph, the reading student should ask the listening student a question or two about what he or she has just heard. Students may ask their partner to summarize the paragraph in his or her own words.

GIFTED & TALENTED

Write a Modern Tale Have students find a copy of *The Thousand and One Nights* at the library or online. Tell each student to choose one tale and rewrite it so it takes place in the present day. Have students read their tales aloud to the class.

Press **mt** *in the Student eEdition for modified text.*

See the Chapter Planner for more strategies for differentiation.

ANSWERS

1. Islamic mosques are topped by a large dome and have one or more minarets.

2. Statues would not be found in a mosque because Muslim artists do not portray people or animals. According to an interpretation of the Qur'an, doing so would imitate God's act of creation and might encourage the worship of images.

3. Answers will vary. Sample response: I like the calligraphy and the arabesques. I find the significance of the arabesque interesting.

3.4 ISLAMIC ART

Islamic art features cultural influences from across vast empires. More importantly, it reflects the values and teachings of Islam. Muslim artists initially created calligraphy to beautify the Qur'an. The intricate floral and geometric patterns of arabesque emerged partly in response to an interpretation of the Qur'an. That interpretation discouraged the depiction of people and animals in art.

Mihrab
This archway comes from a mosque in Iran built in the 1300s. It features a mosaic of colorful tiles decorated with arabesque and calligraphy.

Caftan
This caftan, a long garment, belonged to Bayezid II, an Ottoman sultan who ruled from 1481 to 1512.

Ceramic Plate
This decorated plate was made in the 1700s in Morocco.

Stained Glass
This stained glass window appears in the Blue Mosque, which was built in the 1600s in Istanbul, Turkey.

Calligraphy
This page of calligraphy comes from a Qur'an produced in Cairo, Egypt, around 1310.

Tile
This Turkish tile from about 1530 features floral patterns.

The Islamic World **397**

PLAN

OBJECTIVE

Identify different examples of art from medieval Muslim civilization.

CRITICAL THINKING SKILLS FOR LESSON 3.4

- Identify
- Make Inferences
- Analyze Visuals

ESSENTIAL QUESTION

What major contributions did medieval Muslim leaders and scholars make to world civilization?

Medieval Muslim dynasties produced a variety of art forms. Lesson 3.4 gives examples of different types of Islamic art.

BACKGROUND FOR THE TEACHER

The Blue Mosque is the mosque of Ahmed I, an Ottoman sultan from 1603 to 1617. Its architect was Mehmed Aga, the royal architect of the Ottoman court. The design of the mosque is symmetrical with a large center dome and four semidomes surrounded by a number of smaller domes. The mosque got its name from its beautiful blue tiles. More than 250 windows let light into the mosque. Many people at the time were upset that the Blue Mosque had six minarets instead of the usual four. They thought this was an attempt to make the Blue Mosque as great as the mosque in Mecca.

DIGITAL RESOURCES myNGconnect.com

TEACHER RESOURCES & ASSESSMENT

 Reading and Note-Taking

 Vocabulary Practice

 Section 3 Quiz

STUDENT RESOURCES

 NG Chapter Gallery

INTRODUCE & ENGAGE

HISTORY THROUGH OBJECTS

Ask students to form small groups and brainstorm a list of different forms of art they know about. Reconvene as a class and ask the groups to share their lists. Use the group lists to create a master list on the whiteboard. Tell students they will learn about different pieces of art from medieval Islamic civilization. **0:05** minutes

TEACH

GUIDED DISCUSSION

1. **Identify** For what reason did Muslim artists initially create calligraphy? (*They initially created calligraphy to make the Qur'an look beautiful.*)

2. **Make Inferences** What might the caftan indicate about the importance of sultans in Ottoman society? (*Answers will vary. Possible response: The caftan is elaborate and it looks like it is made of rich fabrics. It would indicate that the sultans were important and powerful in Ottoman society.*)

ANALYZE VISUALS

Have students write two adjectives to describe each of the art pieces shown in the lesson. Then have students take turns sharing their adjectives with the class. **0:10** minutes

ACTIVE OPTIONS

On Your Feet: Question and Answer Chain Divide the class into groups of six. Have each group sit in a circle or around a table. One student starts the activity by asking the student to the right a question about one of the art objects shown in this lesson. The student to the right answers the question and then turns to the student on her or his right and asks a new question. Students continue until each student has asked and answered a question. **0:10** minutes

NG Learning Framework: Give a Presentation

ATTITUDE: Curiosity
SKILL: Communication

Have students search local libraries for interesting books about Islamic art and architecture. Have them choose a building or art object to present to the class. Encourage them to include images with their presentation. **0:10** minutes

DIFFERENTIATE

INCLUSION

Identify Art Objects Pair students so that there is a proficient reader in each pair. Have the proficient reader read each caption aloud. Then have the other student point to each image and describe the object.

PRE-AP

Design a Web Site Have students work in small groups to design a Web site about the Blue Mosque. Have them design a home page as well as supporting pages. The Web site should include information about where, when, and how the mosque was built, its size, religious significance, and features on its architecture.

Press **mt** *in the Student eEdition for modified text.*

See the Chapter Planner for more strategies for differentiation.

VOCABULARY

Use each of the following vocabulary words in a sentence that shows an understanding of the word's meaning.

1. oasis
An oasis was the only source of water for traders crossing the vast desert.

2. medieval

3. mosque

4. pilgrimage

5. caliph

6. sultan

7. janissary

8. minaret

READING STRATEGY

9. IDENTIFY MAIN IDEAS AND DETAILS If you haven't already, complete your web with details that illustrate the legacy of Islamic culture. Then answer the question.

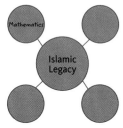

How is the influence of Islamic culture apparent in the present day?

MAIN IDEAS

Answer the following questions. Support your answers with evidence from the chapter.

10. How were the Bedouin in Arabia organized in the 600s? **LESSON 1.1**

11. Who was Muhammad? **LESSON 1.2**

12. What happened to the Muslim state after Muhammad's death in 632? **LESSON 1.5**

13. Why did Muslims split into two main sects in the late 600s? **LESSON 2.1**

14. What dynasty transformed Muslim Spain into a center of Islamic culture between 756 and 1031? **LESSON 2.2**

15. Who ruled the Ottoman Empire at its peak, and what were his major achievements? **LESSON 2.4**

16. What major contributions did medieval Muslim scholars make to the field of mathematics? **LESSON 3.1**

17. What are the advantages of the medical invention Hayat Sindi promotes? **LESSON 3.2**

CRITICAL THINKING

Answer the following questions. Support your answers with evidence from the chapter.

18. DRAW CONCLUSIONS What is one major way in which medieval Muslim scholars helped build a foundation for modern civilization?

19. ANALYZE CAUSE AND EFFECT How did the Qur'an affect the development of Islamic art?

20. MAKE INFERENCES How did its geographic location contribute to the growth of the Savafid Empire?

21. YOU DECIDE Which of the Muslim empires was the greatest? Be sure to explain what you mean by "great."

INTERPRET MAPS

Study the map that shows the spread of Islam. Then answer the questions that follow.

SPREAD OF ISLAM, 632–750

22. Across what region had Islam spread by the time of Muhammad's death in 632?

23. To what continents had Islam spread by 661?

ANALYZE SOURCES

Read this part of an oath that was written by Moses Maimonides, a physician in Muslim Spain. Then answer the question that follows.

> May I never see in the patient anything but a fellow creature in pain. Grant me the strength, time and opportunity always to correct what [learning] I have acquired, always to extend its domain [sphere]; for knowledge is immense and the spirit of man can extend indefinitely to enrich itself daily with new requirements. . . . Oh, God, Thou has appointed me to watch over the life and death of Thy creatures; here am I ready for my vocation and now I turn unto my calling.

24. How do Maimonides' ideas about knowledge reflect achievements in Muslim Spain during its golden age?

WRITE ABOUT HISTORY

25. INFORMATIVE Write a brief encyclopedia article that compares the main beliefs of Islam with those of Judaism and Christianity.

TIPS

- Take notes on the beliefs of Islam described in Lesson 1.3.
- State the main idea about the similarities among the beliefs of Islam, Judaism, and Christianity in your beginning sentence.
- Develop the main idea by using relevant, well-chosen facts about the beliefs of each religion.
- Use appropriate transition words, such as *likewise*, *similarly*, and *also*, to clarify the similarities among the three religions' beliefs.
- Provide a concluding statement that follows from and supports the facts you have presented on the three religions' beliefs.

VOCABULARY ANSWERS

Sentences will vary. Sample responses are given.

1. An oasis was the only source of water for traders crossing the vast desert.

2. The years from the 500s to the 1500s were medieval times.

3. At the center of the Islamic community is the mosque, which is the Muslim place of worship.

4. Being a devout Muslim, the boy planned to make the hajj—the pilgrimage to Mecca—after he finished college.

5. After Muhammad's death, Abu Bakr was appointed as the first caliph, or successor, to the prophet.

6. Suleyman I was a powerful sultan, or Muslim leader, who ruled the Ottoman Empire at its peak.

7. Ferocious soldiers who were greatly feared made up the sultan's janissary corps of the army.

8. An extremely tall tower called a minaret rises above the mosque.

READING STRATEGY ANSWER

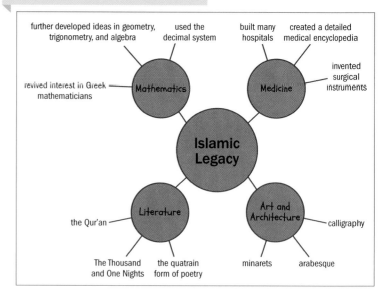

9. The influence of Islamic culture is apparent in the present day in the areas of math, medicine, art, and literature. Mathematical concepts such as the decimal system are used widely, and many medical procedures developed by Muslim physicians are still used today. People today also still use calligraphy as a style of elegant writing, and tales from Muslim literature, such as *The Thousand and One Nights*, are part of many world cultures.

MAIN IDEAS ANSWERS

10. The Bedouin were organized into tribes based on clans. The tribes were headed by an elected sheik.

11. Muhammad was the prophet of Islam.

12. After Muhammad's death, the Muslim state almost collapsed because his followers disagreed over how to choose a successor. Then a few leading Muslims appointed Muhammad's father-in-law, Abu Bakr, as caliph. He united all of Arabia under Islam and crushed rebellions.

13. Unpopular actions by the Umayyad—establishing a hereditary system of succession and moving the capital to Damascus—caused Islam to split into two opposing sects in the late 600s. The Sunni believed any Muslim could be caliph, while the Shi'ite believed only Muhammad's descendants could be caliph.

14. The Umayyad dynasty transformed Muslim Spain into a center of Islamic culture between 756 and 1031.

15. Suleyman I ruled the Ottoman Empire at its peak. He conquered vast swathes of northern Africa and eastern Europe. He inspired a cultural blossoming that made Istanbul the artistic center of the Islamic world. He commissioned the restoration of the Grand Mosque in Mecca. He built magnificent mosques and palaces in Istanbul.

16. They revived interest in the works of such Greek mathematicians as Euclid and Archimedes and further developed their ideas in geometry, trigonometry, and algebra. They promoted the adoption of the decimal number system as the world's standard.

17. The invention is small, inexpensive, easy to interpret, and can be used to diagnose a range of medical conditions.

CRITICAL THINKING ANSWERS

18. Medieval Islamic scholars translated the works of ancient Greece, Persia, and India into Arabic, further developed many of the ideas, and spread the knowledge throughout much of the world.

19. According to an interpretation of the Qur'an, the depiction of human figures and animals in art is forbidden, and so Muslim artists developed the abstract designs of arabesque. Muslim artists developed calligraphy to beautify the Qur'an.

20. The Safavid Empire was located at the center of international trade routes, resulting in the development of a strong economy. The Safavids used their wealth to build palaces, mosques, schools, hospitals, roads, and bridges. They made Persia into a cultural center.

21. Answers will vary. Students should support their opinions with evidence from the text.

INTERPRET MAPS ANSWERS

22. Islam had spread across much of Arabia by the time of Muhammad's death.

23. Islam had spread to Asia, Africa, and Europe by 661.

ANALYZE SOURCES ANSWER

24. In his oath, Maimonides describes knowledge as immense and always open to being corrected and extended. He also depicts the acquisition of knowledge as a way for people to extend and enrich their spirits. This view of knowledge and learning reflects the great emphasis on learning in Islamic Spain during its golden age and the many advances made in science, philosophy, medicine, and the arts.

WRITE ABOUT HISTORY ANSWER

25. Students' encyclopedia articles will vary, but students should present the information clearly, accurately, and logically.

ON **LOCATION**
WITH Jodi

MAGNESS

NATIONAL GEOGRAPHIC GRANTEE

▶ Check out more on myNGconnect

Archaeologist Jodi Magness stands
on the eastern wall of the synagogue
her team unearthed in the ancient
village of Huqoq in Galilee, Israel.

EXPLORING IN ISRAEL

I was just 12 when I decided I wanted to become an archaeologist. It is a passion I'm lucky enough to pursue as my career. I've taken part in over 20 excavations around the Mediterranean Sea. I now specialize in the history of ancient Palestine, the area that includes modern Israel, Jordan, and the Palestine territories. It's a land rich in history, and it's allowed me to study the city of Jerusalem, the fortress of Masada, and the Roman Army. But things really took off in 2011 when I came to study the ancient village of Huqoq (hoo-KOKE) in Galilee, Israel.

We were hunting for the remains of a fifth century synagogue. It was a big, overgrown site but our very first sounding came down right on the synagogue's eastern wall. We weren't able to use technologies like ground-penetrating radar to find the synagogue because it is covered by the bulldozed ruins of a modern village. We remove one rock at a time and record everything we do because you can never put the stones back the way they were.

HIDDEN MOSAICS

This is especially important because of what we are finding—mosaic floors made up of thousands of tiny cubes of stone. The very first mosaic that peered out of the dirt was the face of a woman. We've also uncovered spectacular mosaics depicting stories from the Hebrew Bible. We found a beautiful depiction of Sampson taking revenge on

Jodi Magness and her team are challenged by the summer heat, scorpions, and snakes in Huqoq.

the Philistines using foxes to carry torches and set fire to their fields. There's another mosaic showing Samson carrying the gate of Gaza in an incredible act of strength. We've even found one mosaic with elephants (see pages 344–345), which indicates that this is not a story from the Hebrew Bible. It might tell the story of Alexander the Great. So far, we have only uncovered a small part of the synagogue, and we hope our continued excavation will reveal more mosaics.

WHY STUDY HISTORY ❓

❝ The mosaics we are uncovering in Huqoq are not only beautiful, they are helping other archaeologists, scholars, and the general public to *better understand ancient Judaism*. Every year we come back and discover more, so it's really an extraordinary experience. ❞ —Jodi Magness

NATIONAL GEOGRAPHIC

The Stolen Past

BY KAREN LANGE

Adapted from "The Stolen Past," by Karen Lange,
in *National Geographic*, December 2008

For a thousand years, the ruins of Khirbet Tawas, a Byzantine jewel, stood southwest of Hebron. Then, in 2000, the second intifada began. As Palestinians fought Israeli troops, the West Bank became all but ungovernable. Soon the Israelis set up a web of security checkpoints, sealed off the region, and barred most Palestinians from working inside Israel. Jobless men looked for cash wherever they could find it. Armed with shovels, a small band descended on Khirbet Tawas. The looters searched for anything they could sell: Byzantine coins, clay lamps, glass bracelets.

Looters have overrun not just Khirbet Tawas but countless other archaeological sites located in the West Bank. They attack ancient sites with backhoes and small bulldozers, scraping away the top layer of earth across areas the size of several football fields. Guided by metal detectors—coins often give away the location of other goods—they take anything of value.

The West Bank is a cradle of civilization and a crossroads of empires. For Jews, Christians, and Muslims, it is sacred ground. Yet this priceless legacy is swiftly being lost. Archaeologist Salah Al-Houdalieh says, "They are destroying a cultural heritage that belongs to every Palestinian, to every human being."

Few jobs, inadequate law enforcement by both Palestinian and Israeli authorities, and demand for artifacts just across the border in Israel have created the perfect storm for looting.

Some looted artifacts are bought by middlemen who supply shops in Israel. Tourists eager to take home a piece of the Holy Land unknowingly support the trade. Other artifacts are smuggled into Jordan, then on to dealers elsewhere, who in turn sell the artifacts to outlets in Israel.

Alarmed by the spike in looting, Palestinian lawmakers have proposed increasing the maximum prison sentence for damaging archaeological sites from three years to five. Yet political circumstances and deep mutual distrust continue to hamper police on both sides of the border.

For more from National Geographic
Check out "The Wells of Memory" on myNGconnect

UNIT INQUIRY: MAKE AN IDEA MAP

In this unit, you learned about many cultural contributions of the Byzantine Empire and medieval Islamic civilizations. Based on your understanding of the text, what impact did these cultural contributions have on civilization as they spread throughout the world? How do medieval cultural contributions continue to make a major impact on our civilization today?

ASSIGNMENT Create an idea map that illustrates the cultural impact one of the major contributions of the Byzantine Empire or medieval Islamic civilizations has had (and continues to have) on our civilization today. Be prepared to present your idea map to the class and explain how the contribution or achievement is an example of cultural diffusion from medieval civilization to today.

Plan As you create your idea map, think about the many cultural achievements and contributions made by the Byzantine Empire and medieval Islamic civilizations. Select one major contribution or achievement that you think has had an impact on today's civilization. You might want to use a graphic organizer to help organize your thoughts. ▶

Produce Use your notes to produce descriptions of different ways the contribution or achievement you selected has impacted the world today. You might want to write them in outline or paragraph form.

Present Choose a creative way to present your idea map to the class. Consider one of these options:

- Create a multimedia presentation using photos to illustrate different ways the medieval contribution/achievement impacts our civilization today.

- Write an introduction to your idea map that explains the significance of cultural diffusion in medieval civilization and the modern world.

- Draw a physical map to show the location where the contribution/achievement originated.

Major Contribution or Achievement:
_____

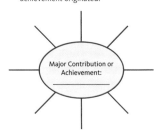

RAPID REVIEW
UNIT 5

BYZANTINE AND ISLAMIC CIVILIZATIONS

TOP TEN

1. Byzantium was a center of trade and learning and the largest city in the medieval world.
2. The Roman Catholic Church split with the Eastern Orthodox Church in 1064.
3. Muhammad was a political and religious leader who founded Islam.
4. Islam spread across Southwest Asia, North Africa, India, and Europe through conquest and trade.
5. Islamic scholars made important advances in mathematics, astronomy, medicine, science, art, architecture, and literature.

6-10. **NOW IT'S YOUR TURN** Complete the list with five more things to remember about Byzantine and Islamic civilizations.

RAPID REVIEW

POSSIBLE RESPONSES

Possible responses for the remaining five things to remember include the following:

6. Islam was ruled by a caliph, which means "successor."

7. After the collapse of the Western Roman Empire, the Byzantines continued Roman traditions for another 1,000 years.

8. Byzantines, proficient in Greek and Latin, helped preserve Greek and Roman knowledge.

9. Muslims believe Muhammad to be the last prophet, and their faith is based on the Qur'an.

10. Emperor Justinian developed the Justinian Code, the basis of many European laws today.

UNIT INQUIRY PROJECT RUBRIC

ASSESS

Use the rubric to assess each student's participation and performance.

SCORE	ASSIGNMENT	PRODUCT	PRESENTATION
3 GREAT	• Student thoroughly understands the assignment. • Student participates fully in the project process. • Student works well independently.	• Idea map contains many details. • Idea map clearly illustrates the cultural impact of a contribution. • Final description reflects the idea map.	• Presentation is clear, concise, and logical. • Presentation does a good job explaining the impact of the contribution. • Presentation engages the audience.
2 GOOD	• Student mostly understands the assignment. • Student participates fairly well in the project process. • Student works fairly independently.	• Idea map contains a fair amount of details. • Idea map somewhat illustrates the cultural impact of a contribution. • Final description somewhat reflects the idea map.	• Presentation is fairly clear, concise, and logical. • Presentation does an adequate job of explaining the impact of the contribution. • Presentation somewhat engages the audience.
1 NEEDS WORK	• Student does not understand the assignment. • Student minimally participates or does not participate in the project process. • Student struggles to work independently.	• Idea map contains few details. • Idea map does not illustrate the cultural impact of a contribution. • Final descriptions do not reflect the idea map.	• Presentation is not clear, concise, or logical. • Presentation does not adequately explain the impact of the contribution. • Presentation does not engage the audience.

AFRICAN
CIVILIZATIONS

NATIONAL GEOGRAPHIC

ON **LOCATION** WITH

Christopher DeCorse
Archaeologist

The story of Africa is an ancient one. The natural resources and movement of people across this huge continent have made the exchange of goods and ideas a major theme throughout its long history. Crossing the vast Sahara and sailing the waters of the Indian Ocean, Africans created some of the most successful trading networks in history. I'm Christopher DeCorse, and I'm an archaeologist and National Geographic Grantee. Join me on a journey to explore the civilizations of Africa!

< CRITICAL VIEWING Ships like this African dhow carried goods in and out of coastal trading cities. Why would a ship like this be good for sailing the open sea?

African Civilizations

c. A.D. 100
Aksum emerges as a prosperous trading kingdom in present-day Ethiopia.

c. 500 B.C.
The Nok people develop iron tools and terra cotta sculpture. *(terra cotta Nok head sculpture)*

c. 300
The introduction of camels in North Africa allows for trans-Saharan trade.

A.D. 100

c. 1000 B.C.
The Bantu begin their slow migration across sub-Saharan Africa.

552 B.C.
ASIA
Confucius is born in northeast China.

1000 B.C.

c. 500 B.C.
AMERICAS
The Zapotec build the city of Monte Albán overlooking the Oaxaca Valley. *(statuette of a Zapotec god)*

The World

What two cultures had become highly developed by about 500 B.C.?

1324
Mansa Musa makes his pilgrimage to Egypt. *(illustration of Mansa Musa from an illuminated map)*

c. 1300
East African city-states, including Kilwa, arise along the East African coast.
(ruins at Kilwa)

c. 1230
The empire of Mali is founded by Sundiata Keita.

c. 500
The trading kingdom of Ghana emerges west of the Sahara.

1400
The kingdom of Kongo emerges in the rain forests south of the Congo River.

1250

1500

1095
EUROPE
Pope Urban II initiates the first crusade to the Holy Land.

1453
ASIA
Ottoman Turks capture Constantinople, ending the Byzantine Empire.

330
EUROPE
Emperor Constantine makes Constantinople the capital of the Eastern Roman Empire.
(profile of Constantine on a gold coin)

407

AFRICA Land Use & Resources
2014

Africa is a huge land area that encompasses a wide variety of physical features and cultures. Trade has long been a part of many of these cultures, fueling the rise of kingdoms across the continent. West African civilizations were built on the trade of gold, salt, and slaves. The Indian Ocean trade made the ancient kingdom of Aksum a mighty power and later helped found the great city-states of East Africa.

With its plentiful natural resources, Africa plays a major role in international trade today. The highly detailed National Geographic map on the next page shows the continent's resources and land use systems. Many African nations are important trading partners of the United States. The graph below shows how much the United States spends on goods received from Africa (imports) and how much it earns on goods sent to Africa (exports).

What natural resources are found in West Africa?

+ POSSIBLE RESPONSE
Bauxite, diamonds, copper, other minerals, and fish are found in West Africa.

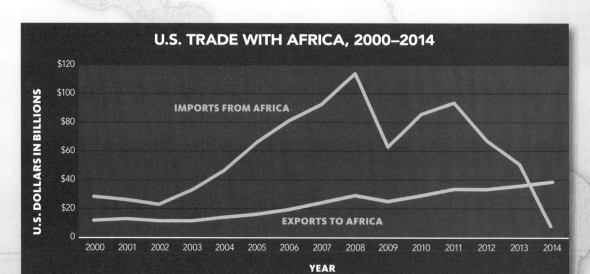

U.S. TRADE WITH AFRICA, 2000–2014

IMPORTS FROM AFRICA

EXPORTS TO AFRICA

U.S. DOLLARS IN BILLIONS: $120, $100, $80, $60, $40, $20, 0

YEAR: 2000 2001 2002 2003 2004 2005 2006 2007 2008 2009 2010 2011 2012 2013 2014

Imports Oil is among the top items imported to the United States from Africa, including that drilled from this oil rig in South Africa.

Exports The top items exported to Africa from the United States are machinery and equipment, including agricultural machines.

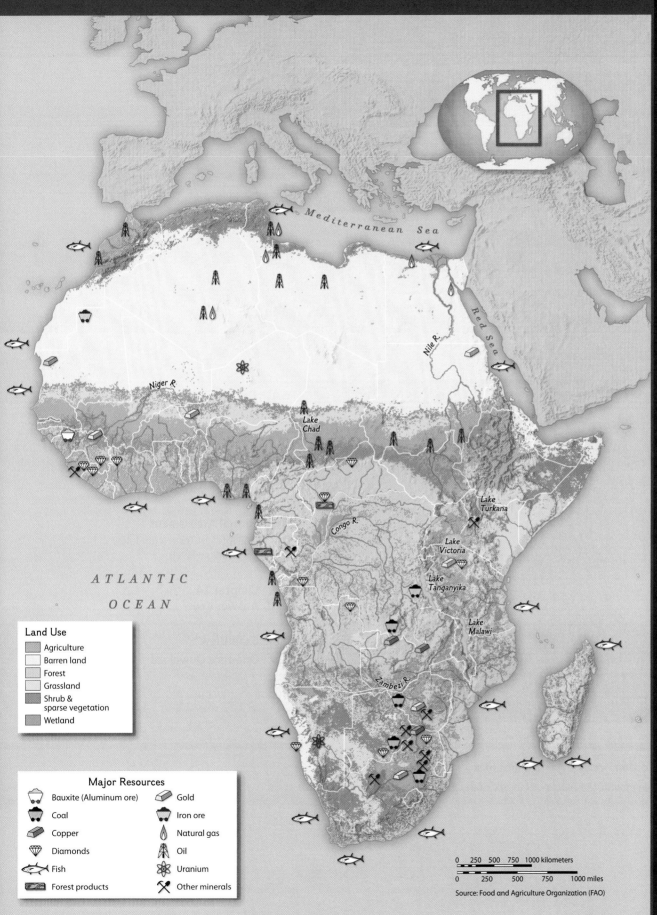

Land Use

- Agriculture
- Barren land
- Forest
- Grassland
- Shrub & sparse vegetation
- Wetland

Major Resources

- Bauxite (Aluminum ore)
- Coal
- Copper
- Diamonds
- Fish
- Forest products
- Gold
- Iron ore
- Natural gas
- Oil
- Uranium
- Other minerals

Source: Food and Agriculture Organization (FAO)

Mediterranean Sea

Red Sea

Nile R.

Niger R.

Lake Chad

Congo R.

Lake Turkana

Lake Victoria

Lake Tanganyika

Lake Malawi

Zambezi R.

ATLANTIC OCEAN

0   250   500   750   1000 kilometers

0   250   500   750   1000 miles

UNIT RESOURCES

On Location with National Geographic Grantee Christopher DeCorse
Intro and Video

Interactive Map Tool

News & Updates

Available on myNGconnect

Unit Wrap-Up:
"Archaeology in Africa"
Feature and Video

"The Telltale Scribes of Timbuktu"
National Geographic Adapted Article

"Rift in Paradise"
National Geographic Adapted Article
Student eEdition exclusive

Unit 6 Inquiry:
Create a Local Trade Exchange

CHAPTER RESOURCES

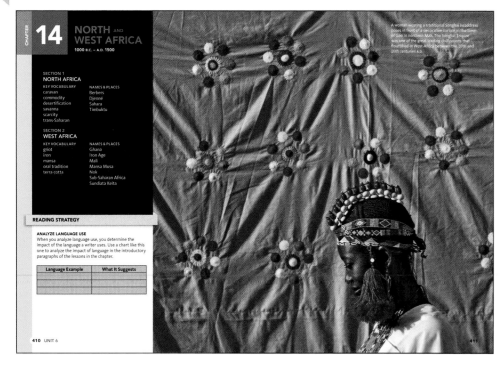

TEACHER RESOURCES & ASSESSMENT
Available on myNGconnect

Social Studies Skills Lessons
• Reading: Analyze Language Use
• Writing: Write a Narrative

Formal Assessment
• Chapter 14 Tests A (on-level) & B (below-level)

Chapter 14 Answer Key

ExamView®
One-time Download

STUDENT BACKPACK *Available on myNGconnect*

• **eEdition** *(English)*   • **eEdition** *(Spanish)*   • **Handbooks**   • **Online Atlas**

For Chapter 14 Spanish resources, visit the Teacher Resource Menu page on myNGconnect.

SECTION 1 RESOURCES

NORTH AFRICA

 Reading and Note-Taking

 Vocabulary Practice

☑ **Section 1 Quiz**

Available on myNGconnect

LESSON 1.1 A VAST AND VARIED LAND
• Critical Viewing: NG Chapter Gallery
• On Your Feet: Inside-Outside Circle

LESSON 1.2 TRANS-SAHARAN TRADE

Active History: Interactive Whiteboard Activity
Map Historic Trade Routes

Active History
Map Historic Trade Routes

Available on myNGconnect

• On Your Feet: Create a Concept Web

LESSON 1.3 GOLD, SALT, AND SLAVES
• Critical Viewing: NG Chapter Gallery
• On Your Feet: Card Response

LESSON 1.4 ISLAM SPREADS TO AFRICA
• Critical Viewing: NG Chapter Gallery
• On Your Feet: Traveling Around the World

SECTION 2 RESOURCES

WEST AFRICA

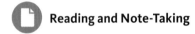 **Reading and Note-Taking**

 **Vocabulary Practice**

 ☑ **Section 2 Quiz**

Available on myNGconnect

LESSON 2.1 NOK CULTURE AND IRON TECHNOLOGY
• Critical Viewing: NG Chapter Gallery
• On Your Feet: One-on-One Interviews

LESSON 2.2 THE KINGDOM OF GHANA

| **NG Learning Framework:**
Learn About the Nok and the Berbers

• On Your Feet: Stage a Quiz Show

LESSON 2.3 THE EMPIRE OF MALI

 Biography
Mansa Musa   *Available on myNGconnect*

• Critical Viewing: NG Chapter Gallery
• On Your Feet: Fishbowl

LESSON 2.4 THE ORAL TRADITION

 Biography
Sundiata Keita   *Available on myNGconnect*

| **NG Learning Framework:**
Think About Sundiata

• On Your Feet: Create a Concept Web

DOCUMENT-BASED QUESTION
LESSON 2.5 TRANS-SAHARAN TRAVELERS

 Biography
Ibn Battuta   *Available on myNGconnect*

• Critical Viewing: NG Chapter Gallery
• On Your Feet: Two Options

CHAPTER 14 REVIEW

STRATEGY ①

Play "ABC Brainstorm"

To elicit prior knowledge before reading, allow students to work in pairs to brainstorm words relating to Africa. Have them begin by making a chart that lists each letter of the alphabet. Tell them to try to list at least one word starting with that letter next to the letter. You may ask students to keep their lists and add words to them as they progress through the lessons.

Use with All Lessons

STRATEGY ②

Preview Text

Help students preview each section in the chapter. For each section, have them read the lesson titles, lesson introductions, Main Idea statements, captions, and section headings. Then have them list the information they expect to find in the text. Have students read a lesson and discuss with a partner what they learned and whether or not it matched their list.

Use with All Lessons

STRATEGY ③

Use a Word Sort Activity

Write these words on the board and ask students to sort them into four groups of three related words each. Then have them use each group of words in a paragraph that shows how they are related.

griot	salt	clay pipes
caravan	iron	trader
trans-Saharan	smelting	gold
commodity	oral tradition	storytelling

Use with All Lessons

Press **mt** *in the Student eEdition for modified text.*

STRATEGY ①

Preview Maps

Preview the maps with students. Explain that maps show different kinds of information. For example, political maps show country boundaries and capitals. Physical maps highlight geographic features such as mountain ranges and bodies of water. Tell students that the maps in Chapter 14 are thematic maps, which show specialized information. Point out that the title of the map and the map legend indicate the type of information shown.

Use with Lessons 1.2 and 2.2 *For Lesson 1.2, have students identify the two main types of information shown on the map (trade routes and commodities). For Lesson 2.2, have students compare the main type of information shown (empires) and contrast it with the area that has a different label in the legend.*

STRATEGY ②

Use Echo Reading

Pair each student with a proficient reader. Have the proficient reader read aloud the Main Idea statement at the beginning of a lesson. Have the student "echo" by reading the same statement. Repeat for all lessons in a section.

Use with All Lessons *Encourage the proficient reader to identify the focus, such as geographic or economic, of each Main Idea.*

STRATEGY ①

Use a Round-Robin Activity

After students have completed a lesson, divide the class into small groups and conduct a round-robin activity to review the factual material students have learned. Write the topic of the lesson on the board and have groups generate facts for about three to five minutes, with all students contributing. Then have one student from each group share the group's responses without repeating any fact already stated by another group. Write the facts on the board.

Use with All Lessons

STRATEGY 2
Use Pronunciation Keys

Preteach the meaning and pronunciation of vocabulary words before beginning each lesson. Give a brief definition or example for each word, and then pronounce it slowly and clearly several times. Have students repeat after you. Then have students create a pronunciation key for each word.

After each lesson, have students write simple sentences using each word (e.g., A *griot* is an African storyteller.) Have students refer to their pronunciation keys to help them say the words correctly.

Use with All Lessons

STRATEGY 3
Pair Partners for Dictation

After students read each lesson in the chapter, have them write a sentence summarizing its main idea. Have students get together in pairs and dictate their sentences to each other. Then have them work together to check the sentences for accuracy and spelling.

Use with All Lessons

GIFTED & TALENTED

STRATEGY 1
Develop a Model

Encourage students to extend their understanding of desertification. Have students study the process of desertification by researching the topic in the library or on the Internet. Then have studetns create a diagram or a 3-D model that illustrates the process. Have students share their findings with the class.

Use with Lesson 1.1 *Have students answer the following: How much larger is the Sahara becoming each year due to desertification? How is desertification affecting Africa's people?*

STRATEGY 2
Act Out a Scene

Have students act out a scene based on Al-Umari's account of Mansa Musa's visit to Cairo (Document One in Lesson 2.5). They should provide costumes and use classroom furniture as a set. After the performance, discuss the attributes portrayed by Mansa Musa, as well as his objectives. Why were his actions considered to be extraordinary?

Use with Lesson 2.5

PRE-AP

STRATEGY 1
Write an Essay

Have students write an essay explaining the impact of the trans-Saharan trade. Copy the following categories on the board and tell students to include them in their essay.

> Economic
>
> Governmental
>
> Intellectual
>
> Linguistic
>
> Religious

Use with All Lessons

STRATEGY 2
Create a Group Presentation

Have students work in small groups to discuss how living in a desert influences the development of a culture. Students should focus on topics such as clothing, housing, food, customs, and livelihoods. Then have groups create a visual report to present to the class. Encourage groups to use visual props such as photos and samples of clothing or food.

Use with Lessons 1.1–2.4 *Have each group assign specific roles to group members, such as researchers and presenters.*

A woman wearing a traditional Songhai headdress poses in front of a decorative curtain in the town of Gao in northern Mali. The Songhai Empire was one of the great trading civilizations that flourished in West Africa between the 10th and 16th centuries A.D.

14

NORTH AND WEST AFRICA

1000 B.C. – A.D. 1500

SECTION 1
NORTH AFRICA

KEY VOCABULARY	NAMES & PLACES
caravan	Berbers
commodity	Djenné
desertification	Sahara
savanna	Timbuktu
scarcity	
trans-Saharan	

SECTION 2
WEST AFRICA

KEY VOCABULARY	NAMES & PLACES
griot	Ghana
iron	Iron Age
mansa	Mali
oral tradition	Mansa Musa
terra cotta	Nok
	Sub-Saharan Africa
	Sundiata Keita

READING STRATEGY

ANALYZE LANGUAGE USE
When you analyze language use, you determine the impact of the language a writer uses. Use a chart like this one to analyze the impact of language in the introductory paragraphs of the lessons in the chapter.

Language Example	What It Suggests

TEACHER BACKGROUND

INTRODUCE THE PHOTOGRAPH

Have students study the photograph. Explain that the traditional headdress and necklace the woman is wearing and the handwork decorating the curtain are reflective of West African culture. Tell students that in this chapter they will learn about factors that contributed to the rise and development of West African empires. **ASK:** Why do people choose to wear traditional clothing? *(Possible response: They are proud of their culture and wish to participate in it.)*

SHARE BACKGROUND

The intricate beadwork displayed in the photograph is just one example of West African bead artistry. West African cultures have used beads as a material of adornment for hundreds of years. African bead makers have traditionally used a variety of materials, including clay, stone, and shells, to produce tiny works of art. The earliest examples of African beads date back to around 10,000 B.C. and were made from ostrich eggshells. Perhaps a lesser-known role of beads in Africa is that of a trade commodity. Glass beads produced in Europe were uncommon in Africa and therefore valued as a means of trade.

DIGITAL RESOURCES myNGconnect.com

TEACHER RESOURCES & ASSESSMENT

 Social Studies Skills Lessons
- Reading: Analyze Language Use
- Writing: Write a Narrative

 Formal Assessment
- Chapter 14 Tests A (on-level) & B (below-level)

ExamView®
One-time Download

A Chapter 14
Answer Key

STUDENT BACKPACK

- **eEdition** (English)
- **eEdition** (Spanish)
- **Handbooks**
- **Online Atlas**

For Chapter 14 Spanish Resources, visit the Teacher Resource Menu page.

INTRODUCE THE ESSENTIAL QUESTION

WHAT IMPACT DID TRADE AND TECHNOLOGY HAVE ON NORTH AND WEST AFRICA?

Four Corner Activity: Effects of Trade and Technology This activity introduces students to four effects of trade and technology on North and West Africa. Post the four signs shown in the list below. Ask students to choose the aspect of trade or technology that they think had the greatest impact on North and West Africa.

A. Geography Trade routes gradually extended across the Sahara.

B. Government Great empires emerged in West Africa, first in Ghana and then in Mali.

C. Technology Iron smelting produced strong tools.

D. Culture Islam spread throughout North and West Africa.

0:15 minutes

INTRODUCE THE READING STRATEGY

ANALYZE LANGUAGE USE

Remind students that analyzing how language is used can help them better understand what they are reading. Model completing the Language Chart by reading the introductory paragraph in Lesson 1.2 and entering the last sentence in the left column. Interpret its meaning in the right column.

Language Example	What It Suggests
The caravan is a merchant's ticket to profit, but first the merchant must survive the journey.	The trip across the Sahara was very dangerous.

INTRODUCE CHAPTER VOCABULARY

KNOWLEDGE RATING

Have students complete a Knowledge-Rating Chart for Key Vocabulary words. Have them list words and fill out the chart. Then have pairs share the definitions they know. Work together as a class to complete the chart.

KEY VOCAB	KNOW IT	NOT SURE	DON'T KNOW	DEFINITION
caravan				
commodity				
desertification				
griot				

KEY DATES	
5300 B.C.	Desertification of the Sahara begins
500 B.C.	Nok begin smelting iron
A.D. 400	Trans-Saharan trade develops
A.D. 500	Ghana emerges as a great trading empire
A.D. 642	Arabs conquer Egypt
A.D. 1076	Almoravids capture Koumbi-Saleh
A.D. 1307	Mansa Musa becomes king of Mali
Early 1900s	Writing down of oral history begins

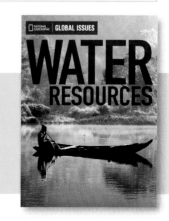

For articles about the importance of water resources in a desert environment, see *GLOBAL ISSUES WATER RESOURCES.*

A Vast and Varied Land

The way that some modern maps are drawn magnifies the size of countries in the Northern Hemisphere. This projection disguises the huge scale of Africa, which is larger than the United States, Europe, Japan, and China combined. North Africa alone is a huge area that includes the Sahara, the world's largest desert.

MAIN IDEA

North Africa has a variety of landforms, including the vast Sahara.

THE LARGEST DESERT IN THE WORLD

The northern part of Africa borders the Mediterranean Sea. (See the map in Lesson 1.2.) At the entrance to the Mediterranean, North Africa lies only ten miles south of Europe. Lining the coast of North Africa are the rugged Atlas Mountains. For centuries, people have lived in villages scattered throughout these mountains.

South of the Atlas Mountains lies the **Sahara**, an important geographic feature of North Africa. Sahara, which means "desert," is the largest desert in the world. It stretches more than 3,000 miles across North Africa, spanning the continent from the Red Sea in the east to the Atlantic

Ocean in the west. Covering 3.5 million square miles, the Sahara is about the size of the continental United States, Alaska, and Hawaii combined. With its hot summers and warm winters, the Sahara is one of the hottest and driest places on Earth.

The Sahara's soaring mountains and vast seas of shifting sand provide a dramatic contrast to the desert's mostly flat and rocky terrain. In addition to the Atlas Mountains, two other mountain ranges, the Ahaggar and Tibesti, rise in the Sahara's interior.

For thousands of years, people found the Sahara almost impossible to cross. As a result, the peoples of North Africa, with their Mediterranean and Southwest Asian influences, developed independently from those living on the rest of the continent.

THE GREEN SAHARA

The hot, dry Sahara seems an unlikely place to find fossils of fish and rock paintings of lakes, forests, and herds of cattle. However, the Sahara has both, which offer clues to its past. The Sahara was not always a desert. Thirty million years ago, the Sahara was an ocean full of fish and whales. Over time, climate change drained the seas to leave lush tropical grasslands called the **savanna**. Many thousands of years ago, the Sahara was green. People farmed there and herded cattle.

Beginning around 5300 B.C., seasonal rains shifted southward. The Sahara's lakes, rivers, and grasslands dried up. As rain became scarce and temperatures soared up to 130°F, the Sahara's fertile soil dried, baked, and became unproductive. This process, called **desertification**, created the desert that exists today.

People and animals began migrating to better land with steady water supplies. Some people moved north, others south. Still others headed east toward the Nile River Valley, where they built one of Africa's greatest civilizations—Egypt, which you learned about in Chapter 4.

+ POSSIBLE RESPONSE

The Niger River would provide a source of irrigation for growing crops, while trees would offer shade from the heat of the day.

Critical Viewing The Gao region of Mali is located in the southern Sahara along the Niger River, shown here. What traits of this area might enable people to live here?

REVIEW & ASSESS

1. **READING CHECK** What major landforms are found in North Africa?

2. **IDENTIFY MAIN IDEAS AND DETAILS** Why did North Africa develop independently from the rest of the African continent?

3. **ANALYZE CAUSE AND EFFECT** What effect did climate change have on the geography and climate of the Sahara?

PLAN

OBJECTIVE

Identify the Sahara and other landforms that characterize North Africa.

CRITICAL THINKING SKILLS FOR LESSON 1.1

- Identify Main Ideas and Details
- Monitor Comprehension
- Analyze Cause and Effect
- Sequence Events

ESSENTIAL QUESTION

What impact did trade and technology have on North and West Africa?

The Sahara is the defining landform in North Africa. Lesson 1.1 describes the Sahara as a basis for understanding the challenges of trade in the region.

BACKGROUND FOR THE TEACHER

North Africa has some of the most extreme topography in the world, including the Sahara. Dry for most of its history, the Sahara undergoes a humid period every 100,000 years. Variations in Earth's tilt and orbit cause changes in how sunlight hits the planet. The humid periods last about 5,000 years, followed by transition back to desert, which is its current state. The challenges of developing trade across this vast desert will be a recurring theme in this chapter.

TEACHER RESOURCES & ASSESSMENT

 Reading and Note-Taking   **Vocabulary Practice**   **Section 1 Quiz**

STUDENT RESOURCES

 NG Chapter Gallery

INTRODUCE & ENGAGE

ACTIVATE PRIOR KNOWLEDGE

Provide each student with a K-W-L Chart like the one below. Have students use their prior knowledge to brainstorm with each other about the physical geography of North Africa. Then ask students to write questions that they would like to have answered as they study the lesson. **0:05** minutes

K What Do I Know?	W What Do I Want To Learn?	L What Did I Learn?

TEACH

GUIDED DISCUSSION

1. **Sequence Events** What was the Sahara like 30 million years ago? How did it transform into what it is today? *(The Sahara was once an ocean. Then climate change drained the ocean and created the savanna. Desertification created the desert that exists today.)*

2. **Analyze Cause and Effect** How did the desertification of the Sahara shape settlement patterns? *(As the Sahara dried out, many of the people living in the Sahara migrated. Some moved north, others south. Those who moved east built Egypt, one of Africa's great civilizations.)*

MORE INFORMATION

Gao The town of Gao, Mali, was one of West Africa's early trading centers. Located on the Niger River, Gao was founded by fishermen who reaped the benefits of the river's bounty. As the trans-Saharan trade developed, Gao became an important stop for trading gold, salt, slaves, and copper. Today Gao serves as a final destination for ships traveling on the Niger River. The river also serves as a source of irrigation for crops such as rice, wheat, and sorghum, from which a syrup is made.

ACTIVE OPTIONS

Critical Viewing: NG Chapter Gallery Invite students to explore the Chapter Gallery to examine the images that relate to this chapter. Have them select one of the images and do additional research to learn more about it. Ask questions that will inspire additional inquiry about the chosen gallery image, such as: What is this? Where and when was this created? By whom? Why was it created? What is it made of? Why does it belong in this chapter? What else would you like to know about it? **0:10** minutes

On Your Feet: Inside-Outside Circle Have students stand in concentric circles facing each other. Students in the outside circle ask questions about North Africa's landforms, and students inside answer. On a signal, students rotate to create new partnerships. On another signal, students trade inside/outside roles. **0:10** minutes

DIFFERENTIATE

GIFTED & TALENTED

Compare Desert Formation Have students conduct Internet research on a desert area that used to be green and lush in the United States or in another country. For example, fossils of rain forest plants have been found in some deserts in the United States. Encourage students to answer the following questions. How does the desert compare with the region at an earlier time? How did scientists learn how the region used to be? Tell students to summarize their findings in a brief report and encourage them to share their reports with the class.

ENGLISH LANGUAGE LEARNERS

Summarize This lesson has seven paragraphs (not including the introductory paragraph). Have students work in pairs and assign each pair one paragraph to read together. Then each pair should summarize their paragraph in one or two sentences. Encourage students to take notes to help them organize the information they encounter in their assigned paragraphs.

Press **mt** *in the Student eEdition for modified text.*

See the Chapter Planner for more strategies for differentiation.

REVIEW & ASSESS

ANSWERS

1. The Atlas Mountains, the Sahara, and the Ahaggar and Tibesti mountains are major landforms of North Africa.

2. North Africa developed independently because the Sahara cut it off from the rest of continent.

3. Climate change caused the Sahara's lakes, rivers, and grasslands to dry up and the soil to become unproductive.

Trans-Saharan Trade

The camel caravan snakes back and forth for miles across the desert. Thousands of camels trudge surefooted across the Saharan sand despite being loaded down with Mediterranean goods for trade. The caravan is a merchant's ticket to profit, but first the merchant must survive the journey.

MAIN IDEA

As North Africa developed a strong economy, trade between native and foreign communities brought the riches of the Sahara to Europe.

BERBER TRADERS

Trade in North Africa began with the **Berbers**. They were native to the region, and they lived in communities spread throughout areas in present-day Egypt, Libya, Tunisia, Algeria, and Morocco. Most Berbers farmed or herded cattle. Others lived as desert nomads or dwelled in the mountains. Despite these differences, they shared a broad Berber culture.

Around 800 B.C., the Phoenicians and Greeks arrived in North Africa and founded cities on the coast. The Phoenicians used these cities as staging areas for trade with Spain. One such city, Carthage, increasingly controlled Berber lands and peoples. Numidia, an early Berber kingdom, reacted to this invasion by helping the Romans overthrow Carthage.

Although clashes between Berbers and foreign rulers continued, trade relationships developed between the people of the desert and the people of the North African coast. The Berbers took an active role in this trade. Traveling along routes in the Sahara, they transported slaves, salt, semiprecious stones, and other goods for the Mediterranean market. In exchange, they received food, cloth, horses, weapons, and other manufactured goods.

A DIFFICULT PASSAGE

Carrying goods on trade routes in the desert was difficult and dangerous. Historians believe that around A.D. 300, the introduction of camels began to transform trade in North Africa, and the animals started to make large-scale **trans-Saharan** trade possible. That is, trade now crossed the Sahara. Camels were able to carry heavy loads over long distances and difficult terrain. They also needed little food and water.

Many independent merchants sought safety in numbers by traveling in a group called a camel **caravan**. Caravans had hundreds or even thousands of camels. Led by highly paid Berber guides, caravans would set off from North African cities and head into the Sahara. To avoid the worst of the desert heat, caravans only traveled in winter and most often at night.

Few merchants crossed the entire Sahara. Instead they exchanged their goods at an oasis, where they could find water. From there, other merchants would take the goods to the next oasis, and so on across the desert. In this way, trade routes connecting North and West Africa developed across the Sahara. The oases grew into towns and cities that became wealthy as centers of trade. However, the dangers of caravan travel remained. The possibility of dying from getting lost or from being caught in a sandstorm was just as real as the threat of attack by desert nomads. Trans-Saharan trade was a risky business.

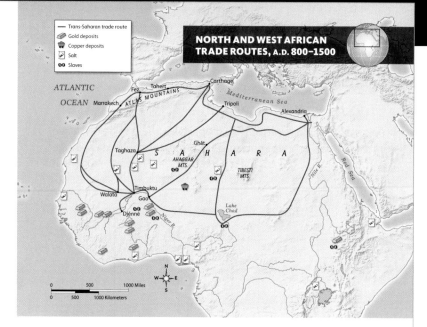

NORTH AND WEST AFRICAN TRADE ROUTES, A.D. 800–1500

- Trans-Saharan trade route
- Gold deposits
- Copper deposits
- Salt
- Slaves

TODAY'S MOUNTAIN BERBERS

Berbers now living in urban areas often lose touch with their traditions. However, the way of life of Berbers living in the Atlas Mountains of North Africa has remained basically unchanged for centuries.

Mountain Berber homes are simple structures of stone and wood. The ground floor is most often a stable, perhaps housing a cow or a few chickens. Their owners occupy the floor above. Instead of power tools, farmers use scythes and other hand tools. They plow using mules and harvest by hand.

Although mountain Berbers see few strangers, they are friendly and hospitable. They often greet Westerners with the ancient term *Arrumi*, meaning "Roman."

REVIEW & ASSESS

1. **READING CHECK** What was trans-Saharan trade?

2. **FORM AND SUPPORT OPINIONS** Was travel by caravan worth the risk? Support your opinion.

3. **INTERPRET MAPS** What valuable goods were exchanged on the trans-Saharan trade routes?

PLAN

OBJECTIVE

Summarize the development of trade in North Africa and across the Sahara.

CRITICAL THINKING SKILLS FOR LESSON 1.2

- Identify Main Ideas and Details
- Monitor Comprehension
- Form and Support Opinions
- Interpret Maps
- Synthesize
- Summarize

ESSENTIAL QUESTION

What impact did trade and technology have on North and West Africa?

Trade relationships developed between cultures on the North African coast and in the desert. Lesson 1.2 discusses how trans-Saharan trade became possible.

BACKGROUND FOR THE TEACHER

Prior to its downfall at the hands of the Romans, the ancient city of Carthage was one of the world's richest cities, mostly as a result of trade. Carthage traded in perishable goods, such as textiles and foodstuffs. Like other cities located on North Africa's Mediterranean coast, Carthage became an important location on trans-Saharan trade routes. Carthage and the Mediterranean cities of Alexandria and Tripoli were shipping ports that made it possible to extend North African trade to Europe.

DIGITAL RESOURCES myNGconnect.com

TEACHER RESOURCES & ASSESSMENT

 Reading and Note-Taking

 Vocabulary Practice

 Section 1 Quiz

STUDENT RESOURCES

 Active History

PROFILE A TRADE ROUTE

Tell students to imagine that they are traveling across the Sahara on a camel caravan. Have them brainstorm and list the sights they might see and the experiences they might have. Encourage them to include the physical environment, the advantages of camel travel, and the potential rewards and dangers of the trip. **0:05 minutes**

TEACH

GUIDED DISCUSSION

1. **Synthesize** What role did camels and oases play in the development of trans-Saharan trade? *(Camels were able to cross the desert carrying heavy loads. Caravans of camels enabled merchants to travel the desert in groups. Oases served as points for the exchange of goods so that merchants could trade without traveling an entire route.)*

2. **Summarize** How did Berbers contribute to the development of trade? *(Berbers transported goods for the Mediterranean market. They guided caravans into the Sahara.)* How did Berbers benefit from trade? *(Berbers received trade goods and were well paid as guides.)*

INTERPRET MAPS

Direct students' attention to the North and West African Trade Routes map in Lesson 1.2. Direct them to consider the size and location of the Sahara. **ASK:** Based on what you notice on the map and what you have read in the text, how might the size and location of the Sahara have made trade difficult? *(Responses will vary, but students should note that the vast expanse of the Sahara coupled with intense heat and sparse settlement would have made trade difficult and dangerous.)* Tell students to identify three cities on the Mediterranean that served as trade route destinations. They should also identify centers of trade and nearby resources within the Sahara. **0:10 minutes**

ACTIVE OPTIONS

Active History: Map Historic Trade Routes Extend the lesson by using either the PDF or Whiteboard version of the activity. These activities take a deeper look at a topic from, or related to, the lesson. Explore the activities as a class, turn them into group assignments, or even assign them individually. **0:15 minutes**

On Your Feet: Create a Concept Web Have students form groups of three around a section of a bulletin board or a table. Provide each group with a large sheet of paper. Have group members take turns contributing a concept or phrase to a Concept Web with the words *Trans-Saharan Trade* at the center. When time for the activity has elapsed, call on volunteers from each group to share their webs. **0:10 minutes**

STRIVING READERS

Complete Sentence Starters Provide these sentence starters for students to complete after reading. You may also have students preview to set a purpose for reading.

- The people who began trade in North Africa were the _____.

- The animals that helped make trans-Saharan trade possible were _____.

- *Caravan* means _____.

- Two dangers of caravan travel were _____ and _____.

INCLUSION

Identify Compass Points Have students of different abilities pair up, and make a simple line drawing of a compass rose with the words *North, South, East, West* written at the appropriate points. Have students use the drawing to help them identify the correct directions in statements such as these related to the map in Lesson 1.2: Alexandria is (*east*) of Tripoli. The Nile River is (*west*) of the Red Sea.

Press **mt** *in the Student eEdition for modified text.*

See the Chapter Planner for more strategies for differentiation.

ANSWERS

1. Trans-Saharan trade was trade that crossed the Sahara.

2. Possible response: Travel by caravan was worth the risk when it led to the acquisition of wealth.

3. Gold, copper, salt, and slaves were valuable goods exchanged on the trans-Saharan trade routes.

Gold, Salt,
and Slaves

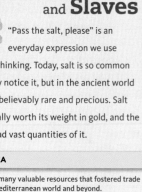

"Pass the salt, please" is an everyday expression we use without thinking. Today, salt is so common we hardly notice it, but in the ancient world it was unbelievably rare and precious. Salt was literally worth its weight in gold, and the Sahara had vast quantities of it.

MAIN IDEA

Africa had many valuable resources that fostered trade with the Mediterranean world and beyond.

Critical Viewing A camel caravan moves through the desert. What does the image show about how camels are useful to traders?

➕ POSSIBLE RESPONSE

Camels are useful to traders because they serve as pack animals and carry large loads.

PRECIOUS RESOURCES

SALT

Too much salt is unhealthy, but a limited amount is crucial to a healthy body.

Salt assists in hydration, circulation, muscle contraction, and digestion. It's important to replace salt lost through perspiration.

Two of Africa's most valuable **commodities**, or trade goods, were gold and salt. Beginning in the 400s, these goods were traded for hundreds of years. The Western Sudan, the name for all of northern Africa west of Lake Chad, was especially rich in gold deposits.

Each year, perhaps a ton of gold crossed the Sahara, finding its way to Europe and Asia. African gold stimulated the flow of silk from China and spices from India. European kings used African gold to make coins.

Salt was worth almost as much as gold. Before there were refrigerators to keep food cold, people used salt to preserve meat and other foods. In some areas of the world, preservation with salt is still practiced. In much of the ancient world, salt was rare. Its **scarcity**, or small supply, made salt valuable. Africa, though, had large salt deposits, thanks to the Sahara. The desert had once been a shallow sea. As its waters dried up, salt deposits were left, especially in western Africa. Laborers extracted, or dug out, 200-pound slabs of salt, which they carved into blocks. Camels carried salt blocks hundreds of miles to be traded at a huge profit.

AFRICAN SLAVE TRADE

The labor needed for mining gold and salt came largely from slaves, who were traded across the desert beginning in the 600s. Like the Atlantic slave trade that would emerge in the 1500s, the trans-Saharan slave trade was a harsh and horrible business. Most slaves came from the Niger Delta region. (See the map in Lesson 1.2.) Once captured, they were chained together and forcibly marched through the desert.

The slave trade increased dramatically when Muslim traders arrived in North Africa in the 600s. However, the desert's vast expanse always limited the slave trade. Many slaves died during the terrible journey. The survivors were exchanged for trade goods, especially horses. A good horse was extremely valuable in the desert and cost a large number of slaves.

While some slaves were sold for labor, others satisfied a growing demand for slaves in the Mediterranean world. There, slaves were likely to become domestic servants, soldiers, artisans, or even important government officials. Nonetheless, these people had been taken from their families and cruelly treated, with little hope of ever returning home. It was a particularly brutal aspect of Africa's history.

REVIEW & ASSESS

1. **READING CHECK** Why were salt and gold such valuable resources?

2. **SEQUENCE EVENTS** What happened to greatly increase the slave trade?

3. **IDENTIFY MAIN IDEAS AND DETAILS** According to the text, what happened to slaves who reached North Africa?

PLAN

OBJECTIVE

Analyze the importance of gold, salt, and slaves as commodities of trade.

CRITICAL THINKING SKILLS FOR LESSON 1.3

- Identify Main Ideas and Details
- Monitor Comprehension
- Sequence Events
- Analyze Cause and Effect
- Draw Conclusions
- Make Predictions

ESSENTIAL QUESTION

What impact did trade and technology have on North and West Africa?

Trade increased the demand for gold, salt, and slaves in North and West Africa. Lesson 1.3 discusses the sources and demand for these commodities.

BACKGROUND FOR THE TEACHER

Gold was a desirable trading commodity for a number of reasons. Gold was minted into coins and used to finance trading caravans. In time, the kingdom of Ghana, which arose in West Africa, became known as the "Land of Gold." The geographer al-Bakri described an 11th-century court in Ghana where gold was used on everything from embroidered caps to swords and dog collars. To enhance gold's value, Ghanian rulers attempted to keep the sources of their gold a secret.

DIGITAL RESOURCES myNGconnect.com

TEACHER RESOURCES & ASSESSMENT

 Reading and Note-Taking

 Vocabulary Practice

 Section 1 Quiz

STUDENT RESOURCES

 NG Chapter Gallery

EXPLORE USES OF SALT

Have students work in teams to brainstorm ways in which salt is important to individuals and communities, both today and in the past. Provide each team with an Idea Web and have them list specific uses of salt. **ASK:** Why do you think salt was such an important trade commodity prior to the invention of refrigeration? *(Salt was used to preserve food.)* **0:05 minutes**

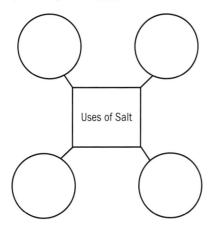

Uses of Salt

TEACH

GUIDED DISCUSSION

1. **Analyze Cause and Effect** How did abundant resources in West Africa help shape the nature of trans-Saharan trade? *(West Sudan had rich deposits of gold that it was able to trade for other commodities. Western Africa had large salt deposits that could be mined and sold to people who lived in regions where salt was scarce. Both gold and salt mines required labor, which resulted in a demand for slaves.)*

2. **Draw Conclusions** How might scarcity increase the value of a commodity such as salt or gold? *(When people need a commodity that is scarce or in short supply, they generally bid to obtain it, which drives up the price.)*

MAKE PREDICTIONS

Tell students that in some areas of Africa, laborers still use traditional methods in the salt flats. They extract the salt by hand and deliver it to market using camels. Have students consider how modern technologies, such as the building of roads or mechanized excavators, might affect workers who use traditional means of mining and transportation. **0:10 minutes**

ACTIVE OPTIONS

Critical Viewing: NG Chapter Gallery Invite students to explore the NG Chapter Gallery and create a list of favorites by choosing the images they find the most interesting. Then encourage them to select the image they like best and do further research on it. **0:10 minutes**

On Your Feet: Card Response Divide the class in half and then have one half write ten true-false questions about the commodities of gold, salt, and slaves. Have the other half create answer cards, writing "True" on one side and "False" on the other side. Students from the first group take turns asking their questions. Students from the second group hold up their cards, showing either "True" or "False." **0:15 minutes**

STRIVING READERS

Summarize Have students work in pairs or small groups to read the lesson and then create a 5Ws Chart like the one shown below. Have the pairs or groups share their charts with the others and add any important information they missed to their own charts.

What?
Who?
Where?
When?
Why?

Press **mt** *in the Student eEdition for modified text.*

See the Chapter Planner for more strategies for differentiation.

ANSWERS

1. Both salt and gold were used in trade to obtain other commodities. Salt was needed to preserve meat and other foods.

2. The arrival of Muslim traders in North Africa greatly increased the slave trade.

3. Slaves who reached North Africa often became domestic servants, soldiers, artisans, or government officials.

1.4

Islam Spreads to Africa

The mighty Muslim general Uqba fought his way across North Africa during the A.D. 600s. After his great triumphs, he rode his horse into the Atlantic Ocean, saying, "Oh God, if the sea had not prevented me, I would have galloped on forever . . . upholding your faith and fighting the unbelievers." Such determination helped assure the place of Islam in Africa.

MAIN IDEA

Islam spread through North and West Africa, affecting African culture.

MALI'S ANCIENT MANUSCRIPTS

Timbuktu and Djenné are home to hundreds of thousands of manuscripts dating back to the 1100s. These handwritten works contain invaluable insight into the history of Africa and Islam.

CONQUEST AND TRADE

After the prophet Muhammad's death in A.D. 632, Islam spread from its origins on the Arabian Peninsula to many other parts of the world. By 642, Arab armies had conquered Egypt. Over the next several centuries, Muslims would spread Islam throughout North and West Africa. At first, few Berbers converted to Islam, but eventually many did so. In time, most North Africans were Muslim. During the 1000s and the 1100s, first the Almoravids (al-muh-RAH-vuhdz) and then the Almohads (al-muh-HAHDZ) founded Berber dynasties that united northwestern Africa.

When the Arabs invaded North Africa, trans-Saharan trade with West Africa expanded greatly. Using camel caravans, Berber merchants carried their goods and religion across the Sahara. Many West African merchants saw a trading advantage and converted to Islam.

By the 1000s, West African rulers also began to convert to Islam, as did some of their subjects. Others continued their traditional beliefs, sometimes mixing them with Islamic practices. Muslim merchants established Islam as far away as the East African coast. By 1500, Islam had spread across North Africa, West Africa, and along the coast of East Africa.

THE IMPACT OF ISLAM

As Islam spread, so did Islamic culture. By the 1300s, Muslim leaders ruled several empires, and mosques were common in North and West Africa. Traditional mosque architecture was cleverly adapted to Africa's climate and materials. Builders used mud and even salt blocks. They created impressive buildings like the mud-built mosque in **Djenné** (jeh-NAY), shown opposite. Builders also designed rectangular mud-brick houses with flat roofs.

The Arabic language also spread. Literacy increased through the teaching of the Qur'an, and mosques became important centers of learning. Scholarship thrived. Cities like **Timbuktu** and Djenné became famous centers for Muslim art, literature, and science. Scholars in Timbuktu collected and wrote down Islamic teachings in many fields of knowledge, including astronomy, medicine, law, and mathematics.

+ POSSIBLE RESPONSE

The mosque appears to be made of earth, with wooden beams sticking out of some of its walls. Tops of the walls are adorned with features that point skyward.

Critical Viewing The Great Mosque of Djenné, Mali, is an architectural wonder. What distinctive features does the image show?

REVIEW & ASSESS

1. **READING CHECK** How did Islam spread throughout North and West Africa?

2. **MAKE INFERENCES** Why might West African merchants have viewed conversion to Islam as a trading advantage?

3. **ANALYZE LANGUAGE USE** How does the phrase "cleverly adapted" help explain the use of traditional mosque architecture in Africa?

418 CHAPTER 14

419

PLAN

OBJECTIVE

Explain how Islam spread throughout North and West Africa.

CRITICAL THINKING SKILLS FOR LESSON 1.4

- Identify Main Ideas and Details
- Monitor Comprehension
- Make Inferences
- Analyze Language Use
- Identify
- Make Predictions
- Analyze Visuals

ESSENTIAL QUESTION

What impact did trade and technology have on North and West Africa?

As trade continued to grow throughout North and West Africa, so did Islam. Lesson 1.4 discusses the cultural impact of Islam on the region.

BACKGROUND FOR THE TEACHER

Market days in the square of the Great Mosque of Djenné are a common occurrence. Vendors sell everything from cattle and vegetables to household goods. Much in the tradition of trans-Saharan trade, sellers and buyers negotiate for the price of goods. Since 1240, a mosque has always stood on the site. The current mosque, completed in 1907, was built entirely of mud. It replaced an earlier mosque that had fallen into disrepair. Each year the entire community gathers to make repairs and maintain the current structure.

DIGITAL RESOURCES myNGconnect.com

TEACHER RESOURCES & ASSESSMENT

 Reading and Note-Taking

 Vocabulary Practice

 Section 1 Quiz

STUDENT RESOURCES

 NG Chapter Gallery

INTRODUCE & ENGAGE

THINK, PAIR, SHARE

Have students work in pairs to brainstorm reasons that the people of a region might decide to change their religious identities. Members of each pair should think about the idea separately at first and then discuss their different ideas. Tell them to develop a final list of reasons and then invite one member from each pair to share those ideas with the class. **0:10** minutes

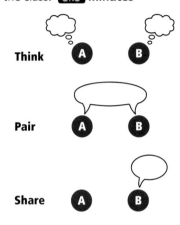

Think **A** **B**

Pair **A** **B**

Share **A** **B**

TEACH

GUIDED DISCUSSION

1. **Identify** What outside influence affected the culture of North and West Africa? What areas of culture were affected? *(Islam greatly influenced the culture of North and West Africa. Islam influenced religion, architecture, language, literacy, and the fields of art and science.)*

2. **Make Predictions** Without Arab influence, how might the history of North and West Africa have been different? *(Islam might not have become a major religion. The Arabic language would not have become widespread. Culture would have developed differently.)*

ANALYZE VISUALS

Have students examine the photograph of the Great Mosque of Djenné. Direct them to make inferences about how members of the community incorporate their cultural heritage into their daily lives. Tell them to think about elements in the photograph that might be historic, modern, or both. **0:10** minutes

ACTIVE OPTIONS

Critical Viewing: NG Chapter Gallery Have students explore the NG Chapter Gallery and choose two of the items to compare and contrast, either in written form or verbally with a partner. Ask questions that will inspire this process, such as: How are these images alike? How are they different? Why did you select these two items? How do they relate in history? **0:10** minutes

On Your Feet: Traveling Around the World Have two students stand in a corner of the room. Ask them a question about the lesson. Whoever first answers the question correctly becomes the "traveler" and moves to another corner to stand with a new partner, while the first partner sits down. Repeat the process. A traveler who correctly answers one question in each corner has gone "around the world." **0:15** minutes

DIFFERENTIATE

ENGLISH LANGUAGE LEARNERS

Identify Main Ideas and Details Have students work in pairs and assign each pair a paragraph from the lesson. Have them use a chart like the one shown to identify key details in their paragraph. Then tell them to work together to write the main idea based on those details. Have pairs practice their pronunciation by reading the details and main idea sentences aloud.

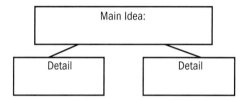

GIFTED & TALENTED

Create Models Have students work in pairs to create a model of the Great Mosque or another mosque in Mali. Tell them to conduct Internet research to locate images and information on the structure. Suggest building materials such as paper, cardboard, or clay. Encourage students to label and display their models once they have completed them.

Press **mt** *in the Student eEdition for modified text.*

See the Chapter Planner for more strategies for differentiation.

REVIEW & ASSESS

ANSWERS

1. After the Arabs invaded North Africa, Berber merchants began converting to Islam. Then West African rulers and merchants also began converting to Islam.

2. Having the same religion as Berber merchants might facilitate trade.

3. It explains that builders considered the effects of climate and used local materials to create structures in a traditional style.

NOK TERRA COTTA SCULPTURES

These heads were sculpted out of terra cotta by the Nok. The first such head was discovered in the small Nigerian town of Nok in 1943. Some archaeologists think the heads were once attached to bodies sculpted in standing, sitting, or kneeling positions.

2.1 Nok Culture and Iron Technology

You put more wood into the blazing furnace and blow into it through long clay tubes. The injection of air makes the fire burn even hotter, and your body is almost scalded by the heat. But the results will be worth it when you succeed in extracting precious iron from rock.

MAIN IDEA

The Nok developed art forms and iron tools that brought great changes to West Africa.

THE NOK

West Africa juts out like the hump of a camel into the Atlantic Ocean. The region is part of **Sub-Saharan Africa**, which stretches south of the Sahara to the southern tip of the continent.

The **Nok** people settled in what is now the country of Nigeria. (See the map in Lesson 2.2.) Around 500 B.C., the Nok were among the first in West Africa to make tools from **iron**, a metal that is found in rock.

Nok artists also used **terra cotta**, which is fire-baked clay, to create unusual sculptures of humans. The sculpted heads of Nok figures, which are about 12 inches high and cone-shaped, are all that remain. These sculptures are the oldest known figurative sculptures south of the Sahara. They have elaborate hairstyles, triangular eyes, oversized features, and exaggerated expressions. This style heavily influenced West African art for centuries.

AFRICA'S IRON AGE

What archaeologists call the **Iron Age** was an important period during which the use of superior iron tools and weapons began and spread. The Nok were probably the first sub-Saharan people to smelt iron. They may have developed smelting independently or learned it through contact with other cultures.

Smelting is the process used to extract iron from a type of rock called iron ore. Using extraordinarily high temperatures, the iron is literally melted out of the rock. The Nok built clay furnaces with two chambers, one for the fire and the other for the ore. Smelters used clay pipes to blow air into the fire and increase its heat. Then they drained the liquid iron into stone molds to make strong iron tools and weapons.

The Nok used iron axes, picks, and hoes to clear huge areas of land for farming. With an increased food supply, the population grew.

At its peak, Nok culture covered about 350,000 square miles. However, deforestation, or cutting down forests, damaged the local ecosystem. At the same time, overuse made the soil infertile. Due to these geographic changes, Nok culture declined after about A.D. 200.

REVIEW & ASSESS

1. **READING CHECK** What Nok developments brought change to West Africa?

2. **ANALYZE CAUSE AND EFFECT** How did the use of iron tools affect Nok culture?

3. **DRAW CONCLUSIONS** How did the Nok use raw materials to advance their culture?

PLAN

OBJECTIVE

Identify and explain the importance of terra cotta and iron smelting to Nok civilization.

CRITICAL THINKING SKILLS FOR LESSON 2.1

- Identify Main Ideas and Details
- Monitor Comprehension
- Analyze Cause and Effect
- Draw Conclusions
- Evaluate
- Sequence Events

ESSENTIAL QUESTION

What impact did trade and technology have on North and West Africa?

The Nok people of West Africa were probably the first culture to smelt iron. Lesson 2.1 discusses how this technology affected the Nok.

BACKGROUND FOR THE TEACHER

Archaeologists have discovered examples of Nok terra cotta sculpture over a wide range of what is today Nigeria. Bernard Fagg, the first archaeologist to discover Nok sculpture, learned that people in the region had been finding fragments for years. Fagg used carbon dating of plant material embedded in the terra cotta and determined that the sculptures dated from 500 B.C. to A.D. 200. At one site, the archaeologist found iron furnaces with terra cotta figures both in and around the furnaces. Carbon analysis of the site revealed bits of charcoal that date from 280 B.C. Fagg concluded that the terra cotta objects were sacred and believed their purpose was to aid in the smelting.

DIGITAL RESOURCES myNGconnect.com

TEACHER RESOURCES & ASSESSMENT

 Reading and Note-Taking

 Vocabulary Practice

 Section 2 Quiz

STUDENT RESOURCES

 NG Chapter Gallery

INTRODUCE & ENGAGE

ACTIVATE PRIOR KNOWLEDGE

Ask students to consider how advances in technology can affect a culture. Have them consider, for example, how advances in agriculture technology might affect a population. Tell them to consider both positive and negative aspects of farming technology. *(The use of new and better fertilizers may result in greater food production but may also damage the soil.)* Tell students they will learn how a different technological advance—smelting iron ore—affected the Nok. **0:10** minutes

TEACH

GUIDED DISCUSSION

1. **Identify Main Ideas and Details** What was a key development in Nok technology? *(iron smelting)* How did this technology result in a population increase? *(Iron tools enabled the Nok to clear more land for farming. The increased supply of food led to a population increase.)*

2. **Evaluate** Was the creation of iron tools of benefit to the Nok or did it prove to be a disadvantage? *(At first it was beneficial because the use of iron farming tools resulted in the clearing of more land on which to raise food. Later, it was a disadvantage, because the clearing of so much land resulted in deforestation and poor soil.)*

SEQUENCE EVENTS

As a class, review the events that enabled the development of iron technology. Have one or two volunteers track the class responses on the board. Work toward the sequence below. **ASK:** What does this sequence of events demonstrate? *(The development of a technology can impact the surrounding environment.)* **0:10** minutes

smelting iron tools ⟶ land cleared for agriculture ⟶ population grows ⟶ deforestation ⟶ population declines

ACTIVE OPTIONS

Critical Viewing: NG Chapter Gallery Ask students to choose one image from the Chapter Gallery and become an expert on it. They should do additional research to learn all about it. Then, students should share their findings with a partner, small group, or the class. **0:10** minutes

On Your Feet: One-on-One Interviews Group students in pairs. Have each pair write three questions about Nok culture and technology based on the information they learned in Lesson 2.1. Have students conduct interviews with each other as if on a talk news show and then have them take questions from the "audience." Students' answers should demonstrate an understanding of Nok sculpture and iron technology. **0:20** minutes

DIFFERENTIATE

STRIVING READERS

Strengthen Vocabulary Ask students to write the words *terra cotta* in a Word Square and then write its definition and characteristics. Have students provide examples and non-examples of it. After students complete the Word Square, ask them to create a Word Square for the word *smelting*.

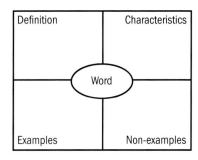

Definition	Characteristics
	Word
Examples	Non-examples

PRE-AP

Create a Presentation Imagine that you are the first to discover a Nok sculptured head. Conduct Internet research to learn about this discovery. Use the information to create a presentation to share with the class. Include when, where, and how you found the artifact. Explain your initial reaction to the discovery and include details about the site and any associated discoveries.

Press **mt** *in the Student eEdition for modified text.*

See the Chapter Planner for more strategies for differentiation.

REVIEW & ASSESS

ANSWERS

1. Iron smelting and the clearing of land brought change to West Africa.

2. Iron tools enabled the Nok to clear land to grow more food. As a result, the Nok population expanded.

3. The Nok used clay to create a distinctive form of sculpture.

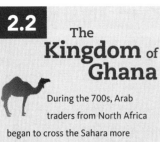

The Kingdom of Ghana

During the 700s, Arab traders from North Africa began to cross the Sahara more frequently. When they reached West Africa, they talked glowingly of a "land of gold," where the king wore a hat made of gold and the horses were draped in stunning gold cloth. This was the land of Ghana, and for centuries, it was the wealthiest kingdom in West Africa.

MAIN IDEA

Trade, especially in gold, spurred the development of the powerful kingdom of Ghana in West Africa.

A KINGDOM OF GOLD

South of the Sahara was a region of grasslands that was ideally suited for agriculture. Iron tools helped the farmers grow more food, which fed more people and allowed the population to increase. The people lived in villages, each of which had its own chief. Over time, the villages banded together to form the kingdom of **Ghana**.

By A.D. 500, Ghana had become the first great trading state in West Africa. Traders arrived there bringing salt and other commodities. The capital of Ghana,

Koumbi-Saleh (KUHM-bee SAHL-uh), stood midway between Africa's main sources of salt, most of which were in the Sahara, and West Africa's gold mines, which Ghana controlled. This control and a favorable location made Ghana's traders the ideal middlemen for trans-Saharan trade. (Middlemen are people who buy goods from one person and sell them to another.) The trade brought Ghana's traders wealth and power.

Ghana's kings made their money by taxing salt and other trade goods as they entered and departed Ghana. Ghana's rulers also strictly controlled the flow of gold. All gold nuggets automatically belonged to the king, and only gold dust could be traded. These rules ensured that gold remained scarce, which kept gold prices high. Trade goods also included textiles, weapons, horses, and even bananas. As trans-Saharan trade expanded, caravans carrying goods grew longer, sometimes numbering several hundred camels.

THE COMING OF ISLAM

Like all societies, Ghana was affected by outside influences. During the 700s, Arab traders brought Islam and Islamic laws to West Africa. Traders and others learned to speak and write in Arabic. Up to that point, people living in West Africa had not had a written language.

Around 1050, the Almoravids, whom you learned about earlier in this chapter, attacked Ghana and tried to force the leaders to become Muslims. The leaders fought back, but they had been greatly weakened by constant war. In 1076, the Almoravids captured Koumbi-Saleh.

In addition, Ghana's soil was worn out and could no longer support the population. By the early 1200s, Ghana's traders and farmers were migrating to richer lands to the south and west. The kingdom of Ghana had come to an end. However, Ghana's "land of gold" had played a major role in the development of trade and civilization in West Africa.

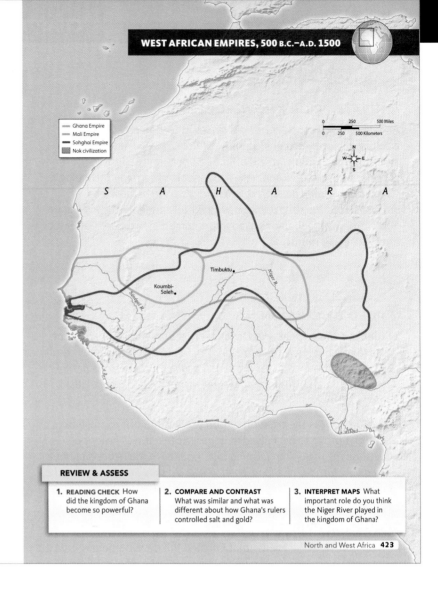

WEST AFRICAN EMPIRES, 500 B.C.–A.D. 1500

Ghana Empire
Mali Empire
Songhai Empire
Nok civilization

SAHARA

Timbuktu
Koumbi-Saleh
Niger R.
Senegal R.

REVIEW & ASSESS

1. **READING CHECK** How did the kingdom of Ghana become so powerful?

2. **COMPARE AND CONTRAST** What was similar and what was different about how Ghana's rulers controlled salt and gold?

3. **INTERPRET MAPS** What important role do you think the Niger River played in the kingdom of Ghana?

PLAN

OBJECTIVE

Describe the rise of the kingdom of Ghana and the events that led to its decline.

Trade was a key factor in Ghana's development as a powerful empire. Lesson 2.2 discusses how trade and other influences affected the kingdom of Ghana.

CRITICAL THINKING SKILLS FOR LESSON 2.2

- Identify Main Ideas and Details
- Monitor Comprehension
- Compare and Contrast
- Interpret Maps
- Analyze Cause and Effect
- Draw Conclusions

BACKGROUND FOR THE TEACHER

Although their names are the same, the kingdom of Ghana and the modern nation called Ghana are only slightly related. The Ghana Empire was located about 400 miles northwest of present-day Ghana. The origins of Ghana are somewhat murky, although one prominent theory is that a number of Soninke clans united under a single ruler who was considered to be semi-divine. The clans may have united to withstand attacks from nomads seeking new territory. Thanks largely to Arab writers, the kingdom's wealth is well documented.

ESSENTIAL QUESTION

What impact did trade and technology have on North and West Africa?

DIGITAL RESOURCES myNGconnect.com

TEACHER RESOURCES & ASSESSMENT

 Reading and Note-Taking

 Vocabulary Practice

 Section 2 Quiz

STUDENT RESOURCES

 NG Chapter Gallery

INTRODUCE & ENGAGE

CITE ADVANTAGES AND DISADVANTAGES

Pose this situation to students: A religious army has invaded a wealthy kingdom. Have students form teams and have each team brainstorm the advantages and disadvantages that each side in the conflict would have. After a few minutes of brainstorming, make a list of students' ideas. Revisit the list after reading the chapter and apply it to the Almoravids' attack on Ghana. Point out the disadvantages that Ghana experienced relative to the attack. **0:10** minutes

TEACH

GUIDED DISCUSSION

1. **Analyze Cause and Effect** What was one effect of Ghana taxing the gold and salt trade? *(Ghana became wealthy from taxing trade within its borders.)*

2. **Draw Conclusions** In addition to spreading Islam, how might Arabs have affected the culture of Ghana? *(Arabs brought Islamic law. Traders and others learned to speak and write in Arabic.)*

INTERPRET MAPS

Have students examine the map of West African empires. Tell them to notice how the empires largely overlap one another and have them draw conclusions about which empire developed first, second, and last. Tell them that the two cities on the map were capitals of one or more empires and have them identify the empire or empires to which each belonged. **0:10** minutes

ACTIVE OPTIONS

NG Learning Framework: Learn About the Nok and the Berbers

ATTITUDE: **Curiosity**
KNOWLEDGE: **Our Human Story**

Have students revisit Lessons 1.2 and 2.1, specifically the information about the Berbers and the Nok. They should work in pairs to create a list of observations about the Berber people and the Nok and how the lives of each were impacted by their environment and nature. Once they have completed their list of observations, each pair should exchange lists with another pair and discuss the new list. **0:10** minutes

On Your Feet: Stage a Quiz Show Have each student write one question about the kingdom of Ghana. Then have groups of five students take turns coming to the front of the class to take part in a quiz. Pose a few of the questions to each group. Students should signal their readiness to answer by raising their hands. **0:20** minutes

DIFFERENTIATE

INCLUSION

Work in Pairs Pair special needs students with students at a higher proficiency level or with a teacher's aide. Have students trace the boundaries of each West African empire and also identify the Nok civilization. Have students count the empires. Make sure they understand the difference between an empire, where one country or kingdom rules others, and a civilization.

STRIVING READERS

Pose and Answer Questions Have students work in pairs to read the lesson. Instruct them to pause after each paragraph and ask one another *who, what, when, where,* or *why* questions about what they have just read. Advise students to read more slowly and focus on specific details if they have difficulty answering the questions or to reread a paragraph to find the answers.

Press **mt** *in the Student eEdition for modified text.*

See the Chapter Planner for more strategies for differentiation.

REVIEW & ASSESS

ANSWERS

1. Ghana became powerful through trade.

2. Ghana's rulers controlled trade of both salt and gold. They controlled gold by controlling the mines and salt by taxing it.

3. It was a natural barrier to Ghana's south and a mode of transportation and trade to other regions.

2.3

The Empire of Mali

"This man flooded Cairo with his [gifts]. He left no . . . holder of a royal office without the gift of a load of gold." This man, Mansa Musa, gave away so much gold that it led to a decline in the precious metal's value and ruined the Egyptian economy! African kings could grow unbelievably rich.

MAIN IDEA

Like Ghana, the powerful empire of Mali was built on trade and gold.

Most people lived in houses made of brick. Living quarters were dark and stuffy.

The Great Mosque, built by Mansa Musa after his pilgrimage to Mecca, had enough prayer space for 2,000 people.

Approximately 25,000 students were taught at the city's 180 schools and 3 universities.

A traveler's inn, or funduq, provided food and water for merchants and their animals.

Camel caravans brought goods such as salt, cloth, copper, and books to trade for gold.

THE EMERGENCE OF MALI

When Ghana declined in the 1200s, it left West Africa without a major power. Then a new power arose—the empire of **Mali**. Like Ghana, Mali built its wealth on gold, but it also boasted great achievements in culture and the arts. Word of Mali's achievements reached as far as Europe.

Located along the west coast of Africa, Mali had several geographic advantages. Much of the land was a savanna. The region received plenty of rain, so farmers could easily grow rice, millet, and other grains. Agricultural surpluses allowed Mali to engage in trade, acquire art, and construct impressive buildings.

MALI'S GREAT LEADERS

Mali was also fortunate because it had some very effective leaders. Popular legend claims extraordinary things of **Sundiata Keita** (sun-JAHT-ah KAY-tah), who founded the mighty empire. He brought peace and tolerance, as well as law and order, to his lands. Sundiata ruled from 1230 to 1255 and became incredibly rich by taxing trade. However, it was **Mansa Musa** (MAHN-sah MOO-sah) who introduced Mali to the world.

A descendant of Sundiata, Mansa Musa became **mansa**, or king, of Mali in 1307. Musa enlarged the empire and controlled trans-Saharan trade. Under his rule, Mali's population grew to about 40 million. Subject kings paid him tribute, and merchants

paid him taxes. Musa owned all of Mali's abundant gold and was fabulously wealthy.

A devout Muslim, Musa provided strong support for the arts, learning, and Islam. He encouraged the trading city of Timbuktu to develop as a center of Islamic learning. He oversaw the construction of the city's Great Mosque, one the oldest mosques in Sub-Saharan Africa. Musa

laid the groundwork for Timbuktu's emergence in the 1500s as the scholarly and religious center of West Africa. Although Musa ably ruled his vast empire, his successors were weak. As a result, Mali shrank to almost nothing as smaller kingdoms broke away and Berber nomads captured Timbuktu. One of the newly independent kingdoms, Songhai, eventually surpassed Mali in size and splendor.

REVIEW & ASSESS

1. **READING CHECK** In what ways were Mali and Ghana similar and different?

2. **DRAW CONCLUSIONS** What enabled Mansa Musa to support the arts and learning?

3. **SEQUENCE EVENTS** What events led to the decline of Mali?

PLAN

OBJECTIVE

Explore the factors that helped the empire of Mali become powerful.

CRITICAL THINKING SKILLS FOR LESSON 2.3

- Identify Main Ideas and Details
- Monitor Comprehension
- Draw Conclusions
- Sequence Events
- Make Inferences
- Analyze Visuals

ESSENTIAL QUESTION

What impact did trade and technology have on North and West Africa?

Trade and technology supported the development of great empires in West Africa. Lesson 2.3 describes the empire of Mali.

BACKGROUND FOR THE TEACHER

Timbuktu was a great center of learning. During the 1500s, the historic mosque of Sangore was the center of the city's Islamic scholarly community. There were no prescribed courses of study, although the primary focus was the teaching of the Qur'an. Other courses included history, astronomy, and logic. Courses were held in private residences, as well as in the courtyards of mosques. One aspect of the city's development as a center of learning was its trade in manuscripts as well as other commodities, such as salt, gold, grain, and cattle.

DIGITAL RESOURCES myNGconnect.com

TEACHER RESOURCES & ASSESSMENT

 Reading and Note-Taking

 Vocabulary Practice

 Section 2 Quiz

STUDENT RESOURCES

 Biography

INTRODUCE & ENGAGE

IDENTIFY STRUCTURES

Ask students to identify the kinds of structures a city in the desert would include if it were a powerful cultural and economic center. Encourage students to think about both public and private structures and to make a list of their ideas. At the conclusion of the lesson, revisit and revise the list as necessary. `0:05` minutes

TEACH

GUIDED DISCUSSION

1. **Identify Main Ideas and Details** Who was most influential in the rise of Mali as a powerful kingdom? *(Mansa Musa was the leader most responsible for Mali's rise to greatness.)*

2. **Make Inferences** What might be the disadvantages of a wealthy kingdom such as Mali in terms of its continued existence? *(Invaders might try to conquer it. Loss of wealth might weaken it.)*

ANALYZE VISUALS

Direct students' attention to the illustration of Timbuktu in Lesson 2.3. Tell them to consider how the physical characteristics of the land influenced how people lived, as well as the structures they built. **ASK:** Based on what you see in the illustration, how do you think people in Timbuktu may have adapted to their environment? *(They used mud and sand as building materials for structures; they built single-story homes to keep them cooler.)* As a class, make a list on the board of the different ways the residents of Timbuktu adapted to their environment. `0:10` minutes

ACTIVE OPTIONS

Critical Viewing: NG Chapter Gallery Invite students to explore the NG Chapter Gallery and choose one image that they feel best represents their understanding of the chapter. Have students provide a written explanation of why they selected the image they chose. `0:10` minutes

On Your Feet: Fishbowl Have students form an inner and outer circle, both facing the center. Use a Fishbowl strategy to have them pose questions and take notes about the emergence of the kingdom of Mali. Then have students switch places to pose questions and take notes about Mansa Musa. `0:20` minutes

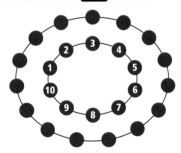

DIFFERENTIATE

ENGLISH LANGUAGE LEARNERS

Identify Main Ideas and Details Have students work with a partner to complete a Main Idea Cluster of the main ideas and details of the lesson using the diagram below. Point out that the main idea is often written in the first sentence of each paragraph, and that details support, or give further description of, the main idea.

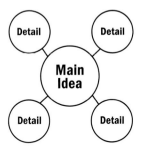

PRE-AP

Explore an Industry Have students conduct Internet research to create a presentation on gold mining in present-day West Africa. Tell students to include locations of major mines, how the gold is extracted, and current markets for gold. Encourage them to download and include appropriate images. Have students make their presentation to the class.

Press (**mt**) *in the Student eEdition for modified text.*

See the Chapter Planner for more strategies for differentiation.

REVIEW & ASSESS

ANSWERS

1. Ghana and Mali were similar in that both had great wealth. However, Mali also produced agricultural surpluses and boasted great achievements in culture and the arts.

2. Mansa Musa's great wealth allowed him to support the arts and learning.

3. Mali declined because Musa's successors were weak rulers. Smaller kingdoms broke away from the empire and Berbers attacked Timbuktu.

The Oral Tradition

You are exploring the past by reading this book. Written history is often considered the most accurate. But until very recently, people in much of the world, including Africa, didn't write down their history. Instead, special performers spoke or sang stories of the past, passing them from generation to generation.

MAIN IDEA

Africa has a rich tradition of oral history.

AN EPIC OF OLD MALI

One of the most famous griot stories is *Sundiata: An Epic of Old Mali*. This epic describes how Sundiata, the Lion King, defeated his enemies to found the empire of Mali. There is good evidence to suggest that at least some of the story is true.

ORAL HISTORY

Most early African civilizations, such as Ghana and Mali, did not develop a writing system until Muslim traders brought the Arabic language and writing system. Before the arrival of these traders, Africans passed on histories and stories orally, a method that historians call the **oral tradition**. In this manner, history, culture, and social values were transmitted from one generation to the next.

A class of special storytellers emerged to relate the stories of villages, families, and kings. Known in West Africa as **griots** (GREE-ohz), they spent years painstakingly memorizing family trees and learning stories.

Griots dramatically told their tales at public ceremonies, where excited crowds gathered to listen and learn. Stories about their ancestors and the exploits of kings were especially popular. Much of what historians know about early African history has been passed down through this oral tradition. It was not until the early 1900s that scholars wrote down these stories, fables, songs, and poems.

GRIOT TRADITION

Griots were highly respected members of African society who carried out many different roles. Most were men, but some were women. Griots served as historians, educators, and advisors. They also served as genealogists, or people who know how family members are related to one another and to their ancestors.

Griots were accomplished performers who could captivate their audiences. They often played drums or stringed instruments, such as the 21-string kora. Other musicians sometimes accompanied them as they told their stories.

Some griots wore costumes and masks. As the stories unfolded, actors and dancers sometimes interpreted the action. These dramatic aspects of griot performances added to the tales' excitement and helped make them more memorable.

In West Africa, the griot tradition is still very much alive. Famous griots are treated like rock stars, and the tradition has had a huge influence on modern West African music. In Western countries, young musicians with African roots are making the tradition their own.

Critical Viewing: The griot is seated before a percussion instrument called a balafon. What instruments popular in the West are similar to the balafon?

+ POSSIBLE RESPONSE

The marimba and the vibraphone are similar to the balafon.

Balafon
The balafon is a traditional African instrument made of wood and gourds.

Kora
The Kora is a stringed instrument with a rounded back similar to that of a mandolin.

Koni
The koni has two strings and is made of wood and leather.

REVIEW & ASSESS

1. **READING CHECK** Why was oral tradition important in West Africa?

2. **ANALYZE LANGUAGE USE** How does the word *captivate* describe the ability of griots to perform?

3. **DRAW CONCLUSIONS** What might be the advantages and disadvantages of passing down history through oral tradition?

PLAN

OBJECTIVE

Explain the contribution of oral history and the griot tradition in North and West African cultures.

CRITICAL THINKING SKILLS FOR LESSON 2.4

- Identify Main Ideas and Details
- Monitor Comprehension
- Analyze Language Use
- Draw Conclusions
- Identify and Explain
- Sequence Events
- Analyze Visuals

ESSENTIAL QUESTION

What impact did trade and technology have on North and West Africa?

Trade and technology shaped the development of culture in North and West Africa. Lesson 2.4 discusses how cultural aspects have been handed down through the oral tradition.

BACKGROUND FOR THE TEACHER

Although the griot is most often described as a storyteller or historian, there is no comparable word in English to describe the griot's role. Griots serve in many capacities, including as ambassadors, advisors, and masters of ceremonies. Traditionally, the role of griot passed from father to son and it emphasized verbal and musical arts. Although fewer in number, women may also become griots, or griottes. Today a number of schools offer training in the griot arts. Although a griot may serve many roles, the most important one is keeping the past alive.

DIGITAL RESOURCES myNGconnect.com

TEACHER RESOURCES & ASSESSMENT

 Reading and Note-Taking

 Vocabulary Practice

 Section 2 Quiz

STUDENT RESOURCES

 Biography

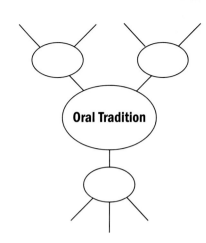

INTRODUCE & ENGAGE

ACTIVATE PRIOR KNOWLEDGE

Ask students to work in groups and discuss their previous associations with African music. Invite them to share their reactions to specific performers, such as Youssou N'Dour or Miriam Makeba. Ask them to discuss their knowledge or ideas about the influence of African music on American music. Call on volunteers from each group to report on the discussion for their group. **0:10** minutes

TEACH

GUIDED DISCUSSION

1. **Identify and Explain** What is oral tradition and how is it important to the history of West Africa? *(Oral tradition is the telling of history or a story through speech and song. It is important because until the arrival of the Arabs and their written language, it was the only way to record and pass along the region's history.)*

2. **Sequence Events** Although spoken and written Arabic eventually spread in West Africa, the oral tradition continued. **ASK:** Why do you think the art of the griot continues to this day? *(The griot belongs to the culture of West Africa and continues to offer a popular form of entertainment.)*

ANALYZE VISUALS

Have students examine the photograph of the griot. Direct them to consider visual elements that enhance the griot's role as being part of a long tradition. **0:10** minutes

ACTIVE OPTIONS

NG Learning Framework: Think About Sundiata

ATTITUDE: **Empowerment**
SKILL: **Problem-Solving**

Have students read the story of Sundiata as told in *Sundiata: An Epic of Old Mali* and imagine that they are in Sundiata's place. **ASK:** How would you have done things differently from Sundiata? How might those changes have affected both Mali and your life? **0:10** minutes

On Your Feet: Create a Concept Web Have students form groups of four around a section of a bulletin board or a table. Provide each group with a large sheet of paper. Have group members take turns contributing a concept or phrase to a Concept Web with the words *oral tradition* at the center. When time for the activity has elapsed, call on volunteers from each group to share their webs. **0:10** minutes

DIFFERENTIATE

STRIVING READERS

Use Sentence Starters Provide these sentence starters for students to complete after reading:

- The job of a griot is _____.
- In West Africa, the oral tradition transmitted _____.
- Griots often played _____.
- The griot tradition has had a major influence on modern _____.

ENGLISH LANGUAGE LEARNERS

Create an Oral History Ask students to think of one tradition in their family or in their local community that they would like to see preserved for future generations. Pair each student with a proficient speaker and have the proficient speaker listen as the student explains the tradition and why it is so important to him or her. The proficient speaker should ask questions to clarify meaning and correct any errors in grammar or usage.

Press **mt** *in the Student eEdition for modified text.*

See the Chapter Planner for more strategies for differentiation.

REVIEW & ASSESS

ANSWERS

1. Oral tradition was important because most early African civilizations had no writing system.

2. *Captivate* suggests that griots were able to completely command the attention of their audience.

3. Possible advantage: Oral tradition ensures that history is not lost when a civilization has no written language. Possible disadvantage: As stories are passed down from one generation to the next, they may become distorted.

Trans-Saharan
Travelers

Written accounts of early Africa have largely come from Muslim sources. Many manuscripts were kept in cities like Timbuktu and are still waiting to be studied. These accounts, written by people who were actually there, offer insights into early Africa and its place in the world.

ANSWERS

DOCUMENT 1
Mansa Musa gave loads of gold and valuables to Egypt's treasury. He wanted only to focus on his pilgrimage rather than on politics.

DOCUMENT 2
Mansa Musa is featured on the map, indicating that he was very important to West Africa.

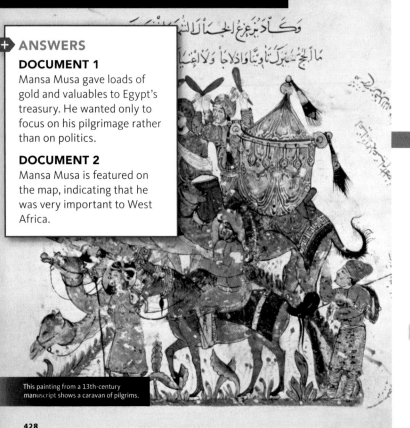

This painting from a 13th-century manuscript shows a caravan of pilgrims.

DOCUMENT ONE

Primary Source: Historical Account

from Al-Umari's account of Mansa Musa's visit to Cairo in 1324

Al-Umari, an Arabic historian, visited Egypt not long after Mansa Musa's famous visit. He was able to interview many firsthand witnesses to the event. His descriptions of Mansa Musa and his enormous wealth have greatly contributed to our knowledge of Mali. In this passage, Al-Umari recounts the experience of a government official who met the legendary ruler.

CONSTRUCTED RESPONSE What evidence from the text demonstrates that Mansa Musa was an immensely wealthy and religious man?

From the beginning of my coming to stay in Egypt I heard talk of the arrival of this sultan Musa on his Pilgrimage.... I asked the emir Abu ... and he told me of the opulence [wealth], manly virtues, and piety of his sultan. "When I went out to meet him [he said] on behalf of the mighty sultan al-Malik al-Nasir, he did me extreme honour and treated me with the greatest courtesy.... Then he forwarded to the royal treasury many loads of unworked native gold and other valuables. I tried to persuade him to ... meet the sultan, but he refused persistently saying: 'I came for the Pilgrimage and nothing else. I do not wish to mix anything else with my Pilgrimage.'"

DOCUMENT TWO

Primary Source: Atlas

from the *Catalan Atlas*, c. 1375

Mansa Musa's pilgrimage to Mecca literally put West Africa on the map. Stories of his extraordinary wealth stimulated international interest in West Africa, the land of gold. This made it a feature of medieval maps such as the *Catalan Atlas*, which gives West Africa considerable prominence. Abraham Cresques, a mapmaker, created the atlas in Majorca, an island that is part of Spain.

CONSTRUCTED RESPONSE Based on the map, what can you conclude about Mansa Musa's importance to West Africa?

Detail showing West Africa and Mansa Musa (right)

SYNTHESIZE & WRITE

1. **REVIEW** Review what you have learned about West Africa and Mansa Musa in this chapter.

2. **RECALL** On your own paper, write down the main idea expressed in each primary source.

3. **CONSTRUCT** Write a topic sentence that answers this question: How did Mansa Musa affect Mali and the rest of the world?

4. **WRITE** Using evidence from the sources, write an argument to support the answer to the question in Step 3.

PLAN

OBJECTIVE
Synthesize information about trans-Saharan travel from primary source documents.

CRITICAL THINKING SKILLS FOR LESSON 2.5
- Synthesize
- Form and Support Opinions
- Identify
- Evaluate

ESSENTIAL QUESTION
What impact did trade and technology have on North and West Africa?

Trade and technology opened trade routes across the Sahara.

Lesson 2.5 provides information on trans-Saharan travel from primary sources.

BACKGROUND FOR THE TEACHER

Mansa Musa was the tenth emperor of Mali. The writings of Arab scholars, including those of Al-Umari and Ibn Battuta, are the main source of information about Mali's emperors. When the emperor who preceded Musa left to explore the Atlantic Ocean, Musa was appointed his deputy. Musa became emperor when his predecessor failed to return. Musa made his pilgrimage to Mecca in 1324. His huge entourage is said to have included 60,000 men and 12,000 slaves. Eighty camels carried bags of gold dust. Musa distributed gold to the cities on his route and also traded gold for souvenirs.

TEACHER RESOURCES & ASSESSMENT

 Reading and Note-Taking   **Vocabulary Practice**   **Section 2 Quiz**

STUDENT RESOURCES

 Biography

PREPARE FOR THE DOCUMENT-BASED QUESTION

Before students begin the activity, briefly preview the two documents. Remind students that a constructed response requires full explanations in complete sentences. Emphasize that students should use their knowledge of Mansa Musa and the history of Mali in addition to the information in the documents. **0:05** minutes

GUIDED DISCUSSION

1. **Form and Support Opinions** Do you think that Al-Umari's account provides reliable information about Mansa Musa's visit to Cairo? Support your answer with examples from the document. *(In this passage, Al-Umari served as a reporter. He directly quotes the government official, which suggests that the account is accurate.)*

2. **Identify** Who is shown in the right of the Catalan Atlas detail? What is he holding and what might be its significance? How does the portrayal of each man suggest the role of each? *(Mansa Musa is at right. He holds a piece of gold, which might be a gift or a trade good. Mansa Musa, a ruler, wears a crown and sits on a throne, while the other man, most likely a trader, is mounted on a camel.)*

EVALUATE

After students have completed the "Synthesize & Write" activity, allow time for them to exchange paragraphs and read and comment on the work of their peers. Guidelines for comments should be established prior to this activity so that feedback is constructive and encouraging in nature. **0:15** minutes

ACTIVE OPTIONS

Critical Viewing: NG Chapter Gallery Have students examine the contents of the Chapter Gallery for this chapter. Then invite them to brainstorm additional images they believe would fit within the Chapter Gallery. Have them write a description of these additional images and provide an explanation of why they would fit within the Chapter Gallery. Then instruct them to do online research to find examples of actual images they would like to add to the gallery. **0:10** minutes

On Your Feet: Two Options Label two locations in the room with the name of one of the documents featured in the lesson. Have students reread the lesson and walk to the corner of the room labeled with the document that most furthered their interest in Mansa Musa's travels. Have students who chose the same document discuss why they made their selection. Then have volunteers from each group explain what their document is, and offer some of the group's reasons for choosing it. **0:20** minutes

INCLUSION

Synthesize Help students minimize distractions by photocopying or printing the documents in Lesson 2.5 for them. Give students highlighters and tell them to highlight words that they do not understand and concepts that confuse them. Pair these students with proficient readers who can help them understand the content.

PRE-AP

Research Mansa Musa Encourage students to explore the character of Mansa Musa further by having them conduct research on him, either in the library or on the Internet. Tell them to explore biographies of Mansa Musa as well as histories of the Mali. Students may wish to work in pairs as they research and gather information. Once they complete their research, have students write a brief report. Ask students to explore how their research coincides with or differs from the documents in Lesson 2.5.

Press **mt** *in the Student eEdition for modified text.*

See the Chapter Planner for more strategies for differentiation.

ANSWERS

1. Responses will vary.

2. Responses will vary.

3. Possible response: Mansa Musa drew the world's attention to Mali by distributing his wealth in North and West Africa.

4. Students' arguments should include their topic sentence from Step 3 and provide several details from the documents to support the sentence.

VOCABULARY

Match each word in the first column with its definition in the second column.

WORD	DEFINITION
1. desertification	a. a tradable good
2. trans-Saharan	b. an area of lush tropical grasslands
3. caravan	c. the practice of passing stories by spoken voice
4. commodity	d. across the Sahara
5. scarcity	e. a West African storyteller
6. savanna	f. the process by which fertile land becomes a desert
7. griot	g. people traveling together
8. oral tradition	h. a shortage of something

READING STRATEGY

9. **ANALYZE LANGUAGE USE** If you haven't already, complete your chart to analyze language in at least three introductory paragraphs. Then answer the question.

Language Example	What It Suggests
The caravan is a merchant's ticket to profit, but first the merchant must survive the journey.	The trip across the Sahara was very dangerous.

How does the writer's use of language in these examples help you understand what life was like in North and West Africa between 1000 B.C. and A.D. 1500?

MAIN IDEAS

Answer the following questions. Support your answers with evidence from the chapter.

10. How did the geography and climate of the Sahara change over a long period of time? **LESSON 1.1**

11. What impact did the development of trade between early colonists and Berbers have on North Africa? **LESSON 1.2**

12. What valuable resources in Africa fostered trade? **LESSON 1.3**

13. How did Islam spread throughout North and West Africa? **LESSON 1.4**

14. What new technology was developed by the Nok people of West Africa? **LESSON 2.1**

15. What factors led to the emergence of the powerful kingdom of Ghana? **LESSON 2.2**

16. Why does Africa have a rich tradition of oral history? **LESSON 2.4**

CRITICAL THINKING

Answer the following questions. Support your answers with evidence from the chapter.

17. **SYNTHESIZE** How did technology contribute to both the rise and the decline of Nok culture?

18. **ANALYZE CAUSE AND EFFECT** What effect did desertification have on the people and animals who inhabited the Sahara?

19. **SEQUENCE EVENTS** How did vast salt deposits develop in the Sahara?

20. **DRAW CONCLUSIONS** What was the cultural legacy of the spread of Islam in North and West Africa?

21. **YOU DECIDE** If you were a trader in West Africa, would you rather have a pound of salt or a pound of gold? Support your opinion with evidence from the chapter.

INTERPRET MAPS

Study the map that shows the spread of ironworking in Africa. Then answer the questions that follow.

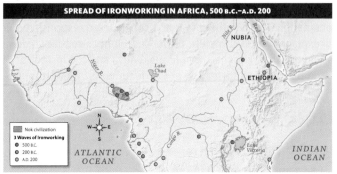

SPREAD OF IRONWORKING IN AFRICA, 500 B.C.–A.D. 200

22. In what areas of Africa did people develop ironworking at the same time as the Nok?

23. Where did ironworking spread between 500 B.C. and 200 B.C?

ANALYZE SOURCES

Alvise Cadamosto was an Italian explorer who wrote one of the earliest known accounts of West Africa. Read his description of the salt-gold trade in the 1450s.

> Having reached these waters [the upper Niger] with the salt, they proceed in this fashion: all those who have the salt pile it in rows, each marking his own. Having made these piles, the whole caravan retires half a day's journey. Then there come another [group] who do not wish to be seen or to speak . . . they place a quantity of gold opposite each pile and then turn back, leaving salt and gold. When they have gone [those] who own the salt return: if they are satisfied with the quantity of gold, they leave the salt and retire with the gold. . . . In this way, by long and ancient custom, they carry on their trade without seeing or speaking to each other.

24. What is distinctive about how transactions in the salt-gold trade were carried out?

WRITE ABOUT HISTORY

25. **NARRATIVE** Suppose you were able to travel to the trading city of Timbuktu at the time of its greatest influence and importance. Write a brief account of your time there and describe what you see.

TIPS

- Take notes from the lesson about the empire of Mali.
- Select relevant, well-chosen facts, concrete details, and examples that will be the basis of your narrative.
- Use transitions to make your account of your trip clear to readers.
- Use vocabulary from the chapter as appropriate.

VOCABULARY ANSWERS

WORD	DEFINITION
1. desertification f.	a. a tradeable good
2. trans-Saharan d.	b. an area of lush tropical grasslands
3. caravan h.	c. the practice of passing stories by spoken voice
4. commodity a.	d. across the Sahara
5. scarcity c.	e. a West African storyteller
6. savanna e.	f. the process by which fertile land becomes a desert
7. griot b.	g. people traveling together
8. oral tradition g.	h. a shortage of something

READING STRATEGY ANSWER

Students' language examples will vary but should be examples of colorful description.

Language Example	What It Suggests
The caravan is a merchant's ticket to profit, but first the merchant must survive the journey.	The trip across the Sahara was very dangerous.

9. The writer's use of language helps me understand what life was like in this period. By using descriptive words and stories, the writer paints a picture of the rich culture and economy of North and West Africa.

MAIN IDEAS ANSWERS

10. The Sahara drained to become a savanna and then dried up to become a desert.

11. Trade allowed North Africa to prosper and some of that wealth began to move from the coastal regions to the interior of Africa.

12. Gold, salt, and slaves were valuable resources that fostered trade.

13. Arab armies brought Islam to North Africa. Traders spread the religion throughout West Africa.

14. Iron smelting was developed by the Nok people.

15. Ghana had a favorable location that made it an ideal trade center. Ghana's rulers controlled West Africa's gold mines and taxed salt and other trade goods. These factors combined to make Ghana a powerful kingdom.

16. Before the arrival of the Arabs, Africa had no written language. Oral history was the only way to preserve Africa's past.

CRITICAL THINKING ANSWERS

17. Smelting enabled the Nok to produce iron tools, which in turn enabled them to clear more land for farming. At first this led to increased population. However, such clearing eventually led to deforestation and the population declined.

18. Desertification led to the migration of people and animals migrating to more hospitable regions with reliable water resources.

19. Salt deposits formed when a shift in rains caused the Sahara to dry up.

20. The Arabic language spread. Literacy increased. Centers of learning sprang up, where people could study the Qur'an and areas of knowledge such as astronomy, medicine, law, and mathematics.

21. Possible response: That depends on the resource available. The value of a pound of salt was about equal to a pound of gold. Either could be traded for other commodities.

INTERPRET MAPS ANSWERS

22. People developed ironworking at the same time as the Nok on the Nile River in Nubia, on the west bank of the Red Sea, and on the west coast of Lake Victoria.

23. Ironworking spread to the west branch of the Nile, the Atlantic coast, the Congo River, and northwest of Lake Chad.

ANALYZE SOURCES ANSWER

24. Based on this document, it seems traders go to great lengths to avoid interacting directly with one another.

WRITE ABOUT HISTORY ANSWER

25. Students should include information from the text about Timbuktu's importance as a center of learning. They should list types of structures found in the city and generally describe the architecture. Students' narratives should do the following:

- introduce the topic clearly
- contain relevant details and concrete examples
- incorporate chapter vocabulary
- include a concluding statement

UNIT RESOURCES

On Location with National Geographic Grantee Christopher DeCorse
Intro and Video

Interactive Map Tool

News & Updates

Available on myNGconnect

Unit Wrap-Up:
"Archaeology in Africa"
Feature and Video

"The Telltale Scribes of Timbuktu"
National Geographic Adapted Article

"Rift in Paradise"
National Geographic Adapted Article
Student eEdition exclusive

Unit 6 Inquiry:
Create a Local Trade Exchange

CHAPTER RESOURCES

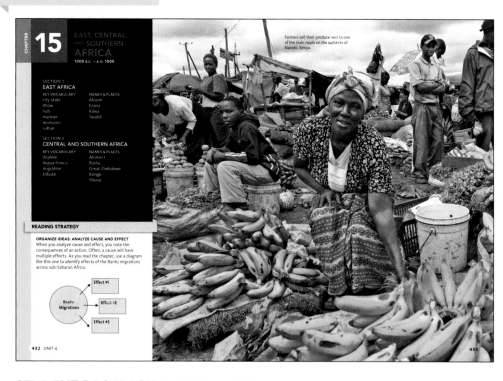

CHAPTER 15
EAST, CENTRAL, AND SOUTHERN AFRICA
1000 B.C. – A.D. 1500

SECTION 1
EAST AFRICA
KEY VOCABULARY
city-state
dhow
hub
mariner
monsoon
sultan

NAMES & PLACES
Aksum
Ezana
Kilwa
Swahili

SECTION 2
CENTRAL AND SOUTHERN AFRICA
KEY VOCABULARY
deplete
lingua franca
migration
tribute

NAMES & PLACES
Afonso I
Bantu
Great Zimbabwe
Kongo
Shona

READING STRATEGY

ORGANIZE IDEAS: ANALYZE CAUSE AND EFFECT
When you analyze cause and effect, you note the consequences of an action. Often, a cause will have multiple effects. As you read the chapter, use a diagram like this one to identify effects of the Bantu migrations across sub-Saharan Africa.

Bantu Migrations → Effect #1, Effect #2, Effect #3

Farmers sell their produce next to one of the main roads on the outskirts of Nairobi, Kenya.

432 UNIT 6   433

TEACHER RESOURCES & ASSESSMENT

Available on myNGconnect

 Social Studies Skills Lessons
• Reading: Analyze Cause and Effect
• Writing: Write an Informative Outline

 Formal Assessment
• Chapter 15 Tests A (on-level)
& B (below-level)

A **Chapter 15 Answer Key**

 ExamView®
One-time Download

STUDENT BACKPACK *Available on myNGconnect*
• **eEdition** *(English)*   • **eEdition** *(Spanish)*   • **Handbooks**   • **Online Atlas**
For Chapter 15 Spanish resources, visit the Teacher Resource Menu page on myNGconnect.

SECTION 1 RESOURCES

EAST AFRICA

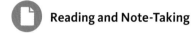 **Reading and Note-Taking**

Vocabulary Practice

☑ **Section 1 Quiz**

Available on myNGconnect

LESSON 1.1 THE KINGDOM OF AKSUM
- Critical Viewing: NG Chapter Gallery
- On Your Feet: Inside-Outside Circle

LESSON 1.2 INDIAN OCEAN TRADE
NG Learning Framework:
Learn About Indian Ocean Trade

- On Your Feet: Which Way the Wind Blows

LESSON 1.3 EAST AFRICAN CITY-STATES
Active History: Interactive Whiteboard Activity
Map the Swahili Language

Active History
Map the Swahili Language

Available on myNGconnect

- On Your Feet: Pick a Side

SECTION 2 RESOURCES

CENTRAL AND SOUTHERN AFRICA

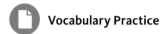 **Reading and Note-Taking**

Vocabulary Practice

☑ **Section 2 Quiz**

Available on myNGconnect

LESSON 2.1 BANTU MIGRATIONS
- Critical Viewing: NG Chapter Gallery
- On Your Feet: Rotating Discussion

LESSON 2.2 GREAT ZIMBABWE
NG Learning Framework:
Learn About Peoples from Across Africa

- On Your Feet: Think, Pair, Share

LESSON 2.3 THE KINGDOM OF KONGO
 Biography
Afonso I   *Available on myNGconnect*

- Critical Viewing: NG Chapter Gallery
- On Your Feet: Numbered Heads

CHAPTER 15 REVIEW

STRATEGY ❶

Activate Prior Knowledge

Display the following words and ask students to use what they learned in earlier chapters to write a sentence for each term. Have students share their sentences orally and check for accuracy.

    port

    city-state

    migration

    monsoon

    sultan

    tribute

Use with Lessons 1.2, 1.3, 2.1, and 2.3

STRATEGY ❷

Create a 3-2-1 Summary

After they read a lesson, direct students to create a 3-2-1 summary by writing three important ideas under the number 3, two Key Vocabulary words and their definitions under the number 2, and one main idea question to ask another student. Students can share their summaries in pairs and answer each other's questions.

Use with All Lessons

STRATEGY ❸

Play the "I Am . . ." Game

To reinforce the meanings of key terms and names, assign every student one term or name that appears in boldface in the chapter and have them write a one-sentence clue beginning with "I am." Have students take turns reading clues and calling on students to guess answers.

Use with All Lessons

Press (mt) *in the Student eEdition for modified text.*

STRATEGY ❶

Modify Main Idea Statements

Provide these modifications of the Main Idea statements at the beginning of each lesson:

1.1   The kingdom of Aksum was in East Africa.

1.2   The Indian Ocean was important for trade in East Africa.

1.3   East Africa had many different city-states.

2.1   The Bantu people spread throughout Africa.

2.2   Great Zimbabwe was a wealthy empire that had large stone structures.

2.3   The kingdom of Kongo grew rich from gold.

Use with All Lessons

STRATEGY ❷

Use Supported Reading

In small groups, have students read aloud the chapter lesson by lesson. At the end of each lesson, have them stop and use these frames to tell what they comprehended from the text:

This lesson is about _____ .

One detail that stood out to me is _____ .

The vocabulary word _____ means _____ .

I don't think I understand _____ .

Guide students with portions of text they do not understand. Be sure all students understand a lesson before moving on to the next one.

Use with All Lessons

Press (mt) *in the Student eEdition for modified text.*

STRATEGY ❶

Use Photographs to Predict Content

Direct students to look at each photograph in the chapter and write one sentence predicting what the caption will be about. After reading, you may wish to have students verify their predictions and reword any sentences if necessary.

Use with Lessons 1.1, 1.3, and 2.2 *Ask for volunteers to hold one-minute discussions of each photograph. They should explain what they had predicted about the photograph and what the photograph actually depicts. Point out that the photographs shown in these lessons show different styles of architecture.*

STRATEGY ②
Pair Partners for Dictation

After reading a lesson, direct each student to write one sentence about a main idea from the reading. Pair students and let them take turns dictating their sentences to each other. Then allow them to work together to check spelling and accuracy of sentences.

Use with All Lessons

STRATEGY ③
Review Vocabulary

After reading, write the following words on the board and ask students to write a phrase and draw a picture to describe each word. Then have volunteers use each word in an oral sentence.

    deplete

    dhow

    hub

    lingua franca

    mariner

Use with Lessons 1.1, 1.2, 2.1, and 2.2

Press (mt) *in the Student eEdition for modified text.*

GIFTED & TALENTED

STRATEGY ①
Explain the Significance

Allow students to choose one term below to investigate and design a presentation that explains the significance of the term to the history of Africa.

- King Ezana
- Swahili
- The Bantu
- Afonso I

Use with Lessons 1.1, 1.3, 2.1, and 2.3

STRATEGY ②
Research Word Origins

Several words in the English language were adopted from languages of Bantu origin (examples include *safari, tote,* and *chimpanzee*). Have students perform research to discover these words along with the history behind each word. Students should consider the following questions as they perform their research: Does the word have the same meaning in English as it did in the original language? How did the word enter the English language? Have students present their findings to the class.

Use with Lessons 1.3, 2.1, 2.2, and 2.3

PRE-AP

STRATEGY ①
Annotate a Time Line

Have students annotate a time line of the history of Africa. Students should include content from Chapters 4, 14, and 15 on their time line. Tell students to include details such as names, dates, and places.

Use with All Lessons

STRATEGY ②
Analyze Effects

Students may work individually or in pairs to research and examine the long-term effects of the Bantu migrations. As an alternative, assign teams and have each team choose one of the following aspects on which to focus:

- trade
- technology
- language
- government

Suggest that students develop a graphic organizer to display the results of their investigation.

Use with Lesson 2.1

15

EAST, CENTRAL, AND SOUTHERN AFRICA

1000 B.C. – A.D. 1500

SECTION 1
EAST AFRICA

KEY VOCABULARY	NAMES & PLACES
city-state	Aksum
dhow	Ezana
hub	Kilwa
mariner	Swahili
monsoon	
sultan	

SECTION 2
CENTRAL AND SOUTHERN AFRICA

KEY VOCABULARY	NAMES & PLACES
deplete	Afonso I
lingua franca	Bantu
migration	Great Zimbabwe
tribute	Kongo
	Shona

READING STRATEGY

ORGANIZE IDEAS: ANALYZE CAUSE AND EFFECT
When you analyze cause and effect, you note the consequences of an action. Often, a cause will have multiple effects. As you read the chapter, use a diagram like this one to identify effects of the Bantu migrations across sub-Saharan Africa.

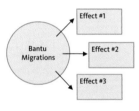

Farmers sell their produce next to one of the main roads on the outskirts of Nairobi, Kenya.

TEACHER BACKGROUND

INTRODUCE THE PHOTOGRAPH

Have students study the photograph of the produce market outside of Nairobi, Kenya. Explain that Kenya is a financially poor country, but it has a rich cultural legacy and great sense of national pride. **ASK:** What crops do you see in the photograph? *(bananas, potatoes, cabbage and parsley)* What can you infer about Kenya's economy? *(that it is based on agriculture)*

SHARE BACKGROUND

The modern history of sub-Saharan Africa has been volatile. Point out to students that this volatility is largely a result of European colonialism. While there is no guarantee that Africans would not have faced problems without European interference, history has shown that European colonialism devastated the African continent and the effects are still visible today. But who were the peoples of Africa before European interference? Tell students that this chapter and its lessons aim to answer that question.

DIGITAL RESOURCES myNGconnect.com

TEACHER RESOURCES & ASSESSMENT

 Social Studies Skills Lessons
- Reading: Analyze Cause and Effect
- Writing: Write an Informative Outline

 Formal Assessment
- Chapter 15 Tests A (on-level) & B (below-level)

 ExamView®
One-time Download

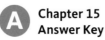 **Chapter 15 Answer Key**

STUDENT BACKPACK

- **eEdition** *(English)*
- **eEdition** *(Spanish)*
- **Handbooks**
- **Online Atlas**

For Chapter 15 Spanish resources, visit the Teacher Resource Menu page.

INTRODUCE THE ESSENTIAL QUESTION

HOW DID TRADE INFLUENCE THE GROWTH AND CULTURE OF EAST, CENTRAL, AND SOUTHERN AFRICA?

Think, Pair, Share Activity: The Impact of Trade Have students think about possible answers to the Essential Question. Allow them to look through the chapter, looking for clues in the photographs, maps, titles, and subheadings. Then have students discuss their ideas with a partner. Tell them to focus on each of the following aspects of the question:

- How trade might influence how and where civilizations grow
- How trade can influence cultures
- How trade might influence political decisions

Finally, call on individual students to share their ideas with the rest of the class. **0:20** minutes

INTRODUCE THE READING STRATEGY

ORGANIZE IDEAS: ANALYZE CAUSE AND EFFECT

Remind students that when they analyze cause and effect, they are looking for the consequences of a specific action. Model completing the Cause and Effect Web by reading aloud the following paragraph and adding an effect to the first box:

> The Bantu were people who migrated from West Africa into sub-Saharan Africa. These migrations began more than two thousand years ago. Arab merchants encountered the descendants of the Bantu when they settled in East African towns. These merchants adopted the Swahili language, which derived from the Bantu, and it became the widespread language of trade.

As an extension, point out that the effects of one cause can become the cause of new effects.

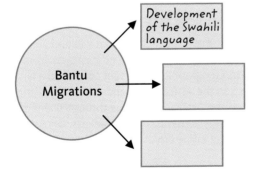

INTRODUCE CHAPTER VOCABULARY

VOC STRATEGY

A VOC strategy is a student-centered approach to vocabulary learning. This strategy helps students analyze word meanings from context and use sensory connections that are associated with their particular learning styles. Have students analyze each of the Key Vocabulary words from several angles by following these steps:

1. Write the sentence in which the word appears in the text.

2. Study how the word is used. What do you think it means?

3. Now look up the word in the dictionary or use the glossary.

4. Use the word in a sentence of your own.

5. To help you remember the meaning, draw a picture or a quick sketch that relates to the word; you might think of an action the word suggests or connect the word to a story or a news report.

6. Tell why you chose this way of representing the meaning.

KEY DATES	
2000 B.C.–A.D. 500	Bantu migration across sub-Saharan Africa
500 B.C.	Founding of Aksum in modern Ethiopia
A.D. 800	African sailors cross Indian Ocean
C. A.D. 1300	Trading cities exist along the East African coast
A.D. 1400	Emergence of the kingdom of Kongo in West Africa
A.D. 1450	Decline of Great Zimbabwe
A.D. 1483	Arrival of the Portuguese in Kongo

For more on modern human migration, see *GLOBAL ISSUES MIGRATION.*

The Kingdom of Aksum

Around A.D. 250, a Persian prophet listed the four great empires in the world: Rome, Persia, China, and Aksum. Two thousand years ago, Aksum was the jewel of East Africa. It was an organized and prosperous kingdom built on trade.

MAIN IDEA

The prosperous kingdom of Aksum rose to power in East Africa.

IVORY TRADE

Ivory comes from the tusks of animals, especially elephants. Ivory exports, such as this mask, brought the African elephant close to extinction. Today these exports are regulated, but illegal trade still threatens elephants.

THE RISE OF AKSUM

The geography of East Africa made it ideally suited for trade. The region is shaped like a rhinoceros horn, earning it the nickname the Horn of Africa. The Red Sea connects East Africa with the Persian Gulf, the Mediterranean Sea, and the Indian Ocean. These bodies of water can carry Africa's vast resources around the world. From very early times, trade was central to East Africa's development.

Aksum (AHK-soom) began around 500 B.C. in what is now Ethiopia. By A.D. 100, Aksum had emerged as a prosperous trading kingdom. Its territory stretched from the Sahara to the Red Sea, where ports enabled it to dominate trade with Arabia, Persia, India, China, and Europe.

Around A.D. 350, King **Ezana** (AY-zah-nah) of Aksum conquered its great trading rival, Kush (which you read about in Chapter 4), and seized control of the valuable ivory trade. He also converted to Christianity and made it the official religion of Aksum. Ezana declared his faith on a solid stone pillar called a stela (STEE-luh). Aksum's kings built these monuments as symbols of their power.

TRADE AND ISOLATION

Aksum's location made it a major international trading **hub**, or center. The kingdom's economy grew through the trade of ivory, spices, and slaves. Aksum spent its wealth on textiles, metal, and olive oil from its trading partners. Its wealth also fueled cultural achievements. Artisans produced luxury goods, and the kingdom minted its own coins. Aksum developed a written language, which was used to create a rich body of literature. However, this time of prosperity did not last.

Beginning in the A.D. 500s, regional wars and Arab expansion closed off some of Aksum's key trade routes. The kingdom also suffered the effects of deforestation, droughts, and overfarming, which reduced the availability of food. Aksum declined, and Muslim invaders shrank its borders. Christian Aksum became surrounded by Muslim territories.

By A.D. 800, Christians in the region had retreated into the mountains of Ethiopia. Isolated, the Christians were mostly left alone, and their legacy still thrives there today.

Giant stelae from the kingdom of Aksum can still be seen today in Ethiopia.

EAST AFRICAN TRADE, c. A.D. 100

REVIEW & ASSESS

1. **READING CHECK** Why was East Africa a good location for trade?

2. **MAKE INFERENCES** How did King Ezana of Aksum help spread Christianity throughout the region?

3. **INTERPRET MAPS** What bodies of water were important to trade routes that extended from East Africa to Europe, India, and the African interior?

PLAN

OBJECTIVE

Examine the role of trade in the development of Aksum.

CRITICAL THINKING SKILLS FOR LESSON 1.1

- Identify Main Ideas and Details
- Monitor Comprehension
- Make Inferences
- Interpret Maps
- Summarize
- Sequence Events

ESSENTIAL QUESTION

How did trade influence the growth and culture of East, Central, and Southern Africa?

Aksum was a powerful African trading empire that reached its height between the third and sixth centuries. Lesson 1.1 discusses how geography and trade supported the development of Aksum.

BACKGROUND FOR THE TEACHER

Aksum was a self-made local power that wielded great regional influence. By and large, Aksum derived its power from its position as a trading state. Geographically, Aksum controlled a large part of the Red Sea coast on the African side, and essentially controlled a portion of the coast on the Arabian Peninsula through economic dominance. This provided ready access to Indian markets, whose goods they could trade north to Byzantine Egypt and even on to Europe.

DIGITAL RESOURCES myNGconnect.com

TEACHER RESOURCES & ASSESSMENT

 Reading and Note-Taking

 Vocabulary Practice

 Section 1 Quiz

STUDENT RESOURCES

 NG Chapter Gallery

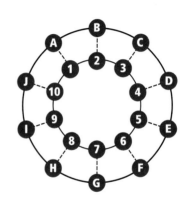

INTRODUCE & ENGAGE

ACTIVATE PRIOR KNOWLEDGE

Review with students Lesson 3.4 from Chapter 4 about the Nubian kingdom of Kush. Remind students that the kingdom conquered ancient Egypt and grew powerful through the trade of gold and iron. Tell students that in this lesson they will learn about Aksum, a rival kingdom that eventually conquered Kush. `0:05` minutes

TEACH

GUIDED DISCUSSION

1. **Summarize** What were the positive effects of a strong and prosperous trading network on Aksum's culture? *(When any society is financially prosperous and able to ward off threats, that society can focus on other aspects of its culture. For Aksum, this can be seen in a thriving artisan community and the development of its own written language and literature.)*

2. **Sequence Events** What were key dates and events in the history of Aksum? *(500 B.C.—Aksum begins in the area of modern Ethiopia; A.D. 100—Aksum has become a strong trading kingdom; 350—Aksum conquers Kush, and King Ezana converts to Christianity; c. 500—warfare and natural crises begin to shrink Aksum's territory; c. 800—Aksum's Christians retreat to the mountains.)*

INTERPRET MAPS

Have students study the East African Trade map. **ASK:** What was the strategic city that could distribute goods from the African interior north to Egypt or east to Aksum's port cities? *(Meroë)* `0:10` minutes

ACTIVE OPTIONS

Critical Viewing: NG Chapter Gallery Have students explore the NG Chapter Gallery and choose two of the items to compare and contrast, either in written form or verbally with a partner. Ask questions that will inspire this process, such as: How are these images alike? How are they different? Why did you select these two items? How do they relate in history? `0:10` minutes

On Your Feet: Inside-Outside Circle Have students stand in concentric circles facing each other. Students on the outside should ask questions related to the lesson and those on the inside should answer. On a signal, students should rotate to create new partnerships. On another signal, students should trade inside/outside roles. `0:10` minutes

DIFFERENTIATE

INCLUSION

Interpret Maps Provide questions to help students describe the map: What is the topic of the map? *(East African trade in the kingdom of Aksum)* What world regions are indicated as an extension of Aksum's trade routes? *(Europe, India, and the African interior)* What river is shown as a trade route on the map? *(the Nile)* What body of water does the kingdom of Aksum cross? *(the Red Sea)*.

GIFTED & TALENTED

Write Feature Articles Assign students the role of journalists reporting on the great trading kingdom of Aksum. Show examples of feature articles from a major newspaper. Have students use the library or the Internet to learn more about Aksum. Tell students to look at cause-and-effect relationships and to consider the empire as a whole—not just an isolated aspect of the kingdom taken out of context.

Press **(mt)** *in the Student eEdition for modified text.*

See the Chapter Planner for more strategies for differentiation.

REVIEW & ASSESS

ANSWERS

1. East Africa was a good location for trade because the Red Sea connected it with the Persian Gulf, the Mediterranean Sea, and the Indian Ocean. These bodies of water could carry Africa's vast resources around the world.

2. King Ezana made Christianity the state religion of Aksum. By doing so, Ezana no doubt encouraged many of his citizens to become Christians, too.

3. Bodies of water important to trade routes included the Arabian Sea, the Mediterranean Sea, the Nile River, and the Red Sea.

1.2
Indian Ocean Trade

In 1980, an adventurer recreating the legendary voyage of Sinbad the Sailor came to a halt near the island of Sri Lanka. The winds propelling his ship suddenly stopped, and for 35 days he went nowhere. Ancient East African sailors could have predicted this occurrence because they understood exactly when the Indian Ocean's winds blew—and when they did not.

MAIN IDEA

The Indian Ocean was a key part of East Africa's far-reaching trade network.

MONSOON WINDS

The East African coast became important for trade because the area could easily be reached by land or sea. Traders could bring goods from inland areas and load them onto ships in the Red Sea. However, even experienced sailors clung to coastlines because their ships and navigational skills were not good enough to sail safely out to sea. Beginning around A.D. 800, however, East African **mariners**, or sailors, developed the skills and ships to cross the Indian Ocean, which is the world's third largest ocean. They also learned how to use the wind to carry them all the way to India and back—if they timed it right.

From April to October, strong winds called **monsoons** blow northeast from Africa toward India. Between November and March, the winds reverse direction and blow southwest from India to Africa. They are extremely reliable and make it possible for a sailing ship to make the long journey from Africa to India and back. Even with the winds, however, the round trip could take as long as a full year.

Sailors learned to predict these winds and plan their journeys around them. Merchants who needed to move their goods between Africa and India hired experienced sailors who knew the winds. This trade across the Indian Ocean helped the economic development of both regions.

INDIAN OCEAN TRADE NETWORK

Over time, mariners and merchants continued working together to create an extensive trade network around the Indian Ocean. This network directly linked East Africa with Arabia, Persia, India, and Southeast Asia. Traders could transport goods to Europe, the Middle East, and even China.

New sailing technology made the trade network possible. Trading goods across the ocean required a sturdy ship that could carry a large amount of goods. In the Indian Ocean trade, that ship was called a **dhow** (dow). Dhows not only carried goods, but they also transported important elements of culture, such as language and religion.

With the expansion of trade, more Muslim merchants settled on the East African coast and married into local ruling families. Coastal villages grew into important trading towns controlled by Muslim rulers called **sultans**. As Muslim sailors and merchants traveled for trade, they introduced Islam to people throughout East Africa. As a result, the region developed a distinctive African-Arabic culture. It was an example of how people from other regions would influence Africa.

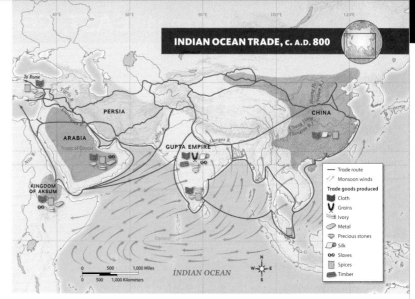

INDIAN OCEAN TRADE, c. A.D. 800

DHOW SHIPS

Dhows typically had long, thin hulls and triangular sails that were good at catching the monsoon winds. The winds were critical for successful voyages.

The early dhows were able to carry relatively large shipments of trade goods. They would travel across the Indian Ocean, trade their cargo, and return to Africa with silks and other valuables.

Today many types of dhows are still used along the East African coast.

REVIEW & ASSESS

1. **READING CHECK** How did monsoon winds affect trade between Africa and India?

2. **IDENTIFY MAIN IDEAS AND DETAILS** How did trade networks across the Indian Ocean develop?

3. **INTERPRET MAPS** What products did East Africans produce to trade with other countries?

PLAN

OBJECTIVE

Analyze the importance of monsoon winds and advances in sailing technology to East African trade.

CRITICAL THINKING SKILLS FOR LESSON 1.2

- Identify Main Ideas and Details
- Monitor Comprehension
- Interpret Maps
- Make Connections
- Describe

ESSENTIAL QUESTION

How did trade influence the growth and culture of East, Central, and Southern Africa?

The Indian Ocean trade moved a variety of goods, people, and

cultures around the Indian Ocean. Lesson 1.2 illustrates how people found a harmony between nature and technology that created a thriving trade network.

BACKGROUND FOR THE TEACHER

The triangular, or lateen, sail found on dhows was not a new development in the Indian Ocean trade, but it was a vital piece of technology. The lateen sail probably first developed around the 2nd century in the Mediterranean, possibly imported from Egypt or Persia. Its development was a reaction to earlier square sails that required a tail wind. The lateen sail could catch the wind on either side of the boat. Thus, a dhow could make forward progress into a head wind by zigzagging, or tacking, back and forth. This was a significant improvement over the square sail.

DIGITAL RESOURCES myNGconnect.com

TEACHER RESOURCES & ASSESSMENT

 Reading and Note-Taking

 Vocabulary Practice

 Section 1 Quiz

STUDENT RESOURCES

 NG Chapter Gallery

PREVIEW AND PREDICT

Have students preview the Indian Ocean Trade map. **ASK:** Why do you think water trade routes were so important to East African merchants in particular? *(Water trade routes were much shorter for East African merchants and they were generally more economical.)* **0:05** minutes

TEACH

GUIDED DISCUSSION

1. **Make Connections** Why were the wind patterns and ocean currents so vital to the Indian Ocean trade at this time in history? *(Without engines, the only way that ships could move over long distances was through the natural propulsion provided by wind and ocean currents.)*

2. **Describe** What was the relationship between merchants and sailors? Why was the relationship mutually beneficial? *(Merchants were the people who bought and sold goods, and sailors knew how to move goods across the water.)*

INTERPRET MAPS

Have students analyze the Indian Ocean Trade map. **ASK:** What group seemed to have the widest variety of goods to offer? *(the Gupta Empire)* What African goods might the Gupta Empire have been most interested in? *(African spices and metals)* **0:10** minutes

ACTIVE OPTIONS

NG Learning Framework: Learn About Indian Ocean Trade

ATTITUDE: **Curiosity**
KNOWLEDGE: **Our Human Story**

Have students select one of the groups shown on the map that they are curious about. Instruct them to write a short paper about this group and their role in the Indian Ocean trade using information from the chapter and additional source material. **0:15** minutes

On Your Feet: Which Way the Wind Blows Tell students to review the months of the year that correspond to the different monsoon wind patterns relative to East Africa. *(April to October, the winds blow from Africa toward India; November to March, the winds blow from India toward Africa.)* Designate one wall of the room as India's western shoreline. Have all students begin by facing India's western shoreline. Tell the students a month and then on the count of three they either continue facing the wall or they turn around. **0:05** minutes

INCLUSION

Identify Cardinal Points Pair students to make a simple line drawing of a compass rose with the words *North, South, East, West* written appropriately at the points. Ask students to use the drawing to help them identify the correct directions in statements such as these related to the map in Lesson 1.2: China is *(east)* of the Gupta Empire. The Kingdom of Aksum controlled territory farther *(south)* than the other groups shown on the map.

GIFTED & TALENTED

Write a Travel Log Have students write a travel log as a sailor on a trade ship in the Indian Ocean. They should review the map in the lesson to:

- Pick a starting port.
- Identify their stops along the way.
- Choose their destination.
- Determine the length of their voyage.

Once they have determined those elements, they should use the library or Internet to research the places on their route to add appropriate details to their travel log. Ask volunteers to present their work to the class.

Press **mt** *in the Student eEdition for modified text.*

See the Chapter Planner for more strategies for differentiation.

ANSWERS

1. Because monsoon winds are very reliable, sailors and merchants planned their journeys around them, making the long journey from Africa to India and back to Africa in one year, thus stimulating the economies of both countries.

2. Trade networks developed not only through the movement of goods but through the movement of cultural and religious ideas. As cultural and religious understanding and, sometimes, assimilation occurred, trade ties were often strengthened.

3. East Africans produced cloth, spices, metals, ivory, and slaves.

East African City-States

The streets of Kilwa were packed with a diverse mix of people from all over the world. Their different clothing, customs, and languages made for an exciting atmosphere. Trade brought all these influences to this vibrant city-state.

MAIN IDEA

City-states with a distinctive culture developed in East Africa.

Habari
"Hello"

SWAHILI TODAY

Today, Swahili is an official language of Tanzania and a common language among many East African peoples. There are about 15 major Swahili dialects, or variations of the language. More than 30 million people speak Swahili. The word above is Swahili for "hello."

TRADE ON THE COAST

As Arab merchants settled in East African towns, they brought Islam. As you have read, these Arabic immigrants married local ruling families, and Muslims came to control trade.

The Arabs encountered Africans who spoke Bantu languages. The Bantu, whom you will learn more about in the next lesson, were people who migrated from West Africa into sub-Saharan Africa. These migrations began more than two thousand years ago. The Bantu established trade networks. In time, their trade networks grew.

As a result, East Africa had a rich mix of cultures. The East African and Arabic Muslim cultures combined to form the unique **Swahili** (swah-HEE-lee) culture.

Swahili became the name used to describe the African-Arabic people of East Africa. Swahili is also the name of their language, which became the language of trade and a common language of all East Africans. The Swahili language and culture, together with the widespread adoption of Islam, helped unify the people of East Africa.

The Swahili people also developed a political system based on independent **city-states**. These are cities that control the surrounding villages and towns. By 1300, there were at least 35 trading cities along the coast. These strongly Islamic cities felt more closely connected to their foreign trading partners than to their non-Muslim African neighbors. Although they were not interested in territorial expansion, East African city-states fought to control as much trade as possible.

KILWA

One of the richest and most powerful city-states in Africa was **Kilwa**. (See the map in the Chapter Review.) It was located on an island that was as far south along the East African coast as trading ships could reach in one season. Any merchants from southern Africa had to come to Kilwa if they wanted foreign goods. Africa's main sources of gold were also south of Kilwa, which meant that the city-state controlled the overseas trade in gold.

To reinforce its control of the gold trade, Kilwa took over the port of Sofala. Sofala was farther south than Kilwa, but Sofala was closer to the gold mines. By controlling Sofala, Kilwa could more easily move gold to its ports for the arrival of seasonal trading ships.

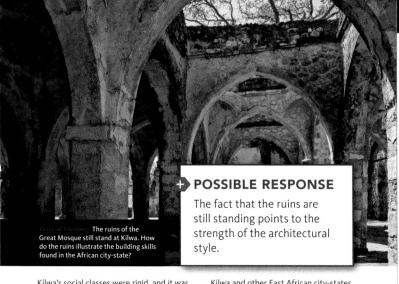

Critical Viewing: The ruins of the Great Mosque still stand at Kilwa. How do the ruins illustrate the building skills found in the African city-state?

+ POSSIBLE RESPONSE

The fact that the ruins are still standing points to the strength of the architectural style.

Kilwa's social classes were rigid, and it was difficult to move from one class to another. This was true for most East African city-states. Kilwa's sultan stood at the top of the society. Below the sultan were Muslim merchants, who were taxed heavily by the sultan but still grew rich. Merchants built ornate palaces, mosques, and homes of coral stone. Below the merchants were the majority of the townspeople, who were artisans, officials, and sailors. At the bottom of society were non-Muslim farmers, fishers, and, below them, slaves.

Kilwa and other East African city-states thrived for centuries until the arrival of the Portuguese in the late 1400s. These European explorers and traders stumbled upon the previously unknown East African trade network. They quickly recognized that the network moved a great deal of wealth. Just as quickly, they decided they wanted a piece of that wealth. Through political pressure and sometimes direct force, the Portuguese gained increasing control over East Africa's city-states, coastline, and commerce.

REVIEW & ASSESS

1. **READING CHECK** What effect did trade have on the culture of East African city-states?

2. **ANALYZE CAUSE AND EFFECT** What factors helped Kilwa become one of the richest and most powerful city-states in Africa?

3. **ANALYZE LANGUAGE USE** The text uses the word *stumbled* to describe how the Portuguese discovered Kilwa's trade network. What does this word suggest about this discovery?

PLAN

OBJECTIVE

Describe the culture that developed in East African city-states.

CRITICAL THINKING SKILLS FOR LESSON 1.3

- Identify Main Ideas and Details
- Monitor Comprehension
- Analyze Cause and Effect
- Analyze Language Use
- Make Inferences
- Explain
- Make Generalizations

ESSENTIAL QUESTION

How did trade influence the growth and culture of East, Central, and Southern Africa?

East African city-states were great centers of trade and a vibrant community that blended aspects of African and Arab culture. Lesson 1.3 looks at East African culture and the city-state of Kilwa in particular.

BACKGROUND FOR THE TEACHER

Kilwa remains a significant place in the study of East African history. Kilwa was an active trade center from the 9th to the 19th centuries. As such, it contains artifacts and buildings that paint a rich portrait of life in an East African trading town. Kilwa's Great Mosque was built in the 1100s and enlarged in the 1300s. Kilwa was placed on the UNESCO World Heritage list in 1981. Excavations and studies of the site continue to provide researchers with valuable context for understanding the rich history of Kilwa.

DIGITAL RESOURCES myNGconnect.com

TEACHER RESOURCES & ASSESSMENT

 Reading and Note-Taking

 Vocabulary Practice

 Section 1 Quiz

STUDENT RESOURCES

 **Active History**

INTRODUCE & ENGAGE

KEYS TO SUCCESS

Tell students that the success of trading city-states on the East African coast was not guaranteed. Have students make an Idea Web of four factors that would contribute to having a successful trading city-state. After students have completed their webs, discuss some of their suggestions. Students can revisit and revise their webs after reading the lesson. **0:05** minutes

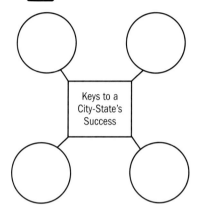

Keys to a City-State's Success

TEACH

GUIDED DISCUSSION

1. **Make Inferences** Why might the social classes of East African city-states have been so rigid and difficult to move between? *(Possible response: Those in power controlled the money and made the laws. Keeping the lower social classes down helped them maintain power and control.)*

2. **Analyze Cause and Effect** What caused the decline of the East African city-states. *(Portuguese interference and eventual control of the Indian Ocean trade meant the loss of power by African leaders.)*

3. **Explain** Why did Kilwa want control of Sofala? *(Sofala was closer to the gold fields of Southern Africa. Gold is heavy and more easily transported by ship than over land. By controlling Sofala, Kilwa could more easily bring gold to Kilwa for trade.)*

MAKE GENERALIZATIONS

The text states that there were many successful trading city-states along the East African coast. Ask students to come up with a general statement that describes what these city-states had in common. *(Possible response: East African city-states were largely Muslim, fought fiercely to control trade, if not land, and served as way-points for the riches of the African interior.)*

ACTIVE OPTIONS

Active History: Map the Swahili Language Extend the lesson by using either the PDF or Whiteboard version of the activity.

These activities take a deeper look at a topic from, or related to, the lesson. Explore the activities as a class, turn them into group assignments, or even assign them individually. **0:20** minutes

On Your Feet: Pick a Side Place signs on three sides of the room: Language, Religion, and Money. Point out to students that three factors that bound the East African city-states together were their language, religion, and wealth. Ask students the following questions and have them move to the sign that represents their answer. Call on a volunteer to explain why they made the choice they did.

- Which factor was the strongest uniting force for East African city-states?
- Which factor had the most lasting impact?
- Which factor was most responsible for the success of the East African city-states?

0:10 minutes

DIFFERENTIATE

INCLUSION

Question and Answer Pair seeing students with visually impaired students. The seeing students can read questions aloud and, after discussion, record their partner's response. Suggest that they read the response back to the visually impaired student to give him or her an opportunity to revise or expand upon it.

GIFTED & TALENTED

Present Information Visually Have students use the chapter and other resources to draw a map of the East African coast and illustrate why Kilwa's location was critical to its success and its role in the Indian Ocean trade. Have them present their maps to the class.

Press **mt** *in the Student eEdition for modified text.*

See the Chapter Planner for more strategies for differentiation.

REVIEW & ASSESS

ANSWERS

1. Trade led to the combination of East African and Arabic Muslim cultures forming the unique Swahili culture.

2. Kilwa's position geographically and its later control of Sofala helped Kilwa become one of the richest and most powerful city-states in Africa.

3. It suggests that the discovery was not planned.

Bantu Migrations

More than two thousand years ago, people in western Africa started migrating east and south, spreading their language and culture. These were the Bantu-speaking people, and their migration is one of the great stories in African history. They have played a major role in the development of sub-Saharan Africa—and they show the role that migration has played in world history.

MAIN IDEA

The Bantu populated much of Africa.

MOVEMENTS EAST

Bantu means "people" and is a general name for many different peoples of Africa who speak more than 500 different languages yet share a common ancestry. By studying the different Bantu languages, linguists, people who study human speech, know that the Bantu originated in western Africa around present-day Nigeria and Cameroon.

The **migration**, or movement, of the Bantu people was slow through the dense forest at the equator but accelerated across the open savanna. By the end of the A.D. 300s, Bantu speakers dominated all of sub-Saharan Africa except in the southwest, where the dry and hot climate was much more harsh.

The earliest Bantu speakers were probably fishers and farmers. Along the way, they learned how to work metals to create tools and weapons. The Bantu carried their metalworking skills with them. They traveled in small family groups and chose the best land for farming.

The Bantu's numbers grew, thanks to their mastery of iron, which allowed them to prepare land for planting crops. They relied on a method in which they used iron tools and fire to clear land for cultivation. They adapted the environment to better suit their needs. When the soil was exhausted, they simply moved to the next fertile area.

One crop that became widespread actually originated from Indonesia—bananas. Bananas became a staple crop in East Africa, where more varieties have developed than anywhere else in the world. Communities had rapid population growth if they had good growing conditions, plentiful rainfall, and an absence of the disease-carrying tsetse flies.

The Bantu spread across Africa in phases. Their migration was not constant and the speed of their migration could be altered by many factors including vegetation, disease, and climate.

IMPACT OF THE MIGRATIONS

At the time the Bantu began migrating, hunter-gatherers populated most of Africa, but both populations remained relatively low. As a result, there was plenty of room for the Bantu and hunter-gathers to coexist peacefully—or to avoid each other if they wanted.

At times, the Bantu and the people they encountered even helped each other by exchanging information. One skill the Bantu learned along the way was how to raise animals. When arguments over territory did occur, however, the Bantu's iron weapons gave them a clear and deadly advantage.

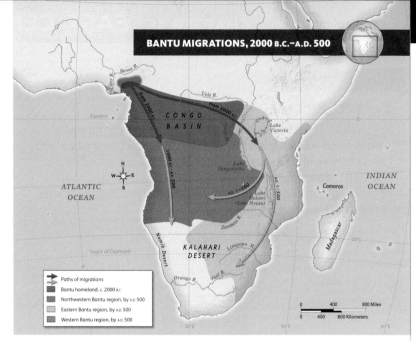

As they migrated, the Bantu had a great impact on the people of eastern and western Africa. They married into local families and spread the technology of making weapons and tools from iron, bronze, and copper. They also affected how people organized and governed themselves. Some of these influences are felt in Africa even today.

At the same time, the Bantu who migrated down the east coast of Africa also absorbed the influences of Arabic settlers. As you have read, this led to the region's distinctive African-Arabic culture and the Swahili language. Swahili became the widespread language of trade and a **lingua franca** (LING-gwuh FRANG-kuh), or a language commonly used by many different groups of people.

REVIEW & ASSESS

1. **READING CHECK** What is one impact the Bantu-speaking people had on Africa?

2. **COMPARE AND CONTRAST** In what ways were the Bantu different from other groups of people who lived in Africa at this time?

3. **INTERPRET MAPS** What physical features may have limited Bantu migration into the far south and southwest?

PLAN

OBJECTIVE

Understand the movement of the Bantu peoples and the lasting effect they had on sub-Saharan Africa.

CRITICAL THINKING SKILLS FOR LESSON 2.1

- Identify Main Ideas and Details
- Monitor Comprehension
- Compare and Contrast
- Interpret Maps
- Identify
- Make Inferences

ESSENTIAL QUESTION

How did trade influence the growth and culture of East, Central, and Southern Africa?

The Bantu migrations spread language, crops, and technology across sub-Saharan Africa. Lesson 2.1 describes the migration and its effects.

BACKGROUND FOR THE TEACHER

The history of the Bantu-speaking peoples of Africa is very difficult to trace. Linguists and historians generally accept a common area of origin around present-day Nigeria and Cameroon. They also believe that before the Bantu migrations, other groups dominated sub-Saharan Africa. As to how and why the migrations began, however, there is little hard evidence. It is clear that today, Bantu speakers are a very diverse group. It is estimated that some 85 million people speak a Bantu-based language and that there are more than 500 such languages.

DIGITAL RESOURCES myNGconnect.com

TEACHER RESOURCES & ASSESSMENT

 Reading and Note-Taking

 Vocabulary Practice

 Section 2 Quiz

STUDENT RESOURCES

 NG Chapter Gallery

UNDERSTAND MIGRATION

Point out to students that people have historically migrated for a variety of reasons. Raise the idea of push and pull factors as they relate to migration. Ask students to pay attention to the theories behind Bantu migration and identify them as push or pull. **0:05** minutes

TEACH

GUIDED DISCUSSION

1. **Identify** What conditions helped Bantu communities grow? *(iron tools for working the land; good growing conditions; plentiful rainfall; absence of disease-carrying insects)*

2. **Make Inferences** What might have helped the Bantu to become the dominant group over Africa's hunter-gatherers? *(The Bantu's technological superiority gave them an advantage over the hunter-gatherers.)*

INTERPRET MAPS

Point out to students that the Bantu generally moved south. Ask students to use their prior knowledge to speculate what geographic reasons might be behind this. *(Responses will vary but should acknowledge the existence of the Sahara north of where the speculated Bantu homeland was.)* **0:05** minutes

ACTIVE OPTIONS

Critical Viewing: NG Chapter Gallery Ask students to choose one image from the Chapter Gallery and become an expert on it. They should do additional research to learn all about it. Then students should share their findings with a partner, a small group, or the class. **0:20** minutes

On Your Feet: Rotating Discussion Have students form a large circle, facing inward. Ask a question about the lesson and then toss a beanbag to a student who must answer the question. After answering, the student asks a question of his or her own and tosses the beanbag to another student. Remind students to support their responses with information from the text. **0:10** minutes

INCLUSION

Complete a 5Ws Chart Guide students in completing a 5Ws Chart to help them understand the text. Review vocabulary words that students might have difficulty comprehending. Review each "W" of the chart as students work through the lesson.

What?
Who?
Where?
When?
Why?

PRE-AP

Bantu Legacy The story of tracing the Bantu homeland using linguistics is fascinating. Have students work in pairs to research the topic and write an essay about it. As an extension, have the pairs add two additional paragraphs about why preserving languages is important based on what they learned while doing their research about locating the Bantu homeland.

Press **mt** in the Student eEdition for modified text.

See the Chapter Planner for more strategies for differentiation.

ANSWERS

1. Possible responses: The Bantu spread knowledge of metalworking; they expanded the cultivation of bananas; and they married into local families.

2. The Bantu had the important knowledge and skill of ironworking, which allowed them to use iron tools to clear land for cultivation.

3. The Kalahari and Namib deserts may have limited migration to the far south or southwest.

2.2
Great Zimbabwe

Meeting Great Zimbabwe's king means walking a narrow path between towering stone walls. Reaching out, you can easily touch each wall, but the sky is just a sliver high above you. You feel closed in, fearful, and very, very small. And that's the idea. These imposing stone structures express the enormous power of the king.

The massive circular wall in Great Zimbabwe surrounds an area known as the Great Enclosure.

MAIN IDEA

Great Zimbabwe was a wealthy trading empire that expressed its power through enormous stone structures.

A SOUTHERN TRADING CITY

One group of the Bantu-speaking migrants that you learned about in the previous lesson settled on a plateau between two rivers in southern Africa. They were the **Shona** (SHOH-nuh), who established **Great Zimbabwe**. The site of their capital was probably chosen for its climate and agricultural potential. But it was also on the route traders used to carry gold to the coast, where Kilwa was located. (See the map in the Chapter Review.) Great Zimbabwe and Kilwa thrived and grew together. Great Zimbabwe's rulers grew rich and powerful by taxing trade goods. They controlled a vast empire with more than 300 towns.

GREAT STONE HOUSES

Great Zimbabwe's rulers expressed their power and wealth through extraordinary stone structures. *Zimbabwe* means "place of stone houses" in Bantu, and over 300 zimbabwes are scattered throughout southern Africa.

The ruins of Great Zimbabwe are still impressive today. The Great Enclosure is an imposing circular wall over 30 feet tall and 15 feet thick. The stones are cut so carefully and wedged in so tightly that they hold together without mortar. Behind the wall lived Great Zimbabwe's elite, separated from the ordinary people.

After A.D. 1450, however, Great Zimbabwe declined and was abandoned. The arrival of Portuguese traders on the coast shifted the gold trade away from Great Zimbabwe, which led to a decrease in wealth. Historians also theorize that the city's citizens may have **depleted**, or used up, the local resources, such as soil, water, and wood.

SHONA SCULPTURE

The only surviving sculptures from Great Zimbabwe are stylized birds carved out of soapstone. The bird was adopted as the symbol of present-day Zimbabwe. Modern Shona have revived traditional sculpture by carving pieces influenced by their Great Zimbabwe traditions.

REVIEW & ASSESS

1. **READING CHECK** What was the source of Great Zimbabwe's wealth?

2. **DESCRIBE GEOGRAPHIC INFORMATION** How did the location of Great Zimbabwe affect its role as a trading civilization?

3. **IDENTIFY MAIN IDEAS AND DETAILS** According to the text, what key factors probably led to the decline and abandonment of Great Zimbabwe?

442 CHAPTER 15

East, Central, and Southern Africa **443**

PLAN

OBJECTIVE

Analyze the importance of Great Zimbabwe's location in its development as a trading empire.

CRITICAL THINKING SKILLS FOR LESSON 2.2

- Identify Main Ideas and Details
- Monitor Comprehension
- Describe Geographic Information
- Explain
- Make Inferences
- Analyze Visuals

ESSENTIAL QUESTION

How did trade influence the growth and culture of East, Central, and Southern Africa?

Great Zimbabwe rose to power in large part by taxing the gold trade between the interior and the coast. Lesson 2.2 describes the rise of Great Zimbabwe and its role in trade.

BACKGROUND FOR THE TEACHER

Great Zimbabwe was at its height between the 11th and 15th centuries, but there is evidence that the site was inhabited as early as 900. Abandoned in the 16th century, Great Zimbabwe was "rediscovered" in the 19th century by Europeans. For many years, Europeans could not believe that Africans had created Great Zimbabwe and attributed the ruins to other ancient civilizations such as Greece or Phoenicia. It was not until the early 20th century that Great Zimbabwe was accepted as a wholly African site.

DIGITAL RESOURCES myNGconnect.com

TEACHER RESOURCES & ASSESSMENT

 Reading and Note-Taking

 Vocabulary Practice

 Section 2 Quiz

STUDENT RESOURCES

 NG Chapter Gallery

INTRODUCE & ENGAGE

CREATE IDEA WEBS

Remind students that in this chapter and in the previous chapter they have learned about a variety of early kingdoms and empires in Africa. Suggest that they create an Idea Web to track dates and other details about each empire. Have them add "Great Zimbabwe" and "Kongo" to their webs and explain that they will learn about these kingdoms in this lesson and the next lesson. **0:10** minutes

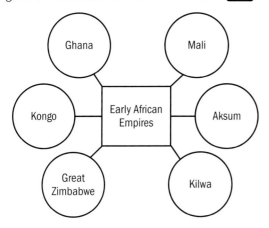

TEACH

GUIDED DISCUSSION

1. **Explain** What was the purpose of the Great Enclosure? *(It separated Great Zimbabwe's elite from the ordinary people who lived there.)*

2. **Make Inferences** Why is taxing trade goods very profitable? *(There is minimal overhead. The government is not incurring the cost of acquiring or transporting goods. They are merely taxing the traders that are moving the goods through their territory.)*

ANALYZE VISUALS

Ask students to examine the photograph of Great Zimbabwe and find more images on their own. **ASK:** To you, what is the most impressive part of these ruins? *(Possible responses: the fact that mortar was not used to hold the stones together; the scale of the structure given the tools available; how the structure was built for dramatic effect.)* **0:05** minutes

ACTIVE OPTIONS

NG Learning Framework: Learn About Peoples from Across Africa

SKILL: Communication
KNOWLEDGE: **Our Human Story**

Have students review the chapter and look for examples of interaction between Africans and people from other parts of the world. Instruct them to write a short essay comparing and contrasting the experiences in different regions of Africa. **0:20** minutes

On Your Feet: Think, Pair, Share Give students a few minutes to think about the following question: *What was the effect of the Great Enclosure on ordinary members of the society?* Then have students chose partners and talk about the question for five minutes. Finally, allow individual students to share their ideas with the class. **0:15** minutes

DIFFERENTIATE

STRIVING READERS

Create a Word Square Have students complete a Word Square for the word *deplete*.

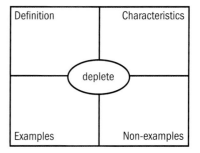

PRE-AP

Dry-Stone Building Dry-stone building is one of the oldest construction techniques in the world. Have groups research an ancient dry-stone site such as Great Zimbabwe, Machu Picchu, Saksaywaman in Peru, or Tiwanaku in Bolivia. Have the groups present their findings to the class.

Press **mt** *in the Student eEdition for modified text.*

See the Chapter Planner for more strategies for differentiation.

REVIEW & ASSESS

ANSWERS

1. The taxing of trade goods was the source of Great Zimbabwe's wealth.

2. Great Zimbabwe was located along the route between the gold mines and Kilwa, which meant its fortunes as a trading civilization rose and fell with the success of the mines and the costal trade cities.

3. The arrival of the Portuguese along the coast and possibly the local depletion of natural resources both led to the decline and abandonment of Great Zimbabwe.

This Portuguese map from the mid-1500s shows how European countries viewed Africa—as territory to be used. The flags across Africa represent areas claimed by European countries.

2.3 The Kingdom of Kongo

"Great and powerful, full of people, having many vassals [loyal landowners]." This is how Portuguese explorers described the African kingdom of Kongo. They were soon responsible for changing every bit of that description.

MAIN IDEA

Kongo grew rich on the gold trade but would lose everything to the Europeans.

KINGDOM OF THE RAIN FOREST

The kingdom of **Kongo** emerged in the rain forests south of the Congo River around 1400. Like other regions of Africa, Kongo was influenced by migrating Bantu speakers who took advantage of the area's fertile soil. The people also knew how to make weapons and tools from iron and copper. They eventually formed a loose partnership of farming villages. Wise kings known as *manikongo* (MA-nuh-kahng-go) led the people and united the kingdom, which expanded through conquest, marriages, and treaties.

By the 1480s, the *manikongo* ruled more than half a million people in a large and well-ordered state. The *manikongo* grew wealthy through an organized tribute system. In this system, local rulers took **tribute**, or goods and services, from their subjects and passed them on to the king and his royal court. The tribute system actually increased trade and strengthened the economy.

The people of Kongo were not only good farmers, but they were also skilled metalworkers, potters, and weavers. Kongo's kings also sought to improve their understanding of science and the arts. When the Europeans arrived, the *manikongo* saw it as an opportunity to make great leaps in understanding. They were wrong.

THE ARRIVAL OF THE PORTUGUESE

In 1483, the Portuguese arrived in Kongo. An alliance was arranged, and, eight years later, the king converted to Christianity. The king's son, **Afonso I** (uh-FOHN-soo), became *manikongo* in 1509. He was a devout Christian and strongly pro-Portuguese. With Portuguese soldiers and weapons, Afonso extended his kingdom and took many prisoners, who were sold to the Portuguese as slaves.

However, the Portuguese wanted more than Kongo's many natural resources. They wanted cheap labor and began enslaving the people of Kongo. Afonso tried to resist slavery, but despite his best efforts, the slave trade grew. The drain of people, especially the agricultural workforce, greatly weakened the kingdom. For the next four centuries, European and American slavery would have a devastating impact on all of Africa.

REVIEW & ASSESS

1. **READING CHECK** What caused the kingdom of Kongo to weaken and lose its wealth and power to Portugal?

2. **DESCRIBE GEOGRAPHIC INFORMATION** What role did the location of Kongo play in the kingdom's settlement and prosperity?

3. **SEQUENCE EVENTS** Describe the turning points in the interaction between Kongo and Portugal.

PLAN

OBJECTIVE

Examine the kingdom of Kongo's growth and interaction with Portugal.

CRITICAL THINKING SKILLS FOR LESSON 2.3

- Identify Main Ideas and Details
- Monitor Comprehension
- Describe Geographic Information
- Sequence Events
- Summarize
- Make Generalizations
- Analyze Visuals

ESSENTIAL QUESTION

How did trade influence the growth and culture of East, Central, and Southern Africa?

Kongo was a West African kingdom that was not part of an international trading network. Lesson 2.3 describes how Kongo rose to power and was then torn apart by the Portuguese.

BACKGROUND FOR THE TEACHER

The kingdom of Kongo was in western Africa. The map in the Chapter Review shows its location. Point out to students that unlike the trading city-states along the East African coast, Kongo's wealth and stability came from within its own borders.

DIGITAL RESOURCES myNGconnect.com

TEACHER RESOURCES & ASSESSMENT

 Reading and Note-Taking

 Vocabulary Practice

 Section 2 Quiz

STUDENT RESOURCES

 Biography

INTRODUCE & ENGAGE

TURN AND TALK

Have students share their expectations of this lesson with a classmate. They should discuss the lessons they have covered to this point and write down three things they would like to know about the Kingdom of Kongo. At the end of the lesson, they should go back to their questions and see if they can answer them. If not, they can do independent research to find the answers **0:10** **minutes**

TEACH

GUIDED DISCUSSION

1. **Summarize** What factors made Kongo successful? *(good soil for farming, knowledge of metalworking, good leadership and organization)*

2. **Make Generalizations** Based on what you've read in this lesson and your knowledge of history, what was the result of interactions between Africans and Europeans? *(Responses will vary, but they should acknowledge that European explorers and traders who went to Africa did not see Africans as equals.)*

ANALYZE VISUALS

Ask students to examine the photograph of the Portuguese map. **ASK:** How does this map support the conclusion that Europeans did not see Africans as equals? *(The flags represent European nations and what Europeans believed was theirs to claim without regard for the people living there.)*

ACTIVE OPTIONS

Critical Viewing: NG Chapter Gallery Invite students to explore the NG Chapter Gallery and choose one image from the gallery they feel best represents their understanding of the chapter. Have students provide a written explanation of why they selected the image they chose. **0:10** **minutes**

On Your Feet: Numbered Heads Have students get into groups of four and number off within each group. Tell the groups to discuss what makes a good leader. After ten minutes, call a number and have a student from each group with that number share a summary of their discussion with the class. **0:20** **minutes**

DIFFERENTIATE

INCLUSION

Traits of the Kingdom of Kongo Pair students who have visual or learning disabilities with partners who are proficient readers. Have the proficient student read the section titled "Kingdom of the Rain Forest" aloud. After each sentence, the reader should stop so the

partner can discuss whether a trait of Kongo was mentioned. If it was, the pair should list it on an Idea Web similar to the one shown here. Explain that students may add more circles to the Idea Web if needed.

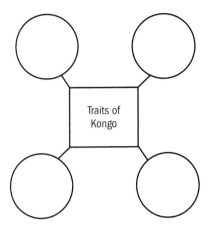

PRE-AP

Write a Feature Article Have students prepare a feature article that compares the West African kingdom of Kongo with one of the East African city-states, such as Kilwa. Encourage them to use the text and other documented sources for their research. They should look for similarities and differences and use evidence to support any conclusions they make.

Press **mt** in the Student eEdition for modified text.

See the Chapter Planner for more strategies for differentiation.

REVIEW & ASSESS

ANSWERS

1. The growing slave trade drained Kongo of its people—particularly the agricultural workforce—and greatly weakened the kingdom, which became dominated by Portugal.

2. Bantu speakers were able to settle and establish the kingdom of Kongo because of the fertile soils in the location south of the Congo River. The fertile soils enabled them to develop prosperous farming villages that they united into a single kingdom.

3. At first, when the Portuguese arrived in 1483, Kongo and Portugal had a mutually beneficial relationship based on the trade of goods. With the aid of Portugal, Afonso I was able to extend his kingdom. But the growth of the slave trade and Portugal's demand for even more slaves caused conflict and hurt relations between Kongo and Portugal.

CHAPTER 15 Review

VOCABULARY

Use each of the following vocabulary words in a sentence that shows an understanding of the term's meaning.

1. hub
Aksum's prime location made it a hub of international trade.

2. monsoon

3. dhow

4. city-state

5. migration

6. deplete

7. lingua franca

READING STRATEGY

8. ORGANIZE IDEAS: ANALYZE CAUSE AND EFFECT If you haven't already, complete your diagram to identify effects of the Bantu migrations across sub-Saharan Africa. Then answer the question.

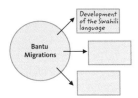

How did the Bantu migrations affect culture in sub-Saharan Africa?

MAIN IDEAS

Answer the following questions. Support your answers with evidence from the chapter.

9. Why was East Africa a good location for trade? **LESSON 1.1**

10. What helped sailors navigate across the Indian Ocean? **LESSON 1.2**

11. How did Kilwa become an important trading city? **LESSON 1.3**

12. How did the Bantu come to populate much of sub-Saharan Africa? **LESSON 2.1**

13. What was the purpose of Great Zimbabwe's imposing stone structures? **LESSON 2.2**

14. What effect did the arrival of the Portuguese have on the kingdom of Kongo? **LESSON 2.3**

CRITICAL THINKING

Answer the following questions. Support your answers with evidence from the chapter.

15. IDENTIFY MAIN IDEAS AND DETAILS What evidence demonstrates that Aksum made many cultural achievements while it was an international trading hub?

16. ANALYZE CAUSE AND EFFECT How did advances in sailing make long-distance trade across the Indian Ocean possible?

17. DRAW CONCLUSIONS In what way was Swahili the result of the blending of cultures?

18. MAKE INFERENCES How did their method of farming influence the Bantu's movement across Africa?

19. ANALYZE CAUSE AND EFFECT What impact did Portugal have on the development of the kingdom of Kongo?

20. YOU DECIDE What was the greatest cultural achievement of eastern, central, and southern Africa? Support your opinion with evidence from the chapter.

INTERPRET MAPS

Study the map that shows the location of kingdoms and city-states in sub-Saharan Africa. Then answer the questions that follow.

SUB-SAHARAN KINGDOMS, c. 1400

21. What do trading city-states—such as Sofala and Kilwa—have in common?

22. What rivers could traders from Great Zimbabwe have used to trade with Mbanza?

WRITE ABOUT HISTORY

24. INFORMATIVE Write an outline of the causes and effects of the slave trade between the kingdom of Kongo and Portugal.

ANALYZE SOURCES

Look at the photograph below of one of the 11 medieval Christian churches of Lalibela, Ethiopia, all of which were carved and chiseled out of rock. Known as House of St. George, this church is isolated from the other 10 churches.

23. What is unique about the construction of this church?

TIPS

- Take notes from the lesson about the kingdom of Kongo.
- List your topic at the beginning of the outline.
- Create two sections under the topic: one to focus on causes and another to focus on effects.
- List relevant facts, concrete details, and examples under each section of the outline.
- Use at least two vocabulary words from the chapter in your outline.

VOCABULARY ANSWERS

1. Aksum's prime location made it a hub of international trade.

2. Trade across the Indian Ocean was made possible in part by the monsoon winds.

3. The ship that African sailors used to carry goods was called a dhow.

4. Along the East African coast trade was controlled by numerous city-states.

5. The Bantu people began their migration across sub-Saharan Africa from the area around present-day Nigeria and Cameroon.

6. African farmers would often move their fields when they had depleted the soil.

7. Swahili became the lingua franca of trade along the East African coast.

READING STRATEGY ANSWER

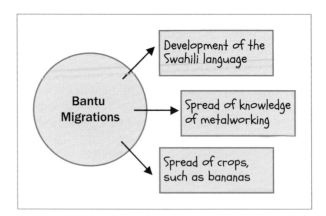

8. As the Bantu migrated across sub-Saharan Africa, they brought with them their ironworking skills, which spread Iron Age technology across Africa. They also interacted with Arabic settlers and traders, leading to a distinctive African-Arabian culture as well as the development of the Swahili language, which is still spoken in the region today.

MAIN IDEAS ANSWERS

9. East Africa is located on the Red Sea, connecting Africa with the Persian Gulf, the Mediterranean, and the Indian Ocean—all of which were vital seas in the trade network and through which Africa's vast resources traveled around the world. Because of this strategic location, prosperous trading kingdoms and nations developed, beginning with the kingdom of Aksum, which controlled the Red Sea ports.

10. Sturdy ships known as dhows and the monsoon winds helped sailors cross the Indian Ocean.

11. Kilwa became an important trading city because it was the port city farthest south that ships from India could reach. Gold from the mines of southern Africa was sent to Kilwa and loaded onto ships for the return voyage.

12. Small groups of Bantu-speaking people moved from their homeland in West Africa in a series of migrations that took place over hundreds of years. They eventually spread to the south, east, and west until they populated much of sub-Saharan Africa.

13. The imposing stone buildings and walls of Great Zimbabwe expressed the enormous power of the king and were meant to intimidate those entering the empire.

14. The growing slave trade drained Kongo of its people as Portugal demanded more and more slaves. Ultimately, this led to the decline of Kongo and its domination by Portugal.

CRITICAL THINKING ANSWERS

15. Because of the wealth it generated as an international trading hub, Aksum made many important cultural achievements. A beautiful kingdom, Aksum had a prosperous urban community, where craftsmen produced luxury goods for trade. Throughout Aksum, there were massive stelae, fortresses, palaces, and tombs, as well as the church of St. George in Lalibela. Aksum minted its own coins and developed its own writing system, which led to a rich literature. Another important cultural achievement was the development of advanced farming techniques, which supported Aksum's growing population.

16. The development of the ship called the dhow made long-distance trade across the Indian Ocean possible. The dhow's long, thin hulls and triangular sails caught the monsoon winds well, so the ship was able to carry large cargoes across the Indian Ocean.

17. The Swahili language was the result of a blending of cultures because it developed over many generations as Bantu and Arabic traders intermingled and Bantu speakers added Arabic words to their language. Today, Swahili is the common language—the lingua franca—of more than 30 million East African people.

18. The Bantu used iron tools and fire to clear land for cultivation. However, this method of farming exhausted the fertile soil, so once they used up the soil in one area, groups of Bantu needed to move to another area with fertile soil.

19. Portugal altered the development of the kingdom of Kongo completely. Kongo King Afonso I was a devout Christian who was raised in the presence of the Portuguese. Afonso adopted many European ways, made Christianity the state religion, and used Portuguese soldiers and weapons to extend his kingdom. Ultimately, however, Afonso was unable to resist the Portuguese demand for slaves and the kingdom was greatly weakened.

20. Students' responses will vary. Students should associate a cultural achievement with the correct region and use evidence to support why they think that achievement is the greatest.

INTERPRET MAPS ANSWERS

21. They are located on the eastern coast of Africa, which made them important ports for trading ships arriving and departing from the Indian Ocean.

22. Traders may have been able to use the Zambezi and Congo rivers to move goods to Mbanza.

ANALYZE SOURCES ANSWER

23. Students' responses will vary. Sample response: The House of St. George is unique because of the tremendous effort and skill needed to create it—chiseling and carving such a structure from rock. The cross-shape of its form is also unique and reinforces the structure's purpose.

WRITE ABOUT HISTORY ANSWER

24. Students' outlines will vary, but they should clearly illustrate the causes and effects of the slave trade between the kingdom of Kongo and Portugal.

ON LOCATION WITH Christopher DeCorse

ARCHAEOLOGIST AND NATIONAL GEOGRAPHIC GRANTEE

▶ Check out more on myNGconnect

When not working at his dig site in Elmina, Ghana, Dr. Chris DeCorse visits other countries along the African coastline, including Morocco, where this mosque is located.

EARLY INTEREST

Who isn't fascinated by archaeology? Lost civilizations, undisturbed tombs, and golden idols captivate us all! When I was five years old, my grandfather took me to museums and I was entranced by the models and displays. My parents indulged my interest with family trips to archaeological sites, taking the bus in our muddy field clothes with our digging equipment—people thought we were nuts. By sixth grade I had decided to be an archaeologist in Africa.

Chris DeCorse and his team visit Freetown, Sierra Leon, the capital city and a major African port in the Atlantic Ocean.

EXCAVATING ELMINA

Africa is believed to be the place where humankind likely emerged, but many parts of the vast continent remain largely unexplored by archaeologists. Given the lack of early written information about most of sub-Saharan Africa, archaeology is the key to revealing a relatively unknown past. I really want to know what the civilizations and societies of the region were like before the Europeans arrived in the 15th century. I'd also like to know how this area was changed by the Atlantic trade, and especially the slave trade that brought millions of Africans to the Americas. Archaeology holds the answers to these questions.

My research into the African settlement of Elmina in coastal Ghana allows me to examine the interactions and exchanges of Africans and Europeans over the past 500 years. In 1482, the Portuguese built a castle next to an existing African settlement. It was the first and largest European outpost in sub-Saharan Africa, and a center of European trade for the next four centuries. By studying the growth of the African settlement of Elmina from a small village to a town of perhaps 20,000, we can chart the changes in the lives of its inhabitants.

Previous studies had suggested there would be few traces of the early Elmira settlement, but I discovered a remarkably preserved site filled with intact artifacts from the town's occupants. While the vast majority of archaeological artifacts are rarely exciting to the average person, every bit of broken pottery or fragment of iron has a story to tell and forms part of the bigger story of how this West African trading city developed. Elmina was part of a changing landscape that marks the emergence of the modern world.

WHY STUDY HISTORY ❓

❝ *History is part of modern life;* **it shaped the world we live in and it continues to influence the present in a myriad of ways. Sites like Elmina are a testament to the exchanges that have shaped the modern world. ❞** —Christopher DeCorse

The Telltale Scribes of Timbuktu

BY PETER GWIN

Adapted from "The Telltale Scribes of Timbuktu," by Peter Gwin, in *National Geographic*, January 2011

Abdel Kader Haidara is one of Timbuktu's leading historians. He is also a man obsessed with the written word. Books, he said, are part of his soul, and books, he is convinced, will save Timbuktu. Words form the muscle that hold societies upright, Haidara argues. Consider the Koran, the Bible, the American Constitution, but also letters from fathers to sons, last wills, or blessings. Thousands of words infused with emotions fill in the nooks and corners of human life. "Some of those words," he says triumphantly, "can only be found here in Timbuktu."

Haidara's family controls Timbuktu's largest private library. The collection of around 22,000 manuscripts dates back to the 11th century. Most are written in Arabic, but some are in Haidara's native Songhai. Others are written in Tamashek, the Tuareg language.

The mosaic of Timbuktu that emerges from its manuscripts describes a city made wealthy by its position at the intersection of the trans-Saharan caravan routes and the Niger River. As its wealth grew, the city built grand mosques, attracting scholars who formed academies and imported books from throughout the Islamic world. New books arrived, and scribes copied facsimiles for the private libraries of local teachers and their wealthy patrons.

Timbuktu's downfall came when one of its conquerors valued knowledge, too. When the Moroccan army arrived in 1591, its soldiers looted the libraries and sent the books back to the Moroccan ruler. The remaining collections were scattered. Scholars estimate many thousands of manuscripts lie buried in the desert or forgotten in hiding places, slowly yielding to heat, rot, and bugs.

Three new state-of-the-art libraries have been constructed to collect, restore, and digitize Timbuktu's manuscripts. Haidara heads one of these new facilities. When asked about tensions in the region, he points to pages riddled with tiny holes and remarks, "Criminals are the least of my worries. Termites are my biggest enemies."

For more from National Geographic
Check out "Rift in Paradise" on **myNGconnect**

UNIT INQUIRY: CREATE A LOCAL TRADE EXCHANGE

In this unit, you learned how trade influenced the growth and cultures of African civilizations. Based on your understanding of the text, what natural resources were Africa's most valuable commodities? For what other goods were these commodities traded? How did Africa's valuable resources stimulate trade in the region and throughout the world?

ASSIGNMENT Create a local trade exchange that focuses on selling a commodity that is plentiful in your local area in exchange for goods and/or services that are needed in your local area. Be prepared to present your trade exchange plan to the class and explain how it will benefit the growth of your community.

Plan As you create your local trade exchange, think about some of the trade items that were highly valuable to African trading kingdoms—salt, for example. To begin creating your local trade exchange, identify trade items (goods and services) that are plentiful in your community, as well as goods and services that are needed. You might want to use a graphic organizer to help organize your thoughts. ▶

Produce Use your notes to produce descriptions of the goods and services you will sell and buy through your local trade exchange. Think about the value of these goods and services and why they are important to your community.

Present Choose a creative way to present your local trade exchange to the class. Consider one of these options:

- Create a multimedia presentation to promote the local goods and services for sale on your trade exchange.

- Write an advertisement for a media site that describes your local trade exchange and its importance to the community.

- Draw a map of your community and provide icons in the map key to identify commodities that are traded on the exchange.

Trade Commodities

Goods and Services to Sell	
Goods and Services to Buy	

RAPID REVIEW
UNIT 6

AFRICAN CIVILIZATIONS

TOP TEN

1. Berbers from North Africa established profitable trans-Saharan trade routes with West Africa for gold, salt, and slaves.
2. The Nok people were the first to raise cattle and use iron, and they dominated West Africa.
3. The empires of Ghana and Mali grew powerful by controlling trans-Saharan trade routes.
4. Wealthy civilizations emerged on the East African coast as the monsoon winds helped a sea trade develop in the Indian Ocean.
5. Groups of people in Central Africa migrated east and south, carrying with them their Bantu language and iron making skills.

6-10. **NOW IT'S YOUR TURN** Complete the list with five more things to remember about African civilizations.

RAPID REVIEW

POSSIBLE RESPONSES

Possible responses for the remaining five things to remember include the following:

6. Bantu speakers settled in southern Africa and established the powerful city of Great Zimbabwe.

7. The kingdom of Kongo ruled Central Africa, but the arrival of Portuguese slave traders led to its collapse.

8. The trans-Saharan slave trade provided slaves from West Africa to the Mediterranean region.

9. Great kingdoms emerged in Africa including Aksum, Kilwa, Great Zimbabwe, and Kongo.

10. By 1500, Islam had spread to North Africa by conquest and to East Africa by trade.

UNIT INQUIRY PROJECT RUBRIC

ASSESS

Use the rubric to assess each student's participation and performance.

SCORE	ASSIGNMENT	PRODUCT	PRESENTATION
3 GREAT	• Student thoroughly understands the assignment. • Student engages fully with the project process. • Student works well independently.	• Trade exchange is well thought out. • Trade exchange includes many commodities and needed goods. • Descriptions of goods are thorough.	• Presentation is clear, concise, and logical. • Presentation does a good job of creatively explaining the trade exchange and its goods and services. • Presentation engages the audience.
2 GOOD	• Student mostly understands the assignment. • Student engages fairly well with the project process. • Student works fairly well independently.	• Trade exchange is somewhat thought out. • Trade exchange includes some commodities and needed goods. • Descriptions of goods are somewhat thorough.	• Presentation is fairly clear, concise, and logical. • Presentation does an adequate job of creatively explaining the trade exchange and its goods and services. • Presentation somewhat engages the audience.
1 NEEDS WORK	• Student does not understand the assignment. • Student minimally engages or does not engage with the project process. • Student struggles to work independently.	• Trade exchange is not well thought out. • Trade exchange does not contain commodities or needed goods. • Descriptions of goods are not thorough or are nonexistent.	• Presentation is not clear, concise, or logical. • Presentation does not creatively explain the trade exchange and its goods and services. • Presentation does not engage the audience.

AMERICAN
CIVILIZATIONS

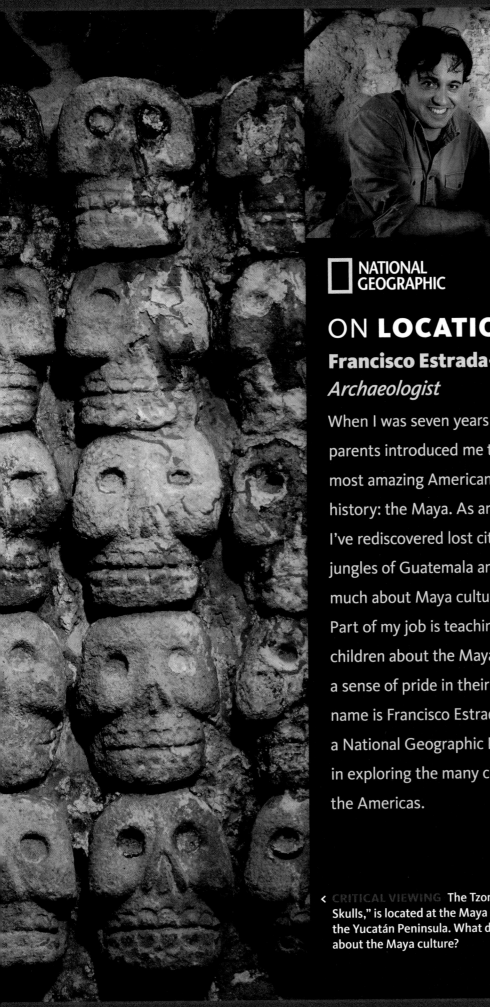

NATIONAL GEOGRAPHIC

ON **LOCATION** WITH

Francisco Estrada-Belli
Archaeologist

When I was seven years old, my parents introduced me to one of the most amazing American civilizations in history: the Maya. As an archaeologist, I've rediscovered lost cities in the jungles of Guatemala and have learned much about Maya culture and history. Part of my job is teaching Guatemalan children about the Maya and instilling a sense of pride in their homeland. My name is Francisco Estrada-Belli, and I'm a National Geographic Explorer. Join me in exploring the many civilizations of the Americas.

‹ CRITICAL VIEWING The Tzompantli, or "Wall of Skulls," is located at the Maya site of Chichén Itzá on the Yucatán Peninsula. What does this carving tell you about the Maya culture?

American
Civilizations

A.D. 250
The Maya Classic
Period begins.
*(carving on a
Maya stele)*

500 B.C.
The Zapotec build
Monte Albán.

900
The ancient
Pueblo build
Pueblo Bonito.

1200 B.C.
The Olmec
civilization begins
in Mesoamerica.

A.D. 500

1200 B.C.

**476
EUROPE**
The Western Roman
Empire falls.

**1045 B.C.
ASIA**
Zhou dynasty begins
800-year rule in China.

**500 B.C.
ASIA**
Buddhism
emerges in
India. *(Indian
Buddha sculpture)*

The
World

How long after the Olmec arose did the Zhou dynasty begin in China?

POSSIBLE RESPONSE
The Zhou dynasty began in China 155 years after the Olmec arose.

1325
The Aztec found Tenochtitlán and build a great civilization.
(clay vessel of Aztec maize goddess)

1450
The Inca build Machu Picchu in the Andes Mountains.

1200
More than 20,000 people live in the Mississippian city of Cahokia.

1519
Spanish conquistadors arrive in the Aztec Empire.

1300

1000

1600

1324
AFRICA
Mali king Mansa Musa makes a pilgrimage to Mecca.

1347
EUROPE
Rats carry the Bubonic plague through Europe.

1405
ASIA
Zheng He begins the first of seven voyages from China, exploring Asia and Africa.

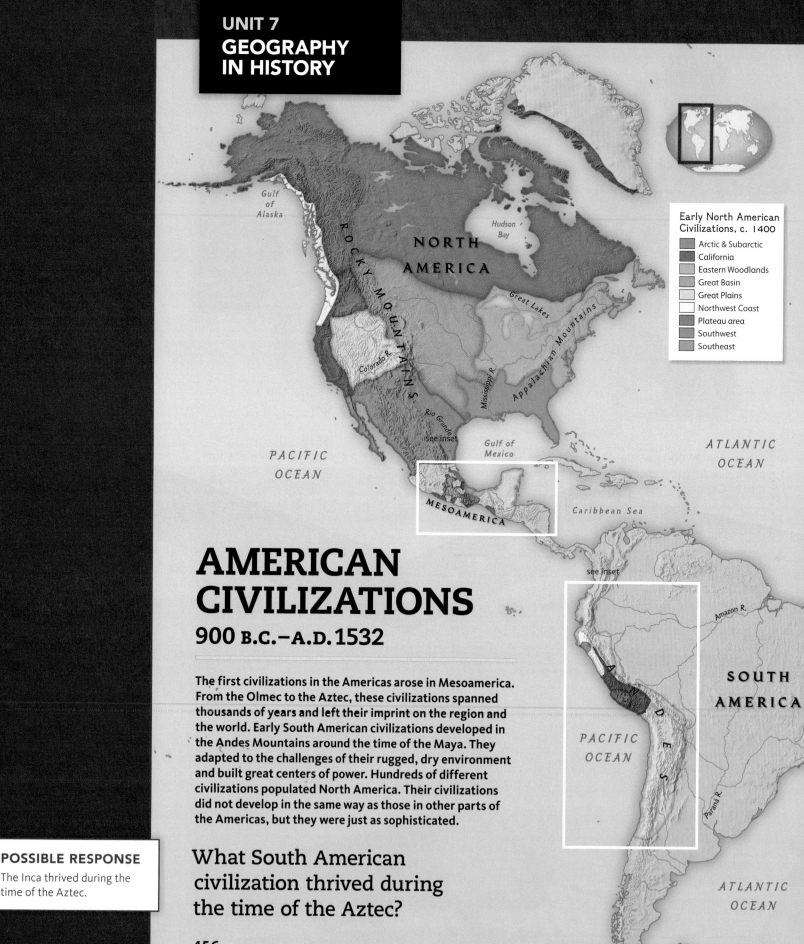

NORTH AMERICA

Gulf of Alaska

Hudson Bay

ROCKY MOUNTAINS

Great Lakes

Colorado R.

Mississippi R.

Appalachian Mountains

Rio Grande

see inset

Gulf of Mexico

PACIFIC OCEAN

MESOAMERICA

Caribbean Sea

ATLANTIC OCEAN

Early North American Civilizations, c. 1400

- Arctic & Subarctic
- California
- Eastern Woodlands
- Great Basin
- Great Plains
- Northwest Coast
- Plateau area
- Southwest
- Southeast

see inset

Amazon R.

SOUTH AMERICA

ANDES

PACIFIC OCEAN

Paraná R.

ATLANTIC OCEAN

AMERICAN CIVILIZATIONS
900 B.C.–A.D. 1532

The first civilizations in the Americas arose in Mesoamerica. From the Olmec to the Aztec, these civilizations spanned thousands of years and left their imprint on the region and the world. Early South American civilizations developed in the Andes Mountains around the time of the Maya. They adapted to the challenges of their rugged, dry environment and built great centers of power. Hundreds of different civilizations populated North America. Their civilizations did not develop in the same way as those in other parts of the Americas, but they were just as sophisticated.

What South American civilization thrived during the time of the Aztec?

+ POSSIBLE RESPONSE
The Inca thrived during the time of the Aztec.

EARLY MESOAMERICAN CIVILIZATIONS

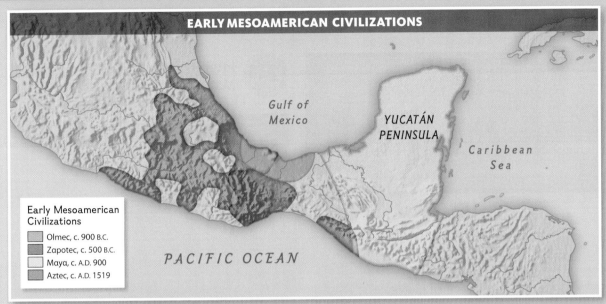

Gulf of Mexico

YUCATÁN PENINSULA

Caribbean Sea

PACIFIC OCEAN

Early Mesoamerican Civilizations
- Olmec, c. 900 B.C.
- Zapotec, c. 500 B.C.
- Maya, c. A.D. 900
- Aztec, c. A.D. 1519

EARLY SOUTH AMERICAN CIVILIZATIONS

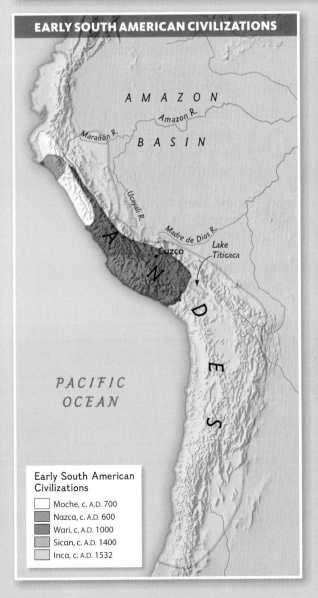

AMAZON

Amazon R.

Marañón R.

BASIN

Ucayali R.

Madre de Dios R.

A N D E S

Cuzco

Lake Titicaca

PACIFIC OCEAN

Early South American Civilizations
- Moche, c. A.D. 700
- Nazca, c. A.D. 600
- Wari, c. A.D. 1000
- Sican, c. A.D. 1400
- Inca, c. A.D. 1532

INCA BY THE NUMBERS

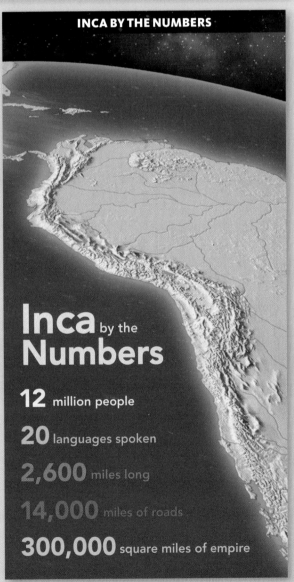

Inca by the Numbers

12 million people

20 languages spoken

2,600 miles long

14,000 miles of roads

300,000 square miles of empire

UNIT RESOURCES

On Location with National Geographic Grantee Francisco Estrada-Belli
Intro and Video

Interactive Map Tool

News & Updates

Available on myNGconnect

Unit Wrap-Up:
"Connecting Past and Present"
Feature and Video

"Unburying the Aztec"
National Geographic Adapted Article

"People of the Horse"
National Geographic Adapted Article
Student eEdition exclusive

Unit 7 Inquiry:
Design an Adaptation Strategy

CHAPTER RESOURCES

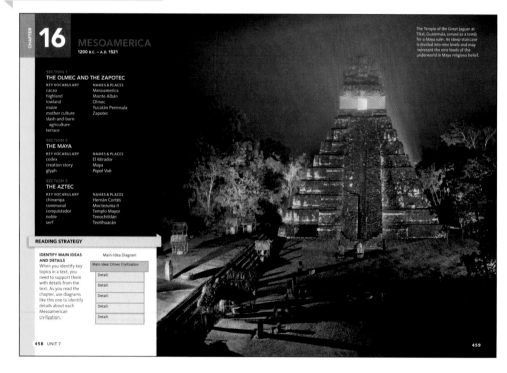

CHAPTER
16
MESOAMERICA
1200 B.C. – A.D. 1521

SECTION 1
THE OLMEC AND THE ZAPOTEC

KEY VOCABULARY	NAMES & PLACES
cacao	Mesoamerica
highland	Monte Albán
lowland	Olmec
maize	Yucatán Peninsula
mother culture	Zapotec
slash-and-burn agriculture	
terrace	

SECTION 2
THE MAYA

KEY VOCABULARY	NAMES & PLACES
codex	El Mirador
creation story	Maya
glyph	*Popol Vuh*

SECTION 3
THE AZTEC

KEY VOCABULARY	NAMES & PLACES
chinampa	Hernán Cortés
communal	Moctezuma II
conquistador	Templo Mayor
noble	Tenochtitlán
serf	Teotihuacán

READING STRATEGY

IDENTIFY MAIN IDEAS AND DETAILS
When you identify key topics in a text, you need to support them with details from the text. As you read the chapter, use diagrams like this one to identify details about each Mesoamerican civilization.

Main-Idea Diagram
Main Idea: Olmec Civilization
Detail:
Detail:
Detail:
Detail:
Detail:

458 UNIT 7
459

The Temple of the Great Jaguar at Tikal, Guatemala, served as a tomb for a Maya ruler. Its steep staircase is divided into nine levels and may represent the nine levels of the underworld in Maya religious belief.

TEACHER RESOURCES & ASSESSMENT

Available on myNGconnect

Social Studies Skills Lessons
• Reading: Identify Main Ideas and Details
• Writing: Write an Explanation

Formal Assessment
• Chapter 16 Tests A (on-level) & B (below-level)

Chapter 16 Answer Key

ExamView®
One-time Download

STUDENT BACKPACK *Available on myNGconnect*

• **eEdition** *(English)*   • **eEdition** *(Spanish)*   • **Handbooks**   • **Online Atlas**
For Chapter 16 Spanish Resources, visit the Teacher Resource Menu page on myNGconnect.

SECTION 1 RESOURCES

THE OLMEC AND THE ZAPOTEC

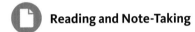 **Reading and Note-Taking**

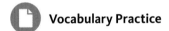 **Vocabulary Practice**

 **Section 1 Quiz**

Available on myNGconnect

LESSON 1.1 THE GEOGRAPHY OF MESOAMERICA
- Critical Viewing: NG Chapter Gallery
- On Your Feet: Team Word Webbing

LESSON 1.2 OLMEC CULTURE
NG Learning Framework:
Learn About Olmec Artists

- On Your Feet: Inside-Outside Circle

LESSON 1.3 THE ZAPOTEC AND MONTE ALBÁN
- Critical Viewing: NG Chapter Gallery
- On Your Feet: Question and Answer

SECTION 2 RESOURCES

THE MAYA

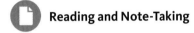 **Reading and Note-Taking**

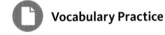 **Vocabulary Practice**

 **Section 2 Quiz**

Available on myNGconnect

LESSON 2.1 MAYA SOCIAL STRUCTURE
NG Learning Framework:
Learn About Maya Gods

- On Your Feet: Model Maya Society

LESSON 2.2 MAYA CITIES
NG Learning Framework:
Learn About Maya Daily Life

- On Your Feet: Numbered Heads

NG EXPLORER WILLIAM SATURNO
LESSON 2.3 UNCOVERING MAYA MURALS
NG Learning Framework:
Learn About William Saturno

- On Your Feet: Three-Step Interview

LESSON 2.4 LEGACY OF THE MAYA
- Critical Viewing: NG Chapter Gallery
- On Your Feet: Turn and Talk on Topic

DOCUMENT-BASED QUESTION
LESSON 2.5 CREATION STORIES
- Critical Viewing: NG Chapter Gallery
- On Your Feet: Jigsaw Strategy

SECTION 3 RESOURCES

THE AZTEC

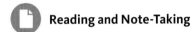 **Reading and Note-Taking**

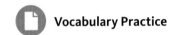 **Vocabulary Practice**

 **Section 3 Quiz**

Available on myNGconnect

LESSON 3.1 TENOCHTITLÁN: AN AZTEC CITY
 **Active History: Interactive Whiteboard Activity**
Create a Sketch Map of Tenochtitlán

 **Active History**
Create a Sketch Map of Tenochtitlán

Available on myNGconnect

- On Your Feet: Tell Me More

LESSON 3.2 AZTEC CULTURE
- Critical Viewing: NG Chapter Gallery
- On Your Feet: Word Chain

LESSON 3.3 AZTEC DEFEAT AND LEGACY
 **Biography**
Hernán Cortés

 **Biography**
Moctezuma II

Available on myNGconnect

- Critical Viewing: NG Chapter Gallery
- On Your Feet: Prepare a Script

CHAPTER 16 REVIEW

STRATEGY ❶
Use a Word Splash

Present the words on the board in a random arrangement (splash) as shown, and ask students to choose three pairs of words that are related to each other. Have students use this sentence starter to write how each pair of words is related.

_____ and _____ are related because . . . .

Use with Lessons 3.1–3.3

STRATEGY ❷
Build an ABC Summary

For a review of the reading, suggest that students write important words from the lessons that begin with each letter of the alphabet starting with A and working through to Z, filling in as many letters as they can. Students can compare summaries.

ABC SUMMARY CHART MESOAMERICA	
A	C
B	D

Use with All Lessons *Encourage students to look beyond Key Vocabulary words and proper nouns. For example, the word influenced in Lesson 1.1 might help students think about how the Mesoamerican cultures developed.*

STRATEGY ❸
Make a "Top Five Facts" List

Assign a lesson to be read. After reading, have students write in their own words five important facts that they have learned. Let them meet with a partner to compare lists and consolidate the two lists into one final list. Call on students to offer facts from their lists.

Use with All Lessons

Press **mt** *in the Student eEdition for modified text.*

STRATEGY ❶
Provide Terms and Names on Audio

Decide which of the terms and names are important for mastery and have a volunteer record the pronunciations and a short sentence defining each word. Encourage students to listen to the recording as often as necessary.

Use with All Lessons *You might also use the recordings to quiz students on their mastery of the terms. Play one definition at a time from the recording and ask students to identify the term or name described.*

STRATEGY ❷
Modify Main Idea Statements

Provide these modifications of the Main Idea statements at the beginning of each lesson:

1.1 Geography had a big impact on Mesoamerican civilizations.

1.2 The Olmec civilization was one of Mesoamerica's earliest civilizations. It influenced cultures that came later.

1.3 The Zapotec started their civilization in the Oaxaca Valley. They controlled the area for more than 1,000 years.

Use with Lessons 1.1–1.3

STRATEGY ❶
Set Up a Word Wall

Work with students to choose three words from each lesson to display in a grouping on a Word Wall. It might be useful to choose words that students are likely to encounter in other contexts, such as *terrace* or *noble*. Keep the words displayed throughout the lessons and discuss each one as it comes up during reading. Have volunteers add words, phrases, and examples to each word to develop understanding.

Use with All Lessons

STRATEGY ❷
PREP Before Reading

Have students use the PREP strategy to prepare for reading. Write this acrostic on the board:

PREP
- **P**review title.
- **R**ead Main Idea statement.
- **E**xamine visuals.
- **P**redict what you will learn.

Have students write their prediction and share it with a partner. After reading, ask students to write another sentence that begins, "I also learned . . ."

Use with All Lessons

STRATEGY ❸
Illustrate a Word Tree

Write the following word tree on the board to help students understand the relationship among the groups. Then ask them to copy and draw pictures to illustrate each branch of the tree.

king
priests warriors
merchants merchants craftspeople craftspeople
farmers farmers farmers slaves slaves slaves

Use with Lesson 2.1 *You might also have students write sentences explaining the relationships.*

GIFTED & TALENTED

STRATEGY ❶
Teach a Class

Before beginning the chapter, allow students to choose one of the lessons listed below and prepare to teach the content to the class. Give them a set amount of time in which to present their lesson. Suggest that students think about any visuals or activities they may want to use when they teach.

Use with Lessons 1.3, 2.2–2.4, and 3.3

STRATEGY ❷
Interview a Historical Figure

Allow students to work in teams of two to plan, write, and perform a simulated television interview with Moctezuma II or with Hernán Cortés. Tell students that the purpose of the interview is to focus on the achievements, actions, and goals of the historical figure.

Use with Lesson 3.3 *Invite students to do research to learn more about the historical figure they have chosen. Encourage them to elicit in-depth answers by asking the historical figures why and how they did the things they did.*

PRE-AP

STRATEGY ❶
Profile a King

Have students work in groups to learn about Maya king Pacal. Have them create a profile of Pacal and illustrate it with images they find on reliable online sites.

Use with Lessons 2.1–2.5 *Encourage students to discuss Pacal's long reign, his building projects, and his tomb.*

STRATEGY ❷
Form a Thesis

Have students develop a thesis statement for a specific topic related to each of the lessons in the chapter. Be sure the statements make a claim that is supportable with evidence either from the lesson or through further research. Then have students get together in pairs to compare their statements and determine which make the strongest or most supportable claims.

Use with All Lessons

MESOAMERICA

1200 B.C. – A.D. 1521

The Temple of the Great Jaguar at Tikal, Guatemala, served as a tomb for a Maya ruler. Its steep staircase is divided into nine levels and may represent the nine levels of the underworld in Maya religious belief.

SECTION 1
THE OLMEC AND THE ZAPOTEC

KEY VOCABULARY	NAMES & PLACES
cacao	Mesoamerica
highland	Monte Albán
lowland	Olmec
maize	Yucatán Peninsula
mother culture	Zapotec
slash-and-burn agriculture	
terrace	

SECTION 2
THE MAYA

KEY VOCABULARY	NAMES & PLACES
codex	El Mirador
creation story	Maya
glyph	*Popol Vuh*

SECTION 3
THE AZTEC

KEY VOCABULARY	NAMES & PLACES
chinampa	Hernán Cortés
communal	Moctezuma II
conquistador	Templo Mayor
noble	Tenochtitlán
serf	Teotihuacán

READING STRATEGY

IDENTIFY MAIN IDEAS AND DETAILS
When you identify key topics in a text, you need to support them with details from the text. As you read the chapter, use diagrams like this one to identify details about each Mesoamerican civilization.

Main-Idea Diagram

Main Idea: Olmec Civilization
Detail:
Detail:
Detail:
Detail:
Detail:

TEACHER BACKGROUND

INTRODUCE THE PHOTOGRAPH

Have students study the photograph of the Maya temple in Tikal, Guatemala. Explain that the Maya and other cultures developed advanced civilizations in a region called Mesoamerica. Tell students that, in this chapter, they will learn about the rise and fall of these civilizations and their lasting legacies. Then read aloud the image caption to the class.

ASK: What feelings might this temple have inspired in Maya worshippers? (*Possible responses: awe, fear, devotion, calm*)

SHARE BACKGROUND

The Temple of the Great Jaguar was built around A.D. 700. The very steep staircase in the center of the pyramid leads to a shrine at the top of the temple. After the decline of the Maya civilization around 900, this temple and many others were hidden by dense jungle growth for centuries. The Temple of the Great Jaguar was finally uncovered by European archaeologists in the 1800s.

DIGITAL RESOURCES myNGconnect.com

TEACHER RESOURCES & ASSESSMENT

 Social Studies Skills Lessons
- Reading: Identify Main Ideas and Details
- Writing: Write an Explanation

 Formal Assessment
- Chapter 16 Tests A (on-level) & B (below-level)

 ExamView®
One-time Download

 Chapter 16 Answer Key

STUDENT BACKPACK

- **eEdition** (*English*)
- **eEdition** (*Spanish*)
- **Handbooks**
- **Online Atlas**

For Chapter 16 Spanish resources, visit the Teacher Resource Menu page.

INTRODUCE THE ESSENTIAL QUESTION

HOW DID MESOAMERICAN CIVILIZATIONS ADOPT AND ADAPT THE CULTURES OF EARLIER CIVILIZATIONS?

Four Corner Activity: Spread of Culture This activity allows students to discuss the ways in which culture spreads. Post the following four signs in the corners of the classroom: Immigration, Trade, Technology, War. Divide the class into four groups and have each group meet at one of the corners. Assign the following questions to the groups:

1. **Immigration:** How do immigrants spread their culture?

2. **Trade:** What types of goods and ideas can be spread by trade?

3. **Technology:** How has technology made culture spread faster?

4. **War:** How might war introduce new cultures?

Have students in each corner discuss their question. When they have finished their discussion, ask a representative from each group to summarize that group's answers. **0:15** minutes

 1's
 3's
 2's
 4's

INTRODUCE THE READING STRATEGY

IDENTIFY MAIN IDEAS AND DETAILS

Remind students that identifying main ideas and details will help them get more out of a text. Model completing the Main Idea and Details List by reading the second paragraph under "Agriculture" in Lesson 1.1 and writing "Agricultural Practices" under Main Idea, and "irrigation in drier areas" under the first Detail. Then have students identify the other details in the paragraph.

Main Idea: Agricultural Practices
Detail: *irrigation in drier areas*
Detail:
Detail:
Detail:
Detail:

INTRODUCE CHAPTER VOCABULARY

KNOWLEDGE RATING

Have students complete a Knowledge-Rating Chart for Key Vocabulary words. Have students list words and fill out the chart. Then have pairs share the definitions they know. Work together as a class to complete the chart.

KEY VOCAB	KNOW IT	NOT SURE	DON'T KNOW	DEFINITION
cacao				
chinampa				
codex				
communal				

KEY DATES

C. 1300 B.C.	San José Mogote emerges as the Zapotec center of power
C. 1200 B.C.	Olmec culture begins to develop
C. 500 B.C.	The Zapotec build Monte Albán
C. 400 B.C.	Olmec civilization disappears
C. A.D. 250	The Maya Classic Period begins
C. 900	The Maya abandon many of their cities
1325	The Aztec found Tenochtitlán
1521	Spanish soldiers conquer the Aztec

EXPLORE THE MAYA

For more information on Maya civilization, check out *EXPLORE THE MAYA.*

1.1
The Geography of
Mesoamerica

You walk among the ruins, gazing at the remains of temple complexes, carved stone sculptures, and towering pyramids. Are you visiting a city that thrived during the time of ancient Egypt? No. You're in the middle of a jungle in a region of North America known as Mesoamerica.

MAIN IDEA

Geographic factors greatly influenced the development of civilizations in Mesoamerica.

HIGHLANDS AND LOWLANDS

Thousands of years ago, advanced civilizations arose in **Mesoamerica**, which stretches from southern Mexico into part of Central America. The region's climate and fertile land helped the civilizations thrive.

Mesoamerica's landscape is divided into two main geographic areas: **highlands**, or land high above the sea, and **lowlands**, or land that is low and level. The highlands lie between the mountains of the Sierra Madre, a mountain system in Mexico, and consist of fairly flat and fertile land. This land was good for agriculture, but it also posed some challenges for its early residents. They were rocked from time to time by volcanic eruptions and powerful earthquakes. The lowlands are less active. They lie along the coast of the

Gulf of Mexico. They are also found in the jungles of the **Yucatán** (you-kuh-TAN) **Peninsula**, which is located between the Gulf of Mexico and the Caribbean Sea.

If you hiked from the lowlands to the highlands, you would experience a wide variety of climates, from tropical rain forests to very cold, dry zones in the higher mountains. In general, the climate in the highlands is cooler and drier than that in the lowlands, where it can rain more than 100 inches a year. The lowlands are also crisscrossed by many rivers. Some of these rivers flood during heavy seasonal rains and wash fertile silt onto their floodplains.

AGRICULTURE

Early Mesoamerican farmers learned what crops would grow well in the different climates of the highlands and lowlands. In the drier highland areas, the main crops included **maize** (also known as corn), squash, and beans. These three crops are often called the Three Sisters because they benefit from being planted close together. The beans grow up the maize stalks, while the squash spreads over the ground, preventing the growth of weeds. Farmers in the lowlands grew these three crops as well as palm, avocado, and **cacao** (kuh-COW) trees. Cacao beans were used to make chocolate. Sometimes the beans were even used as money.

Mesoamerica's farmers developed different agricultural practices in the region's varied landscapes. In drier areas, farmers redirected the course of streams to irrigate their fields. In the dense lowland jungles, farmers cleared fields through a technique known as **slash-and-burn agriculture**, shown on the opposite page. These agricultural techniques helped ancient cultures produce food surpluses and allowed people to do jobs other than farming. As a result, civilizations began to arise in Mesoamerica more than 3,000 years ago—first the Olmec and later the Zapotec.

EARLY MESOAMERICAN CIVILIZATIONS, 900–500 B.C.

- Olmec civilization, 900 B.C.
- Major Olmec center
- Zapotec civilization, 500 B.C.
- Major Zapotec center
- Limit of Mesoamerica

SLASH-AND-BURN AGRICULTURE

1 Slash
Wooded areas and jungles are too thick to plant crops. Farmers slash, or cut down, trees.

2 Burn
Fallen trees and leaves are burned to clear the land. Ash produced by the fires is used as fertilizer.

3 Fertilize and Plant
Cleared land is fertilized with ash. Farmers plant crops such as maize and squash.

4 Migrate
Farmers move on to new locations after soil on cleared land becomes less productive.

REVIEW & ASSESS

1. **READING CHECK** What geographic factors influenced the development of civilizations in Mesoamerica?

2. **INTERPRET MAPS** Why do you think the Olmec and Zapotec civilizations developed along coastal areas?

3. **COMPARE AND CONTRAST** How did agricultural techniques differ in Mesoamerica's highlands and lowlands?

PLAN

OBJECTIVE

Discuss how geographic factors influenced the development of civilizations in Mesoamerica.

CRITICAL THINKING SKILLS FOR LESSON 1.1

- Identify Main Ideas and Details
- Monitor Comprehension
- Interpret Maps
- Compare and Contrast
- Summarize

ESSENTIAL QUESTION

How did Mesoamerican civilizations adopt and adapt the cultures of earlier civilizations?

Mesoamerica has a varied landscape, with some areas experiencing occasional volcanic eruptions and earthquakes. Lesson 1.1 describes how Mesoamerican farmers developed different agricultural practices to adapt to their environment and thrive.

BACKGROUND FOR THE TEACHER

Corn, often eaten as a vegetable, is actually a grain related to other cereal plants such as wheat and rice. Originating in the Americas, it has spread around the world and become a food staple.

The maize that was first domesticated in Mesoamerica did not look exactly like the corn we eat today. Early maize plants produced many branches on the stalks and ears that were quite small. Over time, Mesoamerican farmers learned to suppress the growth of branches, which resulted in a lower number of larger ears. Today, maize plants produce just a few ears of corn growing on a single stalk.

DIGITAL RESOURCES myNGconnect.com

TEACHER RESOURCES & ASSESSMENT

 Reading and Note-Taking

 Vocabulary Practice

 Section 1 Quiz

STUDENT RESOURCES

 NG Chapter Gallery

INTRODUCE & ENGAGE

INTRODUCE & ENGAGE

ANALYZE VISUALS

Have students study the illustrations of slash-and-burn agriculture. Read aloud each caption in the illustrations. **ASK:**

- How are the people using the tools in the first illustration? *(They are chopping down trees.)*
- What tasks are they doing in the second and third illustrations? *(They are burning trees and plants. They are planting crops.)*
- Why are the farmers walking away in the fourth illustration? *(The soil is not productive anymore.)*

Tell students that, in this lesson, they will learn how Mesoamerican farmers used this technique to grow abundant food. **0:05 minutes**

TEACH

GUIDED DISCUSSION

1. **Compare and Contrast** How does the climate of Mesoamerica's highlands and lowlands differ? *(The climate in the highlands is generally cooler and drier than that in the lowlands, where it can rain more than 100 inches a year.)*

2. **Summarize** How did Mesoamerican farmers adapt to their environment? *(They learned what crops would grow well in the different climates. They planted crops that benefited from being planted close together. They learned how to irrigate their crops and clear their fields.)*

INTERPRET MAPS

Have students study the map of early Mesoamerican civilizations. Point out the yellow coloring that indicates the limit of Mesoamerica. Have students trace the area with a finger on the map. Tell them that the Sierra Madre del Sur, on the southwestern edge of Mexico, and the Sierra Madre Oriental, on the eastern edge, are mountain ranges. Then point out the areas where the Olmec and Zapotec civilizations arose. **ASK:** How would you describe their location in relation to each other? *(The civilizations developed very close to each other.)* Why do you think that is so? *(They both developed in advantageous areas: near the coast and in mountain valleys.)* **0:10 minutes**

ACTIVE OPTIONS

Critical Viewing: NG Chapter Gallery Invite students to explore the Chapter Gallery to examine the images that relate to Chapter 16. Have them select one of the images and do additional research to learn more about it. Ask questions that will inspire additional inquiry about the chosen gallery image, such as: What is this? Where and when was this created? By whom? Why was it created? What is it made of? Why does it belong in this chapter? What else would you like to know about it? **0:10 minutes**

On Your Feet: Team Word Webbing Divide the class into four groups and have them gather at desks in the four corners of the room. Give each group a large sheet of paper and different colored markers. Assign each group one of these topics: highlands, lowlands, climates, slash-and-burn agriculture. Then have the groups create a Word Web for their topic. Have them write words for their topic, adding as many circles as they need. Tell them to pass the paper to each group member and rotate it as they add to the Word Web. **0:20 minutes**

DIFFERENTIATE

STRIVING READERS

Identify Main Ideas and Details Allow students to form two groups and give each group a copy of a Main Ideas and Details List. Assign each group one of the two subsections of the lesson. Have them work together to identify the main idea in their assigned section and the details that support that idea. Then guide groups in constructing a one- or two-sentence statement that unites the two main ideas. *(Sample statements: Mesoamerica is divided into highlands and lowlands, which have a variety of climates and geographic features. Mesoamerican farmers learned to adapt to their environment and lay the foundation for thriving civilizations.)*

ENGLISH LANGUAGE LEARNERS

Make Vocabulary Cards Have students use flash cards to learn and practice unfamiliar words they encounter in this lesson. On one side of each card, they should write the target word. On the other, they should write related words they are familiar with, draw or paste images that will help them recall the meaning of the target word, or write out other mnemonic devices. Encourage students to use their flash cards for review.

Press **mt** *in the Student eEdition for modified text.*

See the Chapter Planner for more strategies for differentiation.

REVIEW & ASSESS

ANSWERS

1. Geographic factors that influenced the development of civilizations in Mesoamerica include the flat, fertile land in the highlands, the rainy climate of the lowlands, and the fertile floodplains of the lowlands.

2. The Olmec and Zapotec civilizations developed along coastal areas in order to be close to water sources.

3. In the drier highlands, fields were irrigated by diverting nearby streams. In the lowlands, slash-and-burn agriculture was used to clear fields in the dense jungles.

Olmec Culture

After a long search, the foreman has finally found the right rock. It's huge and heavy. He directs his men to begin their work. Their task: to haul the rock 50 miles through the jungle to the city where an artist will carve it into a sculpture. Their challenge: to move the rock without using a wheeled cart or animals. Welcome to the world of the Olmec.

MAIN IDEA

The Olmec civilization that arose in Mesoamerica was one of the region's earliest civilizations and influenced later cultures.

JAGUAR GOD
The Olmec worshipped many gods, but one of the most important was the jaguar god. When Olmec priests visited the spirit world, the priests believed they transformed into powerful jaguars.

OLMEC CITIES

The **Olmec** (AHL-mehk) culture began along Mexico's Gulf Coast around 1200 B.C. The development of this culture led to the birth of Mesoamerica's first civilization.

Like the ancient civilizations of Mesopotamia, Egypt, India, and China, the Olmec emerged on the floodplains of rivers. Heavy rains caused these rivers to flood and deposit fertile silt on their plains. The rich soil allowed farmers to grow abundant crops. In time, the culture's economy expanded and cities, including San Lorenzo, La Venta, and Tres Zapotes, began to develop. (See the map in Lesson 1.1.)

Olmec cities contained pyramids and temples built on earthen mounds. The Olmec also built courts where athletes played a game that was a sort of combination of modern soccer and basketball. You will learn more about this game later in the chapter.

Archaeologists have also found extraordinary works of art in Olmec cities. Chief among these are the huge stone heads the Olmec carved out of rock. The heads stand as tall as 10 feet and can weigh up to 20 tons. They are believed to represent different Olmec rulers.

DAILY LIFE AND LEGACY

Workers, including those who hauled the rocks for the stone sculptures, and farmers made up most of Olmec society. They were at the bottom of the civilization's class structure. Rulers were at the top, followed by priests, merchants, and artists. The farmers and workers lived in simple houses made of wood or mud. The upper classes lived in more elaborate stone structures and wore fine clothes and precious jewelry.

Archaeologists are not sure why, but around 400 B.C., the Olmec civilization disappeared. However, elements of the civilization's legacy can be seen in later civilizations. The Olmec had established an extensive trade network. In addition to the exchange of goods, the trade routes carried Olmec culture throughout Mesoamerica. As new civilizations arose, their people were influenced by Olmec art and religious practices. As a result, many archaeologists consider the Olmec to be the **mother culture** of Mesoamerica.

Critical Viewing The rock this head was carved out of may have been rolled onto a log raft and floated downriver. Why might Olmec laborers have chosen to use this method to move the head?

+ POSSIBLE RESPONSE

It would have much easier to transport the huge block of stone on a raft rather than push and haul it by hand.

REVIEW & ASSESS

1. **READING CHECK** What geographic features played a key role in the development of Olmec civilization?

2. **INTERPRET VISUALS** What does the stone head suggest about the power and authority of Olmec rulers?

3. **DRAW CONCLUSIONS** What conclusions can you draw about daily life for most of the Olmec people?

PLAN

OBJECTIVE

Discuss the Olmec civilization and explain how it influenced later cultures.

CRITICAL THINKING SKILLS FOR LESSON 1.2

- Identify Main Ideas and Details
- Monitor Comprehension
- Interpret Visuals
- Draw Conclusions
- Compare and Contrast
- Make Inferences

ESSENTIAL QUESTION

How did Mesoamerican civilizations adopt and adapt the cultures of earlier civilizations?

The Olmec developed Mesoamerica's first civilization and built elaborate cities and created great works of art. Lesson 1.2 explains how the Olmec, with their extensive trade network, spread their culture and became the mother culture of Mesoamerica.

BACKGROUND FOR THE TEACHER

Only 17 stone Olmec heads have been uncovered, 10 of which were found in San Lorenzo and La Venta. Archaeologists have determined that each head was carved from a single basalt boulder. Experts theorize that sculptors only depicted the head because, according to Mesoamerican culture, the head was believed to be where the soul resided. Originally, the heads were probably painted in bright colors, but these have long since worn off.

DIGITAL RESOURCES myNGconnect.com

TEACHER RESOURCES & ASSESSMENT

 Reading and Note-Taking

 Vocabulary Practice

 Section 1 Quiz

STUDENT RESOURCES

 NG Chapter Gallery

DISCUSS TERMS

Draw an Idea Web on the board and write *culture* in the center square. Ask students to volunteer what comes to mind when they hear the word *culture* and add their ideas to the web. Then tell them that the Olmec civilization became a mother culture to later Mesoamerican civilizations. Discuss the term and encourage students to identify other civilizations that have been so influential that they might be considered mother cultures. **0:10** minutes

TEACH

GUIDED DISCUSSION

1. **Compare and Contrast** How was the emergence of the Olmec similar to the rise of the ancient civilizations of Mesopotamia, Egypt, India, and China? *(Like these civilizations, the Olmec emerged on the floodplains of rivers.)*

2. **Make Inferences** Which classes of Olmec society probably lived in the cities? *(probably only the upper classes, including rulers, priests, merchants, and artists)*

INTERPRET VISUALS

Have students examine the image of the Olmec head. Discuss the size, facial features, and head covering of the head. **ASK:** How would you describe the expression carved on the head? *(Possible responses: stern, serious, angry)* What might have been the purpose of the heads? *(Possible responses: to celebrate Olmec rulers, to frighten enemies, to inspire awe and respect for the rulers)* **0:10** minutes

ACTIVE OPTIONS

On Your Feet: Inside-Outside Circle Have students form concentric circles facing each other. Allow students time to write questions about the geography, cities, culture, and society of the Olmec. Ask students in the inside circle to pose questions to students in the outside circle. Then have students switch roles. Students may ask for help from other students in their circle if they are unable to answer a question. **0:20** minutes

NG Learning Framework: Learn About Olmec Artists

SKILL: Communication
KNOWLEDGE: **Our Human Story**

Have students imagine they are workers hauling rocks to the city so that Olmec artists can create stone heads. Ask students to write journal entries about the difficulties and challenges they encounter as they drag the rocks through the jungle. Suggest, too, that they record their experiences and conversations with the other workers. **0:10** minutes

STRIVING READERS

Pose and Answer Questions Have students work in pairs to read the lesson. Instruct them to pause after each paragraph and ask each other *who, what, where, when,* or *why* questions about what they have just read. Suggest students use a 5Ws Chart to help organize their questions and answers.

```
┌─────────────────────────────────┐
│                                 │
│  Who?   _____  │
│                                 │
│  What?  _____  │
│                                 │
│  Where? _____  │
│                                 │
│  When?  _____  │
│                                 │
│  Why?   _____  │
│         _____  │
│         _____  │
│                                 │
└─────────────────────────────────┘
```

GIFTED & TALENTED

Prepare an Interview Have pairs of students use online sources to learn more about the Olmec civilization. Then ask them to imagine that they could interview an Olmec man or woman living in an Olmec city or on a farm. Have them come up with ten questions to ask about Olmec culture and prepare the answers. Pairs should then take turns sharing several of their questions and answers with the class.

Press **mt** *in the Student eEdition for modified text.*

See the Chapter Planner for more strategies for differentiation.

ANSWERS

1. A geographic feature that played a key role in the development of Olmec civilization includes the floodplains of rivers, where heavy rains caused rivers to flood and deposit fertile silt along the plains.

2. The head suggests that Olmec rulers were powerful and revered.

3. Since most of the Olmec people were farmers and workers, their daily lives were probably filled with hard work and deprivation.

1.3 The **Zapotec** and **Monte Albán**

As the Olmec declined, the Zapotec people were developing an advanced society to the southwest. Although their culture reflected Olmec influence, the Zapotec developed their own distinct and powerful civilization. They became a leading player in Mesoamerica.

MAIN IDEA

The Zapotec established a civilization and controlled the Oaxaca Valley for more than 1,000 years.

PEOPLE OF THE VALLEY

The **Zapotec** people would build one of the first major cities in Mesoamerica, but their beginnings were humble. They developed their society in the Oaxaca (wuh-HAH-kah) Valley, a large, open area where three smaller valleys meet. (See the map in Lesson 1.1.) This fertile area, with its river, mild climate, and abundant rainfall, proved excellent for growing crops, especially maize.

For centuries, the Zapotec lived in farming villages located throughout the Oaxaca Valley. Then, around 1300 B.C., a settlement called San José Mogote (san ho-ZAY moh-GOH-tay) emerged as the Zapotec center of power. Leaders built temples there and had artists decorate them with huge sculptures. In time, nearly half of the Zapotec people lived in San José Mogote.

URBAN CENTER

Around 500 B.C., the center of power shifted when the Zapotec built a city known now as **Monte Albán** (MAHN-tay ahl-BAHN) high atop a mountain. The site overlooked the Oaxaca Valley. Its location helped the Zapotec defend themselves against their enemies. Monte Albán must have been a spectacular sight. The city's rulers flattened the top of the mountain and built great plazas on it filled with pyramids, palaces, and even an astronomical observatory.

Monte Albán became the center of the Zapotec civilization. There, the Zapotec built magnificent tombs in which they buried the bodies of wealthy people wearing their gold jewelry. The Zapotec believed the deceased would carry the jewelry into the afterlife. Artificial **terraces**, or stepped platforms built into the mountainside, provided additional area for building and agriculture.

Around A.D. 750, Monte Albán's power began to weaken. By 900, the city had disappeared. Economic difficulties may have caused the decline, but no one knows for sure. Like the fall of the Olmec, the decline of the Zapotec civilization remains a mystery.

POSSIBLE RESPONSE

Members of the upper class are being served by those of the lower and wear fancy clothes, elaborate headdresses, and shoes. Members of the lower classes kneel before those of the upper class, wear simple and minimal clothing, and are barefoot. The artists, who rank above the workers, wear more clothing as well as some pieces of jewelry.

Critical Viewing This mural by Mexican artist Diego Rivera shows Zapotec artists at work. What details in the mural convey class differences in the society?

REVIEW & ASSESS

1. **READING CHECK** What geographic features of the Oaxaca Valley encouraged the development of the Zapotec civilization?

2. **MAKE INFERENCES** How do you think the location of Monte Albán helped the Zapotec defend themselves from their enemies?

3. **DETERMINE WORD MEANINGS** What does *deceased* mean in the phrase, "the deceased would carry the jewelry into the afterlife"?

OBJECTIVE

Explain how the Zapotec established a civilization and controlled the Oaxaca Valley for more than 1,000 years.

CRITICAL THINKING SKILLS FOR LESSON 1.3

- Identify Main Ideas and Details
- Monitor Comprehension
- Make Inferences
- Determine Word Meanings
- Draw Conclusions
- Analyze Visuals

ESSENTIAL QUESTION

How did Mesoamerican civilizations adopt and adapt the cultures of earlier civilizations?

The Zapotec developed a powerful civilization in the Oaxaca Valley. Lesson 1.3 explains that the Zapotec adopted aspects of Olmec culture but went on to develop their own distinct civilization.

BACKGROUND FOR THE TEACHER

Monte Albán was the first true urban center in the Americas. In 200 B.C., it was home to 15,000 people. At its peak, about 25,000 people lived in the city. Remains of the city of Monte Albán still stand. Archaeologists have studied what's left of its magnificent temples, ball courts, tombs, and works of art.

Experts have also admired Monte Albán's advanced plan and design. The city was laid out in a sophisticated grid pattern, with buildings following a strict and harmonious design.

DIGITAL RESOURCES myNGconnect.com

TEACHER RESOURCES & ASSESSMENT

 Reading and Note-Taking   **Vocabulary Practice**   **Section 1 Quiz**

STUDENT RESOURCES

 NG Chapter Gallery

INTRODUCE & ENGAGE

BUILD A CITY

Ask students to imagine that they are rulers of a developing civilization and want to build a great city to demonstrate their power. Have them discuss the following questions:

- Where would you want to build the city? Encourage students to think about the need for water sources, a good climate, and natural defenses.

- What types of buildings would your city contain? Remind students that the buildings should include those used for government, work, recreation, and residence.

- What infrastructure would the city have? Tell students that infrastructure includes roads, transportation and communication services, energy sources, and schools.

When the discussion has concluded, tell students that, in this lesson, they will learn about the Zapotec civilization, whose rulers built a city on a mountaintop that became the first urban center in Mesoamerica. **0:10** minutes

TEACH

GUIDED DISCUSSION

1. **Make Inferences** Why was Monte Albán probably a good place to build an astronomical observatory? *(The city was built on top of a mountain, so astronomers would have had a good, clear view of the stars and other heavenly bodies.)*

2. **Draw Conclusions** What aspects of Olmec culture did the Zapotec adopt? *(Like the Olmec, the Zapotec grew maize, built temples, pyramids, and ball courts, and created huge sculptures.)*

ANALYZE VISUALS

Have students examine the mural. Make sure students understand which members of society the different figures represent. **ASK:** Who are the artists? *(The artists are the modestly clothed figures who mostly appear seated in the foreground of the mural.)* What are the artists creating? *(headdresses and, possibly, paintings)* Which figures probably belong to a class beneath the artists? How can you tell? *(the figures helping the artists and kneeling in front of the figures in the background; They appear to be more subservient and are dressed only in a type of loincloth.)* What level of society do the figures trying on the headdresses probably belong to? How can you tell? *(the upper classes; They are elegantly dressed and are being waited on.)* **0:10** minutes

ACTIVE OPTIONS

Critical Viewing: NG Chapter Gallery Ask students to choose one image from the Chapter Gallery for Section 1 and become an expert on it. They should do additional research to learn all about it. Then have students share their findings with a partner, a small group, or the class. **0:10** minutes

On Your Feet: Question and Answer Have half the class write true-false questions based on information in the lesson. Ask the other half to create answer cards, with "True" written on one side and "False" on the other. As each question is read aloud, students in the second group should stand and hold up the correct answer to the question. When discrepancies occur, review the question and discuss which answer is correct. **0:15** minutes

DIFFERENTIATE

INCLUSION

Discuss Key Events Have students conduct roundtables in groups of four. Students should take turns identifying key events that shaped the rise, dominance, and fall of the Zapotec civilization. **ASK:** How would you summarize the course of the Zapotec civilization?

> The Zapotec civilization developed in the Oaxaca Valley and grew to become a leading player in Mesoamerica until it mysteriously began to decline around A.D. 750.

PRE-AP

Compare and Contrast Have students conduct online research to learn more about the Olmec and Zapotec and compare the two cultures. Have them address the following questions:

- What were some of the two cultures' religious beliefs?

- What, if any, writing system did they have?

- What artwork did they produce?

- What scientific studies did they pursue?

Ask students to present their findings to the class.

Press **mt** *in the Student eEdition for modified text.*

See the Chapter Planner for more strategies for differentiation.

REVIEW & ASSESS

ANSWERS

1. The Oaxaca Valley had fertile soil, a mild climate, adequate rainfall, and access to water provided by a river running through the valley.

2. From their position high atop the mountain, the Zapotec could see the enemy advancing and had time to prepare their defense.

3. The word *deceased* means "dead people."

Maya
Social Structure

Can people be made of corn? According to Maya tradition, they can. But it took the Maya gods a while to figure out how to do it. At first, they made people out of things like mud and wood, but these creatures couldn't speak. Finally, the gods mixed their blood with maize flour. The result? Walking, talking human beings. No wonder the early Maya called themselves "the people of the maize."

MAIN IDEA

Maya society was structured according to a class system, and religion shaped daily life.

CLASS SYSTEM

The **Maya** emerged around the same time as the Zapotec. Their culture began to develop to the east of the Zapotec in areas of present-day southern Mexico and Central America around 1500 B.C. These areas included lowlands in the north, highlands in the south, the forests of the Yucatán Peninsula, and the tropical jungles of Mexico and Guatemala.

Like Olmec farmers, Maya farmers developed successful agricultural practices. They produced surpluses of crops, including beans, chili peppers, cacao beans, and, of course, maize, which the Maya considered sacred. These surpluses allowed some people to become priests, merchants, and craftspeople and some villages to gain great wealth. Wealthier villages with religious ceremonial centers arose around 500 B.C. In time, these villages grew into cities.

The development of Maya cities produced a class system with four main classes. At the top was the king, who performed religious ceremonies and was believed to have descended from the gods. Next came priests and warriors. The priests decided when farmers could plant and when people could marry. They also conducted important religious rituals and ceremonies. Warriors were well respected and well trained.

Merchants and craftspeople followed these upper classes. Craftspeople made articles out of pottery and designed buildings and temples. The merchants sold and traded goods—often with buyers in other Maya cities. Finally, farmers—who made up the majority of the population—and slaves were at the bottom of the heap. Most of the slaves were prisoners of war. They were given the worst jobs and were often killed when their masters died.

DAILY LIFE

Class determined where people lived and how they dressed. People who belonged to the upper classes lived in stone buildings and wore colorfully decorated clothes and jewelry. Farmers wore plain clothes and lived in mud huts.

While the wealthy enjoyed a comfortable lifestyle, farmers worked hard in the heat to grow their crops. On hillsides they carved out terraces on which to grow their maize, cacao beans, and chili peppers. In drier areas they dug channels that carried river water to their fields. In addition to doing their own work, sometimes farmers had to tend the king's fields and build monuments and temples in his cities.

MAYA MAIZE GOD

The maize god was one of the most important Maya gods. The god often appeared as a handsome young man with hair made of maize silk. The god represented the cycle of life (birth, death, rebirth) as well as the cycle of maize (planting, harvesting, replanting).

MAYA CIVILIZATION, A.D. 250–900

Eventually the Maya learned how to track seasonal changes. This knowledge helped them predict the best time to plant and harvest their crops. You will learn more about how the Maya measured time later in the chapter.

Above all, however, the farmers looked to their gods to control the weather and increase their harvests. Religion was central to everyone's lives, and the Maya worshipped many gods, including the gods of fire, sun, war, rain, and maize. (You can learn more about the importance of the maize god in the feature above.) All of these gods were thought to influence every aspect of the people's lives—in both good and bad ways.

To please the gods, the Maya made frequent offerings of food, animals, plants, and precious objects. As you have already learned, the Maya believed that the gods had given their blood to create people. In return, the Maya sometimes offered their own blood or made human sacrifices to honor the gods. Just as maize nourished people, the Maya believed that blood nourished the gods. Rather than sacrifice one of their own, however, the Maya often sacrificed a member of the lowest class in their society: a slave.

REVIEW & ASSESS

1. **READING CHECK** What were the four main classes of early Maya society?

2. **INTERPRET MAPS** On what geographic landform were many of the major Maya cities located?

3. **COMPARE AND CONTRAST** How did the daily life of farmers differ from that of people belonging to the wealthier classes?

PLAN

OBJECTIVE

Describe the class system in Maya society and the importance of religion in daily life.

CRITICAL THINKING SKILLS FOR LESSON 2.1

- Identify Main Ideas and Details
- Monitor Comprehension
- Interpret Maps
- Compare and Contrast
- Make Inferences
- Draw Conclusions

ESSENTIAL QUESTION

How did Mesoamerican civilizations adopt and adapt the cultures of earlier civilizations?

The Maya developed a social structure and worshipped many different gods. Lesson 2.1 describes the development of Maya civilization, which was similar to that of the Olmec and Zapotec.

BACKGROUND FOR THE TEACHER

Chac, the Maya god of rain and lightning, was an important god because the Maya could not survive without rain. The god was especially revered in the Yucatán Peninsula, where rain tends to be unpredictable. However, the Maya also somewhat feared Chac, who was believed to live in the underworld. Because the Maya thought caves provided a doorway to the underworld, they often made offerings to Chac in caves. Some of these offerings were in the form of human sacrifices. Modern Maya still sometimes appeal to Chac, particularly in times of drought. Of course, they no longer offer sacrifices to the god. Instead, they often mix water with ground corn and drink it.

TEACHER RESOURCES & ASSESSMENT

 Reading and Note-Taking

 Vocabulary Practice

 Section 2 Quiz

STUDENT RESOURCES

 NG Chapter Gallery

INTRODUCE & ENGAGE

PREVIEW WITH THE VISUAL

Have students study the photograph of the Maya maize god. Read the caption aloud to the class. Explain that maize silk refers to the soft, glossy strands that surround and cling to a fresh ear of corn. Encourage students to discuss and describe the maize god. Then ask students why they think the Maya worshipped a maize god. Point out that, in this lesson, students will learn about Maya gods and religious practices. **0:05** minutes

TEACH

GUIDED DISCUSSION

1. **Make Inferences** Why do you think priests occupied such a high place in the Maya class system? *(because the Maya gods were central to Maya life and priests conducted the rituals and ceremonies honoring the gods)*

2. **Draw Conclusions** Why was it important to the Maya to please their gods? *(because the gods could influence every aspect of people's lives in both good and bad ways)*

INTERPRET MAPS

Have students study the Maya Civilization map. Point out the Yucatán Peninsula and remind students that a peninsula is a body of land that is bordered by water on three sides. Point out the major cities and archaeological sites shown on the map. Explain that dots represent the cities and small squares represent the sites. **ASK:** Which major city is located far away from most of the other cities? *(Chichén Itzá)* Between which two cities are the two archaeological sites located? *(between El Mirador and Tikal)* Tell students that they will learn about these Maya cities and archaeological sites in the next few lessons. **0:15** minutes

ACTIVE OPTIONS

On Your Feet: Model Maya Society Have students model Maya society. Have one student stand at the front of the class to represent the king. Place two students representing the priests and two students representing warriors behind the king. Next, place six students representing merchants and craftspeople after the priests and warriors. Finally, have all remaining students stand at the back of the classroom. Tell these students that they represent the farmers and slaves in Maya society.

While standing in this pyramid formation, students should describe their places in Maya society. Ask the student who holds the highest position in the society to raise his or her hand. *(the king)* Ask students who hold the lowest position to raise their hands. *(farmers and slaves)* **ASK:** What inequalities in the society do you see? *(Most of the people belong in the bottom class and have no power.)* **0:20** minutes

NG Learning Framework: Learn About Maya Gods

ATTITUDE: Curiosity
SKILLS: Communication, Collaboration

Have groups of five students research to learn about five important Maya gods. Each student in a group should then pick one of the gods and take turns presenting him or her to the class. Students should provide the god's name, explain what the god represented, and tell how the god was worshipped. **0:10** minutes

DIFFERENTIATE

STRIVING READERS

Take Notes Have students take notes as they read the lesson by completing a chart like the one shown below. Allow students to compare their completed charts in small groups and make any necessary corrections. Then call on volunteers to use their charts to summarize what they know about Maya society and daily life.

	Class and Role	Daily Life
King		
Priests and Warriors		
Merchants and Craftspeople		
Farmers and Slaves		

ENGLISH LANGUAGE LEARNERS

Read in Pairs Pair English language learners with native English speakers and have them read the lesson together. Instruct the native speakers to pause whenever they encounter a word or sentence construction that is confusing to their partners. Suggest that the native speakers point out context clues to help their partners understand the meanings of unfamiliar terms. Encourage English language learners to restate sentences in their own words.

Press **mt** *in the Student eEdition for modified text.*
See the Chapter Planner for more strategies for differentiation.

REVIEW & ASSESS

ANSWERS

1. The four main classes included the king, priests and warriors, merchants and craftspeople, and farmers and slaves.

2. Many were located on the Yucatán Peninsula.

3. Wealthy people lived in stone buildings and wore colorfully decorated clothes and jewelry. Farmers wore plain clothes and lived in mud huts. While the wealthy enjoyed a comfortable lifestyle, farmers worked hard to grow their crops.

Maya Cities

In the 1800s, explorers battled mosquitoes, illness, and thick jungle growth in their search for the ruined remains of the Maya civilization. Their efforts paid off. When they came upon the half-buried monuments in the ancient Maya city of Copán, one of the explorers—John Lloyd Stephens—was so fascinated by what he saw that he purchased the site on the spot.

MAIN IDEA

The Maya built sophisticated cities that contained impressive structures and artwork.

CLASSIC PERIOD

Many of the great Maya cities lay hidden beneath the jungle growth for centuries. One of the earliest of these cities was **El Mirador**, which has been called the "cradle of the Maya civilization." (See the map in Lesson 2.1.) The city flourished from about 300 B.C. to A.D. 150 and was home to as many as 200,000 people. Most Maya cities, however, developed during the Classic Period, which lasted between A.D. 250 and 900. These cities included Copán (koh-PAHN), Tikal (tee-KAHL), Chichén Itzá (chee-CHEHN ee-TSAH), and Palenque (pah-LEHNG-keh). Although

each was an independent city-state ruled by a king, trade linked the city-states. Merchants from the cities exchanged goods such as salt and jade jewelry and often paid for them with cacao beans.

Most Maya cities followed a similar layout. A large plaza in the center of the city served as both a public gathering place and market. Each city also contained a palace for the king, administrative buildings, temples, and stepped pyramids. The pyramids rose hundreds of feet in the air and were lined with steep staircases. Many of the pyramids featured platforms at the top. Priests conducted ceremonies on the platforms so that the entire population could witness them.

The Maya built temples on the top of some of the pyramids. A huge ball court was constructed at the foot of at least one of these pyramids in each city to allow athletes to play the sacred Mesoamerican ball game. The Maya played this game, which began with the Olmec, to honor their gods. The illustration on the opposite page shows Maya athletes in action on the court.

CULTURE AND ART

Like the ball game, many other aspects of Maya culture and art were linked to religion. Artists made sculptures that honored and brought to life the various Maya gods. They also carved stone slabs called stelae to honor their kings. Artists carved a king's likeness on the slab and recorded his actions on it as well—actually setting his story in stone.

All of these stories were probably passed down orally from generation to generation. This oral tradition continued long after the great Maya civilization had come to an end. It may have been weakened by war, food shortages, or overcrowding. For whatever reason, by A.D. 900, the Maya had abandoned many of their cities. When Spanish conquerors arrived in the 1500s, only weakened city-states had been left behind—a shadow of their former glory.

MESOAMERICAN BALL GAME

The game the Maya and other Mesoamerican peoples played on a court like this one was much more than a game. It was often a matter of life and death. The captain of the losing Maya team probably climbed the temple steps to be sacrificed to the gods.

Players weren't allowed to touch the ball with their hands. They could only bounce the ball off their knees, hips, and elbows.

The solid ball was hard enough to break bones, so the players wore some heavy padding.

The goal of the game was to launch the ball through a stone ring. Since this wasn't easy, a game could go on for days.

REVIEW & ASSESS

1. **READING CHECK** What was the layout of most of the great Maya cities?

2. **INTEGRATE VISUALS** Based on the illustration and what you have learned about the Mesoamerican ball game, what qualities were probably necessary to play the game?

3. **MAKE INFERENCES** How do you think the Maya reacted as they witnessed a religious ceremony performed at the top of a towering pyramid?

PLAN

OBJECTIVE

Describe the cities, structures, and art of the Maya in the Classic Period.

The Maya built sophisticated cities and created impressive artwork. Lesson 2.2 describes the influence of the Olmec on Maya structures and culture.

CRITICAL THINKING SKILLS FOR LESSON 2.2

- Identify Main Ideas and Details
- Monitor Comprehension
- Integrate Visuals
- Make Inferences
- Draw Conclusions
- Sequence Events

ESSENTIAL QUESTION

How did Mesoamerican civilizations adopt and adapt the cultures of earlier civilizations?

BACKGROUND FOR THE TEACHER

The Mesoamerican ballgame, sometimes called pok-a-tok, may have been the first team sport in human history. The game was played on an I-shaped court painted in bright colors. When the ball players made their ceremonial entrance onto the court, they wore fine clothing: elaborate headdresses, animal skins, and jewelry. To play the game, however, they wore minimal clothing—just enough to protect them from the hard rubber ball. The life-and-death game was surrounded by religious ritual and symbolism. The Maya believed that sacrificing a member of the losing team would help ensure plentiful crops or rain.

DIGITAL RESOURCES myNGconnect.com

TEACHER RESOURCES & ASSESSMENT

 Reading and Note-Taking

 Vocabulary Practice

 Section 2 Quiz

STUDENT RESOURCES

 NG Chapter Gallery

INTRODUCE & ENGAGE

ACTIVATE PRIOR KNOWLEDGE

Invite students to share what they know about the pyramids of ancient Egypt from their knowledge of world history. Ask these questions and write students' responses on the board:

- What did the pyramids in ancient Egypt look like?
- Where were they located?
- What were the pyramids used for?
- What happened to the pyramids after the power of ancient Egypt declined?

Then ask students if they know about pyramids located in other places. Tell them that they will learn about the pyramids built by the Maya in this lesson. **0:10** minutes

TEACH

GUIDED DISCUSSION

1. **Draw Conclusions** Why do you think the market occupied a central place in most Maya cities? *(because trade was so important to the Maya)*

2. **Sequence Events** What happened around A.D. 900? *(The Maya abandoned many of their cities.)*

INTERPRET VISUALS

Review the illustration of the Mesoamerican ball game with students in class. Read aloud the introduction and captions. Have students study the stone ring in the illustration and invite students to imagine how difficult it must have been to launch a ball through it. Then point out the athlete in the illustration bouncing the hard rubber ball off of his hip. Remind students that, in an earlier lesson, they learned that the Mesoamerican ball game has some aspects in common with basketball and soccer. **ASK:** In what ways is the Mesoamerican game similar to basketball and soccer? *(In basketball, players try to throw a ball through a hoop. In soccer, most players are not allowed to touch the ball with their hands.)* **0:10** minutes

ACTIVE OPTIONS

On Your Feet: Numbered Heads Organize students into groups of four. Tell students to think about and discuss a response to this question: *What were important elements of Maya civilization?* Then call a number and have the student from each group with that number report for the group. **0:15** minutes

NG Learning Framework: Learn About Maya Daily Life

SKILLS: Observation, Collaboration
KNOWLEDGE: **Our Human Story, Our Living Planet**

Have students revisit Lessons 2.1 and 2.2 to put together a complete picture of the Maya. Ask students to focus on the following topics: geographic challenges, agriculture, class system,

daily life, cities, religion, and art. Students should work in groups, with each member choosing a topic. Have students become an expert in their chosen topic and then take turns presenting what they've learned to the class. **0:10** minutes

DIFFERENTIATE

STRIVING READERS

Summarize Have students complete a graphic organizer like the one shown to keep track of important details about Maya cities as they read the lesson. Then have students form pairs and use their completed charts to summarize what they learned about Maya cities.

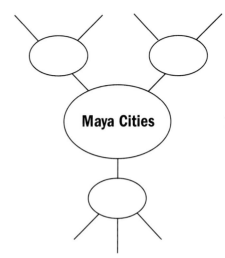

PRE-AP

Create a Multimedia Presentation Have students research to find information about some aspect of the Maya, such as religion, architecture, the writing system, or the Mesoamerican ball game. Tell students to create a multimedia display that uses text and images to describe their findings. Allow them to draw the images if they wish. Encourage students to share their presentations with the class.

Press **mt** *in the Student eEdition for modified text.*

See the Chapter Planner for more strategies for differentiation.

REVIEW & ASSESS

ANSWERS

1. Most Maya cities included a palace for the king, administrative buildings, temples, and stepped pyramids.

2. Qualities such as exceptional athletic skill, endurance, strength, bravery, intense religious feeling, and self-sacrifice were probably necessary.

3. The people were probably awestruck, deeply inspired, and made more devout by the spectacle.

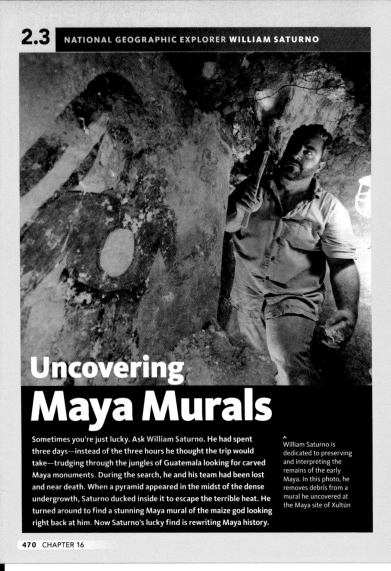

Uncovering
Maya Murals

Sometimes you're just lucky. Ask William Saturno. He had spent three days—instead of the three hours he thought the trip would take—trudging through the jungles of Guatemala looking for carved Maya monuments. During the search, he and his team had been lost and near death. When a pyramid appeared in the midst of the dense undergrowth, Saturno ducked inside it to escape the terrible heat. He turned around to find a stunning Maya mural of the maize god looking right back at him. Now Saturno's lucky find is rewriting Maya history.

^ William Saturno is dedicated to preserving and interpreting the remains of the early Maya. In this photo, he removes debris from a mural he uncovered at the Maya site of Xultún

MAIN IDEA

Archaeologist William Saturno's discoveries have challenged ideas about the early Maya and provided insight into their way of thinking.

A LUCKY FIND

National Geographic Explorer William Saturno has spent his life studying the Maya and searching out the civilization's secrets. His greatest discovery occurred in 2001, when he found the mural at a site he later named San Bartolo.

Saturno spent several years excavating the wall painting, which represented the Maya creation story in graceful and sophisticated detail. However, when Saturno dated the work of art, he found that it had been created around 100 B.C.—more than 300 years before the Maya Classic Period had even begun. As Saturno says, "Clearly Maya painting had achieved glory centuries before the great works of the Classic Maya."

The far end of the mural revealed another surprise—the portrait of a king. "Some scholars thought that at this early stage in Maya history, the Preclassic, city-states had not yet evolved into full-fledged monarchies, with all the trappings seen later," explains Saturno. "But here was a king, named and titled, receiving his crown. In short, this one chamber upended much of what we thought we knew about the early Maya."

ROOM OF WONDER

About ten years later and just five miles from San Bartolo, Saturno got lucky again. He was digging under a mound in the Maya site of Xultún (shool-tuhn) when a

Portrait of a scholar in the San Bartolo mural

student assistant claimed he'd found traces of paint on a wall. "I was curious," Saturno says. "So I excavated to the back wall, and I saw a beautiful portrait of a king. There he was in Technicolor, with blue feathers."

After more painstaking work, Saturno uncovered an entire room with paintings of other figures and a wall covered with columns of numbers. He thinks that mathematicians had been using the walls like a whiteboard to see whether the movements of the moon and planets matched the dates they had calculated. The mural and numbers dated back to about A.D. 750, around the time Xultún was beginning to decline.

According to Saturno, the Maya knew the collapse of their city had begun. Still, as he says, "They wanted to tie events in their king's life to larger cosmic cycles. They wanted to show that the king would be okay and that nothing would change. We keep looking for endings. It's an entirely different mind-set. I would never have identified this nondescript [uninteresting] mound as special. But this discovery implies that special things are everywhere."

REVIEW & ASSESS

1. **READING CHECK** Why are William Saturno's discoveries so remarkable?
2. **DRAW CONCLUSIONS** Saturno emphasizes the luck he's had in his explorations, but what other qualities must he possess to carry out his work?
3. **ANALYZE LANGUAGE USE** Saturno says that the Maya had "an entirely different mind-set." What do you think he is suggesting about how the Maya viewed the world?

PLAN

OBJECTIVE

Discuss how archaeologist William Saturno's discoveries are challenging ideas about the early Maya.

CRITICAL THINKING SKILLS FOR LESSON 2.3

- Identify Main Ideas and Details
- Monitor Comprehension
- Draw Conclusions
- Analyze Language Use
- Summarize
- Synthesize

ESSENTIAL QUESTION

How did Mesoamerican civilizations adopt and adapt the cultures of earlier civilizations?

William Saturno discovered early Maya murals that had been hidden for many centuries. Lesson 2.3 describes the ways in which Saturno's findings have provided insight into Maya culture and their view of the world.

BACKGROUND FOR THE TEACHER

William Saturno believes that the Maya artists who painted the murals at San Bartolo began their artistic training when they were young. They would have been schooled at an early age in the art of making the sacred Maya stories come to life.

When the artists finished, their murals covered at least two walls of a room at the pyramid's base. Saturno says, "The masterpiece had two purposes: to honor the gods and to illustrate that the king derived his power from those gods."

DIGITAL RESOURCES myNGconnect.com

TEACHER RESOURCES & ASSESSMENT

 Reading and Note-Taking   **Vocabulary Practice**   **Section 2 Quiz**

STUDENT RESOURCES

 NG Chapter Gallery

INTRODUCE & ENGAGE

DISCUSS IMPORTANT FINDINGS

Initiate a class discussion about findings—their own and those in history. Ask students to think of a time when they found something that had been missing or lost or that had meaning for them. Invite them to share how they felt when they made their discovery. Then see if students can identify some important findings in history, such as the discovery of King Tut's tomb in Egypt or Columbus' voyage to the Americas. Tell students that, in this lesson, they will learn about an archaeologist who uncovered Maya murals that had been hidden for centuries. **0:05** minutes

TEACH

GUIDED DISCUSSION

1. **Summarize** What did Saturno's findings at the archaeological site of San Bartolo reveal about the Maya? *(They had been creating great works of art and were under the rule of monarchs before the Maya Classic Period.)*

2. **Draw Conclusions** What do the columns of numbers Saturno uncovered at Xultún suggest about Maya mathematicians? *(They were very advanced.)*

SYNTHESIZE

Divide the class into groups of four students. Each group should analyze Saturno's explorations in San Bartolo and Xultún, synthesizing information in Lesson 2.3. Have students record their findings in a chart like the one shown and use the information to answer the "Reading Check" question in Review & Assess. **0:10** minutes

SAN BARTOLO	XULTÚN

ACTIVE OPTIONS

On Your Feet: Three-Step Interview Have students work in pairs to discuss the third question in Review & Assess. Ask students what they think William Saturno means when he says that the Maya had "an entirely different mind-set." As pairs conduct their interviews, tell them to use more detailed questions about the quotation. For example: "What do you think *mind-set* means?" "What is our modern mind-set?" "What was the Maya mind-set?" Remind students to listen closely as their partner answers so that they can report what they hear to the rest of the class. **0:20** minutes

NG Learning Framework: Learn About William Saturno

ATTITUDE: Curiosity
KNOWLEDGE: Our Human Story

Have students learn more about William Saturno. Instruct them to write a short biography about the archaeologist using information from the chapter and additional source material. **0:10** minutes

DIFFERENTIATE

INCLUSION

Clarify Text Have visually impaired students work with sighted partners. As they listen to an audio recording of the text, have the visually impaired students indicate if there are words or passages they do not understand. Their partners can clarify meaning by repeating passages, emphasizing context clues, and paraphrasing.

GIFTED & TALENTED

Write an Explorer Blog Ask students to imagine that they are archaeologists exploring Maya archaeological sites where they make a great discovery. Ask them to write a brief blog about their experiences at the site, the challenges they face searching for it, and their thoughts and emotions when they make their discovery.

> Just made the discovery of a lifetime!

Press **mt** *in the Student eEdition for modified text.*

See the Chapter Planner for more strategies for differentiation.

REVIEW & ASSESS

ANSWERS

1. Before the discovery at San Bartolo, archaeologists had thought that great works of Maya art had only been produced during the Classic Period. Archaeologists also didn't believe that city-states had evolved into monarchies before the Classic Period.

2. Possible responses include intelligence, a deep interest and love of the past, perseverance, skill, patience, enthusiasm, tenacity, empathy, and optimism.

3. He is suggesting that the Maya believed the world would continue, that there would be cycles—new beginnings, but never endings.

Legacy of the Maya

In 2012, the prediction went viral: On December 21, the world was going to end. The prediction was based on the Maya calendar, which some people claimed would end on that day. But the date simply marked the completion of a 5,125-year cycle. The Maya had calculated that a new cycle would begin on the 22nd.

MAIN IDEA

Important advances in mathematics, astronomy, and writing allowed the Maya to create their calendar.

The Maya calendar is actually a system of several calendars used together to track days and cycles. Glyphs, like those you see here, represent days and months in the complex calendar.

MAYA NUMBERS

0	1
2	5
6	10

The Maya represented numbers using only three symbols: a shell for zero, a dot for one, and a bar for five. A few of the numbers are shown above. Try using the symbols to create some simple subtraction problems.

MATH AND ASTRONOMY

The Maya were superb mathematicians. Like the people of ancient India, they developed the concept of zero. They also developed a sophisticated number system using positions to show place value and to calculate sums up to the hundreds of millions.

Such calculations were used to record astronomical observations as well. Maya astronomers observed the sun, moon, planets, and stars and were able to predict their movements with great accuracy—all without the aid of any instruments. Instead, they studied the sky from temples and observatories. Astronomers used their observations to calculate the best times for planting and harvesting crops and for religious celebrations.

These astronomical observations and calculations were used to develop an elaborate 365-day calendar that was nearly as accurate as our own. Remember the room that William Saturno uncovered in Xultún? The mathematical calculations on its walls were probably used to work out dates in the calendar.

WRITING SYSTEM AND BOOKS

Archaeologists gained a better understanding of the Maya people's scientific achievements and culture once they began to crack the code of their writing system. The Maya used symbolic pictures called **glyphs** (glihfs) to represent words, syllables, and sounds that could be combined into complex sentences.

The Maya carved glyphs into their monuments, stelae, and tombs. Maya writers, called scribes, also used them to record their people's history in a folded book made of tree-bark paper called a **codex**. The Spanish conquerors destroyed most of the codices in the 1500s. However, after the Spanish arrived, the Maya wrote other books in which they recorded Maya history and culture. The most famous of these books is called the *Popol Vuh*, which recounts the Maya creation story.

As you've already learned, the Maya civilization had greatly declined by A.D. 900. However, Maya people today still keep their culture alive. Many of them speak the Maya languages and tell their ancestors' stories. They are a living legacy of the Maya civilization.

REVIEW & ASSESS

1. **READING CHECK** What important mathematical ideas did the Maya develop?

2. **IDENTIFY MAIN IDEAS AND DETAILS** According to the text, why did Maya astronomers study the sun, moon, planets, and stars?

3. **ANALYZE CAUSE AND EFFECT** What breakthrough helped archaeologists gain a better understanding of Maya history and culture?

PLAN

OBJECTIVE

Describe the important advances the Maya made in mathematics, astronomy, and writing.

The Maya left a great legacy in mathematics and science. Lesson 2.4 describes the Maya number system and the accuracy of the observations made by Maya astronomers.

CRITICAL THINKING SKILLS FOR LESSON 2.4

- Identify Main Ideas and Details
- Monitor Comprehension
- Analyze Cause and Effect
- Make Inferences
- Summarize

BACKGROUND FOR THE TEACHER

Before archaeologists cracked the code of the Maya writing system, many researchers believed the ancient civilization was a peaceful one. They believed the Maya were farmers who were ruled by wise astronomer-priests. Once archaeologists learned to read the glyphs, however, they discovered that the Maya were as warlike and political as any civilization. New technologies are helping them learn even more. In time, they hope that all their questions about the Maya will be answered.

ESSENTIAL QUESTION

How did Mesoamerican civilizations adopt and adapt the cultures of earlier civilizations?

DIGITAL RESOURCES myNGconnect.com

TEACHER RESOURCES & ASSESSMENT

 Reading and Note-Taking

 Vocabulary Practice

 Section 2 Quiz

STUDENT RESOURCES

 NG Chapter Gallery

INTRODUCE & ENGAGE

CALCULATE LIKE THE MAYA

Copy the Maya numbers from the lesson on the board and explain them to the class. Then jot down a couple of simple addition and subtraction problems using the numbers and challenge students to solve them. Finally, ask volunteers to write their own math problems on the board using the Maya numbers. Invite other students to come up and write the answers. **0:10** minutes

TEACH

GUIDED DISCUSSION

1. **Make Inferences** Why do you think the Maya recorded their history and culture after the Spanish conquered them? *(They didn't want their culture to disappear without a trace.)*

2. **Summarize** Where have archaeologists found Maya glyphs? *(on Maya calendars, monuments, stelae, tombs, and in codices)*

MORE INFORMATION

December 21, 2012 The world didn't come to an end on this date, but it was still a very important one for the Maya. They believed that, on that day, the gods who created the world would return. The gods would conduct certain rites and set space and time in order. In other words, the Maya believed the world would be renewed on December 21, 2012, not destroyed.

ACTIVE OPTIONS

Critical Viewing: NG Chapter Gallery Invite students to explore the Chapter 16 Gallery to examine the images that relate to this section. Have them select one of the images and do additional research to learn more about it. Ask questions that will inspire additional inquiry about the chosen gallery image, such as: What is this? Where and when was this created? By whom? Why was it created? What is it made of? Why does it belong in this chapter? What else would you like to know about it? **0:10** minutes

On Your Feet: Turn and Talk on Topic Have students form four lines. Give each line the same topic sentence: *The Maya civilization left a great legacy.* Tell groups to build a paragraph on that topic by having each student in each line add one sentence about a different achievement of the Maya civilization. Finally, have groups present their paragraphs to the class, with each student reading his or her sentence. **0:15** minutes

DIFFERENTIATE

STRIVING READERS

Create Charts Provide students with a three-column chart with the heads *Math, Astronomy,* and *Writing,* similar to the one shown below. Have them work in pairs to fill out the chart with information from the lesson on Maya achievements in these areas.

MATH	ASTRONOMY	WRITING

ENGLISH LANGUAGE LEARNERS

Use Sentence Strips Choose a paragraph from the lesson and make sentence strips out of it. Read the paragraph aloud, having students follow along in their books. Then have students close their books and give them the set of sentence strips. Students should put the strips in order and then read the paragraph aloud.

Press **mt** *in the Student eEdition for modified text.*

See the Chapter Planner for more strategies for differentiation.

REVIEW & ASSESS

ANSWERS

1. They developed the concept of zero and a sophisticated number system using positions to show place values.

2. They studied the sun, moon, planets, and stars to calculate the best times for planting and harvesting crops and for religious celebrations. They used this information to develop their elaborate calendar.

3. Cracking the code of the Maya writing system helped them gain a better understanding of Maya history and culture.

Creation Stories

Every culture has a **creation story**: an account that explains how the world began and how people came to exist. Creation stories are often considered sacred and are usually passed down by oral tradition before they are written down. Like the excerpts you are about to read, creation stories often begin by describing how a god or gods brought order to the universe.

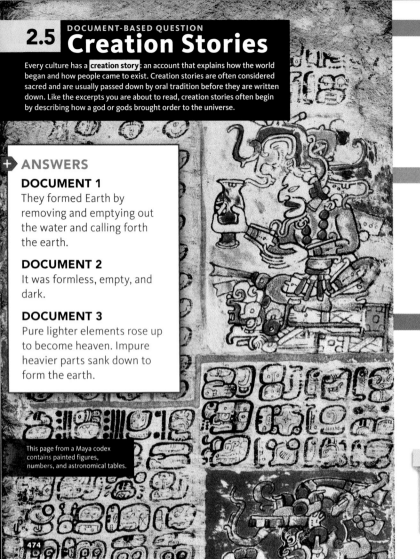

This page from a Maya codex contains painted figures, numbers, and astronomical tables.

+ ANSWERS

DOCUMENT 1
They formed Earth by removing and emptying out the water and calling forth the earth.

DOCUMENT 2
It was formless, empty, and dark.

DOCUMENT 3
Pure lighter elements rose up to become heaven. Impure heavier parts sank down to form the earth.

474

DOCUMENT ONE
Primary Source: Sacred Text

from the *Popol Vuh*,
translated by Dennis Tedlock
Spanish conquerors destroyed much of Maya culture in the 1500s. To preserve their sacred stories for future generations, Maya scribes wrote them down in the *Popol Vuh*. In this passage, two Maya gods form Earth from a world that contains only the sea.

CONSTRUCTED RESPONSE According to this passage, how did the Maya gods form Earth?

"Let it be this way, think about it: this water should be removed, emptied out for the formation of the earth's own plate and platform . . ." they said. And then the earth arose because of them, it was simply their word that brought it forth. For the forming of the earth they said, "Earth." It arose suddenly, just like a cloud, like a mist, now forming, unfolding.

DOCUMENT TWO
Primary Source: Sacred Text

from the Book of Genesis
Genesis is the first book of the Hebrew Bible, a collection of sacred Jewish texts. It is also the first book of the Old Testament in the Christian Bible. Followers of both religions believe in a single God. In this passage from Genesis, which means "the origin, or beginning," God creates night and day.

CONSTRUCTED RESPONSE In this excerpt, what was the world like before God brought light to the earth?

When God began to create heaven and earth—the earth being unformed and void [empty]. . .—God said, "Let there be light"; and there was light. God saw that the light was good, and God separated the light from the darkness. God called the light Day, and the darkness He called Night. And there was evening and there was morning, a first day.

DOCUMENT THREE
Primary Source: Myth

from *Pan Gu Creates Heaven and Earth*,
translated by Jan and Yvonne Walls
Pan Gu is a god in an ancient Chinese creation story that has been told and passed down for more than 2,000 years. According to the story, Pan Gu created heaven and earth. In this passage, Pan Gu bursts from a disordered universe that is shaped like an egg.

CONSTRUCTED RESPONSE In this myth, what elements formed heaven and what elements formed the earth?

Pan Gu, an enormous giant, was being nurtured [cared for] in the dark chaos of that egg. . . . Then one day he woke and stretched himself, shattering the egg-shaped chaos into pieces. The pure lighter elements gradually rose up to become heaven and the impure heavier parts slowly sank down to form the earth.

SYNTHESIZE & WRITE

1. **REVIEW** Review what you have learned about the creation stories and religious beliefs of early civilizations.

2. **RECALL** On your own paper, write down the main idea expressed in each document.

3. **CONSTRUCT** Write a topic sentence that answers this question: What are some common characteristics of creation stories?

4. **WRITE** Using evidence from the documents, write a paragraph to support your answer in Step 3.

PLAN

OBJECTIVE

Synthesize information about creation stories from three sacred texts.

CRITICAL THINKING SKILLS FOR LESSON 2.5

- Synthesize
- Identify
- Compare and Contrast
- Make Connections
- Evaluate

ESSENTIAL QUESTION

How did Mesoamerican civilizations adopt and adapt the cultures of earlier civilizations?

Every culture has a creation story that explains how the world began and people came to exist. Lesson 2.5 provides creation stories from three different cultures.

BACKGROUND FOR THE TEACHER

According to the *Popol Vuh*, the first four humans who could speak were given godlike powers. The people could speak the language of the gods. They could also see beyond Earth to the heavens and knew what had happened at the beginning of time and would occur at its end. Soon, however, the gods decided that they didn't want humans to be their equals. As a result, the gods limited human speech, sight, and knowledge.

DIGITAL RESOURCES myNGconnect.com

TEACHER RESOURCES & ASSESSMENT

 Reading and Note-Taking

 Vocabulary Practice

 Section 2 Quiz

STUDENT RESOURCES

 NG Chapter Gallery

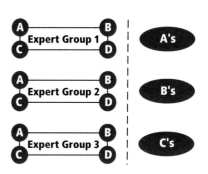

INTRODUCE & ENGAGE

PREPARE FOR THE DOCUMENT-BASED QUESTION

Before students start on the activity, briefly preview the three documents. Remind students that a constructed response requires full explanations in complete sentences. Emphasize that students should use what they have learned about the Maya in addition to the information in the documents. **0:05** minutes

TEACH

GUIDED DISCUSSION

1. **Identify** According to the excerpt from the *Popol Vuh*, what did Earth look like as it arose? *(like a mist or cloud unfolding)*

2. **Compare and Contrast** How is God's formation of light in the Bible excerpt similar to how the Maya gods form Earth in the *Popol Vuh? (Both light and Earth are formed when the words are spoken.)*

3. **Make Connections** What does the description in the Chinese creation story of Pan Gu's bursting from an egg remind you of? *(Possible response: of a chick being hatched from an egg; of birth; of life)*

EVALUATE

After students have completed the "Synthesize & Write" activity, allow time for them to exchange paragraphs and read and comment on the work of their peers. Guidelines for comments should be established prior to this activity so that feedback is constructive and encouraging in nature. **0:15** minutes

ACTIVE OPTIONS

Critical Viewing: NG Chapter Gallery Have students examine the contents of the Chapter Gallery for this chapter. Then invite them to brainstorm additional images they believe would fit within the Chapter Gallery. Have them write a description of these additional images and provide an explanation of why they would fit within the Chapter Gallery. Then instruct them to do online research to find examples of actual images they would like to add to the gallery. **0:10** minutes

On Your Feet: Jigsaw Strategy Organize students into three "expert" groups and have students from each group analyze one of the documents and summarize the main ideas of the teaching in their own words. Then have the members of each group count off using the letters A, B, C, and so on. Regroup students into three new groups so that each new group has at least one member from each expert group. Have students in the new groups take turns sharing the simplified summaries they came up with in their expert groups. **0:10** minutes

DIFFERENTIATE

INCLUSION

Put It Together Help students minimize distractions by typing the three excerpts on one sheet of paper. Give photocopies of these to students along with highlighters. Tell students to highlight important words that appear in all three documents. Then have them write a summary sentence using several of the words.

PRE-AP

Research Creation Stories Ask students to research the creation stories of other cultures. For example, students might study the creation stories of Native American tribes, including the Hopi and Cherokee. They might also read creation stories from Japan and India. Encourage students to find similarities between the creation stories they find and those in this lesson. Students should share the results of their research with the class.

Press (**mt**) *in the Student eEdition for modified text.*

See the Chapter Planner for more strategies for differentiation.

SYNTHESIZE & WRITE

ANSWERS

1. Responses will vary.

2. Responses will vary.

3. Possible response: In many creation stories, gods form Earth out of emptiness, darkness, or chaos.

4. Students' paragraphs should include their topic sentence from Step 3 and provide several details from the documents to support the sentence.

3.1

Tenochtitlán: An Aztec City

Thriving cities, massive temples, fierce warriors, strong armies. These are only a few characteristics of the Mesoamerican civilization called the Aztec. The Aztec were nomads from a mysterious land known as Aztlán—the origin of the name *Aztec*. Starting from only an island city in a swamp, the Aztec founded a powerful empire.

MAIN IDEA

The Aztec developed a mighty empire in central Mexico.

SETTLING IN CENTRAL MEXICO

Around A.D. 1300, Aztec nomads migrated into the Valley of Mexico, a thriving and populous region in the central part of Mexico. When the Aztec arrived, the valley was dominated by rival city-states. The Aztec settled there, adopted local ways, and served powerful kings as farmers and warriors. Then, in 1325, the Aztec founded their own city, **Tenochtitlán** (tay-nohch-teet-LAHN). Today Tenochtitlán is known as Mexico City.

The Aztec built Tenochtitlán on two islands in a swamp in the western part of Lake Texcoco. To feed their growing population, they constructed artificial fields called **chinampas** (chee-NAHM-pahz). Chinampa farmers piled layers of mud and vegetation to raise the soil level above the water. Then they planted trees alongside to mark off planting areas. Finally, they covered the areas with more soil, dug up from the bottom of the lake. Farmers planted maize, beans, and different kinds of squash on the chinampas. These remarkable fields produced many crops, and the Aztec population thrived.

One advantage of living in a lake was that canoes made transport easy, so trade flourished. In time, the Aztec established a twin city called Tlatelolco (tlaht-el-OHL-koh) in the northern part of Lake Texcoco. Tlatelolco had a huge marketplace. Every day, thousands of people crossed the lake in canoes and visited Tlatelolco's bustling market.

BUILDING AN EMPIRE

The Aztec developed into skilled warriors. At first they fought for other kings, but then they overthrew their masters and began fighting for themselves. They allied with two other cities, Texcoco and Tlacopan (tlaht-oh-PAHN), to form a powerful Triple Alliance that the Aztec would control by 1428. Well-trained Aztec armies marched steadily through Mesoamerica, forcing hundreds of small city-states to surrender to Aztec rule.

Aztec bureaucrats, or government officials, kept order and enforced the supply of tribute to Tenochtitlán. Tribute, or a payment for protection, was made in food, raw materials, goods, or labor. Over time, the Aztec grew rich and commanded a vast empire stretching from the Pacific Ocean to the Gulf of Mexico. Around six million people lived in the Aztec Empire at its height.

By 1519, about 200,000 people lived in Tenochtitlán, which had become the largest city in Mesoamerica. It was one of the most magnificent cities of its time. The pyramid of **Templo Mayor**, or the Great Temple, towered above the city. Dozens more temples and many beautiful palaces surrounded Templo Mayor. Four roads divided the city into quarters, each with distinct neighborhoods, leaders, farmland, markets, and temples. The island city was crisscrossed by canals and connected to the mainland by long causeways, or roads across the water. When Spanish explorers arrived in 1519, they marveled at Tenochtitlán's size and splendor.

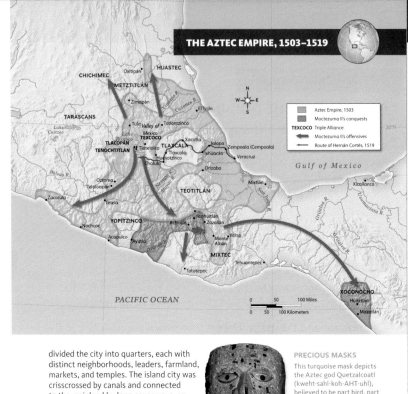

THE AZTEC EMPIRE, 1503–1519

Aztec Empire, 1503
Moctezuma II's conquests
TEXCOCO Triple Alliance
Moctezuma II's offensives
Route of Hernán Cortés, 1519

PRECIOUS MASKS

This turquoise mask depicts the Aztec god Quetzalcoatl (kweht-sahl-koh-AHT-uhl), believed to be part bird, part snake. Aztec sculptors carved masks from volcanic rock and precious stones such as turquoise and jade.

REVIEW & ASSESS

1. **READING CHECK** What features made Tenochtitlán an awe-inspiring city?

2. **ANALYZE CAUSE AND EFFECT** How were the Aztec able to develop productive farm fields in the swampy lands around Tenochtitlán?

3. **INTERPRET MAPS** Use the map scale to determine how far the Aztec Empire extended from north to south in 1503.

PLAN

OBJECTIVE

Explain how the Aztec built a mighty empire in central Mexico.

CRITICAL THINKING SKILLS FOR LESSON 3.1

- Identify Main Ideas and Details
- Monitor Comprehension
- Analyze Cause and Effect
- Interpret Maps
- Make Inferencess

ESSENTIAL QUESTION

How did Mesoamerican civilizations adopt and adapt the cultures of earlier civilizations?

The Aztec settled in central Mexico and founded a great empire there.

Lesson 3.1 describes the splendor of the Aztec city of Tenochtitlán, which contained pyramids and temples similar to those built by other Mesoamerican civilizations.

BACKGROUND FOR THE TEACHER

According to Aztec legend, the Aztec were led to Tenochtitlán by their god, Tenoch. This god, they believed, had told them to look for a place where an eagle would be perched on a cactus, eating a snake. The Aztec searched for the place for hundreds of years. Finally, they found what they had been looking for on Lake Texcoco. There they saw a cactus growing on an island in the lake with an eagle perched atop it, devouring a snake. Obeying their god, the Aztec began building their city on the location and called it Tenochtitlán.

DIGITAL RESOURCES myNGconnect.com

TEACHER RESOURCES & ASSESSMENT

 Reading and Note-Taking

 Vocabulary Practice

 Section 3 Quiz

STUDENT RESOURCES

 Active History

INTRODUCE & ENGAGE

REVIEW EMPIRE

Tell students that they are about to read about the Aztec, who built an empire in Mesoamerica. Point out that the other civilizations they have read about in this chapter did not build empires. Help students recall what they have learned about empires. **ASK:** What ancient civilizations built great empires? *(Possible responses: Egypt, Rome, China)* Then ask students to name the words and ideas they associate with the word *empire*. Record their responses in an Idea Web. **0:10** minutes

TEACH

GUIDED DISCUSSION

1. **Make Inferences** What might have been an advantage of building the Aztec capital city on islands rather than on the mainland? *(The city would be easier to protect because any invasion would be by water. Also, the water around the city could be used for transportation as well as trade.)*

2. **Identify Main Ideas and Details** How did the Aztec expand their empire? *(Their armies forced city-states in Mesoamerica to surrender to Aztec rule, and government officials exacted tribute from these city-states in exchange for protection.)*

INTERPRET MAPS

Have students study the map of the Aztec Empire. Have them find the three cities of the Triple Alliance on the map. **ASK:** Why do you think these cities formed an alliance? *(They're located very close together.)* Then point out that the empire didn't include many other big cities. **ASK:** What does this suggest about the Aztec? *(The Aztec Empire might have been more centralized or focused on building the three large cities of the alliance.)* Finally, tell students that Moctezuma II became the Aztec emperor in 1502 and that Hernán Cortés led Spanish soldiers against the Aztec in 1519. Let students know that they will learn about these historical figures in another lesson. **0:10** minutes

ACTIVE OPTIONS

Active History: Create a Sketch Map of Tenochtitlán Extend the lesson by using either the PDF or Whiteboard version of the activity. These activities take a deeper look at a topic from, or related to, the lesson. Explore the activities as a class, turn them into group assignments, or even assign them individually. **0:10** minutes

On Your Feet: Tell Me More Have students form three teams and assign each team one of the following topics: Aztec agriculture; the Aztec capital city; Aztec empire-building. Each group should write down as many facts about their topic as they can. Have the class reconvene, and have each group stand up, one at a time. The rest of the class calls out, "Tell me more about [the topic]!" The group recites one fact. The class again calls, "Tell me more!" until the group runs out of facts to share. Then the next group presents its facts. Keep track of which group has shared the most facts on their topic. **0:15** minutes

DIFFERENTIATE

STRIVING READERS

Complete Sentence Starters Provide these sentence starters for students to complete after reading. You may also have students preview the starters to set a purpose for reading.

- The Aztec founded a city called _____.

- To grow their crops, Aztec farmers made _____.

- The Aztec built a great empire in _____.

- The temple that towered above the Aztec capital is called _____.

GIFTED & TALENTED

Create Models Invite groups of students to research to learn more about a chinampa and then make a model of the artificial field. Students may draw a detailed model or make the model out of clay or cardboard. Once students have completed their model, have them present it to the class. Ask them to use the model to explain how a chinampa was made and be prepared to answer their classmates' questions.

Press **mt** *in the Student eEdition for modified text.*

See the Chapter Planner for more strategies for differentiation.

REVIEW & ASSESS

ANSWERS

1. Features include the Templo Mayor, other temples, palaces, the grid pattern, and causeways.

2. They were able to develop productive farm fields by constructing artificial fields called chinampas to grow their crops.

3. It extended about 600 miles from north to south in 1503.

Aztec Culture

In any big city, you will find people from all walks of life. The same was true for the great Aztec city of Tenochtitlán, where you might have met nobles, priests, soldiers, artisans, and slaves.

MAIN IDEA

Class structure and religious practices defined Aztec society.

+ POSSIBLE RESPONSE

It probably sent the message that the Aztec were fearful warriors and would show no mercy to their enemies.

CLASS STRUCTURE

The emperor was the most powerful person in Aztec society. He controlled all political and spiritual matters and served for life. Below him were the **nobles**. Nobles were the smallest but most powerful class. They inherited their status and held the top jobs as generals, priests, tax collectors, and judges. Some nobles even governed cities for the Aztec emperor.

Most Aztec belonged to the commoner class, which included merchants and artisans, farmers, and soldiers. Merchants and artisans were highly respected, and they lived in their own communities. Merchants traveled throughout the empire, trading goods. Artisans made and sold jewelry, ornaments, and clothes. Many Aztec were farmers who worked **communal**, or shared, land and had to give part of their harvest as a tax to the empire. Others were professional soldiers, some of whom gained wealth and privilege by distinguishing themselves on the battlefield.

Serfs and slaves occupied the lowest level of Aztec society. **Serfs** lived and worked on the private land of nobles. In addition to providing agricultural labor, serfs performed household tasks for landowners. Slaves were considered property and were usually prisoners of war. Slave status was not based on race, and children of slaves were born free.

AZTEC GODS

Religion was central to all classes of Aztec society. The Aztec were polytheistic. They worshipped as many as 1,000 gods and built hundreds of magnificent temples and religious structures in Tenochtitlán to honor those gods. Though people's individual homes were simply constructed, they almost always featured a shrine to the gods.

The Aztec followed many traditions that they shared with other Mesoamerican cultures. They believed they could please the gods with offerings and sacrifices. Some of these sacrifices were human.

Most of the human sacrifices were prisoners of war. The Aztec considered themselves "the People of the Sun" and believed they nourished the sun with these sacrifices.

An important site for the Aztec was **Teotihuacán** (tay-oh-TEE-wah-khan), or "the place where the gods were born." Teotihuacán was located north of Tenochtitlán and built by an earlier people. This once-great city became sacred to the Aztec, who came later. The Aztec built onto the ruins they found there and revived worship at its many temples, including two vast pyramids dedicated to the sun and moon.

WARRIOR SCHOOLS

This Aztec sculpture depicts an Eagle Warrior. Much of the success of the Aztec Empire was due to its fierce warriors. All boys attended military training schools from a young age. At these schools, boys learned to fight in formation and use weapons.

REVIEW & ASSESS

1. **READING CHECK** Which social class in Aztec society had the most members?

2. **DRAW CONCLUSIONS** Why do you think merchants and artisans were highly respected members of the commoner class?

3. **COMPARE AND CONTRAST** In what ways were some Aztec religious practices similar to practices of other Mesoamerican cultures?

PLAN

OBJECTIVE

Explain how class structure and religious practices defined Aztec culture.

CRITICAL THINKING SKILLS FOR LESSON 3.2

- Identify Main Ideas and Details
- Monitor Comprehension
- Draw Conclusions
- Compare and Contrast
- Make Inferences
- Analyze Visuals

ESSENTIAL QUESTION

How did Mesoamerican civilizations adopt and adapt the cultures of earlier civilizations?

In Aztec society, everyone belonged to a well-defined class and followed the same religious practices. Lesson 3.2 describes the class structure and religious practices of the Aztec, which had much in common with those of other Mesoamerican cultures.

BACKGROUND FOR THE TEACHER

Aztec pyramids often contained temples. For example, the Templo Mayor was Tenochtitlán's main religious building. The pyramid had two temples on the top. One of the temples was dedicated to the Aztec god of the sun and war. The other temple was dedicated to the god of rain. Both gods, archaeologists believe, required many human sacrifices. Researchers have found evidence suggesting that, during the temple's final phase of construction, thousands were sacrificed.

DIGITAL RESOURCES myNGconnect.com

TEACHER RESOURCES & ASSESSMENT

 Reading and Note-Taking

 Vocabulary Practice

 Section 3 Quiz

STUDENT RESOURCES

 NG Chapter Gallery

INTRODUCE & ENGAGE

FILL OUT A K-W-L CHART

As a class, complete a K-W-L Chart to help students remember what they have already learned about the Aztec and to get them to think about what more they would like to learn. Write students' responses and ideas on the board in a chart like the one shown here. Give students the opportunity to return to the chart and review what they have learned after reading the lesson. **0:10** minutes

K What Do I Know?	W What Do I Want To Learn?	L What Did I Learn?

TEACH

GUIDED DISCUSSION

1. **Draw Conclusions** Why couldn't a farmer in Aztec society hope to rise to become a judge or general? *(because only nobles could hold these positions, and they inherited their status)*

2. **Make Inferences** Why do you think Aztec society included so many prisoners of war? *(because the Aztec fought and won many wars)*

ANALYZE VISUALS

Have students examine the photograph of the skulls while you read aloud the caption. **ASK:** What is being shown in the photo? *(skulls)* To whom did the skulls belong? *(sacrificed prisoners of war)* Where was the photo taken? *(in Templo Mayor)* Then discuss the answer to the "Critical Viewing" question. **0:10** minutes

ACTIVE OPTIONS

Critical Viewing: NG Chapter Gallery Have students explore the entire Chapter 16 Gallery and choose two images: one illustrating some aspect of the Maya civilization and the other illustrating a similar aspect of the Aztec civilization. Then have students compare and contrast the images, either in written form or verbally with a partner. Ask questions that will inspire this process, such as: How are these images alike? How are they different? Why did you select these two items? How do they relate in history? **0:10** minutes

On Your Feet: Word Chain Have students form three lines. Hand a piece of paper to the first person in each line with one of these words from the lesson: *classes, slaves, religion.* The first student adds a word to the list that relates to the word based on what they've learned about the Aztec. Students then pass the paper from person to person in a line, each one adding a word they associate with the previously written word. Have a volunteer from each group read off the word chain. Ask the rest of the class to listen for any words that were used in more than one chain or any that may not connect correctly with the original word. **0:20** minutes

DIFFERENTIATE

ENGLISH LANGUAGE LEARNERS

Analyze Vocabulary Point out the context clues given in the lesson that help define the word *communal.* Tell students that *communal* can also be defined as something "in common use." Then provide additional help with the following questions:

- What other word or words does *communal* remind you of? *(community, commune)*
- How does the word *community* relate to what is being described in the lesson? *(In a community, people often share common goals and interests. The text discusses Aztec farmers who worked communal, or shared, land.)*
- What other examples of something that can be described as communal can you think of? *(communal living, communal kitchen)*

PRE-AP

Present a Poster Have students research to learn about the two pyramids dedicated to the sun and moon in Teotihuacán. Ask them to find and photocopy images of the two pyramids and present them, along with informative captions, on a poster that can be displayed in the classroom.

Press **mt** *in the Student eEdition for modified text.*

See the Chapter Planner for more strategies for differentiation.

REVIEW & ASSESS

ANSWERS

1. The commoner class had the most members.
2. They were highly respected because they enriched the empire; artisans made the goods that merchants traded throughout the empire.
3. Like other Mesoamerican cultures, the Aztec worshipped many gods. Like the Maya, the Aztec sometimes made human sacrifices to their gods.

3.3

Aztec
Defeat and Legacy

The Aztec founded thriving cities, developed rich cultures, and built a strong military. However, their empire lasted barely 200 years. It came to a sudden end when the Spanish arrived in the early 1500s.

MAIN IDEA

European invaders defeated the Aztec, who left behind a rich cultural legacy.

END OF THE EMPIRE

Aztec power depended on the empire's huge military, which conquered many people and then demanded tribute from defeated populations. Constant wars and regular rebellions, though, kept the Aztec Empire unstable. The unrest in the empire was made worse by the rule of **Moctezuma II** (mok-tih-ZOO-muh), who became emperor in 1502. He considered himself an equal to the gods. He also kept pressuring defeated peoples for more and more tribute to pay for his luxurious, wasteful lifestyle. Until 1519, he crushed one rebellion after another. Then the unthinkable happened.

That year **conquistadors** arrived from Europe. Conquistadors were Spanish conquerors who were greedy for gold and other riches from South and Central America. Although few in number, they were able to overpower the Aztec with superior weapons, such as guns and cannons, as well as horses. Aztec warriors armed with spear throwers and swords were no match for Spanish conquistadors. Spanish invaders also brought diseases such as smallpox that would eventually kill millions of native people throughout the Americas.

Believing the Spanish would liberate them from the tyranny of their rulers, some Aztec joined the conquistadors' leader, **Hernán Cortés**, in his battles. (See Cortés' route on the map in Lesson 3.1.) The conquest ended with a great siege of Tenochtitlán in 1521. The Spanish surrounded and systematically destroyed the great city. They rebuilt over the ruins, and that city became present-day Mexico City, Mexico.

AZTEC LEGACY

Because of their ruthless approach to conquest, the Spanish destroyed Aztec buildings, art, and literature. However, some Aztec ruins, artifacts, and writings survived the conquest. Archaeologists and historians study them to learn more about the Aztec.

The Aztec built huge monuments, especially temples for their gods. Aztec temples were positioned to line up with the sun and stars. The Aztec were skilled astronomers who could predict the movements of the sun, moon, planets, and stars. Like the Maya, the Aztec believed these movements directly affected their lives. They also used complex calendars to chart and record events, such as important religious rituals and the planting and harvesting of crops.

Aztec writing also gives archaeologists and historians a picture of their society. The Aztec recorded historical events, and they wrote inspiring speeches, poetry, legends, and prayers to their gods. Glyphs represented words that were painted into codices. Although few of the original codices survived, many were copied and translated by Spanish scholars. These colorful books offer a detailed and artistic picture of Aztec society.

This painting of Moctezuma II reflects how Europeans viewed him. Moctezuma expanded the Aztec Empire and made Tenochtitlán its capital city.

Portrait of Montezuma II, European School, 16th century

REVIEW & ASSESS

1. **READING CHECK** What factors caused instability and unrest in the Aztec Empire?

2. **DRAW CONCLUSIONS** How were the Spanish conquistadors able to defeat the powerful Aztec?

3. **MAKE INFERENCES** Why are Aztec codices important to archaeologists and historians?

480 CHAPTER 16

481

PLAN

OBJECTIVE

Describe the defeat of the Aztec and the rich cultural legacy they left behind.

CRITICAL THINKING SKILLS FOR LESSON 3.3

- Identify Main Ideas and Details
- Monitor Comprehension
- Draw Conclusions
- Make Inferences
- Analyze Cause and Effect
- Form and Support Opinions
- Make Connections

ESSENTIAL QUESTION

How did Mesoamerican civilizations adopt and adapt the cultures of earlier civilizations?

Spanish conquerors defeated the Aztec, but archaeologists have been able to learn about the civilization from the ruins, artifacts, and writings that survived the conquest. Lesson 3.3 describes the legacy of the Aztec in building, astronomy, and the arts.

BACKGROUND FOR THE TEACHER

Three things linked the Aztec god Quetzalcoatl to Cortés. First of all, one myth said that the god had left Mexico by sea, journeying to the east—the direction from which Cortés came. Second, the god was supposed to return in the very year that Cortés arrived in Mexico. Third, Quetzalcoatl was sometimes depicted as a man with a beard, like the conquistador. Perhaps the Aztec who joined Cortés in his battles did so because they believed the Spanish leader was Quetzalcoatl in disguise.

DIGITAL RESOURCES myNGconnect.com

TEACHER RESOURCES & ASSESSMENT

 Reading and Note-Taking   **Vocabulary Practice**   **Section 3 Quiz**

STUDENT RESOURCES

 Biography

480 CHAPTER 16

INTRODUCE & ENGAGE

MAKE PREDICTIONS

Remind students that the Aztec Empire expanded mainly by conquering small city-states in Mesoamerica and forcing the defeated peoples to pay tribute. **ASK:** What do you think the conquered peoples might have done when an outside force arrived to conquer the Aztec? *(They might have wanted to provide assistance to the outside force.)* Can you think of other disadvantages to building an empire through military conquest? *(Possible response: fear of rebellion by the people and the need to always maintain a large military force)* `0:10` **minutes**

TEACH

GUIDED DISCUSSION

1. **Analyze Cause and Effect** Why did some Aztec rebel against Moctezuma II? *(because he considered himself an equal to the gods, exacted more and more tribute from defeated peoples, and lived a wasteful, luxurious lifestyle)*

2. **Form and Support Opinions** What attitude do you think the conquistadors had toward the Aztec? Explain. *(Possible response: The conquistadors probably thought they were superior because they had superior weapons and took over Aztec lives and land.)*

MAKE CONNECTIONS

Have students discuss some of the similarities between the Aztec and the Maya relative to the following:

- astronomy and calendars
- temples and religion
- writing and writing system
- defeat and destruction

`0:10` **minutes**

ACTIVE OPTIONS

Critical Viewing: NG Chapter Gallery Invite students to explore the Chapter Gallery and choose one image from the gallery they feel best represents their understanding of Chapter 16. Have students provide a written explanation of why they selected that particular image. `0:10` **minutes**

On Your Feet: Prepare a Script Divide the class into groups of six. Assign each group member one of the following questions: *Who? What? Where? When? Why?* or *How?* Have the groups use their assigned question to write sentences for a script about the conquest of the Aztec and the legacy they left behind. Each group member should contribute his or her information at the appropriate time in the script. `0:20` **minutes**

DIFFERENTIATE

STRIVING READERS

Sequence Events To focus on the events described and their connections to each other, have students use a Sequence Chain like the one below to record the sequence of events beginning with the rule of Moctezuma II and ending with the destruction of Tenochtitlán. Tell students to add ovals if necessary. Allow them to work in pairs or groups, or assign parts of the lesson to individuals or groups and have them fill in their portion of the Sequence Chain.

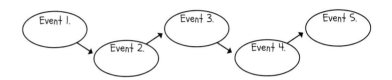

GIFTED & TALENTED

Write Dialogue Have student pairs imagine and write a dialogue that might have taken place in a meeting between Moctezuma and Cortés. Students might have Moctezuma and Cortés discuss their goals or provoke each other to fight. Encourage students to capture both men's sense of superiority in the dialogue. Ask volunteers to read their dialogue to the class.

Press **(mt)** *in the Student eEdition for modified text.*

See the Chapter Planner for more strategies for differentiation.

REVIEW & ASSESS

ANSWERS

1. Factors that caused instability and unrest include constant war, regular rebellions, and Moctezuma's rule.

2. They were able to defeat the Aztec by overpowering them with superior weapons, such as guns and cannons, as well as horses.

3. Codices provide archaeologists and historians with firsthand descriptions of events in Aztec history, culture, and daily life.

VOCABULARY

On your paper, match the vocabulary word in the first column with its definition in the second column.

WORD	DEFINITION
1. terrace	**a.** a civilization that greatly influences other civilizations
2. mother culture	**b.** a stepped platform built into a mountainside
3. codex	**c.** a symbolic picture used to represent a word, syllable, or sound
4. glyph	**d.** a Spanish conqueror who overpowered the Aztec
5. chinampa	**e.** a folded book made from tree-bark paper
6. conquistador	**f.** an artificial field

READING STRATEGY

7. IDENTIFY MAIN IDEAS AND DETAILS If you haven't already, complete your diagram for each Mesoamerican civilization. Then answer the question.

Main-Idea Diagram

Main Idea: Olmec Civilization
Detail: *Developed along a floodplain*
Detail:
Detail:
Detail:
Detail:

What feature do you think was the greatest legacy of each civilization? Explain.

MAIN IDEAS

Answer the following questions. Support your answers with evidence from the chapter.

8. Why is the Olmec civilization considered to be Mesoamerica's mother culture? **LESSON 1.2**

9. Why is Monte Albán considered one of the first major cities in Mesoamerica? **LESSON 1.3**

10. Which groups of people made up the largest social class in the Maya civilization? **LESSON 2.1**

11. During what time period did most of the great Maya cities develop? **LESSON 2.2**

12. What did the Maya use to develop their elaborate 365-day calendar? **LESSON 2.4**

13. Describe the class structure of society in the Aztec Empire. **LESSON 3.2**

14. How did instability contribute to the end of the Aztec Empire? **LESSON 3.3**

CRITICAL THINKING

Answer the following questions. Support your answers with evidence from the chapter.

15. ANALYZE CAUSE AND EFFECT What happened as a result of the Olmec's trade network?

16. DRAW CONCLUSIONS What conclusions can you draw about cacao beans based on the fact that the Maya often used them to pay for goods?

17. COMPARE AND CONTRAST What are some of the similarities surrounding the decline of the Zapotec and Maya civilizations?

18. COMPARE AND CONTRAST What distinguishes the Aztec from the early river valley civilizations of Mesopotamia, Egypt, India, and China?

19. FORM AND SUPPORT OPINIONS In your opinion, was Moctezuma II an effective leader of the Aztec Empire? Why or why not?

20. YOU DECIDE What do you think is the Maya civilization's greatest legacy? Support your opinion with evidence from the chapter.

INTERPRET VISUALS

Study the images of a Maya pyramid and an ancient Egyptian pyramid. Then answer the questions that follow.

Maya pyramid

Egyptian pyramid

21. How are the pyramids alike, and how do they differ?

22. What challenges did both pyramid styles present to the people who built them?

ANALYZE SOURCES

This jade mask was placed over the face of King Pacal, a great ruler of Palenque, when he died. The mask shows the king's own features.

23. The Maya highly valued jade and often used it to represent the maize god. Study the mask. Why do you think the Maya associated jade with the maize god?

WRITE ABOUT HISTORY

24. EXPLANATORY How were the Olmec, Zapotec, Maya, and Aztec civilizations similar? How did they differ? Write a paragraph comparing and contrasting the civilizations for tourists who are planning to visit some of the civilizations' archaeological and historic sites. Consider such aspects of the civilizations as religion, art, architecture, daily life, social structure, and the sciences.

TIPS

- Take notes from the lessons about the Olmec, Zapotec, Maya, and Aztec civilizations. You might jot down your comparisons in a chart using the aspects listed above as headings in the chart.

- State your main idea clearly at the beginning of the paragraph. Support your main idea with relevant facts, details, and examples.

- Use vocabulary from the chapter in your paragraph.

- Provide a concluding statement about the similarities and differences among the Olmec, Zapotec, Maya, and Aztec civilizations.

VOCABULARY ANSWERS

WORD	DEFINITION
1. terrace b	**a.** a civilization that greatly influences other civilizations
2. mother culture a	**b.** a stepped platform built into a mountainside
3. codex e	**c.** a symbolic picture used to represent a word, syllable, or sound
4. glyph c	**d.** a Spanish conqueror who overpowered the Aztec
5. chinampa f	**e.** a folded book made from tree-bark paper
6. conquistador d	**f.** an artificial field

READING STRATEGY ANSWER

Main-Idea Diagram

Main Idea: Olmec Civilization
Detail: *Developed along a floodplain*
Detail: *Became Mesoamerica's first civilization*
Detail: *Built cities with pyramids, temples, and ball courts*
Detail: *Civilization mysteriously disappeared*
Detail: *Considered mother culture of Mesoamerica*

7. Students' responses will vary. Possible response: The greatest legacy of the Olmec were their religion and art. The greatest legacy of the Zapotec was Monte Albán. The greatest legacy of the Maya were their advances in mathematics. The greatest legacy of the Aztec were their temples and pyramids.

MAIN IDEAS ANSWERS

8. It is considered to be Mesoamerica's mother culture because later Mesoamerican civilizations adopted and adapted many aspects of Olmec civilization, including religion and art.

9. It is considered one of the first major cities because it was a major center of power, because it contained many monumental structures, and because it had such a big population.

10. Farmers and slaves made up the largest social class.

11. Most of the great Maya cities developed during the Classic Period, which lasted from about A.D. 250 to 900.

12. They used astronomical observations and mathematical calculations.

13. The emperor was the most powerful person. Below him were the nobles, commoners, serfs, and slaves.

14. War and rebellions distracted the emperor and spread the army too thin.

CRITICAL THINKING ANSWERS

15. The trade routes spread Olmec civilization throughout Mesoamerica. As later civilizations arose, their people adopted aspects of Olmec culture.

16. Possibly because the trees were hard to grow or produced few beans, cacao beans were considered as valuable as money.

17. The causes for the declines are not known, and both civilizations fell at around the same time.

18. The Aztec began to develop in swampland around Lake Texcoco rather than along a river valley.

19. Students' responses will vary. Some students may say Moctezuma was an effective leader because he extended the Aztec Empire. Others may say he was not effective because his actions created instability in the empire that helped the conquistadors defeat the Aztec.

20. Students' responses will vary. Some students may say that introducing the concept of zero to the Americas is the Maya's greatest legacy.

INTERPRET VISUALS ANSWERS

21. The pyramids have the same shape, with outer surfaces forming triangles. The Egyptian pyramid has smooth sides and comes to a point at the top. The Maya pyramid has steep outer steps on each side, and its top is flat.

22. Complex mathematical calculations had to be made to get the proportions right. Both pyramid styles were built without the use of machines. People had to haul and raise the building materials by hand and using ropes.

ANALYZE SOURCES ANSWER

23. Students' responses will vary. Possible response: The green color of the jade may have reminded them of young, growing corn.

WRITE ABOUT HISTORY ANSWER

24. Students' paragraphs should do the following:

- compare and contrast aspects of the Olmec, Zapotec, Maya, and Aztec civilizations
- support the comparison with relevant facts, details, and examples
- be written in a formal style
- include vocabulary words from the chapter
- provide a concluding statement about the similarities and differences among the civilizations

UNIT RESOURCES

On Location with National Geographic Grantee Francisco Estrada-Belli
Intro and Video

Interactive Map Tool

News & Updates

Available on myNGconnect

Unit Wrap-Up:
"Connecting Past and Present"
Feature and Video

"People of the Horse"
National Geographic Adapted Article
Student eEdition exclusive

"Unburying the Aztec"
National Geographic Adapted Article

Unit 7 Inquiry:
Design an Adaptation Strategy

CHAPTER RESOURCES

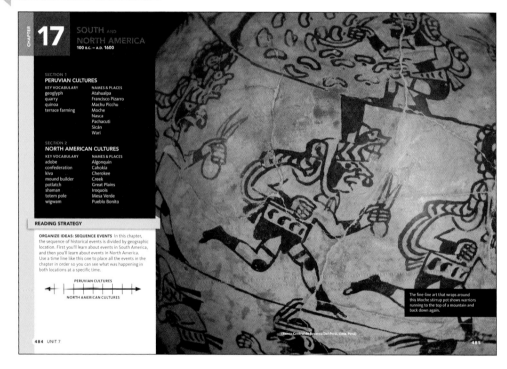

CHAPTER 17
SOUTH AND NORTH AMERICA
100 B.C. – A.D. 1600

SECTION 1
PERUVIAN CULTURES

KEY VOCABULARY
geoglyph
quarry
quinoa
terrace farming

NAMES & PLACES
Atahualpa
Francisco Pizarro
Machu Picchu
Moche
Nasca
Pachacuti
Sicán
Wari

SECTION 2
NORTH AMERICAN CULTURES

KEY VOCABULARY
adobe
confederation
kiva
mound builder
potlatch
shaman
totem pole
wigwam

NAMES & PLACES
Algonquin
Cahokia
Cherokee
Creek
Great Plains
Iroquois
Mesa Verde
Pueblo Bonito

READING STRATEGY

ORGANIZE IDEAS: SEQUENCE EVENTS In this chapter, the sequence of historical events is divided by geographic location. First you'll learn about events in South America, and then you'll learn about events in North America. Use a time line like this one to place all the events in the chapter in order so you can see what was happening in both locations at a specific time.

PERUVIAN CULTURES

NORTH AMERICAN CULTURES

The fine-line art that wraps around this Moche stirrup pot shows warriors running to the top of a mountain and back down again.

(Banco Central de Reserva Del Perú, Lima, Perú)

484 UNIT 7
485

TEACHER RESOURCES & ASSESSMENT

Available on myNGconnect

Social Studies Skills Lessons
• Reading: Sequence Events
• Writing: Write an Informative Paragraph

Formal Assessment
• Chapter 17 Tests A (on-level) & B (below-level)

A Chapter 17 Answer Key

ExamView®
One-time Download

STUDENT BACKPACK *Available on myNGconnect*

• **eEdition** *(English)*   • **eEdition** *(Spanish)*   • **Handbooks**   • **Online Atlas**

For Chapter 17 Spanish resources, visit the Teacher Resource Menu page on myNGconnect.

SECTION 1 RESOURCES

PERUVIAN CULTURES

 Reading and Note-Taking

 Vocabulary Practice

 Section 1 Quiz

Available on myNGconnect

LESSON 1.1 PRE-INCA CULTURES
• On Your Feet: Four Corners

NG Learning Framework:
Think Like an Archaeologist

HISTORY THROUGH OBJECTS
LESSON 1.2 PERUVIAN GOLD
• On Your Feet: Create an Exhibition
• Critical Viewing: NG Chapter Gallery

LESSON 1.3 INCA SOCIETY AND GOVERNMENT
 Biography
Pachacuti   *Available on myNGconnect*

• On Your Feet: Running an Empire

NG Learning Framework:
Farming in the Empire

LESSON 1.4 INCA ARCHITECTURE
 Active History: Interactive Whiteboard Activity
Create a Sketch Map of Machu Picchu

 Active History
Create a Sketch Map of Machu Picchu

Available on myNGconnect

• On Your Feet: Compare Engineering Feats

MOMENTS IN HISTORY
LESSON 1.5 THE INCA AND SPANISH MEET
 Biography
Atahualpa   *Available on myNGconnect*

• On Your Feet: Team Word Webbing

NG Learning Framework:
Research Conquistadors

SECTION 2 RESOURCES

NORTH AMERICAN CULTURES

 Reading and Note-Taking

 Vocabulary Practice

 Section 2 Quiz

Available on myNGconnect

LESSON 2.1 NORTHWEST COAST CULTURES
• On Your Feet: Fishbowl
• Critical Viewing: NG Chapter Gallery

LESSON 2.2 THE ANCIENT PUEBLO
• On Your Feet: Choose Your Home
• Critical Viewing: NG Chapter Gallery

LESSON 2.3 PEOPLES OF THE GREAT PLAINS
• On Your Feet: Inside-Outside Circle

NG Learning Framework:
Buffalo in Trouble

LESSON 2.4 THE MOUND BUILDERS AND CAHOKIA
• On Your Feet: Cahokia Roundtable
• Critical Viewing: NG Image Gallery

LESSON 2.5 CULTURES IN THE EAST AND SOUTHEAST
• On Your Feet: Four Corners
• Critical Viewing: NG Chapter Gallery

CHAPTER 17 REVIEW

STRATEGY 1

Complete a Summary Chart

Students can take notes on different cultures in this chapter by completing a summary chart. Tell students to add notes to their charts after reading each lesson. Some lessons will require multiple rows in students' charts.

LESSON	CULTURES	TWO FACTS
1.1		
1.2		
1.3		
1.4		
1.5		
2.1		
2.2		
2.3		
2.4		
2.5		

Use with All Lessons

STRATEGY 2

Play "Who Are We?"

Choose from the names below and distribute a list to students. Have them make game cards with the culture on the front and a clue to the group's identity on the back. For example, for Mound Builders, students might write, "built Cahokia." Use the cards to play a whole-group, small-group, or partner review game.

Moche	Nasca	Wari
Sicán	Inca	Northwest Coast Cultures
Ancient Pueblo	Great Plains Tribes	Mound Builders
Cherokee	Creek	Algonquin
Iroquois		

Use with All Lessons

STRATEGY 3

Build an ABC Summary

To help students review the reading, suggest that they write important words from the lessons that begin with each letter of the alphabet starting with *A* and working through to *Z*, filling in as many letters as they can. Tell students to compare their summaries.

Use with All Lessons *Encourage students to look beyond Key Vocabulary words and proper nouns. For example, the word* construct *in Lesson 1.4 might help students think about the buildings created by different cultures.*

Press *in the Student eEdition for modified text.*

INCLUSION

STRATEGY 1

Modify Vocabulary Lists

Provide two separate colors of index cards for students: one for Section 1, South America, and one for Section 2, North America. Limit the number of vocabulary words that students will be required to master. As they read, have students create a vocabulary card for each word in the modified list, making sure that they write the words on the correctly colored card to keep them straight. Students may create pictures to illustrate words or write definitions, synonyms, or examples. Encourage students to refer to their vocabulary cards often as they read.

Use with All Lessons

STRATEGY 2

Provide a Summary Chart

Provide a summary of Inca achievements for students to use to preview Lessons 1.3 and 1.4. Explain that they will be learning about the ways in which the Inca lived in a challenging environment and how they built a large empire.

INCA ACHIEVEMENTS	
Government	• Large empire • Well organized
Farming	• Terrace farming • Irrigation system
Building/Engineering	• Suspension bridges • System of roads • Machu Picchu

Use with Lessons 1.3 and 1.4

ENGLISH LANGUAGE LEARNERS

STRATEGY 1
Provide Sentence Frames

Have pairs of students read the lessons and complete the sentences below.

1.1 The Nasca drew huge designs called _____ on the ground.

1.2 Pre-Inca Peruvian cultures created beautiful masks and jewelry from _____ .

1.3 The Inca Empire expanded when _____ became the emperor.

1.4 The Inca built a city in the mountains called _____ that still exists.

1.5 The Inca Empire collapsed when the Spanish conquistador _____ defeated Atahualpa.

For Section 2, have students work in pairs to write their own sentence frames for each lesson. Pairs can then trade sentence frames with another pair and complete them together.

Use with All Lessons

STRATEGY 2
Use Either/Or Questions

After reading, ask students either/or questions to reinforce meanings. You may also give copies of the questions to students to answer or to quiz each other.

- Is a geoglyph a drawing or a building?

- Did pre-Inca artists work with wood or gold?

- Did the Inca farm using terrace farming or dry farming?

- Were homes in Mesa Verde built on flat plains or underneath cliffs?

- Did Great Plains cultures hunt buffalo or raise cattle?

- Did mound builders use stone or earth?

- Was the Iroquois League a group of allied tribes or a group of builders?

Use with All Lessons *You may wish to place students in groups with various levels of language proficiency and have more proficent students write more either/or questions to ask beginning students.*

STRATEGY 3
Illustrate Culture Groups

To help students organize information about the cultures explored in this chapter, have them visualize a way to remember each culture group. Provide students with index cards. Tell them to draw a sketch to remember the group on one side and the name of the group on the other side. For example, for the Nasca students could sketch a geoglyph. For the ancient Pueblo, they could draw homes underneath cliffs.

Use with All Lessons

GIFTED & TALENTED

STRATEGY 1
Sketch a Flip Chart

Tell students that all the civilizations in this chapter are distinctive, both in their histories and in their artisanship. Have them create flip charts by sketching a symbol for each culture group. Tell them not to label their symbols. Then have them make a review game out of their flip charts, quizzing classmates on which symbol goes with what culture.

Use with All Lessons

STRATEGY 2
Find Examples of Artisanship

Civilizations in South and North America produced artisans who created extraordinary gold and silver jewelry, elaborately decorated vessels, wood carvings, and baskets. Tell students to research examples of the art of their favorite culture in this chapter. Then have students create a poster of artwork created by the culture they choose.

Use with All Lessons

PRE-AP

STRATEGY 1
Write a Summary

Remind students of the Essential Question introduced at the beginning of the chapter: In what ways do civilizations adapt to the environments in which they live? Tell students to review all the lessons and identify ways each culture adapted to its environment. Then have students write a summary essay using examples they identify to answer the Essential Question.

Use with All Lessons

CHAPTER

17 SOUTH AND NORTH AMERICA

100 B.C. – A.D. 1600

SECTION 1
PERUVIAN CULTURES

KEY VOCABULARY	NAMES & PLACES
geoglyph	Atahualpa
quarry	Francisco Pizarro
quinoa	Machu Picchu
terrace farming	Moche
	Nasca
	Pachacuti
	Sicán
	Wari

SECTION 2
NORTH AMERICAN CULTURES

KEY VOCABULARY	NAMES & PLACES
adobe	Algonquin
confederation	Cahokia
kiva	Cherokee
mound builder	Creek
potlatch	Great Plains
shaman	Iroquois
totem pole	Mesa Verde
wigwam	Pueblo Bonito

READING STRATEGY

ORGANIZE IDEAS: SEQUENCE EVENTS In this chapter, the sequence of historical events is divided by geographic location. First you'll learn about events in South America, and then you'll learn about events in North America. Use a time line like this one to place all the events in the chapter in order so you can see what was happening in both locations at a specific time.

PERUVIAN CULTURES

NORTH AMERICAN CULTURES

The fine-line art that wraps around this Moche stirrup pot shows warriors running to the top of a mountain and back down again.

(Banco Central de Reserva Del Perú, Lima, Perú)

484 UNIT 7

485

TEACHER BACKGROUND

INTRODUCE THE PHOTOGRAPH

This Moche stirrup vessel is a type of pot with two handles that come together in a single spout that pours in both directions. The Moche used fine-line art on vessels to tell stories. This particular vessel shows warriors in headdresses running to the top of a mountain and then back down again. It is much like a comic strip and to see the whole scene, you have to follow the runners around the pot. The oval shapes at the top represent lima beans, which the Moche used in farming and as fertility symbols in ceremonies. **ASK:** How would you describe the decorations on this pot? *(Possible responses: realistic, detailed, well proportioned, full of action)*

SHARE BACKGROUND

The Moche civilization flourished in South America from A.D. 100 to 700. The Moche had no writing system but they were master craftspeople. The fine-line art on their vessels and murals portrayed animals, people, plants, gods, and stories. Some vessels were designed for burial and other ceremonial purposes, but many were created for everyday use.

DIGITAL RESOURCES myNGconnect.com

TEACHER RESOURCES & ASSESSMENT

Social Studies Skills Lessons
- Reading: Sequence Events
- Writing: Write an Informative Paragraph

Formal Assessment
- Chapter 17 Tests A (on-level) & B (below-level)

STUDENT BACKPACK

- **eEdition** *(English)*
- **eEdition** *(Spanish)*
- **Handbooks**
- **Online Atlas**

ExamView®
One-time Download

Chapter 17 Answer Key

For Chapter 17 Spanish Resources, visit the Teacher Resource Menu page.

484 CHAPTER 17

INTRODUCE THE ESSENTIAL QUESTION

IN WHAT WAYS DO CIVILIZATIONS ADAPT TO THE ENVIRONMENTS IN WHICH THEY LIVE?

Roundtable Activity: Environments of the Americas This activity asks students to think about the variety of environments that make up South and North America. Students should specifically think about geography, climate, and landforms. Have students sit around tables in groups of four. Ask them to describe different geographic areas of South and North America. Each student around the table should identify and describe a different environmental area somewhere in the two continents. When they finish, have each group report on how many different climates and environments they described. **0:20** minutes

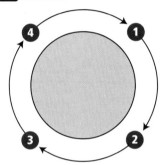

INTRODUCE THE READING STRATEGY

ORGANIZE IDEAS: SEQUENCE EVENTS

Model completing the time line for students. Draw and label a time line on the board like that on the student page. Then read aloud the first paragraph in Lesson 1.1. Above the time line, at the first hash mark write *A.D. 100 The Moche civilization began to flourish.* Then read aloud the third paragraph in Lesson 2.1 and below the time line write *A.D. 500: The Tlingit developed tools for splitting and carving wood.*

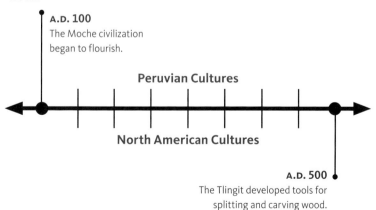

A.D. 100
The Moche civilization
began to flourish.

Peruvian Cultures

North American Cultures

A.D. 500
The Tlingit developed tools for
splitting and carving wood.

INTRODUCE CHAPTER VOCABULARY

KNOWLEDGE RATING

Have students complete a Knowledge-Rating Chart for Key Vocabulary words. Have students list words and fill out the chart. Then have pairs share the definitions they know. Work together as a class to complete the chart.

KEY VOCAB	KNOW IT	NOT SURE	DON'T KNOW	DEFINITION
adobe				
confederation				
geoglyph				
kiva				

KEY DATES

1000 B.C.–A.D. 500	Adena and Hopewell build mounds in North America
A.D. 100–700	Moche and Nasca flourish in mountains and deserts of Peru
A.D. 500	Tlingit develop tools for carving wood in Pacific Northwest
A.D. 800–1400	Sicán thrive in northern Peru; Mississippians build Cahokia
A.D. 850–1200	Ancient Pueblo construct Pueblo Bonito and Mesa Verde
A.D. 1450	Inca build Machu Picchu in Peru
A.D. 1500s	Iroquois League forms
A.D. 1532	Spanish conquer the Inca

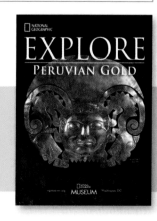

To read more about pre-Inca and Inca civilizations, check out *EXPLORE PERUVIAN GOLD.*

Pre-Inca
Cultures

Humans have treasured gold for centuries. When people mold gold into necklaces and bracelets, the beautiful finish outshines all other metals. In the northern and western parts of South America, four cultures developed extraordinary skill in working with gold and other precious metals. These cultures lived in present-day Peru, which the Inca would dominate by A.D. 1400.

MAIN IDEA

Beginning around A.D. 100, four complex cultures thrived in Peru.

THE MOCHE AND THE NASCA

On the northwest coast of South America, the **Moche** (MOH-chay) culture flourished between A.D. 100 and 700. Their land was harsh—a desert that was squeezed between the Andes Mountains to the east and the Pacific Ocean to the west. Like other pre-Inca cultures and the Inca who came later, the Moche showed great creativity in adapting to this challenging environment. To irrigate the farm fields in their arid region, they built complex irrigation systems. They also developed a strong military and ruled nearly 400 miles of the Peruvian coast.

The Moche were also artists, as shown by the artifacts archaeologists have discovered. Moche artisans created beautiful ceramics, or bowls, statues, and other objects made from clay and then hardened under intense heat. The artisans decorated the vessels with detailed line drawings of animals and people, such as rulers and warriors. Just as impressive was Moche artists' work with gold, which they shaped into exquisite jewelry. One pair of solid gold peanuts looked just like the real things—except they were three times larger.

In south Peru, the **Nasca** culture thrived from about A.D. 200 to 600. It was one of the earliest complex cultures in South America. Nasca artisans were as highly skilled as those of the Moche culture, creating magnificent jewelry from gold, silver, and copper. They also formed ceramic pottery and decorated it with intricate designs from nature, such as birds and fish.

The Nasca left behind a mystery, though. They created enormous **geoglyphs**, or large geometric designs and shapes drawn on the ground. The shapes often took the form of animals or birds. The dry climate where the Nasca lived helped preserve the geoglyphs. However, archaeologists are still not absolutely certain what the purpose of the designs was.

THE WARI AND THE SICÁN

The greatest military power among pre-Inca cultures was the **Wari** culture, which dominated the high desert of central Peru from about A.D. 500 to 1000. With their strong military, the Wari overran the Nasca and other people and established the first empire in the region of the Andes Mountains. The Wari were also skilled farmers. To cultivate crops on the rugged terrain of the Andes, they created terraced fields, or flat fields dug out of the sides of hills.

In a recent find at El Castillo, a Wari city along the Peruvian coast, archaeologists

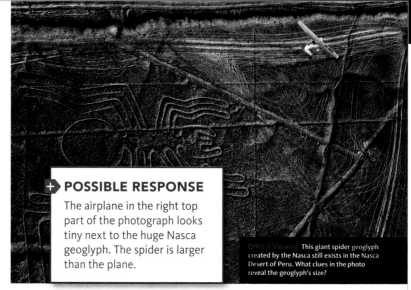

+ POSSIBLE RESPONSE

The airplane in the right top part of the photograph looks tiny next to the huge Nasca geoglyph. The spider is larger than the plane.

Critical Viewing This giant spider geoglyph created by the Nasca still exists in the Nasca Desert of Peru. What clues in the photo reveal the geoglyph's size?

unearthed a royal tomb that revealed a great deal about Wari culture. The tomb contained the remains of four queens or princesses and other members of the nobility. Buried with the remains were golden earrings, copper axes, and silver bowls. The discovery indicates that not only did the Wari worship their ancestors but they were, like other pre-Inca cultures, gifted artisans with precious metals.

While the Wari ruled central Peru, the **Sicán** culture flourished in the mountains of northern Peru from about A.D. 800 to 1400. The Sicán created delicate jewelry from gold, silver, and copper. They perfected a technique of pounding gold into extremely thin sheets. Archaeologists found two strips of metal that were only 0.006 inches thick—almost as thin as a piece of paper.

The Sicán showed great respect for the creatures of the natural world. Artists created a mural that was decorated with waves, fish, the sun, and the moon. When the Sicán buried the dead, they prepared them for the next world by burying them with gold, copper, and shells to carry water. This practice revealed their belief in an afterlife.

REVIEW & ASSESS

1. **READING CHECK** Where did the pre-Inca cultures live?

2. **SUMMARIZE** What have discoveries of tombs revealed about pre-Inca cultures?

3. **COMPARE AND CONTRAST** In what ways were these four pre-Inca cultures similar?

PLAN

OBJECTIVE

Explore pre-Inca civilizations in South America.

CRITICAL THINKING SKILLS FOR LESSON 1.1

- Identify Main Ideas and Details
- Monitor Comprehension
- Summarize
- Compare and Contrast
- Identify
- Synthesize

ESSENTIAL QUESTION

In what ways do civilizations adapt to the environments in which they live?

Lesson 1.1 describes four pre-Inca cultures in Peru that adapted farming methods to irrigate desert areas, farm mountainous areas, and build terraced fields in the sides of hills.

BACKGROUND FOR THE TEACHER

In order to piece together the histories of pre-Inca cultures, archaeologists and historians rely on artifacts uncovered in archaeological digs. So when sites are looted or destroyed, we lose important evidence of the past. Experts in the fields of archaeology, history, and cultural studies work hard to make sure sites are protected to ensure that valuable and irreplaceable artifacts are not being looted and sold on the black market. Unmanned aircraft called drones are helping with this cause, too. They can gather photos and data of sites to help prevent looting and the destruction of cultural heritage.

DIGITAL RESOURCES myNGconnect.com

TEACHER RESOURCES & ASSESSMENT

 Reading and Note-Taking

 Vocabulary Practice

 Section 1 Quiz

STUDENT RESOURCES

 NG Chapter Gallery

ROUNDTABLE

Divide students into groups of four. **ASK:** How do artisans create fine jewelry from precious metals such as gold, silver, and copper? Tell groups to explore the question. Encourage each student to contribute what he or she knows about how artisans create a piece of jewelry, such as a necklace or bracelet. Encourage groups to share their answers with the class when they are finished with their roundtable discussions. `0:05` minutes

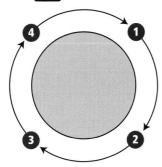

TEACH

GUIDED DISCUSSION

1. **Identify** What methods did the different cultures use to farm their land in such a harsh environment? *(They built irrigation systems in the desert and created terraced fields on hills and mountains.)*

2. **Synthesize** Archaeologists have concluded that the pre-Inca cultures described in Lesson 1.1 were excellent artisans. What led them to that conclusion? *(They found gold, silver, and copper jewelry; ceramic pottery; geoglyphs that were large geometric designs; and thin delicate gold jewelry in tombs for the dead.)*

MORE INFORMATION

Nasca Geoglyphs The Nasca geoglyphs take the shape of many different kinds of species. Archaeologists have discovered fish, birds, spider monkeys, lizards, plants, and even a whale. Archaeologists believe that these figures could have represented different meanings based on the social structure of the Nasca. They think that the Nasca placed much importance on the mountain gods who they believed watched over them and had control of the weather.

ACTIVE OPTIONS

On Your Feet: Four Corners Designate four corners of the classroom with signs labeled *Moche, Nasca, Wari,* and *Sicán.* Have students separate into equal groups to act as experts on the culture in their corner. Have them reread the text about their culture and do extra research to find out more. Then tell students to work together to prepare and give an oral presentation about their group. `0:10` minutes

NG Learning Framework: Think Like an Archaeologist

ATTITUDE: Curiosity
SKILL: Observation

Explain to students that archaeologists follow very strict procedures when they excavate a site to ensure that no information is lost. Since the archaeologists don't know what might be important, they have to treat everything as important. They also have to make sure that in digging, they don't destroy or ruin some object or piece of art. Have students work together in groups of four. They should pretend that they are in charge of digging the sites of these pre-Inca cultures. Have them work together to make a list of "dos" and "don'ts" for the archaeological digging crew. Let them share their lists when finished. `0:10` minutes

STRIVING READERS

Create a Culture Chart Help students organize information about different cultures discussed in Lesson 1.1 by having them record facts in a chart. Have students work in pairs to write two facts about each of the four cultures described in the lesson. Then have student pairs trade charts to check their facts.

MOCHE	NASCA	WARI	SICÁN

Press **mt** in the Student eEdition for modified text.

See the Chapter Planner for more strategies for differentiation.

ANSWERS

1. The Moche lived on the northwest coast. The Nasca were in southern Peru. The Wari lived in the high desert of central Peru. The Sicán were in northern Peru.

2. Archaeologists have found the remains of people who were buried with jewelry and pottery, reflecting the high level of respect that the people had for their ancestors.

3. All four of the cultures excelled at metalworking, particularly in gold. The cultures were different in how they adapted to their environments. For example, the Moche build complex irrigation systems, while the Wari built terraces. The Nasca created geoglyphs of animals in their environment. The Sicán created murals that reflected their environment.

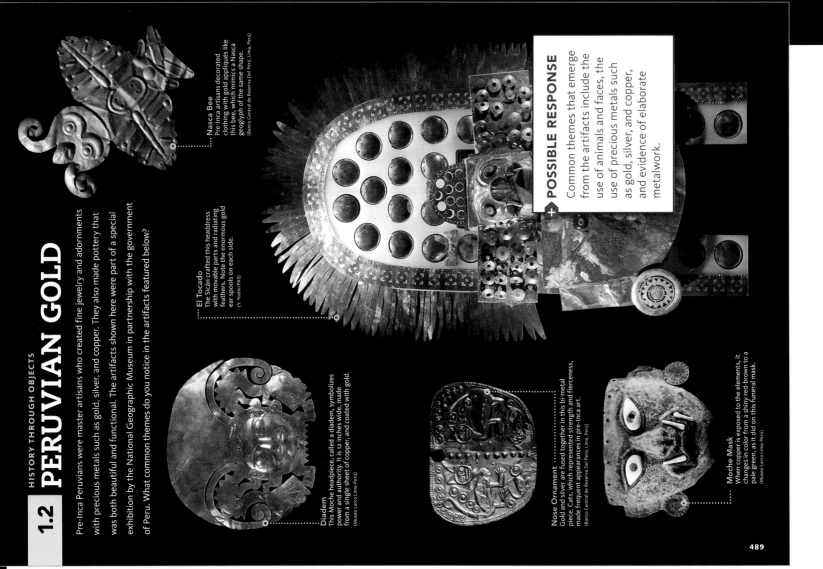

1.2 PERUVIAN GOLD

Pre-Inca Peruvians were master artisans who created fine jewelry and adornments with precious metals such as gold, silver, and copper. They also made pottery that was both beautiful and functional. The artifacts shown here were part of a special exhibition by the National Geographic Museum in partnership with the government of Peru. What common themes do you notice in the artifacts featured below?

Nasca Bee
Pre-Inca artisans decorated clothing with gold appliqués like this bee, which mimics a Nasca geoglyph of the same shape.
(Banco Central de Reserva Del Perú, Lima, Perú)

El Tocado
The Sicán crafted this headdress with movable parts and radiating feathers. Note the enormous gold ear spools on each side.
(Y. Yoshii/PAS)

Diadem
This Moche headpiece, called a diadem, symbolizes power and authority. It is 12 inches wide, made from a single sheet of copper, and coated with gold.
(Museo Larco Lima-Perú)

Nose Ornament
Gold and silver are fused together in this bi-metal piece. Cats, which represented strength and fierceness, made frequent appearances in pre-Inca art.
(Banco Central de Reserva Del Perú, Lima, Perú)

Moche Mask
When copper is exposed to the elements, it changes in color from a shiny red-brown to a pale green, as it did on this funeral mask.
(Museo Larco Lima-Perú)

POSSIBLE RESPONSE
Common themes that emerge from the artifacts include the use of animals and faces, the use of precious metals such as gold, silver, and copper, and evidence of elaborate metalwork.

PLAN

OBJECTIVE

Learn about the extraordinary artisanship of pre-Inca cultures.

CRITICAL THINKING SKILLS FOR LESSON 1.2

- Identify
- Sequence Events
- Analyze Visuals

ESSENTIAL QUESTION

In what ways do civilizations adapt to the environments in which they live?

Pre-Inca civilizations used precious metals such as gold, silver, and copper to make beautiful and lasting objects. Lesson 1.2 introduces students to such artisanship through artifacts created from the raw materials pre-Inca cultures mined in the Andes Mountains.

BACKGROUND FOR THE TEACHER

Peruvians have been mining gold, silver, and copper for centuries. Ancient Peruvians took gold from deposits in the rivers in the Andes Mountains as early as 1200 B.C. Goldsmiths have been working gold in this area for as long as 2,500 years. In the Mediterranean region, after the fall of the Roman Empire, little gold was discovered for almost 1,000 years. However, gold, silver, and copper were continuously mined in South America. Because Spanish conquistadors were seeking treasures, the availability of precious metals in South America became one factor that led to the downfall of the Inca.

DIGITAL RESOURCES myNGconnect.com

TEACHER RESOURCES & ASSESSMENT

 Reading and Note-Taking

 Vocabulary Practice

 Section 1 Quiz

STUDENT RESOURCES

 NG Chapter Gallery

INTRODUCE & ENGAGE

PREVIEW WITH VISUALS

Have students preview the artifacts featured in Lesson 1.2. Tell students that these objects were part of a museum exhibition at the National Geographic Museum that was a joint venture between the National Geographic Society and the government of Peru. Explain to students that the artifacts in the exhibition represent civilizations that emerged around A.D. 500 **ASK:** Approximately how old are these artifacts? *(about 1,500 years old)* `0:05` **minutes**

TEACH

GUIDED DISCUSSION

1. **Identify** What features appear on the pre-Inca artifacts? *(All have faces and eyes and look somewhat realistic. Some artifacts reflect insects, such as the bee, or animals, such as cats. Other features found on the artifacts include large teeth, feathers, geometric patterns, and movable parts.)*

2. **Sequence Events** Consider the artifacts in Lesson 1.2. What processes would people have to go through to create such artifacts, from beginning to end? Start with prospecting for gold. *(Possible responses: discovering gold deposits, mining or extracting the gold, cleaning and smelting the gold, pounding gold into thin sheets, creating the jewelry or coating it onto copper)*

ANALYZE VISUALS

Have students focus on the El Tocado, meaning "the headdress." List the separate parts they see that must have been soldered together. *(Examples include feathers; circles of gold at the top; the strip holding the feathers; the bird face in the strip across the head; circular button-like pieces on the lower crown, eyes, nose, lower face, ears, and earrings. Students may name other parts.)* `0:15` **minutes**

ACTIVE OPTIONS

On Your Feet: Create an Exhibition Have students work in small groups to create an exhibition that represents their school. Some students can play the role of curator, collecting artifacts for the exhibitions. Others can write labels for the artifacts that will appear in the exhibition. Some students can be designers, creating a space in the classroom to display the artifacts. Other students can advertise the exhibition and lead tours. Encourage students to play different roles in this project. You might even want to invite a museum professional to the classroom to speak about the exhibition-building process. `0:15` **minutes**

Critical Viewing: NG Chapter Gallery Invite students to explore the Chapter Gallery to examine the images that relate to this chapter. Have them select one of the images and do additional research to learn more about it. Ask questions that will inspire additional inquiry about the chosen gallery image, such as: What is this? Where and when was this created? By whom? Why was it created? What is it made of? Why does it belong in this chapter? What else would you like to know about it? `0:10` **minutes**

DIFFERENTIATE

INCLUSION

Categorize Artifacts Students who are visual learners may benefit from grouping and categorizing the artifacts presented in Lesson 1.2. Students might group artifacts by metal, by shape, or by type of animal or face. Have students work in pairs to make their groupings. Then have pairs compare their categories with other pairs.

GIFTED & TALENTED

Compare and Contrast Jewelry Have students research images of ancient Egyptian jewelry. Working in pairs, have them compare and contrast the types and style of the Egyptian jewelry with the jewelry of pre-Inca Peruvians. Ask them to come up with two or three generalizations. Encourage them to reproduce copies of the Egyptian jewelry to compare visually with the pieces in this lesson and to present their findings to the rest of the class.

Press **(mt)** *in the Student eEdition for modified text.*

See the Chapter Planner for more strategies for differentiation.

Inca Society and Government

The civilization known as the Inca began as a small mountain culture that lived high in the Andes Mountains. In only a few hundred years, the Inca had conquered large parts of South America and governed a huge empire.

MAIN IDEA

The Inca created and controlled a large empire in South America.

ORGANIZED EMPIRE

About the same time as the Aztec emerged in Mesoamerica, the Inca began their conquest of western South America. In A.D. 1200, the Inca were one of many small states occupying the Urubamba Valley, high in the Andes Mountains of present-day Peru. By 1440, the Inca ruled the region.

Under the leadership of the emperor **Pachacuti** (pah-chah-KOO-tee), the empire expanded rapidly. The name *Pachacuti* means "he who changed the world"—and this ambitious man certainly did that. Pachacuti conquered and ruled widespread areas through a powerful military and a strong central government. He also transformed the Inca capital, Cusco (KOO-skoh), into an impressive stone city of 100,000 people.

The Inca Empire stretched 2,600 miles from present-day Colombia to Argentina and included about 12 million people who spoke more than 20 languages. Despite its size, the Inca Empire was well organized. The hierarchy of Inca society helped rulers maintain tight control of the large empire.

At the top, the emperor had absolute power. Below him, four regional officials called prefects oversaw provincial governors, district officers, and local chiefs. Foremen supervised ten families each and helped carry out the policies of the emperor. The Inca government viewed the empire's subjects as a resource, like gold or timber. It demanded that whole populations relocate if the state needed their labor elsewhere. Commoners farmed communal land and worked on state-owned farms while also serving in the army or on building projects.

In order to manage the many details involved in running an empire, the Inca also had a large bureaucracy, or system of state officials. In fact, for every 10,000 Inca, there were 1,331 administrators. These administrators kept detailed records about all parts of the empire, from population to farm animals to trade.

MOUNTAIN LIFE

Like other early civilizations, the Inca Empire was built on agriculture. However, farming was difficult in the steep Andes. The Inca made up for the lack of flat farmland with a type of farming called **terrace farming**. They cut flat steps, or terraces, on the sides of mountains and then built stone walls to keep the terraces in place. Terrace farming produced potatoes, maize, and **quinoa** (KEEN-wah), a high-protein grain native to the Andes. In addition to farming, the Inca raised llamas and alpacas for meat and wool and for transporting goods and people across the mountains.

Inca religious rituals centered on the need to guarantee a good harvest. The Inca worshipped their emperor as the son of Inti, the Sun God, and believed the emperor helped humans communicate with the gods.

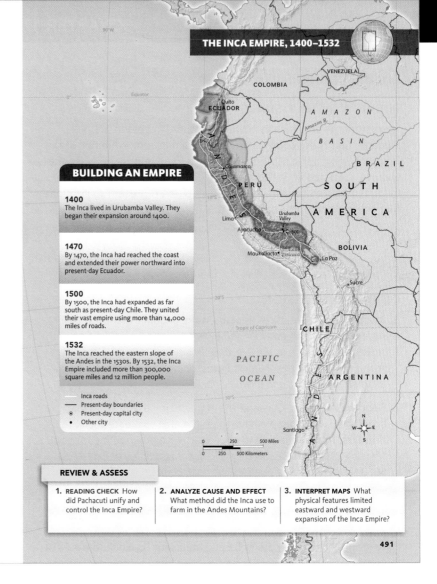

THE INCA EMPIRE, 1400–1532

BUILDING AN EMPIRE

1400
The Inca lived in Urubamba Valley. They began their expansion around 1400.

1470
By 1470, the Inca had reached the coast and extended their power northward into present-day Ecuador.

1500
By 1500, the Inca had expanded as far south as present-day Chile. They united their vast empire using more than 14,000 miles of roads.

1532
The Inca reached the eastern slope of the Andes in the 1530s. By 1532, the Inca Empire included more than 300,000 square miles and 12 million people.

- Inca roads
- Present-day boundaries
- Present-day capital city
- Other city

REVIEW & ASSESS

1. **READING CHECK** How did Pachacuti unify and control the Inca Empire?

2. **ANALYZE CAUSE AND EFFECT** What method did the Inca use to farm in the Andes Mountains?

3. **INTERPRET MAPS** What physical features limited eastward and westward expansion of the Inca Empire?

PLAN

OBJECTIVE

Examine the Inca Empire in South America.

Lesson 1.3 describes how the Inca adapted to a mountainous environment and built a complex civilization and empire.

CRITICAL THINKING SKILLS FOR LESSON 1.3

- Identify Main Ideas and Details
- Monitor Comprehension
- Analyze Cause and Effect
- Interpret Maps
- Identify Problems and Solutions
- Make Inferences
- Draw Conclusions

BACKGROUND FOR THE TEACHER

The Inca did not have a system of writing, and no portraits have been found of their rulers. The Spanish later destroyed the ruins of the Inca's past. However, now archaeologists are discovering thousands of new sites and gathering evidence of the wars that the Inca kings fought to expand their empire. They grew their empire village by village, sometimes by marriage and bribery and sometimes by military force. They built a strong army while others were farming their lands.

ESSENTIAL QUESTION

In what ways do civilizations adapt to the environments in which they live?

TEACHER RESOURCES & ASSESSMENT

 Reading and Note-Taking

 Vocabulary Practice

 Section 1 Quiz

STUDENT RESOURCES

 Biography

INTRODUCE & ENGAGE

THINK, PAIR, SHARE

Tell students to think about what qualities the leader of an empire might need to have to rule effectively. Have them discuss those qualities with a partner. Then encourage student pairs to share their ideas with the class. Finally, tell them to look for those qualities when they read about the man who founded the Inca Empire, Pachacuti. `0:05` **minutes**

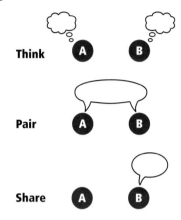

Think   A   B

Pair   A   B

Share   A   B

TEACH

GUIDED DISCUSSION

1. **Identify Problems and Solutions** Why was a large bureaucracy needed to run the empire? *(The empire was huge. It covered 300,000 square miles and held 12 million people who spoke 20 languages. The government needed many officials to manage all the details and keep the population unified.)*

2. **Make Inferences** Describe the Inca government's attitude toward the people. *(The bureaucrats supervised them closely, viewed them as a resource, and made them obey and even move if needed.)*

DRAW CONCLUSIONS

Tell students to consider the geography of the Inca Empire based on their understanding of both the map and the text. **ASK:** Why were roads so important to the Inca? *(Between the mountains, desert, and ocean, they needed a way to get from one part of the empire to another. The roads allowed them to travel to and communicate with all parts of the empire.)* `0:10` **minutes**

ACTIVE OPTIONS

On Your Feet: Running an Empire Have students work in teams of four. Tell them that they are in charge of the Inca Empire, and they need to appoint officials to help them keep order and keep the empire together. Have them list and come to an agreement on what jobs they need to give the officials below them. For example, one official might be the Road Manager. Tell them to limit their lists

to ten people. When they have finished, have them share their lists with other teams. `0:10` **minutes**

NG Learning Framework: Farming in the Empire

SKILLS: Observation, Collaboration
KNOWLEDGE: **Our Living Planet**

Have students revisit Lessons 1.1 and 1.3, specifically for the information about the geography of the Inca Empire. They should work in pairs to create a list of observations about the difficulties of farming this area. Then they should list observations about how the Inca and earlier civilizations figured out ways to farm successfully. Once they have completed their list of observations, each pair should exchange lists with another pair and discuss the new list. `0:10` **minutes**

DIFFERENTIATE

STRIVING READERS

Preview Text Help students preview Lesson 1.3. Point out the text features, such as the lesson title, Main Idea, subheadings, and the annotated map. **ASK:** Based on the lesson title and subheadings, what do you expect this lesson to be about? Take time to review the map and its color-coordinated legend. **ASK:** What does this map show? As students begin reading, help them confirm their understandings of each paragraph before moving on to the next one.

PRE-AP

Create an Annotated Time Line Have students do library or Internet research to build an annotated time line of the Inca Empire. Tell them to include dates, descriptions of significant events, and visuals to represent their dates and events. Encourage students to use the map in Lesson 1.3 as a reference. Students might organize their time lines either horizontally or vertically. Ask students to share their annotated time lines with the class.

Press **mt** in the Student eEdition for modified text.

See the Chapter Planner for more strategies for differentiation.

REVIEW & ASSESS

ANSWERS

1. Pachacuti introduced a strong central government, ruled with a powerful military supporting him, and made Cusco an important city.

2. The Inca used the method of terrace farming, which involved building terraces into the mountainsides and holding them in place with stone walls.

3. The Pacific Ocean prevented expansion to the west, while the Andes Mountains prevented expansion to the east.

Inca Architecture

What do you do when you are faced with a problem? The Inca met the challenge of mountain living head-on by building some of the most remarkable structures you can imagine.

MAIN IDEA

The Inca used their building skills to adapt to their mountain surroundings.

MOUNTAIN BUILDERS

The Inca were gifted engineers and builders. They built an extensive network of roads that helped them transport people and goods. Bridges built of wood, stone, and even thick rope helped them cross rivers and deep canyons. Inca stone architecture was even more impressive. The Inca constructed walls, buildings, and entire cities out of enormous blocks of stone. They **quarried**, or extracted, the stone in the Andes without the use of iron or steel tools.

Machu Picchu (MAH-choo PEE-choo) sits high on a mountain in Peru. Built around 1450, this stone city survived Spanish conquest in the 1530s because the Spanish never found it. Machu Picchu included religious temples, royal residences, and homes for workers as well as waterworks and terraces for farming. Aqueducts made of stone carried water to the city—just as aqueducts carried water in ancient Rome.

Critical Viewing Machu Picchu sits 8,000 feet above sea level. Why might the Inca have built this city in such a remote place?

+ POSSIBLE RESPONSE

The Inca built Machu Picchu high in the Andes Mountains for several reasons. They wanted a place that was remote and safe from invaders, and its high and spectacular location helped create a space for ceremonies and the worship of Inca gods.

REVIEW & ASSESS

1. **READING CHECK** Why are the Inca known as highly skilled engineers and builders?

2. **MAKE INFERENCES** How did bridges and roads help the Inca manage their empire?

3. **DRAW CONCLUSIONS** Why did Machu Picchu survive the Spanish conquest?

492 CHAPTER 17

493

PLAN

OBJECTIVE

Discover the Inca's extraordinary building skills in mountain surroundings.

CRITICAL THINKING SKILLS FOR LESSON 1.4

- Identify Main Ideas and Details
- Monitor Comprehension
- Make Inferences
- Draw Conclusions
- Compare and Contrast
- Analyze Visuals

ESSENTIAL QUESTION

In what ways do civilizations adapt to the environments in which they live?

The Inca adapted to life high in the Andes Mountains through ingenious building techniques. Lesson 1.4 describes Inca architecture.

BACKGROUND FOR THE TEACHER

The Inca had no iron, no steel, nor even the wheel when they built Machu Picchu. The stones are laid so tightly together that even a knife cannot get through; they used no mortar to cement them. Scholars think that this tremendously difficult building feat was created for fewer than 1,000 people who lived there. Its purpose could have been a military base, a site for ceremonies, or a retreat for the rich. Because the Inca left no written records, we may never know.

DIGITAL RESOURCES myNGconnect.com

TEACHER RESOURCES & ASSESSMENT

 Reading and Note-Taking

 Vocabulary Practice

 Section 1 Quiz

STUDENT RESOURCES

 Active History

COMPLETE A K-W-L CHART

Provide each student with a K-W-L Chart. Have students brainstorm what they know about the engineering and building skills of the Inca. Then ask them to write questions that they would like to have answered as they study the lesson. Allow time at the end of the lesson for students to fill in what they have learned. `0:05` minutes

K What Do I Know?	W What Do I Want To Learn?	L What Did I Learn?

TEACH

GUIDED DISCUSSION

1. **Compare and Contrast** What challenges did Inca engineers face that the Roman engineers did not have to face? *(They had to build roads and bridges in high mountains filled with stone; the Romans had a much flatter land and used a lot less stone for building. The Inca had a longer empire to connect with roads than the Romans did. Roads were already built in much of the Roman Empire. The Romans had iron tools to use, while the Inca did not.)*

2. **Make Inferences** Machu Picchu is 8,000 feet above sea level. What do you think the climate and weather would be like there? *(Possible responses: usually chilly, lots of clouds, thin air because of its high altitude)*

ANALYZE VISUALS

Have students study the photograph of Machu Picchu and answer the following questions:

- Why does Machu Picchu look undamaged? *(It is made of stone, which holds up well through the centuries. It is also an important site, carefully preserved by Peruvians.)*
- What keeps the terraces from falling down or eroding? *(stone walls)*
- What are the buildings made of? *(stone)*

- Why would it be hard for an enemy to invade Machu Picchu? *(It's located on top of a mountain. There is no easily visible path to it. It's almost impossible to attack from the bottom of the mountain.)* `0:15` minutes

ACTIVE OPTIONS

Active History: Create a Sketch Map of Machu Picchu Extend the lesson by using either the PDF or Whiteboard version of the activity. These activities take a deeper look at a topic from, or related to, the lesson. Explore the activities as a class, turn them into group assignments, or even assign them individually. `0:10` minutes

On Your Feet: Compare Engineering Feats Divide the class into three groups and assign each group a culture: Egyptians, Greeks, and Romans. Have them look back at other chapters to find photographs of stone architecture or art from their assigned culture. Tell groups to compare and contrast their stone sculptures or buildings with Machu Picchu. Have them list some similarities and differences they find between the two styles, such as materials, size, features, subjects, purpose, or other details. Have them share their findings with the other two groups. `0:10` minutes

DIFFERENTIATE

ENGLISH LANGUAGE LEARNERS

Identify Details Have students work in pairs to find details in the two paragraphs that make up the body of the lesson. **ASK:** What did the Inca build, and what materials did they use? *(Answers should include bridges, roads, walls, buildings, cities, temples, homes, waterworks, terraces for farming, and aqueducts. Materials were stone, wood, and thick ropes.)* Have students keep a running list of words related to building and materials. Encourage them to look up definitions for words they don't know.

Press (mt) *in the Student eEdition for modified text.*

See the Chapter Planner for more strategies for differentiation.

REVIEW & ASSESS

ANSWERS

1. The Inca built bridges and impressive stone architecture without the use of iron or steel tools.

2. The Inca built an extensive network of roads to transport people and goods throughout the empire. They built bridges of wood, stone, and rope to cross the rivers and canyons in the mountains.

3. Machu Picchu survived the Spanish conquest because it was so remote the Spanish never found it.

+ POSSIBLE RESPONSE

Details in the mural that convey Atahualpa's power include attendants carrying Atahualpa on a litter, or chair. He is richly dressed and has a sun medallion around his neck and is holding a staff signifying power.

1532

This 20th-century mural in Cajamarca, Peru, depicts the 1532 meeting of the Spanish conquistador **Francisco Pizarro** and **Atahualpa** (ah-tah-WAHL-pah), the Inca emperor. Pizarro had just 180 men with him, but they had the advantage of horses and superior metal weapons. Shortly after the meeting, Pizarro's men captured Atahualpa and killed his unarmed attendants. The Spanish ruled the Inca through Atahualpa for almost a year—and then executed him. By 1539, the Spanish had conquered the territory of the fallen empire. What details in the mural convey Atahualpa's power as emperor?

495

OBJECTIVE

Identify how the Spanish defeated the Inca and conquered their empire.

CRITICAL THINKING SKILLS FOR LESSON 1.5

- Analyze Visuals
- Analyze Cause and Effect
- Sequence Events

ESSENTIAL QUESTION

In what ways do civilizations adapt to the environments in which they live?

The Inca had adapted very well to their environment, but could not adapt to an outside threat. Lesson 1.5 explains how the Spanish defeated the Inca and took over their empire.

BACKGROUND FOR THE TEACHER

The title *conquistador* means "conqueror" and refers to the Spanish conquerors of Mexico and Peru. Two famous ones were Hernán Cortés, who conquered the Aztec, and Francisco Pizarro, who conquered the Inca. As explorer Vasco Núñez de Balboa's chief lieutenant, Pizarro helped "discover" the Pacific Ocean and the western coast of South America. He tried twice to conquer the Inca before succeeding. He was motivated to keeping trying to conquer the Inca because of the gold that he knew existed in the Andes.

DIGITAL RESOURCES myNGconnect.com

TEACHER RESOURCES & ASSESSMENT

 Reading and Note-Taking

 Vocabulary Practice

 Section 1 Quiz

STUDENT RESOURCES

 Biography

INTRODUCE & ENGAGE

THINK, PAIR, SHARE

Ask students to think about the fact that even though the Inca Empire was so powerful and well organized, it was ultimately defeated by the Spanish. Ask students to consider factors that cause empires to fall or disappear. After individuals have time to think about the topic, tell them to discuss their ideas with a partner. Then have a discussion as a class about reasons that empires disappear. Tell students that they will learn what happened to the Inca Empire in Lesson 1.5. **0:05** minutes

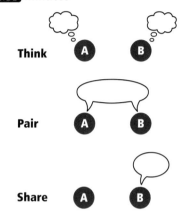

TEACH

GUIDED DISCUSSION

1. **Analyze Visuals** Why might present-day Peruvians have a mural like this one showing a defeated emperor? *(Even though Atahualpa was defeated and executed by Pizarro, he was an important figure in Inca history. Today, Peruvians acknowledge Inca and Spanish influences on their culture.)*

2. **Analyze Cause and Effect** What advantage did the Spanish have over the Inca? *(The Spanish had horses and superior metal weapons; the Inca had no horses and used weaker weapons.)*

SEQUENCE EVENTS

Have students complete a Sequence Chain that shows the events surrounding the Spanish conquest of the Inca. **0:15** minutes

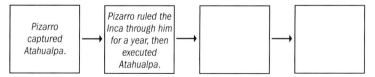

ACTIVE OPTIONS

On Your Feet: Team Word Webbing Arrange teams of students around a large piece of paper. Give each team member a different colored marker. **ASK:** Why did Pizarro capture Atahualpa? Have students write a reason on the part of the web nearest to them. On your signal, have students rotate the paper and each student writes on the nearest part again. When finished, tell students to compare their answers. Encourage team members to share their answers about Pizarro's motives with the class. **0:10** minutes

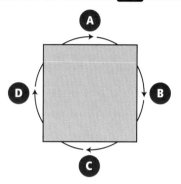

NG Learning Framework: Research Conquistadors

ATTITUDE: **Curiosity**
KNOWLEDGE: **Our Human Story**

Have students research Francisco Pizarro and another Spanish conquistador who explored South America. Instruct them to write a short report that compares Pizarro and their additional conquistador. Encourage students to explore suitable research sites online. **0:10** minutes

DIFFERENTIATE

STRIVING READERS

Make a Top Five Facts List Tell students to reread Lesson 1.5 and to take a few minutes to study the mural featured in the lesson. Then have students write down five facts that they remember from the text. Have students meet with a partner to compare lists and consolidate the two lists into one final list. Encourage student pairs to offer facts from their lists.

GIFTED & TALENTED

Present a Skit Tell students to research the encounter of Atahualpa and the Inca with Pizarro and his soldiers. Have them use what they learn to write a short skit about the historic meeting. Encourage students to consider writing two different endings: one that reflects the historical events, and one that imagines a different outcome. Encourage students to present their skits to the class and to perform both endings.

Press (**mt**) *in the Student eEdition for modified text.*

See the Chapter Planner for more strategies for differentiation.

Northwest Coast Cultures

North America is made up of vastly different landscapes, including rain forests, mountains, deserts, prairies, and woodlands. The hundreds of Native American cultures varied as much as North America's geography. In the Pacific Northwest, the forests and seacoast provided a hospitable environment for several cultures.

MAIN IDEA

Native American cultures of the Pacific Northwest thrived in a land of plentiful rainfall and dense forests.

NORTHWEST COAST TRIBES

Thirty distinct cultures lived in the Pacific Northwest region. This narrow strip of mountains and woodland followed the coast from present-day northern California to Alaska. It was one of the most densely populated parts of North America. The lakes, rivers, and ocean provided fish, shellfish, and whales. The forests offered plentiful plants and game. With such abundance, populations grew, and complex societies developed without any need to farm.

Along the southern coast of what is now the state of Alaska, the Tlingit (KLING–kit) people developed a thriving culture that was closely tied to the Pacific Ocean and

the many rivers. In fact, the word *Tlingit* means "the People of the Tides." The Tlingit were superb sailors and fishers, and their most important food was salmon.

Because the Pacific Northwest receives ample rainfall, forests carpet the region. As a result, wood was central to Tlingit culture. Around A.D. 500, the Tlingit developed tools for splitting and carving wood. With those tools, they built permanent homes and crafted everyday necessities such as plates and utensils. They also used tools and fire to carve dugout canoes from logs. The canoes, some as long as 60 feet, were seaworthy and could sail for miles into the Pacific Ocean, allowing the Tlingit to hunt for whales.

Two other important Northwest Coast tribes—the Kwakiutl (kwahk-ee-YOU-tuhl) and the Haida (HIGH-dah)—lived south of the Tlingit. Both lived by hunting and gathering but settled in permanent villages. They used the forests' cedar trees to build large family houses. Like the Tlingit, they also built excellent seagoing canoes.

These tribes also traded extensively with neighboring cultures. Over time, trade allowed some families to become wealthy, and social classes developed. Social rank became hereditary and certain families had great influence based on their wealth and ancestry. These families demonstrated and shared wealth through gift-giving ceremonies called **potlatches**, in which they gave away gifts and food to their communities.

TOTEM POLES AND MASKS

The skillful wood carvings of Northwest Coast cultures reveal their relationship to the natural world and their belief in a spirit world. One example of their artistry is found in the intricate masks they carved and painted and then wore at ceremonies. A **shaman**, or a person who is believed to be able to help others communicate with the spirit world, guided the mask carving and led the ceremonies.

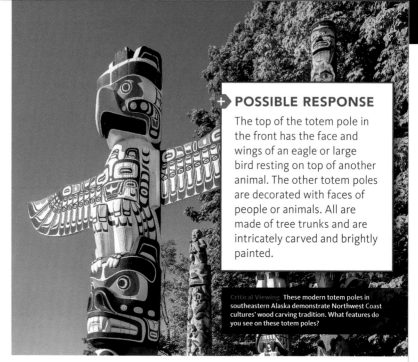

POSSIBLE RESPONSE

The top of the totem pole in the front has the face and wings of an eagle or large bird resting on top of another animal. The other totem poles are decorated with faces of people or animals. All are made of tree trunks and are intricately carved and brightly painted.

Critical Viewing These modern totem poles in southeastern Alaska demonstrate Northwest Coast cultures' wood carving tradition. What features do you see on these totem poles?

Totem poles are another example of Northwest Coast wood carving artistry. Totem poles are tall, elaborately carved and painted tree trunks that honor a revered being or guardian associated with a family. Totem pole carvings included colorful representations of animals of the region, such as bears, whales, and eagles. Other carvings included human figures, such as chiefs or ancestors and supernatural spirits. Totem poles told stories and legends as well as family and tribal histories. Wood rots easily in the region's damp climate, so few totem poles have survived more than 100 years. However, totem pole carving remains a Northwest Coast tradition today.

REVIEW & ASSESS

1. **READING CHECK** In what ways did the geography of the Pacific Northwest influence the culture of the Tlingit people?

2. **DRAW CONCLUSIONS** What was the function of the potlatch in the Kwakiutl and Haida societies?

3. **EVALUATE** What role did totem poles and masks play in the cultures of Pacific Northwest tribes?

PLAN

OBJECTIVE

Explore the Native American cultures of the Northwest Coast.

CRITICAL THINKING SKILLS FOR LESSON 2.1

- Identify Main Ideas and Details
- Monitor Comprehension
- Draw Conclusions
- Evaluate
- Compare and Contrast
- Summarize

ESSENTIAL QUESTION

In what ways do civilizations adapt to the environments in which they live?

The Northwest Coast cultures used the resources of their environment for food, shelter, and travel. Lesson 2.1 explains how these cultures adapted to their ocean and forest environment.

BACKGROUND FOR THE TEACHER

Today, the Tlingit live mostly along the southern coast of Alaska and the west coast of Canada. In the late 18th and early 19th centuries, the Tlingit struggled with Russian fur traders, battling with them for land and resources. The Tlinglit were pushed away from their land for 20 years by the Russians but were eventually able to return. The Tlingit experienced health problems after they were exposed to European diseases, alcohol, and tobacco. Though some Tlinglit still speak their native language, most speak English and their native language is in danger of dying out.

DIGITAL RESOURCES myNGconnect.com

TEACHER RESOURCES & ASSESSMENT

 Reading and Note-Taking

 Vocabulary Practice

 Section 2 Quiz

STUDENT RESOURCES

 NG Chapter Gallery

INTRODUCE & ENGAGE

ACTIVATE PRIOR KNOWLEDGE

Draw a large Word Web on the board with *Northwest Coast* in the center. Show the area of the Northwest Coast on a North American map, including upper California, Oregon, Washington, and Alaska. Ask students to volunteer what they know about the climate and geography of the Northwest Coast. Write students' descriptive phrases on the spokes of the web. **0:05** minutes

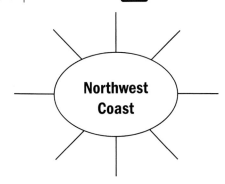

Northwest
Coast

TEACH

GUIDED DISCUSSION

1. **Compare and Contrast** How were the materials available to the Northwest Coast tribes different from the materials available to the Inca? (*The Northwest Coast tribes had abundant wood, plants, wild game, and an ocean full of fish. The Inca had to use stone for building, needed to conserve water, and farmed on terraces for food.*)

2. **Summarize** Give examples that show the complexity of the Northwest Coast cultures. (*Possible responses: They had permanent villages and social classes based on wealth and ancestry; they produced intricate wood carvings; and they developed a spiritual tradition with professional shamans.*)

MORE INFORMATION

Totem Poles The carved animals and figures of a totem pole represent a family's achievements, social standing, and real and mythical ancestors. The word *totem* comes from a Native American word meaning "kinship group." Totem poles often display the animal that serves as the emblem, or crest, of a family. The traditional process of carving a totem pole begins with stripping the bark from a cedar log and flattening one side of the log. The carver then uses a variety of chisels, knives, and hammer-like tools called adzes to carve the designs. If a figure or animal has wings or other appendages, the carver attaches them using mortise-and-tenon joints, a common woodworking process still used today.

ACTIVE OPTIONS

On Your Feet: Fishbowl Have part of the class sit in a close circle facing inward; the other part of the class sits in a larger circle

around them. Students on the inside discuss what they have learned about the Northwest Coast cultures. They should describe how the different tribes lived, including their diets, homes, and survival skills. Those on the outside should listen for new information and decide what might have been omitted from the discussion. Then groups reverse positions and the new inner circle discusses the same topic. **0:10** minutes

Critical Viewing: NG Chapter Gallery Have students examine the contents of the Chapter Gallery for this chapter. Then invite them to brainstorm additional images they believe would fit within the Chapter Gallery. Have them write a description of these additional images and provide an explanation of why they would fit within the Chapter Gallery. Then instruct them to do online research to find examples of actual images they would like to add to the gallery. **0:10** minutes

DIFFERENTIATE

INCLUSION

Monitor Comprehension Have students work in small groups, reading aloud the text paragraph by paragraph. At the end of each paragraph, have them stop and use these sentence frames:

- This paragraph is about _____.
- One detail that stood out to me was _____.
- The word _____ means_____.
- I don't think I understand _____.

Encourage students to help each other with any part of the text that they do not understand.

Press **mt** *in the Student eEdition for modified text.*

See the Chapter Planner for more strategies for differentiation.

REVIEW & ASSESS

ANSWERS

1. The Tlingit took advantage of the ocean and the forests by fishing for salmon, hunting for whales, and using wood for shelter and the necessities of daily life, such as utensils.

2. The potlatch was a ceremony at which people exchanged gifts and gave gifts to their communities. It was an opportunity to show generosity and the unity of the community.

3. The totem poles and masks were expressions of respect for ancestors and the spirits that were important to the culture. Totem poles could tell stories or legends about a family. People wore masks during ceremonies to celebrate ancestors.

The Ancient Pueblo

The American Southwest could not be more different from the Pacific Northwest. The Southwest is a harsh land of mountains and deserts, where temperatures can reach a scorching 120 degrees Fahrenheit. In this forbidding land, the ancient Pueblo developed a vibrant culture that was closely tied to the land.

MAIN IDEA

The ancient Pueblo adapted to their environment by farming the arid land and building complex structures.

DESERT DWELLERS

As early as 1000 B.C., the ancient Pueblo began to farm in various parts of the arid Southwest desert. They inhabited the Four Corners region, where present-day Arizona, Colorado, Utah, and New Mexico come together. Little by little, they began to build villages with permanent structures on high plateaus or in canyons. Some structures were dwellings made of stone and **adobe**, a clay used for building. Farm fields surrounded the villages. Using a technique called dry farming, the ancient Pueblo grew crops on the dry land, using very little water. The three staples of their diet were corn, beans, and squash.

The ancient Pueblo were skilled artisans who created baskets and pottery that were beautiful yet practical. They wove lightweight baskets and threaded together different materials to create brightly colored patterns. They used the baskets to carry objects and even to cook by placing hot stones in the baskets to heat the food. As they settled in permanent villages, the ancient Pueblo began to create extraordinary pottery, which was heavier but more permanent than baskets. They molded clay into jars, bowls, and pitchers.

PUEBLO BONITO AND MESA VERDE

One of the most impressive ancient Pueblo settlements was **Pueblo Bonito**, located in Chaco Canyon in northern New Mexico. It housed as many as 1,200 people and had more than 600 rooms and 30 kivas. **Kivas** were circular-shaped chambers in the ground used for ceremonies and social gatherings. Construction on Pueblo Bonito began around A.D. 850 and continued for another 200 years. The ancient Pueblo abandoned Pueblo Bonito sometime during the 1200s. Archaeologists are not sure why, but they believe that a severe drought may have forced people to migrate to other parts of the Southwest.

By 1200, the ancient Pueblo who lived in present-day southwestern Colorado built a series of dwellings into the sides of cliffs at **Mesa Verde**. They did this to defend themselves from invaders and provide protection from rain and the intense sun. Using advanced architectural skills, they built structures with several stories underneath cliff overhangs. The largest dwelling, Cliff Palace, featured more than 200 rooms and housed about 250 people. In all, the dwellings at Mesa Verde sheltered as many as 5,000 people.

The ancient Pueblo abandoned Mesa Verde by about 1300. In the late 1800s, two local ranchers discovered the ruins there, and in 1906, it became a U.S. National Park.

+ **POSSIBLE RESPONSE**

The buildings at Pueblo Bonito and Mesa Verde were close together in compact spaces, connected, possibly for protection against invaders.

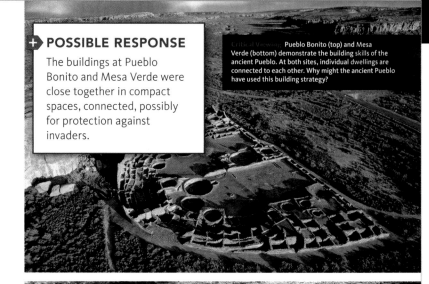

Critical Viewing Pueblo Bonito (top) and Mesa Verde (bottom) demonstrate the building skills of the ancient Pueblo. At both sites, individual dwellings are connected to each other. Why might the ancient Pueblo have used this building strategy?

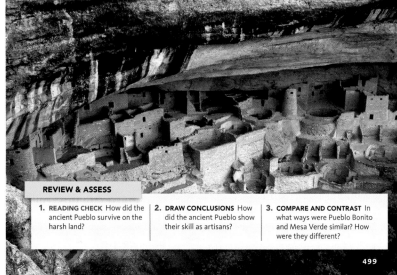

REVIEW & ASSESS

1. **READING CHECK** How did the ancient Pueblo survive on the harsh land?

2. **DRAW CONCLUSIONS** How did the ancient Pueblo show their skill as artisans?

3. **COMPARE AND CONTRAST** In what ways were Pueblo Bonito and Mesa Verde similar? How were they different?

PLAN

OBJECTIVE

Explore the ancient Pueblo of the Southwest.

CRITICAL THINKING SKILLS FOR LESSON 2.2

- Identify Main Ideas and Details
- Monitor Comprehension
- Draw Conclusions
- Compare and Contrast
- Analyze Cause and Effect
- Describe
- Analyze Visuals

ESSENTIAL QUESTION

In what ways do civilizations adapt to the environments in which they live?

The ancient Pueblo adapted to living in the arid Southwest desert. Lesson 2.2 explains how they built homes from adobe, built dwellings underneath cliffs, and learned to farm on dry land.

BACKGROUND FOR THE TEACHER

Some ancient Pueblo lived on plateaus at high altitudes with steep canyons near them, depending on snow for water. Summer rains could be destructive, causing wind and water erosion, and the rains were unreliable. All lived with the threat of drought. No one knows why Pueblo Bonito or Mesa Verde were abandoned. Experts believe that drought and providing food for so many exhausted the soil and destroyed the forests. The environment could not sustain the population any longer, so the ancient Pueblo left.

DIGITAL RESOURCES myNGconnect.com

TEACHER RESOURCES & ASSESSMENT

 Reading and Note-Taking

 Vocabulary Practice

 Section 2 Quiz

STUDENT RESOURCES

 NG Chapter Gallery

INTRODUCE & ENGAGE

TEAM WORD WEBBING

Divide the class into teams of four to recall the characteristics of deserts. They should cover the geography, climate, and weather. The teams should sit around a large piece of paper. Each team member has a different colored marker. Each student adds to the part of the web nearest to him or her. On your signal, students rotate the paper and each student adds to the nearest part again. When finished, have different teams share what they have recalled about deserts. Explain that Lesson 2.2 explores the ancient Pueblo of the American Southwest. **0:05** minutes

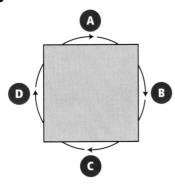

TEACH

GUIDED DISCUSSION

1. **Analyze Cause and Effect** How did living underneath cliffs protect the ancient Pueblo? (*Their cliff homes protected them from snow and heavy rains and was hidden to protect them from other invaders.*)

2. **Describe** What did the shift from baskets to pottery likely indicate? (*Once the ancient Pueblo began to make pottery, they were likely more settled and less nomadic, because pottery was heavier and more fragile than baskets.*)

ANALYZE VISUALS

Have students study the second photograph and imagine the cliffs before the ancient Pueblo built Mesa Verde. **ASK:** What difficulties might the ancient Pueblo have had while building the cliff dwellings? (*They had to bring all their materials to the area; they had to build on rocky and uneven terrain; they had to work little by little, probably going from inside to outside and extending outside as far as they could; workers faced the danger of falling.*) **0:10** minutes

ACTIVE OPTIONS

On Your Feet: Choose Your Home Label one corner of the room Pueblo Bonito and another corner Mesa Verde. Remind students that Pueblo Bonito was built in a canyon and Mesa Verde was built underneath cliffs. Have students study the photos and text and think about what each settlement had to offer its inhabitants in terms of desert living. Have students imagine living in both places. Then have them choose which area they would have preferred to live in and why. Tell them to go to that corner of the room. Finally, ask the groups in each corner to explain their choices. **0:10** minutes

Critical Viewing: NG Chapter Gallery Ask students to choose one image from the Chapter Gallery and become an expert on it. They should do additional research to learn all about it. Then, students should share their findings with a partner, small group, or the class. **0:10** minutes

DIFFERENTIATE

ENGLISH LANGUAGE LEARNERS

Make Vocabulary Cards Have students use flash cards to learn and practice unfamiliar words they encounter in this lesson and other lessons in this section. On one side of each card, they should write the target word. On the other, they should write related words they are familiar with, draw or paste images that will help them recall the meaning of the target word, or write out other mnemonic devices. Encourage students to use their flash cards for review.

GIFTED & TALENTED

Create a Poster Direct students to research more information on and photos of Mesa Verde. Tell them to reproduce their findings on a poster. Have students write informative captions for the photos they select and include odd or interesting facts they come across in their research. Encourage students to share their posters with the class.

Press (**mt**) *in the Student eEdition for modified text.*

See the Chapter Planner for more strategies for differentiation.

REVIEW & ASSESS

ANSWERS

1. The ancient Pueblo developed techniques of farming in which they used little water, and they used materials such as clay to construct adobe buildings.

2. They created brightly colored patterns in the baskets they wove and beautiful pottery. They made clay jars, bowls, and pitchers.

3. Similarities: At both sites, the dwellings were connected and close together. Both have round kivas for ceremonies and many rooms that held many people. Differences: Pueblo Bonito was out in the open; Mesa Verde was built underneath cliffs.

2.3

Peoples of the Great Plains

Hunting might be a sport for some people in the 21st century, but for early Great Plains cultures, hunting was key to survival. Farming on dry grasslands did not always produce good harvests. So Great Plains tribes relied on other natural resources, such as the buffalo.

MAIN IDEA

Native Americans on the Great Plains depended on the land and especially on the buffalo for survival.

PLAINS DWELLERS

The **Great Plains** is a wide area of flat, windswept grasslands that stretches north from present-day Texas into Canada. Early tribes settled along the region's major rivers and established permanent villages.

To survive the bitter winters, some tribes built earth lodges out of soil and grasses to house whole families. They relied mostly on hunting, gathering, and fishing because farming was not easy on the dry grasslands of the plains.

The different tribes of the Great Plains each had their own spiritual beliefs and traditions. Many homes had altars for burning incense during prayers. Farming communities practiced religious ceremonies centered on a good harvest. Hunting tribes had ceremonies focused on visions and spirit beings that might enhance their hunting abilities. For example, young men participated in vision quests where they put their bodies through strenuous ordeals. The goal was to achieve a trancelike state and have a vision—often of an animal. Shamans would interpret their visions.

Another important spiritual practice for Great Plains people was the Sun Dance. The Sun Dance was an annual ceremony of drumming, dancing, singing, and praying for harmony among people and giving thanks for prosperity.

BUFFALO HUNTERS

One animal was central to the livelihood and the culture of the Great Plains people— the buffalo. Large herds grazed on the wide-open grasslands, and nomadic tribes followed their migrations. These tribes had no horses, so they traveled on foot.

Because buffalo are more aggressive than cattle, they will attack if provoked. Hunting buffalo was a risky business. Hunters agitated the herd into a thunderous stampede. Then they drove the buffalo over cliffs or into corrals where they killed the animals with arrows or spears.

Buffalo were a useful resource. Great Plains people ate buffalo meat raw, roasted, or as smoked jerky. They used buffalo skins for clothes and tents, bones for tools, sinew, or tendons, for bowstrings, boiled hooves for glue, and even buffalo dung for fuel.

In the 1500s, the Spanish introduced horses to North America, and some Great Plains people began to use them to hunt. Horses allowed the tribes to follow buffalo migrations across the plains. As hunting became more efficient, more tribes moved to the plains and became buffalo hunters. White settlers in the 1800s also hunted the buffalo, resulting in its near extinction.

Critical Viewing Before 1500, about 50 million buffalo roamed freely on the plains. By 1889, commercial hunting with horses and guns had reduced buffalo numbers to just 1,000. How might this overhunting have affected tribes on the Great Plains?

+ POSSIBLE RESPONSE

Overhunting of the buffalo affected tribes on the Great Plains because as their central source of livelihood, the buffalo was threatened with extinction after commercial hunting decreased their numbers in the 1800s.

REVIEW & ASSESS

1. **READING CHECK** Why were buffalo important to the people of the Great Plains?

2. **ANALYZE CAUSE AND EFFECT** How did the introduction of the horse to North America affect life for tribes on the Great Plains?

3. **COMPARE AND CONTRAST** How were the religious practices of Great Plains tribes similar? How did they differ?

PLAN

OBJECTIVE

Explore cultures that lived on North America's expansive plains.

CRITICAL THINKING SKILLS FOR LESSON 2.3

- Identify Main Ideas and Details
- Monitor Comprehension
- Analyze Cause and Effect
- Compare and Contrast
- Make Inferences

ESSENTIAL QUESTION

In what ways do civilizations adapt to the environments in which they live?

Peoples of the Great Plains relied on hunting rather than farming for survival and made homes out of grass and earth. Lesson 2.3 describes several Great Plains cultures.

BACKGROUND FOR THE TEACHER

Hunting buffalo on foot was a dangerous task. Buffalo can weigh up to 2,000 pounds or more. They are herbivores, meaning they eat grasses and not other animals, and they spend most of their time grazing. These animals can run 35 to 40 miles an hour and jump 6 feet in the air. Today, buffalo are raised in herds for their meat, which tastes similar to beef but has less cholesterol and more protein.

DIGITAL RESOURCES myNGconnect.com

TEACHER RESOURCES & ASSESSMENT

 Reading and Note-Taking

 Vocabulary Practice

 Section 2 Quiz

STUDENT RESOURCES

 NG Chapter Gallery

THINK, PAIR, SHARE

Allow students time to think about what they know about Great Plains cultures and the type of hunting they did to survive. Have them discuss the topic with a partner. Then have them share what they know with the class. Explain that Lesson 2.3 explores Great Plains cultures and their hunting practices. **0:05** minutes

TEACH

GUIDED DISCUSSION

1. **Make Inferences** Why was hunting buffalo on foot so dangerous and difficult? *(Buffalo are aggressive and fast; they would charge and kill people. Hunters on foot had to start a stampede and drive buffalo over cliffs or into corrals before they could spear them or kill them with arrows.)*

2. **Compare and Contrast** How and why were the homes of the Plains peoples different from those of the ancient Pueblo? *(Plains peoples built earth lodges out of soil and grasses because they lived on flat grasslands. The ancient Pueblo lived in cliffs, on plateaus, or in canyons and used adobe they could make from desert soils.)*

MORE INFORMATION

Vision Quests One of the common purposes of vision quests was for young people to learn more about themselves and their place in the tribe and in the world. Vision quests had great spiritual and religious significance. Many involved leaving home and living in the wilderness alone for a few days. The youth would fast—from food and possibly water. A tribal leader would guide the youth in preparing for the quest and might also watch over the youth from a distance. During a vision quest, the youth would have a vision or a dream in which a spirit would reveal something. The spirit might take the form of an animal or a process of nature. A member of the tribe would then help the youth interpret the vision. Afterward, the youth would take steps to gain the skills or knowledge needed to follow the path indicated by the vision. For example, a youth might begin to study and work with the tribe's shaman.

ACTIVE OPTIONS

On Your Feet: Inside-Outside Circle Have students stand in concentric circles facing each other. Direct students in the outside circle to ask questions about the hunting and the hunters of the Plains peoples. Students on the inside answer. On a signal, students rotate to create new partnerships. On another signal, students trade inside/outside roles. **0:10** minutes

NG Learning Framework: Buffalo in Trouble

SKILL: Collaboration
KNOWLEDGE: **Critical Species**

Have students review the caption about the near extinction of the buffalo. They should work in pairs to write the facts presented and then do research to find out how many buffalo there are today and how numbers were restored. Have the pairs prepare an oral report that gives a short history of the buffalo and discusses how herds were restored. Encourage students to share their reports with the class. **0:10** minutes

DIFFERENTIATE

STRIVING READERS

Use Topics to Take Notes Help students take notes by providing them with the list of topics below. Tell students to search for the topics as they read. Then have students write at least one note for each topic they locate. Review students' notes to ensure that they understand the content of the lesson.

- Geography
- Dwellings
- Spiritual beliefs
- Sun Dance
- Buffalo
- Hunting buffalo on foot
- Buffalo as a resource
- Horses to hunt buffalo

PRE-AP

Research Horses in North America Have students research the first horses that were brought to the Plains by the Spanish. Students should also explore how the Plains peoples became a horse culture as time passed. Tell pairs of students to prepare a visual presentation to share with the class. Direct their attention to the *National Geographic* adapted article, "People of the Horse," listed in the Chapter Planner for content, ideas, and illustrations.

Press **mt** *in the Student eEdition for modified text.*

See the Chapter Planner for more strategies for differentiation.

REVIEW & ASSESS

ANSWERS

1. The vast herds of buffalo that grazed on the plains made life possible for the nomadic tribes, who hunted the buffalo and used its meat and skins to survive.

2. With the introduction of the horse, nomadic tribes on the Great Plains could follow buffalo migrations across the plains, making the buffalo easier to hunt. The horse also made it more practical for other tribes to move to the plains and become nomadic buffalo hunters.

3. In general, Great Plains cultures had practices that focused on the prosperity of their tribes. In the farming communities, those practices centered on fertility and a good harvest, while in the hunting tribes the practices focused on visions and spirit beings that would enhance their hunting abilities.

The Mound Builders and Cahokia

The Mississippi River Valley and prairies and woodlands further east supported many different Native American cultures. Some built mounds, others built cities—including one of the largest cities in North America.

MAIN IDEA

Native Americans from the Great Lakes to the Gulf of Mexico developed complex societies, large cities, and organized governments.

MOUND BUILDERS

East of the Mississippi River, woodlands and prairies covered the lands that stretch between the Great Lakes and the Gulf of Mexico. Between 1000 B.C. and A.D. 500, the Adena and then the Hopewell lived in this region. They are known as **mound builders** because they built huge mounds of earth. The mounds served religious and ceremonial purposes. Some mounds, such as the Great Serpent Mound built by the Adena in southern Ohio, formed the shape of animals.

The mound builders relied mostly on hunting and gathering, but they also tamed wild plants and farmed crops such as barley. Maize—called corn today—appeared around A.D. 100, probably brought there by traders. The Adena and Hopewell cultures developed highly organized and complex societies. Living in villages that dotted the region, they hunted, farmed, and traded. The Hopewell culture collapsed by A.D. 500 for reasons that remain unknown.

From 800 to 1700, a different mound building culture—the Mississippians—emerged in the Mississippi River Valley. The Mississippians eventually populated the region from present-day Ohio, Indiana, and Illinois, south to the Gulf of Mexico. Like the Adena and Hopewell, Mississippians built mounds that had sloping sides, steps, and flat tops. However, the Mississippians built their mounds around a central plaza, where they held feasts and ceremonies.

The fertile floodplains of the Mississippi River Valley supported farming. Because of the fertility of their lands, the Mississippians grew ample quantities of maize, beans, and squash. They also hunted, skillfully using bows and arrows. Because of their plentiful food, Mississippian settlements supported large populations. In fact, they were the most populous Native American settlements north of Mexico.

CAHOKIA

The largest and most complex city that the mound builders created was at **Cahokia**, in southwest Illinois. Cahokia contained more than 120 mounds covering 6 square miles and supported more than 30,000 people. A series of stockades surrounded much of the city and a grand plaza provided space for ceremonies and celebrations.

The centerpiece of Cahokia was Monks Mound, which rose 100 feet above the flat prairie and covered 16 acres. This mound contained 814,000 cubic yards of soil—enough to fill 45,000 dump trucks. The Cahokians moved all this earth without the use of dump trucks, though. They used baskets instead.

Building the mounds required a highly organized society. A powerful chief who lived in a palace on top of one of the mounds ruled the city. Archaeologists believe that

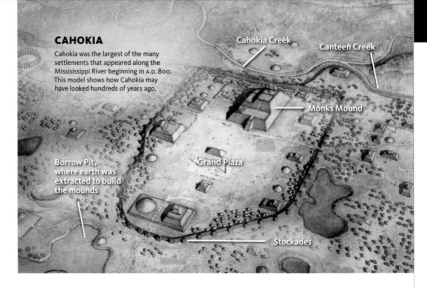

CAHOKIA

Cahokia was the largest of the many settlements that appeared along the Mississippi River beginning in A.D. 800. This model shows how Cahokia may have looked hundreds of years ago.

Cahokia Creek

Canteen Creek

Monks Mound

Borrow Pit, where earth was extracted to build the mounds

Grand Plaza

Stockades

when the chief died, the people destroyed the palace, added more earth to the mound, and built a new palace for the next ruler.

Cahokians engaged in widespread trade with other Mississippian cities and towns. Using the Mississippi River and other waterways, they exchanged freshwater pearls, silver, copper, beads, and pottery.

By 1400, Cahokia had been abandoned. Archaeologists are not sure why, but many think this once-mighty city may have been weakened by less abundant crop production, disease, overpopulation, or warfare.

Archaeologists found this artifact, called the Rattler Frog Pipe, in a burial mound near Cahokia. They think it may represent a shaman in an amphibian disguise.

REVIEW & ASSESS

1. **READING CHECK** What purposes did mounds serve in the Adena, Hopewell, and Mississippian cultures?

2. **DRAW CONCLUSIONS** How was agriculture important to the way of life of Mississippian cultures?

3. **ANALYZE VISUALS** Based on the text and illustration of Cahokia, what purpose might the stockades have served?

PLAN

OBJECTIVE

Explore the mound builders of the Mississippi River Valley and the city of Cahokia.

CRITICAL THINKING SKILLS FOR LESSON 2.4

- Identify Main Ideas and Details
- Monitor Comprehension
- Draw Conclusions
- Analyze Visuals
- Make Inferences
- Form and Support Opinions

ESSENTIAL QUESTION

In what ways do civilizations adapt to the environments in which they live?

The mound builders lived in fertile river valleys where they could both hunt and farm, which provided plenty of food. They used soil to build mounds. Lesson 2.4 describes the culture and settlements of the mound builders.

BACKGROUND FOR THE TEACHER

Cahokia National Park is located in southern Illinois, just across the Mississippi River from St. Louis, Missouri. During its height, Cahokia represented one of the largest populations in North America, second only to the civilizations that dominated what is now Mexico. At its peak, Cahokia covered almost six square miles and contained about 120 earthen mounds. Today, Cahokia is the largest and most complex archaeological site in North America that is located north of Mexico.

DIGITAL RESOURCES myNGconnect.com

TEACHER RESOURCES & ASSESSMENT

 Reading and Note-Taking

 Vocabulary Practice

 Section 2 Quiz

STUDENT RESOURCES

 NG Chapter Gallery

PREVIEW CONTENT WITH MAPS

Use a map to introduce the physical geography of the environment in which the mound builders lived. Have students look at a physical map of North America. Tell them to focus on the part of the continent that stretches from the Great Lakes to the Gulf of Mexico, along the Mississippi River. Assign students to one of four groups: Rivers, Landforms, Coasts, or Climate. Allow students time to consider their group's topic. Then tell the groups to identify details about their topic. Finally, have representatives from each group report their groups' findings. **0:05** minutes

TEACH

GUIDED DISCUSSION

1. **Make Inferences** What facts show the complexity of the mound builders' culture? *(The settlements were so populous that they must have had good organization to be able to feed and house so many. Many people carrying baskets of dirt built the mounds; building so many huge mounds required a great deal of organization, planning, and supervision. Cahokia was as large as a modern city and lasted hundreds of years.)*

2. **Form and Support Opinions** Archaeologists do not know why the mound builders disappeared, but one reason might be that they could not grow or find enough food to feed their large populations. Do you agree with this possible explanation? Explain why or why not. *(Students' responses should include evidence from the reading and reflect an understanding of the lesson. Possible response: Yes, the environment cannot sustain overfarming, and the populations were very large. They might have moved to other places. No, disease or other tribes could have wiped them out.)*

ANALYZE VISUALS

Have students study the model of Cahokia and answer the following questions.

- Where did the majority of people live, inside or outside the stockade? *(outside)*
- Aside from the mound, did people live on flat or mountainous land? *(flat)*
- Since the Mississippi River and other rivers were nearby, what natural disasters could happen in this area? *(flooding; drought)* **0:15** minutes

ACTIVE OPTIONS

On Your Feet: Cahokia Roundtable Have students hold a roundtable discussion to compile details about Cahokia. Arrange students around tables or in circles in groups of four. Each student around the table gives a different detail about Cahokia. Allow some students to draw their answers. Afterwards, have groups share their details and sketches. **0:10** minutes

Critical Viewing: NG Image Gallery Have students explore the entire NG Image Gallery and choose two of the items to compare and contrast, either in written form or verbally with a partner. Ask questions that will inspire this process, such as: How are these images alike? How are they different? Why did you select these two items? How do they relate in history? **0:10** minutes

INCLUSION

Analyze Visuals Provide concrete questions to help students understand the different parts of the illustration and the photograph in Lesson 2.4.

- What does the illustration show?
- What two creeks can you identify?
- What mound appears to be the biggest mound at Cahokia?
- What was the Borrow Pit?
- What purpose do you think the stockades served?
- What does the photograph show?
- Why might the artifact be surrounded by corn?

GIFTED & TALENTED

Build a Cahokia Model Encourage students to make a 3-D model of Cahokia out of clay or some other malleable substance. Tell them to include mounds, the stockades, the borrow pit, and the creeks. Students should label different parts of their models. If they modeled Machu Picchu in Lesson 1.4, have them compare and contrast the two models.

Press **mt** in the Student eEdition for modified text.

See the Chapter Planner for more strategies for differentiation.

ANSWERS

1. The Adena and Hopewell built their mounds to serve ceremonial and religious purposes. In the Mississippian culture, the mounds also served political purposes and were the sites of palaces for a city's chief.

2. The Mississippians were able to use the fertile soil to grow maize, beans, and squash. Because they had ample food, the population grew, and Mississippian settlements were the largest in North America north of Mexico.

3. The stockades might have been built to protect the mounds against invaders or flooding from surrounding creeks and rivers.

Cultures in the East and Southeast

Like cultures in the Pacific Northwest, Native Americans who lived on the opposite side of North America relied on the plentiful wood and game from the forests and woodlands that surrounded them. Over time, they developed sophisticated ways of governing themselves.

MAIN IDEA

Native American cultures in the East and Southeast developed complex political organizations.

THE CHEROKEE AND THE CREEK

The **Cherokee** lived in the forests of the present-day states of Georgia, Tennessee, North Carolina, and South Carolina. They built permanent log cabins using the wood from the forests that surrounded them. The Cherokee hunted deer, elk, and bear, and they also farmed, growing crops such as corn, beans, and squash.

Individual Cherokee villages formed complex alliances with each other and with other cultures. During wartime, some villages were known as "red towns," where the people held war councils and ceremonies. Other villages were considered "white towns," or towns devoted to peace. Spanish explorers arrived in the mid-1500s, and

British colonists moved into the region in the 1700s. The Cherokee traded extensively with both groups, exchanging furs and animal hides for horses, fabrics, and firearms.

The **Creek** lived south and west of the Cherokee, in what are now the states of Alabama, Mississippi, Florida, Georgia, South Carolina, and Tennessee. Like the Cherokee, the Creek formed alliances with different tribes that spoke related languages.

The Creek had great respect for fire. Each settlement had a permanent fire, which the people believed was a symbol of the life-giving powers of the sun. The female head of each household lit a fire from the village's flame and then carried it to her family. With this custom, the Creek developed a strong sense of unity within the community.

An important custom that the Cherokee and the Creek shared was the Green Corn Ceremony. Corn was an important crop for both groups. The Cherokee and Creek held this ceremony when their corn first ripened, in early to mid-summer. Over a period lasting from four to eight days, they feasted, held dances, and repaired buildings. At the height of the ceremony, they relit the sacred fire at the center of the village's plaza.

THE ALGONQUIN AND THE IROQUOIS

The **Algonquin** and **Iroquois** dominated the woodlands of the Northeast, in present-day southern Canada, upper New York, and Pennsylvania. Each culture included different tribes with their own languages and customs. The woodlands provided wood, plants, and animals, but they could not support enough farming to sustain large cities.

Instead, farmers in temporary villages relied on slash-and-burn techniques. Algonquin and Iroquois farmers burnt fields out of the forests and grew crops such as corn, beans, and squash until the soil was exhausted, or depleted of nutrients. Entire villages would then move on and create new fields elsewhere.

This reproduction shows what an Iroquois longhouse may have looked like. Like wigwams, longhouses had domed roofs and were covered with tree bark for protection.

The Algonquin lived in **wigwams**, or domed huts built on a framework of poles and covered with skins or bark. Wigwams could be quickly moved and easily adapted to the changing weather. The Algonquin farmed for much of the year, but in winter moved around because they were hunting game. Chiefs led villages made up of related families. Villages traded and formed loose **confederations**, or groups of allies, to help each other through war or hardship.

In contrast to the Algonquin, the Iroquois developed a more formal political structure. They called themselves the "people of the longhouse." They lived in villages of longhouses, in which as many as 10 families lived. Iroquois tribes fought each other until the 1500s, when they formed the Iroquois League. This agreement formally bound together five tribes—Onondaga, Seneca, Mohawk, Oneida, and Cayuga—in a representative and democratic alliance.

REVIEW & ASSESS

1. **READING CHECK** What was the function of the Green Corn Ceremony in Cherokee and Creek culture?

2. **COMPARE AND CONTRAST** How did the political structures of the Algonquin and Iroquois differ?

3. **MAKE INFERENCES** How might the Iroquois League have helped end fighting among the Iroquois tribes?

OBJECTIVE

Explore Native American cultures in the East and Southeast.

CRITICAL THINKING SKILLS FOR LESSON 2.5

- Identify Main Ideas and Details
- Compare and Contrast
- Analyze Cause and Effect
- Monitor Comprehension
- Make Inferences
- Analyze Visuals

ESSENTIAL QUESTION

In what ways do civilizations adapt to the environments in which they live?

Native Americans in the East and Southeast hunted and farmed in the forests and woodlands in which they lived. Lesson 2.5 describes cultures in the East and Southeast.

BACKGROUND FOR THE TEACHER

In the Iroquois League, each tribe got one vote and decisions had to be unanimous. The leaders were village and clan chiefs, and peace chiefs at each tribe kept the tribes running. The Iroquois League was better organized and more effective than other leagues. It had rituals for the selection of leaders and decision-making. In 1722, one more tribe joined the league so its name changed to Six Nations. In the 1600s, the Iroquois lived mostly in upper New York State. The united groups eventually fought against the Mohawk, Huron, Mohican, Algonquin, and French.

DIGITAL RESOURCES myNGconnect.com

TEACHER RESOURCES & ASSESSMENT

 Reading and Note-Taking

 Vocabulary Practice

 Section 2 Quiz

STUDENT RESOURCES

 NG Chapter Gallery

INTRODUCE & ENGAGE

COMPLETE A K-W-L CHART

Provide each student with a K-W-L Chart. Have students brainstorm what they know about cultures in the East and Southeast, such as the Cherokee, Creek, Algonquin, and Iroquois. Then ask them to write questions that they would like to have answered as they study the lesson. Allow time at the end of the lesson for students to fill in what they have learned. **0:05** minutes

K What Do I Know?	W What Do I Want To Learn?	L What Did I Learn?

TEACH

GUIDED DISCUSSION

1. **Analyze Cause and Effect** What factors helped the Cherokee become a prosperous culture? *(They hunted and farmed, lived in permanent cabins, had complex alliances with each other, and traded with both the Spanish and the British.)*

2. **Compare and Contrast** In what ways did the geography and climate of the East and Southeast help cultures who lived there succeed? *(Because these tribes could use forests for hunting and they could farm, they had plenty of food. They used forest wood to make homes. The temperate climate varied but it was not extreme.)*

ANALYZE VISUALS

Have students study the photograph in Lesson 2.5. Explain that the photograph is of a reproduction of a longhouse, not an actual structure that people lived in. **ASK:** Why does the photograph show a reproduction instead of a real one, such as the structures of the ancient Pueblo or Inca? *(Longhouses were made of wood and would not last over time; the wood would rot and disintegrate, unlike the stone or bricks of the others.)* **0:15** minutes

ACTIVE OPTIONS

On Your Feet: Four Corners Label the four corners of the classroom: *Cherokee, Creek, Algonquin,* and *Iroquois.* Allow students time to write down what they know about all four cultures. Then

have individual students move to a corner of their choice and discuss the culture they chose. Finally, have at least one student from each corner share a summary of the corner discussion. **0:10** minutes

Critical Viewing: NG Chapter Gallery Have students examine the contents of the Chapter Gallery for this chapter. Then invite them to brainstorm additional images they believe would fit within the Chapter Gallery. Have them write a description of these additional images and provide an explanation of why they would fit within the Chapter Gallery. Then instruct them to do online research to find examples of actual images they would like to add to the gallery. **0:10** minutes

DIFFERENTIATE

ENGLISH LANGUAGE LEARNERS

Make a Summary Chart Help students keep track of the four tribes discussed by having them copy the chart below. They can write a few phrases under each tribe to help them review and remember information in Lesson 2.5.

CHEROKEE	CREEK	ALGONQUIN	IROQUOIS

Press (**mt**) *in the Student eEdition for modified text.*

See the Chapter Planner for more strategies for differentiation.

REVIEW & ASSESS

ANSWERS

1. Through the Green Corn Ceremony, the Cherokee and the Creek brought renewal to their villages by feasting, dancing, and relighting the fire at the center of each village. The fire symbolized the life-giving powers of the sun.

2. Algonquin villages were made up of related families led by a chief; these villages traded and formed a loose confederation to help one another during times of hardship or war. In contrast, the Iroquois developed a more formal political structure and lived in villages of longhouses, each housing up to 10 families. Unlike the Algonquin, who helped one another, the Iroquois tribes fought each other until they formed the Iroquois League.

3. The Iroquois League helped to end fighting among the different Iroquois tribes by formally joining together the five main tribes in a representative democratic alliance.

(Banco Central de Reserva Del Perú, Lima, Perú)

VOCABULARY

Use each of the following vocabulary words in a sentence that shows an understanding of the term's meaning.

1. quinoa
The Inca grew quinoa, a high-protein grain native to the Andes Mountains.

2. wigwam

3. totem pole

4. terrace farming

5. adobe

6. confederation

7. potlatch

8. quarry

9. geoglyph

READING STRATEGY

10. ORGANIZE IDEAS: SEQUENCE EVENTS
If you haven't already, complete your time line to sequence events that occurred in civilizations in South and North America. Then answer the question.

A.D. 100
The Moche civilization began to flourish.

PERUVIAN CULTURES

NORTH AMERICAN CULTURES

A.D. 500
The Tlingit developed tools for splitting and carving wood.

What event affected civilizations in both South and North America in the 1500s?

MAIN IDEAS

Answer the following questions. Support your answers with evidence from the chapter.

11. What have archaeologists learned about pre-Inca cultures from various discoveries in Peru? **LESSON 1.1**

12. Why did the Inca Empire develop rapidly under the leadership of Pachacuti? **LESSON 1.3**

13. What factors helped Machu Picchu survive the Spanish conquest? **LESSON 1.4**

14. On what natural resources did Northwest Coast cultures rely? **LESSON 2.1**

15. How did the beginning of pottery making signal a shift in ancient Pueblo culture? **LESSON 2.2**

16. Why were buffalo important to the people of the Great Plains? **LESSON 2.3**

17. What made it possible for the Mississippi River Valley to support large cities? **LESSON 2.4**

CRITICAL THINKING

Answer the following questions. Support your answers with evidence from the chapter.

18. EVALUATE Were the cultures in South and North America successful in adapting to their environments? Explain your answer.

19. COMPARE AND CONTRAST Consider what you have learned in previous chapters of this book. What distinguishes the Inca from the early river valley civilizations of Mesopotamia, Egypt, India, and China?

20. MAKE INFERENCES Why was a network of roads important to the success of the Inca Empire?

21. ANALYZE CAUSE AND EFFECT How were complex societies in the Pacific Northwest able to develop and grow without farming?

22. YOU DECIDE Did the size of the Inca Empire contribute to its fall? Support your opinion with evidence from the chapter.

INTERPRET VISUALS

Study the photograph showing farming terraces built by the Inca. Then answer the questions that follow.

23. Use details in the photo to describe the method of terrace farming the Inca used.

24. Why might Inca farmers have preferred flat surfaces on which to grow crops?

ANALYZE SOURCES

While on an expedition in the Andes in 1911, American explorer Hiram Bingham and his guide discovered a city that had been hidden for nearly 400 years: Machu Picchu. Read the passage and then answer the question.

> We were confronted with an unexpected sight, a great flight of beautifully constructed stone-faced terraces, perhaps a hundred of them, each hundreds of feet long and ten feet high. . . . The flowing lines, the symmetrical arrangement of the [large stones], and the gradual gradation of the [layers], combined to produce a wonderful effect, softer and more pleasing than that of the marble temples of the Old World.
>
> from *Lost City of the Incas*, by Hiram Bingham, 1952

25. What were Bingham's impressions of the architecture at Machu Picchu?

WRITE ABOUT HISTORY

26. INFORMATIVE Suppose you are contributing to a booklet about Native American cultures. Write a paragraph that explores the impact of the Spanish use of guns and horses on either the Inca or the people of the Great Plains.

TIPS

- Take notes from the lessons about the Inca or the Great Plains peoples.

- Begin the paragraph with a clear topic sentence.

- Develop the paragraph with supporting details and examples of the impact of Spanish guns and horses on your chosen group.

- Use vocabulary from the chapter as appropriate.

- Conclude with a sentence about how changes resulting from the introduction of guns and horses affected the Inca or people of the Great Plains.

VOCABULARY ANSWERS

1. The Inca grew quinoa, a high-protein grain native to the Andes Mountains.

2. Wigwams were domed huts built on a framework of poles and covered with skins or bark.

3. Northwest Coast cultures carved totem poles out of huge tree trunks.

4. The Inca developed terrace farming in order to grow crops in the Andes.

5. The ancient Pueblo sometimes used adobe to build houses.

6. Algonquin villages formed different confederations with each other to get through hard times.

7. Families in Northwest Coast cultures shared wealth through potlatches.

8. In order to build Machu Picchu, the Inca had to quarry a large amount of stone.

9. The Nasca culture left behind many interesting geoglyphs.

READING STRATEGY ANSWER

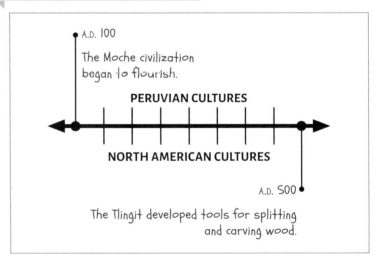

A.D. 100

The Moche civilization began to flourish.

PERUVIAN CULTURES

NORTH AMERICAN CULTURES

A.D. 500

The Tlingit developed tools for splitting and carving wood.

10. One event that affected civilizations in both South and North America in the 1500s was the arrival of the Spanish. In South America, the Spanish conquered the Inca Empire. In North America, the Spanish introduced the horse and eventually conquered much of the southwestern part of the continent.

MAIN IDEAS ANSWERS

11. Archaeologists have learned that pre-Inca cultures, including the Moche, Nasca, Wari, and Sicán, were complex. They adapted to their environments, and they produced extraordinary ceramic, gold, silver, and copper artifacts.

12. The Inca Empire developed rapidly under the leadership of Pachacuti because he introduced a strong central government, transformed the capital city of Cusco, and built an efficient network of roads that connected the vast empire.

13. Machu Picchu was built in a remote location high up in the Andes Mountains. The Spanish never found it, so it survived conquest.

14. Northwest Coast cultures used the forests for plants and hunting game. They used the wood for making seagoing canoes and houses. They traveled the ocean, fishing and hunting whales.

15. As the ancient Pueblo began living in more permanent settlements, they shifted from using mostly baskets to using pottery. This shift indicates a more settled population because pottery is heavier and more fragile than baskets and would only be practical for a settled community.

16. The vast herds of buffalo that grazed on the plains made life possible for the nomadic tribes, who hunted the buffalo and used its meat and all other body parts for food, clothing, tools, ropes, and fuel.

17. The fertile floodplains of the Mississippi River Valley supported intensive agriculture and large, settled populations.

CRITICAL THINKING ANSWERS

18. Possible response: They were very successful. They used the materials around them for housing and learning to farm creatively in their environment. The large, complex civilizations that developed and the length of time they lived there proved how successful they were.

19. The Inca lived in a very difficult and harsh environment of mountains and desert land. The other civilizations were in river valleys. The Inca learned to farm on mountains, and they conquered and ruled a larger physical area and more people than the other civilizations did.

20. The extensive network of 25,000 miles of roads was essential to the success of the Inca Empire because it connected distant subjects and allowed communication, troops, and trade to travel quickly over the mountainous terrain.

21. Because of the region's bountiful natural resources, populations grew and complex societies emerged without any need to farm.

22. Students' responses will vary. Students should clearly state their opinion regarding whether the size of the Inca Empire contributed to its fall and support that opinion with evidence from the chapter.

INTERPRET VISUALS ANSWERS

23. The photo shows the flat terraces cut into the mountainside, as well as the supporting rock walls.

24. Growing crops on sloped mountainsides would be very difficult, if not impossible, so Inca farmers would prefer the flat surfaces of terraces.

ANALYZE SOURCES ANSWER

25. Students' responses will vary. Sample response: Bingham seems amazed by the unexpected sight, but then he describes it with the detail and clarity of a historian, comparing the stonework of Machu Picchu to that of the Old World and concluding he is looking at the finest stonework in the world.

WRITE ABOUT HISTORY ANSWER

26. Students' informative paragraphs should do the following:
- contain a topic sentence that introduces the main idea
- support the topic sentence with facts, details, and examples from the chapter
- include vocabulary words from the chapter
- present the information in a clear, logical manner
- contain a concluding statement

ON LOCATION WITH Francisco ESTRADA-BELLI

ARCHAEOLOGIST AND NATIONAL GEOGRAPHIC GRANTEE

▶ **Check out more on myNGconnect**

Francisco Estrada-Belli examines the ancient stucco sculpture he discovered in the buried foundations of a rectangular pyramid in Holmul, Guatemala.

HIDDEN CITIES

Exploring lost Mayan cities hidden deep in the jungles of Guatemala—that's my job! Every year we discover additional sites to explore to learn more about the Maya civilization, which thrived in Central America for nearly 1,500 years. It seems incredible, but in Guatemala you can still hack your way through the vegetation and come face-to-face with a long lost city.

As a child I visited the magnificent Mayan ruins of Tikal. I had so many questions! How did the Maya build such a great civilization in a jungle? Why did they leave their city? That's why I became an archaeologist: to try and answer some of those questions. I wanted to shed light on the beginnings of Maya civilization, so I chose to study the buried Maya city of Holmul, which had been partially excavated a hundred years ago and then forgotten. It was a good place to start. Exploring nearby, I found another lost Maya city called Cival. This turned out to be one of the earliest cities the Maya built, around 800 B.C. This was over 1,000 years before classic Maya civilization blossomed in cities like Tikal. By showing the complexity and innovation of early Maya settlements, including their architecture, our findings challenge the common belief that the early Maya were simple village farmers.

BURIED SCULPTURES

We've made many important discoveries, including a massive sculpture buried beneath a temple's rubble at Holmul. The site already had been ransacked by looters,

Archaeology can be messy. Here, Estrada-Belli uses a tractor to tow a car through the muddy Guatemalan jungle.

and if they had dug for another ten minutes, they might have found the sculpture. It's amazingly well-preserved—it even has a little color left on it—and it had almost been lost forever. That makes me feel as if we really rescued the past. I feel like I have made a really important contribution.

I love sharing all this new knowledge with others, not just academics but ordinary people and students. I want to help the modern Maya who live in the area, especially the children, reconnect with their glorious Maya past. Right now, they have little or no knowledge of their heritage, and I believe that people who know their past can live a better life.

WHY STUDY HISTORY ❓

❝ The past is irreplaceable, but the past is disappearing because of development, looting, and erosion. I study history because *the past is not a luxury, but instead a necessity* for cultures and for humanity as a whole to be able to live in peace. ❞   — Francisco Estrada-Belli

NATIONAL GEOGRAPHIC

Unburying the Aztec

BY ROBERT DRAPER

Adapted from "Unburying the Aztec" by Robert Draper, in National Geographic, November 2010

Archaeologists reassemble an earth goddess monolith at Templo Mayor.

Archaeologist Leonardo López Luján might be on the verge of a major discovery. Since the Spanish conquest of Mexico in 1521, no Aztec emperor's remains have been discovered. Yet historical records say that three Aztec rulers were cremated and their ashes buried at the foot of Templo Mayor, in present-day Mexico City.

In 2008, López Luján unearthed a 12-ton monolith representing an earth goddess near Templo Mayor. Immediately, López Luján noticed that the monolith depicted a figure holding a rabbit, with ten dots above it. In the Aztec writing system, 10-Rabbit is 1502—the year that the empire's most feared ruler, Ahuitzotl (ah-WEE-tzoh-tuhl), died. López Luján is convinced that Ahuitzotl's tomb is somewhere near where the monolith was found.

Aztec power was fleeting. They ruled their empire for less than a century before the Spanish demolished it. The Aztec maintained what some scholars call "a cheap empire." The conquered were allowed to continue governing themselves as long as they paid tribute.

Ahuitzotl assumed the throne in 1486. As the eighth emperor, he stretched the empire to its breaking point. His armies made 45 conquests over 16 years, conquering areas along the Pacific coast, down into present-day Guatemala. He also sealed off trade from rivals to the west and increased control over subjugated territories. "He was more forceful, more brutal," says archaeologist Raúl Arana. "When people didn't want to pay tribute, he sent in the military. With Ahuitzotl, the Aztec went to the maximum expression of everything. And perhaps it was too much. All empires have a limit."

López Luján's work at the Templo Mayor site is slow, partly because of the challenges excavating in a modern city. Urban archaeologists have to dig around sewer and subway lines, avoid underground telephone, fiber optic, and electric cables, and maintain security for a dig in the middle of a city. "Sooner or later, we'll find Ahuitzotl's tomb," López Luján hopes. Whether or not he does, the Aztec mystique will continue to occupy modern Mexico's imagination.

For more from National Geographic
Check out "People of the Horse" on myNGconnect

UNIT INQUIRY: DESIGN AN ADAPTATION STRATEGY

In this unit, you learned how civilizations in North and South America adapted to the environments in which they lived. Based on your understanding of the text, what were the environments like in which these different civilizations lived? In what ways did people adapt to survive or become better suited to their environment?

ASSIGNMENT Design an adaptation strategy that you think would be helpful to people moving to a new environment. The strategy should identify the specific environment, such as a new school, neighborhood, or city. The strategy should also include a series of actions/steps people could take to adapt to their new environment. Be prepared to present your strategy to the class and explain how it will help people adapt successfully to their new environment.

Plan As you design your strategy, think about the role adaptation has played in the survival and success of past civilizations. Adaptation—no matter when and where it occurs—does not happen overnight. Think about the steps that would ensure successful adaptation in a new environment today. You might want to use a graphic organizer to help organize your thoughts. ▶

Produce Use your notes to produce descriptions of the elements of your adaptation strategy. You might want to write them in outline or paragraph form.

Present Choose a creative way to present your strategy for adaptation to the class. Consider one of these options:

- Create a multimedia presentation using photos to illustrate the series of actions/steps in your strategy.

- Write a slogan for your strategy that communicates the importance of successful adaptation in a new environment.

- Describe how a potential problem or difficulty in the new environment might be turned into an opportunity.

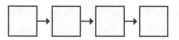

RAPID REVIEW
UNIT 7

AMERICAN CIVILIZATIONS

TOP TEN

1. The Maya developed an advanced writing system, and they studied mathematics and astronomy.

2. The Aztec Empire grew powerful through conquest by its formidable army.

3. Spanish conquistadors used steel weapons and horses to overthrow the Aztec and the Inca.

4. The Inca established a massive empire that included more than 12 million people.

5. The Mississippians built many cities in the Mississippi River Valley, including Cahokia.

6-10. **NOW IT'S YOUR TURN** Complete the list with five more things to remember about American civilizations.

RAPID REVIEW

POSSIBLE RESPONSES

Possible responses for the remaining five things to remember include the following:

6. The ancient Pueblo built Pueblo Bonito and Mesa Verde.

7. Northwest Coast cultures relied on the abundant resources of the forests and coasts.

8. Nomadic tribes on the Great Plains hunted the buffalo to survive.

9. Successful agriculture turned prosperous Maya villages into powerful city-states ruled by kings.

10. The Olmec, Mesoamerica's mother culture, influenced later civilizations such as the Zapotec.

UNIT INQUIRY PROJECT RUBRIC

ASSESS

Use the rubric to assess each student's participation and performance.

SCORE	ASSIGNMENT	PRODUCT	PRESENTATION
3 GREAT	• Student thoroughly understands the assignment. • Student engages fully with the project process. • Student works well independently.	• Adaptation strategy is well thought out. • Adaptation strategy takes into account the challenges and benefits of moving to a new environment. • Adaptation strategy contains all of the key elements listed in the assignment.	• Presentation is clear, concise, and logical. • Presentation does a good job of creatively explaining the adaptation strategy. • Presentation engages the audience.
2 GOOD	• Student mostly understands the assignment. • Student engages fairly well with the project process. • Student works fairly well independently.	• Adaptation strategy is fairly well thought out. • Adaptation strategy considers the challenges and benefits of moving to a new environment. • Adaptation strategy contains some of the key elements listed in the assignment.	• Presentation is fairly clear, concise, and logical. • Presentation does an adequate job of creatively explaining the adaptation strategy. • Presentation somewhat engages the audience.
1 NEEDS WORK	• Student does not understand the assignment. • Student minimally engages or does not engage with the project process. • Student struggles to work well independently.	• Adaptation strategy is not well thought out. • Adaptation strategy does not take into account the challenges and benefits of moving to a new environment. • Adaptation strategy contains few or none of the key elements listed in the assignment.	• Presentation is not clear, concise, or logical. • Presentation does not creatively explain adaptation strategy. • Presentation does not engage the audience.

TURN AND TALK
One of the themes in this Why Study History? text is "global citizenship." Pair students and ask them to write about what this concept means to each of them. Then ask them to discuss their written responses. Finally, ask student pairs to discuss how trade affected and/or created global citizens throughout history.

WHY STUDY HISTORY ?

TO UNDERSTAND THE SIMILARITIES AND DIFFERENCES AMONG CIVILIZATIONS

You just plowed through five units introducing civilizations with similar but different languages, cultures, and religions. As global citizens, our call to action is to understand that each civilization has its own unique identity. Recognizing the inherent worth and equality of all civilizations and cultures—and, in fact, of all people—is at the heart of global citizenship.

On the Framework of World History chart at the beginning of this text, the civilizations in Units 3, 4, and 5 fall under "World Systems." The Greek, Roman, Byzantine, and Islamic civilizations continued to build on the foundations that early civilizations had established. Some of the civilizations in Africa and the Americas fall under the second and third levels of that chart. Yet all these civilizations established sophisticated cultures. Understanding the similarities and differences among them is one reason we study history.

Fred Hiebert
▶ Watch the Why Study History video

WHAT COMES NEXT? PREVIEW UNITS 8–9

PREVIEW UPCOMING UNITS
Have students examine the images at the bottom of the Why Study History? spread, and read the labels on each photograph. Invite volunteers to make observations and predictions about what the upcoming units (8-9) will bring.

8

HORSE RACE, MONGOLIA

9

SAN GIOVANNI

EMPIRES OF ASIA
Follow the inventions and advancements in technology that would open the globe to exploration and trade, cause an explosion in communication, and make human conflict more deadly.

MEDIEVAL & RENAISSANCE EUROPE
Learn how the cultures and empires of medieval and Renaissance Europe further developed technology and artistic expression to set the stage for today's modern, global world.

KEY TAKEAWAYS UNITS 3–7

PATTERNS IN HISTORY: SIMILAR DEVELOPMENTS ACROSS LOCATIONS

- Continued environmental adaptations in Africa and the Americas improve agricultural production.
- Trade takes off on a global scale, including trans-Saharan movement of gold and salt and Indian Ocean trade between East Africa and Asia.

GOVERNMENT

- In Europe, emphasis shifts to protecting ordinary people, with the development of democracy in ancient Greece and Rome.
- Mighty empires form in Mali and Aksum in Africa.
- In the Americas, the Maya and Inca rise to power.

MOVEMENT OF PEOPLE AND IDEAS

- Hellenistic culture spreads through the empire-building of Alexander the Great.

- Roman culture spreads through colonization and trade.
- Islamic culture spreads through trade and conquest.

ARTISTIC EXPRESSION

- In Europe, new art forms include more realistic "selfies" in statues from ancient Greece; mosaics and frescoes of ancient Rome; and calligraphy and arabesques of Islam.
- The Nok in Africa produce terra cotta sculptures.

TECHNOLOGY & INNOVATION

Engineering and architectural developments include

- columns and temples from ancient Greece
- improved concrete and arches from ancient Rome
- the iron technology of the Nok
- the monumental structures of the Maya, Aztec, and Inca

These massive Roman aqueducts in Segovia, Spain, are evidence of ancient Roman technological advances in arch-building.

AS YOU READ ON

You've got a whole backdrop of complex civilizations to draw on as you read about key civilizations in Asia in Unit 8. Think about how these civilizations helped set the stage for the deep changes that would occur by the 1600s (Unit 9).

Remember that as global citizens, you know that throughout history all civilizations made enduring contributions to the human community. The diversity of those cultures and their contributions is what makes our world a rich and exciting place to live.

+ GUIDED DISCUSSION

In Units 3–7, students learned about five different civilizations with their own cultures, languages, and religions.

1. **Time Out for a Definition!**
   The concept of "trade" is something students are likely familiar with, but one that should be examined in terms of its evolution and impact throughout history. Ask students to note examples of trade in the units they have completed. Consider the differences between local and global trade, the types of transportation required for each type, and how trade impacted the countries, regions, or cultures involved. Post examples of the types of trade students have read about on sheets of paper on a wall for discussion. As a class, sort the examples chronologically and according to similarities or differences.

2. **Compare and Contrast**
   As a class, use a chart to compare and contrast different civilizations from Units 1–7. Discuss how influences such as geography and technology affected these cultures differently.

+ REFLECT ON UNITS 8 AND 9

As they read Units 8 and 9 in their textbook, have students complete pages 37–44 in their Field Journal to process the material in these units. Remind students that they will use their Field Journal as they read each Why Study History? section and explore the historical record. They will record their thoughts about what they've read and fit them into the larger picture of world history. They will also use the journal to consider how they fit into that big picture and what it means to be a global citizen.

EMPIRES OF ASIA

NATIONAL GEOGRAPHIC

ON **LOCATION** WITH

Albert Lin
Research Scientist/Engineer

Looking for the unknown burial ground of the Mongol emperor Genghis Khan is a big challenge. The vast and unending steppe landscape of Mongolia makes it hard to know where to search. Add to that the fact that the Mongolians consider the tomb of their great leader to be sacred and off-limits to the traditional methods of archaeology—digging in the earth. I'm Albert Lin, and I'm using innovative technology such as satellite imagery and remote sensors to search for Genghis Khan's tomb without ever touching a shovel.

< CRITICAL VIEWING Children race horses across Central Mongolia during a summer festival. What can you infer about the geography of this region?

POSSIBLE RESPONSE
The geography is relatively flat and wide open.

UNIT 8
TIME LINE OF WORLD EVENTS

Asian Civilizations
China, Japan, Korea, and Southeast Asia

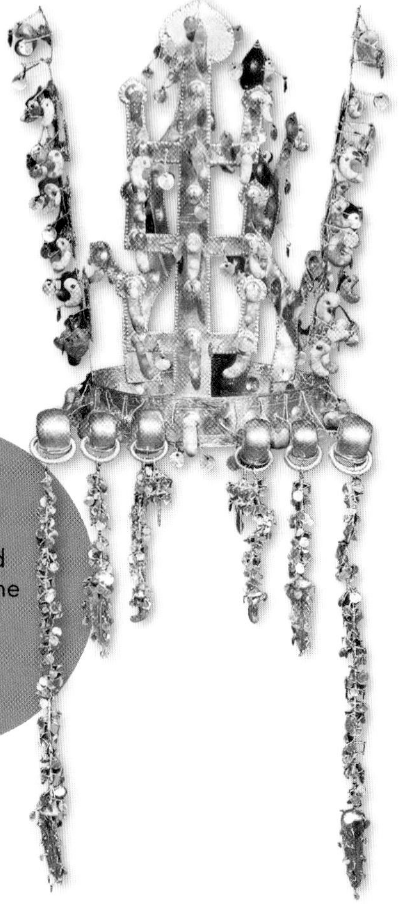

676
Korea is united for the first time under the Silla kingdom.
(Silla crown)

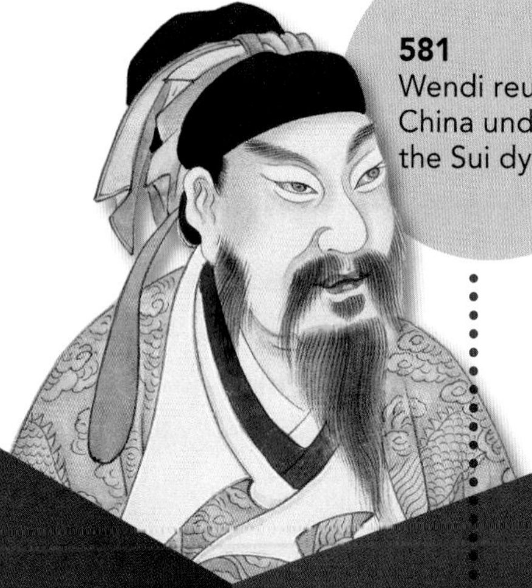

581
Wendi reunifies China under the Sui dynasty.

938
The Dai Viet state (Vietnam) gains independence from China.

500

900

1000

c. 570
ASIA
The prophet Muhammad is born in Mecca.

800
EUROPE
Charlemagne becomes the first Holy Roman Emperor.

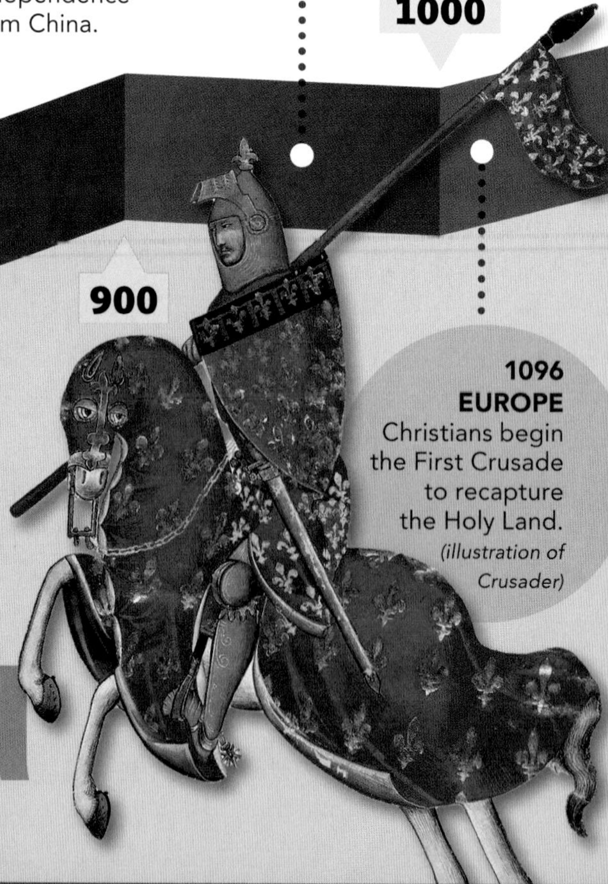

1096
EUROPE
Christians begin the First Crusade to recapture the Holy Land.
(illustration of Crusader)

The World

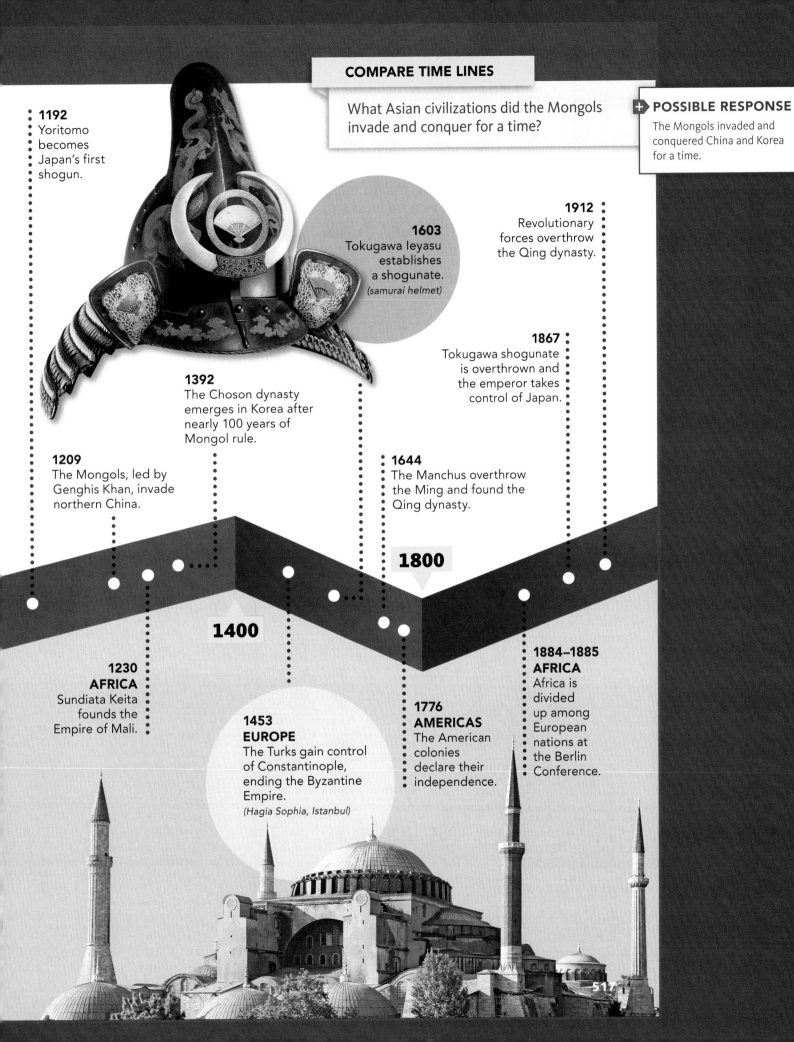

What Asian civilizations did the Mongols invade and conquer for a time?

1192
Yoritomo becomes Japan's first shogun.

1603
Tokugawa Ieyasu establishes a shogunate.
(samurai helmet)

1912
Revolutionary forces overthrow the Qing dynasty.

1867
Tokugawa shogunate is overthrown and the emperor takes control of Japan.

1392
The Choson dynasty emerges in Korea after nearly 100 years of Mongol rule.

1644
The Manchus overthrow the Ming and found the Qing dynasty.

1209
The Mongols, led by Genghis Khan, invade northern China.

1800

1400

1230
AFRICA
Sundiata Keita founds the Empire of Mali.

1453
EUROPE
The Turks gain control of Constantinople, ending the Byzantine Empire.
(Hagia Sophia, Istanbul)

1776
AMERICAS
The American colonies declare their independence.

1884–1885
AFRICA
Africa is divided up among European nations at the Berlin Conference.

517

Empires of Asia
1100–1200

Between 1100 and 1200, many great empires existed almost side by side in Asia. The Song dynasty, with its many inventions and booming economy, made China the world's most advanced society of the time. Chinese ideas had influenced kingdoms on the Korean Peninsula for centuries. However, the Koryu dynasty adapted Chinese practices, including the idea of a centralized government, to meet their own needs. In the 1200s, both China and the Koryu were conquered by the Mongols, who would establish the largest land empire in history.

East of the Korean Peninsula lay Japan, which was under military rule in the 1100s. In the strictly structured society of Japan at that time, armies of samurai fought to protect their ruler. Far to the south, the Khmer empire dominated much of Southeast Asia. Intensive rice production was the foundation of Khmer prosperity and power. Only the Dai Viet also ruled in the region. This state began a thousand years of independence for Vietnam.

Where were most of the Asian empires located?

POSSIBLE RESPONSE
Most of the Asian empires were located along the Pacific Ocean and other bodies of water.

Architecturally, the Song were famous for their pagodas.

Tea, sipped from bowls like this one, became popular under the Song, and rice became an important crop.

Ba
of
Beng

Karakorum● **MONGOL HOMELAND**

G O B I

Huang He (Yellow R.)

KORYU DYNASTY (KOREA)

Sea of Japan

JAPAN

Heian (Kyoto)●

Huang He (Yellow R.)

●Kaifeng

Yellow Sea

●Yangzhou

SONG DYNASTY (CHINA)

Chang Jiang (Yangtze R.)   *Chang Jiang (Yangtze R.)*

Yangtze R.

Mekong R.

●Hangzhou

East China Sea

DAI VIET (VIETNAM)

●Hanoi

●Guangzhou

Hainan

KHMER

●Angkor

Mekong R.

South China Sea

Philippines

PACIFIC OCEAN

Empires of Asia

- Japan, 1100
- Khmer, 1100
- Koryu Dynasty (Korea), 1100
- Mongol homeland, 1200
- Song Dynasty (China), 1100
- Da Viet (Vietnam), 1200
- ⌐∟⌐ Grand Canal
- ⌐∟⌐ Great Wall

0 200 400 600 800 kilometers
0 200 400 600 800 miles

Borneo

Sumatra

Celebes

UNIT RESOURCES

On Location with National Geographic Emerging Explorer Albert Lin
Intro and Video

Unit Wrap-Up:
"The Search for Genghis Khan"
Feature and Video

"Divining Angkor"
National Geographic Adapted Article

"The Forgotten Road"
National Geographic Adapted Article
Student eEdition exclusive

Unit 8 Inquiry:
Leave a Legacy of Innovation

Interactive Map Tool

News & Updates

Available on myNGconnect

CHAPTER RESOURCES

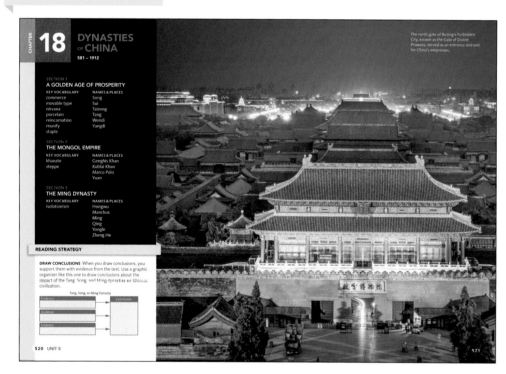

TEACHER RESOURCES & ASSESSMENT

Available on myNGconnect

Social Studies Skills Lessons
• Reading: Draw Conclusions
• Writing: Write an Expository Paragraph

Formal Assessment
• Chapter 18 Tests A (on-level)
  & B (below-level)

Chapter 18 Answer Key

ExamView®
One-time Download

STUDENT BACKPACK *Available on myNGconnect*
• **eEdition** *(English)*   • **eEdition** *(Spanish)*   • **Handbooks**   • **Online Atlas**
For Chapter 18 Spanish resources, visit the Teacher Resource Menu page on myNGconnect.

SECTION 1 RESOURCES

A GOLDEN AGE OF PROSPERITY

 Reading and Note-Taking

 Vocabulary Practice

 Section 1 Quiz

Available on myNGconnect

LESSON 1.1 REUNIFICATION UNDER THE SUI DYNASTY

NG Learning Framework:
Learn About the Construction of the Grand Canal

• On Your Feet: Compare Canals

LESSON 1.2 THE SPREAD OF BUDDHISM

• Critical Viewing: NG Image Gallery
• On Your Feet: Team Word Webs

LESSON 1.3 TANG AND SONG DYNASTIES

NG Learning Framework:
Write a Biography

• On Your Feet: Create a Time Line

LESSON 1.4 THE LEGACY OF CHINESE INVENTIONS

 Active History: Interactive Whiteboard Activity
Evaluate China's Inventions

 Active History
Evaluate China's Inventions

Available on myNGconnect

• On Your Feet: Explore Movable Type

SECTION 2 RESOURCES

THE MONGOL EMPIRE

 Reading and Note-Taking

 Vocabulary Practice

 Section 2 Quiz

Available on myNGconnect

BIOGRAPHY:
LESSON 2.1 GENGHIS KHAN

 Biography
Kublai Khan

Available on myNGconnect

NG Learning Framework:
Learn About Genghis Khan

• On Your Feet: Conduct an Interview

LESSON 2.2 LIFE IN YUAN CHINA

 Biography
Marco Polo

Available on myNGconnect

• Critical Viewing: NG Chapter Gallery
• On Your Feet: Role-Play Different Social Classes

DOCUMENT-BASED QUESTION
LESSON 2.3 TRAVELS ON THE SILK ROADS

• Critical Viewing: NG Chapter Gallery
• On Your Feet: Create a Passport Medallion

SECTION 3 RESOURCES

THE MING DYNASTY

 **Reading and Note-Taking**

 **Vocabulary Practice**

 **Section 3 Quiz**

Available on myNGconnect

LESSON 3.1 RETURN TO CHINESE RULE

• Critical Viewing: NG Image Gallery
• On Your Feet: Design a Palace

LESSON 3.2 ZHENG HE'S EXPLORATIONS

NG Learning Framework:
Learn About Zheng He

• On Your Feet: Role-Play Exploration

LESSON 3.3 CHINA TURNS INWARD

NG Learning Framework:
Learn About Different Dynasties

• On Your Feet: Name That Dynasty

NG EXPLORER CHRISTINE LEE
LESSON 3.4 EXPLORING CHINA'S DIVERSE CULTURES

NG Learning Framework:
Learn About Archaeology

• On Your Feet: Guess the Culture

CHAPTER 18 REVIEW

STRATEGY 1
Preview Text

Help students preview each section in the chapter. For each section, have them read the lesson titles, lesson introductions, Main Idea statements, captions, and subheadings. Then have them list the information they expect to find in the text. Have students read a lesson and discuss with a partner what they learned and whether or not it matched their list.

Use with All Lessons

STRATEGY 2
Build a Time Line

Select key events, naming dynasties and emperors, from Lessons 1.1 and 1.3. Then have students use the events to start a time line on the board. Students will add to the time line as they read the chapter.

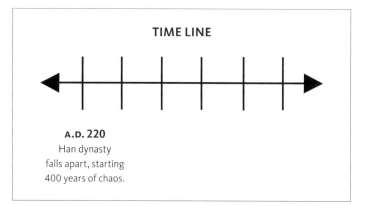

TIME LINE

A.D. 220
Han dynasty
falls apart, starting
400 years of chaos.

Use with All Lessons *For example, key events from Lesson 1.3 might include "A.D. 618: Beginning of the Tang dynasty," "A.D. 626: Taizong is emperor of Tang dynasty."*

STRATEGY 3
Use a Word Sort Activity

Display these words and tell students to sort them into groupings and label each group by category. Then have students write a sentence that explains how each group of words is connected.

Tang	Forbidden City	Ming	Taizong
Grand Canal	movable type	Wu Zhao	Genghis Khan
Yongle	Wendi	gunpowder	Yuan
compass	Song	Great Wall	porcelain

Use with All Lessons

STRATEGY 1
Preview Visuals to Predict

Ask students to preview the title and visuals in each lesson. Then have students tell what they think the lesson will be about. After reading, ask them to repeat the activity to see whether their predictions were confirmed.

Use with All Lessons *Invite volunteers to describe the visuals in detail to help visually impaired students see them.*

STRATEGY 2
Use Dynasty Flashcards

Distribute index cards to students and have them create flash cards for the dynasties of China mentioned in this chapter. On one side of each card, students should write *Sui, Tang, Song, Yuan,* and *Ming.* On the other side, they should list a fact or two about the leader and the dynasty. Then have student pairs take turns reading the facts on one side of the card and challenging their partner to identify the dynasty written on the other.

Use with Lessons 1.1, 1.3, 2.1, 2.2, 3.1, and 3.3

STRATEGY 1
Find Someone Who Knows

Give students copies of the questions below and have them find seven different classmates to answer them.

1. Who made seven voyages to show foreigners China's wealth and power? *(Zheng He)*

2. What was the name of the trade routes that connected China and other countries? *(Silk Roads)*

3. What religion from India did many Chinese adopt to provide comfort and a clear path from suffering? *(Buddhism)*

4. What leader of the Mongols conquered China and became their emperor? *(Genghis Khan)*

5. Whose teachings influenced China's government and people for centuries? *(Confucius)*

6. What is the other name for the Imperial Palace built during the Ming dynasty? *(Forbidden City)*

7. What are four inventions created by the Chinese during this time? *(movable type, porcelain, gunpowder, magnetic compass)*

Use with All Lessons

Press (mt) *in the Student eEdition for modified text.*

STRATEGY 2
Set Up a Word Wall

Work with students to choose one to three words from each lesson to display in a grouping on a Word Wall. It might be useful to choose words that students are likely to encounter in other contexts, such as *tolerance* or *conquest*. Keep the words displayed throughout the lessons and discuss each one as it comes up during reading. Have volunteers add words, phrases, and examples to each word to develop understanding.

Use with All Lessons

STRATEGY 3
Use Pronunciation Keys

Preteach the meaning and pronunciation of vocabulary words before beginning each lesson. Give a brief definition or example for each word, and then pronounce it slowly and clearly several times. Have students repeat after you. Then have students create a pronunciation key for each word.

After each lesson, have students write simple sentences using each word (e.g. "To *reunify* is to join again." "Buying and selling is *commerce*.") Have students refer to their pronunciation keys to help them say the words correctly.

Use with All Lessons

GIFTED & TALENTED

STRATEGY 1
Create a Chinese Art Gallery

Have students research and find a picture of a piece of art created in each of the dynasties of this chapter: Tang, Song, Yuan, Ming, and Quin. They should find several examples and choose the piece that they like best from each dynasty. The art can be a sculpture or statue, painting, vase, plate, urn, embroidery, or anything an artisan made. Encourage them to reproduce the picture, label it, and learn as much as they can about that piece. They can create an art gallery to display as the class reads the chapter.

Use with All Lessons

STRATEGY 2
Assign an Investigation

Each of the structures below took years to build and underwent many changes over the course of Chinese history. Allow students to choose one structure and investigate the history of its building. Suggest that they produce a presentation that both shows and tells that structure's history. Encourage them to add a time line to their presentation.

- the Great Wall
- the Grand Canal
- the Forbidden City

Use with All Lessons

PRE-AP

STRATEGY 1
Use the "Persia" Approach

Have students write an essay that traces life in China today back to its rich history. Students should learn as much as they can about China today and think about what traditions and attitudes came from the period of dynasties covered in this chapter. For example, they should think about isolationism, religion, art, economic ties, and so on. Copy the following mnemonic on the board and tell students to use the "Persia" strategy:

    Political

    Economic

    Religious

    Social

    Intellectual

    Artistic

Use with All Lessons

STRATEGY 2
Consider Both Sides of an Issue

Suggest that students make a list of both positives and negatives for the rule of one of the emperors of China, such as Genghis Khan or Yongle. Then have them analyze their list and write a paragraph stating their own judgment about this emperor. They should present both positive and negative sides of the emperor's rule, tell their conclusion, and offer evidence supporting their conclusion. Then have pairs compare their paragraphs and determine which judgment is the most convincing based on the evidence.

Use with All Lessons

The north gate of Beijing's Forbidden City, known as the Gate of Divine Prowess, served as an entrance and exit for China's empresses.

SECTION 1
A GOLDEN AGE OF PROSPERITY

KEY VOCABULARY	NAMES & PLACES
commerce	Song
movable type	Sui
nirvana	Taizong
porcelain	Tang
reincarnation	Wendi
reunify	Yangdi
staple	

SECTION 2
THE MONGOL EMPIRE

KEY VOCABULARY	NAMES & PLACES
khanate	Genghis Khan
steppe	Kublai Khan
	Marco Polo
	Yuan

SECTION 3
THE MING DYNASTY

KEY VOCABULARY	NAMES & PLACES
isolationism	Hongwu
	Manchus
	Ming
	Qing
	Yongle
	Zheng He

READING STRATEGY

DRAW CONCLUSIONS When you draw conclusions, you support them with evidence from the text. Use a graphic organizer like this one to draw conclusions about the impact of the Tang, Song, and Ming dynasties on Chinese civilization.

Tang, Song, or Ming Dynasty

Evidence → Conclusion
Evidence →
Evidence →

TEACHER BACKGROUND

INTRODUCE THE PHOTOGRAPH

Have students study the photograph of the Gate of Divine Prowess and its surroundings at the Forbidden City in Beijing. Explain that the word *prowess* means "distinguished bravery." Tell students that the Forbidden City was the imperial palace in China's capital of Beijing and is the largest palace in the world. Explain that in this chapter, students will learn about the dynasties that ruled China and what led up to the building of the Forbidden City.

ASK: What does the name of the gate in the photo suggest about the values of imperial China? *(Possible response: It suggests that military strength and extreme bravery were important values.)*

SHARE BACKGROUND

The Forbidden City was built in the early 1400s and stood as China's seat of power for 500 years. It is a whole complex of incredibly beautiful architecture that housed the imperial family and more than 100,000 servants. More than a million workers built it over a 14-year period during the Ming dynasty under emperor Yongle.

DIGITAL RESOURCES myNGconnect.com

TEACHER RESOURCES & ASSESSMENT

Social Studies Skills Lessons
· Reading: Draw Conclusions
· Writing: Write an Expository Paragraph

ExamView®
One-time Download

Formal Assessment
· Chapter 18 Tests A (on-level) & B (below-level)

Chapter 18
Answer Key

STUDENT BACKPACK

· **eEdition** *(English)*   · **Handbooks**
· **eEdition** *(Spanish)*   · **Online Atlas**

For Chapter 18 Spanish Resources, visit the Teacher Resource Menu page.

INTRODUCE THE ESSENTIAL QUESTION

WHAT LEGACY DID CHINA LEAVE TO THE MODERN WORLD?

Roundtable Activity: Legacy of China Review the concept of *legacy* with students: A legacy is something handed down from the past, or inherited from our ancestors. A legacy can be an idea, an object, a custom, a way of operating, wealth, arts, an invention, or a religion. Have students sit around tables in groups of four. Tell them to think of a legacy that came to us from China. Each student around the table should name a different legacy that the modern world has gotten from China's past. One student per group should record the answers. After groups finish, collect the papers and save them until students have read the chapter. Then have them add or correct information. **0:15** minutes

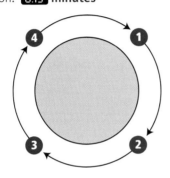

INTRODUCE THE READING STRATEGY

DRAW CONCLUSIONS

Remind students that when they draw conclusions, they need to support them with evidence from the text. Model completing the Draw Conclusions Organizer by reading aloud the first paragraph under the subheading "The Tang Dynasty" in Lesson 1.3 and adding the phrase "encouraged economic growth through agriculture and trade" as an example of evidence.

Tang Dynasty

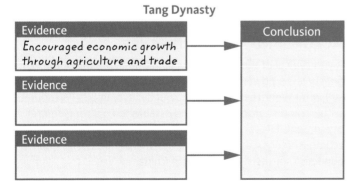

INTRODUCE CHAPTER VOCABULARY

DEFINITION MAP

Have students work together to create Definition Maps for Key Vocabulary words. Have pairs of students make a map for each word, fill in what they know about a word before reading and then add to or correct the map during reading. Show the example below on the board.

KEY DATES	
A.D. **581**	Wendi begins Sui dynasty, reunifies China
A.D. **618**	Tang dynasty expands empire; Taizong is succeeded by Empress Wu Zhao
A.D. **960**	Song dynasty has glorious period; economy booms
A.D. **1206**	Genghis Khan unites Mongols, begins conquering China and central Asia
A.D. **1264**	Kublai Khan starts Yuan dynasty, controlled by Mongols
A.D. **1368**	Hongwu, a Chinese peasant, starts Ming dynasty; Yongle builds Forbidden City
A.D. **1405**	Zheng He begins seven sea voyages, sails 40,000 miles to many countries
A.D. **1644–1912**	Manchus start the Qing dynasty, last dynasty

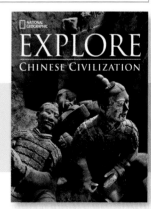

For more information about China, check out *EXPLORE CHINESE CIVILIZATION.*

Reunification
Under the
Sui Dynasty

A famous Chinese proverb says, "After a long split, a union will occur; after a long union, a split will occur." This saying reflects the belief that Chinese history has been a series of cycles alternating between strength and weakness. After a period of unrest, a strong leader establishes a powerful dynasty. It flourishes and then eventually declines until the people rebel and a new dynasty gains power. This dynastic cycle is a repeating theme in Chinese history.

MAIN IDEA

The short-lived Sui dynasty reunified China after centuries of civil war.

WENDI'S RULE

The Han dynasty, which began its rule of China in 206 B.C., ruled China for centuries, until weak rulers, rebellions, and powerful warlords caused its collapse in A.D. 220. China was plunged into nearly 400 years of civil war among many small kingdoms. The state belief system of Confucianism declined, though its ethical ideals and Chinese culture survived.

Then, in 581, the dynastic cycle turned again. A general named **Wendi** seized power and established a new dynasty called the **Sui** (sway). Wendi's conquests allowed him to **reunify**, or join together again, northern and southern China. He then faced the enormous challenge of restoring order across a vast and culturally diverse land.

To reunify China, Wendi strengthened the central government, limiting the power of local nobles and the bureaucracy. The government selected new officials by written examination and made sure they better reflected China's diverse ethnic groups. The military was organized and brought under Wendi's control.

Wendi also issued a new law code that combined northern and southern traditions. He gave farming land to former soldiers, established agriculture in the border regions of the empire, and extended the canal system. Wendi encouraged religious tolerance but also promoted the popular religion of Buddhism. When he died unexpectedly in 604, he left a strong empire for his son and successor, **Yangdi**.

THE GRAND CANAL

Yangdi loved luxury and built extravagant palaces in his new eastern capital at Luoyang (lu-WOH-YAHNG). Yangdi extended some of his father's useful public projects, such as restoring and expanding the Great Wall to help protect China's long and vulnerable northern border, and building state granaries to protect the food supply.

He also built the Grand Canal, connecting the southern Chang Jiang with the northern Huang He. This incredible 1,200-mile waterway had a road alongside it and became a vital communication link. It united China's economy, allowing southern China's plentiful resources to flow north where the government and armies were located. However, it came at a cost. Millions of peasants were forced to work on it, and many of them died.

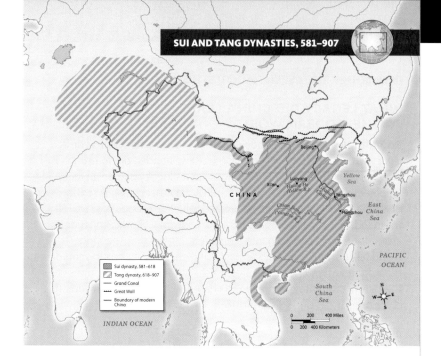

SUI AND TANG DYNASTIES, 581–907

Legend:
- Sui dynasty, 581–618
- Tang dynasty, 618–907
- Grand Canal
- Great Wall
- Boundary of modern China

The people of China hated this forced labor and the high taxes imposed by both Wendi and Yangdi to pay for such projects. Yangdi also launched expensive and unsuccessful wars against Korea. The military campaign required more money and service from his unhappy subjects.

Yangdi grew increasingly unpopular until, in 611, a famine finally pushed the people to rebel. It was the dynastic cycle at work. Rich and poor rose up against Yangdi's harsh rule, and he was assassinated. The Sui dynasty proved to be short-lived. In 618, a new dynasty—the Tang—rose to power. These leaders would continue to unify China.

REVIEW & ASSESS

1. **READING CHECK** What is the Sui dynasty known for?

2. **MAKE INFERENCES** How did the Sui dynasty reflect the pattern of the dynastic cycle?

3. **INTERPRET MAPS** How might the Grand Canal have improved China's trade network?

OBJECTIVE

Explain how the Sui Dynasty reunited China and helped it flourish.

CRITICAL THINKING SKILLS FOR LESSON 1.1

- Identify Main Ideas and Details
- Monitor Comprehension
- Make Inferences
- Interpret Maps
- Identify
- Evaluate

ESSENTIAL QUESTION

What legacy did China leave to the modern world?

To reunite China, Wendi created a strong central government, established a written exam for China's officials, and embraced the diversity of China's population. Lesson 1.1 also describes how the Grand Canal improved China's economy by enabling communication and commerce.

BACKGROUND FOR THE TEACHER

As was typical of the dynastic cycle in China, the fall of the Han dynasty left a power vacuum for almost 400 years, filled with civil wars, until Wendi established the Sui dynasty in 581. Wendi reunited northern and southern China and established a strong central government. His successor was his son Yangdi, whose greatest accomplishment was completing the 1,200-mile Grand Canal that connected southern and northern China.

DIGITAL RESOURCES myNGconnect.com

TEACHER RESOURCES & ASSESSMENT

 Reading and Note-Taking

 Vocabulary Practice

 Section 1 Quiz

STUDENT RESOURCES

 NG Chapter Gallery

UNITED OR DIVIDED?

Ask students what war in the United States almost separated the country into two parts. *(the Civil War)* Have them suggest ways life in America would be different if we were two nations instead of one. Point out that after the fall of the Han dynasty in A.D. 220, China broke into two separate parts due to fighting and corruption for almost 400 years. Tell students that they will read about how China was reunited, or made one again, by the Sui dynasty. **0:05** minutes

TEACH

GUIDED DISCUSSION

1. **Identify** In what ways did Wendi try to strengthen the new government? *(He limited the power of nobles, gave tests to select administrators, hired diverse people to reflect the population, organized the military, and issued a new fairer law code.)*

2. **Evaluate** How did the new Grand Canal both help and hurt China? *(Help: It connected the north and south; it helped the people communicate through travel; it made trade much easier, thus helping the economy. Hurt: Millions of peasants were forced to work on it and died, and all had to pay high taxes for it.)*

INTERPRET MAPS

Have students study the map of the Sui and Tang dynasties. Point out that the area controlled by the Tang dynasty included the land controlled by the Sui dynasty. **ASK:** About how much bigger was the Tang dynasty than the Sui dynasty? *(about double in size)* What two rivers did the Grand Canal connect? *(the Chang Jiang and the Huang He)* Have students observe the position of the Great Wall relative to the land controlled by the Sui dynasty; point out that it protected China from northern invaders. **0:10** minutes

ACTIVE OPTIONS

On Your Feet: Compare Canals Divide the class into four teams and assign one canal to each team: Grand Canal, Suez Canal, Panama Canal, Erie Canal. Each team should find out the length of their canal, its geographic location, and the two bodies of water it connects. Have each team make a sign naming their canal, its length, its location, and the bodies of water it connects. Then have the canal teams line up according to the length of their canals, shortest canal to longest canal. **0:10** minutes

NG Learning Framework: Learn About the Construction of the Grand Canal

ATTITUDE: Responsibility
SKILL: Communication
KNOWLEDGE: Our Human Story

Have students imagine that they are one of the peasants who were forced to work on the Grand Canal. Encourage them to write a story from the peasant's point of view. What happened to you? How did you feel? What was your new working life like? Let students share their stories aloud. **0:10** minutes

STRIVING READERS

Visualize a Dynastic Cycle Help students understand the dynastic cycle by drawing a big donut on the board. Put #1 Strong Dynasty at the top with an arrow pointing to the right. Have students tell where on the edge of the circle each of these phrases should fall:

- A strong dynasty is backed by the people.
- The dynasty is overthrown.
- People believe gods don't approve of the dynasty.
- A new dynasty comes to power.
- The dynasty weakens and disasters occur.

GIFTED & TALENTED

Map the Great Wall The Great Wall was a work in progress over several dynasties. Have students follow its progress in this chapter and do extra research on it. Challenge them to present it visually on a map using different colors to show different times it was lengthened or strengthened. Encourage them to add artistic touches or add present-day photographs to make an interesting and informative poster.

Press **mt** *in the Student eEdition for modified text.*

See the Chapter Planner for more strategies for differentiation.

ANSWERS

1. The Sui dynasty reunited a divided China.

2. China was in chaos because of wars between small kingdoms; then Wendi took over and established a strong government in the Sui dynasty; his son Yangdi kept it strong for awhile, but it declined, the people rebelled, and a new dynasty took power.

3. The Grand Canal became a vital communication link and increased trade; resources went from southern China to the north; people used the canal to transport goods more easily.

The Spread of Buddhism

When bad things happen, it's common to question our beliefs and re-examine our understanding of the world. In trying to make sense of the suffering, we might find comfort in the spirituality of religion—the belief that a higher power can end the misery. The Chinese people found comfort in religion when they most needed it.

MAIN IDEA

In troubled times, many Chinese turned to Buddhism.

BUDDHISM IN CHINA

The collapse of the Han dynasty in A.D. 220 plunged China into chaos for a period that would last hundreds of years. In such troubled times, many Chinese turned from the practical belief system known as Confucianism to a new, more spiritual religion—Buddhism.

As you learned in Chapter 6, Buddhism was based on an understanding of life founded by Siddhartha Gautama in India around 500 B.C. He taught that the keys to a good life were revealed in the Four Noble Truths: Life is full of suffering; the cause of suffering is desire and ignorance; to end the cycle of desire is to end suffering; and one can be free of desires by following the Eightfold Path. The path promoted a balanced life in which the sum of a person's deeds, or karma, results in **reincarnation**, or rebirth, into another life. Through good karma over successive lifetimes, a person could reach the state of **nirvana**—an end of reincarnation and the suffering of life.

Foreign traders and missionaries brought Buddhism to China during the first century A.D. During the collapse of the Han dynasty and the civil war that followed, Buddhism's teachings provided comfort and offered a clear path beyond suffering. Buddhist texts were translated, and Buddhist practices were adapted into a distinctive Chinese form, which became very popular among all classes of people.

Over the following centuries, Buddhism's popularity rose and declined, but emperors often promoted it to gain the people's support, as Wendi had done. This promotion included building magnificent monuments and not taxing Buddhist religious lands. Meanwhile, Buddhism continued to spread rapidly across the east and southeast areas of Asia, especially Korea and Japan.

IMPACT ON CONFUCIANISM

After the chaotic period of civil war ended, Confucianism made a comeback during the 600s. The government reintroduced traditional Confucian-style tests for the civil service. Confucian principles of respect, responsibility, loyalty, and duty to family and the state became popular once again.

In contrast, Buddhism encouraged moral behavior but played down the importance of obedience to outside authority in favor of inner guidance. Daoism, which emphasized our essential unity with nature, also had a strong following. These three competing belief systems became interwoven. Confucianism's concern with earthly duty influenced the religious spirituality of Buddhism and Daoism. As a result, Confucianism once more emerged as an important part of Chinese society.

Critical Viewing This Buddhist cave painting from China shows a seated figure meditating. What do the details in this painting suggest about Buddhism?

+ POSSIBLE RESPONSE

Bright colors and the smile on the figure's face suggest happiness and hope. The robe and the throne are very detailed and colorful. Two robed people are offering the central figure food or drink; he is likely a person of importance. The small figures around his head, which are both male and female, are meditating also, and suggest that Buddhism is for everyone.

REVIEW & ASSESS

1. **READING CHECK** After the collapse of the Han dynasty, why did many Chinese turned to Buddhism?

2. **SEQUENCE EVENTS** How was Buddhism first introduced in China?

3. **COMPARE AND CONTRAST** How do the main principles of Confucianism and Buddhism differ?

PLAN

OBJECTIVE

Describe why Buddhism took a strong hold in China.

CRITICAL THINKING SKILLS FOR LESSON 1.2

- Identify Main Ideas and Details
- Monitor Comprehension
- Sequence Events
- Compare and Contrast
- Make Inferences
- Draw Conclusions

ESSENTIAL QUESTION

What legacy did China leave to the modern world?

The Chinese embraced both Buddhism as a popular religion and Confucianism as a moral philosophy. Lesson 1.2 compares these two belief systems and their influence on early China.

BACKGROUND FOR THE TEACHER

Buddhism, originating in India, became more popular in China after the fall of the Han dynasty but did not displace Confucianism completely. Both Buddhism and Confucianism are belief systems; however Buddhism is considered a religion because of its spiritual nature, while Confucianism is a philosophy and code for moral conduct. The goal of Buddhism is to attain enlightenment and eventually to be released from cycles of reincarnation to reach nirvana. The goal of Confucianism is to achieve a structured, moral society.

DIGITAL RESOURCES myNGconnect.com

TEACHER RESOURCES & ASSESSMENT

 Reading and Note-Taking

 Vocabulary Practice

 Section 1 Quiz

STUDENT RESOURCES

 NG Chapter Gallery

INTRODUCE & ENGAGE

ACTIVATE PRIOR KNOWLEDGE

Have students name the major religions of the world as you list them on the board. *(Buddhism, Christianity, Hinduism, Islam, Judaism, and Sikhism)* Help them distinguish between major religions and branches of Christianity, such as Baptists or Catholics. Point out that there are many other belief systems or religions, not all classified as major or as religions. Confucianism is a philosophy, or a way of conducting oneself in the world. Religions (such as Buddhism) promote spirituality, belief in a god or gods, or an afterlife in another world. Many people around the world believe in parts of several religions, and some believe in no religion at all. **0:05** minutes

TEACH

GUIDED DISCUSSION

1. **Make Inferences** Wendi used both Confucianism and Buddhism to make a strong reunited China. How did he use each? *(He embraced Buddhism because the people needed and liked the spiritualism and hope it offered; he built monuments and did not tax religious lands. He used Confucianism to make his administration strong by employing civil service tests and emphasizing duty to family and state.)*

2. **Draw Conclusions** Why might Chinese citizens embrace both Confucianism and Buddhism? *(Confucianism's moral code emphasized how people live in relation to each other; Buddhism emphasized their inner lives and how they could achieve life after reincarnation and reach nirvana. The beliefs were compatible because the code of behavior was similar.)*

MORE INFORMATION

Chinese Buddhism The branch of Buddhism mainly practiced in East Asia is Mahayana Buddhism, which teaches that ordinary people can be released from suffering without having to become monks or nuns. Buddhists in East Asia created many large sculptures of the Buddha and other wise beings called bodhisattvas (bah-dee-SAHT-vahs). Buddhist temples are similar to Confucian and Daoist temples, and many contain deities from both Buddhist and Daoist traditions. Many Chinese Buddhist temples feature pagodas.

ACTIVE OPTIONS

Critical Viewing: NG Image Gallery Invite students to explore the entire NG Image Gallery to examine images that concern East Asian religions, including Confucianism. Have them select one of the images and do additional research to learn more about it. Ask questions that will inspire additional inquiry about the image, such as: What is this? What religion or philosophy does it represent? Where, when, and by whom was this created? Why was it created? What is it made of? What else would you like to know about it? **0:10** minutes

On Your Feet: Team Word Webs Divide the class into two teams. Give each team a sheet of paper, one with the key term "Confucianism," and the other with the term "Buddhism." Give students a few minutes to create a team Word Web about their term. Then have students share their web with the other team. Suggest that they circle any phrases that appear on both webs. **0:10** minutes

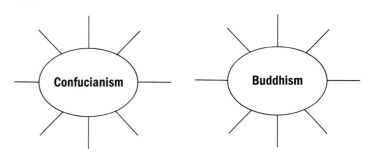

DIFFERENTIATE

ENGLISH LANGUAGE LEARNERS

Use Word Parts Write the following terms on the board: *Buddhism, Confucianism, Daoism, Hinduism,* and *Judaism.* Underline the suffix *-ism* in each word. Explain that this word ending is often used to indicate a system of belief. Then show how the parts of *Confucianism* mean "belief in Confucius." Finally, write the word *monotheism,* underlining *mono-* and *-ism.* Explain that *mono-* means "one." Monotheism is the belief in one god.

GIFTED & TALENTED

Create a Graph Remind students that China today has diverse religions. Challenge students to research the numbers and create a graph showing how many Chinese follow these religions: Buddhism, Christianity, Islam, Shintoism, Daoism, no religion (atheism), and other (such as Confucianism and folk religions).

Press **mt** *in the Student eEdition for modified text.*

See the Chapter Planner for more strategies for differentiation.

REVIEW & ASSESS

ANSWERS

1. Buddhism brought them comfort and hope for a better future life after great suffering.

2. Foreign traders and missionaries brought Buddhism from India in the first century A.D.

3. Confucianism promotes principles of respect, responsibility, loyalty, and duty to family and to the state; Buddhism promotes good moral behavior from inner guidance, not obedience to outside authority. Confucianism concerns earthly behavior, while the more spiritual Buddhism offers hope about a better future after death.

Tang and Song Dynasties

A picture is worth a thousand words—but it often does not last as long. Only words remain to capture the brilliance of Chinese painting from this era. For example, legend tells how the acclaimed Tang artist Wu Daozi (woo dow-dzuh) painted a mural that was so lifelike, he walked into it and disappeared forever.

MAIN IDEA

Under the Tang and Song dynasties, China grew and prospered.

THE TANG DYNASTY

Although unpopular, the Sui dynasty established solid foundations of government for future dynasties to build on. After the rulers of the **Tang** dynasty seized power in 618, they continued the Sui policy of tolerance toward China's many religions and cultures. They encouraged economic growth through agricultural reform and trade. The dynasty also strengthened the government by using civil service examinations to select government officials. These well-educated scholar-officials carried out government policy. They helped keep the government stable from one emperor to the next.

These reforms helped the Tang expand the empire into central and southern Asia.

(See the map in Section 1.1.) Meanwhile, literature and art flourished in a golden age. Few paintings survive, but beautiful sculptures reveal the talent of the artists of this period. Also, around 48,000 poems exist from this time. Tang officials were encouraged to write poetry.

Taizong (ty-johng) was the second Tang emperor and an admired figure in Chinese history. From 626 to 649, he used Confucian ideas to organize his government. Later, Wu Zhao (woo jow), the wife of Taizong's son and successor Gaozong, became China's only official female emperor by ruthlessly eliminating her rivals, including her own children. Despite the stormy succession, Wu Zhao had inherited a peaceful and well-run country. Her policies were sensible, improved the life of the people, and helped strengthen the empire. Later Tang emperors were less successful. Political instability sparked a long civil war in which millions died. Poor rulers, corruption, and rebellion weakened Tang authority until the dynasty lost power in 907. Once again, China plunged into chaos.

THE SONG DYNASTY

In 960, over 50 years later, the **Song** dynasty restored order. Though the Song rulers did not expand the territory of the empire, they introduced domestic improvements that made Song China the world's most advanced society of the time. Confucianism again became the state philosophy. Art and literature thrived while technology led to new inventions. Agriculture expanded with new techniques in drainage, irrigation, and terrace farming. Strains of rice from Southeast Asia doubled the harvest, and rice became China's **staple**, or main crop. In a short period, from 750 to 1100, China's population doubled to 100 million.

Meanwhile, this growth led to more rapid trade, and China's economy boomed. Farmers grew sugar cane, tea, bamboo, and hemp for trade, and the traditional crafts of

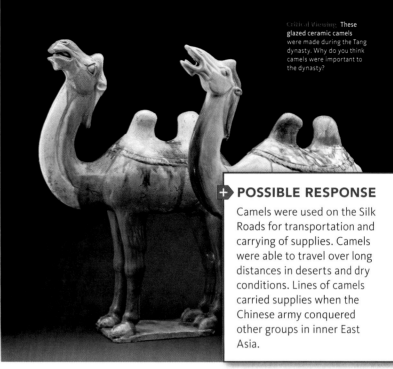

Critical Viewing These glazed ceramic camels were made during the Tang dynasty. Why do you think camels were important to the dynasty?

+ POSSIBLE RESPONSE

Camels were used on the Silk Roads for transportation and carrying of supplies. Camels were able to travel over long distances in deserts and dry conditions. Lines of camels carried supplies when the Chinese army conquered other groups in inner East Asia.

silk, paper, and ceramics grew in popularity. Improved roads and canals carried goods within China, while bigger ships carried exports overseas. For the first time, the state made more money from trade than from agriculture. Because of the strong economy, China started banks and printed the world's first paper money. Economic prosperity led to the growth of cities, which became busy centers of culture and **commerce**, or the buying and selling of goods.

REVIEW & ASSESS

1. **READING CHECK** How did China change during the Song dynasty?

2. **MAKE INFERENCES** How did reforms introduced under the Tang dynasty contribute to China's golden age?

3. **ANALYZE CAUSE AND EFFECT** How did the growth of trade during the Song dynasty affect China?

PLAN

OBJECTIVE

Identify ways in which China grew and prospered under the Tang and Song dynasties.

CRITICAL THINKING SKILLS FOR LESSON 1.3

- Identify Main Ideas and Details
- Monitor Comprehension
- Make Inferences
- Analyze Cause and Effect
- Identify
- Summarize
- Draw Conclusions

ESSENTIAL QUESTION

What legacy did China leave to the modern world?

During this era, the Chinese created great art and literature.

Lesson 1.3 describes how China flourished under the Tang and Song dynasties.

BACKGROUND FOR THE TEACHER

The Tang and Song dynasties were the most glorious periods in Chinese history. Many regard Taizong as China's greatest emperor. Not only did he expand the Chinese empire greatly, but he improved its economy and governed the country extremely well. His reign resulted in a long peaceful period in which poetry and the arts flourished.

After the Tang Dynasty declined, the Song Dynasty took over, and China became the most advanced society of its time. Creativity flourished in all areas.

DIGITAL RESOURCES myNGconnect.com

TEACHER RESOURCES & ASSESSMENT

 Reading and Note-Taking

 Vocabulary Practice

 Section 1 Quiz

STUDENT RESOURCES

 NG Chapter Gallery

INTRODUCE & ENGAGE

BRAINSTORMING

Ask students to brainstorm all the ways in which people are creative. List their answers on the board. Push them to think of not only the arts, but also other fields such as cooking, technology, agriculture, business, inventions, and so forth. Then tell them that they will be reading about China's most creative period. As they read, have them look for new ideas and products that came out of this time period. **0:05** minutes

TEACH

GUIDED DISCUSSION

1. **Identify** What creative products and ideas came out of the Tang and Song dynasties? *(paintings, sculptures, poetry, agricultural techniques, technology, inventions, paper, banks, paper money)*

2. **Summarize** What accomplishments caused this period of time to be called "glorious"? Consider aspects of China's military, government, economy, agriculture, and arts. *(military: doubled the size of the empire; government: well run and caused peace; economy: trade grew to become more profitable than farming; agriculture: irrigation and other techniques caused tremendous growth in productivity; arts: poetry, sculpture, paintings, and music flourished)*

DRAW CONCLUSIONS

The emperors during the Tang and Song dynasties used Confucian techniques to run their governments. Why did this result in such prosperity? *(Government officials were tested and qualified, rather than friends of the emperors, and ruled with fairness. Good government resulted in peace and lack of corruption, so the people could concentrate on things other than their safety. They had time to become creative and solve problems, leading to innovation in all fields.)* **0:10** minutes

ACTIVE OPTIONS

On Your Feet: Create a Time Line Put students in teams of four. Challenge students to create a time line of dynasties and their accomplishments, including the Sui, Tang, and Song dynasties. While half of each team creates the time line, the other should record two or three accomplishments that happened during each dynasty and add them to the time line. Have teams share their finished time lines. **0:10** minutes

NG Learning Framework: Write a Biography

ATTITUDE: **Curiosity**
KNOWLEDGE: **Our Human Story**

Have students select one of the people from the chapter that they are still curious about. Instruct them to write a short biography about this person using information from the chapter and additional source material. Possibilities include Taizong, Empress Wu, Wendi, Yangdi, Siddhartha Gautama, Confucius, or someone else. **0:10** minutes

DIFFERENTIATE

STRIVING READERS

Chart Tang and Song Dynasties Have students divide their paper into two columns, one side labeled *Tang* and the other *Song*. As they read, have them write three details about each dynasty. Then have them pair up and copy details from each other's charts to create a more complete list of details.

GIFTED & TALENTED

Map an Empire Taizong expanded China to become the largest nation in the world at that time. Under him China grew to include most of present-day China, Vietnam, and most of Central Asia. Give students a current map of East Asia. Have them use the map of the Sui and Tang dynasties in Lesson 1.1 and further research to visually map out the Chinese empire during Taizong's reign. Have them share the finished map on a bulletin board.

Press **mt** *in the Student eEdition for modified text.*
See the Chapter Planner for more strategies for differentiation.

REVIEW & ASSESS

ANSWERS

1. Agriculture expanded, rice became the staple crop, the population doubled to 100 million, technology took huge gains, the economy boomed, banks were started, paper money was printed, new things were invented, and trade surpassed agriculture as the source of China's wealth.

2. The reforms led to a period of peace and stability, which allowed people to focus on creativity.

3. Trade became more profitable than agriculture for China; the economy improved so much that the Chinese invented banks and paper money to avoid carrying coins.

The Legacy of Chinese Inventions

Imagine using dimes to buy a car. Maybe you'd start counting but soon give up. Dollar bills are far more convenient. Printed money was a Chinese invention, as were printed books, porcelain, navigational compasses, and gunpowder. All these new inventions were created during the Tang and Song dynasties. It's difficult to imagine our world without these items.

MAIN IDEA

Chinese inventions have helped shape the world we live in today.

PRINTING AND PAPER MONEY

The Chinese had invented paper around A.D. 100. About five hundred years later, they contributed another bookmaking breakthrough—block printing. This technique involved carving the text in reverse to stand out on a block of wood. The block was painted with ink and pressed onto paper to create a printed page. Carving the blocks for each page of each book was a long process.

Around 1041, the innovation of **movable type**, which used individually carved characters, made it easier and cheaper to print books. The new widespread distribution of books helped spread government regulations, literature, and the ideas of Confucianism and Buddhism.

Meanwhile, China's booming population and economy created a large demand for coins—by 1085 six billion coins were minted per year. The coins were too bulky for large transactions, so merchants began exchanging paper notes as IOUs. The money stayed in a bank but was owned by whoever held the note. Around 1100, the first government-backed currency was issued. Over time, the use of bank seals and increasingly complex designs helped discourage counterfeiting.

GUNPOWDER, THE MAGNETIC COMPASS, AND PORCELAIN

Gunpowder was an accidental discovery by Chinese alchemists attempting to turn worthless metals into gold. These early chemists found that sulfur, saltpeter, and charcoal made a powerful explosive when mixed together. The military found that gunpowder confined in an iron tube could shoot objects great distances. This discovery led to the development of cannons, guns, and fireworks. Later, Chinese armies used gunpowder in Central Asia, and the secret spread.

The Chinese had long used magnetic compasses for ceremonies, but in the 1100s they began using them for navigation. A sliver of magnetized iron hanging from a silk thread or floating in water would point north and south. This property allowed sailors to tell their direction without the sun or stars. Longer sea journeys also became possible, which increased China's maritime trade.

One especially prized trade item was **porcelain**—a strong, light, and nearly see-through ceramic. Porcelain's closely guarded secret was the blending of unique minerals and a glaze at very high temperatures. Because of these secret techniques, porcelain—or china, as it came to be called—was incredibly rare and precious.

CHINESE INVENTIONS

Antique block characters for printing

Movable Type
The Chinese created block characters for use in movable type, a development that made printing easier. Artisans carved characters as individual clay tablets that could be arranged on a board to form text. After printing, the characters could be reused.

Song porcelain vase with celadon glaze

Porcelain
Techniques for creating porcelain were perfected during the Tang dynasty and reached the height of artistry under the Song. The formula used to create porcelain was a closely guarded secret.

Ancient Chinese nautical compass

Compass
The ancient Chinese had developed a compass that was used in rituals. During the Song dynasty, they discovered the secret to making a magnetic compass used for navigation.

Fireworks display

Gunpowder
After the invention of gunpowder, the military experimented with explosive arrows, grenades, rockets, and land mines, and finally developed firearms and fireworks.

REVIEW & ASSESS

1. **READING CHECK** What inventions occurred during the Tang and Song dynasties?

2. **DRAW CONCLUSIONS** Why did the invention of movable type help increase the spread of ideas?

3. **ANALYZE CAUSE AND EFFECT** How did the use of magnetic compasses for navigation affect China's trade?

PLAN

OBJECTIVE

Identify how Chinese inventions have shaped our own world.

CRITICAL THINKING SKILLS FOR LESSON 1.4

- Identify Main Ideas and Details
- Monitor Comprehension
- Draw Conclusions
- Analyze Cause and Effects
- Summarize
- Compare and Contrast
- Evaluate

ESSENTIAL QUESTION

What legacy did China leave to the modern world?

China left the inventions of paper, paper money, movable type for printing books, porcelain, gunpowder, and the magnetic compass for navigation.

BACKGROUND FOR THE TEACHER

Most ceramics are made from a single type of clay. True porcelain is made from a mixture of kaolin, a white clay made from the mineral feldspar, and petuntse, another type of feldspar that is found only in China. Korea learned to make porcelain in the 1100s and Japan began making it in the 1500s. The demand for porcelain increased in the 1600s, as more Europeans started drinking coffee, tea, and chocolate.

DIGITAL RESOURCES myNGconnect.com

TEACHER RESOURCES & ASSESSMENT

 Reading and Note-Taking

 Vocabulary Practice

 Section 1 Quiz

STUDENT RESOURCES

 Active History

WHAT IF?

Ask students to check their pockets or purses and pull out some coins or change. Then show them a twenty-dollar bill. Have them figure out how many quarters you would need to carry to equal $20. *(80)* How many dimes? *(200)* **ASK:** What is the problem with using quarters or dimes instead of paper money? *(weight, bulk, awkwardness)* What does a new car cost, approximately? *(somewhere north of $20,000)* How many quarters would you need? *(80,000)* Explain that we can thank the Chinese for inventing paper money so that we can carry the money to buy things. `0:05` minutes

TEACH

GUIDED DISCUSSION

1. **Summarize** How did inventions related to printing affect Chinese society? *(The inventions of movable type and printing allowed the Chinese to produce books in quantity to spread ideas, and paper money to replace coins, which made buying things simpler, improved trade, and helped expand the economy.)*

2. **Compare and Contrast** Contrast today's use of these inventions with the past. What modern technology and usage are gradually replacing the following: paper money *(plastic credit cards)*, magnetic compasses *(radar)*, printed books *(digital books)*, porcelain/China dishware *(plastic and paper)*?

EVALUATE

The invention of gunpowder allowed the Chinese to create explosions, cannons, guns, and fireworks. What are some positive and negative effects of each of these? (There may be disagreement about whether these are positive or negative.) *(Possible responses: explosions —positive = destroy old buildings; negative = kill/ injure people; cannons—positive = useful for armies; negative = kill many people; guns—positive = shoot enemies, protect individuals, hunt animals; negative: kill people, animals; fireworks—positive = celebrations, add excitement, fun, beauty: negative: can injure people, can pollute atmosphere)* `0:10` minutes

ACTIVE OPTIONS

Active History: Evaluate China's Inventions Extend the lesson by using either the PDF or Whiteboard version of the activity. These activities take a deeper look at the inventions discussed in the lesson. Explore the activities as a class, turn them into group assignments, or even assign them individually. `0:10` minutes

On Your Feet: Explore Movable Type Have students work in small groups to explore the process of setting movable type. Give each group a pile of letter tiles from a spelling game or have students make their own tiles using small squares of paper or cardboard. Remind students to use blank tiles to create spaces between words. Have one group come to the front of the class and use the tiles to form a sentence. Students can construct a sentence from the lesson or create a sentence about Chinese inventions. Then have the other groups take turns coming to the front of the class to form their own sentences. Students should move around the previous group's tiles and add their own. After all groups have had a turn, invite students to discuss how this process would have been faster and more flexible than carving a full page of text on a wooden block. `0:25` minutes

DIFFERENTIATE

STRIVING READERS

Create Charts Have students complete a chart like the one below as they read the lesson. Have students work in pairs to read and take notes in the chart. Then instruct them to use the chart to help them evaluate the positive and negative effects of each invention and decide which invention they think had the greatest impact on society.

Invention	Date	Effects

GIFTED & TALENTED

Describe Inventions Have students think of their own inventions. They might come up with a new electronic device, vehicle, or concept or an item that simply makes everyday life easier. Ask students to write a description of their invention and share it with the class.

Press **mt** *in the Student eEdition for modified text.*

See the Chapter Planner for more strategies for differentiation.

REVIEW & ASSESS

ANSWERS

1. Inventions include movable type, paper money, banks, gunpowder, cannons, guns, fireworks, magnetic compasses, and porcelain.

2. Movable type made it easier and cheaper to print books.

3. Magnetic compasses made it possible to tell direction without the sun or stars, so sailors could take longer sea voyages and trade in many distant places new to them.

GENGHIS
KHAN A.D. 1162 – 1227

Forget Rome or Britain. It was the Mongols who ruled the largest land empire in history. It stretched from present-day Korea to Hungary and included more than 100 million people of widely differing cultures. And the Mongols conquered all this territory in less than 100 years, thanks to the determination of one man—Genghis Khan.

💼 **Job:** Universal ruler
📖 **Education:** His harsh childhood
🌐 **Home:** Near the Onon River
Real Name: Temujin

FINEST HOUR

When he died, Genghis Khan had united the nomadic tribes, conquered China, and extended his rule over all of central Asia.

WORST MOMENT

The death of his father, a defeated Mongol chieftain, left young Temujin and his mother to eke out a living on the harsh steppe.

FRIENDS

Jamuka was a friend and rival whom Temujin later defeated to become universal ruler.

TRIVIA

It is said that Temujin was born grasping a clot of blood in his hand, which has been viewed throughout history as a mixed sign—an omen of his future fame (and notoriety).

THE MONGOL CONQUEST

The Mongols were a loose collection of independent nomadic tribes from the **steppes**—or vast, grassy plains—of northwest China. They spent their lives roaming, raiding, herding, and fighting across this landscape.

A child named Temujin (TEH-moo-juhn) was born on this landscape. He was the son of a defeated Mongol chieftain, and his childhood was harsh. However, Temujin was ambitious, clever, charismatic, and a great warrior. He became a tribal leader and, in 1206, the Mongol people gave him the title **Genghis Khan** (JEHNG-gihs KAHN), meaning "universal ruler."

Despite conflicts among the tribes, there was one thing they all needed—more grazing lands. Genghis Khan organized the diverse bands into a powerful military machine that would sweep mercilessly across Asia in one of history's most impressive conquests.

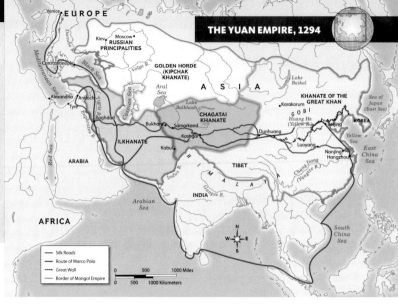

THE YUAN EMPIRE, 1294

Silk Roads
Route of Marco Polo
Great Wall
Border of Mongol Empire

0   500   1000 Miles
0   500   1000 Kilometers

In 1212, Genghis Khan and the Mongols invaded northern China, destroying more than 90 cities and killing their inhabitants. Turning west, he destroyed an empire in what is now Iran. He then invaded southern Russia and, in 1215, destroyed China's capital.

When Genghis Khan died around 1226, he had conquered much of central Asia. Four of his sons shared his vast empire, dividing it into four **khanates**, or regions, and expanded their rule into Europe and southern China.

KUBLAI KHAN

China's next great leader was Genghis Khan's grandson, **Kublai Khan** (KOO-bluh KAHN). He rose to become leader of the Mongol Empire in 1264. Kublai Khan was determined to add to his empire by conquering all of southern China. By 1271, he had succeeded, giving the Mongols control over most of China. That year he declared himself emperor, adopting the dynastic name **Yuan** (yoo-ahn) and preparing to help his army meet new challenges.

REVIEW & ASSESS

1. **READING CHECK** How did the Mongols gain power?

2. **COMPARE AND CONTRAST** How were Genghis and Kublai Khan alike?

3. **INTERPRET MAPS** Which cities in the northwest were part of the Mongol Empire?

PLAN

OBJECTIVE

Describe how Genghis Khan, the Mongol ruler, conquered China and created the largest land empire in history.

CRITICAL THINKING SKILLS FOR LESSON 2.1

- Identify Main Ideas and Details
- Compare and Contrast
- Analyze Cause and Effect
- Monitor Comprehension
- Interpret Maps
- Make Inferences

ESSENTIAL QUESTION

What legacy did China leave to the modern world?

Genghis Khan, a Mongol, conquered and ruled the largest empire in history. Lesson 2.1 discusses his powerful military machine and the vast empire he and his son, Kublai Khan, created.

BACKGROUND FOR THE TEACHER

Genghis Khan, as a ruthless military conqueror, may have caused the deaths of as many as 40 million people. However, as a ruler he did some good things. He granted freedom of religion to his diverse subjects; he created an international postal system; he adopted a system of writing; he held regular censuses; he abolished torture; and he encouraged trade. He also fathered hundreds of children, leading modern genealogists to believe that currently 0.5 percent of males in the world, or over 16 million men, are direct descendants.

DIGITAL RESOURCES myNGconnect.com

TEACHER RESOURCES & ASSESSMENT

 Reading and Note-Taking

 Vocabulary Practice

 Section 2 Quiz

STUDENT RESOURCES

 Biography

PREVIEW THE MAP

Have students preview the map of the Yuan Empire and look at the green line around the Mongol Empire. Ask them to name as many modern countries as they can that were inside, or had been conquered by, the Mongol Empire at that time. *(Russia, China, Iran, Korea, Hungary, Mongolia, Kazakhstan, Ukraine, Romania, and so on)* Explain that they are about to read about the largest land empire in the world's history. **ASK:** How do you think one group of people could conquer all this vast land? *(by force, with a strong army)*
0:05 minutes

TEACH

GUIDED DISCUSSION

1. **Analyze Cause and Effect** What personality traits and abilities did Genghis Khan have that enabled him to become the "universal ruler?" *(Possible responses: great military ability, strong, ruthless, organized, good leader, ambitious, intelligent, cruel)*

2. **Make Inferences** What did Kublai Khan accomplish? *(He conquered all of southern China to add to the empire and ran the whole Mongol Empire well.)* Why did he declare himself the dynastic emperor Yuan? *(He had complete control of China and used their method of establishing dynasties.)*

INTERPRET MAPS

Have students examine the map of the Yuan Empire in the lesson. **ASK:** What do the different colors within the green line mean? *(The empire was divided into four khanates among Genghis Khan's four sons; each color is a different khanate.)* Which one contained most of China? *(Khanate of the Great Khan)* **0:10** minutes

ACTIVE OPTIONS

On Your Feet: Conduct an Interview Divide the class into four groups and have them choose one of the following to act out an interview: Taizong, Empress Wu, Genghis Khan, or Kublai Khan. Have the teams prepare questions and answers for two of their members to act out for the class. Remind them that the interviewees should reflect the personality and know the accomplishments of each leader. Then allow teams to present their interview to the class. **0:10** minutes

NG Learning Framework: Learn About Genghis Khan

ATTITUDE: **Empowerment**
SKILL: **Problem-Solving**

Invite students to revisit the biography of Genghis Khan in this lesson and imagine that they were in his place. Have them break into groups and discuss these questions: How would you have done things differently from Genghis Khan? How do you feel these changes would have affected both China and the empire he ruled?
0:10 minutes

ENGLISH LANGUAGE LEARNERS

Understand Vocabulary Students may be unfamiliar with adjectives used to describe Genghis Khan, such as *ruthless, merciless, ambitious, clever,* and *charismatic.* Write the definitions below on the board and have students read and discuss them and copy them into their vocabulary notebooks. Then have them tell you which words are positive, which are negative, and why.

ruthless = without pity; cruel

merciless = without mercy or pity

ambitious = wanting to get power, wealth, success

clever = mentally bright, having sharp intelligence

charismatic = having great charm or appeal

GIFTED & TALENTED

Research the Mongolian Army The Mongolian army did incredible feats and conquered a huge amount of the world. How did they do it? The Internet contains many articles on the Mongolian army. Have students research how the army worked and why it was so successful. Suggest that students divide up the topics: training, weapons, mobility, organization, strategy, and ground tactics. They should organize their findings into a presentation for the class.

Press **(mt)** in the Student eEdition for modified text.

See the Chapter Planner for more strategies for differentiation.

ANSWERS

1. The Mongol tribes united into a strong military and invaded and destroyed cities in China, central Asia, and Europe. They conquered all the lands of the empire by force.

2. Both were strong, ambitious, ruthless, and willing to kill countless people to expand the empire. Neither trusted the Chinese, and both treated them badly. Both ran the empire successfully without Chinese bureaucrats.

3. Moscow and Kiev were part of the empire.

2.2
Life in Yuan China

You love your country but hate your rulers.

The Mongols are in charge, and they discriminate against you. You pay higher taxes than foreigners, receive less justice, and are excluded from the best jobs—all because you're Chinese.

MAIN IDEA

The Mongols set up strict rules to control China.

YUAN GOVERNMENT

Kublai Khan adopted a less destructive approach to governing than that of his predecessors, trying to win over the Chinese people and preserve conquered towns instead of destroying them. Even so, any resistance was brutally punished. During the 1270s, Song loyalists continued to fight the Mongols in southern China. The Mongols defeated the Song uprising of 200,000 troops—and then killed the entire population of Hangzhou (hahng-joh) city. To avoid further suffering, remaining officials of the Song dynasty surrendered in 1279.

Kublai Khan was now ruler of all China—the first to unite all China since the end of the Tang dynasty, which ended in 907—and its first foreign ruler ever. He would rule for 15 years, until his death in 1294. His Yuan dynasty led China for a century, but it was not an easy time for the Chinese.

The Mongols were more used to fighting than governing, and controlling a country as large and sophisticated as China demanded a highly organized government. Under the Yuan dynasty, Chinese government continued much as before, with a strong central state built around a bureaucracy with Confucian rituals and ceremonies.

The big difference was that the Mongols excluded Chinese people from higher positions to stop them from having too much power. Instead, Mongols and foreigners, especially Muslims, received the top jobs. Foreigners migrated to China, including the famous Italian merchant **Marco Polo**, who served as a tax collector and special envoy to the emperor. However, Chinese scholars still had a strong unofficial influence, and Kublai Khan relied on Chinese advisors.

SOCIAL CLASSES

Most Chinese hated living under the Mongols, who treated them as second-class citizens in their own country. Society was divided into four classes. At the top were the Mongols, followed by non-Chinese foreigners. Then came the northern Chinese, who had lived longest under Yuan rule. At the very bottom of society were the southern Chinese, who made up 80 percent of the population.

Many peasant farmers in the bottom bracket of society were forced off their land when they could not pay their taxes. Unable to feed their families, many sold themselves into slavery far from home. The government forced peasants to work on extravagant imperial projects. The Yuan dynasty rebuilt Beijing as a wealthy city filled with magnificent palaces and pleasure gardens enjoyed by rich foreigners.

All this luxury came at a cost for the Chinese. The Mongols feared rebellion because of the pressures they placed on the Chinese. Looking for signs of revolt, agents working for the government kept a close eye on neighborhoods. They forced

People in China still use the Grand Canal, shown in this photograph, to move goods up and down the river.

every ten Chinese families to share a single knife. The government banned meetings and fairs and prevented the Chinese from going out at night or playing sports, thinking it was too much like military exercise.

The Yuan dynasty did make significant contributions, though. During its reign, trade and agriculture expanded. The Yuan built roads and extended the Grand Canal. The Mongol postal service provided efficient communication, and the government introduced an accurate calendar of 365.2 days. Also, with many Chinese scholars out of work, they had more time to write, and Chinese literature flourished.

Still, the Chinese remained hostile to Mongol rule and formed secret societies to plot rebellions. After Kublai Khan's death in 1294, the Yuan dynasty gradually declined. There were seven emperors in 40 years, none of them as gifted as Kublai Khan. Rebellions started to break out, and, by 1368, China was poised for yet another change in dynasties.

REVIEW & ASSESS

1. **READING CHECK** How did the Mongols treat the Chinese under their rule?

2. **MAKE INFERENCES** Why did Kublai Khan exclude the Chinese from important jobs in government?

3. **ANALYZE CAUSE AND EFFECT** Under the Yuan dynasty, how did the Mongols open China to foreigners?

PLAN

OBJECTIVE

Identify how the Mongols ruled China.

CRITICAL THINKING SKILLS FOR LESSON 2.2

- Identify Main Ideas and Details
- Monitor Comprehension
- Make Inferences
- Analyze Cause and Effect
- Identify

ESSENTIAL QUESTION

What legacy did China leave to the modern world?

The Yuan dynasty introduced the international postal service to China as well as an accurate 365-day calendar. Lesson 2.2 explains these and other innovations that developed under Yuan rule.

BACKGROUND FOR THE TEACHER

Under Kublai Khan, the Mongols ruled China as the Yuan dynasty. Kublai Khan reunited China under his reign by totally destroying and killing the inhabitants of at least one city. The Mongols replaced or killed the Chinese rulers. Then the Mongols and non-Chinese foreigners ran the government to keep power away from the Chinese. Society was divided into classes with Mongols at the top, non-Chinese foreigners next, northern Chinese next, and southern Chinese (80% of the Chinese) at the bottom.

The Yuan dynasty expanded trade and agriculture, lengthened the Grand Canal, and added in other ways to Chinese progress. Chinese literature flourished since scholars were no longer involved in governing. At this time Marco Polo, a wealthy Italian merchant, visited China and later achieved fame for writing about his travels.

DIGITAL RESOURCES myNGconnect.com

TEACHER RESOURCES & ASSESSMENT

 Reading and Note-Taking

 Vocabulary Practice

 Section 2 Quiz

STUDENT RESOURCES

 Biography

WALK IN THEIR SHOES

Present a "what-if" scenario to students: Suppose another country defeated the United States and took over the government. What if the foreign country's people were in charge and Americans had to obey their wishes? How would you feel? How would your life change? After students discuss the changes and their feelings, tell them that when the Mongols took over China, that's what happened to the Chinese. `0:05` **minutes**

TEACH

GUIDED DISCUSSION

1. **Identify** How did Kublai Khan keep the Mongols in power in China? Give examples of how he gained power and how he kept it. *(He defeated the Song army, killed off the entire population of Hangzhou city, took the Chinese out of positions in the government, got foreigners to run the country, taxed peasants out of their land, and forced the Chinese to obey the Mongols.)*

2. **Analyze Effects** What good things did the Yuan dynasty accomplish for China? *(Trade and agriculture expanded, the Grand Canal was extended, roads were built, a postal service was established, an accurate calendar was introduced, and Chinese literature flourished.)*

ANALYZE CAUSE AND EFFECT

Discuss with students the effects of Mongol rule on the Chinese people. **ASK:** What caused the Mongols to fear that the Chinese would rebel? *(They treated the Chinese poorly and feared the Chinese would fight back.)* What was the effect of the Mongols' fear on the Chinese? *(The Mongols placed even tighter controls on the Chinese: ten Chinese families had to share one knife; no one was allowed to go out at night or to play sports; they could hold no meetings or fairs.)* `0:10` **minutes**

ACTIVE OPTIONS

Critical Viewing: NG Chapter Gallery Have students examine the contents of the Chapter Gallery for Chapter 18. Then invite them to brainstorm additional images they believe would fit within the Chapter Gallery. Have them write a description of these additional images and provide an explanation of why they would fit within the Chapter Gallery. Then instruct them to do online research to find examples of actual images they would like to add to the gallery. `0:10` **minutes**

On Your Feet: Role-Play Different Social Classes In groups of four, have students discuss how individuals in each of the four social classes would behave and act. Then have each role-play an individual in one of those classes. After teams have practiced, let them role-play for the class and have other teams guess to which class each individual belongs. `0:10` **minutes**

STRIVING READERS

Chart Social Classes Have students pair up to read the lesson. Then have them make a list of the four social classes in the Yuan dynasty. Ask them to describe the difficulties that the bottom class faced.

GIFTED & TALENTED

Discover Marco Polo Encourage interested students to research the life and works of Marco Polo. Some can focus on his biography, others on his writings, and others on his value to the world at that time. Have them create a poster to present what they learned in a visual form to share with the class.

Press **mt** in the Student eEdition for modified text.

See the Chapter Planner for more strategies for differentiation.

ANSWERS

1. The Mongols made the Chinese second-class citizens. They took away all governmental power; they forced peasants off their land and forced them to work on government projects; they distrusted the Chinese and guarded them closely, denying them basic freedoms.

2. Kublai Khan did not want the Chinese to regain any power that would threaten his rule.

3. The Mongols gave foreigners top government jobs; they admitted many Muslims and they welcomed foreign immigrants.

Travels on the Silk Roads

Under the Mongols, China continued to produce goods that were popular all around the world, especially silk and porcelain. The Mongols wanted to encourage commerce, and their control of China and all the lands that connected it to Europe helped trade flourish. The ancient trade routes, the Silk Roads, were revitalized, and new routes reached north to the Mongol capital of Karakorum. From here, great caravans could now travel in safety and ease across the lush plains that had previously been too dangerous because of tribal wars and banditry.

ANSWERS

DOCUMENT 1
Until Genghis Khan changed the routes, the people on the steppes had not been included in the Silk Roads trade because caravans were afraid to go there. Now they were able to buy the silks and other materials from merchants and sell some of their own products. They would also be exposed to people from other areas, get news, and learn new things.

DOCUMENT 2
Experts knew the value of the materials, preventing fraud, trickery, and ignorance of the real value of items. Haggling over price would be limited.

DOCUMENT 3
Marco Polo brought goods from China back to Europe and interested Europeans in buying them. He also traveled through many other lands and marketed his knowledge with many other individuals.

In this illustration from Marco Polo's book of his travels, traders bring spices from the western part of the Mongol empire to the east.

from *Book of the Wonders of the World* by Marco Polo and Rustichello, 15th century

DOCUMENT ONE
Secondary Source: History Text

from *Genghis Khan and the Making of the Modern World* by Jack Weatherford
Anthropologist Jack Weatherford presents a fairly positive view of the rule of the Mongols. Silk was one of China's most valued exports, and here Weatherford notes how Genghis Khan shaped its distribution.

CONSTRUCTED RESPONSE Why might the people living on the steppes benefit from Genghis Khan's rerouting of exports through their territory?

> A river of brightly colored silk flowed out of China. It was as though Genghis Khan had rerouted all the different twisting channels of the Silk Route, combined them into one large stream, and redirected it northward to spill out across the Mongol steppes.

DOCUMENT TWO
Primary Source: Travel Account

from *Travels* by Marco Polo
Marco Polo was a merchant from Venice whose adventures in Asia have become the most celebrated of the medieval world. His colorful descriptions of life in Mongol China paint a vivid picture of the court of Kublai Khan.

CONSTRUCTED RESPONSE Why would using experts to determine prices make trade fairer and easier?

> Several times a year, parties of traders arrive with pearls and precious stones and gold and silver and other valuables, such as cloth of gold and silk, and surrender them all to the Great [Kublai] Khan. The Khan then summons twelve experts . . . and bids them examine the wares that the traders have bought and pay for them what they judge to be their true value.

DOCUMENT THREE
Primary Source: Artifact

Passport Medallion, c. 1300
Kublai Khan issued a medallion like the one at right to Marco Polo before he set off on his travels. It acted as a passport, helping Marco Polo access difficult areas and secure help and supplies from subjects of the Khan.

CONSTRUCTED RESPONSE How might Marco Polo have helped expand China's foreign contact and trade during the Mongol Empire?

SYNTHESIZE & WRITE

1. **REVIEW** Review what you have learned about the Mongol Empire.

2. **RECALL** On your own paper, write down the main idea expressed through each document and artifact.

3. **CONSTRUCT** Write a topic sentence that answers this question: During the Mongol Empire, how did Genghis Khan and Kublai Khan promote and increase trade?

4. **WRITE** Using evidence from the documents and artifact, write an informative paragraph to support the answer to the question in Step 3.

PLAN

OBJECTIVE
Synthesize information about the travels on the Silk Roads from primary and secondary source documents.

CRITICAL THINKING SKILLS FOR LESSON 2.3
- Synthesize
- Identify
- Make Inferences
- Describe
- Evaluate

ESSENTIAL QUESTION
What legacy did China leave to the modern world?

The Mongols revitalized the Silk Roads, thus enabling Chinese goods, especially silk and porcelain, to be traded all over the world. Travelers also spread Chinese culture and spread ideas from foreign cultures to China. Lesson 2.3 provides information on the Silk Roads trade from primary and secondary sources.

BACKGROUND FOR THE TEACHER
The Silk Roads were ancient routes for travel and trade. In the 1300s, before Genghis Khan took over, though, they were becoming increasingly dangerous for merchants and were used less often. When the Mongols took over, they eliminated crime on the routes and made the journeys much safer. Because the Mongols ruled so many lands, interaction between the Chinese and foreigners grew greatly during this period. Europeans were able to get Chinese goods more easily, and Marco Polo was a great marketer for Chinese goods.

DIGITAL RESOURCES myNGconnect.com

TEACHER RESOURCES & ASSESSMENT

 Reading and Note-Taking

 Vocabulary Practice

 Section 2 Quiz

STUDENT RESOURCES

 NG Chapter Gallery

INTRODUCE & ENGAGE

PREPARE FOR THE DOCUMENT-BASED QUESTION

Before students start on the activity, briefly preview the three documents. Remind students that a constructed response requires full explanations in complete sentences. Emphasize that students should use their knowledge of the Mongolian rulers, the Silk Roads, Marco Polo, and Chinese culture in addition to the information in the documents. **0:05 minutes**

TEACH

GUIDED DISCUSSION

1. **Identify** To what does Jack Weatherford compare the new routes of the Silk Roads? *(a river or stream made up of silk, spilling on the steppes)*

2. **Make Inferences** Kublai Khan summoned twelve experts to evaluate the goods brought by the merchants. What does this tell you about his opinion of merchants? *(He didn't trust them.)* Why would this method save time? *(It limited haggling over price.)*

3. **Describe** How did the passport medallion from Genghis Khan help Marco Polo? *(It protected him from danger since most were afraid of Genghis Khan, and it opened doors for him. It assured people that Genghis Khan knew and respected him.)*

EVALUATE

After students have completed the "Synthesize & Write" activity, allow time for them to exchange paragraphs and read and comment on the work of their peers. Guidelines for comments should be established prior to this activity so that feedback is constructive and encouraging in nature. **0:15 minutes**

ACTIVE OPTIONS

Critical Viewing: NG Chapter Gallery Ask students to choose one image from the Chapter Gallery and become an expert on it. They should do additional research to learn all about it. Then, students should share their findings with a partner, small group, or the class. **0:10 minutes**

On Your Feet: Create a Passport Medallion Have students study the medallion Genghis Khan gave to Marco Polo. Allow them to work with clay to create a medallion of their own that would give them "safe passage" through the school. They could use your name as the "emperor"; they can carve their own name in the medallion as well, using a pen or pointed instrument. **0:20 minutes**

DIFFERENTIATE

INCLUSION

Work in Pairs If some students have disabilities, consider pairing them with other students who can read the documents aloud to them. You may also want to give students the option of recording their responses.

PRE-AP

Research Marco Polo's Book Ask students to research *The Travels of Marco Polo*. They may be able to find and copy other pictures from the book to explain and share with the class. They should report on how the book was written and what people learned from it, true or false.

Press **mt** *in the Student eEdition for modified text.*

See the Chapter Planner for more strategies for differentiation.

SYNTHESIZE & WRITE

ANSWERS

1. Responses will vary.

2. Responses will vary.

3. Possible response: By revitalizing the Silk Roads and using foreigners to advertise Chinese products, the Khans promoted and increased trade.

4. Students' paragraphs should include their topic sentence from Step 3 and provide several details from the documents to support the sentence.

3.1 Return to Chinese Rule

After a challenging period of Mongol rule, the Chinese people found an unlikely rescuer in a peasant who led China's rebellion. China's next two emperors set out to restore the country to greatness. The Ming dynasty's capital was a spectacular new seat of power that would be used continuously for 500 years.

MAIN IDEA

The Ming dynasty restored China to greatness.

A NEW LEADERSHIP

By the 1360s, Mongol rule had weakened and rebellions broke out. The son of a peasant, Zhu Yuanzhang (joo yoo-ahn-jahng), emerged as a leader. In 1368, the rebels began driving the Mongols north of the Great Wall, eventually bringing an end to Mongol rule. Zhu declared himself **Hongwu** (hung-woo), or the first emperor of the **Ming** dynasty.

The Chinese again ruled China, and Hongwu set out to restore the country to greatness. He could be paranoid, controlling, and cruel, but he worked hard to improve the lives of peasants. Hongwu rebuilt China's agriculture system and supported the growth of manufacturing. He cut government spending and established efficient taxation. He based his rule on the principles of the Tang and Song dynasties, restoring Confucian values. Notices in villages outlined government policy and expectations of moral behavior.

Hongwu's son **Yongle** (yung-loh) was, like his father, a suspicious, ruthless, and tyrannical ruler. However, he also effectively continued his father's work rebuilding China. Yongle sponsored sea expeditions and encouraged local governments to build schools for commoners. He also sponsored great literary works and led armies to suppress China's neighbors.

IMPERIAL PALACE

Like many Chinese emperors, Yongle moved the imperial capital—this time north, to Beijing. This location placed Yongle near his supporters and closer to his armies guarding China's borders. Beijing was well organized. It was laid out in a grid aligned with the points of the compass and surrounded by 14 miles of 40-foot walls. To feed the vast numbers of people who flocked to the capital, Yongle extended the Grand Canal even farther, using advanced engineering to carry boats uphill.

At Beijing's heart was the Imperial Palace, or Forbidden City—so named because few were admitted and only with the emperor's permission. The Forbidden City would be the center of imperial power and government for the next 500 years. It took an estimated one million workers nearly 15 years to complete the palace, which was an architectural marvel. The huge complex boasted hundreds of buildings that towered over Beijing. It included luxurious private residences for the imperial family and more than 100,000 servants. The city's rectangular, symmetrical, and compass-aligned design was said to be in perfect harmony with the world. It remains the world's largest palace—the perfect place for the emperor to fulfill his role as a connection between the will of heaven and the practical rule of Earth.

FORBIDDEN CITY

Governments are often housed in imposing buildings that reflect the power of politics. But few are as impressive as the Imperial Palace in Beijing.

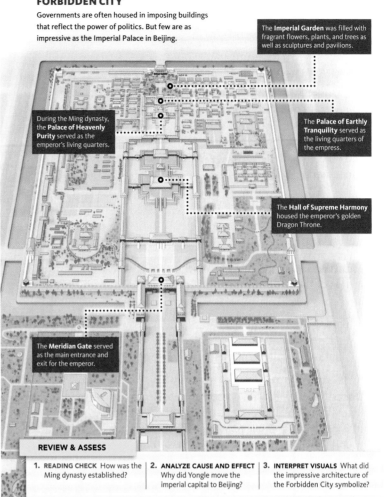

The **Imperial Garden** was filled with fragrant flowers, plants, and trees as well as sculptures and pavilions.

During the Ming dynasty, the **Palace of Heavenly Purity** served as the emperor's living quarters.

The **Palace of Earthly Tranquility** served as the living quarters of the empress.

The **Hall of Supreme Harmony** housed the emperor's golden Dragon Throne.

The **Meridian Gate** served as the main entrance and exit for the emperor.

REVIEW & ASSESS

1. **READING CHECK** How was the Ming dynasty established?

2. **ANALYZE CAUSE AND EFFECT** Why did Yongle move the imperial capital to Beijing?

3. **INTERPRET VISUALS** What did the impressive architecture of the Forbidden City symbolize?

537

PLAN

OBJECTIVE

Identify how the Ming dynasty restored China's greatness.

CRITICAL THINKING SKILLS FOR LESSON 3.1

- Identify Main Ideas and Details
- Monitor Comprehension
- Analyze Cause and Effect
- Interpret Visuals
- Make Inferences
- Compare and Contrast

ESSENTIAL QUESTION

What legacy did China leave to the modern world?

The Ming dynasty restored the Chinese to power and encouraged the growth of education, literature, and the arts. Lesson 3.1 also describes improvement in the lives of peasants and a renewed respect for agriculture.

BACKGROUND FOR THE TEACHER

A Chinese peasant, Zhu Yuanzhang, led a long but successful rebellion against the Mongols and eventually ousted them, starting the Ming Dynasty. Hongwu, as he called himself, set out to rebuild China. His was a very autocratic reign, but he supported and improved the lives of peasants and restored the government back to Confucian values.

Hongwu's son Yongle succeeded him and continued the rebuilding of China. He sponsored Zheng He's sea expeditions (Lesson 3.2) and encouraged education and writing literature. He also changed the capital to Beijing, where he had the Forbidden City built.

DIGITAL RESOURCES myNGconnect.com

TEACHER RESOURCES & ASSESSMENT

 Reading and Note-Taking   **Vocabulary Practice**   **Section 3 Quiz**

STUDENT RESOURCES

 NG Chapter Gallery

INTRODUCE & ENGAGE

COMPARE AND CONTRAST

Ask students if any have visited the White House or the U.S. Capitol in Washington, D.C. Encourage them to give a brief description of each. **ASK:** Who lives in a palace? *(kings, queens, royalty)* **ASK:** Why doesn't our U.S. president live in a palace? *(Possible response: The founders of the United States did not want leaders to be royalty, but elected by the people. A palace suggests power that they did not want to give the president.)* Have students preview the illustration of the Forbidden City in the lesson. **0:05 minutes**

TEACH

GUIDED DISCUSSION

1. **Make Inferences** Write these adjectives on the board and discuss their meanings with students: *paranoid, controlling, cruel, suspicious, ruthless,* and *tyrannical.* Tell students that these words describe the personalities of both Hongwu and Yongle. **ASK:** How do you think the leaders became that way? *(Possible responses: Mongol rule had been repressive; Hongwu's life had been very rough; they needed to be tough and ruthless to defeat the Mongols and to keep power.)*

2. **Compare and Contrast** If you were a peasant, how might your life have changed since the Ming dynasty got rid of Mongol rule? *(It would be much improved; the Mongols were cruel and taxed peasants heavily, pushing many off their land; the Ming dynasty improved peasants' lives, established schools for commoners, and rebuilt the agriculture system.)*

INTERPRET VISUALS

Have students examine the illustration of the Forbidden City. Point out the symmetry and the compass-aligned design. Have volunteers read aloud the captions. **ASK:** Who lived in the Forbidden City? *(the royal family and their 100,000 servants)* Remind students that the Imperial Palace is still the largest palace in the world. Encourage students to give their opinions about both the architecture and the entire complex. **0:10 minutes**

ACTIVE OPTIONS

Critical Viewing: NG Image Gallery Have students explore the entire NG Image Gallery for images of palaces, monuments, large statues, or manmade architectural wonders and choose two of the items to compare and contrast, either in written form or verbally with a partner. Ask questions that will inspire this process, such as: How are these monuments or palaces alike? How are they different? Where and when were they built? Why did you select these two items? **0:10 minutes**

On Your Feet: Design a Palace Point out the luxury and perfection of the Forbidden City. Encourage students to think about what they would want their own palace to look like and contain. Have

students design their own palace, either an overview of the grounds and buildings similar to the illustration in the lesson, or particular buildings or special parts. Remind them that cost is not a problem. They can make a map, an architectural blueprint, or a drawing or painting of a finished palace. Allow them to share their dream palaces with the class. **0:10 minutes**

DIFFERENTIATE

STRIVING READERS

Play the "I Am . . ." Game Individually and quietly assign two students the name "Hongwu" and two others "Yongle." Have each student write a one-sentence clue beginning with "I am." Have students take turns reading clues and calling on other students to guess which emperor each speaker is pretending to be.

GIFTED & TALENTED

Research the Forbidden City Have students choose one part of the Forbidden City to research on the Internet. Their assignment is to provide more visual detail about that part of the city. They can focus on a particular building or on the layout of an area. They can sketch, diagram, or print out pictures of the building or area. Have them label and hang the visuals around the classroom for viewing.

Press **mt** in the Student eEdition for modified text.

See the Chapter Planner for more strategies for differentiation.

REVIEW & ASSESS

ANSWERS

1. Hongwu led a long rebellion and drove the Mongols north of the Great Wall. He declared himself emperor and started the Ming dynasty.

2. Beijing was closer to his supporters and armies; it was farther north and closer to the border.

3. It symbolized perfect harmony with the world, so the emperor could be the connector between the will of heaven and the ruling of Earth.

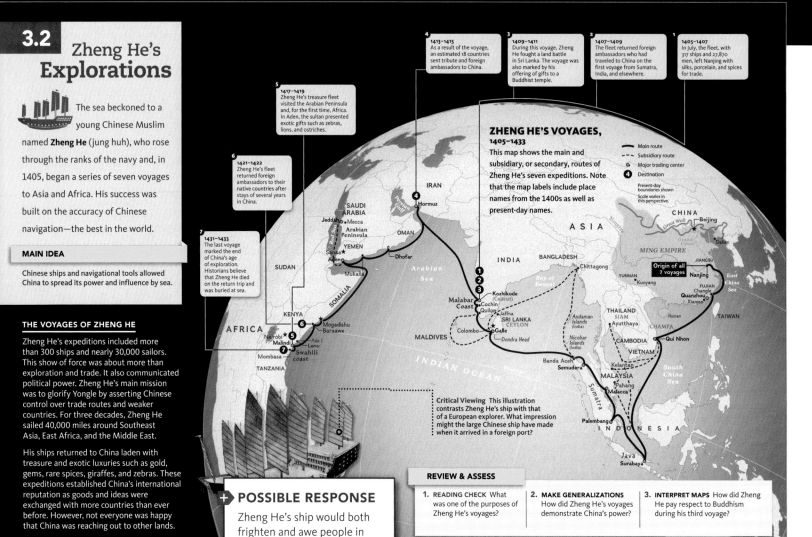

3.2

Zheng He's Explorations

The sea beckoned to a young Chinese Muslim named **Zheng He** (jung huh), who rose through the ranks of the navy and, in 1405, began a series of seven voyages to Asia and Africa. His success was built on the accuracy of Chinese navigation—the best in the world.

MAIN IDEA

Chinese ships and navigational tools allowed China to spread its power and influence by sea.

THE VOYAGES OF ZHENG HE

Zheng He's expeditions included more than 300 ships and nearly 30,000 sailors. This show of force was about more than exploration and trade. It also communicated political power. Zheng He's main mission was to glorify Yongle by asserting Chinese control over trade routes and weaker countries. For three decades, Zheng He sailed 40,000 miles around Southeast Asia, East Africa, and the Middle East.

His ships returned to China laden with treasure and exotic luxuries such as gold, gems, rare spices, giraffes, and zebras. These expeditions established China's international reputation as goods and ideas were exchanged with more countries than ever before. However, not everyone was happy that China was reaching out to other lands.

538 CHAPTER 18

5 1417–1419
Zheng He's treasure fleet visited the Arabian Peninsula and, for the first time, Africa. In Aden, the sultan presented exotic gifts such as zebras, lions, and ostriches.

6 1421–1422
Zheng He's fleet returned foreign ambassadors to their native countries after stays of several years in China.

7 1431–1433
The last voyage marked the end of China's age of exploration. Historians believe that Zheng He died on the return trip and was buried at sea.

4 1413–1415
As a result of the voyage, an estimated 18 countries sent tribute and foreign ambassadors to China.

3 1409–1411
During this voyage, Zheng He fought a land battle in Sri Lanka. The voyage was also marked by his offering of gifts to a Buddhist temple.

2 1407–1409
The fleet returned foreign ambassadors who had traveled to China on the first voyage from Sumatra, India, and elsewhere.

1 1405–1407
In July, the fleet, with 317 ships and 27,870 men, left Nanjing with silks, porcelain, and spices for trade.

ZHENG HE'S VOYAGES, 1405–1433

This map shows the main and subsidiary, or secondary, routes of Zheng He's seven expeditions. Note that the map labels include place names from the 1400s as well as present-day names.

- Main route
- Subsidiary route
- Major trading center
- **4** Destination

Present-day boundaries shown
Scale varies in this perspective.

Critical Viewing This illustration contrasts Zheng He's ship with that of a European explorer. What impression might the large Chinese ship have made when it arrived in a foreign port?

+ POSSIBLE RESPONSE

Zheng He's ship would both frighten and awe people in the countries he visited.

REVIEW & ASSESS

1. **READING CHECK** What was one of the purposes of Zheng He's voyages?

2. **MAKE GENERALIZATIONS** How did Zheng He's voyages demonstrate China's power?

3. **INTERPRET MAPS** How did Zheng He pay respect to Buddhism during his third voyage?

539

PLAN

OBJECTIVE

Identify how Chinese spread their influence across the world by sea.

CRITICAL THINKING SKILLS FOR LESSON 3.2

- Identify Main Ideas and Details
- Monitor Comprehension
- Make Generalizations
- Interpret Maps
- Identify
- Evaluate

ESSENTIAL QUESTION

What legacy did China leave to the modern world?

Zheng He's voyages spread Chinese influence and trade throughout the world, and he brought back foreign influence, ideas, and goods to China. Lesson 3.2 describes the ships and routes Zheng He took to travel farther and to more places than anyone had gone before.

BACKGROUND FOR THE TEACHER

Zheng He's wooden treasure ships were first developed in the 11th century. Some were 440 feet long and 185 feet across with multiple decks and watertight compartments below decks. The ships were designed with a deep keel, a very large rudder in the stern, and a complex system of rigging in the sails.

INTRODUCE & ENGAGE

ACTIVATE PRIOR KNOWLEDGE

Invite students to share what they know about European explorers from their knowledge of U.S. and European history. Ask these questions and write students' responses on the board:

- Which explorers have you studied?
- What countries did they come from?
- What areas did they explore?
- What reasons did they have for exploring?

Then ask students if they know of any Asian explorers. Tell them that they will learn about a Chinese explorer who commanded a larger fleet than later European explorers. **0:10 minutes**

TEACH

GUIDED DISCUSSION

1. **Identify** What did Zheng He bring back to China from his voyages? *(tribute from foreign countries, people, ideas, and goods, such as gold, gems, spices, plants, and animals)*

2. **Evaluate** What were Zheng He's noteworthy accomplishments? *(Possible responses: He traveled 40,000 miles to more countries than had ever been visited; he had the largest ships with the best navigation tools; he opened trade to many countries; he showed off China's power and luxurious goods; he commanded 300 ships with 30,000 sailors in seven trips; he brought back tributes.)* Which accomplishment do you think was most important to Emperor Yongle? *(Possible response: showing off China's power)*

INTERPRET MAPS

Have students study the map of Zheng He's voyages, paying particular attention to his destinations and the heavy line that shows his main route. Conduct a class Map Bee to see who can answer these questions accurately and quickly:

- What present-day country did he reach on his first three voyages? *(India)*
- What islands did he visit on the way? *(Java, Sumatra, Malaysia, Sri Lanka)*
- What was the destination of the fourth voyage? *(Iran and the Red Sea)*
- Why would Zheng He take a side trip to Mecca off the Red Sea? *(Mecca is sacred to Muslims)*
- What continent did he visit for his last three voyages? *(Africa)*

0:10 minutes

ACTIVE OPTIONS

On Your Feet: Role-Play Exploration Station some students around the classroom to represent different places where Zheng

He stopped on his voyages. Have other students represent Zheng He and his fleet and travel around the classroom, moving from right to left and stopping at each location. Students should role-play the encounters between Zheng He and the people he met on his travels. **0:10 minutes**

NG Learning Framework: Learn About Zheng He

ATTITUDE: **Curiosity**
SKILL: **Observation**
KNOWLEDGE: **New Frontiers**

Ask students to choose one destination of Zheng He's voyages and find out what he might have seen and experienced in that place and at that time. They should research the people and culture of that destination. Then they should write up their observations as Zheng He might have written in a journal. **0:10 minutes**

DIFFERENTIATE

INCLUSION

Read the Map Have students study the map of Zheng He's voyages. Help them understand the map and its captions. Point out that Zheng He traveled west from the point where he started in China. Explain that the callouts are in chronological order, but, like the map, need to be read from right to left. Call on volunteers to read each callout and point to the places referred to on the map.

GIFTED & TALENTED

Write Travel Tweets Ask students to imagine that they are living in one of the countries visited by Zheng He. Have them write a series of tweets to a friend about Zheng He, his fleet, and the goods he is carrying. You might label the walls of the classroom with some of Zheng He's destinations and post the tweets on the appropriate wall.

> Amazing ships! Makes ours look tiny. LOL!

Press (mt) *in the Student eEdition for modified text.*

See the Chapter Planner for more strategies for differentiation.

REVIEW & ASSESS

ANSWERS

1. Possible responses include the following: to show China's political power; to glorify Yongle; to explore and establish control over trade routes; to collect tribute; to sell China's goods; and to establish an international reputation.

2. The size and quality of the ships, the distances he traveled, the many countries he visited, and the tributes he collected showed China's political power.

3. He offered gifts to a Buddhist temple in Sri Lanka.

China Turns Inward

An ostrich is believed to bury its head in the sand to avoid seeing its enemies. But that doesn't stop its enemies from seeing it—or attacking it. China could have learned a valuable lesson on what not to do from this bird.

MAIN IDEA

China isolated itself from the world, but foreign influences still brought the downfall of the dynastic system.

ISOLATION POLICY

China's great explorer, Zheng He, died during his seventh voyage and was buried at sea. His death marked the end of China's maritime expeditions. There were competing government factions for and against exploration, and when the emperor Zhengtong (jung-tung) took power in 1435, he stopped all future voyages, claiming that they were too expensive and they imported dangerous foreign ideas.

The Chinese considered themselves the most civilized people on Earth. They felt they were surrounded by barbarians and did not need the rest of the world. After a period of foreign rule and much instability in their history, it was understandable that the Chinese reacted this way. However, the effect of Zhengtong's decision was to surrender control of the region's seas and trade to ambitious European nations and Japanese pirates.

In the following centuries, China entered a long period of **isolationism**, during which it rejected foreign contact and influences. The government took up a defensive attitude and geared the economy toward self-sufficiency. Rulers banned foreign trade, kicked out foreigners, and tried to eliminate foreign influences from Chinese society.

Symbolic of this effort was the extension of the Great Wall, which the government rebuilt entirely in stone and completed with 25,000 watchtowers along its 5,500-mile length. The wall was a formidable physical sign of China's defensive isolation.

THE LAST DYNASTY

The world, however, would not leave China alone. Starting in the mid-1500s, the Ming dynasty faced more and more challenges. Pirate raids were common along the southeast coast. The Mongols invaded the north, and Japan conquered Chinese-protected Korea. The cost of these wars, on top of a lavish imperial lifestyle and corruption at court, spelled financial difficulties. The peasants paid taxes for all this while they were already coping with widespread crop failures, famine, and disease. The people rebelled, and Ming authority crumbled.

In 1644, rebels took over Beijing. In despair, the last of the Ming emperors hanged himself from a tree. Tribes north of the wall, the **Manchus**, united and took advantage of the confusion to seize power. They easily defeated the rebels and founded the **Qing** (chihng) dynasty.

China would remain under the Qing's foreign rule for nearly 300 years. The Qing kept native customs and the Ming government structure but also introduced some of their own traditions. They forced Chinese men to wear their hair as the Qing did, in a long braid. The Qing continued

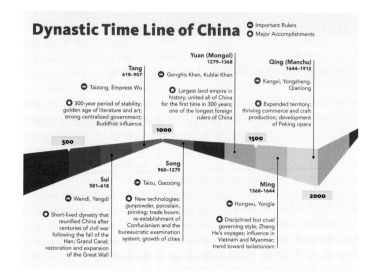

Dynastic Time Line of China

- 🔵 Important Rulers
- 🔵 Major Accomplishments

Tang 618–907
- 🔵 Taizong, Empress Wu
- 🔵 300-year period of stability; golden age of literature and art; strong centralized government; Buddhist influence

Yuan (Mongol) 1279–1368
- 🔵 Genghis Khan, Kublai Khan
- 🔵 Largest land empire in history; united all of China for the first time in 300 years; one of the longest foreign rulers of China

Qing (Manchu) 1644–1912
- 🔵 Kangxi, Yongzheng, Qianlong
- 🔵 Expanded territory; thriving commerce and craft production; development of Peking opera

500 **1000** **1500**

Sui 581–618
- 🔵 Wendi, Yangdi
- 🔵 Short-lived dynasty that reunified China after centuries of civil war following the fall of the Han; Grand Canal; restoration and expansion of the Great Wall

Song 960–1279
- 🔵 Taizu, Gaozong
- 🔵 New technologies: gunpowder, porcelain, printing; trade boom; re-establishment of Confucianism and the bureaucratic examination system; growth of cities

Ming 1368–1644
- 🔵 Hongwu, Yongle
- 🔵 Disciplined but cruel governing style; Zheng He's voyages; influence in Vietnam and Myanmar; trend toward isolationism

2000

China's isolationism, although they did embark on some successful wars that expanded the empire by the end of the 18th century. With peace and prosperity, the population started to increase again, reaching 300 million by 1800. At that time, many Chinese began to migrate to new lands that the Ming had conquered earlier.

Since 1514, European traders had been traveling to China. The Europeans were building strong trading colonies across Asia. The Qing tried to restrict European trade and refused to buy European goods. During the late 1700s, frustrated British merchants began smuggling the drug opium into China. They soon had a successful trade, but addiction ruined countless Chinese lives. The resulting Opium Wars weakened China internally and internationally. European powers seized Chinese territories and took control of the economy. After 1850, a string of rebellions weakened China, and, in February 1912, revolutionary forces overthrew the Qing dynasty. Two thousand years of imperial rule had come to a decisive end.

REVIEW & ASSESS

1. **READING CHECK** How did China try to isolate itself from foreign influences?

2. **COMPARE AND CONTRAST** How did China's policy toward the outside world at the beginning of the Ming dynasty differ from that at the end of the Ming Dynasty?

3. **INTEGRATE VISUALS** How does the time line illustrate the recurring theme of the "dynastic cycle" in Chinese history?

PLAN

OBJECTIVE

Identify how China isolated itself and eventually lost its dynastic system.

CRITICAL THINKING SKILLS FOR LESSON 3.3

- Identify Main Ideas and Details
- Monitor Comprehension
- Compare and Contrast
- Integrate Visuals
- Analyze Cause and Effect

ESSENTIAL QUESTION

What legacy did China leave to the modern world?

China's isolationism in this period limited its influence on the modern world, but foreigners continued to visit China. Lesson 3.3 explains how European powers eventually opened China up to foreign trade.

BACKGROUND FOR THE TEACHER

Most of the official records of Zheng He's voyages were destroyed after his death. New laws made it illegal to build large ships to sail the oceans. The Chinese still exported silk, porcelain, and tea, but they stopped importing European goods and thought Western influence would weaken their culture. As a result, European and Japanese merchants and pirates took control of the seas. More foreign visitors and missionaries began coming to China in the mid-1500s.

DIGITAL RESOURCES myNGconnect.com

TEACHER RESOURCES & ASSESSMENT

 Reading and Note-Taking

 Vocabulary Practice

 Section 3 Quiz

STUDENT RESOURCES

 NG Chapter Gallery

INTRODUCE & ENGAGE

ANALYZE SYMBOLS

Ask a volunteer to describe the Statue of Liberty or show a picture of it. **ASK:** What is the function of this statue? What is its message to the world? *(It is a symbol of our invitation to people from other countries to come to our country and experience freedom; its message is "Welcome.")* **ASK:** What function did China's Great Wall serve? What is its message to the world? *(Its function is protection from foreign invaders; its message is "Keep out.")* Explain that during this next period in China's history, the Great Wall was rebuilt in stone and extended even farther; most of it still exists today. Point out that both the Statue of Liberty and the Great Wall are symbols that have opposite messages for the world. Finally, introduce the word *isolationism,* meaning "the belief that a country should keep itself separate from other countries." **0:05** minutes

TEACH

GUIDED DISCUSSION

1. **Analyze Causes** Point out that the causes of the fall of dynasties were similar. **ASK:** What led to the fall of the Ming dynasty? *(pirate raids from Japan, wars with the Mongols and Japan, crop failures, famine, rebellions, cost of wars, weak leadership)*

2. **Analyze Effects** In what ways did isolationism help China? How did it hurt China? *(Help: It initially prevented foreign powers from taking over China. It allowed China to become more self-sufficient economically. Hurt: It caused them to lose power in the seas; it made China a target for foreign merchants; it allowed European countries to create trade colonies across Asia; it led to the Opium Wars.)*

MORE INFORMATION

The Opium Wars Chinese merchants had to be paid in silver, which was hard for European countries that had gone to the gold standard. The British started smuggling opium to China when they couldn't sell other products. Opium went from being a medicinal product to a recreational drug and caused the addiction and deaths of many Chinese. China fought this trade in a series of wars called the Opium Wars that were costly and weakened the Qing dynasty.

ACTIVE OPTIONS

On Your Feet: Name That Dynasty Have three or four volunteers use the time line to write individual facts about each dynasty on separate slips of paper. For example, they can write "Yangdi" or "short-lived dynasty" on the top of the paper, "Sui Dynasty" on the bottom of the paper. Each of the 6 dynasties should have three to four slips of paper telling one fact about it.

Divide the class into small groups and have them play "Name That Dynasty." Designate each volunteer as an emcee; give that person a set of the paper clues. The other students in each group will guess the dynasty. Whoever guesses correctly gets the slip of paper; at the end whoever has most slips is the winner. **0:10** minutes

NG Learning Framework: Learn About Different Dynasties

SKILL: Problem-Solving
KNOWLEDGE: **Our Human Story**

Challenge pairs of students to create a pie chart out of the time line in the lesson. They need to look at the years covered by each dynasty and figure out how to show the percentage of time each took in relation to the rest. They should color their charts and make sure to label each section of the chart with its dynasty. **0:10** minutes

DIFFERENTIATE

ENGLISH LANGUAGE LEARNERS

Analyze Word Roots Students may benefit from an introduction to the Latin word *insula,* meaning "island." Remind them an island is separate from a mainland. Display the word *isolate* and explain that it means "to keep separate". Then display the word *isolation* and explain that it means "the state of being separate." Finally, remind students that the word part *ism* indicates a belief. Therefore, *isolationism* means "the belief in keeping separate." Tell them that the Chinese during this period believed that isolationism would keep out foreign influences and strengthen their country.

Press (**mt**) *in the Student eEdition for modified text.*

See the Chapter Planner for more strategies for differentiation.

REVIEW & ASSESS

ANSWERS

1. Rulers stopped funding sea voyages to foreign lands, banned foreign trade, kicked out foreigners, extended and rebuilt the Great Wall, discouraged foreign influences, adopted a defensive attitude, and tried to make their economy self-sufficient.

2. At the beginning of the Ming dynasty, Zheng He's voyages caused great commerce with many foreign nations, including ideas, goods, and people; by the end of the dynasty, China isolated itself from foreign influence, trade, ideas, and people.

3. At the beginning of each new dynasty, strong rulers united parts of China and inspired progress. Later instability and problems would set in, causing the dynasty to fall apart until a new strong leader took over, repeating the cycle. The dynasties lasted many years but in each case only lasted for two or three strong rulers.

Exploring China's
Diverse Cultures

"When I was little I would identify the pieces of our Thanksgiving turkey and then reassemble the bones after the meal," laughs Christine Lee, a bioarchaeologist and a National Geographic Explorer. "My parents thought I was going to be a doctor!" Instead, she entered a relatively new science, bioarchaeology, which combines biology and archaeology, using the tools of both sciences to find out about the way ancient people lived.

^
This pit of human skulls was found during the excavation of Zhengzhou, a city from the Shang period about 3,750 years ago. Burial customs varied among several distinct cultures in early China.

MAIN IDEA

Bioarchaeology is providing insights into ancient China and Mongolia.

SKELETAL SECRETS

Christine Lee uses biological techniques to examine human skeletons found in archaeological sites. These new techniques allow researchers to piece together clues that tell the stories of long-dead individuals and groups. It is amazing what Dr. Lee can learn from even a single tooth.

A skeleton reveals even more. "Bones can tell me a person's sex, age, and whether they worked hard or had an easy life," she says. "Were they right- or left-handed, did they walk long distances, ride horses, or spend lots of time kneeling? Did they have arthritis, leprosy, tuberculosis? Did they get kicked by a cow, fall off a horse, break their nose in a fight? Bones show me all this and more," says Dr. Lee. By comparing particular skeletal characteristics across populations, she can see how ancient peoples were connected. She can also find details that provide clues to ancient people's ancestral origins, movements, and marriages.

Dr. Christine Lee in the field

PUZZLES FROM THE PAST

Dr. Lee has worked all over the world but has a particular interest in Asia. In Mongolia, she was the lead bioarchaeologist on a team excavating a cemetery of the Xiongnu (shung-noo) people. These were the nomads whose raids drove China to build the 2,000-mile-long Great Wall to keep them out. The dig site was in the middle of the desert, a thousand miles from the Mongolian capital. "We stopped in a village and asked for directions and

were told the site was cursed," she says. "When we got there it was eerily quiet . . . I always said if I ever felt the skeletons didn't want me there I would leave. I decided we could study the skeletons when they were brought to the museum—then we left."

Back at the museum, Dr. Lee's studies highlighted cultural differences between the ancient Xiongnu and their Chinese neighbors to the south. "The ancestors of today's Mongolians rode horses, ate meat, and had a certain cowboy wildness compared to the rigid society and structure on the other side of the Great Wall," she notes. This cultural contrast was reinforced by her excavations of another independent kingdom, the Dian (dee-ahn), a city society of farmers and fishers in southern China. Dr. Lee's findings suggest that the Xiongnu and the Chinese had very little interaction and almost never intermarried.

Dr. Lee feels a responsibility to uncover the stories of these cultures in China's history: "When I look at a 2,000-year-old skull it's like I'm saying, 'Don't worry. I will tell the world about you—I'll describe what your life was like and prove it had meaning.'"

REVIEW & ASSESS

1. **READING CHECK** How is bioarchaeology helping scientists gain insights into ancient China and Mongolia?

2. **IDENTIFY MAIN IDEAS AND DETAILS** What can Dr. Lee tell about ancient people's lives from their bones?

3. **COMPARE AND CONTRAST** According to Dr. Lee's studies, what important cultural differences existed between the Xiongnu people and their Chinese neighbors?

OBJECTIVE

Explain how bioarchaeology helps people learn about ancient China and Mongolia.

CRITICAL THINKING SKILLS FOR LESSON 3.4

- Identify Main Ideas and Details
- Compare and Contrast
- Evaluate
- Ask Questions
- Monitor Comprehension
- Make Inferences

ESSENTIAL QUESTION

What legacy did China leave to the modern world?

Bioarcheologists are uncovering secrets about the many cultures incorporated into China's diverse population. Lesson 3.4 describes the work of Dr. Christine Lee in learning more about the Xiongnu people in Mongolia.

BACKGROUND FOR THE TEACHER

The term *bioarchaeology* came into use in 1972 as an offshoot of zooarchaeology, the study of animal bones as part of archaeology. Now the term extends to studying human bones. To learn more about ancient peoples, bioarchaeologists study burials, diets, teeth, health, nutrition, paleodemography (demographics of ancient peoples), paleogenetics, occupations, and behaviors.

DIGITAL RESOURCES myNGconnect.com

TEACHER RESOURCES & ASSESSMENT

 Reading and Note-Taking

 Vocabulary Practice

 Section 3 Quiz

STUDENT RESOURCES

 NG Chapter Gallery

INTRODUCE & ENGAGE

BRAINSTORM ETHNIC GROUPS

Have students work in groups of four to identify different ethnic groups that are part of their community. Record those listed by one group and see if any group has more ethnic groups to add. Then ask students how closely these groups interact—Do they live near one another, or do they maintain their different spaces? Are they tolerant of each other, all mixed together, or do they practice different ways of living? Remind students that in China's long history, people from different ethnic groups ruled some dynasties. Explain that there are 56 officially recognized ethnic groups in China today, with the Han Chinese being the largest group (90 percent). `0:05` minutes

TEACH

GUIDED DISCUSSION

1. **Make Inferences** Dr. Lee discovered that two ancient ethnic groups did not interact very much. Why do you think the Xiongnu and Chinese did not interact more? *(They had different lifestyles, valued different things, had little in common, and were not interested in each other.)*

2. **Evaluate** Dr. Lee left an eerie burial site that she had heard was cursed. Do you agree with her actions? Why or why not? *(Responses will vary.)*

ASK QUESTIONS

Have students study the picture of the burial pit and ask them what is unusual about it. *(It contains only human skulls.)* **ASK:** If you were an archaeologist, what questions might you have about this gravesite? *(Possible responses: Why are only skulls here? How were the skulls separated from the skeletons? To whom did these skulls belong? How did these people die?)* `0:10` minutes

ACTIVE OPTIONS

On Your Feet: Guess the Culture Divide the class into three groups. One group should brainstorm details that might describe the culture of the Xiongnu and write them individually on slips of paper; the second group should write details that might describe the culture of the Chinese neighbors in the south. Mix up the two groups' clues. Let volunteers read the clues to the last group, the guessing group, to see if they correctly guess the culture. `0:10` minutes

NG Learning Framework: Learn About Archaeology

ATTITUDE: **Curiosity**
KNOWLEDGE: **Our Human Story**

Have students work together to research career choices in the fields of archaeology and science. They should find out what the job is like, what and how much education is necessary, what salary it yields, and where the person would work. Have them create a "Career Wheel" from these facts. They should write succinctly about each career separately on a 3" x 5" index card. The cards can be hole-punched and put together on a spindle to be shared. `0:10` minutes

DIFFERENTIATE

STRIVING READERS

Build a Cluster Map Post the words "Skeletal Secrets" in a large circle on the board. Ask students to look for what Dr. Christine Lee learns from ancient bones. They should write words or phrases that they find in the "Skeletal Secrets" subheading of the lesson. Then have volunteers help create a Word Web by drawing lines from the circle and copying a word or phrase that they read. When finished, have students copy the web as a way to take notes.

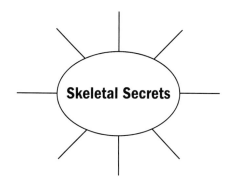

GIFTED & TALENTED

Archeological Finds Have interested students look up recent archaeological finds in China, such as the tomb of the emperor Yangdi or ancient bridges on the Wei River. They can use the Internet to gather information and pictures, if possible, about one such find. Let them share their information and pictures with the class.

Press **mt** *in the Student eEdition for modified text.*

See the Chapter Planner for more strategies for differentiation.

REVIEW & ASSESS

ANSWERS

1. By using modern biology to study ancient remains, bioarchaeology allows scientists to discover physical details about individuals within an ancient culture, including how they lived and interacted with other cultures.

2. Bones can tell her about people's sex, age, the physical hardness of their lives, diseases or injuries they had, their diet, their ancestry, travels, and marriages.

3. The Xiongnu were a little wild, riding horses, eating meat, and living outdoors. The Chinese led much more structured lives, were citified, and lived in a more rigid society.

VOCABULARY

On your paper, write the vocabulary word that completes each of the following sentences.

1. General Wendi's conquests managed to _____ north and south China and establish a strong new dynasty called the Sui.

2. During the Song dynasty, agricultural techniques improved and rice became China's _____.

3. A strong, nearly see-through ceramic called _____ was an especially valuable trade item.

4. The Mongols were a loose collection of nomadic tribes who roamed, raided, herded, and fought across the vast _____ of northwest China.

5. During Emperor Zhengtong's rule, China pursued a policy of _____, rejecting foreign contact and influences.

6. Shortly after Zheng He's voyages, China entered a long period of _____, during which it rejected foreign contact and influences.

READING STRATEGY

7. **DRAW CONCLUSIONS** If you haven't already, complete your graphic organizer to draw conclusions about the impact of the Tang, Song, and Ming dynasties on Chinese civilization. Then answer the question.

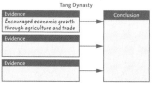

Which dynasty do you think had the greatest impact on Chinese civilization? Explain your reasoning.

544 CHAPTER 18

MAIN IDEAS

Answer the following questions. Support your answers with evidence from the chapter.

8. What happened after the collapse of the Han dynasty in A.D. 220? LESSON 1.1

9. Why did many Chinese turn away from traditional Confucianism and embrace Buddhism? LESSON 1.2

10. What factors contributed to China's growth during the Tang and Song dynasties? LESSON 1.3

11. How did the Mongols gain power in China? LESSON 2.1

12. During the Yuan dynasty, how did the Mongols treat the Chinese under their rule? LESSON 2.2

13. How did the Ming dynasty restore Chinese rule to China? LESSON 3.1

14. What were the goals of Zheng He's voyages through Asia and Africa? LESSON 3.2

15. Why did China adopt a policy of isolationism during the Ming dynasty? LESSON 3.3

CRITICAL THINKING

Answer the following questions. Support your answers with evidence from the chapter.

16. **ANALYZE CAUSE AND EFFECT** Why was Wendi able to win the support of China's population?

17. **ANALYZE CAUSE AND EFFECT** How did Buddhism and Daoism influence Confucianism?

18. **EVALUATE** Which ancient Chinese invention benefitted people most: moveable type, porcelain, gunpowder, or the compass?

19. **SEQUENCE EVENTS** Describe the order of events in the Mongol creation of the world's largest empire.

20. **MAKE INFERENCES** How did Zheng He's maritime expeditions expand Chinese influence and demonstrate China's power and wealth?

21. **YOU DECIDE** Was Mongol rule good or bad for China? Support your opinion with evidence from the chapter.

INTERPRET VISUALS

Study the photograph of the seated Buddha statues in the Yungang Grottoes, a UNESCO World Heritage site in the Shanxi province of China. Then answer the questions that follow.

22. What spiritual qualities are conveyed through these statues of Buddha?

23. Why do you think these statues were carved in such a large scale?

ANALYZE SOURCES

Read the following poem, written by Li Po, one of the most popular Chinese poets of the Tang dynasty.

Zazen on Ching-t'ing Mountain

The birds have vanished down the sky.
Now the last cloud drains away.

We sit together, the mountain and me,
Until only the mountain remains.

24. What is one Daoist or Buddhist ideal that is reflected in this poem?

WRITE ABOUT HISTORY

25. **EXPOSITORY** Suppose you are a historian being interviewed about China. The interviewer asks you, "How did the Great Wall become a symbol of China's policy of isolationism at the end of the Ming dynasty?" Write your answer in a brief paragraph.

TIPS
- Take notes from Lesson 3.3, "China Turns Inward."
- Begin the paragraph with a clear topic sentence.
- Develop the paragraph with supporting details and examples of the steps China took to pursue its policy of isolationism, particularly the expansion and fortification of the Great Wall.
- Use at least two vocabulary terms from the chapter.
- Conclude with an explanation of why the Great Wall became a symbol of China's policy of isolationism.

Dynasties of China **545**

VOCABULARY ANSWERS

1. reunify
2. staple
3. porcelain
4. steppes
5. isolationism
6. isolationism

READING STRATEGY ANSWER

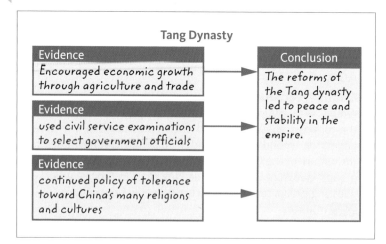

7. The Tang dynasty had the greatest impact on Chinese civilization. The peace and stability that were brought about due to Tang reforms allowed the empire to expand and a golden age to occur.

MAIN IDEAS ANSWERS

8. China had civil wars among its small kingdoms for 400 years following the collapse of the Han dynasty, until Wendi took over and started the Sui dynasty.

9. The Chinese people suffered greatly during the chaotic civil wars and needed a spiritual lift to get them through tough times. Buddhism offered comfort and hope for a better life after a cycle of reincarnation. Confucianism helped structure society through obedience to higher authorities and following a good moral code. During civil wars, there were no authority figures worth obeying and no structure.

10. Factors include a strong, stable government run by Confucian-style bureaucracy, tolerance for religions and cultures, agricultural improvements, the growth of trade yielding a strong economy, and technology leading to new inventions.

11. Genghis Khan united the Mongol tribes, creating a powerful army that conquered China by destroying cities and killing inhabitants.

12. The Mongols treated the Chinese as second-class citizens, gave them no power in the government, forced peasants off the land by taxation, and established a class system with the Chinese at the bottom.

13. The Chinese once again ruled their country, restoring Confucian values in government and society. Hongwu improved peasants' lives and rebuilt the agricultural system. Yongle sponsored sea voyages that increased trade and established Chinese power around the world.

14. Zheng He's goals were to glorify Yongle and China and to assert Chinese control over trade routes and weaker countries.

15. Rulers felt that foreigners and their ideas were dangerous to China and that China should become self-sufficient. They felt superior and did not need foreign influence.

CRITICAL THINKING ANSWERS

16. China had been in chaos for 400 years filled with civil wars. Wendi restored order, reunified northern and southern China, strengthened the government, established a new law code, established agriculture, and promoted Buddhism.

17. Buddhism and Daoism were spiritual and focused on inner guidance and good karma to achieve nirvana; Confucianism was a philosophy that focused on earthly behavior in society, especially obedience. Confucianism was useful especially for running the government, while ordinary people needed Buddhism and Daoism to offer hope for the future.

18. Responses will vary but should be accompanied by good reasons. Many will say movable type.

19. Genghis Khan united Mongol tribes into a powerful army; (in 1212) the army conquered northern China and then Iran; (in 1215) the Mongols destroyed China's capital and went on to conquer most of Asia; Kublai Khan conquered southern China (by 1271) and declared himself emperor, starting the Yuan dynasty.

20. Zheng He's huge ships sailed for 30 years to Southeast Asia, East Africa, and the Middle East. He impressed all countries with his powerful armada, established trade links and routes, brought back tribute, traveled to more countries than anyone had before, and established China's international reputation as the world's biggest traders.

21. Responses will vary, but most will say "bad." Bad: Chinese were no longer in charge of their own country; the social classes elevated foreigners and hurt the Chinese, especially peasants; peasants lost their land because of taxes; Mongol rulers wasted money on imperial projects; the Mongols were paranoid so the Chinese were very repressed. Good: the Mongols reunited all of China, expanded trade and agriculture, built roads and extended the Grand Canal, provided a postal service and an accurate calendar, and caused unemployed Chinese scholars to write more literature.

INTERPRET VISUALS ANSWERS

22. Inner peace, hope, calm, and good karma are conveyed through the statues.

23. They were large enough to be seen by many; they were an invitation to join Buddhism or a reminder to practice it; they advertised Buddhism.

ANALYZE SOURCES ANSWER

24. Responses will vary, but could include serenity, a deep connection with nature, or the shortness of human life.

WRITE ABOUT HISTORY ANSWER

25. Students' paragraphs should do the following:
   - start with a clear topic sentence
   - contain details about the extension and fortification of the Great Wall
   - contain examples of other ways China tried to achieve isolationism
   - conclude with an explanation of why the Great Wall symbolized isolationism
   - be written in a formal style

UNIT RESOURCES

On Location with National Geographic Emerging Explorer Albert Lin
Intro and Video

Interactive Map Tool

News & Updates

Available on myNGconnect

Unit Wrap-Up:
"The Search for Genghis Khan"
Feature and Video

"Divining Angkor"
National Geographic Adapted Article

"The Forgotten Road"
National Geographic Adapted Article
Student eEdition exclusive

Unit 8 Inquiry:
Leave a Legacy of Innovation

CHAPTER RESOURCES

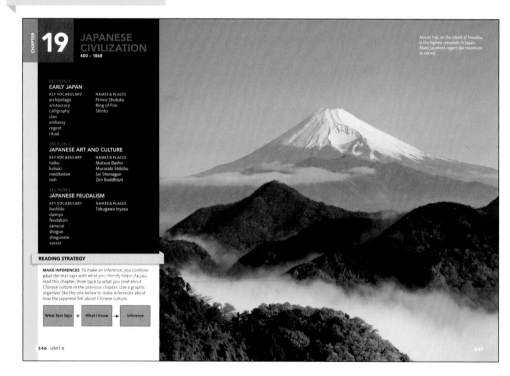

TEACHER RESOURCES & ASSESSMENT

Available on myNGconnect

Social Studies Skills Lessons
- Reading: Make Inferences
- Writing: Write an Informative Article

Formal Assessment
- Chapter 19 Tests A (on-level) & B (below-level)

Chapter 19 Answer Key

ExamView®
One-time Download

STUDENT BACKPACK *Available on myNGconnect*

- **eEdition** *(English)*   - **eEdition** *(Spanish)*   - **Handbooks**   - **Online Atlas**

For Chapter 19 Spanish resources, visit the Teacher Resource Menu page on myNGconnect.

SECTION 1 RESOURCES

EARLY JAPAN

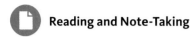 **Reading and Note-Taking**

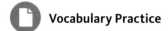 **Vocabulary Practice**

 **Section 1 Quiz**

Available on myNGconnect

LESSON 1.1 THE GEOGRAPHY OF JAPAN

- On Your Feet: Team Word Webbing
- **NG Learning Framework:** Team Island Experts

LESSON 1.2 EARLY BELIEFS AND CULTURES

- Critical Viewing: NG Chapter Gallery
- On Your Feet: Three-Step Interview

LESSON 1.3 PRINCE SHOTOKU

 **Biography** Prince Shotoku

Available on myNGconnect

- Critical Viewing: NG Image Gallery
- On Your Feet: Create a Character Map

LESSON 1.4 INFLUENCES FROM CHINA

- **NG Learning Framework:** Tell a Story
- On Your Feet: Write in Calligraphy

SECTION 2 RESOURCES

JAPANESE ART AND CULTURE

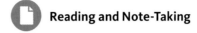 **Reading and Note-Taking**

 **Vocabulary Practice**

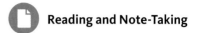 **Section 2 Quiz**

Available on myNGconnect

LESSON 2.1 LITERATURE AND THE ARTS

 **Biography** Murasaki Shikibu

Available on myNGconnect

- Critical Viewing: NG Chapter Gallery
- On Your Feet: Write a Haiku

DOCUMENT-BASED QUESTION
LESSON 2.2 POETRY AND PROSE

- **NG Learning Framework:** Write a Biography
- On Your Feet: Three Options

LESSON 2.3 ZEN BUDDHISM

- Critical Viewing: NG Image Gallery
- On Your Feet: Fishbowl

SECTION 3 RESOURCES

JAPANESE FEUDALISM

 **Reading and Note-Taking**

 **Vocabulary Practice**

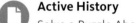 **Section 3 Quiz**

Available on myNGconnect

LESSON 3.1 SAMURAI AND SHOGUNS

 **Active History: Interactive Whiteboard Activity** Solve a Puzzle About Feudal Japan

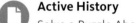 **Active History** Solve a Puzzle About Feudal Japan

Available on myNGconnect

- On Your Feet: Warrior Comparison

HISTORY THROUGH OBJECTS
LESSON 3.2 TOOLS OF THE SAMURAI

- On Your Feet: Weapons of War
- Critical Viewing: NG Image Gallery

LESSON 3.3 UNIFICATION AND ISOLATION

- **NG Learning Framework:** Geographic Effects
- On Your Feet: Two Corners

CHAPTER 19 REVIEW

STRATEGY ❶
Turn Titles into Questions

To help students set a purpose for reading, have them read the title of each lesson in a section and then turn that title into a question they believe will be answered in the lesson. Students can record their questions and write their own answers, or they can ask each other their questions.

Use with All Lessons *For example, in Lesson 1.2, the question could be, "What were the beliefs and cultures of the early Japanese?" For Lesson 1.3, the question could be, "Who was Prince Shotoku and what did he do?"*

STRATEGY ❷
Write Titles for Visuals

Have students look at the visuals as they read each lesson. Tell them to read the captions carefully. Then ask them to write a short, clear title for each visual, lesson by lesson. Their list can serve as the beginning of an outline to review later.

Use with All Lessons *For example, for Lesson 1.2, they could write, "A Shinto Shrine," or for Lesson 2.1, they could write, "Kabuki Theater."*

STRATEGY ❸
Use a Word Sort Activity

Write these words on the board and ask students to sort them into four groups of three related words each. Then have them use each group of words in a paragraph that shows how they are related.

Shinto	daimyo	Zen Buddhism	shogun
tsunami	typhoon	volcano	Confucianism
kabuki	noh	samurai	haiku

Use with Lesson 3.1

Press (mt) *in the Student eEdition for modified text.*

STRATEGY ❶
Use Echo Reading

Pair each student with a proficient reader. Have the proficient reader read aloud the Main Idea statement at the beginning of each lesson. Have the student "echo" by reading the same statement. Repeat for all the lessons in a section.

Use with All Lessons

STRATEGY ❷
Use Supported Reading

In small groups, have students read aloud the chapter lesson by lesson. At the end of each lesson, have them stop and use these frames to tell what they comprehended from the text:

- This lesson is about _____.
- One detail that stood out to me is _____.
- The vocabulary word _____ means _____.
- I don't think I understand _____.

Guide students with portions of text they do not understand. Be sure all students understand a lesson before moving on to the next one.

Use with All Lessons

STRATEGY ❶
PREP Before Reading

Have students use the PREP strategy to prepare for reading. Write this acrostic on the board:

PREP	**P**review title.
	Read Main Idea statement.
	Examine visuals.
	Predict what you will learn.

Have students write their prediction and share it with a partner. After reading, ask students to write another sentence that begins "I also learned . . ."

Use with All Lessons

STRATEGY ❷
Use Sentence Stems

Before reading, provide students with the two sentence stems for the lessons listed below. Call on volunteers to read the stems orally and explain any unclear vocabulary. After reading, have students complete the stems in writing and compare completed sentences with a partner.

1.1 **a.** Because Japan lies on the Ring of Fire, it has lots of _____ and _____.

   b. Japan is an archipelago, or a _____.

1.2 **a.** The early religion called _____ was a belief that spiritual powers lived in nature.

   b. Clans were groups of _____ who shared the same ancestor.

1.3 **a.** Clans battled each other until Yamato won by fighting while riding _____.

   b. Prince Shotoku created Japan's first _____.

1.4 **a.** Japan sent embassies to _____ to learn new ideas.

   b. From China, the Japanese learned to write beautifully, using _____.

Use with 1.1–1.4

STRATEGY ❸
Use Either/Or Questions

After reading, ask students either/or questions to reinforce meanings. You may also give copies of the questions to students to find and write the answers or to quiz each other.

- Is an *archipelago* made up of islands or peninsulas?
- Is *kabuki* a form of writing or theater?
- Is a *samurai* a soldier or a farmer?
- Were the *daimyo* poor or rich?
- Is *bushido* a code of behavior or a weapon?
- Is a *haiku* a family group or a poem?
- Does the *Ring of Fire* have many earthquakes or shiny jewels?
- Is *Shinto* a famous Japanese person or a Japanese religion?

Use with All Lessons *You may wish to place students in groups with various levels of language proficiency and have advanced students write more either/or questions to ask beginning students.*

STRATEGY ❶
Create a Haiku Library

Have students research, find, and copy as many Japanese haiku as they can. In addition, they can write some of their own haiku. Then have them illustrate the haiku using ink paintings, watercolors, charcoal drawings, or photography. Have them set up their display in a corner of the room or library for all to enjoy.

Use with Lessons 2.1 and 2.2

STRATEGY ❷
Model Japanese Samurai vs. European Knight Armor

Have students figure out how to show the difference between Japanese and European warriors' armor. Students can draw, use papier-mâché, dress up toy soldiers, or dress themselves in fabrics to show their versions of the protective armor. They can model their outfits if they are wearable or show small versions that they have made.

Use with Lessons 3.1 and 3.2

STRATEGY ❶
Write an Essay

Have students write an essay explaining the significance of Shinto and Zen Buddhism to the Japanese. Have them get to the basics of both religions and then show how they affected all parts of Japanese culture.

Use with All Lessons

STRATEGY ❷
Debate

Have students act as two different groups: the foreigners who wanted to trade and visit with Japan and the Japanese allied with Tokugawa Ieyasu. Acting as one or the other side, have them debate the wisdom of Japan's closed-door policy. All arguments should be supported with good reasons.

Use with Lesson 3.3

19 JAPANESE CIVILIZATION
400 – 1868

Mount Fuji, on the island of Honshu, is the highest mountain in Japan. Many Japanese regard the mountain as sacred.

SECTION 1
EARLY JAPAN

KEY VOCABULARY	NAMES & PLACES
archipelago	Prince Shotoku
aristocracy	Ring of Fire
calligraphy	Shinto
clan	
embassy	
regent	
ritual	

SECTION 2
JAPANESE ART AND CULTURE

KEY VOCABULARY	NAMES & PLACES
haiku	Matsuo Basho
kabuki	Murasaki Shikibu
meditation	Sei Shonagon
noh	Zen Buddhism

SECTION 3
JAPANESE FEUDALISM

KEY VOCABULARY	NAMES & PLACES
bushido	Tokugawa Ieyasu
daimyo	
feudalism	
samurai	
shogun	
shogunate	
vassal	

READING STRATEGY

MAKE INFERENCES To make an inference, you combine what the text says with what you already know. As you read this chapter, think back to what you read about Chinese culture in the previous chapter. Use a graphic organizer like the one below to make inferences about how the Japanese felt about Chinese culture.

What Text Says	+	What I Know	→	Inference

547

TEACHER BACKGROUND

INTRODUCE THE PHOTOGRAPH

Have students study the photograph of Mount Fuji. **ASK:** Based on the nearby vegetation, what time of year was this photograph probably taken? *(Possible responses: late spring or summer since the trees have full leaves that have not turned color yet).* Why is Mount Fuji covered with snow? *(It is so high that the temperature is cold and snow remains year-round.)*

SHARE BACKGROUND

Mount Fuji is actually a volcano that last erupted in 1707. It lies about 60 miles southwest of Tokyo. It rises to an elevation of 12,388 feet and is 78 miles in circumference. Its perfect symmetrical shape makes it highly revered in Japan. Yearly, between 100,000 and 200,000 people climb the mountain, most of them Japanese. It is Japan's most visited tourist attraction. Mount Fuji is also represented in Japanese art quite often and is considered holy by most of the Japanese religions.

DIGITAL RESOURCES myNGconnect.com

TEACHER RESOURCES & ASSESSMENT

Social Studies Skills Lessons
- Reading: Make Inferences
- Writing: Write an Informative Article

ExamView®
One-time Download

Formal Assessment
- Chapter 19 Tests A (on-level) & B (below-level)

Chapter 19 Answer Key

STUDENT BACKPACK

- **eEdition** *(English)*
- **eEdition** *(Spanish)*
- **Handbooks**
- **Online Atlas**

For Chapter 19 Spanish Resources, visit the Teacher Resource Menu page.

INTRODUCE THE ESSENTIAL QUESTION

HOW WAS JAPANESE CIVILIZATION INFLUENCED BY NEIGHBORING CULTURES?

Four Corner Activity: Factors of Influence This activity introduces students to four factors that were highly influential in Japan's early history. Have students choose which factor they think was the most influential. Post the four signs shown in the list below. Ask students to choose the factor that they think had the highest impact on early Japan, go to that corner, and then explain why.

A. Geography Japan is a mountainous island country separated from nearby countries. It suffers from frequent volcanic activity as well as oceanic activity.

B. Arts and Culture Japanese authors, poets, artists, and even gardeners found beauty in simple things and created their own artistic style.

C. Military Japan developed a class of fierce samurai warriors that held a highly respected position in Japan's feudal society, united under the military rule of the shogun.

D. Philosophy or Religion Japanese culture combined parts of Shinto, Buddhism, and Confucianism. Even soldiers searched for self-discipline and inner peace. **0:15** minutes

INTRODUCE THE READING STRATEGY

Make Inferences Remind students that when they make an inference, they combine what the text says with what they already know. Give the students an example to work through. Read aloud to them "The Japanese added new characters to the Chinese alphabet, which made writing Japanese much easier." Ask what they know about the Chinese alphabet from previous chapters. They should know that the Chinese created the alphabet to correspond to the Chinese language. Therefore, students should infer that the Japanese adopted the Chinese system of writing but adapted it for their own language and use.

What Text Says		What I Know		Inference
The Japanese added new characters to the Chinese alphabet.	+	The Chinese had developed an alphabet for the Chinese language.	→	

INTRODUCE CHAPTER VOCABULARY

KNOWLEDGE RATING

Have students complete a Knowledge-Rating Chart for Key Vocabulary words. Have students list words and fill out the chart on their own paper. Then have pairs share the definitions they know. Work together as a class to complete the chart.

KEY VOCAB	KNOW IT	NOT SURE	DON'T KNOW	DEFINITION
archipelago				
aristocracy				
bushido				
calligraphy				

KEY DATES	
8000 B.C.	The Jamon emerge as the first culture in Japan
300 B.C.	The Yayoi arrive from mainland Asia
A.D. 400s	The Yamato unite Japan's clans and take control
A.D. 593	Prince Shotoku takes over as regent
607–839	Japan sends embassies to China
1192	Yoritomo becomes Japan's first shogun
1274–1281	First and second Mongol invasions end in a Japanese victory
1467–1568	The "Warring States" period occurs
1603	Takugawa Ieyasu unites Japan under his shogunate
1639–1854	Japan closes its doors to foreigners

EXPLORE EXTREME WIND & WATER

For more information about Japan, specifically its devastating 2011 tsunami, check out *EXPLORE EXTREME WIND AND WATER.*

The Geography of Japan

From studying its geography, no one would expect Japan to have become the industrial superpower it is today. This small country consists of thousands of isolated, mostly mountainous islands. Japan has little land for agriculture and few natural resources or navigable rivers. In addition, catastrophic natural disasters are common.

MAIN IDEA

Japan's geography has greatly affected its historical and cultural development.

AN ISLAND NATION

Japan is an **archipelago** (AHR-kuh-peh-luh-goh), or group of islands, located in the vast Pacific Ocean. The country's thousands of islands stretch out in a long arc along the east coast of Asia.

Most of Japan's population lives on four main islands: Hokkaido (hah-KY-doh), Honshu (HAHN-shoo), Shikoku (shih-KOH-koo), and Kyushu (kee-OO-shoo). These four islands have a total area of about 145,000 square miles—roughly the size of the state of Montana—and thousands of miles of coastline. Honshu is by far Japan's largest island. Along with Kyushu, it has

been the historic heartland of political, economic, and social development in Japan.

Japan's neighbor, South Korea, is more than 120 miles away. China is about 500 miles away. Japan's isolation has had a huge impact on its culture. For much of its history, Japan was far enough away from mainland Asia to escape invasions and major migrations. As a result, the Japanese nation developed largely from one ethnic group. This common ethnicity gave the Japanese a strong sense of unity.

However, Japan's nearest neighbors still influenced the country's culture. Japan imported many ideas and institutions from China and Korea and adapted them to form a unique Japanese culture. You will learn more about China's influence on Japan later in this chapter.

A MOUNTAINOUS LAND

The islands of Japan are actually the peaks of mostly submerged mountains and volcanoes. Japan lies along the **Ring of Fire**, an area of intense earthquakes and volcanic activity that arcs around the basin of the Pacific Ocean. About 1,500 earthquakes and thousands of volcanic eruptions rock Japan every year.

Because of underwater earthquakes, Japan also is at risk from huge ocean waves called tsunamis (su-NAH-mees). In addition, destructive storms called typhoons (ty-FOONS) are common. In the Atlantic Ocean, these storms are called hurricanes.

Japan's mountainous terrain limits the amount of space available for farming and for building homes. Only about 12 percent of the country's land can be farmed, and Japan's population is crowded onto a few coastal plains.

Apart from seafood and vast forests, Japan lacks any important natural resources, such as metals or coal. However, its geographic difficulties have helped make the Japanese a hardy people.

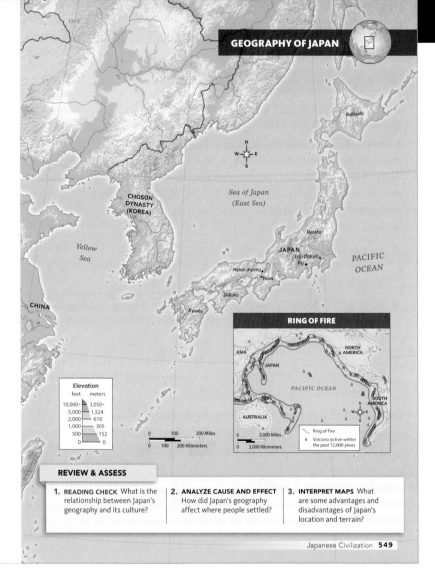

GEOGRAPHY OF JAPAN

REVIEW & ASSESS

1. **READING CHECK** What is the relationship between Japan's geography and its culture?

2. **ANALYZE CAUSE AND EFFECT** How did Japan's geography affect where people settled?

3. **INTERPRET MAPS** What are some advantages and disadvantages of Japan's location and terrain?

PLAN

OBJECTIVE

Discover how Japan's geography affected its historical and cultural development.

CRITICAL THINKING SKILLS FOR LESSON 1.1

- Identify Main Ideas and Details
- Monitor Comprehension
- Analyze Cause and Effect
- Interpret Maps
- Compare and Contrast

ESSENTIAL QUESTION

How was Japanese civilization influenced by neighboring cultures?

Even though it was relatively isolated, Japan was still influenced by China and Korea—its closest neighbors. Lesson 1.1 describes Japan's geography and how it affected the country's cultural development.

BACKGROUND FOR THE TEACHER

The Ring of Fire around the Pacific Rim is approximately 25,000 miles long and extends from New Zealand north to Japan, east across the Pacific Ocean, and then south along the western coasts of North America and South America. The Ring of Fire experiences thousands of earthquakes a year. It also has approximately 350 active volcanoes, including Japan's Mount Fuji.

DIGITAL RESOURCES myNGconnect.com

TEACHER RESOURCES & ASSESSMENT

 Reading and Note-Taking

 Vocabulary Practice

 Section 1 Quiz

STUDENT RESOURCES

 NG Chapter Gallery

PREVIEW THE MAP

Direct students to look at the map showing Japan. As a class, ask them to volunteer words and phrases that describe Japan's position and geography as the map shows it. List their descriptions on the board. After they have read the lesson, ask for any other descriptive phrases they have learned and add them to the list. `0:05` minutes

TEACH

GUIDED DISCUSSION

1. **Compare and Contrast** How and why is Japan's culture so different from that of the United States? (*Japan had one ethnic group, basically one culture, and it was totally isolated; no other groups invaded or migrated to Japan. The United States has many ethnic groups, mixes of all cultures, and welcomes many peoples from around the world. Its culture is a complete mix.*)

2. **Analyze Cause and Effect** What dangers do the Japanese face as a result of Japan's geography? (*earthquakes, volcanic eruptions, tsunamis caused by underwater earthquakes, typhoons*)

INTERPRET MAPS

Have students study the Ring of Fire inset map. **ASK:** Which areas in the Ring of Fire seem to have had the most volcanic eruptions in the past 12,000 years? (*Japan, the area between Asia and North America, the area to the northeast of Australia, and southeastern coast of South America*) `0:10` minutes

ACTIVE OPTIONS

On Your Feet: Team Word Webbing Have students work in teams of three, sitting around a large piece of paper. Each team member has a different colored marker. Tell them to write *Ring of Fire* in the middle of a web. Have each student write something they know about the Ring of Fire to the nearest part of the web. On a signal, students rotate the paper and each student adds to the nearest part again. When finished, have teams share the phrases they wrote. `0:10` minutes

NG Learning Framework: Team Island Experts

ATTITUDE: **Curiosity**
SKILL: **Collaboration**
KNOWLEDGE: **Our Living Planet**

Divide students into four teams and assign each team one main island of Japan: Hokkaido, Honshu, Shikoku, or Kyushu. Have the teams work together to research their island. Tell them to look for facts about the population, size, geography, important people, and any historical facts about their island that they can find. They should devise a way to visually present their island. When finished, have them give an oral presentation about their island to the other teams. `0:10` minutes

ENGLISH LANGUAGE LEARNERS

Sentence Frames Provide sentence frames like the ones below and let students complete them to help them understand the geography of Japan.

- Japan consists of _____ main islands.
- The islands of Japan are made up of the peaks of underwater _____ and _____.
- Because Japan is an island country far away from other countries, it is alone, or _____.
- Underwater earthquakes cause Japan to have huge waves or _____.
- Storms from the sea in Japan are called _____.

PRE-AP

Research Japan's Physical Disasters Have each student pick a different category to research from this list:

- earthquakes
- volcanic eruptions
- tsunamis
- typhoons

Have students use the library or the Internet to research these physical events in Japan's history, focusing on one disaster, and make a fact sheet about that disaster to share with the class.

Press (**mt**) *in the Student eEdition for modified text.*

See the Chapter Planner for more strategies for differentiation.

ANSWERS

1. As an island nation in the vast Pacific Ocean, Japan was isolated from its nearest neighbors in its early history. This isolation limited major migrations of foreigners to Japan, so its people remained ethnically homogenous.

2. Because Japan is extremely mountainous, most people settled on Japan's coastal plains.

3. Answers may vary. Sample response: Advantages—Japan's island location kept the country safe from invasion during its early history, while the ocean has provided a source of food. Disadvantages—Japan's mountainous terrain limits the amount of land available for farming. Its location along the Ring of Fire makes it prone to earthquakes and volcanic eruptions.

1.2 Early Beliefs and Cultures

Many people feel a great sense of awe when they witness a vibrant sunset, a stunning mountain view, or another wonder of nature. In early Japan, the beauty of the natural world became the basis of a religion.

MAIN IDEA

Religion was at the center of a society organized into family groups in early Japan.

+ POSSIBLE RESPONSE

Each has a pair of gates close to each other and is painted red, with a curved black top. They have Japanese writing on them. They are not covered and do not block the natural view. They are very symmetrical and have a simple architectural design.

Critical Viewing Fushimi Inari Shrine in Kyoto, Japan, is noted for its many entrance gates, called torii. What are some distinctive features of the torii?

TRADITIONAL RELIGION

With its rugged mountains and lush forests, Japan has an especially beautiful landscape. Its breathtaking views inspired Japan's most ancient religion, **Shinto** (SHIHN-toh), which means "way of the gods."

Shinto is based on the belief that spiritual powers reside in nature. Followers of Shinto worship divine spirits or gods called *kami*. The religion recognizes millions of kami, ranging from the sun, moon, and storms to individual animals, trees, streams, and rocks. Anything in nature that inspires a sense of religious wonder is considered a kami or the home of a kami. Followers of Shinto regard mountains as especially important homes for Shinto gods. Perhaps because of its size, Mount Fuji, near Tokyo, has long been considered particularly sacred.

Shinto has no founder, no holy scriptures, no moral code, and no clear date of origin. It also does not have elaborate temples. Instead, worshippers focus on simple shrines, or places that are considered sacred. Gates called torii (TAWR-ee-ee) often mark a shrine's entrance.

Shinto worship is relatively simple. Worshippers typically visit a shrine, purify themselves by washing, clap their hands to attract the god's attention, and then whisper a short prayer. Shinto priests perform more elaborate **rituals**, or religious ceremonies, that often involve bells, music, and dancing.

SOCIAL STRUCTURE

People from Siberia and Korea first settled Japan about 30,000 years ago. The first culture, the Jomon (JOH-mahn), emerged about 10,000 years ago. The Jomon people were hunters, gatherers, and fishers who lived in caves and shallow pit dwellings. They made simple pottery, baskets, and clothes from natural materials. Around 3000 B.C., they began basic farming.

About 300 B.C., a new wave of immigrants with a significantly more advanced culture—the Yayoi (YAH-yoy)—arrived from mainland Asia. They knew how to grow rice, work metal, and weave. Their skills changed Japan dramatically. As farming flourished, people built villages that grew into larger communities.

A powerful **clan** ruled each community. A clan is a group of families who share a common ancestor. Each clan had a chief who was a religious leader or a mighty warrior. The chief, who could be male or female, headed a social class system in which a small **aristocracy**, or group of wealthy people, was supported by many farmers, artisans, and slaves.

After A.D. 300, the power of the aristocracy increased. This growth in power was reflected in the large tombs built for people of high social status. Vast earthen mounds covered the tombs. The largest of these tombs rivals Egypt's great pyramids in scale.

The Shinto religion served as a strong unifying factor in early Japanese society. The worship of particular gods bound together families, clans, and regions. Later, Shinto would help unite Japan's many independent kingdoms under a single leader.

REVIEW & ASSESS

1. **READING CHECK** What inspired the development of the ancient Japanese religion called Shinto?

2. **DESCRIBE** What are some distinctive features of the Shinto religion?

3. **ANALYZE CAUSE AND EFFECT** How did the Yayoi culture affect Japan?

PLAN

OBJECTIVE

Identify how the Shinto religion tied Japan together and the society became organized into family groups.

CRITICAL THINKING SKILLS FOR LESSON 1.2

- Identify Main Ideas and Details
- Monitor Comprehension
- Describe
- Analyze Cause and Effect
- Compare and Contrast
- Draw Conclusions
- Create Graphic Organizers

ESSENTIAL QUESTION

How was Japanese civilization influenced by neighboring cultures?

Several different groups settled in early Japan. Lesson 1.2 describes how a group called the Yayoi changed the ancient Japanese culture by adding skills and a social structure organized around family groups.

BACKGROUND FOR THE TEACHER

Shinto, the ancient religion that developed in Japan, is still practiced today by at least five million people. It does not contradict other religions, so people can believe in Shinto and still follow Buddhism or other more modern religions. Because it is based on nature and has many gods, it is somewhat similar to traditional religions in other parts of the world that are also based on nature, such as animism in parts of sub-Saharan Africa.

DIGITAL RESOURCES myNGconnect.com

TEACHER RESOURCES & ASSESSMENT

 Reading and Note-Taking

 Vocabulary Practice

 Section 1 Quiz

STUDENT RESOURCES

 NG Chapter Gallery

INTRODUCE & ENGAGE

Roundtable Discussion Ask students to think about all the religions that they know. Mention Christianity, Judaism, Islam, and Buddhism. Have them work in small groups around a table to answer this question: *What do most religions have in common?* After they share their answers, tell them that they will read about a religion that is a bit different from these modern ones. `0:05` minutes

TEACH

GUIDED DISCUSSION

1. **Compare and Contrast** How did the power structure change in Japan after the Yayoi came? *(The Yayoi introduced a social structure that gave power to the chief and the wealthy aristocrats at the top. Before that, everybody seemed to be equal.)*

2. **Draw Conclusions** From what you know of the Shinto religion, why would Mount Fuji be considered sacred? *(It was the highest mountain; followers of Shinto worshipped beautiful, individual parts of nature; it would be the largest and most obvious natural thing they could worship.)*

CREATE GRAPHIC ORGANIZERS

As a class, complete a Concept Cluster to highlight traits and beliefs of the Shinto religion. `0:10` minutes

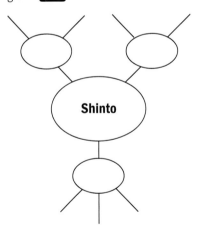

ACTIVE OPTIONS

Critical Viewing: NG Chapter Gallery Invite students to explore the Chapter Gallery to examine the images that relate to this chapter. Have them select one of the images and do additional research to learn more about it. Ask questions that will inspire additional inquiry about the chosen gallery image, such as: What is this? Where and when was this created? By whom? Why was it created? What is it made of? Why does it belong in this chapter? What else would you like to know about it? `0:10` minutes

On Your Feet: Three Step Interview Tell students that they are going to describe the clan system that developed in early Japan. Have students form pairs. Tell them that one partner interviews the other about the clans. Then the partners reverse roles. Finally, both students share the information they gathered from each other with the class. `0:10` minutes

DIFFERENTIATE

STRIVING READERS

Build Cluster Maps Have students work in pairs to complete a Word Web for the terms *Shinto* and *clan*.

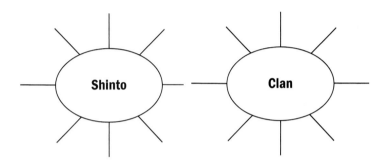

GIFTED & TALENTED

Compare Tombs Have students use the library or Internet research to find pictures of the tombs covered by earthen mounds for the rich mentioned in the lesson. They should look up Kofun tombs. Have them gather some pictures of these tombs and find out about their construction. If possible, have them compare the Kofun tombs to pictures of Egyptian tombs. They can make a short visual presentation to the rest of the class.

Press **mt** *in the Student eEdition for modified text.*

See the Chapter Planner for more strategies for differentiation.

REVIEW & ASSESS

ANSWERS

1. Japan's beautiful landscape of rugged mountains and lush forests inspired the development of the ancient Japanese religion called Shinto.

2. Shinto followers worship millions of sacred spirits or gods called kami. Anything in nature that inspires a sense of religious wonder is considered a kami. Shinto has no founder, scriptures, moral code, or temples.

3. The Yayoi culture brought advanced farming, metalworking, and weaving skills to Japan. As farming flourished, villages grew into hundreds of small kingdoms, each ruled by a powerful clan.

This bronze statue stands before the entry gate of Horyu-ji, a Buddhist religious center founded by Prince Shotoku in the 600s.

1.3 Prince Shotoku

"In a country, there are not two lords; the people have not two masters. The sovereign is the master of the people of the whole country." In this strong statement, **Prince Shotoku** (shoh-toh-ku) of Japan sent a clear message to the people. He wanted them to know that Japan was now a united nation under a single ruler, or sovereign.

MAIN IDEA

Between 593 and 622, Prince Shotoku unified Japan under a Chinese model of centralized government and promoted other Chinese ideas.

A POWERFUL CLAN

Before the 400s, hundreds of Japan's independent clans ruled their own territories and often battled one another. Amid the many clans, one grew increasingly powerful: the Yamato (YAH-mah-toh). The Yamato rode into battle on horses, recently introduced from Korea. With their military superiority, they won control over many of the clans. By the 400s, these clans had united under the leadership of a Yamato emperor and his successors. To support the idea that they were the rightful rulers of Japan, the Yamato claimed their line of emperors was directly descended from the chief Shinto deity, the sun goddess Amaterasu (ah-mah-teh-RAH-soo). The Yamato effectively established a hereditary monarchy, in which rule passes from one member of a royal family to another.

In 593, Japan took another political leap. Empress Suiko (soo-EE-koh) won the throne and named her 21-year-old nephew, Prince Shotoku, as her **regent**. A regent is a person who rules when a monarch or emperor is unable to do so. However, Shotoku held most of the real power in Japan. He established the Japanese practice of having both a ruler in name only and an actual ruler. Between 593 and 622, Shotoku and Suiko laid the foundations of Japanese government.

CENTRALIZED GOVERNMENT

Greatly impressed by China's culture, Prince Shotoku introduced Chinese ideas and practices to help unite the Japanese people and strengthen imperial control over them. The religion of Buddhism and a centralized government were among these ideas and practices.

In 604, Shotoku issued Japan's first constitution, which skillfully mixed Confucian and Buddhist ideas. The constitution emphasized obedience to the emperor and the emperor's duty to care for his subjects. Shotoku introduced ideas for Japanese government that lasted for centuries.

REVIEW & ASSESS

1. **READING CHECK** How did Prince Shotoku unify the Japanese people?

2. **MAKE INFERENCES** Why do you think Prince Shotoku stressed the fact that Japan had only one ruler?

3. **FORM AND SUPPORT OPINIONS** What do you consider to be Prince Shotoku's greatest accomplishment? Why?

PLAN

OBJECTIVE

Identify how Prince Shotoku unified Japan using a Chinese model of centralized government.

CRITICAL THINKING SKILLS FOR LESSON 1.3

- Identify Main Ideas and Details
- Monitor Comprehension
- Make Inferences
- Form and Support Opinions
- Analyze Cause and Effect
- Summarize
- Analyze Visuals

ESSENTIAL QUESTION

How was Japanese civilization influenced by neighboring cultures?

Prince Shotoku unified Japan under his rule. Lesson 1.3 explains how he borrowed governing ideas from the Chinese and adapted them for Japan.

BACKGROUND FOR THE TEACHER

Prince Shotoku was a very bright youngster who read extensively as a child. The story goes that he once listened to eight people at once and understood all that they said, eventually giving him the nickname "the prince of eight ears." After the emperor died, there was infighting over who would take over. Eventually Shotoku's aunt, Empress Suiku, became emperor; she appointed her 21-year-old nephew, rather than her own sons, to become the regent. She may have appreciated his knowledge, intellect, and wisdom.

DIGITAL RESOURCES myNGconnect.com

TEACHER RESOURCES & ASSESSMENT

 Reading and Note-Taking   **Vocabulary Practice**   **Section 1 Quiz**

STUDENT RESOURCES

 Biography

INTRODUCE & ENGAGE

THINK, PAIR, SHARE

Have students think about the qualities they would expect to be necessary for a strong leader of a country. Then have them pair with a partner to discuss the qualities they think such a ruler would have. Finally, have the pairs share their ideas with the rest of the class. `0:05` minutes

TEACH

GUIDED DISCUSSION

1. **Analyze Cause and Effect** How did the Yamato get control over the other clans? *(They conquered the other clans militarily with the use of horses from Korea. Then they declared that their clan was descended from the chief Shinto deity, the sun goddess Amaterasu.)*

2. **Summarize** What ideas did Prince Shotoku borrow from the Chinese and what new ideas did he implement himself to solidify the Japanese government? *(He borrowed the religion of Buddhism and a centralized system of government from the Chinese; he created a constitution for Japan that combined Confucian and Buddhist ideas. He also said the emperor should care for the people, and they should obey him.)*

ANALYZE VISUALS

Have students study the photograph of the bronze statue in the lesson. **ASK:**

- What feeling do you get from this statue? *(ferocity, authority, a demand for obedience)*
- What details contribute to that feeling? *(the angry facial expression, piercing eyes, angry mouth, raised fist, and physical strength and fitness of the man)*
- What might be ironic, or not quite fitting, about the placement of this statue in front of a Buddhist center? *(He looks ready to do battle, not to be gentle, loving, and contemplative as the Buddha would be.)*

`0:10` minutes

ACTIVE OPTIONS

Critical Viewing: NG Image Gallery Have students explore the entire NG Image Gallery and choose an item related to Shinto and an item related to another religion (e.g., Christianity, Islam, Judaism, or Hinduism). They can compare and contrast the two either in written form or verbally with a partner. Ask questions that will inspire this process, such as: How are these images alike? How are they different? Why did you select these two? How are the impressions or moods they give alike or different? `0:10` minutes

On Your Feet: Create a Character Map Have students sit in groups of four. Tell them to think about how powerful Prince Shotoku became. Have them consider both his positive and negative qualities. Half of the group should talk about and write down his positive qualities. The other half should talk about and write down possible negative qualities. Then as a group, evaluate his motives. Was he more interested in improving Japan or in having power for himself? Groups should share their judgment with the rest of the class. `0:10` minutes

DIFFERENTIATE

ENGLISH LANGUAGE LEARNERS

Categorize Vocabulary Write the following three lists of words on the board or give students the lists separately. Tell them to make a heading for each list. (What kinds of words is each list about?) Finally, go over the words in each list and make sure students know or understand those terms.

sovereign	archipelago	shrine
ruler	typhoon	religion
emperor	volcano	ritual
dictator	mountain	scripture
king	tsunami	ceremony
regent	island	

GIFTED & TALENTED

Give a Speech Based on this lesson and other research they might do, have students act as if they were Prince Shotoku. As the Prince, who was also a politician, they should write a speech for the Japanese people in which they explain how and why things are going to change in Japan, starting with the new government and constitution. Suggest that they work in pairs to write the speech. Suggest that the speaker should show the same attitude that Prince Shotoku would have taken when giving the speech. Have speakers give their speeches to the class; let the class vote on the speech that would be most like one that Prince Shotoku would give.

Press (**mt**) *in the Student eEdition for modified text.*

See the Chapter Planner for more strategies for differentiation.

REVIEW & ASSESS

ANSWERS

1. Prince Shotoku unified the Japanese people by introducing ideas, institutions, and practices that formed the basis of Japanese government and society for centuries.

2. Prince Shotoku probably had to stress the fact that Japan had only one ruler because many people retained an allegiance to their clan chief.

3. Possible response: Prince Shotoku's greatest accomplishment was establishing a centralized form of government. This action helped Japan emerge as a nation.

Influences from China

When you see a hairstyle you like, you might decide to copy it. But you might change it slightly to fit your own taste, type of hair, or facial shape. In a similar way, the Japanese copied aspects of Chinese culture but adapted them to suit Japan's culture.

MAIN IDEA

From the early 600s to the 800s, Japan adopted ideas from China's civilization and adapted them to fit Japanese culture.

SPREADING NEW IDEAS

To learn about Chinese culture, Japan sent many embassies to China. An **embassy** is a group of official representatives from one country who have been sent on a mission to another country. Between 607 and 839, Japan sent hundreds of people on more than 12 official missions to China. They brought back knowledge that influenced many aspects of Japanese life, including agriculture, art, government, religion, and technology.

As a result, China's influence extended to such everyday practices as drinking tea, cooking, and gardening. Even the name the Japanese use to refer to their country, *Nippon*, comes from the Chinese language. *Nippon* means "Land of the Rising Sun" and refers to Japan's location east of China—toward the rising sun.

China had a major impact on Japanese writing, even though the Japanese and Chinese languages are completely unrelated. For example, most Chinese words are just one syllable, while Japanese words combine many syllables. The differences made it extremely difficult to write Japanese using the Chinese alphabet, so at first the Japanese wrote in the Chinese language. Later, the Japanese added new characters to the Chinese alphabet, which made writing Japanese much easier.

The Chinese also influenced how the Japanese viewed writing. Initially, the Japanese considered writing to be a purely functional activity, useful for such purposes as keeping records. Japanese aristocrats did not bother to learn to write. However, interaction with China encouraged writing for cultural reasons, such as telling stories. The Japanese began to use writing to create religious, philosophical, and literary works. They also adopted the practice of **calligraphy**, or beautiful writing, from China.

ADAPTING INFLUENCES

The Japanese did not simply imitate everything Chinese. They carefully selected what suited them and then adapted it to their own needs, which led to a distinctive Japanese culture. For example, the Japanese copied the Chinese civil service system, which established a hierarchy, or ranking, of government officials. In China, government officials earned their positions based on examinations and good work. However, members of Japan's aristocracy wanted to keep power to themselves. In Japan, the emperor appointed government officials based on heredity, not on ability.

Japan continued adopting and adapting Chinese practices into the early 800s. By then, however, Japan's own culture was flourishing. After 839, Japan no longer sent any major missions to China. Nevertheless, China's influence on Japanese culture can still be seen today.

These students are participating in an annual calligraphy contest in Tokyo.

REVIEW & ASSESS

1. **READING CHECK** How does Japan's name reflect the influence of the Chinese?

2. **MAKE INFERENCES** How does the Japanese system of writing demonstrate Japan's tendency to adopt—and adapt—ideas from China?

3. **COMPARE AND CONTRAST** What was a major difference between the civil service systems in China and Japan?

PLAN

OBJECTIVE

Identify the ideas that the Japanese borrowed from China and adapted to fit their own culture.

CRITICAL THINKING SKILLS FOR LESSON 1.4

- Identify Main Ideas and Details
- Monitor Comprehension
- Make Inferences
- Compare and Contrast
- Draw Conclusions
- Analyze Cause and Effect
- Analyze Visuals

ESSENTIAL QUESTION

How was Japanese civilization influenced by neighboring cultures?

The Japanese visited China and brought back many ideas, adapting them to fit their own needs. Lesson 1.4 highlights several of these influences.

BACKGROUND FOR THE TEACHER

The Japanese written language has three different character sets: *hiragana*, *katakana*, and *kanji*. These are mixed together. Kanji is borrowed from Chinese and is used with Hiragana to form sentences. Katakana is used mostly for foreign words. Some characters represent syllables and some represent words. Because of these complications, Japanese is one of the hardest languages to learn to write.

DIGITAL RESOURCES myNGconnect.com

TEACHER RESOURCES & ASSESSMENT

 Reading and Note-Taking   **Vocabulary Practice**   **Section 1 Quiz**

STUDENT RESOURCES

 NG Chapter Gallery

MAKE A CHOICE

ASK: Besides our own country, what country do you admire? What country would you visit if you had a chance? Have students write down the name of the country. After students have done this without talking, take a poll. Group those students who have chosen the same country. Have them list as many reasons for visiting the country as they can. Then let them share their lists with the students who chose other countries. Tell them that they will read about the Japanese visiting another country to learn about its customs and ways of operating. **0:05** minutes

GUIDED DISCUSSION

1. **Draw Conclusions** Japan sent embassies to China. What does that show about Japan's attitude toward other countries? *(The Japanese were eager to learn new things from other countries and adapt ideas to their own needs. They were open to ideas from others.)*

2. **Analyze Cause and Effect** How did the Chinese influence Japanese literature? *(Before going to China, the Japanese thought writing was strictly utilitarian, just for practical purposes, used only by record keepers. Later they realized that they could write literature, religious works, and philosophy. Educated aristocrats learned how to write and began writing literature.)*

ANALYZE VISUALS

Have students study the photograph of the calligraphy contest. **ASK:** Why might it be hard to win such a contest? *(The brushes are big, perhaps giving less control to the writer. Ink could drip on the paper. The paper could tear. The ink could run. The writer's hand has to be steady.)* Ask how many students would like to participate in such a contest. **0:10** minutes

ACTIVE OPTIONS

On Your Feet: Write in Calligraphy Encourage students to try their own hands at calligraphy. They can use calligraphy pens, paintbrushes, markers, gel pens, or regular ballpoint pens. Let them choose their own word, phrase, or sentence to copy. When finished, have them vote on the three cleanest, neatest, and nicest examples. Tell them that people pay professionals in our own country to write invitations, signs, t-shirt logos, and so on using calligraphy. **0:10** minutes

NG Learning Framework: Tell a Story

ATTITUDE: **Responsibility**
SKILL: **Communication**
KNOWLEDGE: **Our Human Story**

Have students imagine that they are Americans in an embassy going to Japan, just like the Japanese embassies went to China to learn

about Chinese culture. Encourage them to think about what they might learn of the Japanese culture. Have them write a journal entry or story about one custom or sight that they encounter in Japan. Urge them to use descriptive words so that the reader can imagine what they are experiencing. Have them share their writing when finished. **0:10** minutes

ENGLISH LANGUAGE LEARNERS

Complete Sentence Frames Provide sentence frames like the ones below and let students complete them to help them understand concepts in the lesson.

- The purpose of Japan's embassies to China was to _____.

- For writing, the Japanese used the _____ alphabet.

- The Chinese taught the Japanese to use writing for _____.

- The Japanese adapted the Chinese civil service system for hiring _____.

- The practice of beautiful writing is called _____.

GIFTED & TALENTED

Research Japanese Characters Have interested students research a word, phrase, or saying written in Japanese to find out what it means. Then have the student copy the word in Japanese, using calligraphy, and translate it into English, also using calligraphy. Let them display their phrases or sayings around the room.

Press (**mt**) *in the Student eEdition for modified text.*

See the Chapter Planner for more strategies for differentiation.

ANSWERS

1. *Japan* is the Chinese pronunciation of *Nippon*, a Japanese word meaning "Land of the Rising Sun."

2. The Japanese used the Chinese alphabet but added new characters to make writing Japanese easier.

3. In China, government officials earned seniority through examinations and good work. In Japan, the emperor appointed officials to positions based on heredity, not on the officials' merits or talents.

Literature and the Arts

If you look at a time line of early English literature, you'll notice that all the best known authors—like William Shakespeare—are male. That's *not* the case with early Japanese literature. Two of the most famous authors are female, and one introduced a new form of literature to the world.

MAIN IDEA

Japan's rich cultural heritage includes unique forms of literature and art.

BONSAI

The Japanese imported the tradition of bonsai (bohn-SY) from China. To create a bonsai, a gardener painstakingly prunes and trains an ordinary plant to grow into a miniature tree that perfectly reflects its full-size relative.

LITERATURE AND DRAMA

A Japanese woman named **Murasaki Shikibu** (MOO-rah-SAH-kee SHEE-kee-boo) wrote the world's first novel in the 1000s. Her novel, *The Tale of Genji*, paints a vivid picture of life at the emperor's court. Her much admired masterpiece is still read today.

Another female writer of the same time, **Sei Shonagon** (SAY SHOW-nah-gohn), wrote a collection of reportedly true stories about court life called *The Pillow Book*. The book's title probably comes from the practice of keeping paper by the bedside for writing down thoughts.

Other Japanese writers developed a form of poetry called **haiku** (HY-koo), which has 17 syllables in three unrhymed lines of 5, 7, and 5 syllables. Traditional haiku evokes aspects of nature and often employs striking comparisons. One of the great masters of haiku was **Matsuo Basho** (MAHT-soo-oh bah-SHAW). In 1666, he abandoned his warrior life to write verses inspired by Buddhism. His poetry provided deep insights into human nature, turning haiku into a popular and beloved art form.

In the field of drama, Japan developed two forms that are still popular today. **Noh** (noh) emerged in the 1300s and **kabuki** (kuh-BOO-kee) in the 1600s. Noh grew out of Shinto rituals and often retold well-known folktales. Performing on a simple wooden stage, the actors wore elaborate masks and many layers of clothing to appear larger than life. Their movements were deliberately slow and choreographed to music to create a powerful effect.

Kabuki developed as a contrast to noh and was more lively and understandable. The actors performed on a large stage with trapdoors, revolving sections, and a raised walkway for dramatic effects. They wore luxurious costumes that reflected their characters' status. Their elaborate makeup highlighted important facial expressions, such as smiling or frowning.

PAINTING AND GARDENING

As you have learned, the Japanese adopted the Chinese art of calligraphy, which is traditionally produced with a brush and ink. China also influenced painting in Japan. Japanese artists adapted a form of Chinese ink painting to create paintings called *suiboku*

Critical Viewing In kabuki, actors wear elaborate makeup and costumes. What emotion is emphasized by the makeup on the actor in the foreground?

+ POSSIBLE RESPONSE

The actor looks angry, unhappy, and fierce.

(soo-ee-BOH-koo), using bold strokes of black and white ink. Artists later created vibrant watercolors and prints. Early Japanese painting focused on religious subjects, but landscapes, scenes of daily life, legends, and battles also became popular.

Following the Shinto tradition of seeking harmony with nature, the Japanese became dedicated gardeners. They developed various types of gardens with the aim of creating symbolic miniature landscapes. Paradise gardens re-created the Buddhist idea of paradise. Dry-landscape gardens consisted of carefully chosen stones arranged in raked gravel as a focus for meditation. Stroll gardens featured carefully designed landscapes along a walking path. Tea gardens had neatly trimmed plants along a short path leading to a special house for drinking tea.

REVIEW & ASSESS

1. **READING CHECK** What new forms of literature and drama did the Japanese develop?

2. **COMPARE AND CONTRAST** How are the literary works of Murasaki Shikibu and Sei Shonagon similar?

3. **MAKE GENERALIZATIONS** How did Japanese gardens reflect both Shinto and Buddhist ideas?

PLAN

OBJECTIVE

Describe the new forms of literature and art that Japan developed.

CRITICAL THINKING SKILLS FOR LESSON 2.1

- Identify Main Ideas and Details
- Monitor Comprehension
- Compare and Contrast
- Make Generalizations
- Contrast
- Make Inferences

ESSENTIAL QUESTION

How was Japanese civilization influenced by neighboring cultures?

The Japanese borrowed the concepts of literature and calligraphy from China but went on to develop their own forms of literature, drama, arts, and gardening. Lesson 2.1 explores Japan's unique forms of literature and art.

BACKGROUND FOR THE TEACHER

Noh theater is drama put to music; historically, it retold a few folktales and was performed for the upper class. Only men were actors. Kabuki theater, however, is lively and exciting. It combines dance, music, and drama and often features sword fights and high action. Historically, the lower classes attended and would often shout with excitement as the drama unfolded. This is still the most popular form of theater in Japan.

DIGITAL RESOURCES myNGconnect.com

TEACHER RESOURCES & ASSESSMENT

 Reading and Note-Taking

 Vocabulary Practice

 Section 2 Quiz

STUDENT RESOURCES

 Biography

INTRODUCE & ENGAGE

ACCESS PRIOR KNOWLEDGE

Invite students to share what they know about poetry. Record student responses in a Concept Cluster on the board. Then call on volunteers to use the completed cluster to summarize the class discussion. Tell students that they will read about new forms of literature and theater in this lesson. **0:05** minutes

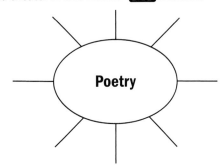

TEACH

GUIDED DISCUSSION

1. **Contrast** How are the dramatic forms of noh and kabuki theater different? *(Noh is set on a simple stage; it's very slow and choreographed to music; it's usually about Shinto rituals or folktales; and the actors wore masks. Kabuki is lively; it's performed on large stage sets with trapdoors and walkways; and it's more exciting and understandable. Kabuki actors wore fancy costumes and heavy makeup.)*

2. **Make Inferences** Why would Japanese gardeners focus on creating miniature trees, such as the bonsai, and miniature landscapes? *(They had only a small amount of land to use, and they liked imitating nature in a smaller way that would be convenient for their space and use.)*

ANALYZE VISUALS

Have a volunteer reread the description of kabuki from the text. **ASK:** How does the photo of the kabuki actors reflect the elements of kabuki. *(The actors are wearing luxurious costumes and elaborate makeup that emphasizes their facial features.)* **0:10** minutes

ACTIVE OPTIONS

Critical Viewing: NG Chapter Gallery Have students examine the contents of the Chapter Gallery for this chapter. Then invite them to brainstorm additional images they believe would fit within the Chapter Gallery. Have them write a description of these additional images and provide an explanation of why they would fit within the Chapter Gallery. Then instruct them to do online research to find examples of actual images they would like to add to the gallery. **0:10** minutes

On Your Feet: Write a Haiku Change the classroom atmosphere for students; you might take them outdoors, to the library, or to another quiet place in the school. Tell them that they are going to write their own haiku. Remind them that haiku is a simple form of poetry that has 3 lines that do not rhyme. The first line has 5 syllables, the second 7 syllables, and the third 5. Suggest that they look at Document Three in the next lesson to get the idea. Suggest that they imagine one natural item or living thing. Let them write their poems, decorate them if desired, and share them in class. **0:10** minutes

DIFFERENTIATE

STRIVING READERS

Classify Terms Help students keep track of all the terms and names in this lesson. Have them work with a partner to put the following terms in their proper column in a chart like the one below. Encourage them to add notes from the lesson about each topic or term.

haiku	suiboku	Murasaki Shikibu	tea gardens
noh	bonsai trees	paradise gardens	watercolors
kabuki	Sei Shonagon	landscape scenes	masks

Literature	Drama	Painting	Gardening
(haiku)	(noh)	(suiboku)	(bonsai trees)
(Murasaki Shikibu)	(kabuki)	(landscape scenes)	(paradise gardens)
(Sei Shonagon)	(masks)	(watercolors)	(tea gardens)

GIFTED & TALENTED

Create Suiboku Have students do research online or in the library to look at a few Japanese suiboku paintings, which are black and white ink paintings. Encourage students to draw their own black ink paintings, with pen or brush. Have them share their work if desired.

Press **mt** *in the Student eEdition for modified text.*

See the Chapter Planner for more strategies for differentiation.

REVIEW & ASSESS

ANSWERS

1. The Japanese developed the first novel; two new types of drama, noh and kabuki; and a short form of poetry called haiku.

2. The literary works of both Murasaki Shikibu and Sei Shonagon deal with court life in Japan.

3. Japanese gardens aimed to express harmony with nature—a Shinto tradition—and to create a beautiful, peaceful place for meditation—a Buddhist practice.

Poetry and Prose

During the Heian (HAY-ahn) period, from 794 to 1185, Japan enjoyed a golden age in literature. The ruling class in the capital city of Heian, modern Kyoto (kee-OH-toh), filled their time with cultural pursuits. Both male and female aristocrats, including warriors, engaged in writing as a cultural activity. The common literary subjects of nature and beauty had wide appeal to Japanese audiences. Literature also flourished during the later Edo (eh-doh) period, from 1603 to 1867.

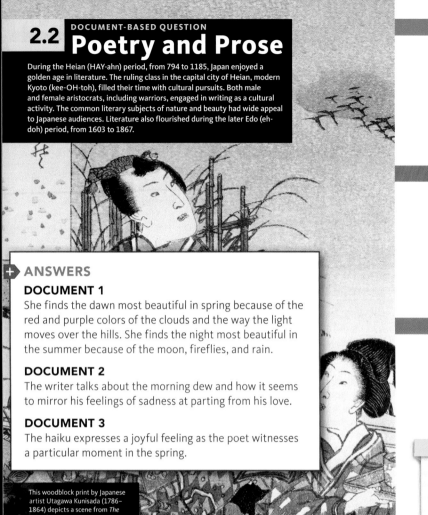

This woodblock print by Japanese artist Utagawa Kunisada (1786–1864) depicts a scene from *The Tale of Genji*.

558

DOCUMENT ONE
Primary Source: Diary

from *The Pillow Book* by Sei Shonagon
In keeping with the traditional Japanese love of nature, artists and writers found a source of inspiration in the changing seasons. Here, Sei Shonagon paints a timeless portrait of the seasons to set the scene at the start of *The Pillow Book*.

CONSTRUCTED RESPONSE Which parts of the day does Sei Shonagon find most beautiful in the spring and summer seasons? Why?

> In spring, the dawn [is most beautiful]— when the slowly paling mountain rim is tinged with red, and wisps of faintly crimson-purple cloud float in the sky.
>
> In summer, the night—moonlit nights, of course, but also at the dark of the moon, it's beautiful when fireflies are dancing everywhere in a mazy [confused] flight.

DOCUMENT TWO
Primary Source: Novel

from *The Tale of Genji* by Murasaki Shikibu
Prince Genji is the central character in Murasaki's novel. Although most of the story is told in prose, Murasaki includes many poems that are spoken by the characters. Here, the writer sets the scene as Genji says farewell to a former love.

CONSTRUCTED RESPONSE How does the writer use images of nature to express Genji's feelings?

> No one could ever convey all that passed between those two [Genji and the lady], who together had known such uncounted sorrows. The quality of a sky at last touched by dawn seemed meant for them alone.
>
> "Many dews attend any reluctant parting at the break of day but no one has ever seen the like of this autumn sky," Genji said.

DOCUMENT THREE
Primary Source: Poetry

Haiku by Matsuo Basho
A traditional haiku has 17 syllables, arranged in three lines of 5, 7, and 5 syllables, though the syllable count is sometimes lost in translation, as in the one shown here. In the 1600s, Matsuo Basho developed haiku into a distinct art form.

CONSTRUCTED RESPONSE What feelings about nature does this haiku express?

> The quiet pond
>   A frog leaps in,
>   The sound of water

SYNTHESIZE & WRITE

1. **REVIEW** Review what you have learned from this chapter about Japanese literature.

2. **RECALL** On your own paper, write down the main idea expressed in each document above.

3. **CONSTRUCT** Write a topic sentence that answers this question: What can you infer about early Japanese authors' relationship to nature?

4. **WRITE** Using evidence from the documents, write a paragraph that supports your topic sentence in Step 3.

ANSWERS

DOCUMENT 1
She finds the dawn most beautiful in spring because of the red and purple colors of the clouds and the way the light moves over the hills. She finds the night most beautiful in the summer because of the moon, fireflies, and rain.

DOCUMENT 2
The writer talks about the morning dew and how it seems to mirror his feelings of sadness at parting from his love.

DOCUMENT 3
The haiku expresses a joyful feeling as the poet witnesses a particular moment in the spring.

PLAN

OBJECTIVE

Appreciate the examples of literature excerpted in three primary source documents written in Japan's golden age of literature during the Heian period.

CRITICAL THINKING SKILLS FOR LESSON 2.2

- Synthesize
- Compare
- Identify
- Evaluate

ESSENTIAL QUESTION

How was Japanese civilization influenced by neighboring cultures?

Japan learned from China to use writing to create literature. Lesson 2.2 provides examples of how the Japanese developed their own unique literature.

BACKGROUND FOR THE TEACHER

The Tale of Genji is about an illegitimate son of an emperor who is quite a ladies' man. He is expelled from court and has many amorous adventures while trying to get back into the court. Over time, his children and grandchildren help restore him to the court. The tale is one of intrigue, adventure, jealousy, and the desire for power.

DIGITAL RESOURCES myNGconnect.com

TEACHER RESOURCES & ASSESSMENT

 Reading and Note-Taking

 Vocabulary Practice

 Section 2 Quiz

STUDENT RESOURCES

 NG Chapter Gallery

INTRODUCE & ENGAGE

PREPARE FOR THE DOCUMENT-BASED QUESTION

Before students begin the activity, briefly preview the three documents. Remind students that a constructed response requires full explanations in complete sentences. Emphasize that students should use their knowledge of Japanese culture in addition to the information in the documents. **0:05** minutes

TEACH

GUIDED DISCUSSION

1. **Compare** How do all three excerpts focus on nature? *(The first talks about dawn and summer nights; the second describes dawn and dew in autumn; the third describes a quiet pond with a frog.)*

2. **Identify** Poetry usually appeals to the senses. Which of the senses—sight, hearing, taste, touch, or smell—does each excerpt appeal to? *(Document 1: sight; Document 2: sight; Document 3: hearing)*

EVALUATE

After students have completed the "Synthesize & Write" activity, allow time for them to exchange paragraphs and read and comment on the work of their peers. Guidelines for comments should be established prior to this activity so that feedback is constructive and encouraging in nature. **0:15** minutes

ACTIVE OPTIONS

On Your Feet: Three Options Label three locations in the room with the name of one of the documents featured in the lesson. Have students reread the lesson and walk to the corner of the room labeled with the poetic description that appealed to them the most. Have students who chose the same document discuss why they made their selection. Then have volunteers from each group explain what their document is and offer some of the group's reasons for choosing it. **0:20** minutes

NG Learning Framework: Write a Biography

ATTITUDE: **Curiosity**
KNOWLEDGE: **Our Human Story**

Have students select one of the people they are still curious about after learning about this individual in the chapter. Instruct them to write a short biography about this person using information from the chapter and additional source material. **0:20** minutes

DIFFERENTIATE

INCLUSION

Work in Pairs Pair visually impaired students with well-sighted students, and have the sighted students read the documents aloud. You may also want to give students the option of recording their responses.

GIFTED & TALENTED

Create a Photo Gallery Challenge students to find examples of Japanese art and Japanese haiku that they can copy. Have students work together to create a photo gallery. They should label the pictures and the haiku with information about its origin or interesting facts about its creation. Have them display their gallery in the classroom.

Press **(mt)** *in the Student eEdition for modified text.*

See the Chapter Planner for more strategies for differentiation.

SYNTHESIZE & WRITE

ANSWERS

1. Responses will vary.

2. Responses will vary.

3. Possible response: Early Japanese authors greatly admired and respected nature.

4. Students' paragraphs should include their topic sentence from Step 3 and provide relevant concrete details from the documents to support the sentence.

Zen Buddhism

The world's religions prescribe a variety of ways for people to seek salvation, enlightenment, or meaning in life. Many encourage followers to study holy books, perform rituals, say prayers, and do good deeds. A religion called **Zen Buddhism**, which took root in Japan in the 1100s, takes a different approach. Its followers focus on clearing their minds and simplifying their lives.

MAIN IDEA

In the 1100s, Zen Buddhism developed a small but elite following that allowed it to greatly influence Japanese culture.

A NEW FORM OF BUDDHISM

Buddhism originally spread to Japan in the 500s. Over time, many sects, or forms, of Buddhism emerged, the best-known being Zen Buddhism. This sect arrived from China in the 1100s.

While traditional Buddhists sought salvation by studying scriptures, performing rituals, and doing good deeds, Zen Buddhists focused on **meditation**. In fact, *Zen* is the Japanese pronunciation of the Chinese word *Ch'an*, which roughly translates as

"meditation." In meditation, a person remains still and enters a trancelike state of thought. True meditation requires self-discipline and concentration. For Zen Buddhists, the goal is to achieve inner peace and to realize that there is something divine in each person. To help focus and escape worldly distractions, Zen Buddhists embrace simplicity in all things, including home furnishings, food, clothing, and art.

INFLUENCE ON CULTURE

Zen Buddhism influenced Japanese culture far more than any other form of Buddhism. Many Japanese poets and artists, for example, embraced the religion's guiding principles of simplicity, understatement, and grace. The content and form of haiku reflect not only these principles but also the religon's focus on the present moment. Artists inspired by Zen Buddhism challenged themselves to convey complex natural scenes with as few brushstrokes as possible, using only black ink on white paper. A typical painting might capture the essence of a mountain-filled landscape.

You read about the different types of Japanese gardens in a previous lesson. These gardens were all influenced by Zen Buddhism. For example, the religion inspired gardeners to create dry-landscape gardens, also called viewing gardens, that represented the world in miniature. In these gardens, simple objects typically stood for something much bigger. An arrangement of rocks might convey a waterfall, or a collection of pebbles might depict a stream. Ryoanji (ree-OHN-gee) Temple in Kyoto has a celebrated Zen viewing garden. It consists of a rectangle of raked sand and 15 pebbles surrounded by clay walls and tall trees.

The main purpose of Zen viewing gardens was to promote a calm state of mind for meditation. As a result, the gardens made a perfect setting for the highly ritualized Zen tea ceremony. This ceremony involved drinking bitter tea in precisely

Critical Viewing: A Buddhist monk meditates by a Zen viewing garden. What mood or state of mind might such a garden inspire?

⊕ POSSIBLE RESPONSE

The simplicity and symmetry of the garden inspires calm, contemplation, and serenity.

three and a half sips while sitting on the floor of a bare hut. The simplicity of the tea ceremony focused attention on the beauty of an everyday activity.

Many people considered Zen Buddhism a difficult religion to practice. However, Zen Buddhism won a strong following among

the warrior class that was developing in Japan. The religion's focus on simplicity, self-discipline, and the contemplation of life and death appealed to warriors, who regularly faced deadly challenges on the battlefield. Their support ensured Zen Buddhism an important place in Japanese society.

REVIEW & ASSESS

1. **READING CHECK** Which guiding principles of Zen Buddhism had an impact on Japanese society and culture?

2. **COMPARE AND CONTRAST** How do traditional Buddhism and Zen Buddhism differ?

3. **MAKE INFERENCES** How do Zen viewing gardens reflect the values of Zen Buddhism?

PLAN

OBJECTIVE

Identify how Zen Buddhism was adopted by many and influenced Japanese culture.

CRITICAL THINKING SKILLS FOR LESSON 2.3

- Identify Main Ideas and Details
- Monitor Comprehension
- Compare and Contrast
- Make Inferences
- Draw Conclusions
- Form and Support Opinions
- Analyze Visuals

ESSENTIAL QUESTION

How was Japanese civilization influenced by neighboring cultures?

Zen Buddhism came from China in the 1100s and was widely embraced by the Japanese. It has influenced Japanese culture more than traditional Buddhism. Lesson 2.3 outlines the basic philosophy and beliefs of Zen Buddhism.

BACKGROUND FOR THE TEACHER

Zen Buddhism is not a typical religion. It does not have a scripture or moral code or leader; it is an experience of looking inside oneself. Zen Buddhists try to achieve a trance-like state through meditation. It has become popular for individuals in all countries, especially as a way to stay calm in a fast and crazy world. Apple cofounder Steve Jobs practiced Zen Buddhism, as have other celebrity figures.

DIGITAL RESOURCES myNGconnect.com

TEACHER RESOURCES & ASSESSMENT

 Reading and Note-Taking

 Vocabulary Practice

 Section 2 Quiz

STUDENT RESOURCES

 NG Chapter Gallery

INTRODUCE & ENGAGE

INTRODUCE & ENGAGE

THINK, PAIR, SHARE

Tell students to think about the topic of meditation. They can jot down what they know about it. Then they should pair up with a classmate and discuss the act of meditation. Finally, have them individually share information with the class. **0:05** minutes

TEACH

GUIDED DISCUSSION

1. **Make Inferences** Why would Zen Buddhism appeal to the warriors in Japan? *(Their working lives would be filled with chaos, high action, war, noise, and quick decision-making. The simplicity and calmness of meditative practice would contrast with their lives and settle them down, giving them peace.)*

2. **Draw Conclusions** From what you have read about the practice of Zen, why does it require self-discipline and concentration? *(To meditate, the person cannot be distracted by what's going on in the world but has to focus on the inner self. The person has to focus his or her thoughts totally on the present moment. This would not be easy for most people. The tea ceremony even dictates how many sips a person takes.)*

3. **Form and Support Opinions** Would you find Zen Buddhism appealing to yourself or people you know? Why or why not? *(Responses will vary but should be backed by reasons.)*

ANALYZE VISUALS

Have students study the photograph of the Buddhist monk meditating. **ASK:**

- Describe the monk's posture. *(straight back, sitting on knees, head up, arms hanging)*
- What does the placement of the gravel suggest to you? *(Responses will vary; some might say waves or water.)*
- Why do you suppose there are no flowers in the garden? *(Flowers might be distracting, and they change over time. Bushes and mosses remain mostly the same, which inspires calm.)*

0:10 minutes

ACTIVE OPTIONS

Critical Viewing: NG Image Gallery Invite students to explore the entire NG Image Gallery and choose one image from the gallery they feel best represents their understanding of this chapter or lesson. Have students provide a written explanation of why they selected the image they chose. **0:10** minutes

On Your Feet: Fishbowl Have part of the class sit in a closed circle facing inward, and have the other part of the class sit in a larger circle around them. Tell students on the inside to discuss Zen Buddhism and contrast it with religions they have studied in

other chapters. Those in the outside circle should listen for new information. Then have the groups reverse positions and continue the discussion. **0:10** minutes

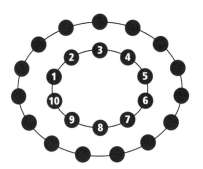

DIFFERENTIATE

STRIVING READERS

Write Paragraph Summaries Have students work with a partner to write a short summary of each paragraph. Students should come up with six statements that summarize the whole lesson.

PRE-AP

Make Connections Have students write a short essay on why they think that Zen Buddhism was so easily adopted by the Japanese people. Suggest that students review the last few lessons and look for patterns in what they read. They can make generalizations about what the Japanese people valued as shown in different ways in their culture. Have students read each other's essays later and see how much they agreed.

Press **mt** *in the Student eEdition for modified text.*

See the Chapter Planner for more strategies for differentiation.

REVIEW & ASSESS

ANSWERS

1. Zen Buddhism's guiding principles of simplicity, understatement, and grace had a major impact on Japanese society and culture and are reflected in the art, literature, and such everyday practices as gardening.

2. Traditional Buddhism and Zen Buddhism differ in their approach to salvation or enlightenment. Followers of traditional Buddhism study scriptures and perform religious rituals and good deeds, while followers of Zen Buddhism practice meditation to achieve inner peace and enlightenment.

3. The use of gravel and a few rocks in Zen viewing gardens reflects the Zen values of simplicity and understatement.

Samurai
and Shoguns

The year is 1195. A Japanese warrior strides confidently past a group of peasant farmers.

He looks magnificent in his colorful and decorative armor. But with his swords and spears, he is also deadly. The warrior hardly notices the peasants, but they bow their heads anyway. They know their place in Japanese society.

MAIN IDEA

Between 1192 and 1867, powerful military families ruled Japan with the support of armies of hired warriors.

FEMALE WARRIORS

Some Japanese women were well-trained, skillful fighters. Women of the samurai class were expected to defend their homes from attack by enemy warriors. A few female warriors also rode into battle.

+ POSSIBLE RESPONSE

The enemy would probably be frightened or feel challenged.

Critical Viewing Samurai line up for battle in this scene from the 2003 movie *The Last Samurai*. How might an enemy facing these samurai feel?

A STRUCTURED SOCIETY

By the mid-1000s, the power of the central government in Japan was fading. The emperor's responsibilities were limited to religious functions. The real rulers of Japan were the **daimyo** (DY-mee-oh), the leaders of large landowning families.

As the power of the central government decreased, the daimyo grew stronger and more independent. They transformed their local estates into self-governing states, wielding the power of life and death over those under them.

Each daimyo had an army of hired warriors called **samurai** (SAM-uh-ry). Individual samurai swore allegiance to a daimyo and were duty-bound to fight for their lord. In return, the samurai received money and land. The samurai were **vassals** of the daimyo. A vassal is a person who receives land from a feudal lord in exchange for obedience and service.

This order of allegiance, called **feudalism**, was the main system of government in medieval Europe as well as Japan. The greatest daimyo came to command the allegiance of many lesser lords and their armies, creating powerful rival groups that battled for control of Japan.

MILITARY RULE

Japan's daimyo fought one another until the Minamoto (MEE-nah-moh-toh) family defeated them all. In 1192, the family's leader, Yoritomo (yoh-REE-toh-moh), became **shogun**, which means "general." As shogun, Yoritomo effectively governed Japan, and the emperor became a figurehead. The Minamoto family began a long line of hereditary rulers. The dynasty held power until the 1300s.

The warrior culture of this period was based on a strict code of behavior called **bushido** (BUSH-ih-doh), or "the way of the warrior." Bushido fused aspects of three religions: Shinto's devotion to family and ruler, Zen Buddhism's focus on inner peace and fearlessness, and Confucianism's service to state and country. The code promoted loyalty, bravery, and honor, much like the code of chivalry followed by knights, a warrior class that arose in Europe around the 800s.

REVIEW & ASSESS

1. **READING CHECK** What were the roles of the emperor, the daimyo, and the samurai in feudal Japan?

2. **IDENTIFY PROBLEMS AND SOLUTIONS** What problem in Japan's central government did feudalism help solve?

3. **MAKE INFERENCES** What were some benefits and drawbacks of being a samurai?

PLAN

OBJECTIVE

Identify how large landowning families ruled Japan using armies of samurai warriors.

CRITICAL THINKING SKILLS FOR LESSON 3.1

- Identify Main Ideas and Details
- Monitor Comprehension
- Identify Problems and Solutions
- Make Inferences
- Form and Support Opinions
- Draw Conclusions
- Analyze Visuals

ESSENTIAL QUESTION

How was Japanese civilization influenced by neighboring cultures?

Although the samurai warriors were uniquely Japanese, their spiritual training and self-discipline had been borrowed and adapted from ideas brought from China. Lesson 3.1 explores the feudal society, including samurai culture, that developed in Japan.

BACKGROUND FOR THE TEACHER

Samurai warriors started training as children. They had physical training and learned about Bushido and Zen Buddhism, Chinese studies, poetry, and spiritual discipline.

The samurai's life of discipline and order was inspired by the teachings of Buddhism, Shinto, and Confucianism. These teaching helped the samurai stay calm and focused in the midst of any challenges and to connect with nature.

DIGITAL RESOURCES myNGconnect.com

TEACHER RESOURCES & ASSESSMENT

 Reading and Note-Taking   **Vocabulary Practice**   **Section 3 Quiz**

STUDENT RESOURCES

 **Active History**

INTRODUCE & ENGAGE

ACCESS PRIOR KNOWLEDGE

Divide the class into teams of four. Challenge them to remember all they can about medieval knights in Europe. Have each team fill out a Word Web to recall details about how the knights fought, their code of chivalry, how they were paid, what they wore, and so on. When teams are finished, have them read some of their facts aloud and allow other teams to add forgotten facts to their own webs. Have them save the charts for use in the "On Your Feet" activity later in the lesson. `0:05` minutes

TEACH

GUIDED DISCUSSION

1. **Form and Support Opinions** In your opinion, was the code of bushido that the samurai followed good or bad for the general population of Japan? Support your opinion with reasons. *(Most will say it was a good thing because it caused the warriors to be on their best behavior. Keeping armed men or warriors on good behavior saves lives.)*

2. **Draw Conclusions** When the shogun took over the power from the emperor, how did it change the leadership of the country? *(It became a country ruled by the military, not run by a civilian. War would be much more likely when the military took over.)*

ANALYZE VISUALS

Have students study the film still from the movie *The Last Samurai*. **ASK:** Do you think this movie scene shows a realistic picture of the samurai? Why or why not? *(Most will say the photo is realistic based on what they've read about bushido in the lesson.)* `0:10` minutes

ACTIVE OPTIONS

Active History: Solve a Puzzle About Feudal Japan Extend the lesson by using either the PDF or Whiteboard version of the activity. These activities take a deeper look at a topic from, or related to, the lesson. Explore the activities as a class, turn them into group assignments, or even assign them individually. `0:10` minutes

On Your Feet: Warrior Comparison Have students form teams of four. Tell them that they are going to create a visual display that compares the medieval knights of Europe with the samurai of Japan. They will need pictures or drawings of both types of warriors, and they should list similarities and differences between the two groups. Remind them to plan their display ahead and prepare what they will write on the display. Urge them to work together as a team to achieve the best displays. Have them present their displays to the class and find a place to show them. `0:10` minutes

DIFFERENTIATE

ENGLISH LANGUAGE LEARNERS

True or False Provide true-false statements like the ones below to check students' understanding of the vocabulary in this lesson. Ask students to correct the false statements.

- A shogun is a military general. *(true)*
- Bushido is a type of literature. *(false: code of behavior)*
- The daimyo were the leaders of the large landowning families. *(true)*
- Vassals had no land and worked for farmers. *(false: had land, worked for daimyo)*
- The system of government in Japan at this time was feudalism. *(true)*
- Japan's military warriors were called knights. *(false: samurai)*

PRE-AP

Write a Samurai Blog Invite students to imagine that they are samurai and have them write a blog about their daily life. Students might write about their bravery in battle and loyalty to their lords, and include examples of their artwork. Ask bloggers to share their writing with the rest of the class. Encourage readers to interact with the bloggers by contributing comments.

Press (**mt**) *in the Student eEdition for modified text.*

See the Chapter Planner for more strategies for differentiation.

REVIEW & ASSESS

ANSWERS

1. The Japanese emperor was mostly a figurehead, holding little political power. The daimyo were rulers of their own independent estates. The samurai fought for the daimyo in exchange for money and land.

2. Feudalism solved the problem of a weak central government by providing structure, order, and protection for people within independent, self-governing states.

3. Possible response: Benefits—Samurai enjoyed respect and status and received money and land. They had a clear-cut way of life. Drawbacks—Samurai could be injured in battle or lose their lives.

3.2 TOOLS OF THE SAMURAI

A samurai riding into battle on horseback must have been quite a sight. The colorful, complicated armor was made to be both beautiful and useful. The armor included metal or leather scales laced together to protect the warrior's body while allowing quick, easy movement. A samurai was armed with two swords, a long curved one and a short one, as well as a spear or gun.

Armor
A great deal of care and effort went into making the elaborate armor for a samurai.

Coat
This surcoat from the 1700s was made to be worn over armor.

Helmet Crest
The creature depicted in this helmet crest has the head of a tiger and the body of a fish.

Spear
This spear from the 1800s is made of iron, wood, and crushed mother of pearl.

Sword
Samurai highly valued their razor-sharp swords.

Gun
The Portuguese introduced the first guns into Japan in the 1500s.

Face and Neck Guard
Samurai wore terrifying masks like this one.

Helmet
This helmet from about 1550 is made of iron, wood, leather, gilt copper, and lacing.

565

PLAN

OBJECTIVE

Identify the weapons and protection that the samurai wore in battle.

CRITICAL THINKING SKILLS FOR LESSON 3.2

- Describe
- Analyze Visuals
- Compare and Contrast

ESSENTIAL QUESTION

How was Japanese civilization influenced by neighboring cultures?

The behavior code and the studies of the samurai were influenced by the Chinese, but the samurai warriors were unique to Japan. Lesson 3.2 shows and explains the use of various samurai equipment.

BACKGROUND FOR THE TEACHER

The name "samurai" comes from a word meaning "to serve." The samurai were totally loyal to their daimyo and would fight to the death, even committing suicide if they failed. They were experts with bows and arrows, spears, and hand-to-hand combat, but their chief weapon and their pride and joy was their sword. People today are still buying Samurai swords. However, when guns became available in later years, the samurai readily adopted these new weapons.

DIGITAL RESOURCES myNGconnect.com

TEACHER RESOURCES & ASSESSMENT

 Reading and Note-Taking   **Vocabulary Practice**   **Section 3 Quiz**

STUDENT RESOURCES

 NG Chapter Gallery

INTRODUCE & ENGAGE

THREE STEP INTERVIEW

Before students look at the visual, have them sit with a partner. Have Student A interview Student B to describe the weapons and protective gear that he or she thinks the samurai used and wore. Then partners reverse roles. Both partners can share their ideas with the class. Then let them look at the visual and see how close their guesses and memories were. **0:10** minutes

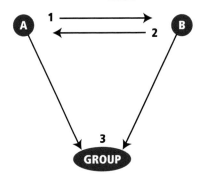

TEACH

GUIDED DISCUSSION

1. **Describe** What combination of materials were used to make the weapons and pieces of armor both strong and flexible? *(iron, wood, crushed mother of pearl, leather, gilt copper, and lacing)*

2. **Analyze Visuals** How is the samurai's horse protected? *(a leather cover for nose, protection near its eyes, a gold chain cover for its chest and neck)*

COMPARE AND CONTRAST

If possible, have students look at the "History Through Objects" feature on medieval knights in Chapter 21, Lesson 1.5. Have students compare the outfits of the knights and the samurai. **ASK:**

- How do the materials used for the samurai's protection differ from that used for the medieval European knights? *(The knights' outfits were made from metal; the samurai's outfit seemed to be principally leather.)*
- How would this affect the wearer? *(The knights' armor would be heavier and hotter than the samurai's leather armor; however the knights might have had stronger protection from spears.)*

0:10 minutes

ACTIVE OPTIONS

On Your Feet: Weapons of War Have students work in teams of four to fill out two Concept Clusters, one naming the weapons of war that the samurai used, the other naming the weapons of war that today's soldiers use. When teams are finished, have them share their charts. **0:05** minutes

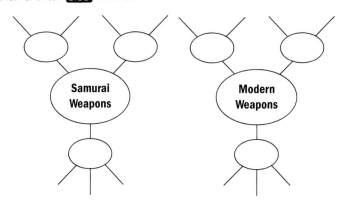

Critical Viewing: NG Image Gallery Have students explore the entire NG Image Gallery and choose two of the items to compare and contrast, either in written form or verbally with a partner. Ask questions that will inspire this process, such as: How are these images alike? How are they different? Why did you select these two items? How do they relate in history? **0:10** minutes

DIFFERENTIATE

INCLUSION

Describe Lesson Visuals Pair visually challenged students with well-sighted students. Have the well-sighted students read the captions and describe the details of the weapons and protective clothing to their partners.

PRE-AP

Samurai Swords Challenge students to research samurai swords. Students should report on the swords of the ancient samurai as well as what is sold today. Have them give an oral report about their findings to the rest of the class.

Press **mt** *in the Student eEdition for modified text.*

See the Chapter Planner for more strategies for differentiation.

3.3 Unification and Isolation

In some developing countries today, people protest against Western influence on their cultures. They fear losing their own unique cultures as their countries become more and more westernized. In the 1600s, Japan's rulers not only complained, they did something. They closed the country's doors to foreigners.

MAIN IDEA

After centuries of intense power struggles, Japan was reunified in the 1600s under a strong central government that rejected contact with foreigners.

THE WARRING STATES PERIOD

Japan faced a major threat in 1274: invasion by the Mongols, the great Asian superpower you learned about in the previous chapter. The Mongols had already conquered China and Korea. Now the Mongol leader Kublai Khan wanted to control Japan, too. In their initial attack, the Mongols captured many outlying islands. Then they retreated after a typhoon wrecked many of their ships.

Kublai Khan did not launch another invasion of Japan until 1281. However, this time he assembled the largest seaborne invasion force the world had yet seen—4,400 ships

carrying about 150,000 men. The daimyo put aside their differences and focused all their resources on defeating the Mongols. The Japanese warriors fought the invaders for about two months. Then a typhoon smashed into the Mongol fleet, killing tens of thousands. Japan claimed that heaven had saved the country by sending a *kamikaze*, or "divine wind," to stop the Mongols.

Instead of unifying Japan, however, this victory against the Mongols tore the country apart. A vast amount of money had been spent on the defense, but the Japanese gained no valuable rewards to repay the nobles and warriors. This inability to pay undermined the shogun's authority. Steadily, the daimyo seized control of their regions and then ruled them independently. Japan became divided among some 300 daimyo, all plotting and fighting for power.

This period of the "Warring States" lasted from 1467 until 1568. Then a powerful leader named Oda Nobunaga (oh-dah noh-boo-nah-gah) brought most of Japan under his control. In 1603, a leader named **Tokugawa Ieyasu** (toh-koo-gah-wah ee-yeh-yah-soo) finally broke the power of the daimyo and reunified all of Japan under a **shogunate**, or rule by a shogun.

THE TOKUGAWA SHOGUNATE

Ieyasu's rule ushered in a period of stability and peace that lasted nearly 300 years. Ieyasu and his successors feared that foreign contact was corrupting the people and upsetting the traditional balance of power. As a result, by 1639, the shoguns had begun a national policy of isolation and cut Japan off from outside influence. They stopped almost all foreign trade and travel and expelled certain groups of foreigners, including Europeans and Christians. Japan's isolation continued for more than 200 years. Then, in 1854, the United States pressured Japan to reopen for foreign trade. In 1867, the Tokugawa shogunate was overthrown and the emperor took control of Japan.

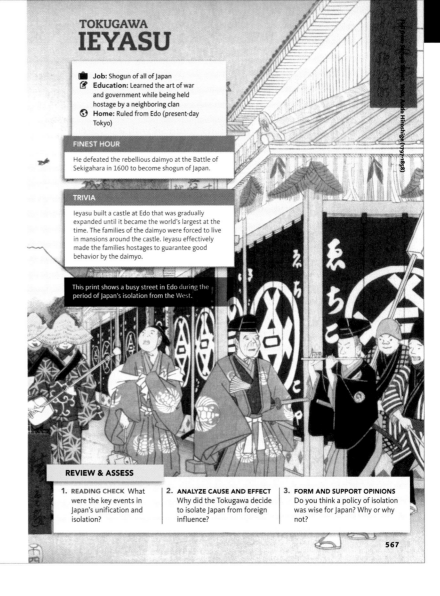

TOKUGAWA IEYASU

- **Job:** Shogun of all of Japan
- **Education:** Learned the art of war and government while being held hostage by a neighboring clan
- **Home:** Ruled from Edo (present-day Tokyo)

FINEST HOUR

He defeated the rebellious daimyo at the Battle of Sekigahara in 1600 to become shogun of Japan.

TRIVIA

Ieyasu built a castle at Edo that was gradually expanded until it became the world's largest at the time. The families of the daimyo were forced to live in mansions around the castle. Ieyasu effectively made the families hostages to guarantee good behavior by the daimyo.

This print shows a busy street in Edo during the period of Japan's isolation from the West.

REVIEW & ASSESS

1. **READING CHECK** What were the key events in Japan's unification and isolation?

2. **ANALYZE CAUSE AND EFFECT** Why did the Tokugawa decide to isolate Japan from foreign influence?

3. **FORM AND SUPPORT OPINIONS** Do you think a policy of isolation was wise for Japan? Why or why not?

566 CHAPTER 19

567

PLAN

OBJECTIVE

Identify how Japan became reunified but isolated from foreign contact.

CRITICAL THINKING SKILLS FOR LESSON 3.3

- Identify Main Ideas and Details
- Monitor Comprehension
- Analyze Cause and Effect
- Form and Support Opinions
- Make Inferences
- Evaluate
- Analyze Visuals

ESSENTIAL QUESTION

How was Japanese civilization influenced by neighboring cultures?

Japan fought to protect itself from Mongols. Lesson 3.3 explains how Japan became divided and reunited after the Mongol threat subsided.

BACKGROUND FOR THE TEACHER

During the time of the Tokugawa Shogunate, Edo, which today is called Tokyo, became a very lively political and cultural center. It featured shopping, theaters, a busy nightlife, streets filled with pedestrians, peace and prosperity for all. Before Tokugawa took it over, it had been a little fishing village. Edo became so prosperous that this period of time was called the "Edo period."

DIGITAL RESOURCES myNGconnect.com

TEACHER RESOURCES & ASSESSMENT

 Reading and Note-Taking

 Vocabulary Practice

 Section 3 Quiz

STUDENT RESOURCES

 NG Chapter Gallery

PREVIEW THE TITLE

Write the title of this lesson on the board, *Unification and Isolation.* Draw two Word Squares on the board, one for the word *unification* and the other for *isolation.* Have volunteers give definitions of each word. Ask for antonyms, or opposites, of each word. Finally, ask for examples of countries that have unified after being split apart. Then ask for examples of countries that seem isolated from the rest of the world. **0:05** minutes

TEACH

GUIDED DISCUSSION

1. **Analyze Cause and Effect** How did Japan avoid being captured by the Mongols twice? *(In both cases, typhoons smashed the Mongol fleets.)*

2. **Make Inferences** Why do you think the defeat of the Mongol fleets split up Japan's united clans rather than keeping them together after a victory? *(Possible response: The daimyos had all lost money on the war and the government couldn't help, so they fought each other for money and power.)*

3. **Evaluate** How did Ieyasu keep control of the daimyos after he became shogun of Japan? What do you think of this method? *(He made the families live near the castle, keeping them as hostages to make the daimyos behave. Opinions will vary. It was effective but unfair to the families.)*

ANALYZE VISUALS

Have students study the print of Edo. What details make the town look prosperous? *(Many people are walking the street, buildings are decorated, people are wearing nice clothing, people are carrying musical instruments and batons, and people look happy.)* **0:10** minutes

ACTIVE OPTIONS

On Your Feet: Two Corners Label two corners of the room with signs: *Isolation = Good Idea, Isolation = Bad Idea.* Begin the activity by having students sit with a partner and make a chart like the one below. Have them list positives and negatives for Japan isolating itself from all foreign influence, called a closed-door policy. When the partners have completed their charts, they should evaluate their list and choose one of the two corners to stand in. When all have chosen, have each corner defend its choice using the reasons they have listed. **0:10** minutes

POSITIVE	NEGATIVE

NG Learning Framework: Geographic Effects

SKILL: Observation
KNOWLEDGE: Our Living Planet

Have small teams of students work together. They should look back through this chapter to find ways that geography and physical events of nature affected Japan's history. They should list positive and negative effects from Japan's point of view. Have them write a short paragraph to summarize their findings. **0:10** minutes

STRIVING READERS

Keep Track of Events Help students keep track of the many events and dates in this lesson. Have them look for dates in each paragraph and make notes to fill out the chart below:

DATE	EVENT
1274	*(Typhoon wrecks Mongol ships, ending invasion)*
1281	*(Typhoon wrecks Mongol ships again, ending invasion)*
1467–1568	*(Period of Warring States)*
1568	*(Oda Nobunaga brings most of Japan under control)*
1603	*(Tokugawa Ieyasu reunifies Japan under his shogunate)*
1639	*(Japan begins period of isolation)*

Press (**mt**) *in the Student eEdition for modified text.*

See the Chapter Planner for more strategies for differentiation.

ANSWERS

1. After the Warring States period, a leader named Oda Nobunaga brought most of Japan under his control. Then in 1603, Tokugawa Ieyasu broke the power of the daimyo and reunified all of Japan under his shogunate. Ieyasu and his successors instituted a national policy of isolation for over 200 years.

2. Ieyasu and his successors feared that foreign contact was corrupting the people and upsetting the balance of power.

3. Possible responses: Yes, it was wise because the shogun could focus on internal problems, which led to a period of peace and stability that lasted nearly 300 years. No, it was not wise because the Japanese missed out on innovation that was occurring in other parts of the world.

VOCABULARY

Use each of the following vocabulary words in a sentence that shows an understanding of the word's meaning.

1. **archipelago**
   Japan is an archipelago, or chain of islands, located in the Pacific Ocean.

2. **daimyo**
3. **clan**
4. **regent**
5. **haiku**
6. **samurai**
7. **shogun**
8. **bushido**

READING STRATEGY

9. **MAKE INFERENCES** If you haven't already, complete the graphic organizer to make inferences about how the Japanese viewed Chinese culture. Then answer the question.

What Text Says
The Japanese added new characters to the Chinese alphabet.

+

What I Know
The Chinese had developed an alphabet for the Chinese language.

↓

Inference

Based on what you've read, how did the Japanese view Chinese culture? Support your response with evidence from the chapter.

MAIN IDEAS

Answer the following questions. Support your answers with evidence from the chapter.

10. In what ways did Japan's geography affect its sense of unity? LESSON 1.1

11. What belief forms the basis of Japan's ancient religion of Shinto? LESSON 1.2

12. What ideas did Japan borrow from China's civilization? LESSON 1.4

13. What new forms of literature and drama did the Japanese develop? LESSON 2.1

14. What is the goal of meditation in Zen Buddhism? LESSON 2.3

15. How did Japan come to be ruled by powerful military families between 1192 and 1867? LESSON 3.1

16. How was Japan reunified after the Warring States period? LESSON 3.3

CRITICAL THINKING

Answer the following questions. Support your answers with evidence from the chapter.

17. **MAKE INFERENCES** How does the Zen tea ceremony reflect the religion's value of simplicity?

18. **ANALYZE CAUSE AND EFFECT** Why was the Shinto religion a strong unifying factor in early Japanese society?

19. **DRAW CONCLUSIONS** Which government probably had more qualified officials—the Chinese or the Japanese? Why?

20. **COMPARE AND CONTRAST** How did Japan open itself to other cultures? How did it close itself off?

21. **MAKE GENERALIZATIONS** How did feudalism benefit both the daimyo and vassals?

22. **YOU DECIDE** Was China's influence on Japan beneficial or harmful? Support your opinion with evidence from the chapter.

INTERPRET CHARTS

Study this chart, which illustrates Japan's society in the feudal period. Then answer the questions that follow.

HIERARCHICAL SOCIETY IN FEUDAL JAPAN
- Emperor
- Shogun
- Daimyo
- Samurai
- Peasants & Artisans

23. Who held the real power in feudal Japan's military society?

24. Which class of people probably created the most wealth for feudal Japan? Why?

ANALYZE SOURCES

Read the following haiku written by a modern Japanese poet. Then answer the question that follows.

I kill an ant . . .
and realize my three children
were watching
—Shuson Kato (1905–1993)

25. What enduring values of Japanese culture are reflected in this haiku?

WRITE ABOUT HISTORY

26. **INFORMATIVE** Write a short encyclopedia article for fellow students comparing or contrasting the rule of Prince Shotoku and the rule of Tokugawa Ieyasu.

TIPS
- Take notes on each ruler from Lessons 1.3 and 3.3.
- State your main idea about the similarities or differences between the two rulers in your beginning sentence.
- Develop the main idea with relevant facts, details, or examples about the rule of each leader.
- Use transitions, such as "in a similar way" or "unlike," to clarify the relationships between ideas.
- Provide a concluding statement that follows from and supports the information presented.

VOCABULARY ANSWERS

Sentences may vary. Sample sentences are given.

1. Japan is an archipelago, or chain of islands, located in the Pacific Ocean.

2. The daimyo, or leaders of large landowning families, ruled like kings of their estates.

3. In the Yayoi culture, each small kingdom was ruled by a powerful clan, whose members shared a common ancestor.

4. Empress Suiko appointed her nephew, Prince Shotoku, as her regent, which meant he was the real power behind the throne.

5. Matsuo Basho was a great master of haiku, a poem of exactly 17 syllables.

6. In Japan, the samurai were a distinct warrior class that swore allegiance to noble families and served as their army.

7. A shogun was a Japanese military ruler who held real power, while the emperor was just a figurehead.

8. The samurai followed a strict code of behavior called bushido, which centered on the values of bravery, honor, and loyalty.

READING STRATEGY ANSWER

What Text Says
The Japanese added new characters to the Chinese alphabet.

+

What I Know
The Chinese had developed an alphabet for the Chinese language.

↓

Inference
The Japanese believed they could adapt and improve Chinese culture for their own use.

9. The Japanese viewed Chinese culture as something they could adapt and improve upon for their own culture. For instance, the

Japanese took the Chinese alphabet and added characters to make it easier to write Japanese words. They also copied the Chinese civil service system but appointed officials based on heredity instead of on ability—this practice fit better within Japan's hierarchical society.

MAIN IDEAS ANSWERS

10. As an island nation in the Pacific Ocean, Japan was relatively isolated from its nearest neighbors, China and Korea, and so its population grew from largely one ethnic group and developed a strong sense of unity.

11. The Shinto religion is based on the belief that spiritual powers reside in nature.

12. Japan borrowed China's system of writing and its civil service system.

13. The Japanese developed the novel and haiku as well as two new types of drama—noh and kabuki.

14. The goal of meditation in Zen Buddhism is to achieve inner peace and realize the divine aspect in each person.

15. By the mid-1000s, Japanese emperors had become figureheads with little political control. The daimyo, supported by armies of samurai, ruled their estates and fought one another to gain control of Japan. By 1192, the Minamoto family gained control and established the rule of shoguns.

16. After the Warring States period, a powerful daimyo named Oda Nobunaga brought most of Japan under his control and restored strong centralized government. Another leader named Tokugawa Ieyasu unified all of Japan under his sole rule.

CRITICAL THINKING ANSWERS

17. The Zen tea ceremony is conducted in a bare hut with participants sitting on the floor. The tea drinkers take exactly three and a half sips. They drink bitter, not sweetened, tea. The tea, number of sips, and surroundings are all simple, thus reflecting Zen's value of simplicity.

18. The Shinto religion was a strong unifying factor in early Japanese society because families, clans, and regions worshipped a particular kami. Eventually, Shinto helped unite Japan under a single leader, an emperor who claimed descent from Shinto's chief deity, the sun goddess.

19. The Chinese government probably had more qualified officials because they earned their positions through examinations and good work, while the appointment of Japanese officials was based on heredity.

20. Between 607 and 839, Japan opened itself to other cultures by sending missions to China to learn everything about Chinese

culture. Between 1639 and 1854, Japan closed itself off by instituting a national policy of isolation, stopping almost all foreign trade and travel and expelling certain groups of foreigners.

21. The daimyo gained military power, and the vassals gained land and money.

22. Students' responses may vary. Sample response: China's influence on Japan was mostly beneficial because it helped unify the country and give the people a national identity. In addition, China's influence helped advance Japan's agriculture, technology, literature, and arts.

INTERPRET CHARTS ANSWERS

23. In feudal Japan's military society, the real power was held by the shogun.

24. The peasants and artisans probably created the most wealth for feudal Japan because they were the ones who produced food and goods for trade.

ANALYZE SOURCES ANSWER

25. Possible response: This haiku reflects the high value that the Japanese place on nature by attaching importance to even the life of an ant. The simplicity of the poem itself reflects the value that the Japanese place on simplicity. The poem also suggests that even our simplest acts are important.

WRITE ABOUT HISTORY ANSWER

26. Students' encyclopedia articles should do the following:
- clearly state the main idea
- develop the main idea with relevant facts, details, or examples about each ruler
- include transitions to clarify relationships between ideas
- end with a concluding statement that supports the information presented

UNIT RESOURCES

On Location with National Geographic Emerging Explorer Albert Lin
Intro and Video

Interactive Map Tool

News & Updates

Available on myNGconnect

Unit Wrap-Up:
"The Search for Genghis Khan"
Feature and Video

"Divining Angkor"
National Geographic Adapted Article

"The Forgotten Road"
National Geographic Adapted Article
Student eEdition exclusive

Unit 8 Inquiry:
Leave a Legacy of Innovation

CHAPTER RESOURCES

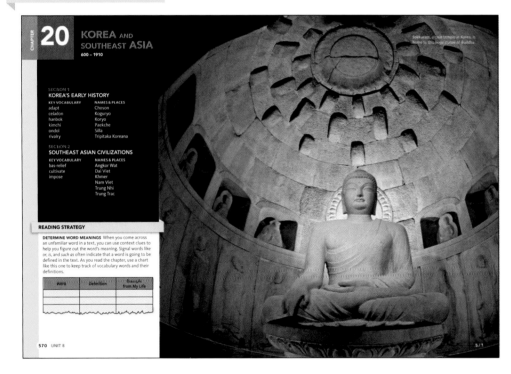

CHAPTER
20 **KOREA** AND **SOUTHEAST ASIA**
600 – 1910

Sokkuram, a cave temple in Korea, is home to this huge statue of Buddha.

SECTION 1
KOREA'S EARLY HISTORY

KEY VOCABULARY	NAMES & PLACES
adapt	Choson
celadon	Koguryo
hanbok	Koryo
kimchi	Paekche
ondol	Silla
rivalry	Tripitaka Koreana

SECTION 2
SOUTHEAST ASIAN CIVILIZATIONS

KEY VOCABULARY	NAMES & PLACES
bas-relief	Angkor Wat
cultivate	Dai Viet
impose	Khmer
	Nam Viet
	Trung Nhi
	Trung Trac

READING STRATEGY

DETERMINE WORD MEANINGS When you come across an unfamiliar word in a text, you can use context clues to help you figure out the word's meaning. Signal words like *or*, *is*, and *such as* often indicate that a word is going to be defined in the text. As you read the chapter, use a chart like this one to keep track of vocabulary words and their definitions.

Word	Definition	Example from My Life

570 UNIT 8

TEACHER RESOURCES & ASSESSMENT

Available on myNGconnect

Social Studies Skills Lessons
• Reading: Determine Word Meanings
• Writing: Write a Narrative

Formal Assessment
• Chapter 20 Tests A (on-level) & B (below-level)

Chapter 20 Answer Key

ExamView®
One-time Download

STUDENT BACKPACK *Available on myNGconnect*
• **eEdition** *(English)*   • **eEdition** *(Spanish)*   • **Handbooks**   • **Online Atlas**
For Chapter 20 Spanish resources, visit the Teacher Resource Menu page on myNGconnect.

SECTION 1 RESOURCES

KOREA'S EARLY HISTORY

 Reading and Note-Taking

 Vocabulary Practice

 Section 1 Quiz

Available on myNGconnect

LESSON 1.1 THE THREE KINGDOMS
- Critical Viewing: NG Chapter Gallery
- On Your Feet: Question and Answer

HISTORY THROUGH OBJECTS
LESSON 1.2 KOREAN ARTIFACTS
- Critical Viewing: NG Chapter Gallery
- On Your Feet: Descriptive Words

LESSON 1.3 KORYO AND CHOSON DYNASTIES
- Critical Viewing: NG Chapter Gallery
- On Your Feet: Inside-Outside Circle

LESSON 1.4 KOREAN CULTURE

 Active History: Interactive Whiteboard Activity
Categorize Korea's Society Levels

 Active History
Categorize Korea's Society Levels

Available on myNGconnect

- On Your Feet: Turn and Talk on Topic

SECTION 2 RESOURCES

SOUTHEAST ASIAN CIVILIZATIONS

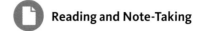 **Reading and Note-Taking**

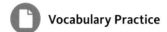 **Vocabulary Practice**

 **Section 2 Quiz**

Available on myNGconnect

LESSON 2.1 VIETNAMESE KINGDOMS
- Critical Viewing: NG Image Gallery
- On Your Feet: Card Responses

LESSON 2.2 THE KHMER EMPIRE

NG Learning Framework:
Make Observations

- On Your Feet: Tell Me More

LESSON 2.3 ANGKOR WAT
- Critical Viewing: NG Image Gallery
- On Your Feet: One-on-One Interviews

CHAPTER 20 REVIEW

STRATEGY ❶
Write a Tweet

Direct students to read a lesson and write a tweet in their own words that explains the main idea of each paragraph. Have pairs of students compare their tweets and agree on a final version.

Use with Lessons 1.1, 1.3, and 1.4

STRATEGY ❷
Ask Questions

Have pairs of students follow the instructions below as they read a lesson.

1. Pairs read the lesson and formulate one question that will help them understand it.

2. Pair One begins by asking Pair Two their question about the lesson. Pair Two answers the question.

3. Pair One confirms the answer.

4. Pair Two chooses Pair Three to answer their question, and so on.

Use with Lessons 2.1–2.3

STRATEGY ❸
Preview Text

Help students preview each section in the chapter. For each section, have them read the lesson titles, lesson introductions, Main Idea statements, captions, and subheadings. Then have them list the information they expect to find in the text. Have students read a lesson and discuss with a partner what they learned and whether or not it matched their list.

Use with All Lessons

Press (mt) *in the Student eEdition for modified text.*

STRATEGY ❶
Use Supported Reading

In small groups, have students read aloud the chapter lesson by lesson. At the end of each lesson, have them stop and use these frames to tell what they comprehended from the text:

This lesson is about _____ .

One detail that stood out to me is _____ .

The vocabulary word _____ means _____ .

I don't think I understand _____ .

Guide students with portions of text that they do not understand. Be sure all students understand a lesson before moving on to the next one.

Use with All Lessons

STRATEGY ❷
Preview Visuals to Predict

Ask students to preview the title and visuals in each lesson. Then have students tell what they think the lesson will be about. After reading, ask them to repeat the activity to see whether their predictions were confirmed.

Use with All Lessons *Invite volunteers to describe the visuals in detail to help visually impaired students see them.*

STRATEGY ❶
PREP Before Reading

Have students use the PREP strategy to prepare for reading. Write this acrostic on the board:

PREP	**P**review title.
	Read Main Idea statement.
	Examine visuals.
	Predict what you will learn.

Have students write their prediction and share it with a partner. After reading, ask students to write another sentence that begins "I also learned . . ."

Use with All Lessons

STRATEGY ❷
Pair Partners for Dictation

After students read each lesson in the chapter, have them write a sentence summarizing its main idea. Have students get together in pairs and dictate their sentences to each other. Then have them work together to check the sentences for accuracy and spelling.

Use with All Lessons

STRATEGY ❸
Use a Pair-Share Strategy

After reading, have students work in pairs. The first student reads aloud the Main Idea statement of the lesson and gives one example from the lesson that expands on or illustrates the main idea. Then the second student rereads the Main Idea statement and gives a different example.

Use with All Lessons

GIFTED & TALENTED

STRATEGY ❶
Teach a Class

Before beginning the chapter, allow students to choose one of the two-page lessons listed below and prepare to teach the contents to the class. Give them a set amount of time in which to present their lesson. Suggest that students think about any visuals or activities they want to use when they teach.

Use with Lessons 1.1, 1.3, 1.4, 2.1, 2.2, and 2.3

STRATEGY ❷
Annotate a Time Line

Suggest that students annotate a time line of events during the period of Korea's Three Kingdoms or during the Koryo and Choson dynasties. Students should use the information in the chapter as well as Internet research. Tell students to include details such as dates, locations, and important people. Students might also include illustrations with their time lines. Have students share their time lines with the class.

Use with Sections 1.1 and 1.3

PRE-AP

STRATEGY ❶
Create a Travel Brochure

Have students imagine that they are living during the time of the early kingdoms of Vietnam or during the time of the Khmer Empire. Tell students to choose a target audience of visitors and do research to prepare a travel brochure illustrating and describing places these visitors should not miss.

Use with Lessons 2.1–2.3

STRATEGY ❷
Form a Thesis

Have students develop a thesis statement for a specific topic related to one of the lessons in the chapter. Be sure the statement makes a claim that is supportable with evidence either from the chapter or through further research. Then have pairs compare their statements and determine which makes the strongest or most supportable claim.

Use with All Lessons

Sokkuram, a cave temple in Korea, is home to this huge statue of Buddha.

CHAPTER 20

20 KOREA AND SOUTHEAST ASIA

600 – 1910

SECTION 1
KOREA'S EARLY HISTORY

KEY VOCABULARY	NAMES & PLACES
adapt	Choson
celadon	Koguryo
hanbok	Koryo
kimchi	Paekche
ondol	Silla
rivalry	Tripitaka Koreana

SECTION 2
SOUTHEAST ASIAN CIVILIZATIONS

KEY VOCABULARY	NAMES & PLACES
bas-relief	Angkor Wat
cultivate	Dai Viet
impose	Khmer
	Nam Viet
	Trung Nhi
	Trung Trac

READING STRATEGY

DETERMINE WORD MEANINGS When you come across an unfamiliar word in a text, you can use context clues to help you figure out the word's meaning. Signal words like *or*, *is*, and *such as* often indicate that a word is going to be defined in the text. As you read the chapter, use a chart like this one to keep track of vocabulary words and their definitions.

Word	Definition	Example from My Life

TEACHER BACKGROUND

INTRODUCE THE PHOTOGRAPH

Ask students to study the photograph of Sokkuram and read the caption. Encourage students to notice details in the photo. **ASK:** How would you describe the temple and statue? *(Possible response: The statue is large, and intricately engraved figures surround the temple.)* What does the fact that this statue is displayed in the temple tell you about Korean culture? *(Possible response: Buddhism was likely an important aspect of Korean culture.)*

SHARE BACKGROUND

Sokkuram is a Buddhist cave temple situated at the foot of Mount Tohamsan in South Korea. Built in the 8th century, the structure is made of granite blocks. The large statue of Buddha sits on an elevated lotus pedestal. The statue is about 12 feet high and is carved out of a single block of granite. The sculpture is one of the finest achievements of Buddhist art in East Asia.

DIGITAL RESOURCES myNGconnect.com

TEACHER RESOURCES & ASSESSMENT

 Social Studies Skills Lessons
- Reading: Determine Word Meanings
- Writing: Write a Narrative

 Formal Assessment
- Chapter 20 Tests A (on-level) & B (below-level)

ExamView®
One-time Download

 **Chapter 20 Answer Key**

STUDENT BACKPACK

- **eEdition** *(English)*
- **eEdition** *(Spanish)*
- **Handbooks**
- **Online Atlas**

For Chapter 20 Spanish Resources, visit the Teacher Resource Menu page.

HOW DID KOREA AND SOUTHEAST ASIA ADAPT TO OUTSIDE INFLUENCES?

Roundtable Activity: Types of Influence This activity will allow students to explore the Essential Question by categorizing types of influence. Divide the class into groups of four or five students. Have the groups move desks together to form a table where they can all sit. Hand each group a sheet of paper with this question at the top: *What types of influence can one country have over another?* The first student in each group should write an answer and then pass the paper clockwise to the next student, who may add a new answer. The paper should be circulated around the group until the time is up. Students may pass at any time. After ten minutes, ask for volunteers to read their group's answers to the class. **0:20 minutes**

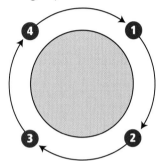

DETERMINE WORD MEANINGS

Remind students that they can use context clues to help them figure out a word's meaning. Tell students that context clues are hints that help define a word. The clue can appear within the same sentence as the word or it may appear in a sentence before or after the word that is being defined. Model completing the chart by reading aloud the first paragraph under "Rivalry" in Lesson 1.1 and adding the term *rivalry* under the column labeled "Word" and the definition *competition* under the column labeled "Definition." Then ask students to provide examples of rivalry from their own life and add them to the column labeled "Example from My Life."

WORD	DEFINITION	EXAMPLE FROM MY LIFE
rivalry	competition	

KNOWLEDGE RATING

Have students complete a Knowledge-Rating Chart for Key Vocabulary words. Have students list words and fill out the chart. Then have pairs share the definitions they know. Work together as a class to complete the chart.

KEY VOCAB	KNOW IT	NOT SURE	DON'T KNOW	DEFINITION
adapt				
bas-relief				
celadon				
cultivate				

KEY DATES	
c. 108 B.C.	Chinese Han dynasty conquers northwest Korea
57 B.C.	Silla kingdom forms
37 B.C.	Koguryo kingdom emerges
18 B.C.	Paekche kingdom founded
A.D. 668	Korea is unified
935	Koryo dynasty begins rule of Korea
1100s	Temple complex of Angkor Wat is built
1392	Choson dynasty replaces Koryo dynasty
1471	Vietnam is created
1910	Korea formally becomes part of Japan

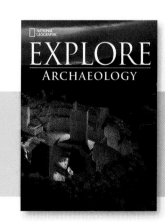

For more information on archaeological finds like Angkor Wat, check out *EXPLORE ARCHAEOLOGY.*

The **Three Kingdoms**

What might happen if your teachers lost control of your school? Groups of friends would stick together and do their own thing. Some small groups might band together to form larger ones based on shared friends and interests. In time, the whole school might be split into a few large groups ruling themselves and maybe even trying to control their rivals. This is what happened in Korea.

MAIN IDEA

Three kingdoms with strong Chinese cultural influences ruled early Korea.

FORMATION OF KOREA

Korea is a large, mountainous peninsula that juts out from the Asian continent. Its population became concentrated in the coastal plains and river valleys, where the land was fertile and could be cultivated.

Korea's nearest neighbors are China and Japan. The three countries have always influenced one another, both culturally and politically. In 108 B.C., the Chinese Han dynasty conquered northwest Korea. Chinese settlers followed, bringing their culture with them. But as the Han dynasty declined, its grip on Korea weakened. Korea's scattered native tribes began taking control of their lands and gradually formed three kingdoms.

Tradition claims that the **Silla** (SIHL-uh) kingdom was formed in southeast Korea around 57 B.C. About 37 B.C., the **Koguryo** (koh-gur-YOO) kingdom emerged in the north. Then, around 18 B.C., the **Paekche** (pahk-chay) kingdom was founded in the southwest. For centuries, the three kingdoms grew, developed, and fought one another for control of Korea. At first, Koguryo was by far the strongest, even as it fought off Chinese invasions. But by the A.D. 300s, Koguryo had managed to dominate most of the peninsula. Paekche's strength was largely economic due to extensive trade. Over time, Silla increased its political, military, and economic power.

RIVALRY

Despite their bitter **rivalry**, or competition, the three kingdoms had very similar cultures. They each developed feudal-style societies, with kings commanding a warrior aristocracy and an educated bureaucracy. Poor peasants provided the labor for agriculture. The kingdoms shared a common language and adopted Chinese writing. Their economies were similar as well. All three exported leather goods, tools, and wool clothing in exchange for Chinese paper, porcelain, silk, and weapons.

Chinese culture greatly influenced Korea in the areas of art, architecture, literature, government, and religion. From China, the kingdoms imported the Buddhist religion, as well as Confucian ideas for government and society. They also adopted Chinese writing. Despite these strong Chinese influences, Korea managed to maintain its own distinct culture.

In A.D. 660, the Silla king entered into an alliance with the Tang dynasty in China. Together, Silla and the Tang conquered Paekche in A.D. 660 and Koguryo in A.D. 668. For the first time, Korea was unified.

THE THREE KINGDOMS OF KOREA, A.D. 500s

KOGURYO

CHINA

Sea of Japan (East Sea)

Yellow Sea

• Kongju

SILLA

PAEKCHE

• Kyongju

JAPAN

• Kyota

• Osaka

Some historians see Silla's alliance with Tang China as a national betrayal that encouraged China's ambition to control the peninsula. Nevertheless, the alliance turned out to be a brilliant move for Silla. After the two allies conquered Paekche, the Tang seized complete control of the conquered lands and reduced the Silla king's powers. Silla waited patiently for revenge. It did not have long to wait.

Following the alliance's defeat of Koguryo, Silla took control of Paekche. Then China tried to depose the Silla king, an action that led to war between the two former allies. After a series of battles, Silla defeated the Chinese army in A.D. 675 and then fought off the Chinese navy the following year. China withdrew from the peninsula in A.D. 676, leaving Silla in control of a unified Korean kingdom.

REVIEW & ASSESS

1. **READING CHECK** How did China influence early Korea?

2. **SYNTHESIZE** What political goal did Silla, Koguryo, and Paekche have in common?

3. **INTERPRET MAPS** Why has human movement between China and Korea been relatively easy throughout history?

PLAN

OBJECTIVE

Identify the Chinese cultural influences on the three kingdoms of early Korea.

CRITICAL THINKING SKILLS FOR LESSON 1.1

- Identify Main Ideas and Details
- Monitor Comprehension
- Synthesize
- Interpret Maps
- Compare and Contrast
- Make Inferences
- Sequence Events

ESSENTIAL QUESTION

How did Korea and Southeast Asia adapt to outside influences?

The location of the Korean peninsula near China led to China's influence over the area. Lesson 1.1 identifies the ways in which Chinese culture influenced the Three Kingdoms of Korea.

BACKGROUND FOR THE TEACHER

During the time of the Three Kingdoms, Buddhism became the state religion and Confucianism provided the basis for government. The time period saw an interest in literature and the arts and an interest in the writing of national histories. A writing system that used Chinese characters to symbolize spoken Korean was also established. In the Silla kingdom, the aristocracy enjoyed many privileges. Aristocrats held all the important official positions and lived in luxury.

DIGITAL RESOURCES myNGconnect.com

TEACHER RESOURCES & ASSESSMENT

 Reading and Note-Taking

 Vocabulary Practice

 Section 1 Quiz

STUDENT RESOURCES

 NG Chapter Gallery

INTRODUCE & ENGAGE

MAKE CONNECTIONS

Hold a class discussion in which students point out influences in their community that come from other countries. Write students' responses on the board. Students might point out ethnic restaurants, language, or traditions they have. Tell students that in this lesson they will learn how Chinese culture influenced the early kingdoms of Korea. **0:05** minutes

TEACH

GUIDED DISCUSSION

1. **Compare and Contrast** How were the cultures of the Silla, Koguryo, and Paekche kingdoms similar? (*All three kingdoms developed feudal-style societies, kings oversaw a warrior aristocracy and an educated bureaucracy, peasants provided labor for agriculture, had a common language, adopted Chinese writing, and had similar economies.*)

2. **Make Inferences** Why do you think the Silla kingdom originally entered into an alliance with the Tang dynasty? (*Possible response: Silla originally entered into an alliance with China in order to have the strength to conquer the other two kingdoms.*)

SEQUENCE EVENTS

Have students use a Sequence Chain to record the actions of the Silla kingdom that left Silla in control of a unified Korea. They should build their chain to include actions up to unification. Remind students to use the information in the lesson and to add boxes if necessary. **ASK:** What could have prevented Silla from gaining control of Korea? (*Possible response: if Silla were not able to defeat the Chinese army or navy*) **0:20** minutes

ACTIVE OPTIONS

Critical Viewing: NG Chapter Gallery Ask students to choose one image from the Chapter Gallery and become an expert on it. They should do additional research to learn all about it. Then, students should share their findings with a partner, a small group, or the class. **0:10** minutes

On Your Feet: Question and Answer Have half the class write true-false questions based on information in Lesson 1.1. Ask the other half to create answer cards with "True" written on one side and "False" on the other. As each question is read aloud, students in the second group should display the correct answer to the question. When discrepancies occur, review the question and discuss which answer is correct. **0:15** minutes

DIFFERENTIATE

STRIVING READERS

Summarize Read the lesson aloud while students follow along in their books. At the end of each paragraph, ask students to summarize what you read in a sentence. Allow them time to write the summary on their own paper.

ENGLISH LANGUAGE LEARNERS

Find Main Idea and Details Have students form two groups. Give each group a piece of construction paper or a flip chart with the main idea of the lesson written on it: *Identify the Chinese cultural influences on the three kingdoms of early Korea.* Ask each group to list as many details from the lesson as they can to support the main idea. They should write their details on the flip chart or construction paper. Then have the two groups compare their lists.

Press **mt** in the Student eEdition for modified text.

See the Chapter Planner for more strategies for differentiation.

REVIEW & ASSESS

ANSWERS

1. China influenced almost every aspect of Korean life.

2. Each kingdom wanted control of Korea.

3. Korea is a peninsula that extends from China, making human movement and cultural influences between the two countries relatively easy throughout history.

HISTORY THROUGH OBJECTS

1.2 KOREAN ARTIFACTS

Archaeologists have discovered many beautiful artifacts from early Korea. These artifacts range from pottery to jewelry to religious figures. In Silla, sometimes called "the land of gold," artisans often used gold to create precious objects, including a number of gold crowns. Uniquely Korean, the crowns' designs incorporate chains with mirrors or jewels as well as elements of trees and antlers.

Crown of Silla
This ornate crown of gold was discovered in the tomb of a Silla king and queen.

Vase
Tiny figures of animals decorate this gray stoneware vase.

Dragon's Head
This gilded bronze dragon's head reflects the skill of Silla artisans.

Gogok
This jade teardrop, or gogok, probably once adorned a crown, belt, or bracelet.

Earrings
This pair of gold earrings from the early 400s were probably worn by a Silla noblewoman.

Tile
The monster mask on this roof tile was thought to ward off evil spirits.

Necklace
This ornate gold necklace is adorned with a jade gogok.

Bodhisattva
This statue of an enlightened being, or bodhisattva, is made of gilded bronze.

PLAN

OBJECTIVE

Describe the style of and materials used in Korean artifacts.

CRITICAL THINKING SKILLS FOR LESSON 1.2

- Draw Conclusions
- Make Generalizations
- Analyze Visuals

ESSENTIAL QUESTION

How did Korea and Southeast Asia adapt to outside influences?

Artisans in early Korea created a variety of artifacts. Lesson 1.2 describes the styles and materials used in Korean artifacts.

BACKGROUND FOR THE TEACHER

Most of the Silla artifacts were excavated from the tombs of Silla aristocrats. They provide a look into the practices surrounding burials and people's ideas about the afterlife. Items including gold jewelry, crowns, clay vessels and weapons were found in the tombs, indicating the people's desire to have a lavish afterlife.

DIGITAL RESOURCES myNGconnect.com

TEACHER RESOURCES & ASSESSMENT

 Reading and Note-Taking   **Vocabulary Practice**   **Section 1 Quiz**

STUDENT RESOURCES

 NG Chapter Gallery

INTRODUCE & ENGAGE

MAKE CONNECTIONS

Ask students to recall artifacts of ancient civilizations they have learned about. Students might recall the cuneiform tablets of the Sumerians, the statues of Egyptian gods, the artifacts found in King Tut's tomb, or Athenian pottery. Discuss with students how artifacts help people learn about the ancient civilizations. Have students review the photos of the Korean artifacts in this lesson. Ask what the artifacts tell about the Silla kingdom. **0:05** minutes

TEACH

GUIDED DISCUSSION

1. **Draw Conclusions** What kind of materials did artisans in the Silla kingdom have access to? *(gold, jade, bronze, stone)*

2. **Make Generalizations** What generalization can you make about the artifacts created by Silla artisans? *(Possible response: The artifacts were luxurious, using the finest materials, and likely used by Korean leaders and aristocrats.)*

ANALYZE VISUALS

Have students examine the photos of the Korean artifacts. Have them identify the various elements they see in each image. List students' responses on the board. Discuss with students what the artifacts indicate about the artisans' skills in creating the objects. **0:10** minutes

ACTIVE OPTIONS

Critical Viewing: NG Chapter Gallery Have students examine the contents of the Chapter Gallery for this chapter. Then invite them to brainstorm additional images they believe would fit within the Chapter Gallery. Have them write a description of these additional images and provide an explanation of why they would fit within the Chapter Gallery. Then instruct them to do online research to find examples of actual images they would like to add to the gallery. **0:10** minutes

On Your Feet: Descriptive Words Hand out two sticky notes to each student. Have students examine the details in the photographs of the Korean artifacts. Then have them write a word or phrase on each sticky note that describes the artifacts. Have students place their sticky notes on the board and discuss their descriptions. **0:10** minutes

DIFFERENTIATE

INCLUSION

Describe Details in a Photo Pair students who are visually impaired with students who are not. Ask the latter to be their partners' "eyes" and describe the details in the photos of Korean artifacts. Students should read the captions of the callouts to the visually impaired students before they describe the details in each one.

GIFTED & TALENTED

Create an Advertisement Have students write an advertisement piece urging people to view a museum exhibit of Korean artifacts. Direct students to use the information in the lesson as well as Internet research to write the advertisement. Encourage students to use photos in their advertisements. Have students display their advertisements in the class.

Press **(mt)** *in the Student eEdition for modified text.*

See the Chapter Planner for more strategies for differentiation.

Koryo and Choson Dynasties

After the decline of Silla in the 700s, two new dynasties rose to power. During the Koryo and Choson dynasties, Korea enjoyed proud independence. Then new rulers forbade Koreans from meeting freely, speaking their mind, practicing their culture, or even using their family name.

MAIN IDEA

Two great dynasties ruled for nearly a thousand years before Korea lost its independence.

KORYO

In the 700s, after a golden age, Silla began to decline. Its rulers fought among themselves. Nobles seized large areas of farmland, while peasants rebelled against poor government. In A.D. 918, General Wang Kon founded a rival dynasty called the **Koryo**. After a long war, the Silla king surrendered in 935. Then, for more than 450 years, Korea was ruled by the Koryo, from which Korea takes its name.

Chinese ideas and practices continued to flow south, although they were **adapted**, or changed, to meet Koryo's own needs. For example, Koryo adapted Chinese-style centralized government but gave special preference to aristocrats. As a result, Koryo's professional bureaucracy came almost entirely from its hereditary

nobility. Koryo potters also imported advanced Chinese techniques but again developed a uniquely Korean style.

Yet Chinese influence remained strong. As in China, Buddhism greatly inspired art. Korea's literary language remained Chinese for centuries, and Chinese poetry was much imitated. Even the oldest surviving book on Korea's history, the *Samguk Sagi*, mentions almost twice as many Chinese sources as Korean.

CHOSON

In 1231, the Mongols invaded Koryo and took control. The Mongols were harsh rulers. They demanded tribute from the Koryo rulers, who had to send them a million soldiers and 20,000 horses. Mongol domination ended in 1336. Soon, a new dynasty arose.

In 1392, the **Choson** dynasty replaced the Koryo dynasty. Choson ruled Korea for the next 518 years. Like Koryo, Choson adapted many elements of Chinese culture. Choson rulers created a strong, centralized Confucian-style government with a strict political and social hierarchy. However, over the following centuries, Korea developed its own alphabet, artistic styles, and other distinctive cultural characteristics.

Then, in 1894, disaster struck. Both China and Japan invaded Korea to help crush a people's rebellion. The rebels quickly surrendered, but Japan fought on and won control of the peninsula. In 1910, Korea was formally made part of Japan, which imposed a harsh military rule.

The Japanese occupied Korea until 1945. During this occupation, life in Korea contrasted sharply with life during the Choson dynasty. The Japanese required Koreans to adopt Japanese culture and even to use Japanese-style names. Koreans considered this a heartbreaking betrayal of their ancestry and a bitter end to Korean independence.

Critical Viewing This detail from an 18th-century silk banner shows a group of women during the Choson Dynasty. What indicates that the women are from different social classes?

+ POSSIBLE RESPONSE

The women appear to be of different social classes because the two women on the left appear to be shading the women on the right; the women on the right have more elaborate clothing and hairstyles.

REVIEW & ASSESS

1. **READING CHECK** What common influence helped shape the Koryo and Choson dynasties?

2. **CATEGORIZE** During the Choson dynasty, which cultural characteristics were distinctively Korean?

3. **ANALYZE CAUSE AND EFFECT** What caused the end of Korean independence in 1910?

PLAN

OBJECTIVE

Describe the rule of the Koryo and Choson dynasties before Korea's loss of independence.

CRITICAL THINKING SKILLS FOR LESSON 1.3

- Identify Main Ideas and Details
- Monitor Comprehension
- Categorize
- Analyze Cause and Effect
- Draw Conclusions
- Make Inferences

ESSENTIAL QUESTION

How did Korea and Southeast Asia adapt to outside influences?

After the decline of Silla, two new dynasties rose to power.

Lesson 1.3 describes the events in Korea during the rule of the Koryo and Choson dynasties.

BACKGROUND FOR THE TEACHER

During the period of the Choson dynasty, landowners became the ruling class known as the *yangban*. This group was anti-Buddhist, and their lack of support for the Buddhists led to the decline of Buddhism in Korea. The *yangban* took on the attitudes expressed in Confucianism. These attitudes reflected the idea that levels of superiority and inferiority existed in most relationships, including those between ruler and subject, father and son, and husband and wife. As a result, a rigid class system developed, with little social mobility.

DIGITAL RESOURCES myNGconnect.com

TEACHER RESOURCES & ASSESSMENT

 Reading and Note-Taking   **Vocabulary Practice**   **Section 1 Quiz**

STUDENT RESOURCES

 NG Chapter Gallery

INTRODUCE & ENGAGE

ACTIVATE WORD KNOWLEDGE

Ask students if they know what the word *adapt* means. Write students' responses on the board. Explain that one meaning of *adapt* is "to change or modify something to better suit a different purpose." Ask students to give examples of adapting something. *(Students might indicate adapting traditions to better fit new situations or adapting styles of clothing.)* Point out to students that adapting does not involve complete change, but keeping some parts and changing others. Tell students that in this lesson they will learn how Chinese ideas and practices were adapted by two Korean dynasties. **0:10 minutes**

TEACH

GUIDED DISCUSSION

1. **Draw Conclusions** Why did life in Korea change during Japanese occupation? *(The Japanese required Koreans to adopt Japanese culture, even using Japanese-style names.)*

2. **Make Inferences** How did Korea's geographic location contribute to ending Korea's independence? *(Answers will vary, but students might indicate that having China on its western border and Japan located to the east made it easier for both countries to invade Korea.)*

MORE INFORMATION

Art During the Choson Dynasty During the time of the Choson dynasty, the spread of Confucianism led to a renewal of the arts. The decline of Buddhism as the dominant religion resulted in more secular themes in Korean painting. Although paintings still imitated Chinese styles, Korean painters also developed a distinct Korean style. They began to use non-Chinese techniques and to paint scenes of the Korean landscape and Korean daily life.

ACTIVE OPTIONS

Critical Viewing: NG Chapter Gallery Invite students to explore the Chapter Gallery to examine the images that relate to this chapter. Have them select one of the images and do additional research to learn more about it. Ask questions that will inspire additional inquiry about the chosen gallery image, such as: What is this? Where and when was this created? By whom? Why was it created? What is it made of? Why does it belong in this chapter? What else would you like to know about it? **0:10 minutes**

On Your Feet: Inside-Outside Circle Arrange students in concentric circles facing each other. Have students in the outside circle ask the students in the inside circle a question about the lesson. Then have the outside circle rotate one position to the right to create new pairings. After five questions, have students switch roles and continue. **0:15 minutes**

DIFFERENTIATE

INCLUSION

Use Supported Reading Have students work in pairs, and assign each pair one paragraph to read aloud together. At the end of each paragraph, have them use the following sentence frames to tell what they do and do not understand:

This paragraph is about _____.

One fact that stood out to me is _____.

_____ is a word I had trouble understanding, so I figured it out by _____.

Be sure students understand the content before moving on to the next paragraph.

PRE-AP

Give Oral Reports Have students do Internet research to find more information on the Koryo or Choson dynasty. Information can pertain to the following areas:

- role of Confucianism
- type of government
- foreign policy
- art styles
- scientific advances

Students can then prepare oral reports to share with the class.

Press (**mt**) *in the Student eEdition for modified text.*

See the Chapter Planner for more strategies for differentiation.

REVIEW & ASSESS

ANSWERS

1. Chinese culture helped make the Koryo and Choson dynasties great.

2. During the Choson dynasty, Korea developed its own alphabet, artistic styles, and other distinctive cultural characteristics.

3. China and Japan invaded Korea to help crush a people's rebellion. However, after the rebellion ended, Japan continued fighting and won control of the Korean Peninsula, making Korea part of Japan in 1910.

1.4
Korean Culture

When we pose for a picture, we say "cheese" to produce a smile. In Korea, they say "kimchi"—a word that ends with a similar sound. Koreans have been making kimchi for hundreds of years. It is one of many examples of Korea's distinctive culture.

MAIN IDEA

Korea developed their own culture despite many Chinese influences.

+ **POSSIBLE RESPONSE**

It most likely indicates the general description of the content of the woodblock.

Critical Viewing A monk holds a Tripitaka Koreana woodblock. What does the writing on each block's end most likely indicate?

RELIGION, POTTERY, AND PRINTING

While Chinese ideas and practices were certainly influential, Korea developed its own culture. Chinese Confucianism and Buddhism were adapted to Korean needs. Inspired by Song China's advanced glazed ceramics, Korean potters developed **celadon** (SEH-luh-dahn), a type of pottery with a unique blue-green color. Korean celadon is considered among the finest porcelain in the world.

Similarly, Chinese woodblock printing reached new heights in Korean hands. Korean monks spent years painstakingly carving Buddhist teachings onto more than 80,000 wooden blocks known collectively as the **Tripitaka Koreana**. After the blocks were burned during the Mongol invasion in 1231, Buddhist monks made and recarved all new blocks, which are kept at Haeinsa Temple in present-day South Korea.

Built in the 1400s, the complex of four buildings that house the Tripitaka Koreana is also remarkable. These structures create an environment that has preserved the woodblocks for centuries. The floor contains a mixture of soil, charcoal, salt, clay, sand, and plaster powder that regulates moisture, while strategically placed windows ensure consistent air quality.

In 1377, Korea produced *Jikji*, the world's oldest book printed with movable metal type. Reusable metal characters arranged on a board created a printing plate that was tough and flexible, allowing for mass printing. Korea used metal type 78 years before it was first used in Europe.

FOOD, CLOTHING, AND HEATING

Other aspects of daily life illustrate Korea's distinctive culture. **Kimchi**, for example, is Korea's national dish. This dish is made of spicy pickled vegetables and is as full of flavor as it is rich in vitamins and minerals. People began making kimchi as a way of preserving vegetables, especially cabbage. Once sliced and seasoned, the vegetables were placed in large jars of salt water and buried. About a month later, the kimchi was ready to eat. Today, there are more than 160 varieties of kimchi.

For centuries, Koreans wore traditional clothing called **hanbok**. A woman's hanbok included seven layers of undergarments covered by a long billowing skirt and a short, tight-fitting jacket. Men wore full-length pants and a long jacket with wide sleeves. The material ranged from hemp to silk but was usually brightly colored with beautiful designs. Today, most Koreans wear hanbok only on special occasions.

From as early as the first century, Korean homes benefited from a unique system of heating called **ondol**. Hot air from fireplaces was drawn through passageways beneath the floors. The heated air warmed both the floors and the rooms above. Even today, Koreans use an updated version of ondol.

REVIEW & ASSESS

1. **READING CHECK** What aspects of Chinese culture did Koreans adapt to develop their own distinct culture?

2. **ANALYZE CAUSE AND EFFECT** Why were the Tripitaka woodblocks carved a second time?

3. **DETERMINE WORD MEANINGS** In the phrase "the complex of four buildings," what does the word *complex* mean?

PLAN

OBJECTIVE

Describe the distinctive culture developed in Korea.

CRITICAL THINKING SKILLS FOR LESSON 1.4

- Identify Main Ideas and Details
- Monitor Comprehension
- Analyze Cause and Effect
- Determine Word Meanings
- Form and Support Opinions
- Make Connections

ESSENTIAL QUESTION

How did Korea and Southeast Asia adapt to outside influences?

The Chinese culture influenced several aspects of Korean culture. Lesson 1.4 describes how Korea developed its own culture despite the Chinese influences.

BACKGROUND FOR THE TEACHER

As the depository for the Tripitaka Koreana, the Haeinsa Temple is included on the World Heritage Site list. The Tripitaka Koreana is one of the most complete bodies of Buddhist texts in the world. The buildings that house the woodblocks are remarkable in how well they have preserved the blocks. More than 800 years later, the blocks on which the texts are engraved are in almost perfect condition. The engravings of these Buddhist manuscripts are the oldest example of this kind of artwork in the world.

DIGITAL RESOURCES myNGconnect.com

TEACHER RESOURCES & ASSESSMENT

 Reading and Note-Taking

 Vocabulary Practice

 Section 1 Quiz

STUDENT RESOURCES

 Active History

INTRODUCE & ENGAGE

POSE AND ANSWER QUESTIONS

As a class, complete a K-W-L Chart exploring what students know and what they would like to learn about the Korean culture. Write students' ideas on the board in a chart like the one shown here. Give students the opportunity to return to the chart and review what they have learned after they have read the lesson. **0:15** minutes

K What Do I Know?	W What Do I Want To Learn?	L What Did I Learn?

TEACH

GUIDED DISCUSSION

1. **Identify Main Idea and Details** Why has the complex that houses the Tripitaka Koreana been able to preserve the woodblocks for centuries? *(The floor of the structures contains a mixture of soil, charcoal, salt, clay, sand, and plaster powder that regulates moisture; strategically placed windows ensure consistent air quality.)*

2. **Form and Support Opinions** Which of the Korean achievements discussed in this lesson do you think is the most important? Why do you think so? *(Answers will vary. Students should provide reasons for their opinions.)*

MAKE CONNECTIONS

Focus students' attention on the photo in this lesson and review the information about the Tripitaka Koreana. **ASK:** How are manuscripts and other ancient items preserved today? *(in libraries and museums)* Then hold a class discussion about why they think efforts have been made and continue to be made to preserve ancient manuscripts and other items and why they think it is or is not important to do so. **0:10** minutes

ACTIVE OPTIONS

Active History: Categorize Korea's Society Levels Extend the lesson by using either the PDF or Whiteboard version of the activity. These activities take a deeper look at a topic from, or related to, the lesson. Explore the activities as a class, turn them into group assignments, or even assign them individually. **0:10** minutes

On Your Feet: Turn and Talk on Topic Have students form four lines. Give each line the same topic sentence: *The Koreans developed their own distinct culture and achievements.* Tell the groups to build a paragraph on that topic by having each student in the line add one sentence about a different Korean achievement. Finally, have groups present their paragraphs to the class, with each student reading his or her sentence. **0:15** minutes

DIFFERENTIATE

STRIVING READERS

Read and Recall Allow students to work in groups of two to four. First have each student read the same lesson independently. After reading, students should meet without the text and share ideas they recall. One person should take notes. As a group, students should look at the lesson and decide what should be added or changed in the notes.

GIFTED & TALENTED

Assign an Investigation Point out to students that the Haeinsa Temple in present-day South Korea is the repository for the Tripitaka Koreana. It has been designated a UNESCO World Heritage Site. Have students investigate why it deserves that title and share the information with the class.

Press **mt** *in the Student eEdition for modified text.*

See the Chapter Planner for more strategies for differentiation.

REVIEW & ASSESS

ANSWERS

1. Koreans adapted many aspects of Chinese culture to develop their own distinct culture, including Confucianism and Buddhism; ceramic art; and woodblock printing.

2. The first set was burned in 1232 during the Mongol invasion.

3. In this sentence, *complex* means "a group of similar buildings on the same site."

Vietnamese Kingdoms

Are there people you admire but also dislike? Perhaps you appreciate their skill in sports but dislike their superior attitude in the classroom. Vietnam appreciated Chinese culture but hated Chinese domination.

MAIN IDEA

Vietnam followed more than a millennium of foreign occupation with a thousand years of independence.

CHINESE RULE

Although the origins of modern Vietnam are shrouded in myth, Vietnamese history most likely began with the migration of settlers from southern China into the Red River delta. As in Korea, Vietnam's challenge was maintaining political and cultural independence from China, its powerful neighbor.

In 207 B.C., an ambitious Chinese governor incorporated the Red River delta into his breakaway kingdom of **Nam Viet**. Barely a century later, in 111 B.C., the Han Chinese seized control of Nam Viet, and it became a Chinese-ruled province for more than a thousand years. The province provided China with valuable ports for traders sailing to India and Southeast Asia.

Nam Viet's Chinese rulers increasingly **imposed**, or forced, Chinese culture onto

the Nam Viet people. Yet the harder China pushed, the more the people resisted, which led to many violent uprisings. The most famous was in A.D. 39, when sisters **Trung Trac** and **Trung Nhi** led a rebellion against Chinese rule. Having raised an army, the sisters rode into battle on the backs of elephants. Within a year, the two women and their allies had driven out the Chinese. The sisters ruled for three years before being defeated by Chinese forces. Today the Trung sisters are still honored as national heroes.

DAI VIET

In A.D. 938, Ngo Quyen (noh kwehn) led an uprising that finally defeated the Chinese. In a decisive battle, he sank China's warships by planting iron-tipped stakes in a riverbed. China acknowledged the independence of the new **Dai Viet** state in exchange for tribute payments. This began a thousand years of independence for Vietnam.

The Ly dynasty's strong leadership from 1009 to 1225 moved the Vietnamese capital to what is now Hanoi, established a strong central government, and built an effective road network. Ly rulers reinforced Buddhism as the state religion and promoted Confucian values in government and society. They developed a code of law and recruited a professional army.

From 1225 to 1400, the equally dynamic Tran dynasty further reformed the administration, agriculture, and economy. Tran rulers succeeded in fighting off a major Mongol invasion in 1257 and expanded south into the rival kingdom of Champa. Then, in 1407, the Ming Chinese invaded and brutally enforced Chinese culture.

When, in 1428, Le Thanh Tong restored native rule, he actively promoted China's government systems as well as its language, art, and literature. His reforms may have had a greater effect on making Vietnam Chinese than a thousand years of occupation. In 1471, Dai Viet reconquered Champa, creating what is now recognized as Vietnam.

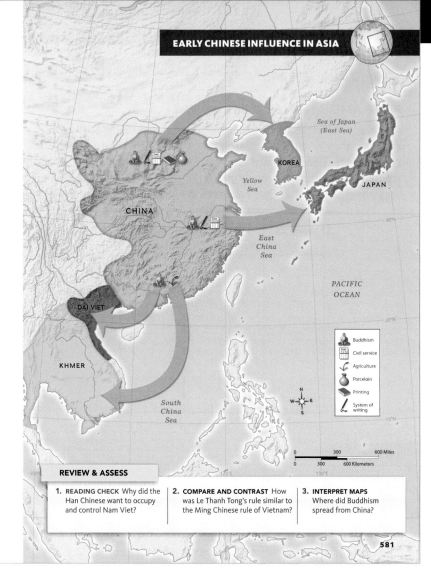

EARLY CHINESE INFLUENCE IN ASIA

Map legend:
- Buddhism
- Civil service
- Agriculture
- Porcelain
- Printing
- System of writing

REVIEW & ASSESS

1. **READING CHECK** Why did the Han Chinese want to occupy and control Nam Viet?

2. **COMPARE AND CONTRAST** How was Le Thanh Tong's rule similar to the Ming Chinese rule of Vietnam?

3. **INTERPRET MAPS** Where did Buddhism spread from China?

PLAN

OBJECTIVE

Explain how Vietnam experienced a thousand years of independence after more than a thousand years of foreign occupation.

CRITICAL THINKING SKILLS FOR LESSON 2.1

- Identify Main Ideas and Details
- Monitor Comprehension
- Compare and Contrast
- Interpret Maps
- Analyze Cause and Effect
- Summarize
- Create Time Lines

ESSENTIAL QUESTION

How did Korea and Southeast Asia adapt to outside influences?

Vietnam's history likely began with the migration of settlers from China. Lesson 2.1 discusses Chinese rule of Vietnam and the events that led to Vietnam's independence from foreign rule.

BACKGROUND FOR THE TEACHER

Trung Trac and Trung Nhi were the daughters of a powerful lord. Trung Trac, the older sister, was also the widow of a powerful lord in northern Vietnam who had been assassinated by the Chinese for planning to overthrow them. After his death, Trung Trac took over leadership of the movement. She and her sister gathered an army to drive the Chinese from their lands. The Trung sisters chose several women and trained them to be generals. Together they liberated 65 fortresses and drove the Chinese out of Vietnam. The sisters became the symbols of the first resistance to the Chinese occupation. Today they are honored by the Vietnamese people, who celebrate their memory annually with a national holiday.

DIGITAL RESOURCES myNGconnect.com

TEACHER RESOURCES & ASSESSMENT

 Reading and Note-Taking

 Vocabulary Practice

 Section 2 Quiz

STUDENT RESOURCES

 NG Chapter Gallery

INTRODUCE & ENGAGE

INTERPRET MAPS

Direct students to the map in this lesson. Have students identify the map title and the places shown on the map. **ASK:** How is color used in this map? (*It is used to distinguish the places on the map.*) What do the arrows on the map signify? (*They show the products and ideas that have spread from China to other places in Asia.*) What does the map tell you about the significance of China in Asia at the time? (*Possible response: It shows that China had a great influence over other Asian kingdoms.*) **0:05** minutes

TEACH

GUIDED DISCUSSION

1. **Analyze Cause and Effect** What caused many violent uprisings by the Nam Viet people against the Chinese? (*The forced imposition of Chinese culture onto the Nam Viet people caused the Nam Viet people to revolt against the Chinese.*)

2. **Summarize** What were some of the achievements of the Ly dynasty in Vietnam? (*The Ly dynasty moved the Vietnamese capital to what is now Hanoi, established a strong central government, constructed an effective road network, reinforced Buddhism as the state religion, promoted Confucian values in government and society, developed a code of law, and recruited a professional army.*)

CREATE TIME LINES

Have students work in pairs to create a time line of events in this lesson. Instruct students to include the dates as discussed in the text and a key event for each date. Work with students to space their dates appropriately on the time line. **0:15** minutes

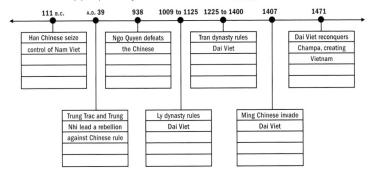

ACTIVE OPTIONS

Critical Viewing: NG Image Gallery Have students explore the entire NG Image Gallery and choose two of the items to compare and contrast, either in written form or verbally with a partner. Ask questions that will inspire this process, such as: How are these images alike? How are they different? Why did you select these two items? How do they relate in history? **0:10** minutes

On Your Feet: Card Responses Have students work in groups to create a quiz about what they learned in Lesson 2.1. Students can write true-false, fill-in-the-blank, or short-answer questions. Have groups trade sets of questions and answer them. Encourage groups to check answers against the text. Have students keep track of group scores. **0:20** minutes

DIFFERENTIATE

STRIVING READERS

Create Graphic Organizers Have students work in pairs. Give each pair a Main Idea diagram like the one shown. Instruct them to write the main idea of the lesson in the top rectangle. Then have them record details from the lesson that support that main idea. Tell them to add more detail boxes if necessary.

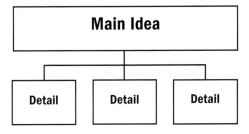

ENGLISH LANGUAGE LEARNERS

Summarize Lesson 2.1 has seven paragraphs. Have students work in pairs or small groups, and assign each pair or group one paragraph to read together. Then each group should summarize their paragraph in one or two sentences for the class.

Press **mt** *in the Student eEdition for modified text.*

See the Chapter Planner for more strategies for differentiation.

REVIEW & ASSESS

ANSWERS

1. The Han Chinese wanted access to trade in India and Southeast Asia; Nam Viet provided China with valuable ports for traders sailing to those locations.

2. Both rulers increasingly imposed aspects of Chinese culture on the Vietnamese, which led to many violent uprisings.

3. Buddhism spread from China to Korea, Japan, Khmer, and Dai Viet.

The **Khmer** Empire

Dark and threatening skies mean the monsoon is coming. However, you are confident that the efficient network of dams, dikes, and canals will save your rice paddy from flood damage. Rice is the backbone of the Khmer economy.

MAIN IDEA

Rice agriculture helped the Khmer dominate Southeast Asia for centuries.

INDIAN AND CHINESE INFLUENCES

Present-day Cambodia was the heartland of one of Southeast Asia's most powerful states. The **Khmer** (kuh-MAIR) people migrated south from China. By A.D. 500, they were founding small city-states known collectively as Chenla. To their south lay the powerful trading kingdom of Funan, which was probably founded by Indian traders who valued its strategic location between India and China. Funan introduced many Indian influences to Cambodia, including irrigation, centralized government, the Sanskrit language, and the Hindu religion.

In the mid-600s, Chenla extended into Funan. Threatened by strong island nations like Java, the Chenla kingdoms rallied together for protection. In 802, they formally united under the "universal ruler" Jayavarman II (JEYE-ah-var-mahn). This was the beginning of the Khmer Empire, which dominated Southeast Asia until 1431.

THE ANGKOR ERA

The Khmer established their capital in Angkor, which means "city." The city's art and architecture were Indian in style, and the layout reflected the Hindu vision of the universe. Khmer religious beliefs were a complex mixture of Hinduism, Buddhism, and native religions. The Khmer adopted the Indian idea of kings as gods who ruled with divine authority.

A large central bureaucracy governed the Khmer Empire, which included vassal states. These states paid tribute, which, along with trade, contributed to the empire's economy. Yet the mainstay of the Khmer economy was rice.

The Khmer were skilled rice farmers, having learned how to grow rice from the Chinese. The Khmer region's many wet and fertile river deltas were ideal for **cultivating**, or growing, rice. Khmer farmers built a brilliant water-management system to control and harness the heavy monsoon rains. The system combined immense storage tanks with canals, dikes, and dams. As a result, farmers were able to produce three or four rice harvests a year. By 1250, rice fed Angkor's population of 1.5 million and produced a huge surplus for export. This intensive rice cultivation was the foundation of Khmer prosperity, stability, and power, which expanded across Southeast Asia.

The Khmer Empire reached its peak under Jayavarman VII, who ruled from 1181 to 1218. Jayavarman VII built roads and a new capital city called Angkor Thom. He also supported Buddhism by building an estimated 20,000 Buddhist shrines. Under his rule, the state supported 300,000 monks and priests. Pouring resources into religious monuments strained the economy to the breaking point. Over the next two centuries, wars further weakened the Khmer Empire. In 1431, a Thai army seized Angkor itself. Though the empire shifted south, its power declined and its capital was abandoned.

A farmer in Cambodia harvests rice by hand.

REVIEW & ASSESS

1. **READING CHECK** How did rice agriculture lead to prosperity and power for the Khmer Empire?

2. **ANALYZE CAUSE AND EFFECT** How did India influence the culture of the Khmer?

3. **IDENTIFY MAIN IDEAS AND DETAILS** What two factors led to the downfall of the Khmer Empire?

PLAN

OBJECTIVE

Explain how rice agriculture helped the Khmer dominate Southeast Asia.

CRITICAL THINKING SKILLS FOR LESSON 2.2

- Identify Main Ideas and Details
- Monitor Comprehension
- Analyze Cause and Effect
- Draw Conclusions
- Summarize
- Analyze Visuals

ESSENTIAL QUESTION

How did Korea and Southeast Asia adapt to outside influences?

Both the Chinese and Indian cultures influenced the culture of the Khmer Empire. Lesson 2.2 explains the importance of rice agriculture to the Khmer people.

BACKGROUND FOR THE TEACHER

The Khmer Empire was divided into approximately 23 provinces with a complex administration. At its height, Angkor was the biggest city in the world, covering an area of about 400 square miles and a population of approximately one million. The Khmer people were festive, taking part in many celebrations year round. Horse races, wrestling, music, and dancing were an essential part of their celebrations and culture.

DIGITAL RESOURCES myNGconnect.com

TEACHER RESOURCES & ASSESSMENT

 Reading and Note-Taking

 Vocabulary Practice

 Section 2 Quiz

STUDENT RESOURCES

 NG Chapter Gallery

INTRODUCE & ENGAGE

MAKE CONNECTIONS

Write the word *rice* on the board. Ask students to describe meals they have or have had in which rice is one of the items. Have students also indicate whether having rice as part of a meal is a regular occurrence or an infrequent one. Tell students that in this lesson they will learn about the significance of rice cultivation to the Khmer Empire. **0:05 minutes**

TEACH

GUIDED DISCUSSION

1. **Draw Conclusions** How did the geography of the Khmer Empire make it ideal for rice cultivation? *(The wet and fertile river deltas made the region ideal for rice cultivation; farmers built a water-management system to control and harness the region's monsoon rains.)*

2. **Summarize** What achievements did Jayavarman VII make as the ruler of the Khmer Empire? *(Jayavarman VII built roads, the capital city of Angkor Thom, and around 20,000 Buddhist shrines.)*

ANALYZE VISUALS

Have students examine the photo of the Cambodian farmer. Have them read the caption. **ASK:** What is the farmer wearing? *(a wide-brimmed hat and a long-sleeved shirt)* What might be the reason for wearing this type of clothing? *(The hat protects the farmer's head and face from the sun, and the long-sleeved shirt protects the arms from the sun and possibly from being irritated by the stalks as they are being cut.)* Discuss with students how they would describe the process of harvesting rice by hand. Make a list of descriptions as students provide them. **0:10 minutes**

ACTIVE OPTIONS

On Your Feet: Tell Me More Have students form three teams and assign each team one of the following topics: Chenla; the Khmer economy; or Jayavarman VII. Each group should write down as many facts about their topic as they can. Have the class reconvene and have each group stand up, one at a time. The rest of the class calls out "Tell me more about [the topic]." The group recites one fact. The class again requests a fact until the group runs out of facts to share. Then the next group presents its facts. **0:10 minutes**

NG Learning Framework: Make Observations

ATTITUDE: **Curiosity**
SKILLS: **Observation, Collaboration**
KNOWLEDGE: **Our Living Planet**

Have students revisit the information in Lesson 2.2, particularly the information about rice cultivation. Students should work in pairs to create a list of observations about the Khmer people and how they used their environment to cultivate rice and how having a rice surplus led to prosperity for the empire. Once they have completed their list of observations, each pair should exchange lists with another pair and discuss the new list. **0:10 minutes**

DIFFERENTIATE

INCLUSION

Clarify Text Have visually-impaired students work with sighted partners. As they listen to an audio recording of the text, have the visually-impaired students indicate if there are words or passages they do not understand. Their partners can clarify meaning by repeating passages, emphasizing context clues, and paraphrasing.

PRE-AP

Research and Report Have students research and report about the road system in the Khmer Empire. Students might find out about the materials used, the extent of the system, and the facilities constructed along the roads for travel. Students should also include information about the importance of the roads to the trade and economy of the Khmer Empire. Encourage students to create visuals to accompany their reports.

Press **mt** *in the Student eEdition for modified text.*

See the Chapter Planner for more strategies for differentiation.

REVIEW & ASSESS

ANSWERS

1. The Khmer practiced intensive rice cultivation that advanced the empire's prosperity, stability, and population growth, leading to its powerful presence in Southeast Asia.

2. The Khmer adopted many Indian ideas and practices, including irrigation, a centralized government, the Sanskrit language, and Hinduism.

3. Under the rule of Jayavarman VII, the Khmer Empire became weak because of the economic strain caused by his ambitious programs in the promotion of Buddhism over Hinduism. Arguments and wars led to the further weakening of the once powerful empire, until a Thai army seized the capital of Angkor.

Angkor Wat

With its dramatic jungle setting and fantastic architecture, the temple city of Angkor Wat is the classic image of a lost city. Remote and mysterious, it has been the spectacular backdrop for many Hollywood movies.

MAIN IDEA

Khmer culture peaked with the building of Angkor Wat.

+ POSSIBLE RESPONSE

It illustrates how large and elaborate the temple is, and it illustrates why it is thought of as representing the peak of Khmer artistic achievement.

Critical Viewing Buddhist monks stand in a doorway of Angkor Wat in present-day Cambodia. What does this image add to the text's description of the temple?

A GREAT TEMPLE COMPLEX

The Khmer capital city of Angkor is actually a series of cities and temples spread over more than 300 square miles. For almost 500 years, Angkor was the political and religious heart of the Khmer Empire and the largest city in the world. Each king added to its glory by building beautiful temples and even a whole new city within the city. In the 1100s, however, King Suryavarman II built Angkor's most celebrated addition—the temple complex of **Angkor Wat**.

Angkor Wat means "city that is a temple." Its complex of interconnected buildings covers 244 acres, making it the largest religious monument in the world. Built to honor the Hindu god Vishnu, the temple has at its center a vast five-towered pyramid. Each tower is shaped like a lotus bud. In Hinduism, the lotus flower represents beauty and purity while the tower symbolizes the

legendary home of the Hindu gods. An outer wall and a wide moat represent mountains at the edge of the world and the ocean that lies beyond. Indeed, every feature of Angkor Wat has a symbolic meaning.

The temple represents the peak of Khmer artistic achievement. Among its most admired features are its extraordinarily intricate carvings. These include hundreds of dancers, each one unique. Another outstanding feature is a 1,970-foot stretch of **bas-reliefs** (slightly raised figures on a flat background) that show scenes from Hindu legends.

Angkor Wat was also built to be Suryavarman's tomb and possibly an astronomical observatory as well. There is some evidence that it is oriented to align with certain stars. Unlike most other Khmer temples, Angkor Wat faces west, toward the setting sun, which symbolizes death.

CHANGES AND RESTORATION

After the Khmer's switch to Buddhism, Angkor Wat became a Buddhist shrine. When the Khmer Empire collapsed, Angkor fell to its enemies. By the 1600s, it was largely abandoned. The jungle quickly consumed its wooden structures and covered its stone buildings.

Then, in 1860, the French explorer Henri Mouhot encountered the "lost" world of Angkor and Angkor Wat. Mouhot brought the site to the attention of westerners. Sadly,

visitors and thieves began removing its treasures. Indeed, Angkor Wat has suffered terribly from looters, uncontrolled tourism, and even poorly performed restoration.

Fortunately, in 1992, it became a UNESCO World Heritage Site with carefully planned measures to protect it for future generations. Today Angkor Wat is Cambodia's main tourist attraction with over 2 million visitors every year. It is so important to the country that it forms the centerpiece of the Cambodian flag.

REVIEW & ASSESS

1. **READING CHECK** Why was Angkor Wat built?

2. **IDENTIFY MAIN IDEAS AND DETAILS** Why is Angkor Wat often thought of as representing the peak of Khmer artistic achievement?

3. **SEQUENCE EVENTS** What changes did Angkor Wat undergo during its long history?

PLAN

OBJECTIVE

Describe how the Khmer culture peaked with the building of Angkor Wat.

CRITICAL THINKING SKILLS FOR LESSON 2.3

- Identify Main Ideas and Details
- Monitor Comprehension
- Sequence Events
- Make Generalizations
- Analyze Visuals

ESSENTIAL QUESTION

How did Korea and Southeast Asia adapt to outside influences?

Angkor was the heart of the Khmer Empire and the largest city in the world. Lesson 2.3 explains why the Khmer culture peaked with the building of the impressive Angkor Wat.

BACKGROUND FOR THE TEACHER

Scientists are still learning new things about Angkor Wat. Scans conducted by the space shuttle *Endeavor* in 1994 and from other remote sensors showed that the complex had hidden buildings and structures that were part of the water management system. Some scientists now suggest that cutting down too many trees and overuse of the land led to excessive flooding and the buildup of silt, which led to the abandonment of the complex.

DIGITAL RESOURCES myNGconnect.com

TEACHER RESOURCES & ASSESSMENT

 Reading and Note-Taking

 Vocabulary Practice

 Section 2 Quiz

STUDENT RESOURCES

 NG Chapter Gallery

POSE AND ANSWER QUESTIONS

As a class, complete a K-W-L Chart exploring what students know and what they would like to learn about Angkor Wat. Write students' ideas on the board in a chart like the one shown here. Give students the opportunity to return to the chart and review what they have learned after they have read the lesson. `0:15` minutes

K What Do I Know?	W What Do I Want To Learn?	L What Did I Learn?

TEACH

GUIDED DISCUSSION

1. **Identify Main Idea and Details** What are the symbolic meanings of some of the features of Angkor Wat? *(Each tower of the temple is shaped like a lotus bud, which represents beauty and purity in Hinduism; the tower symbolizes the legendary home of the Hindu gods; an outer wall and moat represent mountains and the ocean that lies beyond.)*

2. **Make Generalizations** Why do you think Angkor Wat is Cambodia's main tourist attraction today? *(Responses will vary, but students might indicate that people marvel at the beauty of the massive structure and are drawn to the archaeological and artistic achievements of earlier civilizations.)*

ANALYZE VISUALS

Have students examine the photograph of Angkor Wat. Have them identify the various elements they see in the photo. List students' responses on the board. Discuss with students what they think were the reactions of explorers who came upon the structure in the 1800s. `0:10` minutes

ACTIVE OPTIONS

Critical Viewing: NG Image Gallery Invite students to explore the entire NG Image Gallery and choose one image from the gallery they feel best represents their understanding of the chapter. Have students provide a written explanation of why they selected the image they chose. `0:10` minutes

On Your Feet: One-on-One Interviews Group students into pairs. Have both students in each pair write three questions about Angkor Wat. Start with one student using his or her questions to interview the other student "expert" about Angkor Wat. Students' answers should show an understanding of the material from the lesson. Once the interview is complete, students should reverse roles. `0:15` minutes

STRIVING READERS

Preview Text Help students preview Lesson 2.3. Point out the text features, such as the lesson title, Main Idea statement, and headings. **ASK:** Based on the headings, what do you expect this lesson to be about? As students begin reading, help them confirm their understanding of each paragraph before moving on to the next one.

GIFTED & TALENTED

Portray Cultural Achievement Have students use Internet research to find out more about Angkor Wat and its features. Then have students use one of the arts to portray this Khmer cultural achievement. They might consider one of these options:

- drawing or sculpting an image (such as the bas-reliefs of the temples)
- making a model of the structure
- writing a poem describing the structure and its significance

Have them share their presentation with the rest of the class.

Press (**mt**) *in the Student eEdition for modified text.*

See the Chapter Planner for more strategies for differentiation.

ANSWERS

1. Angkor Wat was built to honor the Hindu god Vishnu.

2. Its intricate carvings and bas-reliefs represent the peak of Khmer artistic achievement.

3. It became a Buddhist temple. After the empire collapsed, it was largely abandoned and consumed by jungle overgrowth. It was rediscovered in the 1850s. In the 1990s, it became a UNESCO World Heritage Site.

VOCABULARY

On your paper, write the vocabulary word that best completes each of the following sentences.

1. Korea's three early kingdoms had a bitter _____, so they fought one another for control of Korea.

2. Korean potters developed _____, which was known for its bluish-green color.

3. The Korean national dish is called _____, which is made with spicy pickled cabbage and other vegetables.

4. For centuries, the traditional _____ worn by Korean men included full-length pants and a long jacket with wide sleeves.

5. Early Koreans invented a unique system of heating called _____, which is still used in Korean homes today.

6. As Chinese rulers tried to _____ Chinese culture on the people of Nam Viet, violent uprisings occurred.

7. The Khmer took advantage of the wet and fertile river deltas to _____ rice successfully, which led to their prosperity.

READING STRATEGY

8. **DETERMINE WORD MEANINGS** If you haven't already, complete the chart for at least three vocabulary words. Then use each word in a paragraph about the history of Korea or Southeast Asia.

Word	Definition	Example from My Life
rivalry	competition	

MAIN IDEAS

Answer the following questions. Support your answers with evidence from the chapter.

9. How did the Silla kingdom triumph to unify Korea? **LESSON 1.1**

10. What borrowed aspects of Chinese culture helped the Koryo and Choson dynasties rule Korea for nearly a thousand years? **LESSON 1.3**

11. Despite strong Chinese influences, how did Korea develop a distinct culture? **LESSON 1.4**

12. Why did the Han Chinese want to occupy and control Nam Viet? **LESSON 2.1**

13. Why was rice farming important to the Khmer people? **LESSON 2.2**

14. What purposes did Angkor Wat serve? **LESSON 2.3**

CRITICAL THINKING

Answer the following questions. Support your answers with evidence from the chapter.

15. **COMPARE AND CONTRAST** How were the cultures of the three early Korean kingdoms—Silla, Koguryo, and Paekche—alike?

16. **ANALYZE CAUSE AND EFFECT** What effect did the Japanese occupation have on Korea?

17. **DRAW CONCLUSIONS** Why was the Korean invention of movable metal type a pioneering breakthrough in printing?

18. **MAKE INFERENCES** How did the Khmer's hierarchical society reflect the influence of Indian ideas?

19. **ANALYZE CAUSE AND EFFECT** What factors led to the Khmer's success in growing rice?

20. **YOU DECIDE** Which do you think was the greater Korean cultural achievement, the development of celadon or the creation of the Tripitaka Koreana? Support your opinion with evidence from the chapter.

INTERPRET MAPS

Study the map of Southeast Asia as it was in 1895. Then answer the questions that follow.

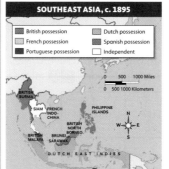

SOUTHEAST ASIA, c. 1895

- British possession
- French possession
- Portuguese possession
- Dutch possession
- Spanish possession
- Independent

21. Based on the map, how would you describe foreign rule of Southeast Asia around 1895?

22. Which European countries held the most territory in Southeast Asia around 1895?

23. **MAP ACTIVITY** Sketch a map of Southeast Asia as it is today. Then compare it with Southeast Asia as it appeared in 1895. What similarities and diferences do you notice between borders of territories in 1895 and countries in the present day?

ANALYZE SOURCES

Read the following paragraph about the Trung sisters. Then answer the question that follows.

In A.D. 40, the Trung sisters set up an army with the aid of the Vietnamese lords. Fighting fearlessly, they expelled the Chinese and established their own kingdom. In A.D. 43, however, the Chinese quelled [put down] the rebellion. To avoid capture, the sisters committed suicide by jumping into the Hat River. Centuries later, stone figures of two women washed up on a sandbank in the Red River. Believed to be the earthly remains of the Trung Sisters, petrified and turned into statues, they were taken to Dong Nhan village and installed in a temple there.

24. The Trung sisters are still honored today in Vietnam. What qualities do you think the Vietnamese admire in the two sisters?

WRITE ABOUT HISTORY

25. **NARRATIVE** Suppose you are taking tourists on a tour of Angkor Wat. Write a paragraph in which you explain to them how Angkor Wat represents the peak of Khmer artistic achievement.

TIPS

- Take notes from the lesson about Angkor Wat.
- Introduce the topic clearly.
- Develop the topic with supporting details and examples about the temple and its layout, relationship to Hinduism, and artistic features and symbolic meanings.
- Use two or three vocabulary terms from the chapter.
- Provide a concluding statement that summarizes the significance of the temple.

VOCABULARY ANSWERS

1. rivalry
2. celadon
3. kimchi
4. hanbok
5. ondol
6. impose
7. cultivate

READING STRATEGY ANSWER

Word	Definition	Example from My Life
rivalry	competition	
adapt	change	
celadon	type of pottery	

8. Sample paragraph: Three kingdoms formed in Korea. Although there was *rivalry* among the kingdoms, all three were strongly influenced by Chinese culture. Chinese culture also influenced the Koryo, a later Korean dynasty. However, the Koryo *adapted* Chinese practices to meet their own needs. Korea also developed its own culture. For example, Korean potters developed *celadon*, which was a type of pottery with a unique blue-green color.

MAIN IDEAS ANSWERS

9. The Silla king allied with Tang China to conquer the other two kingdoms—Paekche and Koguryo. The Silla king turned on his Tang allies and drove them out of all but northwest Korea, unifying Korea under the Silla kingdom.

10. Both dynasties adapted and implemented elements of Chinese government that established strong, centralized governments with a strict political and social hierarchy.

11. Koreans were able to develop their own distinct culture by adapting Chinese ideas and practices to suit their own needs and uses. By adapting these ideas and practices, Koreans made many advances and improvements, such as the development of celadon.

12. The Han Chinese wanted access to trade in India and Southeast Asia; by occupying and controlling Nam Viet, China had access to Nam Viet's valuable ports for traders sailing to and from India and Southeast Asia.

13. Rice farming was the basis of the Khmer's economy, and its success helped them grow into an empire that dominated Southeast Asia for centuries.

14. Angkor Wat was a Hindu temple, a Buddhist temple, a royal tomb, and an astronomical observatory.

CRITICAL THINKING ANSWERS

15. The three kingdoms all developed feudal hierarchical societies, spoke the same Korean language, adopted the Chinese writing system, imported and adapted ideas from Buddhism and Confucianism, and shared similar economies.

16. Japan's conquest and occupation of Korea not only ended its independence but had detrimental effects on Korea. The Japanese imposed a harsh military rule and forced Koreans to adopt Japanese culture, including giving up their family names and taking Japanese-style names.

17. The Korean invention of movable metal type was a pioneering breakthrough in printing because it enabled mass printing, which would not only lower printing costs, but allow for texts to have multiple printings and reach a far larger audience, thus further spreading ideas in religion, arts, philosophy, and so on.

18. The Khmer's hierarchical society reflects the Indian idea of kings as gods, ruling their hierarchical society with unquestioned divine authority.

19. Many factors contributed to the Khmer's success in growing rice. First, the region had many wet and fertile river deltas that were ideal for cultivating rice. But the Khmer built on that good fortune by developing advanced water management that allowed them to control, harness, and store the water from the monsoon rains. This advanced water management system also included the building of canals, dikes, and dams. These advancements meant the Khmer could produce three or four rice harvests per year, feed their growing population, and produce a huge surplus for export.

20. Students' responses will vary. Students should present evidence from the chapter to support their opinion about which Korean cultural achievement was the greater achievement.

INTERPRET MAPS ANSWERS

21. The theme of colonial occupation and rule is common in the history of Southeast Asia.

22. The French, British, and Dutch held the most territory in Southeast Asia around 1895.

23. Students' responses will vary. Students might indicate that the borders of the present-day countries generally align with the borders of the territories in 1895. French Indo-China today is divided between Laos and Vietnam.

ANALYZE SOURCES ANSWER

24. Students' responses will vary. Sample response: The Vietnamese people—then and now—most likely admire qualities such as bravery, fearlessness, selflessness, pride, and strength in the Trung sisters, who drove the Chinese out of Vietnam.

WRITE ABOUT HISTORY ANSWER

25. Students' paragraphs will vary, but students should present the information in a clear, logical manner that explains and describes how Angkor Wat represents the peak of Khmer artistic achievement.

NATIONAL
GEOGRAPHIC

ON **LOCATION** WITH

Albert Lin

Research Scientist/Engineer
and National Geographic Emerging Explorer

▶ Check out more on myNGconnect

Albert Lin, pictured here in the forests of Mongolia,
teams up with other National Geographic Explorers
as part of the Valley of the Khans Project to hunt
for the tomb of Genghis Khan.

TWO PATHS

Society often encourages us to choose a single path in life, but I've always been interested both in the sciences and the humanities. Turning my education in engineering into one of the greatest adventures of my life has been a huge journey. The idea to search for the tomb of Genghis Khan occurred to me while backpacking in Mongolia. I wanted to do something that everyone thought was impossible.

Genghis Khan united Mongolia's feuding tribes and led them on a campaign of conquest unequalled in world history. He died in 1227, but the location of his tomb remains a mystery. In fact, Mongolian custom warns that disturbing Genghis Khan's burial site will unleash a curse that could end the world. With a cultural taboo as strong as that, you can't just start digging—you have to get smart.

USING TECHNOLOGY

There are many ways to look under the ground without having to touch it. I use non-invasive computer based technologies to gather, synthesize, and visualize data without ever digging a hole. Satellite imagery, ground-penetrating radar, and remote sensors let me explore places and make archaeological discoveries while respecting the traditional beliefs of indigenous people.

The real trick is synthesizing the vast amounts of information we collect into something that can be understood. We program billions of individual data bits into a file that allows us

Albert Lin examines a digital projection of northern Mongolia from inside the StarCAVE, a 3D virtual environment.

to re-render it into a digital 3D world. And then we have some fun in the StarCAVE, a virtual reality room that lets us manipulate our way through images projected on the ground, walls, and on every surface. Special glasses create the 3D effect so we can "fly" over the landscape. For example if a mountain is described in an old text, I can go into the StarCAVE and travel around that region to see if it actually exists. Technology like this lets us conduct a non-invasive search for Genghis Khan in a way that is respectful to the Mongolians. We can try to solve this ancient mystery without overstepping cultural barriers.

WHY STUDY HISTORY ?

" The Mongols created a lot of what we know of as our modern history, but their story hasn't been fully told and their contributions have been underestimated. *Sharing the true history of the foundation of our cultural past is crucial.* **"** —Albert Lin

NATIONAL GEOGRAPHIC

Divining Angkor

BY RICHARD STONE

Adapted from "Divining Angkor," by Richard Stone,
in *National Geographic*, July 2009

The Khmer kingdom lasted from the 9th to the 15th centuries. At its height it dominated a wide swath of Southeast Asia. Angkor, its capital, was the most extensive urban complex of the preindustrial world. As many as 750,000 people lived there. By the late 16th century, the once-magnificent capital was in decline.

Angkor became a powerhouse thanks to a sophisticated system of canals and reservoirs. Over several centuries, teams of laborers constructed hundreds of miles of canals and dikes. The city could hoard water in dry months and get rid of excess water during the rainy season.

The ability to divert and collect water would have afforded a measure of protection from floods, as well as a steady water supply. But forces beyond Angkor's control threw this system into disarray. Archaeologist Roland Fletcher was baffled when his team unearthed a vast structure in the waterworks and found that it had been destroyed, apparently by Angkor's own engineers.

These ruins are a vital clue to an epic struggle that unfolded as generations of Khmer engineers coped with an increasingly complex water system. "They probably spent vast portions of their lives fixing it," says Fletcher. Any deterioration of the waterworks would have left Angkor vulnerable to a natural disaster.

Starting in the 1300s, Europe endured a few centuries of unpredictable weather marked by harsh winters and chilly summers. Now it appears that Southeast Asia, too, experienced climatic upheaval. Extreme weather could have been the final blow to a vulnerable civilization. Prolonged and severe droughts, punctuated by torrential downpours, "would have ruined the water system," says Fletcher.

Angkor's end is a sobering lesson in the limits of human ingenuity. "Angkor's hydraulic system was an amazing machine," Fletcher says. Its engineers managed to keep the civilization's signal achievement running for six centuries—until, in the end, a greater force overwhelmed them.

For more from National Geographic
Check out "The Forgotten Road" on myNGconnect

UNIT INQUIRY: LEAVE A LEGACY OF INNOVATION

In this unit, you learned about Chinese, Japanese, and Korean civilizations. Based on your understanding of the text, what new products, methods, and ideas did these civilizations invent or develop? Which of these innovations do you think has made a lasting legacy on the modern world?

ASSIGNMENT Choose an innovation that you think our modern civilization will leave as a legacy for a future civilization. The innovation you choose should come from the 20th and 21st centuries. Be prepared to present your legacy to the class and explain why you chose it.

Plan As you choose your innovation, think about how other innovations—such as the Chinese invention of paper—dramatically changed and influenced many civilizations past and present. Make a list of the ways in which the innovation you selected has affected or changed the modern world. You might want to use a graphic organizer to help organize your thoughts.

Produce Use your notes to produce detailed descriptions of the impact your innovation has made on modern civilization and what impact you envision it having on a future

civilization. You might want to write your descriptions in outline or paragraph form.

Present Choose a creative way to present your innovation to the class. Consider one of these options:

- Create a multimedia presentation using photos to illustrate different ways your innovation has affected or changed modern civilization.

- Design an advertisement for your innovation, providing a "before" and "after" view of our civilization with and without the innovation.

- Write a paragraph describing how you envision this innovation will impact a future civilization and why.

Innovation	Effects

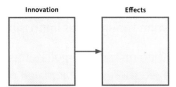
RAPID REVIEW

POSSIBLE RESPONSES

Possible responses for the remaining five things to remember include the following:

6. The Silla kingdom unified Korea and drove out the Chinese, but Korea's Koryo and Choson dynasties remained heavily influenced by Chinese culture.

7. The Khmer Empire, more influenced by India than China, dominated the Southeast Asian mainland until 1431.

8. China experienced the rise and fall of many dynasties such as the Sui, Tang, and Song.

9. Japan's location inspired its fierce isolationism and the Shinto religion based on natural spirits.

10. The Japanese adapted Chinese culture into unique forms of art, literature, drama, gardening, government, and religion.

UNIT INQUIRY PROJECT RUBRIC

ASSESS

Use the rubric to assess each student's participation and performance.

SCORE	ASSIGNMENT	PRODUCT	PRESENTATION
3 GREAT	• Student thoroughly understands the assignment. • Student engages fully with the project process. • Student works well independently.	• Innovation choice is well thought out. • Innovation choice takes into account how it has affected or changed the modern world. • Innovation choice contains a detailed description of its impact on a future civilization.	• Presentation is clear, concise, and logical. • Presentation does a good job of creatively explaining the innovation and its impact on modern and future civilizations. • Presentation engages the audience.
2 GOOD	• Student mostly understands the assignment. • Student engages fairly well with the project process. • Student works fairly well independently.	• Innovation choice is fairly well thought out. • Innovation choice somewhat takes into account how it has affected or changed the modern world. • Innovation choice contains a somewhat detailed description of its impact on a future civilization.	• Presentation is fairly clear, concise, and logical. • Presentation does an adequate job of creatively explaining the innovation and its impact on modern and future civilizations. • Presentation somewhat engages the audience.
1 NEEDS WORK	• Student does not understand the assignment. • Student minimally engages or does not engage with the project process. • Student struggles to work independently.	• Innovation choice is not well thought out. • Innovation choice does not take into account how it has affected or changed the modern world. • Innovation choice contains few or no details to describe its impact on a future civilization.	• Presentation is not clear, concise, or logical. • Presentation does not creatively explain the innovation and its impact on modern and future civilizations. • Presentation does not engage the audience.

MEDIEVAL AND RENAISSANCE EUROPE

NATIONAL GEOGRAPHIC

ON **LOCATION** WITH

Maurizio Seracini
Cultural Heritage Engineer

Europe experienced a "rebirth" around the 1300s, a time when writing, thinking, and the arts flourished. This movement, known as the Renaissance, began in Italy, and artists like Leonardo da Vinci, Raphael, and Michelangelo were hugely influential. I'm Maurizio Seracini, and I use technology to study priceless European works of art—and seek out ones that haven't been seen for centuries. Join me on an exploration of medieval and Renaissance Europe.

< CRITICAL VIEWING? The Baptistery of Saint John in Florence, Italy, dazzles visitors with its mosaics and fine artwork. What types of imagery can you identify and what does it reveal about this time period?

POSSIBLE RESPONSE

There are images of Jesus, saints, and angels. It indicates that people were very religious—Christian—during this time period.

593

Medieval and Renaissance Europe

1096
The Crusades begin.
(illustration of Crusaders in Jerusalem)

768
Charlemagne becomes king of the Franks and, in time, unites much of Western Europe. *(bust of Charlemagne)*

1215
King John seals the Magna Carta.

c. 1300
The Renaissance begins in Italy.

1200

700

1192
ASIA
Military rule under leaders called shoguns begins in Japan.

1325
THE AMERICAS
Aztecs establish their capital in Tenochtitlán, present-day Mexico City.
(Aztec calendar)

610
ASIA
Muhammad begins to spread Islam.

The World

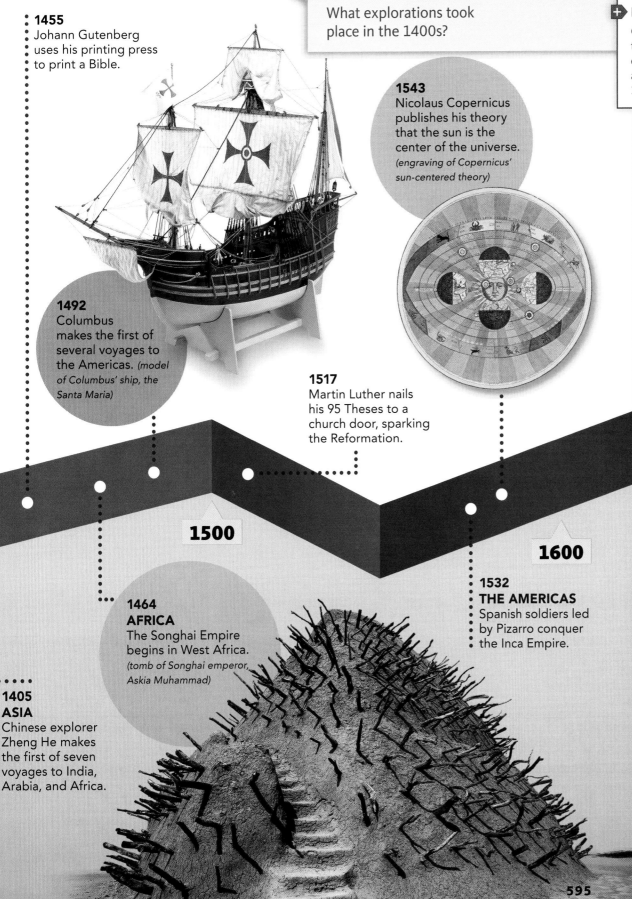

What explorations took place in the 1400s?

POSSIBLE RESPONSE
Columbus' explorations of the Americas and Zheng He's explorations of India, Arabia, and Africa took place in the 1400s.

1455
Johann Gutenberg uses his printing press to print a Bible.

1543
Nicolaus Copernicus publishes his theory that the sun is the center of the universe. *(engraving of Copernicus' sun-centered theory)*

1492
Columbus makes the first of several voyages to the Americas. *(model of Columbus' ship, the Santa Maria)*

1517
Martin Luther nails his 95 Theses to a church door, sparking the Reformation.

1500

1600

1464
AFRICA
The Songhai Empire begins in West Africa. *(tomb of Songhai emperor, Askia Muhammad)*

1532
THE AMERICAS
Spanish soldiers led by Pizarro conquer the Inca Empire.

1405
ASIA
Chinese explorer Zheng He makes the first of seven voyages to India, Arabia, and Africa.

595

Europe
c. 1600

Europe, c. 1600
- Austrian-Habsburg possessions
- Spanish-Habsburg possessions
- Papal states
— Holy Roman Empire

EUROPEAN STATES

By the 1600s, Europe was divided into many states. One of these, the Holy Roman Empire, began in the 800s, when a Germanic king named Charlemagne united many other kingdoms under his rule. Charlemagne was a Christian and a strong supporter of the pope in Rome. He spread his faith throughout his empire.

However, over time, a revolution in thought led people to question the Roman Catholic Church. Some Europeans broke away from the Church and developed their own Christian religions, which soon spread over Europe.

What religions were practiced in the Holy Roman Empire?

POSSIBLE RESPONSE

Roman Catholicism, Lutheranism, and Calvinism were practiced in the Holy Roman Empire.

0 100 200 300 400 kilometers

0   100   200   300   400 miles

Renaissance Gallery

In the 1300s, an explosion in art called the Renaissance began in Italy and spread through Europe. Some of the greatest Renaissance artists created the works shown here.

Giotto: The Mourning of Christ (c. 1305)

Jan van Eyck: The Arnolfini Portrait (c. 1434)

Christianity in Europe, c. 1600

- Church of England
- Calvinist
- Lutheran
- Roman Catholic
- Holy Roman Empire

0 100 200 300 400 kilometers

0 100 200 300 400 miles

RUSSIA

SWEDEN

DENMARK-NORWAY

Baltic Sea

Prussia

POLAND-LITHUANIA

North Sea

SCOTLAND

IRELAND

ENGLAND

London

NETHERLANDS

Elbe BRANDENBURG

SMALL STATES

SAXONY

Wittenberg

HOLY

ROMAN

EMPIRE

Rhine

Worms

Augsburg

BAVARIA

Danube

AUSTRIA

HUNGARY

Seine

FRANCE

SWISS CONFEDERATION

Trent

SAVOY

Danube

OTTOMAN EMPIRE

Adriatic Sea

Aegean Sea

ATLANTIC

OCEAN

Avignon

PAPAL STATES

Corsica

Rome

Naples

PORTUGAL

Madrid

SPAIN

Balearic Islands

Sardinia

Mediterranean Sea

Sicily

Crete

Leonardo da Vinci: The Last Supper (c. 1498)

Durer: Four Horsemen of the Apocalypse (c. 1498)

Michelangelo: Moses (c. 1515)

UNIT RESOURCES

On Location with National Geographic Fellow Maurizio Seracini
Intro and Video

Interactive Map Tool

 STORIES MAKING HISTORY **News & Updates**

Available on myNGconnect

Unit Wrap-Up:
"Using Technology to See the Past"
Feature and Video

"Brunelleschi's Dome"
National Geographic Adapted Article

"Lady with a Secret"
National Geographic Adapted Article
Student eEdition exclusive

Unit 9 Inquiry:
Map the New Worldview

CHAPTER RESOURCES

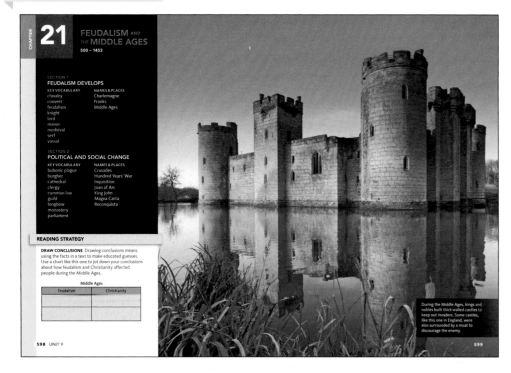

CHAPTER 21
FEUDALISM AND THE MIDDLE AGES
500 – 1453

SECTION 1
FEUDALISM DEVELOPS

KEY VOCABULARY
chivalry
convert
feudalism
knight
lord
manor
medieval
serf
vassal

NAMES & PLACES
Charlemagne
Franks
Middle Ages

SECTION 2
POLITICAL AND SOCIAL CHANGE

KEY VOCABULARY
bubonic plague
burgher
cathedral
clergy
common law
guild
longbow
monastery
parliament

NAMES & PLACES
Crusades
Hundred Years' War
Inquisition
Joan of Arc
King John
Magna Carta
Reconquista

READING STRATEGY

DRAW CONCLUSIONS Drawing conclusions means using the facts in a text to make educated guesses. Use a chart like this one to jot down your conclusions about how feudalism and Christianity affected people during the Middle Ages.

Middle Ages

Feudalism	Christianity

During the Middle Ages, kings and nobles built thick-walled castles to keep out invaders. Some castles, like this one in England, were also surrounded by a moat to discourage the enemy.

598 UNIT 9

599

TEACHER RESOURCES & ASSESSMENT

Available on myNGconnect

 Social Studies Skills Lessons
• Reading: Draw Conclusions
• Writing: Write an Informative Paragraph

 Formal Assessment
• Chapter 21 Tests A (on-level) & B (below-level)

A **Chapter 21 Answer Key**

ExamView®
One-time Download

STUDENT BACKPACK *Available on myNGconnect*

• **eEdition** *(English)* • **eEdition** *(Spanish)* • **Handbooks** • **Online Atlas**
For Chapter 21 Spanish resources, visit the Teacher Resource Menu page on myNGconnect.

SECTION 1 RESOURCES

FEUDALISM DEVELOPS

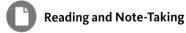 **Reading and Note-Taking**

Vocabulary Practice

☑ **Section 1 Quiz**

Available on myNGconnect

LESSON 1.1 MEDIEVAL EUROPE
- Critical Viewing: NG Chapter Gallery
- On Your Feet: Create a Kingdom

BIOGRAPHY
LESSON 1.2 CHARLEMAGNE
| **NG Learning Framework:**
Write a Biography
- On Your Feet: Fishbowl Discussion

NG WRITER CAROLINE ALEXANDER
LESSON 1.3 INVESTIGATING A MYSTERIOUS TREASURE
| **NG Learning Framework:**
Evaluate Treasure
- On Your Feet: Bury a Time Capsule

LESSON 1.4 FEUDAL SOCIETY
| **NG Learning Framework:**
Write a Description
- On Your Feet: Four Corners

HISTORY THROUGH OBJECTS
LESSON 1.5 MEDIEVAL KNIGHTS
- Critical Viewing: NG Image Gallery
- On Your Feet: Weapons Experts

LESSON 1.6 THE MANOR SYSTEM
| **NG Learning Framework:**
Castles and Manor Houses
- On Your Feet: Three-Step Interview

SECTION 2 RESOURCES

POLITICAL AND SOCIAL CHANGE

 **Reading and Note-Taking**

Vocabulary Practice

☑ **Section 2 Quiz**

Available on myNGconnect

LESSON 2.1 CHURCH AND CROWN
| **NG Learning Framework:**
Write a Biography
- On Your Feet: Think, Pair, Share

LESSON 2.2 KING JOHN AND THE MAGNA CARTA
| **NG Learning Framework:**
Role-Play
- On Your Feet: Numbered Heads

DOCUMENT-BASED QUESTION
LESSON 2.3 CHARTERS OF FREEDOM
- Critical Viewing: NG Image Gallery
- On Your Feet: Three Options

LESSON 2.4 THE CRUSADES
- On Your Feet: Jigsaw

LESSON 2.5 WAR AND PLAGUE
| **NG Learning Framework:**
Make Observations
- On Your Feet: Role-Play

MOMENTS IN HISTORY
LESSON 2.6 THE BUBONIC PLAGUE
- Critical Viewing: NG Chapter Gallery
- On Your Feet: Interpret a Painting

LESSON 2.7 GROWTH OF TOWNS
- Critical Viewing: NG Image Gallery
- On Your Feet: Create a Concept Web

CHAPTER 21 REVIEW

STRATEGY 1

Use a K-W-L Chart

Before beginning each lesson, have students work in pairs to preview the lesson title and complete these steps:

1. Write one fact that they already know about the topic.
2. Write one question to which they want to know the answer.
3. After reading, answer the question they asked or discuss how they can find the answer.

K What Do I Know?	W What Do I Want To Learn?	L What Did I Learn?

Use with All Lessons

STRATEGY 2

Use a Word Sort Activity

Write these words and names on the board and ask students to sort them into four groups of three related words. Then have them use each group of words in a paragraph that shows how they are related.

lord	pope	shield
helmet	monastery	cathedral
serf	church	long sword
clergy	bishop	vassal

Use with Lesson 2.1

Press (mt) *in the Student eEdition for modified text.*

STRATEGY 3

Play "Who Am I?"

Choose from the names below and distribute a list to students. Have them make game cards with a name on the front and a clue to the person's identity on the back. For example, for King John, students might write, "sealed the Magna Carta." Use the cards to play a whole group, small group, or partner review game.

Charlemagne	Joan of Arc	King John
King Henry IV	Pope Gregory	Ferdinand and Isabella
Clovis	Pope Leo III	William of Normandy

Use with Lessons 1.1, 1.2, and 2.1–2.5

STRATEGY 1

Preview Visuals to Predict

Ask students to preview the title and visuals in each lesson. Then have students tell what they think the lesson will be about. After reading, ask them to repeat the activity to see whether their predictions were confirmed.

Use with All Lessons *Invite volunteers to describe the visuals in detail to help visually impaired students see them.*

STRATEGY 2

Make Word Connections

Have students write a Key Vocabulary word from each lesson in the center of a sticky note or index card and display it on their desk as that lesson is read and discussed. As they read, have students write words from the text or other words they know that are associated with the vocabulary word.

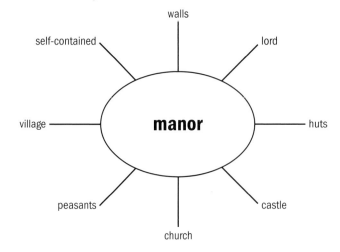

Use with All Lessons

ENGLISH LANGUAGE LEARNERS

STRATEGY ❶
Preview Visuals

Before reading Section 1, have students look at all the visuals. Lead students in creating labels that identify important features in each picture. Encourage students to label words that will support their understanding of the lesson, such as *castle* or *knight*. Repeat before reading Section 2.

Use with All Lessons *For their labels, students may use sticky notes or index cards. Labels may be reused across lessons.*

STRATEGY ❷
Illustrate a Word Tree

Write the following word tree to help students understand the relationship of the feudal classes. Then ask them to copy and draw pictures to illustrate each branch of the tree.

king

lord   lord   lord

vassal   vassal   vassal   vassal

peasant   peasant   peasant   peasant   peasant

serf   serf   serf   serf   serf   serf   serf   serf   serf   serf   serf

Use with Lesson 1.4 *You might also have students write sentences explaining the relationships.*

STRATEGY ❸
Use Either/Or Sentences

After reading, ask students either/or questions to reinforce meanings. You may also give copies of the questions to students to find and write the answers, or to quiz each other.

- If a person is *converted*, does he change his religion or his country?
- Was a *serf* more like a king or a slave?
- Was a *knight* an expert soldier or a Church official?
- Were the *Crusades* fought between two kingdoms or between religious enemies?
- Is a *parliament* part of a government or part of the church?

Use with All Lessons *You may wish to place students in groups with various levels of language proficiency and have advanced students write more either/or questions to ask beginning students.*

GIFTED & TALENTED

STRATEGY ❶
Create a Model

Encourage interested students to create a model of a feudal manor. Their model can be a diorama, made from clay or papier-mâché, ice pop sticks, cardboard, or anything else they think of to use. They can imitate the diagram in Lesson 1.6 or others that they research.

Use with Lesson 1.6

STRATEGY ❷
Act Out a Scene

This chapter describes several confrontations or meetings between kings or between kings and the Church. Have pairs of students select one scene from the following list. Tell them to imagine the scene, write out a script, and then act out their scene for the class.

- Henry IV and Pope Gregory VII
- King John and the barons
- Ferdinand and Isabella about the Inquisition
- Joan of Arc and Charles of France

Use with Lessons 2.1, 2.2, 2.4, and 2.5

PRE-AP

STRATEGY ❶
Use the "Persia" Approach

Have students write an essay explaining the significance of the Middle Ages. Copy the following mnemonic on the board, and tell students to use the "Persia" strategy to look at the period.

Political

Economic

Religious

Social

Intellectual

Artistic

Use with All Lessons

STRATEGY ❷
Form and Support Opinions

Ask students to decide which ruler made the greatest impact on history: Charlemagne, King John, or Ferdinand and Isabella. Have them develop a thesis statement that explains their decision and write an essay that supports it.

Use with Lessons 1.2, 2.2, 2.3, and 2.4

FEUDALISM AND THE MIDDLE AGES
500 – 1453

SECTION 1
FEUDALISM DEVELOPS

KEY VOCABULARY	NAMES & PLACES
chivalry	Charlemagne
convert	Franks
feudalism	Middle Ages
knight	
lord	
manor	
medieval	
serf	
vassal	

SECTION 2
POLITICAL AND SOCIAL CHANGE

KEY VOCABULARY	NAMES & PLACES
bubonic plague	Crusades
burgher	Hundred Years' War
cathedral	Inquisition
clergy	Joan of Arc
common law	King John
guild	Magna Carta
longbow	Reconquista
monastery	
parliament	

READING STRATEGY

DRAW CONCLUSIONS Drawing conclusions means using the facts in a text to make educated guesses. Use a chart like this one to jot down your conclusions about how feudalism and Christianity affected people during the Middle Ages.

Middle Ages

Feudalism	Christianity

During the Middle Ages, kings and nobles built thick-walled castles to keep out invaders. Some castles, like this one in England, were also surrounded by a moat to discourage the enemy.

TEACHER BACKGROUND

INTRODUCE THE PHOTOGRAPH

Have students study the photograph of the castle. Explain that the Middle Ages was a time of much warfare between kings and nobles. This castle is typical of a royal castle built by the Normans for William of Normandy. Tell students that in this chapter, they will learn about many power struggles during the Middle Ages.

ASK: In what ways does the castle look safe from intruders? *(Possible responses: It is made of stone, tall towers have areas from which soldiers can shoot arrows, windows are very small, it is surrounded by a moat, no doors are visible.)*

SHARE BACKGROUND

Most large castles in England were built after William of Normandy conquered England in 1066. The Normans built castles of stone for the best protection in warfare. These castles were sturdier than those built by earlier lords. Many castles were built in England after the Norman invasion, but most have deteriorated. Royal castles were built for the king, but barons or lords also built their own castles. Today those that are left are used as tourist attractions.

DIGITAL RESOURCES myNGconnect.com

TEACHER RESOURCES & ASSESSMENT

 Social Studies Skills Lessons
- Reading: Draw Conclusions
- Writing: Write an Informative Paragraph

ExamView®
One-time Download

 Formal Assessment
- Chapter 21 Tests A (on-level) & B (below-level)

A **Chapter 21 Answer Key**

STUDENT BACKPACK
- **eEdition** *(English)*
- **eEdition** *(Spanish)*
- **Handbooks**
- **Online Atlas**

For Chapter 21 Spanish Resources, visit the Teacher Resource Menu page.

INTRODUCE THE ESSENTIAL QUESTION

HOW DID EUROPE CHANGE DURING THE MIDDLE AGES?

Four Corners Activity: Factors of Impact This activity introduces students to four factors that affected Europeans in the Middle Ages and allows them to choose which had the greatest impact on people. Post the four signs shown in the list below in the four corners of the classroom. Ask students to choose the factor that they think had the greatest effect on ordinary people, go to that corner, and explain why.

A. Religion The Roman Catholic Church dominated people's lives, sent armies on Crusades, and expelled many Muslims and Jews from parts of Europe.

B. Disease The bubonic plague was a deadly and contagious disease that wiped out about one-third of Europe's population.

C. War Many wars were waged between kingdoms; one between France and England lasted for over 100 years.

D. Society Under feudalism, peasants and serfs had to obey their lords and farm the lords' land. They had little freedom and little possibility of changing their lives. `0:15` minutes

INTRODUCE THE READING STRATEGY

DRAW CONCLUSIONS

Remind students that when they draw conclusions, they use facts in a text to make educated guesses. Model filling out the Conclusions Chart by reading aloud the following paragraph and discussing it with students.

> It is hard for people today to understand the extraordinary power Christianity had in the Middle Ages. The Roman Catholic Church was the strongest unifying force in medieval Europe. The Church baptized, married, pardoned, and buried everyone from serfs to kings. It promised that good people would go to heaven and the wicked would be punished after death.

Work with students to come up with the conclusion that Christianity dominated people's lives during the Middle Ages.

Middle Ages

Feudalism	Christianity
	The Church dominated people's lives.

INTRODUCE CHAPTER VOCABULARY

KNOWLEDGE RATING

Have students complete a Knowledge-Rating Chart for Key Vocabulary words. Have students list words and fill out the chart. Then have pairs share the definitions they know. Work together as a class to complete the chart.

KEY VOCAB	KNOW IT	NOT SURE	DON'T KNOW	DEFINITION
bubonic plague				
burgher				
cathedral				
chivalry				

KEY DATES

486	Clovis, king of the Franks, converts to Christianity and unites other kingdoms
800	Charlemagne becomes emperor of the Holy Roman Empire
800s	Feudalism becomes Europe's political and social system
1066	William, Duke of Normandy, conquers England
1075	Pope Gregory VII keeps control of religious appointments, defeating King Henry IV
1215	King John seals the Magna Carta in England
1295	King Edward I assembles first representative parliament in England
1096–1291	Crusades are fought to save Palestine; Muslims defeat Christians
1000–1492	Reconquista drives Muslims away from Iberian Peninsula; Ferdinand and Isabella use Inquisition to defeat and expel all Muslims and Jews
1337–1453	Hundred Years' War is fought between England and France; Joan of Arc leads France to victory
1347–1350	Bubonic plague kills one-third of Europe's population

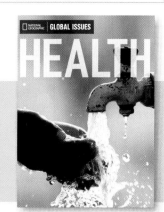

For more information on pandemics like the bubonic plague and other health issues, check out *GLOBAL ISSUES: HEALTH.*

1.1

Medieval Europe

The Germanic tribes that caused the fall of the Western Roman Empire in A.D. 476 didn't just devastate towns and kill many of their inhabitants. They destroyed a way of life. For hundreds of years, the Roman Empire had united much of Europe. With the empire no longer in control, "Now what?" could well have been the question on almost everyone's mind.

MAIN IDEA

After Rome fell, Western Europe underwent many political and cultural changes.

AFTER THE FALL OF ROME

What came next is a period historians call the **Middle Ages**. This era lasted from about 500 to 1450 in Western Europe and is also called the medieval period. **Medieval** comes from the Latin words *medium*, meaning "middle," and *aevum*, meaning "age."

During the early part of this period, Western Europe was very different from what it had been under Rome's strong central government and powerful army. After Rome fell, Germanic leaders seized power, and much of the region became divided into small kingdoms that were almost constantly at war. As a result of this widespread warfare, one of the greatest challenges

facing leaders was to keep their people safe and secure. This challenge would help shape stronger governments over time.

It was a violent time, yet many kingdoms thrived. Thanks to the region's mostly moderate climate and rich soil, farmers could grow crops and feed themselves and their livestock. Abundant forestland provided wood for building, and mountains containing a wealth of minerals—particularly iron—allowed the Germanic peoples to make all the weapons they needed to fight their foes. In addition, Western Europe's long coastline and major rivers gave people access to the sea and plentiful supplies of fish.

POLITICAL AND CULTURAL CHANGES

The region's many waterways offered ideal routes and networks for trading. However, unlike the Romans, the Germanic peoples who migrated to Western Europe were not interested in trade. The tribes that settled in Roman lands in the early part of the Middle Ages preferred their own traditions to Roman ways.

For example, the new settlers had their own ideas about government. Tribes such as the **Franks** united to form powerful kingdoms but didn't create large centralized governments or write down their laws, as the Romans had. Instead, the people obeyed the unwritten rules and traditions of their king. They lived in small villages where they worked the land and tended their herds. As trade began to disappear in the region, so did many cities.

Just about the only force that helped unite Western Europe in the early Middle Ages was Christianity, which survived the fall of Rome. Before the 500s, most Germanic peoples, including the Angles, Jutes, and Saxons, practiced their traditional religions and worshipped many gods. After the Germanic leaders came to power, however, many of them **converted**, or changed their religion, to Christianity.

MEDIEVAL EUROPE, A.D. 500

SAXONS, ANGLES, etc. Major tribe

The first leader to convert was Clovis, who ruled the Franks. After Clovis defeated Roman Gaul (now France) in 486, he went on to conquer other weaker kingdoms. When he converted to Christianity, many of his subjects did, too. As a result of his conversion and that of other rulers, Christianity spread and increased in influence. Even though the Western Roman Empire had disappeared, the city of Rome itself retained a certain amount of power and strength. It remained the home of the pope as well as the center of Christianity.

REVIEW & ASSESS

1. **READING CHECK** How did government change in Western Europe after the fall of Rome?

2. **INTERPRET MAPS** Which of the six kingdoms labeled on the map might have been most exposed to attack from other kingdoms? Explain why.

3. **COMPARE AND CONTRAST** How did Western European culture in the early Middle Ages differ from culture during the Roman Empire?

PLAN

OBJECTIVE

Identify how Western Europe changed after Rome fell.

CRITICAL THINKING SKILLS FOR LESSON 1.1

- Identify Main Ideas and Details
- Monitor Comprehension
- Interpret Maps
- Compare and Contrast
- Identify
- Analyze Cause and Effect

ESSENTIAL QUESTION

How did Europe change during the Middle Ages?

After the Western Roman Empire fell, Europe broke up into small kingdoms ruled by Germanic kings. Lesson 1.1 explains the many

political and cultural changes that occurred after the fall of the Roman Empire.

BACKGROUND FOR THE TEACHER

During the medieval period, Germanic tribes created their own small kingdoms and ruled Europe. The Franks settled in what is now France. Clovis started taking over the Frankish tribes when he was just 16. He ruled the kingdom for 30 years, making it strong militarily and converting his subjects to Christianity.

Other tribes included the Visigoths and the Ostrogoths. The Visigoths sacked Rome and put an end to the Western Roman Empire. The Visigoths eventually settled in what is now Spain. The Ostrogoths, under Theodoric the Great, took over what is now Italy.

DIGITAL RESOURCES myNGconnect.com

TEACHER RESOURCES & ASSESSMENT

 Reading and Note-Taking

 Vocabulary Practice

 Section 1 Quiz

STUDENT RESOURCES

 NG Chapter Gallery

INTRODUCE & ENGAGE

MAKE PREDICTIONS

Ask students to look at the map of medieval Europe. **ASK:** Based on the map, what do you think happened in Europe after the Western Roman Empire collapsed? Record students' responses on an Idea Web like the one shown below. After students have read the lesson, revisit the Idea Web and add to it or correct any misconceptions they may have had. **0:05** minutes

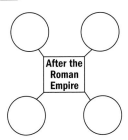

After the Roman Empire

TEACH

GUIDED DISCUSSION

1. **Identify** What was the only thing that united the Germanic kingdoms? *(Christianity)*

2. **Analyze Cause and Effect** Why was the early Middle Ages so violent? *(Small kingdoms were constantly fighting each other.)*

ANALYZE CAUSES

Remind students that, during the early Middle Ages, cities disappeared. Have students discuss what caused this to happen. List student responses in a chart like the one shown. *(Most people lived in small villages; kingdoms were at war with each other; people didn't travel outside their kingdom; groups stopped trading; kingdoms became self-sufficient.)* **0:15** minutes

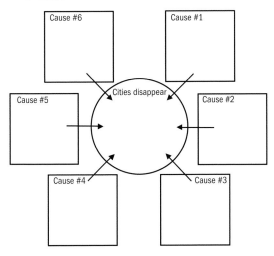

ACTIVE OPTIONS

Critical Viewing: NG Chapter Gallery Invite students to explore the Chapter Gallery to examine the images that relate to this

chapter. Have them select one of the images and do additional research to learn more about it. Ask questions that will inspire additional inquiry about the chosen gallery image, such as: What is this? Where and when was this created? By whom? Why was it created? What is it made of? Why does it belong in this chapter? What else would you like to know about it? **0:10** minutes

On Your Feet: Create a Kingdom Have students get together in teams of four. Tell them that each group is its own kingdom and will make decisions about its kingdom. Decisions include choosing a name, describing their activities, explaining how they will protect themselves from other kingdoms, and deciding how they will rule their subjects. After the groups have recorded their decisions, call on volunteers from each group to share their ideas. **0:10** minutes

DIFFERENTIATE

STRIVING READERS

Chart Changes Have students use a chart like the one below to compare Western Europe under the Romans with life in medieval Europe. Encourage students to work in pairs or small groups to complete the chart.

	Roman Empire	Medieval Europe
Government		
Laws		
Daily LIfe		
Religion		

GIFTED & TALENTED

Clovis Biography Clovis was quite young when he combined the Franks into one fighting force. Have interested students research and write a short biography of his life, using the format used in Lesson 1.2 for Charlemagne. Display the biographies in the classroom.

Press **mt** *in the Student eEdition for modified text.*

See the Chapter Planner for more strategies for differentiation.

REVIEW & ASSESS

ANSWERS

1. After the fall of Rome, Western Europe was no longer controlled by a central government but was instead divided into many small kingdoms.

2. The Burgundian kingdom might have been most vulnerable because it was surrounded on all sides by three other powerful kingdoms.

3. In the Middle Ages, people didn't trade. They lived in small villages and obeyed unwritten rules and traditions. Learning wasn't emphasized, and cities largely disappeared.

CHARLEMAGNE
c. 742 – 814

He was a man of contrasts. He ruthlessly destroyed his enemies but loved learning. He was a tall, commanding figure but usually wore simple clothing. He received fabulous gifts from foreign kings but collected songs of ancient Germanic heroes. In spite of—or maybe because of—these contradictions, he became the first emperor in Western Europe since the fall of the Western Roman Empire. They didn't call this king of the Franks Charlemagne—or Charles the Great—for nothing.

In this painting, Pope Leo III crowns Charlemagne emperor of the Romans before an audience of Church officials.

Job: First emperor of the Holy Roman Empire

Home: Kingdom of the Franks

FINEST HOUR

After Charlemagne conquered and united the Germanic kingdoms of Western Europe, the pope placed a crown on Charlemagne's head, proclaiming him emperor of the Romans.

HOBBIES

He enjoyed hunting and swimming and often made his friends and nobles swim with him.

TRIVIA

He could get by on little sleep and sometimes woke his officials to hear the latest report or charge them with a new task.

DEATH

After swimming in one of his favorite springs, he came down with a fever and died a week later.

A MIGHTY RULER

More than 200 years after Clovis died, **Charlemagne** (SHAHR-luh-mayn) became the Frankish king in 768 and proved to be a natural leader. He had a vision for his reign. Charlemagne wanted to unite under his rule all of the Germanic kingdoms shown on the map in the previous lesson. To achieve that goal, the Frankish king battled such tribes as the Slavs, the Lombards, and the Saxons, who reigned in what is now Germany. In the end, Charlemagne succeeded. He brought many of the Germanic tribes together as one people and became the strongest leader in Western Europe.

While Charlemagne was doing battle with the Saxons and other powerful Germanic tribes, he ably administered his kingdom. He established new laws to keep order and appointed officials to run faraway regions of his realm. Each year, Charlemagne called the officials to his court to keep tabs on them. He also took care of his subjects. He founded schools and protected the weak against injustice. Above all, he wanted to strengthen Christianity throughout his kingdom.

A CHRISTIAN EMPIRE

Like all Frankish kings since the 500s, Charlemagne was a Christian. In fact, his wars against the Germanic tribes had been fought not only to unite the tribes but also to spread his faith. After he conquered the Saxons, he declared that he would put to death anyone who refused to convert to Christianity. Since Charlemagne had already proved how ruthless he could be by slaughtering more than 4,000 Saxons who had fought against him, those who remained offered no further resistance.

Charlemagne was also a loyal defender of the pope at the time, Pope Leo III. After the pope passed laws that chipped away at the power of the nobles of Rome, they rebelled against him in 800. Leo asked for Charlemagne's help, and the king put the uprising down.

To express his gratitude, Leo crowned Charlemagne emperor of the Romans during a Christmas service in Rome. Charlemagne became the first German emperor of what would later be called the Holy Roman Empire. The title recognized Charlemagne as a guardian of Christianity. It also fueled his passion to strengthen the Church. By the time Charlemagne died in 814, he had created a strong Christian empire.

REVIEW & ASSESS

1. **READING CHECK** What were Charlemagne's two main goals during his reign?

2. **SEQUENCE EVENTS** What happened after Charlemagne put down the uprising in Rome?

3. **MAKE INFERENCES** How was Charlemagne a stabilizing, or steadying, force in Western Europe?

PLAN

OBJECTIVE

Discuss Charlemagne's rule and empire.

CRITICAL THINKING SKILLS FOR LESSON 1.2

- Identify Main Ideas and Details
- Monitor Comprehension
- Sequence Events
- Make Inferences
- Summarize
- Form and Support Opinions
- Analyze Visuals

ESSENTIAL QUESTION

How did Europe change during the Middle Ages?

Charlemagne united the Germanic kingdoms under his rule. Lesson 2.2 explores the rule of Charlemagne and the Christian empire he created.

BACKGROUND FOR THE TEACHER

Charlemagne was a skilled military strategist who was ruthless when it came to conquering the various Germanic tribes in Western Europe. Much of his rule was spent in warfare against the Saxons. He reportedly massacred about 4,500 of them, forcing the rest to convert to Christianity. He became the first German emperor of the Holy Roman Empire by protecting Pope Leo and the Christians in Rome.

DIGITAL RESOURCES myNGconnect.com

TEACHER RESOURCES & ASSESSMENT

 Reading and Note-Taking

 Vocabulary Practice

 Section 1 Quiz

STUDENT RESOURCES

 NG Chapter Gallery

INTRODUCE & ENGAGE

MAKE GENERALIZATIONS

Have students compare leaders today with those of the Middle Ages. **ASK:** What qualities characterize great leaders today? What qualities do you think leaders in the Middle Ages possessed? Write students' responses in a T-chart on the board. Then have the class look for any words and phrases that leaders from both periods have in common. Explain that this lesson is about Emperor Charlemagne, or Charles the Great, a leader during the Middle Ages. **0:05** minutes

TEACH

GUIDED DISCUSSION

1. **Summarize** What achievements did Charlemagne accomplish? *(Possible responses: He united the Germanic tribes into one empire, conquered the Saxons, stabilized Europe, kept order, established laws, promoted education, established a Christian empire, and protected Pope Leo III.)*

2. **Form and Support Opinions** Some of Charlemagne's achievements were good for the Franks but not for other people. What do you think of his methods and his goals? In your opinion, was Charlemagne "great"? Support your opinion with reasons. *(Opinions will vary; some may say that in the Middle Ages, a strong leader had to be ruthless. Others may think that Charlemagne should not have killed so many or forced Christianity on them.)*

ANALYZE VISUALS

Have students examine the painting of Charlemagne being crowned emperor. Have them make observations about the people attending the event and discuss who they might be. Have students also describe the hall and its decorations. Ask them why the painter might have included all these details. **0:10** minutes

ACTIVE OPTIONS

NG Learning Framework: Write a Biography

ATTITUDE: **Curiosity**
KNOWLEDGE: **Our Human Story**

Have students select one of the people they are still curious about after reading this lesson. Instruct them to write a short biography about this person using information from the chapter and additional source material. **0:20** minutes

On Your Feet: Fishbowl Discussion Have half the class sit in a circle with the other half of the class sitting around them. Both circles should be facing inward. Have the inner circle discuss Charlemagne. After ten minutes, have the groups switch places and let the new inside circle continue the discussion. Have students discuss the following:

- What did Charlemagne achieve?
- What methods did he use to succeed?
- Could he have achieved his results any other way?
- How does he compare with other rulers?

0:10 minutes

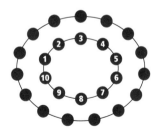

DIFFERENTIATE

ENGLISH LANGUAGE LEARNERS

Provide Sentence Frames Have pairs of students read the lesson and complete the sentences below.

1. In English, the name *Charlemagne* means "Charles _____." *(the Great)*

2. Charlemagne conquered the Germanic tribes and _____ them into one large _____. *(united, empire)*

3. When Pope Leo crowned Charlemagne, he became _____. *(emperor)*

4. Charlemagne's empire was eventually called _____. *(the Holy Roman Empire)*

5. Charlemagne forced everyone in his empire to become _____. *(Christian)*

GIFTED & TALENTED

Draw Parallels to Today's World Have students think about Charlemagne's reign and compare events then to current events. Have them list specific similarities and differences.

Press **mt** *in the Student eEdition for modified text.*

See the Chapter Planner for more strategies for differentiation.

REVIEW & ASSESS

ANSWERS

1. Charlemagne wanted to unite all the Germanic tribes under his rule and spread Christianity.

2. He was crowned emperor of the Romans by Pope Leo III.

3. He established an organized government and instituted new laws to keep order, appointed officials to oversee regions of the empire, took care of his subjects, and spread Christianity.

NATIONAL GEOGRAPHIC WRITER **CAROLINE ALEXANDER**

Investigating a
Mysterious Treasure

People carefully combing every inch of a stretch of beach with a metal detector may dream of striking it rich, but they usually just find a few dollars in change. Who knows what Terry Herbert dreamed of finding with his metal detector as he searched a field in the English county of Staffordshire in 2009? The farmer who owned the land hoped Herbert would uncover his missing wrench. Instead, as Caroline Alexander has reported, he found a mysterious stash of long-ago buried treasure.

^ This gold sword hilt, or handle, was among the treasure found in Staffordshire. The hilt is inlaid with red gemstones called garnets. If you look closely, you can see traces of soil on the gems

MAIN IDEA

Archaeologists are trying to figure out who buried a great treasure in England in the late 600s and why.

BURIED TREASURE

Remember reading about the Angles and Saxons in the first two lessons of this chapter? Not all members of these powerful tribes lived in Germany. The Anglo-Saxons—made up mostly of Angles, Saxons, and Jutes—settled in England in the 400s and ruled there for about 600 years. Archaeologists know that the treasure Herbert uncovered in Staffordshire was buried during the Anglo-Saxons' rule. They have also determined that most of the Staffordshire Hoard, as it came to be called, consists of military items. (*Hoard* is just another word for a mass or collection of something.) The only nonmilitary items are a quotation from the Bible, inscribed on a thin strip of gold, and two golden crosses.

What archaeologists don't know is who hid the hoard and why. Was the treasure buried by Anglo-Saxon soldiers or thieves? Did those who hid the treasure want to keep it safe from enemy hands? Did they plan to come back for it? Questions like these captured the imagination of National Geographic writer Caroline Alexander. As she points out in a 2011 issue of *National Geographic* magazine, "The Staffordshire Hoard was thrilling and historic—but above all it was enigmatic [mysterious]."

MYSTERIES AND MAGIC

Alexander believes the key to understanding the mystery of the hoard lies in understanding the importance of magic

STAFFORDSHIRE, ENGLAND

at that time. The Anglo-Saxons deeply believed in magic and certain supernatural creatures. For example, as Alexander writes, "Misfortune was commonly attributed to tiny darts fired by elves." Gold was thought to have magical properties that could please these creatures. So the hoard might also have been meant to ward off misfortune—particularly in battle.

But what about the Christian items? You've learned that many Germanic peoples converted to Christianity after the fall of Rome. This may explain the quotation from the Bible on the strip of gold and the two crosses. However, many of the new converts blended Christianity with their traditional beliefs. Some early Germanic Christian kings called on God to help them in battle. They also believed that biblical quotations could give them magical power in battle.

So was the hoard buried as an offering for the gods, the Christian God, or supernatural creatures? Perhaps it was a combination of all three. Or maybe it was none of the above. As Alexander admits, "Odds are we will never know the story behind the Staffordshire Hoard, but in a world without magic spells or dragons, would we understand it if we did?"

REVIEW & ASSESS

1. **READING CHECK** What treasure was discovered in a field in Staffordshire?

2. **IDENTIFY MAIN IDEAS AND DETAILS** Who were the Anglo-Saxons?

3. **DRAW CONCLUSIONS** Why does Caroline Alexander think we may never understand the story behind the Staffordshire Hoard?

PLAN

OBJECTIVE

Discuss who buried a great treasure in England in the late 600s and why.

CRITICAL THINKING SKILLS FOR LESSON 1.3

- Identify Main Ideas and Details
- Draw Conclusions
- Summarize
- Make Inferences
- Analyze Visuals
- Monitor Comprehension

ESSENTIAL QUESTION

How did Europe change during the Middle Ages?

The Anglo-Saxons settled in England in the 400s and ruled for 600 years. Lesson 1.3 describes the discovery of a mysterious treasure that dates from this time.

BACKGROUND FOR THE TEACHER

The Saxons were Germanic peoples whom the Romans had used as mercenaries in England before the empire fell. The Angles and Jutes came from what is now Denmark. After the Romans withdrew from England, the Angles and Jutes took over the area and ruled it for 600 years. The treasure found by archaeologists was mainly military equipment, which would have meant a great deal to these people. The Bible quotation and crosses add to the mystery surrounding the treasure.

DIGITAL RESOURCES myNGconnect.com

TEACHER RESOURCES & ASSESSMENT

 Reading and Note-Taking
 Vocabulary Practice
 Section 1 Quiz

STUDENT RESOURCES

 NG Chapter Gallery

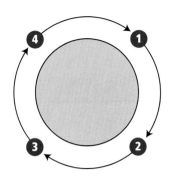

INTRODUCE & ENGAGE

CONNECT TO WHAT YOU KNOW

Tell students that a superstition is the belief that supernatural beings can cause something to happen. Have students get together in small groups and brainstorm superstitions they have heard. Encourage students to discuss any superstitions they themselves might believe in. Then tell students that, in this lesson, they will learn about some of the superstitious beliefs held during the Middle Ages. **0:05** minutes

TEACH

GUIDED DISCUSSION

1. **Make Inferences** Why would Anglo-Saxons consider military items to be valuable? *(They were a fighting people who valued good weapons and might decorate them with gold and gems.)*

2. **Summarize** What are Caroline Alexander's theories about who buried the treasure and why? *(The hoard could have been buried as an offering for the gods, or for the Christian God, or for supernatural creatures to help people gain magical power in battle.)*

ANALYZE VISUALS

Have students examine the photo of the gold sword hilt. **ASK:** Approximately how old is the hilt? *(about 1,400 years old)* Why is it so well preserved? *(It remained underground all that time.)* What does the hilt suggest about the skill of the artisan who created it? *(It suggests that the artisan was greatly skilled.)* **0:10** minutes

ACTIVE OPTIONS

NG Learning Framework: Evaluate Treasure

SKILL: Collaboration
KNOWLEDGE: **Our Human Story**

Invite students to work in groups to discuss the contents of the Anglo-Saxon treasure. Ask them to decide what ordinary people living at that time would have thought of the treasure if they had found it. Would they have stolen it or added other items to the treasure? Encourage students to think like people who lived during the Middle Ages. **0:10** minutes

On Your Feet: Bury a Time Capsule Tell students that this treasure serves as a time capsule and gives us a hint about how the Anglo-Saxons lived and what they valued. Have students conduct a roundtable discussion to discuss what they would include in a time capsule today. Each student should contribute an idea. Let all groups share their best ideas in a class discussion. **0:10** minutes

DIFFERENTIATE

STRIVING READERS

Answer Questions Have students work together to come up with answers to the questions listed below. Remind them that there are no right or wrong answers.

- Who buried the treasure? *(Anglo Saxons or thieves)*
- To whom might the treasure have been meant to bring good luck? *(Anglo-Saxon soldiers in battle)*
- Why were Christian items buried with the rest of the hoard? *(to obtain God's help or that of supernatural creatures in battle)*

GIFTED & TALENTED

Magic and Superstition Interested students might enjoy researching the role of magic and superstition during the early Middle Ages. Have them work in pairs to create a poster that reflects their findings. Encourage students to present their posters to the rest of the class.

Press **mt** *in the Student eEdition for modified text.*

See the Chapter Planner for more strategies for differentiation.

REVIEW & ASSESS

ANSWERS

1. A valuable Anglo-Saxon treasure of military and nonmilitary items was discovered in a field in the county of Staffordshire in England.

2. The Anglo-Saxons were warlike Germanic people who settled in England and ruled the country for six centuries.

3. Caroline Alexander thinks we may never understand the story behind the Staffordshire Hoard because we may never fully understand the culture, beliefs, and motivations of the people who buried it.

FEUDAL SOCIETY

In feudal society, everyone knew his or her place. Feudalism created an economy based on the possession of land. The upper three classes held all the power, and peasants and serfs had few rights.

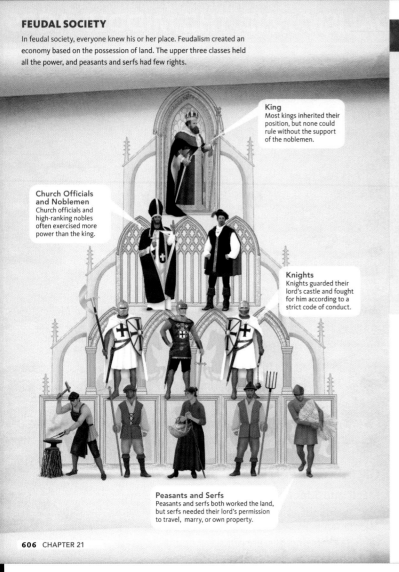

King
Most kings inherited their position, but none could rule without the support of the noblemen.

Church Officials and Noblemen
Church officials and high-ranking nobles often exercised more power than the king.

Knights
Knights guarded their lord's castle and fought for him according to a strict code of conduct.

Peasants and Serfs
Peasants and serfs both worked the land, but serfs needed their lord's permission to travel, marry, or own property.

1.4 Feudal Society

The united Europe that Charlemagne had fought so hard to establish didn't last very long. About 30 years after his death in 814, his empire was divided into three kingdoms. Frankish rule grew weak, and Western Europe fell back into disorder. Once again, the Germanic kingdoms competed for power.

MAIN IDEA

In the Middle Ages, feudalism grew out of the need to provide security and defense.

A NEW SYSTEM

Kings in Western Europe and England could not defend their vast kingdoms on their own. To help them hold on to their land and protect their subjects, a political and social system called **feudalism** developed by the 800s. In this system, kings gave pieces of their land to noblemen known as **lords**. A lord, in turn, granted parts of this land, called fiefs (feefs), to lesser noblemen called **vassals**. The vassals paid taxes on the land and pledged their military service to the lord. This meant that a vassal had to organize his own army of fighting men. Many vassals were themselves soldiers in the army and served as **knights**, who were warriors on horseback. The lord protected his vassals in exchange for their service.

Vassals were supposed to be loyal to the king, but many vassals switched their allegiance to their lord. This was the man who guarded their families, after all. As a result, lords were supreme rulers in their own territory.

A NEW SOCIAL ORDER

The new system created a social order that was as tightly structured as a pyramid. At the very top sat the king. Next came the church officials and noblemen, who included lords and some vassals. Lords lived in fortified castles that were guarded by knights, the third class in feudal society.

Relatively few people belonged to the upper three classes. The great majority of people in the Middle Ages found themselves at the bottom of the social heap. This class included peasants and serfs. Although some peasants worked as artisans and merchants, most were farmers and laborers. **Serfs**, however, were tied to the land and gave their lord most of whatever they produced. In return, their lord gave them shelter and protection. Serfs weren't quite slaves. They were allowed to buy their freedom. Yet with no skills or education to help them earn money, they were basically powerless to change their condition.

REVIEW & ASSESS

1. **READING CHECK** What role did vassals play in the feudal system?

2. **INTERPRET VISUALS** How does the illustration show that peasants and serfs made up the largest class in society and had little power?

3. **MAKE INFERENCES** How did the relationship between a lord and his vassals affect that between vassals and the king?

PLAN

OBJECTIVE

Describe feudalism and how it developed.

CRITICAL THINKING SKILLS FOR LESSON 1.4

- Identify Main Ideas and Details
- Monitor Comprehension
- Interpret Visuals
- Make Inferences
- Explain
- Analyze Cause and Effect

ESSENTIAL QUESTION

How did Europe change during the Middle Ages?

Feudalism became the political, economic, and social system in Western Europe. Lesson 1.4 explains the reasons for the development of feudalism and its resulting new social order.

BACKGROUND FOR THE TEACHER

Feudalism was a political, economic, and social system based on land ownership and military allegiance. Under this system, land replaced money as the main currency. The system served as a method of providing defense and security, and it provided a role in society for everyone from the top to the bottom.

DIGITAL RESOURCES myNGconnect.com

TEACHER RESOURCES & ASSESSMENT

 Reading and Note-Taking

 Vocabulary Practice

 Section 1 Quiz

STUDENT RESOURCES

 NG Chapter Gallery

INTRODUCE & ENGAGE

ANALYZE VISUALS

Have students study the diagram of feudal society. **ASK:**

- What is the shape of the diagram? *(a triangle or pyramid)*
- How many people are in each layer? *(one to five)*
- What can you infer about power and wealth from this diagram? *(A few at the top have more power and wealth than the many at the bottom.)*

Tell students that the feudal system was Europe's social, economic, and political system for about six centuries. **0:05** minutes

TEACH

GUIDED DISCUSSION

1. **Explain** Why was a serf's life especially hard? *(Serfs were tied to the land, worked hard, and gave what they produced to the lord. They couldn't make money or save for themselves, and they had to get the lord's permission even to marry.)*

2. **Make Inferences** What does the position of the church officials in the pyramid show about the Church's power during this time? *(They were equal to lords, right under the king, but above everyone else. The Church was very powerful.)*

ANALYZE CAUSE AND EFFECT

Have students think about why the feudal system developed. What responsibilities did kings have after the Western Roman Empire fell apart? Why was there so much need for protection? Have students fill out a chart like the one below. You might give them the causes and let them come up with the effects. **0:10** minutes

Cause	Effect
The Roman Empire broke up.	
Kingdoms fought other kingdoms and protected their people.	
Kingdoms needed to pay their armies.	
Lords gave land to vassals for military help.	
Everyone needed food.	
Peasants needed protection.	

ACTIVE OPTIONS

NG Learning Framework: Write a Description

ATTITUDE: **Curiosity**
KNOWLEDGE: **Our Human Story**

Have students select one of the classes of feudal people they are still curious about after reading this lesson. Instruct them to write a short description of the everyday lives of these people using information from the chapter and additional source material. **0:20** minutes

On Your Feet: Four Corners Post signs in the four corners of the room labeled as follows: 1—King, 2—Church Officials and Noblemen, 3—Knights, 4—Peasants and Serfs. Have students count off from 1 to 4, and send them to their appropriate corners. Have students in each corner describe and record details about their lives and the problems they face. Then call on volunteers from each group to share their descriptions and problems. Point out that, like the people in feudal society, the students could not choose which group they belonged to. **0:10** minutes

DIFFERENTIATE

STRIVING READERS

Make a Chart Have students record the classes of feudal society and one fact about each class, using a chart like the one shown below. Ask them to share their charts and add details with a partner.

King	
Church Officials and Noblemen	
Knights	
Peasants and Serfs	

GIFTED & TALENTED

Legends of King Arthur Have interested students read about King Arthur and the Knights of the Round Table. Tell them that these stories are fictional but will give them some insight into the Middle Ages. Advanced readers might read T.H. White's *The Once and Future King*. Others might watch the movie *Camelot* or read other shorter legends about King Arthur.

Press **mt** *in the Student eEdition for modified text.*

See the Chapter Planner for more strategies for differentiation.

REVIEW & ASSESS

ANSWERS

1. Vassals paid taxes on the land to their lord and attended him at his court. They also pledged their loyalty and military service to the lord.

2. Peasants and serfs are shown in the biggest number and placed at the bottom of the illustration.

3. Vassals probably felt greater loyalty to their lord than to the king.

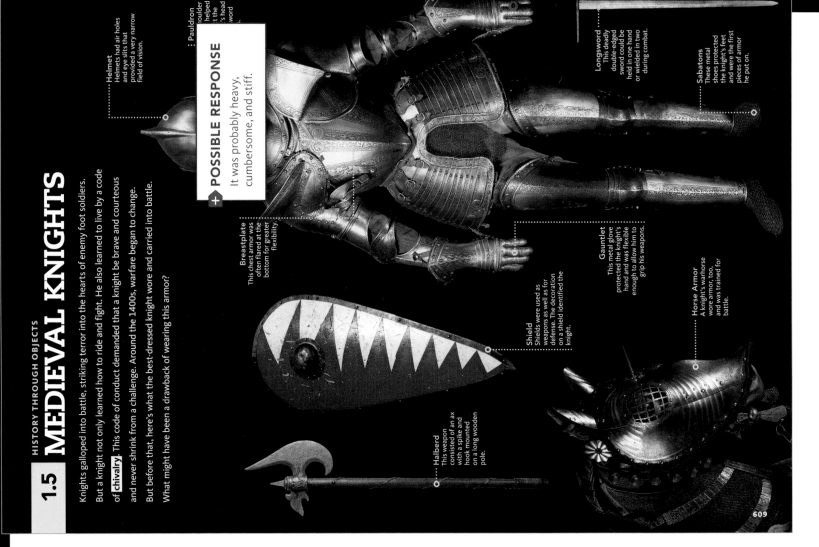

1.5 MEDIEVAL KNIGHTS

Knights galloped into battle, striking terror into the hearts of enemy foot soldiers. But a knight not only learned how to ride and fight. He also learned to live by a code of **chivalry**. This code of conduct demanded that a knight be brave and courteous and never shrink from a challenge. Around the 1400s, warfare began to change. But before that, here's what the best-dressed knight wore and carried into battle. What might have been a drawback of wearing this armor?

+ POSSIBLE RESPONSE

It was probably heavy, cumbersome, and stiff.

Helmet
Helmets had air holes and eye slits that provided a very narrow field of vision.

Pauldron
...oulder ...helped ...t the ...'s head ...word

Longsword
This deadly double-edged sword could be held in one hand or wielded in two during combat.

Sabatons
These metal shoes protected the knight's feet and were the first pieces of armor he put on.

Breastplate
This chest armor was often flared at the bottom for greater flexibility.

Gauntlet
This metal glove protected the knight's hand and was flexible enough to allow him to grip his weapons.

Horse Armor
A knight's warhorse wore armor, too, and was trained for battle.

Shield
Shields were used as weapons as well as for defense. The decoration on a shield identified the knight.

Halberd
This weapon consisted of an ax with a spike and hook mounted on a long wooden pole.

609

OBJECTIVE

Identify the equipment medieval knights wore and carried into battle.

CRITICAL THINKING SKILLS FOR LESSON 1.5

- Make Inferences
- Describe
- Analyze Visuals

ESSENTIAL QUESTION

How did Europe change during the Middle Ages?

Knights became the fighting military force during the Middle Ages. Lesson 1.5 shows the equipment that knights wore and carried into battle.

BACKGROUND FOR THE TEACHER

A knight's armor was heavy, weighing in at a total of 45 to 55 pounds, including the helmet, which weighed from 4 to 8 pounds. Armor worn in jousting tournaments was heavier, partly because knights wore it for a limited period of time, not on the battlefield.

Many people believe that a knight's movements were severely restricted by the armor, but it's not true. The pieces of the armor were made separately to fit different body parts. They were then linked together in a harness of leather straps, so a knight's limbs could move easily.

DIGITAL RESOURCES myNGconnect.com

TEACHER RESOURCES & ASSESSMENT

 Reading and Note-Taking

 Vocabulary Practice

 Section 1 Quiz

STUDENT RESOURCES

 NG Chapter Gallery

HISTORY THROUGH OBJECTS

Ask students to discuss what they have learned about knights through books, television, movies, and online sources. **ASK**: What was a knight's role in medieval society? What do you know about the code knights lived by? What was the armor like that they wore into battle? What kind of weapons did they use? Then tell students that, in this lesson, they will see and learn about a knight's armor and weapons. **0:05** minutes

TEACH

GUIDED DISCUSSION

1. **Describe** Describe the weapons a knight carried and explain their use. *(The longsword had two sharp edges and could be swung at the enemy with one hand. The halberd was an ax with a spike mounted on a long pole; the knight could chop or swing this ax at the enemy.)*

2. **Analyze Visuals** Have students look at each labeled part of the suit of armor. Ask what protection each part gives and what problems each part might cause. *(The helmet protects the head, but it is heavy and confining, it's hard to see through the eye slits. The pauldron protects the shoulders and neck, but it probably puts a lot of weight on the shoulders. The breastplate protects the chest but is heavy, confining, and hot to wear. The gauntlet protects the hand like a glove but is stiff and heavy. The sabatons protect the feet, keeping them warm like socks, but they are heavy and hot to wear and hard on the feet.)*

MORE INFORMATION

Medieval Armor Knights were not the only people who wore armor or who fought in battle. Many other people fought in the battles, including foot soldiers, such as crossbowmen or archers and, occasionally, women. Some of these people fashioned their own armor. The armor shown in this lesson would have been very expensive and may have been worn by an important knight. Not all armor was as valuable. Its cost varied according to the wealth of the kingdom and status of the knight.

ACTIVE OPTIONS

Critical Viewing: NG Image Gallery Have students explore the entire NG Image Gallery and choose two of the items to compare and contrast, either in written form or verbally with a partner. Have interested students look for warriors or soldiers and weapons from different ages and places. Ask questions that will inspire this process, such as: How are these images alike? How are they different? How are the weapons or protective clothing similar and different? Why did you select these two items? How do they relate in history? **0:10** minutes

On Your Feet: Weapons Experts The lesson shows only two types of weapons, but knights had many other choices. Have students work in teams to research other weapons and obtain pictures or make drawings of them. They can choose among daggers, lances, maces, flails, and different types of swords such as the broadsword, claymore, falchion, sabre, or arming sword. Have each team show and describe their weapons to the class. **0:10** minutes

DIFFERENTIATE

INCLUSION

Read Captions and Visuals Pair students who are visually impaired with students who are not. Ask the latter to read the captions and point out the features of the armor and the weapons described. Then have the partners review the purpose of each piece of armor together.

PRE-AP

Code of Chivalry The knights in feudal society pledged to obey a code of chivalry. Have students research the chivalric code and give an oral presentation describing it to the rest of the class.

Press **mt** *in the Student eEdition for modified text.*

See the Chapter Planner for more strategies for differentiation.

The Manor System

You're cold, tired, hungry, and dirty before you even start work. And no wonder. You get up before dawn to work the land, haul rocks, or do whatever your lord tells you to do. About 16 hours later, you retire to the comforts of your one-room home and huddle with your family around a smoky fire pit. Finally, you call it a night and fall asleep on the floor. At least you've got a sack for a blanket.

MAIN IDEA

Life on the manor was hard for most people but provided nearly everything they needed, including security.

A SELF-CONTAINED WORLD

The rough accommodations of peasants and serfs were part of everyday life in Europe's feudal society. The homes were part of the manor system, which tied the lowest class of people to the land and their lord. The **manor** was the system's basic unit, a walled-in, self-contained world located on land belonging to a lord.

A typical manor included a manor house, a church, a village, and lands with meadows, forests, pastures, and farms. The village provided such necessary businesses as a mill, bakery, and forge where metal was worked into tools. The manor's farmland was divided into strips: one for the lord, one for the church, and the rest for the peasants and serfs. These laborers farmed the lord's lands as well as their own. They paid the lord rent for their land and fees for almost everything they used on the manor, including the woods and meadows.

LIFE ON THE MANOR

Life for peasants and serfs on the manor was hard. Their average lifespan was 30 years, and that was if they survived infancy. One out of six children did not. Those who grew into adulthood spent their lives performing hard physical labor and got by on a diet of bread, cheese, and vegetables. Peasants and serfs did get time off, though, on Sundays and religious holidays. With the lord's permission, they could even attend nearby fairs and markets.

While workers lived in one-room huts with dirt floors, the lord and his family lived much more comfortably in the manor house. The rooms in this fortified stone house had tiled floors, tapestries on the walls, and fine furnishings. After managing his lands, judging court cases, or hunting wild game, the lord would feast on meat, fish, bread, cheese, and fruit in his large dining room.

Peasants and serfs were sometimes admitted to the manor house on holidays or when the estate was under attack, but the church was the center of life on the manor. Church officials conducted religious services and also cared for the sick and needy. Some educated priests even instructed children in the Bible. The church required peasants and serfs to work its land for free and give one-tenth of their produce to the church, but workers did this willingly. They believed that doing these things was the key to escaping eternal punishment and attaining a better life after death.

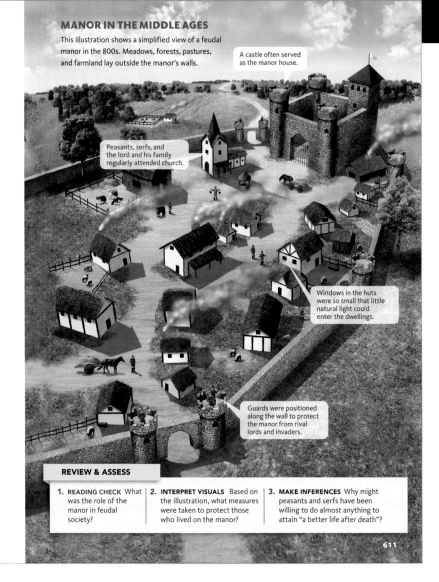

MANOR IN THE MIDDLE AGES

This illustration shows a simplified view of a feudal manor in the 800s. Meadows, forests, pastures, and farmland lay outside the manor's walls.

A castle often served as the manor house.

Peasants, serfs, and the lord and his family regularly attended church.

Windows in the huts were so small that little natural light could enter the dwellings.

Guards were positioned along the wall to protect the manor from rival lords and invaders.

REVIEW & ASSESS

1. **READING CHECK** What was the role of the manor in feudal society?

2. **INTERPRET VISUALS** Based on the illustration, what measures were taken to protect those who lived on the manor?

3. **MAKE INFERENCES** Why might peasants and serfs have been willing to do almost anything to attain "a better life after death"?

PLAN

OBJECTIVE

Describe what life was like on a medieval manor.

CRITICAL THINKING SKILLS FOR LESSON 1.6

- Identify Main Ideas and Details
- Monitor Comprehension
- Interpret Visuals
- Make Inferences
- Compare and Contrast
- Summarize

ESSENTIAL QUESTION

How did Europe change during the Middle Ages?

The manor was a self-contained world that belonged to a lord and provided security for his peasants. Lesson 1.6 describes the medieval manor system.

BACKGROUND FOR THE TEACHER

The lands of a manor in the Middle Ages generally covered about 1,200 to 1,600 acres, and a lord often owned several manors in different places around the country. The lord's manor was his domain. Food grown near the manor was destined for the lord. The rest of the land was divided into strips that the peasants rented from the lord and farmed. Meadows and forests were common land; peasants could use some of the land to graze their farm animals, but their use was limited. They could cut only a certain amount of meadow hay for their animals or wood from the forest for heating and building.

DIGITAL RESOURCES myNGconnect.com

TEACHER RESOURCES & ASSESSMENT

 Reading and Note-Taking   **Vocabulary Practice**   **Section 1 Quiz**

STUDENT RESOURCES

 NG Chapter Gallery

INTRODUCE & ENGAGE

CONNECT TO MODERN LIFE

Ask students to name various ways that people try to protect their homes today and make a class list of their responses. *(Possible responses: guard dogs, fences, alarm systems, security guards)* Remind students that in the Middle Ages there was no strong central government to keep peace and order. Ask students to predict what people did to protect themselves from the surrounding invading kingdoms. **0:05** minutes

TEACH

GUIDED DISCUSSION

1. **Compare and Contrast** How did the life of a serf differ from that of a lord? Have students name many ways their lives were different. Suggest they fill out a chart like the one below.

SERFS	LORDS
Lived in a tiny hut	*Lived in a castle*
Worked day and night for the lord	*Worked for himself as little as he wanted*
Did physical labor	*Was a manager, judge, general*
Owned nothing and had no way of getting more	*Owned the land and could invade other kingdoms to take more*

2. **Summarize** In what ways were the manors self-sufficient? *(Most had housing within the manor; peasants grew their own food, had access to a village and church, and were protected. The people provided everything they needed themselves.)*

ANALYZE VISUALS

Have students examine the diagram of the manor. **ASK:** Where is the safest place in the manor? *(the castle)* Why do you think the church is positioned close to the castle? *(safety for church officials; the lord and his family can get to church easily)* To whom do the animals shown belong? *(the lord and his family)* How would you describe the peasants' huts? *(small, dark, and probably dirty inside)* **0:10** minutes

ACTIVE OPTIONS

NG Learning Framework: Castles and Manor Houses

ATTITUDE: **Curiosity**
KNOWLEDGE: **Our Human Story**

Have students reread the paragraph about the manor house or castle. Invite them to research manor houses and castles to become experts. Encourage them to reproduce representations of various castles, using photographs or sketches, and put together a poster. Tell them to label the parts and include interesting facts about castles. **0:20** minutes

On Your Feet: Three-Step Interview Have students choose a partner. One student should interview the other on the following question: *Would you have liked to live in the Middle Ages? Why or why not?* Then they should reverse roles. Finally, each student should share the results of his or her interview with the class. **0:20** minutes

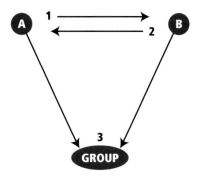

DIFFERENTIATE

ENGLISH LANGUAGE LEARNERS

Give a Thumbs Up or Thumbs Down Write a set of true-false statements about the lesson, such as, "The serfs lived inside the castle." Read the lesson aloud with students following along. Then have them close their books and listen as you read the true-false statements. Students should give a thumbs up if a statement is true and a thumbs down if a statement is false.

GIFTED & TALENTED

Model a Castle Working as a team, have students research medieval castles and choose a way to make a model of a castle. They might make a diorama or use papier-mâché or clay to make a three-dimensional replica. Display the finished models in class.

Press **mt** *in the Student eEdition for modified text.*

See the Chapter Planner for more strategies for differentiation.

REVIEW & ASSESS

ANSWERS

1. The role of the manor in feudal society was to provide the lord, priest, peasants, and serfs with everything they needed and to provide security against attacks by rival lords.

2. Fortified walls surrounding the village, watchtowers with guards, and an iron gate before the manor house were among the measures taken to protect those who lived on the manor.

3. Because their life on Earth was so hard, peasants and serfs would have clung to the promise of going to heaven after death and done anything to realize it.

2.1

Church and Crown

Light streams through stained-glass windows in the great church, inspiring worship. The ceiling seems to rise to heaven. It took decades and even centuries to construct cathedrals in the Middle Ages—some bigger than a king's castle. They were built for the greater glory of God. But they were also meant to inspire awe in the wealth and power of the Church.

MAIN IDEA

In the Middle Ages, the Church controlled lives and challenged the authority of kings.

THE ROLE OF THE CHURCH

It is hard for people today to understand the extraordinary power Christianity had in the Middle Ages. The Roman Catholic Church dominated people's lives from the cradle to the grave. It was the strongest unifying force in medieval Europe. The Church baptized, married, pardoned, and buried everyone from serfs to kings. It promised that good people would go to heaven and the wicked would be punished after death.

The religious leaders who oversaw these ceremonies and delivered the teachings formed the **clergy**. The pope led this group, which included bishops and priests. While a priest was in charge of a single church,

a bishop oversaw a group of churches. Bishops exercised their authority from towering churches called **cathedrals**, the skyscrapers of their day.

Some Christians withdrew from medieval society to live in religious communities called **monasteries**. Monks, the people who lived in a monastery, spent much of their day praying, reading the Bible, and meditating. In addition, rulers and high-ranking clergy sometimes had monks make copies of ancient Greek and Roman texts. As a result, monks helped keep knowledge alive, and monasteries became centers of learning.

STRUGGLE FOR POWER

If anything, the power and wealth of the Church began increasing in the 1000s—in part because it received free land from nobles. At the same time, however, kings began to regain their former authority. The kings' return to power was largely because of the growth of towns and trade, which you will learn more about later. The kings' rise weakened the feudal structure, but it also led to a power struggle between kings and the Church.

The struggle came to a head in 1075. The German king Henry IV was next in line to become Holy Roman Emperor. Like Charlemagne, the first Holy Roman Emperor, Henry ruled over a multi-ethnic group of territories in central Europe, an empire that would continue until it dissolved in 1806. Henry had appointed his own priests to become bishops, but Pope Gregory VII claimed that these were religious appointments and should be his decision.

The conflict raged until Gregory shut Henry out of the Church, forcing the king to back down. Henry knew that if he did not, he would lose his throne. In those days, no one would have anything to do with a king who had been banished from the Church. Gregory got his way and lifted the ban. He then regained full control of religious appointments.

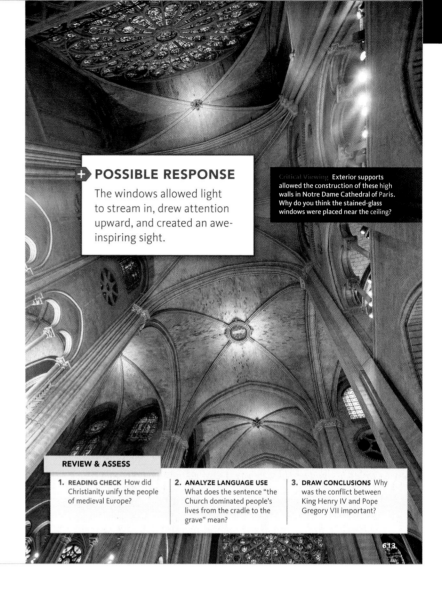

+ POSSIBLE RESPONSE

The windows allowed light to stream in, drew attention upward, and created an awe-inspiring sight.

Critical Viewing Exterior supports allowed the construction of these high walls in Notre Dame Cathedral of Paris. Why do you think the stained-glass windows were placed near the ceiling?

REVIEW & ASSESS

1. **READING CHECK** How did Christianity unify the people of medieval Europe?

2. **ANALYZE LANGUAGE USE** What does the sentence "the Church dominated people's lives from the cradle to the grave" mean?

3. **DRAW CONCLUSIONS** Why was the conflict between King Henry IV and Pope Gregory VII important?

PLAN

OBJECTIVE

Explain that, during the Middle Ages, the Church controlled lives and challenged the authority of kings.

CRITICAL THINKING SKILLS FOR LESSON 2.1

- Identify Main Ideas and Details
- Monitor Comprehension
- Analyze Language Use
- Draw Conclusions
- Explain
- Analyze Visuals
- Compare and Contrast

ESSENTIAL QUESTION

How did Europe change during the Middle Ages?

The Roman Catholic Church grew in power during the Middle Ages. Lesson 2.1 explains how the Church challenged the authority of kings.

BACKGROUND FOR THE TEACHER

During the 1000s, a power struggle erupted between the Church and King Henry IV. Henry had built his empire through wars and had become the Holy Roman Emperor. However, his power was challenged by Pope Gregory VII, who believed that he should appoint bishops, not the king. As the struggle escalated, Henry even attempted to kidnap the pope. Finally, Henry was threatened with being shut out of the Church, and he backed down. As a result, Pope Gregory succeeded in establishing the Church as stronger than the king.

DIGITAL RESOURCES myNGconnect.com

TEACHER RESOURCES & ASSESSMENT

 Reading and Note-Taking

 Vocabulary Practice

 Section 2 Quiz

STUDENT RESOURCES

 NG Chapter Gallery

INTRODUCE & ENGAGE

ACCESS PRIOR KNOWLEDGE

Initiate a class discussion on the separation of church and state. **ASK:** Is there one religion in the United States? Do religious leaders have government roles? Do government officials have any power over religious belief? Use a chart like the one below to record students' responses. Then tell students that they will learn about a power struggle in the Middle Ages between Church and state in this lesson. **0:05 minutes**

CHURCH	STATE

TEACH

GUIDED DISCUSSION

1. **Explain** How did both the Church and the kings gain power during this period? *(Nobles gave land to the Church, religious leaders were ranked high in feudal society, and the Church had holdings all over Europe; the kings started to gain more power when towns and trade grew and people gave less allegiance to their lords.)*

2. **Analyze Visuals** What details in the photograph of Notre Dame Cathedral show the Church's wealth? *(gold, beautiful stained-glass windows, carved arches, massive size)*

COMPARE AND CONTRAST

Have students contrast life in our country today with life in the Middle Ages. They should consider the role of religion, government, living conditions for ordinary people, the class system, wealth, agriculture, and so on. Have them work in pairs to write as many differences as they can in a five-minute period of time. Then ask for suggestions and list them on the board. **0:10 minutes**

ACTIVE OPTIONS

NG Learning Framework: Write a Biography

ATTITUDE: **Curiosity**
KNOWLEDGE: **Our Human Story**

Have students select one of the people they are still curious about after learning about this individual in this chapter. Instruct them to write a short biography about this person using information from the chapter and additional source material. Suggest that some research King Henry IV or Pope Gregory VII. **0:10 minutes**

On Your Feet: Think, Pair, Share Have students choose partners. Explain that one student will role-play King Henry IV and the other will role-play Pope Gregory VII while discussing their differences.

Finally, each pair should present the results of their discussion to the class. **0:20 minutes**

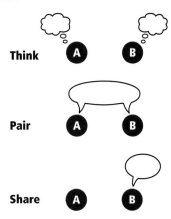

DIFFERENTIATE

ENGLISH LANGUAGE LEARNERS

Vocabulary Word Origins Explain to students that the word *cathedral* comes from the Latin word *cathedra,* meaning "seat." A cathedral was a bishop's seat, or the place from which he exercised his power. Both the word *monk* and the word *monastery* come from the Greek word *mono,* meaning "alone, or separate." The monks left the world to be alone at their religious communities, called *monasteries.*

PRE-AP

Notre Dame Cathedral Have interested groups of students research Notre Dame Cathedral in Paris. Suggest that each student in a group focus on one of the following topics: history of construction, architecture, statues, crypts, bells, gargoyles, and stained-glass windows. Have students present their findings to the class and use visuals in the presentation, if possible.

Press **mt** *in the Student eEdition for modified text.*

See the Chapter Planner for more strategies for differentiation.

REVIEW & ASSESS

ANSWERS

1. People throughout Western Europe shared the same religious beliefs and practices.

2. It means that the Church dominated their lives from birth to death.

3. The conflict determined that the Church had authority over Christendom and its rulers.

2.2

King John and the Magna Carta

Since the 1200s and the sealing of the Magna Carta, Britain's Parliament has met on this site on the Thames River in London. Today, representatives meet in the Houses of Parliament, shown here, next to the clock tower called Big Ben.

Here's a joke told by English schoolchildren: Where did King John sign the Magna Carta? At the bottom. Actually, he was in a meadow called Runnymede, and he didn't sign it—he placed his seal on it. And it was called the Articles of the Barons then. The barons—a group of noblemen—were not amused by the growing authority of the king.

MAIN IDEA

The Magna Carta marked a major step toward democratic government in Western Europe.

THE GREAT CHARTER

In the last lesson, you read that kings were regaining their power. **King John** was one in a long line of powerful English kings that began in 1066. In that year, William, Duke of Normandy—a region in France— invaded England and established a strong, centralized monarchy there. When John rose to the throne in 1199, he ruled England and half of present-day France. However, the king soon weakened his position by waging a series of failed, expensive wars.

A group of local barons took advantage of John's decreased power to stage a rebellion. The barons believed that by raising their taxes the king had violated **common law**. This was a system of law established in the 1100s that sought to ensure that people throughout England received equal treatment.

So, in 1215, the barons forced John to place his seal on their document, which came to be known as the **Magna Carta**, or "Great Charter." It was meant to be just a contract between the king and his nobles. However, the Magna Carta made the king subject to the law of the land and limited his authority.

A STEP TOWARD DEMOCRACY

Although the Magna Carta didn't benefit ordinary English people at the time, its guarantee of certain individual rights would have a great impact on the development of democracy. The document is recognized as the foundation of English law.

A further step toward democracy—in the form of representative government— took place in 1258. Henry III, John's son, was king of England at the time. Like his father, he had angered a group of nobles. The nobles overruled Henry's authority and put together a council of 15 men to advise the king and limit his power. This group of representatives would come to be called a **parliament**.

After King Henry died in 1272, his son Edward I rose to the throne. In 1295, Edward assembled what is considered the first truly representative parliament. The group included two knights from every county and two residents from each town. They passed laws, imposed taxes, and discussed political and judicial matters. From that point on, English kings would have to share their power—whether they liked it or not.

REVIEW & ASSESS

1. **READING CHECK** In what way did the Magna Carta limit the king's authority?

2. **ANALYZE CAUSE AND EFFECT** How did the establishment of a parliament change the government of England?

3. **MAKE INFERENCES** Do you think the Magna Carta affected the lives of ordinary people? Why or why not?

PLAN

OBJECTIVE

Explain how the Magna Carta marked the first step toward democratic government in Western Europe.

CRITICAL THINKING SKILLS FOR LESSON 2.2

- Identify Main Ideas and Details
- Monitor Comprehension
- Analyze Cause and Effect
- Make Inferences
- Summarize
- Create Time Lines

ESSENTIAL QUESTION

How did Europe change during the Middle Ages?

The Magna Carta was a major step toward democratic government in Western Europe. Lesson 2.2 explores the causes and effects of this important document.

BACKGROUND FOR THE TEACHER

King John not only angered his nobles but also antagonized Pope Innocent, the pope at the time. As a result, Innocent excommunicated King John. However, after John complained that he had been forced to seal the Magna Carta, Innocent took the king's side. John's struggle against the document ended with his death in 1216.

DIGITAL RESOURCES myNGconnect.com

TEACHER RESOURCES & ASSESSMENT

 Reading and Note-Taking   **Vocabulary Practice**   **Section 2 Quiz**

STUDENT RESOURCES

 NG Chapter Gallery

INTRODUCE & ENGAGE

ACTIVATE PRIOR KNOWLEDGE

Ask students what they know about Britain's government today. Have them decide if each statement below is true or false:

- The king or queen is elected by the people. *(false, title is inherited)*
- The Parliament is elected by the people. *(true)*
- Parliament has two houses, the House of Lords and the House of Commons. *(true)*
- The prime minister's job is inherited. *(false, he/she is elected)*
- Parliament is similar to the U.S. Congress. *(true)* **0:05 minutes**

TEACH

GUIDED DISCUSSION

1. **Summarize** Who struggled for power in England and who won the battle? *(the king and the barons; The barons won.)*

2. **Analyze Cause and Effect** Why did the barons rebel against King John and King Henry III? *(John lost expensive wars and territory and angered barons by raising taxes. Henry III also angered the barons.)*

3. **Make Inferences** Why was the Magna Carta such an important document? *(It made the king subject to the law of the land and, so, on a more equal footing with the rest of society.)*

CREATE TIME LINES

Have pairs of students work together to create a time line of the sealing of the Magna Carta, the battle between kings and barons, and England's steps toward democratic government. They should label the time line with the dates and people discussed in the lesson. Have students begin their time lines with 1066 and end with 1300. **0:10 minutes**

England's Kings vs. Barons

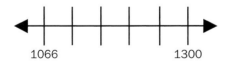

1066   1300

ACTIVE OPTIONS

NG Learning Framework: Role-Play

ATTITUDE: **Curiosity**
SKILL: **Communication**
KNOWLEDGE: **Our Human Story**

Invite students to research to find out more about King John and his relationship with the barons. Then have pairs act out the sealing of the Magna Carta, with one student role-playing King John, while the other role-plays one of the barons. **0:10 minutes**

On Your Feet: Numbered Heads Have students form groups of four and number off within each group. Tell the groups to list as many ways as they can to show how England's government changed between 1066 and 1300. After ten minutes, call a number. A student from that group should read his or her group's list. Compile a list on the board that incorporates all the groups' ideas. **0:10 minutes**

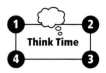

DIFFERENTIATE

STRIVING READERS

Who Am I? Help students sort through the names in this lesson by playing "Who Am I?" After they read the lesson, give them these clues and ask which of these kings each clue refers to: William Duke of Normandy, King John, Henry III, or Edward I.

- I came from France, took over England in 1066, and put a strong central government in place. *(William Duke of Normandy)*
- I angered the nobles and they started a representative council. *(King Henry III)*
- I lost expensive wars and sealed the Magna Carta. *(King John)*
- I started the first parliament composed of knights and townspeople. *(King Edward I)*

GIFTED & TALENTED

Historical Tapestry Have students find out about the Bayeaux Tapestry, an embroidered tapestry made in England in 1050 that shows 50 scenes of the Norman conquest of England. Ask them to research the tapestry's history and show selected images of it to the class, explaining what each scene depicts.

Press (**mt**) *in the Student eEdition for modified text.*

See the Chapter Planner for more strategies for differentiation.

REVIEW & ASSESS

ANSWERS

1. It made him subject to the law of the land and limited his authority.

2. It forced the king to share power with a group of representatives.

3. No, the document only dealt with the concerns of the upper classes in medieval society.

Charters of Freedom

By setting down individual rights in the Magna Carta, the barons—unknowingly—laid the groundwork for the development of democracy. The Parliament members who penned the English Bill of Rights and the American Founders who wrote the U.S. Bill of Rights found inspiration in the Great Charter. So the next time you speak your mind or celebrate a religious holiday, you might remember the documents on the next page. They helped make such freedoms possible.

ANSWERS

DOCUMENT 1
The rights to life, property, and a fair trial according to the law of the land are guaranteed in this article of the Magna Carta.

DOCUMENT 2
Parliament wanted to ensure that its members showed allegiance to those who elected them and not to those who appointed them. They wanted to be free to express opinions that might have been critical of the king.

DOCUMENT 3
Without a written document that explicitly states and guarantees personal freedoms, individuals might be subject to abuses of government power.

DOCUMENT ONE
Primary Source: Legal Document

from the Magna Carta
Most of the Magna Carta's 63 articles deal with the relationships among the king, nobles, and clergy and largely ignore the rights of the lower classes. However, the principles expressed in the following article are significant today for all free men—and women.

CONSTRUCTED RESPONSE What individual rights are protected in this article from the Magna Carta?

> 39. No freeman shall be taken, imprisoned, disseised [stripped of property], outlawed, banished, or in any way destroyed, nor will We proceed against or prosecute him [put him on trial], except by the lawful judgment of his peers [equals] or by the law of the land.

DOCUMENT TWO
Primary Source: Legal Document

from the English Bill of Rights
Concern over the increasing power of monarchs led Parliament to pass the English Bill of Rights in 1689. However, instead of focusing on the rights of nobles, the English Bill of Rights focuses on the rights of Parliament.

CONSTRUCTED RESPONSE Why do you think Parliament insisted on the free election and free speech of its members?

> 8. That election of members of Parliament ought to be free.
>
> 9. That the freedom of speech, and debates or proceedings in Parliament, ought not to be impeached [charged as a crime] or questioned in any court or place out of Parliament.

DOCUMENT THREE
Primary Source: Legal Document

from the U.S. Bill of Rights
The U.S. Bill of Rights took the documents above a step or two further. Adopted in 1791, the Bill of Rights—the first ten amendments to the Constitution—guarantees personal freedoms, like these, that had previously not been clearly stated.

CONSTRUCTED RESPONSE Why do you think the American Founders insisted on having these freedoms clearly stated in the Bill of Rights?

> 4. The right of the people to be secure in their persons, houses, papers, and effects, against unreasonable searches and seizures, shall not be violated . . .
>
> 6. In all criminal prosecutions, the accused shall enjoy the right to a speedy and public trial, by an impartial [fair to both sides] jury . . .

SYNTHESIZE & WRITE

1. **REVIEW** Review what you have learned about the Magna Carta and the development of democratic ideas in England.

2. **RECALL** On your own paper, write down the main idea expressed in each document.

3. **CONSTRUCT** Write a topic sentence that answers this question: How do the Magna Carta, English Bill of Rights, and U.S. Bill of Rights promote democratic ideas?

4. **WRITE** Using evidence from the documents, write a short essay to support your answer to the question in Step 3.

PLAN

OBJECTIVE
Synthesize the democratic ideas expressed in three important primary documents from England and the United States.

CRITICAL THINKING SKILLS FOR LESSON 2.3
- Synthesize
- Identify
- Evaluate

ESSENTIAL QUESTION
How did Europe change during the Middle Ages?

The Magna Carta marked the first step toward democratic government in England. Lesson 2.3 presents three documents that were influenced by the Magna Carta.

BACKGROUND FOR THE TEACHER
The rights listed in the Magna Carta refer only to the barons. Those in the English Bill of Rights have to do with Parliament's rights. The rights listed in the U.S. Bill of Rights refer to all individuals, not just the elected few. Democracy in America is not class-oriented. The U.S. founders rejected the class system and guaranteed individual liberties when they framed the Bill of Rights.

DIGITAL RESOURCES myNGconnect.com

TEACHER RESOURCES & ASSESSMENT

 Reading and Note-Taking

 Vocabulary Practice

 Section 2 Quiz

STUDENT RESOURCES

 NG Chapter Gallery

INTRODUCE & ENGAGE

PREPARE FOR THE DOCUMENT-BASED QUESTION

Before students start on the activity, briefly preview the three documents. Remind students that a constructed response requires explanations in complete sentences. Emphasize that students should use their knowledge of medieval history and the history of the American Revolution in addition to the information in the documents. **0:05 minutes**

TEACH

GUIDED DISCUSSION

1. **Identify** What words in each document identify or name the persons whose rights are being defended? *(Document 1 = freemen; Document 2 = members of Parliament; Document 3 = people)*

2. **Identify** What rights that we have today are named in these three documents? *(right to trial by jury of peers, freedom of speech, free elections, safety against unreasonable search and seizure, speedy and public trial)*

EVALUATE

After students have completed the "Synthesize & Write" activity, allow time for them to exchange paragraphs and read and comment on the work of their peers. Guidelines for comments should be established prior to this activity so that feedback is constructive and encouraging in nature. **0:15 minutes**

ACTIVE OPTIONS

Critical Viewing: NG Image Gallery Invite students to explore the entire NG Image Gallery and choose one image from the gallery they feel best represents their understanding of this chapter. Have students provide a written explanation of why they selected the image they chose. **0:10 minutes**

On Your Feet: Three Options Label three locations in the room with the name of one of the documents featured in the lesson. Have students reread the lesson and walk to the corner of the room with the document that names a democratic right that is important to that student. Have students who chose the same document discuss why that right is so important to them. Then have volunteers from each group explain what their document is and offer some of the group's reasons for choosing it. **0:20 minutes**

DIFFERENTIATE

STRIVING READERS

Provide Sentence Frames Have students read in pairs. Provide these sentence frames to help them understand the rights described in the documents.

- **Document 1** Freemen accused of crimes will have a lawful _____ and be judged by their _____ . *(trial, peers)*
- **Document 2** Elections to Parliament should be _____ . *(free)* Members of parliament shall have freedom of _____ and not be punished. *(speech)*
- **Document 3** People shall be safe against _____ . *(unreasonable searches and seizures)* People who are accused of crimes shall have a _____ and _____ trial. *(speedy, public)*

PRE-AP

Compare to Current Events Tell students that the protection of individual civil rights is still important to Americans today. Have students think about recent instances in which people believe their civil rights were violated. Have interested students choose one of these instances and research the arguments on both sides of the issue. Invite students to present the issue to the class, explaining the reasoning on both sides.

Press **mt** *in the Student eEdition for modified text.*

See the Chapter Planner for more strategies for differentiation.

SYNTHESIZE & WRITE

ANSWERS

1. Responses will vary.

2. Responses will vary.

3. The Magna Carta, the English Bill of Rights, and U.S. Bill of Rights protect the rights of individuals and guarantee equality under the law.

4. Students' paragraphs should include their topic sentence from Step 3 and provide several details from the documents to support the sentence.

The Crusades

In 1095, Pope Urban II condemned a group of people who had "invaded the lands of the Christians." The people Urban referred to were Muslims, and he called on Christians to wage war against them. Kings had regained a good bit of their authority, but the Church and the pope still had plenty of power—certainly enough for the pope to gather armies to fight the spread of Islam.

MAIN IDEA

Christians in Europe fought non-Christians to conquer Palestine and retake Spain.

BATTLE FOR PALESTINE

Specifically, the people Urban had condemned were Seljuk Turks, Muslim rulers who had seized control of Jerusalem in 1071. Their takeover had made Christian pilgrimages to the Holy Land—also called Palestine—almost impossible. The Holy Land included Jerusalem and the area around the city, sites that were sacred to Christians, Jews, and Muslims.

The Seljuks had also begun to attack the Christian Byzantine Empire, once the eastern half of the Roman Empire. When the Byzantine emperor asked for help, Pope

Urban seized his chance to rally Christians against the growing power of Islam. His words had the desired effect. In 1096, Christian armies set off to fight a series of wars called the **Crusades** to reclaim the Holy Land. Christian leaders and soldiers were motivated by a desire to protect Christians and to slow the spread of Islam.

Peasants, knights, and foot soldiers joined the fight, and they achieved victory. In 1099, the army retook Jerusalem and divided the Holy Land into four Crusader states. But the triumph was short-lived. In 1144, the Muslims fought back and conquered Edessa, one of the Crusader states. Soon after, a new pope launched the Second Crusade, but this ended in disaster for the Europeans. A Third and Fourth Crusade were fought, but these also failed to defeat the enemy. By 1291, the Muslims had defeated the Crusaders and taken control of Palestine. The Crusades were over.

A SPANISH CRUSADE

The Crusades had an unexpected impact on Europe. During the wars, trade between Europe and the eastern Mediterranean region greatly increased because of greater contact between the two regions. After the wars, ideas as well as goods were exchanged. The trade led to the rise of a merchant class in Europe and the further decline of feudalism.

Still, crusading fever didn't die, and hostility toward any non-Christians increased. As soldiers galloped toward the Holy Land, they killed Jews in Europe as well as those in Palestine. After the Crusades, many Jews were expelled from England and France. The greatest expulsion effort, however, took place on the Iberian Peninsula, which includes present-day Spain and Portugal. In the 700s, Muslims had conquered almost the entire peninsula. When Islamic rule weakened in the 1000s, Christian kings began a long war, called the **Reconquista** (ray-cone-KEY-stah), to drive the Muslims off the peninsula.

THE CRUSADES, 1096–1204

Christian lands
Muslim lands
First Crusade, 1096–1099
Second Crusade, 1147–1149
Third Crusade, 1189–1191
Fourth Crusade, 1202–1204

King Ferdinand and Queen Isabella of Spain stepped up the war. They used a powerful court known as the **Inquisition** to punish non-Christians. The court ordered the torture and execution of many Muslims and Jews who would not convert or who had converted but secretly practiced their former religion. In 1492, Ferdinand and Isabella finally defeated and expelled the last of the Muslim rulers and their followers from Spain and Portugal. They also drove out about 200,000 Jews. Unlike the Crusades, the Reconquista had achieved its goal—but at the cost of many human lives.

FERDINAND AND ISABELLA
The Reconquista ended when the Spanish army conquered Granada, a city in Spain. When the Muslim ruler handed over the keys to his palace, the Alhambra, Ferdinand and Isabella swore that Muslims would always be able to follow their faith in Spain. They broke that promise a few years later when they ordered Muslims to convert to Christianity or leave the country.

REVIEW & ASSESS

1. **READING CHECK** Why did Pope Urban II encourage Christians to begin a series of wars against Muslims?

2. **INTERPRET MAPS** Which Crusade involved much of Western Europe?

3. **SEQUENCE EVENTS** What efforts to drive Muslims from Europe were undertaken after the Crusades ended?

PLAN

OBJECTIVE

Discuss the steps Christians in Europe took to conquer Palestine and retake Spain.

CRITICAL THINKING SKILLS FOR LESSON 2.4

- Identify Main Ideas and Details
- Monitor Comprehension
- Interpret Maps
- Sequence Events
- Analyze Cause and Effect
- Make Inferences

ESSENTIAL QUESTION

How did Europe change during the Middle Ages?

During the Crusades, Europeans united to try to defeat the Muslims in Palestine and recover the Holy Lands for Christianity. Lesson 2.4 describes the Crusades and other events that sought to make Christianity the sole religion of Europe.

BACKGROUND FOR THE TEACHER

The majority of the Reconquista in the Iberian Peninsula took place from the mid-11th century to the mid-13th century. Muslim strength had weakened, and Spanish Christians pushed out both Muslims and Jews. Those who stayed were forced to convert to Christianity. The Spanish Inquisition tried those whom the monarchs did not believe had really converted. They called people heretics when they did not adhere to the letter of Catholic teachings. They tortured and killed thousands of non-Christians during the Inquisition.

DIGITAL RESOURCES myNGconnect.com

TEACHER RESOURCES & ASSESSMENT

 Reading and Note-Taking

 Vocabulary Practice

 Section 2 Quiz

STUDENT RESOURCES

 Active History

INTRODUCE & ENGAGE

PREVIEW WITH A MAP

Have students preview the map of the Crusades. Explain that the lines represent the routes of the Christian armies during all four Crusades. Have students trace the route of the First Crusade by finding Paris on the map and then following the purple line to Jerusalem. Ask the following questions:

- About how far did the Christians travel from Paris to Jerusalem? *(nearly 2,500 miles)*
- How did people travel in those days? *(by foot, on horses, or by boats)*
- About how long might such a journey take? *(many months)*

Tell students that, in this lesson, they will read about the Crusades and what took place in Europe afterward. **0:05 minutes**

TEACH

GUIDED DISCUSSION

1. **Analyze Cause and Effect** What caused so many people to fight wars in the Holy Land? *(to save the Holy Land for Christianity, to get a chance to fight and travel to new places, to change their own lives, to gain wealth)*

2. **Make Inferences** How might the Crusades have motivated Christians in the Iberian Peninsula to push Muslims and Jews out during the Reconquista? *(They were even more hostile toward non-Christians after losing the Crusades.)*

MORE INFORMATION

The Children's Crusade The Children's Crusade supposedly occurred in 1212. A 12-year old French boy, Stephen of Cloyes, believed that Jesus told him to form a crusade of children to peacefully retake Jerusalem. He amassed an "army" of 30,000 children. Stephen also believed that God would part the seas for them at Marseilles, France, so that they could walk to Palestine. When the sea did not part, they boarded seven boats. They were never seen again after they boarded the ships. Historians believe the boats either sank or were captured by pirates, who may have sold the children into slavery.

ACTIVE OPTIONS

Active History: Categorize Effects of the Crusades Extend the lesson by using either the PDF or Whiteboard version of the activity. This activity takes a deeper look at the Crusades and their effects. Explore the activity as a class, turn it into a group assignment, or even assign it individually. **0:10 minutes**

On Your Feet: Jigsaw Group students into three "expert" groups and assign each group one of the following topics: Crusades, Reconquista, Inquisition. Students should study their assigned topic in depth. Then have students regroup so that each new group has at least one member from each expert group. Have students in each new group share what they learned about their topic. **0:10 minutes**

DIFFERENTIATE

STRIVING READERS

Three Webs Have students draw three webs with the following words in the middle: Crusades, Reconquista, and Inquisition. Have them read the lesson in pairs and take notes by adding circles to the appropriate web. Have students share their webs with the rest of the class and add any information they might have missed to their own webs.

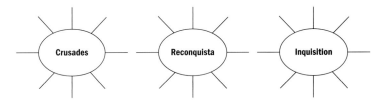

PRE-AP

The Pit and the Pendulum Challenge students to read Edgar Allan Poe's short story, "The Pit and the Pendulum," which is set during the Spanish Inquisition. The story reflects the horrors of the Inquisition. Have them discuss the story among themselves when they have finished.

Press **mt** *in the Student eEdition for modified text.*

See the Chapter Planner for more strategies for differentiation.

REVIEW & ASSESS

ANSWERS

1. Pope Urban II encouraged Christians to unite in a crusade to wrest the Holy Land from its Muslim rulers and protect the Byzantine Empire from the growing power of Islam.

2. The Third Crusade involved much of Western Europe.

3. The Reconquista and the Inquisition were undertaken to drive Muslims from Europe.

War and Plague

Shattered buildings and churches, deserted villages, and abandoned fields—these formed the landscape of Europe after war and disease swept through the continent in the 1300s. Both catastrophes brought suffering and death to millions and, like the Crusades, greatly weakened the feudal way of life.

MAIN IDEA

War and disease devastated Europe in the 1300s and brought about fundamental changes to society.

WAR BETWEEN ENGLAND AND FRANCE

The roots of the war were established long before the 1300s. As you may remember, William, Duke of Normandy, conquered England in 1066 and became its king. William and the Norman kings who came after him were vassals to the French kings. However, they also ruled over England in their own right. This created a tense relationship between England and France. Kings from both countries were very powerful and competed for territory in France. In time, they also competed over who would be king of France.

The situation came to a head in 1328 when the king of France died. Edward III of England believed he should succeed him, but French nobles crowned a Frenchman instead. In 1337, Edward invaded France to claim the throne. His actions began the **Hundred Years' War** between England and France. This was not a continuous conflict but rather a series of wars that dragged on for 116 years.

Between the beginning of the war in 1337 and its end in 1453, the English won many important victories. The French cause seemed hopeless until rescue came from an unexpected source. A French peasant girl called **Joan of Arc** claimed that Christian saints had told her to save her country. She impressed Charles, the ruler of France, and was given command of his army in 1429. Her religious and patriotic passion inspired her soldiers to win a battle that turned the tide of the war. The English captured and executed Joan, but they had lost the war. By 1453, the French had driven the English out of their lands.

Both sides were aided in their fight by deadly new weapons. The powerful **longbow** allowed archers to fire arrows with enough force to pierce a knight's armor. Cannons, made possible by the invention of gunpowder, could blast through castle walls. These weapons changed the nature of European warfare and made knights and castles, the symbols of feudalism, almost powerless.

DISEASE SPREADS OVER THE WORLD

As if war and its new weapons weren't enough, medieval Europeans suffered from widespread disease. Poor diet, filthy living conditions, and a lack of medicine made sickness common.

In 1347, however, a devastating disease known as the **bubonic plague** swept through Europe. Infected rats carried fleas that spread the disease to humans along land and sea trade routes from Asia to Europe and Africa. Unfortunately, no one at the time understood that the plague was caused by bites from these fleas.

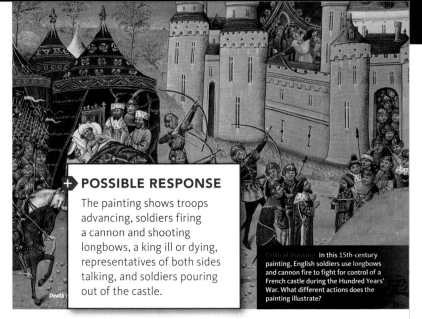

+ **POSSIBLE RESPONSE**

The painting shows troops advancing, soldiers firing a cannon and shooting longbows, a king ill or dying, representatives of both sides talking, and soldiers pouring out of the castle.

Critical Viewing In this 15th-century painting, English soldiers use longbows and cannon fire to fight for control of a French castle during the Hundred Years' War. What different actions does the painting illustrate?

Instead, many people believed the plague was a punishment from God. Some Christians believed the Jews had caused the plague by poisoning town wells. As a result, they destroyed entire Jewish communities. By the early 1350s, the worst of the plague was over in Europe, but by then it had killed about one-third of the continent's population. The deaths of so many people—from disease and war—led to major social and economic changes that would finally bring an end to feudalism.

JOAN OF ARC

After the English captured Joan of Arc, she was tried by the Inquisition and found guilty of being a witch. The court believed that the voices she claimed to hear were those of the devil. In 1431, Joan was burned at the stake. She was about 19 years old. Twenty-five years later, another court pardoned her. In 1920, the Catholic Church declared Joan a saint.

REVIEW & ASSESS

1. **READING CHECK** What impact did the Hundred Years' War and the bubonic plague have on medieval Europe?

2. **ANALYZE CAUSE AND EFFECT** How did events in 1066 lead to the Hundred Years' War?

3. **MAKE INFERENCES** How did the rats that carried plague-infected fleas probably travel along the trade routes?

PLAN

OBJECTIVE

Discuss how war and disease killed so many Europeans in the 1300s and fundamentally changed society.

CRITICAL THINKING SKILLS FOR LESSON 2.5

- Identify Main Ideas and Details
- Monitor Comprehension
- Analyze Cause and Effect
- Make Inferences
- Draw Conclusions
- Create Time Lines

ESSENTIAL QUESTION

How did Europe change during the Middle Ages?

The Hundred Years' War between England and France changed the nature of European warfare and rendered knights and castles almost powerless. Meanwhile, the bubonic plague ravaged the European population. Lesson 2.5 explains how both events led to the end of feudalism.

BACKGROUND FOR THE TEACHER

In 1347, twelve trading ships arrived in Genoa, Italy, from the Black Sea and brought the plague to Europe. The bubonic plague, also called the Black Death, was spread by rats and killed one-third of the population of Europe. The disease was called the Black Death because of the black boils that erupted on people's skin. Healthy people could die overnight if they were exposed to it.

DIGITAL RESOURCES myNGconnect.com

TEACHER RESOURCES & ASSESSMENT

 Reading and Note-Taking   **Vocabulary Practice**   **Section 2 Quiz**

STUDENT RESOURCES

 Biography

INTRODUCE & ENGAGE

MAKE PREDICTIONS

Tell students to preview the headings, vocabulary words, and pictures in this lesson and the next one. Have them make predictions about what the lessons will cover. Then ask them to predict how war and plague probably affected people in the Middle Ages. Tell them that they will be reading about a time that included a long war and the bubonic plague, both of which killed millions of people. **0:05** minutes

TEACH

GUIDED DISCUSSION

1. **Analyze Cause and Effect** Why were Jewish communities destroyed during the plague? *(Christians blamed Jews for poisoning wells to cause the plague.)*

2. **Draw Conclusions** What events helped put an end to feudalism during this time and why? *(Both the Hundred Years' War and the plague killed many people. These deaths led to major social and economic changes.)*

CREATE TIME LINES

Have students work together in groups to create a time line of the events discussed in this lesson. Suggest that students record events about the Hundred Years' War above the time line, and events about the bubonic plague below the line. When they finish, have them share their time lines with other groups and add entries as needed. **0:10** minutes

ACTIVE OPTIONS

NG Learning Framework: Make Observations

ATTITUDE: **Curiosity**
SKILL: **Observation**
KNOWLEDGE: **Our Human Story**

Have students work in pairs to research and create a list of observations about the plague and how it impacted the lives of Europeans. Once they have completed their list, have pairs exchange lists and discuss their findings. **0:10** minutes

On Your Feet: Role-Play Have students work in groups of four to role-play the concerns that people must have had about their families during the spread of the plague. Ask the groups to create short skits in which families discuss their concerns. Then have groups take turns presenting their skits. **0:10** minutes

DIFFERENTIATE

STRIVING READERS

Key Words and Phrases Have students read the lesson in pairs. As they read, have them record notes about each name or phrase below. They should then reread and add notes as their understanding increases.

What	When	What Happened
Hundred Years' War		
Joan of Arc		
Bubonic Plague		

GIFTED & TALENTED

Research the Bubonic Plague Have students read different accounts and articles about the Black Death to learn new facts about the plague. Then have them assemble their facts and share them with the class.

Press (**mt**) *in the Student eEdition for modified text.*

See the Chapter Planner for more strategies for differentiation.

REVIEW & ASSESS

ANSWERS

1. Both catastrophes killed many people and weakened the feudal system.

2. After William of Normandy became king of England in 1066, the Norman leaders and kings who came after him became vassals to the king of France. This created a tense relationship between England and France. Kings from both countries competed for territory in France and even over who would be king of that land. In time the competition erupted in war.

3. They probably stowed away among the merchants' goods and rode on their carts and ships.

POSSIBLE RESPONSE

The victims belong to every class in medieval society: peasants, clergy, nobles, and kings.

OCTOBER 1347

In a port in Italy, workers unload a ship's cargo and also release rats covered in fleas carrying the bubonic plague. According to an old legend, a childhood rhyme was said to describe the plague. The rhyme begins with "Ring around the rosie," which may refer to the red blisters caused when the fleas bit their victims. "A pocket full of posies" was said to be the flowers people carried to ward off the disease. When the flowers failed as a cure, "we all fall down," or die. In this painting, called *The Triumph of Death*, death is represented by skeleton figures. What generalization can you make about death's victims?

622 CHAPTER 21   623

PLAN

OBJECTIVE

Analyze a painting that demonstrates the impact of widespread death in the Middle Ages.

CRITICAL THINKING SKILLS FOR LESSON 2.6

- Analyze Visuals
- Make Inferences
- Draw Conclusions

ESSENTIAL QUESTION

How did Europe change during the Middle Ages?

The bubonic plague devastated the population of Europe. Lesson 2.6 shows an artistic interpretation of the effect of such widespread death.

BACKGROUND FOR THE TEACHER

Pieter Bruegel the Elder, a Flemish artist, painted *The Triumph of Death* around 1562. The painting hangs in the Prado in Madrid, Spain. In the painting, Bruegel personified death as skeletons actively killing people. The skeletons wear the clothing of those they killed. The barrenness of the land and fires in the background reflect the theme of death.

DIGITAL RESOURCES myNGconnect.com

TEACHER RESOURCES & ASSESSMENT

 Reading and Note-Taking   **Vocabulary Practice**   **Section 2 Quiz**

STUDENT RESOURCES

 NG Chapter Gallery

INTRODUCE & ENGAGE

CONNECT TO TODAY

Tell students that a contagious disease is one that can spread from person to person. Have students think about recent disease scares in the United States and around the world, such as Ebola, measles, AIDS, the flu, and others. **ASK:** How do diseases spread today? How do we fight contagious diseases? Which ones have we successfully fought? Which ones still need cures? **0:05** minutes

TEACH

GUIDED DISCUSSION

1. **Analyze Visuals** Examine the details of this painting that show the consequences of the bubonic plague. Tell students that the skeletons represent death. What kinds of people were victims of the plague, as the artist showed? *(Possible responses: wealthy lords, poor people, church people, military people, men and women)*

2. **Make Inferences** Notice the land and sea in the background. What details illustrate that the devastation caused by the plague did not only affect people? *(barren land, no greenery, fires in the background, starving animals in the foreground)*

3. **Draw Conclusions** What does the title of this painting, *The Triumph of Death,* mean? *(A triumph is a victory. Death conquers everyone. In this case, it conquered everyone at the same time.)*

MORE INFORMATION

The Spread of the Plague For two years before the plague, cold weather and terrible rains had destroyed much of Europe's grain crops. The shortage of food caused many people to move to the cities, which became crowded and very unsanitary. The crowded and filthy conditions allowed the plague to spread quickly.

ACTIVE OPTIONS

Critical Viewing: NG Chapter Gallery Invite students to explore the Chapter Gallery to examine the images that relate to this chapter. Have them select one of the images and do additional research to learn more about it. Ask questions that will inspire additional inquiry about the chosen gallery image, such as: What is this? Where and when was this created? By whom? Why was it created? What is it made of? Why does it belong in this chapter? What else would you like to know about it? **0:10** minutes

On Your Feet: Interpret a Painting On a large sheet of paper or on a whiteboard, create a chart like the one pictured below. As a class, re-examine *The Triumph of Death.* Have volunteers describe a detail in the painting and where it is in the painting. Then have them draw a conclusion about why the painter added that detail. Record students' observations in the chart. **0:15** minutes

Detail	Where in Painting	Painter's Reason

DIFFERENTIATE

STRIVING READERS

Analyze Visuals Provide questions to help students of different ability levels interpret the painting. **ASK:** How does the painter show death? *(skeletons)* How does he show that different classes of people died? *(nobles wear fancy clothing, some poor people wear rags, some wear religious attire, soldiers have weapons)* Encourage students to point to things they don't understand about the painting, and help them frame questions about these details.

GIFTED & TALENTED

Study an Artist Pieter Bruegel the Elder painted many other paintings. Invite interested students to find other examples of his paintings, either online or in art history books and select one. Have them share the painting with the class and provide background and information on the work of art.

Press **mt** *in the Student eEdition for modified text.*

See the Chapter Planner for more strategies for differentiation.

Growth of Towns

In the late Middle Ages, a saying started making the rounds: Town air makes you free. In the towns, you could work at a job and keep all your wages. You could go where you wanted without having to ask anyone's permission because you were no longer bound to a landowning lord or vassal. In fact, you answered to no one but the king.

MAIN IDEA

The growth of towns and trade led to economic, political, and cultural changes that brought the Middle Ages to an end.

All Souls College, at England's University of Oxford, was founded in the 1400s during Europe's revival of learning.

ECONOMIC OPPORTUNITIES ARISE

People had been moving to towns since about 1000, but the bubonic plague greatly accelerated this movement. With about a third of the workforce wiped out by the disease, employers desperate for help increased wages to attract workers. Many peasants, and many serfs as well, left the manor to apply for jobs in the towns. As a result, the manor system began to fall apart.

After life on the manor, the bustling, exciting towns might have made a welcome change. Towns held weekly markets where local produce was sold, while town fairs brought in trade goods from other places.

In time, a merchant class composed of traders and craftspeople arose. Wealthy town-dwelling merchants, known as **burghers**, could be elected to sit on governing councils. Groups of craftspeople, such as shoemakers or silversmiths, joined together to form **guilds**, which helped protect and improve the working conditions of their members.

THE MIDDLE AGES END

The growth of towns and their prosperous trade further helped kings regain their authority. By taxing the towns within his realm, a king earned money to pay for his army. A strong army brought peace and stability to his land. Increasingly, power and people's loyalty shifted from local lords to their king.

Europe experienced cultural changes as well as economic and political ones. You may remember that the Crusades brought European traders into contact with the civilizations of Islam and Byzantium. These civilizations had preserved the writings of ancient Greek and Roman philosophers in their libraries. As the Middle Ages came to a close, people became eager to gain knowledge. Universities were founded to satisfy this desire for learning. Monasteries were no longer the only centers of education. After centuries of war, instability, and fear, Europe was more than ready to embark on a new age of creativity.

REVIEW & ASSESS

1. **READING CHECK** What economic opportunities did towns offer ordinary people?

2. **ANALYZE CAUSE AND EFFECT** How did the growth of towns affect monarchs?

3. **MAKE INFERENCES** Why do you think learning was revived at the end of the Middle Ages?

PLAN

OBJECTIVE

Discuss how the growth of towns and trade led to changes that brought the Middle Ages to an end.

After the plague, people moved from the manors to the towns to make a better living. Lesson 2.7 explores the growth of towns and how they led to the end of the Middle Ages.

CRITICAL THINKING SKILLS FOR LESSON 2.7

- Identify Main Ideas and Details
- Analyze Cause and Effect
- Compare and Contrast
- Monitor Comprehension
- Make Inferences
- Analyze Visuals

BACKGROUND FOR THE TEACHER

Guilds in the Middle Ages were like trade unions for craftspeople. The name *guild* came from *gilden,* the fee that craftspeople paid the guild for protection. The guild tried to keep the taxes their members had to pay low. Guilds also offered protection from unfair competition.

ESSENTIAL QUESTION

How did Europe change during the Middle Ages?

DIGITAL RESOURCES myNGconnect.com

TEACHER RESOURCES & ASSESSMENT

 Reading and Note-Taking

 Vocabulary Practice

 Section 2 Quiz

STUDENT RESOURCES

 NG Chapter Gallery

INTRODUCE & ENGAGE

THREE-STEP INTERVIEW

Ask the class to think about whether they would rather live in the city, suburbs, or in the country. Then have pairs of students take turns explaining their answer. Finally, have pairs summarize their discussion with the class. **0:05** minutes

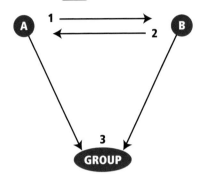

TEACH

GUIDED DISCUSSION

1. **Compare and Contrast** In what ways did life in town differ from life on a manor? *(On a manor, peasants and serfs worked for their lord with little compensation. In town, they worked for wages that they kept. They could also do different types of work, meet other people, and come and go as they pleased.)*

2. **Make Inferences** What might be the negative effects of living in towns? *(more vulnerable to disease, crowding, less freedom, more exposure to dangerous people, less sanitary)*

ANALYZE VISUALS

Have students examine the photo of All Souls College. **ASK:** What aspects of the college look similar to the architecture of castles, cathedrals, and manors of the Middle Ages? *(spires, large castle-like buildings made of stone, long windows, decorated arches)* **0:10** minutes

ACTIVE OPTIONS

Critical Viewing: NG Image Gallery Invite students to explore the entire NG Image Gallery and choose one image from the gallery they feel best represents their understanding of this chapter. Have students provide a written explanation of why they selected the image they chose. **0:10** minutes

On Your Feet: Create a Concept Web Have students form groups of four around a section of a bulletin board or a table. Provide each group with a large sheet of paper. Have group members take turns contributing a concept or phrase to a Concept Web with the phrase *Middle Ages* at the center. When time for the activity has elapsed, call on volunteers from each group to share their webs. **0:10** minutes

DIFFERENTIATE

STRIVING READERS

Fill in a Cause-Effect Chart Have students work together to fill in the chart below. Help them understand how all these causes and effects led to the end of the Middle Ages.

Cause	Effect
	Town employers needed more workers.
Jobs were offered in town.	
	Manor system fell apart.
People became loyal to kings, not lords.	

GIFTED & TALENTED

Medieval Art Have interested students research different aspects of medieval art. Have them select from these choices: bronze art, illuminated manuscripts, silver and gold work, frescoes, paintings, embroidery, ceramics, panel painting, mosaics, stained glass, or sculptures. Suggest that they pick a favorite to learn about and share with the class.

Press (**mt**) *in the Student eEdition for modified text.*

See the Chapter Planner for more strategies for differentiation.

REVIEW & ASSESS

ANSWERS

1. The towns offered higher wages for work and the chance to become a merchant or craftsperson.

2. By taxing the towns within his realm, a king earned money to pay for his army, which brought peace and stability to his land. Increasingly, power and people's loyalty shifted from local lords to their king.

3. People felt more secure and had more time and money to do something besides work.

VOCABULARY

Use each of the following vocabulary words in a sentence that shows an understanding of the word's meaning.

1. **medieval**
   The Middle Ages is also known as the medieval period, which was a time of many political, economic, and cultural changes in Western Europe.
2. **monastery**
3. **feudalism**
4. **manor**
5. **serf**
6. **parliament**
7. **cathedral**
8. **longbow**
9. **bubonic plague**
10. **guild**

READING STRATEGY

11. **DRAW CONCLUSIONS** If you haven't already, complete your chart to draw conclusions about how feudalism and Christianity affected people during the Middle Ages. Then answer the question.

Middle Ages

Feudalism	Christianity
People's loyalties were divided between their king and their lord.	The Church dominated people's lives.

What impact did the power struggles between kings and lords and between kings and the Church have on people during the Middle Ages?

MAIN IDEAS

Answer the following questions. Support your answers with evidence from the chapter.

12. What helped many small kingdoms thrive after the fall of Rome? LESSON 1.1
13. Why did the pope crown Charlemagne emperor of the Romans? LESSON 1.2
14. What led to the emergence of feudalism in Europe? LESSON 1.4
15. What did a typical manor include? LESSON 1.6
16. How did the Church become more powerful and wealthy in the 1000s? LESSON 2.1
17. How did the Magna Carta affect the development of democracy in Western Europe? LESSON 2.2
18. In what way did the Crusades help weaken feudalism? LESSON 2.4
19. How did the bubonic plague contribute to the growth of towns? LESSON 2.7

CRITICAL THINKING

Answer the following questions. Support your answers with evidence from the chapter.

20. **EVALUATE** How did a code of conduct help the knights do their job?
21. **COMPARE AND CONTRAST** How did manor life differ for workers and the lord of the manor?
22. **ANALYZE CAUSE AND EFFECT** What happened as a result of King John's weakened power?
23. **MAKE INFERENCES** Why do you suppose the ruler of France and his soldiers believed Joan of Arc could save their country?
24. **YOU DECIDE** Do you think feudalism benefited the lives of ordinary people or made them worse? Support your opinion with evidence from the chapter.

INTERPRET CHARTS

Study this chart, which compares the feudal structure in medieval Europe with that in medieval Japan. Then answer the questions that follow.

Feudal Structure in Europe and Japan	Europe	Japan
Ruler	King	Emperor
Landowners	Nobles and Church	Daimyo
Warriors	Knights	Samurai
Lower Classes	Peasants and serfs	Peasants, artisans, and merchants

25. How was the feudal structure in Europe similar to that in Japan?
26. How did the makeup of the lower classes in the two regions differ?

ANALYZE SOURCES

A Frankish scholar named Einhard was a trusted friend and adviser of Charlemagne and wrote a biography about his king. Read this excerpt from Einhard's biography of Charlemagne. Then answer the question that follows.

> He cherished the Church of St. Peter the Apostle at Rome above all other holy and sacred places, and heaped its treasury with a vast wealth of gold, silver, and precious stones . . . [T]hroughout his whole reign the wish that he had nearest at heart was to re-establish the ancient authority of the city of Rome . . . and protect the Church of St. Peter.

27. What does the excerpt suggest about Charlemagne's feelings toward the Church?

WRITE ABOUT HISTORY

28. **INFORMATIVE** What events brought about the downfall of feudalism and ended the Middle Ages? Write a paragraph for a children's encyclopedia, summarizing these events and explaining how they brought about the end of feudalism and the Middle Ages. You might create a chart or web diagram to organize your ideas and details.

TIPS
- Take notes from the lessons on the Crusades, the increasing power of the Church, the Hundred Years' War, and the growth of towns.
- State your main idea clearly at the beginning of the paragraph.
- Support your main idea with relevant facts, details, and examples.
- Use vocabulary from the chapter.
- Provide a concluding statement about the end of feudalism and the Middle Ages.

VOCABULARY ANSWERS

1. The Middle Ages is also known as the medieval period, which was a time of many political, economic, and cultural changes in Western Europe.

2. During the Middle Ages, some Christians lived in religious communities called monasteries.

3. A political and social system called feudalism provided stability and protection from the constant warfare during the early Middle Ages.

4. The manor was a self-contained world located on land belonging to a lord.

5. On the manor, serfs belonged to their lord, worked his land, and gave him most of whatever they produced.

6. In 1264, the group of representatives who got together to rule in King Henry III's place came to be called a parliament.

7. Bishops exercised their authority from towering churches called cathedrals.

8. During the Hundred Years' War, archers used a powerful weapon called the longbow, which could pierce a knight's armor.

9. The bubonic plague was a devastating disease that swept through Europe and killed millions of people.

10. As towns grew, groups of craftspeople joined together to form guilds, which helped them protect and improve the working conditions of their members.

READING STRATEGY ANSWER

Middle Ages

Feudalism	Christianity
• People's loyalties were divided between their king and their lord. • Kings and lords competed for power. • People were protected by the feudal system.	• The Church dominated people's lives. • The Church competed with kings for power. • The Church united people.

11. As warfare raged and lords, kings, and the Church struggled for power, people were protected by the feudal system and united by Christianity.

MAIN IDEAS ANSWERS

12. They had a moderate climate and rich soil, abundant forestlands, a wealth of minerals, and access to the sea and rivers.

13. The pope crowned Charlemagne emperor of the Romans because he had put down a rebellion waged against the pope and because Charlemagne was a staunch Christian.

14. After the death of Charlemagne, Europe again fell into chaos and conflict. With its strict hierarchical structure, feudalism emerged as a new social order that provided security and defense.

15. A typical manor included a manor house, a church, a village, and lands with meadows, forests, pastures, and farms.

16. The Church became more powerful and wealthy in the 1000s from the free land the Church received from nobles.

17. It guaranteed certain individual rights and is considered the world's first written constitution.

18. The Crusades resulted in increased trade between Europe and the Eastern Mediterranean, which led to the rise of a merchant class in Europe.

19. After the bubonic plague killed about a third of Europe's workforce, those who survived were in great demand by employers who offered increased wages.

CRITICAL THINKING ANSWERS

20. It probably made them proud to be knights and kept them focused on their task. Because of the code, they also knew what to do and what was expected of them.

21. Peasants and serfs lived in one-room huts, worked all day, and ate the simplest of foods. The lord lived in a comfortable, relatively spacious manor house, performed no physical labor, and feasted on meat and fish.

22. The barons rebelled and forced John to set his seal to the Magna Carta.

23. Religious faith was so strong during the Middle Ages that people would have believed that Christian saints really were speaking to and guiding her.

24. Students' answer will vary. Some may say that because feudalism provided people with security, food, and a place to live, the system benefited them. Others may say that the feudal system kept people down and prevented them from bettering their lives or those of their children.

INTERPRET MAPS ANSWERS

25. They both had a powerful landowning class and skilled warriors.

26. In Europe, the lower class was made up of farmers and workers, while that in Japan included artisans and merchants, who may have earned a better living.

ANALYZE SOURCES ANSWER

27. He was devoted to the Church, and it was his primary concern.

WRITE ABOUT HISTORY ANSWER

28. Students' paragraphs should do the following:
- discuss the impact of the Crusades, the increasing power of the Church, the Hundred Years' War, and the growth of towns
- contain a clearly stated main idea at the beginning of the paragraph
- support the main idea with relevant facts, details, and examples
- include vocabulary from the chapter
- provide a concluding statement about the end of feudalism and the Middle Ages

UNIT RESOURCES

NATIONAL GEOGRAPHIC

On Location with National Geographic Fellow Maurizio Seracini
Intro and Video

Interactive Map Tool

News & Updates

Available on myNGconnect

Unit Wrap-Up:
"Using Technology to See the Past"
Feature and Video

"Brunelleschi's Dome"
National Geographic Adapted Article

"Lady with a Secret"
National Geographic Adapted Article
Student eEdition exclusive

Unit 9 Inquiry:
Map the New Worldview

CHAPTER RESOURCES

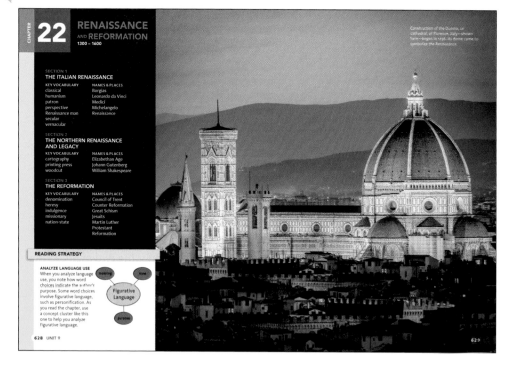

TEACHER RESOURCES & ASSESSMENT

Available on myNGconnect

Social Studies Skills Lessons
• Reading: Analyze Language Use
• Writing: Write an Explanatory Text

Formal Assessment
• Chapter 22 Tests A (on-level) & B (below-level)

Chapter 22 Answer Key

ExamView®
One-time Download

STUDENT BACKPACK *Available on myNGconnect*

• **eEdition** *(English)*   • **eEdition** *(Spanish)*   • **Handbooks**   • **Online Atlas**

For Chapter 22 Spanish resources, visit the Teacher Resource Menu page on myNGconnect.

SECTION 1 RESOURCES

THE ITALIAN RENAISSANCE

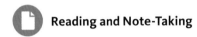 **Reading and Note-Taking**

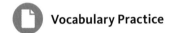 **Vocabulary Practice**

 **Section 1 Quiz**

Available on myNGconnect

LESSON 1.1 RISE OF THE INDIVIDUAL

 **Biography**
Michelangelo
Available on myNGconnect

| **NG Learning Framework:**
Learn More About Marco Polo

• On Your Feet: Three-Step Interview

LESSON 1.2 NEW STYLES AND TECHNIQUES

| **NG Learning Framework:**
Research Renaissance Buildings

• On Your Feet: Renaissance Roundtable

MOMENTS IN HISTORY
LESSON 1.3 RAPHAEL'S *SCHOOL OF ATHENS*

• Critical Viewing: NG Chapter Gallery

• On Your Feet: Inside-Outside Circle

LESSON 1.4 THE MEDICI AND THE BORGIAS

| **NG Learning Framework:**
Learn More About the Borgias

• On Your Feet: Tell Me More

BIOGRAPHY
LESSON 1.5 LEONARDO DA VINCI

• Critical Viewing: NG Chapter Gallery

• On Your Feet: Create a Poster

NG PHOTOGRAPHER DAVE YODER
LESSON 1.6 SEARCHING FOR A LOST DA VINCI

| **NG Learning Framework:**
Learn More About the Painting

• On Your Feet: Fishbowl

SECTION 2 RESOURCES

THE NORTHERN RENAISSANCE AND LEGACY

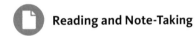 **Reading and Note-Taking**

 **Vocabulary Practice**

 **Section 2 Quiz**

Available on myNGconnect

LESSON 2.1 THE RENAISSANCE MOVES NORTH

| **NG Learning Framework:**
Write a Biography

• On Your Feet: Inside-Outside Circle

BIOGRAPHY
LESSON 2.2 WILLIAM SHAKESPEARE

• Critical Viewing: NG Chapter Gallery

• On Your Feet: One-on-One Interviews

LESSON 2.3 THE PRINTING PRESS

• Critical Viewing: NG Chapter Gallery

• On Your Feet: Build a Paragraph

LESSON 2.4 LEGACY IN THE ARTS AND SCIENCES

| **NG Learning Framework:**
Examine Cartography

• On Your Feet: Quiz Each Other

SECTION 3 RESOURCES

THE REFORMATION

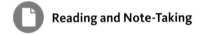 **Reading and Note-Taking**

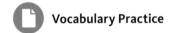 **Vocabulary Practice**

 **Section 3 Quiz**

Available on myNGconnect

LESSON 3.1 PROTESTS AGAINST THE CHURCH

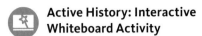 **Biography**
Martin Luther

 **Active History: Interactive Whiteboard Activity**
Map the Protestant Reformation

Active History
Map the Protestant Reformation

Available on myNGconnect
• On Your Feet: Half and Half

DOCUMENT-BASED QUESTION
LESSON 3.2 CONFLICT IN THE CHURCH

• Critical Viewing: NG Chapter Gallery

• On Your Feet: Three Options

LESSON 3.3 THE COUNTER REFORMATION

• Critical Viewing: NG Chapter Gallery

• On Your Feet: Card Responses

LESSON 3.4 THE IMPACT OF THE REFORMATION

| **NG Learning Framework:**
Learn About Nation-States

• On Your Feet: Sequence Events

CHAPTER 22 REVIEW

STRATEGY ❶
Activate Prior Knowledge

Before reading, pose the following questions and have students brainstorm independently or in pairs to list ideas that come to mind. Call on volunteers to share list items as well as any additional information they have about their items.

1. How many Renaissance painters can you name?
2. What are some plays written by William Shakespeare?
3. What do you know about England's King Henry VIII?

Use with Lessons 1.1, 2.2, and 3.1

STRATEGY ❷
Use Paired Reading

Choose two lessons to assign to a pair of students. Each student will read both lessons. Then have students reread and take notes on one lesson and report on it to the other student. Student presenters can also write five questions for the listeners to answer.

Use with All Lessons

STRATEGY ❸
Play "Who Am I?"

Choose from the names below and distribute a list to students. Have them make game cards with a name on the front and a clue to the person's identity on the back. For example, for Leonardo da Vinci, students might write "painted the *Mona Lisa*." Use the cards to play a whole group, small group, or partner review game.

Leonardo da Vinci	Martin Luther
Filippo Brunelleschi	Raphael
Johann Gutenberg	William Shakespeare
Michelangelo	Ignatius of Loyola
Lorenzo de Medici	

Use with All Lessons

Press **mt** *in the Student eEdition for modified text.*

STRATEGY ❶
Modify Vocabulary Lists

Limit the number of vocabulary words, terms, and names students will be required to master. Have students write each word from your modified list on a colored sticky note and put it on the page next to where it appears in context.

Use with All Lessons

STRATEGY ❷
Sequence Events

Write events from Section 3 (The Reformation) on index cards. Read the events aloud and then have students put the cards in chronological order.

Use with Lessons 3.1–3.4

STRATEGY ❶
Create a Word Web

To activate prior knowledge and build vocabulary, work with students to create a Word Web for the word *Renaissance* before beginning Section 1 and the word *Reformation* before beginning Section 3.

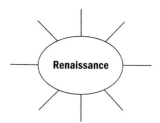

Use with Lessons 1.1 and 3.1

STRATEGY ❷
Provide Sentence Frames

Have pairs of students read the lessons in Section 1 and complete the sentences below.

1.1 _____ is a movement that stressed independence and thinking for oneself.

1.2 New styles and techniques developed in the fields of _____ .

1.3 The people in Raphael's *School of Athens* were _____ .

1.4 Two powerful Renaissance families were _____ .

1.5 Two of Leonardo da Vinci's best-known paintings are _____ .

1.6 National Geographic photographer Dave Yoder is part of a team searching for a lost painting by _____ .

Use with Lessons 1.1–1.6

STRATEGY ③

Ask Yes/No Questions

To reinforce vocabulary meanings after reading, ask the questions below and have students say or write *yes* or *no* in response. Then reread the questions and ask students to correct the information in any sentence that has *no* as an answer *(numbers 1 and 3).*

1. Were followers of humanism inspired by the Renaissance?
2. Were the Medici patrons of Renaissance artists and scholars?
3. Is a Renaissance man someone who is only an artist?
4. Were indulgences given out to people for free?
5. Were Protestants considered guilty of heresy by the Roman Catholic Church?

Use with All Lessons

GIFTED & TALENTED

STRATEGY ①

Complete a Tic-Tac-Toe Project

Give students a choice of completing any three activities that form a tic-tac-toe win. Suggest that students develop a schedule for completing each part by an assigned end date.

Create a display of works of art by famous Renaissance artists.	Read aloud a sonnet by Shakespeare or Petrarch and explain its meaning.	Make a Top-Ten list of the most important buildings of the Renaissance.
Research and write a profile, such as the one for da Vinci in Lesson 1.5 or Shakespeare in Lesson 2.2, for King Henry VIII.	Research and locate the Renaissance artists that appear in Raphael's *School of Athens.*	Act out a scene from one of Shakespeare's plays.
Watch a film version of one of Shakespeare's plays and present an oral summary of it.	Draw a picture that uses perspective to show depth and distance.	Write an essay that compares and contrasts the artistic styles of Michelangelo and Pieter Bruegel the Elder.

Use with All Lessons

STRATEGY ②

Plan an Itinerary

Tell students to imagine that they work for a travel agency that is putting together a European tour to showcase highlights of the Renaissance. Have students create an itinerary for a seven-day trip. They should choose which cities to visit and what to see and do there.

Use with Lessons 1.1–1.6 and 2.1–2.4

PRE-AP

STRATEGY ①

Use the "Persia" Approach

Have students write an essay explaining the significance of the Renaissance or the Reformation. Copy the following mnemonic on the board and tell students to use the "Persia" strategy:

Political

Economic

Religious

Social

Intellectual

Artistic

Use with All Lessons

STRATEGY ②

Support an Opinion

Present a challenge to students to decide whether Leonardo da Vinci or William Shakespeare made a greater impact on history. Have them develop a thesis statement that explains their decision and write an essay that supports it.

Use with Lessons 1.5, 1.6, 2.2, and 2.4

SECTION 1
THE ITALIAN RENAISSANCE

KEY VOCABULARY	NAMES & PLACES
classical	Borgias
humanism	Leonardo da Vinci
patron	Medici
perspective	Michelangelo
Renaissance man	Renaissance
secular	
vernacular	

SECTION 2
THE NORTHERN RENAISSANCE AND LEGACY

KEY VOCABULARY	NAMES & PLACES
cartography	Elizabethan Age
printing press	Johann Gutenberg
woodcut	William Shakespeare

SECTION 3
THE REFORMATION

KEY VOCABULARY	NAMES & PLACES
denomination	Council of Trent
heresy	Counter Reformation
indulgence	Great Schism
missionary	Jesuits
nation-state	Martin Luther
	Protestant
	Reformation

READING STRATEGY

ANALYZE LANGUAGE USE
When you analyze language use, you note how word choices indicate the author's purpose. Some word choices involve figurative language, such as personification. As you read the chapter, use a concept cluster like this one to help you analyze figurative language.

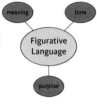

Construction of the Duomo, or cathedral, of Florence, Italy—shown here—began in 1296. Its dome came to symbolize the Renaissance.

TEACHER BACKGROUND

INTRODUCE THE PHOTOGRAPH

Have students study the photo of the Duomo in Florence, Italy. Explain that, during the Renaissance, architects revived ancient Greek and Roman ideas and built structures with domes, arches, and columns. Tell students that, in this chapter, they will learn more about advances in science, art, and architecture during the Renaissance. **ASK:** How does the Duomo resemble buildings you see today? (*Possible response: Many buildings I see today have domes. Some examples are the U.S. Capitol in Washington, D.C., and many state capitol buildings.*)

SHARE BACKGROUND

Many people consider the Duomo in Florence to mark the beginning of the Renaissance. The architect, Filippo Brunelleschi, was one of the most influential architects of the time. After the Duomo was built, it was decorated by artists such as Donatello, Paolo Uccello, and Luca Della Robbia. Brunelleschi's dome still rises above other buildings in Florence. A large statue of Brunelleschi now sits before the Duomo.

DIGITAL RESOURCES myNGconnect.com

TEACHER RESOURCES & ASSESSMENT

Social Studies Skills Lessons
- Reading: Analyze Language Use
- Writing: Write an Explanatory Text

Formal Assessment
- Chapter 22 Tests A (on-level) & B (below-level)

Chapter 22 Answer Key

ExamView®
One-time Download

STUDENT BACKPACK
- **eEdition** (*English*)
- **eEdition** (*Spanish*)
- **Handbooks**
- **Online Atlas**

For Chapter 22 Spanish Resources, visit the Teacher Resource Menu page.

INTRODUCE THE ESSENTIAL QUESTION

HOW DID NEW WAYS OF THINKING TRANSFORM EUROPEAN CULTURE?

Four Corner Activity: Changing Society Post four signs as described below. Tell students to suppose that they are part of a cutting-edge movement that wants to change society for the better. Tell them to choose which of the four influences they will rely on as the inspiration for those changes, move to the appropriate corner, and explain their reasons. Tell students that, in this chapter, they will learn about the influences that transformed Europe beginning in the 1300s.

A. **Foreign Culture**—the art, language, customs, and food from other lands

B. **Religious Tradition**—the core teachings and laws of a particular religion or belief system

C. **Ancient Learning**—the wisdom of an earlier civilization

D. **New Technology**—an invention that improves people's lives in some way

0:15 minutes

INTRODUCE THE READING STRATEGY

ANALYZE LANGUAGE USE

Take a moment to review types of figurative language with students, specifically personification (giving a thing or an idea human qualities), simile (using *like* or *as* to compare two things), metaphor (using something to stand in as a symbol for something else), and idioms (using an expression that means something beyond its literal meaning). Model filling out the Concept Cluster by reading aloud the following paragraph and discussing the author's use of the idiom *clawed their way to the top* to refer to the Medici family.

There were other rich families in Florence, but it was the Medici who clawed their way to the top. Like other great families in the city, the Medici built their fortune as bankers and textile merchants. They were part of a wealthy merchant class that had developed in Italy and gained great power. The family's money bought them so much political power that the Medici ruled Florence during the Renaissance.

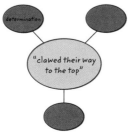

INTRODUCE CHAPTER VOCABULARY

KNOWLEDGE RATING

Have students complete a Knowledge-Rating Chart for Key Vocabulary words. Have students list words and fill out the chart. Then have pairs share the definitions they know. Work together as a class to complete the chart.

KEY VOCABULARY	KNOW IT	NOT SURE	DON'T KNOW	DEFINITION
cartography				
classical				
denomination				
heresy				

KEY DATES

1300	Beginning of Italian Renaissance
1305	Center of Church moved from Rome to Avignon
1378	Two popes elected, one in Rome, one in Avignon
1417	Rome restored as center of Christianity
1455	Printing of the Gutenberg Bible
1517	Publication of Luther's 95 Theses
1545	Beginning of Council of Trent
1558–1603	Elizabethan Age
1618–1648	The Thirty Years' War

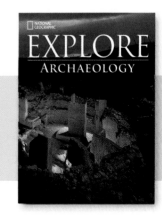

For more information on archaeological wonders like the Duomo, check out *EXPLORE ARCHAEOLOGY.*

Rise of the Individual

In the 1300s, a revolution began to brew in Europe. But this revolution didn't involve weapons and war. This was a movement of ideas. People decided they wanted to enjoy life on Earth—and not just look forward to their reward in heaven. They focused on the individual and believed every person had unlimited possibilities. This was not what the Church had taught in the Middle Ages. The movement was, indeed, revolutionary.

MAIN IDEA

The growth of humanism, with its emphasis on the individual, led to a rebirth of the arts and learning.

THE GROWTH OF HUMANISM

The new movement was called **humanism**. Instead of blindly obeying the authority of a king or the teachings of the Church, the followers of this movement wanted to be independent and think for themselves. Humanists stressed living a Christian life but also sought to explore a new understanding of the individual in relation to God. Humanism inspired a new sense of possibility. People suddenly felt as if they could do anything they chose.

The movement's followers found inspiration in **classical**, or ancient Greek and Roman, writings. Scholars in the Muslim empires had obtained and preserved many classical writings. Growing trade with these empires brought Europeans into greater contact with the texts. Humanists admired what the people of those ancient times had done and said and built.

An Italian poet named Petrarch became an early humanist leader and collected around 200 classical manuscripts. Some of these manuscripts had been hidden away in monastery libraries for centuries. People learned Greek just so they could read them. They began to forget about Charlemagne and wanted to learn more about the great leaders of ancient Greece and Rome.

REBIRTH OF THE ARTS

This rebirth of classical learning led to a movement of great creativity in the arts, writing, and thinking. Historians call the movement the **Renaissance**, which actually means "rebirth" in French. The Renaissance lasted from about 1300 to 1600 and began in Italy.

As the center of the ancient Roman Empire, Italy was well positioned to become the movement's birthplace. In addition, many of its cities—including Florence, Venice, Rome, and Milan—had become wealthy from trade. Ideas as well as goods were traded in these cities, which attracted artists, writers, and scientists.

Italian cities particularly benefited from the reopening of the ancient trade routes of the Silk Roads between Europe and China. Interest in Asian markets had been sparked, in part, by Venetian merchant Marco Polo. He wrote about the wonders he saw as he traveled the Silk Roads from Europe to Central Asia, China, and India.

+ POSSIBLE RESPONSE

Details such as her expression, her eyes, her mouth, her hair, and the folds in her robe make the subject seem lifelike.

Critical Viewing Michelangelo painted this fresco of a woman on the walls of the Sistine Chapel in Rome's Vatican Museums. What details make the subject seem lifelike?

No city in Italy was more influential during the Renaissance than Florence. Artists like **Leonardo da Vinci**, Raphael, and **Michelangelo** came to Florence hoping to make a name for themselves—and they certainly did. Leonardo excelled as a painter, an inventor, and a scientist. You'll read more about the genius of Leonardo later in the chapter. Raphael came to Florence to study the great masters, including Leonardo, and created his own masterpieces. Michelangelo was a painter and sculptor whose muscular subjects convey great intensity and power. These artists and many, many others are counted among the greats of the Italian Renaissance. They were all part of an earthshaking cultural shift that transformed Europe.

REVIEW & ASSESS

1. **READING CHECK** What inspired the development of humanism?

2. **IDENTIFY MAIN IDEAS AND DETAILS** Why did the Renaissance begin in Italy?

3. **ANALYZE LANGUAGE USE** What does the phrase "an earthshaking cultural shift" suggest about the impact of the Renaissance in Europe?

PLAN

OBJECTIVE

Explain how the growth of humanism, with its emphasis on the individual, led to a rebirth of the arts and learning.

CRITICAL THINKING SKILLS FOR LESSON 1.1

- Identify Main Ideas and Details
- Monitor Comprehension
- Analyze Language Use
- Summarize
- Identify
- Analyze Visuals

ESSENTIAL QUESTION

How did new ways of thinking transform European culture?

The movement known as humanism emphasizes the individual.

Lesson 1.1 discusses how humanism led to advances in the arts and learning.

BACKGROUND FOR THE TEACHER

The city of Florence is located about 145 miles northwest of Rome. It lies along the Arno River and is surrounded by rolling hills. Florence was founded as a Roman military colony in the first century B.C. By the 1300s, Florence had become a wealthy city. Much of this wealth was due to its successful textile industry. Florentine merchants sailed to England to get wool, and Florentine artisans wove it into fine cloth. The cloth was sold in Italy, northern Europe, and Asia. Florence also became a center of banking and exerted great influence throughout Europe and beyond.

DIGITAL RESOURCES myNGconnect.com

TEACHER RESOURCES & ASSESSMENT

 Reading and Note-Taking

 Vocabulary Practice

 Section 1 Quiz

STUDENT RESOURCES

 Biography

INTRODUCE & ENGAGE

MAKE CONNECTIONS

Ask students to identify the ways in which literature and art reflect the culture of a society and a time in history. **ASK:** What ideas about religion, politics, and daily life can be communicated through literature and art? What can we learn about the past from literature and art? Make a list of students' responses. Tell students they will learn about the rebirth and growth of the arts in Europe at the time of the Renaissance. `0:05` minutes

TEACH

GUIDED DISCUSSION

1. **Summarize** How did ideas about the individual change during the growth of humanism? *(In the Middle Ages, people blindly obeyed the authority of a king or the teachings of the Church. Although humanists stressed living a Christian life, they wanted to be independent and think for themselves.)*

2. **Identify** What movement resulted from the rebirth of classical learning that began during the time of humanism? *(the Renaissance)*

ANALYZE VISUALS

Expand on the "Critical Viewing" question in the lesson by inviting students to take a closer look at the image of the woman from the fresco in the Sistine Chapel. Have students work in pairs to create a list of details that make the woman seem lifelike. Then have pairs share their details with the class. Record the most common details in a Word Web like the one below. `0:15` minutes

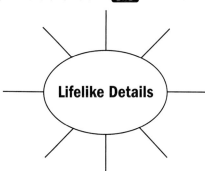

Lifelike Details

ACTIVE OPTIONS

NG Learning Framework: Learn More About Marco Polo

ATTITUDE: **Curiosity**
SKILL: **Communication**
KNOWLEDGE: **Our Human Story**

Have students reread the information in the lesson on Marco Polo. Then have small groups of students do research about Marco Polo's travels. Ask groups to write and present a short skit about the

merchant. Invite them to include characters he might have met and sights he may have seen along the Silk Roads. `0:10` minutes

On Your Feet: Three-Step Interview Have students choose a partner. One student should interview the other on the following question: Would you have liked to live during the time of humanism? Why or why not? Then students should reverse roles. Finally each student should share the results of his or her interview with the class. `0:10` minutes

DIFFERENTIATE

ENGLISH LANGUAGE LEARNERS

Use Sentence Strips Choose a paragraph from the lesson and make sentence strips out of it. Read the paragraph aloud, having students follow along in their books. Have students close their books and give them the set of sentence strips. Students should put the strips in order and then read the paragraph aloud.

PRE-AP

Write a Journal Have students do research to find out more about life in Italy during the Renaissance. Then ask them to imagine that they live in an Italian city at the beginning of the Renaissance movement. Have them write at least five daily entries for a journal. Invite students to write creative descriptions of people they meet and things they see, hear, and experience each day. Encourage students to include entries giving details about specific events that occur.

Press **mt** *in the Student eEdition for modified text.*

See the Chapter Planner for more strategies for differentiation.

REVIEW & ASSESS

ANSWERS

1. Ancient Greek and Roman writings inspired the development of humanism.

2. It was the center of the ancient Roman Empire. Many of its cities had become wealthy from trade. Goods as well as ideas were traded in these cities, which attracted artists, writers, and scientists.

3. It suggests that its vibrations were felt throughout Europe.

New Styles and Techniques

Remember reading in the last chapter about the great stained-glass-filled cathedrals built during the Middle Ages? The walls of these churches seemed to stretch to the sky. But heavy brick blocks were often placed on the outside of a cathedral to support its soaring walls. As you'll see, Renaissance architects would try to find another, less visible means of support.

MAIN IDEA

The Renaissance inspired new forms of expression in art, literature, and architecture.

ART AND LITERATURE

Renaissance architects came up with new building strategies. However, the movement demanded new forms of expression from artists as well. For example, they found ways to show landscapes in a realistic manner by developing a technique called **perspective**

to produce an impression of depth and distance. While art during the Middle Ages appeared flat, perspective allowed Renaissance artists to produce works that looked three-dimensional.

The subjects of the artwork changed, too. Artists including Titian (TIH-shun), a great painter in Venice, still drew inspiration from religious subjects. But **secular**, or nonreligious, subjects also became popular. For example, Sandro Botticelli of Florence painted *La Primavera*, which celebrates the arrival of spring.

New styles in the arts weren't limited to painters and sculptors. Renaissance writers got in on the act as well. Instead of using Latin, the language of the Church, many wrote in the **vernacular**, or their native language. One of the first to do so was the poet Dante, who wrote his masterpiece, *The Divine Comedy*, in Italian in the early 1300s. The work describes Dante's long journey to heaven led in part by the ancient Roman poet Virgil.

ARCHITECTURE

During the Renaissance, architects found inspiration by studying the buildings of ancient Rome. They incorporated classical Roman engineering features such as arches and domes in their own creations. One of the greatest of these architects was Filippo Brunelleschi (brew-nuhl-LESS-key) of Florence, whose impressive dome is illustrated on the opposite page.

It all began with a contest. In 1418, architects were challenged to build a self-supporting dome for the cathedral of

PERSPECTIVE

Renaissance artists often included perfectly proportioned buildings in their paintings. As you can see in this painting, *The Ideal City* by Piero della Francesca, the larger buildings in the foreground and the smaller ones in the background provide the illusion of depth and distance.

BRUNELLESCHI'S DOME

When the dome was completed in 1436, it soared to a height of about 374 feet. Engineers today still do not fully understand how Brunelleschi constructed his masterpiece. It remains the largest brick dome ever built.

Nesting Domes
To prevent the base of the dome from bulging outward, Brunelleschi constructed an inner and an outer dome connected by vertical and horizontal brick ribs.

Building Materials
Beneath the tiles on the dome's exterior lie several million bricks made of different shapes and set either horizontally or vertically depending on where they were used.

Supporting Rings
Experts know that this wooden ring helped hold the dome in place. They believe the two stone rings above may also have been used.

Florence. Brunelleschi won the competition, but at first even he wasn't sure how to build the dome, which had to sit on a base that was about 150 feet wide. Without internal support, how could the dome be prevented from sagging and collapsing? Eventually, inspiration struck. Instead of constructing

massive visible supports, Brunelleschi proposed building two domes, one nested inside the other. The effect would be of a dome rising effortlessly in the air. The dome would come to symbolize the freedom of the Renaissance and of the human spirit. It also inspired other architects and helped make Florence the center of the Renaissance.

REVIEW & ASSESS

1. **READING CHECK** What new techniques did Renaissance artists use?

2. **MAKE INFERENCES** Why do you think some Renaissance writers began expressing themselves in the vernacular?

3. **INTERPRET VISUALS** What difficulties do you think the builders of the dome encountered during its construction?

PLAN

OBJECTIVE

Describe how the Renaissance inspired new forms of expression in art, literature, and architecture.

The Renaissance inspired new styles and techniques in the arts. Lesson 1.2 discusses how art, literature, and architecture changed during the Renaissance.

CRITICAL THINKING SKILLS FOR LESSON 1.2

- Identify Main Ideas and Details
- Make Inferences
- Interpret Visuals
- Identify
- Describe
- Monitor Comprehension

BACKGROUND FOR THE TEACHER

Dante Alighieri was born in Florence in 1265 and died in 1321. Dante's greatest masterpiece is *The Divine Comedy*. The epic poem describes a journey through hell, purgatory, and heaven. The allegory draws on medieval Christian theology and is said to represent the soul's journey toward God. Dante wrote the poem in the vernacular because he believed that the development of a literary Italian language would strengthen Italian culture. In fact, Italian became the literary language in Western Europe for several centuries.

ESSENTIAL QUESTION

How did new ways of thinking transform European culture?

DIGITAL RESOURCES myNGconnect.com

TEACHER RESOURCES & ASSESSMENT

 Reading and Note-Taking

 Vocabulary Practice

 Section 1 Quiz

STUDENT RESOURCES

 NG Chapter Gallery

INTRODUCE & ENGAGE

NUMBERED HEADS

Organize students into groups of four and assign each student a number (one, two, three, or four). Tell students to think about and discuss a response to this question: *What would you like to learn about forms of art, literature, and architecture during the Renaissance?* Then call a number and have the student from each group with that number explain the group's response to the question. Tell students they will learn about how forms of art, literature, and architecture changed during the Renaissance in this lesson. **0:10** minutes

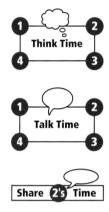

TEACH

GUIDED DISCUSSION

1. **Identify** What classical Roman engineering features were incorporated into buildings built during the Renaissance? *(arches and domes)*

2. **Describe** What is *The Divine Comedy?* *(a work written by the poet Dante that describes his journey to heaven led in part by the ancient Roman poet Virgil)*

INTERPRET VISUALS

Invite students to take a closer look at the painting by Piero della Francesca. Have them discuss in small groups what techniques the artist used to create a sense of perspective. **0:10** minutes

ACTIVE OPTIONS

NG Learning Framework: Research Renaissance Buildings

ATTITUDES: **Curiosity, Responsibility**
SKILLS: **Collaboration, Communication**

Have students work in groups to research another building constructed during the Italian Renaissance. Then have them present their findings to the class. Encourage them to include information about how and when the building was constructed. Ask them to describe interesting characteristics of the building. Students should include images of the building they chose. **0:10** minutes

On Your Feet: Renaissance Roundtable Divide the class into groups of four. Hand each group a sheet of paper with the question *How did the Renaissance influence forms of art, literature, and architecture?* The first student in each group should write an answer, read it aloud, and pass the paper clockwise to the next student. Each student in the group should add at least one answer. The paper should circulate until students run out of answers. At the end of the activity, initiate a class discussion of students' responses. **0:10** minutes

DIFFERENTIATE

STRIVING READERS

Record and Compare Facts After reading the lesson, ask students to write three important facts they learned about Renaissance styles and techniques. Allow pairs of students to compare and check their facts and then combine their facts into one longer list. Ask a volunteer from each group to write the most important fact from each group.

GIFTED & TALENTED

Demonstrate Perspective Have students do research to learn how artists use linear perspective in paintings. Then ask them to make an informational poster by taking a photocopy of a Renaissance work of art, drawing the perspective lines over the image, and then mounting the diagram on a piece of poster board with an explanation beneath. Ask them to use the resulting poster to teach perspective to the rest of the class.

Press **mt** *in the Student eEdition for modified text.*

See the Chapter Planner for more strategies for differentiation.

REVIEW & ASSESS

ANSWERS

1. Renaissance artists used new techniques such as realism and perspective. They also painted more secular subjects and nature.

2. They wanted their works to be more accessible to ordinary people. They wanted to break away from the Church's authority and dominance. They wanted to use the vernacular to express the thoughts and dreams of everyday individuals.

3. They probably encountered difficulties such as transporting heavy materials, lifting materials up to the dome, working on the outside of the dome at dangerous heights, and enduring bad weather conditions.

A.D. **1511**

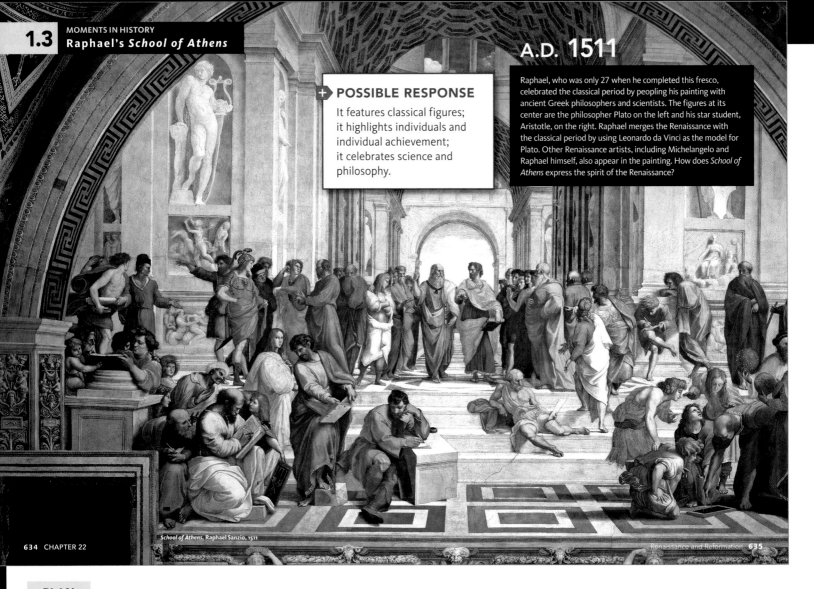

+ POSSIBLE RESPONSE

It features classical figures; it highlights individuals and individual achievement; it celebrates science and philosophy.

Raphael, who was only 27 when he completed this fresco, celebrated the classical period by peopling his painting with ancient Greek philosophers and scientists. The figures at its center are the philosopher Plato on the left and his star student, Aristotle, on the right. Raphael merges the Renaissance with the classical period by using Leonardo da Vinci as the model for Plato. Other Renaissance artists, including Michelangelo and Raphael himself, also appear in the painting. How does *School of Athens* express the spirit of the Renaissance?

School of Athens, Raphael Sanzio, 1511

PLAN

OBJECTIVE

Describe Raphael's fresco *School of Athens*.

CRITICAL THINKING SKILLS FOR LESSON 1.3

- Synthesize
- Analyze Visuals
- Identify

ESSENTIAL QUESTION

How did new ways of thinking transform European culture?

During the Renaissance, there was an explosion in art in Italy. Lesson 1.3 describes one of the most well-known and admired frescoes painted by the Italian artist Raphael.

BACKGROUND FOR THE TEACHER

Raphael Sanzio was born in 1483 in Urbino, Italy. Even as a young artist at the age of 17, he displayed great artistic talent. In about 1504, he moved to Florence where Leonardo da Vinci and Michelangelo were his principal teachers. Raphael became known as one of Italy's best painters and was called to Rome by the pope in 1508. There, he painted many frescoes in the Vatican Palace. He painted *School of Athens*, one of his most famous frescoes, between 1509 and 1511. Raphael died in 1520 in Rome on his 37th birthday.

DIGITAL RESOURCES myNGconnect.com

TEACHER RESOURCES & ASSESSMENT

 Reading and Note-Taking   **Vocabulary Practice**   **Section 1 Quiz**

STUDENT RESOURCES

 NG Chapter Gallery

CREATE AN IDEA WEB

Have students form groups of four around a section of a bulletin board or a table. Provide each group with a large sheet of paper. Have group members take turns contributing a concept or phrase to an Idea Web with the phrase *School of Athens* at the center. Call on volunteers from each group to share their webs. Tell students that after they learn about Raphael's *School of Athens,* they should infer why the words *school* and *Athens* are used in the title of the painting. **0:05** minutes

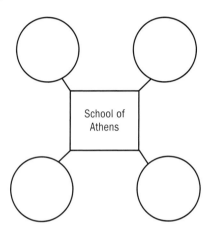

School of Athens

TEACH

GUIDED DISCUSSION

1. **Analyze Visuals** Examine Raphael's fresco *School of Athens.* Why do you think the artist chose to celebrate ancient Greece? *(Responses will vary. Possible response: because ancient Greece witnessed great advances in learning and culture)*

2. **Identify** What two Greek philosophers are depicted at the center of *School of Athens? (Plato and Aristotle)*

MORE INFORMATION

Raphael's Tapestries Pope Leo X hired Raphael to design tapestries to hang on the walls of the Sistine Chapel in the Vatican. Seven of the ten drawings for the tapestries were completed by 1516. The tapestries woven from them were completed by 1519. The tapestries are still in the Vatican today. Seven of Raphael's original drawings are in the Victoria and Albert Museum in London.

ACTIVE OPTIONS

Critical Viewing: NG Chapter Gallery Invite students to explore the Chapter Gallery to examine the images that relate to this chapter. Have them select one of the images and do additional research to learn more about it. Ask questions that will inspire additional inquiry about the chosen gallery image, such as: What

is this? Where and when was this created? By whom? Why was it created? What is it made of? Why does it belong in this chapter? What else would you like to know about it? **0:10** minutes

On Your Feet: Inside-Outside Circle Arrange students in concentric circles facing each other. Have each student in the outside circle ask a question about Raphael's *School of Athens.* Then have each student in the inside circle answer their partner's question. On a signal, have students on the inside circle rotate counterclockwise to meet a new partner and begin again. On a different signal, have students trade roles so those in the inside circle ask the questions and those in the outside circle answer the questions. **0:10** minutes

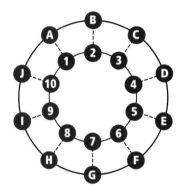

STRIVING READERS

Analyze Visuals Provide concrete questions to help students of different ability levels process and interpret the fresco. **ASK:** What kinds of objects do you see in the painting that would be related to studying or learning? What does the presence of Greek philosophers in the painting suggest? What are some of the figures in the painting doing that could indicate they are studying or learning? How might the figures and objects in the picture relate to the word *school* that is used in the title of the painting? Encourage students to point to things they don't understand about the painting and help them frame questions about these details.

PRE-AP

Write a Biography Have students work in small groups to write a biography of Raphael highlighting some of his major accomplishments. Encourage students to illustrate their biography with photos and drawings. Invite students to share their biography with the class.

Press (**mt**) *in the Student eEdition for modified text.*

See the Chapter Planner for more strategies for differentiation.

1.4

The **Medici** and the **Borgias**

The Medici were like the godfathers, or crime bosses, of the Renaissance. They defeated their rivals by whatever means necessary—including murder. But the Medici family used its wealth and power to support some of the greatest artists in Florence.

MAIN IDEA

Wealthy and powerful families supported Renaissance artists and thinkers in many Italian cities.

WEALTHY FLORENCE

There were other rich families in Florence, but it was the **Medici** (MEH-dee-chee) who clawed their way to the top. Like other great families in the city, the Medici built their fortune as bankers and textile merchants. They were part of a wealthy merchant class that had developed in Italy and gained great power. The family's money bought them so much political power that the Medici ruled Florence during the Renaissance.

But the Medici weren't all about money and political gain. The Renaissance had brought about a renewed sense of pride throughout Italy. Rich families competed to restore the glory of ancient Rome's civilization to their cities and so became patrons of the arts. **Patrons** used some of their wealth to encourage and support artists. This support allowed the artists to create and work full-time on their masterpieces.

The Medici family made sure that Florence became the place to be for the great artists and scholars of the day. They spent fortunes attracting the best and brightest to their city. No member of the Medici family was more successful at bringing artists and scholars to Florence than Lorenzo de Medici, also known as Lorenzo the Magnificent. A poet himself, Lorenzo supported some of the most important artists of the Renaissance, including Leonardo da Vinci and Michelangelo.

POWERFUL ROME

Florence got a head start, but eventually Renaissance ideas and a new flood of people made their way to Rome. The pope, who ruled both Rome and the Catholic Church, rebuilt the city and brought back its authority and importance. In time, Rome became almost as powerful as Florence, and the two cities competed for dominance. When Michelangelo created his statue of the biblical hero David, it was originally placed outside the center of Florence's government. The towering, muscular David stood there, tense and ready for battle, with his eyes looking warningly in the direction of Rome.

The pope had authority over Rome, but the city, like Florence, had its share of patrons. The **Borgia** (BOR-gee-ah) family, originally from Spain, was the most powerful group of patrons in Rome. The Borgias were even more ruthless than the Medici. Since the Church controlled Rome, the Borgias attempted to control the Church. In the 1400s, two members of the family became popes. Another Borgia named Cesare (CHAY-suh-ray) was made a cardinal, a high-ranking member of the clergy, at the age of 17. Like many of the Borgias, Cesare used political methods that were less than honest. However, he did do one thing right: He briefly brought Leonardo da Vinci to Rome.

This museum in Florence, called the Pitti Palace, was built in 1472 for Luca Pitti. However, the palace became the official residence of the Medici in 1550.

REVIEW & ASSESS

1. **READING CHECK** What roles did the Medici play in Florence?

2. **ANALYZE CAUSE AND EFFECT** How did the Medici family become wealthy?

3. **MAKE INFERENCES** Why did some members of the Borgia family want to join the clergy?

PLAN

OBJECTIVE

Tell how wealthy and powerful families supported Renaissance artists and thinkers in many Italian cities.

CRITICAL THINKING SKILLS FOR LESSON 1.4

- Identify Main Ideas and Details
- Monitor Comprehension
- Analyze Cause and Effect
- Make Inferences
- Summarize
- Identify
- Compare and Contrast

ESSENTIAL QUESTION

How did new ways of thinking transform European culture?

The wealthy Medici family in Florence and the wealthy Borgia family in Rome were very powerful. Lesson 1.4 discusses how these families supported artists and scholars during the Renaissance.

BACKGROUND FOR THE TEACHER

Cosimo de Medici, known as Cosimo the Elder, gained great wealth from his success in banking. The leader of the Medici family, he ruled Florence by 1434. He lived an extravagant life. Cosimo hired artists and architects to decorate his magnificent palace and redesign many buildings in Florence. He valued education, built libraries, and collected books and manuscripts. His son, Piero, and his grandson, Lorenzo, continued to follow an aristocratic way of life. Lorenzo successfully invested in the culture of Florence through his patronage of artists, scholars, and architects.

DIGITAL RESOURCES myNGconnect.com

TEACHER RESOURCES & ASSESSMENT

 Reading and Note-Taking   **Vocabulary Practice**   **Section 1 Quiz**

STUDENT RESOURCES

 NG Chapter Gallery

INTRODUCE & ENGAGE

PREVIEW AND PREDICT

Have students read the lesson title, the Main Idea statement, and any text in large blue type. Have students use that information to write sentences that predict what the lesson is about. Allow pairs of students to compare sentences. Then tell students that they will learn about wealthy and powerful families in Italy during the Renaissance in the lesson. **0:05** minutes

TEACH

GUIDED DISCUSSION

1. **Summarize** Why was Lorenzo de Medici known as Lorenzo the Magnificent?
   (He was successful at bringing artists and scholars to Florence.)

2. **Identify** What two cities in Italy competed for dominance during the Renaissance? *(Florence and Rome)*

COMPARE AND CONTRAST

Have students compare and contrast the Medici and the Borgia families. Record similarities and differences in a Venn diagram and use it as a basis for discussion about the lesson. **0:10** minutes

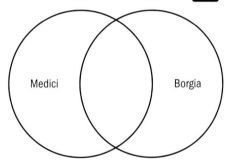

Medici   Borgia

ACTIVE OPTIONS

NG Learning Framework: Learn More About the Borgias

ATTITUDE: **Empowerment**
KNOWLEDGE: **Our Human Story**

Have students revisit the information in the lesson about the Borgia family. Then have them use other resources to learn more about Cesare Borgia. **ASK**: How would you have done things differently from Cesare Borgia? How do you feel these changes would have affected Rome and its citizens? **0:10** minutes

On Your Feet: Tell Me More Have students form two teams and assign each team one of the following topics:

- Florence during the Renaissance
- Rome during the Renaissance

Each group should write down as many facts about their topic as they can. Have the class reconvene and have each group stand up, one at a time. The rest of the class calls out "Tell me more about [Florence or Rome]." The group recites one fact. The class again requests a fact until the group runs out of facts to share. Then the next group presents its facts. **0:10** minutes

DIFFERENTIATE

INCLUSION

Pose and Answer Questions Pair students who have reading or perception issues with stronger readers. Have the pairs work together to read each paragraph of the lesson. After each paragraph, allow the student with reading issues to ask questions for clarification. Have the other student pose one simple recall question for each paragraph.

ENGLISH LANGUAGE LEARNERS

Give a Thumbs Up or Thumbs Down Write a set of true-false statements about the lesson, such as "The Borgia family was the most powerful family in Florence." Read the lesson aloud with students following along in their books. Then have them close the books and listen as you read the true-false statements. Students should give a thumbs up if a statement is true and a thumbs down if a statement is false.

Press **mt** *in the Student eEdition for modified text.*

See the Chapter Planner for more strategies for differentiation.

REVIEW & ASSESS

ANSWERS

1. They ruled the city and were patrons of the arts.
2. They became wealthy through their success in banking and in the textile industry.
3. They wanted to join the clergy because the pope ruled Rome and they wanted to hold that kind of power.

LEONARDO DA VINCI 1452–1519

According to legend, Leonardo's father asked his teenage son to paint a wooden shield. The boy decided to paint a face on the shield—but not a human face. Instead, he collected an assortment of dead animals, including maggots, bats, and lizards, to create the head of a monster belching smoke. When Leonardo's father saw the painting, he was so stunned by its realism that he knew his son would be a painter. He was right. But Leonardo would be so much more.

LEONARDO'S *MONA LISA*

Many mysteries surround the *Mona Lisa*. For one thing, no one really knows the subject's identity, although she is believed to be Lisa Gherardini (gehr-ahr-DEE-nee), the wife of a merchant. (*Mona* means "madame.") But it is her mysterious smile that has captured people's imagination for centuries. What is she smiling about? And what's going on behind those eyes? Leonardo never gave the painting to whoever commissioned it. Instead, he kept it with him all his life. Today the painting hangs in the Louvre, a museum in Paris.

Mona Lisa, Leonardo da Vinci, 1503–1506

Jobs: Painter, sculptor, engineer, scientist, and inventor

Home: He was born near Vinci but made his home wherever he found work—mostly Florence and Milan.

FINEST HOUR

Perhaps the acclaim received by his great painting, the *Mona Lisa*

WORST MOMENT

Seeing his bitter rival, Michelangelo, given the honor of decorating the Vatican, the palace of the pope in Rome

TRIVIA

He was left-handed and wrote backward, either because it was easier or to prevent the curious from reading his notebooks. His writing had to be held up to a mirror to be read.

LEONARDO THE ARTIST

Because of Leonardo da Vinci's obvious talent, he was sent to apprentice under Andrea del Verrocchio (vehr-OAK-ee-oh), a great painter in Florence. Eventually, Leonardo was given the honor of painting an angel in one of his teacher's paintings. It turned out to be the best part of the painting. Soon after, Leonardo left his teacher's studio to strike out on his own.

Word quickly spread about the young painter. Soon, nobles, patrons, and popes engaged Leonardo's services. He would produce several great works, including two very celebrated paintings. One is the *Mona Lisa*, shown here and arguably the most famous painting in the world. The other is *The Last Supper*, one of the best-known frescoes in history. The fresco depicts the final meal that, according to Christian belief, Jesus and his followers ate together. It is admired for the different emotions expressed by the followers and for the use of light and angles to draw attention to Jesus, the central figure.

ULTIMATE RENAISSANCE MAN

Unfortunately for the world, Leonardo produced relatively few paintings—only about 17. He began many other paintings and other works of art but failed to finish them. This failure was probably due to his interest in so many other fields, including engineering and anatomy, or the study of the human body. Leonardo dissected, or cut up, the bodies of dead people, and used what he learned to make remarkably accurate anatomical sketches. These sketches helped him portray people more realistically. He also designed machines, including early forms of a flying machine and a submarine.

Leonardo studied whatever interested him and recorded his observations and sketches in a collection of notebooks. These are works of art themselves but were not widely known until more than 100 years after his death. Many people had considered Leonardo to be solely an artist and so were amazed at the breadth of his knowledge. In fact, with all his talents, Leonardo embodied the well-rounded ideal of Renaissance and humanist thinking. He could do it all. He was a painter, an architect, an inventor, an engineer, and a scientist. All these qualities and many more made Leonardo the ultimate **Renaissance man**.

REVIEW & ASSESS

1. **READING CHECK** Why is Leonardo da Vinci considered a true Renaissance man?

2. **INTERPRET VISUALS** The *Mona Lisa* is said to represent the idea of happiness. What details in the painting do you think make Mona Lisa appear happy?

3. **MAKE INFERENCES** Why do you think Leonardo decided to keep the *Mona Lisa* for himself?

PLAN

OBJECTIVE

Discuss the accomplishments of Leonardo da Vinci in the arts and other fields.

Leonardo da Vinci was a master painter, an architect, and a scientist during the Renaissance. Lesson 1.5 gives an overview of many of da Vinci's accomplishments.

CRITICAL THINKING SKILLS FOR LESSON 1.5

- Identify Main Ideas and Details
- Monitor Comprehension
- Interpret Visuals
- Make Inferences
- Summarize
- Analyze Cause and Effect
- Categorize

BACKGROUND FOR THE TEACHER

Leonardo da Vinci was raised on his father's family's estate. When he was apprenticed to artist Andrea del Verrocchio, he received training in painting and sculpture as well as technical and mechanical subjects. Leonardo worked in Florence until 1481. During that time, he did many pen and pencil drawings, including technical sketches of such objects as pumps, various other machines, and military weapons. Leonardo then moved to Milan, where he had a large workshop and hired many students and apprentices.

ESSENTIAL QUESTION

How did new ways of thinking transform European culture?

DIGITAL RESOURCES myNGconnect.com

TEACHER RESOURCES & ASSESSMENT

 Reading and Note-Taking

 Vocabulary Practice

 Section 1 Quiz

STUDENT RESOURCES

 NG Chapter Gallery

ASK QUESTIONS

Have students form groups of four and come up with a list of three questions about Leonardo da Vinci and his accomplishments. After the lesson, review the questions and have students from each group answer the questions they listed or give them the opportunity to research answers if their particular question was not addressed in the text. Have each group share its questions and answers with the class. **0:05** minutes

TEACH

GUIDED DISCUSSION

1. **Summarize** Why do people admire the painting *The Last Supper* so much? *(People admire the painting for the different emotions conveyed by the followers and for the use of light and angles to draw attention to Jesus, the central figure.)*

2. **Analyze Cause and Effect** What reason probably caused Leonardo to produce relatively few paintings during his life? *(probably his interest in so many other fields, including engineering and anatomy)*

CATEGORIZE

Have students categorize Leonardo da Vinci's many accomplishments. You might have them fill out a chart such as the one below. **0:15** minutes

Leonardo da Vinci's Accomplishments

Art	Engineering	Science
(Mona Lisa)	*(flying machine design)*	*(dissections and sketches of the human body)*
(The Last Supper)	*(submarine design)*	

ACTIVE OPTIONS

Critical Viewing: NG Chapter Gallery Invite students to explore the NG Chapter Gallery and create a Favorites List by choosing the images they find most interesting. If possible, have students copy the images into a document to form an actual list. Then encourage them to select the image they like best and do further research on it. **0:10** minutes

On Your Feet: Create a Poster Encourage students to use knowledge from the lesson to create a poster about Leonardo da Vinci. Before starting on the poster, students should plan the poster and do a rough sketch. Ask students to focus on Leonardo's life, his accomplishments, and his interests. Students should illustrate their posters with photos and drawings. **0:10** minutes

DIFFERENTIATE

STRIVING READERS

Ready, Set, Recall After reading, ask students to work independently to list everything they recall about Leonardo da Vinci, his life, and his accomplishments. Then allow small teams to combine their lists within a given time limit. Finally, have teams contribute one item at a time to a class list on the board until all teams run out of items. (If a team thinks of a new item, the team can get back in.)

GIFTED & TALENTED

Interview Leonardo da Vinci Allow students to work in teams of two to plan, write, and perform a simulated television interview with Leonardo da Vinci. Tell students that the purpose of the interview is to focus on the many achievements of Leonardo during his lifetime.

Press **mt** in the Student eEdition for modified text.

See the Chapter Planner for more strategies for differentiation.

REVIEW & ASSESS

ANSWERS

1. He is considered a true Renaissance man because he was so well-rounded—a gifted painter, architect, inventor, engineer, and scientist.

2. Possible response: Her smile, her eyes, the warm colors, and the beautiful scenery in the background all make Mona Lisa appear happy.

3. He was proud of the painting and fell in love with the subject.

Searching for a
Lost da Vinci

What if there were a painting by Leonardo that was just waiting to be uncovered? Italian engineer Maurizio Seracini is convinced one exists, and he thinks he knows where it is. His obsession has taken him to Florence, where he has conducted extensive research and experienced both triumphs and defeats. Seracini has also gathered a team, including photographer Dave Yoder, to help him find the hidden masterpiece. The question is: Will they find the lost da Vinci?

^ A member of Seracini's team looks on nervously as a probe is inserted in this painting by Giorgio Vasari. Seracini believes Leonardo's missing painting lies hidden behind Vasari's work

Researchers are trying to find a long-lost painting by Leonardo da Vinci.

A CENTURIES-OLD MYSTERY

The object of Seracini's search dates back about 500 years. Around 1505, Leonardo painted a fresco called *The Battle of Anghiari* (ahn-ghee-AHR-ee) on the wall of a room in the Palazzo Vecchio, the town hall of Florence. The fresco depicts four men on horseback, engaged in an intense battle. Leonardo had completed the *Mona Lisa*, but it was *The Battle of Anghiari* that other artists came to admire and copy.

About 50 years later, a Renaissance artist and writer named Giorgio Vasari was asked to redecorate the town hall. However, legend has it that rather than destroy Leonardo's fresco, Vasari built a wall over the painting. He then painted his own battle scene on the new wall. Vasari had preserved other great works in a similar way.

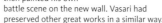
Photographer Dave Yoder

An expert on Leonardo first told Seracini about the lost painting and suggested that he gather a team to look for it. As part of the team, National Geographic photographer Dave Yoder said his challenge was "to find things to photograph about a painting that might or might not be behind a wall." They also weren't sure which wall to look behind.

CLUES AND FINDINGS

But Seracini believes Vasari provided a clue to the painting's whereabouts. On a small flag in his painting, the artist wrote in tiny letters the Italian words *Cerca trova*, which mean "Seek and you shall find." At first Seracini used noninvasive methods to reveal what he called "a subtle gap behind the wall on which Vasari painted, which could have been constructed by Vasari himself to protect Leonardo's masterpiece."

Soon after this discovery, however, officials in Florence had Seracini's team use an endoscope, a more invasive method, to explore the painting. An endoscope is a lighted instrument that can be inserted inside an object to examine it. To reduce the damage, Seracini mostly inserted the endoscope into holes that had already opened in Vasari's painting. Material taken from one hole revealed traces of colors that only Leonardo had used. One black pigment was believed to be the same type used in painting the *Mona Lisa*.

Despite this promising finding, Italian authorities called a halt to further exploration in 2012. Restorers protested the invasion of Vasari's masterpiece. They also didn't believe Seracini's theory. As a result, the holes were filled in, and the scaffolding was taken down. So, is the lost da Vinci lost for good? Both Seracini and Yoder hope not. "I think it's likely that there is at least part of Leonardo's fresco somewhere in the room," says Yoder. "But given the technology we're limited to, we could easily miss it by a few inches, and then the world would never know."

1. **READING CHECK** What does Seracini think is hidden behind Vasari's fresco?

2. **ANALYZE CAUSE AND EFFECT** What event brought the search to a halt?

3. **FORM AND SUPPORT OPINIONS** Do you think the search for the lost da Vinci should continue? Explain why or why not.

PLAN

OBJECTIVE

Describe the efforts of researchers to find a long-lost painting by Leonardo da Vinci.

Dave Yoder was part of a team that searched in Florence for a lost painting by Leonardo da Vinci. Lesson 1.6 describes Yoder's role as photographer and the team's findings.

CRITICAL THINKING SKILLS FOR LESSON 1.6

- Identify Main Ideas and Details
- Monitor Comprehension
- Analyze Cause and Effect
- Form and Support Opinions
- Identify
- Summarize
- Evaluate

BACKGROUND FOR THE TEACHER

Dave Yoder is a National Geographic photographer. He was born in Indiana but grew up in Tanzania in Africa, where he kept pet mongooses and monkeys. Yoder is based in Milan, Italy. In 2006, he read about the possibility of a lost Leonardo painting behind another in Florence's Palazzo Vecchio. Two years later, he suggested to a reporter that they work together on a story about the lost da Vinci painting.

ESSENTIAL QUESTION

How did new ways of thinking transform European culture?

DIGITAL RESOURCES myNGconnect.com

TEACHER RESOURCES & ASSESSMENT

 Reading and Note-Taking   **Vocabulary Practice**   **Section 1 Quiz**

STUDENT RESOURCES

 NG Chapter Gallery

INTRODUCE & ENGAGE

K-W-L CHART

Provide each student with a K-W-L Chart. Have students brainstorm what they know about Leonardo's paintings. Then ask them to write questions that they would like to have answered as they learn about a painting by Leonardo that is thought to be missing. Tell students they will learn about Italian engineer Mauruzio Seracini's theory of what happened to the painting. Students also will learn how Seracini and his team, including photographer Dave Yoder, searched for the lost Leonardo painting. Allow time at the end of the lesson for students to fill in their charts with the information they have learned. **0:05** minutes

TEACH

GUIDED DISCUSSION

1. **Identify** Where did Leonardo paint the fresco *The Battle of Anghiari?* (*on the wall of a room in the Palazzo Vecchio, the town hall of Florence*)

2. **Summarize** Why was an endoscope used to examine the area behind Vasari's painting? (*Seracini used the endoscope to examine the wall behind the Vasari painting.*)

EVALUATE

Expand on the third "Review & Assess" question in the lesson by pairing students and having them complete a Decision Matrix such as the one below. After pairs have completed their matrix, have them share their final decision and reasoning behind it with the rest of the class. **0:15** minutes

Choice	
Pros	Cons
Decision	

ACTIVE OPTIONS

NG Learning Framework: Learn More About the Painting

ATTITUDE: Curiosity
KNOWLEDGE: Our Human Story

Have students review the information about National Geographic photographer Dave Yoder. Then have them do research about

The Battle of Anghiari. **ASK:** Why do some people think it is important to find Leonardo's lost painting? What can people learn about the Renaissance from studying the art of the time? **0:10** minutes

On Your Feet: Fishbowl Have students form an inner and outer circle, both facing the center. Use a Fishbowl strategy to have them pose questions and take notes about the mystery of Leonardo's lost fresco. Then have students switch places to pose questions and take notes about the search by Maurizio Seracini and his team for the long-lost painting. **0:10** minutes

DIFFERENTIATE

INCLUSION

Complete Cloze Statements Provide copies of these cloze statements for students to complete during or after reading.

Legend has it that Giorgio Vasari built a wall over Leonardo's _____, *The Battle of Anghiari.* He painted his own _____ scene on top of the wall. Maurizio Seracini used an instrument called an _____ to explore the painting. Italian authorities called a _____ to exploration.

ENGLISH LANGUAGE LEARNERS

Identify Main Ideas and Details Have students form two groups. Give each group a piece of construction paper or a flip chart with the main idea of the lesson written on it: *Researchers are trying to find a long-lost painting by Leonardo da Vinci.* Ask each group to list as many details from the lesson as they can to support the main idea. They should write their details on the flip chart or construction paper. Then have the two groups compare their lists.

Press **(mt)** *in the Student eEdition for modified text.*
See the Chapter Planner for more strategies for differentiation.

REVIEW & ASSESS

ANSWERS

1. He thinks a lost fresco painted by Leonardo da Vinci is hidden behind Vasari's fresco.

2. The use of invasive methods to search for the lost painting brought the search to a halt.

3. Answers will vary. Some students may say that the search should continue because any means necessary should be undertaken to find a painting by Leonardo. Other students may say that Vasari's own painting is a masterpiece and should not be sacrificed to the search.

The Renaissance Moves North

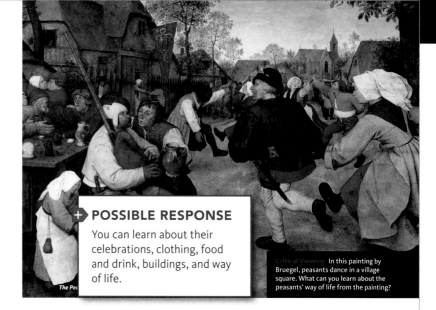

You've heard about the wonders in Italy, but you still can't believe your eyes and ears. In Florence, you marvel at the lifelike, muscular statue of David. You stop on the street in Rome to listen to people discuss the limitless possibility of the individual. In Milan, you gaze at *The Last Supper* and admire its depth and emotional power. You can't wait to get back home to northern Europe and tell everyone what you've seen and heard.

MAIN IDEA

Renaissance ideas spread from Italy and influenced art and literature across northern Europe.

ARTISTIC STYLES

Great ideas cannot be contained. This was true even in the 1400s and 1500s. In time, Italian Renaissance ideas began to influence northern Europe. Trade and the growth of cities spread the ideas to countries such as France, Belgium, the Netherlands, Germany, Spain, and England.

Artists from these countries visited Italy's cities to soak up their rebirth of culture firsthand. Powerful rulers in countries like France and England brought Italian artists to their courts. The kings and queens became the artists' patrons and paid them to create works that became a source of national pride.

While northern European artists were inspired by the Italian Renaissance, many put their own spin on artistic styles. For instance, instead of focusing on classical subjects, artists of the Northern Renaissance often painted scenes of everyday life. A Flemish artist named Pieter Bruegel (BROY-guhl) the Elder demonstrated this style. (*Flemish* refers to people from a region called Flanders, which is in present-day Belgium.) As the painting on the opposite page illustrates, Bruegel often depicted the lives of peasants with remarkable realism.

Another Flemish artist, Jan van Eyck (yahn van EHK), painted detailed, colorful portraits and images of religious subjects. The rich color in his paintings was largely due to his use of oil paint. Artists of the Italian Renaissance had mostly used water-based paints that often faded quickly. When Italian artists visited northern Europe, they eagerly adopted van Eyck's use of oils and brought the style back to Italy. The trade of ideas didn't go in only one direction.

The German artist Albrecht Dürer (DYUR-uhr) is often considered to be the greatest artist of the Northern Renaissance. Dürer had visited Italy and absorbed the styles there. He combined classical ideas, perspective, and great attention to detail to create realistic paintings and **woodcuts**, or images carved on blocks of wood.

SCHOLARS AND WRITERS

The Italian Renaissance and its humanist ideals also influenced the intellectual thinking of northern Europe. As you may recall, Petrarch was an early humanist leader of the Italian Renaissance. The Dutch scholar and priest Desiderius Erasmus (dehz-ih-DEHR-ee-uhs ir-RAZ-muhs) was a key humanist leader of the Northern Renaissance. Erasmus focused on making classical works and Christian texts more accessible to ordinary people. He also criticized some Church practices and called for reform. As you will see later in the chapter, the writings of Erasmus and others would have a big impact on the Church. Another humanist, the English statesman Thomas More, promoted free education for men and women, which was a radical idea at the time.

Unlike Erasmus and More, the best-known writer of the Northern Renaissance did not try to reform society. This author wrote tragic, comic, and historical plays filled with characters that spring to life off the page. Their passions, humor, personalities, and conflicts still capture our imagination today. Many people believe that the man who created these characters—William Shakespeare—is the greatest writer in the English language.

+ POSSIBLE RESPONSE

You can learn about their celebrations, clothing, food and drink, buildings, and way of life.

Critical Viewing In this painting by Bruegel, peasants dance in a village square. What can you learn about the peasants' way of life from the painting?

The Pec...

REVIEW & ASSESS

1. **READING CHECK** How did Renaissance ideas spread from Italy to northern Europe?

2. **COMPARE AND CONTRAST** In what ways did the artistic styles of the Northern Renaissance differ from those of the Italian Renaissance?

3. **SYNTHESIZE** Based on what you have learned about humanism, how did the scholars and writers of the Northern Renaissance reflect its ideals?

PLAN

OBJECTIVE

Describe how Renaissance ideas spread from Italy and influenced art and literature across northern Europe.

CRITICAL THINKING SKILLS FOR LESSON 2.1

- Identify Main Ideas and Details
- Monitor Comprehension
- Compare and Contrast
- Synthesize
- Summarize
- Analyze Visuals

ESSENTIAL QUESTION

How did new ways of thinking transform European culture?

Renaissance ideas spread from Italy to northern Europe. Lesson 2.1 describes how these ideas influenced art and literature as they moved north.

BACKGROUND FOR THE TEACHER

The Hundred Years' War between England and France lasted until 1453. When the war ended, cities in England, France, and other parts of Europe grew, and a wealthy merchant class developed. Prosperous businesspeople began to sponsor writers and artists. In the late 1400s, kingdoms in Italy began fighting with each other. Many Italian artists fled to northern Europe for safety. They began teaching their artistic styles and techniques to local artists. Artists from northern Europe also traveled to Italy, bringing Italian ideas back to their homelands.

DIGITAL RESOURCES myNGconnect.com

TEACHER RESOURCES & ASSESSMENT

 Reading and Note-Taking

 Vocabulary Practice

 Section 2 Quiz

STUDENT RESOURCES

 NG Chapter Gallery

INTRODUCE & ENGAGE

THINK, PAIR, SHARE

Give students a few minutes to think about the following discussion topic: *Suppose you lived in northern Europe in the 1400s. You have heard a lot about the art, literature, and cultural movements in Italy. Would you be interested in moving to Italy to learn more about what was happening there during the Renaissance? Why or why not?* Then have students choose partners and talk about the topic. Finally, allow individual students to share their ideas with the class. Tell students that, in this lesson, they will learn how Renaissance ideas spread through Europe. **0:10** minutes

TEACH

GUIDED DISCUSSION

1. **Summarize** What influence did kings and queens in France and England have on art in their countries during the Renaissance? *(They brought Italian artists to their courts and became the artists' patrons. They paid them to create works that became a source of national pride. Northern European artists were influenced by the art of the Italian Renaissance, but many began to use their own styles for the art they created.)*

2. **Compare and Contrast** How did oil paintings, such as those by van Eyck, differ from watercolor paintings done during the Italian Renaissance? *(The rich color in the paintings of van Eyck was largely due to his use of oil paint. Watercolor-based paints used during the Italian Renaissance often faded quickly.)*

ANALYZE VISUALS

Expand on the "Critical Viewing" question in the lesson by inviting students to take a closer look at the Bruegel painting. Have students work in pairs to create a list of details that contribute to the realism of the painting. Then have pairs share their details with the class. Record the most common details in a Word Web like the one below. **0:15** minutes

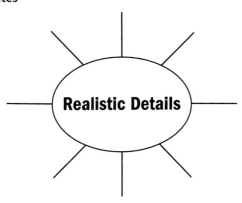

Realistic Details

ACTIVE OPTIONS

NG Learning Framework: Write a Biography

ATTITUDE: **Curiosity**
KNOWLEDGE: **Our Human Story**

Have students select a person from the Northern Renaissance that they are still curious about after reading this lesson. Instruct them to write a short biography about this person using information from the lesson and additional source material. **0:10** minutes

On Your Feet: Inside-Outside Circle Have students stand in concentric circles facing each other. Have students in the outside circle ask students in the inside circle a question about the lesson. Then have the outside circle rotate one position to the right to create new pairings. After five questions, have students switch roles and continue. **0:10** minutes

DIFFERENTIATE

STRIVING READERS

Summarize Read the lesson aloud while students follow along in their books. At the end of each paragraph, ask students to summarize what you read in a sentence. Allow them time to write the summary on their own paper.

PRE-AP

Present a Skit Have students work in pairs to write a skit. One student in each pair should play the role of a tour guide in a museum that has art produced during the Northern Renaissance. The other student should play the role of a visitor to the museum who has many questions about the art, the artists, and the period. Have students include specific information about artists and their works. Invite students to perform their skits for the class. If time permits, have students reverse roles and focus on different artists and works of art.

Press **mt** *in the Student eEdition for modified text.*

See the Chapter Planner for more strategies for differentiation.

REVIEW & ASSESS

ANSWERS

1. They spread through trade, the growth of cities, the movement of people, and the patronage of northern European kings.

2. Instead of focusing on classical subjects, artists of the Northern Renaissance often created detailed images of everyday life. Artists of the Italian Renaissance mostly used water-based paints, while many artists of the Northern Renaissance used oil paints.

3. They focused on the individual and classical works. They criticized the Church.

WILLIAM SHAKESPEARE
1564–1616

Some people don't believe William Shakespeare wrote the works credited to him, in part because he didn't have a university education. These doubters have identified other writers of the time as the authors of Shakespeare's work, but they've never been able to prove their theories. Maybe some people can't believe that a man of humble background could pen some of the greatest plays ever written. But that seems to have been exactly what happened.

Romeo and Juliet is a timeless work. Its themes can be interpreted and expressed in many ways, and the story can be set in many different eras. This film version takes place in the present day and features actors Leonardo DiCaprio and Claire Danes.

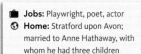

Jobs: Playwright, poet, actor

Home: Stratford upon Avon; married to Anne Hathaway, with whom he had three children

FINEST HOUR
Writing and performing for his patrons—first Queen Elizabeth I and later King James I of England

WORST MOMENT
Perhaps the death of his son, Hamnet, at age 11

DEATH
Unlike many writers of his day, he died a rich man and left most of his possessions to his daughter Susanna.

TRIVIA
Some of the writers of his time didn't respect him and referred to him as an "upstart crow."

THE BARD

The Northern Renaissance was well established in England by the time **William Shakespeare** went to seek his fortune in London around 1585. He began as an actor and apparently had a successful career. In time, he became part owner of a theatrical company known as the Lord Chamberlain's Men and began writing his own plays. By around 1594, the company was mainly performing only Shakespeare's plays, and the playwright acted in many of them himself.

The Bard—or poet—as he is often called, wrote more than 150 poems and 37 plays, including tragedies such as *Romeo and Juliet* and comedies such as *A Midsummer Night's Dream*. Shakespeare's plays have stood the test of time largely because of their insight into human nature. Shakespeare created complex characters with deep emotions and used clever wordplay to make his audience laugh or cry. The plays also reflected the Renaissance mindset.

They dealt with human life rather than religious themes. And many of the plays were based on stories and characters from classical Greek and Latin works.

THE ELIZABETHAN AGE

Most of Shakespeare's plays were written during the **Elizabethan Age**, or the reign of Queen Elizabeth I, which lasted from 1558 to 1603. Elizabeth spoke many languages, wrote poetry, and was a gifted musician. The queen supported the Globe Theater, where many of Shakespeare's plays were performed before people from all walks of life. After Elizabeth died, her cousin James I rose to the throne. James soon became the patron of Shakespeare's theatrical company, which then changed its name to the King's Men. Shakespeare wrote some of his greatest plays, including *Macbeth*, under the king's patronage.

Shakespeare retired from the theater when he was 49 and died three years later. Several years after his death, his plays were collected in a volume. The English playwright Ben Jonson, who had known Shakespeare, understood his friend's genius. In an introduction to the volume, Jonson wrote that Shakespeare "was not of an age, but for all time."

REVIEW & ASSESS

1. **READING CHECK** How did Shakespeare's plays reflect Renaissance ideas?

2. **MAKE INFERENCES** Why do you think Shakespeare's plays appealed to all people, from the very wealthy to the very poor?

3. **ANALYZE LANGUAGE USE** What does the phrase "not of an age, but for all time" suggest about Shakespeare's legacy?

Renaissance and Reformation **645**

PLAN

OBJECTIVE

Summarize the achievements of William Shakespeare and analyze the influence he has had during and after his life.

CRITICAL THINKING SKILLS FOR LESSON 2.2

- Identify Main Ideas and Details
- Monitor Comprehension
- Make Inferences
- Analyze Language Use
- Summarize
- Draw Conclusions

ESSENTIAL QUESTION

How did new ways of thinking transform European culture?

Many people consider Shakespeare to be one of the greatest playwrights of all time. Lesson 2.2 provides an overview of Shakespeare's life and accomplishments.

BACKGROUND FOR THE TEACHER

Shakespeare's plays were performed at the Globe Theater, which was built in London in 1599. The theater accommodated about 3,000 people, who ranged from the wealthy seated in the covered galleries to the "groundlings," who stood around the edges of the stage to watch the performance. Plays were performed every day of the week except Sunday. Color-coded flags were flown from the top of the theater to indicate the type of play being performed. A white flag meant a comedy, a black flag meant a tragedy, and a red flag meant a historical play.

DIGITAL RESOURCES myNGconnect.com

TEACHER RESOURCES & ASSESSMENT

 Reading and Note-Taking

 Vocabulary Practice

 Section 2 Quiz

STUDENT RESOURCES

 NG Chapter Gallery

INTRODUCE & ENGAGE

GIVE IT A TWIRL

Copy the following mnemonic on the board and tell students to use the TWIRL strategy to prepare for the lesson.

Think of a question you would like to ask about William Shakespeare.

Write your question on a piece of paper.

Interact with a partner by discussing your questions and possible answers.

Report details about your discussion with the class.

Listen politely as other students talk about their discussions.

Tell students that, in this lesson, they will learn about the life and accomplishments of William Shakespeare. **0:10** minutes

TEACH

GUIDED DISCUSSION

1. **Summarize** How did William Shakespeare begin his career? *(He began his career as an actor. Then he became part owner of a theatrical company and began writing his own plays.)*

2. **Draw Conclusions** Why were Queen Elizabeth I and King James I important to Shakespeare's life and success? *(Queen Elizabeth I supported the Globe Theater. King James was the patron of Shakespeare's theatrical company.)*

MORE INFORMATION

The Real Shakespeare? Many people have questioned whether William Shakespeare wrote the plays credited to him. During the 19th century, some literary critics suggested that another Renaissance writer, such as Christopher Marlowe or Francis Bacon, was the true author. A more recent theory surfaced during the early 20th century. Put forth by the Shakespeare Oxford Society, this argument suggests that the English aristocrat Edward de Vere, the 17th Earl of Oxford, was the true author of Shakespeare's poems and plays. The society cites such evidence as de Vere's knowledge of aristocratic society, his education, and the similarity in structure between his poetry and that of what's attributed to Shakespeare. The society also believes that Shakespeare did not have the education or literary background needed to create such masterpieces.

ACTIVE OPTIONS

Critical Viewing: NG Chapter Gallery Invite students to explore the Chapter Gallery and choose one image they feel best represents their understanding of the Northern Renaissance. Have students provide a written explanation of why they selected the image they chose. **0:10** minutes

On Your Feet: One-on-One Interviews Group students into pairs. Have both students in each pair write three questions about William Shakespeare. Then have pairs take turns posing and answering the questions. Students' answers should show an understanding of the material from the lesson. **0:10** minutes

DIFFERENTIATE

ENGLISH LANGUAGE LEARNERS

Ask Yes/No Questions Ask the following questions and have students say or write *yes* or *no* in response. Then reread the questions and ask students to correct the information in any sentence that has *no* as an answer *(2, 4, 6, 7, 8).*

1. Did Shakespeare ever work as an actor?

2. Did Shakespeare write only plays?

3. Did Queen Elizabeth I support Shakespeare?

4. Did Shakespeare write mostly about religious themes?

5. Did Shakespeare write tragedies and comedies?

6. Did Shakespeare's friend Ben Jonson write the play *Macbeth?*

7. Did Shakespeare's plays reflect a medieval mindset?

8. Did only wealthy people attend Shakespeare's plays at the Globe Theater?

PRE-AP

Do a Dramatic Reading Have students choose a Shakespearean sonnet. Have them write a short paragraph summarizing the sonnet and its meaning. Tell them to do research to find out about any unfamiliar words. Then have students do a dramatic reading of the sonnet for the class. After the reading, they should share their paragraph about the sonnet.

Press **mt** *in the Student eEdition for modified text.*

See the Chapter Planner for more strategies for differentiation.

REVIEW & ASSESS

ANSWERS

1. They dealt with human life rather than religious themes. Many of the plays were based on stories and characters from classical Greek and Latin works.

2. His plays presented realistic characters, experiences, and emotions that everyone could relate to.

3. It suggests that he was not just appreciated in the time in which he lived but also would continue to be read and admired throughout the centuries.

The Printing Press

Today, ideas can fly around the world at the push of a button or the click of a mouse. In the early days of the Renaissance, however, ideas mostly spread by word of mouth as traders and travelers made their slow way from place to place. But then a German printer came up with an invention that sped up the exchange of ideas. In many ways, it was the Internet of its day.

MAIN IDEA

The printing press greatly quickened the spread of Renaissance ideas and information.

TECHNOLOGICAL ADVANCE

The invention was the **printing press**, and it was developed around 1450 by the German blacksmith, goldsmith, publisher, and printer **Johann Gutenberg**. He developed the press by improving on the Chinese technology of woodblock printing. Chinese printers had carved text onto a wooden block, inked the block, and then pressed it onto paper. Gutenberg developed movable metal type, with a separate piece of type for each letter. Using this technology, printers could arrange the letters any way they liked. They could also use and reuse the pieces. The diagram on the opposite page shows how the printing press worked.

Around the same time, a new technique for making paper was developed, which made paper easier to manufacture. Gutenberg used this paper and his new press to print a Latin Bible in 1455. He tried to keep his printing technique a secret, but his beautiful Bible caught people's attention. Like Renaissance culture, the technology of the new printing press spread quickly.

IMPACT OF PRINTING

It's hard to overestimate the impact of the printing press. It resulted in an information explosion throughout Europe. Before the press, most printers made every copy of a book by hand, which could take a full month. In the same amount of time, Gutenberg's press could produce 500 books. These books were far cheaper than the handmade copies. They also spread ideas much more quickly.

As you know, people had become eager for knowledge by the time of the Renaissance. The printing press only fueled this demand. As more books became available, more people learned to read, and more universities were founded. In addition, libraries became better stocked with reliable information, which helped in the advancement of science, technology, and scholarship.

Many of the first printed books were religious and classical works, but a demand for less scholarly reading soon grew. In response, publishers printed poetry, plays, travel books, and histories. People also wanted to read books in their native language, instead of Latin. Remember that Dante began this trend when he wrote *The Divine Comedy* in Italian. As a result, books began to be printed in the vernacular—even the Bible. This allowed many more people to read the Bible and interpret its teachings for themselves for the first time. As you'll see in the next section, this trend would cause trouble for the Catholic Church. Soon Gutenberg's invention would be printing pamphlets that would question the authority of the pope himself.

PRINTING ON GUTENBERG'S PRESS, STEP BY STEP

4. Press The printer rolls the type box under the press and uses the handle to imprint letters onto the paper.

2. Ink Ball The printer uses the ink ball to apply an oil-based ink onto the type.

1. Type Box The printer arranges the letters in the type box.

3. Paper Holder The printer inserts paper in the holder and folds it onto the inked type.

GUTENBERG'S BIBLE
The Gutenberg Bible, as it came to be called, contained 1,286 pages with about 42 lines on each page. It was remarkable for its neat, even letters and hand-painted illustrations of nature. Gutenberg printed 200 copies of his Bible, of which about 50 survive today.

REVIEW & ASSESS

1. **READING CHECK** How did the printing press help spread information?

2. **INTEGRATE VISUALS** Based on the diagram and what you have learned about the printing press, how do you think the new invention improved printers' lives?

3. **ANALYZE CAUSE AND EFFECT** What happened once the printing press made books more widely available?

PLAN

OBJECTIVE

Describe how the printing press greatly quickened the spread of Renaissance ideas and information.

CRITICAL THINKING SKILLS FOR LESSON 2.3

- Identify Main Ideas and Details
- Monitor Comprehension
- Integrate Visuals
- Analyze Cause and Effect
- Identify
- Make Generalizations
- Make Connections

ESSENTIAL QUESTION

How did new ways of thinking transform European culture?

Gutenberg invented the printing press in 1450. Lesson 2.3 discusses how the invention of the printing press resulted in an information explosion.

BACKGROUND FOR THE TEACHER

Johann Gutenberg was born in 1468 in Mainz, Germany, and came from a wealthy family. From about 1434 to 1444, Gutenberg lived in Strassburg, where he worked as a goldsmith, did gem-cutting, and taught crafts to students. Gutenberg's invention of the printing press revolutionized the printing process. Gutenberg is also credited with the invention of a new kind of ink for his printing press. The ink had to adhere well to the metal type so it needed to be an oil-based ink. This ink was more durable than water-based inks that had previously been used.

DIGITAL RESOURCES myNGconnect.com

TEACHER RESOURCES & ASSESSMENT

 Reading and Note-Taking

 Vocabulary Practice

 Section 2 Quiz

STUDENT RESOURCES

 NG Chapter Gallery

INTRODUCE & ENGAGE

BRAINSTORM INVENTIONS

Have students work in small groups to brainstorm a list of inventions. For each invention, have them write a sentence telling how its development affected society. Have students share their ideas with the class. Tell students that, in this lesson, they will learn how Gutenberg developed the printing press and how the printing press affected the spread of ideas and information. **0:10** minutes

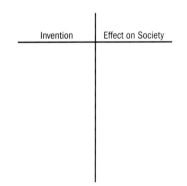

Invention | Effect on Society

TEACH

GUIDED DISCUSSION

1. **Identify** What trend did Dante start when he wrote *The Divine Comedy*? *(writing books in people's native languages)*

2. **Make Generalizations** How did printing the Bible in the vernacular affect the Catholic Church? *(It allowed people to read the Bible and interpret its teachings for themselves. The printing press even printed pamphlets that would question the authority of the pope.)*

MAKE CONNECTIONS

Lead a discussion with students to help them draw parallels between the invention of the printing press and the invention of the Internet, specifically with regard to how each invention changed society. Make a list of parallels and encourage students to add to it as they work through the rest of the chapter. **0:15** minutes

ACTIVE OPTIONS

Critical Viewing: NG Chapter Gallery Ask students to choose one image from the Chapter Gallery and become an expert on it. They should do additional research to learn all about it. Then, students should share their findings with a partner, small group, or the class. **0:10** minutes

On Your Feet: Build a Paragraph Have students form five lines. Give each group the same topic sentence: *The invention of the printing press was one of the most important technological advancements of the Renaissance.* Tell them to build a paragraph by having each student in the line add one sentence that supports the topic. Groups can present their paragraphs to the class with each student reading her or his sentence. **0:10** minutes

DIFFERENTIATE

STRIVING READERS

Write Main Idea Questions As they read the lesson, direct students to look for and take notes on what they think are its key ideas. After reading, tell them to use their notes to write five questions about these key ideas. Allow students to exchange and answer each other's questions.

GIFTED & TALENTED

Build a Social Network Have students do research to learn more about Johann Gutenberg. Then have them design a page for him on a social network site. The page can include images, quotations, and posts about daily activities. Allow students to display their pages to the class.

Press **mt** *in the Student eEdition for modified text.*

See the Chapter Planner for more strategies for differentiation.

REVIEW & ASSESS

ANSWERS

1. Books could be produced more quickly, easily, and cheaply—all of which made books and the knowledge they contained affordable and accessible to more people.

2. They probably welcomed it because the new press made their job easier and they may also have made more money since they produced more texts more quickly and cheaply.

3. More people learned to read, more universities were founded, and libraries became better stocked with reliable information.

Legacy in the Arts and Sciences

Did you know that the Renaissance influenced many modern developments? GPS technology owes a debt to the advances Renaissance scientists made in mapmaking. Studies of the human body in the 1500s paved the way for today's medical-imaging techniques. As for the arts, if you travel to almost any state capitol, you'll see a dome that resembles Brunelleschi's. The Renaissance left us a living legacy.

MAIN IDEA

Renaissance advances in the arts and sciences continue to influence thinking today.

THE ARTS AND ARCHITECTURE

As you have learned, Renaissance architects revived ancient Greek and Roman ideas to build and perfect such structures as domes, arches, and columns. These structures continue to be important elements in architecture today. Similarly, Renaissance artists' realistic portrayal of individuals and use of perspective have influenced modern and contemporary artists.

You've read about William Shakespeare, but the Renaissance also produced such literary figures as Spanish writer Miguel de Cervantes (sehr-VAHN-tez) and Italian historian Niccolò Machiavelli. In Cervantes' masterpiece, the novel *Don Quixote* (key-HOE-tay), the author used humor and insight to tell his tale. The novel has influenced other writers since its publication about 400 years ago. Machiavelli wrote a book on effective leadership called *The Prince*. The book continues to influence leaders—and would-be leaders—today.

IMPACT OF SCIENTIFIC ADVANCES

The Renaissance made its mark on the sciences, too. Some historians say that Gutenberg's printing press is the greatest invention of the past 1,000 years—more significant than the computer or the Internet. The printing press made it possible for people all around the world to share, study, and challenge others' ideas.

In mathematics, Renaissance scholars came up with the idea of using letters in algebraic equations; for example, $x + y = 5$. Renaissance thinkers also became interested in the natural world. Some scientists learned about the metals and minerals that make up Earth's surface. Others studied astronomy and gained new understanding of the wider universe and Earth's place in it.

You've learned about Leonardo da Vinci's anatomical sketches. In 1543, the Belgian physician Andreas Vesalius (vuh-SAHL-ee-us) dissected the bodies of executed criminals and published his findings. As a result of his accurate drawings of the human body, anatomy became a scientific discipline.

Scientific ideas were also applied to **cartography**, or mapmaking, during the Renaissance. Using these new ideas, exploration by men such as Christopher Columbus continued to improve the accuracy of maps. Exploration also opened up new lands to colonization and settlement. The legacy of these events is still felt today.

Statue of Martin Luther King, Jr., at his memorial

Drawing of the skull by Leonardo

Michelangelo's *David*

THEN AND NOW

These images demonstrate the legacy of the Renaissance. Find each work created during the Renaissance and compare it to its modern counterpart. What similarities and differences do you see in each pair?

Dome of St. Peter's Basilica in Rome

X-ray of the skull

Capitol Building dome in Washington, D.C.

REVIEW & ASSESS

1. **READING CHECK** What were some of the important scientific advances made during the Renaissance?

2. **COMPARE AND CONTRAST** In what way was the impact of Gutenberg's printing press similar to that of the Internet?

3. **MAKE CONNECTIONS** How have Renaissance advances in cartography affected modern life?

PLAN

OBJECTIVE

Discuss how Renaissance advances in the arts and sciences continue to influence thinking today.

CRITICAL THINKING SKILLS FOR LESSON 2.4

- Identify Main Ideas and Details
- Monitor Comprehension
- Compare and Contrast
- Make Connections
- Identify
- Form and Support Opinions
- Analyze Visuals

ESSENTIAL QUESTION

How did new ways of thinking transform European culture?

During the Renaissance, many advances were made in the arts and sciences. Lesson 2.4 discusses how many of these advances continue to influence thinking today.

BACKGROUND FOR THE TEACHER

Some Renaissance scientists studied ancient math texts and expanded on the ideas in them. They developed many of the math symbols that people use today. For example, they developed the symbols for positive and negative numbers as well as the square root symbol. They also developed mathematical formulas that helped architects and engineers design stronger buildings. During the Renaissance, scientists also made advances in making clocks that could keep time more accurately than before.

DIGITAL RESOURCES myNGconnect.com

TEACHER RESOURCES & ASSESSMENT

 Reading and Note-Taking

 Vocabulary Practice

 Section 2 Quiz

STUDENT RESOURCES

 NG Chapter Gallery

INTRODUCE & ENGAGE

TEAM WORD WEBBING

Organize students into teams of four and give each team a large sheet of paper with the word *Renaissance* in the center. Provide each student with a different colored marker. Encourage students to write words or phrases about the Renaissance on the paper. Prompt students to rotate the paper clockwise every 60 seconds. After students have written on all four sides of the paper, have a spokesperson from each team summarize what they listed about the Renaissance. Tell students that this lesson deals with Renaissance advances in the arts and sciences that continue to influence people today. **0:10** minutes

TEACH

GUIDED DISCUSSION

1. **Identify** Who were some of the important literary figures during the Renaissance? *(William Shakespeare, Miguel de Cervantes, Niccolò Machiavelli)*

2. **Form and Support Opinions** Do you agree with the idea that Gutenberg's printing press is the greatest invention of the past 1,000 years? Explain your reasoning. *(Possible responses: Yes— because it allowed people all around the world to share, study, and challenge others' ideas, which had never been done before; No—the Internet had an even greater impact in terms of connecting the world and making communication possible.)*

ANALYZE VISUALS

Expand on the question under the "Then and Now" feature by having students work in pairs to choose one of the sets of images and discuss their similarities and differences. Then ask students to come up with additional examples of contemporary examples of the influence of the Renaissance. **0:15** minutes

ACTIVE OPTIONS

NG Learning Framework: Examine Cartography

ATTITUDES: **Curiosity, Responsibility**
KNOWLEDGE: **Our Living Planet**

Have students reread the last paragraph in the lesson on cartography. **ASK:** How did scientific exploration impact cartography? In what ways have accurate maps been important throughout history? How has cartography changed since the Renaissance? What are some examples of times when accurate maps helped you? **0:10** minutes

On Your Feet: Quiz Each Other Divide the class into an even number of groups. Have each group create a matching quiz about important people, events, and terms from the Renaissance. Then have pairs of students exchange papers, take the quizzes, and then check each other's answers. **0:10** minutes

DIFFERENTIATE

STRIVING READERS

Use a Detail Web Have students summarize information using a Detail Web. Provide the following phrase for the center circle: Advances in Arts and Sciences. Have students complete the web using details from the lesson.

Advances in Arts and Sciences

GIFTED & TALENTED

Create a Multimedia Presentation Have students choose a research topic about advances in the arts or sciences during the Renaissance. Then have them create a multimedia presentation on it. Ask students to use photos and art to support their presentation.

Press **mt** in the Student eEdition for modified text.

See the Chapter Planner for more strategies for differentiation.

REVIEW & ASSESS

ANSWERS

1. Important advances were made in the development of the printing press and the study of Earth, anatomy, and cartography.

2. Like the Internet, the printing press made the diffusion of information much faster and easier.

3. Renaissance advancements in cartography made settlement in new lands possible and led to the development of GPS.

3.1

Protests
Against the
Catholic Church

Thanks to Gutenberg's new printing press, the printers quickly finish making copies of the pamphlet a customer brought in. But they're a bit nervous about its contents. The pamphlet, by Martin Luther, contains a list of items criticizing the Church. The printers are used to seeing old ideas challenged, but this list seems to go too far.

MAIN IDEA

In the 1500s, Martin Luther's protests against the Roman Catholic Church led to the Reformation.

HENRY VIII

King Henry VIII of England formed a new branch of Protestantism when the Church refused to grant him a divorce. The king wanted to divorce and marry a woman he hoped would give him a son.

MARTIN LUTHER

As you know, some people had begun to criticize the Church and call for reforms during the Renaissance. In the last chapter, you also learned that the Church became weaker as the authority of kings increased. In 1305, a powerful French king moved the center of the Church from Rome to Avignon (ah-veen-YOHN), in France, and appointed a French pope. Following a struggle for power, two popes were elected in 1378: one in Rome and the other in Avignon. This split in the Church

is known as the **Great Schism** (schism means "split"). Although the Church was unified once again in 1417 and Rome restored as the center of Christianity, the Church had been weakened even further.

The Church needed money to regain its former strength, but some people believed the Church used questionable practices to obtain it. For example, Church officials sold **indulgences**, which relaxed the punishment for a sin. However, sometimes the officials sold an indulgence as forgiveness for a sin, with no punishment imposed. Many people, though, believed that only God could forgive sins. People also objected to paying one-tenth of their income to the Church every year in taxes.

A German monk named **Martin Luther** actively protested against these practices. On October 31, 1517, Luther nailed a list of protests, known as the 95 Theses, to a church door in Wittenberg, Germany. The list included the idea that the Bible was the only source of religious truth and that priests were not needed to interpret its words. Luther further suggested that salvation came through faith in Christ alone. Those who supported Luther's ideas would be called **Protestants**, which comes from the word protest. The reform movement Luther began is known as the **Reformation**.

PROTESTANTISM GROWS

After Luther made the 95 Theses public, Pope Leo X demanded that the monk take back his statements. Luther refused and was excommunicated, or cut off, from the Church. Nevertheless, pamphlets containing Luther's theses were soon printed, and his ideas spread rapidly.

SPREAD OF PROTESTANTISM, 1500s

In response, peasants throughout Europe used Luther's teachings to stage revolts for better wages and living conditions.

Luther's teachings also had a great impact on Christianity. As people interpreted the Bible for themselves, their differing beliefs led to the development of many branches, or **denominations**, of Protestant religions. One branch, called Lutheranism, was inspired by Luther's

teachings. Another, called Calvinism, was led by a French reformer named John Calvin who believed that God chose people for salvation. They could do nothing to earn it. A third branch, called Anglicanism or the Church of England, was begun in England by King Henry VIII. Protestantism would have a lasting impact on Europe. But in the meantime, the Catholic Church began to look for ways to stop its spread.

REVIEW & ASSESS

1. **READING CHECK** What Church practices did Martin Luther protest against?

2. **INTERPRET MAPS** How did the spread of the Lutheran and Calvinist branches of Protestantism differ from that of the Anglican branch?

3. **IDENTIFY MAIN IDEAS** Why did many branches of Protestantism develop?

PLAN

OBJECTIVE

Describe how Martin Luther's protests against the Roman Catholic Church in the 1500s led to the Reformation.

CRITICAL THINKING SKILLS FOR LESSON 3.1

- Identify Main Ideas and Details
- Monitor Comprehension
- Interpret Maps
- Summarize
- Explain
- Synthesize

ESSENTIAL QUESTION

How did new ways of thinking transform European culture?

Martin Luther protested against many practices of the Roman Catholic Church. Lesson 3.1 discusses how his protests led to the Reformation.

BACKGROUND FOR THE TEACHER

In 1520, Martin Luther published "To the Christian Nobility of the German Nation Concerning the Reformation of the Christian Commonwealth." In this piece, he called for a national German Church. He also translated both the New Testament and the Old Testament into German. He believed that the Bible contained all of God's teachings. For that reason, he thought it was important that people be able to read the Bible in their own language.

DIGITAL RESOURCES myNGconnect.com

TEACHER RESOURCES & ASSESSMENT

 Reading and Note-Taking

 Vocabulary Practice

 Section 3 Quiz

STUDENT RESOURCES

 Biography

INTRODUCE & ENGAGE

HOLD A PANEL DISCUSSION

Have students work in groups of five to conduct a panel discussion. Pose the following questions: *What characteristics would you expect a reformer to have? Which, if any, of these characteristics are the most important and why?* Then have students name reformers throughout history. List the names of the reformers on the board. Tell students that, in this lesson, they will learn about Martin Luther, whose protests led to a reform movement. **0:10** minutes

TEACH

GUIDED DISCUSSION

1. **Summarize** What led to the Great Schism? (*In 1305, a French king moved the center of the Church from Rome to Avignon in France and appointed a French pope. Following a struggle for power, two popes were elected: one in Rome and the other in Avignon. This split in the Church is known as the Great Schism.*)

2. **Explain** What were Luther's 95 Theses? (*They were a list of protests against the Catholic Church that Luther nailed to a church door in Wittenberg, Germany.*)

SYNTHESIZE

Have students study the map of the spread of Protestantism and ask them to note which areas of Europe were not affected by the spread of Protestantism. (*Ireland, Spain, Italian States, Papal States, Ottoman Empire*) As a class, come up with a list of reasons why these areas were not affected. Encourage students to draw upon what they learned in earlier chapters when thinking of reasons. **0:15** minutes

ACTIVE OPTIONS

Active History: Map the Protestant Reformation Extend the lesson by using either the PDF or Whiteboard version of the activity. These activities take a deeper look at a topic from, or related to, the lesson. Explore the activities as a class, turn them into group assignments, or even assign them individually. **0:10** minutes

On Your Feet: Half and Half Divide the class in half. Ask one half to discuss the influence of the Renaissance on European culture and the other half to discuss the influence of the Reformation. Then have each team present a report on their topic with visuals. For example, the Renaissance team might use art in their presentation. **0:10** minutes

DIFFERENTIATE

ENGLISH LANGUAGE LEARNERS

Use Sentence Stems Before reading, provide students with the sentence stems listed below. Call on volunteers to read the stems aloud and explain any unfamiliar vocabulary. After reading, have students complete the stems in writing and compare completed sentences with a partner.

1. Two popes were elected in 1305, one in Avignon and one in _____.

2. To forgive a person's sin, the Church sold _____.

3. People who supported Luther's ideas were called _____.

4. The reform movement Luther began was called the _____.

5. Luther was cut off from the Catholic Church, or _____.

6. Anglicanism was begun in England by _____.

PRE-AP

Research and Report Remind students that there have been many famous reformers in history. Some examples are Thomas Jefferson, Martin Luther King, Rosa Parks, and Florence Nightingale. Have students do research and then write a report about a reformer of their choice. Encourage students to include images in their reports. Invite students to present their reports to the class.

Press **mt** *in the Student eEdition for modified text.*

See the Chapter Planner for more strategies for differentiation.

REVIEW & ASSESS

ANSWERS

1. Luther protested against the sale of indulgences and the lavish lifestyle of the pope. Luther also believed that the Bible was the only source of religious truth and that priests were not needed to interpret its words. Luther further suggested that salvation came through faith in Christ alone.

2. The Lutheran and Calvinist branches of Protestantism spread widely throughout Europe, whereas the Anglican branch was confined to England.

3. Many branches developed because people interpreted the Bible differently and had different beliefs.

DOCUMENT-BASED QUESTION
Conflict in the Church

Martin Luther didn't set out to create chaos within the Catholic Church. He nailed his 95 Theses onto the church door to engage scholars at the University of Wittenberg in debate. But Luther hadn't counted on the reaction his ideas would inspire. Within two months, copies of the theses had spread throughout Europe. Within three years, the pope had written a letter condemning the theses. Meanwhile, Luther's followers supported the theses by protesting certain Church practices.

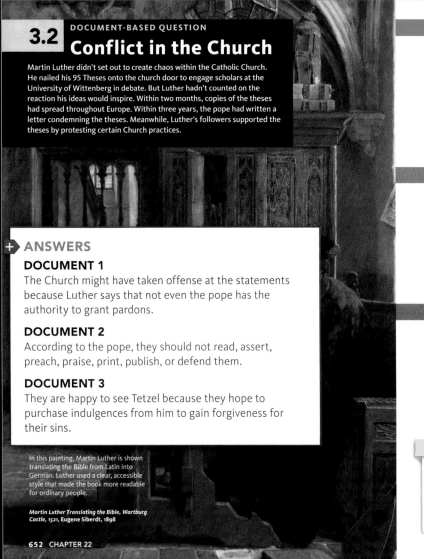

In this painting, Martin Luther is shown translating the Bible from Latin into German. Luther used a clear, accessible style that made the book more readable for ordinary people.

Martin Luther Translating the Bible, Wartburg Castle, 1521, Eugene Siberdt, 1898

+ ANSWERS

DOCUMENT 1
The Church might have taken offense at the statements because Luther says that not even the pope has the authority to grant pardons.

DOCUMENT 2
According to the pope, they should not read, assert, preach, praise, print, publish, or defend them.

DOCUMENT 3
They are happy to see Tetzel because they hope to purchase indulgences from him to gain forgiveness for their sins.

DOCUMENT ONE
Primary Source: Pamphlet

from the 95 Theses
In his 95 Theses, Luther expresses his criticism of the Church in statements that sum up his interpretation of teaching found in the Bible. In the following two theses, Luther presents his idea that letters of pardon, or indulgences, do not make people better and cannot ensure salvation.

CONSTRUCTED RESPONSE Why might the Church have taken offense at these statements?

> 44. . . . Love grows by works of love, and man becomes better; but by pardons man does not grow better, only more free from penalty.
>
> 52. The assurance of salvation by letters of pardon is vain [useless], even though . . . the pope himself were to stake his soul upon it.

DOCUMENT TWO
Primary Source: Letter

from the Papal Bull of Pope Leo X
In 1520, Pope Leo X issued a papal bull, or official letter, giving Luther 60 days to take back his theses. In the following excerpt from the bull, Leo condemns Luther's ideas and tells followers of Catholicism ("the faithful") how to handle them.

CONSTRUCTED RESPONSE According to the pope, how should Catholics deal with Luther's ideas?

> With the advice and consent of these our venerable [respected] brothers, . . . we condemn, reprobate [disapprove], and reject completely each of these theses. . . . We forbid each and every one of the faithful . . . to read, assert, preach, praise, print, publish, or defend them.

DOCUMENT THREE
Primary Source: Leaflet

Leaflet Against Johann Tetzel
Luther's followers distributed this leaflet to protest against the practices of Johann Tetzel, a monk who sold indulgences. Tetzel is said to have written the last two lines in the leaflet: "As soon as gold in the cashbox rings, The rescued soul to heaven springs."

CONSTRUCTED RESPONSE Why do you think the people shown in the leaflet are happy to see Tetzel?

SYNTHESIZE & WRITE

1. **REVIEW** Review what you have learned about the Reformation and protests against the Catholic Church.

2. **RECALL** On your own paper, write down the main idea expressed in each document.

3. **CONSTRUCT** Write a topic sentence that answers this question: How did the Church and Luther's followers react to the 95 Theses?

4. **WRITE** Using evidence from the documents, write a short paragraph to support your answer to the question in Step 3.

PLAN

OBJECTIVE

Synthesize information about the conflict in the Catholic Church during the Reformation from primary source documents.

CRITICAL THINKING SKILLS FOR LESSON 3.2

- Synthesize
- Identify
- Summarize
- Monitor Comprehension
- Evaluate

ESSENTIAL QUESTION

How did new ways of thinking transform European culture?

The excommunication of Martin Luther after he wrote his 95 Theses had a strong impact on Christianity. Lesson 3.2 provides several interpretations of this event from primary sources.

BACKGROUND FOR THE TEACHER

Pope Leo X was born Giovanni di Lorenzo de Medici. He was the son of Lorenzo the Magnificent, who was the ruler of Florence during the Italian Renaissance. Pope Leo X was always looking for new means to raise money. Following the example of his predecessor, Pope Julius II, Pope Leo X granted indulgences to anyone who contributed money toward the construction of St. Peter's Basilica in Rome. It was not until early 1517 that Johann Tetzel, a Dominican monk, began preaching about indulgences in Germany. In response to this preaching, Martin Luther wrote his 95 Theses.

TEACHER RESOURCES & ASSESSMENT

 Reading and Note-Taking

 Vocabulary Practice

 Section 3 Quiz

STUDENT RESOURCES

 NG Chapter Gallery

INTRODUCE & ENGAGE

PREPARE FOR THE DOCUMENT-BASED QUESTION

Before students start on the activity, briefly preview the three documents. Remind students that a constructed response requires full explanations in complete sentences. Emphasize that students should use their knowledge of protests against the Catholic Church in the 1500s in addition to the information in the documents. **0:05** minutes

TEACH

GUIDED DISCUSSION

1. **Identify** For what reason did Luther write his 95 Theses? *(to sum up his interpretation of teaching found in the Bible; to present his idea that indulgences cannot ensure salvation)*

2. **Summarize** What directive did Pope Leo X give to Martin Luther in his papal bull of 1520? *(to take back his theses within 60 days)*

3. **Monitor Comprehension** What do the last two lines in the leaflet against Tetzel mean? *(that as soon as people paid money for indulgences, they were promised salvation)*

EVALUATE

After students have completed the "Synthesize & Write" activity, allow time for them to exchange paragraphs and read and comment on the work of their peers. Guidelines for comments should be established prior to this activity so that feedback is constructive and encouraging in nature. **0:15** minutes

ACTIVE OPTIONS

Critical Viewing: NG Chapter Gallery Have students explore the Chapter Gallery and choose two of the items to compare and contrast, either in written form or verbally with a partner. Ask questions that will inspire this process, such as: How are these images alike? How are they different? Why did you select these two items? How do they relate in history? **0:10** minutes

On Your Feet: Three Options Label three locations in the room with the name of one of the documents featured in the lesson. Have students reread the lesson and walk to the corner of the room with the document that best helped support their understanding or sharpened their interest in the protests against the Church in the 1500s and the Reformation that followed. Have students who chose the same document discuss why they made their selection. Then have volunteers from each group explain what their document is and offer some of the group's reasons for choosing that one. **0:10** minutes

DIFFERENTIATE

INCLUSION

Work in Pairs If some students have disabilities, consider pairing them with other students who can read the documents aloud to them. You may also want to give students the option of recording their responses.

PRE-AP

Write an Essay Have students write an essay explaining the significance of the papal bull written by Pope Leo X in 1520. Ask them to include information about the response of Martin Luther and his followers to the papal bull. Ask them to infer how many other people in Europe may have responded to the papal bull. Encourage students to include ideas about how the papal bull may have influenced the rise of Protestant religions throughout Europe.

Press **mt** *in the Student eEdition for modified text.*

See the Chapter Planner for more strategies for differentiation.

SYNTHESIZE & WRITE

ANSWERS

1. Responses will vary.

2. Responses will vary.

3. Possible response: The Church and Luther's followers had conflicting reactions to the publication of the 95 Theses.

4. Students' paragraphs should include their topic sentence from Step 3 and provide several details from the documents to support the sentence.

The **Counter Reformation**

After the Reformation, the Catholic Church was down but certainly not out. Millions of faithful followers remained loyal. They continued to recognize the pope as their leader and trusted their priests' interpretation of the Bible. But Church officials knew that to keep their members and bring Protestants back to the fold, they had to stop the spread of Protestantism. To do that, they had to make some changes.

MAIN IDEA

Reforms and a new religious order established during the Counter Reformation helped strengthen Catholicism.

REFORM FROM WITHIN

The changes the Catholic Church made were part of a movement called the Catholic Reformation—sometimes also called the **Counter Reformation**. (In this use of the word, *counter* means "against.") A meeting of Church officials and scholars summoned by the pope in 1545 was a key element of the movement.

The meeting, which came to be known as the **Council of Trent**, met for 26 sessions over 18 years, mostly in the northern Italian

city of Trent. During that time, the council worked to define Catholic beliefs and practices and determine how the Church needed to change. Council members also sought to clarify how Catholicism differed from Protestantism. For example, while Protestants believed that the Bible could be understood directly by individuals, the Church taught that it must be interpreted and understood in light of tradition.

To make sure Catholics didn't stray from their faith, the Church also established a Roman Inquisition. Like the Spanish Inquisition discussed in the previous chapter, the Roman Inquisition used harsh methods, including torture, to force a confession and punish **heresy**, or a denial of Church teachings. Protestants were, of course, considered to be guilty of heresy.

In addition, Church officials created a list of books they objected to. Followers of Catholicism were forbidden to read the books, which included Bibles in the vernacular as well as most anything written by Luther, Calvin, and Erasmus. The books were collected by Church clergy and burned.

On the other hand, the Church also applied gentler methods to broaden its appeal. It built new, larger churches to hold more worshippers. In addition, priests sometimes delivered sermons in the vernacular.

A NEW RELIGIOUS ORDER

The struggle to revive Catholicism was aided by the development of a new religious order called the Society of Jesus, whose followers were known as **Jesuits** (JEHZH-oo-ihts). A former Spanish knight named Ignatius of Loyola formed the order, and he insisted on strict obedience.

Beginning in 1540, Ignatius commanded his followers as their "Superior General," and the Jesuits carried out their duties with great discipline. They also took vows of poverty and obedience, promising to fight "for the greater glory of God."

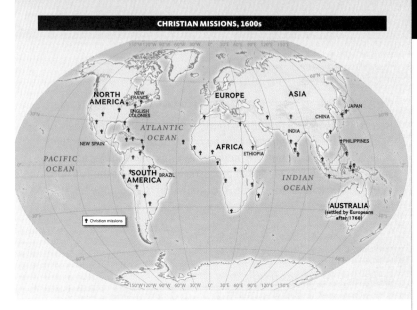

CHRISTIAN MISSIONS, 1600s

From the start, the Jesuits' purpose was to obey the pope and go wherever he thought they were most needed. In time, this meant establishing schools and universities throughout Europe and the world. The Jesuits provided a good education to thousands of men and inspired many to dedicate their lives to the Church.

The Jesuits also worked as **missionaries** by spreading Catholicism to people in Africa, Asia, and the Americas.

To prepare for this task and enable them to communicate their faith to people in other parts of the world, Jesuit priests studied many different languages.

Through their support of the Counter Reformation, the Jesuits and other Catholic reformers helped revitalize the Church. By the end of the 1500s, the Church had regained much of its power. The Church was ready to play an important role in the coming century.

REVIEW & ASSESS

1. **READING CHECK** What were some of the methods used during the Counter Reformation to stop the spread of Protestantism?

2. **MAKE INFERENCES** Why do you think the Church burned certain books?

3. **DRAW CONCLUSIONS** Why was it important to the Catholic Church to establish its own schools and universities?

PLAN

OBJECTIVE

Describe how reforms and a new religious order established during the Counter Reformation helped strengthen Catholicism.

CRITICAL THINKING SKILLS FOR LESSON 3.3

- Identify Main Ideas and Details
- Monitor Comprehension
- Make Inferences
- Draw Conclusions
- Compare and Contrast
- Describe
- Interpret Maps

ESSENTIAL QUESTION

How did new ways of thinking transform European culture?

During the Counter Reformation, the Catholic Church made many changes in order to keep its members. Lesson 3.2 discusses some of these changes and describes how a new religious order helped strengthen the Church.

BACKGROUND FOR THE TEACHER

Ignatius of Loyola was one of the most influential figures in the Counter Reformation in the 1500s. Ignatius was a soldier. While in battle, he was hit by a cannonball that fractured one leg and wounded the other. During his long convalescence, Ignatius read about Jesus and the saints. He decided to emulate the austere lives of the saints to atone for his sins and dedicate his life to God. Ignatius founded the Jesuits as a religious order devoted to serving the pope and the Catholic Church. The Jesuits became leaders of the Counter Reformation.

DIGITAL RESOURCES myNGconnect.com

TEACHER RESOURCES & ASSESSMENT

 Reading and Note-Taking　 **Vocabulary Practice**　 **Section 3 Quiz**

STUDENT RESOURCES

 NG Chapter Gallery

ACTIVATE PRIOR KNOWLEDGE

Remind students that a prefix is a word part placed before a base word that usually changes the meaning of the base word. Discuss what students know about the meaning of the prefix *counter-*. Have students work in small groups to name as many words as they can with the prefix *counter-*. Students may use dictionaries to find words. List the words on the board. Invite students to explain how the prefix affects the meaning of each base word. Tell students that *counter* in the term *Counter Reformation* serves as a prefix. Students will learn about the Counter Reformation and how it strengthened the Catholic Church in this lesson. **0:10** minutes

GUIDED DISCUSSION

1. **Compare and Contrast** How did Catholic and Protestant beliefs about the Bible differ? *(Catholics believed that the Bible should be interpreted and understood in light of Catholic tradition. Protestants believed that the Bible could be understood directly by individuals.)*

2. **Describe** How did the Jesuits prepare to communicate their faith to people all over the world? *(They studied many different languages.)*

INTERPRET MAPS

Have students study the map of Christian missions. Then have them create a list of the continents that had Christian missions in the 1600s. *(North America, South America, Africa, and Asia)* **ASK:** What can you conclude about the success of the Jesuit missionaries? *(They were very successful in establishing missions all over the non-European world.)* **0:15** minutes

ACTIVE OPTIONS

Critical Viewing: NG Chapter Gallery Have students examine the contents of the Chapter Gallery. Then invite them to brainstorm additional images they believe would fit within the gallery. Have them write a description of these additional images and provide an explanation of why they would fit. Then instruct them to do online research to find examples of actual images they would like to add to the gallery. **0:10** minutes

On Your Feet: Card Responses Have half the class write 15 true-false or yes-no questions based on the lesson. Have the other half create answer cards, writing "True" or "Yes" on one side of the cards and "False" or "No" on the other side. Students from the question group should take turns asking their questions. Students from the answer group should hold up their cards, showing the correct answer. Have students keep track of their correct answers. **0:10** minutes

INCLUSION

Use Echo Reading Pair students so that there is a proficient reader in each pair. Have the proficient reader read aloud the Main Idea statement at the beginning of the lesson. Have the other student "echo" the same statement in his or her own words.

PRE-AP

Debate an Issue Have students work in small groups. Ask students to imagine that they are debating an issue at a session of the Council of Trent. Half of the students in each group should take the position that the Catholic Church should change in order to bring Protestants back to the Church. The others in each group should take the position that the Catholic Church is fine as it is and does not need to change. Ask each group to take notes about their meeting and share their notes with the class.

Press (**mt**) *in the Student eEdition for modified text.*

See the Chapter Planner for more strategies for differentiation.

ANSWERS

1. The Council of Trent was established to define Catholic beliefs and practices and determine how the Church needed to change. The Roman Inquisition forced confessions and punished heresy. Church officials created a list of forbidden books. The Jesuits established schools and universities and conducted missionary work to spread Catholicism.

2. Church officials didn't want Catholics to read the books and be swayed by them. They felt the very existence of the books was an affront to God.

3. The Church hoped to draw Catholics to its schools and universities where they would develop a new pride and attachment to the faith. The Church may also have hoped to attract new followers.

3.4

The Impact of the Reformation

The Reformation resulted in a cultural shift. Once people could interpret the Bible for themselves, they formed new ideas about the Christian religion. More Protestant denominations formed as differences in beliefs developed, and new Protestant churches sprang up. Europe would never be the same.

MAIN IDEA

The Reformation had a long-lasting religious, social, and political impact on Europe.

RELIGIOUS EFFECTS

Protestantism flourished. Like Catholics, Protestants founded universities and parish schools to teach their beliefs and gain new followers. As a result, because both Protestants and Catholics wanted to read the Bible, the Reformation increased literacy.

In England, many Anglicans learned to read the Bible but not in the vernacular. They followed the Catholic belief that prohibited reading the Bible in translation. However, reformer William Tyndale believed that Anglicans should reject all Catholic beliefs and practices and so began to prepare an English translation of the New Testament.

Tyndale completed his work in Germany. In time, however, Catholic officials there arrested and executed him for his beliefs.

POLITICAL EFFECTS

The Reformation had both positive and negative political effects. On the positive side, the Reformation influenced the development of democracy and federalism. Protestants who formed a church sometimes governed it themselves. This practice would later encourage religious groups immigrating to the English colonies to form a government with equal and fair laws—an early step toward democracy. In addition, Calvinist churches sometimes allowed church members to share power with the clergy. This practice represented an early form of federalism in which power is shared, like that between a national government and state governments.

On the negative side, the Reformation led to widespread warfare in Europe. In the years after Luther published the 95 Theses, religious wars erupted within countries and between them. The Thirty Years' War, for example, started as a conflict between Catholics and Protestants in Central Europe. The war, which lasted from 1618 to 1648, devastated the German states, killing an estimated seven million people.

Although the Catholic Church had partly recovered from the Reformation, its power in Europe would come to be challenged by powerful kings. These kings worked to bring all of the people within their territory under a unified rule. As a result, powerful modern **nation-states** began to emerge, with their own independent governments and populations united by a shared culture, language, and national pride.

The Catholic Church would also face challenges from another source. Scientists influenced by humanism would begin to question accepted views—including those of the Church. Their discoveries would change the way people looked at the world.

Church towers in the northern European country of Latvia represent three different Christian denominations: (from left to right) Lutheranism, Catholicism, and Anglicanism.

REVIEW & ASSESS

1. **READING CHECK** What were some of the religious effects of the Reformation?

2. **DETERMINE WORD MEANINGS** In the sentence "Because more people wanted to read the Bible, the Reformation also increased literacy," what does *literacy* mean?

3. **ANALYZE CAUSE AND EFFECT** What led to the rise of nation-states?

PLAN

OBJECTIVE

Discuss the religious, social, and political impacts of the Reformation on Europe.

CRITICAL THINKING SKILLS FOR LESSON 3.4

- Identify Main Ideas and Details
- Monitor Comprehension
- Determine Word Meanings
- Analyze Cause and Effect
- Summarize
- Explain
- Categorize

ESSENTIAL QUESTION

How did new ways of thinking transform European culture?

The Reformation had a long-lasting impact on Europe. Lesson 3.4 discusses some of the religious, social, and political changes that resulted from the Reformation.

BACKGROUND FOR THE TEACHER

For centuries, all Christians in Western Europe were Catholic. The Reformation led to a division in Europe between Catholicism and Protestantism, resulting in political conflict. For example, in 1562, a war broke out in France between French Catholics and French Protestants, who were called Huguenots. The war lasted until 1598. In 1618, Protestants in Bohemia—a region in central Europe—revolted against their Catholic king. The rebellion spread throughout the Holy Roman Empire, starting The Thirty Years' War.

TEACHER RESOURCES & ASSESSMENT

 Reading and Note-Taking

 Vocabulary Practice

 Section 3 Quiz

STUDENT RESOURCES

 NG Chapter Gallery

USE AN ANTICIPATION GUIDE

Have students work in small groups. Before reading the lesson, distribute copies of the statements below to students. Read each statement aloud, and have students write A for *Agree* or D for *Disagree* for each one. After reading, have students repeat the activity and explain answers that changed.

1. Protestantism flourished after the Reformation.

2. Eventually, most Protestants in Europe returned to the Catholic religion.

3. Some Protestants helped govern their own churches.

4. Religious disagreements did not have anything to do with political disagreements.

5. Wars broke out in Europe because of religious differences.

6. Most European kings wanted to share their power with the people in their countries.

Tell students that they will learn about the impact the Reformation had on Europe. **0:10** minutes

TEACH

GUIDED DISCUSSION

1. **Summarize** How did the Reformation influence the development of democracy and federalism? *(Protestants who formed a church sometimes governed it themselves. This practice encouraged religious groups immigrating to the English colonies to form a government with equal and fair laws. Calvinist churches sometimes allowed church members to share power with the clergy. This practice represented an early form of federalism in which power is shared.)*

2. **Explain** What challenge did the Catholic Church face from scientists influenced by humanism? *(These scientists began to question views of the Church. Their discoveries would change the way people looked at the world.)*

CATEGORIZE

Have students categorize the effects of the Reformation on Europe. You might have them fill out a chart such as the one below. **0:15** minutes

Impact of the Reformation

Religious	Social	Political
(founding of new universities and schools)	*(questioning accepted views)*	*(development of democracy and federalism)*
(translation of the Bible into the vernacular)	*(scientific discoveries)*	*(religious wars—Thirty Years' War)*
		(emergence of nation-states)

ACTIVE OPTIONS

NG Learning Framework: Learn About Nation-States

ATTITUDES: **Curiosity, Responsibility**
KNOWLEDGE: **Our Human Story**

Have students work in groups to research the rise in nation-states after the Reformation. Have them find out about the role of finances, armies, government structures, and religious control. Ask each group to write a paragraph about a nation-state and present the paragraph to the class. After the presentations, lead a class discussion comparing and contrasting some of the nation-states that were presented. **0:20** minutes

On Your Feet: Sequence Events Write the following events on the board. Have students work in small groups and use chart paper to list the events in order. Students may consult their text if desired.

- Widespread warfare breaks out in Europe.
- The Counter Reformation begins.
- Nation-states begin to emerge in Europe.
- New Protestant denominations develop.

As a class, review the events to determine if the groups have arranged them correctly. If not, have the groups make adjustments. **0:15** minutes

DIFFERENTIATE

STRIVING READERS

Expand Main Idea Statements After reading, direct students to copy the Main Idea statement and write a paragraph that expands on the statement. Use the following starter as an example if needed:

The Reformation had a long-lasting religious, social, and political impact on Europe. One religious effect was _____ . This was important because _____ .

Press (mt) *in the Student eEdition for modified text.*

See the Chapter Planner for more strategies for differentiation.

REVIEW & ASSESS

ANSWERS

1. Both Catholicism and Protestantism flourished and founded schools and universities.

2. *Literacy* means "the ability to read."

3. The decline in the authority of the Church and the rise in power of kings gave rise to nation-states.

VOCABULARY

Complete each of the following sentences using one of the vocabulary words from the chapter.

1. A movement called _____ focused on the potential of the individual.

2. During the Renaissance, artists often painted nonreligious, or _____, subjects.

3. Artists use _____ to produce an impression of depth and distance.

4. Instead of Latin, some Renaissance writers wrote in the _____.

5. Wealthy _____ often supported artists during the Renaissance.

6. Gutenberg's development of the _____ helped spread ideas quickly.

7. The Roman Inquisition punished _____, or a denial of Church policy.

READING STRATEGY

8. **ANALYZE LANGUAGE USE** If you haven't already, complete at least three concept clusters that analyze figurative language. Then use each example of the language in a sentence of your own.

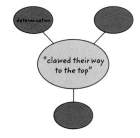

MAIN IDEAS

Answer the following questions. Support your answers with evidence from the chapter.

9. What was the Renaissance? **LESSON 1.1**

10. What artistic subjects became popular during the Renaissance? **LESSON 1.2**

11. Why were the best artists and scholars attracted to Florence during the Renaissance? **LESSON 1.4**

12. Who often served as patrons of Northern Renaissance artists? **LESSON 2.1**

13. How did Gutenberg's printing press improve on Chinese woodblock printing? **LESSON 2.3**

14. Which event triggered the Reformation? **LESSON 3.1**

15. What was the purpose of the Counter Reformation? **LESSON 3.3**

CRITICAL THINKING

Answer the following questions. Support your answers with evidence from the chapter.

16. **COMPARE AND CONTRAST** How did the ideas of humanism differ from those of the Middle Ages?

17. **MAKE PREDICTIONS** What might have happened if wealthy patrons had not supported Renaissance artists?

18. **MAKE INFERENCES** Why do you think art experts become so excited over the prospect of finding a new painting by Leonardo da Vinci?

19. **DRAW CONCLUSIONS** What conclusions can you draw about Shakespeare's career based on the fact that he died a rich man?

20. **SEQUENCE EVENTS** What chain of events followed Martin Luther's publication of his 95 Theses?

21. **YOU DECIDE** What do you think was the most important achievement of the Renaissance? Support your opinion with evidence from the chapter.

INTERPRET VISUALS

Study the paintings below from the Middle Ages and the Renaissance. Then answer the questions that follow.

Medieval painting from Catalan School, Spain

Renaissance painting by Raphael

22. In what ways are the two paintings alike?

23. How do the artistic styles differ in the two paintings?

ANALYZE SOURCES

In 1568, Giorgio Vasari wrote a collection of biographies about the great artists of his day, including Michelangelo. In this excerpt, a high-ranking government official named Piero Soderini has a suggestion for improving Michelangelo's famous sculpture of David.

> While Michelangelo was giving it the finishing touches, [Soderini] told Michelangelo that he thought the nose of the figure was too large. Michelangelo, . . . having quickly grabbed his chisel in his left hand along with a little marble dust, . . . began to tap lightly with the chisel, allowing the dust to fall little by little without retouching the nose from the way it was. Then, looking down at [Soderini] who stood there watching, he ordered: "Look at it now." "I like it better," replied [Soderini]: "you've made it come alive."

24. Based on this story, what were some of Michelangelo's personality traits?

WRITE ABOUT HISTORY

25. **EXPLANATORY** How did the Renaissance affect Europe? Write a paragraph designed to inform museumgoers about the ways in which Renaissance ideas about art, literature, and thinking changed Europe.

TIPS

- Take notes from the lessons on how the Renaissance affected people and events in Europe. You might use a web diagram to organize your notes.
- State your main idea clearly at the beginning of the paragraph.
- Support your main idea with relevant facts, details, and examples.
- Use two or three vocabulary terms from the chapter in your paragraph.
- Provide a concluding statement about the ways in which the Renaissance changed Europe.

VOCABULARY ANSWERS

1. humanism
2. secular
3. perspective
4. vernacular
5. patrons
6. printing press
7. heresy

READING STRATEGY ANSWER

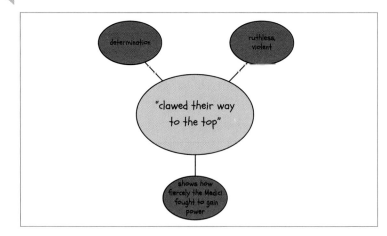

8. Students should identify three examples of figurative language and complete a Concept Cluster for each. Make sure students' sentences reflect an understanding of the language examples.

MAIN IDEAS ANSWERS

9. The Renaissance was a movement of great creativity in the arts, writing, and thinking.

10. In addition to religious subjects, artists depicted nature, real people, and the world around them.

11. The best artists and scholars were drawn to Florence because the Medici sponsored them and funded their achievements.

12. Powerful kings in countries such as France and England often served as patrons of Northern Renaissance artists.

13. It used movable metal type that could be arranged, rearranged, and reused.

14. The posting of Martin Luther's 95 Theses, which criticized certain Church practices, triggered the Reformation.

15. The purpose of the Counter Reformation was to keep people loyal to the Roman Catholic Church, stop the spread of Protestantism, and bring Protestants back to the Church.

CRITICAL THINKING ANSWERS

16. During the Middle Ages, people accepted without question the role of the Church and religion as central to all aspects of life. Humanism shifted that worldview by stressing the importance of individual thought and achievement and focusing on more secular matters.

17. Artists may not have had the money or time to produce their masterpieces.

18. Because Leonardo finished so few paintings, art experts would love to have the opportunity to study and admire others.

19. His plays were very popular, and many people paid to go see them.

20. His ideas spread; people interpreted the Bible for themselves; Protestantism and the Reformation arose; the Counter Reformation arose.

21. Students' answers will vary. Some may say that the printing press was the most important achievement because it was an important factor in the rise of the Reformation, which had a long-lasting religious, social, and political impact on Europe.

INTERPRET VISUALS ANSWERS

22. Both deal with a mother and child; in both, the mother is holding her baby; the figures in both paintings are facing the viewer.

23. The medieval painting is two-dimensional while the Renaissance painting appears to have three dimensions due to the use of perspective. The figures in the medieval painting are stylized and out of proportion. The figures in the Renaissance painting are portrayed with greater realism and human emotion.

ANALYZE SOURCES ANSWER

24. He was confident of his artistic ability. He was disdainful of authority figures and of people who did not understand his work. He was clever and tricky.

WRITE ABOUT HISTORY ANSWER

25. Students' paragraphs will vary, but students should discuss in a clear, logical manner some of the ways in which the Renaissance affected Europe.

UNIT RESOURCES

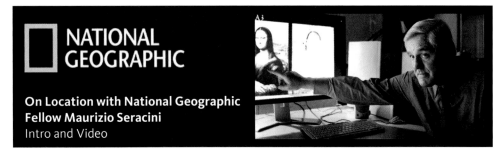

On Location with National Geographic Fellow Maurizio Seracini
Intro and Video

Interactive Map Tool

News & Updates
Available on myNGconnect

Unit Wrap-Up:
"Using Technology to See the Past"
Feature and Video

"Brunelleschi's Dome"
National Geographic Adapted Article

"Lady with a Secret"
National Geographic Adapted Article
Student eEdition exclusive

Unit 9 Inquiry:
Map the New Worldview

CHAPTER RESOURCES

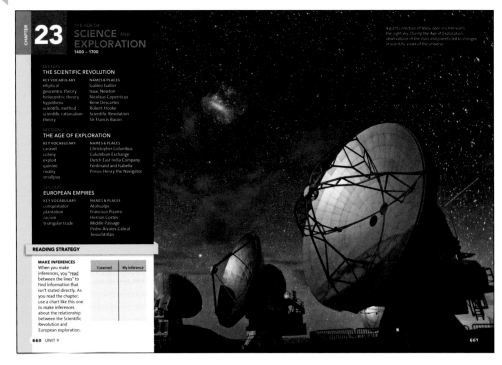

CHAPTER 23
THE AGE OF
SCIENCE AND
EXPLORATION
1400 – 1700

A giant collection of telescopes in Chile scans the night sky. During the Age of Exploration, observations of the stars and planets led to changes in scientific views of the universe.

SECTION 1
THE SCIENTIFIC REVOLUTION

KEY VOCABULARY	NAMES & PLACES
elliptical	Galileo Galilei
geocentric theory	Isaac Newton
heliocentric theory	Nicolaus Copernicus
hypothesis	René Descartes
scientific method	Robert Hooke
scientific rationalism	Scientific Revolution
theory	Sir Francis Bacon

SECTION 2
THE AGE OF EXPLORATION

KEY VOCABULARY	NAMES & PLACES
caravel	Christopher Columbus
colony	Columbian Exchange
exploit	Dutch East India Company
quinine	Ferdinand and Isabella
rivalry	Prince Henry the Navigator
smallpox	

SECTION 3
EUROPEAN EMPIRES

KEY VOCABULARY	NAMES & PLACES
conquistador	Atahualpa
plantation	Francisco Pizarro
racism	Hernán Cortés
triangular trade	Middle Passage
	Pedro Álvares Cabral
	Tenochtitlán

READING STRATEGY

MAKE INFERENCES
When you make inferences, you "read between the lines" to find information that isn't stated directly. As you read the chapter, use a chart like this one to make inferences about the relationship between the Scientific Revolution and European exploration.

I Learned	My Inference

660 UNIT 9

661

TEACHER RESOURCES & ASSESSMENT
Available on myNGconnect

Social Studies Skills Lessons
• Reading: Make Inferences
• Writing: Write an Informative Paragraph

Formal Assessment
• Chapter 23 Tests A (on-level) & B (below-level)

Chapter 23 Answer Key

ExamView®
One-time Download

STUDENT BACKPACK *Available on myNGconnect*
• **eEdition** *(English)*   • **eEdition** *(Spanish)*   • **Handbooks**   • **Online Atlas**
For Chapter 23 Spanish resources, visit the Teacher Resource Menu page on myNGconnect.

SECTION 1 RESOURCES

THE SCIENTIFIC REVOLUTION

 Reading and Note-Taking

 Vocabulary Practice

 Section 1 Quiz

Available on myNGconnect

LESSON 1.1 ROOTS OF THE REVOLUTION
- Critical Viewing: NG Chapter Gallery
- On Your Feet: Inside-Outside Circle

LESSON 1.2 DISCOVERIES AND INVENTIONS

 Biography
Galileo Galilei
Available on myNGconnect

NG Learning Framework:
Write a Biography

- On Your Feet: Turn and Talk on Topic

LESSON 1.3 THE SCIENTIFIC METHOD
- Critical Viewing: NG Chapter Gallery
- On Your Feet: Card Responses

SECTION 2 RESOURCES

THE AGE OF EXPLORATION

 Reading and Note-Taking

 Vocabulary Practice

 Section 2 Quiz

Available on myNGconnect

LESSON 2.1 AN EXPANDING WORLD

NG Learning Framework:
Learn About GPS

- On Your Feet: Thumbs Up/Thumbs Down

LESSON 2.2 EXPLORATION AND COLONIZATION
- Critical Viewing: NG Chapter Gallery
- On Your Feet: Fishbowl

MOMENTS IN HISTORY
LESSON 2.3 COLUMBUS DISCOVERS THE NEW WORLD
- Critical Viewing: NG Chapter Gallery
- On Your Feet: Descriptive Words

DOCUMENT-BASED QUESTION
LESSON 2.4 A NEW WORLD
- Critical Viewing: NG Chapter Gallery
- On Your Feet: Two Options

LESSON 2.5 THE COLUMBIAN EXCHANGE
- Critical Viewing: NG Chapter Gallery
- On Your Feet: Think, Pair, Share

SECTION 3 RESOURCES

EUROPEAN EMPIRES

 Reading and Note-Taking

 Vocabulary Practice

 Section 3 Quiz

Available on myNGconnect

LESSON 3.1 THE SPANISH CONQUEST

NG Learning Framework:
Write a Story

- On Your Feet: Question and Answer

LESSON 3.2 PORTUGAL'S EMPIRE

NG Learning Framework:
Make Observations

- On Your Feet: Roundtable

LESSON 3.3 THE ATLANTIC SLAVE TRADE

 Active History: Interactive Whiteboard Activity
Analyze the Role of Slavery in Brazil

 Active History
Analyze the Role of Slavery in Brazil
Available on myNGconnect

- On Your Feet: Three Corners

CHAPTER 23 REVIEW

STRATEGY ❶
Preview Text

Help students preview each lesson in the chapter. For each lesson, have them read the title, lesson introduction, Main Idea statement, caption, and subheadings. Then have them list the information they expect to find in the text. Have students read a lesson and discuss with a partner what they learned and whether or not it matched their list.

Use with All Lessons

STRATEGY ❷
Use Paired Reading

Pair students and assign each pair two passages in a lesson. Tell them that they will each take one passage, read it, take notes, become an expert on it, and share their expertise with their partner. After students have had time to prepare their passages, have them report on their reading to each other. Tell each listener to write two clarifying questions.

Use with All Lessons

STRATEGY ❸
Turn Lesson Titles into Questions

Before reading each lesson, display the appropriate question based on the lesson title. After reading, have students write the answers to the questions and compare their answers.

1.1   What were the roots of the Scientific Revolution?

1.2   What important discoveries and inventions were made?

1.3   What is the scientific method?

Use with Lessons 1.1–1.3 *Use the same strategy for the titles in Section 3. Tell students to pay careful attention to words in the titles so that their questions are relevant. For Lessons 3.1–3.3, have students share their questions and answers with classmates.*

Press **(mt)** *in the Student eEdition for modified text.*

STRATEGY ❶
Modify Vocabulary Lists

Limit the number of vocabulary words, terms, and names students will be required to master. Have students write each word from your modified list on a colored sticky note and put it on the page next to where it appears in context.

Use with All Lessons

STRATEGY ❷
Preview Visuals to Predict

Ask students to preview the title and visuals in each lesson. Then have students tell what they think the lesson will be about. After reading, ask them to repeat the activity to see whether their predictions were confirmed.

Use with All Lessons *Invite volunteers to describe the visuals in detail to help visually impaired students see them.*

STRATEGY ❶
Use a Pair-Share Strategy

After reading, have students work in pairs. The first student reads aloud the Main Idea statement of the lesson and gives one example from the lesson that expands on or illustrates the main idea. Then the second student rereads the Main Idea statement and gives a different example.

Use with All Lessons

STRATEGY ❷
Find Someone Who Knows

Give students a time limit and tell them to find classmates who can supply the correct answer to each question below. Each person should write the answer and sign his or her name.

1.   Who proposed the heliocentric theory?

2.   Who was the first scientist to describe cells?

3.   What was Tenochtitlán?

4.   What Spanish explorer conquered the Inca Empire?

Use with Lessons 1.2 and 3.1

STRATEGY ❸

Use Pronunciation Keys

Preteach the meaning and pronunciation of vocabulary words before beginning each lesson. Give a brief definition or example for each word, and then pronounce it slowly and clearly several times. Have students repeat after you. Then have students create a pronunciation key for each word.

After each lesson, have students write simple sentences using each word (e.g., "A *theory* is a proposed explanation for a set of facts.") Have students refer to their pronunciation keys to help them say the words correctly.

Use with All Lessons

GIFTED & TALENTED

STRATEGY ❶

Create a Poster

Ask students to research one of the crops that developed in North America, such as corn or potatoes, as part of the Columbian Exchange. Have them find out the impact of the crop on the world today. Direct students to present their findings in a poster. Display completed posters in the classroom and discuss the students' findings.

Use with Lesson 2.5

STRATEGY ❷

Read Historical Biographies

Work with the school librarian to find biographical information about the scientists during the Scientific Revolution or one of the Spanish conquistadors. Allow students to choose one of the scientists or explorers and read a book or story about the individual and design a way to report on the book or story to the class.

Use with Lessons 1.2 and 3.1

PRE-AP

STRATEGY ❶

Support an Opinion

Present a challenge to students to decide which discovery or invention made the greatest impact on European exploration. Have them develop a thesis statement that explains their decision and write an essay that supports it. Ask students to share their essays with the class.

Use with Lessons 1.2–1.3 and 2.1–2.2

STRATEGY ❷

Explain the Significance

Allow students to choose one term below to investigate and design a presentation that explains the significance of the term to the development of European empires in the New World.

> conquistadors
>
> plantation
>
> triangular trade

Use with Lessons 3.1–3.3

23
THE AGE OF
SCIENCE AND EXPLORATION
1400 – 1700

A giant collection of telescopes in Chile scans the night sky. During the Age of Exploration, observations of the stars and planets led to changes in scientific views of the universe.

SECTION 1
THE SCIENTIFIC REVOLUTION

KEY VOCABULARY	NAMES & PLACES
elliptical	Galileo Galilei
geocentric theory	Isaac Newton
heliocentric theory	Nicolaus Copernicus
hypothesis	René Descartes
scientific method	Robert Hooke
scientific rationalism	Scientific Revolution
theory	Sir Francis Bacon

SECTION 2
THE AGE OF EXPLORATION

KEY VOCABULARY	NAMES & PLACES
caravel	Christopher Columbus
colony	Columbian Exchange
exploit	Dutch East India Company
quinine	Ferdinand and Isabella
rivalry	Prince Henry the Navigator
smallpox	

SECTION 3
EUROPEAN EMPIRES

KEY VOCABULARY	NAMES & PLACES
conquistador	Atahualpa
plantation	Francisco Pizarro
racism	Hernán Cortés
triangular trade	Middle Passage
	Pedro Álvares Cabral
	Tenochtitlán

READING STRATEGY

MAKE INFERENCES
When you make inferences, you "read between the lines" to find information that isn't stated directly. As you read the chapter, use a chart like this one to make inferences about the relationship between the Scientific Revolution and European exploration.

I Learned	My Inference

TEACHER BACKGROUND

INTRODUCE THE PHOTOGRAPH

Have students study the photograph of telescopes and read the caption. Point out to students that the telescopes pictured here can see some of the most distant galaxies. Ask students if they have ever viewed the skies with a telescope, and, if they have, ask what they saw. Explain that in this chapter they will learn about the discoveries and inventions that occurred in the 1500s and 1600s and how some of these inventions led to an age of exploration.

SHARE BACKGROUND

The Atacama Large Milimeter/submillimeter Array (ALMA) is the world's most powerful observatory for studying the universe. It was designed to see some of the most distant galaxies ever seen. The observatory is so powerful that it can see a golf ball 9 miles away. It took thousands of scientists and engineers from around the world more than 10 years to construct the observatory. The observatory is located 16,570 feet above sea level, in the Atacama Desert.

DIGITAL RESOURCES myNGconnect.com

TEACHER RESOURCES & ASSESSMENT

 Social Studies Skills Lessons
- Reading: Make Inferences
- Writing: Write an Informative Paragraph

ExamView®
One-time Download

 Formal Assessment
- Chapter 23 Tests A (on-level) & B (below-level)

 Chapter 23 Answer Key

STUDENT BACKPACK
- **eEdition** (English)
- **eEdition** (Spanish)
- **Handbooks**
- **Online Atlas**

For Chapter 23 Spanish Resources, visit the Teacher Resource Menu page.

INTRODUCE THE ESSENTIAL QUESTION

HOW DID NEW IDEAS AFFECT EUROPEANS' VIEWS OF THE WORLD?

Jigsaw Activity: Preview Content Divide the class into seven groups. Assign one of the lesson titles listed below to each group and have group members discuss what they think they'll learn. Ask them to consider the following clues and questions:

Group 1 Lesson 1.1 is about the start of the Scientific Revolution. What was the Scientific Revolution? How did it change Europeans' ideas about science?

Group 2 Lesson 1.2 is about discoveries and inventions. What important discoveries were made in the 1500s and 1600s? How did new technology lead to these discoveries?

Group 3 Lesson 1.3 is about the scientific method. What was the scientific method? Who developed the scientific method?

Group 4 Lesson 2.1 is about European exploration. Why did Europeans begin voyages of exploration?

Group 5 Lesson 2.2 is about European exploration and colonization. What countries established colonies in the New World? How did exploration change the world?

Group 6 Lesson 2.3 is about an important moment in history— October 12, 1492. Why is this date significant?

Group 7 Lesson 2.5 is about the Columbian Exchange. What is the Columbian Exchange? Why is it significant?

`0:20` minutes

INTRODUCE THE READING STRATEGY

MAKE INFERENCES

Remind students that inferences are based on studying what is stated in the material as well as previous knowledge. Read aloud the following passage and guide students to make an inference about the influence of the Scientific Revolution on European exploration.

> Medieval Muslim scholars made significant advances in astronomy. They developed special buildings called observatories for studying the stars. These buildings had scientific instruments that allowed astronomers to accurately plot the locations of stars. As a result, scientists were able to develop more accurate calendars and methods of navigation.

I Learned	My Inference
Observatories helped astronomers accurately plot the locations of stars, which led to better navigation.	Better navigation made it easier for ships to travel far from home.

INTRODUCE CHAPTER VOCABULARY

VOC STRATEGY

Have students use the six steps shown below for five of the chapter vocabulary words. Do the first vocabulary word together as a class. Then have students work in pairs. Invite volunteers to share their work with the class.

Vocabulary Word: _____

1. Write the sentence in which the word appears in the text.

2. Study how the word is used. What do you think it means?

3. Now look up the word in the dictionary or use the glossary.

4. Use the word in a sentence of your own.

5. To help you remember the meaning, draw a picture or a quick sketch that relates to the word; you might think of an action the word suggests or connect the word to a story or news report.

6. Tell why you chose this way of representing the meaning.

KEY DATES	
1419	Prince Henry the Navigator establishes navigation school in Portugal
1492	Columbus lands in the Americas
1494	Treaty of Tordesillas settles land dispute between Spain and Portugal
1519	Spain launches invasion of Mexico
1543	Copernicus publishes his heliocentric theory
c. 1590	Microscope is invented
1633	Catholic Church condemns Galileo's discoveries

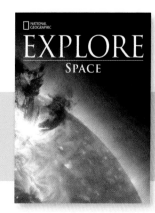

EXPLORE SPACE

For more information on present-day observations of the universe, check out **EXPLORE SPACE.**

Roots of the Revolution

The period following the Middle Ages was one of major changes in Europe. The Renaissance brought an explosion of creativity in art, literature, and architecture. The Reformation transformed people's religious ideas. Another important movement introduced great advances in science. This movement is called the **Scientific Revolution**, and it began in Europe around the mid-1500s.

MAIN IDEA

Before the Scientific Revolution, Europeans generally relied on the works of ancient Greek thinkers and medieval Muslim scholars to answer scientific questions.

ANCIENT GREEK SCIENTISTS

Since earliest times, people have attempted to understand and explain the natural world—sometimes through religion, sometimes through science, and sometimes by combining the two. Early scientists called themselves "natural philosophers," and their methods differed greatly from those of modern scientists.

The ancient Greeks were great thinkers, and they often based their scientific explanations on reasoning rather than

evidence. Indeed, some famous Greek philosophers rejected the need for scientific experiments. They believed that if enough clever men thought for long enough, they would discover the truth. This belief led to some incorrect theories. A **theory** is a proposed explanation for a set of facts.

Two ancient Greek thinkers, Aristotle and Ptolemy, promoted the **geocentric theory**, which placed Earth at the center of the universe. According to this theory, the sun, moon, and planets all moved in a circular path around Earth. This theory later supported the Christian belief that God had created Earth at the center of the universe. Even though the theory was wrong, it influenced scientific ideas about the universe for hundreds of years.

In other areas, however, the ancient Greeks made some valuable contributions to scientific knowledge. For example, the Greek mathematicians Pythagoras, Euclid, and Archimedes (ahr-kuh-MEE-deez) developed theories on which modern mathematics is based.

MEDIEVAL MUSLIM SCHOLARS

After the collapse of the Roman Empire in A.D. 476, most classical knowledge was lost to western Europe. However, it survived in the Muslim empire. Between the 600s and 1100s, Muslim scholars studied Greek scientific theories and combined them with ideas from other regions. From India, for example, they adopted such mathematical concepts as the decimal system, the number zero, and the ten Arabic numerals commonly used today. By bringing together learning from different cultures, Muslim scholars advanced mathematical understanding.

Muslim scholars also made significant advances in astronomy. They developed special buildings called observatories for studying the stars. These buildings had scientific instruments that allowed astronomers to accurately plot the locations of stars. As a result, scientists

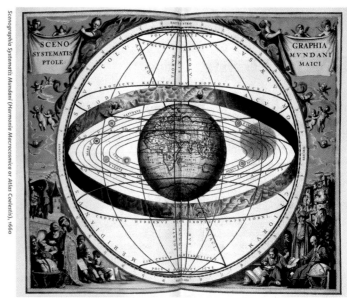

Scenographia Systematis Mundani (Harmonia Macrocosmica or Atlas Coelestis), 1660

were able to develop more accurate calendars and methods of navigation.

The advanced knowledge of the Muslims spread throughout their vast empire and beyond, eventually reaching western Europe after the 1200s. Beginning in the 1500s, European scientists combined this knowledge with new technology and a willingness to challenge long-accepted ideas. These actions sparked a revolution in scientific thinking.

GEOCENTRIC THEORY ^

This illustration from the 1500s depicts the geocentric theory, which incorrectly placed Earth at the center of the universe. The illustration shows the sun, moon, and other planets revolving around a much larger Earth. The surrounding band shows the signs of the zodiac, an imaginary belt in the heavens that encircles the orbits of the planets. The zodiac plays a major role in astrology, the study of how the stars and planets supposedly influence people's lives and events on Earth. In the Middle Ages, astronomy and astrology were closely linked.

REVIEW & ASSESS

1. **READING CHECK** What sources of knowledge did scholars turn to before the Scientific Revolution?

2. **DETERMINE WORD MEANINGS** How do the roots of the words *geocentric* and *observatory* help clarify their meanings?

3. **ANALYZE CAUSE AND EFFECT** How did medieval Muslim scholars help advance the field of mathematics?

PLAN

OBJECTIVE

Describe how Europeans answered scientific questions by relying on the works of ancient Greek thinkers and medieval Muslim scholars.

CRITICAL THINKING SKILLS FOR LESSON 1.1

- Identify Main Ideas and Details
- Monitor Comprehension
- Determine Word Meanings
- Analyze Cause and Effect
- Summarize
- Draw Conclusions
- Analyze Visuals

ESSENTIAL QUESTION

How did new ideas affect Europeans' views of the world?

A revolution in scientific thinking began in Europe around the mid-1500s. Lesson 1.1 describes how Europeans answered scientific questions before the Scientific Revolution.

BACKGROUND FOR THE TEACHER

The geocentric theory dominated ancient and medieval science. Early astronomers believed that evidence pointed to Earth being a stable, motionless body around which the rest of the universe moved. They believed that the sun, the moon, planets, and the stars could be seen moving around Earth in circular paths. Early astronomers also believed that Earth was stationary because nothing seemed to make it move. The fact that objects fell toward Earth provided additional support to early astronomers for the geocentric theory.

DIGITAL RESOURCES myNGconnect.com

TEACHER RESOURCES & ASSESSMENT

 Reading and Note-Taking

 Vocabulary Practice

 Section 1 Quiz

STUDENT RESOURCES

 NG Chapter Gallery

WORD KNOWLEDGE

Ask students if they know what the word *revolution* means. Write students' responses on the board. Point out to students that *revolution* has several meanings, including "an overthrow of a government," "the orbiting of one heavenly body around another," or "a change in the way of thinking." Direct students' attention to the lesson title and ask students which definition of *revolution* the title refers to. *(a change in the way of thinking)* Ask students what they think the lesson, based on the title, will be about. **0:05 minutes**

GUIDED DISCUSSION

1. **Summarize** What was the geocentric theory promoted by Aristotle and Ptolemy? *(The geocentric theory said the sun, moon, and planets all moved in a circular path around Earth.)*

2. **Draw Conclusions** How did the classical knowledge that was lost to western Europeans at the collapse of the Roman Empire survive? *(It survived through the efforts of Muslim scholars and was kept alive in the Muslim empire.)*

ANALYZE VISUALS

Have students focus their attention on the illustration in the lesson. **ASK:**

- What part of the illustration indicates the geocentric theory? *(the part that shows Earth in the center with the planets and the sun orbiting around it)*

- Based on the illustration, what parts of Earth were people aware of at that time? *(Responses will vary, but students might indicate that the continents of Africa, Europe, and Asia were known.)* **0:15 minutes**

ACTIVE OPTIONS

Critical Viewing: NG Chapter Gallery Invite students to explore the Chapter Gallery to examine the images that relate to this chapter. Have them select one of the images and do additional research to learn more about it. Ask questions that will inspire additional inquiry about the chosen gallery image, such as: What is this? Where and when was this created? By whom? Why was it created? What is it made of? Why does it belong in this chapter? What else would you like to know about it? **0:10 minutes**

On Your Feet: Inside-Outside Circle Arrange students in concentric circles facing each other. Have students in the outside circle ask the students in the inside circle a question about the lesson. Then have the outside circle rotate one position to the right to create new pairings. After five questions, have students switch roles and continue. **0:10 minutes**

INCLUSION

Use Supported Reading Have students work in pairs and assign each pair one paragraph to read aloud together. At the end of each paragraph, have them use the following sentence frames to tell what they do and do not understand:

- This paragraph is about _____.

- One fact that stood out to me is _____.

- _____ is a word I had trouble understanding, so I figured it out by _____.

Be sure students understand the content before moving on to the next paragraph.

ENGLISH LANGUAGE LEARNERS

Find Main Ideas and Details Have students form two groups. Give each group a piece of construction paper or a flip chart with the main idea of the lesson written on it: *Before the Scientific Revolution, Europeans generally relied on the works of ancient Greek thinkers and medieval Muslim scholars to answer scientific questions.* Ask each group to list as many details from the lesson as they can to support the main idea. They should write their details on the flip chart or construction paper. Then have the two groups compare their lists.

Press **mt** *in the Student eEdition for modified text.*

See the Chapter Planner for more strategies for differentiation.

ANSWERS

1. Before the Scientific Revolution, scholars relied on the works of ancient Greek thinkers and medieval Muslim scholars.

2. In the word *geocentric*, the root *geo* means "Earth" and *centric* means "at the center," so *geocentric* means "with Earth at the center." In the word *observatory*, the root *observe* leads to the definition "a place to observe the stars and planets."

3. Medieval Muslim scholars advanced the field of mathematics by bringing together learning from different cultures.

Discoveries and Inventions

You are a scientist living in the early 1600s. You spend many hours looking through a telescope, studying the stars and planets. Your observations lead you to believe the planets revolve around the sun. But you are afraid to publicly state this view because it conflicts with the teachings of the powerful Catholic Church. There could be serious consequences if you publish your findings.

MAIN IDEA

Improved technology and a focus on direct observation led to important scientific discoveries from the 1500s through the 1600s.

STRUCTURE OF THE UNIVERSE

The geocentric theory placed Earth at the center of the universe. According to this theory, the sun, planets, and stars revolved around Earth in perfect circles. Some scientists began to doubt this theory, however.

In the early 1500s, a Polish scientist named **Nicolaus Copernicus** was studying the locations of the stars to create a more accurate calendar. He noticed that his mathematical calculations worked better

if he assumed that Earth revolved around the sun. He proposed the **heliocentric theory**, stating that the sun was the center of the universe. Copernicus published his theory in 1543, the year he died. His theory challenged the long-held view of Earth as the center of the universe.

The research of other scientists supported the heliocentric theory. The German scientist Johannes Kepler concluded that Copernicus's basic ideas were correct. Kepler added that the planets had **elliptical**, or oval, orbits rather than perfect circular ones.

Using more powerful telescopes, the Italian scientist **Galileo Galilei** (gal-uh-LAY-oh gal-uh-LAY-ee) made observations that further supported Copernicus's theory. In 1633, the Catholic Church condemned Galileo's discoveries and put him on trial. The church required Galileo to deny support for Copernicus's theory and kept Galileo under house arrest for the rest of his life. Over time, however, the heliocentric theory gained acceptance.

The English scientist **Isaac Newton** further expanded scientific understanding of the universe in the 1600s. He proposed the law of universal gravitation, which holds that all objects in the universe attract one another. With this law and his three laws of motion, Newton created a complete mechanical explanation of motion in the universe. The Royal Society of London, an organization dedicated to advancing and sharing scientific knowledge, helped spread Newton's ideas. His work would provide the foundation of modern physics and lead to scientific advances ranging from steam engines to space rockets.

BIOLOGY AND CHEMISTRY

While some scientists explored the universe, others focused on life on Earth. The invention of the microscope around 1590 allowed biologists to explore a new microscopic world and to observe things that had previously been invisible to them.

TECHNOLOGY OF THE 1600s

Scientists developed new tools and instruments as the Scientific Revolution spread in the 1600s.

Galileo's Pendulum Clock
Galileo Galilei designed a clock operated by a pendulum. This model of Galileo's design was built in the 1800s.

Hooke's Microscope
Robert Hooke was among the first to build a practical compound microscope, which had more than one lens.

Newton's Color Wheel
Isaac Newton experimented with light and invented the first color wheel.

The English scientist **Robert Hooke** used his microscope to produce detailed drawings of tiny creatures, such as fleas. In 1665, Hooke coined the word *cell* to name the microscopic structures he observed in thin slices of cork. Hooke was the first scientist to describe cells.

Hooke worked closely with Irish scientist Robert Boyle. Together, they discovered that air is made up of gases and determined how changes in the volume of a gas affect the gas's pressure. They formed Boyle's Law to describe this relationship. Boyle's work with gases led him to propose that all matter is made up of smaller particles that join together in different ways. Boyle's theory challenged the ideas of Aristotle, who stated that the physical world consisted of the four elements of earth, fire, air, and water. The experimental work and writings of Hooke and Boyle greatly advanced the fields of biology and chemistry.

REVIEW & ASSESS

1. **READING CHECK** How did technology and direct observation help advance science in the 1500s and 1600s?

2. **MAKE INFERENCES** Why did the Catholic Church condemn Galileo's ideas?

3. **DRAW CONCLUSIONS** How did Robert Hooke advance the field of biology?

PLAN

OBJECTIVE

Identify how technology and a focus on direct observation led to important scientific discoveries from the 1500s through the 1600s.

CRITICAL THINKING SKILLS FOR LESSON 1.2

- Identify Main Ideas and Details
- Monitor Comprehension
- Make Inferences
- Draw Conclusions
- Make Generalizations
- Analyze Visuals

ESSENTIAL QUESTION

How did new ideas affect Europeans' views of the world?

Prior to the 1500s, Europeans believed that Earth was the center of the universe. Lesson 1.2 discusses how improved technology and direct observation led to a change in that thinking as well as other important scientific discoveries in the 1500s and 1600s.

BACKGROUND FOR THE TEACHER

Johannes Kepler is best known for his discovery that the orbits of the planets around the sun are elliptical in shape. Many astronomers in Kepler's time believed that the sun was the center of the universe and that Earth turned on its axis. However, they still believed that the planets moved in a circular orbit around the sun, but they could not explain the motions of the planets as seen from Earth. Kepler decided to explain the motions by observing the motion of the planet Mars.

DIGITAL RESOURCES myNGconnect.com

TEACHER RESOURCES & ASSESSMENT

 Reading and Note-Taking

 Vocabulary Practice

 Section 1 Quiz

STUDENT RESOURCES

 Biography

MAKE CONNECTIONS

Write the word *invention* on the board. Ask students if they ever thought of inventing something. Call on volunteers to share their ideas for the invention. Have students indicate what led them to think of the invention and how the invention they would develop would affect their life. Tell students that in this lesson they will learn about inventions that helped advance scientific thought. **0:05** minutes

GUIDED DISCUSSION

1. **Identify Main Ideas and Details** Which two scientists' discoveries advanced the fields of biology and chemistry? *(the work of Robert Hooke and Robert Boyle)*

2. **Make Generalizations** What generalization can you make about the observations and inventions discussed in this lesson? *(Possible response: The observations and inventions greatly advanced the field of science.)*

ANALYZE VISUALS

Have students examine the images in the feature on technology in the 1600s and read the captions. Discuss what each instrument was used for and discuss whether each kind of instrument is still used today in some capacity. **0:10** minutes

ACTIVE OPTIONS

NG Learning Framework: Write a Biography

ATTITUDE: **Curiosity**
KNOWLEDGE: **Our Human Story**

Have students select one of the people they are still curious about after learning about this individual in the chapter. Instruct them to write a short biography about this person using information from the chapter and additional source material. **0:20** minutes

On Your Feet: Turn and Talk on Topic Have students form four lines. Give each line the same topic sentence: *Direct observation led to important scientific discoveries in the 1500s and 1600s.* Tell the groups to build a paragraph on that topic by having each student in the line add one sentence about a direct observation that led to an important scientific discovery. Finally, have groups present their paragraphs to the class, with each student reading his or her sentence. **0:15** minutes

STRIVING READERS

Summarize Read the lesson aloud while students follow along in their books. At the end of each paragraph, ask students to summarize what you read in a sentence. Allow them time to write the summary on their own paper.

PRE-AP

Extend Knowledge Have students conduct Internet research to find out more about the new technology developed in the 1600s. Their findings should include the developer of the technology, its function, and the effect of the technology on scientific knowledge. Ask students to present their findings in an oral report to the class. Encourage students to accompany their reports with illustrations.

Press **mt** *in the Student eEdition for modified text.*

See the Chapter Planner for more strategies for differentiation.

ANSWERS

1. Improvements in telescopes and microscopes allowed scientists to make direct observations that disproved some theories and led to new discoveries.

2. Galileo's ideas challenged old, accepted beliefs promoted by the Catholic Church, such as the idea that Earth was the center of the universe.

3. Hooke built the first practical compound microscope and was the first scientist to describe cells, which advanced biologists' understanding of the microscopic structure of organisms.

The Scientific Method

For more than 2,000 years, European scientists believed that a person's health depended on a balance of four body fluids called *humors*. They thought diseases were caused by an imbalance in these fluids. Even though no evidence supported the theory, European scientists did not question it.

MAIN IDEA

Two European philosophers, Sir Francis Bacon and René Descartes, helped advance a new approach to science in the 1600s.

SIR FRANCIS BACON

How do scientists develop knowledge? Most people would answer that scientists make observations and conduct experiments. But, surprisingly, that approach is relatively new. Before the 1600s, European scholars mainly referred to ancient Greek or Roman writers or to the Bible to decide what to believe. They did not seek answers by carefully observing nature themselves. The Scientific Revolution changed that approach. Scholars began to rely on observations, experiments, evidence, and reasoning in order to understand the natural world.

Galileo was one of the first scientists to actually test scientific ideas through experiments. Along with Copernicus and Kepler, he started a revolution in scientific thinking.

Two important thinkers of the 1600s—**Sir Francis Bacon** and **René Descartes** (reh-NAY day-KAHRT)—promoted ideas that eventually led to an entirely new approach to science. This approach, called the **scientific method**, is a logical procedure for developing and testing ideas. One of the key steps in the procedure is forming a **hypothesis**, an explanation that can be tested.

Sir Francis Bacon was an English philosopher, politician, and writer who had a strong interest in science. He pioneered a different approach to science in 1620 in the book *New Instrument*. Bacon urged scientists to gather data by following specific steps. Bacon's insistence on observation and experimentation as the keys to scientific accuracy became the cornerstone of modern science.

RENÉ DESCARTES

René Descartes was a brilliant French philosopher who shared Bacon's interest in science. But instead of emphasizing experimentation, Descartes relied on logic and mathematics to learn about the world. He agreed with Bacon on the need for proof in answering questions. In fact, Descartes believed that everything should be doubted until it was proved by reason.

Descartes went so far as to declare that the only thing he knew for certain was that he existed. He reasoned, "I think, therefore I am." From this starting point, Descartes used mathematical reasoning and logic to establish other certainties. Descartes argued that in mathematics, the answers were always correct because you began with simple, provable principles and then used logic to gradually build on them.

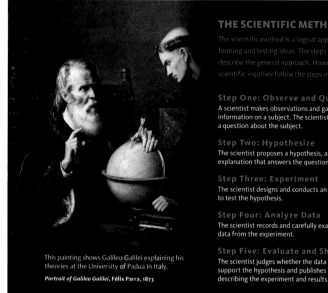

This painting shows Galileo Galilei explaining his theories at the University of Padua in Italy.

Portrait of Galileo Galilei, Félix Parra, 1873

THE SCIENTIFIC METHOD

The scientific method is a logical approach for forming and testing ideas. The steps shown here describe the general approach. However, not all scientific inquiries follow the steps in this exact order.

Step One: Observe and Question
A scientist makes observations and gathers information on a subject. The scientist forms a question about the subject.

Step Two: Hypothesize
The scientist proposes a hypothesis, an idea or explanation that answers the question.

Step Three: Experiment
The scientist designs and conducts an experiment to test the hypothesis.

Step Four: Analyze Data
The scientist records and carefully examines the data from the experiment.

Step Five: Evaluate and Share Results
The scientist judges whether the data do or do not support the hypothesis and publishes an article describing the experiment and results.

The ideas of Bacon and Descartes became known as **scientific rationalism**. In this school of thought, observation, experimentation, and mathematical reasoning replaced ancient wisdom and church teachings as the source of scientific knowledge. Scientific rationalism provided a procedure for establishing proof for scientific theories. It laid a foundation for formulating theories on which other scientists could build.

The influence of scientific rationalism extended beyond science. Bacon was active in politics and government, and he applied the principles of scientific rationalism to government. He argued that the direction of government should be based on actual experience.

Other writers argued that scientific rationalism encouraged people to think for themselves, so people should be allowed to take more control of their own lives. This thinking undermined the authority of the Catholic Church and contributed to the development of democratic government.

REVIEW & ASSESS

1. **READING CHECK** According to Bacon and Descartes, what are the best ways to build knowledge?

2. **EVALUATE** Why is it important to share the results of experiments?

3. **MAKE CONNECTIONS** How has the development of the scientific method affected your life?

OBJECTIVE

Explain how Sir Francis Bacon and René Descartes helped advance a new approach to science in the 1600s.

CRITICAL THINKING SKILLS FOR LESSON 1.3

- Identify Main Ideas and Details
- Monitor Comprehension
- Evaluate
- Make Connections
- Make Inferences
- Form and Support Opinions

ESSENTIAL QUESTION

How did new ideas affect Europeans' views of the world?

The Scientific Revolution changed the way scientists developed knowledge. Lesson 1.3 explains how the work of Sir Francis Bacon and René Descartes helped advance a new approach to science with the development of the scientific method.

BACKGROUND FOR THE TEACHER

René Descartes's work is considered to be the foundation of modern philosophy and modern mathematics. Descartes based his entire philosophical approach to science on the deductive method of reasoning. His philosophical model included four basic parts: accept as true only those things that cannot be doubted, divide every question into smaller manageable parts, begin with the simplest issues and proceed to more complex ones, review frequently enough to synthesize findings and to be certain nothing was omitted.

DIGITAL RESOURCES myNGconnect.com

TEACHER RESOURCES & ASSESSMENT

 Reading and Note-Taking

 Vocabulary Practice

 Section 1 Quiz

STUDENT RESOURCES

 NG Chapter Gallery

INTRODUCE & ENGAGE

CONCEPT EXPLORATION

Write the word *science* in the center circle of an Idea Web. Ask students what they think of when they hear the word *science*. Then divide the class into small groups. Have each group brainstorm what science involves. Possible responses might include such items as experiments, microscopes, and test tubes. Then call on a member from each group to share the group's ideas. Record the responses in one of the circles of the Idea Web. Tell students that in this lesson they will learn about new approaches to science in the 1600s.
0:10 minutes

TEACH

GUIDED DISCUSSION

1. **Make Inferences** How did scientific rationalism undermine the authority of the Catholic Church? *(By promoting the idea that people should think for themselves and take more control over their own lives, scientific rationalism undermined the Catholic Church, which taught that people should follow and not question the teachings of the church.)*

2. **Form and Support Opinions** Do you agree with the idea that scientific rationalism contributed to the development of democratic government? Why do you think so? *(Responses will vary. Students might indicate that a democratic government needs citizens who think for themselves and use facts to voice their opinions. Since scientific rationalism encourages people to think for themselves, it has contributed to the development of democratic government.)*

ACTIVATE PRIOR KNOWLEDGE

Have students focus on the painting of Galileo and the feature on the steps of the scientific method. Ask students to think of a science experiment that they might have run in the past. Have them work in pairs to report how they applied or could have applied the scientific method to their experiment. Ask students to share their procedures with the rest of the class. **0:10 minutes**

ACTIVE OPTIONS

Critical Viewing: NG Chapter Gallery Have students explore the Chapter Gallery and choose two of the items to compare and contrast, either in written form or verbally with a partner. Ask questions that will inspire this process, such as "How are these images alike? How are they different? Why did you select these two items? How do they relate in history?" **0:10 minutes**

On Your Feet: Card Responses Have half the class write 10 true-false or yes-no questions based on the lesson. Have the other half create answer cards, writing "True" or "Yes" on one side of the cards and "False" or "No" on the other side. Students from the question group should take turns asking their questions. Students from

the answer group should hold up their cards, showing the correct answer. Have students keep track of their correct answers.
0:10 minutes

DIFFERENTIATE

ENGLISH LANGUAGE LEARNERS

Summarize Lesson 1.3 has two subsections. Pair students, and assign each pair a subsection of the text to read together. Encourage students to use a Main Idea and Details List such as the one below to make notes about their part of the lesson, including questions they have about vocabulary or idioms. After answering their questions, have each pair write a one- or two-sentence summary of their subsection.

Main Idea:
Detail:
Detail:
Detail:
Detail:
Detail:
Detail:

GIFTED & TALENTED

Find Main Ideas and Details Have students form two groups. Give each group a piece of construction paper or a flip chart with the main idea of the lesson written on it: *Two European philosophers, Sir Francis Bacon and René Descartes, helped advance a new approach to science.* Ask each group to list as many details from the lesson as they can to support the main idea. They should write their details on the flip chart or construction paper. Then have the two groups compare their lists.

Press **(mt)** *in the Student eEdition for modified text.*

See the Chapter Planner for more strategies for differentiation.

REVIEW & ASSESS

ANSWERS

1. According to Bacon and Descartes, the best ways to build knowledge are through observation, experimentation, mathematical reasoning, and logic.

2. It is important to share the results of experiments so that other scientists can evaluate the work and build upon it.

3. Answers may vary. Sample response: The use of the scientific method has resulted in dramatic advances in science, which affect my medical care and life expectancy, the way I travel and communicate, the way I access knowledge, and many other aspects of my life.

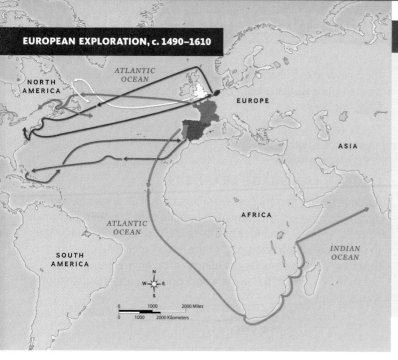

The map above shows a few of the many voyages of exploration that European countries sponsored between the 1400s and 1700s. The chart below describes the voyages shown on the map.

Sponsoring Country	Voyage
Spain	1492 Italian navigator Christopher Columbus lands in the Americas while searching for a western sea route to Asia.
Portugal	1497–1498 Portuguese explorer Vasco da Gama sails to India, establishing a direct sea route to Asia.
England	1497 Italian explorer John Cabot tries to find a northwest passage through North America to Asia. He paves the way for England's colonization of North America.
France	1535 French navigator Jacques Cartier explores the St. Lawrence River, in what is now Canada, hoping it will lead to Asia.
Netherlands	1609 English explorer Henry Hudson sails to the New World and explores the river that will later be named after him.

2.1

An Expanding World

The key to successful trading is being able to supply what people want.

In the 1400s, Europeans wanted Asian spices. But Ottoman Turks controlled the trade routes to Asia, and they charged high prices. European rulers and merchants knew that whoever found an alternative sea route to Asia would become fabulously wealthy.

MAIN IDEA

The desire to control trade encouraged Europeans to explore the world.

THE PUSH TO EXPLORE

For about a thousand years after the fall of the Roman Empire, western Europeans tended to view the rest of the world with hostility and fear. By about 1450, however, the time was right for change. The Renaissance encouraged a spirit of adventure and inspired curiosity about the world. Western Europe's population was booming. Above all, merchants were impatient to find new trading opportunities—and new markets.

In the 1400s, many of Europe's most valuable luxuries, including silk and spices, came from Asia. However, the Ottoman Empire controlled the trade routes. Europe's leaders and merchants wanted a share of this profitable trade, so they sponsored numerous sailing expeditions to search for an alternative sea route to Asia.

AIDS TO EXPLORATION

By 1450, important advances in shipbuilding had made longer sea journeys possible. The Portuguese had pioneered ocean-going ships called **caravels**, which were fast, sturdy, and easy to maneuver. The caravel had triangular sails that enabled it to sail effectively against the wind, which earlier sailing ships could not do.

Along with advances in shipbuilding came improvements in navigational techniques. Greater knowledge of astronomy allowed sailors to steer a course by the stars. In addition, such technological tools as the astrolabe, quadrant, and magnetic compass further improved navigation. These tools also helped explorers draw more accurate maps of their travels.

With the new ability to travel to distant parts of the world, European explorers undertook numerous expeditions in a period of time that came to be known as the Age of Exploration. In less than a century, Europeans greatly extended their geographic knowledge of the continents of Europe, Africa, and Asia—and then North and South America. Their travels brought together the people of many different lands.

REVIEW & ASSESS

1. **READING CHECK** Why did Europeans want to find a sea route from Europe to Asia?

2. **IDENTIFY MAIN IDEAS AND DETAILS** What advances made long sea voyages possible in the 1400s?

3. **INTERPRET MAPS** Which explorer found a direct sea route to Asia? Describe the route.

PLAN

OBJECTIVE

Explain how the desire to control trade encouraged Europeans to explore the world.

CRITICAL THINKING SKILLS FOR LESSON 2.1

- Identify Main Ideas and Details
- Monitor Comprehension
- Interpret Maps
- Analyze Cause and Effect
- Draw Conclusions

ESSENTIAL QUESTION

How did new ideas affect Europeans' views of the world?

Europeans' views of the world as a hostile place and one to be feared changed in the mid-1400s to a curiosity about the world. Lesson 2.1 describes how the desire to establish a profitable trade network led to European voyages of exploration.

BACKGROUND FOR THE TEACHER

Three navigational tools that made exploration of distant lands possible included the astrolabe, the magnetic compass, and the quadrant. The astrolabe was a brass or bronze disk with carefully adjusted rings marked off in degrees. A person held the astrolabe by a ring at the top, while another knelt facing the rim of the astrolabe. That person pointed the pointer at the sun and read the angle from the markings on the disk. In doing so, a sea captain could calculate latitude. The magnetic compass enabled explorers to more accurately track the direction the ship was sailing. The quadrant was another latitude-measuring device.

TEACHER RESOURCES & ASSESSMENT

 Reading and Note-Taking

 Vocabulary Practice

 Section 2 Quiz

STUDENT RESOURCES

 NG Chapter Gallery

MAKE CONNECTIONS

Discuss with students the kinds of explorations that are done today. Students might point to exploration of the universe or underwater explorations. Ask students why they think such explorations are taking place, what the risks are of such explorations, and what benefits such explorations can have for people. Write students' responses on the board as they offer them. Tell students that in this lesson they will learn about European explorations of the world in the 1400s. **0:05** minutes

GUIDED DISCUSSION

1. **Analyze Cause and Effect** What caused Europeans to change their views of the world? *(The causes include the spirit of adventure and curiosity about the world encouraged by the Renaissance and the desire of merchants to find new markets.)*

2. **Draw Conclusions** How did the caravel enable sailors to make longer sea journeys? *(The caravels were fast, sturdy, and easy to maneuver. They also used triangular sails, which enabled them to sail effectively against the wind.)*

INTERPRET MAPS

Point out the European Exploration map in the lesson. Review the map legend with students. Call on volunteers to identify the voyage and explorers shown. **ASK:**

- What was the purpose of the explorations illustrated on the map? *(The purpose was to find a sea route to Asia.)*
- Which exploration actually resulted in reaching Asia? *(the voyage of Vasco da Gama)*

0:10 minutes

ACTIVE OPTIONS

NG Learning Framework: Learn About GPS

ATTITUDES: Curiosity, Responsibility
SKILLS: Observation, Collaboration
KNOWLEDGE: New Frontiers

Have students review the technological advances that improved navigation in Europe in the 1550s. Students should review the purpose of navigation tools such as the astrolabe, quadrant, and magnetic compass. Then have students work with partners to research information about the Global Positioning System (GPS). Have them write a brief description of this modern navigation system. Ask students to share their reports with the rest of the class. **0:10** minutes

On Your Feet: Thumbs Up/Thumbs Down Divide the class into groups and have each group write six true-false statements about the lesson with the correct answers included. Collect the questions. Mix them up and read them aloud to the class, skipping any duplicates. Have students give a "thumbs up" for true statements and a "thumbs down" for false statements. Correct any misconceptions. **0:05** minutes

INCLUSION

Clarify Text Have visually-impaired students work with sighted partners. As they listen to an audio recording of the text, have the visually-impaired students indicate if there are words or passages they do not understand. Their partners can clarify meaning by repeating passages, emphasizing context clues, and paraphrasing.

PRE-AP

Write an Opinion Piece Ask students to do additional research on the technological advancements that led to European exploration. Then have students use that information and the information in the lesson to write an opinion piece on which technological advancement was the most important to European exploration. Have students share their opinion pieces with the class.

Press **(mt)** *in the Student eEdition for modified text.*

See the Chapter Planner for more strategies for differentiation.

ANSWERS

1. Europeans wanted to find a sea route from Europe to Asia so that they could control the profitable trade between Asia and Europe.

2. Advances in shipbuilding and navigation made long sea voyages possible in the 1400s. These advances included the caravel, astrolabe, quadrant, magnetic compass, and more-accurate maps. More-advanced knowledge of astronomy also aided navigation.

3. Portuguese explorer Vasco da Gama found a direct sea route to Asia. He sailed from Portugal, along the western coast of Africa, around the southern tip of Africa, along part of the eastern coast of Africa, and across the Indian Ocean to India.

2.2 Exploration and Colonization

Pedro is just 16 years old when he joins an expedition to sail across the Atlantic Ocean. Bringing just the clothes he's wearing, he climbs aboard a wooden ship to sail off to . . . he's not sure exactly where. He has no idea when he will return. He's excited—and scared, much like the other sailors on European expeditions.

MAIN IDEA

During the Age of Exploration, five western European nations competed for trade, land, and riches.

COMPETITION AMONG NATIONS

Portugal, a great seafaring nation, took the lead in European exploration. In 1419, **Prince Henry the Navigator**, the son of Portugal's king, established a navigation school in Portugal. He began encouraging sailors to explore Africa's western coast, where they soon established trading posts. The Portuguese discovered an eastern sea route to India in 1498 and eventually established a profitable Asian trade.

In 1492, Spain's monarchs **Ferdinand and Isabella** funded an expedition, led by the Italian navigator **Christopher Columbus,** to find a sea route to Asia by sailing west

across the Atlantic Ocean. Although the expedition failed to achieve its goal, reaching the Americas proved to be of great benefit to Spain. The Spanish established colonies in the Caribbean and conquered large areas of the Americas. As you know, a **colony** is a group of people who settle in a new land but keep ties to their native country.

Portugal and Spain developed a heated **rivalry**, or competition, over who would control the newly encountered lands. In 1494, Portugal and Spain agreed to the Treaty of Tordesillas (tawr-day-SEE-yahs) to settle their dispute. The treaty drew an imaginary line through the Atlantic Ocean from north to south. Portugal received the easterly lands, including Brazil, while Spain would receive any newly encountered lands to the west.

The English, Dutch, and French entered the competition for trade and new lands later. The English formed the East India Company in 1600 and established trading posts in India. They established colonies in North America as well. In 1602, the Dutch founded the **Dutch East India Company** to compete for trade in the Indian Ocean. The French joined the exploration race largely to compete with their English rivals.

IMPACT OF EXPLORATION

European exploration changed the world. Trade increased greatly. At trading posts, both goods and ideas were readily exchanged. As trading posts developed into colonies, more and more people moved from Europe to establish farms, towns, and cities in Asia, Africa, and the Americas. These colonies enriched the mother countries, which claimed land and **exploited**, or used to their own advantage, local resources and native people. The colonists brought European culture to places all over the world. As the Age of Exploration turned into a competition for land and riches, Europeans ended up controlling much of the world.

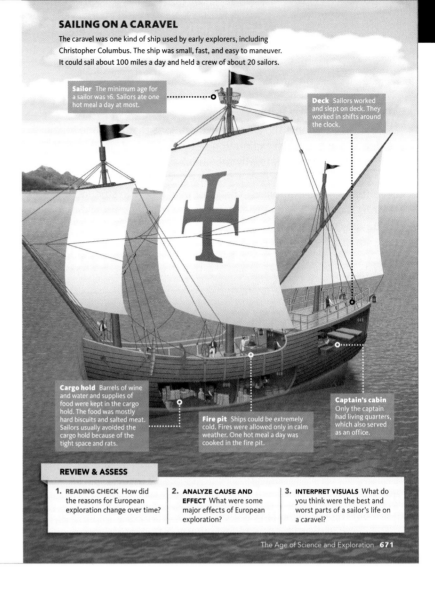

SAILING ON A CARAVEL

The caravel was one kind of ship used by early explorers, including Christopher Columbus. The ship was small, fast, and easy to maneuver. It could sail about 100 miles a day and held a crew of about 20 sailors.

Sailor The minimum age for a sailor was 16. Sailors ate one hot meal a day at most.

Deck Sailors worked and slept on deck. They worked in shifts around the clock.

Cargo hold Barrels of wine and water and supplies of food were kept in the cargo hold. The food was mostly hard biscuits and salted meat. Sailors usually avoided the cargo hold because of the tight space and rats.

Fire pit Ships could be extremely cold. Fires were allowed only in calm weather. One hot meal a day was cooked in the fire pit.

Captain's cabin Only the captain had living quarters, which also served as an office.

REVIEW & ASSESS

1. **READING CHECK** How did the reasons for European exploration change over time?

2. **ANALYZE CAUSE AND EFFECT** What were some major effects of European exploration?

3. **INTERPRET VISUALS** What do you think were the best and worst parts of a sailor's life on a caravel?

PLAN

OBJECTIVE

Identify the five European nations that competed for trade, land, and riches during the Age of Exploration.

CRITICAL THINKING SKILLS FOR LESSON 2.2

- Identify Main Ideas and Details
- Monitor Comprehension
- Analyze Cause and Effect
- Interpret Visuals
- Explain
- Compare and Contrast

ESSENTIAL QUESTION

How did new ideas affect Europeans' views of the world?

With better navigation tools and a new way of viewing the world,

several nations increased exploration voyages. Lesson 2.2 describes how these European nations competed for trade, land, and riches.

BACKGROUND FOR THE TEACHER

The life of sailors on the exploration voyages was difficult. Food was particularly not nutritious and often inedible. The main rations included salt beef or salt pork, cheese, fish, ale, and biscuits. The quality of the food deteriorated during the duration of the voyage because of poor storage problems and lack of ventilation. The quality further deteriorated due to the presence of rats and other pests on the ships. The biscuits were often filled with maggots. Most often, the ship's cook was selected from sailors who were either wounded or maimed and therefore not fit for other duties on the ship.

DIGITAL RESOURCES myNGconnect.com

TEACHER RESOURCES & ASSESSMENT

 Reading and Note-Taking   **Vocabulary Practice**   **Section 2 Quiz**

STUDENT RESOURCES

 NG Chapter Gallery

THREE-STEP INTERVIEW

Ask the class to think about places they would like to explore if they had the chance. Why do they want to go there? Have pairs of students take turns asking each other those questions. Then ask pairs to share their interview results with the class. **0:15** minutes

GUIDED DISCUSSION

1. **Explain** How did Portugal and Spain settle the dispute over who would control newly encountered lands? *(Portugal and Spain agreed to the Treaty of Tordesillas to settle the dispute. The treaty drew an imaginary line through the Atlantic Ocean; Spain would receive newly encountered lands to the west of the line, and Portugal would receive the easterly lands.)*

2. **Compare and Contrast** How were explorations of Portugal similar to those of Spain? How were they different? *(Similar: Both Spain and Portugal wanted to find a sea route to Asia. Different: Portugal discovered an eastern sea route to Asia, while Spain wanted to find a sea route by sailing west across the Atlantic; Portugal established a profitable Asian trade, while the Spanish established colonies in the Caribbean and parts of the Americas.)*

INTERPRET VISUALS

Direct students' attention to the illustration of the caravel. Have them read the captions describing the sections of the ship. **ASK:**

- What was the purpose of the fire pit? *(It was used to provide warmth on cold days when the weather was calm and to cook one hot meal a day.)*
- Why did sailors avoid the cargo hold? *(It was a tight space with rats.)*
- What do you think might have attracted young people to sign on to voyages on a caravel? *(Responses will vary. Students might indicate a desire for adventure or the hope of gaining wealth.)*

0:05 minutes

ACTIVE OPTIONS

Critical Viewing: NG Chapter Gallery Have students examine the contents of the Chapter Gallery for this chapter. Then invite them to brainstorm additional images they believe would fit within the gallery. Have them write a description of these additional images and provide an explanation of why they would fit. Then instruct them to do online research to find examples of actual images they would like to add to the gallery. **0:10** minutes

On Your Feet: Fishbowl Have one half of the class sit in a close circle, facing inward. The other half of the class sits in a larger circle around them. Post the following statement: *Describe how European nations competed with one another during the Age of Exploration.*

Students in the inner circle should discuss the question for 5 minutes while those in the outer circle listen to the discussion and evaluate the points made. Then have the groups reverse roles and continue the discussion. **0:10** minutes

SUMMARIZE

Summarize Have students work in pairs. Assign each pair one of the two sections under the blue headings. Pairs should read their sections together and then write a summary sentence to share with the class. If more than one pair summarizes a particular section, allow them to take turns sharing their section summary before moving to the next section.

ENGLISH LANGUAGE LEARNERS

Match Words and Definitions Give students the following matching exercise. Have them work in pairs to match the words with their definitions and then write a sentence using each one.

1.	exploited (c)	a.	a group of people that settles in a new land but keeps ties to its native country
2.	colony (a)	b.	competition
3.	rivalry (b)	c.	used to their own advantage

Press **mt** *in the Student eEdition for modified text.*

See the Chapter Planner for more strategies for differentiation.

ANSWERS

1. The reasons for European exploration changed from a desire to find a sea route from Europe to Asia in order to control trade to a competition for newly encountered lands and riches.

2. As a result of European exploration, global trade increased; more Europeans moved to Asia, Africa, and the Americas and established farms, towns, and cities; European countries became enriched by exploiting the resources and native people of their colonies; European culture was introduced around the world; and Europeans ended up controlling much of the world.

3. Answers will vary. Sample response: I think the best part of a sailor's life on a caravel was the exposure to new sights and the worst part was the lack of a comfortable, private place to sleep.

OCTOBER 12, 1492

Around 2:00 a.m. on a moonlit night, the Spanish sailor Rodrigo de Triana yelled out the words his fellow sailors were so desperate to hear: "Land! Land!" The three small ships of Christopher Columbus's fleet had finally reached land. But what land? Columbus was aiming for Asia. Convinced that he'd reached it, he called the lands the West Indies and the natives Indians. In fact, Columbus had massively underestimated the size of the planet. He had unexpectedly found an area unknown to Europeans: the Americas or New World. The precise location of this landfall remains a mystery. One possibility is an island in the Bahamas called Samana Cay, which is shown above.

672 CHAPTER 23

673

PLAN

OBJECTIVE

Identify the significance of October 12, 1492, on Europeans' view of the world.

CRITICAL THINKING SKILLS FOR LESSON 2.3

- Analyze Visuals
- Summarize
- Analyze Cause and Effect

ESSENTIAL QUESTION

How did new ideas affect Europeans' views of the world?

When Christopher Columbus finally reached land after sailing west across the Atlantic Ocean, he was convinced that he had reached Asia. However, the moment in history featured in Lesson 2.3 would significantly change Europeans' views of the world.

BACKGROUND FOR THE TEACHER

In October 1986, after a five-year study, the National Geographic Society announced that Samana Cay was the site of Christopher Columbus's first landfall in the New World on October 12, 1492. Before this claim, San Salvador was thought to be the landing site. The National Geographic Society used computer analyses of Columbus's transatlantic route as well as descriptions in Columbus's journal and other evidence to come to its conclusion.

DIGITAL RESOURCES myNGconnect.com

TEACHER RESOURCES & ASSESSMENT

 Reading and Note-Taking   **Vocabulary Practice**   **Section 2 Quiz**

STUDENT RESOURCES

 NG Chapter Gallery

ANALYZE MAPS

Ask students to examine the photograph of Samana Cay. Point out to students that Samana Cay is located in the Bahamas. Provide students with a map of the Bahamas. Students should notice that the Bahamas are made up of several islands and cays. Ask them to locate Samana Cay on the map. Point out to students that Samana Cay was likely the place where Christopher Columbus first made landfall. **0:05** minutes

TEACH

GUIDED DISCUSSION

1. **Summarize** Why did Christopher Columbus call the place where he landed the West Indies? *(He thought he had reached Asia.)*

2. **Analyze Cause and Effect** What was the effect of Columbus's landing on Samana Cay on European nations? *(Columbus's landing led to expeditions by other European nations to find routes to Asia and eventually changed Europeans' views of the world.)*

MORE INFORMATION

The Bahamas The Bahamas is an archipelago that covers an area of about 530 square miles and is located about 60 miles off the southeastern coast of Florida. The Bahamas comprises nearly 700 islands and cays. A cay is a small, sandy island on the surface of a coral reef. Only about 30 of the islands and cays of the Bahamas are inhabited. The Samana Cay is the largest uninhabited cay in the Bahamas.

ACTIVE OPTIONS

Critical Viewing: NG Chapter Gallery Invite students to explore the NG Chapter Gallery and create a Top Five List by choosing the five images they find most interesting. If possible, have students copy the five images into a document to form an actual list. Then encourage them to select the image they like best and do further research on it. **0:10** minutes

On Your Feet: Descriptive Words Hand out two sticky notes to each student. Have students examine the details in the photograph of Samana Cay. Then have them write a word or phrase on each sticky note that describes the physical features of the cay. Have students place their sticky notes on the board and discuss their descriptions. Have them discuss what they think Christopher Columbus thought when he landed here on October 12, 1492. **0:10** minutes

INCLUSION

Describe Lesson Visuals Pair visually impaired students with students who are not impaired. Ask the latter to help their partners "see" the visual in this lesson by describing the elements in the photograph and answering questions the visually impaired student might have.

GIFTED & TALENTED

Write Journal Entries Direct students to focus on the photograph and to read the information about October 12, 1492. Invite students to imagine that they are crew members on Columbus's ships. Ask them to imagine how they felt and what they thought when they finally reached the land pictured here on October 12, 1492. Instruct them to write one or more journal entries describing their experience. Have them consider the following:

- How did they feel when they departed the ship and set foot on the land?
- Was the land they reached what they had expected to find?
- What concerns might they have had about their location?

Ask students to share their journal entries with the class.

Press **mt** *in the Student eEdition for modified text.*

See the Chapter Planner for more strategies for differentiation.

A New World

During the European Age of Exploration, the leaders of many expeditions kept journals, in which they wrote detailed accounts of their voyages. Christopher Columbus kept such a journal. The voyages of Columbus and other explorers changed Europeans' view of the world—and their maps.

DOCUMENT ONE

Primary Source: Journal

from *The Journal of Christopher Columbus*

Christopher Columbus's original journal from his historic voyage in 1492 was lost. Then, in 1790, a full copy was found in the writings of the Spanish historian Bartolomé de Las Casas. In this excerpt from the journal, Columbus addresses his sponsors, the Spanish monarchs Ferdinand and Isabella. He discusses the direction of his voyage and how he intends to record the voyage.

CONSTRUCTED RESPONSE What land was Columbus trying to reach, and what was unusual about his route?

> Your Highnesses . . . determined to send me, Christopher Columbus, to the above-mentioned countries of India . . . and furthermore directed that I should not proceed by land to the East, as is customary, but by a Westerly route, in which direction we have hitherto no certain evidence that any one has gone . . . Moreover, Sovereign Princes, besides describing every night the occurrences of the day, and every day those of the preceding night, I intend to draw up a nautical chart, which shall contain the several parts of the ocean and land in their proper situations; and also to compose a book to represent the whole by picture with latitudes and longitudes.

DOCUMENT TWO

Primary Source: Map

Map from 1513

This map by the German mapmaker Martin Waldseemüller was published in 1513. It was the first printed map to include a part of the New World. It highlights the importance of the islands of the Caribbean. The area labeled with the Latin words *terra incognita*, meaning "unknown land," is present-day Brazil.

CONSTRUCTED RESPONSE What does this map demonstrate about European knowledge of the Western Hemisphere in 1513?

ANSWERS

DOCUMENT 1

Columbus was trying to reach India. He sought a westerly route to India, which no one had ever done before.

DOCUMENT 2

In 1513, Europeans knew that a large landmass existed across the Atlantic Ocean, but they knew no details about its interior.

These ships are replicas of the *Pinta*, the *Santa María*, and the *Niña*, the three ships that made up Columbus's expedition in 1492.

SYNTHESIZE & WRITE

1. **REVIEW** Review what you have learned about the Age of Exploration.

2. **RECALL** Think about your responses to the constructed response questions above.

3. **CONSTRUCT** Write a topic sentence that answers this question: How did European voyages lead to unexpected results?

4. **WRITE** Using evidence from the documents, write an informative paragraph that supports your topic sentence.

PLAN

OBJECTIVE

Synthesize information about the changes in Europeans' view of the world from primary source documents.

CRITICAL THINKING SKILLS FOR LESSON 2.4

- Synthesize
- Summarize
- Draw Conclusions
- Evaluate

ESSENTIAL QUESTION

How did new ideas affect Europeans' views of the world?

The leaders of European voyages during the Age of Exploration kept journals of their explorations. The content of the journals helped change Europeans' views of the world. Lesson 2.4 includes excerpts from Christopher Columbus's journal and a map of the New World.

BACKGROUND FOR THE TEACHER

In 1507, Martin Waldseemüller's map of the world was printed. It reflected the world in light of the results of the explorations of Spain and Portugal. In creating the 1507 map, Waldseemüller likely had access to the letters of Amerigo Vespucci, who concluded that the lands reached by Columbus in 1492 were a new continent, not known to Europeans. To honor this accomplishment, Waldseemüller used Vespucci's name and labeled the continent "America" on the 1507 map. However, by the time Waldseemüller created the 1513 map, he appears to have regretted honoring only Vespucci for his explorations, and the name "America" was replaced with *terra incognita*, meaning "unknown land."

DIGITAL RESOURCES myNGconnect.com

TEACHER RESOURCES & ASSESSMENT

 Reading and Note-Taking   **Vocabulary Practice**   **Section 2 Quiz**

STUDENT RESOURCES

 **NG Chapter Gallery**

INTRODUCE & ENGAGE

PREPARE FOR THE DOCUMENT-BASED QUESTION

Before students start on the activity, briefly preview the two documents. Remind students that a constructed response requires full explanations in complete sentences. Emphasize that students should use their knowledge of the results of European explorations in addition to the information in the documents. **0:05** minutes

TEACH

GUIDED DISCUSSION

1. **Summarize** What does Christopher Columbus discuss in the excerpt in Document One? *(He discusses the direction of his voyage and how he intends to record the voyage.)*

2. **Draw Conclusions** What ocean is shown on Waldseemüller's map in Document Two? *(the Atlantic Ocean)*

EVALUATE

After students have completed the "Synthesize & Write" activity, allow time for them to exchange paragraphs and read and comment on the work of their peers. Guidelines for comments should be established prior to this activity so that feedback is constructive and encouraging in nature. **0:15** minutes

ACTIVE OPTIONS

Critical Viewing: NG Chapter Gallery Ask students to choose one image from the Chapter Gallery and become an expert on it. They should do additional research to learn all about it. Then, students should share their findings with a partner, small group, or the class. **0:10** minutes

On Your Feet: Two Options Label two locations in the room with the name of one of the documents featured in the lesson. Have students reread the lesson and walk to the corner of the room with the document that best helped support their understanding that Europeans' view of the world had changed in the 1500s. Have students who chose the same document discuss why they made their selection. Then have volunteers from each group explain what their document is, and offer some of the group's reasons for choosing that one. **0:20** minutes

DIFFERENTIATE

INCLUSION

Work in Pairs If some students have disabilities, consider pairing them with other students who can read the documents aloud to them. You may also want to give students the option of recording their responses.

PRE-AP

Research Have students conduct Internet research to find out more about either the journals of Columbus or about the life and work of Martin Waldseemüller. Have them report to the rest of the class about what information Columbus's journals provide or about the impact Waldseemüller's work had on people in the 1500s.

Press **mt** *in the Student eEdition for modified text.*

See the Chapter Planner for more strategies for differentiation.

SYNTHESIZE & WRITE

ANSWERS

1. Responses will vary.

2. Responses will vary.

3. Possible response: The discovery of a new land and resources were unexpected results of European voyages.

4. Students' paragraphs should include their topic sentence from Step 3 and provide several details from the documents to support the sentence.

The **Columbian** Exchange

For lunch, a girl in the United States eats an apple and a roast beef sandwich on wheat bread.

A boy in Ireland chows down on a turkey-and-tomato sandwich and some french fries. In 1500, neither person could have eaten this lunch. The two meals are a result of the **Columbian Exchange**—a transfer of foods, plants, animals, and diseases between the Old and New Worlds.

MAIN IDEA

A global exchange of foods, plants, animals, and diseases occurred in the period after Columbus arrived in the Americas, bringing both benefits and disaster.

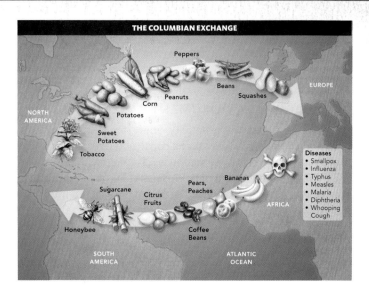

THE COLUMBIAN EXCHANGE

Peppers
Corn
Peanuts
Beans
Squashes
EUROPE
NORTH AMERICA
Potatoes
Sweet Potatoes
Tobacco
Diseases
• Smallpox
• Influenza
• Typhus
• Measles
• Malaria
• Diphtheria
• Whooping Cough
Sugarcane
Citrus Fruits
Pears, Peaches
Bananas
AFRICA
Honeybee
Coffee Beans
SOUTH AMERICA
ATLANTIC OCEAN

EUROPEAN DISEASES

European diseases killed more Native Americans than warfare. The native population of Central America fell from about 25 million to 2.5 million between 1519 and 1565 due to disease.

FROM EAST TO WEST

The European encounter with the New World coincided with improved sea connections within the Old World of Europe, Africa, and Asia. The combined impact was enormous. Places and people that were once isolated from one another became part of a global exchange network. The contact and trade between these far-flung lands helped some people—and harmed others.

European explorers and colonists wanted to re-create their European lifestyles in the New World. They introduced such familiar foods as wheat, barley, oats, grapes, apples, citrus fruits, and olives. They also brought cattle, sheep, pigs, goats, chickens, and horses. These plants and animals flourished in the Americas. Wheat could be grown in places where native crops could not, and it became one of North America's most important crops. The use of horses changed warfare and transportation in the Americas, while other livestock provided new sources of food.

Europeans also brought crops from Africa and Asia to the Americas. These crops included bananas, coffee beans, and sugarcane. Sugarcane grew especially well in the Caribbean climate. Using slave labor, European growers were able to harvest the sugar and sell it at a huge profit in Europe.

Unfortunately, Europeans also introduced deadly new diseases to the Americas. Native people no resistance against such diseases as measles, malaria, and **smallpox**. Smallpox proved to be especially deadly, killing millions of native people across the Americas. Caused by a virus, smallpox is highly contagious. It produces a high fever and small blisters on the skin that leave pitted scars. The virus would finally be eradicated, or eliminated, in the United States in the 1900s.

FROM WEST TO EAST

In the Columbian Exchange, animals and plants also traveled from the Americas to Europe and Africa. Explorers returned to Europe with such exotic foods as turkeys, peppers, corn, tomatoes, potatoes, beans, and squashes. Many of these foods eventually became a regular part of European diets. Other imports were considered luxuries, including tobacco, vanilla, and cacao beans. Vanilla was used as a flavoring, while cacao beans were used to make chocolate drinks, which were sweetened with imported sugar.

The New World also contributed an important medicine called **quinine** to the Old World. Europeans learned about quinine, which comes from the bark of a tree in South America, in the 1600s. For about 300 years, it served as the only effective remedy for malaria, which is carried by mosquitoes. Quinine's use as a treatment for malaria benefitted millions of people and allowed Europeans to colonize malaria-ridden areas of the world.

For better or worse, the Columbian Exchange affected the lives of people throughout the world. About 30 percent of the foods eaten today originated in the Americas. A greater variety of foods helped improve the nutrition of people around the world. However, the effect of the Columbian Exchange on native populations in the Americas was disastrous.

REVIEW & ASSESS

1. **READING CHECK** How did the Columbian Exchange benefit Europeans?

2. **ANALYZE CAUSE AND EFFECT** Why was the Columbian Exchange disastrous for Native Americans?

3. **INTERPRET MAPS** What foods do you eat that came to the Americas in the Columbian Exchange?

PLAN

OBJECTIVE

Describe the effect of a global exchange of foods, plants, animals, and diseases that occurred in the period after Columbus arrived in the Americas.

After Columbus arrived in the Americas, an exchange of foods, plants, and animals developed between the New World and Europe and Africa. Lesson 2.5 describes the benefits and disasters brought about by this exchange.

CRITICAL THINKING SKILLS FOR LESSON 2.5

- Identify Main Ideas and Details
- Analyze Cause and Effect
- Draw Conclusions
- Monitor Comprehension
- Interpret Maps
- Synthesize

ESSENTIAL QUESTION

How did new ideas affect Europeans' views of the world?

BACKGROUND FOR THE TEACHER

At first, some of the foods that were introduced to Europeans from the Americas frightened them. For example, some Europeans thought that tomatoes were poisonous and that potatoes caused leprosy. Corn and potatoes became significant crops to be transferred from the Americas. The two crops were inexpensive to grow and highly nutritious. They became important foods in the diets of many people throughout the world, helping to boost the world's population.

DIGITAL RESOURCES myNGconnect.com

TEACHER RESOURCES & ASSESSMENT

 Reading and Note-Taking

 Vocabulary Practice

 Section 2 Quiz

STUDENT RESOURCES

 NG Chapter Gallery

INTRODUCE & ENGAGE

MAKE CONNECTIONS

Ask students how people around the world are connected today. Students might indicate that the Internet and cell phones have made it easy to connect with people around the world. Also, the ease of travel has connected people around the world. Ask students if some of the foods they eat come from different parts of the world and to share with the class what these foods are. Point out to students that before Columbus's expeditions, the Americas were isolated from the rest of the world. In this lesson they will learn about the exchange of plants, animals, and diseases that occurred after Columbus arrived in the Americas. **0:10** minutes

Think (A) (B)

Pair (A) (B)

Share (A) (B)

TEACH

GUIDED DISCUSSION

1. **Draw Conclusions** Why did Europeans introduce foods such as wheat and apples to the New World? *(European explorers and colonists wanted to re-create their lifestyles back home, including the foods they ate.)*

2. **Synthesize** Why is the Columbian Exchange considered a significant event? *(Responses will vary. Possible response might be that the transfer of foods in the Columbian Exchange brought the Western and Eastern Hemispheres together and affected many of the world's people.)*

INTERPRET MAPS

Have students focus on the Columbian Exchange map. **ASK:** What continents were involved in the Columbian Exchange? *(North America, Europe, Africa, and South America)* Ask students if the source of any of the foods listed surprised them, and if so to explain why. **0:15** minutes

ACTIVE OPTIONS

Critical Viewing: NG Chapter Gallery Invite students to explore the entire NG Image Gallery and choose one image from the gallery they feel best represents their understanding of the section. Have students provide a written explanation of why they selected the image they chose. **0:10** minutes

On Your Feet: Think, Pair, Share Have students use the Think, Pair, Share strategy to develop their ideas about the positive and negative effects of the Columbian Exchange. Have pairs decide what they believe to be the greatest benefit of the exchange to Europe, the Native Americans, and the world, as well as the greatest negative effect on each of the three. **0:15** minutes

DIFFERENTIATE

ENGLISH LANGUAGE LEARNERS

Summarize Lesson 2.5 has seven paragraphs. Have students work in pairs or small groups, and assign each pair or group one paragraph to read together. Then each group should summarize their paragraph in one or two sentences for the class.

PRE-AP

Analyze Effects Assign teams and have each team choose a food or a disease from the Columbian Exchange diagram on which to focus. Teams researching a particular food item can identify the varieties available today. Teams researching a disease should find out how widespread it is today and what treatments are available. Suggest that students develop a graphic organizer to display the results of their investigations.

Press (mt) *in the Student eEdition for modified text.*

See the Chapter Planner for more strategies for differentiation.

REVIEW & ASSESS

ANSWERS

1. Many new foods, plants, and animals were introduced to Europe. Many Europeans grew wealthy by trading and exploiting the resources of the New World.

2. Europeans brought to the Americas many deadly diseases, such as measles, malaria, and smallpox, to which the native populations had no resistance. Many millions of Native Americans died as a result.

3. Answers will vary depending on the foods that students eat. Possible responses include citrus fruits, apples, grapes, bananas, sugar, peaches, pears, olives, rice, wheat, barley, oats, milk, pork, beef, and lamb.

The Spanish Conquest

Two Aztec messengers run to carry an important message to their king: Strangers have invaded their land. The invaders have white skin that looks like that of a ghost. They wear clothes that cover their entire bodies. They sit on deer that carry them wherever they want to go. They have a weapon that shoots a ball of stone, which comes out raining fire and shooting sparks. The messengers' report fills the Aztec king with terror.

MAIN IDEA

Spain created a large American empire that covered parts of the Caribbean and Central and South America by the mid-1500s.

CORTÉS AND THE AZTEC

As you learned earlier, the Treaty of Tordesillas divided the New World between Spain and Portugal. Spain was quick to explore and exploit its new territory. The Spanish established important colonies on several Caribbean islands, including what are now Haiti, the Dominican Republic, and Cuba. Although these islands provided valuable agricultural land, they did not supply the gold so coveted by the Europeans.

Seeking gold, in 1519 the Spanish launched their most daring conquest ever—the invasion of Mexico. The Spanish adventurers who led the conquest of the Americas became known as **conquistadors** (kahn-KEES-tuh-dawrs). A conquistador named **Hernán Cortés** led the invasion of Mexico with about 500 men who had come to the Caribbean to make their fortunes.

After landing on the uncharted coast of Mexico, Cortés learned of the fabulously rich Aztec Empire and marched inland to conquer it. Though outnumbered, Cortés's soldiers had superior steel weapons, devastating cannons, and horses, all unknown in the New World.

On his march to the Aztec capital of **Tenochtitlán** (tay-nohch-teet-LAHN), Cortés was joined by many native tribes who resented the harsh rule of the Aztec. With their support, Cortés fought and defeated the Aztec in a series of battles and a final dramatic siege that destroyed the magnificent city of Tenochtitlán. Its ruins lie buried under what is now Mexico City. The Spanish gained what they wanted—Aztec gold and silver—and they ruled Mexico for the next 300 years.

PIZARRO AND THE INCA

With Mexico conquered, the Spanish then pushed into South America. Sometime between 1530 and 1532, the conquistador **Francisco Pizarro** set off to invade the reportedly rich land of Biru, or what is now Peru. The huge and well-organized Inca Empire was based in Peru.

Pizarro's army had fewer than 200 men, but their steel weapons and horses gave them a deadly advantage. So did their cruelty. When Pizarro arrived, he found the Inca Empire weakened by smallpox and a bitter civil war. Pizarro arranged a meeting with the newly appointed Inca emperor, **Atahualpa** (ah-tah-WAHL-pah), but he had laid a dangerous trap.

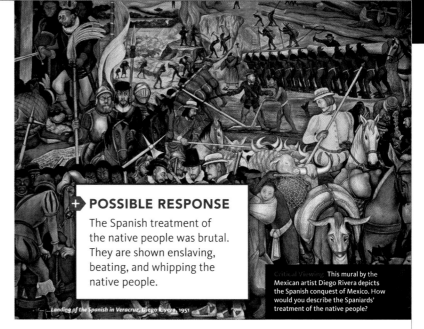

⊕ POSSIBLE RESPONSE

The Spanish treatment of the native people was brutal. They are shown enslaving, beating, and whipping the native people.

Critical Viewing This mural by the Mexican artist Diego Rivera depicts the Spanish conquest of Mexico. How would you describe the Spaniards' treatment of the native people?

Landing of the Spanish in Veracruz, Diego Rivera, 1951

Although Atahualpa was accompanied by between 3,000 and 5,000 attendants, the Spanish cavalry cut a path to the Inca emperor and captured him. They then slaughtered many of his stunned and unarmed followers.

Atahualpa offered the Spanish a roomful of gold and two rooms of silver in exchange for his release. However, after obtaining the gold and silver, the Spanish killed the Inca ruler.

The Spanish went on to conquer much of the vast Inca Empire, which stretched from Ecuador into central Chile. The Inca continued to resist the Spanish until 1572, when the Spanish executed the last Inca ruler. Through military conquest, the Spanish built a large empire that helped make Spain the richest and most powerful country in the world in the 1500s. The Spanish continued to rule over much of South America for centuries.

REVIEW & ASSESS

1. **READING CHECK** What drove the Spanish to invade and conquer large areas of the Americas?

2. **COMPARE AND CONTRAST** How was Pizarro's conquest of the Inca similar to Cortés's conquest of the Aztec?

3. **MAKE INFERENCES** Why were small numbers of the Spanish able to conquer large areas of the Americas?

PLAN

OBJECTIVE

Explain how Spain created a large American empire in parts of the Caribbean and Central and South America by the mid-1500s.

CRITICAL THINKING SKILLS FOR LESSON 3.1

- Identify Main Ideas and Details
- Monitor Comprehension
- Compare and Contrast
- Make Inferences
- Summarize
- Make Generalizations
- Analyze Visuals

ESSENTIAL QUESTION

How did new ideas affect Europeans' views of the world?

Christopher Columbus's expeditions to the Americas led to further explorations by the Spanish. Lesson 3.1 explains how Spain created a large American empire in the mid-1500s.

BACKGROUND FOR THE TEACHER

Tenochtitlán, the capital of the Aztec Empire, was located on the site of present-day Mexico City. It was founded in 1325 in the marshes of Lake Texcoco. The city was surrounded by floating gardens called *chinampas,* on which produce for the city's food supply was grown. The city covered about five square miles and was joined to the mainland by several causeways. By 1519, when the Spanish launched their invasion of Mexico, Tenochtitlán's population was estimated to be about 400,000 people. The Spanish destroyed the capital city in 1521.

DIGITAL RESOURCES myNGconnect.com

TEACHER RESOURCES & ASSESSMENT

 Reading and Note-Taking

 Vocabulary Practice

 Section 3 Quiz

STUDENT RESOURCES

 NG Chapter Gallery

ACTIVATE PRIOR KNOWLEDGE

Ask students to recall what they know about the settlement of the United States by Europeans. Discuss with them how the Europeans treated the Native Americans they encountered there. Tell students that in Lesson 3.1 they will learn about Spain's conquest of the Americas and the Spanish treatment of the native people there. `0:05` minutes

TEACH

GUIDED DISCUSSION

1. **Summarize** What events brought about an end to the Aztec and Inca empires? *(The Aztec Empire ended after a series of battles between Cortés's army and the Aztec and the destruction of the capital city of Tenochtitlán. The Inca Empire came to an end after Francisco Pizarro set a trap to capture the Inca emperor, killed the emperor's followers, conquered much of the Inca Empire, and executed the last Inca ruler.)*

2. **Make Generalizations** How would you describe the character traits of conquistadors such as Cortés and Pizarro? *(Responses will vary. Possible responses: greedy, cruel, deceitful, brave, skilled, strong leaders)*

ANALYZE VISUALS

Have students work with a partner to analyze the mural by artist Diego Rivera in the lesson. Provide students with a 5Ws Chart. Then have them answer these questions: What is being shown in the mural? Who is shown in the mural? Where or in what location does the event in the mural take place? What event is the mural portraying? Why was this painting created? `0:15` minutes

What?
Who?
Where?
When?
Why?

ACTIVE OPTIONS

NG Learning Framework: Write a Story

ATTITUDE: **Curiosity**
SKILL: **Communication**
KNOWLEDGE: **Our Human Story**

Have students select one of the people they are still curious about after learning about this individual in this chapter. Instruct them to use information from the chapter and additional source material to write a story that they could tell about this person. `0:20` minutes

On Your Feet: Question and Answer Have half the class write true-false questions based on information in the lesson. Ask the other half to create answer cards, with "True" written on one side and "False" on the other. As each question is read aloud, students in the second group should display the correct answer to the question. When discrepancies occur, review the question and discuss which answer is correct. `0:10` minutes

STRIVING READERS

Preview Text Help students preview Lesson 3.1. Point out the text features, such as the lesson title, Main Idea statement, and subheadings. **ASK:** Based on the subheadings, what do you expect this lesson to be about? Have them study the mural and its accompanying "Critical Viewing" caption. As students begin reading, help them confirm their understandings of each paragraph before moving on to the next one.

GIFTED & TALENTED

Conduct an Interview Have students imagine that they are news broadcasters covering the Spanish conquest of the Americas. Have students work with partners to create an interview with Hernán Cortés, Francisco Pizarro, or Atahualpa. Student partners should develop questions to ask the interviewee. Then have each pair present their interviews to the class.

Press (mt) *in the Student eEdition for modified text.*

See the Chapter Planner for more strategies for differentiation.

ANSWERS

1. The Spanish launched their invasion and conquest of large areas of the Americas to obtain gold.

2. Both Pizarro and Cortés had a relatively small group of soldiers, but they had weapons that were superior to those of the native people and they had horses, which the native people lacked.

3. Answers may vary. Possible response: The Spanish had superior weapons and horses, the native people were weakened by European diseases, and the Spanish were relentless and brutal.

Portugal's Empire

On the sand of an African beach, your crew carries a huge stone cross and sets it upright. Its design and words stake Portugal's claim to this land where your crew has arrived. Almost all Portuguese explorers carry crosses like the one you've just erected here. These crosses dot the coasts of Africa and other lands.

MAIN IDEA

Portugal built a powerful trading empire that extended along the coast of Africa and reached into areas of the Indian Ocean and South America.

A TRADE NETWORK

In the Middle Ages, Portugal was a relatively small and undeveloped country. However, by focusing on maritime exploration and trade, the country developed a powerful commercial empire by the 1500s.

Beginning in 1415, Portugal's kings encouraged seafarers to explore the west coast of Africa, hoping to find an easterly sea route to tap into the spice trade with Asia. Portuguese explorers systematically advanced along Africa's coastline. By 1460, they had established trading posts that were sending spices, gold, and slaves to European markets.

Portugal's explorers continued around the southern tip of Africa, along its eastern coast, and across the Indian Ocean. They reached India itself in 1498. However, the Muslim merchants who had controlled the region's trade for centuries did not welcome the Portuguese. Portugal fought to gain access to the Indian Ocean trade. With bigger, stronger, and better-armed ships, the Portuguese defeated the Muslim traders.

The Portuguese built strongly fortified trading posts to control important areas, including Goa and Calicut in India and Macao in China. By the 1540s, the Portuguese had reached Japan and completely dominated the Indian Ocean trade. They were unrivaled until the Dutch and English muscled into the Indian Ocean trade in the early 1600s.

SUGAR, GOLD, AND DIAMONDS

The Portuguese stumbled across Brazil when they sailed too far west on a trip to India. In 1500, the Portuguese explorer **Pedro Álvares Cabral** sighted the coast of Brazil and landed for a short time to stake Portugal's claim to the area.

At first, Portugal had limited interest in Brazil, which provided little more than brazilwood, a source of red dye. But after the French began trading with Brazil's native people, Portugal decided to establish a colony to assert its authority over the area. Brazil's scattered tribes offered no organized resistance. Portugal established its first Brazilian colony in 1532 and divided the colony into administrative districts with a governor in charge.

The Portuguese kings encouraged Brazilian colonists to set up large farms, called **plantations**, for growing sugarcane, a plant used to make sugar. In the 1500s, sugar was a rare luxury in Europe, and Portugal expected to make huge profits from its import. However, growing and processing sugarcane was complex and labor-intensive. Sugarcane producers used a huge number of slaves to perform the

+ POSSIBLE RESPONSE

The man's clothing suggests that he needs protection from the sun, insects, and perhaps snakes.

Critical Viewing: This photograph shows a man in present-day Brazil dressed and equipped to harvest sugarcane. What does his clothing suggest about the hazards of the job?

hard and often dangerous work. Over the course of 300 years, Brazil would import nearly 4 million slaves from West Africa.

Then, in 1695, huge quantities of gold were discovered in Brazil, sparking a gold rush. By 1760, gold rivaled sugar as Brazil's main export. The search for

gold led to the discovery of diamonds in the 1720s, adding to the wealth that Portugal gained from Brazil. Almost all the wealth was made possible through a much bigger trade, however—the slave trade. You'll learn more about the Atlantic slave trade in the next lesson.

REVIEW & ASSESS

1. **READING CHECK** How was the relatively small country of Portugal able to build a powerful trading empire?

2. **DRAW CONCLUSIONS** Why did Portuguese kings encourage colonists in Brazil to establish plantations for growing sugarcane?

3. **ANALYZE CAUSE AND EFFECT** How did the sugar trade contribute to the development and growth of the slave trade?

PLAN

OBJECTIVE

Describe how Portugal built a powerful trading empire along the coasts of Africa and South America.

CRITICAL THINKING SKILLS FOR LESSON 3.2

- Identify Main Ideas and Details
- Monitor Comprehension
- Draw Conclusions
- Analyze Cause and Effect
- Evaluate

ESSENTIAL QUESTION

How did new ideas affect Europeans' views of the world?

Although a small country, Portugal focused on maritime exploration and trade. Lesson 3.2 discusses how Portugal built a trading empire.

BACKGROUND FOR THE TEACHER

Pedro Álvares Cabral is credited as the first European to reach Brazil. In 1500, King Manuel I named him commander of the second Portuguese expedition to India. Sailing westward, Cabral sighted the coast of Brazil and named it the True Cross. Eventually, the country took the present-day name, *Brazil,* from a kind of wood called *paubrasil* that is found there. Cabral took formal possession of the country and sent a ship back to Portugal to inform the king. Afterward, maps showed Portugal as the ruler of a great area of land. Later voyages used Brazil as a port of call in the journey from Europe to the Cape of Good Hope in Africa and the Indian Ocean.

DIGITAL RESOURCES myNGconnect.com

TEACHER RESOURCES & ASSESSMENT

 Reading and Note-Taking

 Vocabulary Practice

 Section 3 Quiz

STUDENT RESOURCES

 NG Chapter Gallery

POSE AND ANSWER QUESTIONS

As a class, complete a K-W-L Chart exploring what students know and what they would like to learn about Portugal's trading empire. Write students' ideas on the board in a K-W-L chart. Give students the opportunity to return to the chart and review what they have learned after they have read the lesson. **0:10** minutes

GUIDED DISCUSSION

1. **Identify Main Ideas and Details** Why did Portuguese kings encourage Brazilian colonists to set up plantations for growing sugarcane? *(Sugar was a luxury in Europe, and Portugal expected to make huge profits from its import.)*

2. **Evaluate** In what ways did slave labor benefit the colonial Portuguese economy? *(Possible response: The African slave labor that was used to extract natural resources in South America made the Portuguese very wealthy. The slave trade itself benefited the Portuguese economy as well.)*

MORE INFORMATION

Sugarcane Industry The sugarcane industry continues to be an important part of the Brazilian economy. In 2012 and 2013, Brazil produced 588 million tons of sugarcane, which produced 38 million tons of sugar. That makes Brazil the greatest sugar producer in the world. The industry employs more than one million workers, and salaries for these workers are among the highest in Brazil's agricultural sector.

ACTIVE OPTIONS

NG Learning Framework: Make Observations

ATTITUDE: **Responsibility**
SKILL: **Collaboration**
KNOWLEDGE: **Our Living Planet**

Have students revisit the information about the Portuguese in Brazil. They should work in pairs to create a list of observations about how the natural resources of Brazil contributed to Portugal's interest in Brazil and to Portugal's eventual wealth. Once they have completed their list of observations, each pair should exchange lists with another pair and discuss the new list. **0:10** minutes

On Your Feet: Roundtable Divide the class into groups of four. Have the groups move desks together to form a table where they can all sit. Hand each group a sheet of paper with the following question: *How did Portugal go about building an empire in the New World?* The first student in each group should write an answer, read it aloud, and pass the paper clockwise to the next student. Each student in the group should add at least one answer. The paper

should circulate around the table until students run out of answers. At the end of the activity, initiate a class discussion of students' responses. **0:20** minutes

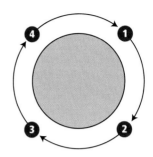

STRIVING READERS

Expand Main Idea Statements After reading the lesson, direct students to copy the Main Idea statement and write a paragraph that expands on the statement. Have students use the following starter:

Portugal built a powerful trading empire that extended along the coast of Africa and reached into areas of the Indian Ocean and South America. First, Portugal _____.

INCLUSION

Sequence Events Write events from the lesson on index cards. Read the events aloud and then have students put the cards in chronological order.

Press **mt** *in the Student eEdition for modified text.*

See the Chapter Planner for more strategies for differentiation.

ANSWERS

1. Even though Portugal was a relatively small country, the Portuguese focused on maritime exploration and trade with the encouragement and support of Portugal's kings.

2. Sugar, which is made from sugarcane, was a rare luxury in Europe, and its import meant huge profits for Portugal and its colonies. Plantations were needed to grow and process large quantities of sugarcane for the lucrative sugar trade.

3. In order to grow sugarcane to make sugar for export to Europe, huge numbers of workers were needed to perform the hard and dangerous work. To meet this demand for labor, slaves were imported from West Africa, contributing to the development and growth of the slave trade.

The Atlantic Slave Trade

You are young and strong. You work more than 18 hours a day, chopping stalks of sugarcane with a machete and loading the stalks onto carts. If you stop to rest, you will be beaten. You're thirsty, but you cannot ask for water. All your muscles ache, and your hands are blistered. You are a slave on a sugarcane plantation in Brazil in 1588. You have no way to escape.

MAIN IDEA

To supply labor on plantations in the New World, Europeans imported and enslaved millions of Africans.

SLAVE LABOR

To increase their profits, the European plantations in the New World wanted a large supply of cheap workers. At first, Europeans believed they could use Native Americans to meet their labor needs. But disease and warfare killed millions of Native Americans, and many who were forced into labor easily escaped into the familiar countryside.

Beginning in the mid-1450s, the Portuguese and Spanish solved the labor-shortage problem by buying and transporting slaves from West Africa. The West Africans were more resistant to European diseases, and they could not easily escape into lands that were largely unknown to them.

Slavery was common in West Africa, and local rulers grew rich by kidnapping and selling their enemies to Europeans. In return for the captives, the rulers received gold, trinkets, and guns. They used the guns to capture more slaves. By 1650, more than 40 trading posts on Africa's west coast were sending slaves to the New World.

These trading posts formed part of a transatlantic trading network known as the **triangular trade**. On the first leg of the triangle, European ships carried cheap manufactured goods to West Africa, where they were used to buy slaves. On the second or middle leg of the triangle, these slaves were brought to the Americas, where they were sold for a huge profit. On the third leg of the triangle, the slave ships returned to Europe laden with valuable sugar, tobacco, coffee, and cotton.

The triangular trade was a massive moneymaking business. Major participating countries—such as Portugal, Spain, Great Britain, France, and the Netherlands—were prepared to fight wars to secure their share of the trade.

IMPACT OF THE SLAVE TRADE

Europeans treated African slaves as property, not people. The slaves had no rights, and their owners could treat them any way they wanted. This system of slavery was based on both custom and **racism**, the belief that some races are better than others. Europeans genuinely believed that they were superior to Africans in every way. Indeed, they justified slavery as a way of civilizing Africans.

The conditions on the slave ships were especially brutal. Up to 600 slaves were chained together in dark, overcrowded holds, where it was impossible to move and difficult to even breathe. The crossing from Africa to the Americas took at least

THE MIDDLE PASSAGE

This illustration shows how enslaved Africans were transported from Africa to the Americas on a European slave ship. The journey could take up to 90 days, depending on the weather.

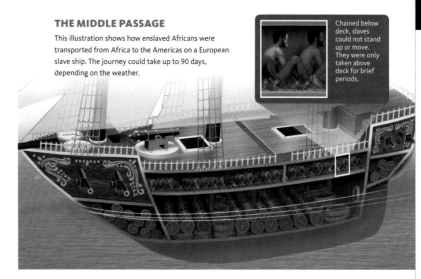

Chained below deck, slaves could not stand up or move. They were only taken above deck for brief periods.

three weeks and often as long as three months. The trip became known as the **Middle Passage** because it was considered the middle leg of the triangular trade. An estimated 13 to 20 percent of slaves died on the voyage from hunger, thirst, disease, suffocation, drowning, and abuse.

For many slaves, conditions in the colonies were little better than on the ships. Some slaveholders believed it was more cost-effective to replace overworked slaves who died than it was to improve conditions so that slaves lived and worked longer. On sugar plantations, death rates were especially high due to overwork, poor nutrition, harsh treatment, and disease. But colonists grew rich by using slaves to produce sugar, tobacco, coffee, and cotton and to mine gold, silver, and diamonds.

The number of people forced into slavery in the transatlantic slave trade is staggering. Slave traders took entire villages and ethnic groups in Africa, destroying whole communities and cultures. Over a period of about 360 years, from 1501 to 1867, more than 12 million Africans were forced into slavery. It was the largest forced migration of people in history.

REVIEW & ASSESS

1. **READING CHECK** How did the transatlantic slave trade affect Africans and Europeans?
2. **IDENTIFY PROBLEMS AND SOLUTIONS** Instead of using slaves, how might Europeans have solved their labor-shortage problem in the New World?
3. **ANALYZE VISUALS** What hardships did African slaves endure on the Middle Passage?

PLAN

OBJECTIVE

Explain why Europeans imported and enslaved millions of Africans in the New World.

CRITICAL THINKING SKILLS FOR LESSON 3.3

- Identify Main Ideas and Details
- Monitor Comprehension
- Identify Problems and Solutions
- Analyze Visuals
- Draw Conclusions
- Synthesize

ESSENTIAL QUESTION

How did new ideas affect Europeans' views of the world?

To increase their profits, European plantations in the New World needed a cheap supply of workers. Lesson 3.3 explains how Europeans imported and enslaved millions of Africans to supply that labor.

BACKGROUND FOR THE TEACHER

According to estimates, more than ten million Africans survived the Middle Passage and were enslaved in the Americas. About nine million were enslaved in South America and the Caribbean islands, while half a million were enslaved in the United States. The majority of enslaved Africans were transported to South America, most to Brazil.

DIGITAL RESOURCES myNGconnect.com

TEACHER RESOURCES & ASSESSMENT

 Reading and Note-Taking

 Vocabulary Practice

 Section 3 Quiz

STUDENT RESOURCES

 Active History

K-W-L CHART

Provide students with a K-W-L Chart like the one below. Have students think about what they know about slavery in the New World and the triangular trade. Then ask them to write questions that they would like to have answered as they study the lesson. Allow time at the end of the lesson for students to fill in what they have learned. `0:10` minutes

What Do You Know?	What Do You Want to Know?	What Did You Learn?

TEACH

GUIDED DISCUSSION

1. **Draw Conclusions** How did racism play a part in the system of slavery? *(As a belief that some races are better than others, racism helped Europeans justify slavery. Europeans genuinely believed that they were superior to Africans in every way, and they justified slavery as a way of civilizing Africans.)*

2. **Synthesize** How was the triangular trade a massive moneymaking business? *(Responses will vary. A possible response might include that each part of the triangle made profits. On the first leg, Europeans brought cheap manufactured goods to West Africa to use to buy slaves. The slaves were brought to the Americas and sold for huge profits. On the third leg, valuable items such as sugar, tobacco, coffee, and cotton were brought to Europe.)*

ANALYZE VISUALS

Have students study the illustration and caption in this lesson. Ask students what the illustration shows. **ASK:** What does the illustration suggest about conditions the enslaved Africans endured on the slave ship? *(Possible response: The enslaved Africans endured horrible conditions. Their location allowed for little air and likely sweltering heat. The lengthy trip and poor sanitary conditions led to disease and death.)* `0:15` minutes

ACTIVE OPTIONS

Active History: Analyze the Role of Slavery in Brazil Extend the lesson by using either the PDF or Whiteboard version of the activity. These activities take a deeper look at a topic from, or related to, the lesson. Explore the activities as a class, turn them into group assignments, or even assign them individually. `0:10` minutes

On Your Feet: Three Corners Have students form three groups, representing the Americas, Europe, and Africa. Have each group prepare a short presentation explaining why it would be to their advantage to stop, continue, or alter the triangular trade. `0:20` minutes

ENGLISH LANGUAGE LEARNERS

Use Sentence Strips Choose a paragraph from the lesson and make sentence strips out of it. Read the paragraph aloud, having students follow along in their books. Have students close their books and give them the set of sentence strips. Students should put the strips in order and read the paragraph aloud.

GIFTED & TALENTED

Create a Multimedia Presentation Have students work in small groups to create a multimedia presentation of the triangular trade route. Assign each person in the group one kind of multimedia to tell the story of the triangular trade. Different forms of media might include a map of the route, an audio explaining the triangular trade, or a chart or graph about some part of the triangular trade. Have groups share their multimedia presentations with the rest of the class.

Press (**mt**) in the Student eEdition for modified text.

See the Chapter Planner for more strategies for differentiation.

ANSWERS

1. Plantation owners, merchants, traders, and Europe's rulers all made money from the transatlantic slave trade. The effects on Africans were disastrous: many died or were subjected to brutal treatment, and whole communities and cultures were destroyed.

2. Answers will vary. Sample response: They might have solved the problem by encouraging immigration and then paying immigrant workers and being content with making lower profits.

3. They were chained closely together and could not stand up or move. They were only taken above deck for brief periods. They had little clothing.

VOCABULARY

Write the vocabulary word that completes each of the following sentences.

1. The _____ incorrectly states that Earth is at the center of the universe.

2. In 1543, Copernicus published the controversial _____, which stated that the sun was the center of the universe.

3. The purpose of an experiment is to test an explanation that is called a _____.

4. Many European explorers sailed on fast, maneuverable ships called _____.

5. Spanish _____ defeated the Aztec and Inca empires.

6. Portuguese colonists in Brazil grew sugarcane on large farms called _____ .

7. In the _____, trade ships traveled from Europe to West Africa to the Americas and back to Europe.

READING STRATEGY

8. MAKE INFERENCES Complete your chart to make inferences about the relationship between the Scientific Revolution and European exploration. Then answer the question.

I Learned	My Inference
Observatories helped astronomers accurately plot the locations of stars, which led to better navigation.	Better navigation made it easier for ships to travel far from home.

How did the Scientific Revolution influence European exploration?

MAIN IDEAS

Answer the following questions. Support your answers with evidence from the chapter.

9. What were the scientific theories of the ancient Greeks based on? **LESSON 1.1**

10. What impact did the invention of the microscope have on scientific discovery? **LESSON 1.2**

11. How did the ideas of Sir Francis Bacon affect the practice of science? **LESSON 1.3**

12. What motivated Europeans to explore the world in the mid-1400s? **LESSON 2.1**

13. How did Prince Henry the Navigator promote exploration in the 1400s? **LESSON 2.2**

14. What were some of the new foods introduced to Europe as part of the Columbian Exchange? **LESSON 2.5**

15. Why did the Spanish invade and conquer large areas of Central and South America? **LESSON 3.1**

16. Why did Europeans ship millions of enslaved Africans to the New World? **LESSON 3.3**

CRITICAL THINKING

Answer the following questions. Support your answers with evidence from the chapter.

17. COMPARE AND CONTRAST How did the geocentric and heliocentric theories of the universe differ?

18. MAKE INFERENCES What did Descartes mean when he said, "I think, therefore I am"?

19. DRAW CONCLUSIONS Why was the first voyage of Christopher Columbus important?

20. ANALYZE CAUSE AND EFFECT How did the Atlantic slave trade affect African families, communities, and cultures?

21. YOU DECIDE Was the Columbian Exchange mainly good or bad for the native people in the Americas? Explain your opinion.

INTERPRET VISUALS

Look closely at the triangular trade map. Then answer the questions that follow.

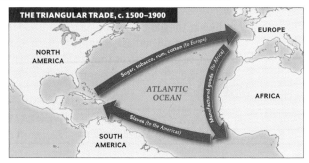

THE TRIANGULAR TRADE, c. 1500–1900

NORTH AMERICA — EUROPE — AFRICA — SOUTH AMERICA — ATLANTIC OCEAN

Sugar, tobacco, rum, cotton (to Europe)

Manufactured goods (to Africa)

Slaves (to the Americas)

22. What goods were shipped from Europe to Africa and exchanged for slaves?

23. Why is the route shown on the map referred to as the triangular trade?

ANALYZE SOURCES

Olaudah Equiano, the son of a village leader in the African kingdom of Benin, was captured and sold into slavery at the age of 11. He later gained his freedom and, in 1789, wrote his autobiography, *The Interesting Narrative of the Life of Olaudah Equiano*. In this excerpt from the autobiography, Equiano describes his voyage on the Middle Passage.

> The closeness of the place, and the heat of the climate, added to the number in the ship, which was so crowded that each had scarcely room to turn himself, almost suffocated us. This produced copious perspirations [a lot of sweat], so that the air soon became unfit for respiration, from a variety of loathsome smells, and brought on a sickness among the slaves, of which many died.

24. How would you describe the treatment of enslaved Africans on the Middle Passage?

WRITE ABOUT HISTORY

25. INFORMATIVE Write an informative paragraph for other students explaining how scientific rationalism changed Europeans' basic approach to science.

TIPS

- Take notes from Lessons 1.1, 1.2, and 1.3 on early Europeans' approach to science.

- State a main idea on how scientific rationalism affected Europeans' practice of science.

- Develop the paragraph with relevant, well-chosen facts, concrete details, or examples about early Europeans' approach to science.

- Use appropriate transitions, such as "because," "in contrast," or "as a result," to clarify the relationships among ideas.

- Use at least two vocabulary terms from the chapter.

- Provide a concluding sentence that follows from and supports the information presented.

VOCABULARY ANSWERS

1. geocentric theory

2. heliocentric theory

3. hypothesis

4. caravels

5. conquistadors

6. plantations

7. triangular trade

READING STRATEGY ANSWER

I Learned	My Inference
Observatories helped astronomers accurately plot the locations of stars, which led to better navigation.	Better navigation made it easier for ships to travel far from home.
The Portuguese built oceangoing ships called caravels.	The new ships were easier to maneuver and could sail against the wind.
Improvements in navigational tools such as the astrolabe, quadrant, and magnetic compass improved navigation.	Explorers used the new tools to draw more accurate maps.

8. The Scientific Revolution resulted in observatories and new navigational techniques and tools. These inventions made exploration easier and allowed explorers to travel to distant parts of the world. This in turn led to European explorers undertaking numerous expeditions and extending their knowledge of the continents.

MAIN IDEAS ANSWERS

9. The scientific theories of the ancient Greeks were based on reasoning.

10. The invention of the microscope enabled scientists to explore a whole new world in microscopic detail and discover many things previously invisible to the naked eye, such as plant cells.

11. Bacon's promotion of observation and experimentation as the basis of scientific knowledge led to the development of the scientific method, which provided a systematic, logical, and detailed process for developing and testing ideas.

12. Europeans wanted to find an alternative sea route to Asia so that they could control the profitable trade in spices and other goods.

13. Prince Henry the Navigator established a navigation school in Portugal and encouraged sailors to explore Africa's western coast.

14. New foods introduced to Europe as part of the Columbian Exchange included potatoes, tomatoes, corn, beans, squashes, peppers, and turkeys.

15. The Spanish invaded and conquered large areas of the Americas in search of gold.

16. Plantations in the New World required a large number of workers, and European diseases had decimated native populations, thus creating a huge labor shortage in the colonies. Enslaved Africans filled that labor shortage.

CRITICAL THINKING ANSWERS

17. The geocentric theory stated that Earth was the center of the universe; the heliocentric theory stated that the sun was the center of the universe. The geocentric theory was proved wrong, and the heliocentric theory was proved correct.

18. In stating "I think, therefore I am," Descartes meant that his ability to think proved he existed.

19. The first voyage of Columbus opened up a whole new part of the world to the people of the Old World.

20. Over 300 years, approximately 12 million Africans were forced into slavery and shipped to the New World, destroying families, whole communities, and cultures.

21. Answers may vary. Most students will probably state that the Columbian Exchange was mainly bad for the native people in the Americas since a majority lost their lives and those who survived lost their land and their way of life.

INTERPRET VISUALS ANSWERS

22. Manufactured goods were shipped from Europe to Africa in exchange for slaves.

23. This route is referred to as the triangular trade because it forms a three-sided voyage from Europe to Africa to the Americas and then back to Europe.

ANALYZE SOURCES ANSWER

24. Answers may vary. Students will probably describe the treatment as cruel and inhumane.

WRITE ABOUT HISTORY ANSWER

25. Students' informative paragraphs will vary, but students should present the information in a clear, logical, and accurate manner.

ON **LOCATION** WITH Maurizio SERACINI

CULTURAL HERITAGE ENGINEER AND NATIONAL GEOGRAPHIC FELLOW

▶ Check out more on myNGconnect

It's not just about the art in museums for Maurizio Seracini, an Italian art expert who uses technology to seek out long-hidden masterpieces no one has seen for centuries.

686 UNIT 9

BELOW THE PAINT

I love the way that technology is helping to write new pages of our history, find hidden treasures, and prove or disprove theories. In art history, for example, new technology has shown that Leonardo da Vinci's acclaimed painting *The Adoration of the Magi* is much more than it appears. It proves that while Leonardo drew the painting's original design, it was actually painted much later by an unknown and inferior artist who changed Leonardo's layout considerably. Technology allows us to peer through the layers of brown paint to reveal over 70 wonderful new images sketched by Leonardo that have not been seen for centuries.

Seracini carefully uses a scope with a tiny camera to examine the surface behind a fresco painted by Vasari.

EVOLVING TECHNOLOGY

Momentous discoveries like this take time and patience. In 1975, I was asked to use technology to solve a 500-year-old mystery about a lost Leonardo da Vinci masterpiece, *The Battle of Anghiari*. This mural painting was supposed to have been painted on the wall of a hall in the Palazzo Vecchio in Florence, Italy. Decades later, the hall was rebuilt and redecorated by another artist, Vasari, and Leonardo's celebrated masterpiece disappeared. We wanted to know if it was gone or if some of it was still there, but the technology of the 1970s wasn't sophisticated enough to tell.

In 2000, we were able to use 3D modeling and thermography to reconstruct the hall at the time of Leonardo. We also learned that in similar projects, Vasari had saved existing artworks by constructing a brick wall in front of them and leaving a small air gap. Maybe Vasari had done the same thing for *The Battle of Anghiari*? We used sophisticated radio antennas to find air gaps in the area where we believed the mural was painted—directly behind a wall with a Vasari fresco on it. But the need to preserve Vasari's work stopped any further investigation.

We returned with new technology in 2011: an endoscope with a 4mm camera, to explore the wall behind the Vasari fresco. We found fragments of red, black, and beige paint. Since we know that no other artist painted on that wall before Vasari sealed it up, those pigments are likely related to mural painting and most likely to da Vinci. If so, we have found one of the most highly praised works of art ever—by far Leonardo's most important commission and the one that made him the top artistic influence of his time.

WHY STUDY HISTORY ❓

❝ What we are doing is rediscovering the spirit of the Renaissance; we are blending art and science. As long as we live a life of *curiosity and passion*, there is a bit of Leonardo in all of us. ❞ —Maurizio Seracini

Brunelleschi's Dome

BY TOM MUELLER
Adapted from "Brunelleschi's Dome,"
by Tom Mueller, in *National Geographic*, February 2014

In 1418, the town fathers of Florence finally addressed a problem they'd been ignoring for decades: the enormous hole in the roof of their cathedral. They announced a contest to design the ideal dome, which would be the cathedral's crowning glory. Leading architects flocked to Florence and presented their ideas. One candidate named Filippo Brunelleschi promised to build not one but two domes, one nested inside the other. He refused to explain how he'd do this because he was afraid that a competitor would steal his ideas. Nevertheless, in 1420 the town fathers agreed to put Brunelleschi in charge of the dome project.

After he assembled the necessary tool kit, Brunelleschi began work on the dome, which he shaped with a series of stunning technical innovations. His double-shell design produced a structure that was far lighter than a solid dome of such size would have been. He also wove regular courses of herringbone brickwork, little known before his time, into the texture of the dome.

Throughout the years of construction, Brunelleschi oversaw the production of bricks of various dimensions and attended to the supply of choice stone and marble. He led an army of masons and stonecutters, carpenters, blacksmiths, and other craftsmen. When they were puzzled by some tricky construction detail, he'd shape a model out of wax or clay or carve up a turnip to illustrate what he wanted.

Brunelleschi and his workmen eventually did their victory dance. On March 25, 1436, the pope blessed the finished cathedral to the tolling of bells and cheering of proud Florentines. A decade later, workmen laid the cornerstone of the lantern, the decorative marble structure that Brunelleschi designed to top his masterpiece.

On April 15, 1446, the great architect died. He was buried in the crypt of the cathedral. A memorial plaque nearby celebrated his "divine intellect." These were high honors but fitting for the architect who had paved the way for the cultural and social revolutions of the Renaissance.

For more from National Geographic
Check out "Lady with a Secret" on myNGconnect

UNIT INQUIRY: MAP THE NEW WORLDVIEW

In this unit, you learned about Europe during the Middle Ages and the Renaissance. Based on your understanding of the text, what new ideas emerged during the Renaissance? How did these new ideas transform, or change, European culture?

ASSIGNMENT Create an idea map of the new worldview that emerged during the Renaissance because of humanism, an intellectual movement that emphasized the individual. The idea map should illustrate how humanism transformed medieval ideas about religion, philosophy, science, art, literature, and education. Be prepared to present your idea map and explain the overall impact of humanism to the class.

Plan As you create your idea map, think about European culture during the Middle Ages. Then think about how Renaissance humanism shifted the focus of European culture from divine matters to human beings and their needs. You might want to use a graphic organizer to help organize your thoughts. ▶

Produce Use your notes to produce detailed descriptions of how humanism transformed European culture. You might want to write the descriptions in outline or paragraph form.

Present Choose a creative way to present your idea map to the class. Consider one of these options:

- Create a multimedia presentation using paintings from the Middle Ages and Renaissance to illustrate how humanism transformed ideas about art.

- Write a monologue for a "Renaissance Man" that describes a day in his/her life.

- Design a brochure for a school that describes all the "new thinking" that will be taught to students.

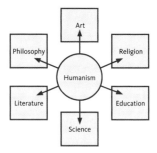

RAPID REVIEW
UNIT 9

MEDIEVAL AND **RENAISSANCE EUROPE**

TOP TEN

1. The collapse of the Roman Empire began a 1,000-year-long period called the Middle Ages in western Europe.
2. Humanism led to a rebirth in classical learning, stimulating a period of great creativity known as the Renaissance.
3. Johann Gutenberg developed the printing press.
4. Martin Luther wrote the 95 Theses, which criticized church practices and launched the Reformation.
5. Europeans explored and colonized much of Africa, Asia, and the Americas, which prompted the exchange of goods, ideas, people, plants, animals, and diseases.

6-10. **NOW IT'S YOUR TURN** Complete the list with five more things to remember about medieval and Renaissance Europe.

RAPID REVIEW

POSSIBLE RESPONSES

Possible responses for the remaining five things to remember include the following:

6. Though the Catholic Church was a powerful institution, some kings began to challenge its authority.

7. The bubonic plague killed many people and resulted in a population shift from the rural countryside to towns.

8. Great advances in scientific thinking during the Scientific Revolution laid the foundation for modern science.

9. The Catholic Church responded to the Reformation with the Counter Reformation.

10. Europe's feudal system was a hierarchy in which knights served a lord who served the king in exchange for land and power.

UNIT INQUIRY PROJECT RUBRIC

ASSESS

Use the rubric to assess each student's participation and performance.

SCORE	ASSIGNMENT	PRODUCT	PRESENTATION
3 GREAT	• Student thoroughly understands the assignment. • Student participates fully in the project process. • Student works well independently.	• Idea map contains many details. • Idea map clearly illustrates how humanism transformed medieval ideas. • Final description is detailed and reflects the idea map.	• Presentation is clear, concise, and logical. • Presentation does a good job explaining how humanism transformed European culture. • Presentation engages the audience.
2 GOOD	• Student mostly understands the assignment. • Student participates fairly well in the project process. • Student works fairly well independently.	• Idea map contains a fair amount of details. • Idea map somewhat illustrates how humanism transformed medieval ideas. • Final description is moderately detailed and somewhat reflects the idea map.	• Presentation is somewhat clear, concise, and logical. • Presentation does an adequate job explaining how humanism transformed European culture. • Presentation somewhat engages the audience.
1 NEEDS WORK	• Student does not understand the assignment. • Student minimally participates or does not articipate in the project process. • Student struggles to work well independently.	• Idea map contains few details. • Idea map does not illustrate how humanism transformed medieval ideas. • Final description is not detailed and does not reflect the idea map.	• Presentation is not clear, concise, or logical. • Presentation does not do an adequate job of explaining how humanism transformed European culture. • Presentation does not engage the audience.

WHY STUDY HISTORY ?

TO IDENTIFY INNOVATIONS AND TECHNOLOGIES THAT SET THE STAGE FOR THE MODERN WORLD

New inventions and technologies are finding their way around the globe, and new trade relationships are beginning to make the world, as shown in Units 8 and 9, more recognizable for us. Understanding the events and developments that laid the groundwork for our society will help you, as global citizens, understand its complexity, promise, and challenges.

Fred Hiebert
▶ **Watch the Why Study History video**

Terra cotta statues surround Chinese emperor Shi Huangdi's tomb and are thought to have helped guide him into the afterlife.

KEY TAKEAWAYS UNITS 8–9

PATTERNS IN HISTORY: SIMILAR DEVELOPMENTS ACROSS LOCATIONS

- Changes in religion, the arts, government, and economics begin to leapfrog each other—a change in one area brings change in others.
- The world economy begins to globalize as communication expands and trade patterns develop.
- With new economic relationships comes increasing conflict between countries and political groups.

GOVERNMENT

- New empires, including the Mongol in East Asia and the Khmer in Southeast Asia, rise to power.
- In Europe, modern nation-states emerge and extend their power.

MOVEMENT OF PEOPLE AND IDEAS

- Trade develops along the Silk Roads during the Mongol Empire.
- The Columbian Exchange is established among Europe, Africa, and the Americas.

ARTISTIC EXPRESSION

- Art reflects changing ideas of human identity.
- Renaissance artists revive classical ideals and depict their subjects more realistically, reflecting the humanist ideal of the individual.

TECHNOLOGY & INNOVATION

- Chinese inventions, including movable type, the compass, and gunpowder, lay the groundwork for European innovations.
- As a result, the invention of the printing press enables widespread communication, while new sailing ships put more explorers on the high seas.
- New weapons like cannons and longbows make conflict more deadly.

IT'S ABOUT BEING A GLOBAL CITIZEN.

As a global citizen, you are empowered to act responsibly in the 21st century by showing empathy and respect for others, making informed decisions and finding your own voice, and actively participating in a rich and diverse environment. Go for it!

+ GUIDED DISCUSSION

In Units 8 and 9, students learned about new empires in Asia and the rise of nation-states in Europe—with the conflicts that those events brought.

1. **Time Out for a Definition!**
   The concept of "conflict" is something students are probably familiar with, both on a personal level and as global citizens. Examining conflict between countries, cultures, and political groups throughout history is one way to understand the world's complexity and challenges. Ask students to list examples of conflicts they are exposed to in daily life. Examples may range from interpersonal conflicts with friends or siblings to wars they see and read about in the media. Then ask volunteers to contribute examples of conflicts they read about in Units 8 and 9. For each one, **ASK:** What caused this conflict? Who participated in this conflict? Why did this conflict occur? Where did it take place? What were the outcomes of this conflict?

2. **Artistic Expression**
   Revisit some of the examples of artwork shown in Units 8 and 9. Encourage students to share their observations about the artwork. Compare it to examples of more modern art from the 20th or 21st century. Invite students to consider what the artwork from each era says about the human identity of that particular time or region.

➡ THINK BACK

Review the Why Study History? sections in the book. Then pose this important question back to the students: Why do YOU think it's important to study history? Ask students to verbally articulate an answer to this question or record an answer in their Field Journal and share it with the class.

STORIES MAKING HISTORY

HISTORY

History is a living thing, and you are part of it.

You've just read about centuries and centuries of events that may seem like they have little connection to your life—but you might be surprised. Those long-gone people and dramatic occurrences have brought us to where we are today, and the things happening all over the world while you sit in class each day will shape your life for years to come. If you don't keep an eye on the issues that will someday become the history of your generation, who will?

As this *World History* book went to the printer, important new National Geographic stories were just hitting the news. So we narrowed them down to the five stories that follow. Remember: These are just a few of the many intriguing stories surfacing around the world, and they're still developing. As a global citizen, it's up to you to ask yourself: What happened next? How did this turn out? **Go find out!**

INTRODUCE STORIES MAKING HISTORY

As you know, part of studying the past is thinking about its implications for the future. Lots of people have repeated what has now become a little cliché: "Those who can't remember the past are condemned to repeat it." That comes from people as varied as Edmund Burke, George Santayana, and Kurt Vonnegut. Using current events in a World History class is a good way to make students aware of the connections among humans across time and place.

National Geographic is a great vehicle to use to bring contemporary stories to the classroom. In Stories Making History, we've offered brief articles on five stories in the headlines when this World History program went to press. Challenge students to follow these stories in online news sources and to identify other important stories that they think will affect their future.

Lead a discussion about the title "Stories Making History." Ask students to use their own words to explain what they think that means. Here are a few strategies to introduce Stories Making History to your class.

1. **Photo Preview** Preview the photos in the opening two pages of this section of the book. Have students identify what they think is shown in each photo and what, if anything, makes the photo particularly interesting or unusual. You might have them write a brief caption for each photo and share as a class.

2. **Read Aloud** Ask for a volunteer to read the two-paragraph introduction to Stories Making History aloud for the class. Ask students to explain in their own words what it means that "the things happening all over the world while [they] sit in class each day will shape [their lives] for years to come." **ASK**: What does that mean to you? Do you want to be part of those events? Discuss the idea of global citizenship (which by this point in the program should be familiar to them).

3. **News Sources** You might provide students with a variety of print news sources or direct them to online sources that they can explore as they read the Stories Making History in their text. What other stories are "making history" in the world today? Which of those stories affect the United States? What stories are important in their local communities? And what would they identify as the important "stories" in their school building and among their peers?

   Help students realize that understanding the events happening at a global level starts by understanding what's happening right around them in school, in their neighborhood, and larger community. Make the point that it's certainly a goal to understand events--but it's also a goal to use their voices to affect change when it's needed.

4. **Jigsaw Activity** Break the class into 5 small groups and assign each group one of the articles in Stories Making History. Have students read the article and work together to create a simple presentation on the article to share with the class. Those same groups can do a little online research to track the status of their article today.

TURN AND TALK

Have students discuss whether they agree with the statement "History is a living thing and you are part of it." Ask them to keep in mind the themes that have been echoing through this World History program:

- the enduring contributions of all civilizations
- the need for empathy and respect for the world's cultures
- the universal need to establish identity
- the role of global citizens
- the importance of preserving the human record
- being empowered to use their voices to speak up for themselves

As they read help them figure out which of these themes connects to each article. And remind them that the kinds of questions they ask—and their determination to keep a dialogue going about history, current events, politics, any issue in the news—will help shape the quality of their lives as adults.

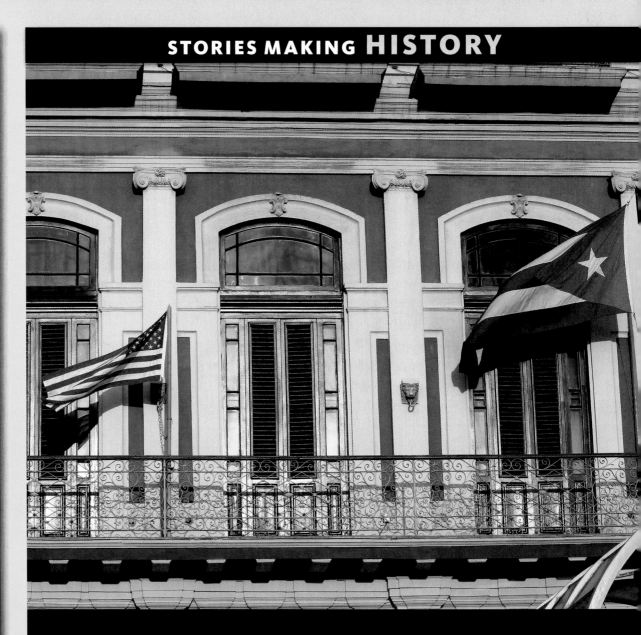

GUIDED DISCUSSION

1. **Why was Juan Valdés so moved by returning to Cuba in 2011?**
   (**Answer:** *Valdés had left Cuba at a very young age because of political changes in Cuba. He had had to leave without his family, and live apart from them for several months. His return no doubt brought back memories of his early years in Cuba as well as renewed his feelings for his country of origin.*)

2. **What events in Cuba in the late 1950s and early 1960s caused famlies like Juan's to flee Cuba for other countries?**
   (**Answer:** *Fidel Castro had come into power. Despite his promises for free elections and other reforms, Castro turned to Communism and formed an alliance with the Soviet Union. People who dld not want to live In a Communist country fled to other countries.*)

3. **What was the Cuban missile crisis?**
   (**Answer:** *The Cuban missile crisis was a confrontation between the United States under President John F. Kennedy and the Soviet Union over the Soviet attempt to move nuclear warheads into Cuba. Castro eventually backed down in the face of a strong U.S. response.*)

Renewing Relationships: Cuba and the United States

Serving as The Geographer for National Geographic's Maps Division is an epic job. On any given day, Juan José Valdés and his team have the monumental task of creating and updating maps in a world where borders change frequently and sometimes without much notice. In 2011, Valdés stood expectantly outside a house in Havana, Cuba; but he wasn't in the country to make a map. He was visiting the place where he was born in 1953, and attempting to reconnect to a country he hadn't entered in 50 years.

^
The national flags of the United States and Cuba fly outside the Cuban hotel where the first U.S. congressional delegation to Cuba stayed in 2015.

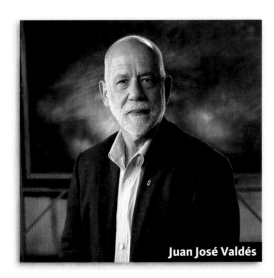
Juan José Valdés

A year later, Juan visited Cuba again and reunited with his remaining family. A cousin approached him saying, "You are Cuban."

"Yes, I am Cuban," Juan answered, his voice trembling with emotion.

Like so many Cuban-Americans, Juan's life has been marked by enormous changes. When he was a child in Havana during the 1950s, a dictator named Fulgencio Batista ruled the country with an iron hand. A young law student and activist named Fidel Castro led rebels who waged a war to end Batista's rule. In 1959, Castro and his forces overthrew Batista.

Castro had promised free elections and other reforms. Yet once he took power, he quickly established a Communist government, in which the state owns or controls factories and other businesses. Castro refused to hold free elections, and he denied Cuban citizens freedom of speech and other rights most Americans take for granted. Castro also formed an alliance with the Soviet Union, in spite of the fact that the United States was in the middle of a Cold War with the Soviets. The U.S. response was swift and severe: diplomatic relations and trade with Cuba ended, and no one could travel between Cuba and the United States.

Hundreds of thousands of Cubans desperately wanted to leave Cuba for other countries like the United States. They didn't want to live in a Communist country. Juan's family could

not leave right away, but they managed to get an airline ticket for Juan in 1961. At the age of seven, he traveled alone on an airplane to Miami, Florida. He lived with an elderly couple in Miami, until several months later, when his parents were able to leave Cuba and join him. Their family was reunited and built a life together in the United States.

Meanwhile, Cuba and the United States remained locked in tension. In April 1961, President John F. Kennedy authorized a group of American-trained Cuban exiles to attack Cuba at the Bay of Pigs and try to overthrow Castro. The invasion was a disaster for the United States. The Cuban exiles were outnumbered and many were captured. In October 1962, the Soviet Union tried to set up missiles with nuclear warheads in Cuba. This dangerous situation, known as the Cuban Missile Crisis, ended only when President Kennedy confronted the Soviets and forced them to remove the missiles.

But the world changes daily. On December 17, 2014, President Barack Obama announced that the United States would work to restore diplomatic and trade relations with Cuba and move to open an embassy in Havana, with Congressional approval. On April 11, 2015, President Obama met with Cuban President Raúl Castro in Panama in the first face-to-face discussion between the leaders of the two countries in more than 50 years. Both leaders expressed hope that the two countries will be able to interact without the tension and restrictions of the past.

This change is important for both nations, but it's also important for people like Juan Valdés who have roots in Cuba. As tensions between the countries continue to subside, Cuban-Americans will be able to travel more easily to Cuba and reconnect with relatives they left behind long ago. Yet change is never without complication. Cubans will have to adjust to the impact the lifted trade embargo has on the local economy they are used to. Others may find it unusual to welcome American tourists to their country after so many decades without them. It's likely that the Cuban people will find themselves and their country in a period of transition and adjustment for years to come.

TURN AND TALK

Conduct a class discussion on the changes that are taking place in the U.S. relationship with Cuba. Encourage students to share their opinions on whether they think these changes are long-lasting and for the good, or whether they suspect the relaxing of restrictions may be fleeting.

Saving Cultural Heritage

Home to some of the oldest cultures on earth and six UNESCO
World Heritage sites, modern-day Syria lies along the eastern coast
of the Mediterranean Sea with Iraq to the east, Turkey to the north,
and Jordan to the south—at the heart of the region referred to as
the Middle East. Syria's modern borders were drawn in the 20th
century, and crossed diverse cultures. This diversity makes it a place
where people from all faiths gather, where cultural heritage is a
part of people's identity, and greatly influences their way of life.

^
Destruction and looting
have drastically altered
the Umayyad Mosque
in Aleppo, Syria, as
seen in these before
and after shots of its
exterior and interior.

696

Salam Al Kuntar
2015 Emerging Explorer

Dr. Salam Al Kuntar, an archaeologist who grew up in Syria, can tell you all about what it's like to live in a place so rich in cultural heritage.

As a young girl picking olives, pistachios, and almonds in her family's orchard in Syria, Al Kuntar also collected pottery shards left behind by ancient cultures. At the time, she dreamed of becoming an astronaut. Today, she laughs as she admits that instead of taking her up into the sky, her career sends her digging below the ground!

Named a National Geographic Emerging Explorer in 2015, Al Kuntar's work has taken on an unexpected urgency. She and a team of experts are working to save ancient evidence of Syria's diverse heritage from the ravages of war. Since civil war erupted in Syria in 2011, violence has sent millions of Syrians fleeing from their homes to live in refugee camps. Years into the conflict, millions of Syrian children are unable to go to school. Instead of focusing on homework assignments, they think about their family's safety and whether or not they'll have enough to eat.

Syria's ancient monuments and museums, too, have been the victims of careless government airstrikes as well as bombing and shelling by various opposition groups.

In the city of Aleppo in April 2013, for example, the minaret, or tower, on the Umayyad Mosque dating from 1090 A.D. was completely destroyed. Other fragile archaeological sites have been damaged, and thieves have been looting antiquities—objects or works of art from the ancient past—and selling them illegally outside of Syria.

Syria's Ma'arra Mosaic Museum, southwest of Aleppo, was once a *caravanserai*, or inn. It holds a collection of Roman and Byzantine mosaics more impressive than any other in the Middle East. The museum was near collapse from damages sustained because of the war until preservationists and volunteers stepped in. Their efforts saved the collection.

The physical destruction of something tangible like Syria's historical monuments actually is intended to rob people of something intangible—their cultural heritage and identity. The impact is deeply felt when people can no longer visit a place or a monument that they have memories of visiting with their grandparents. The stories they've carried with them since childhood become harder to remember and share. Al Kuntar warns that the war "is killing the hope for the future."

But there is still hope even under these difficult circumstances. Salam Al Kuntar's team works closely with local activists to document the destruction of monuments. They map and identify damage, apply a harmless glue to keep the tesserae, or small cubes that make up the mosaics, intact, and use sandbags and wrapping materials to protect them. People sometimes try to escape from the war and seek refuge inside some of the remote ruins. Al Kuntar's team does emergency repairs to shore up crumbling stone so it doesn't crush these frightened and exhausted guests.

As an archaeologist, Al Kuntar knows something very important that keeps her going under dangerous and discouraging conditions: this effort to destroy Syria's cultural heritage ultimately is not going to work. The fact is that their cultural heritage is embedded in the hearts and minds of the Syrian people—in their memories of family and country—and it cannot be destroyed. Salam Al Kuntar describes Syria's diversity as "precious," and is determined to protect it for future generations. ▪

 **TURN AND TALK**

Talk with students about the assertion in the text that attempts to destroy Syria's cultural heritage aren't going to work because "their cultural heritage is embedded in the hearts and minds of the Syrian people." Ask students if they believe that's true in the United States too. What aspects of their own heritage can students identify as most important? Remind them that developing and practicing empathy and respect for all cultures is one reason they are studying world history.

Because artifacts from a number of cultures have been looted and sold across the world, this lesson on the repatriation of stolen artifacts reinforces several points in the chapters. Suggest that students quickly review Chapter 4 Ancient Egypt so they connect what they know about Egypt with the Egyptian repatriation that took place at National Geographic on April 22, 2015.

Chapter 17, Lesson 1.2 History Through Objects: Peruvian Gold also connects well with this article. The textile shown on page 838 was part of the exhibition of Peruvian artifacts that opened at the National Geographic Museum in April 2014.

1. **The text says that the human record—the record of human history on Earth—is a nonrenewable resource. What does that mean? What happens to a cultural artifact when it is damaged or stolen?** (**Answer:** *When an artifact is damaged or stolen, it loses the historical context in which it was found and can't be used to support a research premise. Once an object loses its context, it is in effect lost to history and can never be replaced.*)

2. **What happens when an object is repatriated?** (**Answer:** *It is returned to its country of origin.*)

3. **Explain Fred Hiebert's efforts to fight looting and preserve cultural heritage.** (**Answer:** *Hiebert has developed a process, including conducting emergency inventories, for dealing with smuggled artifacts when they are discovered in suspicious shipments. He also trains customs agents in how to identify and safely handle artifacts, and works with local populations to help them become good stewards of their heritage.*)

STORIES MAKING HISTORY

Our Shared History

Imagine if a symbol of the United States—for example, the Statue of Liberty—was stolen from New York Harbor and whisked away to another country. Most Americans would be angry that part of their history was lost to them. Across the world, this theft of the past happens regularly in areas that have been centers of civilization and are rich with archaeological sites and cultural artifacts. And it results in the same feeling of loss.

^ Top U.S. Customs agents at Dulles Airport in Washington, D.C., examine illegally shipped artifacts.

Bottom Left Head of a lamassu repatriated to Iraq

Bottom Right Paracas textile repatriated to Peru

Cultural artifacts are the little pieces of humanity left behind. They add to what we know of the human record, a non-renewable resource that we all share. When a cultural artifact is damaged or stolen, it is robbed of its identity and can never be replaced. The more conflict a region experiences, the less stable it becomes and the more vulnerable it is to looting, the illegal excavation and smuggling of cultural artifacts.

Some experts now work to help keep artifacts and identities where they belong. Dr. Fredrik Hiebert, National Geographic's Archaeology Fellow and an expert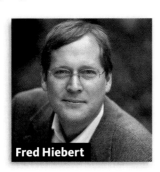

Fred Hiebert

in documenting endangered collections around the world, calls these people "culture heroes" for their dedication to preserving the past. These historians, archaeologists, and anthropologists often support the goal of repatriation, the official returning of looted artifacts to their country of origin. National Geographic has helped bring about repatriations to Afghanistan, Egypt, and Peru.

Afghanistan 2009 Afghanistan was a gathering place for cultures that traded along the Silk Roads. Invasion by the Soviet Union in 1979 began more than three decades of violence that continues today. As a result, Afghanistan's archaeological sites and museums suffered rocket attacks that destroyed cultural artifacts. Such unintended damage is called collateral damage. Other damage is caused intentionally. In 2001, for example, the Taliban used explosives to blow up giant sandstone Buddha statues dating from the 6th century A.D. For years, looting was widespread. More than 1,500 objects spanning thousands of years were confiscated at Heathrow Airport in London and repatriated to Afghanistan in 2009.

Peru 2015 Sometimes what happens to an artifact isn't necessarily the result of violence or war. The 2,300-year-old textile shown

on the opposite page has had numerous adventures on its journey home—yet is still in perfect condition. It was discovered as part of a necropolis, or ancient cemetery, in the 1920s and excavated by the founder of Peruvian archaeology, Julio Tello. The textile was stolen from the National Museum in Lima, Peru, not once, but twice. The second time, it found its way to Texas, where U.S. Customs agents recognized the illegal shipment and returned it to the Peruvian embassy. National Geographic helped return the textile in good condition to the museum in 2015.

Egypt 2010 and 2015 In 2008, U.S. Customs agents in Miami, Florida, became suspicious about a shipment with inconsistencies in the paperwork accompanying it. Two years later, the sarcophagus of a man named Imesy who lived during the 21st dynasty of Egypt was repatriated to the Grand Egyptian Museum in Cairo.

In April 2015, National Geographic hosted a ceremony for dozens more illegally shipped artifacts being repatriated from the United States back to Egypt, including a rare nesting sarcophagus from the 26th dynasty and even some mummy parts. Attended by both the U.S. Customs officers and archaeologists involved in solving the case, the ceremony was a moving recognition of an international effort to stop the looting of cultural artifacts and preserve them for future generations.

Fred Hiebert believes that every country is entitled to its own history. He is part of an effort to develop an "antiquities protocol," a process that can be deployed when smuggled artifacts are discovered in the world's ports. Hiebert conducts emergency inventories of looted artifacts, creating a "passport" or permanent record for these objects. But he claims that education is just as important: training customs agents to safely handle artifacts and teaching local residents to become better stewards for the objects that represent their heritage. "Who owns the past?" Fred Hiebert asks, and he has a ready answer: "All of us."

➕ TURN AND TALK

Lead the class in a discussion about what it means to be a "culture hero." Can they think of someone they would identify as a culture hero? It doesn't have to be someone in a position to physically save an artifact. Make sure they understand that there are other ways to contribute. A culture hero might be someone in the community who makes sure holidays like Diwali or Cinco de Mayo are celebrated along with more traditional American holidays. Challenge them to think of other ways to be a culture hero in one's community.

Into the Okavango Delta: A Live-Data Expedition

Located on the continent of Africa in the northwestern part of Botswana, the Okavango Delta is one of the richest wildlife areas on Earth. Unlike most deltas, it doesn't flow into an ocean or sea—it's an inland delta made up of flat, grassy savannas that are flooded by the Okavango River during the winter. This miraculous ecosystem was declared the 1000th UNESCO World Heritage Site in 2015, in part because its unique, seasonal wetlands give many endangered large mammals salvation after their long migration across the Kalahari Desert.

^
National Geographic Emerging Explorers Steve Boyes and Shah Selbe and their team document and share their experiences with the species of the Okavango Delta.

Visible from space, the Okavango Delta is huge—the size of the state of Texas. It's one of Africa's last truly wild landscapes, like the Sahara, the Serengeti, and the Congo. 100,000 elephants roam free across the land. Lions, leopards, hyenas, rhino, cheetahs, crocodiles, and wild dogs also thrive here, as well as nearly 500 bird species and over 1,000 plants.

Since 2011, an expedition team made up of Ba Yei river bushmen and National Geographic Emerging Explorers Steve Boyes and Shah Selbe and their team has been making annual visits to the remote land of the delta in one of the first "live-data" expeditions. That means the team constantly uploads data from the field to their website—intotheokavango.org—via satellite. This data is also available through a public API, or application program interface, which allows anyone to analyze and examine the collected information. "We're connecting society with the wilderness," explains conservation biologist, and Into the Okavango expedition leader, Steve Boyes.

Every ten seconds, state-of-the-art sensors record personal data about expedition members, including heart rate, the amount of energy they are using, and GPS positional data. Cameras automatically take pictures of the team's current location and record sound clips every ten minutes. Team members also post water quality data, and document their animal and bird sightings. They tweet progress updates constantly for people who are tracking their movements online and analyzing the expedition's data.

This mobile computer station allows sensors to be programmed and data to be posted from the field.

Team members also respond to questions and suggestions from their followers.

The team has crossed the Okavango Delta five times so far in dug-out canoes, the traditional mode of transportation for Ba Yei river bushmen. Their goal is to continue conducting in-depth biodiversity surveys in this delicate ecosystem so that any major changes can be noted and addressed.

"We have unprecedented opportunities to improve the world. But only if we act in time." –Shah Selbe

In 2015, the team's two-month "Source to Sand" expedition includes plans to cover the entire Okavango River system. They'll start at the river's source in Angola and travel 1,000 miles down the river through Namibia's Caprivi Strip, into untouched wilderness in the heart of the Okavango Delta in Botswana.

The team gathers in Okavango after a long trek in 2014.

This Okavango Delta exploration team has made an exciting step forward into expedition technology. For the first time, National Geographic explorers can share their movements, findings, and the sights and sounds of their surroundings, as well as their personal data, thoughts, and emotions in real-time while exploring one of the world's richest wilderness areas. This ground-breaking expedition gives people everywhere the chance to experience— and hopefully support—one of the world's most vibrant and important ecosystems. ▪

➡ **TURN AND TALK**

Encourage students to go online and check out the expeditions website at **intotheokavango.org**. You might set aside a couple of class periods for them to share their findings about the Okavango Delta and the expedition.

GUIDED DISCUSSION

1. **What circumstances led to South Sudan splitting off from the rest of Sudan to become its own country?**
   (**Answer:** *civil wars arising from religious and ethnic conflicts*)

2. **What is the National Geographic Photo Camp?**
   (**Answer:** *It is National Geographic's outreach program in response to the unrest in South Sudan. Twenty university students from different ethnic backgrounds had an opportunity to use photography to tell stories about their lives and community with the help of some National Geographic photographers.*)

3. **One participant in the South Sudan photo camp said the camp was about "how you can look into something differently." What do you think she means by that?**
   (**Answer:** *Answers will vary. She may have meant that using a camera gives the photographer a new angle on a particular subject. Composing a photograph to express an idea or portray a particular subject makes one think about that idea or that subject in a new way.*)

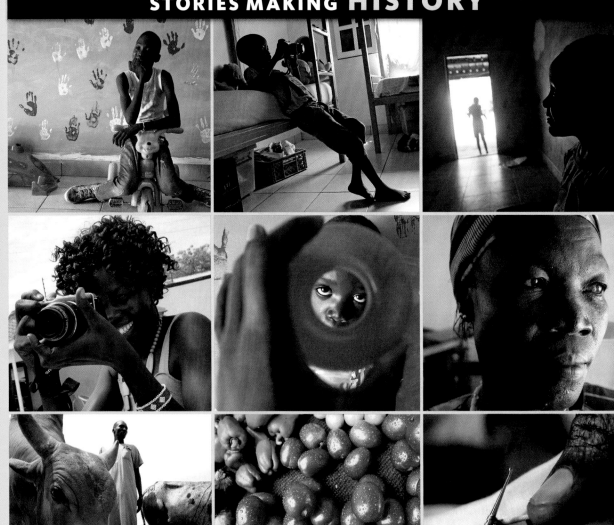

Peacemaking Through Photography

The shifting nature of national boundaries is a theme throughout history as well as in current news stories. The world's newest nation is one of those stories. In July 2011, South Sudan became an independent country after citizens voted to break away from Sudan. Why did one country become two?

^
Photos taken by the students of National Geographic's South Sudan Photo Camp capture friends, family members, and daily life.

For the first half of the 20th century, Sudan was a British colony. During British rule, English-speaking Christians and members of many different tribes lived in the southern part of the country. Arabic-speaking Muslims lived in the northern part. When the British left in 1956, two civil wars took place: one in the 1960s and another in the 1980s. War finally ended, but old wounds and animosities did not disappear. A 2005 peace agreement included an option for independence. In January 2011, southern Sudanese people voted to split from Sudan. South Sudan became the world's newest country in July 2011, with the city of Juba as its capital.

Immediately, the new country faced a number of problems, including border disputes with Sudan. Then, in December 2013, widespread violence broke out between rival political groups. Since then, more than 10,000 South Sudanese have been killed, and 2 million have been internally displaced, or forced to leave their homes. Tens of thousands of South Sudanese have fled the country altogether, and many now live in neighboring Ethiopia as refugees. Both sides are responsible for violence committed against others based on their ethnic and tribal background. The fighting in South Sudan also disrupted farming, and now 11 million people face a serious food crisis.

In September 2014, National Geographic responded to the situation in South Sudan with an outreach program called Photo Camp. This program empowers young people to tell their own stories about their life and community through photography, guided by the mentorship of National Geographic photographers. Over a period of five days, 20 University of Juba students from different ethnic backgrounds learned photography from National Geographic photographers and photo editors. This lively group took nearly 32,000 images, including the ones you see on the left. They also engaged in cross-tribal peace-building activities.

Why photography? National Geographic photographers Ed Kashi, Matt Moyer, and Amy Toensing explain. According to Toensing, the students at Photo Camp are eager to learn about cameras and photography.

Moyer observes, "To see the students take the cameras and go into their communities, document positive things, and see their world with new eyes is just really inspiring."

National Geographic Photo Camp teaches photography skills, but it also encourages storytelling. Ed Kashi says, "I believe in the power of storytelling. And I believe in the importance of bridging these gaps of misunderstanding. Photo Camp represents that spirit, that desire to bring people together to share stories and to try to make the world a better place."

Participants in National Geographic's South Sudan Photo Camp examine the photos they took.

"We are the same—we are all South Sudanese."
—Mabil Dau Mabil, student

South Sudan participants responded to Photo Camp in a number of ways. For Catherine Koro, the benefits reached far beyond photography. She said, "It's about how you can look into something differently." Students saw their communities and each other with new eyes. Mabil Dau Mabil said they purposely avoided identifying themselves as belonging to the Dinka, Bari, Kuku, or Madi tribes.

These budding photographers understand that the story of South Sudan is just beginning. Even in the midst of the country's current turmoil, they remain hopeful. Akuot Chol Mayak predicts, "The world's eyes are on this nation, not because it's special, but because it is the newest. We are still on the move, but we shall reach there."

TURN AND TALK

Encourage students to discuss how photography can open minds to new possibilities. If any of them have experience with cameras, suggest that they try to explain why photography is enjoyable for them. Interested students might create a display of their own photography to share with the class.

Think It Through

The articles in this section focus on history-making events and issues that have a profound effect on people and cultures across the globe. Consider and discuss the questions below to further your understanding of these important topics.

1 Choose one article that connects to your own life and experiences in some way and explain why. How does this article relate to your own personal history?

2 Which of the five articles would be most likely to motivate you to take action as a global citizen? How might you get involved?

3 Which topic are you most interested in finding out more about, and why? How might you seek additional information or updates?

Inquiry Project: Roundtable

Consider each of the newsworthy issues discussed in this section and select the one you feel is the most important or impactful within the world today. Why do you feel your chosen global issue is the most important one?

Assignment Become an expert on the issue you have chosen alongside others who have also chosen that issue. Participate in a roundtable discussion. Articulate why you feel your chosen issue is the most important one, and support your argument.

Plan Connect with other students in your class who share your opinion and discuss what you already know about this issue and what you would like to know. Through research and discussion, develop a solid understanding of the topic.

Produce From your research, develop a list of reasons and arguments to support the notion that your chosen topic has the most impact on the world.

Present Participate in a classroom-wide roundtable discussion. Along with others who share your opinion about the topic you have chosen, work to explain why your topic has the most world impact. Listen respectfully as others present their viewpoints.

THINK IT THROUGH

Answers to all three questions will vary. Lead a discussion of student responses to each of the questions provided. You might also use one or more of the questions as a writing prompt, or for question 2, ask students to debate among themselves which article they found most motivating.

RUBRIC FOR INQUIRY PROJECT: ROUNDTABLE

SCORE	ASSIGNMENT	PRODUCT	PRESENTATION
3 GREAT	• Student thoroughly understands the assignment. • Student participates fully in the project process. • Student works well with team members.	• Research is thorough and appropriate • Reasons and arguments are well thought out and support the notion that student's topic has the greatest impact on the world. • Student's work meets all of the requirements listed in the assignment.	• Student's comments as he/she participates in roundtable discussion are clear, concise, and logical. • Student effectively communicates his or her views and evidence. • Presentation engages other participants and demonstrates student's ability to be an effective listener.
2 GOOD	• Student mostly understands the assignment. • Student participates adequately in the project process. • Student works well with team members most of the time.	• Research is fairly thorough and appropriate • Most reasons and arguments are well thought out and support the notion that student's topic has the greatest impact on the world. • Student's work meets most of the requirements listed in the assignment.	• Student's comments as he/she participates in roundtable discussion are clear, concise, and logical most of the time. • Student is fairly effective in communicating his or her views and evidence. • Presentation engages some of the participants and demonstrates student's ability to be an effective listener most of the time.
1 NEEDS WORK	• Student does not understand most of the assignment. • Student does not fully participate in the project process. • Student struggles to work well with team members.	• Research lacks completeness and/or is inappropriate • Reasons and arguments are not. They do not effectively support the notion that student's topic has the greatest impact on the world. • Student's work does not meet all of the requirements listed in the assignment.	• Student's comments as he/she participates in roundtable discussion are not typically clear, concise, or logical. • Student struggles to effectively communicate his or her views and evidence. • Presentation fails to engage other participants and does not demonstrate student's ability to be an effective listener.

STUDENT REFERENCES

AVAILABLE ONLINE

Skills Handbook
Primary Source Handbook
Geography Handbook
World Religions Handbook
Economics and Government Handbook

GLOSSARY

A

acropolis *n.* the highest point in an ancient Greek city

adapt *v.* to change

adobe *n.* a kind of clay that when dried is used as a building material

agora *n.* an open space in an ancient Greek city that served as a marketplace and social center

agriculture *n.* the practice of growing plants and rearing animals for food

alliance *n.* an agreement between nations to fight each other's enemies; a partnership

anthropologist *n.* a scientist who studies the cultural development of humans

aqueduct *n.* a long stone channel that carries clean water

arabesque *n.* an abstract design made up of patterns or flowers, leaves, vines, or geometric shapes

arch *n.* a curved structure over an opening

archaeologist *n.* a scientist who studies past human life by analyzing fossils and artifacts

archipelago *n.* a collection of islands

aristocracy *n.* an upper class that is richer and more powerful than the rest of society

artifact *n.* an object made by humans from a past culture

artisan *n.* a person skilled at making things by hand

B

barbarian *n.* in this context, a person who lived outside the Roman Empire

barter *v.* to exchange goods

bas-relief *n.* a realistic sculpture with figures raised against a flat background

bubonic plague *n.* a disease that killed more than a third of Europe's population during the Middle Ages

bureaucracy *n.* a system of government in which appointed officials in specialized departments run the various offices

burgher *n.* a wealthy, town-dwelling merchant during the Middle Ages

bushido *n.* a strict code of behavior followed by the samurai in feudal Japan

C

cacao *n.* a bean used to make chocolate

caliph *n.* the title of the chief Muslim leader who was regarded as a successor of Muhammad from A.D. 632 to 1924

calligraphy *n.* a form of elegant writing

caravan *n.* a group of people that travels together

caravel *n.* a small, fast ship used by Spanish and Portuguese explorers

cartography *n.* the study of maps and mapmaking

caste system *n.* a rigid social hierarchy in India that divides people into hereditary classes

catacomb *n.* a hidden underground chamber where people are buried

catapult *n.* a weapon that hurls large stones

cataract *n.* a rock formation that creates churning rapids; also, a large waterfall

cathedral *n.* a towering church built during the Middle Ages; often the place from which a bishop ruled

celadon *n.* a type of Chinese pottery with a unique blue-green color

chinampa *n.* a floating field that supported agriculture

chivalry *n.* a code of conduct for knights

city *n.* a political, economic, and cultural center with a large population

city-state *n.* a self-governing unit made up of a city and its surrounding lands and settlements; a city that controls the surrounding villages and towns

civilization *n.* a society with a highly developed culture and technology

civil war *n.* a war between groups in the same country

clan *n.* a group of families that shares a common ancestor

classical *adj.* relating to ancient Greek and Roman culture

clergy *n.* the religious leaders who oversee ceremonies and deliver teachings of the Christian Church

codex *n.* a folded book made of tree bark paper

colony *n.* a group of people that settles in a new land but keeps ties to its native country

comedy *n.* a humorous form of Greek drama that often mocked famous people

commerce *n.* the buying and selling of goods

commodity *n.* a trade good

common law *n.* a system of law established in England to make sure people received equal treatment

communal *adj.* shared

confederation *n.* a group of allies

conquistador *n.* a Spanish conqueror who sought gold and other riches in the Americas

consul *n.* one of two chief leaders elected yearly in ancient Rome

convert *v.* to change one's religion

cosmopolitan *adj.* worldly

covenant *n.* a religious agreement

creation story *n.* an account that explains how the world began and how people came to exist

creed *n.* a statement of belief

crossroads *n.* the place where two roads meet

cultivate *v.* to grow a crop

cultural diffusion *n.* the process by which cultures interact and ideas spread from one area to another

cultural hearth *n.* a place from which new ideas, practices, and technology spread

culture *n.* a group's way of life, including types of food, shelter, clothing, language, religion, behavior, and ideas

cuneiform *n.* the earliest form of writing, invented by the Sumerians

D

daimyo *n.* a class of large landowning families in medieval Japan

delta *n.* an area where a river fans out into various branches as it flows into a body of water

democracy *n.* a form of government in which citizens have a direct role in governing themselves or elect representatives to lead them

denomination *n.* a branch of one type of religion

deplete *v.* to use something up, such as a resource

desertification *n.* the process by which once fertile land is transformed into a desert

dharma *n.* the Buddha's teachings; divine law

dhow *n.* a ship with a long, thin hull and triangular sails

dictator *n.* a person who rules with total authority

direct democracy *n.* a form of democracy in which citizens gather together to vote on laws and policies

diversity *n.* a range of different things; a variety

divine *adj.* having the nature of a god

domestication *n.* the raising of plants and animals to make them useful to humans

drought *n.* a long period of dry, hot weather

dynastic cycle *n.* the pattern of the rise and fall of dynasties in ancient and early China

dynasty *n.* a series of rulers from the same family

E

elliptical *adj.* oval

embassy *n.* a group of people who represent their nation in a foreign country

emperor *n.* the supreme ruler of an empire

empire *n.* a group of different lands and people governed by one ruler

enlightened despot *n.* an absolute ruler who applied Enlightenment principles to his or her reign

epic poem *n.* a long story in the form of a narrative poem

epistle *n.* a letter

excommunicate *v.* to officially exclude a member of a church from its rituals and membership

exile *n.* the forced removal from one's native country

exploit *v.* to mistreat

F

famine *n.* an extreme lack of crops or food causing widespread hunger

fertile *adj.* encouraging the growth of crops and plants

feudalism *n.* a political and social system in which a vassal receives protection from a lord in exchange for obedience and service

filial piety *n.* the belief that children owe their parents and ancestors respect

fossil *n.* the remains of organisms that lived long ago

fresco *n.* a picture painted directly onto a wall

G

geocentric theory *n.* a theory that places Earth at the center of the universe

geoglyph *n.* a large, geometric design or shape drawn on the ground

gladiator *n.* a man in ancient Rome who fought others for entertainment

global citizen *n.* a person who functions effectively in the interdependent, modern world

glyph *n.* a symbolic picture used to represent a word, syllable, or sound

golden age *n.* a period of great cultural achievement

government *n.* an organization set up to make and enforce rules in a society

griot *n.* a West African storyteller who relates stories through the oral tradition

guild *n.* a group of craftspeople that helped protect and improve the working conditions of its members

H

haiku *n.* a form of Japanese poetry that has 17 syllables in three unrhymed lines of 5, 7, and 5 syllables

hanbok *n.* a traditional Korean jacket and skirt or pant combination

heliocentric theory *n.* a theory that places the sun at the center of the universe

Hellenistic *adj.* relating to Greek history or culture

helot *n.* a state-owned slave who was part of the lowest class of ancient Greek society

heresy *n.* beliefs contrary to Church teachings; opposition to Church policy

hero *n.* a character who faces a challenge that demands courage, strength, and intelligence

hierarchy *n.* a system in which people belong to social classes of different ranks

hieroglyph *n.* a picture representing an object, sound, or idea that was part of the ancient Egyptian writing system

highland *n.* a type of land that is high above the sea

hub *n.* a center

humanism *n.* a movement that focused on the importance of the individual

hunter-gatherer *n.* a human who hunts animals and gathers wild plants to eat

hypothesis *n.* an explanation that can be tested

I

icon *n.* an image of Jesus or a saint

imam *n.* a Muslim religious leader

immortal *adj.* able to live forever

impose *v.* to force someone to do something

indulgence *n.* the release from punishment for sins, sold by papal officials

inoculation *n.* a vaccine containing a mild form of a disease to prevent the development of that disease

iron *n.* a metal that is found in rock

irrigation *n.* the supply of water to fields using human-made systems

isolate *v.* to cut off from the rest of the world

isolationism *n.* a rejection of foreign contact and outside influences

J

janissary *n.* a highly trained and disciplined soldier in the Ottoman army

jury *n.* a group of people chosen to make a decision based on evidence presented in a trial

K

kabuki *n.* a form of Japanese drama that involves luxurious costumes and elaborate makeup

karma *n.* in Hinduism, a state of being influenced by a person's actions and conduct; determines the kind of life into which a person will be reborn

khanate *n.* a region of the Mongol empire

kimchi *n.* a spicy pickled vegetable mix that serves as Korea's national dish

kiva *n.* a circular-shaped chamber built in the ground by the ancient Pueblo

knight *n.* a warrior in medieval Europe

kosher *adj.* specially prepared according to Jewish dietary laws

L

labyrinth *n.* a maze

land bridge *n.* a strip of land connecting two landmasses

legacy *n.* the things, both cultural and technological, left to us from past cultures

legend *n.* a story from the past that is accepted as truth but cannot be proven

legionary *n.* a professional soldier in ancient Rome

lingua franca *n.* a language commonly used by many different groups of people

longbow *n.* a weapon that allowed archers to fire arrows

lord *n.* a nobleman who received land from a king in medieval feudal society

lowland *n.* a type of land that is low and level

M

maize *n.* a type of corn first domesticated by early Mesoamericans

manor *n.* a self-contained world located on land belonging to a lord

mansa *n.* a West African king

mariner *n.* a sailor

maritime *adj.* relating to the sea

matrilineal *adj.* relating to descendants traced through the mother

medieval *adj.* a period in history that spanned from the A.D. 500s to the 1500s; from the Latin *medium* (middle) and *aevum* (age)

meditation *n.* the act of achieving inner peace and an enlightened realization of the divine aspect in each person

megafauna *n.* the large animals of a particular region, habitat, or geological period

mercenary *n.* a hired soldier

metallurgy *n.* the science of obtaining metals in their natural form and preparing them for use

migration *n.* the movement from one place to another

minaret *n.* a tall, slender tower that is part of a mosque

missionary *n.* a person who goes to another country to do religious work; a person who tries to spread Christianity to others

monarchy *n.* a government ruled by a single person, such as a king

monastery *n.* a Christian religious community

monotheism *n.* the worship of a single God

monsoon *n.* a strong seasonal wind in South and Southeast Asia

mosaic *n.* a grouping of tiny colored stone cubes set in mortar to create a picture or design

mosque *n.* a Muslim place of worship

mother culture *n.* a civilization that greatly influences other civilizations

mound builder *n.* a Native American culture that built mounds and cities in the Mississippi River Valley region between 1000 B.C. and A.D. 500

movable type *n.* the individual clay tablets that could be arranged on a board to form text

mummy *n.* the preserved body of a pharaoh or other powerful person in ancient Egypt

myth *n.* an old story told to explain an event or justify a belief or action

mythology *n.* a collection of stories that explains events, beliefs, or actions

N

nation-state *n.* a country with an independent government and a population united by a shared culture, language, and national pride; a political unit in which people have a common culture and identity

nirvana *n.* in Buddhism, a state of bliss or the end of suffering caused by the cycle of rebirth

noble *n.* a member of a high class in society who inherits his or her status

noh *n.* a form of drama that grew out of Japanese Shinto rituals and often retells well-known folktales

nomad *n.* a person who moves from place to place

O

oasis *n.* a fertile place with water in a desert

oligarchy *n.* a government ruled by a few powerful citizens

ondol *n.* a Korean system of heating in which an outside fire heats thick stones set into a floor

oracle bone *n.* an animal bone used to consult with the many gods worshipped by the Shang people

oral history *n.* an unwritten account of events, often passed down through the generations as stories or songs

oral tradition *n.* the passage of spoken histories and stories from one generation to the next

oratory *n.* the art of public speaking

P

pantheon *n.* the gods of a group of people, a religion, or a civilization

papyrus *n.* a paperlike material made from reeds

parable *n.* in the Bible, a simple story to illustrate a moral or spiritual lesson

parliament *n.* a group of representatives who shared power with the English monarch

patriarch *n.* the leader of the Eastern Orthodox Church

patriarchy *n.* a society in which men hold all the power

patrician *n.* a wealthy landowner in ancient Rome

patron *n.* a wealthy person who financially supports and encourages an artist

peasant *n.* a poor farmer

peninsula *n.* a piece of land surrounded by water on three sides

perspective *n.* an artistic technique that produces an impression of depth and distance

phalanx *n.* in ancient Greece and Rome, a battle formation in which soldiers stood close together to protect themselves from enemy attack

pharaoh *n.* an ancient Egyptian ruler

philosophy *n.* the study of the universe and our place in it

pilgrimage *n.* a journey to a holy place

plague *n.* a disease that causes many deaths

planned city *n.* a city built with a specific layout in mind

plantation *n.* a large farm where slaves worked to grow and harvest crops

plebeian *n.* a common person in ancient Rome

polis *n.* a Greek city-state

polytheism *n.* a belief in many gods

pope *n.* the leader of the Roman Catholic Church

porcelain *n.* a strong, light, and translucent ceramic

potlach *n.* a gift-giving ceremony practiced by the Kwakiutl and Haida Native American tribes

primary source *n.* an artifact or piece of writing that was created by someone who witnessed or lived through a historical event

printing press *n.* an invention that used movable metal type to print pages

prophet *n.* a teacher believed to be inspired by God

province *n.* an administrative district of a larger empire or country

pyramid *n.* a massive monumental tomb for a pharaoh

Q

quarry *v.* to extract stone from the earth

quinine *n.* a substance from the bark of a tree that is an effective remedy for malaria

quinoa *n.* a high-protein grain native to the Andes Mountains in South America

R

rabbi *n.* a Jewish spiritual leader

racism *n.* the belief that one race is better than others

raw material *n.* a substance from which other things are made

record keeping *n.* the practice of organizing and storing information

reform *n.* a change to make a situation better

regent *n.* a person who rules when a monarch or emperor is unable to do so

reincarnation *n.* in Hinduism, the rebirth of a person's soul into another body after death

religion *n.* the belief in and worship of one or more gods and goddesses

Renaissance man *n.* a person who has a wide variety of skills and knowledge

representative democracy *n.* a form of democracy in which people are elected to vote on the citizens' behalf

republic *n.* a type of government in which citizens vote for their leaders

reunify *v.* to join together again

ritual *n.* a formal series of acts always performed in the same way; a religious ceremony

rivalry *n.* a competition

S

samurai *n.* a hired warrior in medieval Japan

satrap *n.* a governor of a province in the Persian Empire

savanna *n.* an area of lush tropical grasslands

scarcity *n.* a small supply of something

schism *n.* a separation

scientific method *n.* a logical procedure for developing and testing ideas

scientific rationalism *n.* a school of thought in which observation, experimentation, and mathematical reasoning replace ancient wisdom and church teachings as the source of scientific truth

scribe *n.* a professional writer who recorded official information

secondary source *n.* an artifact or writing created after an event by someone who did not see it or live during the time when it occurred

secular *adj.* nonreligious

serf *n.* a person who lived and worked on the private land of a noble or medieval lord

shah *n.* a ruler of the Safavid Empire; the Persian title for "king"

shaman *n.* a medicine healer in Native American cultures

shari'a *n.* an Islamic system of law that covers all aspects of human behavior

shogun *n.* the military ruler of medieval Japan

shogunate *n.* the rule by a shogun

siege *n.* a military tactic in which troops surround a city with soldiers in an attempt to take control of it

silk *n.* a textile made from the cocoons of silkworms

silt *n.* an especially fine and fertile soil

slash-and-burn agriculture *n.* a method of clearing fields for planting

smallpox *n.* a deadly virus that causes a high fever and small blisters on the skin

social class *n.* a category of people based on wealth or status in a society

specialized worker *n.* a person who performs a job other than farming, such as metalworking or toolmaking

staple *n.* a main crop produced in a specific place

steppe *n.* a vast, grassy plain

subcontinent *n.* a large, distinct landmass that is part of a continent

sultan *n.* a ruler of the Ottoman Empire

surplus *adj.* more than is required or necessary; extra

synagogue *n.* a Jewish place of worship

T

technology *n.* the application of knowledge, tools, and inventions to meet people's needs

temple *n.* a place of worship

terrace *n.* a stepped platform built into a mountainside

terrace farming *n.* a type of farming in which flat steps are cut into a mountain to provide farmland

terra cotta *n.* a fire-baked clay

tetrarchy *n.* a system of rule by four emperors

theory *n.* a proposed explanation for a set of facts

tolerance *n.* the sympathy for the beliefs and practices of others

totem pole *n.* a tall, elaborately carved and painted tree trunk common in Northwest Coast native cultures

trade *n.* the exchange of goods

tragedy *n.* a serious form of Greek drama in which characters endure suffering before an unhappy ending

trans-Saharan *adj.* across the Sahara

triangular trade *n.* a transatlantic trade network formed by Europe, West Africa, and the Americas

tribe *n.* an extended family unit

tribune *n.* a representative who fought to protect the rights of ordinary citizens in ancient Rome

tribute *n.* a tax paid or goods and services rendered in return for protection

trireme *n.* an ancient Greek warship

truce *n.* an agreement to stop fighting

tyrant *n.* in ancient Greek city-states, a ruler who took power illegally

V

vassal *n.* a person, usually a lesser nobleman, who received land and protection from a feudal lord in exchange for obedience and service

vernacular *n.* a person's native language

veto *v.* to reject a decision or proposal made by another government body

vizier *n.* a chief official in ancient Egypt who carried out much of the day-to-day work of governing

W

wigwam *n.* a domed tent used as housing by the Algonquin in North America

woodcut *n.* an image carved on a block of wood

Y

yoga *n.* a series of postures and breathing exercises

Z

ziggurat *n.* a pyramid-shaped temple in Sumerian city-states

absolute *adj.* complete (page 360)

accuracy *n.* the freedom from errors (page 666)

accurate *adj.* without mistakes or errors (page 472)

advance *v.* to move forward (page 238)

ambitious *adj.* having a desire for fame or success (page 530)

appoint *v.* to give someone a particular job or duty (page 354)

benefit *v.* to be helpful to someone or something (page 677)

capacity *n.* the ability to do something (page 15)

coexist *v.* to live peacefully together (page 440)

collide *v.* to crash together (page 145)

commerce *n.* the buying and selling of goods and services (page 282)

commit *v.* to promise to do something (page 306)

communal *adj.* used or shared by a group of people (page 490)

concentrate *v.* to focus on (page 74)

constant *adj.* happening all the time (page 422)

crucial *adj.* extremely important or necessary (page 390)

decline *v.* to worsen in terms of condition or quality (page 434)

depose *v.* to remove someone from power (page 573)

determination *n.* the quality that makes someone continue to try doing a difficult task (page 284)

distinct *adj.* noticeably different or unique (page 496)

distinctive *adj.* different in a noticeable way (page 41)

dominate *v.* to have power over someone or something (page 112)

elaborate *adj.* made with great detail and effort (page 556)

emerge *v.* to rise or appear (page 36)

emphasis *n.* the additional importance given to something (page 380)

ensure *v.* to make something certain (page 386)

eternal *adj.* existing at all times; lasting forever (page 150)

ethical *adj.* following accepted rules or behaviors (page 522)

excel *v.* to be or do better than others (page 631)

flourish *v.* to be successful (page 270)

fortified *adj.* strong, strengthened (page 607)

influence *v.* to affect or change someone or something indirectly (page 170)

interval *n.* the period of time between events (page 308)

intricate *adj.* having many parts or details (page 584)

luxury *adj.* expensive and unnecessary (page 434)

observation *n.* the written descriptions based on something you have watched or seen (page 639)

policy *n.* a set of rules or ideas about how things should be done (page 127)

possession *n.* a personal article or possession (page 181)

predict *v.* to say that something will happen in the future (page 467)

privilege *n.* a right or benefit that only some people receive (page 114)

profit *n.* the money that is made through doing business (page 416)

promote *v.* to encourage (page 154)

prosperous *adj.* successful, usually by making a lot of money (page 209)

radical *adj.* different from what is typical or ordinary (page 643)

reluctantly *adv.* with hesitation or doubt (page 245)

retain *v.* to keep or continue to have (page 601)

revolve *v.* to move or turn around something (page 664)

supervise *v.* to watch and oversee someone or something (page 69)

transform *v.* to dramatically change (page 26)

undermine *v.* to make someone or something weaker (page 566)

wage *n.* the amount of money a worker is paid (page 221)

A

acrópolis *s.* punto más alto en una ciudad griega de la antigüedad

acueducto *s.* canal largo de piedra que transporta agua limpia

adaptar *v.* cambiar

adobe *s.* tipo de arcilla que cuando se seca se usa como material de construcción

ágora *s.* espacio abierto en una ciudad griega de la antigüedad que servía como mercado y centro social

agotar *v.* consumir algo por completo, por ejemplo, un recurso

agricultura *s.* práctica de cultivar plantas y criar animales para obtener alimento

agricultura de tala y quema *s.* método de limpiar los campos para sembrar cultivos

aislacionismo *s.* rechazo al contacto extranjero y a las influencias externas

aislar *v.* apartar del resto del mundo

alianza *s.* acuerdo entre naciones para colaborar en la lucha contra los enemigos; asociación; pacto religioso

alminar *s.* torre alta y angosta que es parte de una mezquita

antropólogo *s.* científico que estudia el desarrollo cultural de los seres humanos

arabesco *s.* diseño abstracto que consiste en patrones o flores, hojas, enredaderas o figuras geométricas

archipiélago *s.* conjunto de islas

arco *s.* estructura curva colocada sobre una abertura

arco largo *s.* arma que permitía que los arqueros dispararan sus flechas

aristocracia *s.* clase alta que es más adinerada y más poderosa que el resto de la sociedad

arqueólogo *s.* científico que estudia el pasado de la vida humana mediante el análisis de fósiles y artefactos

artefacto *s.* objeto hecho por humanos pertenecientes a una cultura del pasado

artesano *s.* persona que se dedica a fabricar objetos de forma manual

B

bajorrelieve *s.* escultura realista que contiene figuras realzadas sobre un fondo plano

bancales *s.* tipo de agricultura en que se cortan escalones planos en una montaña para brindar terrenos de cultivo

bárbaro *s.* en este contexto, una persona que vivía fuera del Imperio Romano

burgués *s.* comerciante rico, citadino, durante la Edad Media; miembro de la clase media

burocracia *s.* sistema de gobierno en que funcionarios designados en departamentos especializados están a cargo de distintas oficinas

bushido *s.* estricto código de comportamiento seguido por los samurái en el Japón feudal

C

caballero *s.* guerrero de la Europa medieval

cacao *s.* grano que se usa para hacer chocolate

califa *s.* título del líder musulmán que era considerado sucesor de Mohammed, desde 632 a 1924 D.C.

caligrafía *s.* forma de escritura elegante

campesino *s.* granjero pobre

carabela *s.* nave pequeña y rápida usada por los exploradores españoles y portugueses

caravana *s.* grupo de personas que viajan juntas

cartografía *s.* estudio de los mapas y de la creación de mapas

catacumba *s.* cámara escondida bajo la superficie en donde se entierra a los muertos

catapulta *s.* arma que lanza piedras enormes

catarata *s.* formación rocosa que crea rápidos agitados; además, una cascada grande

catedral *s.* iglesia alta construida durante la Edad Media; a menudo el lugar en donde gobernaba un obispo

cazador-recolector *s.* ser humano que caza animales y que cosecha plantas silvestres para alimentarse

celadón *s.* tipo de cerámica china con un peculiar color verdeazulado

centro de comercio *s.* núcleo comercial

chamán *s.* curandero de las culturas nativo-americanas

chinampa *s.* campo flotante que sustenta la agricultura

ciclo dinástico *s.* patrón del surgimiento y la caída de las dinastías de la China ancestral y antigua

cieno *s.* suelo especialmente fino y fértil

cisma *s.* separación

ciudad *s.* centro político, económico y cultural con una población grande

ciudad-estado *s.* unidad que se gobierna a sí misma, formada por una ciudad y sus territorios y asentamientos circundantes; ciudad que controla las aldeas y pueblos circundantes

ciudad planificada *s.* ciudad construida con un diseño específico en mente

civilización *s.* sociedad con una cultura y tecnología altamente desarrolladas

clan *s.* grupo de familias que comparten un ancestro en común

clase social *s.* categoría de personas basada en las riquezas o estatus en una sociedad

clásico *adj.* relacionado con la cultura griega y romana antiguas

clérigo *s.* líder religioso que dirige las ceremonias e imparte las enseñanzas de la iglesia cristiana

códice *s.* libro plegado hecho de papel de corteza de árbol

colonia *s.* grupo de personas que se asientan en un nuevo territorio, pero que mantienen sus lazos con su país nativo

comedia *s.* obra de teatro griega con un formato humorístico que solía burlarse de las personas famosas

comercio *s.* intercambio de productos; compra y venta de bienes

comercio triangular *s.* red de comercio transatlántico formado por Europa, África Occidental y las Américas

comunal *adj.* compartido

confederación *s.* grupo de aliados

conquistador *s.* explorador español que buscaba oro y otras riquezas en Centroamérica y América del Sur

constructores de montículos *s.* cultura nativo-americana que construyó montículos y ciudades en la región del valle del río Mississippi entre los años 1000 A.C. y 500 D.C.

cónsul *s.* uno de los dos jefes líderes elegidos cada año en la Antigua Roma

convertirse *v.* cambiar la propia religión

cosmopolita *adj.* internacional

credo *s.* declaración de creencia

crisol cultural *s.* lugar desde el cual se difunden nuevas ideas, prácticas y tecnología

cultivar *v.* sembrar cultivos

cultivo básico *s.* cultivo principal producido en un lugar específico

cultura madre *s.* civilización que tiene una gran influencia sobre otras civilizaciones

cultura *s.* forma de vida de un grupo, que incluye tipos de alimento, vivienda, vestimenta, idioma, religión, comportamiento e ideas

cuneiforme *s.* primera forma de escritura conocida, inventada por los sumerios

D

daimio *s.* clase de familias terratenientes grandes del Japón medieval

delta *s.* área donde un río se divide en distintos brazos a medida que fluye hacia una masa de agua

democracia *s.* forma de gobierno en que los ciudadanos tienen un papel directo para gobernarse a sí mismos o para elegir a representantes que los gobiernen

democracia directa *s.* forma de democracia en que los ciudadanos se reúnen para votar sobre las leyes y las políticas

democracia representativa *s.* forma de democracia en que se eligen personas para que voten en representación de los ciudadanos

denominación *s.* rama de una religión determinada

derecho consuetudinario *s.* sistema legal establecido en Inglaterra para asegurarse de que todas las personas fueran tratadas con igualdad

desertificación *s.* proceso mediante el cual las tierras fértiles se convierten en un desierto

dharma *s.* enseñanzas de Buda; ley divina

dhow *s.* nave con un casco largo y delgado y velas triangulares

dictador *s.* persona que gobierna con total autoridad

difusión cultural *s.* proceso mediante el cual las culturas interaccionan y las ideas se propagan de un área a otra

dinastía *s.* serie de gobernantes de la misma familia

diversidad *s.* rango de cosas diferentes; variedad

divino *adj.* tener la naturaleza de un dios

domesticación *s.* cultivo de plantas y animales de manera que fueran útiles para los humanos

E

edad de oro *s.* período de grandes logros culturales

elíptico *adj.* ovalado

embajada *s.* grupo de personas que representa a su nación en un país extranjero

emperador *s.* gobernante supremo de un imperio

epístola *s.* carta

escasez *s.* suministro pequeño de algo

escriba *s.* escritor profesional que anotaba información oficial

estepa *s.* planicie vasta y cubierta de hierbas

excedente *adj.* más de lo que se requiere o necesita; extra

excomulgar *s.* excluir oficialmente a un miembro de una iglesia de sus rituales y membresía

exilio *s.* expulsión forzada del propio país de origen

explotar *v.* maltratar

extraer *v.* sacar piedras de la tierra

F

falange *s.* en la Antigua Grecia y Roma, formación de batalla en que los soldados se formaban juntos unos de otros para protegerse de los ataques de los enemigos

faraón *s.* gobernante egipcio de la antigüedad

fértil *adj.* que sustenta el crecimiento de cultivos y plantas

feudalismo *s.* sistema político y social en que el vasallo recibe protección de un señor a cambio de obediencia y servicio

filosofía *s.* estudio del universo y de nuestro lugar en él **fósil** *s.* restos de organismos que vivieron hace mucho tiempo atrás

fresco *s.* arte que se pinta directamente sobre una muralla

fuente primaria *s.* artefacto o texto escrito creado por alguien que presenció o vivió un acontecimiento histórico

fuente secundaria *s.* artefacto o texto escrito creado después de un acontecimiento por alguien que no lo vio o presenció durante el tiempo en que ocurrió

G

geoglifo *s.* diseño o forma geométrica grande dibujado sobre el suelo

gladiador *s.* hombre de la Antigua Roma que luchaba contra otros como espectáculo de entretención

glifo *s.* dibujo simbólico usado para representar una palabra, sílaba o sonido

gobierno *s.* organización establecida para hacer y reforzar las reglas de una sociedad

gremio *s.* grupo de artesanos que ayudaron a proteger y a mejorar las condiciones laborales de sus miembros

griot *s.* cuentacuentos del África Occidental que cuenta historias a través de la tradición oral

guerra civil *s.* guerra entre grupos de un mismo país

H

haikú *s.* forma de poesía japonesa que consiste en 17 sílabas organizadas en tres versos no rimados de 5, 7 y 5 sílabas respectivamente

hambruna *s.* escasez extrema de cultivos o de alimentos que causa hambre generalizada

hanbok *s.* combinación coreana de vestimenta tradicional que consiste en una chaqueta con falda o pantalón

helenístico *adj.* relacionado con la historia o cultura griega

herejía *s.* creencias contrarias a las enseñanzas de la iglesia; oposición a las políticas de la iglesia

héroe *s.* personaje que enfrenta un desafío que requiere valentía, fuerza e inteligencia

hidalguía *s.* código de comportamiento de los caballeros

hierro *s.* metal que se encuentra en la roca

hipótesis *s.* explicación que puede ponerse a prueba

historia de la creación *s.* narración que explica cómo comenzó el mundo y cómo nacieron las personas

historia oral *s.* registro no escrito de acontecimientos, que a menudo se transmite de una generación a otra a través de historias o canciones

hombre renacentista *s.* persona con una amplia variedad de destrezas y conocimientos

hueso oracular *s.* hueso de animal usado para consultar a los muchos dioses adorados por el pueblo Shang

humanismo *s.* movimiento que se enfoca en la importancia del individuo

I

ícono *s.* imagen de Jesús o de un santo

ilota *s.* esclavo que poseía el estado que era parte de la clase social más baja en la sociedad griega de la antigüedad

imán *s.* líder religioso musulmán

imperio *s.* conjunto de diferentes tierras y pueblos liderados por un gobernante

imponer *v.* forzar a alguien a hacer algo

imprenta *s.* invento que usaba tipos móviles de metal para imprimir páginas

indulgencia *s.* liberación de los castigos causados por los pecados, vendida por funcionarios papales

inmortal *adj.* que puede vivir para siempre

inoculación *s.* vacuna que contiene una forma leve de una enfermedad para prevenir el desarrollo de dicha enfermedad

intersección *s.* lugar en donde se juntan dos caminos

irrigación *s.* suministro de agua para los campos mediante el uso de sistemas hechos por el hombre

J

jenízaro *s.* soldado altamente entrenado y disciplinado del ejército otomano

jerarquía *s.* sistema en que las personas pertenecen a distintas clases sociales que tienen distintos rangos en la sociedad

jeroglífico *s.* imagen que representa un objeto, sonido o idea y que era parte del antiguo sistema de escritura egipcio

jurado *s.* grupo de personas escogidas para tomar una decisión con base en la evidencia presentada en un juicio

K

kabuki *s.* forma de obra teatral japonesa que incluye disfraces lujosos y maquillaje elaborado

kanato *s.* región del Imperio Mongol

karma *s.* en el hinduismo, estado de estar influenciado por las acciones y el comportamiento; determina el tipo de vida en que una persona volverá a nacer

kimchi *s.* plato nacional de Corea, que consiste en una mezcla de verduras bien condimentadas

kiva *s.* cámara de forma circular construida en el suelo por los indígenas pueblo del pasado

kosher *adj.* preparado especialmente según las leyes dietéticas judías

L

laberinto *s.* lugar formado por encrucijadas, del cual es difícil salir

legado *s.* cosas, tanto culturales como tecnológicas, que nos quedan del pasado

legionario *s.* soldado profesional de la Antigua Roma

lengua franca *s.* idioma que se usa comúnmente entre distintos grupos de personas

leyenda *s.* historia del pasado que se acepta como verdad, pero que no puede probarse

M

maíz *s.* tipo de elote que fue domesticado por los primeros mesoamericanos

mansa *s.* rey de África Occidental

marinero *s.* marino

marítimo *adj.* relacionado con el mar

materia prima *s.* sustancia a partir de la cual se fabrican otras cosas

matrilineal *adj.* relacionado con los descendientes que provienen de la madre

mecenas *s.* persona adinerada que apoya financieramente y promueve a un artista

medieval *adj.* período de la historia que se expandió desde el siglo VI al siglo XVI; del latín *medieum* (medio) y *aevum* (edad)

meditación *s.* acto de alcanzar la paz interior y el entendimiento del aspecto divino en cada persona

megafauna *s.* animales grandes de una región, hábitat o período geológico en particular

mercancía *s.* producto de comercio

mercenario *s.* soldado asalariado

metalurgia *s.* ciencia que consiste en obtener materiales en su forma natural y prepararlos para el uso

método científico *s.* procedimiento lógico para desarrollar y poner a prueba las ideas

mezquita *s.* lugar musulmán de adoración

migración *s.* mudarse de un lugar a otro

misionero *s.* persona que va a otro país para realizar labores religiosas; persona que trata de divulgar la cristiandad a otros

mito *s.* historia antigua contada para explicar un acontecimiento o justificar una creencia o acción

mitología *s.* colección de historias que explica acontecimientos, creencias o acciones

momia *s.* cuerpo preservado de un faraón u otra persona poderosa del Antiguo Egipto

monarquía *s.* gobierno liderado por una sola persona como, por ejemplo, un rey

monasterio *s.* comunidad religiosa cristiana

monoteísmo *s.* alabanza a un solo Dios

monzón *s.* vientos estacionales fuertes en el Sudeste Asiático

mosaico *s.* agrupación de cubitos de piedra coloridos que se colocan sobre argamasa para crear un dibujo o diseño

N

nación-estado *s.* país con un gobierno independiente y una población unida por una cultura compartida, un idioma común y orgullo nacional; unidad política en que las personas tienen una cultura e identidad en común

nirvana *s.* en el budismo, un estado de dicha o del final del sufrimiento causado por el ciclo del renacer

noble *s.* miembro de la clase alta de la sociedad que hereda su estatus de sus antepasados

noh *s.* forma de obra teatral que surgió a partir de los rituales japoneses Shinto y que a menudo relata cuentos folclóricos conocidos

nómada *s.* persona que se muda de un lugar a otro

O

oasis *s.* lugar fértil con agua en un desierto

oligarquía *s.* gobierno liderado por unos pocos ciudadanos

ondol *s.* sistema coreano de calefacción en que una fogata al exterior calienta piedras gruesas que se colocan en el suelo

oratoria *s.* arte del discurso público

P

panteón *s.* dioses de un grupo de personas, una religión o una civilización

papa *s.* líder de la Iglesia Católica Romana

papiro *s.* material parecido al papel que se hace a partir de juncos

parábola *s.* en la Biblia, un relato sencillo que ilustra una moraleja o una lección espiritual

parlamento *s.* grupo de representantes que comparten el poder con el rey inglés

patriarca *s.* líder de la Iglesia Ortodoxa oriental

patriarcal *adj.* dicho de una sociedad en que los hombres tienen todo el poder

patricio *s.* terrateniente rico de la Antigua Roma

península *s.* porción de tierra rodeada por agua en tres de sus costados

peregrinación *s.* viaje a un lugar sagrado

permutar *v.* intercambiar productos

perspectiva *s.* técnica artística que produce una impresión de profundidad y distancia

peste bubónica *s.* enfermedad que mató a más de un tercio de la población de Europa durante la Edad Media

piedad filial *s.* creencia de que los niños le deben respeto a sus padres y ancestros

pirámide *s.* tumba masiva y monumental construida para un faraón

plaga *s.* enfermedad que causa muchas muertes

plantación *s.* granja grande en donde trabajan esclavos para producir y cultivar las siembras

plebeyo *s.* persona común de la Antigua Roma

poema épico *s.* historia larga escrita como un poema narrativo

polis *s.* ciudad-estado griega

politeísmo *s.* creencia en muchos dioses

porcelana *s.* cerámica resistente, liviana y translúcida

potlach *s.* ceremonia de entrega de obsequios practicada por las tribus nativo-americanas kwakiutl y haida

profeta *s.* maestro que se cree es inspirado por Dios

provincia *s.* distrito administrativo de un imperio grande o de un país

puente terrestre *s.* franja de territorio que conecta dos masas terrestres

Q

quinina *s.* sustancia de la corteza de un árbol que es un antídoto efectivo para la malaria

quínoa *s.* grano alto en proteínas originario de las montañas de los Andes en América del Sur

R

rabino *s.* líder espiritual judío

racionalismo científico *s.* escuela de pensamiento en que la observación, experimentación y razonamiento matemático reemplazan el conocimiento ancestral y las enseñanzas de la iglesia como fuente de la verdad científica

racismo *s.* creencia de que una raza es mejor que las otras

reencarnación *s.* en el hinduismo, el renacer del alma de una persona en otro cuerpo después de la muerte

reforma *s.* cambio hecho para mejorar una situación

regente *s.* persona que gobierna cuando un monarca o emperador no puede hacerlo

registros *s.* práctica que consiste en organizar y almacenar la información

religión *s.* creencia en y alabanza de uno o más dioses y diosas

república *s.* tipo de gobierno en que los ciudadanos votan por sus líderes

reunificar *v.* volver a unir

ritual *s.* serie de actos formales que siempre se realizan de la misma manera; ceremonia religiosa

rivalidad *s.* competencia

S

sabana *s.* área de praderas tropicales exuberantes

samurái *s.* guerrero asalariado del Japón medieval

sátrapa *s.* gobernante de una provincia en el Imperio Persa

secular *adj.* no religioso

seda *s.* textil hecho de los capullos de los gusanos de la seda

señor *s.* miembro de la nobleza que recibía tierras de un rey en la sociedad feudal medieval

señorío *s.* mundo autosuficiente ubicado en las tierras que pertenecían a un señor

sequía *s.* período largo de estado del tiempo seco y caluroso

shah *s.* gobernante del Imperio Safávida; título persa para "rey"

shari'a *s.* sistema islámico de leyes que cubre todos los aspectos del comportamiento humano

siervo *s.* persona que vivía y trabajaba en los terrenos privados de un noble o de un señor medieval

sinagoga *s.* lugar de reunión religiosa para los judíos

sistema de castas *s.* jerarquía social rígida en India que divide a las personas en clases sociales hereditarias

sitio *s.* táctica militar en que las tropas rodean una ciudad con soldados en un intento por controlarla

sogún *s.* gobernante militar del Japón medieval

sogunato *s.* gobierno de un sogún

subcontinente *s.* gran masa de tierra que es parte de un continente

sultán *s.* gobernante del Imperio Otomano

T

tecnología *s.* aplicación de conocimiento, herramientas e inventos para satisfacer las necesidades de las personas

templo *s.* lugar de alabanza

teoría *s.* explicación propuesta para un conjunto de hechos

teoría geocéntrica *s.* teoría que posiciona a la Tierra en el centro del universo

teoría heliocéntrica *s.* teoría que posiciona al Sol como el centro del universo

terracota *s.* arcilla cocida al fuego

terrazas *s.* plataformas de estepa construidas en la ladera de una montaña

tetrarquía *s.* sistema de gobierno de cuatro emperadores

tierras altas *s.* terrenos que están sobre el mar

tierras bajas *s.* tipo de terrenos nivelados de poca altura

tipos móviles *s.* tablas de arcilla individuales que podían organizarse sobre un tablero para formar un texto

tirano *s.* en las ciudades-estado de la Antigua Grecia, gobernante que obtenía el poder de forma ilegal

tolerancia *s.* respeto por las creencias y las prácticas de otros

tótem *s.* tronco de árbol alto y elaboradamente tallado y pintado, común en las culturas nativas de la costa noroeste

trabajador especializado *s.* persona que realiza un trabajo que no está relacionado con la agricultura, como en la metalurgia o en la producción de herramientas

tradición oral *s.* transmisión verbal de historias y relatos de una generación a la siguiente

tragedia *s.* obra de teatro griega con un formato serio en que los personajes sufren antes de enfrentar un final triste

transahariano *adj.* que va a través del Sahara

tregua *s.* acuerdo para detener un conflicto

tribu *s.* unidad familiar extendida

tribuno *s.* representante que luchó para proteger los derechos de los ciudadanos comunes en la Antigua Roma

tributo *s.* impuesto pagado o bienes y servicios proporcionados a cambio de protección

trirreme *s.* antigua nave de guerra griega

V

vasallo *s.* persona, usualmente un hombre noble menor, que recibía tierras y protección de un señor feudal a cambio de obediencia y servicio

vernáculo *s.* idioma nativo de una persona

vetar *v.* rechazar una decisión o propuesta hecha por otro cuerpo gubernamental

viruela *s.* virus mortal que causa una fiebre alta y ampollas pequeñas en la piel

visir *s.* oficial jefe en el Antiguo Egipto que realizaba la mayor parte del trabajo de gobernar cotidiano

W

wigwam *s.* tipo de choza con techo en forma de cúpula usada como vivienda por los indígenas algonquinos de América del Norte

xilografía *s.* imagen tallada en un bloque de madera

Y

yoga *s.* serie de posturas y ejercicios de respiración

Z

zigurat *s.* templo con forma de pirámide en las ciudades-estado de Sumeria

absoluto *adj.* completo (pág. 360)

ambicioso *adj.* que desea la fama o el éxito (pág. 530)

asegurar *v.* garantizar algo (pág. 386)

avanzar *v.* moverse hacia adelante (pág. 238)

beneficiar *v.* ayudar a alguien o a algo (pág. 677)

capacidad *s.* habilidad de hacer algo (pág. 15)

coexistir *v.* vivir en paz en conjunto (pág. 440)

colisionar *v.* chocar (pág. 145)

comercio *s.* compra y venta de bienes y servicios (pág. 282)

comprometerse *v.* prometer hacer algo (pág. 306)

comunal *adj.* usado o compartido por un grupo de personas (pág. 490)

concentrar *v.* enfocarse en algo (pág. 74)

constante *adj.* que ocurre todo el tiempo (pág. 422)

crucial *adj.* extremadamente importante o necesario (pág. 390)

decaer *v.* empeorar en términos de condición o de calidad (pág. 434)

designar *v.* dar a alguien un trabajo o responsabilidad determinado (pág. 354)

destituir *v.* remover a alguien del poder (pág. 573)

determinación *s.* cualidad que hace que alguien continúe intentando realizar una labor difícil (pág. 285)

distintivo *adj.* notoriamente diferente o único (pág. 496)

dominar *v.* tener poder sobre alguien o algo (pág. 112)

elaborado *adj.* hecho con mucho detalle y esfuerzo (pág. 556)

énfasis *s.* importancia adicional que se otorga a algo (pág. 380)

eterno *adj.* que existe en todo momento; que dura para siempre (pág. 150)

ético *adj.* que sigue las reglas o comportamientos aceptados (pág. 522)

florecer *v.* tener éxito (pág. 270)

fortificado *adj.* fuerte, resistente (pág. 607)

ganancia *s.* dinero que se gana al hacer negocios (pág. 416)

girar *v.* moverse o rotar alrededor de algo (pág. 664)

influenciar *v.* afectar o cambiar alguien o algo de manera indirecta (pág. 170)

intervalo *s.* período de tiempo entre los acontecimientos (pág. 308)

intrincado *adj.* que contiene muchas partes o detalles (pág. 584)

lujoso *adj.* costoso e innecesario (pág. 434)

observación *s.* descripción escrita con base en lo observado o visto (pág. 639)

peculiar *adj.* diferente de una manera perceptible (pág. 41)

política *s.* conjunto de reglas o ideas sobre cómo deben hacerse las cosas (pág. 127)

posesión *s.* artículo o propiedad personal (pág. 181)

precisión *adj.* sin faltas ni errores (pág. 472)

preciso *s.* libre de errores (pág. 666)

predecir *v.* decir qué sucederá en el futuro (pág. 467)

privilegio *s.* derecho o beneficio que sólo reciben algunas personas (pág. 114)

promover *v.* animar (pág. 154)

próspero *adj.* exitoso, usualmente por ganar mucho dinero (pág. 209)

radical *adj.* diferente de lo que es típico u ordinario (pág. 643)

reaciamente *adv.* con incertidumbre o dudas (pág. 245)

retener *v.* mantener o seguir teniendo (pág. 601)

salario *s.* cantidad de dinero que recibe un trabajador (pág. 221)

sobresalir *v.* ser o desempeñarse mejor que el resto (pág. 631)

socavar *v.* debilitar a alguien o a algo (pág. 566)

supervisar *v.* vigilar y monitorear algo o alguien (pág. 69)

surgir *v.* emerger o aparecer (pág. 36)

transformar *v.* cambiar dramáticamente (pág. 26)

SKILLS INDEX

A

Analyze Cause and Effect, 25, 27, 49, 69, 86, 91, 105, 120, 140, 142, 157, 162, 183, 209, 215, 217, 219, 221, 233, 239, 243, 249, 255, 256, 309, 317, 327, 338, 350, 353, 365, 366, 371, 373, 379, 398, 413, 421, 430, 432, 439, 446, 473, 477, 482, 491, 501, 506, 527, 529, 533, 537, 544, 549, 551, 567, 568, 577, 579, 583, 586, 615, 621, 625, 626, 637, 641, 647, 657, 663, 671, 677, 681, 684

Analyze Language Use, 31, 79, 95, 151, 164, 171, 191, 192, 293, 410, 419, 427, 430, 439, 471, 613, 628, 631, 645, 658

Analyze Sources, 33, 53, 87, 121, 141, 163, 193, 227, 257, 303, 339, 367, 399, 431, 447, 483, 507, 545, 569, 587, 627, 659, 685

Analyze Visuals, 39, 81, 223, 355, 503, 683

C

Categorize, 577

Compare, 101

Compare and Contrast, 10, 23, 31, 32, 41, 52, 91, 97, 109, 125, 162, 171, 181, 192, 206, 211, 223, 226, 231, 237, 251, 254, 255, 268, 275, 279, 289, 297, 302, 335, 389, 393, 423, 441, 461, 467, 479, 482, 487, 499, 501, 505, 506, 525, 531, 541, 543, 555, 557, 561, 568, 581, 586, 601, 626, 643, 649, 658, 679, 684

Compare Time Lines, 7, 61, 203, 265, 347, 407, 455, 517, 595

Contrast, 83

Critical Viewing, 5, 13, 14, 17, 27, 59, 71, 79, 91, 95, 101, 109, 115, 117, 127, 147, 179, 187, 201, 213, 215, 219, 239, 240, 243, 251, 255, 263, 275, 279, 283, 295, 298, 311, 330, 345, 365, 371, 375, 395, 405, 417, 419, 427, 439, 453, 463, 464, 479, 487, 493, 497, 499, 501, 515, 525, 527, 551, 557, 561, 563, 577, 579, 585, 593, 613, 621, 631, 643, 645, 679

D

Describe, 37, 93, 99, 325, 551

Describe Geographic Information, 443, 445

Determine Word Meaning, 13, 17, 41, 71, 119, 149, 177, 215, 228, 239, 256, 279, 361, 465, 570, 579, 586, 657, 663

Distinguish Fact and Opinion, 393

Document-Based Question, 72–73, 130–131, 152–153, 172–173, 240–241, 298–299, 322–323, 376–377, 428–429, 474–475, 534–535, 558–559, 616–617, 652–653, 674–675

Draw Conclusions, 15, 29, 32, 45, 49, 52, 75, 86, 88, 95, 99, 101, 107, 119, 120, 129, 137, 140, 155, 169, 175, 187, 192, 209, 226, 235, 247, 249, 256, 275, 283, 289, 302, 325, 327, 331, 366, 383, 395, 398, 421, 425, 427, 430, 446, 463, 471, 479, 481, 482, 493, 497, 499, 503, 520, 529, 544, 568, 586, 598, 605, 613, 626, 655, 658, 665, 681, 684

E

Evaluate, 52, 140, 162, 226, 256, 338, 381, 395, 497, 506, 544, 626, 667

F

Form and Support Opinions, 107, 159, 213, 338, 415, 482, 553, 567, 641

Form Opinions, 19, 27, 52, 85, 175, 183, 295

I

Identify Details, 135, 373

Identify Main Ideas, 67, 651

Identify Main Ideas and Details, 34, 39, 47, 52, 77, 86, 115, 122, 127, 139, 140, 191, 213, 243, 247, 251, 271, 273, 277, 285, 295, 302, 307, 355, 368, 381, 398, 413, 417, 437, 443, 446, 458, 473, 482, 543, 583, 585, 605, 631, 669

Identify Problems, 133

Identify Problems and Solutions, 329, 389, 563, 683

Integrate Maps, 113, 145

Integrate Visuals, 23, 25, 43, 47, 69, 85, 147, 169, 177, 221, 233, 281, 469, 541, 647

Interpret Charts, 87, 163, 303, 569, 627

Interpret Diagrams, 121, 367

Interpret Maps, 19, 21, 29, 33, 37, 53, 67, 75, 93, 125, 137, 149, 157, 159, 167, 181, 185, 193, 211, 217, 227, 237, 245, 257, 271, 291, 293, 309, 321, 329, 339, 353, 361, 371, 387, 399, 415, 423, 431, 435, 437, 441, 447, 461, 467, 477, 491, 523, 531, 539, 549, 573, 581, 587, 601, 619, 651, 669, 677

Interpret Time Lines, 141

Interpret Visuals, 359, 463, 483, 507, 537, 545, 607, 611, 633, 639, 659, 671, 685

ACKNOWLEDGMENTS

Text Acknowledgments

545 Li Po, "Zazen on Ching-t'ing Mountain" from Crossing the Yellow River: Three Hundred Poems from the Chinese, translated by Sam Hamill. Copyright ©2000 by Sam Hamill. Reprinted with the permission of The Permissions Company, Inc., on behalf of Tiger Bark Press, www. tigerbarkpress.com.

559 Matsuo Basho, "The Quiet Pond..." from The Classic Tradition of Haiku: An Anthology by Faubion Bowers (editor). Dover Publications, Inc., 1996. (Poem translated by Edward G. Seidensticker)

569 Shuson Kato, "I kill and Ant..." from Haiku Mind: 108 Poems to Cultivate and Open Your Heart, by Patricia Donegan, ©2008 by Patricia Donegan. Reprinted by arrangement with The Permissions Company, Inc., on behalf of Shambhala Publications Inc., Boston, MA. www. shambhala.com.

National Geographic Learning gratefully acknowledges the contributions of the following National Geographic Explorers and affiliates to our program:

Salam Al Kuntar, National Geographic Emerging Explorer
Caroline Alexander, National Geographic Writer/Journalist
Nicole Boivin, National Geographic Grantee
Steve Boyes, National Geographic Emerging Explorer
Michael Cosmopoulos, National Geographic Grantee
Christopher DeCorse, National Geographic Grantee
Steven Ellis, National Geographic Grantee
Francisco Estrada-Belli, National Geographic Grantee
Beverly Goodman, National Geographic Emerging Explorer
Fredrik Hiebert, National Geographic Archaeology Fellow
Patrick Hunt, National Geographic Grantee
Louise Leakey, National Geographic Explorer-in-Residence
Christine Lee, National Geographic Emerging Explorer
Albert Lin, National Geographic Emerging Explorer
Jodi Magness, National Geographic Grantee
Sarah Parcak, National Geographic Fellow
Thomas Parker, National Geographic Grantee
William Parkinson, National Geographic Grantee
Matt Piscitelli, National Geographic Grantee
Jeffrey Rose, National Geographic Emerging Explorer
Max Salomon, National Geographic Producer
William Saturno, National Geographic Grantee
Anna Secor, National Geographic Grantee
Shah Selbe, National Geographic Emerging Explorer
Maurizio Seracini, National Geographic Fellow
Hayat Sindi, National Geographic Emerging Explorer
Christopher Thornton, National Geographic Lead Program
    Officer of Research, Conservation, and Exploration
Soultana Maria Valamoti, National Geographic Grantee
Juan José Valdés, National Geographic Geographer
Xiaobai Angela Yao, National Geographic Grantee
Dave Yoder, National Geographic Grantee

Map Credits

Illustrator Credits

OUR HUMAN STORY GLOBAL CITIZENSHIP

EMPATHY

PRESERVING CULTURES

HISTORY THROUGH OBJECTS

WHY STUDY HISTORY?

IDENTITY

CIVILIZATION

WHO OWNS THE PAST?

MOMENTS IN HISTORY

WHY STUDY HISTORY?

EMPATHY

CIVILIZATION

GLOBAL CITIZENSHIP

PRESERVING CULTURES

STORYTELLING

OUR HUMAN STORY

THE HUMAN EPIC

GLOBAL CITIZENSHIP

WHO OWNS THE PAST?

IDENTITY PRESERVING CULTURE

GLOBAL CITIZENSHIP EMPATHY

WHY STUDY HISTORY

STORYTELLING

OUR HUMAN STORY

STORIES MAKING HISTORY

EMPOWERMENT

SAVING OUR PAST

CIVILIZATION

IDENTITY

EMPOWERMENT

EMPATHY

HISTORY THROUGH OBJECTS

EMPOWERMENT

SAVING OUR PAST

STORIES MAKING HISTORY

THE HUMAN EPIC GLOBAL CITIZENSHIP

STORYTELLING

WHY STUDY HISTORY? EMPATHY

IDENTITY CIVILIZATION

STORIES MAKING HISTORY

EMPOWERMENT

SAVING OUR PAST

EMPATHY

HISTORY THROUGH OBJECTS

EMPOWERMENT
PRESERVING CULTURES
SAVING OUR PAST
WHY STUDY HISTORY?
GLOBAL CITIZENSHIP
IDENTITY
THE HUMAN EPIC
STORYTELLING
OUR HUMAN STORY

CIVILIZATION

PRESERVING CULTURES

GLOBAL CITIZENSHIP

PRESERVING CULTURES

EMPATHY

OUR HUMAN STORY

CIVILIZATION THE HUMAN EPIC

WHO OWNS THE PAST?

STORIES MAKING HISTORY

THE HUMAN EPIC STORIES MAKING HISTORY

EMPOWERMENT

GLOBAL CITIZENSHIP

SAVING OUR PAST

EMPOWERMENT

MOMENTS IN HISTORY

IDENTITY SAVING OUR PAST